THE TIMES
ATLAS OF WORLD
HISTORY

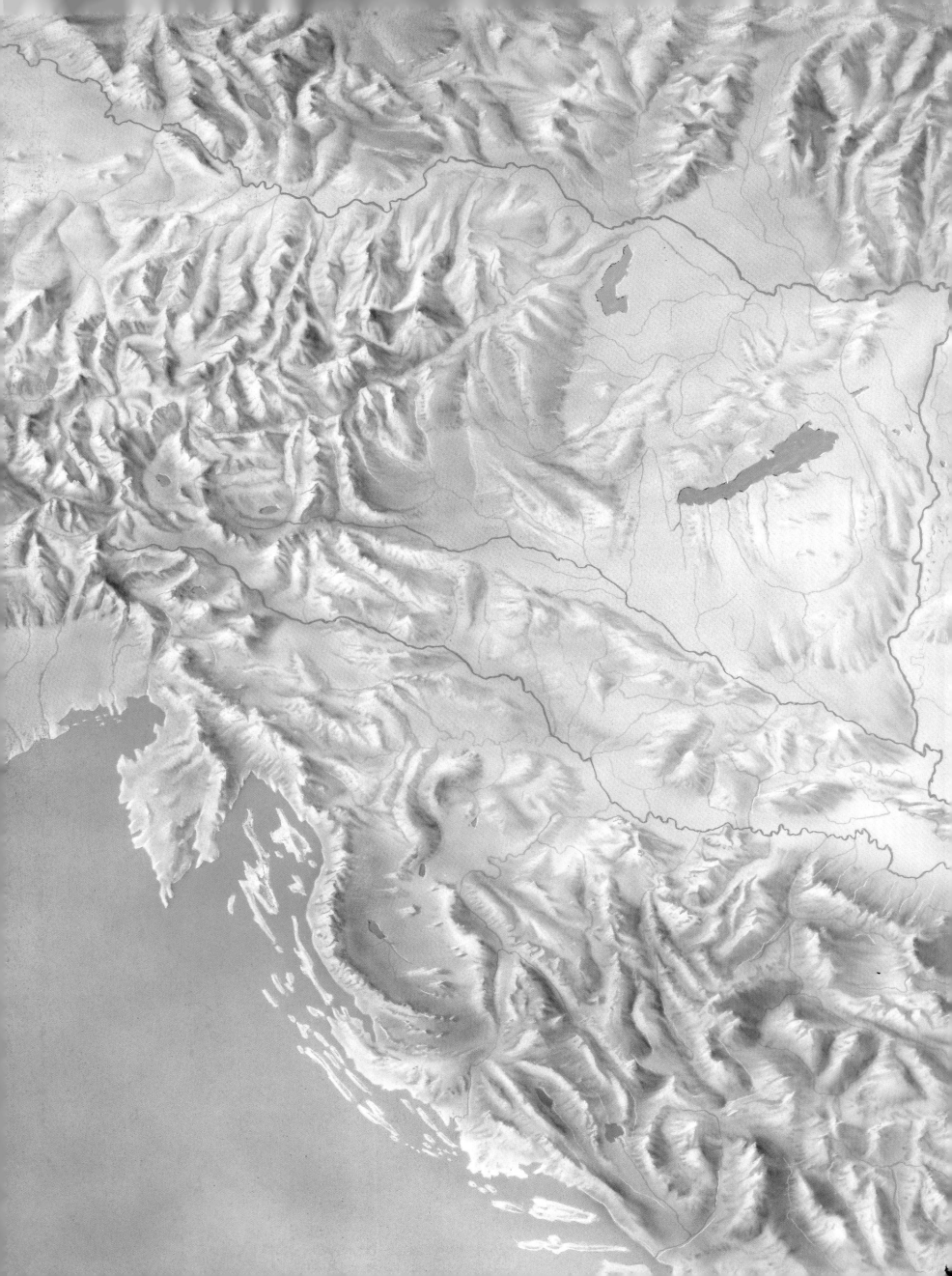

THE ✦ TIMES
ATLAS OF WORLD
HISTORY

EDITED BY GEOFFREY BARRACLOUGH

FOURTH EDITION
Edited by GEOFFREY PARKER

BCA

LONDON   NEW YORK   SYDNEY   TORONTO

This edition published 1994
by BCA by arrangement with
TIMES BOOKS
A Division of HarperCollins*Publishers*
77–85 Fulham Palace Road
Hammersmith
London W6 8JB

First edition published 1978
Reprinted with revisions 1979
Reprinted 1979, 1980, 1981, 1983
Second edition 1984
Reprinted 1985
Reprinted with revisions 1986
Third edition 1989
Reprinted 1992
Fourth edition 1993
Reprinted 1994 (twice)
Copyright © Times Books 1978, 1979,
1984, 1986, 1989, 1993, 1995

Maps:
Duncan Mackay, Norman Michael Fahy, Rex
Nicholls, Sue Paling, Hugh Penfold, Malcolm
Swanston, Cheryl Wilbraham, Alan Wormwell

Editorial Director: Barry Wickleman

Place names consultant: P J M Geelan

Map design and layout: Peter Sullivan

Fourth edition:
Artwork and typesetting by Swanston Graphics
Limited, Derby

Colour separations by City Ensign Limited, Hull

Editorial: Angus Cameron, Cicely Oliver,
Tessa Rose

Picture Research: Anne-Marie Ehrlich

Design and layout:
Ivan Dodd, Tracy Enever, Judith Clarke

Printed and bound in Italy by
Rotolito Lombarda, Milan

CN 5759

In addition to the contributors listed on pages 5 and
6 the publishers would also like to thank the
following for their generous advice and help:
Correlli Barnett, *Fellow and Keeper of the Archives,
Churchill College, Cambridge*; Professor C D Cowan,
*Director, School of Oriental and African Studies,
University of London*; J Morland Craig; Dr Elizabeth
Dunstan, *International African Institute*; Professor
John Erickson, *Director of Defence Studies, University
of Edinburgh*; Professor D W Harding, *Abercromby
Professor of Archaeology, University of Edinburgh*;
Professor David Hawkins, *School of Oriental and
African Studies, University of London*; Thomas M
Jordan, *Department of History, University of Illinois,
Urbana-Champaign*; Morton Keller, *Spector Professor
of History, Brandeis University, Massachusetts*;
Jonathan King *of the Museum of Mankind, London*;
Dr Michael Leifer, *Professor of International
Relations, London School of Economics*; George
Maddocks; Professor Roland Oliver, *School of
Oriental and African Studies, University of London*;
Professor P J Parish, *Emeritus Professor of American
History, Institute of United States Studies, University
of London*; Dr D W Phillipson, *Curator, Museum of
Archaeology and Anthropology, University of
Cambridge*; Professor M C Rickleffs, *Department of
History, Monash University, Australia*; Dr R L Sims,
School of Oriental and African Studies; Peter Sluglett,
*Lecturer in Modern Middle Eastern History, Durham
University*; Denis Mack Smith, *University of Oxford*;
Professor Jan van Houtte, *Department of History,
University of Louvain, Belgium*; Patricia A Wenzel,
*Department of History, University of Illinois, Urbana-
Champaign*; Dr Joachim Whaley, *University of
Cambridge*; Dr L R Wright, *Department of
Archaeology, University of Edinburgh*.

Contributors

Editor:
Geoffrey Barraclough
Late President, Historical
Association
Chichele Professor of
Modern History
University of Oxford

Editor, Third Edition:
Norman Stone
Professor of Modern History
University of Oxford

Editor, Fourth Edition:
Geoffrey Parker FBA
Robert A Lovett
Professor of Military
and Naval History
Yale University

F R Allchin
Emeritus Reader in Indian Studies
University of Cambridge

R W Van Alstyne
Late Distinguished Professor
of History
*Callison College
University of the Pacific, California*

David Arnold
Professor of the History of
South Asia
*School of Oriental and African Studies
University of London*

Anthony Atmore
Research Fellow
*School of Oriental and African Studies
University of London*

John Barber
Fellow of King's College
University of Cambridge

James R Barrett
Professor of History
*University of Illinois at
Urbana-Champaign*

Iris Barry
Formerly Research Student
*Institute of Archaeology
University of London*

Peter Bauer
Professor Emeritus
London School of Economics

Christopher Bayly
Professor of Modern Indian History
University of Cambridge

W G Beasley
Emeritus Professor of the History
of the Far East
*School of Oriental and African Studies
University of London*

Ralph Bennett
President of Magdalene College
University of Cambridge

A D H Bivar
Professor Emeritus
*School of Oriental and African Studies
University of London*

Brian Bond
Professor of Military History
*King's College
University of London*

David Boren
Department of War Studies
*King's College
University of London*

Hugh Borton
Formerly Professor of Japanese
and Director
*East Asian Institute
Columbia University, New York*

David Brading
Reader in Latin American History
University of Cambridge

Warwick Bray
Reader in Latin American
Archaeology
*Institute of Archaeology
University of London*

Michael G Broers
Lecturer in Modern History
University of Leeds

F R Bridge
Reader in International History
University of Leeds

Roy C Bridges
Professor of History
University of Aberdeen

Hugh Brogan
Reader in History
*Department of History
University of Essex*

Tom Brooking
Senior Lecturer in History
University of Otago, New Zealand

Ian Brown
Senior Lecturer in Economic History
*School of Oriental and African Studies
University of London*

Anthony Bryer
Professor of Byzantine Studies
and Director
*Centre of Byzantine,
Ottoman & Modern Greek Studies
University of Birmingham*

Muriel E Chamberlain
Professor of History
*University College of Swansea
University of Wales*

David G Chandler
Head of Department of War Studies
and International Affairs
*The Royal Military Academy,
Sandhurst*

John Channon
Senior Lecturer,
Russian Economic History
*School of Slavonic and
East European Studies
University of London*

Eric Christiansen
Fellow
*New College
University of Oxford*

Peter Coates
Lecturer in American History
University of Bristol

Irene Collins
Honorary Research Fellow in History
University of Liverpool

Jill Cook
Head of Quaternary Section
*Department of Prehistoric and
Romano-British Antiquities
The British Museum, London*

Michael Crawford
Professor of Ancient History
University College, London

James Cronin
Associate Professor of History
University of Wisconsin

Douglas Dakin
Emeritus Professor of History
University of London

John Darwin
Fellow
*Nuffield College
University of Oxford*

Ralph Davis
Late Professor of Economic History
University of Leicester

I E S Edwards
Formerly Keeper of Egyptian
Antiquities
The British Museum, London

Robert Evans
Professor of European History
University of Oxford

John Ferguson
Late President
*Selly Oak Colleges
Birmingham*

Felipe Fernández-Armesto
Faculty of Modern History
University of Oxford

Stefan Fisch
Lecturer in Modern History
University of Munich

David H Fischer
Warren Professor of History
Brandeis University, Massachusetts

John R Fisher
Professor of Modern History and
Latin American Studies and Dean of
the Faculty of Arts
University of Liverpool

Kate Fleet
*The Skilliter Centre for Ottoman
Studies
Newnham College
University of Cambridge*

Michael Flinn
Late President
The Economic History Society

Timothy Fox
Lecturer in Economics with
Reference to Japan
*School of Oriental and African Studies
University of London*

Alan Frost
Professor of History
La Trobe University, Melbourne

W J Gardner
Formerly Reader in History
*University of Canterbury,
New Zealand*

Carol Geldart
Formerly Adviser
*House of Commons
Foreign Affairs Committee*

John Gillingham
Senior Lecturer in Medieval History
*London School of Economics
University of London*

Martin Goodman
Reader in Jewish Studies
*Wolfson College
University of Oxford*

D G E Hall
Late Emeritus Professor of
South East Asian History
University of London

Norman Hammond
Professor of Archaeology
Rutgers University, New Jersey
and Archaeology Correspondent
The Times, London

John D Hargreaves
Emeritus Professor of History
University of Aberdeen

Jonathan Haslam
Fellow
*Corpus Christi College
University of Cambridge*

Ragnhild Hatton
Emeritus Professor of
International History
*London School of Economics
University of London*

M Havinden
Senior Lecturer in Social and
Economic History
University of Exeter

Harry Hearder
Professor Emeritus
University of Wales

W O Henderson
Formerly Reader in International
Economic History
University of Manchester

Colin J Heywood
Lecturer in the History of the Near
and Middle East
*School of Oriental and African Studies
University of London*

Sinclair Hood
Formerly Director
*British School of Archaeology,
Athens*

Albert Hourani
Late Honorary Fellow
*Magdalen and St Antony's Colleges
University of Oxford*

Henry Hurst
Lecturer in Classical Archaeology
University of Cambridge

Jonathan Israel
Professor of Dutch History and
Institutions
University of London

Edward James
Director
*Centre for Medieval Studies
University of York*

Colin Jones
Professor of History
University of Essex

Richard H Jones
Professor of History
Reed College, Oregon

Ulrich Kemper
*University of the Ruhr
Bochum, Germany*

Mark H Leff
Professor of History
*University of Illinois at
Urbana-Champaign*

Colin Lewis
Lecturer in Latin American
Economic History
London School of Economics

Karl Leyser
Formerly Chichele Professor of
Medieval History
University of Oxford

Wolfgang Liebeschuetz
Professor of Classics and
Ancient History
University of Nottingham

D Anthony Low
President of Clare Hall
Smuts Professor of the History of the
British Commonwealth
University of Cambridge

David Luscombe
Professor of Medieval History
University of Sheffield

John Lynch
Emeritus Professor of Latin
American History
University of London

James M McPherson
Professor of History
Princeton University

Isabel de Madriaga
Emeritus Professor of Russian
Studies
University of London

J P Mallory
Lecturer in Archaeology
The Queen's University, Belfast

P J Marshall
Rhodes Professor of Imperial
History
*King's College
University of London*

A R Michell
Lecturer in Economic History
*Department of Economic and
Social History
University of Hull*

Christopher D Morris
Professor of Archaeology
University of Glasgow

A E Musson
Professor of Economic History
University of Manchester

F S Northedge
Professor of International Relations
*London School of Economics
University of London*

D Wayne Orchiston
Senior Lecturer in Museum Studies
*Victoria College
Melbourne, Australia*

David Ormrod
Lecturer in Economic and
Social History
University of Kent at Canterbury

R J Overy
Reader in Modern History
*King's College
University of London*

J H Parry
Late Professor of Oceanic History
Harvard University

Thomas M Perry
Reader in Geography
University of Melbourne, Australia

Sidney Pollard
Honorary Senior Research Fellow
University of Sheffield

Avril Powell
Lecturer in History
*School of Oriental and African Studies
University of London*

T G E Powell
Late Professor of Prehistoric
Archaeology
University of Liverpool

John Poynter
Deputy Vice-Chancellor
University of Melbourne, Australia

Benjamin Ravid
Associate Professor of
Jewish History
Brandeis University, Massachusetts

Tapan Raychaudhuri
Reader in Modern South Asian
History
*St Antony's College
University of Oxford*

B H Reid
Research Associate
*Department of War Studies
King's College
University of London*

Michael Roaf
Senior Research Officer
Oxford Archaeological Unit

A N Ryan
Reader in History
University of Liverpool

Gören Rystad
Professor of History
Lund University, Sweden

H W F Saggs
Professor of Semitic Languages
University College, Cardiff

S B Saul
Vice-Chancellor
University of York

Peter Sawyer
Formerly Professor of
Medieval History
University of Leeds

Chris Scarre
*McDonald Institute
University of Cambridge*

Roger Schofield
Director
*ESRC Cambridge Group for the
History of Population and Social
Structure*

D J Schove
Late Principal
St David's College, Kent

H M Scott
Senior Lecturer in Modern History
*Department of Modern History
University of St Andrews, Scotland*

H H Scullard
Late Emeritus Professor of
Ancient History
*King's College
University of London*

Andrew Sharf
Professor of History
Bar Ilan University, Israel

Andrew Sherratt
Assistant Keeper of Antiquities
Ashmolean Museum, Oxford

R B Smith
Professor of the International
History of Asia
*School of Oriental and African Studies
University of London*

Frank C Spooner
Professor of Economic History
University of Durham

Jocelyn Statler
Adviser
*House of Commons
Foreign Affairs Committee*

L S Stavrianos
Adjunct Professor of History
University of California, San Diego

Zara Steiner
Fellow and College Lecturer
in History
*New Hall
University of Cambridge*

W C Sturtevant
Curator of North American
Ethnology
*Smithsonian Institute,
Washington DC*

Alan Sykes
Lecturer in Modern History
University of St Andrews, Scotland

Denis Taylor
Assistant Foreign Editor
The Times, London

E A Thompson
Emeritus Professor of Classics
University of Nottingham

Hugh Tinker
Formerly Professor of Politics
University of Lancaster

Malcolm Todd
Professor of Archaeology
University of Exeter

R C Trebilcock
Fellow and Director of Studies
*Pembroke College
University of Cambridge*

Hugh R Trevor-Roper
Formerly Master of Peterhouse
University of Cambridge

Denis C Twitchett
Professor of East Asian Studies
Princeton University, New Jersey

Nancy E van Deusen
Department of History
*University of Illinois at Urbana-
Champaign*

Frans von der Dunk
Lecturer
*Department of International Law
University of Leiden*

F R von der Mehden
Albert Thomas Professor of
Political Science
Rice University, Texas

Ernst Wangermann
Reader in Modern History
University of Leeds

Geoffrey Warner
Visiting Senior Fellow
*Department of Political and
International Studies
University of Birmingham*

D Cameron Watt
Stevenson Professor of
International History
University of London

Bodo Wiethoff
Professor of Chinese History
*University of the Ruhr
Bochum, Germany*

D S M Williams
Lecturer in the History of
Asiatic Russia
*School of Slavonic and
East European Studies
University of London*

Glyn Williams
Professor of History
*Queen Mary and Westfield College
University of London*

H P Willmott
Visiting Professor in Naval History
*Department of Military Strategy
and Operations
National War College,
Washington DC*

David M Wilson
Former Director
The British Museum, London

George D Winius
Lecturer in the History of Spain
and Portugal
*Centre of the History of European
Expansion
University of Leiden*

6

Contents

Contents *CONTINUED*

Contents CONTINUED

Contents CONTINUED

Introduction

Significant changes have occurred during the past half century in our conception of the scope and pattern of world history. *The Times Atlas of World History* sets out to reflect these changes and thus to present a view of world history appropriate to the age in which we live.

Most of the hundreds of historical atlases published before 1978 suffered from 'Eurocentricity', that is to say from a tendency to concentrate on the history of Europe (particularly of western Europe) and to refer to other regions or countries only when and where Europe impinged upon them. *The Times Atlas of World History*, first published in 1978, breaks away from this traditional western view because such an approach is both misleading and untenable. It aims instead to present a view of history that is world-wide in conception and presentation and which does justice, without prejudice or favour, to the achievements of all peoples, in all ages and in all quarters of the globe.

As Geoffrey Barraclough wrote in his introduction to the first edition of this Atlas in 1978:

"It is, of course, true that our knowledge of the past is unequal; but while we have tried to avoid the error of allotting less space to the history of the West than its achievements demand, no people has consciously been relegated to the margin of history and none singled out for specially favoured treatment. We have laid particular emphasis upon the great world civilizations and their links and interplay; but we have not neglected the peoples outside the historic centres of civilization – for example, the nomads of central Asia – whose impact on history was more profound than is generally appreciated.

When we say this is an atlas of world history, we mean that it is not simply a series of national histories loosely strung together. In other words, it is concerned less with particular events in the history of particular countries than with broad movements – for example, the spread of the great world religions spanning whole continents. There are many excellent specialized atlases of national history. It is no part of our intention to compete with them; nor would it have been possible to do so, had we wished, without dislocating the balance of the present work.

Any atlas seeking to present a conspectus of world history in approximately 130 plates must be selective. In singling out topics for inclusion we have adhered to the principle of selecting what was important then rather than what seems important now. Any other criterion, we believe, would put history through a distorting mirror.

If we have tried to ensure that the Atlas reflects the relative importance of different civilizations and the balance of world forces at any given moment in time, it is not merely out of piety towards the past but because we believe that, in the world as constituted today, the histories of India, China and Japan, and of other countries in Asia and Africa, are as relevant as the history of Europe. In the same way, and for the same reason, we have tried to hold a balance between eastern Europe and western Europe, and also to do justice to civilizations, such as the Ottoman Empire, which too often are treated as peripheral. It would be vain to hope that we have achieved a balance which all will find acceptable; but we believe that, granted the limits of space, this Atlas can fairly be described as comprehensive and ecumenical. Such, at least, has been our aim and endeavour."

This remains the aim and endeavour for the Fourth Edition of this *Atlas*. In the 15 years since its first appearance, over one-million copies have been sold world-wide in 13 different languages, including Hebrew, Croatian and Chinese. *The Times Atlas of World History* has thus become a publishing classic. However, in spite of the many changes and updates made in the Revised Edition of 1984, carried out under the direction of Geoffrey Barraclough, and in the Third Edition of 1989, superintended by Norman Stone, new material and fresh perspectives have arisen. Every map has therefore once again been re-examined by expert consultants to ensure the highest standard of accuracy, and many thousands of revisions and corrections have been made in order to incorporate the results of the most recent research. The Index of place names has been amplified and re-set, the Chronology updated, and the Glossary revised. New projections have been introduced where appropriate, and maps redrawn.

Particular attention has been paid to the prehistoric section, for archaeology is a vital, living science and its findings constantly modify our historical view of the distant past. At the other end of the time-scale, the plates dealing with the period since 1945 have been radically revised: two entirely new spreads have been added and all the rest have been updated, and in some cases radically altered, to take account of developments since 1978 and to reflect more closely the global situation as we approach the 21st century. But this is in no sense an atlas of current affairs, and it makes no claim to keep up – if that were possible – with the changing panorama of contemporary international politics.

And yet, for all the changes, this Atlas remains essentially the work of the late Geoffrey Barraclough. His energy was formidable; although (or perhaps because) he was a medievalist by training, with classic works of meticulous scholarship to his name, he became increasingly interested in modern times on a world-wide scale. His enthusiasm and the conciseness with which he summed up complicated matters were central to the success of this Atlas. He drew up the original scheme for the Atlas in 1973, following discussions with L S Stavrianos and the late A J Toynbee (from both of whom he received not only advice and criticism but also encouragement), and proceeded to direct the work of almost 100 expert contributors as they strove to present both familiar and unfamiliar material in a new and arresting way. As a result, the plates in this volume are all original and several deal with topics that have never been treated cartographically before.

Historical atlases have traditionally been concerned with political events, wars and changes in political geography. *The Times Atlas of World History* pays considerable attention to such topics, and particularly to economic developments (which are covered in tables and charts as well as in maps). Cultural and intellectual history presents more of a challenge to cartographic treatment and, to quote Professor Barraclough:

"... there are some subjects which ideally we should have wished to include and were forced reluctantly to omit. But we have sought in compensation to indicate the cultural connotations – and at the same time to make the presentation more vivid – by including, where space permits, visual records of the times or of historically significant tools, artifacts and other characteristic products of the peoples or civilizations with which the plates are concerned. Each plate also includes a commentary by a leading expert, providing the background to the maps and diagrams.

All atlases involve a number of specialized skills and disciplines, and none more so than an historical atlas. We have sought to make use of all available cartographic techniques, and in particular to emphasize different historical situations by employing a variety of different projections; thus a map of Islam, to take but one example, has been deliberately centred on Mecca, and the Mediterranean world has been viewed from there – as it might have been viewed by an Arab in the 7th century. In some instances we have used elaborate relief maps; in others we have deliberately simplified, sacrificing geographical detail to bring out the main historical facts. The results may not always be familiar, but we believe they may open new insights."

The essence of history, as Geoffrey Barraclough realized, is change and movement over time; and the historian's principal mission is therefore to discern the static from the dynamic, the aberration from the trend, and the constant from the contingent. So instead of presenting a series of static pictures of particular situations at particular moments in the past, *The Times Atlas of World History* seeks to emphasize change, expansion and contraction. It endeavours to convey a sense of the past as a continuing process and thus provide a fresh perspective on today's world which will meet the requirements and interests of present-day readers in all parts of the globe.

Geoffrey Parker
April 1993

THE following 12 pages present a chronological synopsis of the major events in world history. The entries, necessarily abbreviated, are set out in columns under regional headings which vary from period to period according to shifts in historical geography. A separate column lists important cultural events (in the broadest sense, including not only music, art and literature but also science and technology) in all regions of the world. Together with the Glossary and with the geographical Index, page 335, the Chronology provides a key to the individual plates and maps, designed to help the reader to place the events narrated there in the broader context of world history. It also indicates (in bold type) the key events in different regions at different times, and the specific contributions of each to the development of civilization and of civilized life.

The calendar of events starts with the beginnings of agriculture around the year 9000 BC. For a time-scale of prehistory refer to the time chart on page 36.

A world chronology

Asia excluding the Near East	Europe	Near East and North Africa	Other regions	Culture and technology
		c.9000-8000 Domestication of animals and crops (wheat and barley), **the 'Neolithic Revolution'**, in the Near East; beginning of permanent settlements	**c.9000** Hunters spread south through Americas	
		8350-7350 Jericho founded: first walled town in the world (10 acres)		
		c.7000 Early experiments with copper ores in Anatolia		
		6250-5400 Çatal Hüyük (Anatolia) flourishes: largest city of its day (32 acres)		
	c.6500 First farming in Greece and Aegean; spreads up Danube to Hungary (c.5500), Germany and Low Countries (c.4500) and along Mediterranean coast to France (c.5000). Farmers cross to Britain c.4000	**c.5000** Colonization of Mesopotamian alluvial plain by groups practising irrigation		**c.6000** First known pottery and woollen textiles (Çatal Hüyük)
c.6000 Rice cultivation (Thailand)		**c.5000** Agricultural settlements in Egypt		
		c.4000 Bronze casting begins in Near East; first use of plough		
c.3500 Earliest Chinese city at Liang-ch'eng chen (Lung-shan culture)				**c.3500** Construction of Megalithic tombs and circles in Brittany, Iberian peninsula and British Isles (Stonehenge c.2000)
				c.3500 Invention of wheel and plough (Mesopotamia) and sail (Egypt)
	3200-2000 Early Cycladic civilization in Aegean	**c.3100** King Menes unites Egypt; dynastic period begins		**c.3100** Pictographic writing invented in Sumer
c.3000 Use of bronze in Thailand	**c.3000** Spread of copper-working	**c.3000** Development of major cities in Sumer	**c.3000** Arable farming techniques spread to central Africa	
			c.3000 First pottery in Americas (Ecuador and Colombia)	
c.2750 Growth of civilizations in Indus valley		**c.2685** The 'Old Kingdom' (pyramid age) of Egypt begins (to 2180 BC)		**c.2590** Cheops builds great pyramid at Giza
		2371-2230 Sargon I of Agade founds first empire in world history	**c.2500** Desiccation of Saharan region begins	**c.2500 Domestication of horse** (central Asia)
	c.2000 Indo-European speakers (early Greeks) invade and settle Peloponnese; beginnings of 'Minoan' civilization in Crete	**c.2000** Hittites invade Anatolia and found empire (1650)	**c.2000** First metal-working in Peru	**c.2000** Use of sail on seagoing vessels (Aegean)
		c.1800 Shamshi-Adad founds Assyrian state	**c.2000** Settlement of Melanesia by immigrants from Indonesia begins	
		c.1750 Hammurabi founds Babylonian Empire		
c.1600 First urban civilization in China, Shang Bronze Age culture	**c.1600 Beginnings of Mycenaean civilization in Greece**	**c.1567** Kamose and Amosis I expel Hyksos invaders and inaugurate Egyptian 'New Kingdom' (to 1090 BC)		
c.1550 Aryans destroy Indus valley civilization and settle in N India				**c.1500** Ideographic script in use in China; 'Linear B' script in Crete and Greece; Hittite cuneiform in Anatolia
	c.1450 Destruction of Minoan Crete			**c.1450** Development of Brahma worship; composition of Vedas (earliest Indian literature) begins
				c.1370 Akhenaten enforces monotheistic sun worship in Egypt
			c.1300 Settlers of Melanesia reach Fiji, later spreading to Western Polynesia	
	c.1200 Mycenaean civilization in Greece collapses	**c.1200** Collapse of Hittite Empire		**c.1200 Beginning of Jewish religion (worship of Yahweh)**
		c.1200 Jewish exodus from Egypt and settlement in Palestine		
		1166 Death of Ramesses III, last great pharaoh of Egypt		
		c.1150 King David unites Israel and Judah	**c.1150 Beginning of Olmec civilization in Mexico**	
		c.1100 Spread of Phoenicians in Mediterranean region (to 700 BC)		**c.1100** Phoenicians develop alphabetic script (basis of all modern European scripts)
c.1027 Shang dynasty in China overthrown by Chou; Aryans in India expand eastwards down Ganges valley	**c.1000** Etruscans arrive in Italy			
		c.840 Rise of Urartu	**c.900** Foundation of kingdom of Kush (Nubia)	
c.800 Aryans expand southwards in India		**814** Traditional date for foundation of Phoenician colony at Carthage		**800-400** Composition of Upanishads, Sanskrit religious treatises
771 Collapse of Chou feudal order in China				**776** First Olympic Games held in Greece
	753 Traditional date for foundation of Rome			
	c.750 Greek city states begin to found settlements throughout Mediterranean			**c.750** Amos, first great prophet in Israel
		721-705 Assyria at height of military power		**c.750** Homer's *Iliad* and Hesiod's poetry first written down
	c.700 Scythians spread from central Asia to eastern Europe			
	c.700-450 Hallstatt culture in central and western Europe: mixed farming, iron tools			

Asia excluding the Near East

c.660 Jimmu, legendary first emperor of Japan

c.650 Introduction of iron technology in China

c.500 Sinhalese, an Aryan people, reach Ceylon

403-221 'Warring States' period in China

322 Chandragupta founds Mauryan Empire at Magadha, India

262 Asoka, Mauryan emperor (273-236), converted to Buddhism

221 Shih Huang-ti, of Ch'in dynasty, unites China (to 207)

202 Han dynasty reunites China; capital at Chang-an

185 Demetrius and Menander, kings of Bactria, conquer northwest India

Europe

c.650 Rise of 'Tyrants' in Corinth and other Greek cities

510 Foundation of Roman Republic

c.505 Cleisthenes establishes democracy in Athens

490 Battle of Marathon: Persian attack on Athens defeated

480 Battles of Salamis and Plataea (479): Persian invasion of Greece defeated

478 Foundation of Confederacy of Delos, later transformed into Athenian Empire

c.450 La Tène culture emerges in central and western Europe

431-404 Peloponnesian War between Sparta and Athens

356 Philip II, king of Macedon

338 Battle of Chaeronea gives Macedon control of Greece

290 Rome completes conquest of central Italy

241 First Punic War (264-241) with Carthage gives Rome control of Sicily

218 Second Punic War (218-201): Hannibal of Carthage invades Italy

206 Rome gains control of Spain

168 Rome defeats and partitions Macedonia

146 Rome sacks Corinth; Greece under Roman domination

Near East and North Africa

671 Assyrian conquest of Egypt; introduction of iron-working

612 Sack of Nineveh by Medes and Scythians; collapse of Assyrian power

586 Babylonian captivity of the Jews

c.550 Cyrus II (the Great) of Persia defeats Medes and founds Persian Empire

521 Persia under Darius I (the Great) rules from the Nile to the Indus

c.520 Darius I completes canal connecting Nile with Red Sea

494 Persians suppress Ionian revolt

334 Alexander the Great (of Macedon) invades Asia Minor; conquers Egypt (332), Persia (330) reaches India (329)

323 Death of Alexander: empire divided between Macedon, Egypt, Syria and Pergamum

304 Ptolemy I, Macedonian governor of Egypt, founds independent dynasty (to 30 BC)

247 Arsaces I founds kingdom of Parthia

149 Third Punic War (149-146): Rome destroys Carthage and founds province of Africa

Other regions

c.500 Iron-making techniques spread to sub-Saharan Africa

500-AD200 Period of Nok culture in northern Nigeria

Culture and technology

c.650 First coins: Lydia (Asia Minor) and Greece (c.600)

c.650 Rise of Greek lyric poetry (Sappho born c.612)

585 Thales of Miletus predicts an eclipse: beginnings of Greek rationalist philosophy

558 Zoroaster (Zarathustra) begins his prophetic work

550 Zoroastrianism becomes official religion of Persia

c.540 Deutero-Isaiah, Hebrew prophet, at work during exile in Babylon

c.530 Pythagoras, mathematician and mystic, active

528 Traditional date for death of Mahavira, founder of Jain sect

520 Death of Lao-tzu (born 605), traditional founder of Taoism

c.500 Achaemenid Persians transmit food plants (rice, peach, apricot, etc.) to western Asia

c.500 Caste system established in India

c.500 First hieroglyphic writing in Mexico (Monte Albán)

486 Death of Siddhartha Gautama, founder of Buddhism

479-338 Period of Greek classical culture. Poetry: Pindar (518-438); drama: Aeschylus (525-456), Sophocles (496-406), Euripides (480-406), Aristophanes (c.440-385); history: Herodotus (c.486-429), Thucydides (c.460-400); medicine: Hippocrates (c.470-406); philosophy: Socrates (469-399), Plato (c.427-347), Aristotle (384-322); sculpture: Phidias (c.490-417), Praxiteles (c.364); architecture: Parthenon (446-431)

479 Death of Confucius

350-200 Great period of Chinese thought: formation of Taoist, Legalist and Confucian schools; early scientific discoveries

312/11 Start of Seleucid era; first continuous historical dating-system

c.290 Foundation of Alexandrian library

277 Death of Ch'ü Yüan (born 343), earliest major Chinese poet

Asia excluding the Near East

141 Wu-ti, Chinese emperor, expands Han power in eastern Asia

c.138 Chang Chien explores central Asia

130 Yüeh-chih tribe (Tocharians) establish kingdom in Transoxania

c.112 Opening of 'Silk Road' across Central Asia linking China to West

AD9 Wang Mang deposes Han dynasty in China

AD25 Restoration of Han dynasty; capital at Lo-yang

c.AD60 Rise of Kushan Empire

AD78-102 Kanishka, Kushan emperor, gains control of north India

AD91 Chinese defeat Hsiung-nu in Mongolia

184 'Yellow Turbans' rebellions disrupt Han China

220 End of Han dynasty: China splits into three states

245 Chinese envoys visit Funan (modern Cambodia), first major Southeast Asian state

304 Hsiung-nu invade China; China fragmented to 589

320 Chandragupta I founds Gupta Empire in northern India

c.350 Hunnish invasions of Persia and India

Europe

133-122 Failure of reform movement in Rome, led by Tiberius and Gaius Gracchus

89 All Italy receives Roman citizenship

49 Julius Caesar conquers Gaul

47-45 Civil war in Rome; Julius Caesar becomes sole ruler (45)

31 Battle of Actium: Octavian (later Emperor Augustus) establishes domination over Rome

27 Collapse of Roman Republic and beginning of Empire

AD43 Roman invasion of Britain

AD117 Roman Empire at its greatest extent

165 Smallpox epidemic ravages Roman empire

212 Roman citizenship conferred on all free inhabitants of Empire

238 Gothic incursions into Roman Empire begin

293 Emperor Diocletian reorganizes Roman Empire

330 Capital of Roman Empire transferred to Constantinople

370 First appearance of Huns in Europe

378 Visigoths defeat and kill Roman emperor at Adrianople

406 Vandals invade and ravage Gaul and Spain (409)

410 Visigoths invade Italy, sack Rome and overrun Spain

Near East and North Africa

64 Pompey the Great conquers Syria; end of Seleucid Empire

53 Battle of Carrhae: Parthia defeats Roman invasion

30 Death of Antony and Cleopatra: Egypt becomes Roman province

AD44 Mauretania (Morocco) annexed by Rome

AD 70 Romans destroy the Jewish Temple in Jerusalem

AD116 Roman Emperor Trajan completes conquest of Mesopotamia

132 Jewish rebellion against Rome leads to 'diaspora' (dispersal of Jews)

224 Foundation of Sasanian dynasty in Persia

429 Vandal kingdom in North Africa

Other regions

100 Camel introduced into Saharan Africa

c.AD50 Expansion of kingdom of Axum (Ethiopia) begins

c.150 Berber and Mandingo tribes begin domination of the Sudan

c.250 Kingdom of Axum (Ethiopia) gains control of Red Sea trade

c.300 Rise of Hopewell Indian chiefdoms in North America and of Maya civilization in Mesoamerica; large civilized states in Mexico (Teotihuacán, Monte Albán, El Tajín)

c.300 Settlement of eastern Polynesia

Culture and technology

142 Completion of first stone bridge over river Tiber

79 Death of Ssu-ma Ch'ien, Chinese historian

46 Julius Caesar reforms calendar; Julian calendar in use until AD 1582 (England 1752, Russia 1917)

31-AD14 The Augustan Age at Rome: Virgil (70-19), Horace (65-27), Ovid (43-AD17), Livy (59-AD17)

5 Building of national shrine of Ise in Japan

c.AD30 Jesus of Nazareth, founder of Christianity, crucified in Jerusalem

AD46-57 Missionary journeys of St Paul

c.AD90-120 Great period of Silver Latin: Tacitus (c.55-120), Juvenal (c.55-c. 140), Martial (c.38-102)

AD105 First use of paper in China

c.125 Third Buddhist conference: widespread acceptance of the sculptural Buddha image

150 Earliest surviving Sanskrit inscription (India)

c.150 Buddhism reaches China

c.200 Completion of *Mishnah* (codification of Jewish Law)

c.200 Indian epic poems: *Mahabharata*, *Ramayana* and *Bhagavad Gita*

c.200-250 Development of Christian theology: Tertullian (c.160-220), Clement (c.150-c.215), Origen (185-254)

271 Magnetic compass in use (China)

274 Unconquered Sun proclaimed god of Roman Empire

276 Crucifixion of Mani (born 215), founder of Manichaean sect

285 Confucianism introduced into Japan

c.300 Foot-stirrup invented in Asia

313 Edict of Milan: Christianity granted toleration in Roman Empire

325 Axum destroys kingdom of Meröe (Kush)

350 Buddhist cave temples, painting, sculpture (to 800)

404 Latin version of Bible (Vulgate) completed

413 Kumaragupta; great literary era in India

426 Augustine of Hippo completes *City of God*

Asia excluding the Near East

480 Gupta Empire overthrown

589 China reunified by Sui dynasty

607 Unification of Tibet

617 China in state of anarchy

624 China united under T'ang dynasty

c.640 Empire of Sri Harsha in northern India

645 Fujiwara's 'Taika Reform' remodels Japan on Chinese lines

658 Maximum extension of Chinese power in central Asia; protectorates in Afghanistan, Kashmir, Sogdiana and Oxus valley

665 Tibetan expansion into Turkestan, Tsinghai

676 Korea unified under Silla

712 Arabs conquer Sind and Samarkand

745 Beginnings of Uighur Empire in Mongolia

751 Battle of Talas River: sets boundary of China and Abbasid caliphate

755 An Lu-shan's rebellion in China

794 Japanese capital moved to Kyoto from Nara

c.802 Jayaxarman II establishes Angkorean kingdom (Cambodia)

836 Struggle for control of Indian Deccan

840 Collapse of Uighur Empire

842 Tibetan Empire disintegrates

Europe

449 Angles, Saxons and Jutes begin conquest of Britain

476 Deposition of last Roman emperor in West

486 Frankish kingdom founded by Clovis

493 Ostrogoths take power in Italy

533 Justinian restores Roman power in North Africa and Italy (552)

c.542 Bubonic plague ravages Europe

568 Lombard conquest of north Italy

590 Gregory the Great expands papal power

610 Accession of East Roman Emperor Heraclius; beginning of Hellenization of (East) Roman Empire, henceforth known as Byzantine Empire

680 Bulgars invade Balkans

687 Battle of Tertry: Carolingians dominate Frankish state

711 Muslim invasion of Spain

732 Battle of Poitiers halts Arab expansion in western Europe

751 Lombards overrun Ravenna, last Byzantine foothold in northern Italy

774 Charlemagne conquers northern Italy

793 Viking raids begin

800 Charlemagne crowned emperor in Rome; beginning of new Western (later Holy Roman) Empire

843 Treaty of Verdun: partition of Carolingian Empire

Near East and North Africa

531 Accession of Chosroes I (died 579): Sasanian Empire at its greatest extent

611 Persian armies capture Antioch and Jerusalem and overrun Asia Minor (to 626)

622 *Hegira* of Mohammed; beginning of Islamic calendar

632 Death of Mohammed: Arab expansion begins

636 Arabs overrun Syria

637 Arabs overrun Iraq

641 Arabs conquer Egypt and begin conquest of North Africa

718 Arab siege of Constantinople repulsed

750 Abbasid caliphate established

809 Death of caliph Harun al-Rashid

Other regions

c.600 Apogee of Maya civilization

c.700 Rise of empire of Ghana

c.800 First settlers reach Easter Island and New Zealand (850) from Polynesia

c.850 Collapse of Classic Maya culture in Mesoamerica

Culture and technology

497 Franks converted to Christianity

c.520 Rise of mathematics in India: Aryabhata and Varamihara invent decimal system

529 Rule of St Benedict regulates Western monasticism

534 Justinian promulgates Legal Code

538 Hagia Sophia, Constantinople, consecrated

c.550 Buddhism introduced into Japan from Korea

563 St Columba founds monastery of Iona: beginning of Irish mission to Anglo-Saxons

607 Chinese cultural influence in Japan begins

625 Mohammed begins his prophetic mission

c.645 Buddhism reaches Tibet (first temple 651)

c.690 Arabic replaces Greek and Persian as language of Umayyad administration

692 Completion of Dome of Rock in Jerusalem, first great monument of Islamic architecture

c.700 Buddhist temples built at Nara, Japan

700 Golden age of Chinese poetry: Li Po (701-62), Tu Fu (712-70), Po Chü-i (772-846)

722 St Boniface's mission to Germany

725 Bede (673-735) introduces dating by Christian era

c.730 Printing in China

751 Paper-making spreads from China to Muslim world and Europe (1150)

760 Arabs adopt Indian numerals and develop algebra and trigonometry

782 Alcuin of York (735-804) organizes education in Carolingian Empire: 'Carolingian renaissance'

788 Great mosque in Córdoba

c.800 Temple at Borobudur (Java) constructed by Shailendra kings

853 First printed book in China

Asia excluding the Near East

907 Last T'ang emperor deposed

916 Khitan kingdom in Mongolia founded

918 State of Koryo founded in Korea

939 Vietnam independent of China

947 Khitans overrun northern China, establish Liao dynasty with capital at Peking

967 Fujiwara domination of Japan begins

979 Sung dynasty reunites China

1018 Mahmud of Ghazni sacks Kanauj and breaks power of Hindu states

1018 Rajendra Chola conquers Ceylon

1021 Cholas invade Bengal

1038 Tangut tribes form Hsi-hsia state in northwest China

1044 Establishment of first Burmese national state at Pagan

1126 Chin overrun northern China; Sung rule restricted to south

1170 Apogee of Srivijaya kingdom in Java under Shailendra dynasty

1175 Muizzuddin Muhammad of Ghazni, founds first Muslim empire in India

c.1180 Angkor Empire (Cambodia) at greatest extent

1185 Minamoto warlords supreme in Japan

Europe

862 Novgorod founded by Rurik the Viking

871 Alfred, king of Wessex, halts Danish advance in England

882 Capital of Russia moved to Kiev

911 Vikings granted duchy of Normandy

929 Abdurrahman III establishes caliphate at Córdoba

955 Otto I defeats Magyars at Lechfeld

959 Unification of England under Eadgar

960 Mieszko I founds Polish state

962 Otto I of Germany crowned emperor in Rome

972 Beginning of Hungarian state under Duke Geisa

983 Great Slav rebellion against German eastward expansion

987 Accession of Capetians in France

1014 Battle of Clontarf breaks Viking domination of Ireland

1016 Cnut the Great rules England, Denmark and Norway (to 1035)

1018 Byzantines annex Bulgaria (to 1185)

1031 Collapse of caliphate of Córdoba

1054 Schism between Greek and Latin Christian churches begins

1066 Norman conquest of England

1071 Fall of Bari completes Norman conquest of Byzantine Italy

1073 Gregory VII elected Pope: beginning of conflict of Empire and papacy

1125 Renewal of German eastwards expansion

1154 Accession of Henry II: Angevin Empire in England and France

1198 Innocent III elected Pope

Near East and North Africa

936 Caliphs of Baghdad lose effective power

969 Fatimids conquer Egypt and found Cairo

1055 Seljuk Turks take Baghdad

1056 Almoravids conquer North Africa and southern Spain

1071 Battle of Manzikert: defeat of Byzantium by Seljuk Turks

1096 First Crusade: Franks invade Anatolia and Syria, and found crusader states

1135 Almohads dominant in northwest Africa and Muslim Spain

1171 Saladin defeats Fatimids and conquers Egypt

1188 Saladin destroys Frankish crusader kingdoms

Other regions

c.990 Expansion of Inca Empire (Peru)

c.1000 Vikings colonize Greenland and discover America (Vinland)

c.1000 First Iron Age settlement at Zimbabwe (Rhodesia)

1076 Almoravids destroy kingdom of Ghana

c.1100 Toltecs build their capital at Tula (Mexico)

c.1150 Beginnings of Yoruba city states (Nigeria)

c.1200 Rise of empire of Mali in west Africa

Culture and technology

863 Creation of Cyrillic alphabet in eastern Europe

865 Bulgars and Serbians accept Christianity

c.890 Japanese cultural renaissance: novels, landscape painting and poetry

910 Abbey of Cluny founded

935 Text of Koran finalized

c.1000 Great age of Chinese painting and ceramics

1020 Completion of *Tale of Genji* by Lady Murasaki

1020 Death of Firdausi, writer of Persian national epic, *The Shahnama*

1037 Death of Avicenna, Persian philosopher

c.1045 Moveable type printing invented in China

1094 Composition of old Javanese *Ramayana* by Yogisvara

c.1100 First universities in Europe: Salerno (medicine), Bologna (law). Paris (theology and philosophy)
c.1100 Omar Khayyam composes *Rubaiyyat*

1111 Death of al-Ghazali, Muslim theologian

c.1150 Hindu temple of Angkor Wat (Cambodia) built

1154 Chartres Cathedral begun; **Gothic architecture spreads through western Europe**
c.1160 development of European vernacular verse: Chanson de Roland (c.1100), El Cid (c.1150), Parzifal, Tristan (c.1200)

1193 Zen Buddhist order founded in Japan

1198 Death of Averroës, Arab scientist and philosopher

Asia excluding the Near East

1206 Mongols under Genghis Khan begin conquest of Asia

1206 Sultanate of Delhi founded

c.1220 Emergence of first Thai kingdom

1234 Mongols destroy Chin Empire

1264 Kublai Khan founds Yüan dynasty in China

1279 Mongols conquer southern China

1333 End of Minamoto shogunate: civil war in Japan

c.1341 'Black Death' starts in Asia

1349 First Chinese settlement at Singapore; beginning of Chinese expansion in Southeast Asia

1350 Golden age of Majapahit Empire in Java

1368 Ming dynasty founded in China

1370 Hindu state of Vijayanagar dominant in southern India

1380 Timur (Tamerlane) begins conquests

1392 Korea becomes independent

1394 Thais invade Cambodia; Khmer capital moved to Phnom Penh

1398 Timur invades India and sacks Delhi

c.1400 Establishment of Malacca as a major commercial port of SE Asia.

1405 Chinese voyages in Indian Ocean

1428 Chinese expelled from Vietnam

1471 Vietnamese southward expansion: Champa annexed

Europe

1204 Fourth Crusade: Franks conquer Byzantium and found Latin Empire

1212 Battle of Las Navas de Tolosa

1215 Magna Carta: King John makes concessions to English barons

1236 Mongols invade and conquer Russia (1239)

1241 Mongols invade Poland, Hungary, Bohemia

1242 Alexander Nevsky defeats Teutonic Order

1250 d. of Emperor Frederick II. collapse of Imperial power in Germany and Italy

1261 Greek empire restored in Constantinople

1291 Beginnings of Swiss Confederation

1309 Papacy moves from Rome to Avignon

1314 Battle of Bannockburn: Scotland defeats England

1325 Ivan I begins recovery of Moscow

1337 Hundred Years' War between France and England begins

1348 Black Death from Asia ravages Europe

1360 Peace of Brétigny ends first phase of Hundred Years' War

1361 Ottomans capture Adrianople

1378 Great Schism in West (to 1417)

1386 Union of Poland and Lithuania

1389 Battle of Kosovo: Ottomans gain control of Balkans

1397 Union of Kalmar (Scandinavia)

1410 Battle of Tannenberg: Poles defeat Teutonic Knights

1415 Battle of Agincourt: Henry V of England resumes attack on France

1428 Joan of Arc: beginning of French revival

1453 England loses Continental possessions (except Calais)

1453 Ottoman Turks capture Constantinople: end of Byzantine Empire

1475 Burgundy at height of power (Charles the Bold)

1478 Ivan III, first Russian tsar, subdues Novgorod and throws off Mongol yoke (1480)

Near East and North Africa

1228 Hafsid dynasty established at Tunis

1258 Mongols sack Baghdad; end of Abbasid caliphate

1299 Ottoman Turks begin expansion in Anatolia

1402 Battle of Ankara: Timur defeats Ottomans in Anatolia

Other regions

c.1200 Emergence of Hausa city states (Nigeria)

c.1200 Aztecs occupy valley of Mexico

c.1250 Mayapan becomes dominant Maya city of Yucatán

c.1300 Kanuri Empire moves capital from Kanem to Borno

c.1300 Emergence of empire of Benin (Nigeria)

1325 Rise of Aztecs in Mexico: Tenochtitlán founded

1415 Portuguese capture Ceuta: beginning of Portugal's African empire

1430 Construction of great stone enclosure at Zimbabwe (Rhodesia)

1434 Portuguese explore south of Cape Bojador

c.1450 Apogee of Songhay Empire; university at Timbuktu

c.1450 Monomatapa Empire founded

1470 Incas conquer Chimú kingdom

Culture and technology

c.1215 Islamic architecture spreads to India

1226 Death of St Francis of Assisi

1274 Death of St Thomas Aquinas: his *Summa Theologica* defines Christian dogma

1275 Marco Polo (1254-1324) arrives in China

1290 Spectacles invented (Italy)

c.1320 Cultural revival in Italy: Dante (1265-1321), Giotto (1276-1337), Petrarch (1304-71)

1339 Building of Kremlin (Moscow)

c.1350 Japanese cultural revival

1377 Death of Ibn Battuta (born 1309), Arab geographer and traveller

1387 Lithuania converted to Christianity

1392 Death of Hafiz, Persian lyric poet

1400 Death of Chaucer, first great poet in English

1406 Death of Ibn Khaldun, Muslim historian

1445 Johannes Gutenberg (1397-1468) prints first book in Europe

Asia

1498 Vasco da Gama: first European sea-voyage to India and back

1500 Shah Ismail founds Safavid dynasty in Persia

1511 Portuguese take Malacca

1516 Ottomans overrun Syria, Egypt and Arabia (1517)

1526 Battle of Panipat: Babur conquers kingdom of Delhi and founds Mughal dynasty

1550 Mongol Altan-khan invades northern China; Japanese 'pirate' raids in China

1557 Portuguese established at Macao (China)

1565 Akbar extends Mughal power to Deccan

1581 Yermak begins Russian conquest of Siberia

1584 Phra Narai creates independent Siam

1609 Beginning of Tokugawa shogunate in Japan

1619 Foundation of Batavia (Jakarta) by Dutch: start of Dutch colonial empire in East Indies

Europe

1492 Fall of Granada: end of Muslim rule in Spain; Jews expelled from Spain.

1494 Italian wars: beginning of Franco-Habsburg struggle for hegemony in Europe

1519 Charles V, ruler of Spain and Netherlands, elected emperor

1521 Martin Luther outlawed: **beginning of Protestant Reformation**

1521 Suleiman the Magnificent, Ottoman sultan, conquers Belgrade

1526 Battle of Mohács: Ottoman Turks overrun Hungary

1534 Henry VIII of England breaks with Rome

1541 John Calvin founds reformed church at Geneva

1545 Council of Trent: beginning of Counter-Reformation

1556 Ivan IV of Russia conquers Volga basin

1562 Wars of religion in France (to 1598)

1571 Battle of Lepanto: end of Turkish sea power in central Mediterranean

1572 Dutch Revolt against Spain

1588 Spanish Armada defeated by English

1598 Time of Troubles in Russia

1600 Foundation of English and Dutch (1602) East India Companies

1609 Dutch Republic becomes independent

1618 Outbreak of Thirty Years' War

Africa

1492 Spaniards begin conquest of North African coast

1505 Portuguese establish trading posts in east Africa

1546 Destruction of Mali Empire by Songhay

1571 Portuguese create colony in Angola

1578 Battle of Al-Kasr al-Kebir: Moroccans destroy Portuguese power in northwest Africa

1591 Battle of Tondibi: Moroccans destroy Songhay kingdom

c.1600 Oyo Empire at height of power

1628 Portuguese destroy Mwenemutapa Empire

New World

1492 Columbus reaches America: discovery of New World

1493 First Spanish settlement in New World (Hispaniola)

1493 Treaty of Tordesillas divides New World between Portugal and Spain

1497 Cabot reaches Newfoundland

1498 Columbus discovers South America

c.1510 African slaves to America

1519 Cortés begins conquest of Aztec Empire

1520 Magellan crosses Pacific

1532 Pizarro begins conquest of Inca Empire for Spain

1545 Discovery of silver mines at Potosí (Peru) and Zacatecas (Mexico)

c.1560 Portuguese begin sugar cultivation in Brazil

1571 Spanish conquer Philippines

1607 First permanent English settlement in America (Jamestown, Virginia)

1608 French colonists found Quebec

1620 Puritans land in New England (*Mayflower*)

1625 Dutch settle New Amsterdam

Culture and technology

c.1500 Italian Renaissance: Leonardo da Vinci (1452-1519), Michelangelo (1475-1564), Raphael (1483-1520), Botticelli (1444-1510), Machiavelli (1469-1527), Ficino (1433-99)

1509 Watch invented by Peter Henle (Nuremberg)

c.1525 Introduction of potato from South America to Europe

1539 Death of Kabir Nanak, founder of Sikh religion

1543 Copernicus publishes *Of the Revolution of Celestial Bodies*

1559 Tobacco first introduced into Europe

1598 Shah Abbas I creates imperial capital at Isfahan

c.1603 Beginnings of Kabuki theatre, Japan

1607 Monteverdi's *La Favola d'Orfeo* establishes opera as art form

1609 Telescope invented (Holland)

c.1610 Scientific revolution in Europe begins: Kepler (1571-1610), Bacon (1561-1626), Galileo (1564-1642), Descartes (1596-1650)

1616 Death of Shakespeare (born 1564) and Cervantes (born 1547)

1620 First weekly newspapers in Europe (Amsterdam)

Asia

Europe

Africa

New World

Culture and technology

1630 Gustavus Adolphus of Sweden intervenes in Thirty Years' War

c.1630 Apogee of Netherlands art: Hals (1580-1666), Rembrandt (1606-69), Vermeer (1632-75), Rubens (1577-1640)

1636 Foundation of Harvard College, first university in North America

1638 Russians reach Pacific

1641 Dutch capture Malacca from Portuguese

1642 English Civil War begins

1644 Manchus found new dynasty (Ch'ing) in China

1648 Peace of Westphalia ends Thirty Years' War

1645 Tasman circumnavigates Australia and discovers New Zealand

1649 Russians reach Pacific and found Okhotsk

1649 Execution of Charles I of England; republic declared

c.1650 Beginnings of popular literary culture in Japan (puppet theatre, kabuki, the novel)

1652 First Anglo-Dutch War: beginning of Dutch decline

1652 Foundation of Cape Colony by Dutch

1653 Taj Mahal, Agra, India, completed

1654 Ukraine passes from Polish to Russian rule

1656 St Peter's, Rome, completed (Bernini)

1658 Peace of Roskilde: Swedish Empire at height

1659 French found trading station on Senegal coast

c.1660 Classical period of French culture: drama (Molière, 1622-1673, Racine, 1639-1699, Corneille, 1606-1684), painting (Poussin, 1594-1665, Claude, 1600-1682), music (Lully, 1632-1687, Couperin, 1668-1733)

1662 Battle of Ambuila: destruction of Kongo kingdom by Portuguese

1662 Royal Society founded in London and (1666) Académie Française in Paris

1664 New Amsterdam taken by British from Dutch (later renamed New York)

1674 Sivaji creates Hindu Maratha kingdom

1667 Beginning of French expansion under Louis XIV

1683 Turkish siege of Vienna

1684 La Salle explores Mississippi and claims Louisiana for France

1687 Isaac Newton's *Principia*

1688 'Glorious Revolution'; constitutional monarchy in England

1689 Treaty of Nerchinsk between Russia and China

1689 'Grand Alliance' against Louis XIV

1690 Foundation of Calcutta by English

1693 Gold discovered in Brazil

1690 John Locke's *Essay concerning Human Understanding*

1697 Chinese occupy Outer Mongolia

1699 Treaty of Carlowitz: Habsburgs recover Hungary from Turks

1700 Great Northern War (to 1720)

c.1700 Rise of Asante power (Gold Coast)

c.1700 Great age of German baroque music: Buxtehude (1637-1707), Handel (1685-1759), Bach (1685-1750)

1703 Foundation of St Petersburg, capital of Russian Empire (1712)

1707 Death of Aurangzeb: decline of Mughal power in India

1707 Union of England and Scotland

1709 Battle of Poltava: Peter the Great of Russia defeats Swedes

1709 Abraham Darby discovers coke-smelting technique for producing pig-iron (England)

1713 Treaty of Utrecht ends War of Spanish Succession

1728 Bering begins Russian reconnaissance of Alaska

c.1730 Revival of ancient empire of Borno (central Sudan)

1730 Wesley brothers create Methodism

c.1735 Wahabite movement to purify Islam begins in Arabia

1736 Safavid dynasty deposed by Nadir Shah

1740 War of Austrian Succession: Prussia annexes Silesia

1747 Ahmad Khan Abdali founds kingdom of Afghanistan

1751 China overruns Tibet, Dzungaria and Tarim Basin (1756-9)

1751 French gain control of Deccan and Carnatic

1755 Alaungpaya founds Rangoon and reunites Burma (to 1824)

1756 Seven Years' War begins

1757 Battle of Plassey: British defeat French

1760 New France conquered by British: Quebec (1759) and Montreal (1760)

c.1760 European enlightenment: Voltaire (1694-1778), Diderot (1713-84), Hume (1711-76)

1761 Capture of Pondicherry: British destroy French power in India

1762 J. J. Rousseau's *Social Contract*

1768 Cook begins exploration of Pacific

c.1770 Advance of science and technology in Europe: J. Priestley (1733-1804), A. Lavoisier (1743-94), A. Volta (1745-1827). Harrison's chronometer (1762), Watt's steam engine (1769), Arkwright's water-powered spinning-frame (1769)

1772 First partition of Poland (2nd and 3rd partitions 1793, 1795)

1774 Treaty of Kuchuk Kainarji: beginning of Ottoman decline

1775 American Revolution begins

Asia

Europe

Africa

Americas and Australasia

Culture and technology

1776 American Declaration of Independence

1776 Publication of *The Wealth of Nations* by Adam Smith (1723-90) and *Common Sense* by Tom Paine (1737-1809)

1781 Immanuel Kant's *Critique of Pure Reason*

1783 Russia annexes Crimea

1783 Treaty of Paris: Britain recognizes American independence

1788 British colony of Australia founded

1789 French Revolution begins; abolition of feudal system and proclamation of Rights of Man

1789 George Washington becomes first President of United States of America

c.1790 Great age of European orchestral music: Mozart (1756-91), Haydn (1732-1809), Beethoven (1770-1827)

1791 Russia gains Black Sea steppes from Turks

1792 Cartwright invents steam-powered weaving loom

1792 French Republic proclaimed; beginning of revolutionary wars

1793 Decimal system introduced (France)

1793 Attempts to reform Ottoman Empire by Selim III

1793 Eli Whitney's cotton 'gin' (US)

1796 Jenner discovers smallpox vaccine (UK)

1796 British conquer Ceylon

1798 Napoleon attacks Egypt

1798 Malthus publishes *Essay on the Principle of Population*

1799 Napoleon becomes First Consul and (1804) **Emperor of France**

1803 Louisiana Purchase nearly doubles size of US

1805 Napoleon defeats Austria and (1806) Prussia

1804 Fulanis conquer Hausa

1805 Battle of Trafalgar: Britain defeats French and Spanish fleets

1806 Cape Colony passes under British control

1807 Abolition of serfdom in Prussia

1807 Slave trade abolished within British Empire

1808 Independence movements in Spanish and Portuguese America: 13 new states created by 1828

1812 Napoleon invades Russia

1811 Mohammed Ali takes control in Egypt

1812 Cylinder printing press invented, adopted by *The Times* (London)

1815 Napoleon defeated at Waterloo, exiled to St Helena

1815 Congress of Vienna

1818 Britain defeats Marathas and becomes effective ruler of India

1818 Shaka forms Zulu kingdom in SE Africa

1817 Foundation of Hindu college, Calcutta, first major centre of Western influence in India

1819 British found Singapore as free trade port

1819 US purchases Florida from Spain

c.1820 Romanticism in European literature and art: Byron (1788-1824), Chateaubriand (1768-1848), Heine (1797-1856), Turner (1775-1851), Delacroix (1798-1863)

1821 Greek war of independence

1822 Liberia founded as colony for freed slaves

1823 Monroe Doctrine

1821 Electric motor and generator invented by M. Faraday (Britain)

1824 British begin conquest of Burma and Assam

1822 First photographic image produced by J-N. Niepce (France)

1825-30 Java war: revolt of Indonesians against Dutch

1825 First passenger steam railway: Stockton and Darlington (England)

1830 Russia begins conquest of Kazakhstan (to 1854)

1830 French begin conquest of Algeria

1830 Revolutionary movements in France, Germany, Poland and Italy; Belgium wins independence

1828 Foundation of Brahmo-samaj, Hindu revivalist movement

1832 Death of Goethe (born 1749)

1833 Death of Rammohan Roy (b.1772), father of modern Indian nationalism

1833 Formation of German customs union *(Zollverein)*

1833 First regulation of industrial working conditions (Britain)

1834 First mechanical reaper patented (US)

1835 'Great Trek' of Boer colonists from Cape, leading to foundation of Republic of Natal (1839), Orange Free State (1848) and Transvaal (1849)

1836 Needle-gun invented (Prussia), making breech-loading possible

1837 Pitman's shorthand invented

1838 First electric telegraph (Britain)

1840 Britain annexes New Zealand

1840 First postage stamp (Britain)

1842 Opium War: Britain annexes Hong Kong

1843 British conquer Sind

1845-9 British conquest of Punjab and Kashmir

1845 Irish famine stimulates hostility to Britain and emigration to US

1845 Texas annexed by US

1846 Britain repeals Corn Laws and moves towards complete free trade

1846 Mexican War begins: US conquers New Mexico and California (1848)

1846 Oregon treaty delimits US-Canadian boundary

1848 Revolutionary movements in Europe; proclamation of Second Republic in France

1848 Communist Manifesto issued by Marx (1818-83) and Engels (1820-95)

1849 Death of Chopin (b.1810); apogee of Romantic music with Berlioz (1803-69), Liszt (1811-86), Wagner (1813-83), Brahms (1833-97), Verdi (1813-1901)

1850 T'ai-p'ing rebellion in China — (to 1864), with immense loss of life

1850 Australian colonies and (1856) New Zealand granted responsible government

1851 Great Exhibition in London

1853 First railway and telegraph lines in India

1852 Fall of French republic; Louis Napoleon (Napoleon III, 1808-73) becomes French emperor

1853 Livingstone's explorations begin

1853 Haussmann begins rebuilding of Paris

1854 Perry forces Japan to open trade with US

1854 Crimean War (to 1856)

Asia

1857 Indian Mutiny

1858 Treaty of Tientsin: further Treaty Ports opened to foreign trade in China

1860 Treaty of Peking: China cedes Ussuri region to Russia

1863 France establishes protectorate over Cambodia, Cochin China (1865), Annam (1874), Tonkin (1885) and Laos (1893)

1868 End of Tokugawa Shogunate and Meiji Restoration in Japan

1877 Queen Victoria proclaimed Empress of India

1879 Second Afghan War gives Britain control of Afghanistan

1885 Foundation of Indian National Congress

1886 British annex Upper Burma

1887 French establish Indo-Chinese Union

1891 Construction of Trans-Siberian railway begun

1894-5 Sino-Japanese War: Japan occupies Formosa

1898 Abortive "Hundred Days" reform in China

1900 Boxer uprising in China

1904 Partition of Bengal: nationalist agitation in India

1904-5 Russo-Japanese War; Japanese success stimulates Asian nationalism

Europe

1859 Sardinian-French war against Austria; Piedmont acquires Lombardy (1860): **unification of Italy begins**

1861 Emancipation of Russian serfs

1864 Prussia defeats Denmark: annexes Schleswig-Holstein (1866)

1864 Russia suppresses Polish revolt

1866 Prussia defeats Austria

1867 Establishment of North German confederation and of dual monarchy in Austria-Hungary

1870 Franco-Prussian war

1871 Proclamation of German Empire, beginning of Third French Republic: suppression of Paris commune

1875 Growth of labour/socialist parties: Germany (1875), Belgium (1885), Holland (1877), Britain (1893), Russia (1898)

1878 Treaty of Berlin: Romania, Montenegro and Serbia become independent, Bulgaria autonomous

1879 Dual alliance between Germany and Austria-Hungary

1890 Dismissal of Bismarck; Wilhelm II begins new course

1894 Franco-Russian alliance

1898 Germany embarks on naval building programme: beginning of German 'world policy'

1904 Anglo-French entente

1905 Revolution in Russia, followed by Tsarist concessions

1905 Norway independent of Sweden

Africa

1860 French expansion in West Africa from Senegal

1869 Suez Canal opens

1875 Disraeli buys Suez Canal Company shares to ensure British control of sea route to India

1881 French occupy Tunisia

1882 Revolt in Egypt leading to British occupation

1884 Germany acquires SW Africa, Togoland, Cameroons

1885 King of Belgium acquires Congo

1886 Germany and Britain partition East Africa

1886 Gold discovered in Transvaal; foundation of Johannesburg

1889 British South Africa Company formed by Cecil Rhodes, begins colonization of Rhodesia (1890)

1896 Battle of Adowa: Italians defeated by Ethiopians

1898 Fashoda crisis between Britain and France

1899 Boer War begins

1900 Copper-mining begins in Katanga

Americas and Australasia

1861 Outbreak of American Civil War

1864 War of Paraguay against Argentina, Brazil and Uruguay (to 1870)
1865 End of American Civil War; slavery abolished in US

1867 Russia sells Alaska to US

1867 Dominion of Canada established

1869 Prince Rupert's Land, Manitoba (1870) and British Columbia (1871) join Canada

1876 Porfirio Díaz (1830-1915) gains control of Mexico (to 1911)

1879 War of the Pacific (Chile, Bolivia, Peru)

1885 Completion of Canadian Pacific railway

1898 Spanish-American war: US annexes Guam, Puerto Rico and Philippines

1901 Unification of Australia as Commonwealth

1903 Panama Canal Zone ceded to US

Culture and technology

1856 Bessemer process permits mass-production of steel

1859 Darwin publishes *The Origin of Species*

1859 First oil well drilled (Pennsylvania, US)

c.1860 Great age of European novel: Dickens (1812-70), Dumas (1802-70), Flaubert (1821-80), Turgenev (1818-83), Dostoyevsky (1821-81), Tolstoy (1828-1910)

1861 Pasteur evolves germ theory of disease

1861 Women first given vote (Australia)

1863 First underground railway (London)

1864 Foundation of Red Cross (Switzerland)

1867 Marx publishes *Das Kapital* (vol. 1)

1869 First trans-continental railroad completed (US)

1870 Declaration of Papal infallibility

1874 First electric tram (New York); telephone patented by Bell (US 1876) first electric streetlighting (London 1878)

1874 Emergence of Impressionist school of painting: Monet (1840-1926), Renoir (1841-1919), Degas (1834-1917)

1878 First oil tanker built (Russia)

1879 F. W. Woolworth opened first '5 and 10 cent store'

1882 First hydro-electric plant (Wisconsin, US)

1884 Maxim gun perfected

c.1885 Daimler and Benz pioneer the automobile (Germany)

1888 Dunlop invents pneumatic tyre

c.1890 Beginnings of modern literature in Japan on western models

c.1890 Europe - realistic drama: Ibsen (1828-1906), Strindberg (1849-1912), Chekhov (1860-1904), Shaw (1856-1950)

1895 Röntgen discovers X-rays (Germany); Marconi invents wireless telegraphy (Italy); first public showing of motion picture (France)

1896 Herzl publishes *The Jewish State* calling for Jewish National Home

1898 Pierre and Marie Curie observe radioactivity and isolate radium (France)

1899 Howard's *Garden Cities of Tomorrow* initiates modern city planning

1900 Planck evolves quantum theory (Germany)

1900 Freud's *Interpretation of Dreams*, beginning of psychoanalysis (Austria)

1903 First successful flight of petrol-powered aircraft (Wright Brothers, US)

1905 Einstein's theory of relativity (Germany)

Asia

1908 Young Turk revolution: Ottoman sultan deposed
1910 Japan annexes Korea

1911 Chinese Revolution: Sun Yat-sen first president of new republic; rise to power of Warlords (to 1926)
1914 German concessions in China and colonies in Pacific taken over by Japan, Australia and New Zealand

1917 'Balfour Declaration' promises Jews a National Home in Palestine

1919 Amritsar incident; upsurge of Indian nationalism

1920 Mustafa Kemal (Atatürk) leads resistance to partition of Turkey; Turkish Nationalist Movement
1921-2 Washington Conference attempts to regulate situation in East Asia
1922 Greek army expelled from Turkey; last Ottoman sultan deposed; republic proclaimed (1923)

1926 Chiang Kai-shek begins reunification of China

1931 Japanese occupy Manchuria
1932 Kingdom of Saudi Arabia formed by Ibn Saud

1934 'Long March' of Chinese communists begins

1936 Japan signs anti-Comintern pact with Germany
1936 Arab revolt in Palestine against Jewish immigration
1937 Beginning of full-scale war between Japan and China

1939 Russian forces defeat Japan at Khalkin Gol (Manchuria); Russo-Japanese neutrality pact (1941)

1941 Japan attacks US at Pearl Harbor
1942 Japan overruns SE Asia
1942 Battle of Midway; US halts Japanese expansion
1942 Gandhi and Indian Congress leaders arrested

1945 US drops atom bombs on Japan, forcing surrender
1946 Civil war in China (to 1949)
1946 Creation of Philippine Republic
1946 Beginning of Vietnamese struggle against France (to 1954)
1947 India and Pakistan independent

1948 Burma and Ceylon independent
1948 Establishment of State of Israel; first Arab-Israeli war
1949 Communist victory in China
1949 Indonesia independent
1950 Korean War begins (to 1953)
1951 US ends occupation of Japan

Europe

1907 Anglo-Russian entente
1908 Bulgaria becomes independent; Austria annexes Bosnia and Herzegovina

1912-13 Balkan wars

1914 Outbreak of World War I

1917 Revolution in Russia: Tsar abdicates (March), Bolsheviks take over (Nov.); **first socialist state established**
1918 Germany and Austria-Hungary sue for armistice: end of World War I
1918 Civil war and foreign intervention in Russia
1919 Paris treaties redraw map of Europe

1920 League of Nations established (headquarters Geneva)

1922 Mussolini takes power in Italy

1924 Death of Lenin; Stalin eventually emerges as Soviet leader (1929)
1925 Locarno treaties stabilize frontiers in West

1928 First five-year plan and (1929) collectivization of agriculture in Russia

1931 Collapse of central European banks begins major recession
1933 Hitler made Chancellor in Germany; beginning of Nazi revolution

1936 German reoccupation of Rhineland
1936 Spanish Civil War begins (to 1939)
1936 'Great Terror' launched in Russia
1938 Germany occupies Austria

1938 Munich conference: dismemberment of Czechoslovakia
1939 German-Soviet non-aggression pact; Germany invades Poland; **Britain and France declare war on Germany**
1940 Germany overruns Norway, Denmark, Belgium, Netherlands, France; Italy invades Greece but is repulsed; Battle of Britain
1941 Germany invades Russia; declares war on US

1943 German VI army surrenders at Stalingrad; Italian capitulation
1944 Anglo-American landing in Normandy; Russian advance in E. Europe
1945 Yalta Conference; defeat of Germany and suicide of Hitler

1947 Development of Cold War; Truman Doctrine enunciated
1947 Marshall Plan for economic reconstruction in Europe
1948 Communist takeover in Czechoslovakia and Hungary; Berlin Airlift
1949 Formation of NATO alliance and of COMECON

1953 Death of Stalin; East Berlin revolt crushed

Africa

1908 Belgian state takes over Congo from King Leopold
1910 Formation of Union of South Africa

1911 Italy conquers Libya

1914-15 French and British conquer German colonies except German East Africa

1919 Nationalist revolt in Egypt against British protectorate

1921 Battle of Anual: Spanish army routed by Moroccans

1926 Revolt of Abd-el Krim crushed in Morocco

1934 Italians suppress Senussi resistance in Libya
1935 Italy invades Ethiopia

1936 Anglo-Egyptian alliance; British garrison Suez Canal Zone

1940-1 Italians expelled from Somalia, Eritrea and Ethiopia

1941 Germans conquer Cyrenaica and advance into Egypt (1942)
1942 Battle of El-Alamein; German defeat and retreat
1942 Anglo-American landings in Morocco and Algeria

1949 Apartheid programme inaugurated in S. Africa

1952 Beginning of Mau Mau rebellion in Kenya
1952 Military revolt in Egypt; proclamation of republic (1953)

Americas and Australasia

1907 New Zealand acquires dominion status

1910 Mexican revolution begins

1914 Panama Canal opens

1917 US declares war on Central Powers

1918 President Wilson announces 'Fourteen Points'

1920 US refuses to ratify Paris treaties and withdraws into isolation

1921 US restricts immigration

1923 General Motors established: world's largest manufacturing company

1929 Wall Street Crash precipitates world Depression
1930 Military revolution in Brazil; Vargas becomes president
1933 US President Franklin D. Roosevelt introduces New Deal

1935 Cárdenas president of Mexico: land redistribution and (1938) nationalization of oil
1936 Pan-American congress; US proclaims 'good neighbour' policy

1941 US enters war against Germany and Japan

1945 United Nations established (headquarters New York)
1946 Perón comes to power in Argentina

1948 Organization of American States established

1951 Australia, New Zealand and US sign ANZUS Pact

Culture and technology

1907 Exhibition of Cubist paintings in Paris: Picasso (1881-1973), Braque (1882-1963)
1910 Development of abstract painting: Kandinsky (1866-1944), Mondrian (1872-1944)
1910 Development of plastics

1913 Henry Ford develops conveyor belt assembly for production of Model T automobile (Detroit, US)

1916 First birth control advice centre opened (New York)
1917 First use of massed tanks (Battle of Cambrai)

1919 Rutherford (1871-1937) splits atom (UK)
1919 Bauhaus school of design started by Gropius at Weimar (Germany)
1919 First crossing of Atlantic by air (Alcock and Brown)
1920 First general radio broadcasts (US and UK)
c.1920 Emergence of jazz in US: Louis Armstrong (1900-71), Duke Ellington (1899-1974), Count Basie (1904-1984)

1923 Development of tuberculosis vaccine (France)
1924 Thomas Mann (1875-1955) publishes *The Magic Mountain*
1925 Franz Kafka (1883-1924) publishes *The Trial*; Adolf Hitler publishes *Mein Kampf*
1927 Emergence of talking pictures. Rise of great film makers: D.W. Griffith (1874-1948), Chaplin (1889-1977), John Ford (1895-1973), Eisenstein (1896-1948), Clair (1898-1981), Hitchcock (1899-1980), Disney (1901-66)

1936 First regular public television transmissions (UK)

1937 Jet engine first tested (UK)
1937 Invention of nylon (USA)

1939 Development of penicillin (UK)
1939 Development of DDT (Switzerland)

1942 Fermi builds first nuclear reactor (US)

1945 Atom bomb first exploded (US)

1946 First electronic computer built (US)

1947 First supersonic flight (US)

1948 Transistor invented (US)

1951 First nuclear power stations (US and UK)
1952 Hydrogen bomb first exploded (US)
1952 Contraceptive pill developed (US)

1953 Crick and Watson explain structure of DNA (UK)
1953 Electronic computers

Asia

1954 Geneva conference: Laos, Cambodia and Vietnam become independent states
1955 Bandung Conference
1956 Second Arab-Israeli war

1958 'Great Leap Forward' in China (to 1961)
1959 China reoccupies Tibet
1959 War between North and South Vietnam (to 1975)
1960 Sino-Soviet dispute begins

1961 Increasing US involvement in Vietnam

1962 Sino-Indian war

1965 Indo-Pakistan war
1965 Cultural Revolution in China (to 1969)

1967 Third Arab-Israeli war (Six-Day War)

1971 Indo-Pakistan war leads to breakaway of East Pakistan (Bangladesh)

1973 US forces withdraw from South Vietnam
1973 Fourth Arab-Israeli war; OPEC countries triple price of oil

1975 Civil war in Lebanon: Syria invades (1976)
1975 Communists take over Vietnam, Laos and Cambodia
1976 Death of Mao-Tse Tung; political re-orientation and modernization under Deng Xiao-Ping
1977 Egypt/Israeli peace talks (Camp David Peace Treaty, 1978)
1977 Military coup ends democratic rule in Pakistan
1979 Fall of Shah of Iran, establishment of Islamic Republic under Ayatollah Khomeini (d.1989)
1979 Afghanistan invaded by USSR (to 1989)
1979 Sino-Vietnamese War
1979 Vietnam invades Cambodia, expelling Khmer Rouge government
1980 Outbreak of Iran/Iraq War (to 1988)

1982 Israel invades Lebanon, expulsion of PLO from Beirut
1982 Israel withdraws from Sinai peninsula
1984 Indira Gandhi assassinated

1985 Israel withdraws from all of Lebanon, other than 'buffer zone' in south
1986 Fall of Ferdinand Marcos in the Philippines; Cory Aquino succeeds

1988 Benazir Bhutto restores civilian rule in Pakistan
1988 Palestine uprising (intifada) against Israeli occupied territories. PLO recognizes state of Israel
1989 Death of Ayatollah Khomeini
1989 Student pro-democracy demonstration crushed in Peking

1990 Iraq invades Kuwait

1991 Gulf War: UN Coalition forces led by US attack Iraq and liberate Kuwait
1991 Middle East peace talks begin

Europe

1955 Warsaw Pact signed
1956 Polish revolt, Gomulka in power; Hungarian revolt crushed by Russians
1957 Treaty of Rome: Formation of European Economic Community and (1959) of European Free Trade Association
1958 Fifth Republic in France: de Gaulle first president

1961 East Germans build Berlin Wall (to 1989)

1968 Liberalization in Czechoslovakia halted by Russian invasion
1969 Outbreak of violence in N. Ireland

1973 Oil crisis ends post-war economic boom
1973 Britain, Ireland and Denmark join EC
1974 End of dictatorship in Portugal
1974 Turkish invasion of Cyprus
1975 Death of Franco; end of dictatorship in Spain

1980 Death of Marshal Tito
1980 Creation of independent Polish trade union Solidarity; martial law (1981)
1981 Greece joins EC
1982 Death of USSR President Brezhnev, succession of Y. Andropov (d.1984), then K. Chernenko (d.1985) as USSR leader

1985 M. Gorbachev leader of USSR (to 1991)

1986 Spain and Portugal join EC

1988 Gorbachev moves USSR towards freedom of information and debate (glasnost), and industrial and social re-structuring (perestroika)

1989 Democratic elections for People's Congress held in USSR; Boris Yeltsin, President of Russia, first democratically elected leader; Poland and Hungary move towards political pluralism; popular protest topples communist regimes in E. Germany, Czechoslovakia, Bulgaria and Romania (Ceausescu executed); Berlin Wall demolished
1990 Unification of Germany
1990-1 Nationalism in USSR leads to secession of Baltic republics
1991 Disintegration of Soviet Union
1991 Distintegration of Yugoslavia: Slovenia and Croatia declare independence.
1992 Civil War in Bosnia-Herzegovina: Bosnian Serbs fight Muslims and Croats
1992 Czech Republic and Slovakia emerge as separate states

Africa

1954 Beginnings of nationalist revolt in Algeria (to 1962)

1956 Suez crisis: Anglo-French invasion of Canal Zone
1957 Beginning of **decolonization in sub-Saharan Africa:** Gold Coast (Ghana) becomes independent

1960 'Africa's year'; many states become independent; outbreak of civil war in Belgian Congo
1961 South Africa becomes independent republic

1962 Algeria becomes independent

1965 Rhodesia declares independence

1967 Civil war in Nigeria (secession of Biafra) (to 1970)

1974 Emperor Haile Selasse of Ethiopia deposed by Marxist junta
1975 Portugal grants independence to Mozambique and Angola

1976 Morocco and Mauritania partition Spanish Sahara

1979 Tanzanian forces invade Uganda and expel President Amin

1980 Black majority rule established in Zimbabwe (Rhodesia)

1981 President Sadat of Egypt assassinated

1984 Famine in Sahel and Ethiopia; continuing war against secession
1985 Civil unrest in South Africa. 'State of Emergency' declared, suspending civil rights and press freedom
1986 US bomb Libya in retaliation for terrorist activities

1990 Namibia becomes independent
1990 S. African government moves towards accommodation with ANC, frees Nelson Mandela, and (1991) announces intention to dismantle apartheid

1992 US forces intervene to end Somalia's famine and civil war

Americas and Australasia

1959 Cuban Revolution

1962 Cuba missile crisis
1963 US President Kennedy assassinated; L.B. Johnson succeeds (to 1968)
1964 US Civil Rights Act inaugurates President Johnson's 'Great Society' programme

1966 Eruption of Black American discontent; growth of Black Power

1968 Assassination of Martin Luther King; R.M. Nixon elected US President (to 1974)

1970 Allende elected president of Chile (killed 1973)
1971 US initiates policy of detente with China and USSR
1971 USA abandons Gold Standard and depreciates dollar
1973 Major recession in US triggered by oil crisis

1979 Civil war in Nicaragua (to 1990)
1979 Civil war in El Salvador (to 1992)

1980 Ronald Reagan elected US President (to 1989)

1982 Argentina occupies South Georgia and Falkland Is; surrenders to UK forces
1983 Democracy restored in Argentina
1983 Coup in Grenada; US invades

1985 Democracy restored in Brazil and Uruguay

1987 INF treaty between USSR and USA; phased elimination of their intermediate-range land-based nuclear weapons
1987 US stock market crash

1989 George Bush becomes President of USA (to 1993)

1989-90 US military intervention in Panama; arrest and extradition of Manuel Noriega
1990 Democratic elections in Nicaragua end Sandinista rule

1993 W.F. Clinton becomes US President

Culture and technology

1956 Beginning of rock and roll music (US): Elvis Presley (1935-77)
1957 First space satellite launched (USSR)

1961 First man in space: Gagarin (USSR)
1961 Structure of DNA molecule (genetic code) determined (UK)
1962 Second Vatican Council reforms Catholic liturgy and dogma

1964 Publication of Thoughts of Chairman Mao

1968 World-wide student protest movement
1969 First man lands on moon: Armstrong (US)

1976 1st supersonic transatlantic passenger service begins with Concorde

1980s Computer revolution: spread of computers in offices and homes in Western world
1980s Acquired Immune Deficiency Syndrome (AIDS) spreads throughout Africa, Europe and North America. Massive research and public education programme launched
1981 First re-usable shuttle space flight (USA)

1986 Launch of world's first permanently-manned space station (USSR)
1986 Major nuclear disaster at Chernobyl power reactor (Ukraine)
1987 World population reaches 5 billion

1988 Global recognition that ozone layer is being depleted. Global ban on CFCs (chlorofluoro-carbons) (1990)

1989 Rushdie (British author) condemned to death by Khomeini for blasphemy

1990 Voyager space probe mission completed; last planetary encounter (Neptune)

The geographical background to world history

warm currents
cold currents
Scale 1:71M

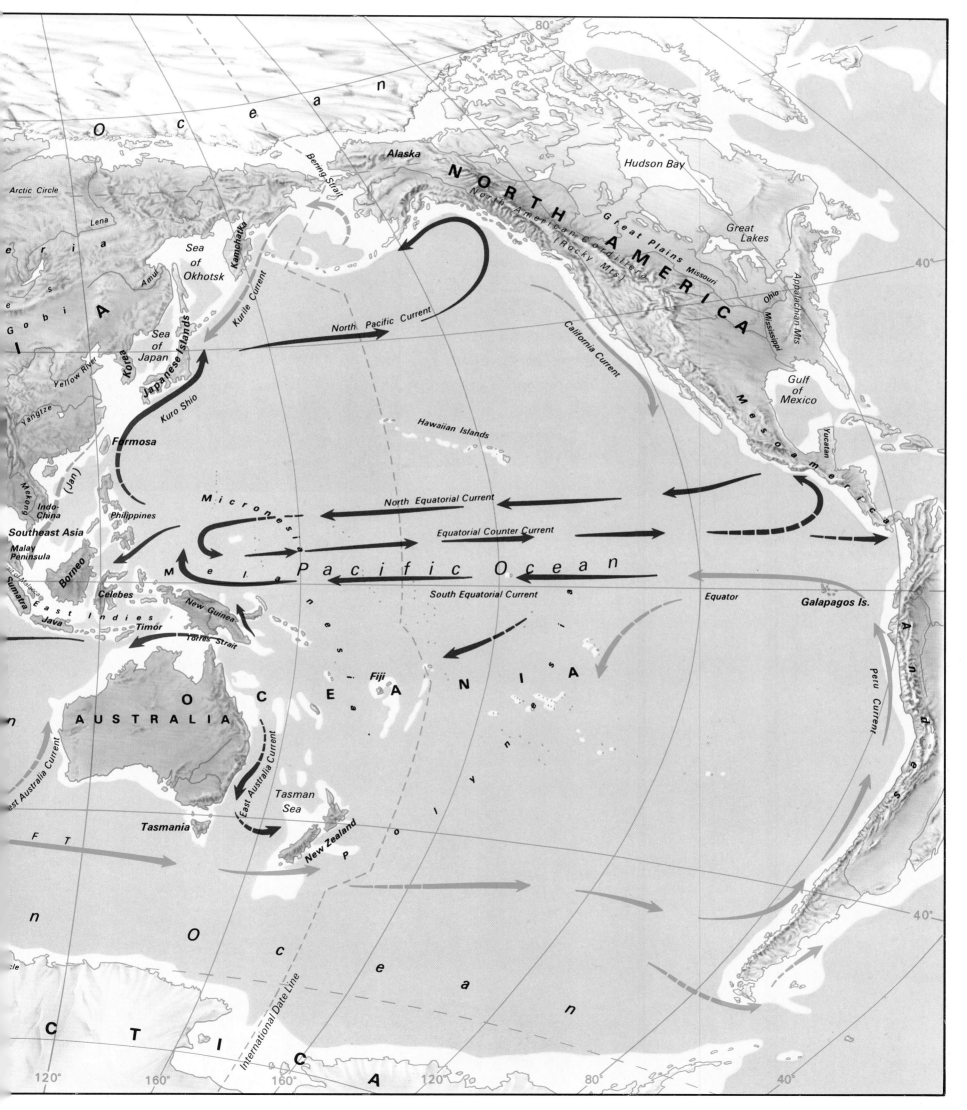

RECORDED history is only the tip of an iceberg reaching back to the first appearance on earth of the human species. Anthropologists, prehistorians and archaeologists have extended our vista of the past by hundreds of thousands of years: we cannot understand human history without taking account of their findings. The transformation of humankind (or, more accurately, of certain groups of humans in certain areas) from hunters and fishers to agriculturists, and from a migratory to a sedentary life, constitutes the most decisive revolution in the whole of human history. The climatic and ecological changes which made it possible have left their mark on the historical record down to the present day.

Agriculture not merely made possible a phenomenal growth of human population, which is thought to have increased some 16 fold between 8000 and 4000 BC, but also gave rise to the familiar landscape of village communities which still characterized Europe as late as the middle of the 19th century and even today prevails in most parts of the world. Nowhere are the continuities of history more visible. The enduring structures of human society, which transcend and outlive political change, carry us back to the end of the Ice Age, to the changes which began when the shrinking ice-cap left a new world to be explored and tamed.

1   Human origins

Stonehenge, Salisbury Plain, Southern England

and early cultures

Human origins

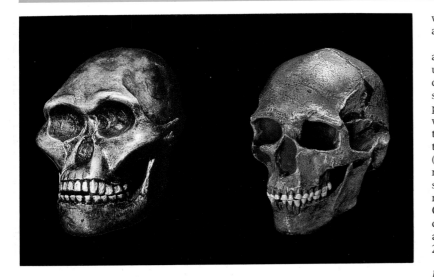

Human ancestors (*above*) *Australopithecus* (*left*) or 'southern ape' was a close relative of our earliest human ancestors. The slender variety, *Australopithecus africanus* had a relatively low skull, a sloping forehead and a protruding mouth equipped with large teeth. Australopithecines had small brains – only about one-quarter that of modern humans – and were about 4 feet (1 m) tall. The crucial feature of subsequent human evolution was not that brain size increased, but that it did so much faster than body size (the modern human brain is over twice as large in relation to body size as that of the Australopithecines). To house their larger brains, modern humans (Cro-Magnon, *right*) have a taller skull and a more steeply rising forehead. Furthermore, the development of tools and cooking methods has made it progressively easier for humans to chew and digest food, taking pressure off the teeth and resulting in a less protruding mouth.

2/Sites in Europe and western Asia (*below*) where fossilized human remains have been found. These sites date from c.700,000 to 14,000 BC. The oldest (700,000-250,000 years old) are associated with the remains of an early form of *Homo sapiens* and the most recent (35,000-14,000 years old) with fully modern humans. Classic Neanderthals have been found at sites dating between 80,000 and 35,000 BC, but some fossils with Neanderthal characteristics date back to nearly 250,000 BC.

WITHIN the animal kingdom, humans are most closely related to the great apes (chimpanzees and gorillas) with whom they share the same basic anatomical structure and similar genetic make-up. These similarities were inherited from a common ancestor which, on the basis of fossil evidence and molecular research, is estimated to have lived about 10 million years ago. Stimulated perhaps by environmental change and other as yet unknown factors, apes and humans diverged onto separate evolutionary courses between 5 and 8 million years ago. Through time, some characteristics of the common ancestor were retained, while others gradually changed to produce the species recognized today.

Fossilized bones and footprints show that the fundamental human adaptation of bipedalism (walking on two legs) had evolved in Africa by 4 million years ago. Remains of the earliest bipedal hominids, the Australopithecines or 'southern apes', were first discovered in southern Africa, mainly in the Transvaal, where they had survived in the debris of former limestone caves. However, the oldest secure evidence of bipedalism was found in East Africa, in the Afar region of Ethiopia. This was the skeleton known as 'Lucy', an Australopithecine female who walked the grasslands of Ethiopia around 3.4 million years ago. Still more remarkable was the discovery of the footprints of two adult Australopithecines accompanied by a single child, preserved by a volcanic ashfall at nearby Laetoli. The find may indicate that our human ancestors were already operating in nuclear family groups as long as 3.8 million years ago.

Australopithecines show a combination of ape and human traits and were widespread in Africa until about 1.7 million years ago. At least four closely related species can be distinguished, some lightly built, others of more robust physique. It is uncertain whether the former, with their small brains, ape-like faces and distinctive pelvic structure, could have been ancestral to humans of our own family or genus, *Homo* (Man); rather, Australopithecines and *Homo* may well represent parallel evolutionary lines stemming from a common ancestor which has not yet been recognized in the fossil record. Clearly, however, the trend away from ape-like characteristics towards ever more modern attributes had certainly begun some time before 2 million years ago.

The oldest fossils attributable to the genus *Homo* have been found in East Africa in areas such as Olduvai Gorge in Tanzania and Koobi Fora in Kenya. The first such fossil discovered at Olduvai was distinguished from the Australopithecines by its larger brain, rounded skull and distinctly human face. These more modern hominids are generally classified as a single species known as *Homo habilis*, meaning 'handy man', or 'man the tool-maker'. The name reflects the fact that simple stone tools sometimes occur alongside the remains of *Homo habilis*, and that these hominids are the earliest of our ancestors to have consciously made and used such tools. They represent a small but crucial first step towards the sophisticated human technology on which we rely so heavily today.

A further stage in the development of more modern anatomical characteristics can be observed in African fossils dating from about 1.7 million years ago to 200,000 BC. Changes in the size and shape of the skull show that these hominids had a larger, more developed brain. The skeleton of a 12-year-old boy found at Nariokotome in Kenya differs only slightly from that of a modern boy, even though it is 1.7 million years old. Fossils of this kind are currently referred to as *Homo erectus*, a name first applied to remains found in Southeast Asia and China. It would be better, however, to regard the African group as an early form of *Homo sapiens* (man the thinker). It is from this stock that the first populations of fully modern humans ultimately derived.

The Australopithecines were restricted to tropical Africa, where they could survive without requiring clothing, shelter or fire. The descendants of *Homo habilis*, however, soon began to spread beyond their original homeland to colonize less hospitable environments in Europe and Asia. To achieve this, they drew upon their greater intelligence which allowed them to build shelters, make clothes and master fire, and enabled them to survive and prosper even when much of the northern world was covered by ice sheets.

The colonization of Europe probably began between 1 million and 700,000 years ago, although the oldest sites with firm evidence of human activity date from about 500,000 BC. Fossilized human remains from sites such as Mauer, Arago and Petralona indicate that the people who adapted to the diverse environments of Europe were an early form of *Homo sapiens*. By about 250,000 BC, this population was beginning to show some of the features which characterize the species *Homo sapiens neanderthalensis* (Neanderthal man). The Neanderthals were well established in Europe and western Asia between about 100,000 BC and 35,000 BC. Their heavily set faces, with large jaws and prominent brow ridges, and the robust muscular bodies of the so-called 'classic' Neanderthals, probably represent a local development of the early *Homo sapiens* stock. They may even have been a specialized adaptation to the cold climates of the last Ice Age.

The earliest known fossils of fully modern type are those from the Omo 1 site in Ethiopia, Klasies River Mouth in South Africa and Qafzeh in Israel, which are dated to between 90,000 BC and 110,000 BC. The earliest modern humans did not immediately replace all earlier forms of human. Although they were present in the Near East alongside the Neanderthals soon after 100,000 years ago, they did not replace the Neanderthals in Europe for over 50,000 years, and in western Europe the first fully modern humans seem to have appeared only about 35,000 years ago. At around the same time fully modern humans appeared in Asia also, developing from or replacing earlier types of hominid including the descendants of those represented in the Chou-k'ou-tien (Zhoukoudian) cave in China.

Much still remains to be discovered about their origins and dispersal, but it is clear that modern humans occupied most of the then habitable world by about 30,000 BC. This included Australia, which was first settled about 50,000 BC by ancestors of the Aborigines who built seacraft to cross the 44 miles (70 km) of open sea between Java, then joined to mainland Southeast Asia, and the uninhabited continent of New Guinea and Australia. The Americas were also populated by waves of people periodically crossing the land-bridge over the Bering Strait, formed at intervals of low sea-level during the last Ice Age around 45,000, 30,000 and 20,000 BC. Such dispersal and adaptation to new environments must be reckoned among the most notable achievements of our early ancestors.

One major aspect of human development from 2.5 million years ago to 10,000 BC is sustained physical change, as small-brained Australopithecines were replaced by early forms of *Homo* and then by fully modern humans. The key to

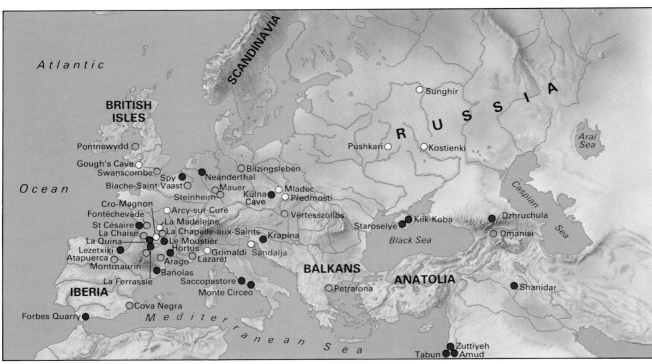

1/Traces of human origins (*right*) Important fossils of humans, and ape and human ancestors have been discovered at sites in Africa, Asia and Australia. The Great East African Rift Valley is a crucial area since fossils found in the stratified deposits here can be reliably dated. The location of the remains suggests that the early humans lived away from the densely populated forests and inhabited the grasslands, where a different range of resources could be exploited with less competition. Even here, however, life was not without danger and some Australopithecine skulls from South African caves show the marks of leopard teeth.

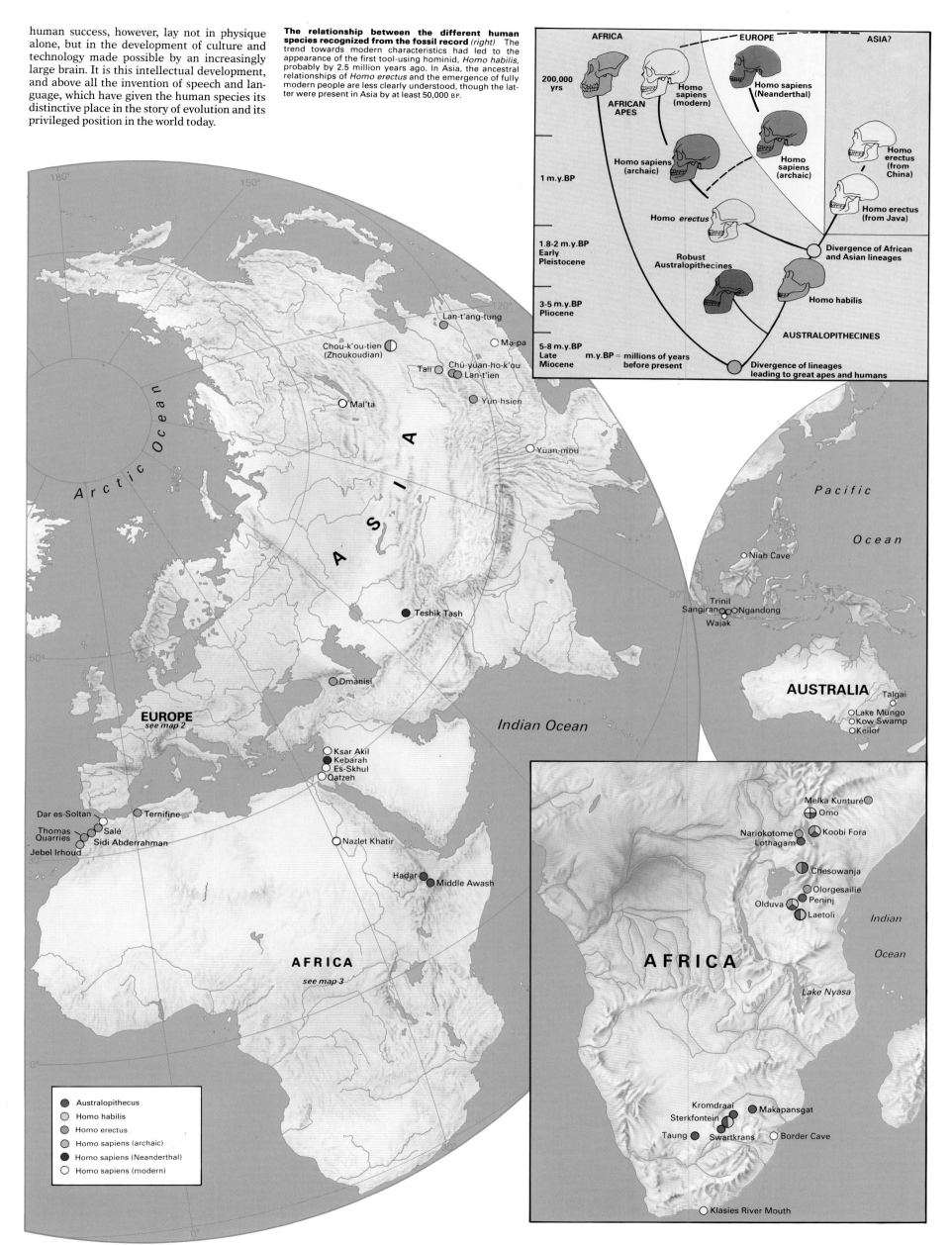

human success, however, lay not in physique alone, but in the development of culture and technology made possible by an increasingly large brain. It is this intellectual development, and above all the invention of speech and language, which have given the human species its distinctive place in the story of evolution and its privileged position in the world today.

The relationship between the different human species recognized from the fossil record (right) The trend towards modern characteristics had led to the appearance of the first tool-using hominid, *Homo habilis*, probably by 2.5 million years ago. In Asia, the ancestral relationships of *Homo erectus* and the emergence of fully modern people are less clearly understood, though the latter were present in Asia by at least 50,000 BP.

AFRICA   EUROPE   ASIA?

200,000 yrs

AFRICAN APES

Homo sapiens (modern)

Homo sapiens (Neanderthal)

Homo erectus (from China)

1 m.y.BP

Homo sapiens (archaic)

Homo sapiens (archaic)

Homo erectus (from Java)

Homo *erectus*

Divergence of African and Asian lineages

1.8-2 m.y.BP Early Pleistocene

Robust Australopithecines

3-5 m.y.BP Pliocene

Homo habilis

AUSTRALOPITHECINES

5-8 m.y.BP Late Miocene

m.y.BP = millions of years before present

Divergence of lineages leading to great apes and humans

Legend:
- ● Australopithecus
- ○ Homo habilis
- ● Homo erectus
- ◓ Homo sapiens (archaic)
- ● Homo sapiens (Neanderthal)
- ○ Homo sapiens (modern)

Hunters and gatherers: the first way of life

THE first humans were creatures of the African savannah. The shape of their teeth and the length of their digestive tract show that they had adapted to eat a mixed diet with a high proportion of seeds and berries. Some meat may also have figured in the diet, growing in importance as better tools and larger body size made them more capable hunters. Thus it was the hunters and gatherers who first colonized the earth. The agricultural way of life with which we are familiar today emerged only after the retreat of the last ice sheets around 10,000 BC. Hence we have been farmers for less than 10,000 years, but hunters and gatherers for at least 2.5 million years, since the development of the first stone tools.

Until the widespread use of metals in relatively recent times, people relied on artefacts of stone, bone and wood for many of their daily tasks. Stone was particularly useful, and since it survives so well it dominates our picture of early human tool-use. Finds of early wooden tools are rare, and bone tools seem to be a relatively recent innovation, beginning only within the last 100,000 years.

The use of tools is a characteristic which distinguishes humans from other primates. Though chimpanzees have been known to split stones and use the sharp edges so formed to break open nuts, there is no chimpanzee tradition of stone tool-making such as we find among our earliest stone-using ancestors. Hence the beginnings of human tool-making around 2.5 million years ago marks a significant watershed in human development. Stone tools can be used to dig up, cut or pulverize plant foods; to cut reeds or strip bark for matting or baskets; and to shape wood, bone and other raw materials into useful artefacts. The dependence on stone implements provided this phase of human cultural development with the name 'Palaeolithic' or 'Old Stone Age'.

Millions of stone tools have survived from the Old Stone Age and attest to the skills of the stone-workers or 'knappers' who often had to work with intractable materials such as quartz, quartzite or lava cobbles. But whether they were using these materials or more suitable rocks such as flint or obsidian which fracture with much greater regularity, the basic technique of the earliest tool-makers remained the same: having selected a suitable nodule of stone, the knapper chipped away at it with another stone, carefully removing flakes to create a sharp cutting edge. This was a process which required forethought and planning, and it is from scant evidence such as this that we must reconstruct the intellectual and manual abilities of our earliest ancestors. By 1.5 million years ago, early chopping tools had given way to a more developed form known as the hand-axe. This became the standard tool of Europe and Africa for over a million years, falling into disuse only 100,000 years ago.

The enormous time-spans involved make it difficult to conceptualize the stages of development in human technology. We do not understand why the hand-axe remained the dominant tool-type for so long, though we do know that it could be used for a number of tasks, including cutting up meat and plant fibres. Its flexibility may have been the key to its success. Aesthetics may also have played a role, since some of the later hand-axes are beautifully fashioned objects, flaked to a symmetrical shape.

At some sites, stone tools and the waste material from their manufacture have remained undisturbed ever since they were dropped by their makers. The distribution of the tools and their relationship to bones, hearths or structures gives a very detailed picture of the activities and shelters of a hunter-gatherer camp. There are traces of a possible brushwood windbreak at the DK site in Olduvai Gorge, which dates back 1.8 million years. At Terra Amata in southern France, the structure was a light brushwood shelter supported on a framework of poles, and at Kostenki in the south Russian plain, the inhabitants provided themselves with much more substantial dwellings made of mammoth bones. Constructions such as these and the use of fire enabled early human populations to spread beyond their tropical homeland and colonize the colder lands of Europe and Asia. In addition to artificial structures, Palaeolithic communities often took advantage of caves and rock overhangs for shelter, and some of these were visited repeatedly over many thousands of years. Their deep accumulations of stratified deposits, each the result of a short period of occupation, provide numerous layers of information about human evolution and cultural change.

Although animal bones found in association with stone tools show that even the earliest tool-makers were meat-eaters, the oldest surviving tool-kits contain no weapons, spears or lance-heads for use in hunting, and these are unknown until after about 200,000 BC. There is a similar lack of hunting equipment in the early stone tool assemblages from Asia and Europe, and this has caused much speculation as to how early humans acquired their meat. It may be that they made weapons from organic materials which have not survived – wooden spears with fire-hardened tips, for example, would have been just as effective as stone-tipped spears – but it is clear that hunting was a skill which our ancestors developed only slowly. The earliest humans, such as *Homo habilis*, were small, slightly built creatures, as much at risk of being eaten as of catching and killing prey themselves. They probably relied largely on plant foods, as hunter-gatherers do in the tropics today. Such meat as they ate would be obtained mostly by scavenging from the carcasses of animals which had died from other causes, including those killed by other carnivores. Full-scale hunting was a later development, associated with the appearance of larger-brained humans and the need to survive in Ice Age environments where plant foods were less abundant.

By the beginning of the Upper Palaeolithic, the last phase of the Old Stone Age (around 35,000 BC in Europe), highly sophisticated stone tools were being manufactured. These were made from long, narrow blades of flint carefully shaped to make spearheads, knives and other tools. In addition to flint, human communities also had an extensive range of bone and antler equipment, including barbed harpoons, fish-hooks, and bone whistles or simple flutes. No longer was it necessary for the hunter to get so near to his prey, since spear-throwers and bows and arrows enabled him to kill with deadly accuracy even from a distance.

The practice of carefully burying the dead also became widespread in Europe, Africa, Asia and Australia during this period. The evidence for intentional burial and the art found on engraved objects and on the walls of caves and rock shelters demonstrate a much richer cultural and spiritual life than at any earlier stage of human development. For the first time we are dealing with individuals with thoughts and feelings very much like our own.

Between 100,000 and 10,000 BC, fully modern humans colonized every continent except Antarctica. Their success derived from their capacity to adapt the hunter-gatherer lifestyle to different environments. In some areas the adaptation was so successful that the lifestyle changed little over many millennia. The success of the hunter-gatherers depended on intelligence and manual dexterity, as well as on the ability to cooperate with, and rely upon, one another. By the time the last Ice Age came to an end around 10,000 BC, modern man was one of the world's most widespread and successful species.

Tools of the early hunters (below) The earliest recognisable stone tools were simply pieces of hard rock (a) from which flakes had been removed to form a crude cutting edge. By 500,000 years ago, flint had become the preferred raw tool material in most parts of the world, owing to the relative ease with which it could be flaked, and the razor-sharp edges it provided. The finest products of this period were the hand-axes (b), carefully shaped implements tapering from rounded butt to pointed tip. These were multi-purpose tools, suitable for cutting vegetable fibres, working wood or butchering an animal carcass. By the end of the Ice Age, heavy stone tools had given way to lighter, more finely worked pieces, such as the Solutrean laurel leaf point (c), which were probably mounted as spearheads.

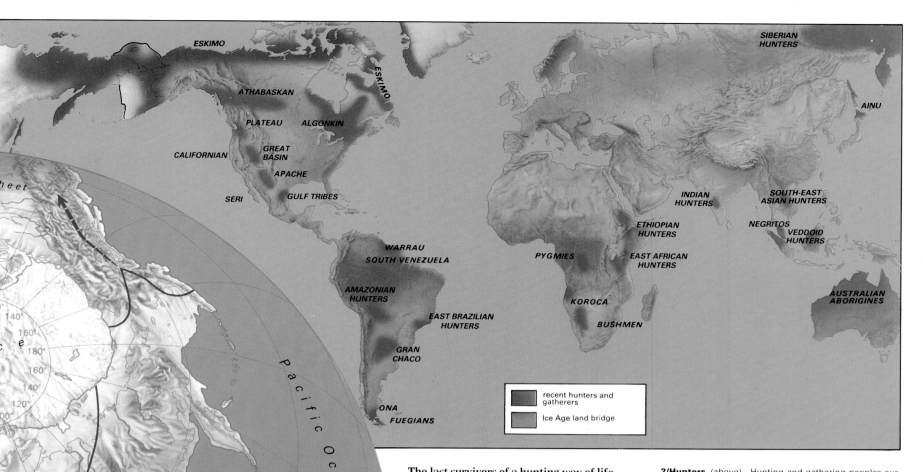

ESKIMO · ATHABASKAN · PLATEAU · ALGONKIN · GREAT BASIN · CALIFORNIAN · APACHE · SERI · GULF TRIBES · ESKIMO · SIBERIAN HUNTERS · AINU · INDIAN HUNTERS · SOUTH-EAST ASIAN HUNTERS · NEGRITOS · VEDDOID HUNTERS · ETHIOPIAN HUNTERS · PYGMIES · EAST AFRICAN HUNTERS · WARRAU · SOUTH VENEZUELA · AMAZONIAN HUNTERS · EAST BRAZILIAN HUNTERS · KOROCA · BUSHMEN · GRAN CHACO · AUSTRALIAN ABORIGINES · ONA · FUEGIANS

ice sheet · ice · Pacific Ocean · Sea of Japan · tundra · Coniferous forest? · forest? · L Balkhash · Desert · Tarim Basin · Oriental forest · Ocean

recent hunters and gatherers

Ice Age land bridge

The last survivors of a hunting way of life
Numerous hunting peoples survived into the 19th and early 20th centuries, long enough to be studied by ethnologists and anthropologists, both physical and social. Today, however, the hunting and gathering way of life is only fully represented by the khoisan, the bushmen, the eskimos and the Australian aborigines, between them totalling only a few hundreds of thousands out of a total world population of nearly 5.5 billion. Nevertheless, they provide a unique and valuable insight into mankind's earlier way of life.

Recent studies reveal the intimacy of the relationship between hunting peoples and their natural environments; the relative simplicity of the material culture (only 94 different artefacts exist among the Kung bushmen); the lack of accumulation of individual wealth; the mobility. The units of society, the bands or hordes, are small: groups of kinfolk and a few friends who can live and work well together. Recent work contradicts the traditional view of hunting life as 'nasty, brutish and short', as a constant struggle against a harsh environment. In fact, bushmen's subsistence requirements are satisfied by only a modest effort – perhaps two or three days' work a week by each adult; they do not have to struggle over food resources; their attitudes towards ownership are flexible; and their living groups admit newcomers from other groups. Such features set hunters and gatherers apart from more technologically developed societies whose very survival depends upon their ability to maintain order and control property.

Evidence suggests that hunting and gathering communities often have a high percentage of old people, and that life expectancy is not necessarily short. Infectious diseases are rare, since people are spread out over the landscape making it more difficult for diseases to pass from group to group. The size of the population is held stable not through high levels of infant mortality so much as through long intervals between births. Breast-feeding infants for long periods has been shown to inhibit pregnancy and is one of the

2/Hunters (above) Hunting and gathering peoples survived into recent times in virtually all the climatic regions of the world. However, the spread of farming and industry has increasingly forced them into marginal environments. The most famous hunter-gatherers of recent times are those of the arid deserts of Australia and the Kalahari, the dense tropical jungles of central Africa and the Amazon, and the frozen wastes of the Arctic.

ways by which this birth-spacing is achieved. Many hunting groups have proved highly adept at population control – not merely in restricting numbers, but in preserving and developing desirable social characteristics, while endeavouring to prevent (often by enforced celibacy) the passing-on of any personal defects that might prevent a member from playing a full part in his or her small community.

Such communities frequently show great robustness and resilience in the face of normal hazards. Illness, accident, climatic change or the migration of food supplies can all be met from within the resources of the group. It is usually outside intruders, especially those introducing modern methods and economic attitudes (not to mention diseases) who shatter the delicate but essential ecological balance between the hunters and their environment. Unfortunately, the massive population explosion of modern times has placed such pressure on land that few hunter-gatherers have survived into the 20th century. Those that have are suffering severe disruption of their traditional lifestyles.

coastline at the height of the last glaciation (Ice Age), 20,000 years ago

modern coastline and rivers

Limits of human occupation in:

lower Palaeolithic
up to 400,000 years ago

middle Palaeolithic
400,000 – 100,000 years ago

upper Palaeolithic
100,000 – 10,000 years ago

1/Hunters colonize the world (above) Tropical Africa was the home of the earliest tool-making hominids, and it was only around 1 million years ago that humans began to colonize adjacent areas of Asia and Europe. By 400,000 years ago, groups of humans were established from the British Isles to northern China and were spreading southwards into India and Southeast Asia. The success of this colonization owed much to the control of fire and the ability to make the shelters and clothing essential in more temperate latitudes. These skills were further developed during the last Ice Age, when groups of hunters penetrated northwards to exploit the rich animal life of the steppe and tundra zones, reaching Siberia and ultimately the New World.

The Altamira bison (right) The polychrome bison painted on the ceiling of the Altamira cave in northern Spain is one of the most vivid images created by the artists of the late Ice Age in western Europe. Many of the paintings at Altamira and other Ice Age sites lie deep inside the caves, accessible only with difficulty. We must, therefore, imagine them as they would have appeared in the dim light of the flickering oil lamps used by the cave artists – mysterious images, lifelike representations of important species such as horse, mammoth and reindeer which roamed the region some 20,000 years ago. Though realistic in themselves, the pictures are never arranged to form scenes, even when they are grouped closely together on cave walls. In many cases, paintings or engravings even overlie each other, suggesting that it was the act of painting itself, rather that the resulting image, that was important to Ice Age communities.

The Ice Age world

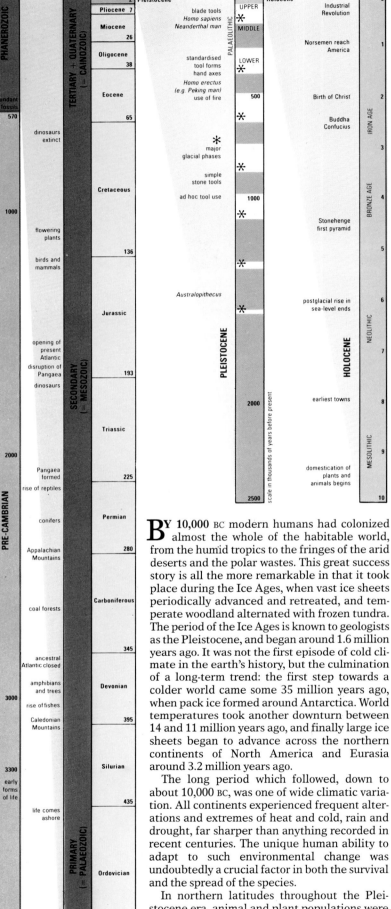

2/Geological periods and the emergence of humans
Using a complex variety of analytical techniques, it is now possible to reconstruct some aspects of the earth's climate as far back as the Pre-Cambrian era, more than 3000 million years ago. The chart sets out the broad patterns of change during the main geological periods from the origins of the earth down to our own period, the Holocene.

BY 10,000 BC modern humans had colonized almost the whole of the habitable world, from the humid tropics to the fringes of the arid deserts and the polar wastes. This great success story is all the more remarkable in that it took place during the Ice Ages, when vast ice sheets periodically advanced and retreated, and temperate woodland alternated with frozen tundra. The period of the Ice Ages is known to geologists as the Pleistocene, and began around 1.6 million years ago. It was not the first episode of cold climate in the earth's history, but it was the culmination of a long-term trend: the first step towards a colder world came some 35 million years ago, when pack ice formed around Antarctica. World temperatures took another downturn between 14 and 11 million years ago, and finally large ice sheets began to advance across the northern continents of North America and Eurasia around 3.2 million years ago.

The long period which followed, down to about 10,000 BC, was one of wide climatic variation. All continents experienced frequent alterations and extremes of heat and cold, rain and drought, far sharper than anything recorded in recent centuries. The unique human ability to adapt to such environmental change was undoubtedly a crucial factor in both the survival and the spread of the species.

In northern latitudes throughout the Pleistocene era, animal and plant populations were seriously affected by the advance and retreat of the glaciers. These frequently covered large parts of Europe, Asia and North America with impenetrable ice sheets, locking up huge quantities of sea water and reducing average temperatures by 50°–54°F (10°–12°C) and ocean levels

by over 450 feet (137 m), far below those of modern times. Only in the interglacial periods, when the ice sheets shrank back and allowed the northward spread of oak and spruce forests and the sub-arctic vegetation on which the mammoths and reindeer browsed, was it possible for early humans to live much outside the equatorial regions; even then it was only the discovery of fire, and the ability to sew warm clothing, which enabled them to survive the cold winters in the rich, but frozen, hunting grounds.

Scientific analysis has shown that sea-bed sediments contain an accurate record of world temperature reaching back more than 2 million years. From this we know that there was an ice advance roughly every 100,000 years, followed in each case by a 10,000-year period known as an interglacial, with warmer conditions similar to those of the present day.

Africa, the original homeland of early humans, lay beyond the reach of the ice sheets, but it was nonetheless severely affected by the dramatic shifts in Ice Age climate. As the expansion and contraction of the icecaps created constantly changing conditions – with expansion of deserts in the cold epochs but increased rainfall in the arid savannahs as temperatures rose again – so humans adapted their lifestyle and tool-kits, taking advantage of favourable conditions. Around 40,000 BC, lighter rainfall led to reduced tropical vegetation and allowed human groups of the large stone tool tradition to expand into the tropical forests. Conversely, during the wet centuries around 20,000 BC bow-and-arrow makers of the Maghreb were able to colonize the previously arid Sahara.

The ability to make and use fire for protection and warmth was particularly important in the process of adapting to cold environments. The use of fire may already have been known in Africa as early as 1.5 million years ago and was certainly being used by the inhabitants of the Chou-k'ou-tien cave in northern China around half a million years ago. When the last ice advance in Europe began around 73,000 BC, the Mousterian cave-dwellers of the Dordogne, with their cooking hearths, their bone needles, and their implements for scraping and shaping furs, were well equipped to survive the bitter conditions of a northern winter. Each time the ice retreated, the peoples of Europe and Asia grew gradually more numerous and more advanced. The water frozen into the ice sheets reduced

sea levels so far that land bridges appeared linking most major areas and many isolated islands into one single continent. As a result, people were first able to reach Australia and Tasmania across a narrow stretch of sea around 50,000 BC. The Bering Strait between eastern Asia and Alaska now became a broad, dry land highway for the migration of peoples and animals of all kinds. The first groups to penetrate the Americas, sometime before 30,000 BC, made little impact on their environment; and then for a time the North American ice sheets expanded and closed off the route south. An ice-free corridor opened up again about 12,000 BC, letting big-game hunters from Siberia through to the rich gamelands of the American plains.

Palaeolithic hunters, now making lethally accurate use of flint-tipped spears and arrows,

1/The world 20,000 years ago *(below)* The world at the height of the last ice age, when the climate was particularly cold. Ice sheets covered most of Canada and much of northern Europe. They also blocked the route between Asia and the plains of North America. Humans had already colonized Australia, Europe, Asia (including Japan) and Alaska, but only a few early hunters had managed to penetrate as far as Central America.

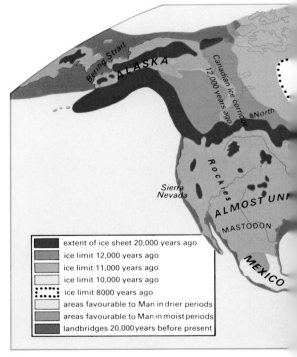

■	extent of ice sheet 20,000 years ago
	ice limit 12,000 years ago
	ice limit 11,000 years ago
	ice limit 10,000 years ago
⋯	ice limit 8000 years ago
	areas favourable to Man in drier periods
	areas favourable to Man in moist periods
	landbridges 20,000 years before present

3/Climatic change and population growth
Population and climate during the Pleistocene are here shown against a logarithmic scale. It should be noted how human population continued to grow even during the pronounced climatic fluctuations of the Ice Ages.

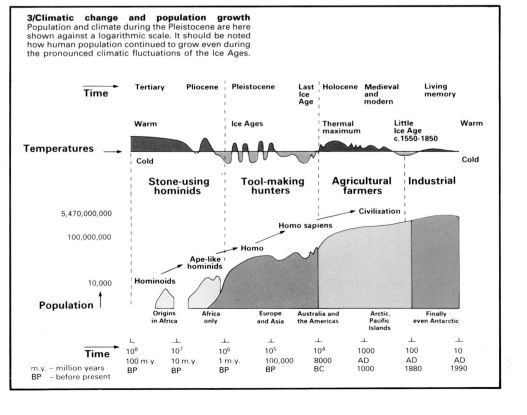

Restoration of *Mammuthus primigenius* (above) The woolly mammoth which lived during the last Ice Age, feeding on tundra vegetation. Mammoth carcasses have been found preserved in frozen Siberian mud, among them the Berezovka mammoth which probably died in a fall from a high river-bank bluff around 40,000 years ago.

had long since begun to reduce once-numerous animal species. The mammoths were well on the way to extinction in northern Eurasia by 15,000 BC, and soon afterwards they became a favourite quarry for the early hunters of North America. Eleven thousand years ago the rolling grasslands of west and southwest North America were teeming with animal life – giant bison with a six-foot (1.8 m) horn spread, towering, beaver-like creatures called casteroides, camels, ground sloths, stag-moose, two types of musk-oxen, several varieties of large, often lion-sized cats, mastodons and three types of mammoths – woolly, Columbian and imperial. The human popula-

tion grew and flourished, but within 1000 years most of these animals were gone – including all the horses, which were reintroduced by Europeans following in the wake of Columbus.

With the disappearance of their customary meat sources such as the mammoth which had weighed a ton or more and sufficed on the frozen tundra to feed a whole tribe for weeks on end, human groups were obliged to devise new subsistence strategies. At the same time, as the world slowly started to warm up again, new opportunities were presented by the spreading forest cover, with its associated fauna of goat and deer. Within a few centuries of the end of the Ice Age, small groups of people all over the world began to domesticate animals and plants, and lay the foundations for the agricultural revolution.

No-one knows to what extent Ice-Age populations were responsible for this wholesale destruction, and there has been no evidence to suggest a climatic or topographical cause. However there are indications, both in cave paintings and in skeletal remains, that many of the now-extinct mammals were attacked by large groups of humans, and sometimes even stampeded in herds over cliffs into swamps.

Whatever the explanation, there is little doubt that the greatly expanded populations of Late Palaeolithic Man, even though their hunting grounds now extended down to the far tip of South America, found their accustomed wild food-plants and wild game far sparser and more difficult to come by as the Pleistocene ice age came to its end, c.10,000 BC.

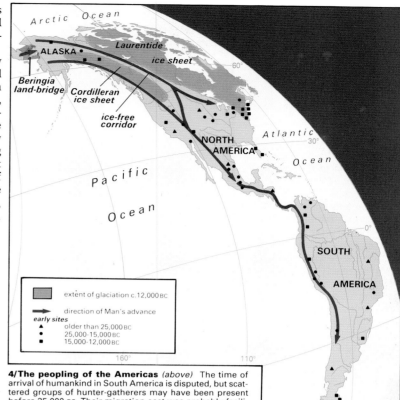

4/The peopling of the Americas *(above)* The time of arrival of humankind in South America is disputed, but scattered groups of hunter-gatherers may have been present before 35,000 BC. Their migration east was probably facilitated by the last ('Wisconsin') glaciation when the growing ice sheets locked up so much water that sea levels fell. The Bering Strait emerged as dry land and as animals colonized it they were followed by hunters, who gradually moved south as the ice melted and the sea levels rose again.

Legend (map 4):
- extent of glaciation c.12,000 BC
- direction of Man's advance
- *early sites*
  - ▲ older than 25,000 BC
  - ■ 25,000-15,000 BC
  - ● 15,000-12,000 BC

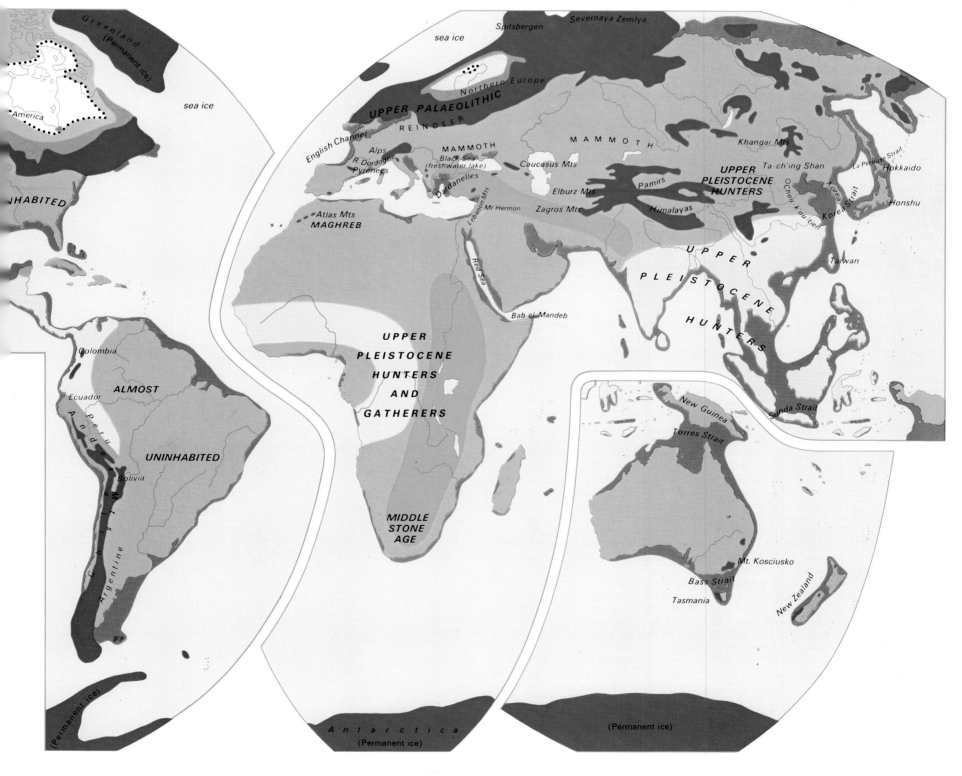

From hunting to farming: the origins of agriculture

THE last 10,000 years, during which present-day climatic conditions have prevailed, is only the last of a dozen or so warmer phases which punctuated the Ice Age. In one respect, however, it is unique: it has seen an unprecedented explosion in the numbers of the human species, and in their impact on the world.

In 8000 BC there were still only small bands of hunters and gatherers, whose lifestyle was little different from that of their predecessors up to 100,000 years before. Within the next 2000 years, however, substantial villages had appeared in certain regions; in another 2000 years, there were towns and cities; 2000 years later, city-states had grown into empires; 2000 years more and technological foundations had been laid for achievements which, in the most recent 2000 years have included the printing press, atomic energy, and man's first moon-landing.

This decisive quickening in the pace of human development can be attributed largely to the beginning of agriculture – the deliberate alteration of natural systems to promote the abundance of an exploited species or set of species. In simple terms, this means the cultivation of crops such as wheat, rice or maize, and the domestication of animals such as cattle, sheep and pigs.

However domestication left some species completely dependent on man's intervention for their survival. This is especially true of the cereals, those species of plant related to wild grasses which more than any other have sustained the tremendous growth of population since the last Ice Age. The yield from cultivated cereals made possible larger settled human communities than ever before, and thus for the first time permitted settlements which can be described as villages or even towns. Because yields came from a limited area of land, it was possible to support a growing population by converting more and more land to crops; and the productivity of this land could be increased by intensive techniques of cultivation, such as terracing in steep-sided valleys, or irrigation in dry regions.

Intensive agriculture demands a high level of social and political organization, and a natural tendency existed for more complex societies to develop as population levels rose. But the actual origins of agriculture are still poorly understood. Certainly, by the end of the last Ice Age, human communities were more complex in their technology and social organization than before, and were thus better equipped to respond to the challenge of environmental change as the ice sheets melted, sea levels rose, and forests recolonized the landscape. Whatever the precise reason, the critical change in human lifestyles was the greater reliance in certain parts of the world on the productive cereal grasses which abounded in the mountain foothills, and the unconscious selection of certain forms which could be grown in lowland habitats and revealed their potential as crops.

Change took place independently in several parts of the world, but earliest and most importantly in the Near East, China, Mesoamerica and Peru. At least three major groups of cereals were involved, each becoming a staple crop and causing fundamental changes in economy and society. In the Near East, and spreading out from there to Europe and the borders of India, wheat and barley formed the basis of village and city life. At the other end of Eurasia, in China, millet was cultivated; and millet and rice (first domesticated in Southeast Asia) have supported the burgeoning communities of India and the Far East to the present day. In Mesoamerica and Peru, maize was the principal cereal crop. Once developed from its tiny wild form to its present size it was able to support the successive civilizations of Central and South America. Everywhere the initial innovation of cereal cultivation had a gradually cumulative effect, for, once

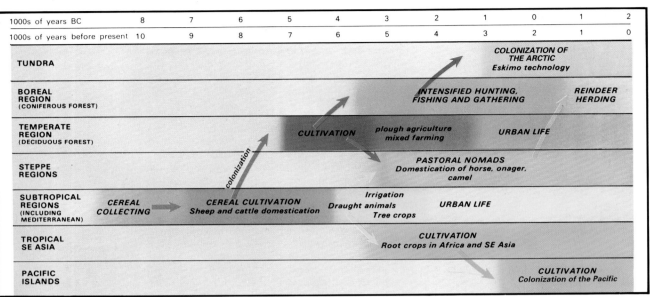

The cumulative consequences of the agricultural revolution (above) This diagram shows how the adoption of plant cultivation and animal husbandry affected the different regions of the Old World. The changes were gradual, but agriculture ultimately transformed human lifestyles wherever it became established.

adopted, there was no easy turning back, and the very success of the new lifestyle induced fundamental changes not only in the economy but in social order, technology and ideology.

In the Old World, the cultivation of plants was complemented by new forms of animal exploitation: sheep, goats, cattle and pigs came to be herded near to the permanent settlements and fields, and became domesticated through isolation from their wild populations. Later it was discovered that some of these animals could be used for wool and milk as well as meat, and also to pull ploughs and carts, so raising agricultural productivity; and that other domesticable species, such as horses and asses, could be used to carry loads and human riders, improving communications and the possibilities of trade and war. With time, also, a wider range of plants came to be used – tree-crops such as figs, dates and olives were taken into cultivation while, as agriculture spread to the tropics, techniques of vegetative propagation were applied to roots and tubers.

In the New World, where few animals were domesticated, the lack of suitable draught animals prevented the development of the plough. Nevertheless, a wide range of plants was domesticated. Many of these were widely adopted in Europe after the discovery of the Americas, and are of worldwide importance today – maize, squashes and beans from Mesoamerica; potatoes, peppers and tomatoes from the tropical region further south. The use of cotton in the New World took the place of wool in the western Old World. The separate development of domestic plants and animals in different parts of the world has provided a valuable pool of diversity, allowing modern man a wide range of choice in selecting appropriate crops and stock for particular situations.

The development of agriculture and domestication was not restricted to those areas where cereal-based urban societies became established. In Africa a wide variety of native species of plants were domesticated in the lands across the southern margin of the Sahara, and in the high grasslands of Ethiopia. Many of these crops, such as sorghum, yams and millet, are still important today, though new introductions (such as maize from the New World) have

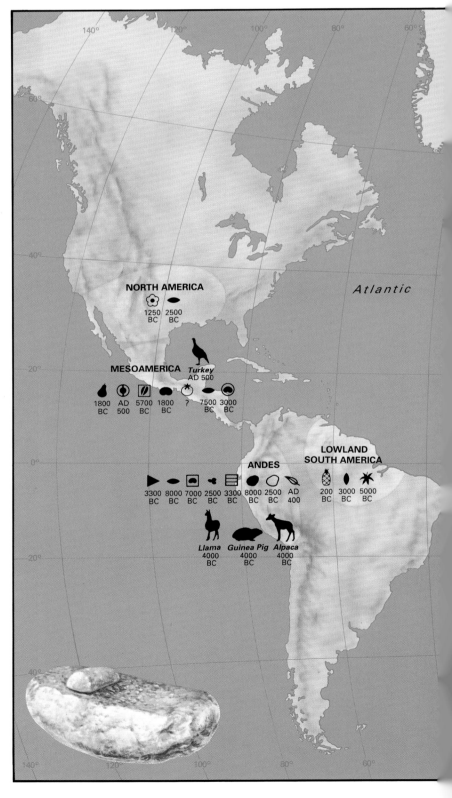

Early milling equipment (right) Found wherever grain crops were cultivated, the simple saddle-quern or flat grinding stone was a basic piece of early agricultural equipment. It was needed to convert the hard seeds to porridge or flour, and appears in early farming contexts both in the Old World and the Americas.

reduced their importance. Over the centuries, farming populations along the southern edge of the Sahara grew, and as they did so gradually expanded southwards, pushing the native hunting groups into more marginal territories. This process eventually brought Bantu farmers to the southernmost parts of the continent, and today the hunter-gatherers are restricted to the dense tropical forests of central Africa and the harsh deserts of the southwest.

On the dry steppe-lands of central Eurasia, animal-keeping was more important than plant cultivation. Here the domestication of the horse gave rise to a specialized lifestyle based on nomadic herding. Further north, the development of more advanced technologies allowed the colonization of the Arctic by specialized Eskimo hunters and fishers, though the climate was too severe for plant cultivation to become established.

By the time of European expansion in the 16th century AD, the world had a roughly zonal arrangement of native economies, ranging from specialized hunter-fishers in the north, through herding groups, societies practising hunting or simple agriculture, complex urban economies based on plough or irrigation-agriculture, to the yam and tuber cultivators of the tropics. Beyond these, in the southern continents, were remaining hunting and gathering populations of South America, southern Africa and Australia – the last surviving examples of the way of life which humankind had followed for thousands of years.

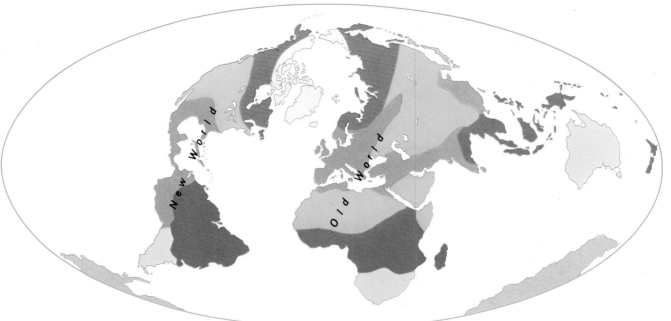

cereal crops
tropical root crops
reindeer hunters and herders
Arctic hunters
hunters and pastoralists
remnant hunting isolates

2/The native economies of the world *(above)* As they developed following the spread of agriculture, the economies of different parts of the world showed a marked zonal pattern. Hunting economies survived at both the northern and at the southern extremes – Inuit peoples in the Arctic, desert hunting groups in central Australia and the Kalahari. Cereal cultivation and root-crop cultivation are characteristic of the temperate and tropical zones respectively, with an emphasis on stock-rearing in the arid zone. Reindeer-hunters of the northern forest/tundra region complete the picture, although – despite close relations between the hunters and their prey – full domestication of the reindeer appears to have been a recent phenomenon and not part of the traditional way of life.

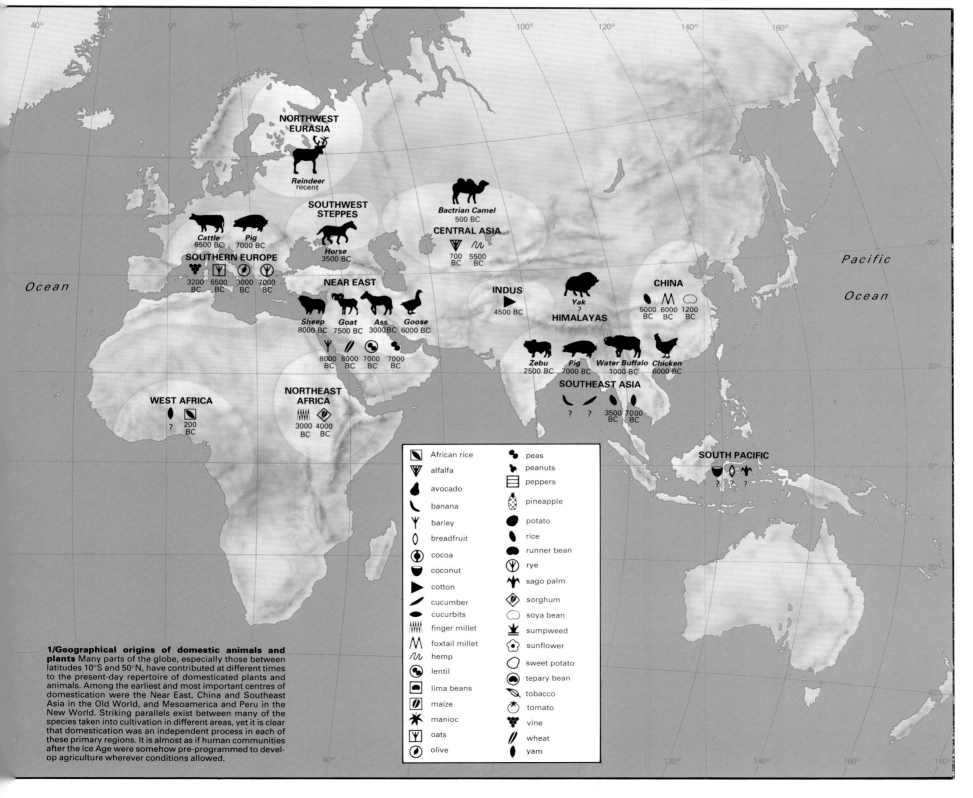

NORTHWEST EURASIA

Reindeer recent

SOUTHWEST STEPPES

Bactrian Camel 500 BC

CENTRAL ASIA

700 BC 5500 BC

Cattle 6500 BC *Pig* 7000 BC

SOUTHERN EUROPE

3200 BC 6500 BC 3000 BC 7000 BC

Horse 3500 BC

NEAR EAST

Sheep 8000 BC *Goat* 7500 BC *Ass* 3000 BC *Goose* 6000 BC

8000 BC 8000 BC 7000 BC 7000 BC

INDUS 4500 BC

Yak ?

HIMALAYAS

Zebu 2500 BC *Pig* 7000 BC *Water Buffalo* 1000 BC *Chicken* 6000 BC

CHINA

5000 BC 6000 BC 1200 BC

SOUTHEAST ASIA

? ? 3500 BC 7000 BC

WEST AFRICA

200 BC ?

NORTHEAST AFRICA

3000 BC 4000 BC

SOUTH PACIFIC

? ? ?

Pacific Ocean

Ocean

Legend

- African rice
- alfalfa
- avocado
- banana
- barley
- breadfruit
- cocoa
- coconut
- cotton
- cucumber
- cucurbits
- finger millet
- foxtail millet
- hemp
- lentil
- lima beans
- maize
- manioc
- oats
- olive
- peas
- peanuts
- peppers
- pineapple
- potato
- rice
- runner bean
- rye
- sago palm
- sorghum
- soya bean
- sumpweed
- sunflower
- sweet potato
- tepary bean
- tobacco
- tomato
- vine
- wheat
- yam

1/Geographical origins of domestic animals and plants Many parts of the globe, especially those between latitudes 10°S and 50°N, have contributed at different times to the present-day repertoire of domesticated plants and animals. Among the earliest and most important centres of domestication were the Near East, China and Southeast Asia in the Old World, and Mesoamerica and Peru in the New World. Striking parallels exist between many of the species taken into cultivation in different areas, yet it is clear that domestication was an independent process in each of these primary regions. It is almost as if human communities after the Ice Age were somehow pre-programmed to develop agriculture wherever conditions allowed.

Before the first cities: the Near East 8000 to 4000 BC

THE beginnings of cereal cultivation in the lowland areas of the Near East during the 9th and 8th millennia BC produced, for the first time, communities which were large and permanent enough to develop brick and stone architecture for both private and public buildings, and a range of arts and crafts to accompany them. The remains of these earliest mudbrick villages – now often forming prominent mounds as a result of rebuilding over hundreds of years – are a common feature of the lowland landscape, especially where abundant springs made the area a first choice for settlement. Most Near-Eastern languages have a word to describe these ancient village mounds: *tell* in Arabic, *hüyük* in Turkish, for instance.

The earliest sites were not far from the mountain ranges which had been the original home of the wild ancestors of wheat and barley, and all lay either within the critical rainfall limit of 12 inches (300 mm) a year, necessary for rain-fed agriculture, or (less commonly) in 'oasis' situations beyond this, where flood plain cultivation was possible. Two of the largest and most developed of these sites are Tell es-Sultan (Jericho) in the Jordan valley and Çatal Hüyük in the central plain of Turkey.

Jericho is by far the older of the two, and in the 8th millennium (when Europe was still only just recovering from the last Ice Age) it was already a settlement of four acres (1.6 ha) defended by a rock-cut ditch and stone wall with a solid circular tower. Pottery had not yet been invented, and the lowest levels of the town are termed 'pre-pottery Neolithic'. Stone bowls served as containers, and obsidian, a volcanic glass from as far afield as Turkey, was used to make cutting tools. Clay ovens were used for cooking. Even at this date public buildings existed, and shrines have been found, some of which contained plaster statues. In addition to these, the inhabitants of early Jericho kept human skulls, modelling the faces naturalistically in plaster and adding cowrie shells for the eyes.

The site of Çatal Hüyük is even more spectacular. Covering 32 acres (13 ha), it was not defended by walls but its tightly packed houses could only be entered through the roof. Here, too, evidence abounds of long-distance trade in desirable materials: obsidian for tools and weapons, for instance, or light-blue apatite for ornaments. House fittings indicate a comparable sophistication: frescoes showing hunting scenes covered some walls, while shrines were adorned with the plastered skulls of wild oxen set into the walls.

Although these two sites were larger than most of their contemporaries, whether they should be described as 'towns' remains uncertain and, although they probably served as important regional centres, they were largely agricultural. Nor is there any continuity between these early centres of population and the temple-based administrative and manufacturing centres of later urban civilization, with their literate elites and monumental architecture. These developments became possible only through more intensive agricultural techniques devised in the intervening millennia.

The settlement at Çatal Hüyük came to an end around 5000 BC, some 2000 years before the earliest writing appeared. Already, however, sophisticated painted pottery was being made, woven textiles were in use, and flax and a full range of food crops were cultivated. But the area of the Near East under farming was small, restricted by the availability of rainfall or natural groundwater. One of the most important changes of the succeeding phase was the development of effective techniques of irrigation, allowing settlement to spread beyond the zone of rain-fed 'dry-farming' and exploit the great rivers which flowed through otherwise semi-desert areas.

The earliest phases of this process occurred in the 5th millennium with the appearance of settlements on slopes where rivers entered plains. Here simple transverse trenches could divert wandering streams into adjacent fields. Such small-scale water-spreading was first used only as an insurance against drought in areas already rain-fed; but during the 5th and 4th millennia it allowed the colonization of arid areas previously beyond the reach of farming communities. As a result, many small settlements appeared on the edges of the riverine plain of Mesopotamia, an area of enormous arable potential, but very poor in basic raw materials such as timber and hard stone for tools and weapons. New settlements had therefore to be supplied with essential materials obtained from distant highland areas. This, in turn, demanded a higher degree of social and economic organization in the villages of the plain. Such pressures set the early farming villages of Mesopotamia on the path to urbanization. Religion played a critical role, and regional religious centres grew into temple-based administrative units. Sites such as Eridu in southern Mesopotamia produced urban, literate cultures in the late 4th and 3rd millennia, and the classic pattern of Near-Eastern civilization was born.

One technological development of this formative period was the beginning of copper metallurgy. While at first of very limited practical significance, metal came to play an increasingly important role as a raw material; and the experience of copper-working led to a knowledge of the properties of other materials. Among the rocks widely traded as ornaments among the Neolithic villages of the Near East as early as the 8th millennium were certain attractive green stones, found only in the highland areas. One such stone was malachite – a pure, high-yielding copper ore. As the technology of early villages already involved the controlled use of heat, either in firing pottery or in baking bread in mudbrick ovens, a combination of raw material and existing skill provided the milieu for man's first experiments with metallurgy. It was not until the 5th millennium, however, that effective techniques of smelting were developed and it first became possible to cast spearheads, axes and the like. Weapons, status symbols and cult objects were the first products of this new technology; useful tools came later.

The output of the early copper industry was sustained by mining the rich surface ores of malachite at places such as Timna, in southern Israel, where the shafts of ancient mines extend over a huge area. Production of finished objects was often promoted by the emerging temple centres, and cult places were adorned by copper objects. The search for ways of moulding complex shapes led to the development of sophisticated casting processes involving wax and clay moulds, and also stimulated an appreciation of the beneficial effects of certain impurities commonly found in the copper ores. Arsenical copper, the first deliberately manufactured alloy known to man, was produced to a consistent recipe for over 1000 years before the rarer but less dangerous metal, tin, became available through trade, and so allowed the production of bronze.

By 4000 BC the foundations of Mesopotamian civilization had been laid. Extensive systems of irrigation canals supported prosperous farming communities, and trade and craftsmanship flourished. It was from these successful and dynamic communities, around the middle of the 4th millennium BC, that the early historic cities of Sumer arose.

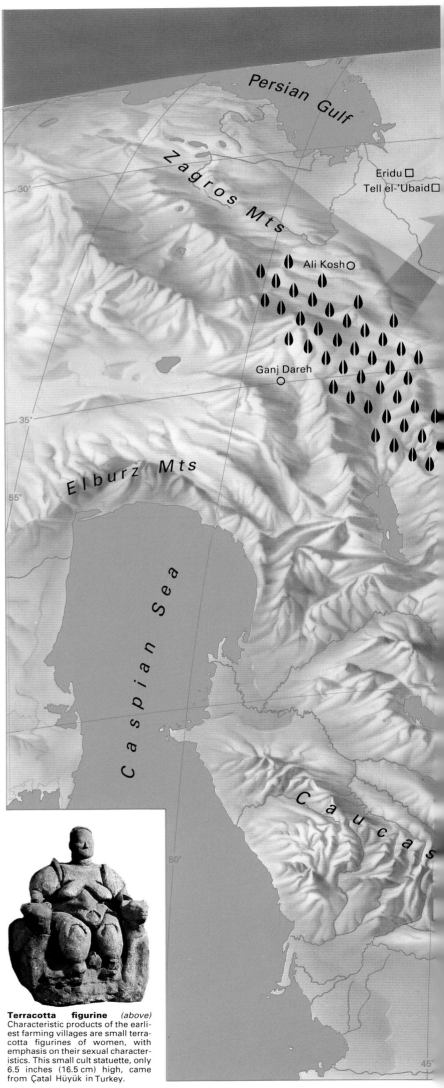

Terracotta figurine *(above)* Characteristic products of the earliest farming villages are small terracotta figurines of women, with emphasis on their sexual characteristics. This small cult statuette, only 6.5 inches (16.5 cm) high, came from Çatal Hüyük in Turkey.

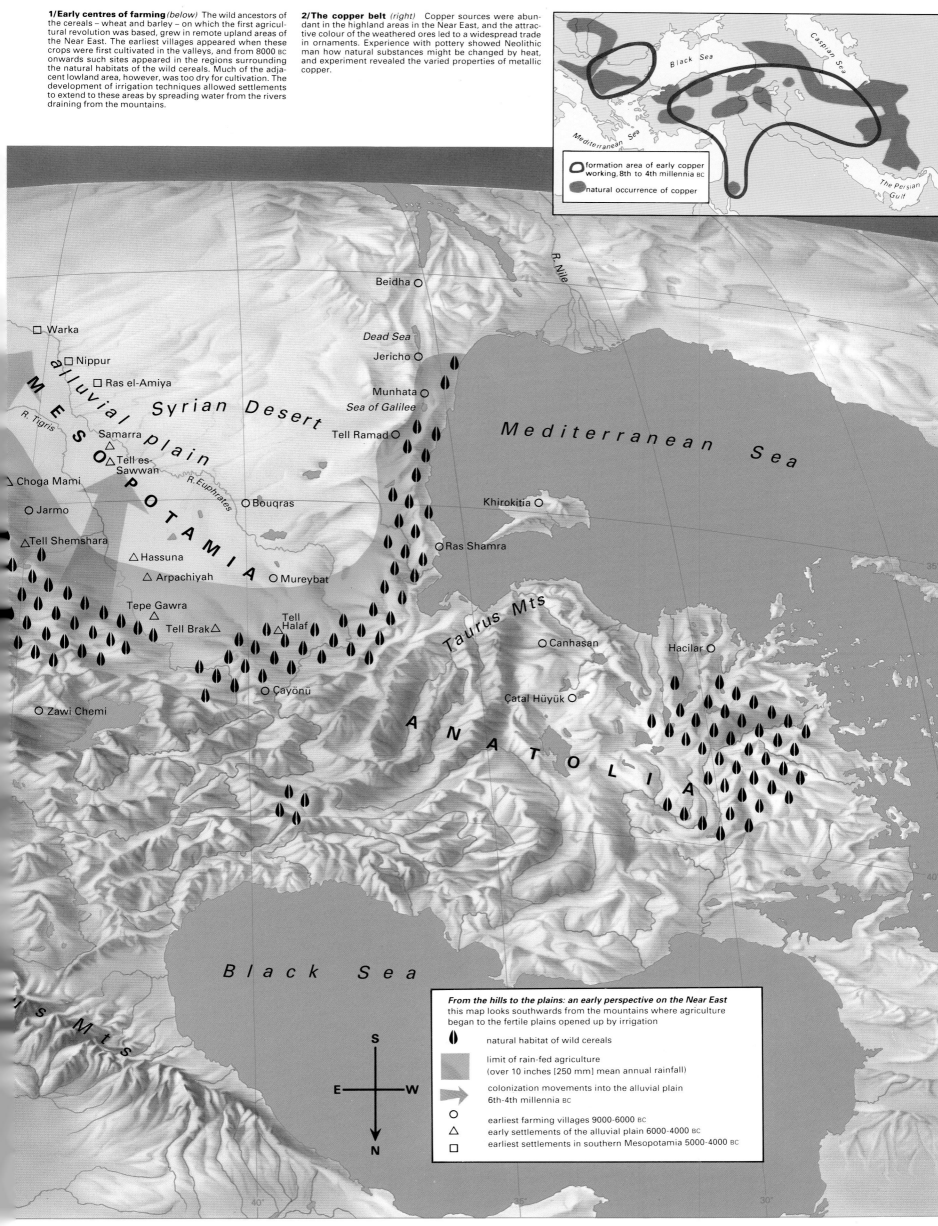

1/Early centres of farming (below) The wild ancestors of the cereals – wheat and barley – on which the first agricultural revolution was based, grew in remote upland areas of the Near East. The earliest villages appeared when these crops were first cultivated in the valleys, and from 8000 BC onwards such sites appeared in the regions surrounding the natural habitats of the wild cereals. Much of the adjacent lowland area, however, was too dry for cultivation. The development of irrigation techniques allowed settlements to extend to these areas by spreading water from the rivers draining from the mountains.

2/The copper belt (right) Copper sources were abundant in the highland areas in the Near East, and the attractive colour of the weathered ores led to a widespread trade in ornaments. Experience with pottery showed Neolithic man how natural substances might be changed by heat, and experiment revealed the varied properties of metallic copper.

Black Sea

Caspian Sea

Mediterranean Sea

The Persian Gulf

◯ formation area of early copper working, 8th to 4th millennia BC

▨ natural occurrence of copper

Beidha ◯

R. Nile

Warka ☐

Dead Sea

Nippur ☐

Jericho ◯

Ras el-Amiya ☐

Munhata ◯

Sea of Galilee

M E S O P O T A M I A

alluvial plain

Syrian Desert

R. Tigris

Samarra △

Tell es-Sawwan △

Tell Ramad ◯

Mediterranean Sea

Choga Mami ↘

R. Euphrates

Bouqras ◯

Khirokitia ◯

Jarmo ◯

Tell Shemshara △

Hassuna △

Arpachiyah △

Mureybat ◯

Ras Shamra ◯

Tepe Gawra △

Tell Brak △

Tell Halaf △

Taurus Mts

Canhasan ◯

Hacilar ◯

Çayönü ◯

Çatal Hüyük ◯

A N A T O L I A

Zawi Chemi ◯

...s Mts

B l a c k   S e a

From the hills to the plains: an early perspective on the Near East
this map looks southwards from the mountains where agriculture began to the fertile plains opened up by irrigation

◗ natural habitat of wild cereals

▨ limit of rain-fed agriculture (over 10 inches [250 mm] mean annual rainfall)

➤ colonization movements into the alluvial plain 6th-4th millennium BC

◯ earliest farming villages 9000-6000 BC

△ early settlements of the alluvial plain 6000-4000 BC

☐ earliest settlements in southern Mesopotamia 5000-4000 BC

S

E — W

N

41

Early Europe: the colonization of a continent 6000 to 1500 BC

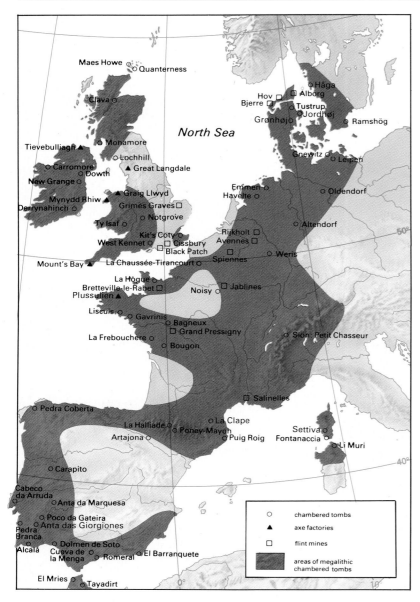

2/Megalithic monuments *(above)* The farmers of the loess-lands built their houses and cult-centres of wood. Further west, while houses continued to be built mostly of wood, public monuments were constructed from large un-dressed boulders or slabs of stone. Such monuments, built to serve many generations, were mainly concerned with mortuary rituals and ancestor-worship. Three or four main areas began independently to build simple structures, but as the monuments grew more elaborate, ideas and techniques were exchanged. By the end of the 4th millennium BC many different kinds of monument were being built over much of western Europe, from simple cists to elaborate chambered tombs.

The cart *(above)* was introduced to Europe from the Caucasus via the steppe region in the 4th millennium BC. This small model is in fact a drinking cup in the shape of a cart. It came from a cemetery at Budakalasz, near Budapest, Hungary, and dates to around 3000 BC.

THE first experiments with the cultivation of cereals and the domestication of animals began in the Near East some 10,000 years ago, and the agricultural way of life was already fully established there when farming villages appeared in adjacent parts of southeast Europe 2000 years later. From there, farming spread rapidly across the more fertile parts of central Europe, reaching the Low Countries by 5000 BC. After a brief pause, the final phase saw the spread of farming to the northern and western fringes of Europe, including Denmark and the British Isles, where it was adopted by existing hunter-gatherer communities in about 4000 BC.

The earliest mudbrick *tell* settlements in Europe, dating to shortly before 6000 BC, stood on the western side of the Aegean, in the plain of Thessaly (e.g. Argissa) and on Crete (e.g. Knossos). Farming spread to these areas from Anatolia, the routes across the Aegean being already well known through the activities of fishing boats and the transport of obsidian to the mainland from the Aegean island of Melos. The material culture of the first European farmers was very similar to that of their contemporaries across the Aegean: they did not at first use pottery, but Anatolian techniques soon spread to the new areas, and both plain and painted vessels were in use in Greece and Bulgaria by 5500 BC. By this time agricultural settlement had spread up the Vardar river valley to the northern Balkans and the lower Danube area. Villages consisted of clusters of square mud-brick buildings, each with an identical layout of hearths, cooking and sleeping areas, though usually with one larger 'club-house' or village shrine. Their economy was based on keeping sheep and cultivating wheat and legumes. Such

villages were situated in the plains, by areas of good soil with a plentiful water supply, and often remained occupied for hundreds of years. Kara-novo in Bulgaria is a good example: the mound of settlement debris is 40 feet (12 m) high.

Villages of this kind spread inland as far as Hungary (e.g. Hódmezövásárhely), but from here northwards a new pattern developed. The square mudbrick dwellings were replaced by wooden longhouses, and villages such as Bylany in Czechoslovakia or Cologne-Lindenthal in Germany therefore did not build up into *tells*. Settlement spread across the whole of Europe, from northeast France to southwest Russia, on the expanses of soil produced by the weathering of loess – a highly fertile wind-blown dust laid down during the Ice Age beyond the southern margins of the glaciers. Over this whole area, the characteristic pottery is decorated with incised lines in spiral or meandering bands. This uniformity of culture reflects the rapid spread of settlement along the main river valleys (especially the Danube and the Rhine) which occurred around 5000 BC. In the eastern part of the area, villages continued to be grouped around a 'club-house'; but in the west, small strings of hamlets consisting of two or three longhouses were often found. Cattle seem to have been more important than sheep in the flat forested interior of Europe, but wheat continued to be the staple crop among the cereals. Where possible, settlements were placed next to small rivers or streams, and almost invariably on loess. Although small stone axes were used, the settlers did not clear wide areas of land away from the watercourses but practised an intensive horticulture in the valleys around their settlements.

This pattern continued, with developments and modifications, down to 4000 BC. By that time, in the Balkans, population density had increased and there had been expansion into the foothills and lower slopes of the mountains. *Tell* settlements multiplied in the plains, and these prosperous communities traded and experimented with a wide range of raw materials for tools or for decorative purposes. Pottery came to be decorated in elaborate multi-coloured paints, using ochre, graphite and manganese. As in the Near East, abundant and easily worked copper ores in the mountains near to permanent settlements provided the opportunity to discover the properties of metals and the techniques of simple smelting and casting. Early metallurgy in Europe was confined to the Balkans and the Carpathian Basin (see map 3), and metal products rarely spread beyond this region. European copper-working appears to have arisen independently from developments in Near-Eastern metallurgy. Using two-piece moulds it produced small ornaments and larger forms such as axes of unalloyed copper – probably as much for prestige as for practical purposes. Gold was also worked at this period, and the appearance of graves especially rich in copper or gold, such as the spectacular gold-rich burials of the Varna cemetery, testifies to the emergence of a stratified society.

Alongside the early agricultural communities, small groups of hunters, fishers and collectors pursued their older way of life in areas untouched by the new economy. Hunting populations were rather sparse in the areas first selected by agriculturalists, and the rapidity with which farming spread across the loess-lands may in part reflect a lack of local competition; but where the forests were more open, hunters became more numerous. They were especially well established in the morainic, lake-strewn landscapes left by the retreating ice sheets around the Alps and on the northern edge of the North European Plain, which were rich in wild animals, fish and edible plants. The early stages of the post-glacial period, as the first

experiments with agriculture took place in the Near East, had been good for the hunters of the European forests. As time wore on, however, life became more difficult: the forest thickened as oak and beech moved northwards, the lakes filled in, and the coastlands were drowned by rising sea levels. As populations grew, many groups found themselves increasingly under stress, and eventually helped to swell the numbers of agriculturalists by adopting the new economy.

In large areas of western Europe farming was first adopted around 4000 BC, and the clearance of fields on the rocky Atlantic shores or amid the stony moraines of northern Europe provided an opportunity for creating more durable monuments as burial places and mortuary shrines for the scattered hamlets of early farmers. Vast unfaced blocks were piled one upon another to create 'megalithic' monuments along the Baltic and Atlantic fringes of Europe (see map 2). Some of the earliest megalithic tombs were built in Brittany and Portugal in about 4500 BC, but particularly elaborate forms were being made in Ireland and Spain up to 2000 years later. Along-side the tombs, other kinds of megalithic monuments came to be constructed in some regions, such as the stone rows of Carnac in Brittany, or the stone circles of the British Isles.

During the period 4000–2500 BC, important developments occurred which were to change the established pattern of life. New areas came into prominence and their innovations in turn affected the older regions. The developing areas included the North European Plain, the south Russian steppes and the Aegean. In the Aegean, fishing and maritime trade swung the emphasis

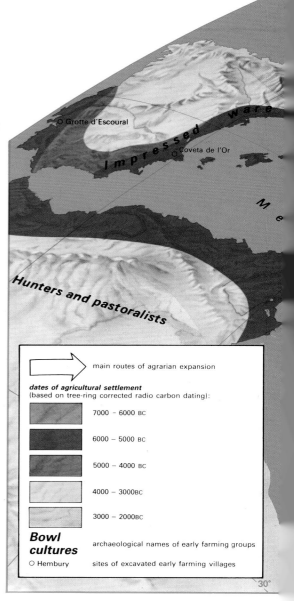

main routes of agrarian expansion

dates of agricultural settlement
(based on tree-ring corrected radio carbon dating):

	7000 – 6000 BC
	6000 – 5000 BC
	5000 – 4000 BC
	4000 – 3000 BC
	3000 – 2000 BC

Bowl cultures   archaeological names of early farming groups

○ Hembury   sites of excavated early farming villages

3/Early metallurgy (right) European copper-working began in the Balkans in the 5th millennium, producing simple objects in one-piece moulds. A similar primitive industry also began in southern Iberia in the early 3rd millennium. A little later Balkan craftsmen learned about alloying and about two-piece moulds from the metal-workers of the Caucasus. The rich metal resources of central Europe and western Britain only came into large-scale use in the early 2nd millennium, when tin was added to the copper to make bronze.

from the inland plains of Greece to the coasts and islands, where the first European civilization was subsequently to develop. In southeast Europe, many of the *tell* settlements came to an end, and in the Carpathian Basin large grave-mounds typical of the steppe area appeared, suggesting the arrival of steppe nomads among the settled farming populations. More definite evidence of eastward links is given by metallurgy, with the appearance of Caucasian designs and techniques.

Wheeled vehicles are evidenced for the first time around 3500 BC. Indeed, draught animals were now used both for carts and for the plough – soils which were in general less productive than loess made the plough an essential aid in cultivating large areas of land. Widespread forest clearance became necessary, and flint mines helped to provide the large quantities of stone needed for axes. The opening up of northern and western Europe in this way produced a change in the cultural configuration of the continent. The importance of the Rhine/Danube axis declined: with the continuing colonization of sandy soils in northern Europe after 2500 BC, the Balkans became something of a backwater between the rapidly developing economy of north-central Europe and the nascent maritime civilization of the Aegean.

1/The colonization of Europe (below) Early farmers spread from one side of Europe to the other by two main routes: the Vardar-Danube-Rhine corridor, and the Mediterranean littoral. The former was the more important. Nonetheless, for thousands of years the most 'developed' part of Europe was the southeast – the first to be settled.

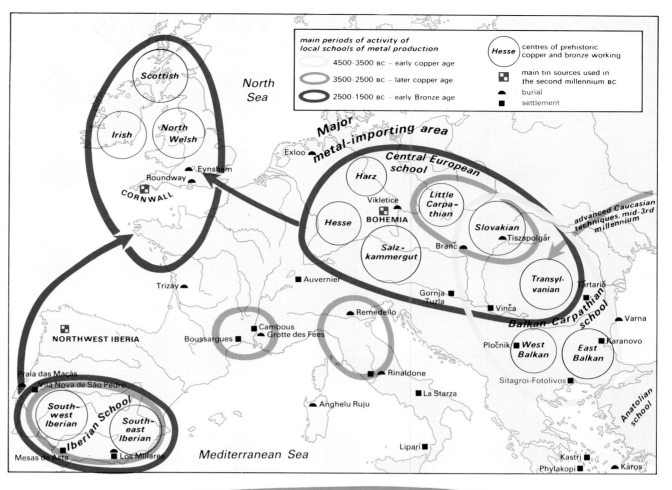

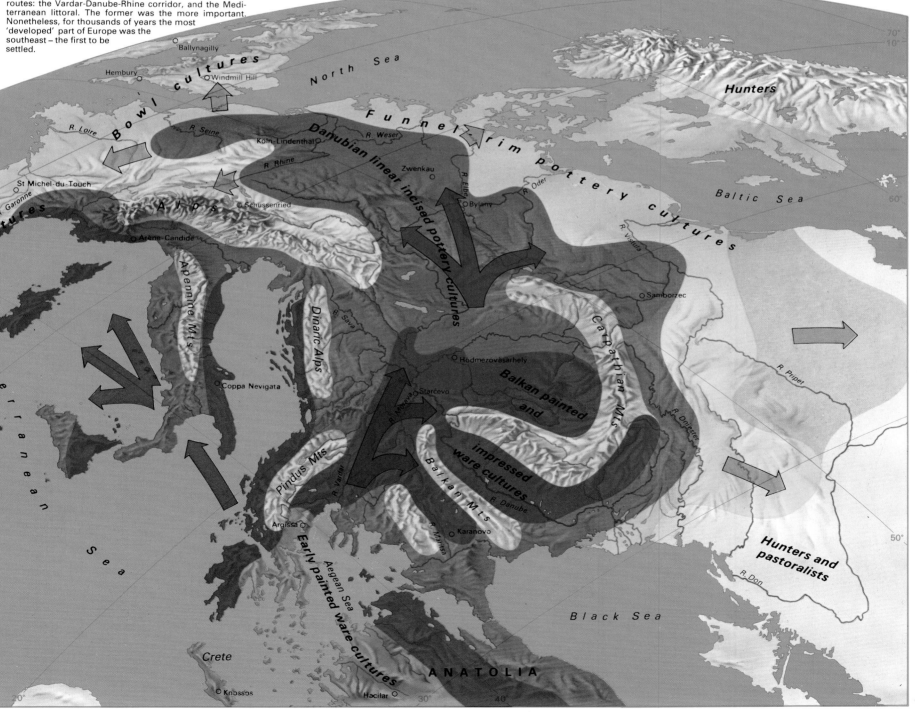

43

African peoples and cultures to AD 1000

AFRICA south of the Equator, though possibly the birthplace of humankind, was long isolated from the technological and intellectual advances that transformed the world elsewhere. North of the Equator, the transition from hunting and gathering to food production began around 8000 BC and quickly gathered momentum; but in the south, cut off from the Mediterranean and the Near East by the Sahara, the equatorial Nile and the almost impenetrable tropical rain forest, settled agriculture only became widespread with the coming of iron at the beginning of the Christian era.

Cereal-growing entered North Africa from western Asia. The earliest sites (7th and 6th millennia BC) show wheat and barley cultivation on the edges of the Nile delta, and cattle-herding near the Hoggar massif in the Sahara, followed by a pronounced wet phase in which much of the present desert was habitable parkland. The discovery of bone harpoons throughout the area attests to a temperate climate.

Desiccation of the Sahara began during the 3rd millennium BC, causing some pastoralists to penetrate the Nile valley and its delta, and others to move south and east. Southward expansion of cereal-growing, however, required the domestication of suitable grains, such as millet and sorghum, which could be grown in the tropics. This probably took place as early as 4000 BC, although there may have been some earlier cultivation of fruits and vegetables, especially yams, in the forest zone, but remains of these soft-bodied plant foods survive only rarely in the archaeological record, making the early history of yam cultivation very difficult to reconstruct. But native populations certainly increased in the Sudanic belt in the last 2 millennia BC thanks mainly to the development of tropical crops.

A few early farmers penetrated the equatorial regions of Africa, particularly in eastern Africa, where a break in the forest enabled herdsmen and perhaps cereal growers to spread down the Rift Valley from Ethiopia into central Kenya and northern Tanzania around 500 BC. Elsewhere the jungle seems to have presented an effective obstacle until the full-scale adoption of iron tools in the last few centuries BC.

To the north, Egyptian civilization developed largely isolated from events south of the Sahara. Copper use began there in the 4th millennium BC, and in the 3rd millennium was superseded by bronze. A few copper and bronze objects have been found along the North African coast, testifying to contacts with the early metal-using societies of southern Europe, but the Sahara prevented any further spread of copper technology southward. Almost everywhere else in Africa iron was the first metal produced in quantity, based on Near-Eastern techniques of iron smelting and working. Occasional objects of native (unsmelted) iron have come from Egyptian royal tombs, notably from that of Tutankhamun (d.1352 BC), but it was only in the 1st millennium that it began to be produced from North-African ore, and in the 6th century BC that it passed into common use in Egypt. At about the same period, iron use also spread from the Near East to the Phoenician and Carthaginian colonies of the North African coast.

Although Egypt's fortunes declined in the 1st millennium BC, when it was conquered by a series of foreign powers, the Kushite state to the south prospered. In the 4th century AD the kingdom of Meroe was overthrown by Axum, a trading state centred on northern Ethiopia. Axum's prosperity derived from maritime trade and exporting African ivory, and by AD 400 its fleet dominated the Red Sea both commercially and militarily; but in the 7th century Axum came into conflict with the rising power of Islam, and in AD 702 its fleet was destroyed by the Arabs, though the city of Axum survived until the late 9th century AD.

Iron use came to sub-Saharan Africa by two routes. Firstly, limited spread occurred along the Nile Valley to Meroe, seemingly an important centre of iron production c.500 BC. The second route took iron-working across the Sahara from the Carthaginian cities to Nigeria, where it is attested by 450 BC at Taruga. The earliest Iron Age sites south of the Equator mark a revolution far more dramatic than that in the north, for here the introduction of iron not only represented an important breakthrough in itself, but was also associated with the earliest cereal agriculture, cattle-keeping and pottery. Almost all sub-Saharan Africa is occupied today by the descendants of these early food producers, speaking the closely related Bantu languages disseminated by the early agriculturalists.

Research suggests that a population of Black farmers, related in language and physical type to the early peoples of West Africa, established itself in the Congo basin in the last few centuries BC, and expanded during the early Iron Age across the rest of southern Africa. The process may have involved intermixture with existing hunter-gatherers and some violence. Ultimately, however, the more numerous Bantu farmers prevailed. They became the dominant linguistic and cultural presence in east and southeast Africa too, and were later responsible for the first trading kingdoms of the region, such as that at Great Zimbabwe.

1/By AD 1000 *(right)* northern Africa had already seen the rise and fall of one of the world's great civilizations, that of ancient Egypt. It had also witnessed the growth of large-scale trade and cultural interchange with Europe and Asia, and the establishment of both Islam and Monophysite Christianity as widespread and influential religions. South of the tropical rain belt, however, the process of transition from hunting and gathering to agriculture had only recently been completed, as the Bantu-speaking food-growers from the Congo spread to dominate the region.

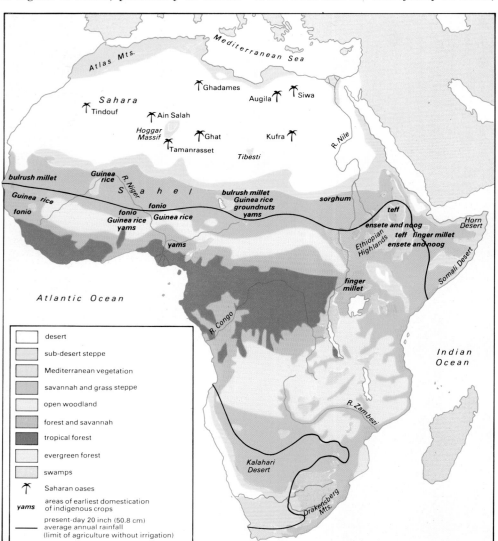

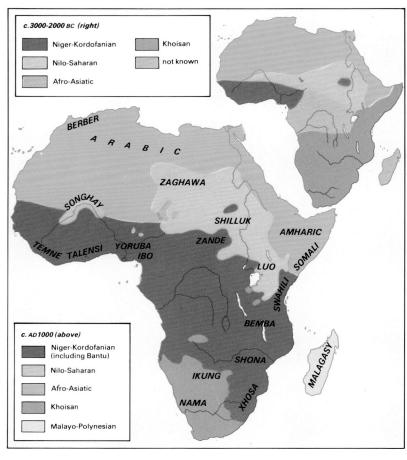

2/Rainfall and vegetation *(left)* The peopling of Africa was crucially determined by the continent's physical constraints. Over large areas the existence of desert and equatorial jungle made agriculture and communication virtually impossible. The areas of light forest and cultivable grassland contracted in the period 2000 BC to AD 1000, forcing major changes in the established methods of food production and food distribution.

3/African languages *(above)* The analysis of languages provides a vital clue to understanding much of early African history, such as the spread of population across the Sudan, the link between Bantu-speakers of the south and their origins north of the Congo, and the overlaying of Bantu upon earlier Khoisan cultures. This linguistic analysis is particularly important in regions which are totally without written records.

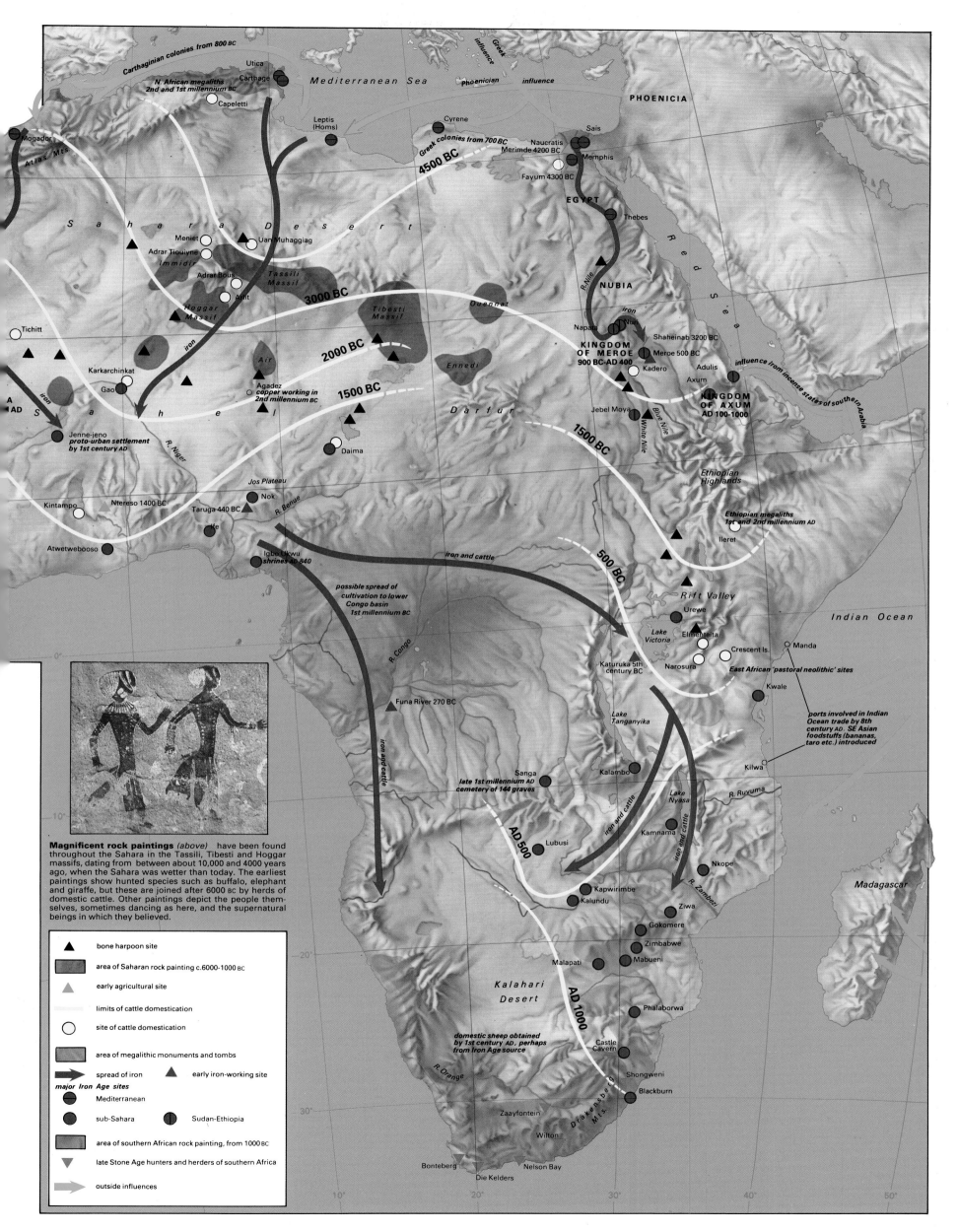

Mediterranean Sea

PHOENICIA

Carthaginian colonies from 800 BC
N. African megaliths
2nd and 1st millennium BC
Utica
Carthage
Capeletti
Leptis (Homs)
Cyrene
Greek colonies from 700 BC
4500 BC
Sais
Naucratis
Merimde 4200 BC
Memphis
Fayum 4300 BC
Thebes
EGYPT

Greek influence
Phoenician influence

Mogador
Atlas Mts.

Sahara Desert

Meniet
Adrar Tiouiyne
Immidir
Uan Muhaggiag
Adrar Bous
Arlit
Tassili Massif
3000 BC
Tibesti Massif
Ouenhat
2090 BC
Ennedi
1500 BC

Tichitt

iron

Karkarchinkat
Gao
Air
Agadez copper working in 2nd millennium BC
Sahel
Darfur

NUBIA
iron
Napata
Nuri
Shaheinab 3200 BC
KINGDOM OF MEROE
900 BC-AD 400
Meroe 500 BC
Kadero
Adulis
Axum
KINGDOM OF AXUM
AD 100-1000

influence from incense states of southern Arabia

iron

Jenne-jeno
proto-urban settlement by 1st century AD
R. Niger

Jebel Moya
White Nile
Blue Nile
1500 BC

Ethiopian Highlands

Kintampo
Ntereso 1400 BC
Jos Plateau
Nok
Taruga 440 BC
Ife
R. Benue
Atwetwebooso

Ethiopian megaliths
1st and 2nd millennium AD
Ileret

500 BC

Igbo Ukwu
shrines AD 840
iron and cattle
possible spread of cultivation to lower Congo basin 1st millennium BC

Rift Valley
Urewe
Lake Victoria
Elmenteita
Crescent Is.
Narosura
Katuruka 5th century BC

Manda

Indian Ocean

East African 'pastoral neolithic' sites
Kwale

ports involved in Indian Ocean trade by 8th century AD. SE Asian foodstuffs (bananas, taro etc.) introduced

R. Congo

Funa River 270 BC

Lake Tanganyika

iron and cattle

Kilwa

Magnificent rock paintings (above) have been found throughout the Sahara in the Tassili, Tibesti and Hoggar massifs, dating from between about 10,000 and 4000 years ago, when the Sahara was wetter than today. The earliest paintings show hunted species such as buffalo, elephant and giraffe, but these are joined after 6000 BC by herds of domestic cattle. Other paintings depict the people themselves, sometimes dancing as here, and the supernatural beings in which they believed.

Sanga
late 1st millennium AD cemetery of 144 graves
Kalambo
Lake Nyasa
R. Ruvuma
Kamnama
Nkope

Lubusi
AD 500
iron and cattle

Kapwirimbe
Kalundu
Ziwa
Gokomere
Zimbabwe
Mabueni
Malapati
R. Zambezi

Madagascar

Kalahari Desert

AD 1000

domestic sheep obtained by 1st century AD, perhaps from Iron Age source

Phalaborwa
Castle Cavern
Shongweni
Blackburn

R. Orange
Zaayfontein
Wilton
Drakensberg Mts.
Bonteberg
Nelson Bay
Die Kelders

▲ bone harpoon site

■ area of Saharan rock painting c.6000-1000 BC

▲ early agricultural site

— limits of cattle domestication

○ site of cattle domestication

■ area of megalithic monuments and tombs

➤ spread of iron   ▲ early iron-working site

major Iron Age sites

● Mediterranean

● sub-Sahara   ◐ Sudan-Ethiopia

■ area of southern African rock painting, from 1000 BC

▼ late Stone Age hunters and herders of southern Africa

➤ outside influences

45

Peoples and cultures of the Americas to AD 900

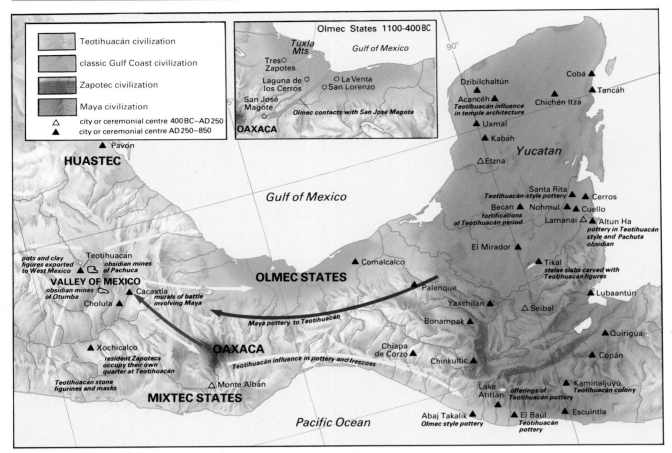

Olmec States 1100–400 BC

Olmec contacts with San José Magote

2/The Classic Period in Meso-america, 400 to 900 (above) During this period Teotihuacán was the dominant civilization of Mesoamerica. Although the area under its direct control may have been limited to central Mexico and parts of Guatemala, the influence of Teotihuacán was felt all over Mesoamerica. Similarly, Maya cultural influence was not limited to the Yucatán peninsula alone.

3/North America 1000 BC to AD 1000 (below) The Adena culture of Ohio developed into the Hopewell, when chiefs obtained ornaments and exotic raw materials from all over North America. By AD 550 Hopewell influence had waned, and by AD 700 the Mississippian culture had arisen in the southwest and southeast, with temple mounds and other features testifying to the influence of Mexican civilization.

HUMANS entered the New World from Siberia some time before 20,000 BC during a period of lowered sea level, when the Bering Strait was dry land. After spending thousands of years as semi-nomadic hunters and collectors of wild plant foods, certain groups of Indians in Mesoamerica and the Andean lands began to experiment around 7000 BC with plant cultivation. By 1500 BC, maize-farming had become the basis of life. Cultivation of tropical root crops may be equally ancient, but archaeological evidence is lacking.

Farmers lived in permanent villages, some of which grew into large towns in the period following 1000 BC. By this time, craftsmen were working luxury materials imported from long distances, and there is evidence for class distinctions between rich and poor, governors and governed. Rather than bands or tribes, communities resembled present-day chiefdoms, with control vested in a chief drawn from a single powerful lineage. Economic power derived from the chief's control over distribution of land, foodstuffs and craft products, and his position was probably reinforced by religious sanctions.

This stage of development was the take-off point for civilization and the growth of true states, with populations numbered in tens of thousands, with a hierarchy of social classes, an efficient civil service, a professional priesthood, and specialists in all kinds of jobs, from manufacturing to commerce, administration and government. Certain peoples (the Olmec of the Mexican Gulf Coast plain, the Zapotec of Monte Albán, and the inhabitants of Chavín in Peru) may have reached this stage by c.1000–600 BC; by the early centuries AD most of Mesoamerica and the Central Andes was 'civilized'.

Around and between these nuclei of civilization, other communities remained at the chiefdom level. Maize, beans and squash were introduced from Mexico into North America, and their arrival initiated a period of rapid development. In Ohio and Illinois, between 300 BC and AD 550, Hopewell chiefs built elaborate burial mounds and maintained trade contacts from Florida to the Rockies. Most American chiefdoms were agricultural, based on plant cultivation, but along the northwest coast unusually rich fishing grounds and an abundance of whales and seals supported large villages and a complex ceremonial life. Towards the extremities of the hemisphere, where conditions were too harsh for farming, populations remained small and the old nomadic and tribal ways of life persisted.

The conventional starting date for the Classic Period of Mesoamerican civilization is AD 250, a time of outstanding intellectual and artistic achievement. At about this date the Maya adopted hieroglyphic writing and began to erect stelae (stone slabs with carved historical or calendrical inscriptions). The Classic Maya were preoccupied with the passage of time. Their astronomers had calculated the exact length of the solar year, the lunar month and the revolution of the planet Venus, and were able to predict eclipses. These calculations demanded advanced mathematical skills, and the Mesoamericans independently invented the idea of place value and the concept of zero.

Classic Maya civilization was not an isolated phenomenon. Important regional civilizations developed elsewhere in Mexico – along the Gulf Coast (El Tajín, etc.), in the Valley of Oaxaca (where Monte Albán became a great city), and at Teotihuacán in the Basin of Mexico. In its prime, around the year AD 600, Teotihuacán was a city of 125,000 people and covered 7.7 square miles (20 km²), laid out according to a precise grid plan. The city's wealth came from agriculture, crafts and trade, in particular the export of obsidian (a natural volcanic glass used for knives and spear points) from the Otumba and Pachuca quarries. Diplomatic and commercial exchanges were kept up with the other civilizations of Mexico, and with the Maya by way of Teotihuacán colonies at Kaminaljuyú and perhaps Escuintla. But this prosperity did not last: Teotihuacán was destroyed and abandoned around AD 750; Monte Albán fell into disrepair during the 10th century; and Classic Maya civilization collapsed, for reasons still not fully understood, between AD 800 and 900.

The Central Andes were the homeland of a second group of interrelated civilizations. Although not in direct contact with Mesoamerica, the level of development was very similar, the main technological difference being that the Andean peoples had determined how to work gold, silver and copper, and used these metals for tools as well as jewellery. This region, with its vast distances and harsh topography, was always difficult to unify under a single state, but the centuries between AD 600 and 1000 saw the rise and fall of a truly imperial power based on Huari (or Wari) in the Peruvian Andes. Many elements of Huari religion and art were first developed at Tiahuanaco in Bolivia, but were quickly adopted in Peru. From Huari, a modified version of the Tiahuanaco cult and its art style was carried by force to many parts of the coast and highlands. For a short time, Huari became the capital of a political state embracing most of Peru, but in about AD 800 the city was overthrown and abandoned forever.

The fragile artificial unity soon broke down, and local states and local art styles reasserted themselves. Not until the Inca conquest of the 15th and 16th centuries was Peru once more unified under the control of a single power.

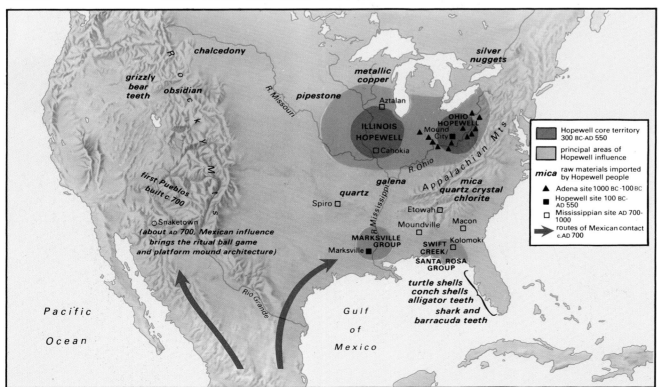

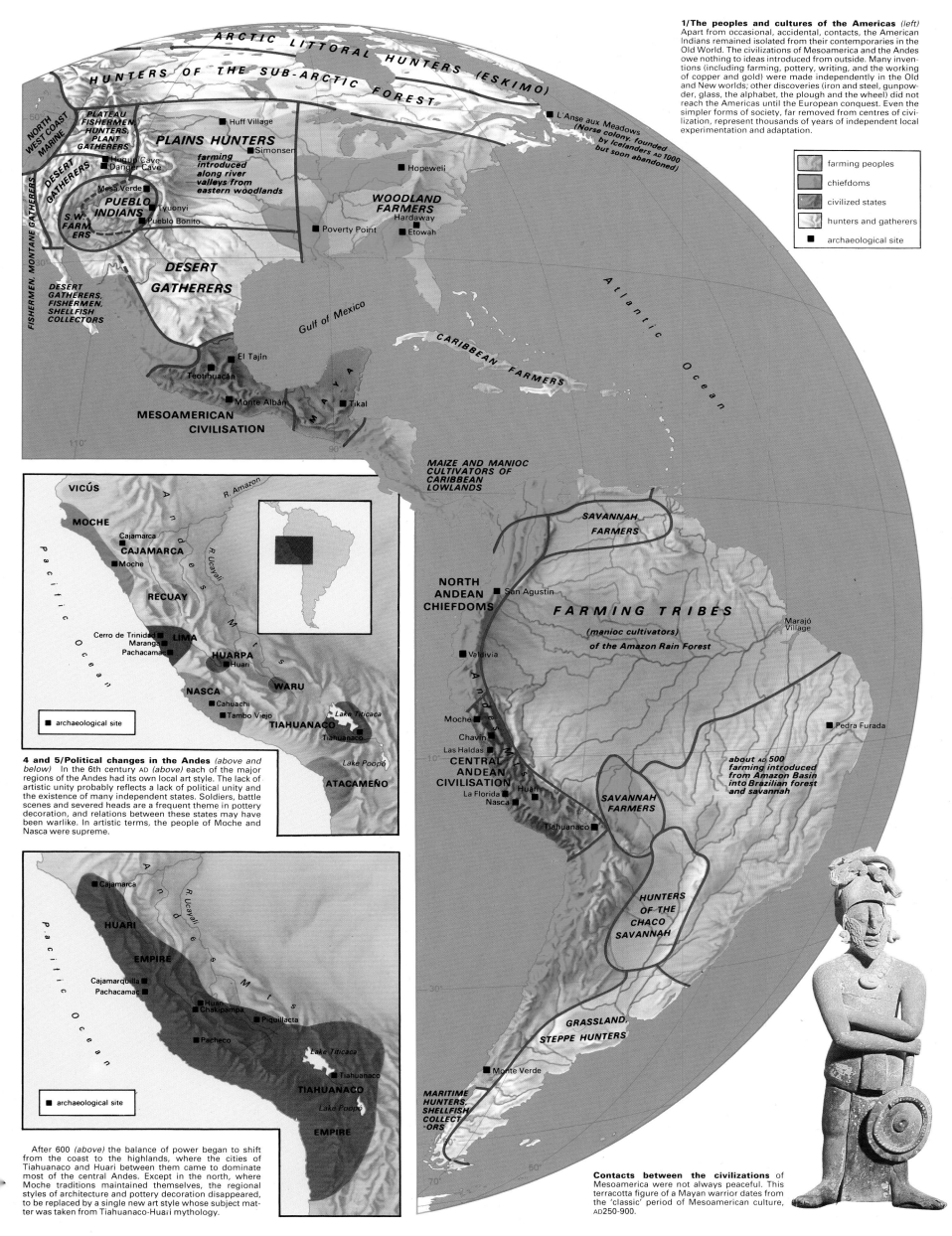

1/The peoples and cultures of the Americas (left)
Apart from occasional, accidental, contacts, the American Indians remained isolated from their contemporaries in the Old World. The civilizations of Mesoamerica and the Andes owe nothing to ideas introduced from outside. Many inventions (including farming, pottery, writing, and the working of copper and gold) were made independently in the Old and New worlds; other discoveries (iron and steel, gunpowder, glass, the alphabet, the plough and the wheel) did not reach the Americas until the European conquest. Even the simpler forms of society, far removed from centres of civilization, represent thousands of years of independent local experimentation and adaptation.

ARCTIC LITTORAL HUNTERS (ESKIMO)

HUNTERS OF THE SUB-ARCTIC FOREST

NORTH WEST COAST MARINE

PLATEAU FISHERMEN, PLANT GATHERERS

DESERT GATHERERS

PLAINS HUNTERS

farming introduced along river valleys from eastern woodlands

■ Huff Village

■ Simonsen

■ Hopewell

■ L'Anse aux Meadows *(Norse colony, founded by Icelanders AD 1000 but soon abandoned)*

FISHERMEN, MONTANE GATHERERS

■ Hogup Cave
■ Danger Cave

■ Mesa Verde

PUEBLO INDIANS

S.W. FARMERS

■ Tyuonyi
■ Pueblo Bonito

WOODLAND FARMERS

■ Hardaway
■ Poverty Point
■ Etowah

DESERT GATHERERS, FISHERMEN, SHELLFISH COLLECTORS

DESERT GATHERERS

Gulf of Mexico

CARIBBEAN FARMERS

Atlantic Ocean

■ El Tajín
Teotihuacán
■ Monte Albán
■ Tikal

MAYA

MESOAMERICAN CIVILISATION

MAIZE AND MANIOC CULTIVATORS OF CARIBBEAN LOWLANDS

SAVANNAH FARMERS

NORTH ANDEAN CHIEFDOMS

■ San Agustín

FARMING TRIBES

(manioc cultivators) of the Amazon Rain Forest

Marajó Village

■ Valdivia

■ Pedra Furada

■ Moche
■ Chavín
■ Las Haldas

CENTRAL ANDEAN CIVILISATION

■ La Florida
■ Huari
■ Nasca

■ Tiahuanaco

SAVANNAH FARMERS

about AD 500 farming introduced from Amazon Basin into Brazilian forest and savannah

HUNTERS OF THE CHACO SAVANNAH

GRASSLAND, STEPPE HUNTERS

■ Monte Verde

MARITIME HUNTERS, SHELLFISH COLLECTORS

R. Amazon
R. Ucayali
Andes
Pacific Ocean

Legend:
- farming peoples
- chiefdoms
- civilized states
- hunters and gatherers
- ■ archaeological site

VICÚS

MOCHE

■ Cajamarca
CAJAMARCA
■ Moche

RECUAY

Cerro de Trinidad ■
Maranga ■ ■ LIMA
Pachacamac ■

HUARPA
■ Huari

NASCA
■ Cahuachi
■ Tambo Viejo

WARU

TIAHUANACO
Lake Titicaca
■ Tiahuanaco

Lake Poopó

ATACAMEÑO

R. Amazon
R. Ucayali
Andes
Pacific Ocean

■ archaeological site

4 and 5/Political changes in the Andes (above and below) In the 6th century AD (above) each of the major regions of the Andes had its own local art style. The lack of artistic unity probably reflects a lack of political unity and the existence of many independent states. Soldiers, battle scenes and severed heads are a frequent theme in pottery decoration, and relations between these states may have been warlike. In artistic terms, the people of Moche and Nasca were supreme.

■ Cajamarca

HUARI EMPIRE

■ Cajamarquilla
■ Pachacamac

■ Huari
■ Chakipampa
■ Piquillacta

■ Pacheco

Lake Titicaca
■ Tiahuanaco

TIAHUANACO EMPIRE

Lake Poopó

R. Ucayali
Andes
Pacific Ocean

■ archaeological site

After 600 (above) the balance of power began to shift from the coast to the highlands, where the cities of Tiahuanaco and Huari between them came to dominate most of the central Andes. Except in the north, where Moche traditions maintained themselves, the regional styles of architecture and pottery decoration disappeared, to be replaced by a single new art style whose subject matter was taken from Tiahuanaco-Huari mythology.

Contacts between the civilizations of Mesoamerica were not always peaceful. This terracotta figure of a Mayan warrior dates from the 'classic' period of Mesoamerican culture, AD 250-900.

Australia and Oceania before European contact

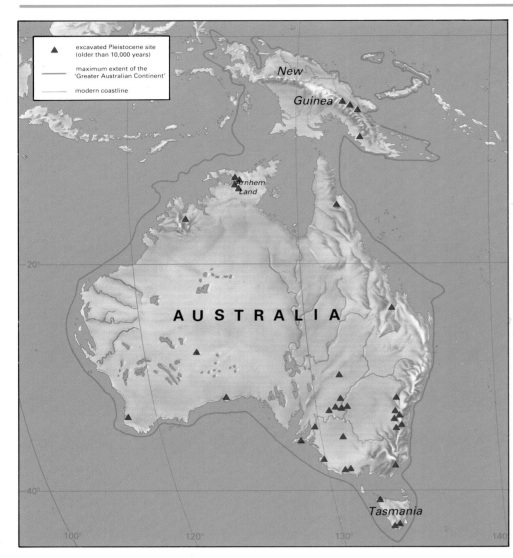

2/**Pleistocene Man in the Greater Australian Continent** (above) During periods of low sea level, New Guinea and Australia (including Tasmania) formed a single large landmass. Settlement was concentrated along the major river systems and the coast, but Pleistocene coastal sites now lie submerged offshore. In this map, the comparative abundance of sites in southeast Australia is simply a result of the greater attention devoted to this region by archaeologists.

Other sites in the highlands of the northwest evidence the widespread distribution of man in New Guinea by 8000 BC. Major changes took place about 6000 years ago with the introduction of domesticated Asian plants and animals, and the creation of drained fields at places such as Kuk Swamp and Mugumamp Ridge. The hunting and gathering tradition of earlier times persisted into recent times, however, alongside agriculture.

Most of island Melanesia (to the east, northeast and southeast of the New Guinea mainland) saw its first occupants during the 2nd and 1st millennia BC, as maritime trading groups bearing domesticated plants and animals spread through the area. These Austronesian people, with their distinctive pottery, belonging to the Lapita tradition (which can be traced back to the Moluccas area of Indonesia), reached Fiji, the eastern boundary of present-day Melanesia, by 1300 BC, and soon after made their way into western Polynesia via Tonga and Samoa. And it was in these two island groups, but particularly in the latter, that a typically Melanesian materi-

Rock art (below) became common in Australia 5000 years ago. This painting shows an ancestral being and a dingo, the descendant of domestic dogs probably introduced from Southeast Asia.

AROUND 60,000 years ago, when lower sea levels linked Tasmania, Australia and New Guinea, man first ventured onto the Greater Australian Continent. That journey, from a Southeast Asian homeland, was a pioneering one, as it involved at least one major sea crossing. The original Australians were therefore among the world's earliest mariners. What a strange new world greeted these newcomers: of enormous size, and ranging from tropical north to temperate south. Admittedly, some of the edible plants found in more northerly latitudes were related to those of Asia and were therefore familiar, but this was not so of the animals. In addition to the mammals which have survived, there was a bewildering assortment of giant forms: ten-foot tall kangaroos, various enormous ox-like beasts, a large native lion, and rangy ostrich-like birds. Despite this terrestrial abundance, it was the plentiful supply of fish and shellfish available along the coasts and in the rivers that drew most attention, and it was in these areas of Australasia that the first human settlements were concentrated. Regrettably, most of the sites are lost to us, for between 60,000 and 5000 years ago the sea was lower than the present level and they now lie offshore, on the continental shelf.

The Pleistocene inhabitants of Australasia used red ochre to create elaborate rock paintings, thus laying the foundations of a rich and long-lived Aboriginal custom. Their stone core implements and crude scrapers belong to what is known as the Australian Core Tool Tradition. This tradition, which underwent remarkably little change in more than 40,000 years, is pan-Australian, but there are a number of regional elements that have links with New Guinea and Southeast Asia. One of these is the edge-ground axe, which has been dated to 22,000 years in Arnhem Land. Similar ground stone tools found in Japan, are up to 30,000 years old. Ground-

stone tools were ultimately developed in most other parts of the world also, but only at a much later period.

Around 5000 years ago the sea rose to its present level, and, while Aboriginal settlements were still concentrated along the coasts, there was a rapid increase in the exploitation of inland resources. At about this time a range of small, finely finished flake implements especially developed for hafting, and known as the Australian Small Tool Tradition, appeared across the continent; the dingo was also introduced.

Political, economic and religious development continued and by the time the first European settlers arrived in the 18th century, there were some 300,000 Aborigines living in around 500 tribal territories.

Although the Aborigines' way of life was still based on hunting and gathering (they never became full-scale agriculturalists), they had developed some very intricate relationships with their environment. In desert areas, small nomadic groups ranged over thousands of square miles, while in richer parts of the continent there were settled, permanent villages. Fish traps were constructed, grasses and tubers replanted to assist nature, and fire was used to burn old vegetation and encourage the growth of rich new plant cover.

New Guinea was first occupied at the same time as Australia. A settlement in northern New Guinea has been dated to at least 40,000 years ago, when it was covered by a deposit of volcanic ash, and New Ireland to the north is known to have been occupied some 33,000 years ago.

al culture gradually evolved into a Polynesian-style one, during more than 1000 years of geographical isolation. Around 150 BC, a time when Lapita pottery was disappearing throughout island Melanesia and western Polynesia, prehistoric Samoans ventured eastward in their canoes and settled the distant Marquesas Islands. After a brief pause, settlers spread to the Hawaiian Islands around AD 400, while at about the same time the first Polynesians reached Easter Island, there to give birth to an extraordinary and impressive culture. All the other major island groups of Polynesia, including New Zealand, were first settled, mainly from Samoa-Tonga or Society Islands–Marquesas, between AD 1000 and 1300, and a multitude of largely independent cultures evolved on these little 'island universes', only to be shattered by the shock of European contact during the 17th, 18th and 19th centuries.

Because of its climatic range, comparative size, and unfamiliar plants and animals, New Zealand presented its initial Polynesian settlers with special adaptive problems. Most of the domesticated plants and animals characteristic of the ancestral homeland were lost en route to New Zealand or else failed to withstand the more rigorous climatic conditions; the only important survivors were the dog and native rat, and the taro, yam and sweet potato (albeit these last three were basically restricted to coastal North Island localities). Nevertheless, the New Zealand environment offered these early settlers unexpected dietary compensation in the

form of a whole suite of giant flightless birds, the best known of which are the moas. The original New Zealanders of North Island and northern South Island (the Maoris) thus became hunter-farmers, and a pattern of seasonal movement was developed to take advantage of local conditions. Settlements were predominantly coastal, and were restricted to several clearly defined regions. Meanwhile, new forms of tools were developed in response to the new environment. During the ensuing centuries the growing population expanded around the coasts of both islands, and inland resources were intensively exploited on South Island.

As hunting and man-made bushfires continued there was a gradual change in the environment, culminating in the 13th and 14th centuries with widespread deforestation, and virtual extinction of large birds. It was probably at about this time that many of the implements derived from ancestral Polynesian types were abandoned, and that distinctly New Zealand artefacts began to emerge. So too did warfare, and with it the appearance of specially developed fortified settlements termed *pa*. By the time of European contact, Cook and other explorers found New Zealand occupied by up to 250,000 Maoris. A hunting-farming lifestyle was still in evidence, except in the southern half of South Island, beyond the limits of horticulture. European contact and settlement soon led to violent confrontation which resulted in the rapid breakdown of traditional Maori society and culture.

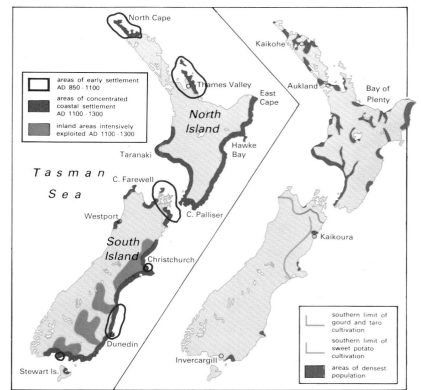

3/Early New Zealand settlement *(above)* New Zealand's early settlers were basically coastal hunter-gatherers, though South Island inland resources were seasonally exploited. Cultivated plants were only grown in sheltered North Island localities.

4/Maori settlement at European contact *(above)* By 1769 most Maoris were settled in North Island, along the coast and rivers. Food obtained by hunting and gathering was in some areas supplemented by horticultural products.

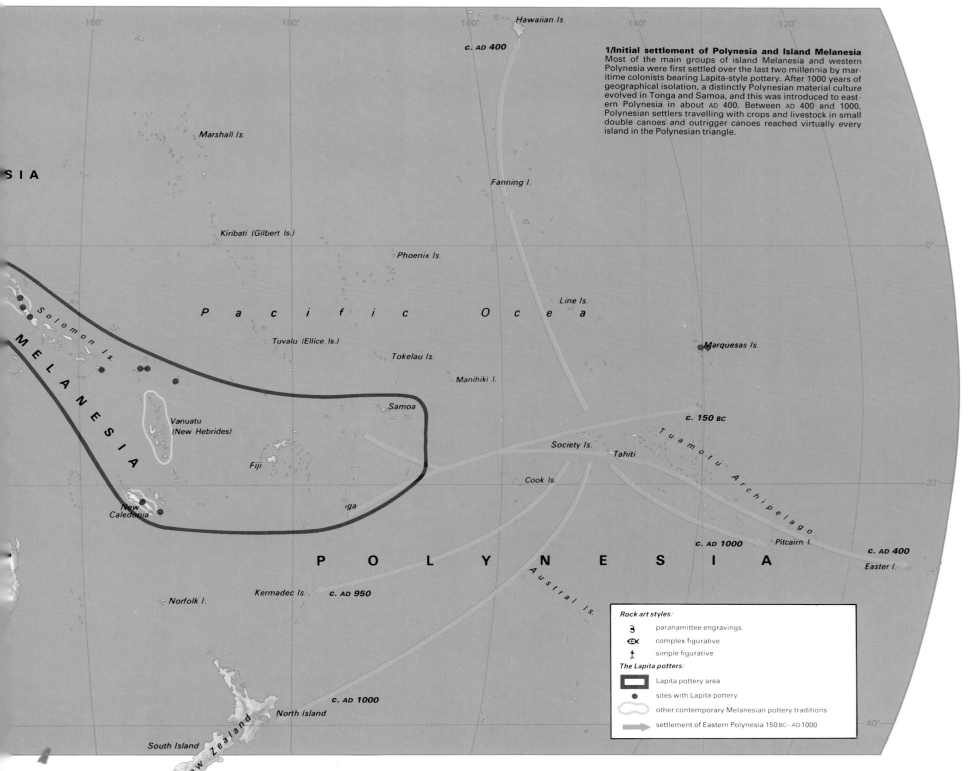

1/Initial settlement of Polynesia and Island Melanesia
Most of the main groups of island Melanesia and western Polynesia were first settled over the last two millennia by maritime colonists bearing Lapita-style pottery. After 1000 years of geographical isolation, a distinctly Polynesian material culture evolved in Tonga and Samoa, and this was introduced to eastern Polynesia in about AD 400. Between AD 400 and 1000, Polynesian settlers travelling with crops and livestock in small double canoes and outrigger canoes reached virtually every island in the Polynesian triangle.

ABOUT 6000 years ago, in a few areas of particularly intensive agriculture, the dispersed villages of Neolithic peoples gave way to more complex societies. These were the first civilizations, and their emergence marks the start of a new phase of world history. They arose, apparently independently, in four widely dispersed areas (the early civilizations of America emerged considerably later): the lower Tigris and Euphrates valleys, the valley of the Nile, the Indus valley around Harappa and Mohenjo-Daro, and the Yellow River around An-yang. The characteristic feature of them all was the city, which now became an increasingly dominant social form, gradually encroaching on the surrounding countryside, until today urban civilization has become the criterion of social progress. But the city possessed other important connotations : a complex division of labour; literacy and a literate class (usually the priesthood); monumental public buildings; political and religious hierarchies; a kingship descended from the gods; and ultimately empire, or the claim to universal rule. A dichotomy already existed between the civilized world and the barbarian world outside. The onslaught of nomadic peoples eager to enjoy the fruits of civilization became a recurrent theme of world history, until the advent of effective firearms in the 15th century AD tilted the balance in favour of the civilized peoples.

2

The first

The pyramids at Giza, Egypt

civilizations

The beginnings of civilization in the Eurasian world 3500 to 1500 BC

THE first civilizations arose in the fertile alluvial basins of the major rivers which drain from the mountain fringes where agriculture began (see page 40) to water the otherwise arid plains of the Near East. More complex societies derived from the increasing organization needed to control the large populations supported by the productive lowland agricultural regimes.

As farming communities spread from the hills to the open alluvial plains, similar hierarchically organized societies evolved in the basins of the Tigris-Euphrates, the Nile, the Yellow River and the Indus. The earliest was that of Mesopotamia, which was in existence by about 3500 BC. Its influence has been identified in early Egypt, which adopted urban civilization in about 3200 BC, and it may also have inspired, albeit indirectly, the Harappan civilization in the Indus Valley in about 2500 BC. Chinese civilization appears to have developed independently early in the 2nd millennium BC.

These societies shared many common features: the development of cities, writing, large public buildings, and the political apparatus of a state. Taken together, they constituted an urban revolution which led to civilization. The large

agricultural surpluses produced by irrigation led to urbanization because it now became possible to employ a large segment of society in activities other than farming, such as manufacture and trade. This led in turn to the emergence of a ruling class which accumulated wealth through the exploitation of labour and the imposition of taxes, and which came to exercise religious, military and political control. The ruler was often the chief priest but, if secular, normally enjoyed the support of the priesthood. In either case the temple centre was an important element of the political system. The centralized control found in these societies fostered a specialized legal system, a standing army, a permanent bureaucracy, and the division of society into distinct classes.

The state also supported scribes, who were usually trained and employed within the temples. The earliest writing was used in administration as a means of keeping track of commodities, wages and taxes, but later developed so that it would be used to record and communicate almost any message.

Monumental public buildings reinforced the authority of the state and formed a visual

reminder to the subjects of the power that controlled their daily life. Long-distance trade was also generally in the hands of the state. Rare, valuable, and luxury goods – metals, wood, and gemstones – were especially in demand and trading expeditions were sent to acquire them. Trade was of particular importance in developing regions since, apart from agricultural produce, the alluvial plains where civilization evolved had few other natural resources.

Luxury goods and raw materials imported from the hinterlands were exchanged for textiles and other manufactured goods from the civilized city-states. This extensive trading activity led to communication between the cities of the alluvial plains and the smaller centres in the river-valleys of the surrounding regions, where similar processes of urbanization were taking place on a smaller scale. It is hard to separate cause and effect in this growing network of trading centres and city-states, which sprang up in a great arc from the eastern Mediterranean to the Indus Valley. Only Chinese civilization developed in relative isolation, sheltered by the Himalayas and the jungles of Southeast Asia, and interacting mainly with neighbouring peasant

1/The spread of civilization (below) As defined by urbanization and writing, civilization began in Mesopotamia and Elam and soon spread to Egypt, the Indus Valley, Crete and parts of Asia Minor. The precondition for civilization was the agricultural surplus which became available through irrigation and intensive cultivation of the fertile alluvial plains created by the major river systems. Trade was a vital ingredient of civilization – the river valleys had few mineral resources – and also helped to disseminate ideas and goods between different regions. Often there is little surviving archaeological evidence for trade, but it is possible to establish the trading patterns for some goods, such as lapis lazuli, which came from Badakhshan in northern Afghanistan and reached Egypt as early as the 4th millennium BC. Although goods could be carried overland using beasts of burden such as cattle, donkeys, horses and camels, bulk trade was more practical using water transport along the major rivers and canals and by sea.

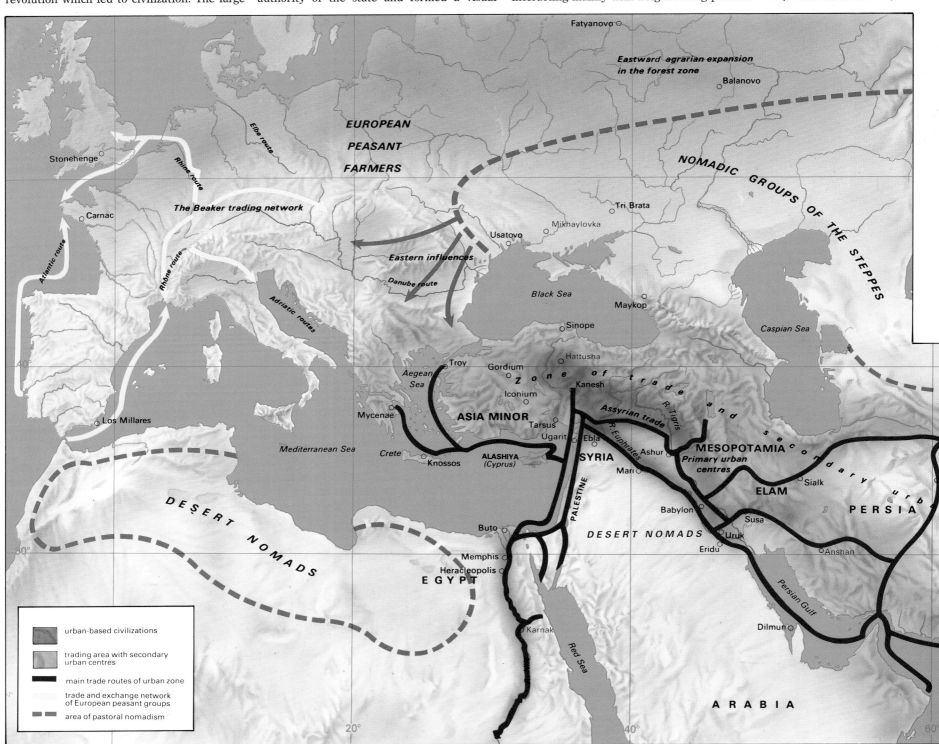

urban-based civilizations

trading area with secondary urban centres

main trade routes of urban zone

trade and exchange network of European peasant groups

area of pastoral nomadism

societies, some of which already practised advanced skills such as bronze-working.

In northern and western Europe, though the working of copper and bronze was practised on a village basis, the population was too small and scattered to necessitate elaborate organization. Nevertheless, there is some evidence of inter-regional links along the major river systems, and also along the coasts, suggesting the importance of boats and fishing. But the wealth of the community was not communally stored, and there was no organization on the scale of the fortified centres of the Near East.

More striking changes, involving the movement of people rather than goods, were taking place in the steppe regions (see page 60), where the horse and the cart gave rise to the mobile way of life of the nomadic pastoralist. At the same time, groups of peasant farmers continued to push eastward along the forest belt of central Russia, penetrating to the southern Urals by 2000 BC. Movements along the forest/steppe margin had opened up one of the earliest routes between China and northwest Eurasia by the end of the 2nd millennium BC.

The contrast between the early civilizations and their neighbours – mobile pastoralists to the north, peasant groups in the forests of Europe and the jungles of Indo-China – lay in the centralization of their economies. As goods were collected and allocated, a permanent record was needed to keep track of them. The development of writing systems is a characteristic feature of early urban societies and the first written records were usually little more than lists of the contents of storehouses. However, once a flexible system of writing had been invented, it was used to record myths, legends and poetry, as well as commercial transactions.

In each region, the earliest script was pictographic or, more precisely, ideographic, with signs for individual words or concepts. This soon became cumbersome, and eventually symbols were used for sounds rather than for ideas. The original pictures thus took on more arbitrary forms and meanings. One of the most successful systems was that evolved in Mesopotamia, where a rectangular-ended stylus was used to inscribe wedge-shaped impressions ('cuneiform') on clay tablets. The earliest inscriptions found at Warka (ancient Uruk) in southern Mesopotamia were ideographic and not phonetic, and although the language in which they were written is not certain some features suggest that it was Sumerian. Later it was adapted to write other languages: Old Akkadian, Eblaite, Amorite, Babylonian, Assyrian, Elamite, Hurrian and Hittite. It was thus used to write Semitic and Indo-European, as well as other languages.

Chinese pictographs were probably an independent invention, although early Mesopot-

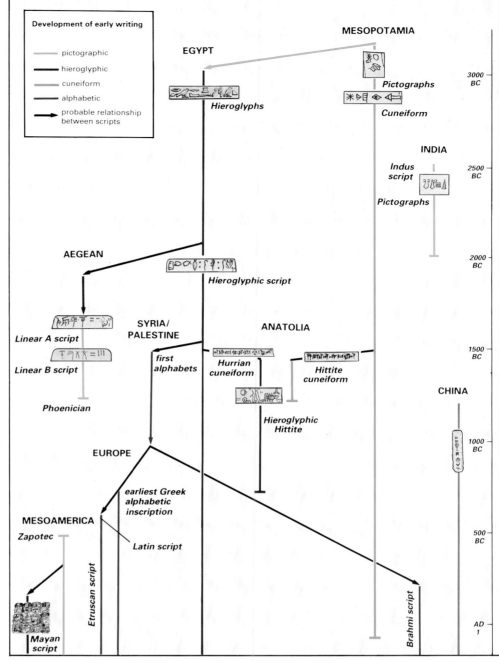

amian writing may have inspired the script used by the Indus civilizations. Egyptian hieroglyphs ('sacred carvings') may similarly owe their initial inspiration to Mesopotamia, but developed their own tradition and may, in turn, have inspired the palace-centres of Crete to develop their scripts: Linear A and Linear B. Scribal inventiveness is best exemplified, however, in the creation of an alphabetic system in the early 2nd millennium BC, which used Egyptian hieroglyphic signs not to represent words, as in Egyptian, but to signify the sound of the initial letter of the word in Canaanite. This alphabet evolved into the Semitic scripts of the Near East – Phoenician, Aramaic, Hebrew and Arabic – and was passed on to the Romans, via the Greeks, to form the basis of most modern European scripts.

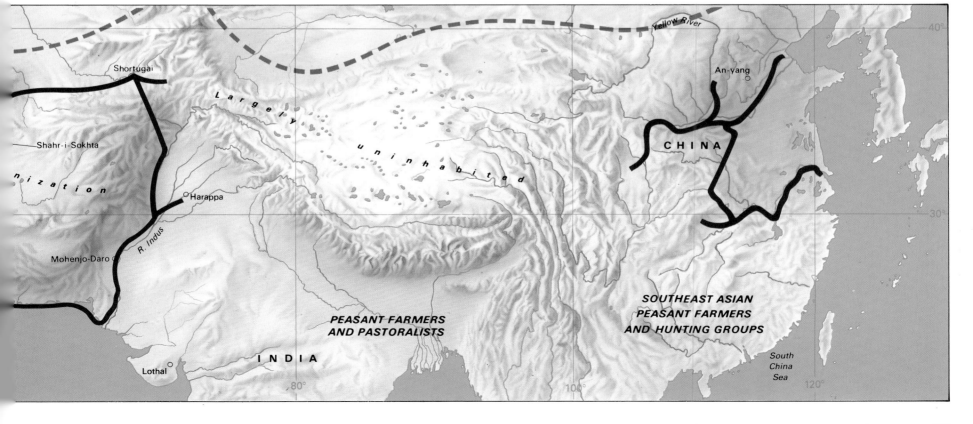

The early empires of Mesopotamia c.3500 to 1600 BC

THE fertile plains and valleys watered by the Tigris and Euphrates offered potentially the richest farming between the Indus and the Nile. But it was a land held in delicate balance, needing defence against nature and human predators alike. Unlike the regular rise and fall of the Nile, the destructive floodwaters of the Mesopotamian rivers, rising in eastern Turkey and western Iran, reached Mesopotamia after the crops had begun growing and, if unchecked, would have drowned them. Furthermore the violent floods of the Tigris devastated large areas. Political organization was required to establish the dykes and canals needed for water control. In meeting this challenge, early communities satisfied many prerequisites of civilization.

Agricultural villages extended from Palestine to the Zagros mountains, within the area where rainfall was sufficient to grow cereals; but irrigation canals enabled settlement to extend into lowland plains where the rainfall was sparse. Favoured locations within this zone, such as Jericho or Çatal Hüyük (see page 40), could support settlements of over 1000 people. But once irrigated, the fertile plains of southern Mesopotamia could support towns of thousands.

In the 4th millennium BC some of these towns became much larger with populations of per-

haps 10,000 or more. From about 3500 BC one site predominated: Warka, ancient Uruk, which occupied 250 acres (100 ha). The success of Uruk was not merely local, for its material culture was exported and characteristic pottery has been found on the Iranian plateau and near the Mediterranean coast. Moreover, the finds from sites such as Susa in Iran or Habuba Kabira in Syria are so similar to those from Uruk itself that they may have been colonized or ruled from Uruk.

Southern Mesopotamia between Nippur and the head of the Gulf was occupied by the Sumerians, with the Akkadians their immediate neighbours to the north. In the first half of the 3rd millennium BC (the Early Dynastic period), the political organization of both was based on city-states – dominated by Uruk, Ur and Kish – with a shifting hegemony among them. Their need for timber, metals, and semi-precious stones led them to exploit the natural resources of the Zagros and Amanus and to develop trade routes by land to distant Iran and Asia Minor, and by sea to Dilmun (Bahrain), Magan (probably Oman) and Meluhha (perhaps the Indus Valley). Similar city-states developed in the outlying regions, in Syria, Turkey and Iran.

The city-states of southern Mesopotamia were

later united under a usurper who chose the name of Sharrukin (Sargon) (c.2334–2279 BC) meaning 'legitimate king'. He built a new capital at Agade (location unknown), and founded the Agade (Akkadian) dynasty. According to his inscriptions, Sargon's conquests reached from the Upper Sea (the Mediterranean) to the

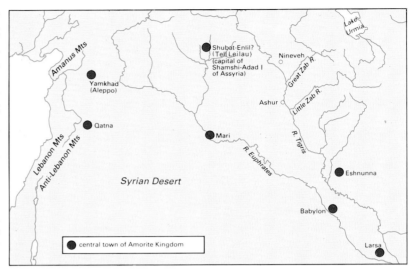

2/ Principal Amorite kingdoms *(above)* 'There is no king who is unquestionably powerful by himself' reported a contemporary of Hammurabi. Ten or 15 kings initially followed Hammurabi, but similar numbers supported rival kings, while 20 backed Yarim-Lim of Yamkhad (Aleppo).

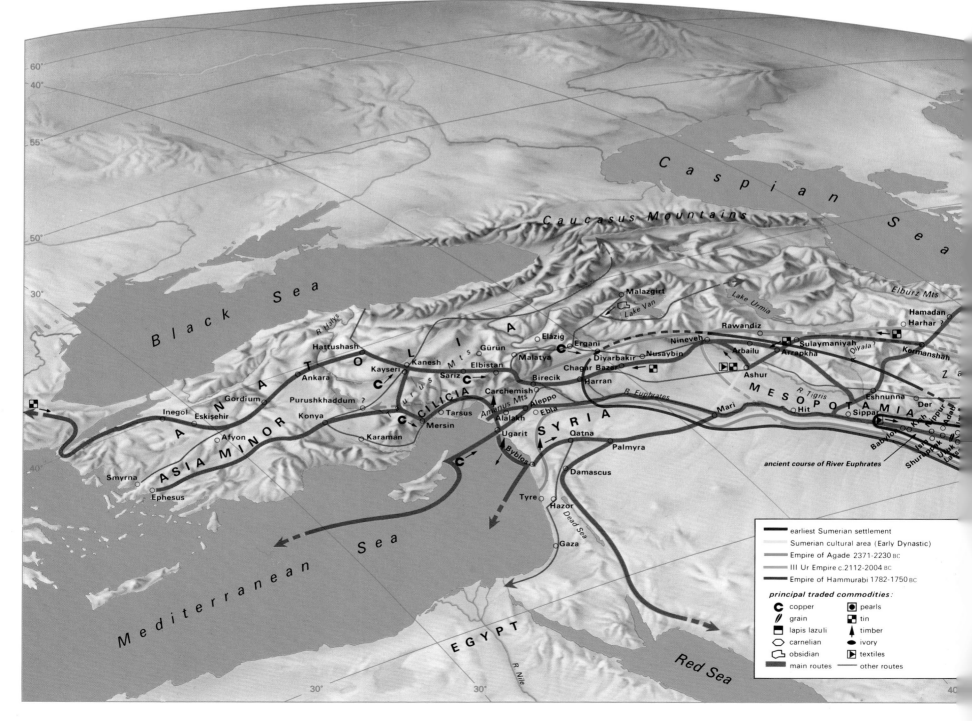

Legend:
- earliest Sumerian settlement
- Sumerian cultural area (Early Dynastic)
- Empire of Agade 2371-2230 BC
- III Ur Empire c.2112-2004 BC
- Empire of Hammurabi 1782-1750 BC

principal traded commodities:
- C copper
- grain
- lapis lazuli
- carnelian
- obsidian
- pearls
- tin
- timber
- ivory
- textiles

main routes — other routes

Lower Sea (the Gulf), while those of his sons and his grandson Naram-Sin (c.2254–2218 BC) extended to Anshan and Marhashi on the Iranian plateau. The nature of Akkadian rule is not known and little evidence exists apart from royal inscriptions, but inscribed objects from northern Mesopotamia indicate that Naram-Sin exercised control over this area.

The Akkadian dynasty fell to invading Gutians from the central Zagros, and was succeeded by a Sumerian dynasty with the city of Ur as the centre of a highly bureaucratic empire, more compact and stable than that of Agade. Known as Ur III, it lasted for little more than a century (2112–2004 BC), but showed all the signs of a fully developed empire, with a core consisting of the city-states of southern Mesopotamia and a periphery consisting of the foothills to the east. These two regions paid different sorts of taxes and were administered in different ways.

Throughout history, Semitic-speaking peoples from the Syrian desert had filtered into Mesopotamia, and at the end of the 3rd millennium the settled city-states were subjected to incursions of Amorites from the west. Ur III collapsed under the pressure of new Semitic invaders, though the *coup de grace* was administered by an invasion of Elamites from Susa.

The Amorites established dynasties from Syria to southern Mesopotamia. Once again Mesopotamia split into rival city-states, which fought continually. The two of greatest eventual significance were Assyria and Babylon. By the death of Shamshi Adad I (c.1780 BC), Assyria had become the most powerful state in Mesopotamia. It was almost immediately succeeded by Babylon, however, with, following the abandonment of the cities of Ur and Nippur, Babylon itself as capital and leading religious centre of Mesopotamia. Babylon's supremacy was to last only 200 years, however, and was ended by the invading Hittites, who in 1595 BC sacked the city and brought the First Dynasty of Babylon to an end.

Limestone stele of Naram-Sin (above) one of the greatest rulers of the third-millennium Agade dynasty which founded the first Mesopotamian empire. It depicts his victory over the Lullubu, a people of the Zagros. The stele, 6.5 feet (2 m) high, taken in antiquity by an Elamite conqueror to Susa in southwest Iran, is now in the Louvre Museum.

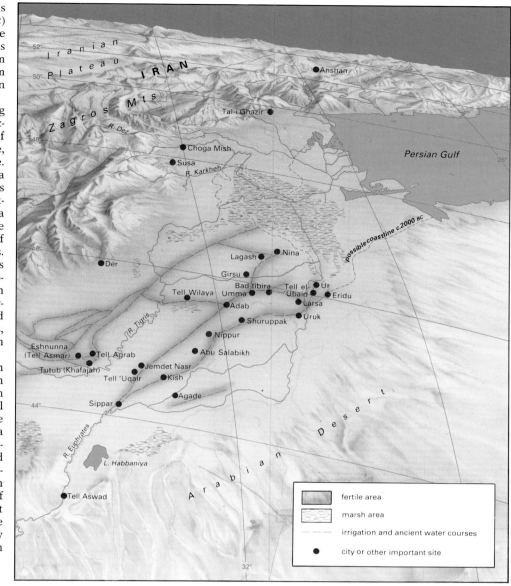

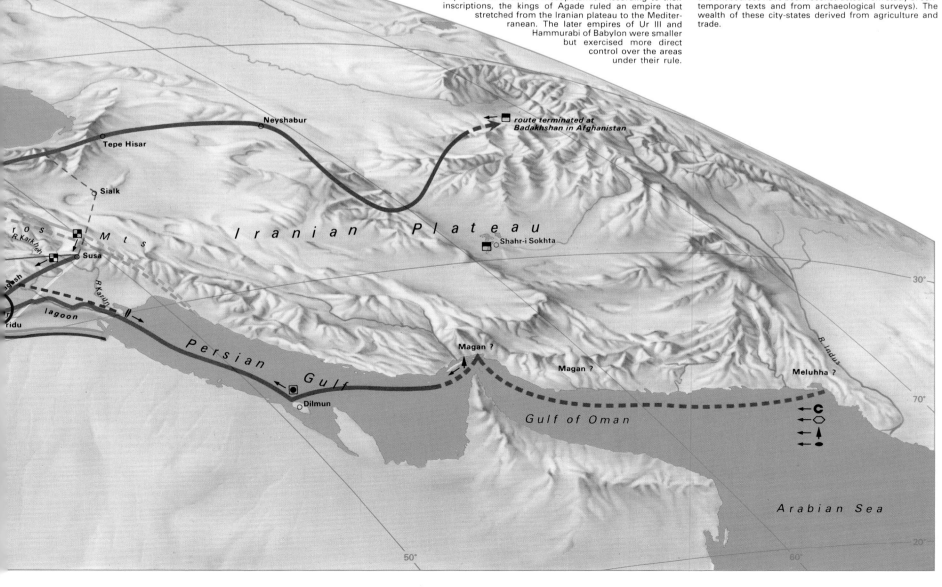

1/The early empires of Mesopotamia (below) The empire of Agade was created by Sargon (d.2279 BC) who expanded its territory far beyond the ancient heartland of city-states in southern Mesopotamia. According to their inscriptions, the kings of Agade ruled an empire that stretched from the Iranian plateau to the Mediterranean. The later empires of Ur III and Hammurabi of Babylon were smaller but exercised more direct control over the areas under their rule.

3/Southern Mesopotamia c.3000-2000 BC (above) During this period the competing Sumerian and Akkadian city-states were linked by a network of rivers and canals (the ancient courses have been reconstructed from study of contemporary texts and from archaeological surveys). The wealth of these city-states derived from agriculture and trade.

Legend:
- fertile area
- marsh area
- irrigation and ancient water courses
- city or other important site

The Near East from the fall of Babylon to the fall of Assyria c.1300 to 612 BC

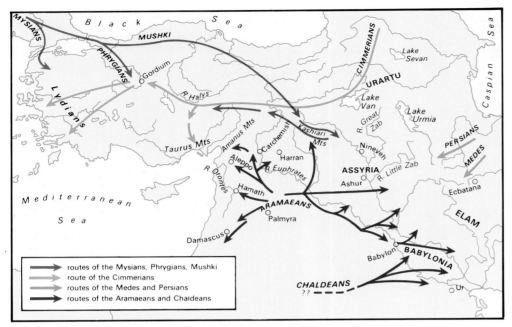

The royal lion-hunt (left) Assyrian kings set up bas-reliefs along the walls of their palaces depicting their military exploits and religious observances. This stone relief from Ashurnasirpal II's palace in Nimrud (ancient Kalhu) shows him shooting lions, trapped and released in a special park, as a royal and religious ritual. In another inscription Ashurnasirpal claimed to have killed some 30 elephants, 250 wild oxen (the extinct aurochs) and 370 lions.

3/Catalysts of civilization (left) The spread and unification of Near Eastern civilization was accelerated by ethnic movements. Particularly significant were the Aramaeans. This Semitic people, the first major users of the camel, were prominent in international trade; their language and script eventually became internationally used for trade and diplomacy.

2/The growth of the Assyrian Empire (top right) The success of Assyria in spreading from its homeland on the middle Tigris to control the Near East from north Egypt to western Iran derived, at least after the 8th century, from skilful administration and diplomacy as much as from military intervention.

A S IT emerged from the 'dark age' of the mid-2nd millennium, the Near East was divided into rival empires, three of which – Mitanni, Egypt and Hatti (Hittites) – vied for control of the Levant and Syria. Mitanni dominated northern Mesopotamia from the Mediterranean to the Zagros Mountains, and numerous smaller kingdoms including Assyria and several Hurrian states, but during the 15th century they retreated to the Euphrates, driven back by martial Egyptian pharaohs who conquered most of Palestine and the Levant (see page 58).

Cuneiform texts from Amarna, the capital of the Egyptian pharaoh Akhenaten, record the diplomatic correspondence of Egypt with its Palestinian vassals and with the rulers of more remote independent kingdoms including Alashiya (Cyprus), Arzawa, Hatti, Mitanni, and Babylonia. During the period covered by this correspondence the kingdom of Mitanni split up largely as a result of Hittite invasions under Suppiluliumas I who took their western lands, while those in the east fell to newly independent Assyria.

The conflict between Hatti and Egypt over the Levant culminated in 1285 BC in the battle of Qadesh where the Egyptian pharaoh Ramesses II faced the Hittite king Muwatallis II. Both sides claimed victory but Muwatallis retained control of the region and in 1269 Egypt and Hatti signed a long-lasting peace treaty.

In about 1200 BC the Hittite Empire collapsed, probably as a result of an invasion by the same Aegean peoples who destroyed the cities of the Levant, stopping only on the borders of Egypt. These peoples appear in Egyptian inscriptions as the 'Peoples of the Sea' and were active during a period of substantial population movement throughout the Near East, putting long-established kingdoms under great pressure.

Further south repeated incursions of Semitic Aramaeans contributed to a significant change in the Near Eastern ethnic and political structure, producing by the end of the millennium (1116–1078 BC) a strong Aramaean element in the Syrian states. Tiglath-Pileser I crossed the Euphrates 28 times to fight the Aramaeans, even managing to reach the Mediterranean and to campaign around Lake Van; but his kingdom shrank and his successors in the 11th and 10th centuries BC controlled little more than the Assyrian heartland around Ashur.

Another Semitic tribe, the Chaldeans, whose earlier history is unclear, settled in south Babylonia and particularly around Ur. It was at this time too that the Israelites invaded Palestine and that the first Iranian tribes, possibly the ancestors of the Medes and Persians,

entered western Iran. After initial encounters in the 9th century BC, the Medes overthrew Assyria in the 7th century (see below), while the Persians conquered Babylonia in the 6th century BC (see page 78).

To the east of Babylonia lay Elam whose kings claimed to rule both Susa in Khuzistan and Anshan in Fars. In the mid-12th century, however, they invaded Babylonia, looted Mesopotamian temples (their booty included the cult statue of Marduk, the chief god of Babylon, the victory stele of Naram-Sin, and the lawcode of Hammurabi) and brought the ruling Kassite dynasty to an end. Babylon revived briefly under Nebuchadnezzar I (1125–1104 BC) who invaded Elam and recovered the statue of Marduk, but nothing further is heard about Elam for another 400 years.

The Near East, like Egypt and Greece, experienced another dark age between 1100 and 900 BC. Very few historical sources survive from the period and it ended only with the rise of Assyria whose armies dominated the region for the next 300 years. For although Assyria possessed fertile corn-plains in the rain belt, these had no natural defence against raids from hill tribes to the north and east. In addition Assyria lacked metal ores and large timber. It responded to these deficiencies by systematically sending armies through the neighbouring states in Syria, in the Taurus, in the Zagros foothills, and in Babylonia to exact tribute in metals, timber and horses.

The greatest expansion of Assyria took place under Ashurnasirpal II (883–859 BC) and his son Shalmaneser III (858–824 BC) whose armies reached as far as the Mediterranean, Lake Van and the Persian Gulf, and incorporated the Aramaean and other states east of the Euphrates into the Assyrian empire. At the battle of Qarqar in 853 BC Shalmaneser fought an alliance including armies from Cilicia, Damascus, Hamath, Israel, Arabia and Egypt, but his long reign finally ended in civil war. A temporary setback followed in Assyria's fortunes, but Tiglath-Pileser III (744–727) and Sargon II (721–705 BC) extended their rule until the empire included Syria, Cilicia and Palestine. Under Esarhaddon (680–669 BC) and Ashurbanipal (668-c.627 BC) Assyria even governed Egypt for a short time.

To the north, the mainly Hurrian people around Lake Van coalesced into a federation of states and then into the kingdom of Urartu. The steep, almost impassable, mountains between Assyria and Urartu confined their conflicts to north Syria on the western side, or to the horse-rearing regions south of Lake Urmia. But the

invasion of Sargon II in 714 and incursions by Cimmerians, migrating hordes from east of the Black Sea, seriously weakened Urartu, removing its threat to Assyria. The Cimmerians also clashed with Assyria in the Taurus and destroyed the kingdom of Phrygia in the early 7th century, but finally lost their momentum in an attack on Lydia a little later.

In response to the seizure of the Babylonian throne by the Chaldeans, Tiglath-Pileser III invaded Babylonia and in 729 BC was crowned king. However Assyrian rule there proved particularly difficult and local rebellions dogged the last century of the Assyrian empire. Sennacherib (704–681) appointed his son king of Babylon only to see him captured in an Elamite invasion. Provoked by this and a subsequent Babylonian rebellion, Sennacherib attacked and after a siege of 15 months Babylon surrendered in 689 BC.

Succession problems plagued Assyria after the reign of Shalmaneser III since the eldest son did not necessarily inherit the throne. Esarhaddon tried to resolve this by making one of his sons, Ashurbanipal, king of Assyria and another, Shamash-shum-ukin, king of Babylon, an arrangement that worked well for more than 15 years until war broke out between the two brothers in 652. After four years of fighting Ashurbanipal was victorious and in 648 and 647 led a successful campaign against Elam which had supported Shamash-shum-ukin; but Assyria had been seriously weakened.

In 626, shortly after Ashurbanipal's death, Nabopolassar (later said to be a Chaldean) seized the throne of Babylon. For the next ten years Babylonians and Assyrians waged war until in 614 an army of Medes struck into the heart of Assyria and sacked the city of Ashur. Two years later the Babylonians and Medes together marched against Assyria and sacked its capital, Nineveh. The last organized Assyrian resistance ended at Harran in 609.

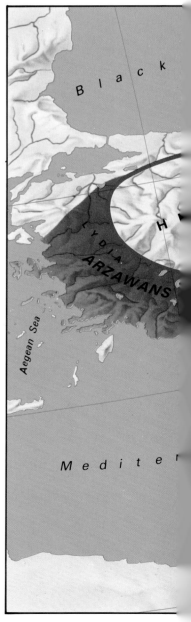

1/Kingdoms and empires c.1600 to 1000 BC (right) The history of this period was shaped by the struggle for control of Syria, first between Egypt and Mitanni and then, with the collapse and disintegration of Mitanni, between Egypt, Assyria and the Hittite Empire (which was dominant from c.1350 BC until its destruction in c.1200 BC). To the southeast lay the kingdoms of Elam, which also exerted control over Anshan on the Iranian plateau, and Babylonia ruled by a Kassite dynasty.

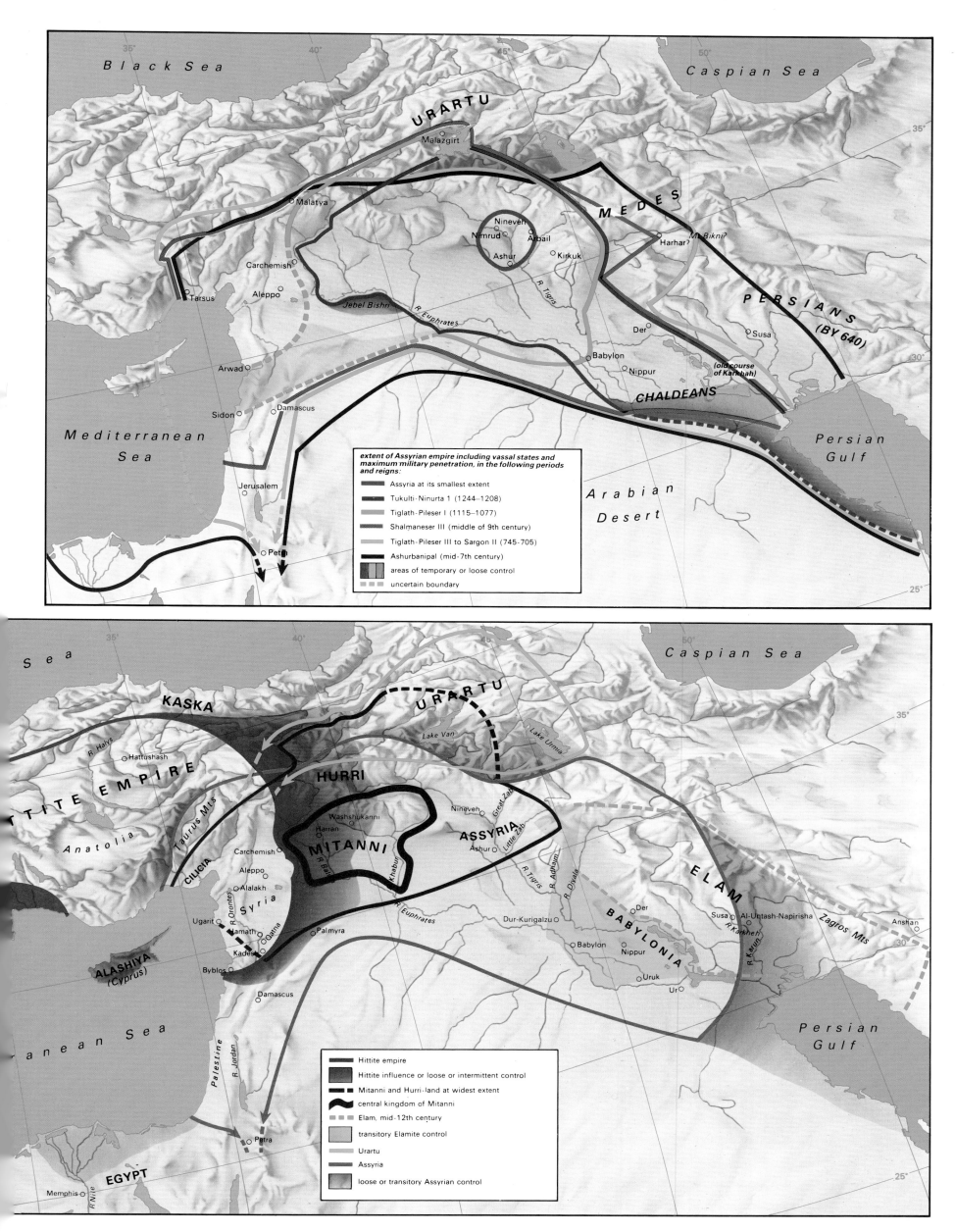

Black Sea

Caspian Sea

URARTU

Malazgirt

MEDES

Malatya

Nineveh

Nimrud Arbail
Ashur

M. Bikni?

Harhar?

Carchemish

Kirkuk

PERSIANS

Aleppo

Jebel Bishri

R Euphrates

(BY 640)

Arwad

R Tigris

Der

Susa

Sidon

Damascus

Babylon

Nippur

(old course
of Karkhah)

CHALDEANS

**Mediterranean
Sea**

**Persian
Gulf**

**Arabian
Desert**

Jerusalem

Petra

*extent of Assyrian empire including vassal states and
maximum military penetration, in the following periods
and reigns:*

Assyria at its smallest extent

Tukulti-Ninurta 1 (1244–1208)

Tiglath-Pileser I (1115–1077)

Shalmaneser III (middle of 9th century)

Tiglath-Pileser III to Sargon II (745-705)

Ashurbanipal (mid-7th century)

areas of temporary or loose control

uncertain boundary

Sea

Caspian Sea

KASKA

URARTU

R. Halys

Hattushash

Lake Van

Lake Urmia

HITTITE EMPIRE

HURRI

Nineveh

Washshukanni

Anatolia

Taurus Mts

Harran

Great Zab

ASSYRIA

Carchemish

MITANNI

Ashur

Little Zab

CILICIA

Aleppo

Khabur

R Balih

R. Adhaim

ELAM

Alalakh

R Orontes

Syria

R. Tigris

R. Diyala

Ugarit

Hamath

Qatna

Palmyra

R. Euphrates

Dur-Kurigalzu

Der

Susa

Al-Untash-Napirisha

Zagros Mts

Anshan

ALASHIYA
(Cyprus)

Kadesh

BABYLONIA

R Karkheh

Byblos

Babylon

Nippur

R. Karun

Damascus

Uruk

Ur

**Persian
Gulf**

anean Sea

Palestine

R. Jordan

Petra

EGYPT

Memphis

R Nile

Hittite empire

Hittite influence or loose or intermittent control

Mitanni and Hurri-land at widest extent

central kingdom of Mitanni

Elam, mid-12th century

transitory Elamite control

Urartu

Assyria

loose or transitory Assyrian control

Ancient Egypt: civilization and empire

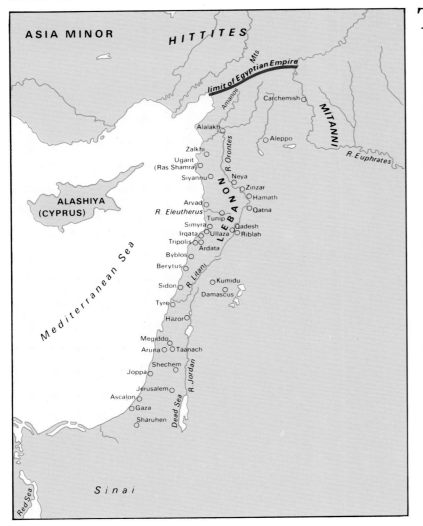

2/Egypt's Asiatic Empire *(above)* The early kings of the VIIIth Dynasty embarked on a policy of expansion into western Asia. Having experienced the rewards of successful conquest, they tried to add to what they had won. The dominion of Tuthmosis I (c.1525-1512 BC) extended from the Euphrates to the Third Cataract in Nubia. His grandson, Tuthmosis III (c.1504-1450 BC) fought 17 campaigns in Palestine and Syria, taking Egypt's empire to its furthest northern limits in the region of Carchemish. After much of this empire had crumbled away in the next 130 years, the campaigns of Seti I (c.1318-1304 BC) and Ramesses II (c.1304-1237 BC) recovered some of the lost territory, but Egyptian armies never again gained control beyond Qadesh on the Orontes.

THE first inhabitants of the Lower Nile valley were semi-nomadic groups of hunter-gatherers who took advantage of the rich natural vegetation of the Nile floodplain and the wild game of the surrounding region, which was more abundant then than today since North Africa was less arid and the desert fringes of Egypt were broken by stretches of grassland. Populations grew after the end of the Ice Age (a period of drought in many tropical latitudes), and early hunters and gatherers began around 6000 BC to cultivate wheat and barley and to herd cattle. Sustained by the annual Nile flood which brought both water and a rich deposit of fertile silt, farming flourished in the Nile valley and village communities grew and prospered.

At first the peasant communities remained largely independent and autonomous, combining only loosely in larger alliances. This situation is reflected in the multiplicity of deities and cults in historical times, many descending from the local deity of an individual village community. When the communities were grouped into larger units (later called *nomes* by the Greeks), they retained much of their religious independence, and local and regional cults remained important when, towards the end of the pre-Dynastic period, the *nomes* became the provinces of two kingdoms with their respective capitals at Hieraconpolis, in Upper Egypt, and Buto in the delta. In c.3100 BC Menes, the king of Upper Egypt, subdued Lower Egypt, united the 'Two Lands' under one crown and built a new capital, later called Memphis, near the junction of the two former kingdoms. It was at about this time that writing in hieroglyphic script was invented, and that many of the conventions employed in Egyptian art for the next 3000 years were adopted. The Ist and IInd Dynasties (c.3100–2685 BC) were the crucial formative age of ancient Egypt, when rapid progress was made in stone-masonry, copper-metallurgy, and technical skills of many kinds. Living conditions improved, and there can be little doubt that there was a considerable growth in the population.

At the beginning of the Old Kingdom (IIIrd-VIth dynasties, c.2685–2180 BC), the immense power and prestige of the Egyptian monarchy was reflected in the construction of the first great pyramid. This, the Step Pyramid of King Zoser at Saqqara, was the first monument in Egypt to be built entirely of hewn stone. So great was the achievement in assembling the necessary skill and manpower that Imhotep, the architect and chief functionary of King Zoser, was in later ages worshipped as a god.

Pyramids of stepped design were superseded at the beginning of the IVth Dynasty (c.2613–2494 BC) by true smooth-faced pyramids, the most outstanding examples being the Great Pyramid of Cheops and that of his son, Chephren, at Giza. Throughout the later Old Kingdom, kings and high officials adorned their temples and tombs with sculptures in relief and in the round which were never surpassed in strength and quality.

By 2400 BC royal power was in decline and the size of the pyramids diminished. Before 2400 BC provincial governors were buried in court cemeteries beside the pyramids of their royal masters. As royal power waned, governors treated their provinces as petty kingdoms, and were buried in impressive rock-cut tombs at provincial centres throughout the Nile Valley, the changed burial practices reflecting their increasing power. But the final blow to the enfeebled monarchy was delivered by the Nile itself. The annual floods were always erratic, and fields bordering the river which were watered and fertilized by the Nile inundations varied. Around 2150 BC, a period of consistently low floods brought half a century of disastrous famine (the First Intermediate Period) which finally tore the old order apart. Nevertheless the norms and values of Egyptian civilization were deeply rooted and enduring: within a century centralized royal power was restored and a new age of stability and prosperity began.

The new era of national unity was brought about by the governors of Thebes, who first gained control of the provinces to the south and then advanced northwards. Mentuhotep II finally emerged victorious, expelling Asiatic and Libyan settlers from the eastern and the western Delta, restoring an effective central government, and laying the foundations for a new age of economic and cultural progress: the Middle Kingdom (XIth and XIIth dynasties, c.2060–1785 BC).

Under the first king of the XIIth Dynasty, Amenemhet I, the capital was moved to Itj-towy

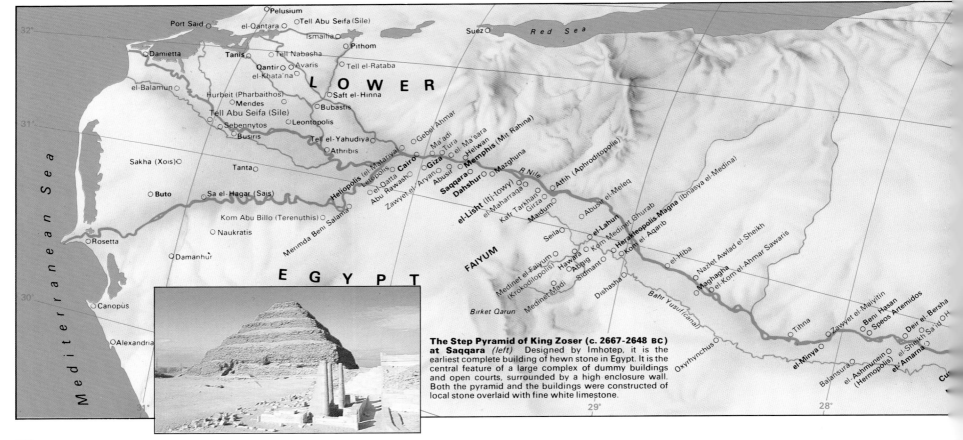

The Step Pyramid of King Zoser (c. 2667-2648 BC) at Saqqara *(left)* Designed by Imhotep, it is the earliest complete building of hewn stone in Egypt. It is the central feature of a large complex of dummy buildings and open courts, surrounded by a high enclosure wall. Both the pyramid and the buildings were constructed of local stone overlaid with fine white limestone.

just south of Memphis and near the entrance to the Faiyum. He and his six successors, three named Amenemhet and three named Senwosret, carried out important land reclamation and irrigation schemes, particularly in the Faiyum. They also campaigned vigorously in the lands south of Egypt, bringing much of ancient Nubia under Egyptian control. The arts flourished, particularly sculpture, jewellery and literature, and the pendants and necklaces found in the royal princesses' tombs beside the pyramids of Amenemhet II at Dahshur and of Senwosret II at el-Lahun are among the very finest surviving examples of ancient Egyptian craftsmanship.

In the unsettled period which followed the XIIth Dynasty (the Second Intermediate Period, c.1785–1570 BC), a succession of ephemeral kings failed to prevent a repetition of the infiltration of Asiatic immigrants into the northeast Delta. This time, moreover, the invaders came in large numbers. Known as the Hyksos, they eventually subjected the Egyptian inhabitants of the Delta and the Nile valley as far as Cusae for more than a century. Farther south, the princes of Thebes ruled as vassals of the Hyksos kings until Kamose in c.1567 BC succeeded in recovering nearly all the occupied territory. His brother, Ahmose I, completed the conquest three years later by capturing Tanis, the Hyksos capital, an event which marks the beginning of the New Kingdom (c.1570–1085 BC).

The traditional representation of Hyksos rule as harsh and oppressive finds little contemporary support. There can be no doubt, however, that it provided later Egyptian rulers with the incentive to safeguard their territory against further foreign domination by embarking on her conquest of neighbouring lands in western Asia. This achievement owed much to the horse-drawn chariot and the composite bow, both of which came to Egypt through the Hyksos.

The six warrior kings of the XVIIIth Dynasty (c.1570–1320 BC) who followed Ahmose (each named either Amenhotep or Tuthmosis), campaigned both in the Levant and Nubia, ultimately controlling an empire which stretched northwards to the Euphrates and southwards to about the Fourth Cataract. Egyptian control over Syria and Palestine, which may partly have been an attempt to shield the Nile Valley from further invasions, in fact brought it into direct conflict with the Hittites of Asia Minor and the Mitannians of north-central Syria. In the 14th century BC the Hittites defeated the Mitannians, who ceased to be a major actors in the struggle for the Levant. This left the Hittites and Egyptians in direct confrontation, but after the drawn battle of Kadesh in 1279 BC Hittites and Egyptians agreed to respect each other's sphere of influence.

For Egypt, the attractions of a Levantine empire were balanced by an interest in the gold deposits of Nubia, and during the 15th century BC the Egyptians extended their control southwards, building a series of forts along the Nile. Even gold, however, was unable to secure the complete allegiance of the Levantine princes, as clay tablets found at the Egyptian capital of el-Amarna illustrate. This group of documents from the state archives consists principally of letters from Palestinian princes to the pharaoh, protesting their loyalty, accusing their neighbours, and beseeching assistance.

The Egyptian pharaohs channelled the profits of empire into vast building programmes, such as the so-called 'Colossi of Memnon' (seated stone figures) built by Amenhotep III at Thebes (1391–1353 BC). Memphis remained the administrative capital, but the power of Thebes as the religious centre of Egypt steadily grew.

There were two further warrior-kings: Merneptah (c.1236–1223 BC) and Ramesses III (c.1198–1166 BC). Their role, however, was not to expand the empire, but to defend Egypt against a series of attacks, sometimes concerted, by Libyans and a mixed army of invaders from Asia Minor and the Aegean, collectively called 'the Sea-Peoples'. Having failed to achieve their aim by military means, the Libyans resorted to peaceful penetration and, some two centuries after the death of Ramesses III, the leader of one group of Libyan settlers in the Nile Valley was able to ascend the throne as the founder of a dynasty of nine Libyan kings (the XXIInd Dynasty, c.935–730 BC).

For the next 700 years, until becoming a province of the Roman Empire in 30 BC, Egypt was ruled by a series of foreign dynasties: Ethiopians from her former province of Nubia (the XXVth Dynasty, 751–656 BC), Persians (525–404 BC and 341–333 BC) and, after the annexation by Alexander the Great in 333 BC, by Macedonians and Greeks. The 200 years during which the country was governed by native kings (the XXVIth Dynasty, c.664–525 BC and the XXVIII-XXXth dynasties, c.404–341 BC) were periods when much attention was paid to the arts, but even under foreign rule the construction of monuments and other creative activities continued without either serious interruption or any fundamental change in character. The same continuity can be observed in religion, government and society, a tribute to the essential worth of Egyptian civilization.

Tutankhamun (c.1361–1352 BC) (below) riding in a chariot and hunting. Among the animals pursued by his hounds through the desert scrub are gazelle, ostriches, wild ass, hartebeest and a striped hyena. Behind the chariot are fan-bearers, courtiers and the king's bodyguard. The scene is painted on a wooden casket found in his tomb in the Valley of the Kings at Thebes.

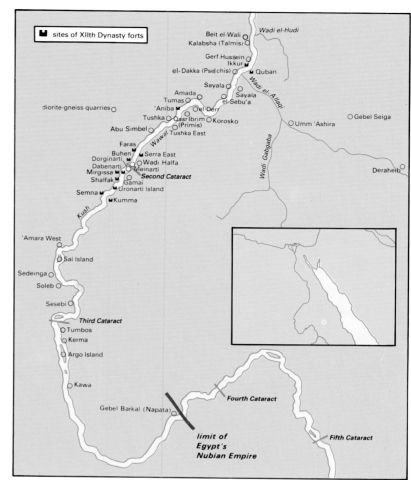

3/Egypt's Nubian conquests (above) Nubia, on Egypt's southern frontier, was an important supplier of certain raw materials, above all of gold from the region of Wadi el-Allaqi and Wadi Gadgaba, and further south between Wadi Halfa and Kerma. During the XIIth Dynasty the whole territory from the First Cataract to Semna was annexed and brick forts were built at strategic points, the most northerly being near Aswan. The XVIIIth Dynasty kings pushed the boundary further south until, under Tuthmosis III, it reached Napata, near the Fourth Cataract.

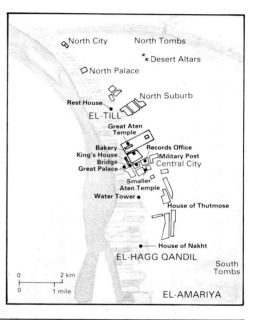

4/El-Amarna (right) Only in one instance has it been possible to reproduce the ground-plan of an ancient Egyptian city and to reconstruct the design of some of its principal buildings. This is Akhetaten, modern el-Amarna, built by Akhenaten as his new capital when he abandoned Thebes. It lies on the east bank of the Nile, approximately half way between Cairo and Luxor, in a natural amphitheatre formed by the cliffs of the high desert, about eight miles (13 km) long and three miles (5 km) wide.

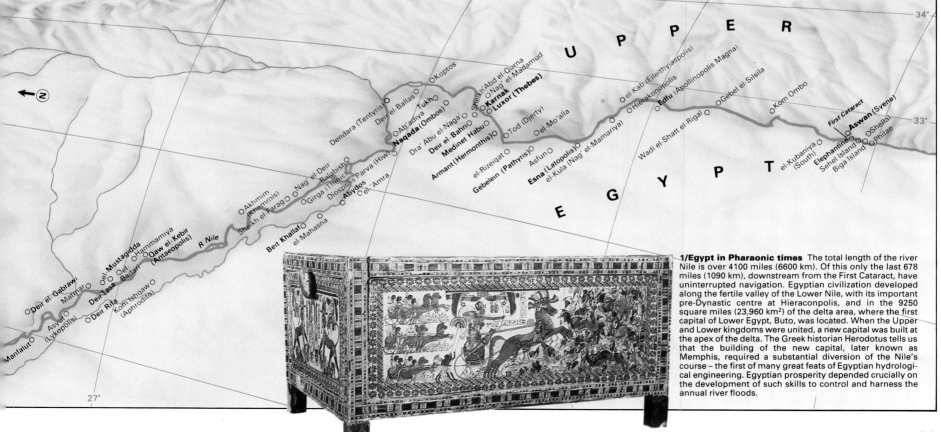

1/Egypt in Pharaonic times The total length of the river Nile is over 4100 miles (6600 km). Of this only the last 678 miles (1090 km), downstream from the First Cataract, have uninterrupted navigation. Egyptian civilization developed along the fertile valley of the Lower Nile, with its important pre-Dynastic centre at Hieraconpolis, and in the 9250 square miles (23,960 km²) of the delta area, where the first capital of Lower Egypt, Buto, was located. When the Upper and Lower kingdoms were united, a new capital was built at the apex of the delta. The Greek historian Herodotus tells us that the building of the new capital, later known as Memphis, required a substantial diversion of the Nile's course – the first of many great feats of Egyptian hydrological engineering. Egyptian prosperity depended crucially on the development of such skills to control and harness the annual river floods.

Language dispersals: Indo-Europeans and Semites

THE study of early languages is one of the most difficult problems faced by archaeologists and historians. In the absence of written records, the only workable approach is to combine archaeological evidence for population continuity – or conversely for invasion and migration – with the distribution of languages at the time they first appear in the historical record. The result is a reconstruction of language history which can usually be regarded only as tentative. Yet the development of the present-day pattern of language distribution is a subject of fundamental importance.

The languages of the modern world are divided into a number of families, including 'Indo-European' which embraces Sanskrit and Persian at one end of the spectrum, and Greek, Latin, French, German and English at the other. The word *father* (Latin *pater*; Sanskrit *pitar*) for instance, is pronounced similarly in member languages of the group. The earliest-known written forms of Indo-European are the 2nd-millennium texts from Greece, written in Mycenaean Linear B, and from Asiatic Turkey (Anatolia), written by peoples such as the Hittites and Luvians. There are also more scattered references in contemporary texts from Mesopotamia which mention a tribe called the Mitanni, and contain Indo-European personal names. Significantly, terms used in the training of horses are also Indo-European. Until recently, it was thought that Indo-European languages had first spread to Europe from the steppes in the 3rd millennium BC, but it now seems more likely that the earliest farmers of Europe already spoke these languages.

The spread of farming in Europe took place in two different ways. In the southeast and in the central plains and river valleys of the Danube and Rhine, it seems that farming groups moved gradually across the landscape, bringing the new economy and the language with them. Thus it is possible that by the 5th millennium BC, Indo-European was already spoken throughout a broad swathe of Europe, from the Balkans to the Low Countries and the Paris Basin. However, in most other parts of Europe – the Baltic lands in the north, Mediterranean Europe in the south, and the Atlantic fringe (including Britain) in the west – farming seems to have been adopted without any significant movement of people. Yet by the Roman period – and perhaps long before – all these areas also spoke principally Indo-European. There must therefore have been a secondary spread of Indo-European from central Europe to the north, south and west. This probably occurred in the 4th and 3rd millennia BC, when a number of important innovations spread from eastern and central Europe: wheeled vehicles, the plough, copper metallurgy and the horse.

The contacts needed to ensure supplies of these and other commodities may have encouraged the adoption of Indo-European languages in western Europe. The continued survival until relatively recently of Pictish in northern Scotland, and of present-day Basque in northeast Spain and southwest France, may represent the last vestiges of the original non-Indo-European speech of western Europe.

A basic division exists between the western Indo-European group, with a stable agricultural life as European farmers, and the eastern Indo-European group, whose members ranged more widely over the steppe and semi-desert areas, and who participated in the expansion of the 'Aryan' peoples into Iran and of Indo-Aryans into northern India. Some authorities have argued that the inhabitants of Indus cities such as Mohenjo-daro and Harappa already spoke an Indo-Aryan language, though most believe that Indo-Aryan reached India some time after the abandonment of these cities in the early 2nd millennium BC. Eastwards, the most far-flung members of the Indo-European groups reached Chinese Turkestan, where the language known as Tocharian was written down in the 8th century AD. Counter-currents also brought eastern Indo-European westwards. Thus, during the 1st millennium BC, groups of peoples known successively as Cimmerians, Scythians and Sarmatians pressed upon the eastern frontiers of Europe, and penetrated over the Caucasus and into northeast Anatolia. Many elements of Iranian art were transmitted westwards in this way, as well as superior kinds of horse-gear.

The eastern and western branches of Indo-European are today separated from one another geographically by a wedge of languages from further east, disseminated during later episodes of expansion and migration across the steppes. Before the birth of Christ, the steppes were dominated by Indo-European tribes; but in the following millennium various tribes from the region of the Altai Mountains in Mongolia also adopted a nomadic way of life, and began to move west. The first to reach Europe were the Huns, followed by their relations the Avars; then came various Turkish tribes, led by the Khazars. The tribes which penetrated Europe were largely driven out or assimilated by Indo-Europeans of the Slav group, but when the Seljuk Turks finally took over the remains of the Byzantine Empire in the Near East, the chain of related languages from Europe to India was severed.

In the zone of urban civilizations on the southern flanks of the Taurus mountains and the rivers running from it, a similar interaction between settled and semi-desert areas produced another set of wide-ranging linguistic relationships, reaching down into Arabia and across into northern Africa. The distribution of the Semitic languages reflects the nomadic character of life in these areas. The earliest urban communities, those of the Sumerians (3rd millennium BC; see page 54) were non-Semitic, but their neighbours and 2nd-millennium successors, the Akkadians and Assyrians, represent the northeast Semitic branch. To their northwest, on the Levantine coast and adjacent areas, were the urbanized Canaanites, including the Aramaeans, Phoenicians and Hebrews, while to the southwest lay the major Hamitic-speaking Egyptian civilization and, to the southeast, the more nomadic Arabs – much later to carry their culture and the Islamic religion from the Atlantic to the Indian Ocean.

Even in the 1st millennium BC, however, Semitic languages and culture were carried well beyond the semi-arid area of the Near East by maritime expansion throughout the Mediterranean. Back in the Bronze Age, in the later 2nd millennium, the Levantine coast had been a noted trading area, and early in the 1st millennium the Phoenicians expanded their maritime trading network, setting up colonies at increasing distances from the homeland. The Greeks, recovering from the post-Mycenaean 'Dark Age', soon followed suit, and great commercial and military rivalry developed. From their Levantine ports of Tyre and Sidon, the Phoenicians sailed beyond the Greek colonial network in the Aegean and Adriatic to found the north African cities of Carthage (814 BC) and Utica, and on to Cádiz in Spain. It was the sea-borne power of these Semitic west Mediterranean colonies that the Romans first encountered in the succession of Punic Wars between 264 and 146 BC.

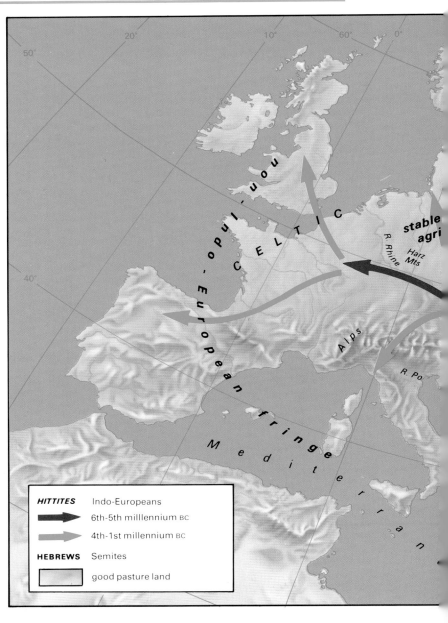

Linear B tablet (*left*) The Linear B tablets provide a unique insight into everyday life in Mycenaean Greece. Most of them contain lists of commodities, sometimes recording the contents of palace stores, in other cases listing payments of rations and raw materials to palace craftworkers.

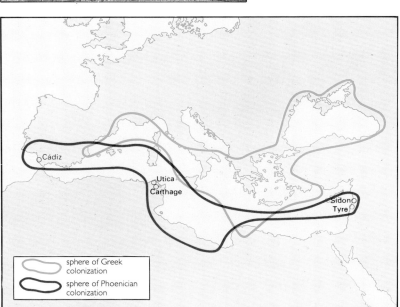

2/Trading hegemonies (*right*) The 1st millennium BC saw a great expansion of maritime activity and the foundation of overseas colonies within the Mediterranean. Bypassing the main areas of Greek influence, the Phoenicians carried Semitic languages and culture to the other end of the Mediterranean world, and even sailed beyond to explore the Atlantic coasts.

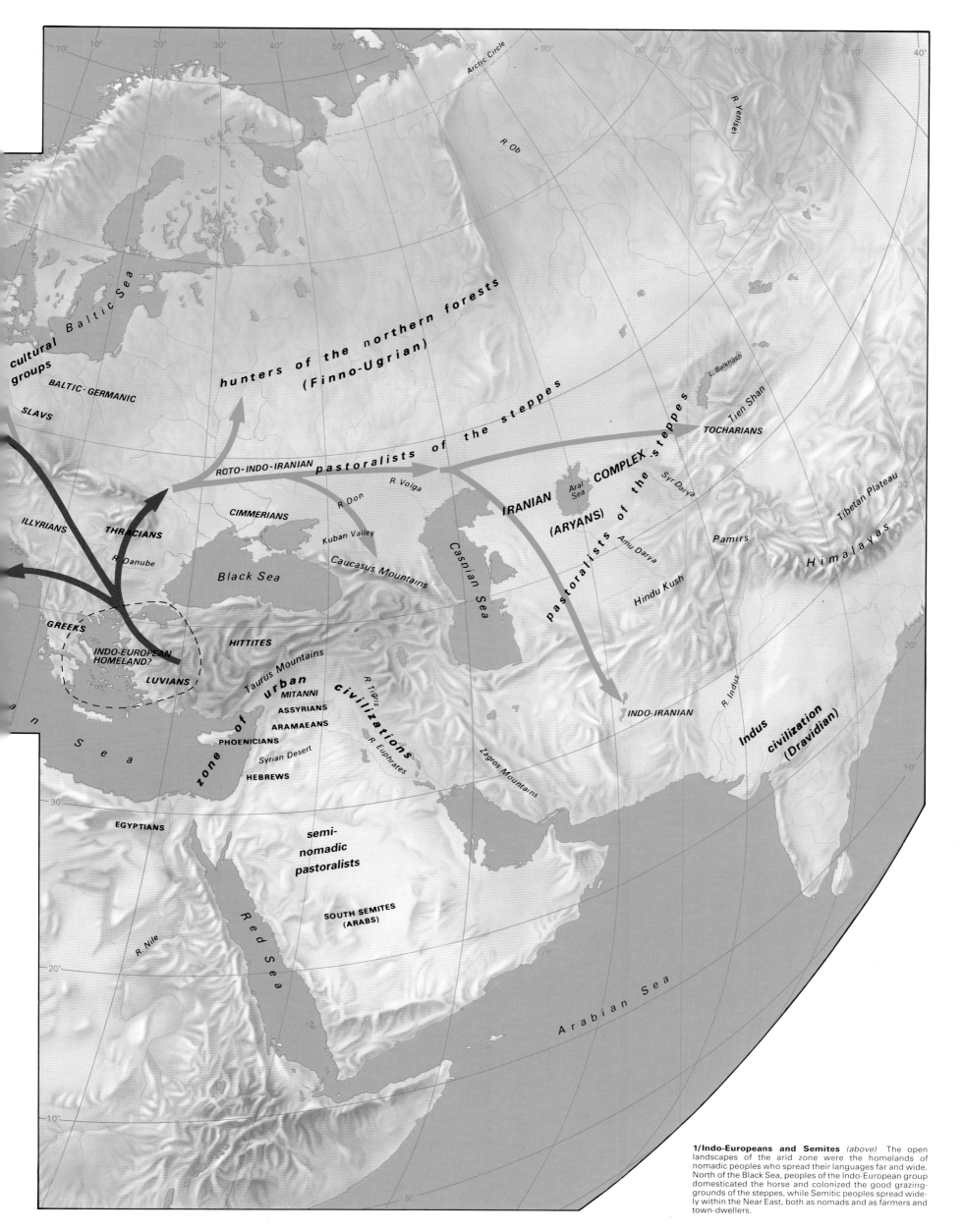

cultural
groups

BALTIC-GERMANIC

SLAVS

Baltic Sea

hunters of the northern forests
(Finno-Ugrian)

R Ob

R. Yenisei

Arctic Circle

ILLYRIANS

THRACIANS

ROTO-INDO-IRANIAN *pastoralists of the steppes*

L. Balkhash

Tien Shan

TOCHARIANS

CIMMERIANS

R. Don

R. Volga

IRANIAN COMPLEX

Aral Sea

Syr Darya

Tibetan Plateau

Kuban Valley

Caspian Sea

(ARYANS)

pastoralists of the steppes

Amu Darya

Pamirs

Hindu Kush

H i m a l a y a s

R. Danube

GREEKS

Black Sea

Caucasus Mountains

INDO-EUROPEAN
HOMELAND?

HITTITES

LUVIANS

Taurus Mountains

urban

MITANNI

ASSYRIANS

ARAMAEANS

PHOENICIANS

Syrian Desert

HEBREWS

R. Tigris

civilizations

R. Euphrates

zone of

Zagros Mountains

R. Indus

INDO-IRANIAN

Indus

civilization
(Dravidian)

EGYPTIANS

*semi-
nomadic
pastoralists*

SOUTH SEMITES
(ARABS)

R. Nile

Red Sea

Arabian Sea

1/Indo-Europeans and Semites *(above)* The open
landscapes of the arid zone were the homelands of
nomadic peoples who spread their languages far and wide.
North of the Black Sea, peoples of the Indo-European group
domesticated the horse and colonized the good grazing-
grounds of the steppes, while Semitic peoples spread widely within the Near East, both as nomads and as farmers and
town-dwellers.

61

The beginnings of Chinese civilization to 500 BC

CHINA has been inhabited continuously by humans since very early times. Remains of early hominids, which are similar to those from Java, have been found in Kwangsi, Yunnan and Shansi. About 500,000 BC Peking Man was living around Peking, in Shansi and possibly in Hupeh and Kwangtung. *Homo sapiens* first appeared in Palaeolithic cultures in the Ordos region, Hopeh, and in the southwest, about 30,000 BC. Later Mesolithic cultures flourished along the northern frontier zone, in the south and southwest, and in Taiwan.

Neolithic agricultural communities, the immediate ancestors of Chinese civilization, arose around 7000 BC in southern China and in the loess-covered lands of the north and northeast, where the well-drained soil of the river terraces was ideal for primitive agriculture. One of the best early sites is Banpo, with round and rectangular houses, as well as pottery kilns and a cemetery area. This contained only adult burials, however; children were buried in pottery urns between the houses. In the valley of the Huang Ho, early Chinese agriculture depended heavily on millet, but farther to the south rice-growing was important and evidence of rice-paddies in the Yangtze delta area dates from the 5th millennium BC. By 3000 BC, more sophisticated farming communities had developed technical skills, including the carving of jade, and settlements became larger and more permanent – small townships rather than villages – sometimes protected by defensive walls of rammed earth construction.

The use of bronze began around 1600 BC, and the beginning of the Bronze Age saw the founding of the first historical dynasty, the Shang. Traditionally a Hsia dynasty preceded the Shang, but the Hsia may have been one of the later Neolithic cultures – certainly none of their sites has yet been identified.

According to tradition, the Shang (1523–1028 or 1751–1111 BC) was a powerful political regime that controlled most of northern China; but more probably it was merely a loose confederation of clan domains, many of them little more than village settlements. The Shang kings moved their capital six times, and two capitals, at Cheng-chou and An-yang, have been excavated: each one, the king's 'Great Domain', contained the court, with many royal functionaries, supported by revenues from an extensive area. The Shang had trade relations with most of northern and central China, and with the steppes to the north and west. Many smaller Shang sites have been found and some are now known from the Yangtze Valley in central China. How far the Shang kings actually controlled these outer areas is uncertain.

In the 11th century BC the Shang were conquered by the Chou, a client people, possibly of different ethnic origin, living on their northwest border. They gradually extended their sovereignty over an area much larger than the Shang, including all of Hopeh, Honan, Shansi, Shantung, much of Shensi, Hupeh and Anhwei, and parts of the middle basin of the Yangtze. At first their capital lay in the vicinity of Hsi-an (Sian), with a secondary capital near Lo-yang. Their state was divided into numerous separate domains. The king himself possessed many of these, especially around the capitals, as a Royal Domain, and granted others as fiefs to members of the royal clan, to the families that had helped the Chou to power, and to the clans of important subjects and office-holders – a system of delegated authority not unlike the later European feudal system.

Until the 8th century BC the Chou kings remained powerful, and constantly extended the area under their control. About 770 BC, however, internal disorders forced them to abandon their homeland in the Wei Valley and move to their eastern capital at Lo-yang, where their power diminished and they soon became mere figureheads. For the next two and a half centuries their former vassals waged constant war until by the 5th century more than 100 petty feudal states had been swallowed up by some 20 of the more powerful kingdoms. Real power was exercised by 'hegemon' states heading temporary alliances: from 667–632 Ch'i was predominant; after 632 Chin; during the 6th century Ch'u. But these alliances did not achieve political stability. Nevertheless, Chou culture and Chinese influence were consolidated and spread far beyond the political borders of early Chou times.

The Shang and early Chou periods were differentiated from their predecessors not only by their political organization and their bronze

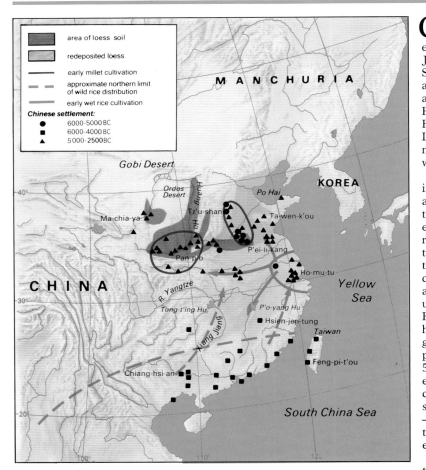

1/Early agriculture *(above)* From around 6000 BC numerous sites in northern China reveal evidence of well-established agriculture based on the cultivation of millet and on domesticated pigs. Further south, rice was the principal crop. Rice grows wild in southern China, but this useful plant was soon being cultivated to the north of its natural range by the early farmers of the Yangtze Valley. In the lower Yangtze area evidence of wet rice cultivation exists from around 5000 BC.

2/Shang China *(below)* By 2500 BC signs of increasing social and cultural complexity appeared among the prosperous farming communities of China, followed during the Lungshan period (2500-1800 BC) by walled settlements and more sophisticated technology, including the potter's wheel. These developments, however, only formed the prelude to the rise of the first Chinese civilization, which is named after the Shang dynasty (c.1600-1028 BC). Extensive walled cities, richly furnished tombs, sophisticated craftsmanship and the earliest Chinese writing all demonstrate the wealth and originality of Shang civilization.

3/Western Chou China: 11th to 9th centuries BC *(below)* The early Chou dominions comprised a very large number of domains. Some remained under royal control, others were granted as fiefs to supporters and servants of the Chou, in a sort of feudal tenure. Much of the area shown on the map was still occupied by peoples of different ethnic origins who were gradually assimilated and conquered by the Chou and their vassals.

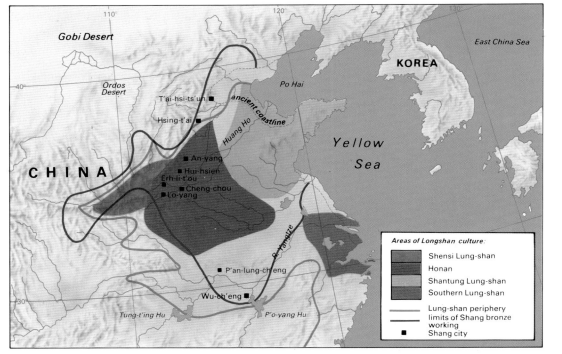

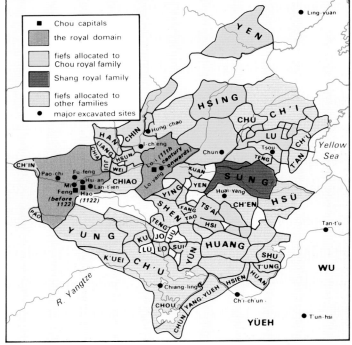

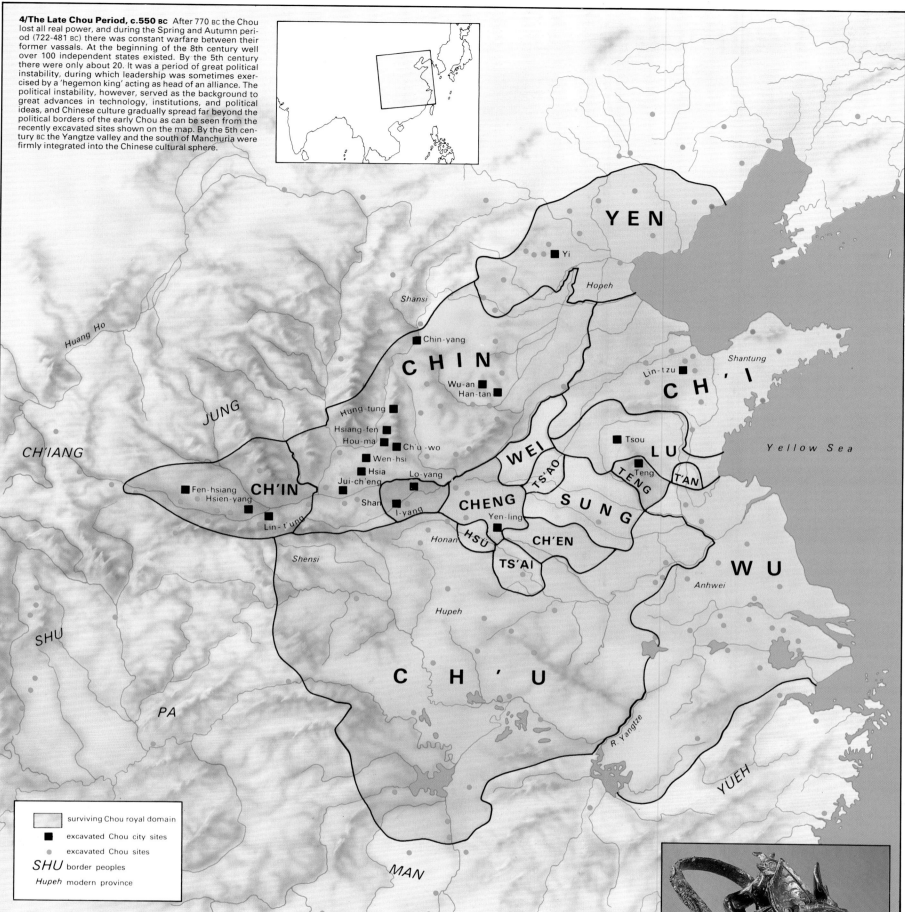

4/The Late Chou Period, c.550 BC After 770 BC the Chou lost all real power, and during the Spring and Autumn period (722-481 BC) there was constant warfare between their former vassals. At the beginning of the 8th century well over 100 independent states existed. By the 5th century there were only about 20. It was a period of great political instability, during which leadership was sometimes exercised by a 'hegemon king' acting as head of an alliance. The political instability, however, served as the background to great advances in technology, institutions, and political ideas, and Chinese culture gradually spread far beyond the political borders of the early Chou as can be seen from the recently excavated sites shown on the map. By the 5th century BC the Yangtze valley and the south of Manchuria were firmly integrated into the Chinese cultural sphere.

surviving Chou royal domain
■ excavated Chou city sites
• excavated Chou sites
SHU border peoples
Hupeh modern province

technology, but also by the use of writing, and their culture was already recognizably 'Chinese'. Their cities maintained a hierarchy of nobles, royal officers and court servants who all engaged in a constant round of warfare, hunting and elaborate religious ritual. They drew support from communities of craftsmen in bronze, jade, wood, stone, ceramics and textiles, many of them slaves, while the peasants working the various royal domains supplied them with revenues and foodstuffs.

Although the court and the nobility enjoyed a sophisticated lifestyle, bronze remained rare and was used almost exclusively for ritual objects rather than practical tools. Farmers working in the fields continued to use stone implements and to lead much the same life as in earlier times, residing in permanent settlements and cultivating lands within a fixed territory with rice, millet, barley and hemp, and raising pigs, poultry and silkworms. Nevertheless culti-vated areas remained relatively few, worked for a few years and then left fallow: the available technology could neither clear the dense woods on the mountains, nor drain and cultivate the heavy lands of the river valleys, so the peasants still depended upon the wild lands surrounding their settlements for much of their food.

Towards the end of the period, the old social order began to collapse. The more powerful states employed bureaucrats rather than the hereditary nobility of older times. Religious observances decayed. A new group of state servants (*shih*) emerged, as military officers and state officials. One of their number, Confucius, formalized many of the ideas current among them, and formulated them into a new ethos, which was to have currency far into the future. He was, however, only one of many thinkers who began to ponder the philosophical and practical problems facing mankind in this period of insecurity and rapid change.

Shang ritual food vessel (14th-11th century BC) *(right)* in Ho or Yu style, in the form of a tiger protecting a man. The vessel is covered with animal motifs related to a fertility cult.

The beginnings of Indian civilization

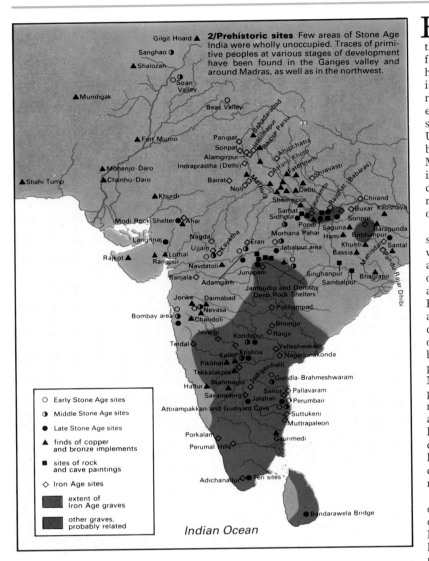

2/Prehistoric sites Few areas of Stone Age India were wholly unoccupied. Traces of primitive peoples at various stages of development have been found in the Ganges valley and around Madras, as well as in the northwest.

○ Early Stone Age sites
◐ Middle Stone Age sites
● Late Stone Age sites
▲ finds of copper and bronze implements
■ sites of rock and cave paintings
◇ Iron Age sites
▨ extent of Iron Age graves
▨ other graves, probably related

Indian Ocean

3/The evidence of pottery Terracotta is the characteristic Harappan material; ochre and red ware testifies to the survival of Neolithic tribes. Painted Grey pottery indicates Aryan occupation, with Black-and-Red emerging in the east. Later Northern Black Polished ware becomes predominant everywhere.

⊕ Black-and-Red ware
● Painted Grey ware
○ Northern Black Polished ware
⊛ sites with both Painted Grey and Northern Black Polished ware

Indian Ocean

HUMANS have inhabited the Indian sub-continent for over 2 million years: some of the oldest stone artifacts so far discovered come from a site near Rawalpindi in Pakistan and have been dated to that period by paleomagnetism (measurement of residual magnetism in rocks). Since then, evidence of human activity exists in almost all parts of South Asia, and stone tools belonging to the Lower, Middle and Upper Paleolithic periods occur in great numbers. The final stage of the Stone Age, the Mesolithic, is likewise widely represented, and in addition to large numbers of microlithic tools, cave sites have been found, some of them decorated with wall paintings of hunting scenes and other human activities.

The earliest evidence of the emergence of sedentary farming settlements comes from the western borders of the Indus valley and dates to around the 8th millennium BC. A long sequence of settlements has been excavated at Mehrgarh and neighbouring sites not far from Quetta. Barley and wheat date from the earliest period, and sheep and goats appear to have been domesticated. At first cattle bones survive in only small quantities, but by around 5000 BC become the dominant animal remains, while pottery first appears at about the same date. Mud-brick houses are present from the earliest period, along with structures consisting of two rows of oblong compartments, since identified as granaries. There is also very early evidence of long-distance trade. This remarkable sequence continues until, in its final stages, a distinctive local culture blended with the emerging Indus civilization in the first half of the 3rd millennium BC.

These developments flowered during the first of the great Indian civilizations which spread out from its leading cities, Harappa and Mohenjo-Daro in the Indus valley, to cover nearly 500,000 square miles (1.3 million km²) of territory and survived for around 1000 years (c.2550 to 1550 BC). The remains of typical Harappan towns, with their high citadels, solid buildings, uniform street grids and elaborate drainage systems, exist as far south as Cutch and Bhagatrav, at the mouth of the Narmada river, as well as at Rupar (Punjab) and Alamgirpur (Uttar Pradesh) in the east, and Judeirjo-Daro (Sind) and the Makran coast to the southwest. The Harappan script, mainly found on seals, is so far undeciphered, but it has been deduced from the vast granaries, the large houses, the proliferation of religious figurines (many of them anticipating Hindu deities) and the absence of royal palaces, that this was essentially a society of priests, merchants and peasant farmers. Many typical Harappan goods have been found in Mesopotamia, and textual references there suggest that the traders of the country known as Meluhha were at this time in regular commercial contact with the Middle East via the land of Dilmun (Bahrein).

The Indus civilization vanished without trace, until archaeological excavations revealed the first of its lost treasures in 1925. Its disappearance is almost certainly linked with the arrival in northwest Pakistan of the 'Aryans', speakers on an Indo-European language. Though some still argue that these were of local origin, they were most probably invaders from Bactria and northern Iran who had broken away earlier from the main nomad hordes in south Russia (see page 60). Their archaeological remains include Iranian funeral furnishings and copper hoards of a 'Caucasian' type, and their likely part in the destruction of Harappa and Mohenjo-Daro is underlined by early Vedic references to hostile, dark-skinned *dasas* (the original untouchables) living in the broken ruins (*armaka*) left behind by the great god Indra, in his role as Purandara, the breaker of cities.

The Vedas, which form the earliest Indian literature, consist largely of hymns to the Aryan gods, but together with the two enormous early Indian epic poems, the *Ramayana* and the *Mahabharata*, the *Rig-veda*, in particular, gives some notion, however selective and stylized, of life in the period from about 1500 BC to 450 BC.

At first the newcomers appear to have been hunters and herdsmen, tending cattle which were already acquiring sacred attributes and breeding the horses which, though unknown to the Harappan painters and sculptors, now figured frequently on the Painted Grey pottery characteristic of early Aryan settlements. Gradually they adopted the techniques of settled farming from the peoples they had conquered and particularly after the advent of iron in about 800 BC, they undertook extensive clearance of the forests then covering northern India. At the same time they evolved a complex and pervasive set of cultural institutions, which in many ways have shaped the sub-continent to the present day. Their language, Sanskrit, formed the basis for a literature as developed as the Greek and Latin to which it is closely related. Their metaphysical subtlety, expressed in the *Upanishads*, held the seeds of many later systems of religious thought. Their emphasis on sacrifice, and the crucial importance which they were already attaching to the notion of caste, set fundamental social patterns and at the same time created objectives of social reform which have continued to shape life in India.

In the first phase of their expansion, down to c.1050 BC, the Rig-vedic Aryans, with their horses and light chariots, extended their domain from Suvastu (the Swat valley in Pakistan) to *Sapta-Sindhava*, the land of the Seven Induses. Thereafter they began to move steadily eastwards towards the Ganges. Painted Grey ware has been found in quantity at the site of Hastinapur, a city largely washed away by a great Ganges flood in about 900 BC. As land clearance then spread eastwards along the valley, the river became a natural trade highway. Ships and voyages figure in the *Rig-veda*, though the Aryans do not seem to have ventured far by sea. Probably after 800 BC they began to penetrate increasingly further south, and though the *Ramayana*'s epic account of their conquest of Sri Lanka, generally believed to be Ceylon, has never been archaeologically substantiated, they undoubtedly moved into the Deccan, which from now on became an increasingly important route between north and south.

The physical geography of India at this time dictated a different form of development for the hilly, much-fragmented lands which make up the southern peninsula. Whereas the great northern plains lent themselves to large-scale agriculture and the growth of substantial kingdoms, the relatively tiny communities of the south evolved their own highly autonomous forms of religious, political and economic life. Distinctive megalithic cultures grew up throughout peninsular India, while the sea-faring peoples of the southern tip continued to cultivate the close maritime ties with the Middle East which had been severed, as far as northern India was concerned, with the eclipse of the Harappans.

From 600 BC to 450 BC the pattern of kingdoms and republics begins to emerge more clearly (see page 82). Archaeological evidence, largely based on pottery styles, suggests that the heartland of the Aryan peoples had by now moved east from the western Punjab to Kurukshetra and the Doab, and the texts refer to land as far eastward as Magadha. Painted Grey ware and the Black-and-Red ceramics of the eastern regions were giving way to a single Black pottery, extending throughout the Indo-Gangetic region. A culturally unified northern India was ready for its first empire, that of Chandragupta Maurya who may have met and been inspired by his contemporary, Alexander the Great.

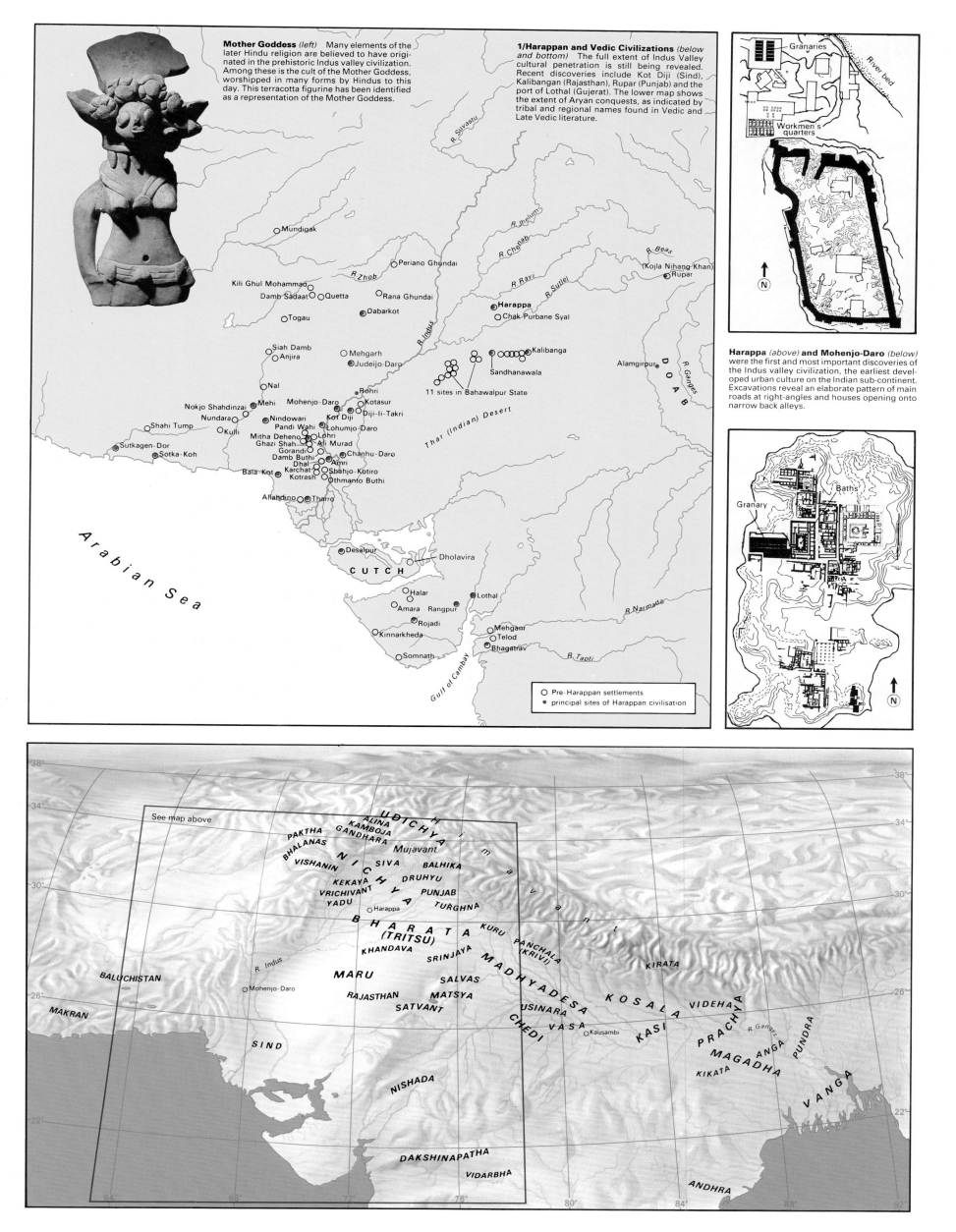

Mother Goddess (left) Many elements of the later Hindu religion are believed to have originated in the prehistoric Indus valley civilization. Among these is the cult of the Mother Goddess, worshipped in many forms by Hindus to this day. This terracotta figurine has been identified as a representation of the Mother Goddess.

1/Harappan and Vedic Civilizations (below and bottom) The full extent of Indus Valley cultural penetration is still being revealed. Recent discoveries include Kot Diji (Sind), Kalibangan (Rajasthan), Rupar (Punjab) and the port of Lothal (Gujerat). The lower map shows the extent of Aryan conquests, as indicated by tribal and regional names found in Vedic and Late Vedic literature.

Harappa (above) and **Mohenjo-Daro** (below) were the first and most important discoveries of the Indus valley civilization, the earliest developed urban culture on the Indian sub-continent. Excavations reveal an elaborate pattern of main roads at right-angles and houses opening onto narrow back alleys.

○ Pre-Harappan settlements

● principal sites of Harappan civilisation

Mediterranean civilizations c.3000 to 950 BC

THE island of Crete, mountainous but fertile, saw the rise of the first major civilization on European soil. Known as the Minoan civilization, it takes its name from Minos, the legendary king of Knossos, and is represented today by the remains of a whole series of palaces, chief among them being Knossos and Mallia in the north, Phaistos in the south, and Zakro in the east of Crete. These appear to have been founded in around 2000 BC, and were rebuilt several times as successive earthquakes struck the island. Each palace was probably the centre of a small kingdom, though we have little evidence of the rulers themselves or their achievements. Later Greek legend made King Minos of Crete a tyrannical ruler who dominated the Aegean with his powerful fleet. It is clear that Minoan seafarers did trade their goods and manufactures with neighbouring states of Egypt and the Near East, but whether Cretan rulers ever exercised any political or military control beyond the island is uncertain. Nevertheless, the cultural influence of Minoan civilization was profound, affecting existing communities throughout the Aegean region.

The Cretans of the palace period were outstanding craftsmen, decorating the palaces with vivid and naturalistic frescoes. They also excelled in pottery manufacture (producing beautiful eggshell-thin vessels), metalworking, the carving of gemstones, and the production of carved stone bowls in attractive variegated materials.

This was evidently a period of flourishing trade. Egyptian stone vases, scarab seals and carved ivories found their way to Crete and were imitated there. Finely decorated pottery from Crete reached Egypt; some of it was recovered from the town of Kahun, built to house workmen and officials engaged in constructing a pyramid

for one of the great pharaohs of the XIIth Dynasty, Sesostris II (c.1906–1888 BC). Much of the trade in these early times was no doubt in raw materials such as copper, and the tin required to mix with it to make bronze. Crete may have imported Egyptian linen, exchanging it for timber and for woollen cloth woven with colourful designs, as depicted in representations of the dress worn by Cretan men and women. Conversely, the painted decoration on the ceilings of some Egyptian tombs from the time of the XIIth Dynasty onwards seems to reflect the influence of imported Cretan textiles.

In the 16th century BC, a second focus of Aegean civilization arose on the Greek mainland, taking its name from the important citadel of Mycenae in the eastern Peloponnese. Six great burial pits, the Shaft Graves, mark the resting places of the rulers who first seem to have made Mycenae a power to be reckoned with. The men in these graves were buried with vast quantities of swords and daggers, their hilts often adorned with gold or precious stones; the richly ornamented dagger blades were inlaid with gold, silver and niello. The more elaborate of the surviving inlays are in the form of pictures, one showing armed men with great body shields (made of ox-hide) combating lions.

The principal centres of Mycenaean Greece were palaces, less elaborate than those of Crete, but mostly sheltered behind massive defensive walls. This was a society geared for war. The graves of local leaders contain weapons and suits of body-armour designed for chariot warfare, and occasionally even chariot models. Chariots also feature on painted pottery, along with scenes showing files of infantry carrying long spears.

The defences of Mycenae and other sites were

probably directed as much against warlike Greek neighbours as against overseas powers, for Mycenaean Greece was divided among a number of independent leaders. (In Homer's epic poem *The Iliad*, Agamemnon of Mycenae is overlord of the other princes, but only in times of war.) This geography is reflected in the distribution of Mycenaean palaces known to archaeologists: each was probably the centre of a small kingdom, in much the same way as Greece in the classical period was divided into city-states.

About 1450 BC, fire destroyed most of the important towns and cities of Crete. The cause of this havoc is unknown, but the consequences are clear and profound, as clay tablets from Knossos show that Greek was now the language of administration, and mainland fashions in pottery, architecture and burial customs henceforth dominated Crete. It seems likely that mainlanders – Mycenaeans – had seized control in Crete, perhaps taking advantage of the disruption following a natural calamity such as an earthquake, or by means of straightforward invasion.

One important innovation adopted from Crete by the Mycenaeans was writing, and clay tablets in their Linear B script have been found at several Mycenaean palaces on the Greek mainland, including Pylos, Tiryns and Mycenae itself. The Linear B script was an early form of Greek, and its decipherment has shown beyond doubt that the Mycenaeans were the direct ancestors of the Greeks of the Classical period. These tablets have also thrown much light on the administration of the Mycenaean palaces, since the great majority of the texts were concerned with accountancy, recording receipts of raw materials and foodstuffs, listing rations to craftsmen and domestics, and detailing the contents of palace storerooms. They reveal a bureaucrat-

Bronze stand *(above)* from Cyprus c.1600-1100 BC showing a man carrying copper or bronze 'oxhide' ingots, so shaped to make them convenient to carry on the shoulders.

3/Trade connections during the Neolithic and Bronze Ages *(below)* Much of the trade in the Aegean world was probably in raw materials, apart from spondylus shells and Melian obsidian.

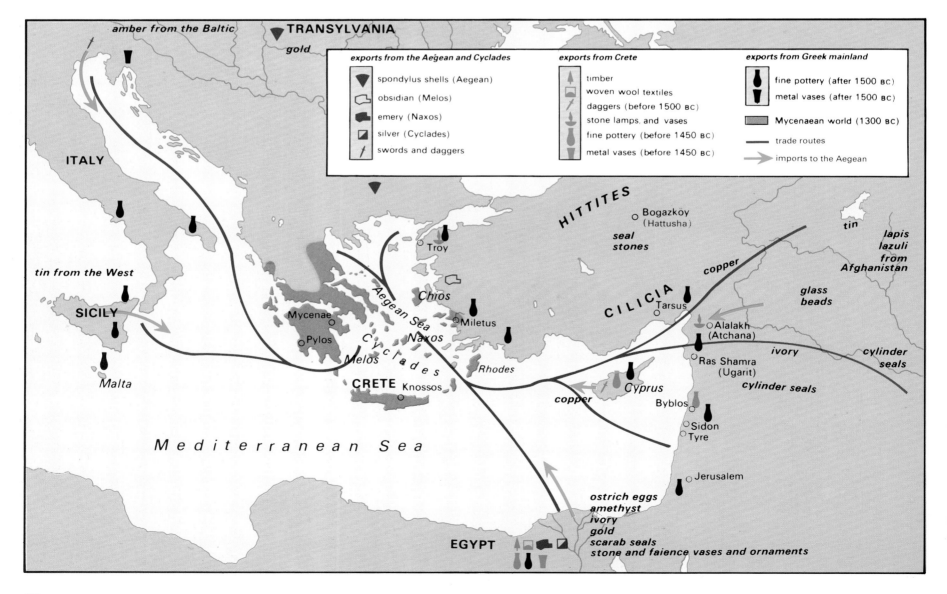

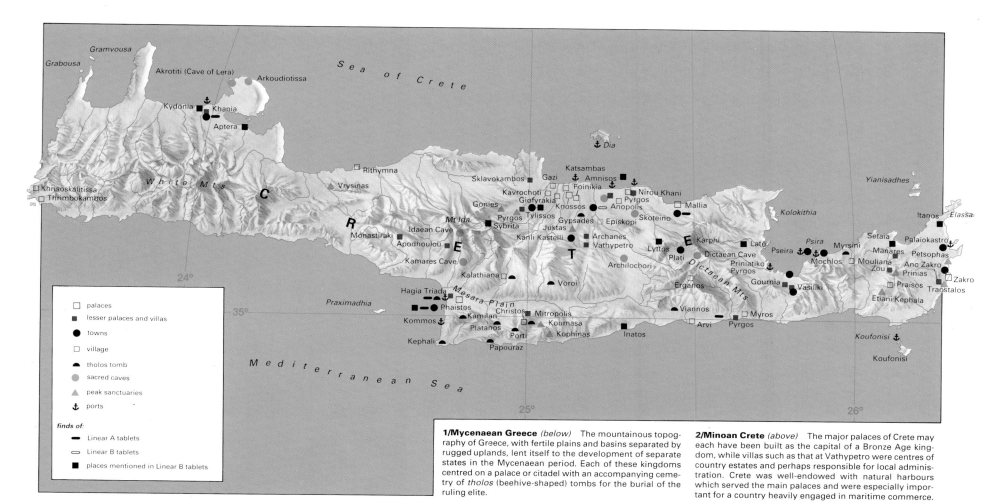

Map 2/Minoan Crete legend:

- □ palaces
- ■ lesser palaces and villas
- ● towns
- □ village
- ◣ tholos tomb
- ● sacred caves
- ▲ peak sanctuaries
- ⚓ ports

finds of:
- ▬ Linear A tablets
- ▱ Linear B tablets
- ■ places mentioned in Linear B tablets

1/Mycenaean Greece *(below)* The mountainous topography of Greece, with fertile plains and basins separated by rugged uplands, lent itself to the development of separate states in the Mycenaean period. Each of these kingdoms centred on a palace or citadel with an accompanying cemetry of *tholos* (beehive-shaped) tombs for the burial of the ruling elite.

2/Minoan Crete *(above)* The major palaces of Crete may each have been built as the capital of a Bronze Age kingdom, while villas such as that at Vathypetro were centres of country estates and perhaps responsible for local administration. Crete was well-endowed with natural harbours which served the main palaces and were especially important for a country heavily engaged in maritime commerce.

ic structure which finds no echo in the memories of the Mycenaean age passed down by Homer.

In the 14th century BC Mycenaean influence spread throughout the Aegean. Knossos appears to have been the only centre of government in Crete after the mainland conquest of c.1450 BC, but eventually the palace there was destroyed, and the whole Aegean may have become a miniature empire ruled from Mycenae, although palaces at Tiryns, Pylos and elsewhere suggest the existence of tributary kings. The story of the siege of Troy in Homer's *Iliad* may enshrine distant memories of the phase of expansion.

The 13th century began with the Mycenaean palaces at the height of their power and prestige, and new building everywhere; but by the end of the century most had perished in flames. Increased feuding between neighbouring states may have been one of the causes; another, perhaps, was revolt by the population at large against the Mycenaean warrior-aristocrats in their sumptuous dwellings. But the Mycenaean kingdoms collapsed, while their mighty neighbours in Anatolia, Egypt, and the rest of the eastern Mediterranean too were struggling against economic disruption and the depredations of roving bands of warriors known as 'the Sea-Peoples', who may have included landless Mycenaean adventurers. The strain was also too much for the Hittite empire, which fell in about 1200 BC (see page 56), and almost too great even for Egypt, which survived only with the loss of its Asiatic possessions. Against the background of these turbulent events and the collapse of the Mycenaean palaces Greece itself entered a Dark Age lasting 400 years, from which it emerged only in the 8th century BC.

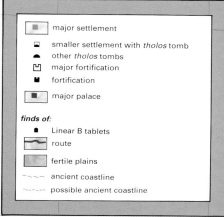

Map 1/Mycenaean Greece legend:

- ▣ major settlement
- ◱ smaller settlement with *tholos* tomb
- ◣ other *tholos* tombs
- ⬚ major fortification
- ■ fortification
- ▪ major palace

finds of:
- ▪ Linear B tablets
- ～ route
- ▦ fertile plains
- ----- ancient coastline
- ∙∙∙∙∙ possible ancient coastline

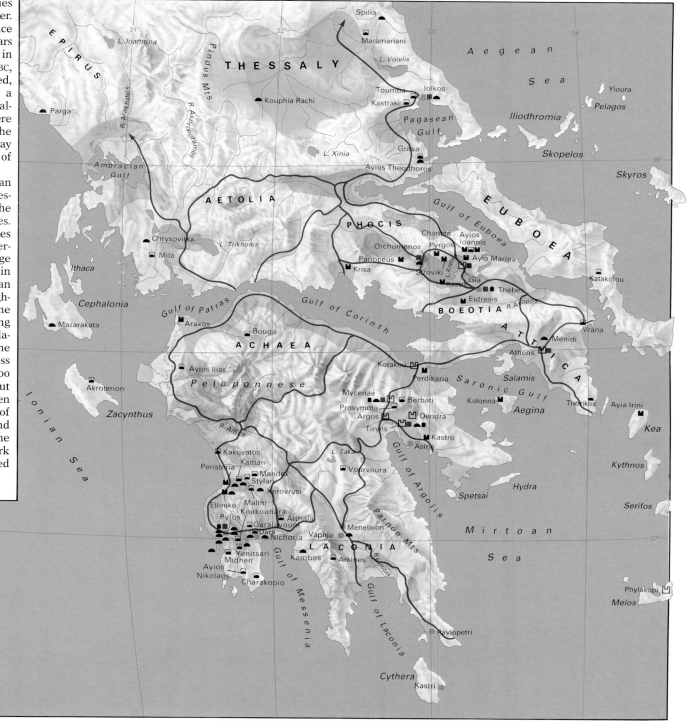

THE earliest civilizations arose at a few scattered points in the vast uninhabited or sparsely inhabited Eurasian landmass. Between 1000 BC and AD 500 the pattern began to change. Although America, Australasia and Africa south of the Sahara still stood outside the mainstream of world history, and were to stay so for a further thousand years, the civilizations of Europe and Asia now formed a continuous belt. By AD 100, when the classical era was at its height, a chain of empires extended from Rome, which encompassed the entire Mediterranean basin, via Parthia and the Kushan Empire to China, constituting an unbroken zone of civilized life from the Atlantic to the Pacific.

This was a new and important fact in the history of the Eurasian world. The area of civilization remained narrow and exposed to unrelenting barbarian pressures, and developments in the different regions remained largely autonomous; but with the expansion of the major civilizations and the elimination of the geographical gaps between them, the way lay open for inter-regional contacts and cultural exchanges which left a lasting imprint. In the west, the expansion of Hellenism created a single cultural area which extended for some time from the frontiers of India to Britain; in the east, the expansion of the Chinese and Indian civilizations resulted in a kind of cultural symbiosis in Indo-China. These wider cultural areas provided a vehicle not only for trade but also for the transmission of ideas, technology and institutions, and above all for the diffusion of the great world religions. Beginning with Buddhism, and continuing later with Judaism, Zoroastrianism, Christianity and Islam, religion became a powerful unifying bond in the Eurasian world, with political and cultural, as well as religious, consequences.

3 The classical

The Acropolis and Parthenon, Athens

civilizations of Eurasia

The commercial and cultural bonds of Eurasia

FEW people in the Near East, let alone in Europe, knew much about eastern Asia until the emergence of Achaemenid Persia in the 6th century BC (see page 78), and China itself remained almost unknown there until shortly before the Christian era. But although little or no evidence exists of face-to-face meetings in the earlier centuries, it is clear that there were important influences and borrowings. Bronze was already giving way to iron in the West when it first appeared in China; and unparalleled technical excellence was soon achieved in the Shang and Chou kingdoms along the Huang Ho (Yellow River). Although the silk-moth was native to Assam and Bengal, it was in northern China that people first learned how to unravel a single, unbroken thread from its cocoon. Jade, the most prized material of the Chinese jewel-carvers, came from the western end of the arid and dangerous Tarim Basin; wheat seeds originated far to the west; water-buffalo and domesticated poultry in Southeast Asia; wet-rice cultivation was common throughout east and Southeast Asia; cowrie shells, the first Chinese money, probably came from the faraway Maldive Islands. All these, it seems, must have been introduced by nomads and itinerant merchants from beyond China's traditionally self-contained borders.

Economic and cultural contact between the extremes of the ancient world reached its height in the 2nd century AD. Although Rome and Han China never established formal diplomatic relations, each was well aware of the other's existence. Luxury goods flowed freely, particularly from East to West, and expensive and non-bulky goods such as silk and spices could be transport-ed by caravan or ship at a cost which was only a small proportion of their market value. In return, gold and silver, mostly in coins, moved in large quantities, both by land and by sea. Between the frontiers of these great classical civilizations, the Kushan Empire of Afghanistan and northern India and the Parthian Empire of Persia both willingly fostered this trade, maintaining and garrisoning the roads, protecting the caravans and thriving on the tolls.

To the south, in the Indian Ocean, up to 120 substantial Greek-owned ships a year plied between the Red Sea ports and India, exploiting the monsoon, while Arab ships traded from port to port along the northwest coast of India, the Persian Gulf, the incense-bearing shore of Arabia and the spice and elephant ivory markets of Abyssinia and Somaliland. The Roman Empire exported glass, copper, tin, lead, red coral, textiles, pottery, and above all currency. The chief imports from the East were Arabian incense, Chinese silk, and from India precious stones, muslin and spices, especially pepper. Other spices reached the Empire from the East Indies via Madagascar and East Africa. Caravans moving between the Empire and the Persian Gulf ports of Charax and Apologos were owned, organized and escorted across the desert by citizens of Palmyra, a city whose role as a desert *entrepôt* earned it the wealth to finance spectacular public buildings, until its power was destroyed by the Romans in AD 273. Farther south, Petra performed the same function for the caravans travelling to and from the Red Sea ports of Leucecome and Arsinoë, and the Persian Gulf port of Gerrha. The most important *entrepôt* of all was Alexandria, a city of up to 1 million inhabitants which received eastern trade goods from the Red Sea ports of Berenice, Myos Hormus and Clysma for shipment to all parts of the Roman Empire. It also exported its own manufactures: linen, processed Arabian drugs and Indian perfumes, papyrus, glassware and – by far the greatest shipment of all – Egyptian grain, which helped to feed the population of Rome.

Ultimately, the horse and the Bactrian camel opened up the central Asian steppes as a great commercial route. During Chinese efforts to control Sinkiang, General Pan Ch'ao, who held the northern and western oases against all comers, defeated a massive Kushan invasion from India in AD 90, led an army across the Pamir mountains to reach the Caspian, and established contact with the Parthians. With the southern and northern silk routes now safe, a Chinese ambassador was sent, in AD 97, to Antioch.

By that time, however, regular caravans had linked the two mighty empires for almost 200 years. Few, if any, went straight through, but there were well-established change-over points where the Greek, Arab, Roman, Iranian and Indian traders of the West exchanged goods with the nomad merchants who undertook the middle stretches of the journey, handing over in turn to the Chinese at the further frontiers.

In the 2nd century AD these trade links were cemented when the Yüeh-chih and the Tocharians combined to create the vast Kushan Empire, extending from the northern half of India to include a great part of the central Asian landmass. Even under the Achaemenids, trade, roads and safe transportation had been matters of prime concern. Darius's Royal Road ran 1677

Ferghana's 'Heavenly Horses'
(right) Ferghana was the home of the horses with which the Chinese were anxious to equip their cavalry to counter the agile ponies of the Hsiung-nu and other nomads north of the Great Wall. The fifth Han emperor, Wu-ti, sent emissaries and armies to Sinkiang to control the source of these horses. China eventually received supplies of Ferghana stallions, and this painting from Tun-huang shows a Chinese official mounted on one of them.

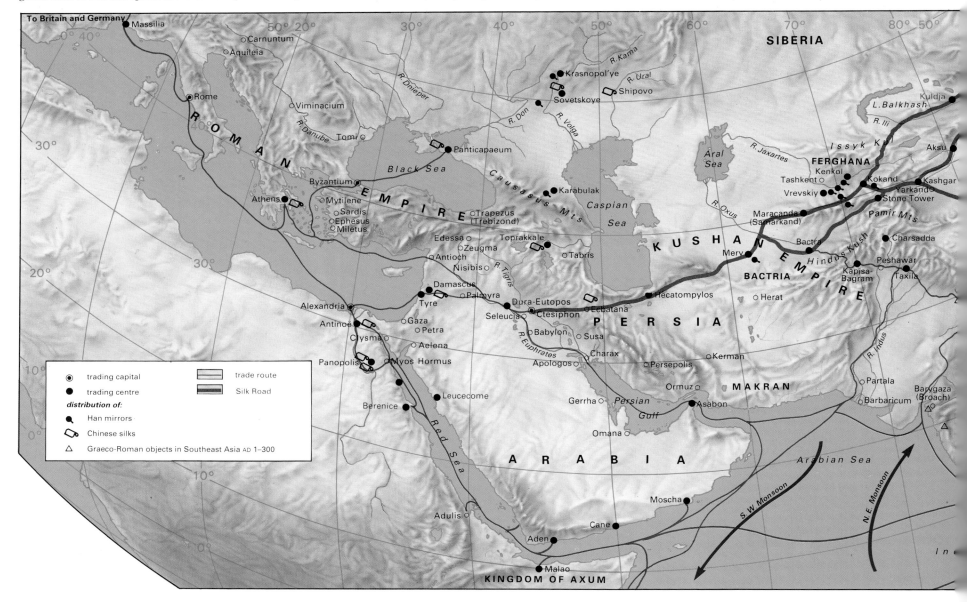

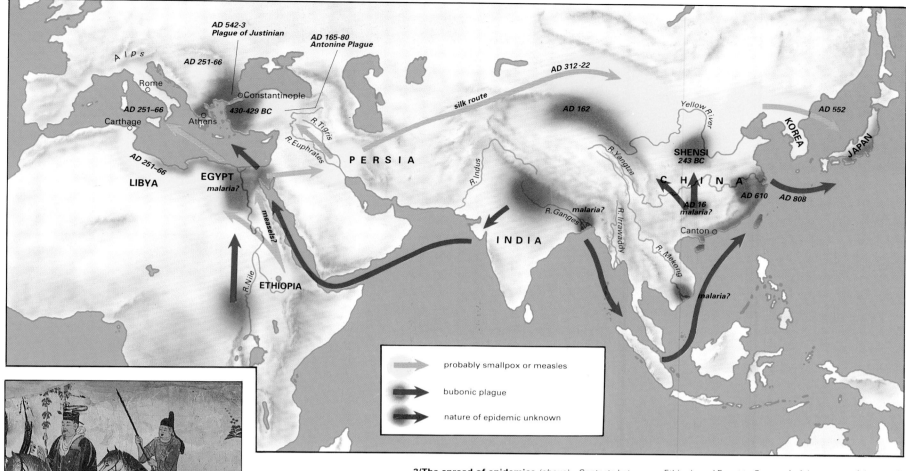

AD 542-3
Plague of Justinian

AD 165-80
Antonine Plague

AD 251-66

AD 312-22

Alps

Rome

○Constantinople

AD 251-66
Carthage

Athens

430-429 BC

silk route

AD 162

Yellow River

AD 552

KOREA

AD 251-66

R. Tigris

R. Euphrates

P E R S I A

R. Indus

SHENSI
243 BC

C H I N A

JAPAN

LIBYA

EGYPT
malaria?

R. Nile

measels?

R. Ganges

malaria?

R. Irrawaddy

R. Yangtze

AD 16
malaria?

AD 610

AD 808

Canton ○

R. Mekong

ETHIOPIA

I N D I A

malaria?

→ probably smallpox or measles

→ bubonic plague

→ nature of epidemic unknown

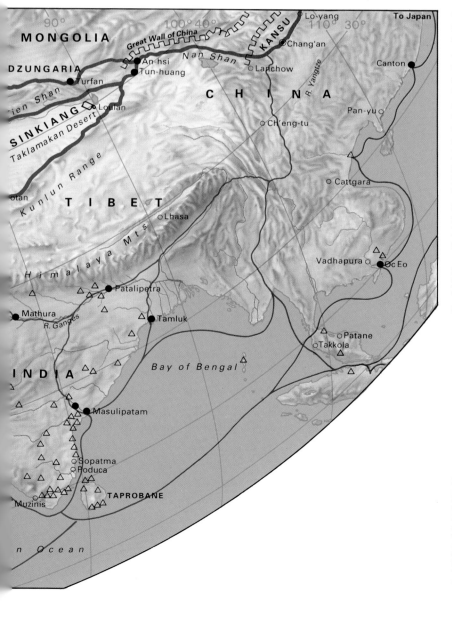

2/The spread of epidemics *(above)* Contacts between India, China and the Mediterranean allowed the interchange of luxury goods, and fostered the spread of the 'world' religions, Buddhism and Christianity. They also carried a less welcome import: disease. Diseases common in some areas could have devastating effects when introduced to populations which had no previous exposure and no inherited resistance to the disease. In many cases the outbreak referred to as 'plague' was in fact another serious epidemic disease such as smallpox or measles. The plague which struck at Athens during the Peloponnesian War (430-429 BC), described in vivid detail by Thucydides, may have been an early manifestation of this pattern, appearing first in Persia, then spreading along the trade routes through Ethiopia and Egypt to Greece. At Athens, tens of thousands died, and the dead lay unburied in the streets. The frequency and intensity of epidemics increased in the first few centuries AD, with virulent outbreaks in the West (251-70), claiming even a Roman emperor, and in China in the early 4th century (312-22). A further severe outbreak afflicted the Byzantine empire during the reign of Justinian (542-3). These outbreaks seriously weakened and demoralized the classical empires of Rome and China, which already faced serious threats from external enemies. Epidemic disease became progressively less common in Europe from the 7th century, until renewed contacts with China in the 14th century brought the Black Death.

well-garrisoned miles (2700 km) from Ephesus to Susa; an even longer route linked Babylon with Ecbatana and Bactra (modern Balkh) in Afghanistan. The Seleucids maintained the tradition, with a major trading network extending across the Persian plateau from their new capital at Seleucia.When Bactria became independent (250–139 BC) it formed the junction for a web of caravan routes joining Siberia and China with India's great trading centre of Taxila and with Persia, the Red Sea, the Persian Gulf and Mediterranean *entrepôt* cities such as Antioch and Alexandria. Great trading concerns centred in Bactria kept branches and agents in China. The Parthians under Tiridates (247–212 BC) deliberately transferred their capital to Hecatompylos on the caravan road from Seleucia to Bactria. Now the Kushans, with their 'thousand cities' of central Asia, completed the chain.

The chain did not hold for long, however. By the opening of the 3rd century AD all parts of the 2500-mile (4000-km) route from Syria to the Tarim were under pressure. The Chinese were driven completely from the Tarim Basin, cutting

the major routes, and both Rome and China found themselves hard pressed by the barbarians to the north (see page 94). The demand for foreign products built up during the years of peace and security did not suddenly vanish, but increasingly it had to be met by the relatively unthreatened – and for bulky cargoes very much more economical – sea route whose traffic had grown rapidly since the Greek pilot Hippalus discovered the monsoon, probably around 100 BC. Since then ships with a carrying capacity of up to 500 tons beat with the monsoon winds across to the Indian ports: Barbaricum at the mouth of the Indus, Barygaza further south and Muziris about 200 miles (320 km) north of the southern tip of India. In winter the winds reversed and the Greek ships returned laden with the products of the east. Occasional Greek merchants may have gone further east than Muziris or Taprobane (Ceylon), but as a rule they did not, instead receiving Chinese wares from Indian merchants. The Chinese Empire now reached as far south as Haiphong; it is likely that Indians and Chinese met at Oc Eo in southern Cambodia. From there the Indians shipped the goods west, portaging them across the Malay Peninsula and the southern tip of India. The development of the sea route greatly reduced the price of silk in the Roman world and significantly increased the use of eastern spices in Roman cookery.

The volume of eastern trade no doubt fluctuated according to the internal conditions of the Roman and Chinese Empires and intervening lands. From time to time war between the Roman and Persian Empires interfered with the land route, while disorders among the Arabs could impede shipping along the Arabian coast. From the 5th century AD the progressive takeover by barbarians of the Western provinces of the Roman Empire reduced – but did not end – the demand for eastern luxuries in those areas. The oriental provinces of the Empire remained prosperous until the end of the 6th century and the age of the Arab conquests.

90°

100° 40°

110° 30°

Lo-yang

To Japan

MONGOLIA

Great Wall of China

KANSU

Chang'an

DZUNGARIA

Nan Shan

An-hsi

Turfan

Tun-huang

Lanchow

Canton

'ien Shan

SINKIANG

Loulan

C H I N A

R. Yangtze

Taklamakan Desert

Ch'eng-tu

Pan-yu ○

'otan

Kunlun Range

Cattgara

T I B E T

Lhasa

Himalaya Mts

Vadhapura

Oc Eo

Patalipetra

Mathura

Tamluk

R. Ganges

Patane

Takkola

I N D I A

Bay of Bengal

Masulipatam

Sopatma

Poduca

Muzinis

TAPROBANE

n Ocean

1/Commercial and cultural bonds *(left)* Extensive links between the major civilizations of Eurasia have been proved by archaeological finds, including huge Roman coin hoards discovered in southern India. Regular journeys from China to the West became possible after the Hsiung-nu had been driven back in the 1st century BC from the desert cities and principalities of Dzungaria. The usual starting point, on the edge of China proper, was Tun-huang, from which the route continued west over the Pamirs to Tashkent, Samarkand and Merv. From the turn of the Christian era an increasing proportion of the trade used the sea-routes of the Indian Ocean, making effective use of the seasonal monsoon winds.

The religious bonds of Eurasia to AD 500

ALL the great world religions originated in Asia, and three of them – Judaism, Christianity and Islam – in a quite small area of western Asia. Equally noteworthy is the concentration of great spiritual leaders in different parts of the world in or close to the 6th century BC, an 'axial' age, in the words of the philosopher Karl Jaspers (*The Origin and Meaning of History*). This was the period of Confucius and perhaps Lao-tzu in China, of Zoroaster in Persia, of Gautama the Buddha in India, of the greatest of the Hebrew prophets, whom we call Deutero- (or second) Isaiah (*Isaiah* 40–55), and of Pythagoras in Greece. Possibly the emergence of civilizations which claimed to be universal called forth universal religions; possibly the new religions responded to tensions within the existing societies, and the need for a spiritual outlet and a faith which transcended a superstitious polytheism. In any case, the movement towards a belief in a single spiritual reality coincided with the search of Greek thinkers for a single principle to explain the material world.

The oldest of the world religions is Hinduism, although narrowly defined it is not a world religion at all but rather the religion of the people of India ('Hindu' means 'belonging to the Indus'). It is comprehensive and enormously complex: it emphasizes 'the right way to live', but embraces vegetarianism and human sacrifice, asceticism and orgy. Its cults express themselves in all the richness of external observance and the devotion of internal meditation, in the simplest beliefs of villagers and the abstruse reasoning of philosophers. Hinduism is not in any real sense a missionary religion.

On the other hand, Buddhism, which began as a reformist movement within Hinduism, is one of the great missionary religions. Ironically, while its outreach has been so successful that it has spread over much of Asia, there are now virtually no Buddhists in India. Gautama, the Buddha (the title means 'Enlightened'), was an Indian prince who lived in the 6th and 5th centuries BC, and gave up his position in the Great Renunciation. Six years later he received enlightenment under the bo tree and attained Nirvana, obliteration of desire. The first great landmark in Buddhist history was the reign of

The 'Golden Hall' of the Horyuji Temple (*below*) Buddhism was introduced into Japan, via China and Korea, in the mid-6th century. The Horyuji at Nara, built in 670, is the oldest surviving Japanese temple. By the 8th century Buddhism was firmly established both as a state religion and as a popular faith in Japan.

the Indian emperor Asoka, 274–232 BC (see page 82). After his conversion to Buddhism, he became a man of peace and high principle of a kind unusual in high places (his conversion stands in marked contrast to that of the Roman emperor Constantine to Christianity). Thereafter, Buddhism soon spread to Ceylon and Burma, and reached China by the 1st or 2nd century AD, Korea in the 4th century, and Japan in the 6th century.

Buddhism is unusual among world religions in that it does not centre upon a god. Its message is one of deliverance from suffering through the annihilation of desire. This is the doctrine which, with the Buddha and the community, form the focal parts of Buddhism. There has been only one great schism in Buddhism, which emerged 500 years or so after the religion was founded: between the more conservative Theravada and the universalist Mahayana. Theravada Buddhism is strong in Ceylon, Burma and Thailand, whereas Mahayana Buddhism tended to have more appeal further east. Buddhism spread along the coast of Southeast Asia and also by the silk route through central Asia.

China itself possessed ancient traditions of ancestor veneration and the worship of spirits of nature. From about the 5th century BC two systems became dominant, at least among the upper classes. One was the ethical system of Kung Futzu or Confucius (551–479 BC), the other the mystical religion of the Tao, associated with the shadowy figure of Lao-tzu. The Tao means 'the way', that is, the way of the universe or humankind's call to be in harmony with the world through the practice of quietude. These two, with Buddhism, constituted the 'three religions' of traditional China. In Japan, Buddhism challenged established Shinto and spirit-worship in the 6th century AD, and it was only towards the end of the Tokugawa era that Shintoism revived as the essence and expression of Japanese national identity.

The Jews were a people, small in number, who according to tradition moved from Mesopotamia to Palestine, and whose documented history began with their escape from oppression in Egypt under a leader named Moses. They attributed their escape to a divine being named Yahweh or the Lord, with whom they made a covenant that they would be his people and he would be their god, a covenant associated with the simple but profound moral demands of the Ten Commandments, the basis of the Torah or Law. They were at first an exclusive people, marked off by their food-laws, circumcision, and other religious observances. The fact that Yahweh was a god who adopted them from outside had in it the seeds of universalism, and a succession of 'prophets' kept the challenge of ethical and religious righteousness before them. The Jews suffered continually from the political and military domination of others, and the consequent dispersion carried them over much of the Mediterranean world as well (see page 102). Later, as a result of Christian persecution, the Jews migrated still further.

Judaism gave birth to Christianity, which spread early over the Roman Empire and later still further afield (see pages 92 and 100). Islam too accepts the traditions of Judaism and Christianity, and sees Mohammed (c.570–632) as one in a line of prophets which includes Moses and Jesus. Islam was also to be a great missionary religion. In one direction it spread across North Africa, through Spain and into Europe; in another it reached India (see page 104).

One other world religion must be mentioned: Zoroastrianism, which started in Persia, and is associated with the name of Zoroaster or Zarathustra, another shadowy figure. It sees life as a battleground between the forces of light and of darkness, and is today represented by the comparatively small Indian sect of the Parsis.

Nevertheless, in the form of Mithraism, it spread through the Roman Empire, until ousted by the rise of Christianity.

Of course, innumerable other creeds failed to make the transition to world religions. The Greek pantheon, adopted and adapted by the Romans, honoured a sky-god, Zeus (Jupiter), and other deities, each with a special function. The Celts (whose priesthood, the druids, was suppressed after charges of human sacrifice), the Scandinavians (whose gods Wotan, Thor and others provided English names for the days of the week), and the Germanic peoples all had their own gods, as did the peoples of Asia Minor. The Egyptian goddess Isis was worshipped even in the Latin west. In the end most of these faiths died out, although they sometimes influenced the religions which superseded them, and their cult-practices occasionally survive today in other religions. But only the world religions provided the bonds that eventualy linked together areas of the world previously separate.

1/The diffusion of religions (below) It is scarcely surprising that the great world religions should be linked with the development of the great riverine civilizations of the Nile, Mesopotamia, the Indus and the rivers of China. However, although world religions might not have emerged without these settled civilizations, rivers were just one factor contributing to religious dissemination.

Expansion generally followed the trade routes. Religions were exported by traders, soldiers, administrators, and ordinary travellers, as well as by missionaries, all naturally using the same routes. Buddhism spread along the coast of Southeast Asia and also by the silk route through central Asia. The Roman and Chinese empires were points of attraction, and peaceable governments helped religious diffusion. Christian writers claim that the peace brought by Rome was providentially designed for the spread of Christianity.

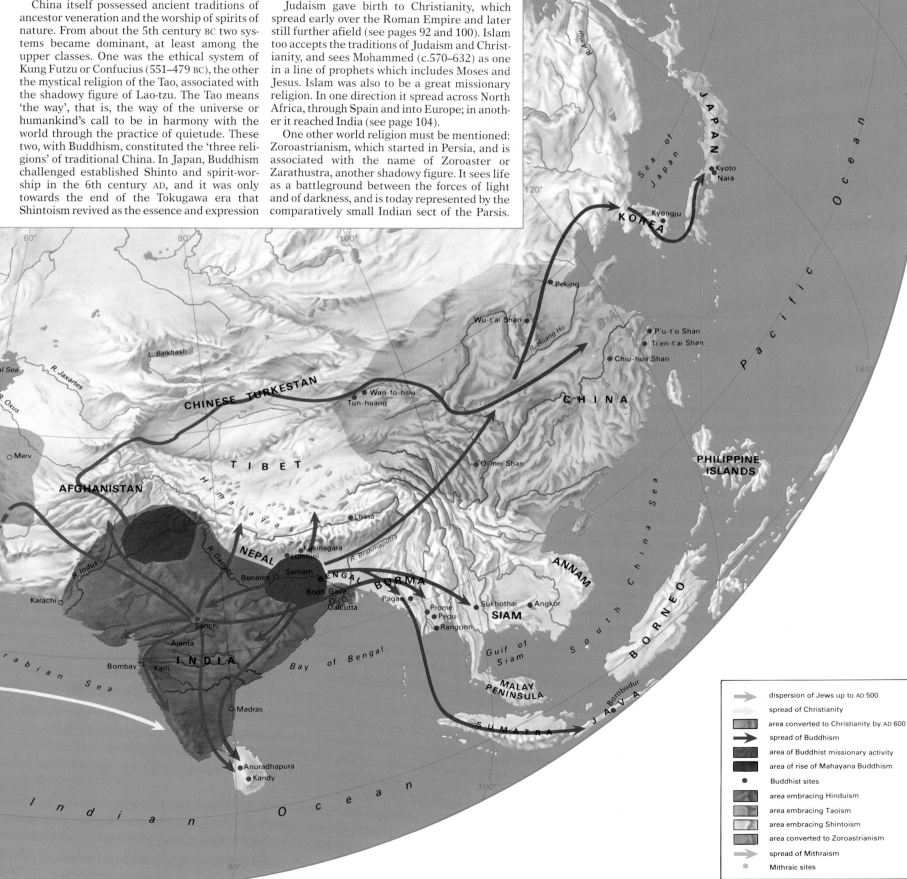

dispersion of Jews up to AD 500

spread of Christianity

area converted to Christianity by AD 600

spread of Buddhism

area of Buddhist missionary activity

area of rise of Mahayana Buddhism

Buddhist sites

area embracing Hinduism

area embracing Taoism

area embracing Shintoism

area converted to Zoroastrianism

spread of Mithraism

Mithraic sites

The spread of Greek civilization

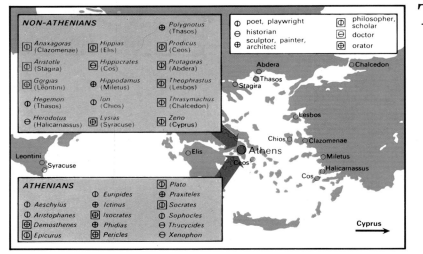

NON-ATHENIANS

⊞ *Anaxagoras* (Clazomenae)	⊟ *Hippias* (Elis)	⊕ *Polygnotus* (Thasos)
		⊟ *Prodicus* (Ceos)
⊡ *Aristotle* (Stagira)	⊞ *Hippocrates* (Cos)	⊟ *Protagoras* (Abdera)
⊟ *Gorgias* (Leontini)	⊟ *Hippodamus* (Miletus)	⊟ *Theophrastus* (Lesbos)
⊟ *Hegemon* (Thasos)	⊟ *Ion* (Chios)	⊟ *Thrasymachus* (Chalcedon)
⊡ *Herodotus* (Halicarnassus)	⊟ *Lysias* (Syracuse)	⊟ *Zeno* (Cyprus)

⊞ poet, playwright		⊟ philosopher, scholar
⊡ historian		⊟ doctor
⊕ sculptor, painter, architect		⊟ orator

ATHENIANS

	⊟ *Euripides*	⊟ *Plato*
⊟ *Aeschylus*	⊕ *Ictinus*	⊟ *Praxiteles*
⊞ *Aristophanes*	⊡ *Isocrates*	⊟ *Socrates*
⊞ *Demosthenes*	⊕ *Phidias*	⊟ *Sophocles*
⊟ *Epicurus*	⊕ *Pericles*	⊟ *Thucydides*
		⊟ *Xenophon*

Cyprus →

2/Athens as a cultural centre in the 5th and 4th centuries (*above*) From about 750 BC the Ionians in Asia Minor led the Greek world in culture; they were soon matched by the Greek colonies in Sicily and southern Italy. When they began to decline, Athens became, in the 5th century, the cultural centre of the Greek world.

THE key to Greek history is the *polis*, or city-state. The *polis* was a limited, independent, self-governing community which commanded the primary loyalty of its members. Its emergence was dictated by geography for Greece, like Asia Minor, is a mountainous country, but the coasts are studded with comparatively small plains, separated by mountain barriers which might be impassable in winter and difficult to traverse at any time. These plains helped to form natural political units, often very small: few would have numbered their people in five figures. (Aristotle argued that a *polis* of 100,000 citizens – that is, of 100,000 free, adult males – would cease to be a *polis*.) In the settlements of Asia Minor the cities protected themselves with walls, but in Greece proper it sufficed for a long time to withdraw to a fortified citadel (*acro-polis*) in an emergency. Around the main centre, farms, hamlets and villages stretched as far as the mountains. The *polis* was both a political and a religious community, and a temple to the principal deity stood at the heart of most Greek

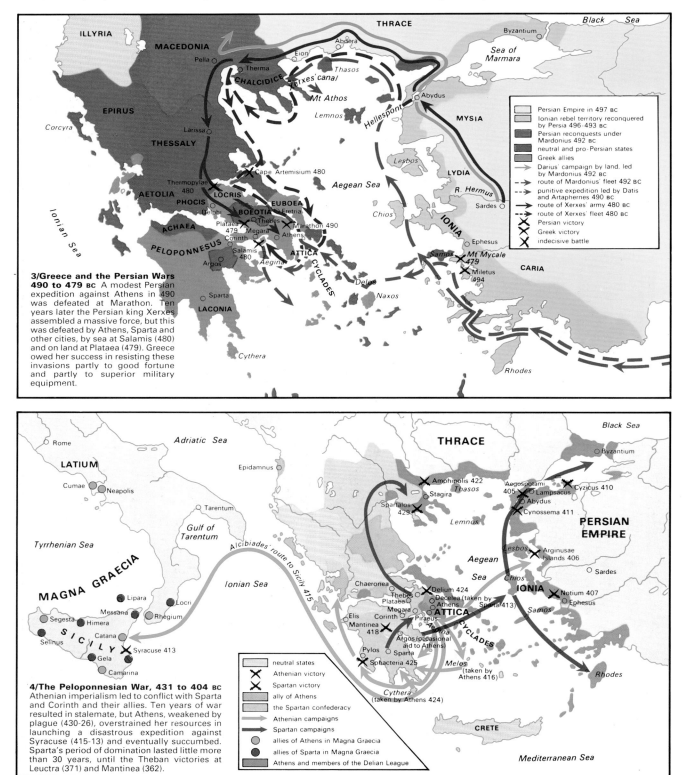

3/Greece and the Persian Wars 490 to 479 BC A modest Persian expedition against Athens in 490 was defeated at Marathon. Ten years later the Persian king Xerxes assembled a massive force, but this was defeated by Athens, Sparta and other cities, by sea at Salamis (480) and on land at Plataea (479). Greece owed her success in resisting these invasions partly to good fortune and partly to superior military equipment.

	Persian Empire in 497 BC
	Ionian rebel territory reconquered by Persia 496-493 BC
	Persian reconquests under Mardonius 492 BC
	neutral and pro-Persian states
	Greek allies
→	Darius' campaign by land, led by Mardonius 492 BC
- →	route of Mardonius' fleet 492 BC
- -	punitive expedition led by Datis and Artaphernes 490 BC
→	route of Xerxes' army 480 BC
- →	route of Xerxes' fleet 480 BC
✕	Persian victory
✕	Greek victory
✕	indecisive battle

4/The Peloponnesian War, 431 to 404 BC Athenian imperialism led to conflict with Sparta and Corinth and their allies. Ten years of war resulted in stalemate, but Athens, weakened by plague (430-26), overstrained her resources in launching a disastrous expedition against Syracuse (415-13) and eventually succumbed. Sparta's period of domination lasted little more than 30 years, until the Theban victories at Leuctra (371) and Mantinea (362).

	neutral states
✕	Athenian victory
✕	Spartan victory
	ally of Athens
	the Spartan confederacy
→	Athenian campaigns
→	Spartan campaigns
●	allies of Athens in Magna Graecia
●	allies of Sparta in Magna Graecia
	Athens and members of the Delian League

cities, symbolizing in its size and splendour the power and self-esteem of the *polis* and its citizens.

The *polis* was essentially a creation of the 8th century, a period which saw a new enlightenment in Greece. Economy and technology flourished, accompanied by major developments in art and culture – above all the alphabet, developed from the Phoenician alphabet in the early 8th century. (*Alpha*, *beta*, *gamma* are not by origin Greek words, but come from Semitic terms for ox, house and camel.) At the same time, the early Greek tradition of oral poetry had its climax in Homer's *Iliad* and *Odyssey*, and in Hesiod's *Works and Days*, the earliest Greek poems to be preserved in writing. This was also the age of the great vases decorated with systematic geometric patterns. Underlying all was the consciousness among the young city-states that they were united by a common blood, a common language, a common culture and a common religion. This found ritual and religious expression in the foundation of the Olympic Games (traditionally in 776 BC), open to all Greeks, and in the new attention paid to the oracle of the god Apollo at Delphi. Throughout

Greek history tension continued between the ideal of panhellenism, as represented at Delphi and Olympia, and the divisiveness of the *polis*.

The 8th century also saw the beginning of 200 years of colonial expansion, encouraged by land-hunger, political disaffection, or the desire for adventure or profit. These were not colonies in the modern sense: they were independent of the mother city, and although exploitation of natives took place it was on a much smaller scale than the land-grabbing of the 19th century. The main colonizing cities were few in number: Eretria and Chalcis in Euboea, Corinth and Megara on the central neck of Greece, Miletus in Asia Minor, the island of Rhodes. They founded settlements of lasting importance: Massilia (Marseilles), Neapolis (Naples, a colony of a colony, being founded from nearby Cumae), Syracuse, Byzantium (later Constantinople, and later still Istanbul).

The 7th and 6th centuries saw new cultural forces especially in the eastern Aegean, at the meeting-point of influences coming up the coast from Egypt and Syria, overland from Mesopotamia and even India. We find the develop-ment of legal structures; a new individualism, especially in poetry, of which Archilochus is the revolutionary forerunner and Sappho the supreme exponent; developments in vase-paint-ing, at first with oriental motifs in bands and then with black figures against a red back-ground; the beginning of stone sculpture; the emergence of coinage, first in Lydia, then in Aegina and Samos; and the first steps towards a scientific philosophy.

In general there was a well-marked pattern of political development. King was challenged by lord; the lords fell out among themselves and a discontented nobleman, perhaps with the back-ing of the populace at large, might establish himself as dictator or 'tyrant'. Good dictators were followed by bad dictators, and revolution by counter-revolution. The 5th century BC saw the Greek world oscillating between oligarchs who wished the power to be confined to a restricted group, and democrats who stood for a wider and more radical extension of power. But democracy was only extended oligarchy: women, aliens and slaves had no political rights, yet the achievements of Classical Greece were based on an economy powered largely by slaves imported in great numbers from Thrace, Asia Minor and the Black Sea region by an army of professional slave traders. Most slaves were non-Greek 'bar-barians', but Greek soldiers captured in war were also put to work as slaves in mines and quarries, often in atrocious conditions. The num-bers involved were substantial – the slaves employed in the notorious Athenian silver mines at Laurion were almost as numerous as the free citizens of Athens themselves.

By the 5th century the situation had polar-ized into a confrontation between Sparta and Athens. Sparta was a militarized state with an archaic constitution. It had retained its mon-archy, power lay with a senate of two kings and 28 elders, guided by five *ephors* or superinten-dents. Athens was a direct democracy, ruled by an assembly in which every male citizen had the right to speak and vote, in which most of the offices were filled by lot from the whole citizen body, and in which a magistrate at the end of his year of office might find himself arraigned before a people's court.

At the beginning of the 5th century these two states stood together to repel the forces of Persia; at the end they fought one another for the mastery of the Greek world in a bitter and bloody war which lasted 27 years (431–404 BC). The Peloponnesian War arose partly from the fear and envy of Spartans and others, generated by the growing power of Athens which had con-verted a free alliance of Greek maritime states into an Athenian empire. Its history was record-ed with incomparable power by Thucydides.

Yet the 5th century also saw, especially in Athens ('the school of Greece' as Pericles called her), an unparalleled flowering of culture: the tragic drama of Aeschylus, Sophocles and Euripides; the comedy of Aristophanes; the his-torians Herodotus and Thucydides; the person-ality of Socrates; the marvellous 'red-figure' vases; the Parthenon; and the sculptures of Phidias and others. In the end it is for these achievements that Greece is of lasting impor-tance. They have had profound and long-lasting impact on European civilization – yet Athens had a population of only 20,000-30,000 free male citizens.

The 4th century saw more jockeying for power, and Persia remained a powerful neigh-bour who did not hesitate to interfere in Greek affairs. Plato and Aristotle produced their great metaphysical constructs, and tried to put the world back to the age of the city-state. Isocrates called vainly for the Greeks to unite. Eventually the unity which they would not find for them-selves was forced upon them by the imperialistic power of Macedonia, their neighbour to the north. Philip of Macedon's crushing victory over the Greek city-states at the battle of Chaeronea (338 BC) was the end of Greek liberty but the beginning, in a sense, of a united Greece.

Bronze statue of Zeus, more than life-size, retrieved from a wreck off Artemisium. It is a superb example of early classical statuary (c.460), embodying the Greek ideals of harmo-ny, strength and moderation.

	extent of Greece in 750 BC
	coast under Greek influence (approximate)
	coast under Phoenician influence
●	Greek parent state or region
◻	Ionian colony
▲	Achaean colony
▼	Aeolian colony
●	Dorian colony founded by Corinth
○	Dorian colony founded by Thera and Rhodes
⊗	Dorian colony founded by Megara or Sparta
⊙	other Greek colonies
⊞	Etruscan city
◻	Punic or Phoenician city
■	Philistine city

1/Greek colonization in the Mediterranean world, 750 to 550 BC Early Greece was not fertile enough to sup-port a fast-growing population. The need for more land, sometimes combined with political oppression by the rul-ing class at home or the attractions of trade, led many Greek cities from c.750 BC onwards to send out colonists to seek new homes overseas. When established, the colonies became independent states. This epoch-making movement changed the whole face of the Mediterranean and spread Greek civilization far and wide. It reached its culmination in the eastward spread of Greek culture in Asia under Alexander the Great.

The Hellenistic world
336 to 30 BC

ALEXANDER the Great transformed the Greek world by opening up for it the resources of the Middle East. In 334 BC he crossed the Hellespont from Europe to Asia, swept through Asia Minor, past Syria to Egypt, then east and southeast down the Tigris and Euphrates, pressing on into the heartlands of Iran, through the Caspian Gates and the Hindu Kush to the neighbourhood of Bukhara and Tashkent. Here he retraced his steps, turned south into Kashmir and east again across the Indus as far as the Beas. He hoped to reach Ocean, the great mythical river which the Greeks believed to encircle the landmass of the world, but his troops would go no further. They turned back along the Indus to its mouth, and marched, with bitter sufferings, northwest to Persepolis and ultimately to Susa.

Alexander died in 323 BC, just before his 33rd birthday, and his mighty empire broke up among his warring generals. Three major powers gradually emerged: one, with its capital at Pella, was the old kingdom of Macedon, shorn of its Asiatic conquests but still dominating Greece proper and exercising substantial authority in Greek affairs, sometimes by diplomacy and sometimes by brute force. In wealthy Egypt, whose capital was now at Alexander's new foundation of Alexandria, an able soldier-historian named Ptolemy (Soter or Saviour) established a new dynasty and extended his interests into Palestine, where he confronted the third of the great kingdoms, the Seleucids.

Seleucus had commanded in Babylonia when Alexander died; from there he extended his power over Syria and established a new capital at Antioch-on-the-Orontes, whence successive sovereigns named Seleucus, Antiochus or Demetrius ruled. These Seleucid kings, like Alexander earlier, founded many Greek cities within their realm. To this triumvirate of kingdoms must be added the breakaway Pergamum, which between 264 and 133 BC maintained an independence which came to overshadow much of Asia Minor, and further east the remarkable kingdom of the Bactrian Greeks who broke away from Seleucid control.

The new developments led to a diffusion of wealth and a great expansion of trade with east Africa, Arabia, India, central Asia, and even, for the first time, with China. Meanwhile Pytheas of Marseilles sailed through the Straits of Gibraltar, circumnavigating Britain, laying the foundations for the Cornish tin trade, and probably reaching Norway and the river Elbe. Within the Mediterranean, silver flowed from Spain, copper from Cyprus, iron from the Black Sea coasts, corn from Egypt, North Africa and the Crimea, olive oil from Athens, dried fruit from Palestine, dried fish from Byzantium, linen, granite and papyrus from Egypt, woollen goods from Asia Minor, timber from Macedon, Asia Minor and the Lebanon, marble from Paros and Athens. Rhodes and Delos prospered as middlemen.

Alexander had flung back the horizons. The Greeks, with their new philosophies and religions, now found themselves members not only of a local community, the *polis*, but of *cosmopolis*, the whole civilized and increasingly Hellenized world. For a century, while Stoics and Epicureans alike proclaimed the brotherhood of man, and the more radical Cynics declared themselves citizens of the universe, the great post-Alexandrian powers maintained an often uneasy, but essentially stable equilibrium. Athens, seized by the Macedonians in the course of Chremonides' War (267 to 262 BC), remained an important cultural centre, but deliberately abdicated any further large-scale political ambitions. The main growth-points were now the newer capitals: Antioch, Pergamum, to some extent Pella, and above all Alexandria. Here the Museum, like the Library of Pergamum, formed

an international centre for higher learning and the arts. Here flourished the great 3rd century poets, Apollonius of Rhodes, Callimachus and Theocritus, and far-reaching advances in medicine, astronomy, mathematics, geography and science were made. It was the age of Eratosthenes and Archimedes.

Greece itself produced a variety of political experiments: different forms of confederation, particularly in the Achaean League; and the attempts by Agis IV and Cleomenes III in Sparta to establish an early form of communism before the regime was smashed by Macedon at Sellasia in 222 BC. To begin with, little of this disturbed the essential underlying balance, which lasted almost throughout the 3rd century. But with Rome's second war against Macedonia (200–197 BC) increasingly significant shifts began to develop, as rulers throughout the eastern Mediterranean were forced to adjust their policies to the rising might of Rome.

Roman imperialism was henceforth to be the crucial factor in the affairs of the Hellenistic kingdoms; but under the late Republic it grew only slowly. Direct annexation, except along the barbarian frontiers, was normally regarded as a policy of last resort, acceptable only when political aims could be achieved by no other means. Not until after 150 BC was there a single Roman governor or permanent army stationed east of the Adriatic. But other forms of intervention grew progressively more forceful.

Philip V of Macedon's provocative alliance with Hannibal in 215 had led to Roman military intervention in Greece which ended in 205 with

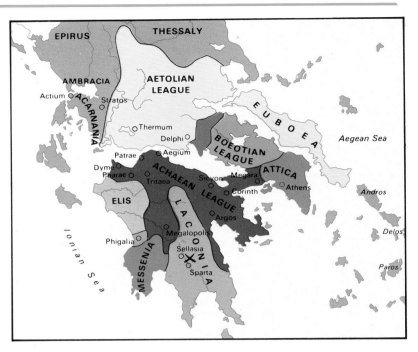

4/The Greek leagues *(above)* Weakness in the 3rd century led to federalism. The Aetolians expanded their influence by force, while an Achaean League expanded by admitting non-Achaean members. Both leagues were normally hostile to Macedon, but later Achaean hostility to Sparta led to reconciliation with Macedon whose king, Antigonus Doson, defeated Sparta at Sellasia (222 BC).

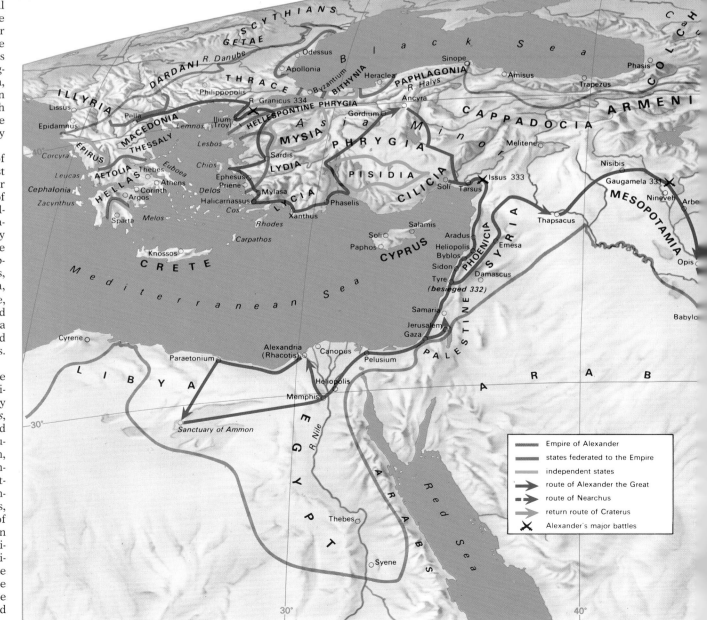

	Empire of Alexander
	states federated to the Empire
	independent states
	route of Alexander the Great
	route of Nearchus
	return route of Craterus
	Alexander's major battles

the Peace of Phoenice, a treaty of mutual co-existence. But Philip's continued expansion, both into Greece, in the Aegean and along the Adriatic, brought retaliatory action, and a heavy defeat by the army of Flamininus at the Battle of Cynoscephalae (197). In 190 BC, the greatest of the Seleucid monarchs, Antiochus III, after invading Greece was similarly humbled at the Battle of Magnesia, and stripped of his possessions in Asia Minor at the Peace of Apemea (188).

From then on, Rome had no serious rival in the Aegean and the Middle East. She could, and did, enhance the power of states like Pergamum and Rhodes and then, just as easily, break them. Even so, it took more than 150 years before the Hellenistic world fell fully under Roman control. Renewed Macedonian aggression, under Philip V's son Perseus, was decisively halted at Pydna (168) and the country divided into four independent territories; it only became a Roman province in 146, after further uprisings. The Seleucid Empire, weakened by internal conflicts and Parthian wars, was finally terminated by Pompey in 64 BC. Pergamum, unexpectedly bequeathed to Rome at the death of Attalus III (133), was only reluctantly accepted by the Senate; and Egypt, bestowed in an even more opulent gesture by Ptolemy Alexander I in 88 BC, was rejected outright. It was only after the defeat of Cleopatra VII, the last of the Ptolemies, at the naval battle of Actium in 31 BC, that Rome legally as well as effectively held the whole of Alexander's heritage. Long before that the framework of Greek civilization had been broken; but its spiritual and intellectual legacy now permeated every aspect of Roman life.

1/The Empire of Alexander (below) The Macedonian conquests stretched to the limits of the known world and beyond, taking Hellenistic civilization decisively beyond the Mediterranean and turning European minds and energies for the first time to the east; they probably also made it more vulnerable to the Roman drive from the west.

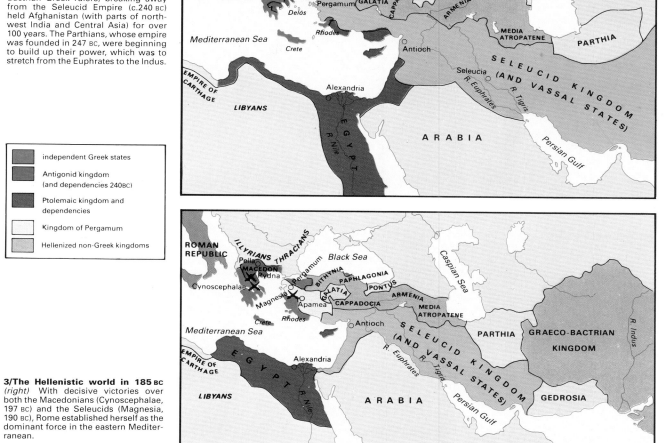

2/The Hellenistic world in 240 BC (right) After two generations of war, the Ptolemies, the Seleucids and the Antigonid kings of Macedon had achieved a sustainable political and military balance. Athens had faded as a political force, but Pergamum, Rhodes, Delos, and Pontus on the Black Sea were all independent rising powers, thanks not least to their commerce. Bactrian Greek rulers, breaking away from the Seleucid Empire (c.240 BC) held Afghanistan (with parts of north-west India and Central Asia) for over 100 years. The Parthians, whose empire was founded in 247 BC, were beginning to build up their power, which was to stretch from the Euphrates to the Indus.

legend:
- independent Greek states
- Antigonid kingdom (and dependencies 240BC)
- Ptolemaic kingdom and dependencies
- Kingdom of Pergamum
- Hellenized non-Greek kingdoms

3/The Hellenistic world in 185 BC (right) With decisive victories over both the Macedonians (Cynoscephalae, 197 BC) and the Seleucids (Magnesia, 190 BC), Rome established herself as the dominant force in the eastern Mediterranean.

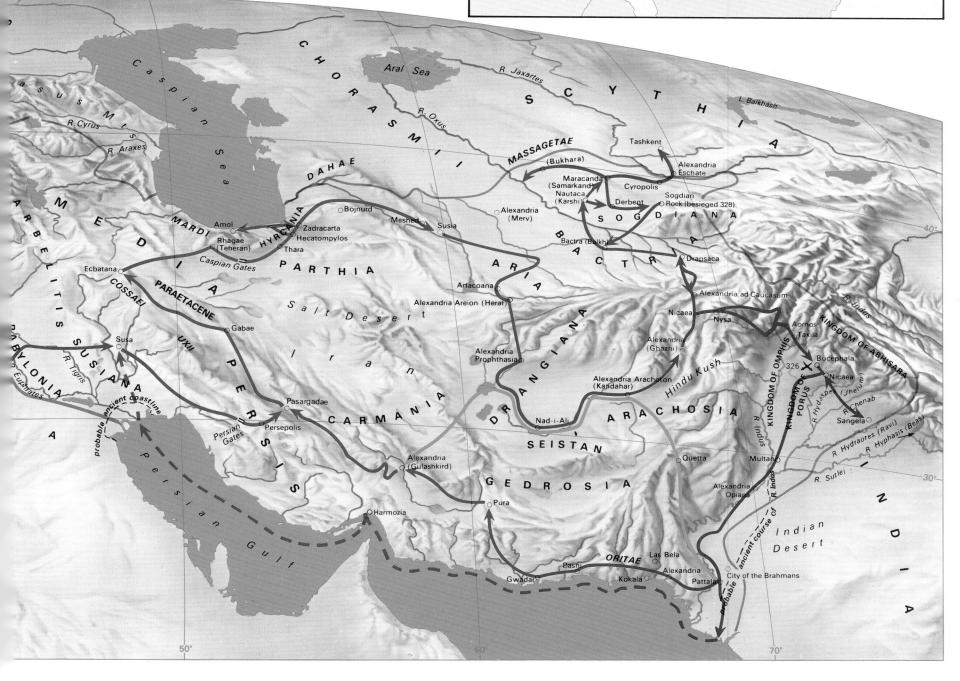

The empires of Persia 550 BC to AD 637

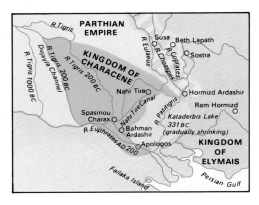

2/The Persian Gulf (above) With the decline of the Seleucids in the 2nd century BC, the kingdoms of Characene and Elymais arose by the Persian Gulf. Here coastlines and river courses underwent continual change. Lake Kataderbis disappeared after 300 BC, and Charax near the Tigris east bank was afterwards the main port.

AFTER the destruction of Assyria and the sack of its capital, Nineveh in 612 BC, Babylon, one of the victors, retained the Mesopotamian lowlands, while the mountain country west of the river Halys (modern Kizil Irmak) was incorporated in the kingdom of its allies the Medes. In 550 BC Cyrus, then Prince of Persia, rebelled, defeated the Median king, Astyages, and welded the Medes and the Persians together to make Iran the dominant power in Asia and the Near East. Its empire, enlarged by successful military campaigns, soon incorporated Lycia, Lydia, the Ionian-Greek settlements of Asia Minor, Babylon and Afghanistan.

The Iranian peoples, newly arrived from central Asia, thus came to dominate the power centres of the Mesopotamian world. Their Iron-Age technology, their ability to exploit the horse for communication and warfare, and above all their vigour and versatility, almost always gave them an edge over the forces of the more ritualized ancient civilizations. Soon after Cyrus's death, while one of his sons, Smerdis, held Iran, the other, Cambyses, defeated the last Egyptian pharaoh, Psamtik III, at Pelusium (525 BC). Later the brothers quarrelled, with fatal results, and a usurper seized the throne. But a cousin of theirs, Darius, led a group of confederates to restore the Achaemenid family line, reorganizing the empire into 20 tribute-paying satrapies and established unified control, with a comprehensive code of laws, a stable currency and an efficient postal service. As organizer and financier, Darius swiftly proved himself as great a genius as his uncle Cyrus had been in military affairs. His administration laid stress on regular, equitable taxes, accurate weights and measures and cautious monetary policies. The Iranians' essentially ethnic religion, Zoroastrianism, sought no converts. Tolerance, whether for Judaism or for the various Greek, Babylonian and Egyptian forms of polytheism, encouraged both communal harmony and loyalty to the king. Martial traditions, artistic sensibility and technical awareness, especially in engineering, all contributed to Iranian success, while an unshakeable national consciousness and an unusual respect for monarchic legitimacy helped the culture to survive repeated invasions.

This strength was soon put to the test. Darius's military enterprises were less uniformly successful than his administrative reforms: he was repulsed by the Scythians of the Ukraine in 513 BC; and his attempts to punish Athens and Eretria for their support of the rebellious Ionians led to a brusque defeat at Marathon in 490 BC. A massive invasion of Greece by his son Xerxes was similarly repulsed, both by sea at Salamis (480 BC) and by land at Plataea the following year.

Persia itself remained impregnable to the Greeks for almost another century. Its weaknesses became apparent when Cyrus the Young-er, the Iranian viceroy in the west, recruited a force of Greek mercenaries, the Ten Thousand, to revolt against his brother the Emperor Artaxerxes II, in 401 BC. The knowledge gained by the Greeks in attacking Babylonia paved the way for the later, devastating onslaughts of Alexander of Macedon, whose defeat of the Persian army at Gaugamela (331 BC) brought the Achaemenid rule to its end.

After the break-up of Alexander's own empire (see page 76) Iran became part of the Seleucid kingdom, remaining so, apart from the appearance of a local dynasty in the region of Persis, until 247 BC. In that year Ptolemy III of Egypt invaded Syria and claimed sovereignty as far east as Bactria. The nomad Parthians on the northern borders took advantage of the resulting upheaval to tear the whole territory of Parthia and Hyrcania away from Seleucid allegiance. Further east, Diodotus, satrap of Bactria, also declared independence, and founded the Graeco-Bactrian kingdom. Valiant efforts in 208 BC by the restored Seleucids, notably Antiochus III the Great, to suppress the Parthians and Graeco-Bactrians achieved little lasting effect, and finally, in 141 BC, Mithridates I of Parthia reversed the situation and entered Seleucia.

Ten years later, however, the situation on Iran's eastern frontiers drastically changed. The Yüeh-chi nomads, or Tocharians, driven back by Huns, clashed with the Scythians beyond the river Jaxartes. The latter then destroyed the Graeco-Bactrian kingdom on their way southward to the Punjab. The Tocharians followed more slowly, by way of northern Afghanistan, sweeping away remaining Hellenic outposts. The brief period of Indo-Parthian dominance in Taxila, the great trading city of north India, itself ended in AD 60 with the rise of the Tocharians' Kushan Empire.

In the west, the Parthian border peoples soon reached the Roman frontier on the Euphrates. Invasions by the elsewhere almost invincible legions failed, and Parthia became the only major state consistently to withstand Roman power. In 53 BC the army of Crassus was destroyed at Carrhae by the relatively modest cavalry forces of a Parthian regional commander. Mark Antony, in 36 BC, led a formidable army from Armenia to Azerbaijan (Atropatene) but quickly encountered difficulties and could barely extricate the survivors of his force. Augustus, seeking better relations, effectively accepted the Euphrates boundary line, and later emperors in the main limited their intervention to dynastic intrigues. It was only in AD 114 that Trajan, exploiting a moment of Parthian weakness, formally annexed Armenia as a Roman province, before advancing down the Euphrates and Tigris to take Seleucia and reach the Persian Gulf. In AD 165, the general Avidius Cassius again sacked Seleucia and also Ctesiphon before being forced to retreat by an attack of smallpox. This feat was repeated by Septimius Severus in AD 198, but such incursions had little lasting effect. The real threat was internal, and came to a head in about 224 when Ardashir Papakan, Prince of Persia and founder of the Sasanian dynasty, defeated his Parthian overlord, Artabanus (Ardavan) V, at Hormizdagan, north of Isfahan.

The new king replaced Parthian feudalism with a highly centralized administration and reorganized the vassal kingdoms (Characene, Elymais, etc.) as provinces, each governed by a Sasanian prince. He crushed the Kushan state to the east and his son, Shapur, pushed the Asiatic frontiers back to Tashkent and Peshawar. Immediately on his accession in 244, Shapur repelled an invasion by the Roman Emperor Gordian III near Meshik on the Euphrates, grandiloquently renaming the place Peroz Shapur. In 253 he smashed a second Roman army at Barbalissus, higher up the Euphrates,

and finally, in 259, defeated and captured the Roman emperor Valerian at Edessa. Annexing Oman on the Arabian shores of the Gulf, he firmly established Sasanian Iran as the strongest power of late antiquity, with an elaborate and efficient bureaucracy, a powerful state religion, Zoroastrianism, and a strong tradition of craftsmanship, especially in the weaving of silk, now widely imported from China.

The peak of Sasanian power and prosperity was reached under Khosrau I Anohshirvan (531–79) when he invaded Syria, captured Antioch and deported its famous metal workers to his own lands. But his son, Khosrau II Panriz (590–628), over-reached himself. Invading the Byzantine Empire, capturing Jerusalem, overrunning Anatolia and Egypt, and camping on the Bosporus facing Constantinople, he was forced to retreat when the Byzantine emperor Heraclius outflanked him and sacked his favourite residence at Dastagerd.

Peace came too late for the two empires, for both quickly fell victim to the newly emergent forces of Islam (see pages 104 and 112). The Arabs scored significant victories at Dhu Qar (c. 611), in the 'Battle of the Chains' and at Ullais, near the Euphrates (633), but the decisive action occurred at Al Qadisiya (637), when they smashed the Persians' metropolitan army and captured the capital, Ctesiphon. Yezdagird III, the last Sasanian king, fled to the Zagros, but further Arab victories at Jalula (637) and Nehavend (642) opened the road to the main Iranian plateau. Within a few years the Muslim armies reached the Oxus, and Iran became part of the Islamic world empire.

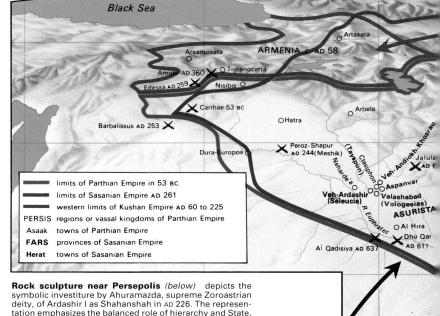

	limits of Parthian Empire in 53 BC
	limits of Sasanian Empire AD 261
	western limits of Kushan Empire AD 60 to 225
PERSIS	regions or vassal kingdoms of Parthian Empire
Asaak	towns of Parthian Empire
FARS	provinces of Sasanian Empire
Herat	towns of Sasanian Empire

Rock sculpture near Persepolis (below) depicts the symbolic investiture by Ahuramazda, supreme Zoroastrian deity, of Ardashir I as Shahanshah in AD 226. The representation emphasizes the balanced role of hierarchy and State, and the importance of the horse for Persian society.

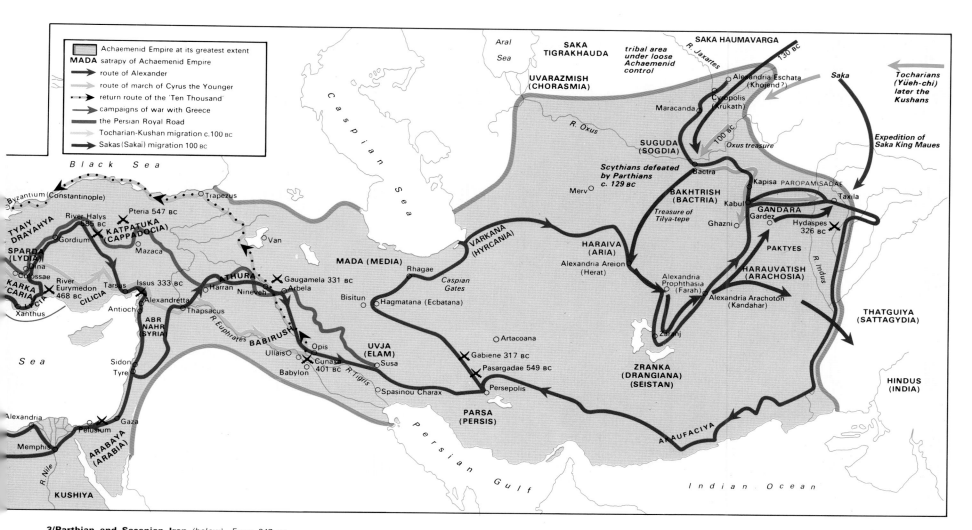

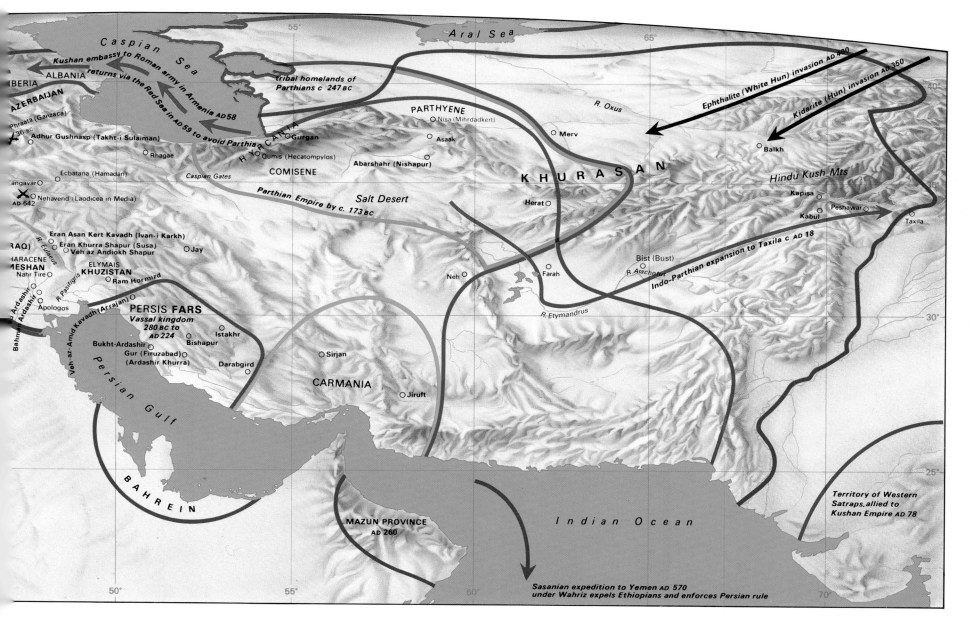

3/Parthian and Sasanian Iran (below) From 247 BC when the nomad Parthians rose, under their chieftain, Arsaces, and seized the Seleucid town of Nisa (Mihrdadkert) until AD 635, when the Arabs clinched their final victory. Iran, though often under attack, remained one of the richest and most powerful regions of the ancient world. The Parthians embraced the whole area from the Euphrates to northern India, but gave way in AD 224 to the Sasanians, a Persian dynasty which only succumbed to the forces of Islam after fighting almost to the death with Byzantium.

1/The Achaemenid Empire (above) The Medes and the Persians were Indo-European peoples from central Asia. The centre of the Medes was founded at Ecbatana, and after the sack of Nineveh in 612 they became the chief power in the East. Their cousins the Persians moved southwards to Fars province (originally Parsa), and won the leadership under Cyrus the Great (550) who extended the rule of his line from the Aegean to the Indus. Under his successors the Empire flourished mightily until 330 BC, when Alexander the Great burnt its capital, Persepolis, to the ground.

The unification of China 350 BC to AD 220

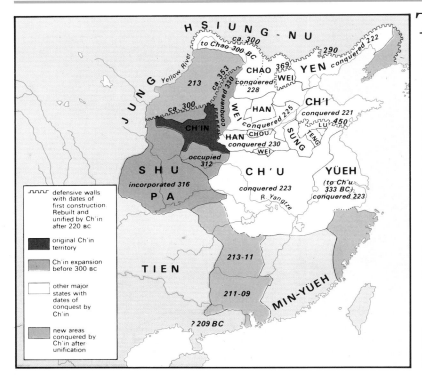

1/The Warring States and the unification of China (left) Ch'in became a serious contender for supremacy over the other major states after her expansion and consolidation in the northwest and west from 328 to 308 BC. Later the other states were eliminated until in 221 BC Ch'in controlled all China. Under Shih Huang-ti the Ch'in expanded its territories to the far south and northeast.

THROUGHOUT the Warring States period (403–221 BC) seven major states contended for supremacy. At first the main rivals were the old-established kingdoms of Ch'i, Ch'u, Han and Wei. Later (328–308 BC) the northwest border state of Ch'in established firm control over the northwest and west, and during the latter half of the 3rd century gradually destroyed its rivals to become master of all China in 221 BC. This was a period of constant warfare, waged on a massive scale by powerful and well-organized kingdoms which began to replace the old feudal social order with a centralized administration staffed by bureaucrats rather than hereditary nobles. They developed effective legal and fiscal systems to provide for their armies and public works.

Their emergence coincided with major economic and social changes. The introduction of iron tools from about 500 BC and the use of animal power for cultivation greatly increased agri-

cultural productivity. The large-scale new states could undertake massive drainage and irrigation projects to bring much new land into cultivation. In these new lands a new social order arose, breaking away from the tight village community of the past. Population multiplied. Commerce and industry flourished as the states built roads and large cities emerged. It was a period of innovation in technology, science and government, and of philosophical ferment, in which the main streams of Chinese thought, Confucianism, Taoism and Legalism, took shape.

In the victorious state of Ch'in the old feudal aristocracy was abolished, and replaced by a rigid centralized bureaucracy. The population was organized in groups of families bearing mutual responsibility, and regimented to provide manpower for construction works and for the army. The new system was enforced through a savage penal code. When the first Ch'in emperor, Shih Huang-ti, unified China, these institutions were extended throughout the country. Although he ruthlessly eliminated all hostile factions, the burdens imposed on the people by his campaigns and vast construction works combined with surviving regional tensions to bring about the collapse of his empire in 206 BC, shortly after his death.

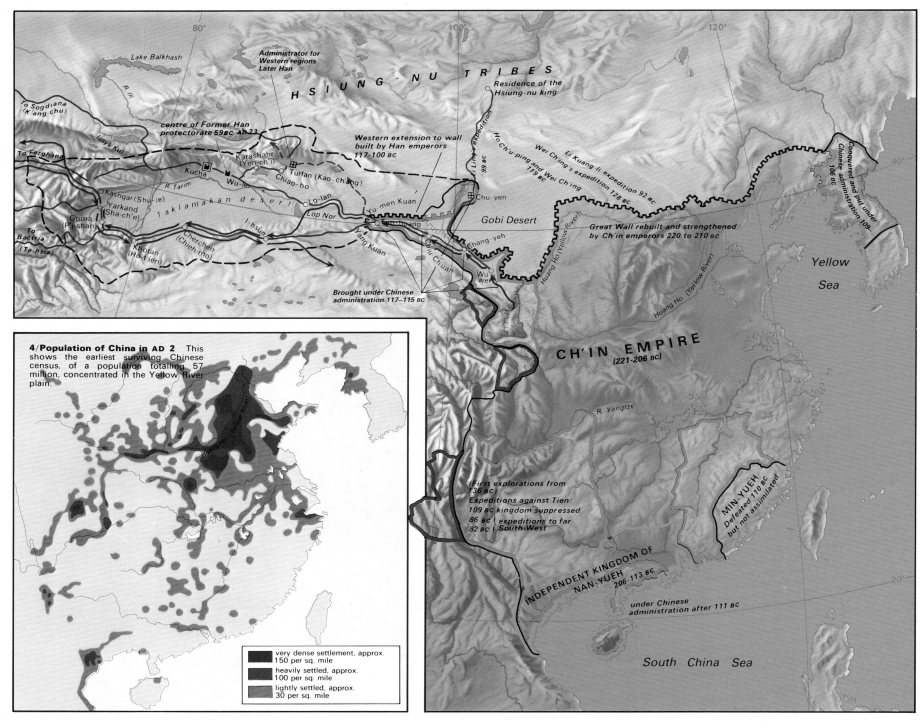

4/Population of China in AD 2 This shows the earliest surviving Chinese census, of a population totalling 57 million, concentrated in the Yellow River plain.

very dense settlement, approx. 150 per sq. mile

heavily settled, approx. 100 per sq. mile

lightly settled, approx. 30 per sq. mile

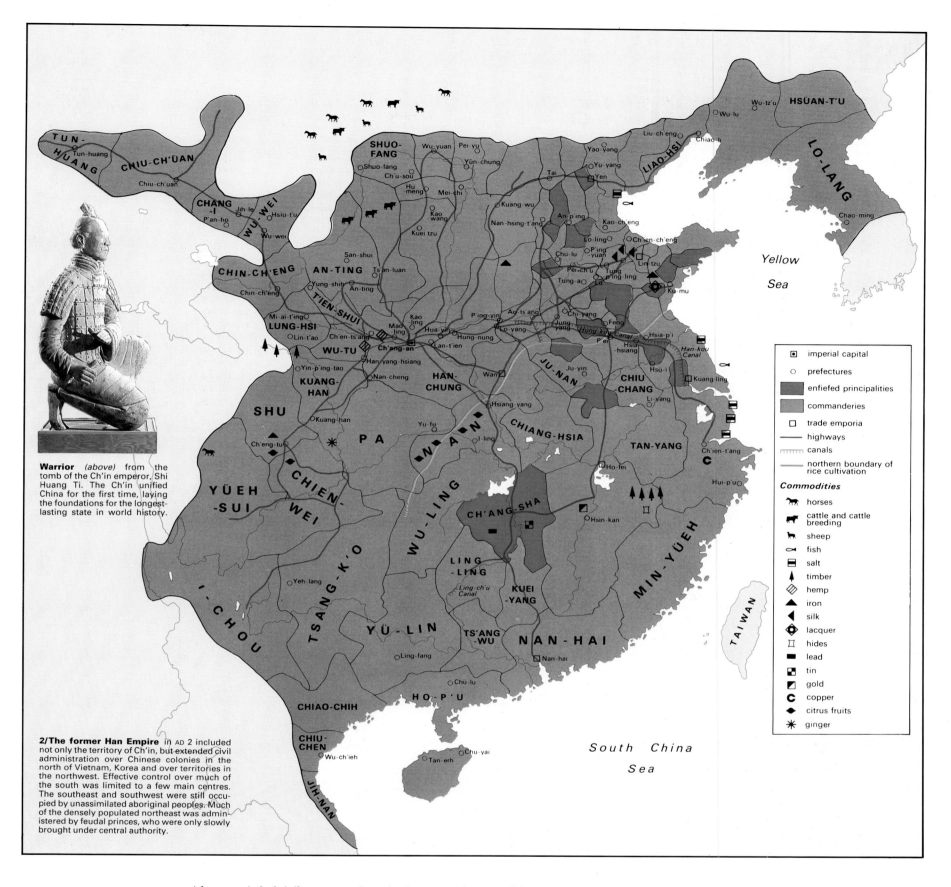

Yellow
Sea

South China
Sea

imperial capital
○ prefectures
■ enfiefed principalities
□ commanderies
□ trade emporia
— highways
≈ canals
— northern boundary of rice cultivation

Commodities
🐎 horses
🐂 cattle and cattle breeding
🐑 sheep
🐟 fish
▲ salt
▲ timber
⬙ hemp
▲ iron
◀ silk
◈ lacquer
□ hides
■ lead
▣ tin
▨ gold
C copper
◆ citrus fruits
✳ ginger

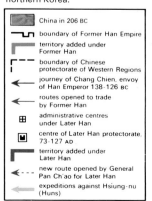

Warrior *(above)* from the tomb of the Ch'in emperor, Shi Huang Ti. The Ch'in unified China for the first time, laying the foundations for the longest-lasting state in world history.

2/The former Han Empire in AD 2 included not only the territory of Ch'in, but extended civil administration over Chinese colonies in the north of Vietnam, Korea and over territories in the northwest. Effective control over much of the south was limited to a few main centres. The southeast and southwest were still occupied by unassimilated aboriginal peoples. Much of the densely populated northeast was administered by feudal princes, who were only slowly brought under central authority.

3/The expansion of Han China
(left) Han expansion began under Wu-ti (140-87 BC), who took the offensive against the Hsiung-nu, and extended the Great Wall far to the northwest to protect the route into central Asia. For a few decades after 59 BC the Chinese controlled the Tarim basin. Missions visited Parthia and Bactria, and extensive trade with the West began. Chinese power was again briefly extended to the west after AD 94. The Han also eliminated the coastal Yüeh kingdoms, occupied north Vietnam and northern Korea.

China in 206 BC
boundary of Former Han Empire
territory added under Former Han
boundary of Chinese protectorate of Western Regions
journey of Chang Chien, envoy of Han Emperor 138-126 BC
routes opened to trade by Former Han
administrative centres under Former Han
centre of Later Han protectorate 73-127 AD
territory added under Later Han
new route opened by General Pan Ch'ao for Later Han
expeditions against Hsiung-nu (Huns)

After a period of civil war a new dynasty, the Han, gained control of all China. Founded by a man of humble origins, the Han were forced to re-introduce a system of feudal principalities allocated to their family and supporters, and these fiefs were not brought under strong central control until about 100 BC. Copying the general outlines of Ch'in government, but softening its harshness, the Han gradually evolved an effective central government and system of local administration.

The Ch'in had taken strong defensive measures against the nomad Hsiung-nu in the north, and had expanded southwards into areas occupied by non-Chinese aboriginal peoples. The Han were at first preoccupied with internal affairs, but under Wu-ti (140-87 BC) China again took the offensive against the Hsiung-nu, rebuilt the Ch'in wall and extended it far to the northwest. They opened up the route to central Asia and after 59 BC briefly exercised control over the oasis states of the Tarim basin. A large export trade, mainly in silk, began to Parthia and to the Roman Empire. The Han also reaffirmed the Ch'in conquests in the Canton region, eliminated the Yüeh kingdoms of the southeast coast at the end of the 2nd century, and occupied north-

ern Vietnam. Chinese armies also drove deep into the southwest, establishing Han control over its native states but apart from a few main centres most of southern China remained in the hands of aboriginal peoples for centuries to come. Wu-ti's armies also occupied and placed under Chinese administration parts of southern Manchuria and northern Korea.

The Han Empire grew extremely prosperous. The rapid growth of the preceding centuries continued and during this period of stability and prosperity China's population reached some 57 million. Many large cities grew up and the largest, the capital, Ch'ang-an, housed a quarter of a million people, and was the centre of a brilliant culture. At the beginning of the Christian era the Han Empire rivalled that of Rome in size and wealth.

Even the riches of the Han Empire, however, were severely taxed by Han Wu-ti's military adventures, and under a series of weak emperors during the latter half of the 1st century BC the authority of the throne was rivalled by the great court families. In AD 9 Wang Mang, an imperial relative by marriage, usurped the throne and set up a brief dynasty (Hsin, AD 9-23) which embarked upon a drastic programme of

reforms. His reign ended in widespread rebellion, and was followed by a restoration of the Han (Later Han, AD 25-220). Since Ch'ang-an had been sacked during the fighting, the capital was moved to Lo-yang and during the Later Han period the northeast of China steadily grew in importance relative to the northwest.

After some decades of consolidation, in the late 1st century the Chinese again began active hostilities against the Hsiung-nu, and in AD 94 again invaded the Tarim basin. But this revival proved short-lived. Trouble with the Chiang tribes of the northwest, the succession of several child-emperors and virulent factionalism at court had seriously weakened the Han state by about AD 160. A wave of agrarian distress culminated in the massive religious uprising of the Yellow Turbans which engulfed China from 184. Some degree of order was eventually restored by various regional warlords and, although the Han survived in name until 220, power in fact lay with these regional commanders. In 220 the last Han emperor abdicated in favour of one of them, and the empire was divided into three independent regional states. China was to remain politically fragmented until 589.

India:
the first empires

By about 600 BC northern India had at least 16 well-articulated political units, some still essentially tribal republics, others already absolute monarchies, established in the rich Gangetic plain. In one of the smaller republics, Kapilavastu, Gautama Buddha, founder of Asia's most pervasive religion, was born c.566 or 466 BC, while on the Ganges itself Mahavira, his near-contemporary, was formulating the teachings of Jainism, the faith still followed by many of India's merchant community.

During the 5th century BC the number of Mahajanapadas, or great realms, gradually diminished to four, and ultimately, after a century of wars, these were all absorbed into the single kingdom of Magadha, with its splendid new capital of Pataliputra (Patna), strategically commanding the Ganges trade route. This was to be the nucleus of the first Indian Empire. When Alexander of Macedon, having conquered Achaemenid Persia, was marching to the Indus in 327 BC, a young adventurer, Chandragupta Maurya, is said to have met him. Shortly after Alexander's invasion of India, Chandragupta seized the Magadhan throne. Then, exploiting

the power vacuum left behind in the northwest after Alexander's departure, Chandragupta annexed all the land east of the Indus, swung south to occupy large parts of central India north of the Narmada river, and in 305 BC decisively defeated Alexander's successor, Seleucus Nicator, who ceded the Greek province of Trans-Indus including a large part of Afghanistan.

The Mauryan Empire, extended by Chandragupta's son Bindusara, reached its zenith under his grandson, the Emperor Asoka, who with the conquest of Kalinga on the Bay of Bengal established his rule over the bulk of the sub-continent. Asoka's India was by this time a land of settled village agriculture, with an elaborate administrative and tax-collecting system, probably described in one of the world's earliest manuals of statecraft, the *Aithasastra*, attributed to Kautilya, Chandragupta's chief minister. Trade flourished and a special group of officials appears to have been made responsible for the building and maintenance of roads, including the Royal Highway (known to modern India as the Grand Trunk Road) from Pataliputra to the northwest. Probably neither Chandragupta nor

his successors practised orthodox Hinduism, although this had now clearly established itself as the predominant religion of the Ganges plain, with the sacerdotal Brahmans the most powerful caste. After the bloody subjection of Kalinga in 260 BC, however, Asoka accepted conversion to Buddhism and abandoned the policy of conquest, *Digvijaya*, in favour of *Dhamavijaya*, the Victory of Righteousness. His ethical teachings are found inscribed on pillars and rockfaces all over India, and his emissaries visited the Hellenistic kingdoms, as well as Ceylon and the far south, to preach the new gospel of peace.

Mauryan rule, however, did not long survive Asoka's death in 232 BC. In the 2nd century BC, the north and northwest were extensively invaded, both by Greeks from Bactria and Parthia, and by new nomad groups on the move from central Asia. In particular the Kushan section of the

Lion capital *(above)* Asoka built the first of these at Sarnath where the Buddha preached. The capital in its original form had a wheel of fortune atop the lions, symbolizing the ascendancy of virtue over worldly pomp and power.

1/The ancient empires *(below)* The warring early kingdoms first gave way to a unified kingdom under Chandragupta Maurya, a contemporary of Alexander. The domain of the Sythian Kushans stretched from Khotan to Benares, but included nothing south of the Vindhyas. In the 4th century AD the Guptas and in the 7th century Sri Harsha established the best-known of the later empires of northern India.

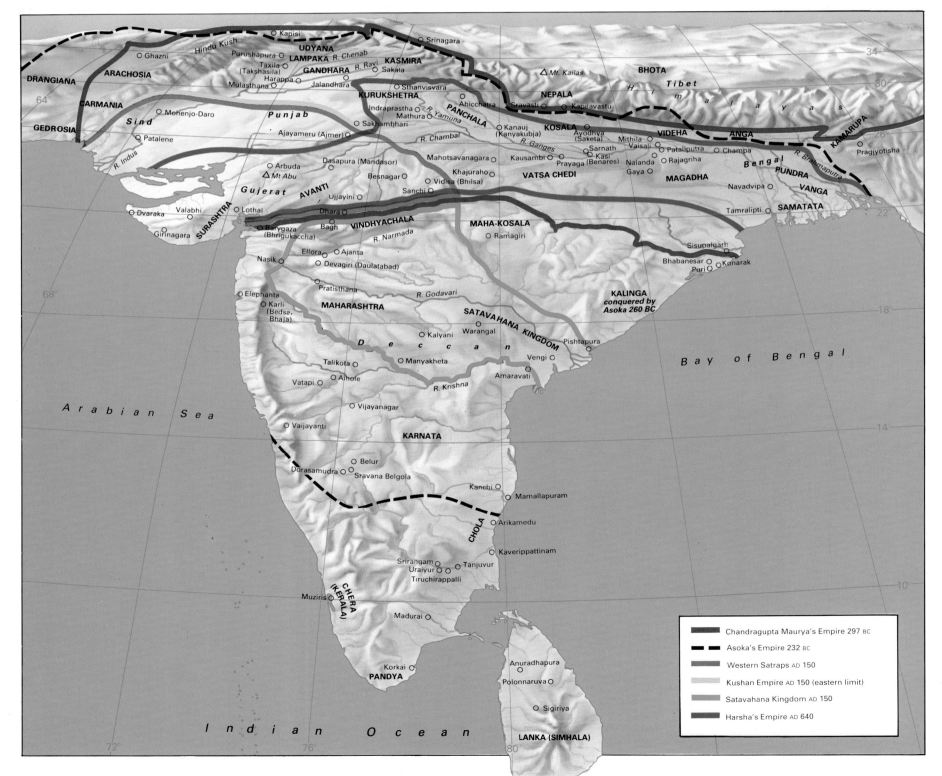

▬▬▬	Chandragupta Maurya's Empire 297 BC
▬ ▬ ▬	Asoka's Empire 232 BC
▬▬▬	Western Satraps AD 150
▬▬▬	Kushan Empire AD 150 (eastern limit)
▬▬▬	Satavahana Kingdom AD 150
▬▬▬	Harsha's Empire AD 640

2/The Mahajanapadas (above) Each of the 16 great realms of early India produced its quota of cities. Others, such as Taxila and the port of Barygaza, were of great trading importance. By the 5th century they were reduced to four major rivals: the three kingdoms of Kasi, Kosala and Magadha, and the republic of the Vrijji, covering parts of modern Nepal and Bihar.

slaves, from Ethiopia, Arabia and the Mediterranean. Indian merchants, seeking spices for the Roman market, opened up agencies throughout Southeast Asia, while much of the Chinese silk traffic (especially during the Roman wars with Parthia) found its way south to the trading city Taxila in Pakistan, before the caravans took it farther west.

By the middle of the 2nd century AD the for-

attempts to force the Deccan were blocked by a powerful southern dynasty, the Chalukyas. For many years Hsüan Tsang, the most famous Chinese traveller to India, lived at Sri Harsha's court, leaving a vivid account of Indian life and politics, and at his death Chinese troops intervened to place a suitable successor on his throne. Very soon, however, India once more relapsed into a tangle of warring states.

3/Alexander's invasion and the Mauryan empire (below) Soon after Alexander's invasion Chandragupta Maurya usurped the Magadha throne. His grandson, Asoka, controlled most of India: his edicts and Buddhist inscriptions are widespread.

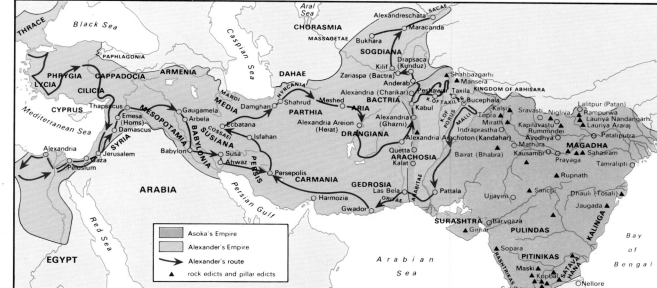

Asoka's Empire
Alexander's Empire
→ Alexander's route
▲ rock edicts and pillar edicts

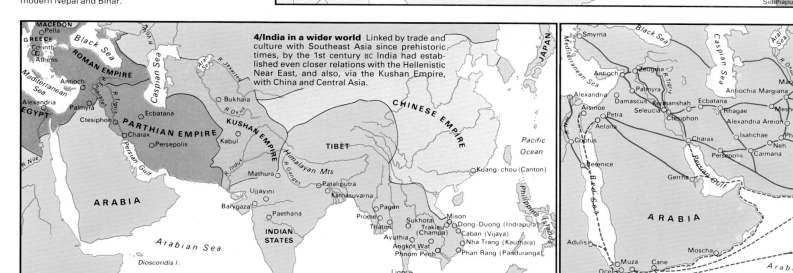

4/India in a wider world Linked by trade and culture with Southeast Asia since prehistoric times, by the 1st century BC India had established even closer relations with the Hellenistic Near East, and also, via the Kushan Empire, with China and Central Asia.

—— trade routes

Yüeh-chih horde (see page 78) who had settled in the Oxus valley after 165 BC, gradually extended their rule inland, reaching Benares in the 1st century AD. Large parts of Afghanistan and Khotan were included in their cosmopolitan empire, which became a melting-pot of cultures – Indian, Chinese, central Asian and Helleno-Roman. Meanwhile, various marauding bands of Greek and Egyptian origin established a number of kingdoms and dynasties in western and central India. Kushan emperors and Greek feudatories adopted Sanskrit names and followed Indian religions; Indian and Hellenistic influences mingled in Gandhara sculpture. Mahayana Buddhism, separating itself at this time from the fundamentalist teachings of the original Theravada, developed a more eclectic outlook, much influenced by non-Indian faith, with a pantheon of deities drawn from many lands. These are now the two great divisions of Buddhism, with Theravada still dominant in Ceylon, Burma and Southeast Asia, and Mahayana the leading sect in India, Tibet, China and Japan.

India's ancient trading links with the Middle East and Egypt were revitalized and greatly extended as the Hellenistic kingdoms gave way before the rising power of Rome. By the 1st century AD, Pliny was complaining that imports from India were costing the Romans 550 million sesterces a year in gold. Ports like Barbaricum, on the Indus delta, and the great *entrepôt* centre of Barygaza (Broach) shipped out turquoise, diamonds, spikenard, indigo, silk yarn and tortoise-shell, receiving in return an immensely varied flow of wine, pearls, copper, dates, gold and

eign kingdoms of the north were in decay, and new, indigenous groupings had begun to emerge. The Tamil-speaking peoples south of Madras had briefly occupied Ceylon and built important harbours on both sides of the southern tip of India, while the Satavahanas of the Deccan had become a formidable force, straddling the peninsula and driving significantly into the northern plain. Then in the 4th century, the native dynasty of the Guptas, based again on Magadha, imposed a new rule which extended, at its furthest stretch, from Sind and the Punjab to Bengal. Their suzerainty was acknowledged in regions even further to the east and the south. This was in many ways the classical age of north Indian civilization, and it survived well beyond the political collapse of the empire, brought about by fresh invasions of Hunnish, or *huna*, nomads in the 5th century.

During this period the Puranas, recording the Hindu version of the Creation and early history of mankind, were composed in their final form, while Vedanta also began its decisive emergence as the dominant system of Hindu thought. But Buddhism, now carried far and wide by Indian merchants and travellers, proved more permanently acceptable beyond the confines of the sub-continent. In 379 it became the state religion of China, and even in Southeast Asia, where Hinduism initially enjoyed much success, it persisted and flourished long after its rival's decline in the 7th and 8th centuries.

In the mid-7th century, the warrior-king Sri Harsha, ruling from Kanauj, once more established a rough feudal unity over an extensive area from Gujerat to east Bengal, but his

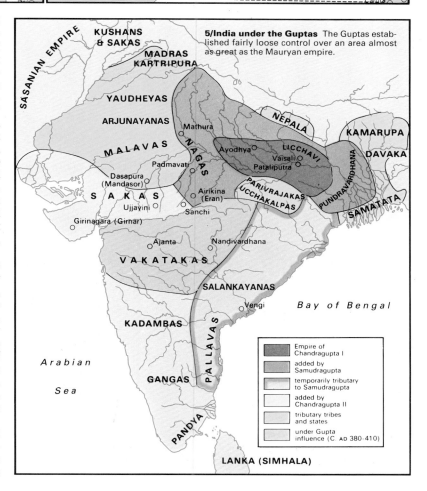

5/India under the Guptas The Guptas established fairly loose control over an area almost as great as the Mauryan empire.

Empire of Chandragupta I
added by Samudragupta
temporarily tributary to Samudragupta
added by Chandragupta II
tributary tribes and states
under Gupta influence (c. AD 380–410)

The peoples of Northern Europe

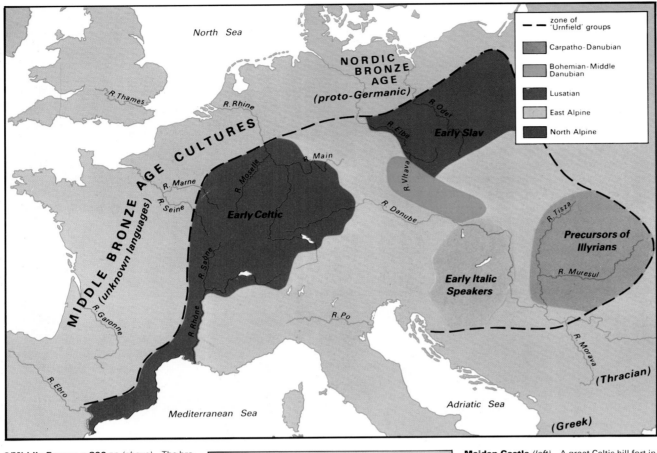

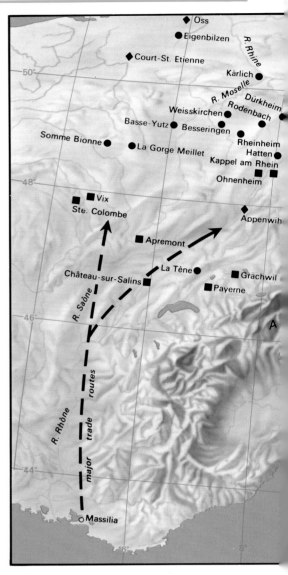

2/Middle Europe c.800 BC *(above)* The broken line encloses the expanding groups of the Late Bronze Age 'Urnfield' complex, characterized by large cemeteries of cremation urns and by unique bronze objects (helmets, breastplates and long slashing swords). The North Alpine group became the Celtic heartland, birthplace of the Celtic culture which dominated central and western Europe in the final centuries before Christ; the Lusatian group was probably ancestral to the Slavs, and the other groups to Illyrians and Italians.

Maiden Castle *(left)* A great Celtic hill fort in Dorset, England, 400-100 BC. It was stormed by the Romans in AD 44.

3/The expansion of the Celts *(below)* From its heartland on the Rhine and Upper Danube, Celtic culture spread to France and Bohemia and Hungary by the 6th century; by the 3rd century Celtic war-bands had replaced the Scythians in the Middle Danube region, and were themselves raiding widely.

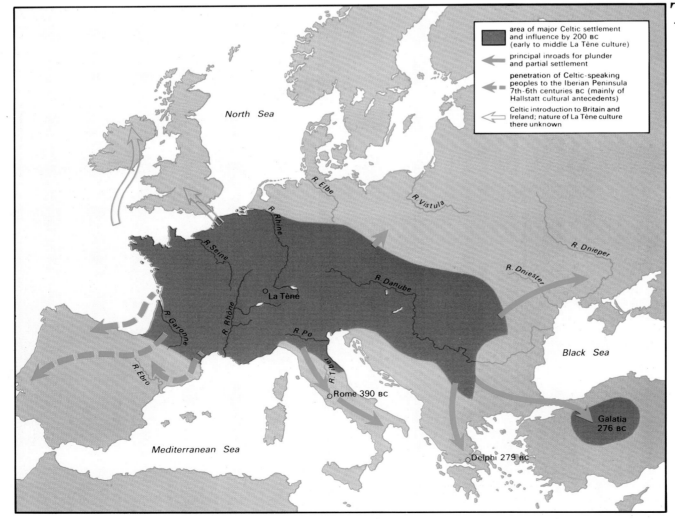

THE 1st millennium before Christ saw a great increase in the population of temperate Europe, north of the Alps. Extensive heavy-soil areas were opened up for the first time to agriculture, and local expansion brought about population movement into peripheral areas. These changes led to a more centralized political system, reflected in the hill forts found in most areas of Europe, dominating the landscape for miles around. Some of these grew to become towns and market-centres in the last two centuries before Christ, a development that facilitated the spread of Roman power by the conquest of one regional centre after another.

The rise in population was evident by the Late Bronze Age, for instance in measures taken to economize in the use of bronze, even though new deep mines for copper had been opened. The adoption of iron-working from the east Mediterranean and Near East in around 800 BC was especially rapid because copper supplies no longer met the growing demand for metal. The main focus of new economic and technical developments lay in central Europe, in the territory of the various branches of the 'Urnfield' culture – a group of related communities with similar culture and burial practices which dominated the Rhine/Danube axis. From about 1000 BC, 'Urnfield' fashions of burial and bronze equipment spread into adjacent areas along the major rivers. Four main branches can be recognized, each ancestral to an important group of historic peoples: Celts in the west, Slavs in the north, Italic speakers in the south, and Illyrians in the southeast.

During the 1st millennium BC, important economic changes began to occur among the Celts as a result of growing contact with the Mediterranean world, for instance via the Greek colony of Massilia (later Marseilles), founded in

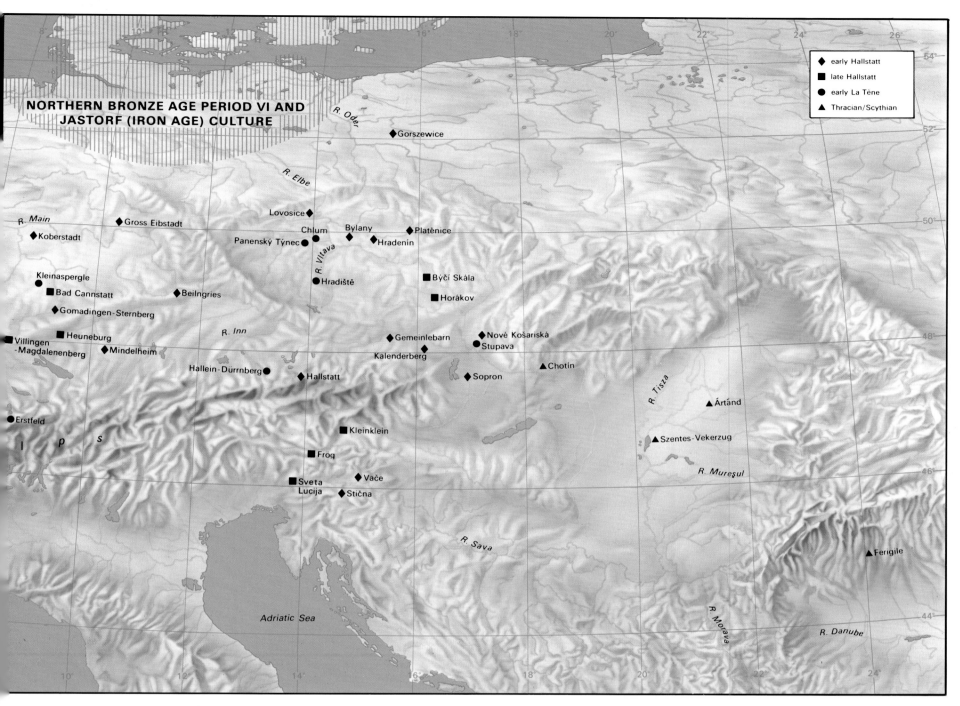

NORTHERN BRONZE AGE PERIOD VI AND JASTORF (IRON AGE) CULTURE

Legend:
- ◆ early Hallstatt
- ■ late Hallstatt
- ● early La Tène
- ▲ Thracian/Scythian

600 BC. Some measure of the importance of commercial relations between the Greeks and their non-Greek 'barbarian' neighbours is given by the magnificent burial of a Celtic princess at Vix near Châtillon-sur-Seine, with a massive ornamented bronze punch-bowl of Italian workmanship, and other pieces of imported finery.

The early Celtic aristocrats lived in hill forts such as the Heuneburg on the Upper Danube, partly designed by a Mediterranean architect, and members of their families were buried with a complete cart bearing their possessions – a burial practice followed all over the Celtic world, from Vix to Lovosice in Bohemia. The breadth of Celtic contacts is best illustrated, however, by the discovery in a burial mound beside the Heuneburg of textiles embroidered with Chinese silk, showing that already in the 6th century BC the trade routes across central Asia were bringing oriental products to markets in the West.

The Celtic Iron Age is divided into two phases, named after the sites of Hallstatt in Austria and La Tène in Switzerland. The La Tène phase (450 BC onwards) was characterized by a dramatic series of Celtic raids on Mediterranean lands: in 390 BC they attacked Rome; in 276 BC they crossed into Asia Minor (where some settled, later to become the 'foolish Galatians' of St Paul's letters); and in 272 BC they sacked the shrine of Apollo at Delphi in Greece. At the same time, a characteristic decorative style known as 'Celtic art' emerged under aristocratic patronage, and spread throughout much of central and western Europe, including the British Isles. The most spectacular pieces are the bronze vessels and gold neck-rings with cast curvilinear decoration which accompany the burials of powerful chieftains in such cemeteries as Rheinheim, Basse-Yutz or Dürkheim.

By the 3rd century BC a clearly defined Celtic culture area extended from the Atlantic to Romania and Anatolia. In some parts the Celts had come as invading war-bands and stayed on as settlers. Other parts, such as Britain and western France, had been absorbed into the Celtic world largely by peaceful means, with the native aristocracies adopting the new continental fashions of art and warfare.

The economic strength of the Celts was based upon growing industrial production. Large numbers of iron ingots show the importance of the Rhineland in primary production, while the light, two-wheeled fighting chariots occasionally buried with the warriors of this phase (e.g. at Somme-Bionne in France) indicate the skills of Celtic craftsmen. These advantages took the Celts eastwards, into territory which in the Hallstatt period had fallen largely under the control of the Scythians – semi-nomadic horsemen and herders whose homeland lay in the steppes of southern Russia – and southwards into Italy, Greece and even Anatolia.

The Celts were the first peoples of temperate Europe to be incorporated within the Roman Empire as it spread beyond the Mediterranean. Already by the end of the 2nd century BC, the Mediterranean part of Gaul was a Roman province; and the intimate links northwards via the Rhone valley led Caesar into a series of campaigns which brought the western Celtic world under Roman control as far as the English Channel by 50 BC. Thus the economically most advanced areas of the barbarian world were rapidly integrated within the Empire. Yet beyond this frontier, and especially in Ireland, Celtic art survived to flower again in the early Middle Ages, in such masterpieces of manuscript illustration as *The Book of Kells* and the *Lindisfarne Gospels*.

4/The prelude to Germanic expansion *(below)* Place-names between the Aller and the Somme show remnants of a language neither Celtic nor German – the last traces of a prehistoric people squeezed between expanding Celtic and Germanic groups. Even this people, however, had already adopted many features of Celtic culture.

1/Middle Europe c.700 to 400 BC *(above)* The map shows important archaeological finds of the Iron Age Celts, and some of their Scythian neighbours to the east, including both richly-furnished graves and large fortified centres. Note the density of finds in the Celtic heartland between the Moselle and the Alps.

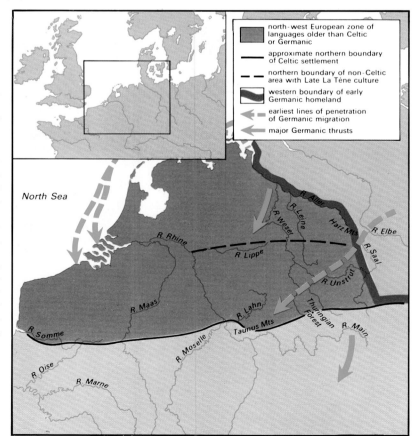

Legend:
- north-west European zone of languages older than Celtic or Germanic
- approximate northern boundary of Celtic settlement
- northern boundary of non-Celtic area with Late La Tène culture
- western boundary of early Germanic homeland
- earliest lines of penetration of Germanic migration
- major Germanic thrusts

The expansion of Roman power in Italy and the Mediterranean to 31 BC

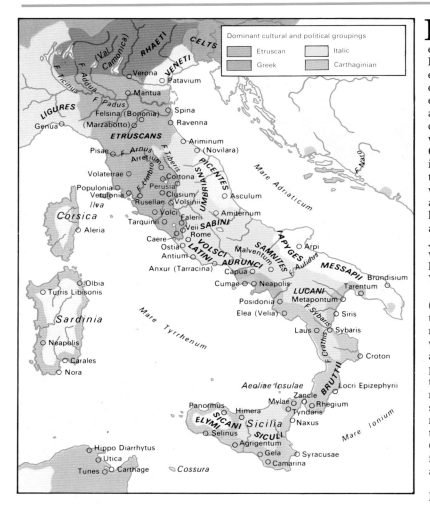

2/The peoples of Italy 500 BC *(above)* During the Bronze and early Iron ages Italy contained many independent tribes, the Etruscans becoming the first to extend their power over a large part of the peninsula. But Etruria proper (Tuscany) was divided into independent city-states and although an Etruscan League was formed, its ties were more religious than political. It thus found concerted action difficult and, assailed by land and sea, the Etruscans were forced back into Etruria around 500 BC, leaving the way open for the more political Romans.

ROME first grew from a cluster of villages into a city in the 7th and 6th centuries BC, influenced by its more civilized overlords, the Etruscans whom the Romans expelled c.510 BC, establishing a republic which gradually expanded its power. Thus while the Greeks repelled the early 5th century Persian invasions and Athens approached its peak under Pericles, the Romans controlled only a small part of central Italy; it was only after the age of Alexander that the Greeks noticed the advance of the 'barbarians' in the west. Equally the Carthaginians, with a trade monopoly and an overseas empire in the western Mediterranean, ignored still agricultural central Italy. Rome could therefore extend her power without much external interference and by 264 BC lead a single Italian confederacy. Just over a century later she dominated the whole Mediterranean, enabling a contemporary historian, Polybius, to write for the first time in Western history of a unified human race.

The early Italian population was very mixed (map 2). The Bronze Age Apennine culture of the central highlands yielded early in the first millennium BC to an Iron Age Villanovan culture which flourished from the Po valley to Etruria and the site of Rome, and even reached Campania. But in the 8th century BC a new and artistically brilliant culture developed in Etruria, reflecting a more complex, centrally organized society, stimulated probably by the development of commercial contacts between Italy and the Greek and Phoenician worlds – from c.750 BC Greek settlers established colonies on the coast from Cumae southwards around the toe of Italy and Sicily.

Etruscan political power declined from the late 6th century onwards as Rome gradually gained the ascendancy, first freeing itself, then achieving mastery over the Latins of central Italy before moving out against the surrounding states: Sabines, Aequi, Volsci and (in the 4th

Julius Caesar formed the First Triumvirate with Pompey and Crassus. He conquered Gaul in 58-50 BC before invading Britain in 55 and 54 BC. After defeating Pompey at Pharsalus in 49-48 BC, he became dictator of Rome in 46 BC but was assassinated two years later.

century BC) the Samnites. During these struggles Rome extended both her territory (*ager Romanus*) and her alliances: by 500 BC she controlled some 350 square miles (907 km²) of territory and by 260 BC some 10,000 square miles (25,900 km²). With conquest went an extension of Roman citizenship, either complete or with limited privileges, while at the same time Rome built up a confederacy with special privileges for the Latins; in all, her allies controlled in 260 BC some 42,000 square miles (108,780 km²), extending effective Roman dominance over some 52,000 square miles (134,680 km² – see map 1). Rome also strengthened her influence by founding strategic colonies in Italy, linked by a network of roads. These colonies comprised either Roman citizens alone or Latins (originally joined by some Romans who surrendered their Roman citizenship): the former were part of the Roman state, the latter independent but privileged allies.

The emergence of this powerful confederacy posed a potential challenge to Carthage, with its commercial interests in the western Mediterranean and its territories in North Africa, Sicily and Sardinia. More by accident than design Rome and Carthage clashed in the First Punic War (264–241). Rome, still essentially agricultural, became a naval power and drove the Carthaginians first from Sicily and then (238) from Corsica and Sardinia, thereby gaining two overseas provinces. In the Second Punic War (218–201), Hannibal invaded Italy from a newly founded Carthaginian empire in Spain but was repulsed and driven from Spain which then

3/The Roman world 264 to 31 BC *(below)* After his death, Alexander the Great's empire split into three, Macedon, Syria and Egypt, whose mutual struggles allowed Carthage to build an empire in the western Mediterranean. Rome and Carthage clashed in Sicily in 264 BC, and after three great wars Rome acquired five overseas provinces: Sicily, Corsica and Sardinia, Spain (two provinces) and Africa (roughly modern Tunisia). In the East, Rome's first annexation was Macedon (146 BC), followed by Asia (western Turkey), Cyrene, Crete, Bithynia, Pontus, Cicilia, Syria and Cyprus. But their administration overstrained the Roman constitution which had not been designed for an overseas empire. The Republic finally collapsed in a series of civil wars, the last of which was won by Octavian (Augustus) over Antony and Cleopatra in 31 BC.

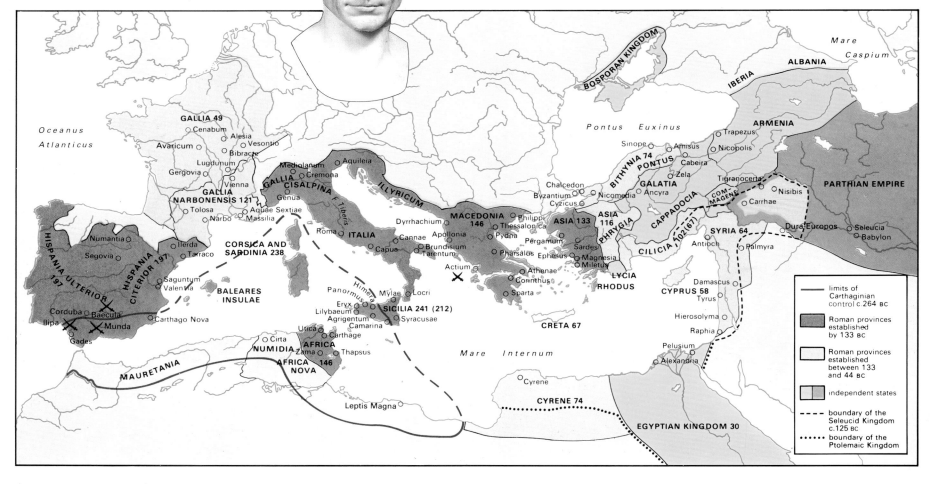

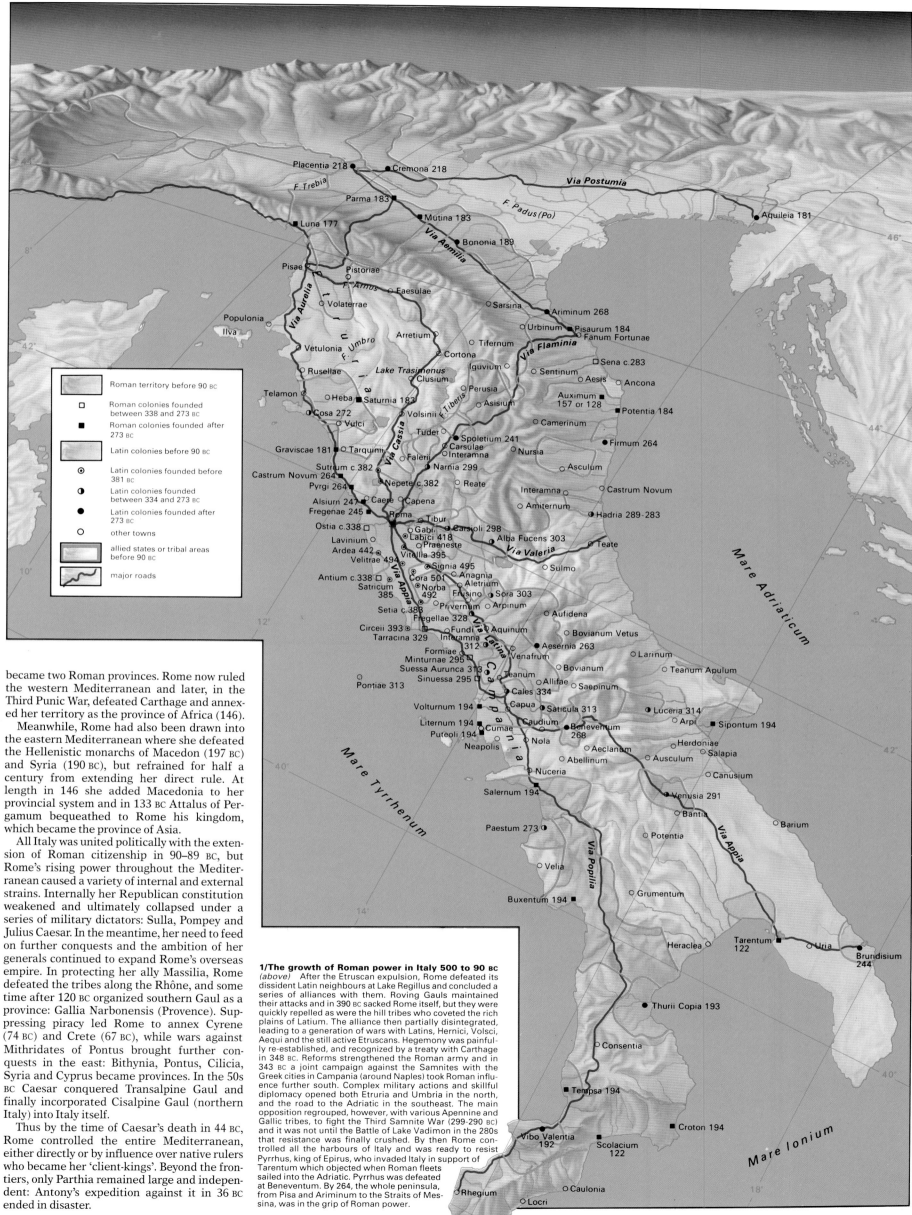

1/The growth of Roman power in Italy 500 to 90 BC
(above) After the Etruscan expulsion, Rome defeated its dissident Latin neighbours at Lake Regillus and concluded a series of alliances with them. Roving Gauls maintained their attacks and in 390 BC sacked Rome itself, but they were quickly repelled as were the hill tribes who coveted the rich plains of Latium. The alliance then partially disintegrated, leading to a generation of wars with Latins, Hernici, Volsci, Aequi and the still active Etruscans. Hegemony was painfully re-established, and recognized by a treaty with Carthage in 348 BC. Reforms strengthened the Roman army and in 343 BC a joint campaign against the Samnites with the Greek cities in Campania (around Naples) took Roman influence further south. Complex military actions and skillful diplomacy opened both Etruria and Umbria in the north, and the road to the Adriatic in the southeast. The main opposition regrouped, however, with various Apennine and Gallic tribes, to fight the Third Samnite War (299-290 BC) and it was not until the Battle of Lake Vadimon in the 280s that resistance was finally crushed. By then Rome controlled all the harbours of Italy and was ready to resist Pyrrhus, king of Epirus, who invaded Italy in support of Tarentum which objected when Roman fleets sailed into the Adriatic. Pyrrhus was defeated at Beneventum. By 264, the whole peninsula, from Pisa and Ariminum to the Straits of Messina, was in the grip of Roman power.

became two Roman provinces. Rome now ruled the western Mediterranean and later, in the Third Punic War, defeated Carthage and annexed her territory as the province of Africa (146).

Meanwhile, Rome had also been drawn into the eastern Mediterranean where she defeated the Hellenistic monarchs of Macedon (197 BC) and Syria (190 BC), but refrained for half a century from extending her direct rule. At length in 146 she added Macedonia to her provincial system and in 133 BC Attalus of Pergamum bequeathed to Rome his kingdom, which became the province of Asia.

All Italy was united politically with the extension of Roman citizenship in 90–89 BC, but Rome's rising power throughout the Mediterranean caused a variety of internal and external strains. Internally her Republican constitution weakened and ultimately collapsed under a series of military dictators: Sulla, Pompey and Julius Caesar. In the meantime, her need to feed on further conquests and the ambition of her generals continued to expand Rome's overseas empire. In protecting her ally Massilia, Rome defeated the tribes along the Rhône, and some time after 120 BC organized southern Gaul as a province: Gallia Narbonensis (Provence). Suppressing piracy led Rome to annex Cyrene (74 BC) and Crete (67 BC), while wars against Mithridates of Pontus brought further conquests in the east: Bithynia, Pontus, Cilicia, Syria and Cyprus became provinces. In the 50s BC Caesar conquered Transalpine Gaul and finally incorporated Cisalpine Gaul (northern Italy) into Italy itself.

Thus by the time of Caesar's death in 44 BC, Rome controlled the entire Mediterranean, either directly or by influence over native rulers who became her 'client-kings'. Beyond the frontiers, only Parthia remained large and independent: Antony's expedition against it in 36 BC ended in disaster.

The Roman Empire from Augustus to Justinian 31 BC to AD 565

The Roman Peace (left) This marble slab from the Altar of Peace (*Ara Pacis*) which Augustus erected in Rome, symbolizes the peace and prosperity which the Roman world enjoyed for two centuries after his death. The central figure is Mother Earth (*Terra Mater*) with fruit, flowers, corn, sheep, children and a bull representing agricultural plenty.

4/The Roman Empire from Diocletian to Justinian
(right) Diocletian's major administrative reforms (see main text) put off the final fragmentation of the Empire which took place when Rome and the West were finally overrun by the barbarians in AD 476. The map shows the reforms (dioceses and prefectures) and the shrinkage that occurred up to the death of Justinian. In the interim, German tribes overran Gaul, Spain, Britain, Italy, North Africa and Pannonia (see page 98). Justinian's partial reconquests from Vandal and Ostrogoth proved ephemeral: three years after his death the Lombards took Italy. Slavs soon poured into Pannonia and a century or so later the Arabs took North Africa and Spain.

BY HIS defeat of Antony and Cleopatra at Actium in 31 BC, Octavian became undisputed master not only of Egypt, which he took as his personal domain, but of the whole Roman world and in 27 BC he accepted the title of Augustus, under which he was to become a Roman god after his death. Without significant political rivals in the Senate and fully supported by his armies, Augustus was able to introduce far-reaching reforms – in taxation, family and social life, the elimination of corruption at home and in provincial administration, the revival of many old Roman and Italian religious cults – which gave the now almost fully consolidated empire a new, intense surge of life. He established himself as First Citizen (*Prínceps*), reshaped the internal constitution, and extended the frontiers to a point where he hoped they would remain unchanged for ever.

While keeping undivided power in his own hands, Augustus allowed the Senate, the old republican magistrates and the business classes (the Equestrian Order) to share with him the task of administering the Empire. Thus in theory 'the Republic was restored', and the government remained in civilian and not military hands. At the cost of some loss of personal liberties, stable government brought most of the civilized western world some two and a half centuries of peace and prosperity, with municipalities throughout the provinces enjoying a considerable degree of local independence, and with the predominantly Latin culture of the west complementing the Hellenism of the east. This more tranquil period was threatened by two brief civil wars (in AD 69 and 193) which emphasized the increasing importance of the army and the dominance of the Princeps. As external pressures on the northern and eastern frontiers

increased, the civilian government collapsed in 235, and armies in different provinces tried to set up their own commanders as emperors (the so-called Thirty Tyrants), shattering economic life. However a series of strong emperors between 268 and 284 turned back the tide of Gothic and other invaders and restored a semblance of orderly government.

In the early days of the Augustan Empire, the long frontiers were defended by a permanent army of some 300,000 men, stationed in camps and mostly deployed in units along the imperial boundaries which at first consisted mainly of natural features such as seas, rivers and mountains. This barrier was backed by an elaborate system of military roads, while naval vessels protected Rome's widespread commercial activity. When expansion ceased under Trajan (d.117), permanent stone barriers were erected to protect the frontiers in northern England and Scotland, beyond the Rhine, along the Danube, in Syria and north Africa. Behind these defences, Roman citizenship gradually spread more widely, and in 212 Caracalla granted it to all free inhabitants. However by the mid-3rd century internal weakness threatened the whole system.

When Diocletian came to power in 284 it was obvious that a single ruler could no longer hold the whole Empire together, so he divided power between himself and a joint Augustus, with two subordinate Caesars, and split the Empire into four prefectura and 12 dioceses. By now the principate was dead: the military had triumphed over the civilian and a new basis had to be found for imperial authority. Under the influence of eastern ideas the Princeps became Dominus (Lord), an absolute ruler, at the head of a vast bureaucracy. In fact the centre of Roman power was shifting eastwards: Constantine established a new capital and a Christian city at Byzantium, later (330) renamed Constantinople.

A new taxation system resulted in an economic revival but further decline was merely postponed, not overcome. Although theoretically governed by joint rulers, the Empire gradually broke into an eastern and western half, while outlying provinces fell to barbarian invaders. Rome itself was sacked by the Visigoth Alaric (410) and the Vandal Gaeseric (455), and in 493 an Ostrogothic kingdom was established in Italy (see page 98). The Western Empire fell to the invaders, and Justinian's attempt in the mid-6th century to reunite the two halves failed to achieve permanent union. Yet in the east the Byzantine Empire survived for another 1000 years, until the capture of Constantinople by the Turks in 1453.

For two centuries after the breakdown of the Western Empire the Byzantine state retained Roman institutions and continued to use Latin in its courts. Although Greek then superseded Latin and the administration became less concentrated, the Eastern Empire compiled the two great monuments of Roman law, the codes of Theodosius and of Justinian.

Further, the east preserved and transmitted to the modern world much of the legacy of the ancient world. Even in the west many Roman traditions survived. The Latin tongue, although widely developing into the derivative 'Romance' languages, remained the language of the Church and of science; Roman law forms the basis of most modern European legal systems; many feats of Roman engineering genius are still visible; the Roman Church lives on as a direct link with the past; and the German kings of the 'Holy Roman Empire' claimed to be Roman rulers.

Detail of the frieze (above) on Trajan's column. Trajan (d.117), the first Roman emperor born outside Italy, came from Italica in Spain, near present-day Seville. His famous column, which still stands in Rome, is a unique work of art, sculptured in the form of a continuous spiral frieze 650 feet (198 m) long, showing arms, armour, fortifications and battle scenes from his two campaigns to conquer Dacia.

2/The frontiers of Germany (left) In 12 BC the Romans finally pushed across the Rhine from Gaul, to reach the Elbe in 9 BC, but failed to establish permanent occupation: a revolt led by Arminius (Herman) in AD 9 ended in the destruction of three legions in the Teutoburg Forest. In AD 74, Vespasian established Roman authority throughout the triangle known as the *Agri Decumates*, lying between the sources of the Rhine and the Danube and stretching to the Black Forest. Under his successor, Domitian, fortifications were erected as far as the Neckar Valley and the Taunus Mountains.

3/The Syrian 'limes' (left) Under Trajan and Hadrian, this once lightly held frontier was equipped with a formidable screen of forts and military roads. It failed, however, to prevent the Sasanians sacking Antioch in AD 260, or to deter the Palmyran 'Empress' Zenobia, who won eastern Syria, Anatolia, Palestine and Egypt before her defeat by Aurelian in 272. The defences were later restored under Diocletian.

1/The Roman Empire from Augustus to c.AD 280
(below) Augustus settled with Parthia, annexed Egypt, Galatia (25 BC) and Judaea (AD 6) and advanced over the Alps to the Danube and the Rhine, adding the provinces of Rhaetia, Noricum, Pannonia and Moesia. Settlement of colonies continued until Hadrian (d.138), after which '*colonia*' became a title for privileged *municipia*. Syria and Cappadocia were extended under the Flavians (69-96) and the German frontier advanced to the Black Forest (*Agri Decumates*). Trajan, whose reign marked the end of the Empire's significant territorial additions, fought wars for the annexation of Dacia (106), Armenia and Assyria (114), and Mesopotamia (115), to join Arabia Petraea, already taken in 106. His successor, Hadrian, decided to abandon these acquisitions, apart from Arabia and Dacia, and to consolidate more defensible frontiers for the Empire.

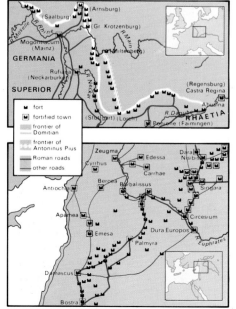

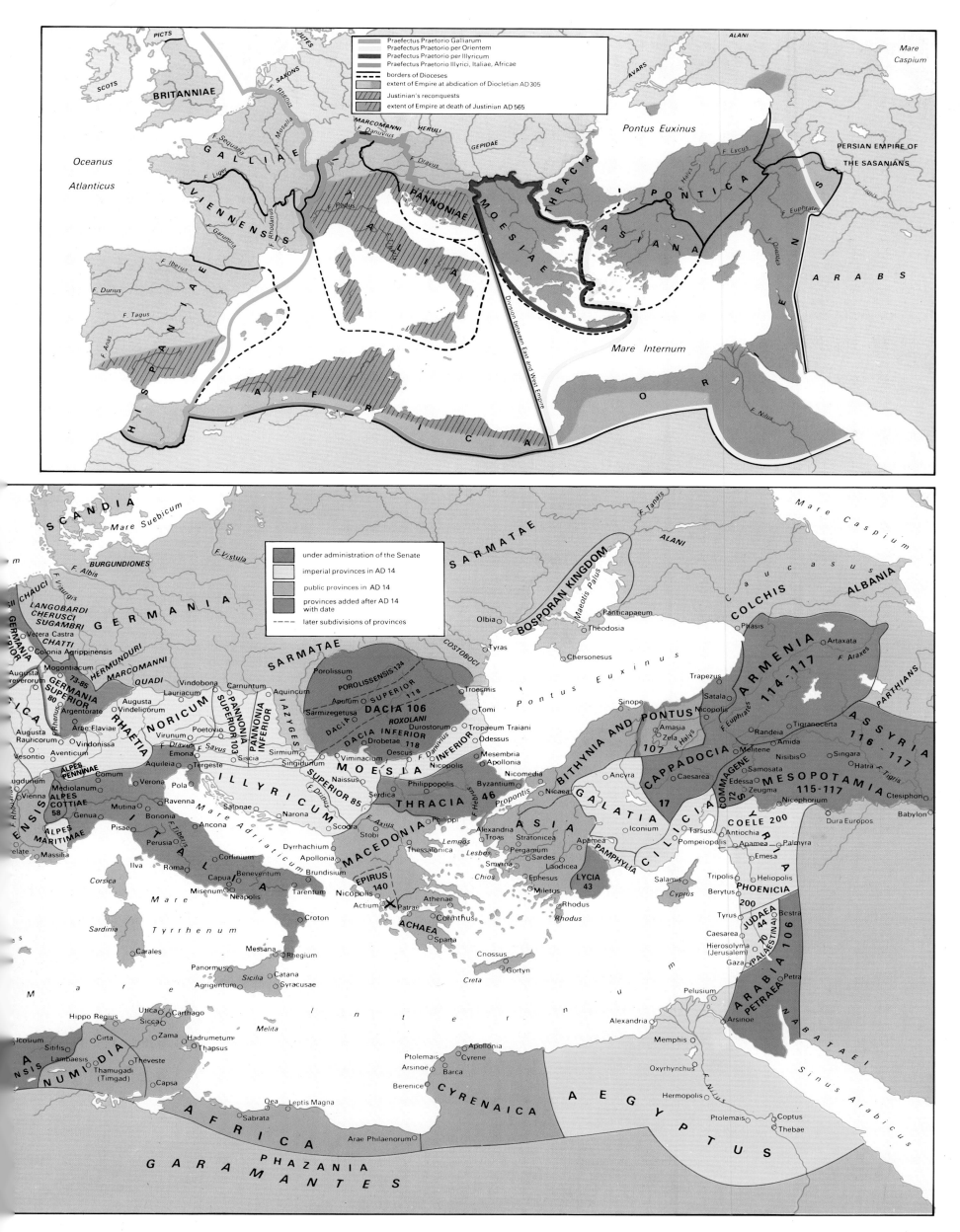

The economy of the Roman world c.AD 200

THE Roman Empire covered a vast area, with a single currency, low customs barriers, and an elaborate network of roads and protected harbours, where neither pirates nor frontiers hindered commerce. Although local agriculture and craftsmanship satisfied the basic needs of most people, Graeco-Roman civilization also involved the long-distance movement of natural products and manufactured goods on a vast scale. Many cities, especially Rome itself, but also a number in Greece and Asia Minor, regularly depended on imported grain, while elsewhere, local crop failures produced a recurrent need for imports. Some parts of the Empire, notably Italy, Greece, Syria, Egypt and Africa (Tunisia) lacked local supplies of essential metals; and a trade developed in wool and linen textiles manufactured on a large scale in different provinces. However luxuries from the East reached all regions – silk clothing was worn as a status symbol by the wealthiest citizens, while spices, especially pepper, seasoned the food of a wider segment of the population – but the same eastern trade caused a drain of currency out of the Empire.

Much of the long-distance movement of goods and products stemmed directly from the existence of the Empire. Wealth was concentrated at Rome itself where a population of around 1 million consumed grain and olive oil imported as taxation in kind, supplemented by further purchases. The main grain-producing areas were Sicily, Africa (Tunisia and Algeria) and Egypt, while most oil came from Spain and Africa. Marble for Roman building schemes and animals for the arena also came from far afield. In addition, the armies stationed in frontier provinces created a large demand for both natural and manufactured products with the result that these areas saw a considerable development in agriculture, mining and manufacture. Army supplies, like other goods, were if possible transported by river, notably the Rhine (Rhenus), Rhône (Rhodanus), Danube (Danuvius) and their tributaries, and a number of large cities, such as Trier (Augusta Treverorum), Lyons (Lugdunum), Aquileia and Antioch, combined the roles of centre of administration and distributor of supplies. In many parts of the Empire, city colonies with attached territory were settled and farmed by retired soldiers. Armies, colonies and the urbanization of the wealthier of their inhabitants all created a new demand in the provinces of western Europe and the Balkans for commodities reflecting the Roman way of life: wine, olive oil, weapons, artistic metalware, fine pottery and glass. In the early 1st century AD Italy supplied these goods as well as pottery from Arezzo (Arretium) to most Mediterranean lands, Gaul, Britain and the western Balkans. (Finds of Arretine pottery have been made as far away as India.) Then the fine pottery industry serving the western provinces gradually moved north to the region of Toulouse (La Graufesenque and other sites), to the Lyons area (Lezoux and other sites) and later still to the Rhineland where glass-making grew up around Cologne (Colonia Agrippina) and a metal industry developed in the hills to the southwest. Spain became a major exporter of metal ores and, under the Empire, also of olive oil and a fish sauce (garum) which filled the amphorae shipped in vast quantities to Rome and to destinations as far away as Britain. From around AD 200 until the late 7th century AD, North Africa served as a large-scale exporter of olive oil and fine pottery to the whole Mediterranean area for by the end of the 2nd century the export trade of Italy had dwindled and large areas of the Empire had become self-sufficient in the items of Roman living.

The distribution of cities reflects the degrees of development of different areas: Asia, Syria, Egypt, Africa (Tunisia), southern Spain, Italy and Provence were the most advanced. In the cities property was unequally divided, and a small group of outstandingly wealthy men financed public building. The permanent army was sometimes employed on the building of roads, bridges or fortifications, especially in frontier regions, but the spectacular nature of Roman remains tends to obscure the economic backwardness of most of the Empire. Wealth generally took the form of land and by far the largest contribution to economic output came from farming by poor people at a low productive level. Despite the fine road system, commerce of any sort was limited by the slowness and expense of land transport which depended on donkeys, mules and oxen, rather than on horses – it was cheaper to ship grain across the Mediterranean than to cart it 80 miles (130 km) by road.

The commercial classes held low social rank, the wealth of even the richest merchant falling below that of the landowning notables or members of the imperial aristocracy. Much trading was carried on by humble men travelling with a small stock of goods and factory production was unknown, even for goods in high demand such as pottery tablewares. Instead, most products were made by craftsmen working on a small scale, sometimes directly for the users of the goods they produced, on estates in the countryside rather than in towns. Sensitive areas of economic production, such as silver-making (to make coins to pay the army and imperial officials) from the lead ores imported from Spain, Greece and Britain were owned directly by the emperor and organized through his officials.

However the political and military crisis of the 3rd century permanently weakened the imperial economy and in order to pay its troops the government gradually debased the silver currency, a debasement accompanied by devaluation and culminating in rapid inflation until around AD 300 Diocletian restored internal stability. Henceforth greater emphasis was placed upon taxation in kind. A new currency based on gold was established, but devaluation of the copper currency continued until the end of the 4th century. The scope of money and the market economy, and thus of the private contractor and merchant, shrank.

Throughout the imperial period slaves formed a significant proportion of the population in many areas of the Empire, providing dependent labour in domestic service, manufacture and agriculture. The managers of farms, workshops, ships or banks, for example, were also normally slaves or freedmen. It is difficult to determine quantitative trends in slave employment, but a gradual decline in the social and legal status of the humbler free population reduced the social and economic distinction between nominal slaves and freemen at the lower levels of society.

Seen in a global perspective, the Roman Empire represented a single economy which was self-sufficient in all essential commodities. Its cohesion was facilitated by geographical factors such as the Mediterranean Sea and the river systems flowing into it. But the development of some areas rather than others and the direction and volume of the movement of goods was largely determined by the political organization of the area. The break-up of the western Empire in the 5th century AD ended the massive government-directed transfer of resources to Rome, Italy and the frontier armies; but the pattern of commercial exchanges in the Mediterranean lasted longer, even though their scale declined gradually. It was only in the 7th century that new patterns began to emerge.

A silver denarius of 44 BC (above) The standard coin of the late Republic and early Empire at first had a very high level of purity, but this fell to 2 per cent by the mid-3rd century.

Amphorae (right) These large two-handled pottery vessels, usually with pointed bases, could be either stood in a rack or stuck in the ground and their shape made them possible to handle when full. They generally held liquids, most commonly wine, olive oil and fish sauce (or salted fish). Their varied shapes, labels and origin-stamps, together with the scientific analysis of the clay from which the vessels were made, provide valuable information about trade.

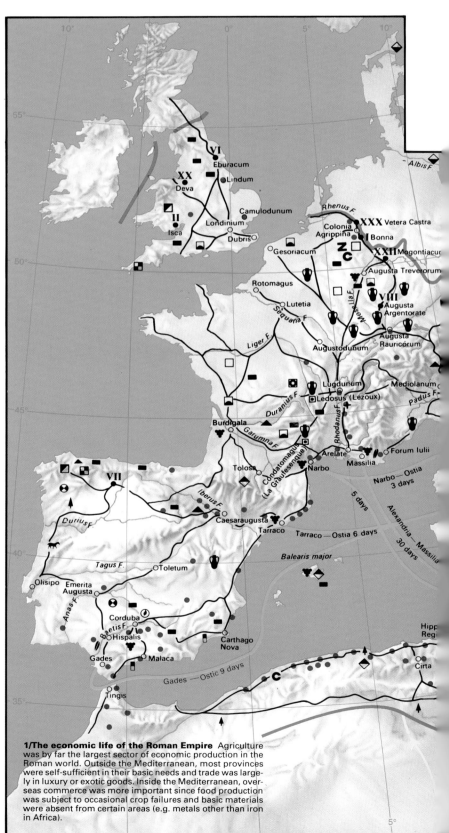

1/The economic life of the Roman Empire Agriculture was by far the largest sector of economic production in the Roman world. Outside the Mediterranean, most provinces were self-sufficient in their basic needs and trade was largely in luxury or exotic goods. Inside the Mediterranean, overseas commerce was more important since food production was subject to occasional crop failures and basic materials were absent from certain areas (e.g. metals other than iron in Africa).

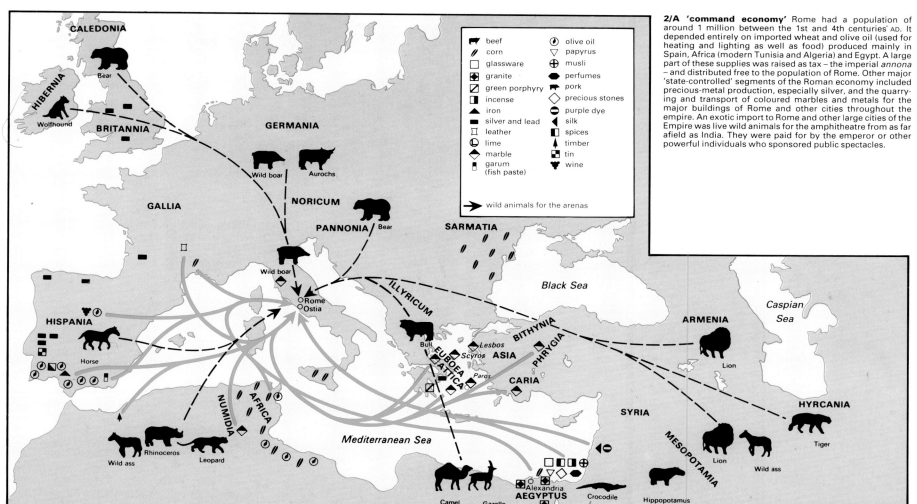

2/A 'command economy' Rome had a population of around 1 million between the 1st and 4th centuries' AD. It depended entirely on imported wheat and olive oil (used for heating and lighting as well as food) produced mainly in Spain, Africa (modern Tunisia and Algeria) and Egypt. A large part of these supplies was raised as tax – the imperial *annona* – and distributed free to the population of Rome. Other major 'state-controlled' segments of the Roman economy included precious-metal production, especially silver, and the quarrying and transport of coloured marbles and metals for the major buildings of Rome and other cities throughout the empire. An exotic import to Rome and other large cities of the Empire was live wild animals for the amphitheatre from as far afield as India. They were paid for by the emperor or other powerful individuals who sponsored public spectacles.

Legend (map 2/A):

beef	olive oil
corn	papyrus
glassware	musli
granite	perfumes
green porphyry	pork
incense	precious stones
iron	purple dye
silver and lead	silk
leather	spices
lime	timber
marble	tin
garum (fish paste)	wine

→ wild animals for the arenas

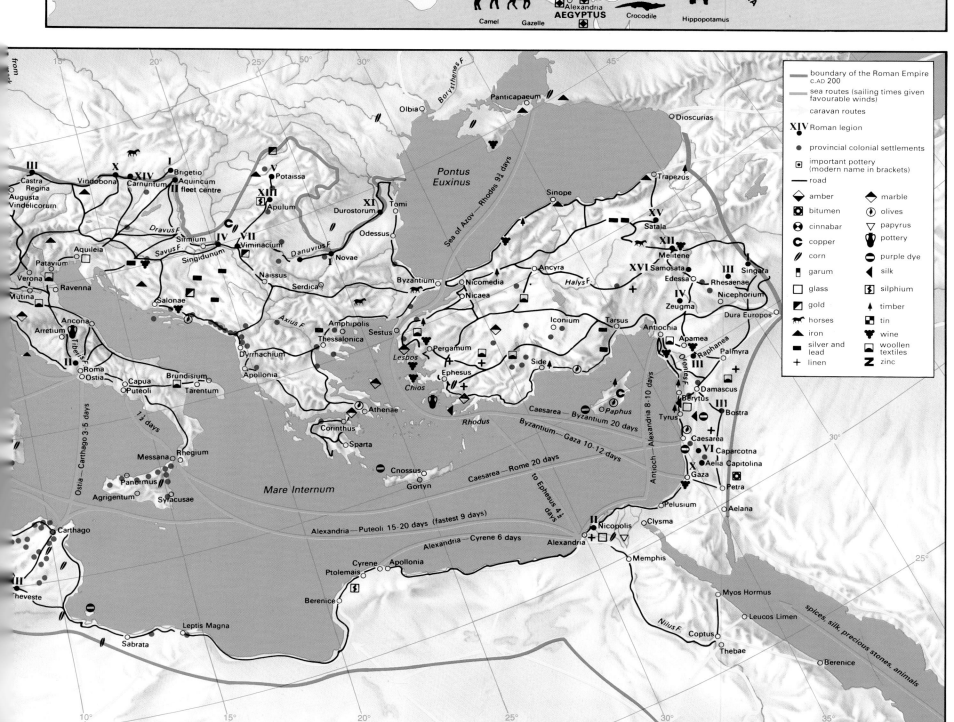

Legend (lower map):

— boundary of the Roman Empire c.AD 200
— sea routes (sailing times given favourable winds)
caravan routes
XIV Roman legion
● provincial colonial settlements
▣ important pottery (modern name in brackets)
— road

amber	marble
bitumen	olives
cinnabar	papyrus
C copper	pottery
corn	purple dye
garum	silk
glass	silphium
gold	timber
horses	tin
iron	wine
silver and lead	woollen textiles
+ linen	**Z** zinc

The rise of Christianity to AD 600

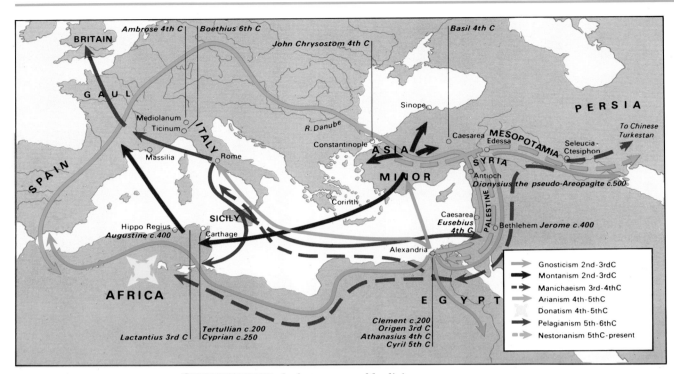

Ambrose 4th C Boethius 6th C John Chrysostom 4th C Basil 4th C

BRITAIN

GAUL

Mediolanum Ticinum

Massilia

ITALY

Rome

R. Danube

Constantinople

Sinope

ASIA

MINOR

Corinth

PERSIA

To Chinese Turkestan

Caesarea MESOPOTAMIA Edessa Seleucia-Ctesiphon

SYRIA

Antioch Dionysius the pseudo-Areopagite c.500

SPAIN

SICILY

Hippo Regius Augustine c.400

Carthage

AFRICA

Caesarea Eusebius 4th C

Alexandria

Bethlehem Jerome c.400

PALESTINE

EGYPT

Lactantius 3rd C Tertullian c.200 Cyprian c.250

Clement c.200 Origen 3rd C Athanasius 4th C Cyril 5th C

Gnosticism 2nd-3rdC
Montanism 2nd-3rdC
Manichaeism 3rd-4thC
Arianism 4th-5thC
Donatism 4th-5thC
Pelagianism 5th-6thC
Nestorianism 5thC-present

2/Writers and heresies (above) As soon as Christianity became a subject of intellectual speculation in the 2nd century AD, it was rent by doctrinal controversies, many of which represented a serious challenge to the Church's traditions and authority. The ideas of theologians such as Donatus, Arius and Pelagius moved men and events almost as powerfully as the Christian revelation itself, and constantly threatened the unity of early Christendom.

The linking of pagan and Christian symbols In the pre-Constantinian inscription (below), the fish, an old religious symbol used because the Greek initial letters of 'Jesus Christ God's Son Saviour' spell ΙΧΘΥΣ, fish, represents Christ; so does the anchor, a firm point in a storm. But DM is a pagan formula, and the laurel is a Roman symbol of triumph. The symbol (above) is from a sarcophagus of about AD 350. Here the Roman laurel wreath is combined with the chi-rho, the first two letters of 'Christ' in Greek, resembling the 'sun-wheel'.

CHRISTIANITY, the last great world religion before Islam, originated in Palestine but little is known of its founder, Jesus of Nazareth, before he began at the age of 30 to preach that 'the kingdom of God is at hand' – a message for which many Jews had waited. Their country, formally annexed by Rome in AD 6, was in turmoil and contained many sects, some chiefly spiritual (like the Essenes), others more political (like those later called the Zealots), which hoped for the long-promised Messiah, or saviour, to liberate them. The crowds at first followed Jesus, seeing in him this Messiah; but the Jewish authorities felt that his message challenged their authority and after three years of teaching and preaching he was handed over to the Roman procurator and crucified as a revolutionary.

However the new faith proved tenacious, despite its founder's early death. His disciples, and even their leader Simon Peter (the Rock), had initially abandoned Jesus but their faith was restored by the Resurrection, when, they claimed, he appeared to them after death and charged them to proclaim the good news of God's supreme power. This revelation was at first presented in a purely Judaic context. Whether Jesus himself believed that God had sent him to convert the Gentiles remains unclear. It was left to Paul, a Jewish convert from Tarsus, to show the power and extent of Christianity's appeal as he preached in the Aegean islands, Asia Minor, Greece, Italy and perhaps as far as Spain. Jewish communities (see page 102) existed in all these areas and the Christian preachers usually began with them, but the Jews in general were not won over; anti-Christian riots broke out, and the gap widened as gentile Christians came to outnumber Jewish believers.

Jesus's teaching appealed particularly to the poor and humble who found in the kingdom of God a message of hope denied to them in the secular world. The number of converts steadily grew and quickly penetrated the educated classes, though more among the urban masses than in the countryside, which long retained its pagan beliefs. Antioch – 'the cradle of gentile Christianity' – spread its influence north and east outside the Empire. One disciple, Philip, is said to have converted an Ethiopian official and there is a persistent tradition that Thomas reached India. At some point before 200, Edessa became a Christian stronghold, while 1st-century churches were established in the west at Puteoli, Rome, and possibly in Spain; by the mid-2nd century many existed in the Empire's eastern provinces and began to spread to the

Rhine valley and North Africa.

By this time Christianity was significant enough to attract the attention of writers like Tacitus and Pliny the Younger – the former described how Nero used the Christians as scapegoats to divert hostility from himself. Nevertheless, conversions continued, despite repression and persecution. The Christians' refusal to worship the emperors, serve as magistrates or carry arms made them officially suspect, but their beliefs appealed to more than the oppressed and insecure: by 230 the Church had penetrated the palace and higher ranks of the army. Pagan reaction, however, resulted in further persecutions in 151 and 303.

Early in the 4th century the Emperor Constantine, whose family had worshipped the Unconquered Sun, decided to accept Christianity and by 324, as sole ruler of the entire Empire, he was sure that he had a divine mission. Recognized by the Edict of Milan (313), Christianity quickly established itself as the emperor's official religion, especially in the new capital, Constantinople. An abortive attempt to put the clock back by the Emperor Julian (361–3) failed, and another tough militarist, Theodosius II (379–95), further strengthened the Church's power. By now Christianity had also reached the barbarians beyond the imperial frontier and soon after 340 Ulfilas converted the Goths near the mouth of the Danube. Many Germanic invaders after 376 were already Christian, though

their preferred Arian beliefs dissented from those defined at the Council of Nicaea (325).

Meanwhile, Christianity became more organized. Gradually those who had placed their faith in the second coming of Christ came to realize that this was not imminent and, by the late 3rd and early 4th centuries, the sheer spread of churches demanded more complex structures to maintain discipline and safeguard doctrinal purity. Authority lay in the Bible, and in the tradition of worship and sacraments safeguarded by bishops (overseers), keeping communion with each other and responsible for the clergy they ordained.

From Paul's time, Christianity included a proportion of the educated elite: the great Alexandrian theologians Pantaenus (d. c.190), Clement (c.150–215) and Origen (c.185–254) had reconciled Christianity with Greek philosophy and made it intellectually respectable. But at the same time they opened the door to acute theological controversy. By the 2nd century, the theosophical beliefs known as Gnosticism had taken hold in Alexandria, while other heresies and schisms which increasingly tended to split the Church were associated with Marcion (d. c.160), who regarded matter as evil; Novatian (d. 257/8) and Donatus (4th century), both strict moralists; Arius (c.250–336), who subordinated the Son to the Father; and Pelagius (d. after 419), a moralist stressing free will. Another threat to Church vitality was the withdrawal of monks and hermits to a life of desert solitude until Pachomius (290–346) and Basil (c.330–77) in the east and Benedict (c.480–550) in the west brought the ascetics together in monastic communities, subject to careful communal rules.

The Christian Church modelled its structure on that of the Roman Empire: the dioceses mirrored the administrative divisions of Diocletian; bishops, based in the chief cities, met in synod in the provincial capitals, and those from the great metropolitan centres were accorded special dignity. Rome, see of Peter and Paul, was granted precedence in 'honour' but not in jurisdiction, and its bishops shared rank and power with those of Antioch and Alexandria, to which were later added Constantinople (381) and Jerusalem (451). Rivalries among 4th-century synods enhanced Roman primacy.

Meanwhile important decisions, particularly the definition of doctrine, were made by the assembled clergy. In the 2nd century local synods were called in Asia Minor to deal with the Montanist heresy, and in 325 the first ecumenical council, representing the whole Church, met at Nicaea, followed by the councils of Constantinople (381), Ephesus (431) and Chalcedon (451).

Theoretically these councils represented the voice of the Church, but in practice Christianity as the state religion was often subjected to imperial constraint. Some emperors – notably Justinian I (527–65) – ruled the Church with a heavy hand, planting the seed of conflict between Church and State, and underlying much of the later tension between Empire and Papacy (see page 118). However, when Rome succumbed to barbarian attack, the Church and its bishops, with their vast estates and pervasive influence, emerged as guardians of the classical tradition, and guided Europe, as well as Christendom, into the new age.

3/Monastic foundations (above) Almost from the beginning, a significant minority of Christians adopted a life of renunciation and withdrawal. By AD 700 monasteries had become centres of piety and learning, as well as great landowners, in every Christian land.

1/The Early Christian churches (below) Starting with the journeys of Paul, Christian churches sprang up throughout the Roman world. By the time of Diocletian's persecutions (AD 304), they were thickly clustered around the Mediterranean and scattered as far apart as Britain and the Nile.

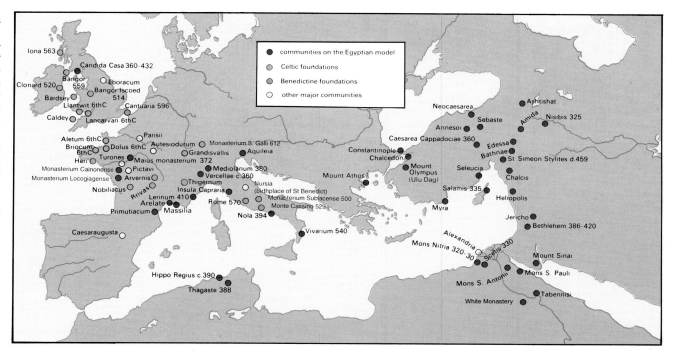

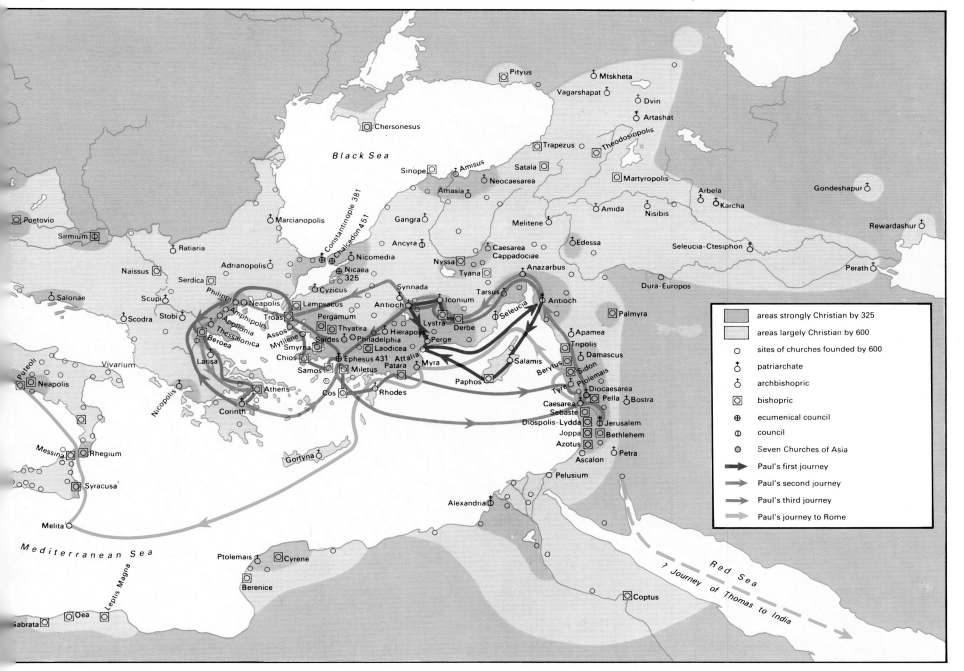

The crisis of the classical world

BY THE 5th century AD the classical empires of Eurasia were deep in crisis. Incursions into northern China in the 1st century AD represented the first in a series of invasions that over the next four centuries threatened the established civilizations of Greece, Rome, northern China, Persia and India. The cause lay in the spread of nomadic peoples from central Asia; the result was a setback to civilization from the Mediterranean to China and the onset of the Dark Ages. China alone successfully resisted the invaders; but even there a period of political fragmentation resulted, which was ended only by the Sui dynasty in AD 589.

The invaders whose incursions produced this crisis were not Indo-Europeans, though they possessed Indo-European subjects and allies, but were northeast Asian peoples linked by common traditions (sometimes reinforced by kinship among their rulers). Unlike the Mongols seven centuries later (see page 126) they lacked any form of central control despite their diffusion from a common geographical area. Their physical type varied but was often Mongoloid; their languages mostly belonged to the Altaic groups of northeast Asia, now represented best by the Turkish dialects; and they all followed the pastoral mode of life. In war they fought as mounted archers, using composite bows made of strips of bone – short, strong and convenient for riders – but also employed sabres at close quarters and, when they acquired taller horses and adopted stirrups, the lance. This light and effective panoply was seldom adequately copied by civilized peoples and accounts for the invaders' successes against them.

The centres of power among these Altaic nomads lay not in arid steppe or desert, but in more favoured regions: along the Great Wall of China, and in Mongolia north of the Gobi Desert. From here they struck both southward and westward, their expansion beginning with the conquests of the people called Hsiung-nu in Chinese sources – a great nomad confederacy, the first to arise in eastern Asia, which grew up in continual rivalry with the Chinese empire of the Han.

Only a vast line of fixed fortifications kept the Hsiung-nu at bay and it was not until the 1st century AD that the Han, using cavalry modelled on that of their adversaries, finally broke their power. But the Hsiung-nu did not vanish from history, and families of the ruling tribes appear to have established themselves in central Asia where they gradually established a new confederacy, now including Iranian nomads and some Mongoloid tribes from the Siberian forests.

The nomad rulers of Mongolia itself initially represented little threat to the Chinese, but they too assaulted China at the beginning of the 4th century AD, after the short period of reunification under the Western Chin (265–317). Setting up an independent state in Shansi and Shensi, they occupied the two traditional capitals, Loyang in 311 and Ch'ang-an in 316. For the next 280 years northern China became the domain of invaders from the steppe, who established a bewildering succession of short-lived dynasties: some by Hsiung-nu leaders, some by the proto-Mongolian Hsien-pi, and others by various Turkic peoples, the Avars, and the Ti and Ch'iang tribes from Tibet's eastern borders.

Most of these groups had long been in contact with the Chinese; a few, like the Hsiung-nu and Ch'iang, even settled inside the Great Wall and served the Chinese as mercenary troops. When they established local states of their own in Chinese territory, however, they lacked the

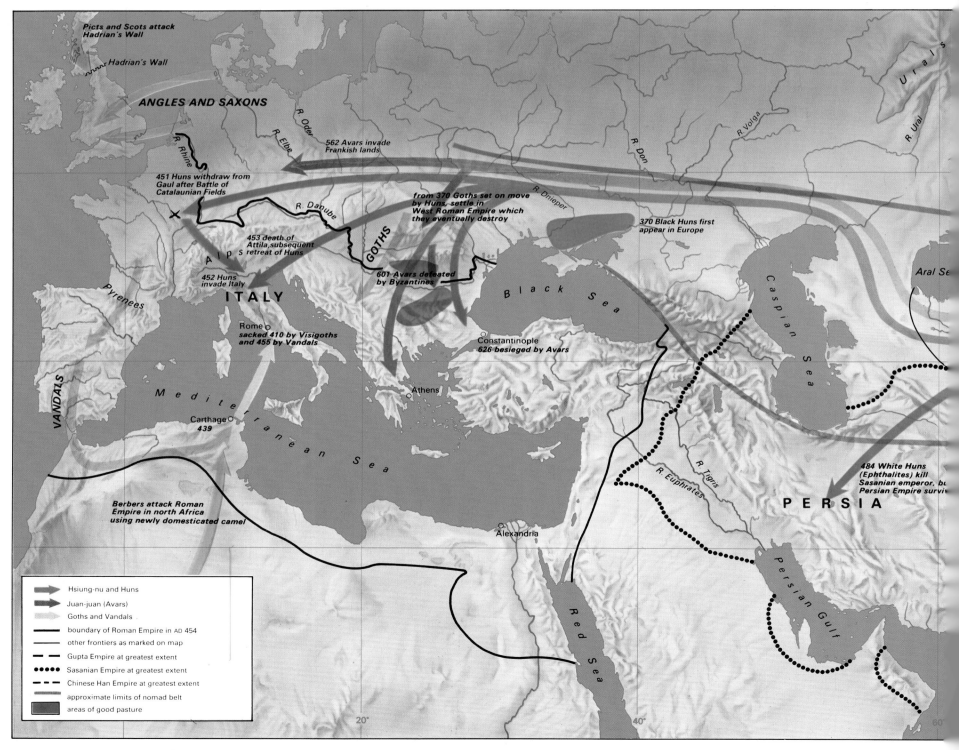

Picts and Scots attack Hadrian's Wall

Hadrian's Wall

ANGLES AND SAXONS

562 Avars invade Frankish lands

451 Huns withdraw from Gaul after Battle of Catalaunian Fields

from 370 Goths set on move by Huns, settle in West Roman Empire which they eventually destroy

370 Black Huns first appear in Europe

453 death of Attila, subsequent retreat of Huns

452 Huns invade Italy

601 Avars defeated by Byzantines

ITALY

Rome sacked 410 by Visigoths and 455 by Vandals

Constantinople 626 besieged by Avars

Athens

Carthage 439

VANDALS

484 White Huns (Ephthalites) kill Sasanian emperor, but Persian Empire survives

Berbers attack Roman Empire in north Africa using newly domesticated camel

PERSIA

Alexandria

GOTHS

Black Sea

Caspian Sea

Aral Sea

Mediterranean Sea

Red Sea

Persian Gulf

R. Rhine
R. Oder
R. Elbe
R. Danube
R. Dnieper
R. Don
R. Volga
R. Ural
Urals
R. Tigris
R. Euphrates
Pyrenees
Alps

- ➤ Hsiung-nu and Huns
- ➤ Juan-juan (Avars)
- ➤ Goths and Vandals
- — boundary of Roman Empire in AD 454
- — other frontiers as marked on map
- ▨ Gupta Empire at greatest extent
- •••• Sasanian Empire at greatest extent
- - - Chinese Han Empire at greatest extent
- ▬ approximate limits of nomad belt
- ▨ areas of good pasture

The Great Wall (below) runs 1500 miles (2415 km) from the Pacific shore to the deserts of central Asia, with an average height of 30 feet (9 m). It was originally begun after 221 BC by the first emperor of a united China, Shih Huang-ti, who conscripted millions of workers to link existing northern defences of his empire into a single system. The wall in its present form was largely constructed under the Ming, who extended and strengthened the system.

experience needed to administer a sedentary agricultural population and were forced to adopt Chinese methods of government and to co-operate with the local Chinese elite families. The tension between the need to adapt tribal customs to Chinese conditions and the desire to preserve their ethnic identity proved fatal to most of these regimes. Eventually a powerful Turkic people, the Toba (northern) Wei, 386–534, succeeded in reunifying northern China, although they did so in the end by becoming Chinese themselves. In the early 6th century this led to civil conflict and their empire fragmented for a time.

During these centuries, not only did the nomadic invaders adopt Chinese customs, literary culture and political institutions, but the Chinese upper class, particularly in northwest China (Kansu, Shensi, Shansi), collaborated widely with them and even intermarried with the Turks and Hsien-pi. A distinctive Sino-nomad aristocracy emerged, many of whom spoke both Chinese and Turkish, with a life-style much influenced by non-Chinese customs, and among whom women played a very powerful role. This aristocratic group evolved into the ruling houses of the Sui (581–617) and T'ang (618–907) dynasties which reunified the whole of China and extended throughout the empire the institutions and style of government developed in the northern successor kingdoms to the Toba Wei. They maintained a distinctive identity as a separate aristocratic group until the late T'ang.

The political chaos of the 4th century, when northern China dissolved into many local states, led to immense physical destruction and wide-spread depopulation with vast numbers of Chinese fleeing to the south where conditions were relatively stable. The flourishing internal and external trade of Han times fell away; the use of money disappeared; trade relied on barter; and the states' finances were collected entirely in commodities. Not until the end of the 5th century did the Toba redistribute land, to bring more of their territory under cultivation, and slowly rehabilitate the economy.

Farther west, the Black Huns of Europe, as they were known, moved into south Russia in the 4th century and advanced in the 5th century into the fertile basin of the Danube, particularly the territories later known as Hungary. From there they threatened both the eastern and western Roman empires until the death of their leader, Attila, in AD 453. The Huns' onslaught eventually destroyed the western Roman Empire, which came under Germanic rule, but in the east the Byzantine Empire survived. Meanwhile, also in the 4th, 5th and 6th centuries AD, the White Huns (Ephthalites) overran much of the Sasanian Empire of Iran in constant wars, and later founded a dynasty in northern India. Byzantine sources and Indian coins represent them as a white, non-Mongoloid people from central Asia, indicating that the name Hun (Khun in Iran, Huna in India) now denoted a political, rather than an ethnic, unity.

The Hsiung-nu and their descendants and successors thus played a leading role in the crisis of established civilizations at the time. Not only did their incursions strain the resources of the states exposed to their attacks, but they also unsettled the tribes through whose territories they passed. It was the Huns who mobilized the Germanic peoples (see page 98), and the withdrawal of garrisons to defend the Rhine frontier left the northern outposts in Roman Britain open to attack by the Picts.

In eastern Asia, the successors of the Hsiung-nu, the Kök Türük (Blue or Celestial Turks) ruled during the 7th and 8th centuries over an empire which reached from Manchuria to the arid steppes west of the Syr Darya, and they appear to have driven other Turks westwards, particularly the tribes of the Ogur, who appear in Byzantine history. They also expelled the Juan-juan of Mongolia, once their rulers, through northern Iran and into the Russian steppes. There the Juan-juan amalgamated with other nomad Turkish or Hunnish tribes to reappear in Hungary as the Avars who threatened Constantinople and western Europe from the 5th to the end of the 8th century, when their empire was destroyed by Charlemagne.

The reasons for these movements among the peoples of central Asia are obscure but they marked the end of one period in world history and set the stage for another.

1/The collapse of the classical world (below) All the great civilizations of the classical world came under pressure from pastoral peoples who formed vast confederacies of mobile cavalry armies. The most dramatic fall was that of the Roman Empire in the west, but China north of the Yangtze was equally devastated, Persia was weakened and Gupta rule in India destroyed.

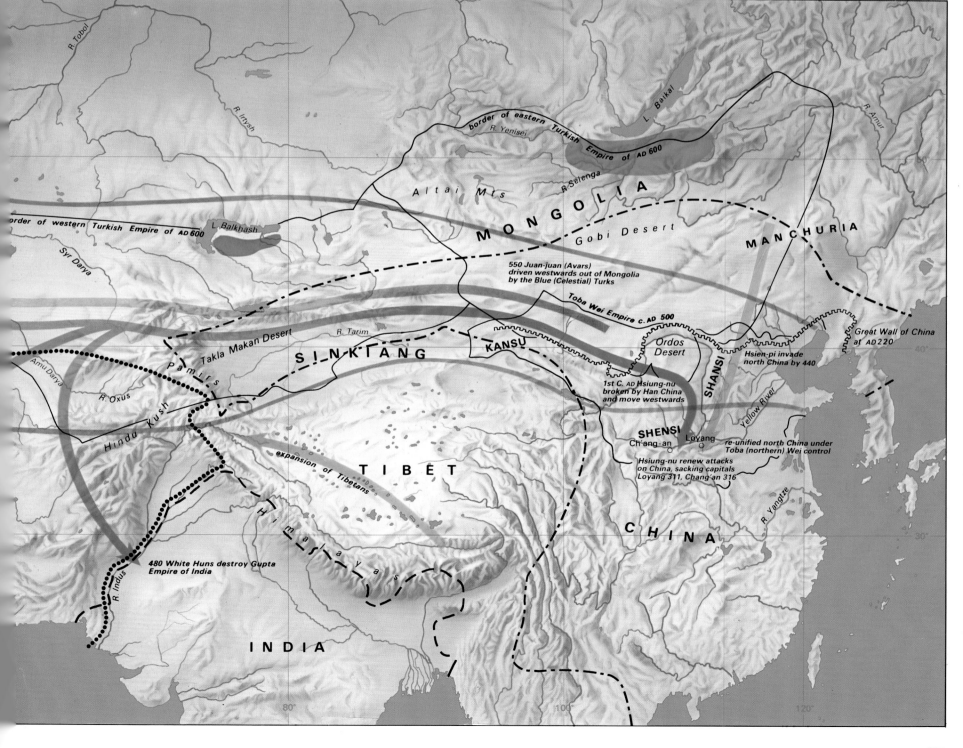

THE period around AD 500 saw upheaval throughout the Eurasian world, when nomads from the steppes of Asia descended upon all the existing centres of civilization. Although the gains of the classical period never entirely disappeared, contacts dwindled between China and the West, between north Africa and Italy, and between Byzantium and the lands of western Europe. For the next few centuries each region was thrown back upon its own resources and forced to fend for itself.

In Western Europe this period is traditionally known as 'the Middle Ages'. This description may be appropriate for European history but it makes little sense in the wider perspective of world history. Here, two outstanding events dominated the scene: first, the rise and expansion of Islam; second, the emergence of the Mongol Empire in the 13th century. At the same time, important developments transformed regions hitherto isolated from the mainstream. The appearance of the Maya, Aztec and Inca civilizations in America, the creation of the empires of Srivijaya and Majapahit in Southeast Asia, and the rise of the empires of Ghana, Mali and Songhai in Africa, all attested to a new vitality and to the expansion of the area of civilized life.

Europe, by comparison, remained backward. Even here, however, it was a formative age, when primitive societies were welded into feudal monarchies. But the process of consolidation was slow, interrupted by barbarian incursions and by economic setbacks. Not until the second half of the 15th century did Europe begin to draw level with the other world civilizations, laying the foundations for overseas expansion with a series of pathbreaking voyages of exploration. Even then, however, for another century it remained overshadowed by the expanding power of the Ottoman Turks.

If a relatively large space in this section is devoted to Europe, it is not so much because of its importance at the time, but rather because this period saw the beginnings of developments in European society which enabled it to advance to centre stage in the following centuries.

4 The world of

The Dome of the Rock, Jerusalem

divided regions

Germanic and Slavonic invasions of Europe

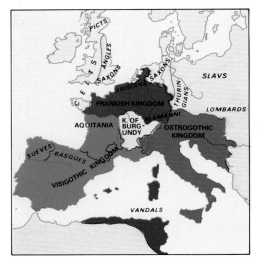

2/**The Germanic kingdom** (*above*) at the accession of Theodoric the Ostrogothic king (493-526), showing the situation before the Byzantine reconquest and the Frankish advance.

THE barbarian invasions of the 4th to 6th centuries and the settlement of Germanic and (later) Slav peoples on the soil of the Roman Empire are the traditional starting point of European history. Roman civilization had been Mediterranean rather than European. With the Arab conquest of Palestine and North Africa (see page 104) and the descent of the Slavs into the Balkans, severing the links between Byzantium and the west, the Mediterranean frame-work of the Roman world was fractured, and the seat of power and influence shifted to the lands north of the Alps. Europe, cut off from the other civilizations of the Near East, began to go its own way under peoples who now moved from the periphery to the centre of the stage.

The Germanic peoples had moved before the Christian era, from Scandinavia to the shores of the Baltic around the mouth of the Vistula. Simultaneously the 'West Germans' were expanding into territory inhabited by the Celts east of the Rhine (see page 84). The 'East Germans' moved south c.AD 150 to the Carpathians and the lands north of the Black Sea. Pressure on both groups on the Roman frontiers began early; but it was the irruption of the Huns from Asia (see page 94) that threw the whole Germanic world into turmoil. First affected (c.370) were the Ostrogoths in the Crimea and the Ukraine. Thrown back across the Dniester, they drove the Visigoths across the Danubian frontier of the Roman Empire into lower Moesia (Bulgaria), where they received permission to settle. Their defeat of the emperor Valens at the battle of Adrianople (378) destroyed Roman powers of resistance and opened the way for other barbarians fleeing westward. The Visigoths themselves first sought to settle in Greece (369-99), then moved on to Italy, when they astonished the civilized world by sacking Rome in 410, but quickly passed over into Aquitaine (418), where they founded the kingdom of Toulouse. They were followed in 406 by Alans, Vandals and Sueves from the Theiss valley and Silesia, who broke across the frozen Rhine frontier near Mainz and ravaged Gaul for three years, until in 409 they crossed the Pyrenees and entered Spain. Behind them came the Burgundians, who founded a kingdom around the city of Worms, but were settled in Savoy in 443, the Huns having destroyed Worms in 437. In Spain the Sueves founded a kingdom in Galicia, which survived from 411 to 585, when it was absorbed into the Visigothic kingdom. The Vandals and Alans crossed from Spain to Africa in 429, and in 442 the imperial government recognized their king, Gaiseric, as an independent ruler. The Vandal kingdom survived until 533, when North Africa was reconquered by Justinian's general, Belisarius. Meanwhile, the defeat of the Huns at the climactic battle of the Catalaunian Fields

near Troyes (451), the death of their leader Attila (453), and their retreat to the Russian plains, released the remaining Germanic tribes on the Danube, and the Ostrogoths moved south into Greece and subsequently into Italy, where they were in control by 493. North of the Alps, Franks and Alemans were infiltrating across the Rhine; while from about 440 Angles and Saxons were occupying the eastern and southern coastal areas of Britain, from which the Roman garrisons had withdrawn some 30 years earlier.

This great movement of peoples did not destroy the fabric of Roman civilization. The Romans had long made a practice of settling barbarian 'confederate troops' within the empire. Salian Franks had been quartered in Belgium since c.360. The Visigoths and others only sought settlement on a larger scale. Except for the Vandals, the Germanic leaders accepted a position within the Roman hierarchy of government. Their object was not to destroy but to share in the benefits of Roman civilization. Their greatest leaders, notably Theoderic the Ostrogoth (493-526), saw it as their task to reconcile Romans and Germans. Nevertheless, except in the Frankish kingdom (see page 106), they did not succeed. The early Germanic kingdoms were inherently unstable. There were many reasons for this, not the least being hostility between the Arian ruling class and their Catholic subjects. But the main weakness was the fact that the warbands (averaging perhaps 80,000, of whom only some 20,000 were warriors), cut off from their homeland, were too small to exercise permanent control. The exceptions were the Franks and Anglo-Saxons, both able to draw on reinforcements from Germany. Otherwise, once Justinian embarked on reconquest in 533, their instability was soon apparent, although the Ostrogoths resisted fiercely from 536 to 554.

Justinian's reconquest was the turning point. Engaged simultaneously in war with Persia, the imperial government was over-extended and unable to restore effective control. The long Gothic wars irretrievably ruined Italy. In 568, only a few years after the capitulation of the last Gothic strongholds, the defenceless country was occupied – apart from the south, which remained Byzantine – by the Lombards, another Germanic people which had moved down from the Elbe to modern Hungary. The destruction of Gothic power, removing the main obstacle to Frankish expansion, also ensured the predominance of the Frankish kingdom in the west. East of the Adriatic the Slav peoples, who had expanded from their home in the region of the Pripet marshes as the Germanic tribes moved west, crossed the Danube c.600 and descended into Greece. Just as the Germans had been propelled by the onslaught of the Huns, so it was the onslaught (beginning c.560) of another Asiatic people, the Avars, which drove the Slavs (and the Lombards) into Roman territory. Apart from Salonika, protected by its walls, Macedonia was permanently occupied by the Slavs; Salona, the Roman capital of Dalmatia, fell to them c.640. Only a few coastal cities of southern Greece and the Peloponnese remained Greek. In the eastern Balkans the Bulgars, an Asiatic people akin to the Huns, ruled over a largely Slav population and were recognized by the imperial government (681). The early history of the peoples of southeast Europe is obscure; but by the end of the 8th century independent Croatian, Serbian and Bulgarian kingdoms were taking shape. Meanwhile Europe had been permanently changed. The three centuries after the battle of Adrianople were a time of desperate confusion and material setbacks; but they were also a period when a new civilization, 'Romano-Germanic' rather then Roman in character, was taking shape. Eventually it was to find its centre in the empire of Charlemagne (see page 106).

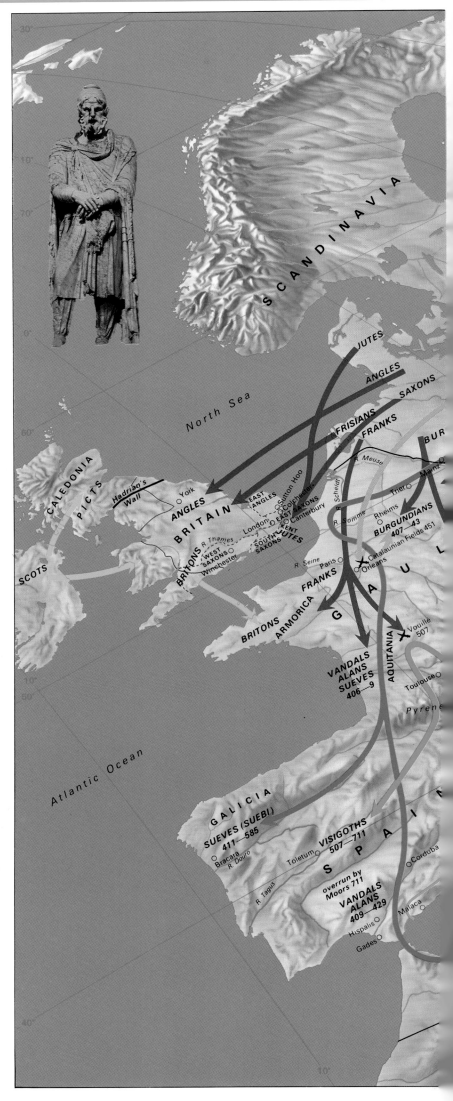

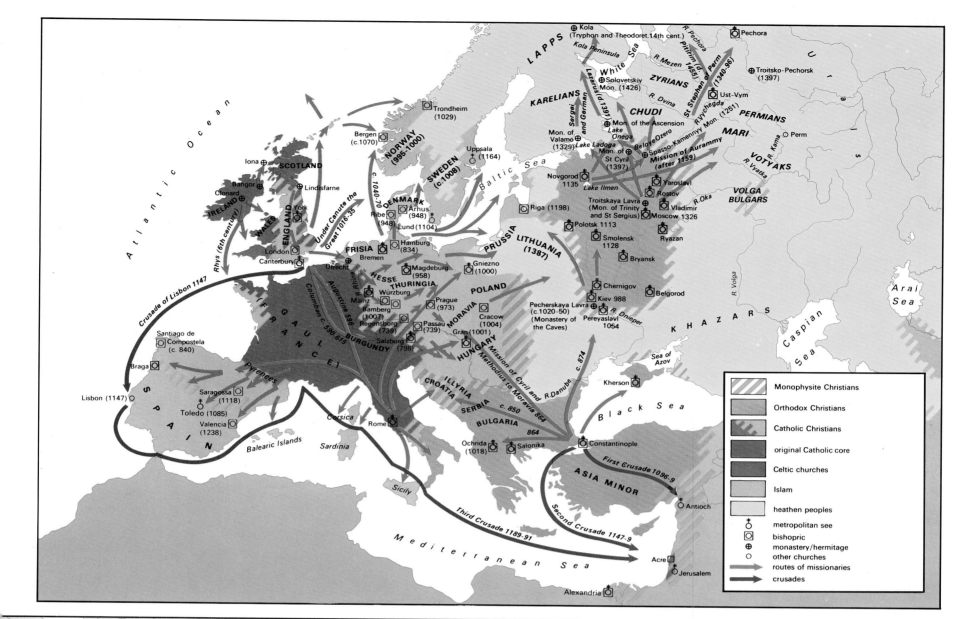

Map 1 legend:

- ⬚ Monophysite Christians
- ▨ Orthodox Christians
- ▤ Catholic Christians
- ▨ original Catholic core
- ▨ Celtic churches
- ▨ Islam
- ▨ heathen peoples
- ✝ metropolitan see
- ◉ bishopric
- ⊕ monastery/hermitage
- ○ other churches
- → routes of missionaries
- → crusades

Place names and labels (Map 1):

LAPPS · Kola (Tryphon and Theodoret, 14th cent.) · Pechora · Pechora
Kola Peninsula · R. Mezen · R. Pechora · Pitirim (d. 1455) · Troitsko-Pechorsk (1397)
White Sea · Solovetskiy Món. (1426) · ZYRIANS · St Stephen of Perm (1340-96) · PERMIANS · Perm
KARELIANS · R. Dvina · Ust-Vym (1251) · R. Vychegda
Trondheim (1029) · Sergei and German (1353) · Mon. of Valamo (1329) · Lake Ladoga · Mon. of the Ascension · R. Kama
Bergen (c.1070) · NORWAY (995-1000) · Lake Onega · Belo Ozero · Spasso Kamennyy Mon. · MARI
SWEDEN (c.1008) · Mon. of St Cyril (1397) · Mission of Auramny (after 1159) · VOTYAKS · R. Vyatka
Uppsala (1164) · Novgorod 1135 · Lake Ilmen · Yaroslavl · Rostov · R. Oka · VOLGA BULGARS
Iona · SCOTLAND · Baltic Sea · Riga (1198) · Troitskaya Lavra (Mon. of Trinity and St Sergius) · Vladimir · Moscow 1326
Bangor · Lindisfarne · Polotsk 1113 · Smolensk 1128 · Ryazan · R. Volga
Clonard · IRELAND · York · DENMARK · Ribe (948) · Arhus (948) · PRUSSIA · Bryansk
WALES · ENGLAND · Under Canute the Great 1016-35 · Lund (1104) · LITHUANIA (1387) · Chernigov · Belgorod
London · Canterbury · FRISIA · Hamburg (834) · Kiev 988 · Aral Sea
Utrecht · Bremen · Gniezno (1000) · Pecherskaya Lavra (c.1020-50) (Monastery of the Caves) · KHAZARS · Caspian Sea
Rhys (6th century) · HESSE · Magdeburg (958) · Pereyaslavl 1054 · R. Dnieper
Mainz · THURINGIA · Würzburg (973) · POLAND · Prague (973)
Columban c. 590-615 · Bamberg (1007) · Passau (739) · MORAVIA · Cracow (1004)
Augustine 596 · Regensburg (739) · Salzburg (798) · Gran (1001) · HUNGARY
Crusade of Lisbon 1147 · Santiago de Compostela (c. 840) · (GAUL) FRANCE · BURGUNDY · Mission of Cyril and Methodius to Moravia 864 · c. 874 · Sea of Azov
Braga · Pyrenees · ILLYRIA · CROATIA · Kherson
Lisbon (1147) · SPAIN · Saragossa (1118) · Corsica · Rome · SERBIA · c. 850 · R. Danube · Black Sea
Toledo (1085) · Valencia (1238) · Balearic Islands · Sardinia · BULGARIA · 864
Ochrida (1018) · Salonika · Constantinople
Sicily · ASIA MINOR · First Crusade 1096-9
Mediterranean Sea · Second Crusade 1147-9 · Antioch
Third Crusade 1189-91 · Acre · Jerusalem
Alexandria

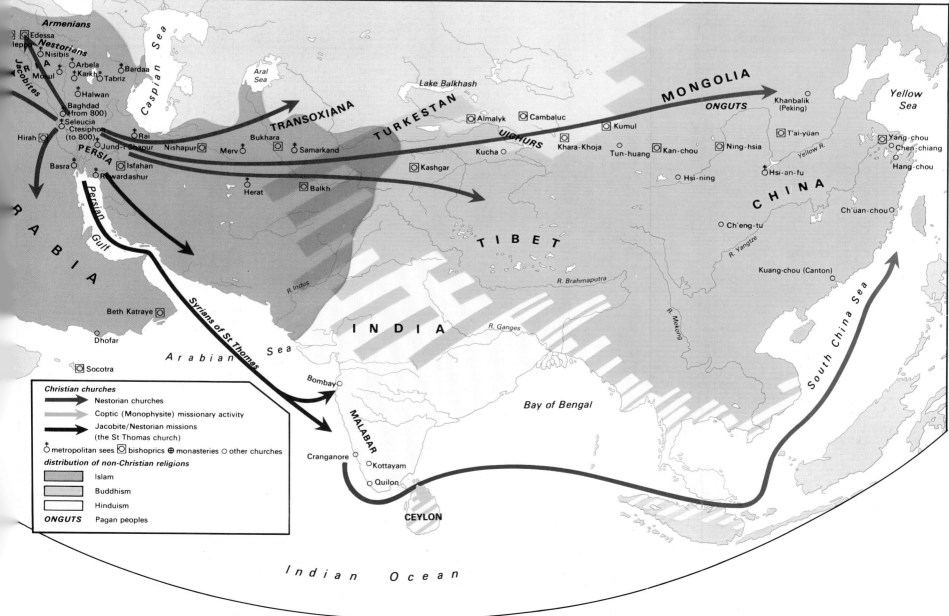

Map 2 legend:

Christian churches
- → Nestorian churches
- → Coptic (Monophysite) missionary activity
- → Jacobite/Nestorian missions (the St Thomas church)
- ✳ metropolitan sees · ◉ bishoprics · ⊕ monasteries · ○ other churches

distribution of non-Christian religions
- ▨ Islam
- ▨ Buddhism
- ▢ Hinduism

ONGUTS Pagan peoples

Place names and labels (Map 2):

Armenians · Edessa · Aleppo · Nestorians · Nisibis · Jacobites · Mosul · Arbela · Karkh · Bardaa · Tabriz · Caspian Sea
Halwan · Baghdad (from 800) · Seleucia-Ctesiphon (to 800) · Rai · Aral Sea · Lake Balkhash · MONGOLIA · ONGUTS · Khanbalik (Peking) · Yellow Sea
Hirah · PERSIA · Jund-i-Shapur · Nishapur · Merv · TRANSOXIANA · TURKESTAN · Almalyk · Cambaluc · Kumul · Yellow R.
Basra · Isfahan · Bukhara · Samarkand · UIGHURS · Kucha · Khara-Khoja · Kan-chou · Ning-hsia · T'ai-yüan · Yang-chou
Rewardashur · Herat · Balkh · Kashgar · Tun-huang · Hsi-ning · Hsi-an-fu · Chen-chiang
Persian Gulf · Hsi-ning · CHINA · Hang-chou
ARABIA · Syrians of St Thomas · TIBET · Ch'eng-tu · R. Yangtze
Beth Katraye · R. Indus · INDIA · R. Ganges · R. Brahmaputra · R. Mekong · Kuang-chou (Canton)
Dhofar · Arabian Sea · Bombay · Bay of Bengal · South China Sea
Socotra · MALABAR · Cranganore · Kottayam · Quilon · CEYLON
Indian Ocean

The Jewish diaspora AD 70 to 1800

F**OR** over 2000 years the history of the Jews has combined external dispersion with internal cohesion. From the time of the destruction of the First Temple and the Babylonian Exile (586 BC), Judaea was absorbed by a succession of powerful empires: Babylon, Persia, the Hellenistic Ptolomies and Seleucids, Rome, Byzantium and finally the Islamic empires, culminating in that of the Ottoman Turks. However, the decisive dispersion of the Jewish people took place under Rome. After a period of growing religious, political and nationalistic tension, the first Jewish Revolt (AD 66–73) briefly broke Roman power in Palestine but soon crumbled. The Roman legions captured Jerusalem in AD 70 and destroyed the Temple; three years later the last stronghold of the zealots, Masada, beside the Dead Sea, fell after a long siege. However the second major Jewish Revolt in AD 132–135, led by Bar Kokhba, did far greater damage to the fabric of Jewish life in Palestine.

Although the revolts and their vigorous suppression, as well as Hadrian's measures to de-Judaize Jerusalem after AD 135, caused rapid deterioration in the position of the Jews in Judaea, elsewhere in the Roman world their legal and economic status and the viability of their communities remained unaffected. This stimulated a constant flow of migration from Palestine where the Jews ceased to be a majority in the 2nd century, and also from the other major Jewish centres in the east, Mesopotamia and Alexandria, to the western and northern shores of the Mediterranean.

The resilience of Judaism after two great defeats at the hands of Rome can be chiefly ascribed to the evolution of the Jewish religion following the destruction of the First Temple in 586 BC, and the gradual emergence of a decentralized faith based on the synagogue and communal prayer. On the one hand, with the synagogue there emerged the new local leaders of Jewish life, the men of learning, or rabbis. On the other, Jewish religious and civil law was gradually codified, first with the *Mishnah*, compiled around AD 200, and then, both in Palestine and Babylonia, with the commentary and discussions systematized as the *Talmud*. Both remain today the basis of Jewish religious and communal life.

Consequently, widely scattered but internally cohesive Jewish communities developed all over the west and north of the Roman empire. A Jewish community appeared in Rome by the 2nd century BC and was firmly established by the 1st century AD. Other communities arose elsewhere in Italy, that of Naples being one of the most important. The earliest evidence of Jews in Spain dates from the 3rd century while, further north, a Jewish community existed in Cologne at least from the early 4th century.

The shift in the centre of gravity in the Jewish world from east to west was a long, slow process culminating during the High Middle Ages as Jews from the Near East and North Africa settled and multiplied in southern Italy, Spain, France, and southern Germany. The golden age of the Jews in Spain began under the first Umayyad caliph of Córdoba, Abd al-Rahman III (912–961), and continued under Christian rule until the devastating anti-Jewish riots of 1391. Jewish life is assumed to have continued uninterrupted along the banks of the Rhine after the fall of the Roman Empire in the west, although no trace of such settlement has been found, and the Jewish community there had clearly assumed significant proportions by the 10th century. Despite the massacre which attended the First Crusade in the 1090s, the 11th and 12th centuries constituted the golden age of medieval German Jewry.

Ultimately, however, the growing presence of the Jews in the west generated a sustained reaction. A variety of factors caused a decline in the economic role of the Jewish communities and, after the Third and Fourth Lateran Councils of 1179 and 1215, the Latin Church both intensified and broadened its traditional hostility to Judaism and Jewish life.

A series of expulsions from western Europe began in England in 1290, though English Jewry was then very small. A more serious blow, with major consequences, was the expulsion from France a century later in 1394. At the same time, recurrent massacres and persecutions in Germany led to a steady migration of German Jews (*Ashkenazim*) from the Rhine valley towards the east, thus laying the foundations of modern central and eastern European Jewry. Prague first became an important Jewish centre in the 11th century and received many immigrants from the western and southern parts of Germany in the 13th. By the 14th century, Vienna had become the leading Jewish centre in the German lands. Jewish communities arose in Cracow, Kalisz, and other towns in western and southern Poland in the 13th century and, further east, at Lvov, Brest-Litovsk, and Grodno, in the 14th. The period of heaviest immigration from the west into Poland-Lithuania came in the late 15th and 16th centuries.

These developments, combined with the 1391 pogroms in Spain, followed by the creation of the Inquisition to tackle crypto-Judaism in Spain, and the general expulsion of the Jews from Spain (1492), Portugal (1497), and Provence (1498), finally tilted the balance back from west to east.

The last stage of this process, in the late 15th and early 16th centuries, was a series of expulsions from German Imperial Free Cities, such as Nuremberg (1499), Ulm (1499) and Regensburg (1519), and Lutheran principalities such as electoral Saxony (1537) and Brunswick and Hanover (1553). The bulk of the exiles from Germany settled in Poland–Lithuania. Most of the expelled Spanish and Portuguese Jews (*Sephardim*) settled in the Ottoman empire and North Africa, though in the late 16th century a trickle migrated to Rome, Venice, Livorno, and other parts of northern Italy.

The Polish, Lithuanian and Ottoman Jewish communities thrived in the 16th and early 17th centuries. Subsequently, conditions deteriorated both in Poland and Turkey but, after the disruption of the Thirty Years' War (1618–48), Jews from east-central and eastern Europe, as well as the Near East, were once again able to settle, with the permission of both trading cities and princely governments, in at least some parts of western Europe.

These new communities in the west arose chiefly in northern Italy, Germany, Holland and, from the 1650s, also in England and the English colonies in the New World (first those in the Caribbean and later also in North America). Small groups also migrated from Germany to Denmark and Sweden. In the central European cities of Vienna, Berlin, Hamburg and Budapest, Jewish communities grew considerably during the 18th and 19th centuries, mainly as a result of immigration from countries further east, especially Poland.

During the 17th and 18th centuries, some of the largest and wealthiest, as well as culturally the most sophisticated communities in the Jewish world existed in Amsterdam, Hamburg, Frankfurt, Livorno, Venice and Rome, followed soon by Berlin and London. Amsterdam, which had substantial Sephardic and Ashkenazic communities, undoubtedly ranked as the leading Jewish centre in the West, especially in the areas of commerce, finance, printing and book production. The Sephardic population of Amsterdam reached a ceiling of about 3000 (1.5 per cent of the city's population) in the late 17th century. The Ashkenazic population overtook the Sephardic in size before 1700 and was over five times as large by the late 18th century when the two Jewish communities amounted to around 10 per cent (20,000) of the city's population.

Nevertheless until the 1940s by far the greater segment of world Jewry continued to live in eastern Europe, with the largest concentrations in eastern Poland and what ultimately became the western fringes of the Soviet empire. Only very small Jewish populations existed in Hungary and Romania in 1700, although in both countries numbers increased rapidly in the 18th and 19th centuries through immigration from Poland and the Czech lands. Under the Tsars, the bulk of the Jewish population in the Russian empire was confined to western areas (the 'Pale of Settlement'), formerly parts of Poland, Lithuania and the Ukraine, Jews being forbidden by law from settling in Russia proper without special permission.

The demographic preponderance of eastern Europe in world Jewry ended with the Nazi occupation and the Holocaust: Jewish life in Poland, Czechoslovakia and the old Pale of Settlement was largely destroyed. Substantial Jewish populations survived only in the interior of the Soviet Union, Romania and Hungary.

2/Judaea in the 1st centuries BC and AD *(right)* In 140 BC an independent Jewish state emerged under Simon the Hasmonean, a brother of Judah Maccabee. It became a Roman protectorate in 63 BC. Subsequently, the Idumaean Herod I (37-4 BC), husband of the Hasmonean princess Miriamme, divided it in his will among his three sons, Archelaus, Herod Antipas and Philip. Judaea was governed by Roman procurators from AD 6 to 66, with a brief interlude when the whole of Herod's kingdom was reunited under his grandson, Agrippa I (AD 41-4). After Agrippa's death, the rule of the procurators provoked an unsuccessful revolt by Jewish nationalists in AD 66-73, who made their last stand at the fortress of Masada.

	area of Roman procuratorial rule in Judaea
	Agrippa II's kingdom, AD 61
	area of major revolt at start of AD 66
	area of revolt at end of AD 69
→	Roman armies

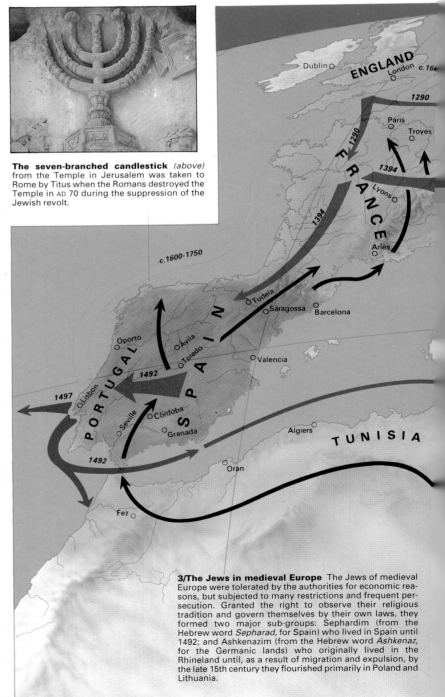

The seven-branched candlestick *(above)* from the Temple in Jerusalem was taken to Rome by Titus when the Romans destroyed the Temple in AD 70 during the suppression of the Jewish revolt.

3/The Jews in medieval Europe The Jews of medieval Europe were tolerated by the authorities for economic reasons, but subjected to many restrictions and frequent persecution. Granted the right to observe their religious tradition and govern themselves by their own laws, they formed two major sub-groups: Sephardim (from the Hebrew word *Sepharad*, for Spain) who lived in Spain until 1492; and Ashkenazim (from the Hebrew word *Ashkenaz*, for the Germanic lands) who originally lived in the Rhineland until, as a result of migration and expulsion, by the late 15th century they flourished primarily in Poland and Lithuania.

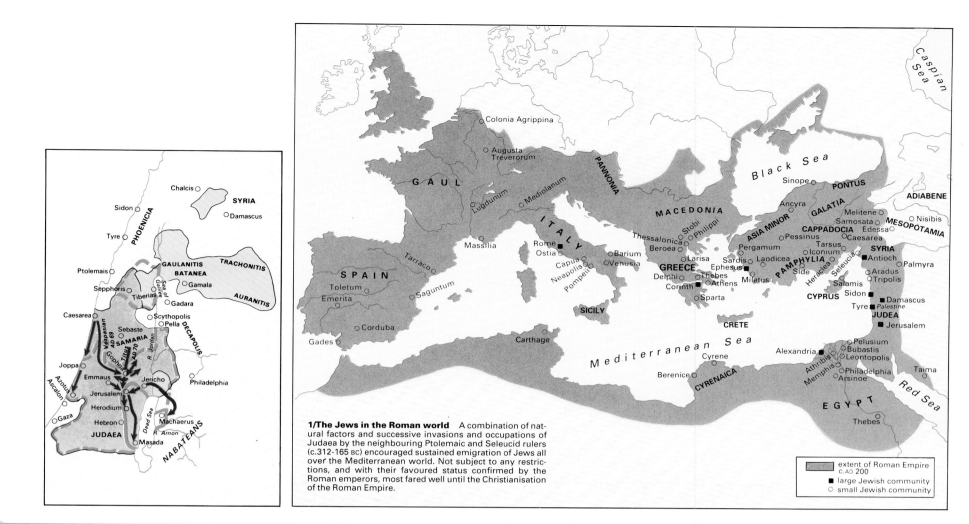

1/The Jews in the Roman world A combination of natural factors and successive invasions and occupations of Judaea by the neighbouring Ptolemaic and Seleucid rulers (c.312-165 BC) encouraged sustained emigration of Jews all over the Mediterranean world. Not subject to any restrictions, and with their favoured status confirmed by the Roman emperors, most fared well until the Christianisation of the Roman Empire.

extent of Roman Empire
c. AD 200
■ large Jewish community
○ small Jewish community

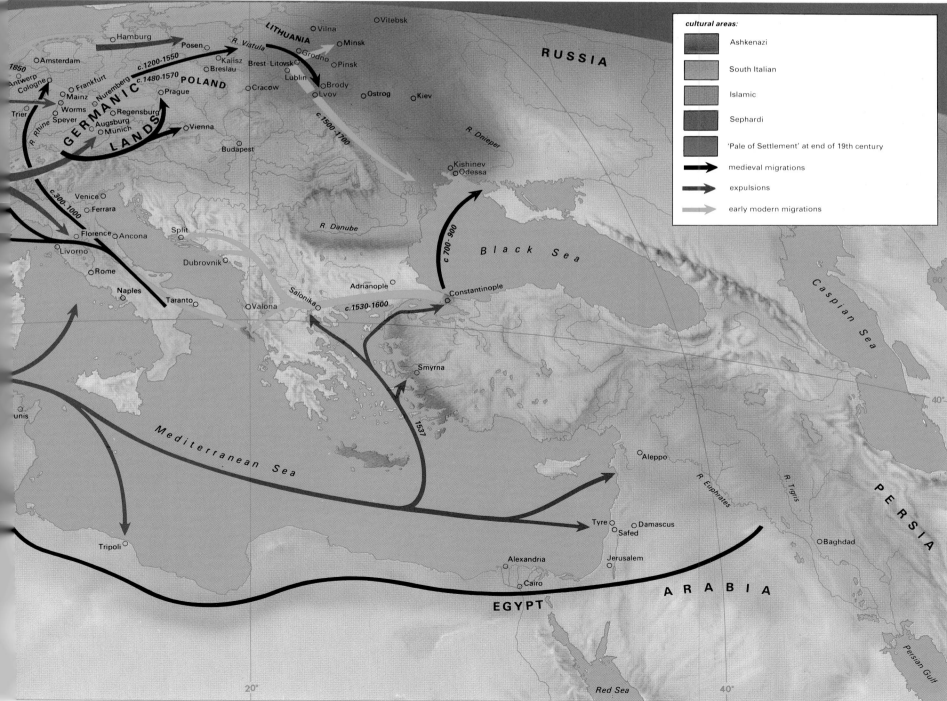

cultural areas:

Ashkenazi

South Italian

Islamic

Sephardi

'Pale of Settlement' at end of 19th century

→ medieval migrations

→ expulsions

→ early modern migrations

The spread of Islam from AD 632

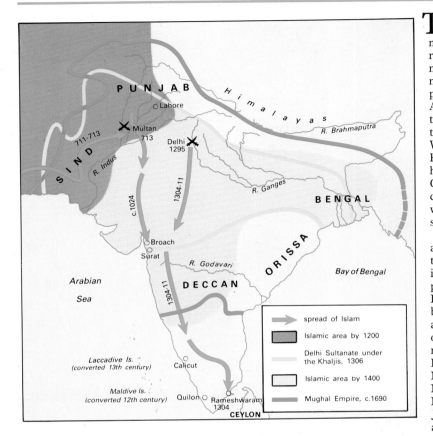

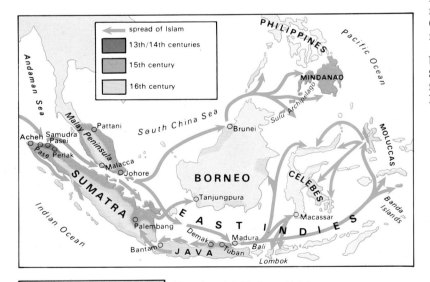

2 and 3/India and Indonesia The spread of Islam in India (above) was partly the result of expansion by successive waves of Muslim conquerors, partly the consequence of conversion by missionaries and traders. Indonesia and the Malay peninsula (below) were converted to Islam by a gradual process of proselytization, beginning in all probability with Muslim traders from Gujerat in India, who had acquired a permanent foothold at Perlak on the northern tip of Sumatra by 1290. From there they spread to Malaya (c.1400), where the new religion quickly took hold, and also to Java and the Moluccas (c.1430-90). By the end of the 16th century most of the islands in the archipelago had accepted Islam, as had the Sulu Archipelago and Mindanao in the Philippines. These gains were maintained despite successive waves of Spanish, Portuguese and Dutch colonization and conquest.

The minaret (left) from which the muezzin chants the call to prayer, is attached to all mosques and is a distinctive feature of Islamic religious architecture. Originally square, the minaret later assumed the slender, lofty, circular form familiar in India and Constantinople. The minaret of the famous mosque of Ahmad ibn Tulun in Cairo, built in 879 and renovated in 1267, combines both forms.

THE rise and expansion of Islam was one of the most significant and far-reaching events in modern history, and its impact continues to reverberate in our own times. Islam means 'submission to the will of God'; God's message to mankind has been expressed through a series of prophets, culminating in Mohammed, the Apostle and Prophet of God. Muslims believe that God has spoken through Mohammed, and that the Koran, which means recitation, is the Word of God. Mohammed is the Seal of the Prophets, and no others will come after him, but he is not of course divine, for divinity belongs to God alone. Mohammed's message to his fellow citizens in the western Arabian city of Mecca was that they should cease to worship idols, and submit instead to the will of Allah.

Mohammed was born in Mecca about AD 570, and was orphaned in early childhood. At that time Mecca was the principal commercial centre in western Arabia, and was also an important pilgrimage centre because of its shrine, the Ka'ba. He received his first revelations in 610, but as his followers grew in number, Mohammed aroused the hostility of the merchant aristocracy of Mecca, who feared that acceptance of his message would pose a threat to the shrine. Hostility developed into persecution, and in 622 Mohammed and his followers withdrew to Medina, some 280 miles (450 km) northeast of Mecca. This 'migration', hijra in Arabic, on 16 July 622, marks the beginning of the Islamic era and thus of the Muslim calendar.

In Medina, Mohammed organized the Muslims into a community, and consolidated his base with the assistance of his Medinan hosts. The Meccans made every effort to dislodge him, but after a series of defeats eventually accepted his message. Mohammed returned to Mecca in triumph in 630 and cast out the idols from the Ka'ba, transforming it into the focal point of the new religion of Islam. When Mohammed died in 632, his authority extended over the Hejaz and most of central and southern Arabia.

Over the next 100 years, the Arab armies brought the religion of Islam as far west as Spain, and as far east as northern India and the frontier of China (thanks to their victory at Talas River in 751). This expansion owed much to the enthusiasm and religious conviction of the conquerors, but it was also facilitated by the war-weariness of the empires of Persia and Byzantium. The first of Mohammed's successors, the caliph Abu Bakr (632–34) completed the conquest of Arabia and entered southern Palestine. His successor Omar (634–44) advanced to Damascus, and victory over the Byzantines at the Yarmuk river in 636 encouraged the Muslims to advance east into Mesopotamia and northwest into Asia Minor. By 643 Persia had been overrun, and the last Persian emperor, Yazdigird, was killed in 651 after his troops had made a final stand at Merv. The conquest of Herat and Balkh (651) and the fall of Kabul (664) opened the way to India; Sind, in northeast India, fell to the Muslims in 712.

Simultaneously, Arab forces pushed west into Egypt, occupying Alexandria in 643, and advancing across North Africa into Cyrenaica. Further progress was held up by Berber resistance, but the advance was resumed after the construction of the fortress city of Kairouan in 670. After the subjection of the Maghreb, Arab forces crossed the Straits of Gibraltar in 711 and conquered Spain. There were further advances into southern France, but Arab troops met with defeat at Poitiers in 732, and in 759 they withdrew south of the Pyrenees. In the late 7th and early 8th centuries attacks were launched against Constantinople, but the Byzantines succeeded in preventing the Arabs from capturing the city and in fact retained control of much of Asia Minor until the 11th century.

Initially, Islam did not particularly encourage, far less insist upon, conversion. The Koran enjoins Muslims to respect the 'people of the book', that is, members of the other monotheis-

1/The spread of Islam outside the Arabian peninsula began almost immediately after the Prophet's death in 632. By 711, Arab armies were simultaneously attacking Sind in northeast India and preparing for the conquest of the Iberian peninsula. In general, the conquests in the east exceeded those in the west in both size and importance. By 750, when the Abbasids ousted the Umayyad dynasty, the empire to which they succeeded was the major civilization west of China.

tic religions with written scriptures, and the existence of substantial Christian (and until comparatively recently, Jewish) communities throughout the Muslim world is ample evidence that this injunction was heeded. However, under the Abbasid dynasty (750–1258), large-scale conversion became common. This was partly because under the Abbasids, when the capital of the empire shifted from Syria to Mesopotamia, power passed from the conquering Arab minority to the non-Arab majority, and non-Arabs were no longer discriminated against as they had been under the Umayyads (661–750).

Although the Muslim world soon lost its first political unity when the Abbasid caliphate began to disintegrate and rival caliphates were established in Cairo and Córdoba in the mid-10th century, it retained a considerable degree of cultural unity, largely through the Arabic language. In many ways, this unity overrode the sectarian divides which had already appeared in the first Islamic century, largely centring on the vexed question of the succession to the caliphate. With the seizure of temporal power by the Buyids in Baghdad in 945, the Abbasid caliphs were largely restricted to their religious functions. The Islamic world had split into local dynastic entities, whose acknowledgement of Abbasid suzerainty was often only nominal.

Although the Islamic empire declined as a theocratic entity, Islam itself continued to expand as a religious force (see maps 2 and 3). This expansion was partly the result of conquest, and partly – particularly in Southeast Asia and West Africa – the result of missionary activity by traders and preachers. The contemporary Islamic world (map 4) covers substantial parts of Asia and Africa, and the events of the 1970s and 1980s have shown that Islam has once more emerged as a decisive factor in world politics.

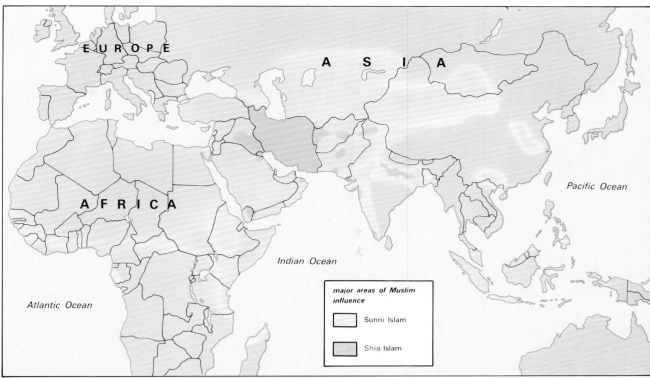

4/Islam today (*above*)   Islam, the most recent of the great world religions, numbers some 400 million adherents, about one-seventh of the total population of the globe. Most Muslims are distributed in a broad band from Morocco to Indonesia, and from northern central Asia to Tanzania. The states with the largest Muslim population are Indonesia (148 million, 90% of total population), Bangladesh (88 million, 80%), Nigeria (81 million, 47%), Pakistan (80 million, 83%), India (70 million, 11%) and Egypt (41 million, 92%). The map shows the relative preponderance of Sunni Muslims, the Shias being mainly found in Iran, Lebanon, southern Iraq, India and Pakistan, with Shias of another kind in Yemen.

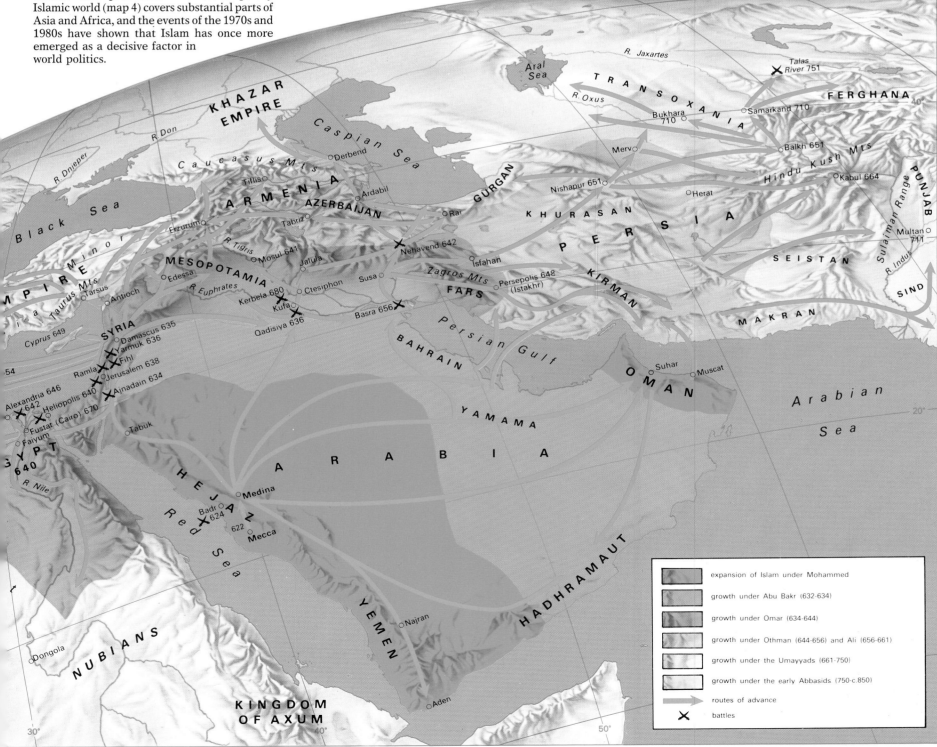

The rise of the Frankish Kingdom 482 to 814

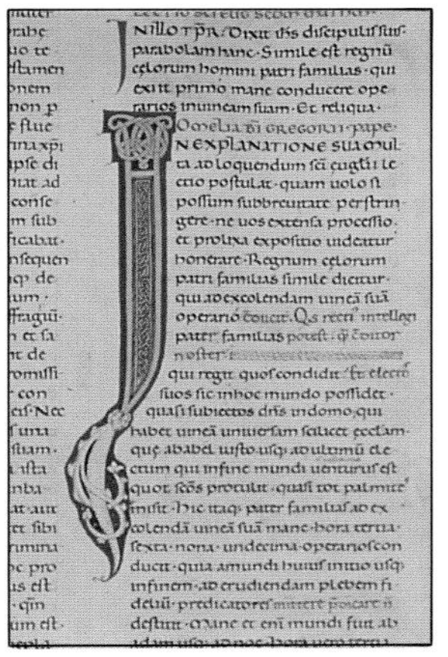

Carolingian script *(above)* A passage from an Italian book of sermons in the script developed in Francia to be easy to write and read. Used in almost all books written in areas under Frankish rule, it eventually provided the basis of modern type.

THE conquests of Clovis (d. 511) and his sons made the Franks the most powerful and important of all the barbarian successors of Rome, and created the basis for the Frankish hegemony that dominated western Europe for more than three centuries. The tomb of Clovis' father, Childeric, discovered in 1653, shows that he was buried with great, but not particularly barbarian, splendour in a Roman cemetery at Tournai, in the heart of the territory seized by the Franks in the 5th century. He was, however, not the only Frankish ruler, for the Franks who lived in the valleys of the Rhine, Mosel and Meuse had other chieftains or kings. Clovis not only destroyed the power of such rivals and so united the Franks under his rule, but also greatly extended his authority over the Thuringians and Alemans in the east and over the Visigoths in the west; while his sons and grandsons not only extended Frankish overlordship in the east as far as the middle Danube, but also conquered the Burgundians and drove the Ostrogoths from Provence.

This expansion was achieved more by conquest than by colonization; some Franks did settle in northern Gaul but most continued to live in the northeast in those areas where Germanic languages have persisted to this day (see map 2). Clovis ruled from Paris, but in Gaul itself there was little displacement of the native population, and the French language has developed from Latin with relatively few German words (e.g. *bleu*). The government largely remained in the hands of bishops and counts drawn from the Gallo-Roman aristocracy who, as a result of Clovis' conversion to Catholic Christianity, were ready to accept Frankish rule in preference to that of Burgundians and Visigoths, who had been converted earlier to the heretical Arian form of the religion.

However valuable Clovis and his successors found such Gallo-Roman support, their power ultimately depended on the Frankish army, and one important motive for the conquests was the need to win booty, land and revenues with which the loyalty of the warriors could be rewarded and maintained. By the middle of the 6th century the first period of expansion was over and Frankish kings now had to reward followers and endow the Church by granting away their own estates and revenues. In so doing, they diminished their resources, and in time their power passed to the many families that had benefitted from royal favour. But by the middle of the 7th century two families had emerged as particularly important and were the principal agents of the kings, holding office as mayors of the royal palace. One family came from Austrasia, the eastern, traditional Frankish lands, while the other was associated with Neustria, the new lands north of the Loire. The conflict between these rivals was ended at the battle of Tertry in 687 when the victor was the Austrasian, Pepin of Herstal. He consequently gained a dominant position in the Frankish kingdom which he retained until his death in 714, and which was quickly re-established by his son Charles Martel, 'the Hammer' (d. 741), who gave his name to the Carolingian family.

These men ruled while the Merovingians, so called because they traced their ancestry back to Clovis' grandfather, Meroveus, continued to reign as kings; but in 751 the situation was transformed when, with the sanction and support of the pope, Charles Martel's son Pepin the Short (d.768) made himself king and so established the new Carolingian dynasty. The Church continued to be a pillar of the monarchy, and Alcuin

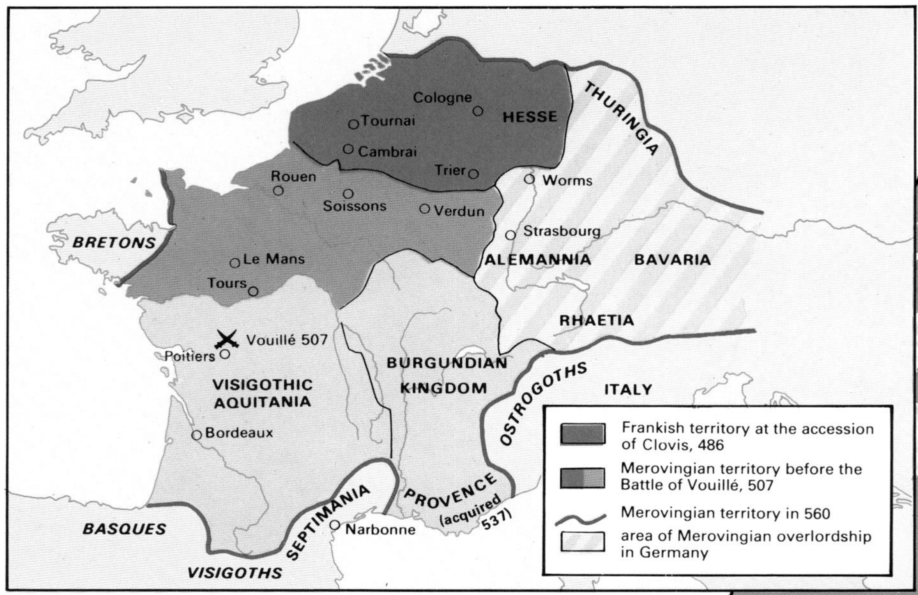
Cologne
Tournai
HESSE
THURINGIA
Cambrai
Trier
Worms
Rouen
Soissons
Verdun
Strasbourg
BRETONS
Le Mans
ALEMANNIA
BAVARIA
Tours
RHAETIA
Vouillé 507
Poitiers
BURGUNDIAN KINGDOM
OSTROGOTHS
ITALY
VISIGOTHIC AQUITANIA
Bordeaux
SEPTIMANIA
PROVENCE (acquired 537)
BASQUES
Narbonne
VISIGOTHS
Frankish territory at the accession of Clovis, 486
Merovingian territory before the Battle of Vouillé, 507
Merovingian territory in 560
area of Merovingian overlordship in Germany

1/Frankish expansion: the first phase *(above)* This map illustrates the remarkable speed with which the Franks under Clovis and his sons extended their kingdom from their homeland near the Rhine at the expense of Roman and barbarian rulers, notably Visigoths and Burgundians. By 540 they were masters of the greater part of Gaul and had extensive protectorates in the east.

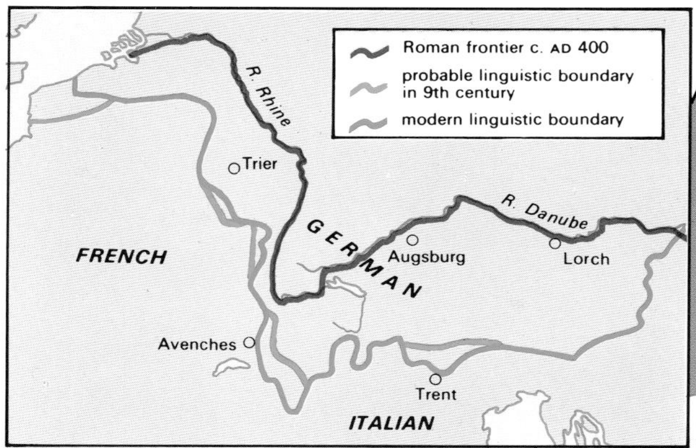
Roman frontier c. AD 400
probable linguistic boundary in 9th century
modern linguistic boundary
R. Rhine
Trier
R. Danube
GERMAN
Augsburg
Lorch
FRENCH
Avenches
Trent
ITALIAN

2/Linguistic frontiers *(above)* Those parts of the former Roman Empire in which German and related languages, such as Dutch and Flemish, are now spoken correspond very closely to the areas that were first conquered and settled by Germanic invaders. Beyond this zone Germanic conquest was not accompanied by such dense colonization and native speech, deriving from Latin, developed into the modern Romance languages. It also survived for a long time around some Roman cities, surrounded by a population which spoke the language of the invaders.

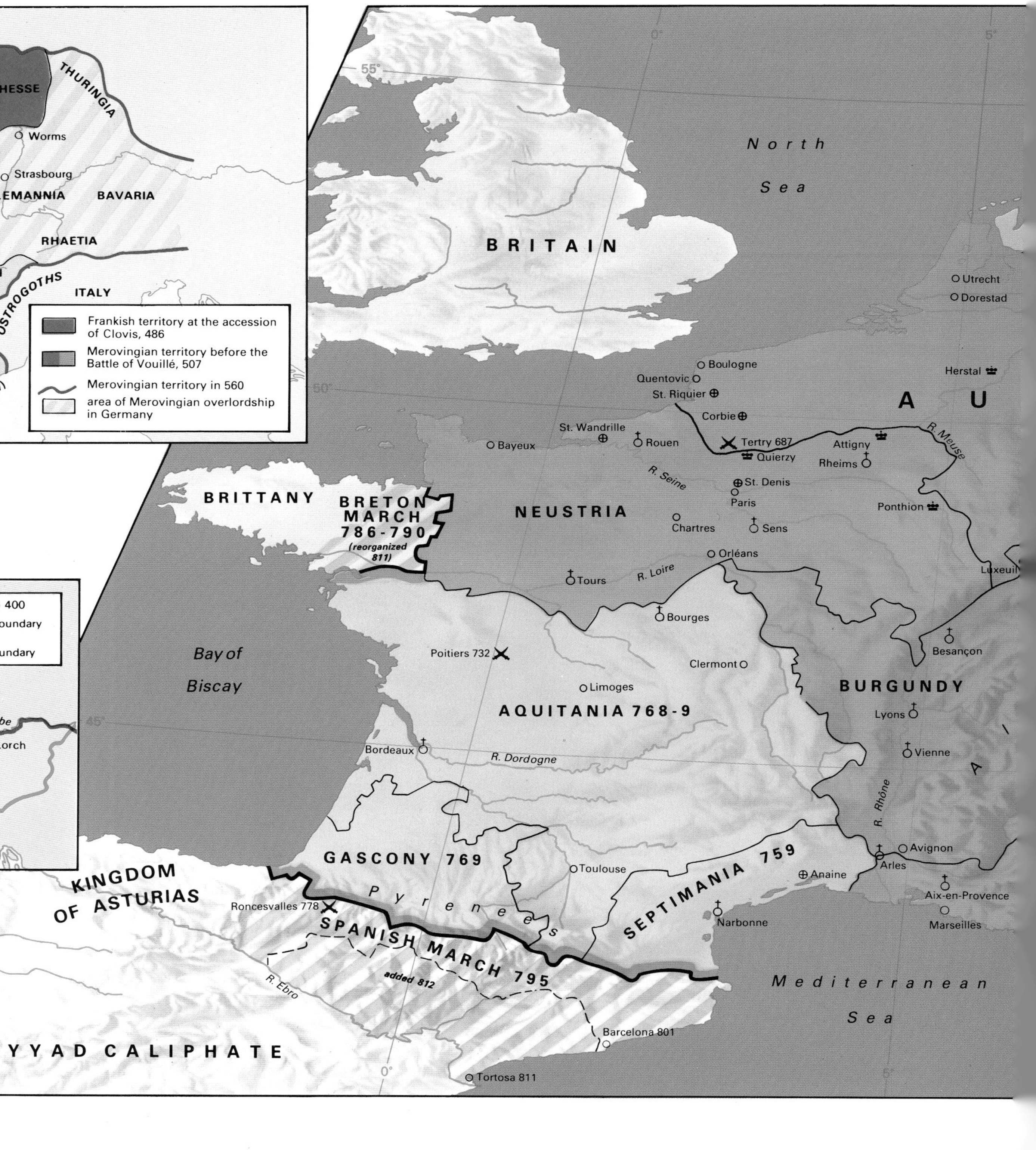
North Sea
BRITAIN
Utrecht
Dorestad
Boulogne
Quentovic
St. Riquier
Herstal
Corbie
A U
St. Wandrille
Bayeux
Rouen
Tertry 687
Quierzy
Attigny
Rheims
R. Meuse
R. Seine
BRITTANY
BRETON MARCH 786-790
(reorganized 811)
NEUSTRIA
St. Denis
Paris
Ponthion
Chartres
Sens
Orléans
Tours
R. Loire
Luxeuil
Bourges
Bay of Biscay
Poitiers 732
Clermont
Besançon
Limoges
BURGUNDY
AQUITANIA 768-9
Lyons
Bordeaux
R. Dordogne
Vienne
R. Rhône
GASCONY 769
Toulouse
Avignon
Arles
KINGDOM OF ASTURIAS
SEPTIMANIA 759
Aniane
Aix-en-Provence
Roncesvalles 778
Pyrenees
Narbonne
Marseilles
SPANISH MARCH 795
added 812
R. Ebro
Mediterranean Sea
Barcelona 801
UMAYYAD CALIPHATE
Tortosa 811

of York became a principal advisor to Pepin's son. Meanwhile, the new dynasty assumed the traditional responsibilities of Frankish rulers, leading expeditions and defending their territory against such old enemies as the Frisians and the Saxons, as well as combating the new threat posed by the Muslim conquerors of Visigothic Spain. Charles Martel's most famous victory was, in fact, the battle of Poitiers in 732 against Muslim raiders, a victory that was remembered as symbolizing the role of the Franks, and of the Carolingians in particular, as defenders of Christendom. That role was first assumed by Clovis and later found its most dramatic expression on Christmas Day 800 at Rome in the imperial coronation of Pepin's son, Charlemagne (Charles the Great), who by conquering and converting the Saxons, by taking over the Lombard kingdom and so liberating the papacy from a persistent threat, and by creating a march, or buffer zone, between the Frankish lands and Muslim Spain, had created a truly imperial and Christian hegemony.

The hegemony was, however, personal. In 806 Charlemagne planned to divide his empire among three sons, a scheme that was frustrated by the death, in his lifetime, of all but one of them, thus making it possible for the survivor, Louis the Pious (814–40) to inherit the whole empire. In providing for such a division Charlemagne was following the Frankish custom of partitioning the royal domain, a custom that had obliged him to share his inheritance for three years with his brother Carloman (see map 4b). This practice can be traced back to the death of Clovis, when his four sons partitioned

their inheritance. The divisions, which could be very complicated, did not mean the dismemberment of the kingdom, which could still be regarded as a unit and was occasionally united, but they did create many opportunities for internal conflict.

Under the Carolingians Frankish expansion was resumed, but it was unlike that of the Merovingians for it led to the displacement of many bishops and counts of Gallo-Roman descent by Franks and Austrasians. The first generations of these Frankish agents of royal government were in general loyal to Pepin and Charlemagne, but their descendants tended to identify with the particular interests of their own localities at the expense of the kingdom and, during the 9th and 10th centuries, as they were able to free themselves from the restraints of royal authority, some established principalities over which the kings could, for a time, claim little more than a theoretical superiority. Frankish hegemony in western Europe was thus disrupted by partition and fragmentation.

4a/Francia in 587 (above) The treaty of 587 was one of many agreements dividing the Frankish kingdom between the descendants of Clovis. Childebert's portion was in effect ruled by his mother, the Visigoth Brunhild, who dominated Frankish politics until she was executed in 613.

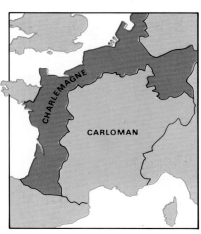

4b/Francia in 768 (above) The custom of partitioning the kingdom was continued by the Carolingians: on the death of Pepin the Short (768) his two sons divided their inheritance. The elder, Charlemagne, held most of the key area of Austrasia until Carloman died (771), when he inherited the whole.

The Chapel at Aachen (right) Charlemagne's vast authority in western Europe was reflected by the construction of a large and complex palace in Aachen which was thought by some contemporaries to be a 'second Rome'. It included this chapel, modelled on the 6th-century church of San Vitale in Ravenna which commemorates Justinian, another great foreign emperor who triumphed in Italy (see page 88).

3/The empire of Charlemagne (below) The Frankish Empire reached its greatest extent around the time of Charlemagne's coronation as Western Emperor in Rome. The Lombard kingdom of Italy had been seized in 774; large parts of Germany were added, in the face of prolonged and determined resistance, between 772 and 804; and a march, or boundary province, was created across the Pyrenees between 795 and 812.

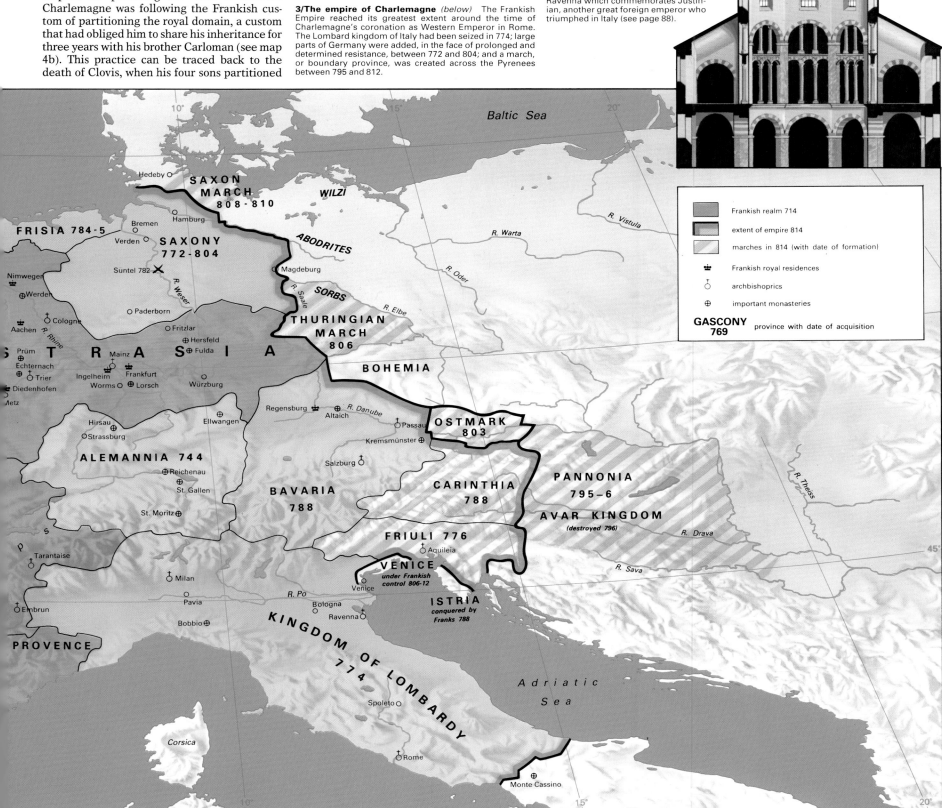

Frankish realm 714

extent of empire 814

marches in 814 (with date of formation)

✠ Frankish royal residences

☩ archbishoprics

✠ important monasteries

GASCONY 769 province with date of acquisition

The Eurasian world in 814

BY 814, the year of the death of the Frankish emperor, Charlemagne, Europe and Asia were recovering from the wave of barbarian invasions which, some four centuries earlier, had disrupted the civilizations of China, Rome and India and severed the trans-Eurasian ties of classical times (see page 94). It was, as events were to prove, a short-lived revival: during the following century all civilizations in Eurasia suffered setbacks, some severe. But the expansion of the area of settled, civilized life proved more than temporary. By 814 a series of powerful empires stretched in unbroken sequence from the Atlantic to the Pacific, and under their shelter new states with a high level of civilization took shape on their southern flank, among them the Srivijayan Empire of Sumatra and the Shailendra Empire of Java. In the far east the boundaries of T'ang China extended to the Tarim basin and the Pamirs: in the west the Franks had reunited the territories north of the Alps formerly part of the Roman Empire. But the decisive factor was the rapid expansion of Islam (see page 104) which carried the dominion of the caliphs to Bukhara and Samarkand by 710 and provided the essential link between Orient and Occident. After the Arab victory over China at Talas River in 751 – one of the decisive battles of history – the two powers, with contiguous frontiers, dominated central Asia. Further north, at the western end of the Eurasian steppe, was the empire of the Khazars, the most civilized state this region had seen since the collapse of Scythian power in the 3rd century BC. Converted to Judaism c.740, the Khazars ruled a vast territory extending west as far as Sambat (the future Kiev) and south to Kherson; and their capital Itil, a populous and highly civilized city, was one of the great commercial centres of the period. Only India, after the collapse of Harsha's short-lived empire (606–47), failed to reconstitute some sort of unity, and the Arabs, who had conquered Sind in 711–12, remained in possession.

More stable conditions were accompanied by a revival of trans-Eurasian relations. China under the T'ang dynasty was unusually open to foreign contacts, and the unification of the vast areas under Arab rule led, particularly after the succession of the Abbasids in 750, to a great expansion of trade. Diplomatic relations also became closer. The caliph, Harun al-Rashid (786–809), who probably sent embassies to Charlemagne in 797 and 801, also despatched envoys to conclude a treaty of alliance with the T'ang emperor in 798. By 758 there was a large establishment of Muslim merchants in Kanfu (Canton) and a century later we hear of Chinese in Baghdad; while in far-away England Offa of Mercia (757–96), who had fairly close diplomatic relations with Charlemagne, issued a gold coin copied from the dinar struck by the Caliph al-Mansur in 774. All this suggests active commerce from one end of the Eurasian heartland to the other. Chinese porcelain, in particular, was prized throughout the Middle East and quantities have been found in 9th-century sites as far afield as Tarsus and Cairo. The art of paper-making, learned from Chinese prisoners taken at Talas in 751, spread rapidly across the Islamic world, reaching Spain by 900; already under Harun al-Rashid the first paper mills were operating in Baghdad.

Although T'ang civilization had passed its peak after 755, the Chinese empire was still pre-eminent in 814. By almost any standard of comparison, China and Islam, even India and the countries of Indo-China, far surpassed Europe in the level of civilization. It is characteristic that, while Chia Tan in 801 was compiling a map of China drawn to a scale of 100 li (⅓ mile, 0.5 km) to an inch (2.5 cm) – a map which measured roughly 30 by 33 feet (9 by 10 m) and covered an area of 10,000 by 11,000 miles (16,000 by 17,700 km) – geographical knowledge in the West was so embedded in myth that Jerusalem was believed to be the centre of the world, and the Nile, Euphrates and Ganges were considered to have a common source in the Garden of Eden.

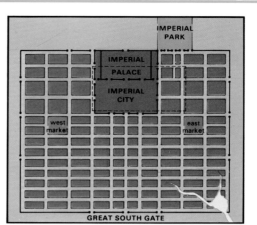

2/Ch'ang-an (left) Planned as a massive rectangle, 5.8 miles (9.4 km) east to west and 5.2 miles (8.4 km) north to south, with 11 great north-south avenues, the main avenue led from the imperial palace to the south gate. It was 500 feet (153 m) wide, intersecting 14 east-west thoroughfares, and dividing the city into 106 wards. Ch'ang-an probably had a million inhabitants within the walls and another million in the suburbs outside. Already by 722 it contained 91 Buddhist and 16 Taoist places of worship, 4 Zoroastrian temples, and 2 Nestorian Christian churches.

3/Constantinople (left) Constantinople never grew beyond the walls of Theodosius II (c.447) and within them there was much vacant space. Historians have tended to exaggerate its population, which at the beginning of the 9th century was probably less than a quarter of a million. Nevertheless it was, with the possible exception of Córdoba, the greatest city of Europe, far excelling any in the Christian west, including Rome, which at this time was in a state of decline.

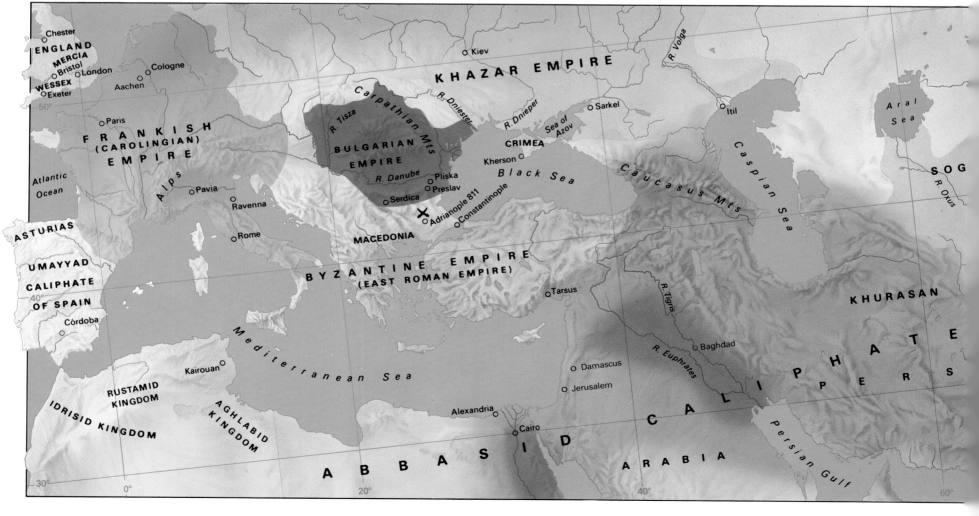

108

4/Baghdad (right) Baghdad was founded in 762 by the caliph al-Mansur, who employed 100,000 men to build it. The circular city, with a diameter of 1.64 miles (2.64 km), surrounded by a rampart with 360 towers, was almost immediately too small for the growing population. By the time of Harun al-Rashid it had expanded south to the suburb of al-Karh, home of commerce and artisans, and east to the residential quarters near the Caliph's new palace (Dar al-Khilafa). By 814 it was probably the world's largest city.

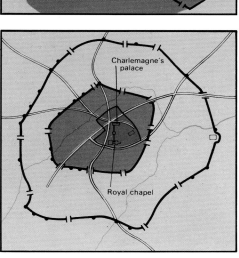

5/Córdoba (right) Córdoba, housing perhaps half a million Muslims, Christians and Jews, was already the leading city west of Constantinople by the late 8th century. Outside the original walled city, planned as a rectangle resting on the river front, with ramparts running about 2.5 miles (4 km), was a series of suburbs. According to a contemporary Arab writer, Córdoba contained 471 mosques, 213,077 houses for workers and traders, 60,000 residences for officials and courtiers, and 80,455 shops. It was also the seat of a university of international repute.

6/Aachen (right) Almost nothing is known of Charlemagne's residence before he built his palace and chapel there in the 790s. It was certainly in no sense a city, though the palace attracted a few Christian and Jewish traders, and some officials had built themselves houses by 828. The massive Romanesque church, 53 yards (48.6 m) long and 38 yards (35 m) wide, is impressive, but with a population probably of no more than two or three thousand, until it was destroyed by the Vikings in the second half of the 9th century. The modern city of Aachen descends from the new foundation of the 12th century.

Cities in comparison (left) This diagram gives some idea of the comparative size of the Eurasian capitals c.814. Clearly Charlemagne's 'royal city' does not compare with the great capitals of the Chinese and Arab empires, or even with Constantinople.

Architecturally, also, no contemporary European building approached in majesty the magnificent temples erected during this period at Prambanan in Java.

The Carolingian Empire, though hardly as large as the area controlled by the Khazars, was impressive in size; but, like the Bulgarian Empire flanking the Byzantine Empire in the north, it was little more than a conquest of a barbarian warband, which fell apart, only 30 years after Charlemagne's death, when its belligerent energies flagged. Such empires could be dangerous militarily, as was seen in 811 when the Bulgarians under Krum (802–14) inflicted a crushing defeat on the Byzantine emperor Nicephorus. But, unlike China and Rome and the Caliphate, they lacked the resources and organization – particularly the financial and bureaucratic organization – to give them stability. The East Roman Empire, hemmed in by Arabs and Bulgars, was weak and ineffective between 780 and 820. After 751, when the Lombards conquered Ravenna and drove out the emperor's viceroy (the Exarch), its authority in Italy was only nominal, making it possible for Charlemagne to usurp the imperial title in 800. But the sound administration inherited from the Heraclian and Isaurian emperors enabled Byzantium not only to survive but to mount a remarkable revival under Basil I (866–86) and Leo VI (886–912). In the West, by contrast, this was the period when feudalism, spreading from northern France, became endemic. Charlemagne had attempted to check the power of the aristocracy by making the counts into removable officials and sending out royal agents (*missi dominici*) to supervise their activities. But the system was too rudimentary to work; within a few years of Charlemagne's death, the relationship of lord and vassal displaced that of ruler and subject as the bond of political society, and royal authority went into eclipse.

The contrast between the civilizations of Eurasia at this period is best illustrated in their capital cities. Characteristically, the Frankish Empire, with its backward agricultural economy, had none. Rome, which Charlemagne never revisited after 800, was in full decline, and there is no sign that he ever thought of reviving it. It is possible that he had a vision of creating a fixed capital at Aachen, where he built himself a palace and a large and impressive chapel (see page 106) modelled upon San Vitale at Ravenna, the last capital of the Roman Empire in

the west. But if so, little came of it. Carolingian writers described Aachen grandiloquently as a 'royal city' (*urbs regalis*), but it is unlikely to have had more than a few thousand inhabitants and did not compare in any way with Constantinople, the capital of the (East) Roman Empire, or with Córdoba, the capital of Umayyad Spain, still less with Ch'ang-an, capital of T'ang China. Even after the foundation of the Abbasid capital, Baghdad, in 762 Ch'ang-an remained the outstanding city of Eurasia, so impressive that the Yamato rulers of Japan used it as a model for their capitals at Nara (710) and Kyoto (794). In the West no city equalled Córdoba, though its period of greatest renown was the 10th century (912–61). But the most astonishing phenomenon was the stupendous growth of Baghdad, which had spilled out by the death of Harun al-Rashid from the original circular city, Madinat as-Salam ('the City of Peace'), and by 814 covered an area of approximately 6.2 by 5.6 miles (10 by 9 km), the equivalent of central Paris. The West had a long way to go to catch up.

The temple of Shiva (above) The great 9th-century temple of Shiva at Prambanan in Java shows both the extension of Hindu influence and the remarkable artistic and architectural achievement of Indonesian civilization at this period. Only the great mosques of Damascus, Kairouan and Córdoba compare in scale and magnificence.

1/Eurasia in 814 The expansion of Islam and the stabilizing influence it exerted in central Asia did much to restore the contacts between the eastern and western halves of the Eurasian heartland which had been disrupted by barbarian invasions in the 4th and 5th centuries. But the west was still on the periphery and its role in the recovery was limited.

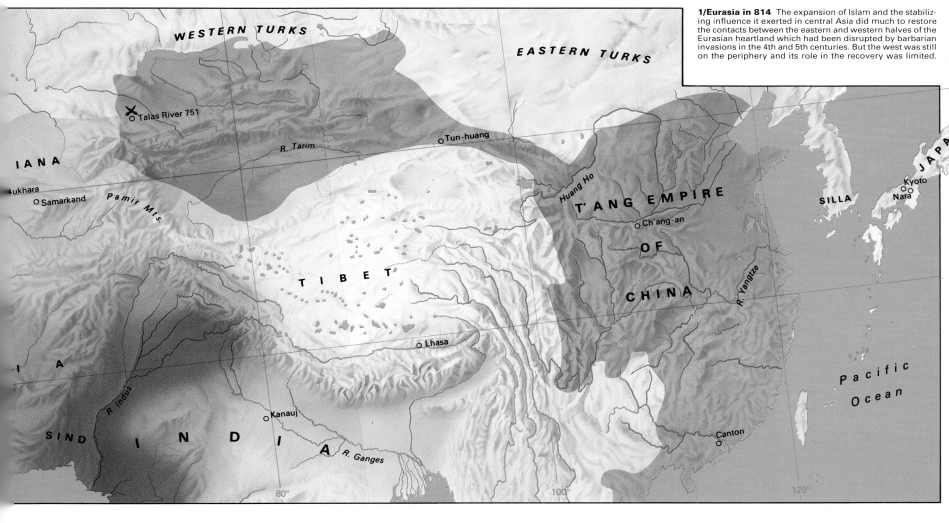

The 9th and 10th century invasions of Europe: Saracens, Magyars, Vikings

2/Scandinavian colonies in Britain and France *(above)* The first Viking colonists were Norwegians; from their new homes they raided the coasts of Western Europe. The Danes, who had tended to raid the rich lowlands of England and Francia, astonished the English in 876 by sharing out some of the conquered land and beginning to farm it, leaving a permanent linguistic mark on eastern and northern areas.

THE relatively effective rule of the Carolingians in western Europe (see page 106) and of the Mercians in England gave some assurance of security from internal attacks to both religious communities and merchants, and by the 8th century abbeys and markets were not fortified and Roman defences were not kept in repair. The accumulations of wealth in such places did, however, offer tempting bait to external raiders, men who accepted neither the religious sanctions that generally protected the holy places of the Christian West nor the authority of Christian kings, and in the 9th and 10th centuries western Europe suffered attacks from three separate groups of such strangers: Saracens, Magyars and Vikings.

The Saracen raids began in the 8th century from Islamic Spain and Africa, and after the occupation of Sicily, completed by 827, Saracen pirates established bases on the coast of southern Italy, and later in southern Gaul, from which they were able to threaten large areas of southern Europe. Corsica and Sardinia were frequently attacked and many monasteries and towns in Italy (including Rome itself) and in Gaul were pillaged, while merchants and pilgrims were robbed or forced to pay large ransoms for their release from captivity. The main credit for driving the pirates from Italy was due to the forces of the Byzantine Empire.

The Magyars posed a different kind of threat. They were horsemen who moved into the Hungarian Plain in the last years of the 9th century and almost immediately began to plunder the neighbouring areas, first northern Italy, then Germany and, on their longest raids, central and southern France. Their advantages of speed and surprise made opposition difficult, and in open country their horsemanship was markedly superior to that of their German or Italian opponents. However, in mountainous country and at river crossings, especially when returning home laden with booty, they were more vulnerable and German rulers had some successes against them. The threat was finally ended by the victory of Otto I at Lechfeld near Augsburg in 955, after which the Magyar leaders were executed

and the assimilation of the Magyars into western Christendom began.

The Vikings also had the advantage of surprise when they descended on the coasts and rivers of western Europe but, unlike the Magyars, they could be colonists as well as raiders. Once the Norwegians had discovered that there were islands in the North Atlantic with an environment very similar to that of their homeland, many were prepared to look for a better life overseas. The Danes also settled abroad, no doubt partly because there were better opportunities for plundering and extorting treasure in western Europe than in Scandinavia. Some Norwegian and Danish leaders of expeditions belonged to extended royal families who, having failed to make themselves kings, hoped to gain both wealth and reputation in the West.

The earliest Viking raids occurred towards the end of the 8th century – the best known, though probably not the first, was on the Northumbrian monastery of Lindisfarne in 793. In the following century several Norwegian bases were established in Ireland, the most famous being Dublin, founded by 841, and from such places warrior chiefs led expeditions to plunder not only the monasteries and other centres in Ireland, but also those in Britain and further afield. The Danish attacks were contained by the Franks from 810 onwards, but the raid on the market of Dorestad in 834 was the first of a series of regular attacks on that place. By the middle of the century bands of Danes were making their way by boat and on foot to attack churches and towns in many parts of Britain and the Frankish Empire. After c.850 they moved on horseback over greater distances. To facilitate these raids they established bases, some of which eventually became centres of permanent Scandinavian settlement, such as the Five Boroughs of the English Midlands. In these colonies the Vikings lost their advantages of mobility and surprise, and were vulnerable to pressures that eventually led them to accept both the overlordship of French and English kings and conversion to Christianity.

While these western enterprises were developing, Swedes were crossing the Baltic to visit markets, notably Bolgar on the middle Volga, in which Muslims were eager to acquire the furs and slaves that the Swedes, and others, could supply from the forests of northern Russia. Swedish leaders who made themselves masters of such places as Kiev and Novgorod were eventually slavicized, but maintained dynastic links with Scandinavia. The rulers of Kiev came into contact with Byzantium but its influence was religious and cultural rather than economic, and the main markets for the produce of the Kiev region continued to be the Islamic east rather than the Byzantine south.

The sudden extension of Scandinavian activity overseas coincided with the growing demand for goods that could only be obtained from the north: walrus tusks were at that time the main source of ivory in Europe, and furs from the arctic regions of Scandinavia and Russia were greatly prized. On the eve of the Viking period there was a growing commerce in coastal markets called *wics*. The greatest of these was the Wijk at Dorestad but there were many others,

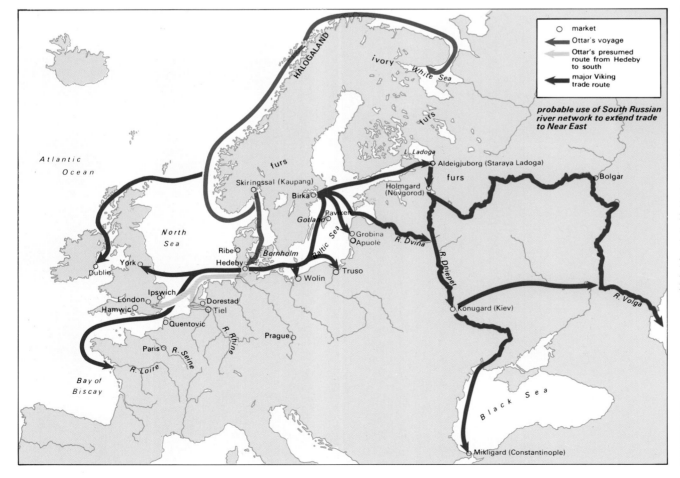

3/Viking trade *(left)* Scandinavia and the lands east of the Baltic were important in the luxury trade of the Dark Ages as the only source of furs and ivory and a good source of slaves. In response to the demand for these goods, first in Western Europe and later in the Muslim east, Scandinavians such as Ottar ventured far afield in search of new supplies.

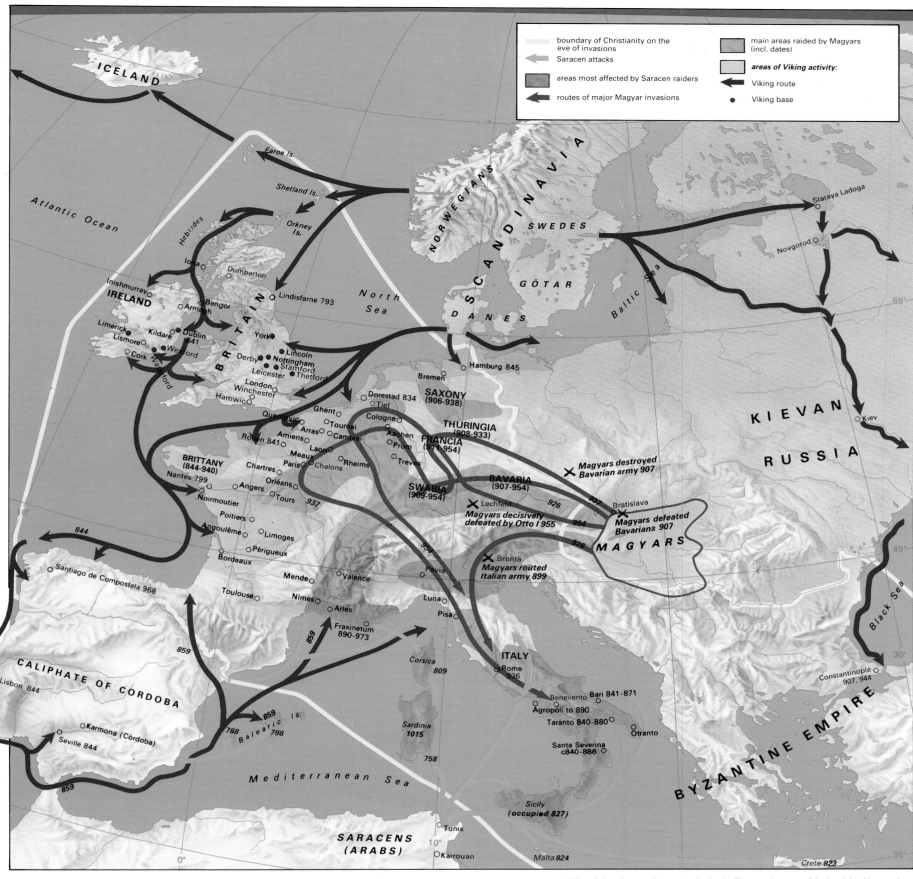

Map labels (clockwise/regional):

ICELAND

Atlantic Ocean

Faroe Is.

Shetland Is.

Orkney Is.

NORWEGIANS

SCANDINAVIA

SWEDES

GÖTAR

DANES

Baltic Sea

Staraya Ladoga

Novgorod

KIEVAN RUSSIA

Kiev

Hebrides

Iona

Dumbarton

Inishmurray

IRELAND

Bangor

Armagh

BRITAIN

Lindisfarne 793

North Sea

Hamburg 845

Bremen

Limerick

Kildare

Dublin 841

Lismore

Cork

Wexford

Waterford

York

Lincoln

Derby

Nottingham

Stanford

Leicester

Thetford

London

Winchester

Hamwic

SAXONY (906–938)

THURINGIA (908–933)

Ghent

Dorestad 834

Tiel

Cologne

Quentovic

Tournai

Aachen

FRANCIA (911–954)

Arras

Amiens

Cambrai

Prüm

Treves

Rouen 841

Meaux

Laon

Rheims

Magyars destroyed Bavarian army 907

BRITTANY (844–940)

Chartres

Paris

Chalons

BAVARIA (907–954)

926

Bratislava

Nantes 799

Angers

Orléans

SWABIA (909–954)

937

Magyars defeated Bavarians 907

Noirmoutier

Tours

937

Lechfeld

954

Poitiers

Magyars decisively defeated by Otto I 955

926

844

Angoulême

Limoges

Périgueux

M A G Y A R S

Santiago de Compostela 968

Bordeaux

Mende

Valence

Brenta

Magyars routed Italian army 899

Pavia

Toulouse

Nimes

Arles

Luna

Pisa

Black Sea

CALIPHATE OF CORDOBA

Fraxinetum 890–973

859

859

ITALY

Rome 936

Lisbon 844

Corsica 809

Benevento

Bari 841–871

Constantinople 907, 944

Karmona (Córdoba)

788

Balearic Is.

798

Agropoli to 890

Seville 844

Taranto 840–880

Otranto

859

Sardinia 1015

Santa Severina c.840–886

BYZANTINE EMPIRE

758

Mediterranean Sea

Sicily (occupied 827)

Tunis

SARACENS (ARABS)

Kairouan

Malta 824

Crete 823

Legend:

boundary of Christianity on the eve of invasions

Saracen attacks

areas most affected by Saracen raiders

routes of major Magyar invasions

main areas raided by Magyars (incl. dates)

areas of Viking activity:

Viking route

Viking base

including Quentovic, near Boulogne, and Hamwic, later to develop into Southampton. Scandinavians were encouraged to search even further afield for fresh supplies of skins, furs and tusks and a contemporary account by a 9th-century Norwegian, Ottar, narrates the voyage he made from his home in northern Norway into the White Sea in search of walrus.

In England the kings of Wessex, particularly Edward the Elder (899–924) and Athelstan (924–39) fought back, while in Gaul the Frankish rulers sometimes had to leave defence to the local magnates. But the result in both areas was the fragmentation of public authority and the strengthening of the local power of military chiefs: in England freemen commended themselves to lords for protection; in Gaul peasant freemen lost status to knights who formed a new 'order' by about 1050. In Germany power devolved into the hands of dukes and margraves who guarded the frontiers. From the beginning of the 10th century, thanks to the destructive energies of the Saracens, Magyars and Vikings, western Europe became an intricate interlacing of counties, communities, principalities and lordships, and remained so for 500 years.

1/The invasions (above) No part of the Christian West was immune from external attack in the 9th and 10th centuries. From their base in the Hungarian Plain the Magyars traversed vast distances, but as they moved fast the disruption they caused was short-lived. Saracens and Vikings established bases in the west and were consequently a more persistent threat; the Saracens were eventually expelled, but the Norwegian and Danish invaders were in time assimilated, as were the Swedes, who had gone east in search of wealth among the Slavs and Finns.

4/The Atlantic settlements (below) The settlement of Iceland by Norwegians began in about 870 and was completed in two generations. Later emigrants travelling in ships such as that illustrated below found limited opportunities there, but after the discovery of Greenland in the last years of the 10th century, some went on to create new settlements which survived for some five centuries. The Vikings later reached Newfoundland, but only temporary settlements have been found there and further south. The location of the 'Vinland' of the sagas is disputed.

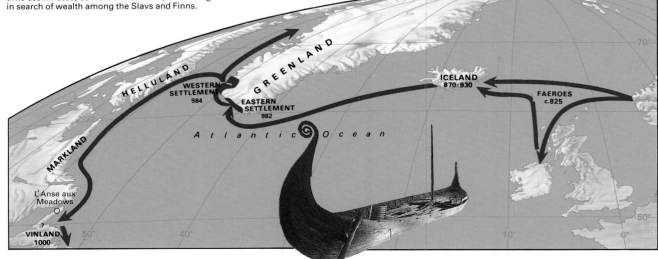

HELLULAND

GREENLAND

WESTERN SETTLEMENT 984

EASTERN SETTLEMENT 982

ICELAND 870–930

FAEROES c.825

MARKLAND

Atlantic Ocean

L'Anse aux Meadows

VINLAND 1000

The Byzantine Empire from Heraclius to the Fourth Crusade: 610 to 1204

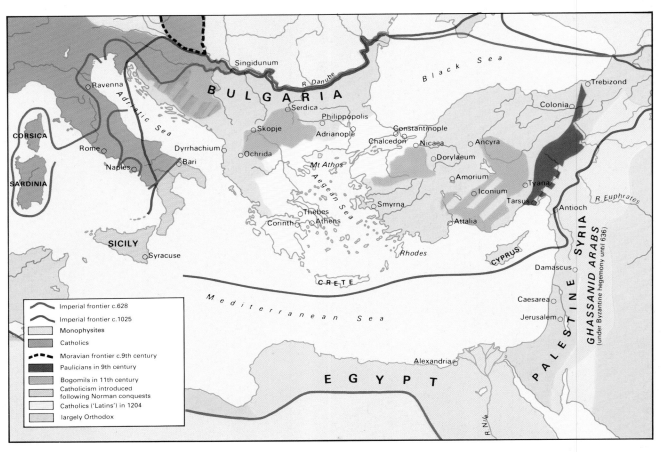

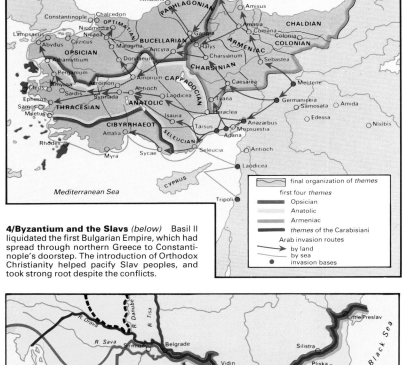

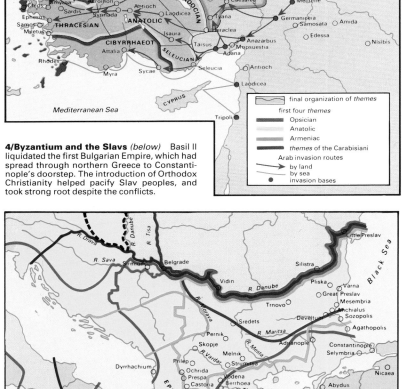

IN MANY ways the reign of Heraclius (610–41) marked the end of the East Roman Empire and the true beginnings of that distinctive, Greek-speaking, Christian, culturally heterogeneous form of civilization known as Byzantine. Although Heraclius ended the struggle with Persia, so long Rome's most formidable rival, with a crushing victory at Nineveh in 628, before his death the southern and eastern frontiers of the empire came under attack as the forces of Islam (see page 104) burst out of Arabia and seized Palestine, Syria and the ruins of Persia before moving into North Africa. For the next two centuries, increasingly isolated from the West, Byzantium was forced to mobilize its whole society for the struggle against Islam.

Constantinople withstood two long Arab sieges, in 674–8 and again in 717–8. But conflicts were not confined to the Arabs. About 680, the Turkic Bulgars flooded into the land now known as Bulgaria. By the 8th century they too constituted a serious threat, with armed outposts less than 60 miles (97 km) from Constantinople itself. Equally seriously, the Empire suffered from grave internal religious dissension. Starting with Leo III, the emperor who forced the Arabs to abandon the second siege of Constantinople, successive rulers imposed a stringent ban on Christian images. Iconoclasm produced a large crop of martyrs and exiles, and lasted, with only one break, from 726 to 843.

Not long after iconoclasm was reversed, under a fresh and vigorous Macedonian dynasty of emperors, Byzantium embarked on a new era of aggressive expansion. Its dominions, which in 610 still stretched from Gibraltar to the Euphrates, had shrunk dramatically. In the west, toeholds remained only in southern Italy, Sicily and along the Dalmatian coast; while Greece, though reconquest had already begun, was still largely in the hands of barbarian Slavs. In the embattled and devastated wastes of Asia Minor the frontier ran roughly from Trebizond to

2/The Conflict of Doctrines (above) Monophysite/Nestorian disputes over the nature of Christ ended with Arab conquests. Paulicians and Bogomils (9th-10th centuries) preached varieties of Manicheism.

3/The 'themes' and Arab invasions (left) The themes were administrative districts in which peasants were granted farms in exchange for service in the local army. They prevented Arab settlement, although they could not stop raids.

4/Byzantium and the Slavs (below) Basil II liquidated the first Bulgarian Empire, which had spread through northern Greece to Constantinople's doorstep. The introduction of Orthodox Christianity helped pacify Slav peoples, and took strong root despite the conflicts.

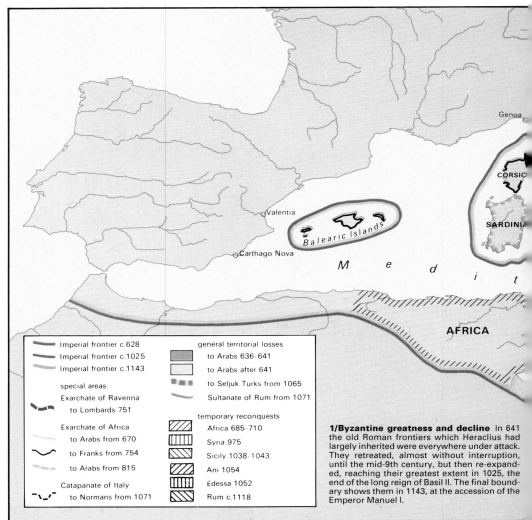

1/Byzantine greatness and decline In 641 the old Roman frontiers which Heraclius had largely inherited were everywhere under attack. They retreated, almost without interruption, until the mid-9th century, but then re-expanded, reaching their greatest extent in 1025, the end of the long reign of Basil II. The final boundary shows them in 1143, at the accession of the Emperor Manuel I.

Tarsus; and apart from Constantinople the great Roman cities of the past – Antioch, Alexandria, Beirut, Caesarea, Gaza – lay under Arab rule. Soon, however, all this was to change. Between 863, when a strong force of Arabs was annihilated at Poson, on the Halys river in Anatolia, and the death of the great warrior-emperor Basil II (976–1025), a series of dramatic victories pushed back the frontiers, often close to where they had been in the heyday of Rome. In the southeast the Arabs at one stage (976) retreated to the very gates of Jerusalem; the Russians were held and routed at Silistra, on the Danube; and Bulgaria, after long, bitter campaigning, became a group of Byzantine provinces. Basil, after defeating Bulgars, Armenians, Georgians, Arabs and Normans, prepared to retake Italy, and possibly Africa beyond.

But it was not to be. Byzantium, outwardly at the height of its prosperity and power, was seriously overextended. Basil, unmarried, was succeeded by women and weaker men. The new frontiers, exhaustingly won, proved indefensible, especially as the previously invincible Byzantine armed forces now found themselves starved of funds by a civilian administration fearful of a military coup. Within 50 years, in 1071, a much weakened Byzantine army was smashed by a force of Seljuk Turks at the battle of Manzikert (see page 134). In the same year, the empire's last Italian possession fell to the Normans; Constantinople's period of greatness, when it ruled the wealthiest and best-governed realm in the Christian world, was at an end.

Paradoxically, the 11th and 12th centuries proved to be among the most fertile in Byzantine history in artistic and theological terms, despite the fact that the social and institutional links which had previously held the multilingual Empire together gradually fell into decay. Indeed, despite the disasters of 1071–81, when the Turks established permanent occupation of the Anatolian plateau and the Normans consolidated their Sicilian gains, it proved possible, under the Comnenian emperors, to sustain the illusion of Byzantium's universal dominion for another 100 years. But for all their genius, Alexius I, John II and Manuel I proved unable to recover much of the vast territory that had been lost; and when they had gone, little spirit remained to resist the final assault.

This came, not from the traditional enemy, the Muslim infidel, but from the Christian West.

The real collapse, however, was from within. Byzantium's strength, apart from its religious cohesion, was two-fold: the *themes* with their independent freeholding peasantry, ready both to farm and to defend its land, and an army and navy often manned by native Asian officers and troops. At least since 1000 these advantages had scarcely existed. In the 11th and 12th centuries, mercenaries (often themselves Seljuk, Muslim or Norman) formed the bulk of the armed forces, and the Empire, whose only hereditary office had been that of the Emperor himself, fell more and more into the ambitious hands of a few rich dynasties. These owed much of their new wealth and power to the Byzantine form of feudalism, the *pronoia* system, under which key state functions, including tax collection, were handed over to large local landowners – originally for their lifetime, but increasingly on a hereditary basis.

Byzantium was already seriously weakened when the First Crusade arrived in 1096, but hopes that Rome and Constantinople could co-exist peacefully were soon dashed. There had been tension, if not actual schism between the Roman and Orthodox churches since 1054 (see

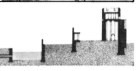
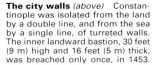

5/The West attacks Byzantium *(above)* Norman invasions and Crusader penetration encouraged western ambitions. Fostered by Venice, eager to destroy her main commercial rival, the Fourth Crusade produced a short-lived Latin Empire (1204-61).

page 100). Both Seljuks and Normans resumed full-scale frontier aggression in the 1170s. By 1180 Serbia was virtually independent; Hungary absorbed Dalmatia; Bulgaria and Wallachia rose; independent feudal rulers detached whole provinces – Cyprus (1184), Eastern Morea (1189); and in 1204 the final blow fell when Constantinople itself was seized and ravaged by the swordsmen of the Fourth Crusade. The immediate beneficiary was the rising power of Venice, whose fleets had carried the Crusaders, but the attempt to set up a Latin Empire in Constantinople proved abortive. Now for the first time, the Greeks constituted a majority within the truncated Empire and in 1261, aided by Genoa, the rival of Venice, they drove out the westerners. But the Greek empire was only a shadow of the Byzantium of the past and, rent by civil war, was no match for the Turks when they advanced into Europe in the 14th century.

The city walls *(above)* Constantinople was isolated from the land by a double line, and from the sea by a single line, of turreted walls. The inner landward bastion, 30 feet (9 m) high and 16 feet (5 m) thick, was breached only once, in 1453.

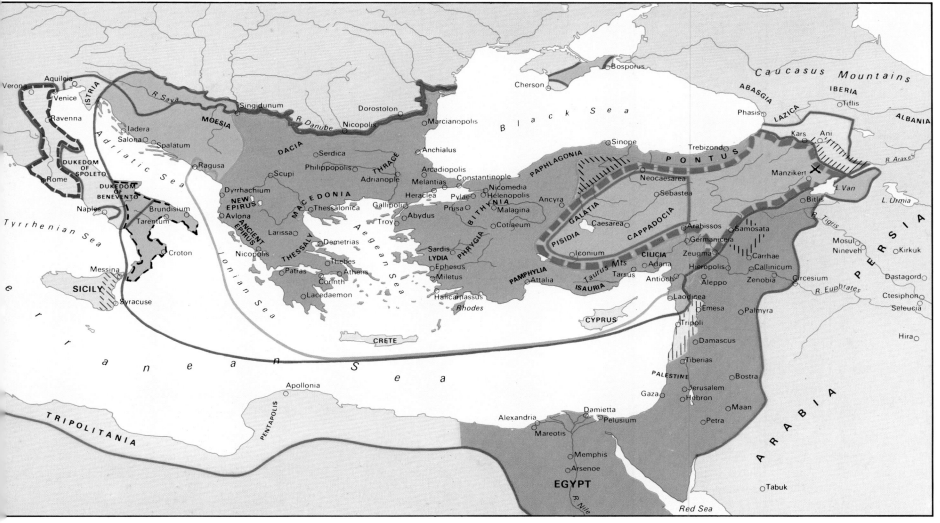

The first Russian state: Kievan Russia 882 to 1242

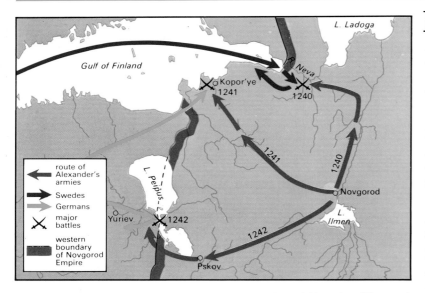

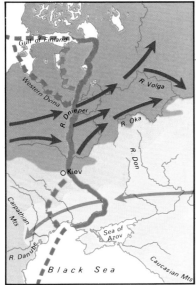

2/The campaigns of Alexander of Novgorod *(above)* An attempt by Swedes and Germans to drive Russia from the Baltic was frustrated. Alexander's decisive victory on the Neva earned him the title 'Nevsky'. Two years later he defeated the Germans.

3/Vegetation belts and early migrations *(left)* The first Russian state was established by the Vikings with the Dnieper as its axis. It lay athwart the northern forest and the southern steppe. Kiev was a natural capital.

▨ forest belt with marshes	⇢ associated waterway trade route
☐ wooded steppe	→ movement of nomadic peoples
☐ open steppe	
➡ Viking route	➡ movements of East Slavs and Russians

4/The Mongol onslaught on Russia *(below)* Until 1236 northern Russia was immune from the steppe nomads' raids, and its centres prospered, but in the winter of 1237-8 the Mongols struck north into the forest and subjugated its princes.

DURING the period 882 to 1242 Russia was subject to powerful external influences: it first emerged as a political unit thanks to the Vikings (known to the Slavs as *Varyagi* or Varangians) from the north; it then received Christianity from Byzantium in the south; and was ultimately overthrown by Mongol Tartars from the east.

The contrast between forest and steppe was of prime importance at this time. Before the arrival of the Vikings in the 9th century, the East Slavs were pushing eastwards from Europe into the woodlands of central Russia, while hordes of nomadic horsemen moved westwards across the southern steppe from Asia. The rivers assumed significance with the coming of the Vikings who established, dominated and exploited trade routes along the waterways; the first Russian state originated in Viking determination to control the lands adjoining them. Because the rivers of Russia flow generally north to south (and south to north), there was great potential for trade between the Baltic and the Black Sea; both the main trade routes and the ensuing political unit therefore ran north and south, across forest and steppe which, however, proved too strong for a north-south alignment based upon the rivers to survive. The history of Kievan Rus, the first Russian state, is dominated by the constant struggle and ultimate failure of the Rus to retain their steppe territory which became once more the undisputed realm of westward-migrating nomads. Instead, they resumed eastward colonization of the forest belt.

The principal waterway route established by the Vikings ran from the Gulf of Finland up the River Neva, through Lake Ladoga, the River Volkhov, thence by portages to the Dnieper, and on across the Black Sea to Byzantium. This was the 'route from the *Varyagi* to the Greeks' mentioned by early writers. As Viking control spread southwards, Novgorod, Smolensk and (in 882) Kiev each became their headquarters. Kiev grew rapidly as the new state's flourishing capital. Its links with Byzantium, its chief trading partner, were strong, and from Byzantium it received the Christian faith during the reign of Vladimir Svyatoslavich (980–1015).

At the time of the Viking incursions the Khazars and their vassals, the Magyars, held the steppes but by the 10th century the formerly nomadic Khazars had largely become merchants and farmers. The Rus were able to hold the lands of the lower Prut, Dniester and Bug, and to control the Dnieper route to the Black Sea and thence to Byzantium. Grand Prince Svyatoslav (962–72) determined to strengthen and expand this Russian grip by crushing the Khazars. But by destroying the relatively peaceful Khazars, Svyatoslav opened the way to the fierce Pechenegs (Turkic nomads) who henceforth dominated the south Russian steppes until displaced by the equally warlike Polovtsy. Vladimir I had some defensive success against the Pechenegs but Kiev was sacked by the Polovtsy in 1093.

Weakened by perpetual conflict with the nomads, the Kievan state after 1054 split into a number of independent and often warring principalities. While the southern lands emptied in the face of pitiless Polovtsy raids, steady colonization of the forest increased the populations of the northern and central principalities, giving them the strength to throw off Kievan suzerainty. Novgorod, which had built up a fur-trading empire reaching to the Urals and beyond, and Vladimir-Suzdal, which contained the fast-growing commercial centre of Moscow (first mentioned in 1147), were the leading forest principalities. On the eve of the Mongol attack of 1237, Vladimir-Suzdal was about to challenge the Voigar Bulgars whose stranglehold on the middle Volga region obstructed further Russian expansion eastward. Nizhniy Novgorod was built as a first move in this campaign.

The Mongol invasion was perhaps the most traumatic event in Russian history. The Mongols had made an exploratory raid into the steppes in 1221, defeating a combined Russian and Polovtsy force at the Kalka River in 1223. In 1237 they returned in strength and struck first at the middle and upper Volga regions, hitherto immune from nomadic attack. In the winter of 1237–8, when the protective rivers were frozen, they overcame the Volga Bulgars and set upon Vladimir-Suzdal, destroying its wealthy towns. Only the approach of spring saved Novgorod, as the invaders dared not be caught by the thaw among its surrounding marshes. In 1239 it was the turn of southwest Russia, which suffered annihilation. Kiev itself was sacked in 1240, along with hundreds of other settlements. Novgorod escaped the Mongol fury but was weakened by incessant attacks from Swedes and Germans in the Baltic region. Prince Alexander Nevsky beat the Swedes decisively on the River Neva in 1240, and the Germans on the ice of Lake Peipus in 1242; yet even he had to recognize Mongol overlordship.

The Mongol invasion had lasting economic, social and political effects. Those peasants who survived, oppressed by the tribute the Mongols exacted, lost all hope of rising above the barest subsistence. The destruction of the leading cities, where handicrafts flourished, reduced life to a barbarous level. The Mongols themselves soon withdrew to the steppes, and although they restricted their direct intervention to punitive expeditions when necessary, and to the appointment of local revenue-collecting agents, their influence was all-pervasive. The elimination of the urban middle classes smoothed the path of an autocracy which imitated its overlords in ruthless terror and efficient extortion.

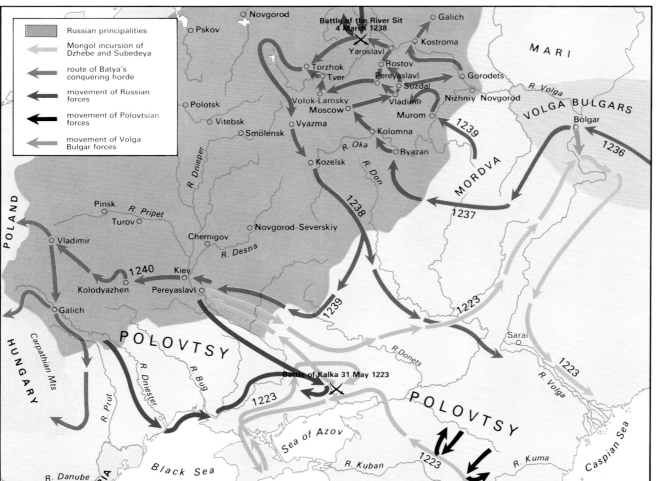

1/Kievan Russia 1054 to 1242 *(right)* In 1054 there was still a unified Russian state but by the early 13th century it had disintegrated. Southern centres, such as Kiev, were weakened by nomadic attack, while northern towns, such as Novgorod, Vladimir and Moscow, exploited their positions on river trade routes in the security of the forest. Novgorod established a vast fur-trading empire stretching to the Arctic and the Urals.

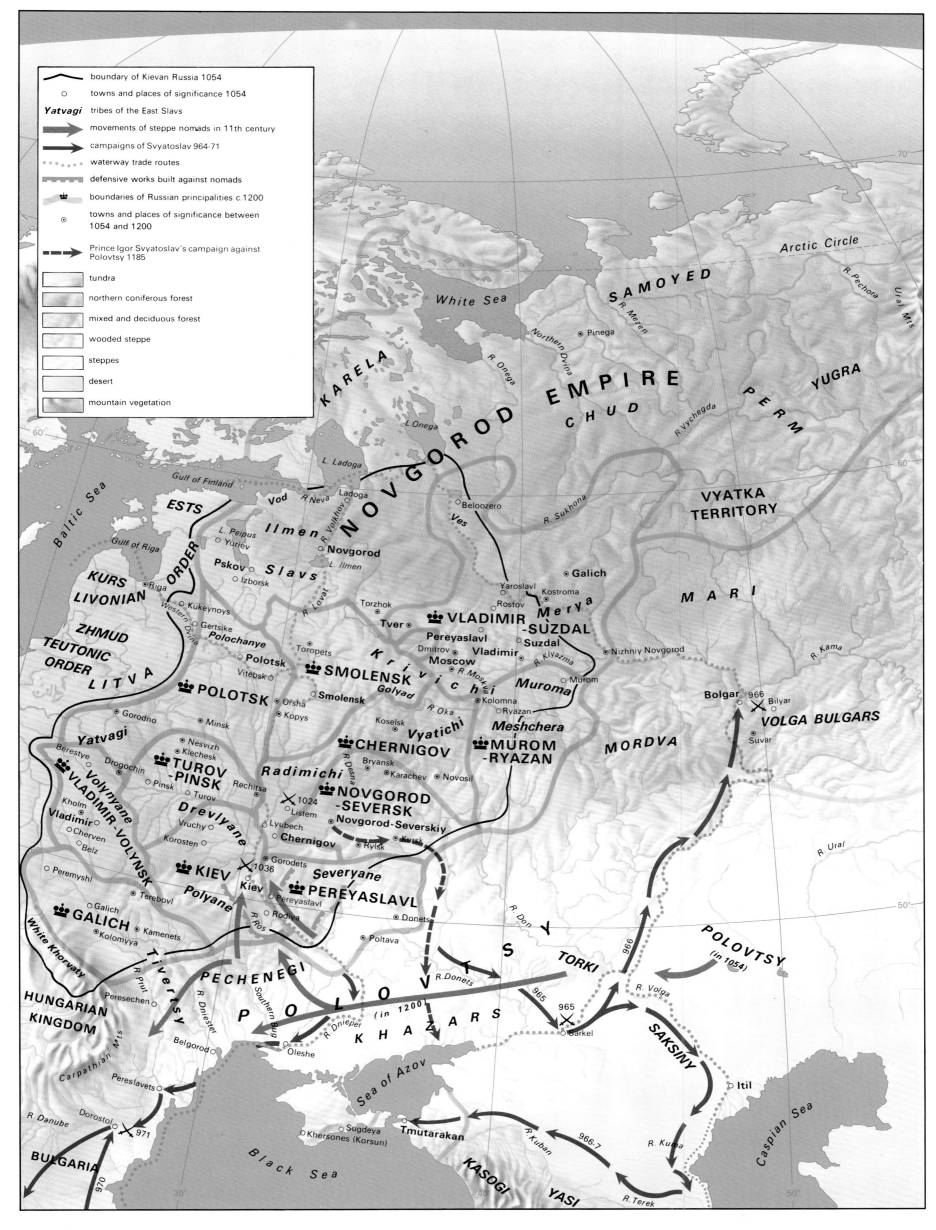

Legend

Arctic Circle

White Sea

KARELA

NOVGOROD EMPIRE

SAMOYED

CHUD

PERM

YUGRA

R. Mezen

R. Pechora

Ural Mts

o Pinega

R. Onega

Northern Dvina

R. Vychegda

VYATKA TERRITORY

L. Onega

o Beloozero

Ves

R. Sukhona

R. Kama

Baltic Sea

Gulf of Finland

L. Ladoga

ESTS

Vod

Ladoga

R. Neva

o Volkhov

ORDER

Ilmen

L. Peipus

o Yüriev

Psków

Slavs

Novgorod

L. Ilmen

o Izborsk

o Galich

MARI

KURS

LIVONIAN

Riga

o Kukeynoys

Western Dvina

o Gertsike

Polochanye

Polotsk

o Vitebsk

R. Lovat

Torzhok

o Toropets

Krivichi

Yaroslavl o Kostroma

o Rostov

Merya

VLADIMIR -SUZDAL

Suzdal

o Nizhniy Novgorod

ZHMUD

TEUTONIC ORDER

LITVA

o Gorodno

o Minsk

o Nesvizh

o Klechesk

Orsha o

SMOLENSK

Smolensk o

Golyad

o Kopys

Tver

Pereyaslavl

Dmitrov o Vladimir

Moscow

R. Moskva

R. Klyazma

o Murom

Muroma

POLOTSK

Vyatichi

Koselsk o

R. Oka

Kolomna

Ryazan

MORDVA

Bolgar 966 Bilyar

VOLGA BULGARS

Suvar

Yatvagi

Berestye

Drogochin

o Pinsk

TUROV -PINSK

o Turov

Rechitsa

Radimichi

CHERNIGOV

o Bryansk

o Karachev o Novosil

Meshchera

MUROM- RYAZAN

VLADIMIR -VOLYNSK

Volynyane

Kholm

Vladimir

o Cherven

o Belz

Drevlyane

o Vruchy

o Korosten

X 1024 Listven

o Lyubech

R. Desna

NOVGOROD- SEVERSK

Novgorod-Severskiy

Chernigov

o Kursk

o Rylsk

o Peremyshl

KIEV

X 1036

o Gorodets

Kiev

Polyane

o Rodnya

Severyane

GALICH

o Galich o Kamenets

o Kolomyya

o Terebovl

PEREYASLAVL

o Pereyaslavl

o Poltava

o Donets

R. Don

R. Ural

White Khorvaty

Tivertsy

o Peresechen

PECHENEGI

R. Ros

o Belgorod

Oleshe

P O L O V (in 1200)

Southern Bug

R. Dnieper

R. Donets

T S Y

TORKI

965

X 965 Sarkel

POLOVTSY (in 1054)

R. Volga

R. Kuban

SAKSINY

HUNGARIAN KINGDOM

o Pereslavets

Carpathian Mts

R. Prut

R. Dniester

K H A Z A R S

Sea of Azov

o Itil

Caspian Sea

R. Danube

Dorostol X 971

970

BULGARIA

Black Sea

o Sugdeya

o Khersones (Korsun)

Tmutarakan

KASOGI

YASI

R. Kuban

966-7

R. Terek

115

The formation of states in northern and eastern Europe 900 to c.1050

THE Carolingian Empire had restored a degree of political order to most parts of western Europe which had formerly belonged to the Roman Empire. In northern and eastern Europe political conditions were different, however, and it was not until the period 850–1050 that certain Scandinavian and Slav states emerged as organized, and aggressive, entities. Their conversions extended the area of Latin Christendom, filled out the political map of Europe, and put pressure on other western European states.

As a result of the initial activity of the early Viking Age, the Scandinavians were by 900 well established in the west. In England the Danelaw was only gradually conquered by Wessex, and although the last Scandinavian king of York, Erik Bloodaxe, was killed in 954, most settlers were apparently able to retain their land, giving a partly Scandinavian character to the customs and place-names of the region. The conquest of the Danelaw, and an expanding economy, paved the way for the unification of 'England' and for the political and religious reforms introduced by Eadgar (959–75).

But the wealth of England soon attracted the Scandinavians again, first as organized military expeditions seeking financial rewards (the Danegeld), then as conquerors, ruling England in tandem with Norway and Denmark under a Danish king, Cnut (Canute). But Cnut's 'northern empire' was short-lived, and with the accession of Edward the Confessor to the English throne (1042), and still more after the Norman Conquest in 1066, England turned away from its ties with northern Europe and aligned itself with the culture of France and the Mediterranean. It was an historic turning-point.

Despite the fall of York, the major ports of Ireland were still held by Scandinavians. These towns had been founded by them in the 9th century, and remained economically under their control, although often politically dominated by the Irish. Like the Welsh, the Irish were divided by many social and political factors: never united, often in disarray, they were slow to develop towns of their own. Indeed, much of this period was dominated by continuous warfare between the various Irish dynasties. Brian Boru may have intended for a few years after 1000 to become overlord of Ireland, but his power lasted only a short time; by 1014 he was dead and his achievement lay in ruins.

Dublin's fortunes fluctuated politically amid the wars, but her function as the chief of the Scandinavian towns is emphasized by the striking of the first Irish coins there in the 990s. From the late 10th century her economic power and international connections grew apace, and the existence of continuous building and growth up to the 12th century bears witness to her prosperity. The town itself served as the chief market for the Isle of Man, the Western Isles of Scotland and the Atlantic islands, all of which remained under Scandinavian control throughout this entire period.

The mainland of Scotland, however, apart from Galloway and the far north, was gradually taken over by the Scots in the course of the 10th and 11th centuries and, by 1050, Scottish influence also extended into the northern counties of modern England. A firm boundary was drawn only in 1237.

Scandinavia was settled by the beginning of the Viking Age, with many peoples speaking a more or less common tongue. Now, powerful 'states' were founded out of the disarray. Denmark under three kings (Gorm, Harald and Sven) became in the course of the 10th century a powerful kingdom and, under Cnut the Great (1014-35), the centre of a great – but impossibly large – Anglo-Scandinavian empire.

After the battle of Hafrsfjord in the 890s much of southern Norway came under the rule of Harald Finehair, but after his death in the

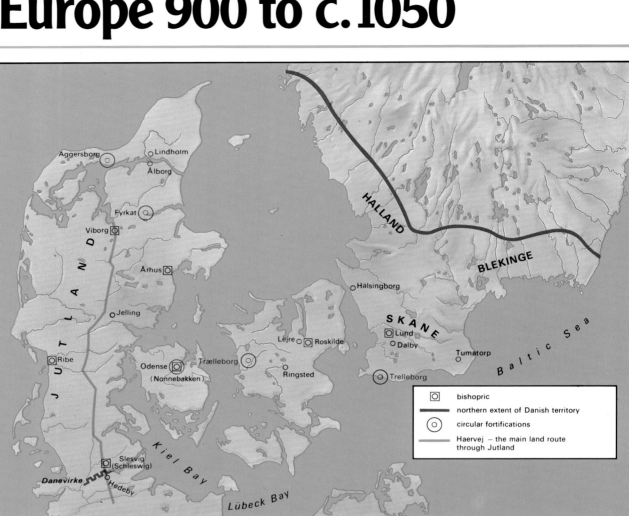

930s, Norway occasionally fell under Danish lordship until the death of Cnut, when a Norwegian king again succeeded. The history of Sweden is more obscure: it was not united under the kings of Uppland until the end of the 11th century. By 930 Iceland was an independent commonwealth (without a king), while Greenland was colonized from about 985. Through the medium of the newly introduced Christianity (brought to Scandinavia by a handful of English and Saxon missionaries during the 10th and 11th centuries) Scandinavia emerged into the community of European Christendom.

Meanwhile, a similar process of consolidation was taking place in eastern Europe. The first organized state in this region, Moravia, was destroyed in 906 by the Magyar invaders, but a new phase of political consolidation began shortly afterwards, probably in response to German pressure under Henry I and Otto I. Although the Slav peoples along the Elbe successfully resisted the Germans in the great Slav revolt of 983, they remained disunited and loosely organized, and it was further east, in Poland, that a major Slav state arose. Mieszko I (960–92) united the tribes of northern Poland, and his son, Bolesław Chrobry (992–1025), extended control to the south. Meanwhile, the Magyars were settling the Hungarian Plain, where a kingdom was established by Duke Geisa (972–97) and his more famous son, King Stephen (997–1038). Bohemia, caught between Germany and Poland, had also emerged as a political unit by the time of Bolesław I (929–67), though the Přemyslid dukes were vassals of the German king and shared power with another dynasty, the Slavniki until the 990s.

The creation of Bohemia, Poland and Hungary – by the Přemyslid, Piast and Árpád dynasties respectively – was founded on agricultural development, suppression of tribal differences and independent tribal aristocracies, and on the organizing and civilizing influence of the Church. At this stage, despite numerous wars (particularly after 1003), there was little racial confrontation between Germans and Slavs. Mieszko I worked closely with Emperor Otto III,

2/The rise of Denmark (above) Denmark was the first Scandinavian kingdom to achieve full statehood in the Latin Christian tradition. Three kings were responsible: Harald Bluetooth (c.958-c.986), Sven Forkbeard (c.986-c.1014) and Cnut the Great (c.1014-35). Harald was instrumental in persuading the Danes to accept Christianity, while politically he countered a German threat and brought Norway under his sway. Sven concentrated largely on warlike campaigns in England from which he drew large amounts of Danegeld. His son, Cnut the Great, eventually came to the throne of England and ruled an 'empire' which stretched, in ˌheory at least, from the North Cape to the Isles of Scilly. Cnut's North Sea empire collapsed at his death, however, and Denmark was subject to the Norwegian king Magnus until 1046, before settling down within what were to become its boundaries for many centuries (including the modern Swedish provinces of Skåne, Blekinge and Halland). In the 10th and early 11th centuries the first towns were founded, the first bishoprics established and a remarkable series of fortifications constructed by the central authority in Denmark – including at least part of the Danevirke (the fortified southern frontier of Denmark) and the fortresses at Trelleborg, Odense, Fyrkat, and Aggersborg.

The Jelling stone (above) is both a symbol and a proof of the unity of Denmark and its official conversion to Christianity in the 10th century. The inscription reads: 'King Harald had this monument made in memory of Gorm his father and in memory of Thyre his mother. That Harald who won for himself all Denmark and Norway, and made the Danes Christian'. Harald died c.986.

Territories from maps 1 and 2
(right and above)

Bohemia Duchy conquered from Slavs by Otto II in 950 and made tributary to Emperor.
Brandenburg (Nordmark and Billungmark) 928 margravate under Empire; 982 reconquered by Slavs.
Brittany Independent Celtic-speaking duchy; 912-37 under Scandinavian control.
Cumbria Kingdom incorporated in Scotland after 1015.
Danelaw Generic term for area of England where 'Danish' customs still prevailed in 12th century: by extension, for area under Scandinavian control in early 10th century.
Dublin Kingdom under Scandinavian control (although political power sometimes in Irish hands).
England Kingdom. North and east under Scandinavian control for much of first half of 9th century. Gradually united under kings of Wessex. 1016-42 under Danish rule.
Hungary Principality. After death of Kursan (904) united under one leader, Árpád. In 1001 Stephen (d.1038) became first king.
Iceland Commonwealth of free landowners.
Ireland Land of petty kings (tuatha). Five main kingdoms to which in this period was added a sixth, Brega. Northern dynasty of Ui Néill most important until Brian Boru produced semi-organized overlordship under Munster in 1002 (see also Dublin).
Man Norse kingdom, including Inner Hebrides; in 10th century under Dublin, 1095-1265 under Norwegian overlordship.
Moravia Empire; 906 fell to Hungarians; 1025 combined with Bohemia after a period in Polish hands.
Normandy Colonized by Scandinavian settlers; ruled by Viking chiefs c.915; by 'Dukes' of Rouen from c.940.
Norway Kingdom. At first very disunited, for some time in late 10th and early 11th centuries under loose Danish control. Finally achieved independence and united under Magnus the Good (1035).
Orkney Earldom under overlordship of Norway. For much of period also probably controlled western islands of Scotland (Nordreyjar and Sudreyjar), Shetland (Hjaltland), and also, for a short period, Man.
Scotland Kingdom centred in east. Edinburgh captured by Indulf (954-62), battle of Carham (1018) added Lothian. Cumbria taken over after death of Owen the Bald (1015). Galloway not properly under Scottish rule; north and west controlled by Norse.
Sweden Political organization divided between Svear and Götar (Swedes and people of Götaland) to c.1100.
Wales Land of petty kings (gwlad). Six main kingdoms struggled for power. After death of Hywel Dda (950) no consolidation until accession of Gruffydd ap Llewelyn of Gwynedd in 1039.
York Norse kingdom until 954.

3/Poland under Bolesław Chrobry (right) After the unification of the tribes of Great (or northern) Poland under Mieszko I, his son Bolesław Chrobry ('The Brave') attempted to create a wider hegemony, including Bohemia and Moravia. Most of the gains were temporary and involved long, debilitating wars on all frontiers; but Little Poland, centred on Cracow, was permanently acquired, and it was to Cracow that Casimir I (1038-58) transferred his residence when he began the restoration of the monarchy after setbacks under Mieszko II (1025-34). Poland was already Christian and a number of bishoprics had been founded. The towns of the Baltic coast came into their own as international trading stations in this period.

and the Bohemian nobility gladly became vassals of Germany when threatened by the Hungarians. Moreover, all three dynasties made use of western institutions (counties, castellanies) to strengthen their position. Bolesław Chrobry had ambitions of founding a personal hegemony from the Baltic to the Danube, including Bohemia and Moravia and certain Russian territories in the east, but the ensuing conflicts (involving wars with Slavs and Hungarians as well as Germans) overtaxed the monarchies and enabled the nobility to assert itself. The result in all three countries was a setback to the authority of the throne.

Nevertheless a foundation had been laid, and none of them henceforth lost its identity, though it was not until the 14th century that a restoration of royal power took place.

1/The emergence of states (below) The 10th century was marked by the emergence of stable political organization in northern and eastern Europe. The marauders of the previous century (the Vikings in the north, the Magyars in the east) formed settled states; in England the successors of Alfred the Great conquered the Danelaw; in Poland the Piasts not only extended their control over Little Poland (around Cracow) but also embarked on expansion at the expense of their Slav neighbours to the south, east and west. In eastern Germany, marches were established to defend the frontiers from incursions from the east.

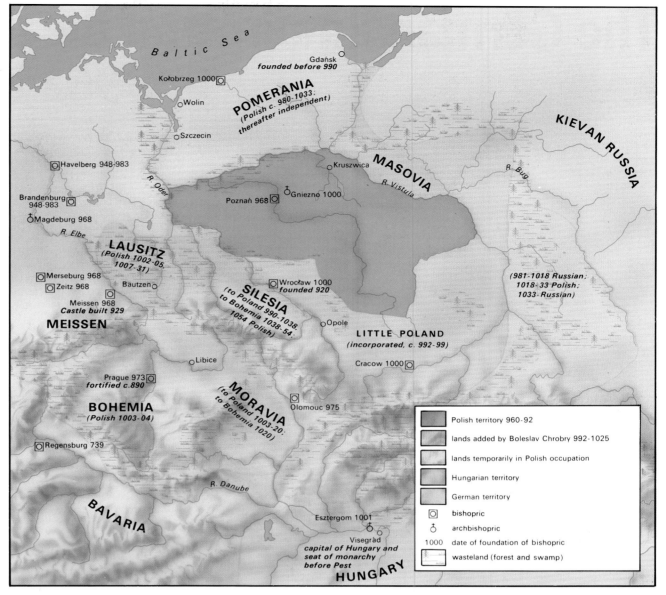

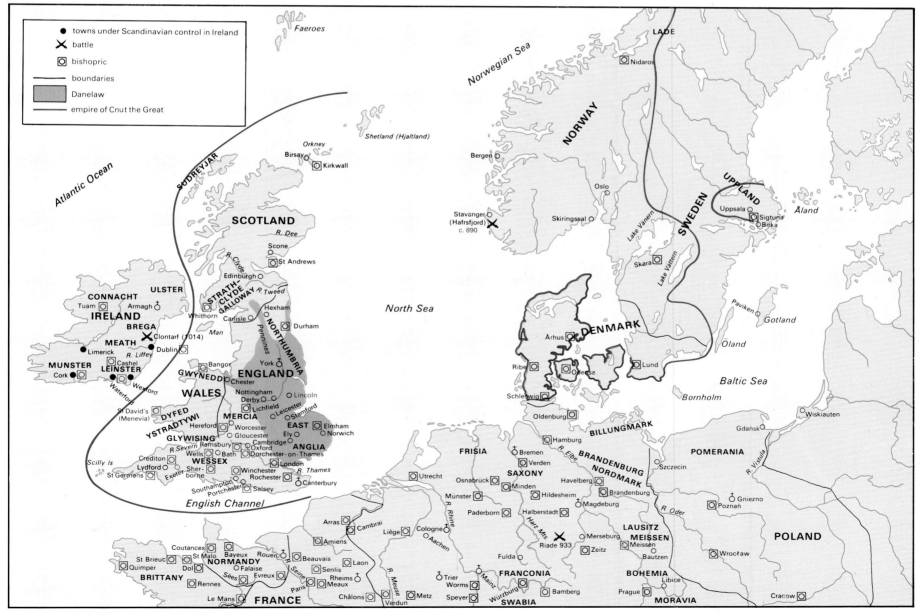

The German Empire and the Papacy 962 to 1250

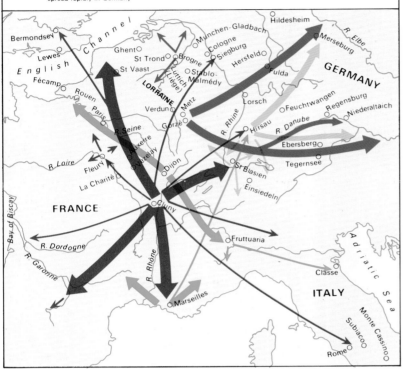

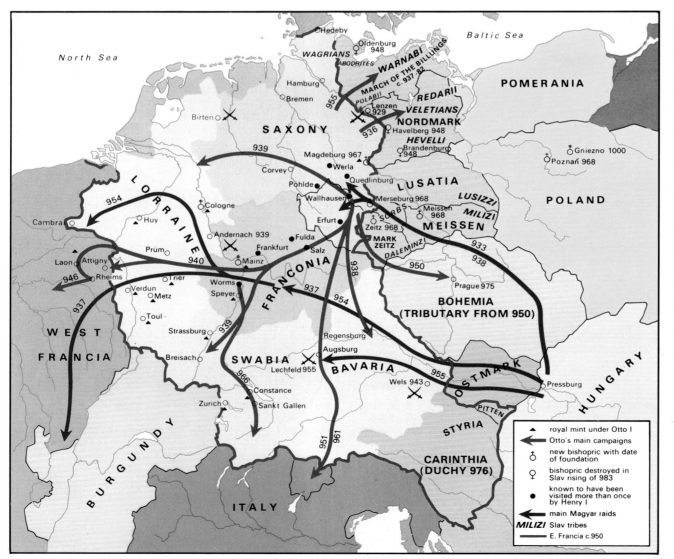

3/Monastic reform *(above)* Reform movements began early in the 10th century, mainly in southeast France and Lorraine. Although the monastery of Gorze influenced 10th-century Germany, monastic reform made no powerful impact east of the Rhine until after 1060. Elsewhere in France, however, movements of dissent (almost unknown in the West since c. 500) spread rapidly in the late 11th century in protest against clerical worldliness. Then, about 1130, doctrinal heresy (Manichaeism) was imported from the Middle East; it took root in southern France. Both movements were repressed but not eradicated by the Albigensian Crusade (1209-13) and the Inquisition (1233 onwards).

2/The East Frankish Kingdom in the reign of Otto I *(below)* Otto I established a firm grip on the East Frankish lands. After the ducal revolts of 938-9 he was able to exercise power even in the more prosperous south and west. Magyar raids were halted. The drive eastward against the Slavs was normally left to the margraves, while Otto himself ranged more widely.

T HE 9th century Viking, Magyar and Saracen invasions (see page 110) shook the foundations of the Carolingian Empire, already weakened by the Frankish custom of partible inheritance. After 887 the West Frankish (French) and East Frankish (German) lands went their own ways, as did Italy. In 919 the East Frankish crown passed to Henry, Duke of the Saxons. This disputed election seemed to mark just another stage in the disintegration of the Carolingian world for Henry's power barely extended beyond the borders of Franconia and southeast Saxony. South of the Alps the imperial crown was now just a prize awarded to the most influential Italian noble, while west of the Rhine the forces of political fragmentation continued to operate for another 200 years (see page 122). But by perseverance, skill and good fortune Henry I's son, Otto I, decisively extended his influence over the German duchies, defeated the Magyars at the Battle of Lechfeld (955), and conquered the kingdom of Italy. His imperial coronation at Rome (962) served to legitimize these vast acquisitions: the Ottonian Empire emerged as the leading power west of the Adriatic.

The Empire's pre-eminence lasted until the death of Frederick II in 1250, although from the mid-12th century, with the recovery of the West Frankish territories and the rise of the Angevin Empire under Henry II of England, the balance was visibly changing.

The Empire's political structure was under-mined gradually by the growth of population and commerce, and by the clearing of waste-lands and forest. From around 1140 internal colonization was reinforced by the eastward expansion of German peasant settlement. But this concerned the eastern frontier princes far more than the emperors: the latter were always more interested in the west, above all in Italy. Only in these economically advanced regions were the profits of lordship sufficient to sustain them and their following. In particular, the urban wealth in Lombardy and Tuscany, the result of an unparalleled rate of economic growth, exerted a magnetic pull. The chroniclers' estimates of Frederick I's income from Italy make it clear that it was this source that made him the equal of the Angevins. The conquest of the Norman Kingdom of Sicily in 1194 made the Hohenstaufen the richest rulers in Europe.

Nevertheless the machinery of government remained inadequate. Only 13th-century Sicily possessed a centralized administrative system. In Germany and northern Italy the kings travelled continually. To enforce their will, the kings had to be on the spot in person. The tremendous accession of landed wealth under Otto I had enabled the Ottonians to stay chiefly in their palaces, supplied by the produce of their estates. But the gradual alienation of royal domains forced their successors to rely more heavily on church lands, particularly on episcopal towns and their developing markets. This meant an increasingly close relationship between king and church – which helps to explain the fierceness of the dispute over investitures.

Kings and emperors had long claimed to rule by divine mandate. Popes challenged this view from at least the 5th century and in the 10th century a movement to free the Church from secular control began in scattered monastic centres in the west, notably at Cluny in Burgundy, and at Brogne and Gorze in Lorraine, spread quickly and finally reached Rome when the emperor Henry III took in hand the reform of the papacy at the Synod of Sutri in 1046.

The connection thus forged between Church reformers and the papal see inaugurated the long struggle of Empire and Papacy, which eventually destroyed the former and fatally impaired the authority of the latter. The conflict came to a head under Gregory VII (1073–85). Gregory excommunicated and deposed the emperor Henry IV in 1076, forced him to perform public penance at Canossa, and allied with the emperor's enemies – the Normans of southern Italy, the recalcitrant German nobility, and a chain of states around the periphery which feared German power. The result was a lasting setback to German monarchy. Although Gregory failed in his immediate objects, the launching of the First Crusade (see page 100) by Urban II (1088–99) testified to the rapid advance of papal authority. But by now both sides were exhausted, and the struggle was settled in 1122 by the Concordat of Worms.

The conflict of Empire and Papacy now deteriorated from an issue of principle to a struggle for control of Italy. The political involvement of the papacy became clear when Alexander III (1154–81) allied with the Lombard League to resist the attempts of Frederick I (1152–90) to restore German imperial authority in Italy. Once again, the issue was settled by a compromise (the Peace of Constance, 1183), but the papacy failed to prevent the Hohenstaufen from acquiring the Norman Kingdom of Sicily. Only the early death of Frederick's son, Henry VI (1190-7) and civil war in Germany (1197-1214) enabled Innocent III (1198-1216) to regain ascendancy for the Church.

Innocent III's pontificate marked a high point for the papacy. He established a papal state in central Italy to protect Rome; he nominated emperors; England bowed to his will; and France

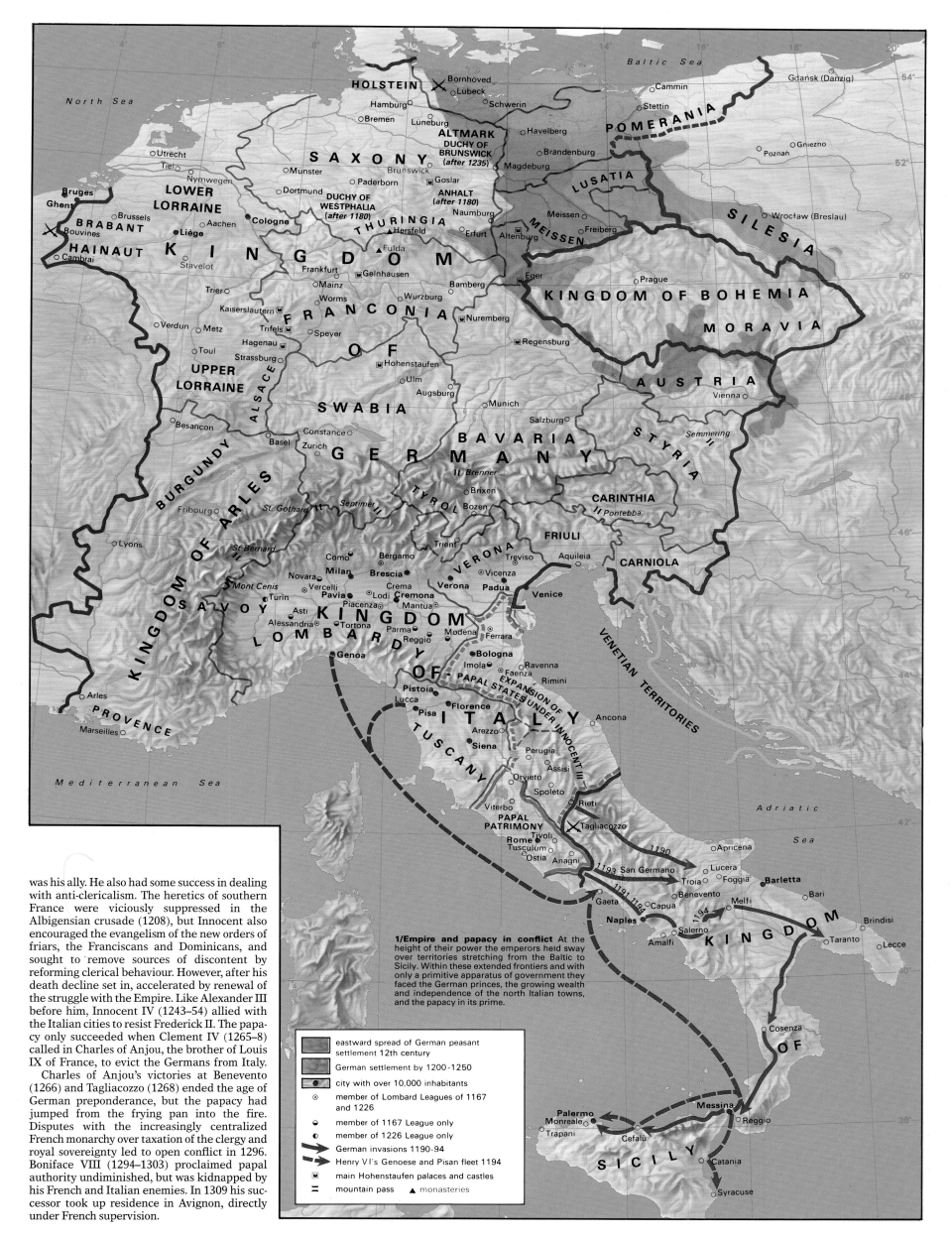

was his ally. He also had some success in dealing with anti-clericalism. The heretics of southern France were viciously suppressed in the Albigensian crusade (1208), but Innocent also encouraged the evangelism of the new orders of friars, the Franciscans and Dominicans, and sought to remove sources of discontent by reforming clerical behaviour. However, after his death decline set in, accelerated by renewal of the struggle with the Empire. Like Alexander III before him, Innocent IV (1243–54) allied with the Italian cities to resist Frederick II. The papacy only succeeded when Clement IV (1265–8) called in Charles of Anjou, the brother of Louis IX of France, to evict the Germans from Italy.

Charles of Anjou's victories at Benevento (1266) and Tagliacozzo (1268) ended the age of German preponderance, but the papacy had jumped from the frying pan into the fire. Disputes with the increasingly centralized French monarchy over taxation of the clergy and royal sovereignty led to open conflict in 1296. Boniface VIII (1294–1303) proclaimed papal authority undiminished, but was kidnapped by his French and Italian enemies. In 1309 his successor took up residence in Avignon, directly under French supervision.

1/Empire and papacy in conflict At the height of their power the emperors held sway over territories stretching from the Baltic to Sicily. Within these extended frontiers and with only a primitive apparatus of government they faced the German princes, the growing wealth and independence of the north Italian towns, and the papacy in its prime.

- ▨ eastward spread of German peasant settlement 12th century
- ▨ German settlement by 1200-1250
- ● city with over 10,000 inhabitants
- ⊙ member of Lombard Leagues of 1167 and 1226
- ◑ member of 1167 League only
- ◐ member of 1226 League only
- ➔ German invasions 1190-94
- ⇒ Henry VI's Genoese and Pisan fleet 1194
- ▣ main Hohenstaufen palaces and castles
- = mountain pass ▲ monasteries

119

The recovery of Europe c.950 to 1150

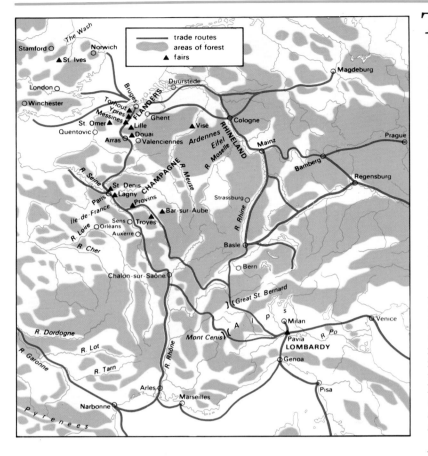

1/Western Europe, c.AD 1000 *(above)*
Before AD 1000 perhaps four-fifths of Europe north of the Alps and Pyrenees was covered by dense forest. The essential work of the next 200 years was to clear the forest and make the land available for human settlement and agriculture. Even in the Rhineland the highlands bounding the river were still largely uninhabited (see map 3). Elsewhere, forests such as the Ardennes and the Eifel constituted an almost impenetrable barrier to communications. At this stage only the western Alpine passes were in regular use. Certain areas – Flanders, Lombardy, and the Rhine valley – were beginning by 1100 to become centres of commercial exchange. But it was only after 1150 that Italian merchants regularly attended the fairs of Champagne (Troyes, Provins, Bar-sur-Aube, Lagny), buying Flemish cloths in exchange for Oriental goods.

THE repulse of the Magyars by Otto I at the battle of Lech in 955 (see page 110) is the conventional date for the beginning of the recovery of Europe from the preceding period of devastation and economic setback. After 950 – a little earlier, perhaps, in some regions, a little later in others – the economic graph of Europe was on an upward curve until around 1300–20 (see pp.140 and 142). This economic recovery, and the sharp rise in population which accompanied it, was a capital fact in European history.

The preceding period had indubitably marked a time of recession. Villages were razed to the ground and cultivated land reverted to waste. Dorestad and Quentovic, leading Carolingian ports, were destroyed, never to be rebuilt; much of Normandy was depopulated when it was handed over to the Viking chief, Rollo, in 911. In the south the cities of Marseilles, Arles, Aix, Fréjus and Genoa, the targets of Saracen raiders, were abandoned.

What is really remarkable, once the invasions were halted, is the speed with which this situation was reversed. The population of Europe in 900 was probably at its lowest level since the fall of the Roman Empire. By 1000 it may have reached a total of 30 million and 150 years later it had probably increased by 40 per cent. Most of this increase was concentrated in western Europe, in France, Germany and England. The development of eastern and northern Europe and the *repoblación* of Spain only got under way after 1150.

The basic factor in this process of recovery was the opening up of new land. In a few regions (e.g. the Po valley of northern Italy, Flanders, the country around the Wash in England) marshes were drained and land reclaimed from the sea. But there is no doubt that the bulk of new land was won by sheer hard work from the vast, impenetrable forests which still covered most of Europe in the year 1000. This is a process which

can only be followed step by step and locality by locality on large-scale maps. It took three main forms: steady encroachment by the peasants of the old villages on the woods which surrounded their fields; the migration of settlers, presumably driven by land-hunger, to the uninhabited uplands and mountains, where they carved out scattered fields and enclosures from the forest and scrub; and planned development by lay lords and monasteries, wealthy promoters and speculators who founded villages and towns, at the foot of a castle or outside a monastery gate, with the aim of increasing their income. All three types of clearing are found juxtaposed in all countries, and their history is revealed by field patterns and by place-names (e.g. Newport, Neuville, Neustadt, Bourgneuf, Nieuwpoort). Occasionally the nomenclature is more fanciful. The small English market town of Baldock (Hertfordshire), founded by the Knights Templar in about 1148, was named optimistically after the great city of Baghdad.

No accurate estimate is possible of the amount of new land which was brought into cultivation in this way, but the effects of the great work of internal colonization are indisputable. First and foremost an agricultural surplus became available for trade, and the result was to stimulate the foundation and growth of towns, markets and fairs.

Historians formerly attributed the recovery of Europe to the revival of long-distance trade at the time of the Crusades. We know today, however, that the basis of recovery was local trade; the fairs (notably the fairs of Champagne) which became internationally renowned after 1150, still essentially served a local market in 1100. The gradual reassertion of European control over the northern shores of the Mediterranean after about 972 was a precondition for the later efflorescence of the Italian cities; but in 1000 Pisa and Genoa were only beginning to emerge

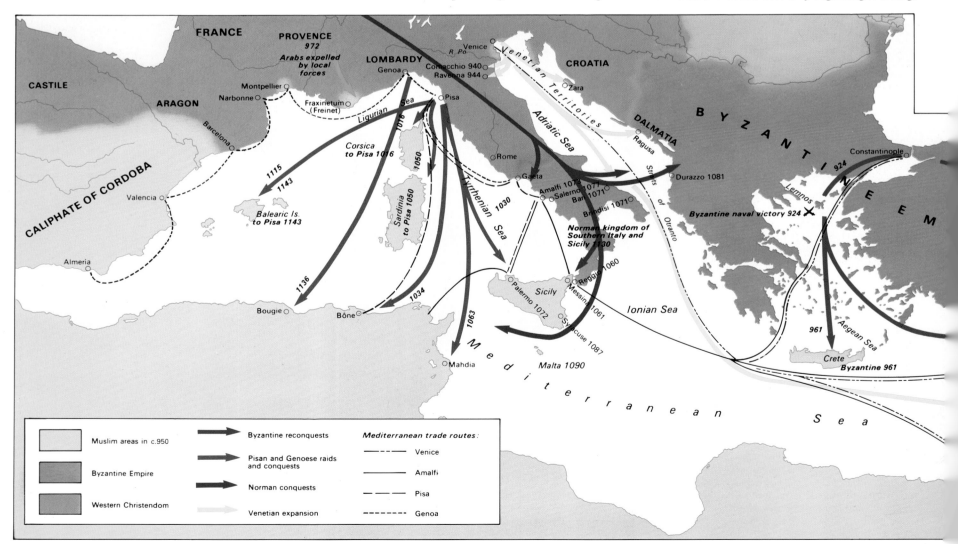

☐ Muslim areas in c.950	→ Byzantine reconquests
☐ Byzantine Empire	→ Pisan and Genoese raids and conquests
☐ Western Christendom	→ Norman conquests
	→ Venetian expansion

Mediterranean trade routes:
– – – – Venice
———— Amalfi
– – – Pisa
– – – – – Genoa

from the setbacks they had suffered at the hands of the Saracens, and Venice alone of the north Italian cities carried on a major overseas trade at the time. Significantly, the first two Crusades (1096–99, 1147–49) proceeded overland to Constantinople; not until the time of the third Crusade (1189–92) did the West possess a fleet capable of transporting a major army the length of the Mediterranean, from Gibraltar to Palestine.

In Europe also, though a few Roman roads remained in partial use, communications were still primitive, and rivers (Rhine, Meuse, Po, Rhône) conveyed bulk transport. Only the western Alpine passes (Mont Cenis, Great St Bernard) were in regular use; the central passes (St Gotthard, Septimer, Splügen) and the Brenner in the east were not developed before the reign of the emperor Frederick I (1155–90) or later. The Mont Cenis and Great St Bernard provided a connection with the Rhineland, and thence with the cloth-towns of Flanders, and also with the Paris region. But the Capetians were still struggling to assert authority in the Ile-de-France, and until this had been achieved the Rhineland remained the focus of artistic and intellectual as well as of economic life. Cologne, in particular, was at the height of its prosperity, but the cathedral-building throughout the region – as at Mainz and Worms – is a testimony to the new-found wealth which 'the great age of clearing' had made available.

2/The reconquest of the Mediterranean *(below left)* In 950 the Mediterranean was almost entirely a 'Muslim lake'. Such trade as there was between western Europe and the Orient was in the hands of the cities of Byzantine Italy: Bari, Amalfi, Gaeta and Salerno. Amalfi, in particular, traded indiscriminately with Muslims (in Sicily and Egypt) and with Constantinople and Antioch. But its connections with northern Europe were at best indirect, and it was Venice that first engaged in trade with Europe north of the Alps, once it had cleared the Adriatic of Dalmatian pirates and fought off the closure of the Straits of Otranto first by Muslims (who occupied Bari from 841 to 871) and then by Norman marauders. In the western Mediterranean trade was virtually at a standstill so long as the Saracens were in control of the Mediterranean islands and, from their base at Fraxinetum, off the Ligurian coast. Their dislodgement from Fraxinetum in 972 was therefore highly significant. By this time Islamic unity was breaking up (see page 132) and this weakening enabled the fleets of Pisa and (later) of Genoa to wrest control of the Ligurian and Tyrrhenian seas from the Saracens. At this stage, however, these cities were freebooters and pirates rather than traders, but the loot from their raids on Saracen shipping provided capital for shipbuilding and eventually for commerce. The first Crusade (1096–99) opened up trading stations in the Levant; but it was only after the great Venetian naval victory off Ascalon in 1123 that the Italian cities came to dominate the Mediterranean from Spain to Syria.

5, 6, 7/Urban development *(right and below)* Throughout western Europe the 12th century was a time of town-foundation. Kings, nobles and ecclesiastics all competed in setting up new towns, hoping for enhanced land values as well as profits from markets and fairs. In England and Wales alone *(right)* more than 100 new towns were founded between 1066 and 1190. By no means all these ventures were a success, and many other urban centres grew from existing villages, while ancient cities such as Cologne (see map 8) got a new lease of life. The counts of Flanders were particularly active in founding new towns; so were the dukes of Zähringen (see map 3). No fewer than nine towns in the northwest of modern Switzerland owe their existence to their initiative *(far right)*. French kings, bishops and princes were equally enterprising. Louis VI (1108-37) and Louis VII (1137-80) planted *villeneuves* (in this case villages rather than towns) the length of the road from Paris to Orléans *(below)*, seeking in this way to consolidate their hold over the region which was the core of their domain.

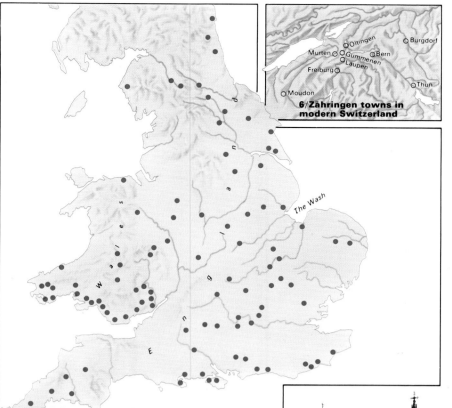

6/Zähringen towns in modern Switzerland

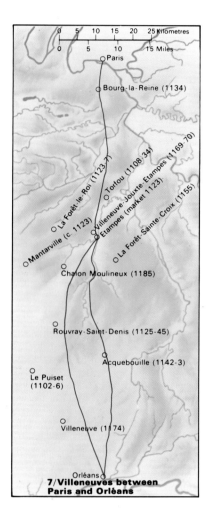

7/Villeneuves between Paris and Orléans

5/New towns in England and Wales, 1066-1190

8/Cologne *(below)*, the Roman Colonia Agrippina, was by the end of the 12th century the largest German city, commanding the trade of the river Rhine. In 900 less than half the area within the Roman walls was occupied, but a merchant quarter, with markets, was growing between the Roman city and the river. In the 10th century (presumably as protection against Viking raiders) this was enclosed by walls. In 1106 the walls were extended, but rapid growth required a new circuit in 1180. This remained the city boundary until the 19th century.

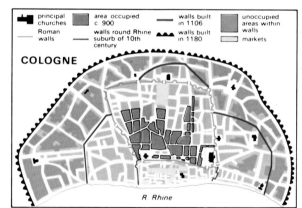

| principal churches | area occupied c 900 | walls built in 1106 | unoccupied areas within walls |
| Roman walls | walls round Rhine suburb of 10th century | walls built in 1180 | markets |

COLOGNE

R. Rhine

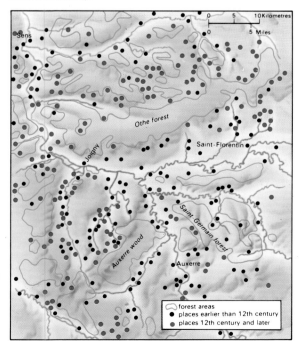

The cathedral of Worms *(above)* The massive Romanesque cathedral illustrates the new wealth generated by the economic recovery of the 11th century.

3/The colonization of the Black Forest *(below)* The Rhineland, a main artery of communications from Roman times, was settled at an early date; but the high, heavily wooded ranges which enclosed it on both sides (Hunsrück, Taunus, Spessart, Odenwald and Black Forest) had to wait until the 11th century before clearing and colonization took place. In the Black Forest settlements of the mountainous areas only took place after c.1075. The agents were the dukes of Zähringen and the monasteries under their control, particularly St Peter (1093) and St Georgen (1114). The Zähringer finally asserted control over the whole region by founding (c.1120) the towns of Freiburg, Villingen and Offenburg, which dominated the few routes traversing the forest. The advance of clearing, from the old-settled areas to the high woodlands, is a classic example of the progress of colonization and settlement.

4/Clearance and settlement in northeastern France *(below)* If in some areas (e.g. the Black Forest) colonization and the clearing of woodland and waste was planned, in others it was the result of piecemeal encroachment by individual peasants on the less fertile uplands and woods. The forest of Othe, southeast of Sens, is an example of this process. Early settlement followed the main river valleys and existing roads; but in the 12th century scores of new settlements opened up the intervening afforested countryside. The result was an increase in the cultivated area assessed at one-third or more for Europe north of the Alps and Pyrenees and west of the Elbe: an accretion of territory and agricultural resources which gave a major impetus to the European economy.

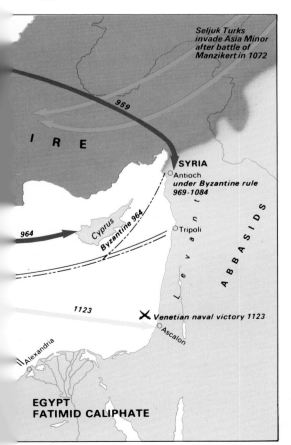

Seljuk Turks invade Asia Minor after battle of Manzikert in 1072

SYRIA

Antioch
under Byzantine rule 969-1084

Cyprus
Byzantine 964

Tripoli

ABBASIDS

1123

✗ *Venetian naval victory 1123*

Ascalon

Alexandria

EGYPT
FATIMID CALIPHATE

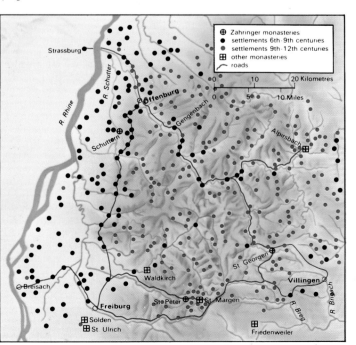

| Zähringer monasteries | settlements 6th - 9th centuries | settlements 9th - 12th centuries | other monasteries | roads |

forest areas
● places earlier than 12th century
● places 12th century and later

Feudal monarchy in western Europe 1154 to 1314

2/Italy disunited *(above)* Papal-Imperial controversy and the wealth of the municipalities inhibited consolidation in Italy. After 1250, public power in independent city states was exercised by republican oligarchies or by despots who often succeeded as alternatives to the factional violence of civic politics.

3/Spain: the Reconquista *(below)* Displaced in Old Castile and León, where Christian freeholders settled, Muslims remained numerous in the Aragonese kingdoms. In Andalusia Christian military leaders, rewarded with great estates, dominated a mixed population.

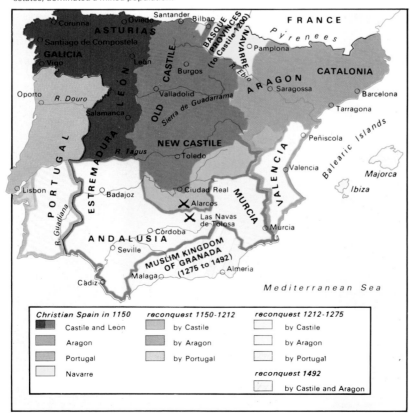

Christian Spain in 1150	reconquest 1150-1212	reconquest 1212-1275
Castile and León	by Castile	by Castile
Aragon	by Aragon	by Aragon
Portugal	by Portugal	by Portugal
Navarre		**reconquest 1492**
		by Castile and Aragon

WESTERN Europe began its slow climb out of political dislocation and feudal anarchy during the 12th century. Viking and Magyar invasions (see page 110) had disrupted royal authority and strengthened local feudatories, but kingship survived. Weak though the king might be in practice, his position was hallowed by religious sanctions, and in the 12th century kings used their position to assert their prerogatives at the head of the feudal hierarchy. They were helped by the reaction against papal attacks on the monarchy during the Investiture Contest (see page 118), when rulers turned to the arsenal of Roman law for weapons to defend their independence. In the hands of the emperor Frederick Barbarossa and later of the French Capetians, Roman law became a powerful instrument of royal authority. But the main weapons used by 12th- and 13th-century kings were feudal: the king's rights as 'liege lord', the duty of tenants-in-chief to render service, the theory that all land was held of the king, and all rights of justice were delegations of royal authority, and therefore reverted, or 'escheated', to the crown in case of abuse or treason. Step by step grave misdemeanours (felonies) were reserved to the king's courts as 'pleas of the crown'. By the beginning of the 13th century, at least in France and England, elective monarchy had been displaced by hereditary monarchy, and the electors, lay and ecclesiastical, shorn of their power. Much of this process was piecemeal; but by the middle of the 13th century the great lawyers (Bracton in England, Beaumanoir in France) had created a systematic theory of royal government, which kings such as Edward I of England (1272–1307) and Philip IV of France (1285–1314) proceeded to implement.

Progress was most rapid in the Norman kingdoms of England and Sicily. Since both were acquired by conquest, the aristocracy was less firmly entrenched than elsewhere and the kings' hands were correspondingly freer. This enabled William the Conqueror (1066–87) to retain and build up the fiscal and jurisdictional prerogatives inherited from his Anglo-Saxon predecessors in England. In Sicily also the great Norman ruler, Roger II, who united Sicily, Apulia and Calabria in 1130, retained the institutions of his Byzantine and Muslim predecessors, particularly their efficient system of taxation. By the end of the 12th century Sicily, with its control of the Mediterranean sea-routes, was the richest, most advanced and tightly organized state in Europe. In France, on the other hand, where the anarchy of the 9th and 10th centuries was greatest, progress was slower. Louis VI (1108–37) spent his reign asserting authority over the petty barons of the Ile de France, and it was scarcely before the reign of Philip Augustus (1180–1223) that expansion of the royal demesne began in earnest. The turning point was the conquest of Normandy in 1204, which effectively meant the destruction of the Angevin Empire, i.e. of the Anglo-Norman dominions across the English Channel. After 1214 English continental possessions were limited to Gascony, and a third of France was now under direct royal control. The defeat of the English also permitted the Capetians to turn their energies elsewhere. Much of Languedoc was subdued in a campaign against the Albigensian heretics (1209–29) and royal authority now extended south of the Loire.

The other area in which monarchy made great strides was the Iberian peninsula. Here the kingdoms of Portugal (independent since 1139), Navarre, Castile and Aragon were creations of the progressive reconquest of the peninsula from the Muslims, whose decisive defeat at Las Navas de Tolosa (1212) led rapidly to the loss of Córdoba (1236), Valencia (1238), Murcia (1243), Seville (1248) and Cádiz (1262). A major role in the reconquest was taken by Castile, originally a tributary of the crown of León, with which it was

permanently united in 1230. By the middle of the 13th century Castile controlled more than half the peninsula and was gradually welded into a monarchical state by Alfonso X (1252–84). In the eastern portion of the peninsula authority was wielded by the crown of Aragon after its union with the county of Catalonia (1137) and the conquest of Valencia (1238). Hemmed in on the west by Castile, Aragon turned its expansionist energies towards the Mediterranean. The Balearics were conquered between 1229 and 1235, and Sicily wrested from Charles of Anjou, in 1282. Though the kingdom's tripartite structure left partial autonomy to the component states, the Aragonese empire was the creation of a powerful monarchy fortified by the commercial wealth of Catalonia and Valencia.

The exceptions to this process of feudal concentration were Germany and Italy. Here, despite the efforts of Frederick Barbarossa (1152–90), the monarchy never fully recovered from its setbacks during the Investiture Contest, and the long interregnum after the death of Frederick's son, Henry VI, in 1197, weakened it still further. Paradoxically, the feudal processes which strengthened monarchy in the west worked to its detriment in central Europe, where power passed to feudal princes or, in Italy, to city magistrates (*podestà*) or increasingly to tyrants (*signori*) who dominated the cities they ruled and the surrounding countryside.

In the west royal supremacy was well established before the end of the 13th century. Kings exercised powers of taxation and legislation (often in consultation with parliaments or 'estates of the realm') and controlled the administration of justice. They also used their authority to assert overlordship over neighbouring territories, where feudalism had resulted in an intricate network of overlapping rights and jurisdictions. Nowhere was the feudal map more complex than in France, where the English possessions at one time stretched from Normandy almost to the Mediterranean coast. The determination of the French kings to assert their overlordship over these lands and over Flanders gave rise to a series of major wars. Meanwhile the English kings were asserting similar claims in Scotland, Wales and Ireland. Henry II's attempt to conquer Ireland (1171) achieved only a precarious foothold, but Edward I subdued Wales, already harassed by marcher lords and the palatine earls of Chester, in 1284. He tried to repeat the process in Scotland in 1296 but met resistance under Wallace and Bruce, and his son Edward II suffered a crushing defeat at Bannockburn in 1314 (see map 140/2).

Edward I's failure in Scotland was matched by Philip IV's failure in Flanders. Defeated by the Flemings at Courtrai (1302), the French king, who had seized Gascony in 1294, was compelled to restore it to the English in 1303. War expenditure and centralization also produced severe internal strains. In Aragon the estates forced the monarchy to grant a General Privilege in 1283. In England Edward I was compelled in 1297 to confirm and extend the concessions wrested from his grandfather, King John, in 1215. In France the States-General met for the first time in 1302. Everywhere, in short, the new monarchies had overreached themselves; the result was a powerful aristocratic reaction. When, after the middle of the 15th century, state-building recommenced (see page 146) the foundations were no longer feudal. Sovereignty had replaced suzerainty, and a new period in the history of western monarchy had begun.

1/The growth of the French and English monarchies *(right)* Early medieval rulers laid claim to supreme power but they depended primarily on personal and feudal allegiances over which not infrequently they had less command than their most powerful subjects. The institutional strength of monarchy, developing in the 12th century, expanded rapidly in the 13th century. By 1300 western kings were no longer primarily feudal overlords but acknowledged executors of effective public authority.

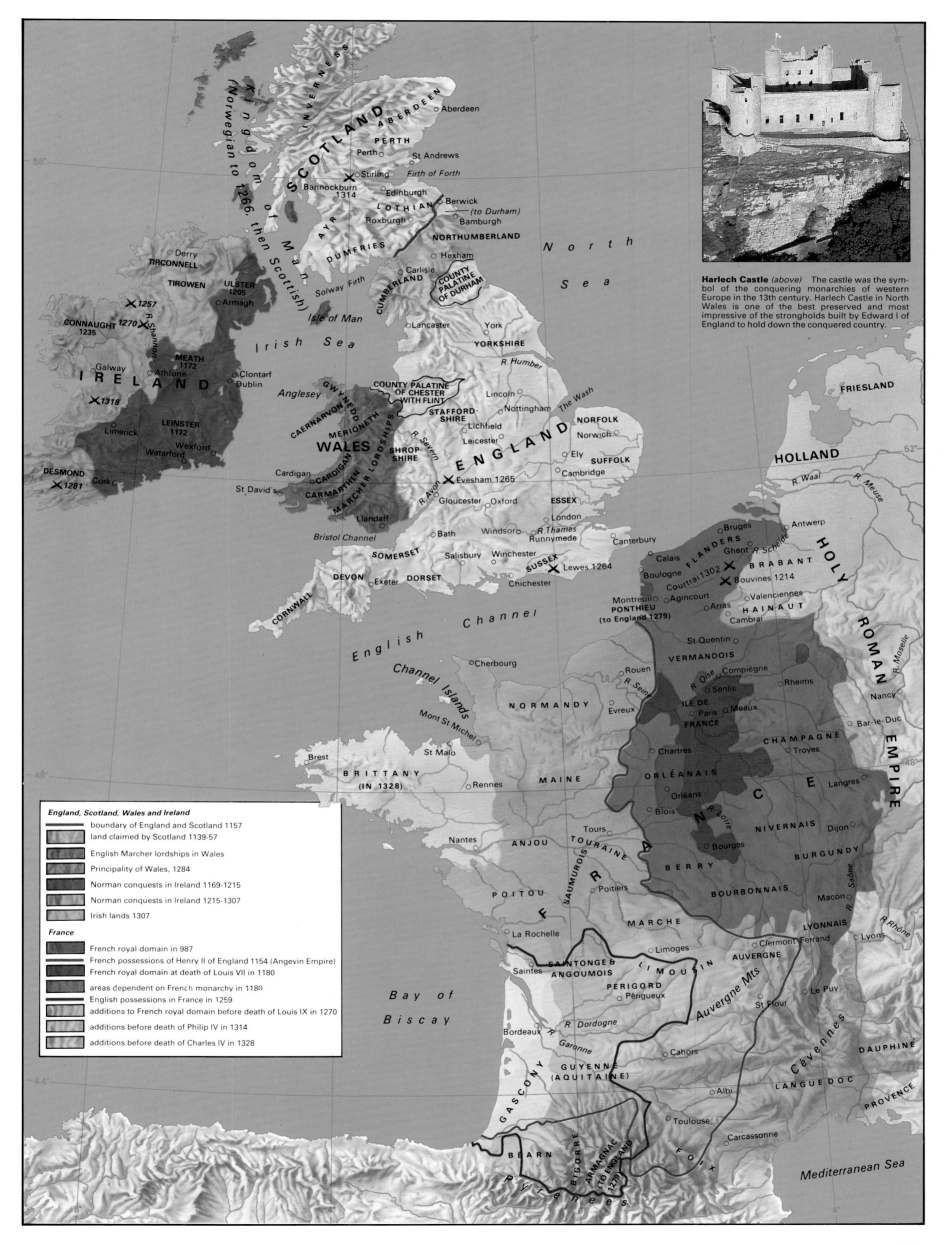

Harlech Castle *(above)* The castle was the symbol of the conquering monarchies of western Europe in the 13th century. Harlech Castle in North Wales is one of the best preserved and most impressive of the strongholds built by Edward I of England to hold down the conquered country.

SCOTLAND
Kingdom of Man (Norwegian to 1266, then Scottish)

INVERNESS
Aberdeen
ABERDEEN
PERTH
Perth
St Andrews
Firth of Forth
Stirling
× Bannockburn 1314
Edinburgh
LOTHIAN
Berwick
Roxburgh
— (to Durham)
Bamburgh
DUMFRIES
NORTHUMBERLAND

North Sea

Derry
TIRCONNELL
TIROWEN
ULSTER 1205
Armagh
× 1257
CONNAUGHT 1235
× 1270
R.Shannon
MEATH 1172
Galway
Athlone
Clontarf
Dublin
IRELAND
× 1318
LEINSTER 1172
Limerick
Wexford
Waterford
DESMOND
× 1281
Cork

Solway Firth
Isle of Man

Irish Sea

Carlisle
CUMBERLAND
COUNTY PALATINE OF DURHAM
Hexham

Lancaster
York
YORKSHIRE
R. Humber

Anglesey
GWYNEDD
CAERNARVONSHIRE
MERIONETH
WALES
CARDIGAN
CARMARTHEN
MARCHER LORDSHIPS
SHROPSHIRE
Cardigan
St David's
Llandaff
Bristol Channel

COUNTY PALATINE OF CHESTER WITH FLINT
STAFFORD-SHIRE
Lincoln
The Wash
Nottingham
Lichfield
Leicester
R. Severn
ENGLAND
Ely
NORFOLK
Norwich
SUFFOLK
Cambridge
× Evesham 1265
R. Avon
Gloucester
Oxford
ESSEX
London
SOMERSET
Bath
Windsor
R.Thames
Runnymede
Canterbury
Salisbury
Winchester
DEVON
DORSET
Exeter
SUSSEX
× Lewes 1264
Chichester
CORNWALL

FRIESLAND

HOLLAND
R. Waal
R. Meuse

HOLY ROMAN EMPIRE

Bruges
Antwerp
Calais
FLANDERS
Ghent R. Schelde
Boulogne
× Courtrai 1302
BRABANT
× Bouvines 1214
Montreuil
Agincourt
Valenciennes
PONTHIEU (to England 1279)
Arras
HAINAUT
Cambrai
St-Quentin
R. Moselle
VERMANDOIS
R. Oise
Compiègne
Rheims
Nancy
Rouen
Senlis
Bar-le-Duc
R. Seine
ÎLE DE FRANCE
Meaux
Paris
CHAMPAGNE
Troyes
Evreux
Chartres
Langres
FRANCE
ORLÉANAIS
NIVERNAIS
Dijon
Orléans
Blois
R. Loire
BURGUNDY
Bourges
BERRY
BOURBONNAIS
Macon
R. Saône
MARCHE
LYONNAIS
R. Rhône
Clermont-Ferrand
Lyons
AUVERGNE
Limoges
LIMOUSIN
Auvergne Mts
PÉRIGORD
Périgueux
St Flour
Le Puy
GUYENNE (AQUITAINE)
Bordeaux
R. Dordogne
R. Garonne
Cahors
DAUPHINE
Cévennes
LANGUEDOC
PROVENCE
GASCONY
Albi
Toulouse
Carcassonne
BÉARN
BIGORRE
ARMAGNAC (TO ENGLAND 1279)
FOIX
Pyrenees
Mediterranean Sea

English Channel
Cherbourg
Channel Islands
NORMANDY
Rouen
Mont St Michel
Brest
St Malo
BRITTANY (IN 1328)
Rennes
MAINE
Nantes
ANJOU
TOURAINE
Tours
SAUMUROIS
POITOU
Poitiers
La Rochelle
SAINTONGE & ANGOUMOIS
Saintes

Bay of Biscay

England, Scotland, Wales and Ireland

boundary of England and Scotland 1157
land claimed by Scotland 1139-57
English Marcher lordships in Wales
Principality of Wales, 1284
Norman conquests in Ireland 1169-1215
Norman conquests in Ireland 1215-1307
Irish lands 1307

France

French royal domain in 987
French possessions of Henry II of England 1154 (Angevin Empire)
French royal domain at death of Louis VII in 1180
areas dependent on French monarchy in 1180
English possessions in France in 1259
additions to French royal domain before death of Louis IX in 1270
additions before death of Philip IV in 1314
additions before death of Charles IV in 1328

Chinese civilization from the T'ang to the Sung 618 to 1278

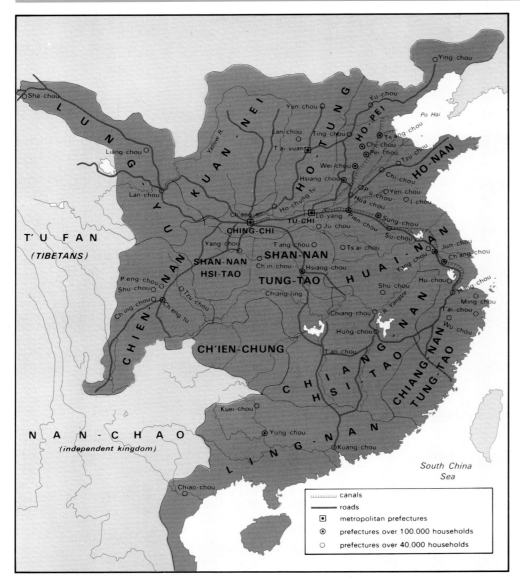

1/T'ang China (above) The whole of China proper, excepting the far southwest, was permanently organized under centralized administration. The empire was linked together by a network of post-roads, while transport of commodities between the rapidly developing regions of the Yangtze valley and the north was provided by an efficient system of canals and waterways. The road system centred on the capital, Ch'ang-an, which remained the political and strategic hub of the empire. However, the eastern plain and the area around the Lower Yangtze were the principal economic centres.

AFTER centuries of disunion (see page 94), China was reunified in 589 by the Sui dynasty (581–617). Their empire was consolidated under the system of centrally codified institutions developed under the northern Wei and their successors, by the state patronage of a style of Buddhism acceptable in north and south alike, and by the construction of a canal system linking the Yangtze with the Yellow River (Huang Ho) and the Peking region. The Sui collapsed, partly from the burden imposed by these public works and by the reconstruction of the Great Wall, partly because of repeated abortive attempts to conquer Koguryŏ (northern Korea).

After some years of widespread rebellions, the Sui were replaced by the T'ang, which was a dynasty of similar social origins and which continued most of their policies. The T'ang state was a strong centralized empire, with a simple but effective administrative system designed to be uniform. At first the system worked well, but after some years of internal consolidation the T'ang began to expand abroad, and in the 8th century the growing complexity of the state and of society, and the costs of defence, produced many changes.

By the 660s Chinese armies had intervened in India, central Asia and Afghanistan, the Chinese had occupied the Tarim Basin and Dzungaria, and briefly set up protectorates in Tukharistan, Sogdiana, Ferghana and eastern Persia. At the same period Koguryŏ was finally conquered and for a few years the T'ang occupied northern Korea. The formidable northern Turks had been defeated in 630, and in the 660s the Chinese Empire reached its greatest extent prior to the Manchu conquests of the 1700s.

While Chinese military force was establishing this vast empire, Chinese culture, its written language and political institutions, were adopted in the states which were growing up around China's eastern periphery – in Silla (Korea), in Japan, in Po-hai (Manchuria) and Nan-chao (Yunnan). Thus began Chinese cultural hegemony in the Far East, which persisted long after T'ang military power had decayed.

In 755 An Lu-shan, a frontier general, began a rebellion which lasted seven years and almost destroyed the T'ang. As a result the Chinese withdrew from central Asia, and the Tibetans and Uighurs occupied their former territories. Islam had meanwhile reached Ferghana and later became the dominant cultural force in Turkestan (see page 108). The deep cultural links between China and central Asia were broken, and China became more inward-looking.

The rebellion also set in motion major social and economic changes. Imperial authority was much reduced, and the uniform centralized policies of the 7th century were abandoned. Power passed to the provinces, and many provincial capitals grew into large and wealthy metropolises. There was a massive movement of population to the fertile Yangtze valley, where new methods of farming produced large surpluses of grain. Trade boomed, and a network of small market towns grew up everywhere.

At the end of the 9th century, however, massive peasant uprisings reduced central authority to a cipher, and power passed to the provincial generals, whose regimes became virtually independent. When in 907 the T'ang finally disappeared, China split into ten separate regional states, and was only reunified by the Sung between 960 and 979. In northern China there was constant warfare, and everywhere it was a period of insecurity, instability and sweeping social change, in which the diversity of China was intensified. During this period of division China lost control of the northeastern area to the Khitan (Liao) who had overwhelmed Po-hai to set up an empire in Manchuria and Inner Mongolia. In the northwest another powerful kingdom, the Hsi-hsia, was founded by the Tanguts in Ningsia and Kansu. These areas remained completely under alien domination until 1368.

The Sung state was organized on less uniform lines than the T'ang. The emperor enjoyed greater power, and military and financial experts were given greater influence. But there was constant and bitter factional strife between those who wished to rationalize government, and the conservatives. This weakened the Sung state, which in spite of its power and resources faced grave external threats. The Sung era was far less cosmopolitan than the T'ang, with China generally on the defensive and suspicious of the outside world. In 1126–7 this attitude hardened when the Chin, who had replaced the Liao in the northeast, overran and conquered all of northern China, with terrible devastation. From 1127 to 1279 the Sung controlled only central and southern China, constantly on the defensive and forced to maintain huge armies and pay vast subsidies to their aggressive neighbours.

Nevertheless, Chinese economic growth continued under the Sung. Between 750 and 1100 the population doubled; trade reached new levels and a great concentration of industries arose around the early Sung capital, K'ai-feng. Even after the loss of the north, Sung China was immensely prosperous. Its southern territories were far more productive than the old northern heartland of China. Population continued to increase rapidly, trade and industry boomed,

2/The Chinese world, 7th-8th centuries (right) During the 660s and 670s Chinese military power reached a peak, and briefly extended the power of the T'ang from Sogdiana to North Korea. The Chinese remained in control of the Tarim Basin and Dzungaria until 756; the Tarim and parts of northwest China fell to the Tibetans in 763-83 after Chinese garrisons were withdrawn. Chinese institutions and literary culture extended over parts of the Far East which were never ruled by China, but still came under Chinese cultural hegemony.

A foreign merchant (above) Most of the trade along the Silk Road was handled not by the Chinese, but by the nomadic peoples of central and western Asia. The T'ang generally regarded them with interested amusement, as is evident in this glazed pottery figure of a camel groom or trader with his exaggeratedly large nose.

3/The fragmentation of China: the Five Dynasties and Ten Kingdoms 910-23 (below) After the widespread peasant rebellions of the 870s, culminating in the Huang Ch'ao uprising, the central power of the T'ang, already weakened since the mid-8th century, speedily collapsed, and a variety of independent local regimes developed on the basis of Late T'ang provincial regional divisions. These were finally reunified by the Sung only in 979.

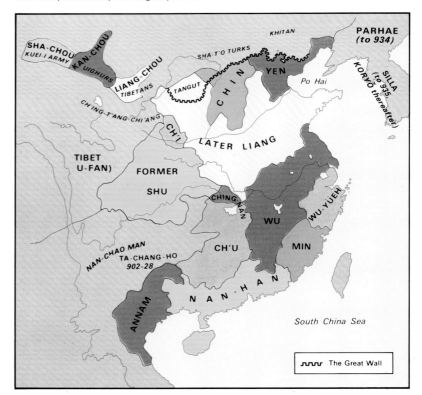

The Great Wall

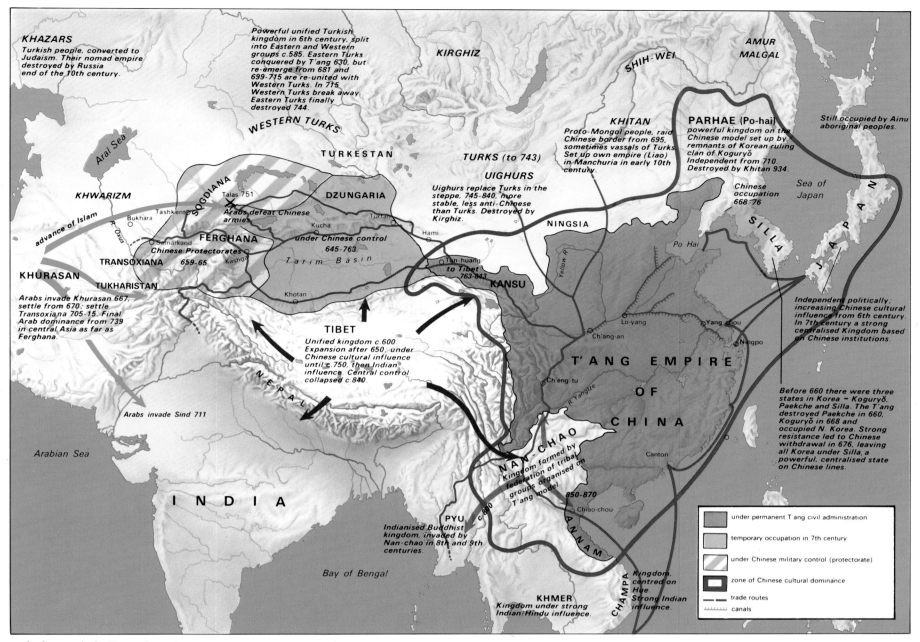

KHAZARS
Turkish people, converted to Judaism. Their nomad empire destroyed by Russia end of the 10th century.

KIRGHIZ

Powerful unified Turkish kingdom in 6th century, split into Eastern and Western groups c.585. Eastern Turks conquered by T'ang 630, but re-emerge from 681 and 699-715 are re-united with Western Turks. In 715 Western Turks break away. Eastern Turks finally destroyed 744.

SHIH-WEI

AMUR MALGAL

WESTERN TURKS

TURKESTAN

KHITAN
Proto-Mongol people, raid Chinese border from 695, sometimes vassals of Turks. Set up own empire (Liao) in Manchuria in early 10th century.

PARHAE (Po-hai)
powerful kingdom on the Chinese model set up by remnants of Korean ruling clan of Koguryŏ. Independent from 710. Destroyed by Khitan 934.

Still occupied by Ainu aboriginal peoples.

KHWARIZM

TURKS (to 743)

UIGHURS
Uighurs replace Turks in the steppe, 745-840, more stable, less anti-Chinese than Turks. Destroyed by Kirghiz.

Chinese occupation 668-76

Sea of Japan

SILLA

JAPAN

Aral Sea

advance of Islam

Tashkent
Talas 751
Arabs defeat Chinese armies
R. Oxus
Bukhara

SOGDIANA

DZUNGARIA

NINGSIA

Po Hai

KHURASAN

Samarkand
Chinese Protectorates
FERGHANA
TRANSOXIANA 659-65

under Chinese control 645-763

Kucha
Turfan
Hami

Kashgar

Tarim Basin

Tun-huang
to Tibet
763-843

KANSU

Lo-yang
Yang-chou

Ch'ang-an

Ningpo

Independent politically; increasing Chinese cultural influence from 6th century. In 7th century a strong centralised Kingdom based on Chinese institutions.

TUKHARISTAN
Arabs invade Khurasan 667, settle from 670; settle Transoxiana 705-15. Final Arab dominance from 739 in central Asia as far as Ferghana.

Khotan

TIBET
Unified kingdom c.600. Expansion after 650, under Chinese cultural influence until c.750, then Indian influence. Central control collapsed c.840.

NEPAL

T'ANG EMPIRE OF CHINA

Ch'eng-tu

R. Yangtze

Before 660 there were three states in Korea – Koguryŏ, Paekche and Silla. The T'ang destroyed Paekche in 660, Koguryŏ in 668 and occupied N. Korea. Strong resistance led to Chinese withdrawal in 676, leaving all Korea under Silla, a powerful, centralised state on Chinese lines.

Arabs invade Sind 711

Arabian Sea

I N D I A

NAN-CHAO
Kingdom formed by federation of tribal groups organised on T'ang model

Canton

850-870

c.810

Chiao-chou

PYU
Indianised Buddhist kingdom, invaded by Nan-chao in 8th and 9th centuries.

Bay of Bengal

ANNAM

CHAMPA
Kingdom, centred on Hué. Strong Indian influence.

KHMER
Kingdom under strong Indian/Hindu influence.

Legend	
	under permanent T'ang civil administration
	temporary occupation in 7th century
	under Chinese military control (protectorate)
	zone of Chinese cultural dominance
	trade routes
	canals

---

and the capital, Hang-chou, became indisputably the world's greatest city. It was also a period of great cultural achievement. In the visual arts, in literature, philosophy, science and technology, new heights were reached. Education became more widespread, aided by the dissemination of printing, which had been invented during the T'ang and was now commonplace. The prosperous cities developed an urban middle class with their own life-style and culture, who became patrons of popular drama and of storytellers.

Society was transformed. State examinations for the recruiting of officials gradually replaced the old ruling aristocratic caste with a mandarinate – a meritocracy of career bureaucrats.

Although merchants were excluded from official service, many became immensely rich and held an important place in society, forming guilds and partnerships and setting up a complex commercial organization with banks, credit systems and paper money. In the countryside the independent peasants of T'ang times, working lands allocated by the state, were replaced by many large estates farmed by tenant farmers and labourers. A free market in land emerged.

Since the old overland routes to central Asia and the Middle East were no longer in Chinese hands, the Chinese slowly became a major sea power. Chinese shipping developed a regular trade with southeast Asia, Indonesia, India and the Persian Gulf. The southern Sung also had a powerful navy.

In the 13th century, after this period of rapid change and growth, the pace of change slowed down markedly. This was partly the result of the immense destruction and social disruption caused by the Mongol conquest (see page 126), but in part because T'ang and Sung China had evolved an abiding social stability, developing conservative and conformist intellectual and political attitudes which militated against change. But in the 13th century China remained far more populous, productive and wealthy, her society far more advanced, than that of contemporary Europe. During this whole period, China was the world's greatest power, and Chinese culture the world's greatest splendour.

5/Sung China *(below)* The Sung suffered considerable losses of territory compared with the T'ang: Vietnam was no longer Chinese territory; in the north, the Khitan state of Liao occupied the border areas to the northeast, and the Tangut state of Hsi-hsia the northwest. The centre of the Sung state was the great commercial city of K'ai-feng, centre of the canal system and of the eastern road network, which grew into the centre of a major complex of industries. The old strategic heartland of the northwest steadily declined in importance.

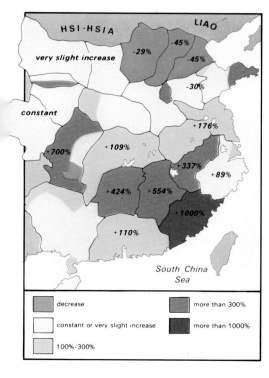

HSI-HSIA **LIAO**

very slight increase

-29% -45% -45%

-30%

constant

-700% +109% -337% +176%

+424% +554% +89%

+110% +1000%

South China Sea

	decrease
	constant or very slight increase
	100%-300%
	more than 300%
	more than 1000%

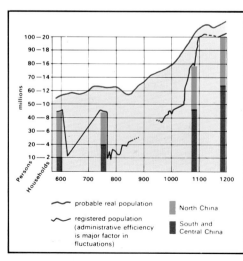

100 — 20
90 — 18
80 — 16
70 — 14
60 — 12
50 — 10
40 — 8
30 — 6
20 — 4
10 — 2

millions

Persons / Households

600 700 800 900 1000 1100 1200

— probable real population
— registered population (administrative efficiency is major factor in fluctuations)

North China
South and Central China

4/Population growth *(above and left)* The period from 750 to 1250 saw a very rapid growth of the Chinese population, which probably doubled. At the same time the distribution of the people completely changed. In the 7th century 73 per cent of the population lived in the northeast of China, and less than a quarter in south and central China. By the 13th century the situation was reversed and China's economic centre of gravity had shifted from the northern plain to the Yangtze valley.

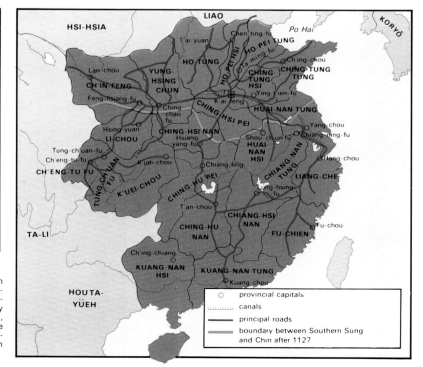

HSI-HSIA **LIAO** **KORYŎ**

Po Hai

T'ai-yuan
Chen-ting-fu

HO TUNG

Lan-chou
YUNG-HSING CHUN
HO PEI HSI
HO PEI TUNG
Ta-ming-fu
CHING-TUNG HSI
CHING-TUNG TUNG
Ch'ing-chou
Ying-t'ien-fu

Feng-hsiang-fu
Ching-chao-fu
K'ai-feng
Ying-t'ien-fu

Hsing-yuan
Hsiang-yang-fu
HUAI-NAN TUNG
Yang-chou
LI-CHOU
Hsiang-yang-fu
CHING-HSI NAN
Shou-ch'un-fu
HUAI-NAN HSI
Chiang-ning-fu

CH'ENG-TU FU
Ch'eng-tu fu
TUNG-CH'UAN FU
K'uei-chou
Chiang-ling
CHING-HU PEI
CHIANG-NAN TUNG
Hang-chou

K'UEI-CHOU
CHIANG-NAN HSI
LIANG-CHE

TA-LI
T'an-chou
CHING-HU NAN
CHIANG-HSI NAN
Fu-chou
FU-CHIEN

Ch'ing-chiang
KUANG-NAN HSI
KUANG-NAN TUNG
Kuang-chou

HOU TA-YÜEH

○	provincial capitals
	canals
	principal roads
	boundary between Southern Sung and Chin after 1127

The Mongol Empire
1206 to 1405

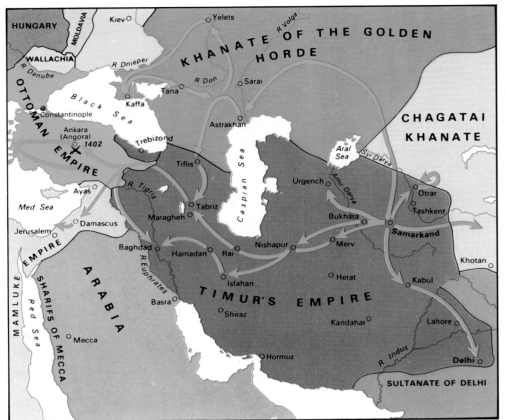

1/The Mongol Empire before 1259 (below) The greatest land empire in world history was conquered by the ruthless and brilliant cavalry armies of Genghis Khan and his successors. It stretched from Java and Korea in the east to Poland in the west, from the Arctic in the north to Turkey and Persia in the south. The armies became expert at siege warfare, learning from the Chinese, and their field intelligence and signals enabled them to mount bewildering flank attacks, encirclements and obstruction of escape routes. Byzantium and western Europe were saved by the death of Ogedei just as his advance guard reached the Adriatic, and Japan by the storms (or *kamikaze*, sacred wind) that destroyed Kublai Khan's navy.

launched against Poland and Hungary. The Oder was passed at Racibórz and the Mongol army swept northwards down the river valley. Breslau was bypassed, and on 9 April 1241 a German/Polish army was annihilated at Legnica. A few days later the second Mongol army routed the Hungarians at Mohi. It is generally believed that only the death of the Great Khan Ogedei in December 1241 saved Europe, for disputes arose over the succession and Batu led the armies back to their old base on the lower Volga in the winter of 1242–3.

If Christian Europe was saved by the death of Ogedei in 1241, the death of the Great Khan Möngke in 1259 saved Muslim Asia. Möngke had resolved to extend the Mongol dominions in the east and west, against the Sung in China, and the Assassins and the Caliphate 'as far as the borders of Egypt'. Möngke himself was to take charge of the Chinese war, while the western campaign was entrusted to his younger

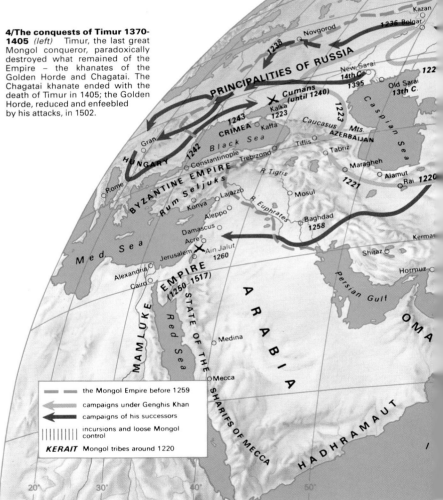

4/The conquests of Timur 1370-1405 (left) Timur, the last great Mongol conqueror, paradoxically destroyed what remained of the Empire – the khanates of the Golden Horde and Chagatai. The Chagatai khanate ended with the death of Timur in 1405; the Golden Horde, reduced and enfeebled by his attacks, in 1502.

T HE Mongols, a pastoralist nomadic people from the depths of Asia, made a tremendous impact on world history. Their conquests were of a scope and range never equalled, stretching from the eastern frontiers of Germany to Korea and from the Arctic Ocean to Turkey and the Persian Gulf. They even attempted seaborne invasions of Japan and Java. This was the last, and most violent, assault by nomadic armies inflicted upon the settled peoples of western Asia, and its effects were enormous. The political organization of Asia and a large part of Europe was altered; whole peoples were uprooted and dispersed, permanently changing the ethnic character of many regions; the strength and distribution of the principal religions of the world were decisively altered; European access to Asia and the Far East, interrupted for 1000 years, became possible again once the transcontinental routes were dominated by a single authority capable of making travel safe.

Ethnically, the most striking result of the Mongol conquests was the wide dispersal of the Turkic peoples over western Asia. Since their barren land could not support a large population, the Mongols were not a numerous people, but from the outset Genghis Khan did not hesitate to augment his armies from Turkish tribes on whose fidelity he could rely, until Turks in the Mongol armies actually out-numbered the native Mongols. Thus the Turkish language advanced across Asia with the Mongol armies, the minority of Mongol speakers was absorbed by the Turkish mass and their language survived only in the original homeland. The Turks had already risen to prominence before the Mongol conquests, but the Mongols, by breaking up the old Seljuk sultanate of Rum, cleared the way for the greatest of Turkish empires – the Ottoman.

In the course of their drive for empire the Mongols came into contact with three religions and their associated cultures – Buddhism, Islam and Christianity. Their attitude towards them was ambivalent: they professed an ancestral shamanism, but felt the powerful attraction of the new creeds which seemed invariably to be associated with higher cultures. Islam at first seemed unfavourably placed. Baghdad itself was captured and sacked and the caliph slain, but the religion of the Prophet slowly established its ascendancy over the conquerors of

that region and a powerful revival began. This revival was closely bound up with the collapse of Asian Christianity, whose prospects had once looked so bright (see page 100). For a time Christianity was widely preached throughout the Asian continent, but the initial promise was never fulfilled. Buddhism, like Islam, emerged from the Mongol experience stronger than it entered it: although it had little success west of the Altai Mountains, in eastern Asia the Mongol dynasty gave it a predominant place in Chinese society.

The early life of Genghis Khan is known from the 13th century *Secret History of the Mongols*. Primitive Mongol-speaking tribes had lived for centuries in the general area of present-day Mongolia, but it took an extraordinary leader to unite the Mongols and transform them into a world power. Temujin (later Genghis Khan) was born probably in 1162, the son of a tribal chief. After many years of struggle he succeeded in uniting all the Mongol tribes by 1206. After subduing other neighbouring tribes, in 1211 he invaded the independent Chin empire in northern China, piercing the Great Wall and opening a struggle that was to continue for 23 years, ending only in 1234, after Genghis' death, with the total destruction of the Chin empire. Peking fell in 1215, but Genghis was then drawn away to the west in campaigns against the Kara-Khitai and Khwarizm – the first Muslim state to experience the full fury of the Mongol onslaught. In spite of bitter resistance, the Mongols overwhelmed the Muslim states of central Asia and reached the Caucasus.

Genghis died in 1227, but his conquests were continued and extended by his successors. Before his death he made provision for the succession, dividing his empire among his four sons. Batu, a grandson of Genghis, directed the invasion of Europe. The northern Russian principalities were smashed in a lightning winter campaign in 1237–8, and the ancient city of Kiev was taken by storm and razed to the ground in 1240. The same year a two-pronged assault was

2/The Mongol invasion of Europe 1237-42 (right) The Mongols conquered Russia in a winter campaign – their cavalry armies moving with great speed on frozen rivers – the only successful winter invasion of Russia in history. A meticulously planned and brilliantly executed campaign against Hungary followed, penetrating from at least three different directions.

The Gagnières-Fonthill Vase
(above) The existence of a direct link between China and the west in the Middle Ages may be proved by objects such as this vase. It was manufactured in China and was recorded in Hungary in the mid-14th century.

brother, Hülegü. The Assassins were exterminated and Baghdad fell early in 1258. However, after the death of Möngke the following year armed conflict broke out between rival claimants, causing Hülegü to concentrate the bulk of his troops in Azerbaijan leaving only a skeleton force in Syria. This soon became known at Cairo, and the Mamluke sultan took the opportunity to march against the pagan enemies of the faith. At Ain Jalut near Nazareth on 3 September 1260 the superior Mamluke army inflicted a crushing defeat. This battle was a turning point in history. The Mongol advance in the west was never seriously renewed, and the spell of their invincibility was shattered for ever.

The death of Möngke also ended the short-lived unity of the Mongol Empire. The direct authority of succeeding Great Khans was confined to the east, while the khanates of Chagatai, Persia (Il-Khan) and the Golden Horde went their several ways as independent states. In the settled kingdoms of Persia and China the Mongol dynasties came to an end in less than a century. In the khanates of the Golden Horde and Chagatai, society was less urbanized and simpler and the population partly nomadic; in consequence Mongol rule lasted longer – in Russia for more than 200 years. Their decline can in fact be dated from the time of Timur (Tamerlane), whose rise to power marks the final phase of the Mongol age of conquests.

The appearance of the Mongols on the world stage was sudden and devastating. Old kingdoms and empires went down before them in monotonous succession. Their success was probably the result of superior strategy, an excellent and highly mobile cavalry, endurance, and a disciplined and co-ordinated manner of fighting. The Mongols even had an organization that in some ways resembled a modern general staff. On the other hand the opposing armies, especially in Europe, were usually cumbersome and unco-ordinated. The invasion of Russia is a good example of Mongol methods. The strongest part of the country was conquered in a few months, and by means of a winter campaign, the Mongol cavalry moving with great speed on the frozen rivers – the only successful winter invasion of Russia in history. The Mongols did not make any startling innovations in the ancient traditions of the steppe nomads. They used the strategy and tactics of the earlier cavalry armies of the steppe peoples, but under a military genius these were brought to the highest pitch of efficiency and produced what was certainly the most formidable instrument of war in the world at that time.

Nevertheless the social and cultural legacy of the Mongol irruption is not easy to trace. Their rule was, in most cases, comparatively brief. In fact the Mongols never succeeded in creating an imperial, enduring civilization. Rather their conquests can be seen as the end of an epoch. From the dawn of civilization, city dwellers and the cultivators of the soil had been menaced by assault from the fierce riders of the steppes. But during the life of the Mongol Empire came the invention of gunpowder and firearms; no longer would battles be decided by endurance and stamina. During the succeeding centuries Russia and China, the two nations which had suffered most from nomad aggression, steadily moved in to contain once and for all the recalcitrant herdsmen of the steppes.

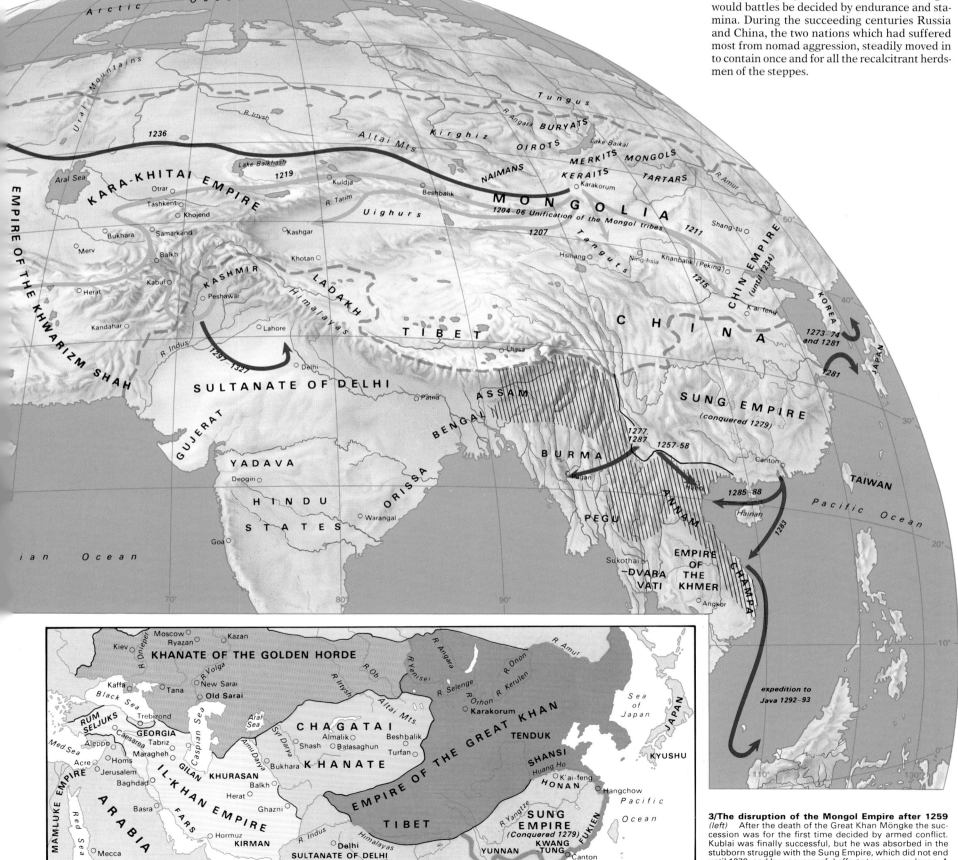

3/The disruption of the Mongol Empire after 1259
(left) After the death of the Great Khan Möngke the succession was for the first time decided by armed conflict. Kublai was finally successful, but he was absorbed in the stubborn struggle with the Sung Empire, which did not end until 1279, and by unsuccessful efforts to conquer Japan. A vast imperial realm comprising nearly all Asia and much of Europe could not be governed by one man.

India: the struggle for power and the Delhi Sultanate

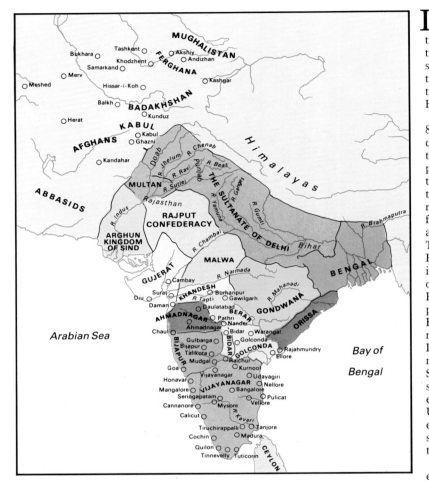

4/India on the eve of Babur's invasion
(above) In 1526, one of the Lodi sultans who had assumed power after Timur's sack of Delhi, held sway in the Punjab, and another controlled the Doab and Bihar. The Bahmani kingdom in the Deccan had broken up into five separate warring sultanates. Rajput dynasties controlled Rajasthan and also territories further to the northwest, including Delhi.

INDIA between the 8th and 13th centuries was characterized by warring regional states, the growth of feudal relations, and the proliferation of castes. Although there was economic stagnation in the traditional urban centres in the north, trade grew with Southeast Asia, thus transmitting culture and religion overseas from Bengal and south India.

Following Harsha's death in c.647 (see page 83), no single contender for power was able to dominate the north. The city of Kanauj became the focus of a struggle for control of the Ganges plain, waged between the Gurjara-Pratiharas, the Palas and the Rashtrakutas. The Rashtrakuta kingdom, founded in the mid-8th century, formed a bridge between north and south from its main power base in the north Deccan, and extended at its peak from south Gujerat to Tanjore. The Pala Empire included Bengal, Bihar, Orissa and the Andhra country. It flourished after a strong king, Gopala, ended a period of political chaos in the 8th century. The Pratiharas originated in Rajasthan and held power from 836 between east Punjab and north Bengal. These three contenders were evenly matched, a situation which ultimately left north India open once more to external invasion. For meanwhile, the arrival of Arab Muslim armies in Sind in the early 8th century had added expansionist objectives in India to the religious influences already at work as a result of Arab trade. Until the 11th century however, Muslim influence was restricted to the lower Indus valley and some trading enclaves on the west coast, with little impact on the Deccan and the south.

The south, like the north, saw continuous efforts to secure regional dominance. Out of the struggles two major powers emerged: the Tamil Cholas in the east and the Chalukyas in the west. The Cholas were well established claimants, first mentioned in the inscriptions of Asoka (page 82). Under Rajaraja (985–1014) and his son Rajendra, they now conquered most of the Tamilnad, eastern Deccan, Ceylon and parts of the Malay Peninsula. Ceylon, involved

in conflicts with assorted enemies (including the Rashtrakutas), finally expelled the Cholas in 1070, but meanwhile the latter had successfully driven north as far as Bengal to participate in the struggle on the northern plains. Rajendra's new capital on the Kaveri River, named Gangaikonda-cholapuram ('city of the Chola conqueror of the Ganges'), commemorates this southern foray into north India. Although retreat from the north followed rapidly, the Cholas had sealed their dominance south of the Narmada river earlier in the 11th century by sacking Kalyani, the capital of their main southern rival, the Chalukyas, until then masters of the western Deccan.

Hindu civilization flourished during this era of conflicting regional kingdoms. There were several attempts to interpret the theology of the ancient Vedic writings. Sankaracharya (c.788–820), a south-Indian brahmin, became the foremost interpreter of Vedanta, which proclaimed that the final object of existence was the union of the individual and the Absolute Soul, and also propagated the monist philosophy of Advaita, holding that the world is an illusion. Further north, the Tantric form of Buddhism and Hinduism, with its emphasis both on magic and on the importance of female as well as male deities, spread its influence to Nepal and Tibet. The famous temples at Tanjore, the exquisite temple sculptures of Khajuraho in central India, and the more monumental style of Bhubaneswar in Orissa, were all built in this period.

From the beginning of the 11th century the north, particularly the Punjab, began to feel the impact of Turkish invaders who turned towards India, first as a source of booty, and later as an extension of expansionist ambitions. The initiator was Mahmud of Ghazni (reigned 998–1030), who brought the Punjab under long-term Muslim sway, but whose motives for the destruction of temples as far distant as Somnath, in Gujerat, have been disputed ever since by historians of the subcontinent. Without doubt Mahmud and successive Turkish-Afghan invaders took advantage of endemic warfare among the northern dynasties, as well as internecine conflict among some recently emerged Rajput clans, to inflict the military victories which prepared the way for Muslim hegemony in the north in the 13th century. In this way the Ghurids, another Turkish family, after seizing the eastern Ghaznavid empire, reconquered the Punjab and then, in 1192, defeated the strongest Rajput contender, Prithviraj, thus allowing Qutbuddin Aibak, a general in the Ghurid service who had risen from slave status, to establish in his own name, the 'sultanate of Delhi'.

Delhi, founded in the 8th century by a Rajput chief, remained the focus of north Indian politics and a centre of Muslim culture, from the 13th until the 19th century. During the Sultanate era (1206–1526), when north India was ruled from Delhi by six successive Muslim dynasties, all of Turkish or Afghan extraction, pretensions to control the Deccan and the south proved unrealizable, partly because of constant threats of further invasions from the northwest. In reality, even the north proved difficult to control. Aibak's son, Iltutmish, claimed by his death in 1235 a coast-to-coast domain from Sind to Bengal, much of which was lost during the conflicts following his daughter, Razziya's, brief reign. Seizure of power by a palace official, Balban, led to a renewed phase of expansion, which was intensified by the seizure of Delhi by

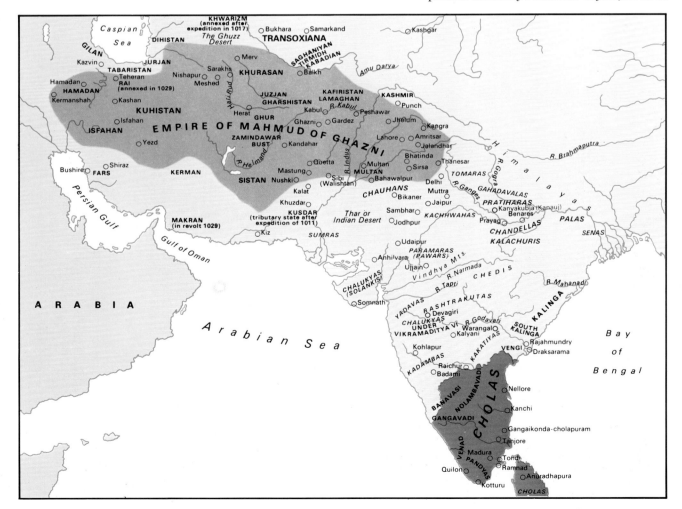

2/India in the 11th century *(left)* The conquests of Sultan Mahmud of Ghazni stretched deep into central Asia. The sub-continent was divided along the line of the Narmada river and the Vindhya mountains. To the south, the Chola Empire, including Ceylon, is shown at its fullest extent. But wars with the Rashtrakutas and others continually abraded the frontiers, both for the Cholas and for the Chalukyas in the west.

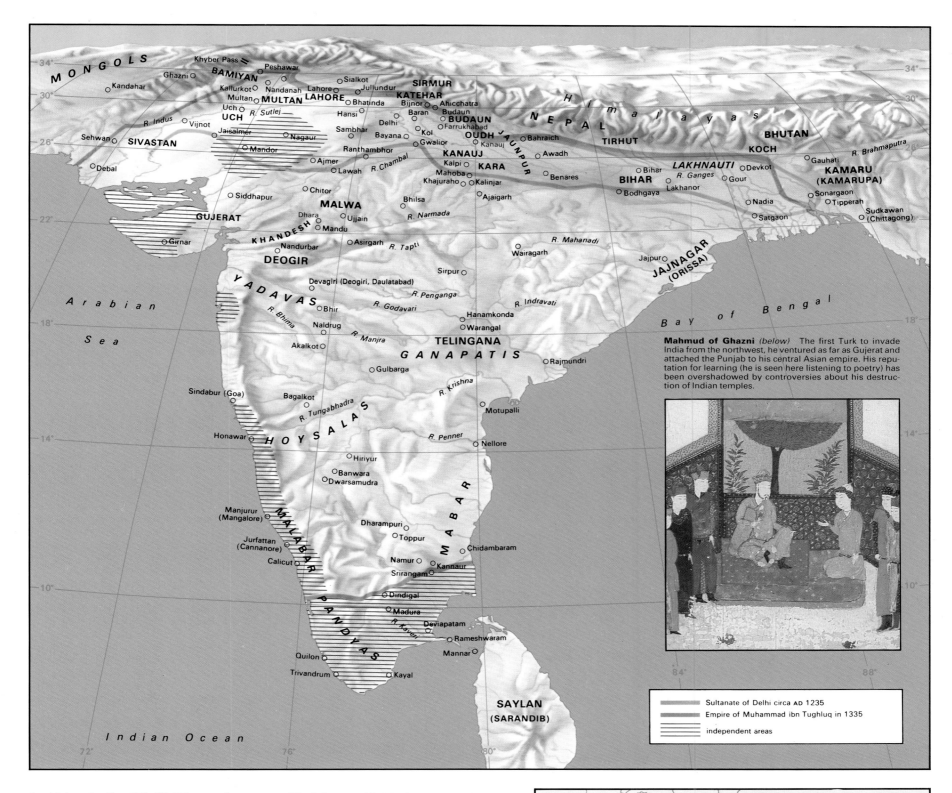

3/The Sultanate of Delhi (above) Turko-Afghan rule in India started in the 12th century and reached its height with the Sultanate under Muhammad ibn Tughluq. However, by 1398 Tughluq rule barely extended beyond Delhi.

Mahmud of Ghazni (below) The first Turk to invade India from the northwest, he ventured as far as Gujerat and attached the Punjab to his central Asian empire. His reputation for learning (he is seen here listening to poetry) has been overshadowed by controversies about his destruction of Indian temples.

▨▨▨	Sultanate of Delhi circa AD 1235
▬▬▬	Empire of Muhammad ibn Tughluq in 1335
⬚⬚⬚	independent areas

the Afghan family of Khalji. Whereas the army of Alauddin Khalji (1296–1316) marched to the southern tip of India to claim tribute from much of the Deccan and the south, his somewhat empty claim was then briefly fulfilled by the Tughluq family, which in turn seized Delhi in 1320. Under Muhammad ibn Tughluq (1325–51) the Sultanate reached its maximum extent, drawing taxes from more than 20 provinces, including some in the extreme south. By this time the Mongol harassment from the northwest had receded, yet controversial decisions by Muhammad (notably an attempt to transfer the population of Delhi to a new capital in the Deccan, and high taxes exacerbated by famine), hastened the disintegration of the empire even as it reached its peak. Bengal broke away in 1341; the Deccan provinces in 1347 to form the Bahmani Sultanate; and Khandesh, Malwa, Jaunpur and Gujerat between 1382 and 1396. The invasion of Timur (Tamerlane) in 1398, when Delhi was razed, ended Tughluq pretensions in all but name, and although two subsequent dynasties (the Sayyids from 1414 to 1445, and the Afghan Lodis, from 1451 to 1526) temporarily revived the Sultanate of Delhi, its age of real greatness was over by the late 14th century.

The Bahmani Sultanate in the Deccan was faced south of the Tungabhadra river by the re-establishment of a strong Hindu polity in the shape of the Vijayanagar Empire, founded in 1336, which under three successive dynasties, dominated south India until the mid-16th century. Recent archaeological discoveries are now throwing new light on many aspects of Vijayanagar's rich civilization.

Whether or not a real *modus vivendi* between Muslims and Hindus gradually evolved during the centuries of Turko-Afghan influence is hotly debated among historians. Certainly a stylistically unified architecture flourished, and a varied local literature grew up in the provincial kingdoms in both north and south. Humbly-born preachers, like Kabir (1440–1518), and Nanak (1469–c.1539), the founder of Sikhism, played down any contradiction between seemingly conflicting ideas of God, and preached social egalitarianism. Bhakti devotionalism spread from south India to Bengal, leading to a revival of Vaishnavism in eastern and northern India. Magnificent temples were built by the Vijayanagar rulers who now led the Hindu revival in the south. Yet in spite of a considerable degree of cultural and religious synthesis, much of India was fragmented into regional kingdoms, intermittently at war with each other. When Timur's descendant, Babur, invaded from Afghanistan in 1526, neither Hindu nor Muslim rulers proved capable of effective resistance.

1/Regional kingdoms and the struggle for empire (right) The fluctuating territories held by the Gurjara-Pratiharas, the Rashtrakutas, the Palas, the Cholas and the Arabs in Sind, as they struggled both on their frontiers and for control of Kanauj from c.750 to 1018.

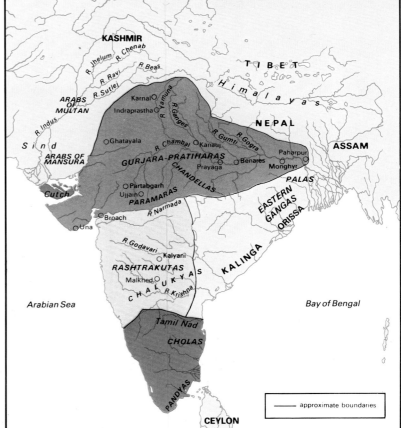

The early civilizations of Southeast Asia to AD 1511

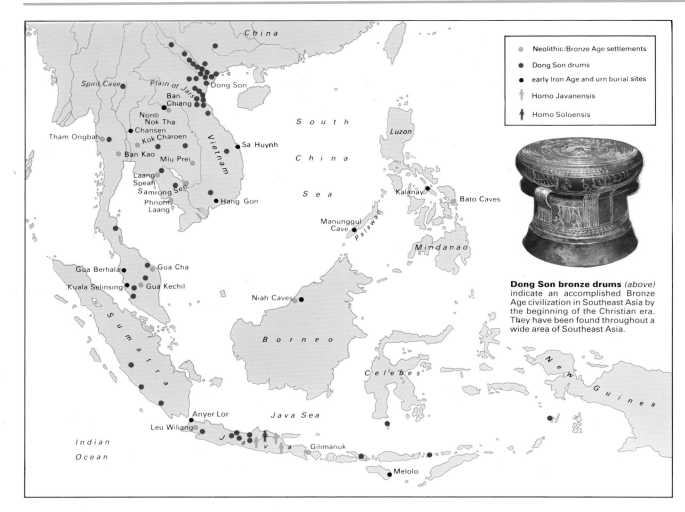

Dong Son bronze drums (above) indicate an accomplished Bronze Age civilization in Southeast Asia by the beginning of the Christian era. They have been found throughout a wide area of Southeast Asia.

1/Prehistoric sites in Southeast Asia (above) Neolithic and early Bronze Age sites indicate developed lowland cultures by the 2nd millennium BC. Later (late 1st millennium BC) we find more advanced cultures, characterized by 'Dong Son' bronze drums or by early Iron Age jar burials, all before the arrival of Indian and Chinese influences in the area.

SITUATED at one of the world's main cross-roads, the countries of Southeast Asia boast a history that reaches back into early prehistory and beyond. 'Java Man', whose remains from the Middle Pleistocene were found in the Solo Valley of central Java, may be related to the culture of 'Peking Man' in China. Java also produced the earliest evidence of *Homo sapiens* in Southeast Asia: remains of c.40,000 BC from the Brantas Valley. A number of Palaeolithic and Mesolithic cultures have been identified in various parts of the region, notably the 'Bacsonian' and 'Hoabinhian' of Vietnam, Siam and Malaya. Early cave sites have been excavated in Sumatra, Borneo, Cambodia and Siam (Thailand), and evidence in one (Spirit Cave, northern Thailand) suggests rice cultivation as early as 6000 BC.

The Neolithic cultures of the region used to be identified by axe types, including the rectangular adze of undoubtedly ancient origin. More recently, the excavation of burial and possible habitation sites has provided information about specific Neolithic cultures and their highly localized pottery traditions. Ban Chiang and Non Nok Tha in northeast Thailand yielded indications of a gradual evolution towards bronze metallurgy (although attempts to date the earliest bronze, by Carbon-14 and thermoluminescence methods, have yielded controversial results: some scholars claim a date earlier than 3000 BC, while others place it nearer to 1000 BC). Evidence of a Neolithic and Early Bronze culture of around 1000 BC has also been found in northern Vietnam. The first use of iron in the region seems to have occurred in central Siam, perhaps as early as 500 BC; spreading to Borneo and Palawan by c.200 BC.

It is thus clear that Southeast Asia had a number of flourishing cultures using bronze and iron before Indian and Chinese influences made themselves felt in the 2nd or 3rd century AD. These influences never obliterated the unique character of Southeast Asian civilization; instead, the next thousand years saw their assimilation to produce distinctive societies in

the area. Chinese influence predominated in Tonking (northern Vietnam), which had its own polity down to c.110 BC but was subsequently annexed to China and ruled as a Chinese province until c.AD 900.

The remainder of the region gradually came under Hindu-Buddhist influences from India, beginning about the 2nd or 3rd century AD. Early trade routes appear to have linked India with southern Burma, central and southern Siam, lower Cambodia and southern Vietnam, where an ancient port city (3rd–6th century) has been excavated at Oc Eo. By the 5th–6th century Buddhist images and votive tablets appeared, and also the earliest Sanskrit inscriptions. Early Indianization occurred in Java and southern Sumatra too. Although Indian in culture, these areas also maintained commercial and political relations with China, which welcomed tribute missions from a growing number of states whose location it is not always easy to identify.

By the 7th century, small Hindu temples were being built in lower Cambodia, notably at Angkor Borei, and also in central Java; other early temples, probably Buddhist, have been excavated in southern Burma at Peikthano and Sri Ksetra. These three areas became the principal centres of temple-building and produced a number of major temple complexes: Borobudur and Prambanan (central Java, 8th–10th centuries); Angkor (9th–13th centuries); and Pagan (11th–13th centuries). All three combined Hindu and Buddhist elements, with Buddhism especially strong at Pagan and Hinduism at Angkor. Another series of temples associated with the Hindu-Buddhist kingdom of Champa was built along the coast of central Vietnam. A centre of Sanskrit culture, Palembang, in southeast Sumatra, emerged perhaps as early as the 7th century as the capital of the maritime empire of Srivijaya, which for centuries controlled international trade passing through the straits of Malacca and Sunda, and across the Isthmus of Kra.

The great temple states fell into decline by the later 13th century. In Java, the area of Prambanan was superseded in importance by eastern Java, where three states developed in succession: Kediri (12th century), Singhasari (13th century) and finally Majapahit (late 13th–early 16th centuries). On the mainland, Pagan was sacked by Mongol invaders and then by Shans (late 13th century), while Angkor fell to Thai attacks from 1369 onwards and was eventually abandoned. Sukhothai, the first of the lowland Thai cities, was itself in decline by the late 14th century. In place of the old temple cities new political centres emerged: in Burma, Ava (1364) on the upper Irrawaddy, Toungoo (1347) on the Sittang, and Pegu (1369), capital of a new Mon kingdom of the south; in Siam, Ayutthaya (1350) and Chiengmai (1296); in Cambodia, Phnom Penh and other capitals along the Mekong; in Laos, Luang Prabang (1353). All were Theravada Buddhist in the Sinhalese tradition, and had stupas, not temples.

Meanwhile, in Vietnam the Chinese failed to reconquer their former province despite invasions in 1075–7 and 1285–8; instead, a new kingdom emerged calling itself Dai Viet, which gradually absorbed the kingdom of Champa and finally annexed its capital, Vijaya, in 1471. In the meantime, Srivijaya declined and at the end of the 14th century Malacca took its place. By that time the east Javanese empire of Majapahit was declining, and the west Javanese kingdom of Pajajaran also collapsed before Muslim pressure from the northern coast ports in the early 16th century.

Political change in the 14th and 15th centuries was accompanied by significant religious developments. Thus while Theravada Buddhism took root on the mainland, Islam, which began to influence northern Sumatra just before 1300,

Ananda Temple, Pagan Built by King Kyanzittha (1084-1112), supposedly in imitation of the great cave temple of Ananta (Orissa), of which, according to the Burmese chronicles, he learned from visiting Indian monks. The massive temple, in the shape of a perfect Greek cross, is crowned with a pinnacle rising to a height of 170 feet (52 m). Inside the temple are four colossal standing Buddha images. The base and terraces are decorated with tiles depicting scenes from classic Buddhist stories.

3/Cultural divisions of Southeast Asia in 1500 *(right)*
By 1500 the modern pattern of polities and cultures had begun to emerge, with the spread of Islam in the islands and Theravada Buddhism on the mainland, while Vietnam remained Confucian and Mahayana Buddhist. Malacca was the centre of a strong maritime, commercial empire which traded with the whole world, and was a main diffusion centre of Islam.

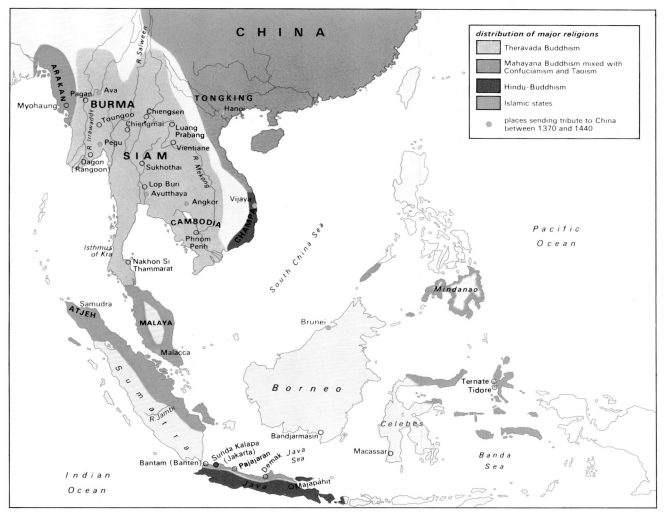

made its first big advances in the archipelago under the patronage of Malacca. From there the faith spread to the north Javanese trading ports and the Spice Islands, and also to north Borneo, and thence in the 16th century to Mindanao in the Philippines. Its advance in that direction was only halted by the Spanish seizure of Manila in 1571, and their introduction of Christianity.

In Vietnam, this period saw the strengthening of Confucian scholarship, despite the repulse of a Chinese attempt at reconquest under the Ming. As before, Chinese cultural influence remained limited to Vietnam, but under the Ming the old system of tributary relationships was revived and strengthened, and a series of important voyages to the southern seas was made by the Muslim admiral, Cheng Ho.

By 1511, when the Europeans took Malacca, Southeast Asia had already begun to take on its modern pattern of cultures and polities.

2/Southeast Asia AD 500-1500 *(below)* Early Buddhist and Hindu images with isolated Sanskrit inscriptions (5th-6th centuries) were succeeded in some areas by temple complexes (8th-13th centuries) denoting major political centres, notably at Pagan and Angkor and in central Java. These were followed by Mon, Thai and Burmese kingdoms on the mainland and Malay sultanates in the maritime areas. Vietnam became Sinicized between the 1st and 9th centuries and subsequently developed as an independent kingdom absorbing the Cham kingdom to the south.

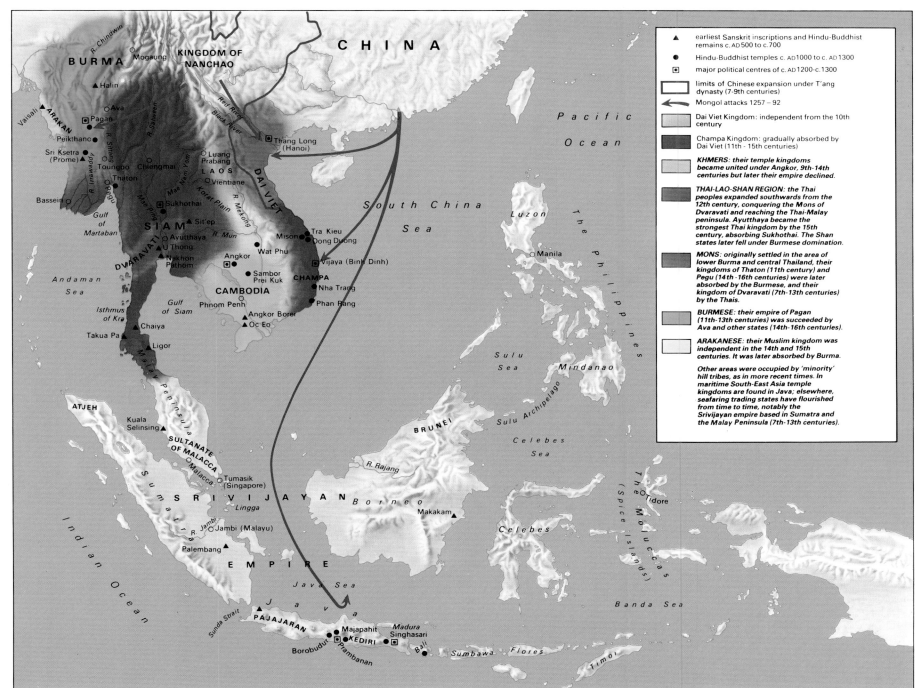

The Muslim world: the Middle East and North Africa 909 to 1517

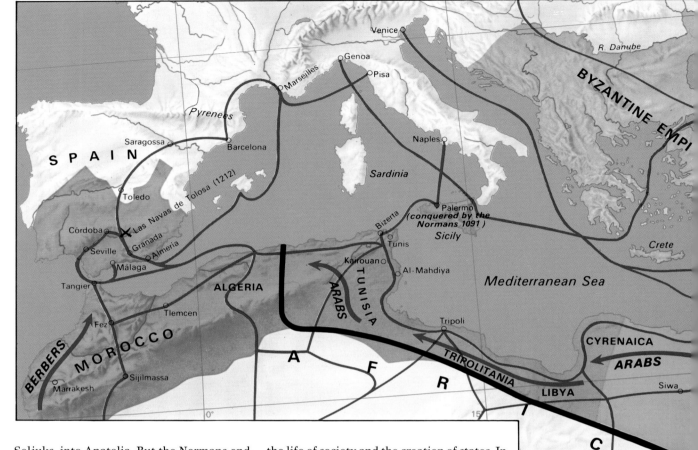

BY THE beginning of the 10th century, the efforts of the Abbasid caliphs to maintain the political unity of the Muslim world were faltering; provincial governors and army commanders were gaining local autonomy, and one military group, the Buyids, established itself in the capital, Baghdad, in 945, and ruled in the name of the Abbasids for more than a century. In some places, the bases of society were weakened; there were movements of social and political unrest, and differences concerning the succession to the caliphate and the nature of authority in Islam. These differences had emerged after Mohammed's death in 632, since the Prophet had left no guidelines for choosing his successor. The group that now forms the majority of Muslims, the Sunnis, claimed that authority passed to the caliphs, leaders whom the community designated, and who exercised supreme power. The Shias, however, believed that Mohammed's authority passed to his cousin and son-in-law Ali. For the Shias the various imams are infallible because of their descent from Ali and from the Prophet's daughter Fatima. In political terms, the Umayyads and the Abbasids were Sunnis while many of the dynasties that challenged their authority were Shia. In the 8th century one of these established a dynasty in Morocco, in the 9th century others created states in eastern Arabia and Yemen, and in the 10th century yet another, the Ismailis, set up a more important state, that of the Fatimids, first in Tunisia and then in Egypt and Syria. They took the title of caliph in opposition to the Abbasids; in opposition to them, so did a branch of the Umayyads which established itself in Spain after defeat by the Abbasids.

In most of the Middle East and North Africa, rainfall is scanty and irregular and vegetation sparse, so settled agriculture depends on strong government and good irrigation. The 10th century saw some disturbance of the settled order, and a shift in the balance between sedentary cultivators and nomadic pastoralists, as Berbers expanded into Morocco, Arabs went west along the North African coast, and Turks spread south and west from central Asia. But pastoral groups also provided the manpower and leadership which made possible a restoration of strong government. In Morocco, two successive movements of religious reform, those of the Almoravids and Almohads, gathered Berber groups around them and formed states; the former spread into Spain, the latter into Algeria and Tunisia. Another group, of Turkish origin, the Seljuks, established themselves in Baghdad. Theirs was the first important example of a new type of Muslim state, based on a partnership between 'men of the sword', mainly of Turkish origin, and bureaucrats and men of the law, Persian or Arab in culture, and on an alliance with the merchant and landowning classes. Officials and officers were paid by being given the right to collect and keep the tax on land in return for service; thus those who might be of alien or nomadic origin were given an interest in the prosperity and stability of society.

The Seljuks were called sultans, not caliphs, and ruled in the name of the Abbasid caliphs. They did not claim universal rule, but their kingdoms existed within a stable, international Islamic order, brought into existence by gradual conversion (although Christian, Jewish and other communities still existed). This order was maintained by a common religion and law, by the Arabic language and by widespread trade.

In the course of time the geographical limits of this society changed. Islam expanded into northern India, and, from the time of the Seljuks, into Anatolia. But the Normans ended Muslim rule in Sicily, and the southward expansion of the Christian states in northern Spain, checked for a time by the coming of the Almoravids and Almohads, continued after the battle of Las Navas de Tolosa (1212), until all that was left of Muslim Spain was the kingdom of Granada (which endured until 1492). In Palestine and Syria, an attempt by Crusaders from western Europe to re-establish Christian rule led to the creation of a number of states in the late 11th century, but a century later they were virtually destroyed by a new government in Egypt and Syria, that of the Ayyubids created by Saladin.

In the 13th century the balance of Muslim society, at least in its eastern part, was again disturbed by a new conquering group, with Mongol leadership and largely Turkish manpower (see page 126): in 1258 they captured Baghdad, ending the Abbasid caliphate. They were gradually converted to Islam and absorbed into Muslim society. The Muslim world was split into clearly defined regions. In the east, there ruled first the Il-khanids, a branch of the conquering Mongol dynasty, and then another dynasty of similar origin, founded by Timur (Tamerlane); to the west, attempts by the Mongols to expand towards the Mediterranean were ended at the battle of Ain Jalut (1260) by a new ruling group in Egypt and Syria, the Mamlukes, from southern Russia and the Caucasus. North Africa fell under the control of two states: the Hafsids in Tunisia and the Marinids in Morocco.

These divisions were more than political. The decline of the irrigation works and a shift in trade routes had weakened the cities of Iraq: the main centres of Muslim society now lay in Persia and the Nile valley. Between these two lay deep differences of culture. The dominant Arabic culture of the west preserved its traditions of law, mysticism and literature but was no longer creative; in the east, the art of the miniature and architecture thrived, and the Persian language, revived in an Islamic form, became the medium of great poetry. In the east, too, Turkish pastoral elements continued to play an important part in the life of society and the creation of states. In Anatolia, Turkish frontier states expanded at the expense of the Byzantines, and in one of them a new dynasty, the Ottomans, emerged.

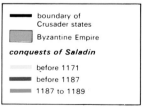

The Crusades made little impact on the Islamic world but they captured Western imagination. The illustration (above) from a manuscript of c.1340 shows Richard I of England defeating Saladin in imaginary combat during the Third Crusade.

▬	boundary of Crusader states
▨	Byzantine Empire

conquests of Saladin

	before 1171
	before 1187
	1187 to 1189

3/The Muslim reconquest of Palestine (left) The Muslim reconquest began when Zengi, a Seljuk officer, built a strong Syrian state and occupied the Crusading county of Edessa in 1144. Saladin, an officer of this state, made himself master first of Egypt, deposing the Fatimids, and then of the interior of Syria. He attacked the Crusaders in 1187, and before his death in 1193 had captured Jerusalem and driven the Crusaders from all but a narrow coastal strip between Acre and Antioch.

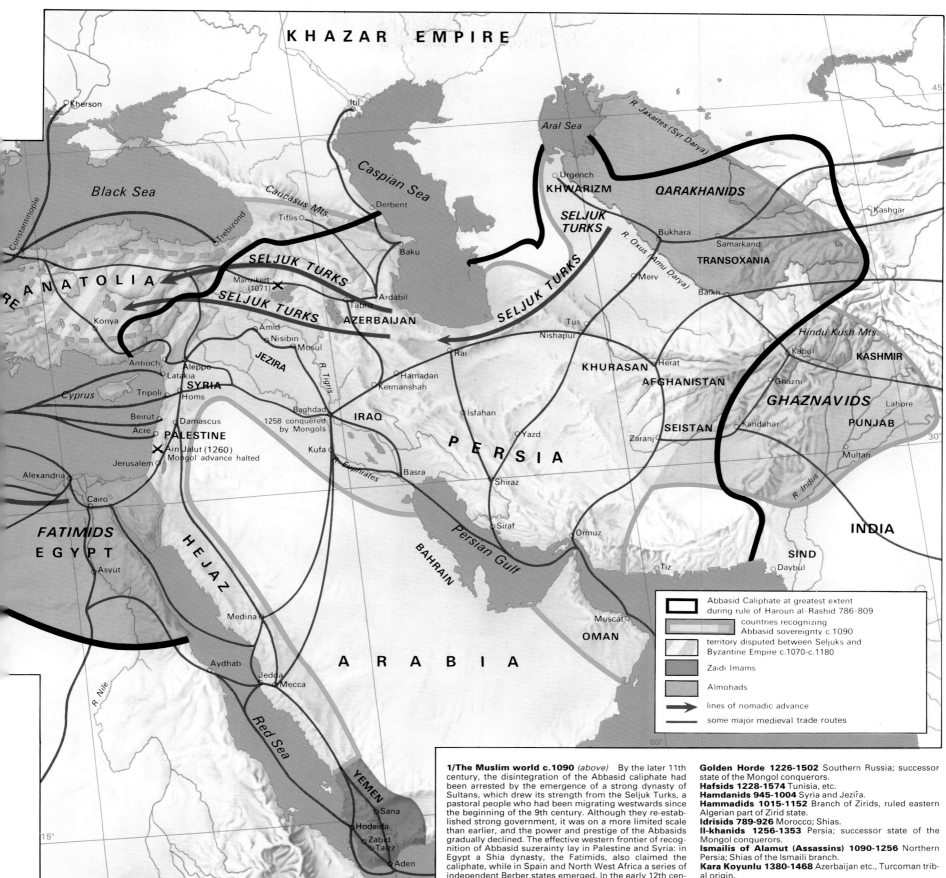

KHAZAR EMPIRE

Black Sea

Caspian Sea

Aral Sea

R. Jakartes (Syr Darya)

QARAKHANIDS

KHWARIZM

SELJUK TURKS

TRANSOXANIA

Caucasus Mts

Kherson

Itil

Derbent

Tiflis

Trebizond

Baku

Ardabil

Tabriz

Urgench

Bukhara

Samarkand

Kashgar

SELJUK TURKS

SELJUK TURKS

Manzikert (1071)

SELJUK TURKS

AZERBAIJAN

Nishapur

Merv

Balkh

Hindu Kush Mts

ANATOLIA

Konya

Amid

Nisibin

Mosul

R. Tigris

Rai

Tus

Hamadan

Kermanshah

KHURASAN

Herat

AFGHANISTAN

Kabul

Ghazni

KASHMIR

GHAZNAVIDS

PUNJAB

Lahore

Antioch

Aleppo

Latakia

JEZIRA

SYRIA

Homs

Tripoli

Cyprus

Beirut

Damascus

Acre

PALESTINE

Jerusalem

Ain Jalut (1260)
Mongol advance halted

Baghdad
1258 conquered
by Mongols

IRAQ

Kufa

Basra

R. Euphrates

PERSIA

Isfahan

Yazd

Shiraz

Siraf

Ormuz

SEISTAN

Zaranj

Kandahar

Multan

R. Indus

SIND

Daybul

INDIA

Alexandria

Cairo

FATIMIDS
EGYPT

HEJAZ

R. Nile

Asyut

BAHRAIN

Persian Gulf

Tiz

Muscat

OMAN

ARABIA

Aydhab

Jedda

Mecca

Medina

Red Sea

YEMEN

Sana

Hodeida

Zabid

Taizz

Aden

Abbasids 750-1258 Ruled Muslim world as caliphs with Iraq as centre; lost power after 945, but retained claim to suzerainty.

Aghlabids 800-909 Ruled in Tunisia, etc., under Abbasid suzerainty.

Ak Koyunlu 1378-1508 Eastern Anatolia, Azerbaijan; based on Turcoman tribesmen.

Almohads 1130-1269 North Africa and Spain; founded by a movement of religious revival.

Almoravids 1056-1147 Morocco, etc., and Spain; originating in a religious movement among Berber nomads.

Ayyubids 1169-1260 Egypt, Syria; founded by Saladin.

Buyids (Buwayhids) 932-1062 Persia, Iraq; Shias, but ruled in the name of the Abbasid caliph.

Carmathians 894-end 11th century Eastern and central Arabia; Shias of the Ismaili branch.

Fatimids 909-1171 Ruled first in North Africa, later in Egypt and Syria; Shias of the Ismaili branch; claimed title of caliph.

Granada, Kingdom of (Nasrids) 1230-1492 Last Muslim state in Spain.

Ghaznavids 977-1186 Khurasan, Afghanistan, northern India; played the main part in the expansion of Islam into India.

Golden Horde 1226-1502 Southern Russia; successor state of the Mongol conquerors.

Hafsids 1228-1574 Tunisia, etc.

Hamdanids 945-1004 Syria and Jezira.

Hammadids 1015-1152 Branch of Zirids, ruled eastern Algerian part of Zirid state.

Idrisids 789-926 Morocco; Shias.

Il-khans 1256-1353 Persia; successor state of the Mongol conquerors.

Ismailis of Alamut (Assassins) 1090-1256 Northern Persia; Shias of the Ismaili branch.

Kara Koyunlu 1380-1468 Azerbaijan etc., Turcoman tribal origin.

Khwarizm-Shahs 1077-1231 Oxus valley; began as Seljuk governors.

Mamlukes 1250-1517 Egypt, Syria, Hejaz; self-perpetuating military elite from southern Russia and Caucasus.

Marinids 1196-1465 Morocco.

Ottomans 1281-1924 See page 136.

Qarakhanids 992-1211 Transoxania (Turkestan).

Rasulids 1229-1454 Yemen.

Saadids 1511-1659 Morocco; claiming descent from the Prophet.

Safavids 1501-1732 Persia, etc.; made Shi'ism the official religion of Persia.

Saffarids 867-1495 Eastern Persia.

Samanids 819-1005 Khurasan and Transoxania; encouraged revival of Persian culture.

Seljuks 1038-1194 Iraq, Persia, etc.; first important Turkish Muslim dynasty, reunited central Abbasid lands under their rule and Abbasid suzerainty, began Muslim conquest of Anatolia.

Seljuks of Rum 1077-1307 Anatolia; offshoot of the main Seljuk state.

Shaybanids 1500-1598 Transoxania; Mongol origin.

Timurids 1370-1506 Transoxania, Persia; successor state of Timur, conqueror of Turco-Mongol origin who built a vast empire.

Tulunids 868-905 Egypt, Syria; virtually autonomous Abbasid provincial governors.

Umayyads of Spain 756-1031 Revival in Spain of dynasty which held the caliphate in the east before the Abbasids; itself later took title of caliph.

Zaidi Imams 860-c.1281 Intermittently, then 1592-1962 Yemen; leaders of Zaidi branch of Shias.

Zangids 1127-1222 Jezira, Syria; at first Seljuk governors, began Muslim counter-attack against Crusader states.

Zirids 972-1148 Berber origin; ruled Tunisia and, for a time, eastern Algeria, at first under Fatimid suzerainty; capital Kairouan.

1/The Muslim world c.1090 (above) By the later 11th century, the disintegration of the Abbasid caliphate had been arrested by the emergence of a strong dynasty of Sultans, which drew its strength from the Seljuk Turks, a pastoral people who had been migrating westwards since the beginning of the 9th century. Although they re-established strong government, it was on a more limited scale than earlier, and the power and prestige of the Abbasids gradually declined. The effective western frontier of recognition of Abbasid suzerainty lay in Palestine and Syria: in Egypt a Shia dynasty, the Fatimids, also claimed the caliphate, while in Spain and North West Africa a series of independent Berber states emerged. In the early 12th century the political and social order of the eastern Muslim countries was disturbed and changed by the Mongol conquest; in the 15th century it was restored in a new form by the rise of great and long-lived empires, those of the Ottomans and Safavids (see pages 136 and 166). The political divisions of the Muslim world during these six centuries are too numerous to be shown on a single map. The following list includes the most important.

Legend:
- Abbasid Caliphate at greatest extent during rule of Haroun al-Rashid 786-809
- countries recognizing Abbasid sovereignty c.1090
- territory disputed between Seljuks and Byzantine Empire c.1070-c.1180
- Zaidi Imams
- Almohads
- lines of nomadic advance
- some major medieval trade routes

Adrianople (Edirne)

Constantinople (conquered by Ottomans 1453)

Black Sea

Trebizond

EMPIRE OF TREBIZOND (conquered 1461)

Aegean Sea

Sea of Marmara

Bosporus

Necaea (Iznik)

Prusa (Bursa)

ANATOLIA

Manzikert (1071)

L. Van

Byzantines defeated by Seljuk Turks

Konya

Antioch

Crete to Venice 1204

Mediterranean Sea

Cyprus independent kingdom 1191-1489

frontier between Byzantine Empire and Abbasid Caliphate c.930

frontier of Byzantine Empire c.1070

controlled by Seljuk Turks c.1070

controlled by Seljuk Turks in early 13th century

frontier between Byzantine Empire and Ottoman Turks 1371-1453

2/The Muslim conquest of Anatolia (above) Under Byzantine rule, Anatolia had survived Arab attacks (see page 112), but the gradual penetration by Muslim armies and Turkish nomadic pastoralists which ended in the establishment of the Ottoman Empire began with the Seljuk defeat of the Byzantine army at the battle of Manzikert.

The emergence of states in Africa 900 to 1500

Africa's golden wealth *(above)* Western Europe ceased to mint gold currency in the Dark Ages, but in the 13th century Italian city states and the Christian Spanish kingdoms began striking gold coins. Up to about 1350 at least two-thirds of the world's supply of gold came from West Africa. Mansa Musa of Mali (shown here holding a glittering coin in the Catalan *World Atlas* of c.1375), epitomized the golden wealth of Africa.

THE period from 900 to 1500 saw the growth of new states over much of the northern part of Africa. Most of them forged trade links with Black Africa, an area about which far less is known, although it is clear that great empires emerged in the western Sudan. South of the Equator, where the consequences of the spread of the Bantu (see page 44) were still being worked out, also saw the development of larger-scale states.

A series of foreign Muslim dynasties – the Fatimids, Ayyubids and Mamlukes – ruled Egypt, and these regimes stimulated commerce in the eastern Mediterranean, the Red Sea and the Arabian Sea. After the decline of Axum, this flow of trade provided the economic basis for the revival of the political power of the Christian empire of Ethiopia, first under the Cushitic-speaking Zagwe dynasty in the 11th century and then, in the 13th century, under the Amharic-speaking Solomonids who later came into conflict with the Muslim coastal states of the Horn of Africa, notably Adal.

By AD 1000 the Maghreb (northwest Africa) had been in Islamic hands for over three centuries and was the site of the great Berber empires of the Almoravids and the Almohads (see page 132). Between 1000 and 1500 Islam spread south: up the Nile into the Christian kingdoms of Nubia; along the northern and eastern coasts of the Horn (which faced southern Arabia); and across the Sahara into the states of the 'Sudanic belt', stretching from Senegal to the Nile. Muslim merchants and travellers crossed the Sahara with caravans of camels which regularly made the hazardous journey from the trading depots on either edge of the desert, such as Sijilmassa, south of the Atlas mountains in Morocco, and Walata in Mali. This dangerous trade carried luxury goods (and, in time, firearms) and salt – a vital element in the diet in tropical countries – to the Black African lands of the south. In exchange, leather-work, slaves and gold went northwards: by 1250 the economies of both the Muslim Middle East and Christian Europe depended upon African gold.

Expanding trans-Saharan trade gave an impetus to the growth of states in the Sudanic belt. Two of the greatest of these, Ghana and Mali, were created by Mande-speaking peoples who had spread across the western part of west Africa. Ghana, which flourished from the 8th to the 11th centuries, was established by the Soninke group of the Mande in the area north of the Senegal and Niger rivers; its successor, Mali, founded by the Malinke Mande, extended from the Atlantic right across the great bend of the Niger. In 1324 the Mali king Mansa Musa went on pilgrimage to Mecca, and took so much gold with his retinue that en route the currency of Cairo was depressed. The empire of Mali gave way to that of Songhay, centred on the Niger cities of Gao and Timbuktu. East of Mali lay the city states of Hausaland, some of which – Zaria, Kano, Katsina – became extremely prosperous, although they never united to form a single Hausa state. Further east stood the Kanuri empire, founded by desert people in Kanem to the east of Lake Chad but by 1300 centred politically at Borno, west of the lake. The Kanuri kings (*mais*) constituted one of the longest surviving dynasties in history until their final overthrow in the 19th century.

By the late Middle Ages, therefore, with western Europe in crisis (see page 140), the Black kingdoms of the western and central Sudan flourished. A number of African kings, among them Mansa Musa and Sonni Ali, enjoyed renown throughout Islam and Christendom for their wealth, brilliance and the artistic achievements of their subjects. Their capitals were large walled cities with many mosques and at least two, Timbuktu and Jenne, had universities that attracted scholars and poets from far and wide. Their power derived from a mixture of military force and diplomatic alliances with local leaders; their judges dispensed justice; their bureaucracies administered taxation and controlled trade, the life-blood of these empires.

To the south of the Sudanic states, Hausa and Malinke merchants (the latter known as Dyula) traded among the peoples on the edge of the tropical forests, especially in the gold-producing regions. By 1500 many notable forest states, such as Oyo, Benin and the Akan kingdoms, had arisen partly as a result of contacts with the northerners. By that time they had also been visited by the first European sailors, mainly Portuguese, who had explored the sea-lanes around west Africa into the Bight of Benin.

Along the east coast, lay a string of Muslim city states where the Swahili people and civilization brought this part of Africa into an Indian Ocean trading complex. Kilwa Kisiwani, with its handsome mosques and palaces, prospered as the *entrepôt* for the gold of Zimbabwe, brought via Sofala. The arrival of Vasco da Gama in 1498 marked the beginning of European encroachment in this lucrative system of oceanic trade.

Meanwhile, in the interior of the southern half of the continent, several African peoples coalesced to form the nucleus of later kingdoms. Iron-working agriculturalists and pastoralists with material cultures (known collectively as Later Iron Age) developed into sophisticated civilizations, many of them Bantu-speaking; while centralized states, with rulers who were held to be divine, emerged in the Kongo region south of the lower Zaire river, in Lubaland (Katanga or Shaba), in Zimbabwe and in the area between the great lakes of east Africa.

1/The great empires *(right)* Africa has few natural harbours south of the Sahara, so internal lines of communication for the passage of commerce and of ideas proved more important than sea routes, with the exception of the Red Sea and parts of the coast of east Africa. In this respect the medieval history of Africa differed profoundly from that of Europe: the great empires of Africa which arose and flourished between 900 and 1500 were all interior states, often lying deep in the heart of the continent for, unlike Europe, Africa tended to develop inwards.

2/The trans-Saharan routes *(below)* Even with camels, introduced into Africa in Roman times, the desert crossing remained extremely hazardous. If the far-spread watering places dried up or if the fiercely independent desert people, the veiled Tuareg, attacked, whole caravans of hundreds of men and beasts perished, their skeletons offering grisly reminders of the dangers. Yet for centuries the great trading system persisted.

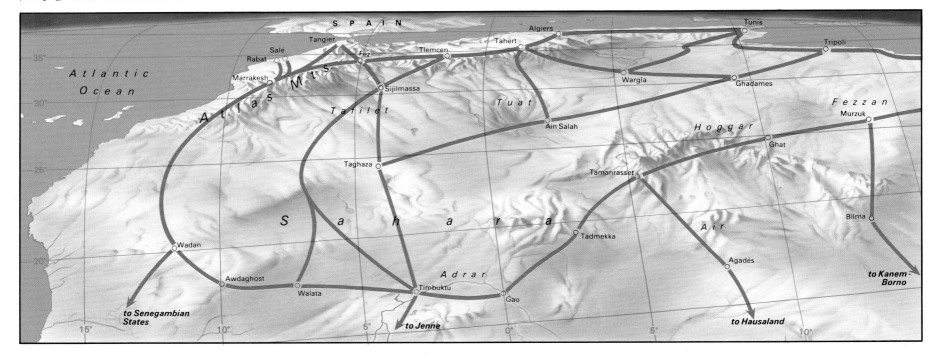

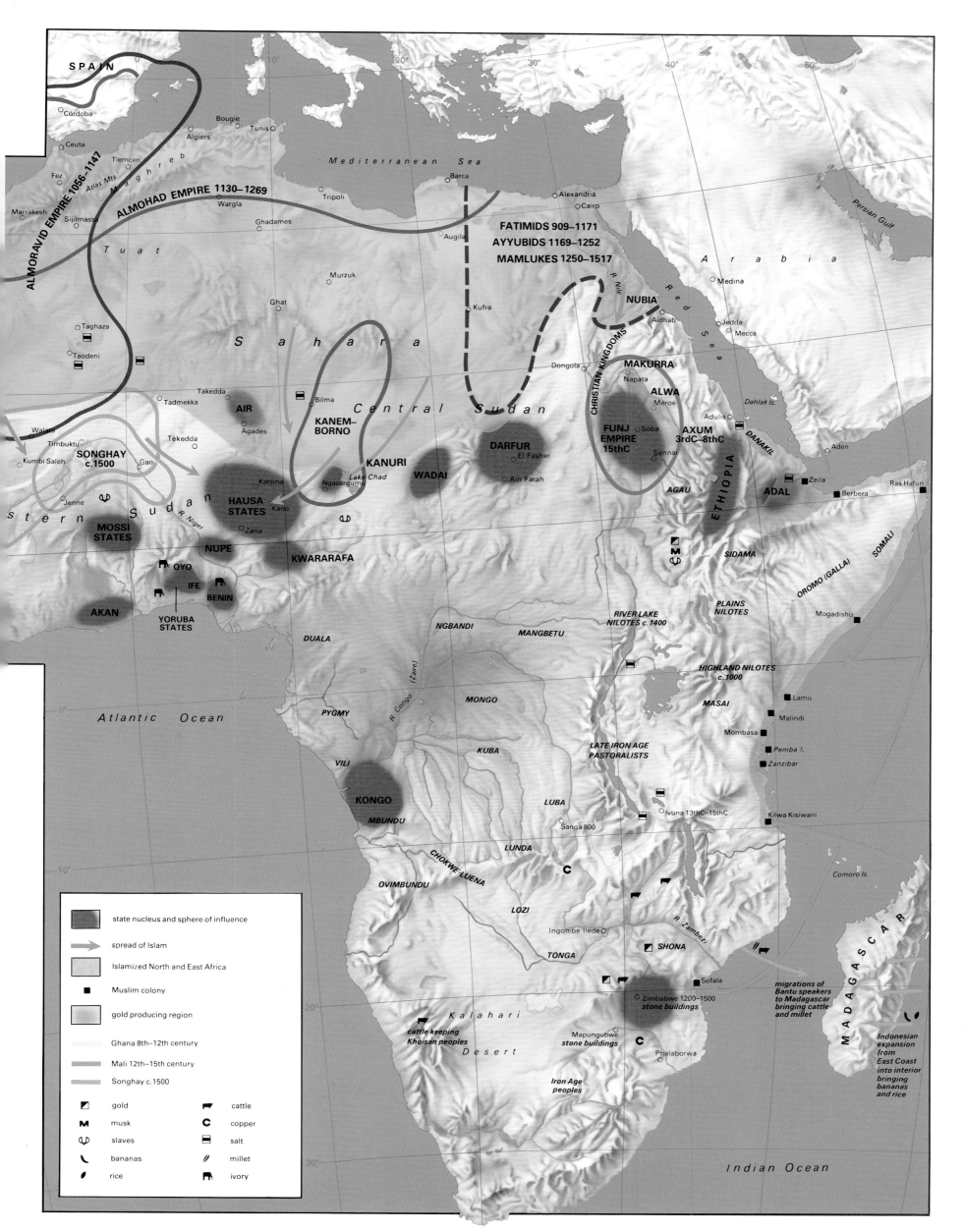

SPAIN

Córdoba
Ceuta
Bougie
Tunis
Tlemcen
Algiers
Fez
Atlas Mts
Maghreb
Marrakesh
Sijilmassa
Wargla
Tripoli
Ghadames

ALMORAVID EMPIRE 1056-1147
ALMOHAD EMPIRE 1130-1269

Mediterranean Sea
Barca
Alexandria
Cairo

FATIMIDS 909-1171
AYYUBIDS 1169-1252
MAMLUKES 1250-1517

Arabia
Medina
Jedda
Mecca

Taghaza
Taodeni
Tuat
Murzuk
Ghat
Kufra
Augila

Sahara

Takedda
Tadmekka
Bilma
Tekedda
AIR
Agadès
KANEM-BORNO
Central Sudan

Walata
Timbuktu
Kumbi Saleh
Gao
SONGHAY c.1500
Jenne
Katsina
Ngazargumu
KANURI
Lake Chad
WADAI
DARFUR
El Fasher
Ain Farah

Nubia
Dongola
MAKURRA
Napata
ALWA
Meroe
CHRISTIAN KINGDOMS
FUNJ EMPIRE 15thC
Soba
Sennar
AXUM 3rdC-8thC
Adulis
Dahlak Is.

R Nile
Red Sea
Aidhab
NUBIA

stern Sudan
MOSSI STATES
HAUSA STATES
Kano
Zaria
NUPE
R Niger
KWARARAFA

OYO
IFE
BENIN
AKAN
YORUBA STATES

AGAU
ETHIOPIA
SIDAMA
ADAL
Zeila
Berbera
Ras Hafun
DANAKIL
Aden

SOMALI
OROMO (GALLA)
Mogadishu

Atlantic Ocean

DUALA
NGBANDI
MANGBETU
PLAINS NILOTES
RIVER LAKE NILOTES c.1400
HIGHLAND NILOTES c.1000
MASAI
Lamu
Malindi
Mombasa
Pemba I.
Zanzibar

PYGMY
MONGO
R Congo (Zaire)

VILI
KONGO
MBUNDU
KUBA
LUBA
LATE IRON AGE PASTORALISTS
Ivuna 13thC-15thC
Sanga 800
Kilwa Kisiwani

CHOKWE-LUENA
LUNDA
OVIMBUNDU
LOZI
Ingombe Ilede
TONGA
SHONA
R Zambezi
Sofala

Comoro Is.

migrations of Bantu speakers to Madagascar bringing cattle and millet

MADAGASCAR

Indonesian expansion from East Coast into interior bringing bananas and rice

Kalahari
cattle keeping Khoisan peoples
Desert
Mapungubwe stone buildings
Phalaborwa
Zimbabwe 1200-1500 stone buildings

Iron Age peoples

Indian Ocean

Legend:
- state nucleus and sphere of influence
- spread of Islam
- Islamized North and East Africa
- Muslim colony
- gold producing region
- Ghana 8th–12th century
- Mali 12th–15th century
- Songhay c.1500

- gold
- cattle
- musk
- copper
- slaves
- salt
- bananas
- millet
- rice
- ivory

The rise of the Ottoman Empire 1301 to 1520

ORIGINALLY a petty principality in Western Anatolia, the Ottoman state rose to become a world empire which lasted, through many vicissitudes, from the late 13th century to 1924. Like that of the Habsburgs, its eventual rival, the Ottoman Empire was dynastic; its territories and character owed little to national or ethnic boundaries, and were determined by the military and administrative power of the dynasty at any particular time.

The rise of the Ottoman state, like that of Islam itself nearly seven centuries earlier, owed much to the weakness of the empires which surrounded it. The damage to the structure of the Byzantine Empire caused by the Fourth Crusade in 1204 facilitated the Ottomans' rapid advance into the Balkans during the 14th century; the defeat of the Seljuks by the Mongols at the battle of Kösedag in 1243 gravely weakened that dynasty's power, and the gradual retreat of the Mongols from Anatolia into Iran created a vacuum in Anatolia which was filled by a number of small Turcoman states, each striving for political supremacy in the area. Ertoghrul, father of Osman, after whom the Ottoman dynasty was named, ruled a small state around the town of Söğüt, then on the 'frontier' between the Seljuks and the Byzantines. On his father's death in about 1281, Osman succeeded and during his reign the territory of the state first underwent significant expansion.

Under Osman I and his successors Orkhan (c.1324–62) and Murad (1362–89), the state gradually expanded: in 1326 Bursa was captured after a long siege, and became the Ottoman capital; the absorption of the emirate of Karasi in 1345 brought the Ottomans to the Dardanelles; and in 1354 they gained their first foothold in Europe with the capture of Gallipoli.

In 1361 the Ottomans took Adrianople (Edirne) and transferred their capital there. Much of the first period of expansion in the Balkans seems to have been undertaken by quasi-independent Turkish warrior leaders rather than by forces directly controlled by the Ottomans, but with the decisive defeat of the Serbians and Bosnians at the battle of Kosovo in 1389, Ottoman supremacy was definitively established. Under Bayezid I (1389–1402) the kingdom of Bulgaria became part of the empire (1393) and most of the independent emirates of Anatolia were absorbed into the Ottoman state, which by 1400 stretched from the Danube to the Euphrates. However, Bayezid's achievement was short-lived – his army was destroyed at Ankara in 1402 by Timur (Tamerlane), the last of the Mongol invaders to reach as far west as Anatolia. There followed an 11-year hiatus between 1402 and 1413, when the Balkan states and the Anatolian emirates took advantage of the opportunity provided by the Mongol victory to shake off Ottoman rule, although further Mongol advance ceased after Timur's death in 1405.

The reconstruction of the Ottoman state by Mehmed I (1413–21) and the revival of the conquests in the reign of his son Murad II (1421–51) again brought most of eastern and central Anatolia and the southern and eastern Balkans under direct or indirect Ottoman control. However, Ottoman rule in the Balkans was far less oppressive than the system it superseded, in which feudal dues and compulsory labour services weighed heavily upon the peasantry; in consequence, the Ottomans were often welcomed as deliverers. The rounding off of these conquests, and the emergence of the Ottoman state as a world power, was the work of Mehmed II al-Fatih, 'The Conqueror' (1451–81), whose conquest of Constantinople in 1453 removed the last major barrier to expansion into northern Anatolia and enabled the Ottomans to dominate the Straits and the southern shore of the Black Sea. The disappearance of the Serbian kingdom, followed by the absorption of Herzegovina and much of Bosnia, left Hungary as the major European power facing the Ottomans. Mehmed's failure to take Belgrade in 1456 left the line of the middle Danube and lower Sava as the Ottoman boundary with Hungary for over 60 years. With the final re-absorption of Karaman in 1468 the last of the independent Anatolian emirates disappeared, leaving the Turcoman confederation of the Ak Koyunlu (White Sheep) as the Ottomans' major opponents in the area until their destruction by the Safavids of Iran in the early 16th century. Further north, Mehmed established a bridgehead in the Crimea by the capture of Caffa (Kefe) from the Genoese in 1475, thus bringing the Khanate of the Crimea, the most important of the successor states of the Golden Horde, under Ottoman control.

In Europe, the middle years of Mehmed's reign saw the ending of Byzantine and Frankish control over the Morea, and the gradual erosion of Venetian and Genoese power in the Aegean and the Black Sea. Mehmed's death in 1481 brought a temporary halt to these advances; and the struggle over the succession between Bayezid II (1481–1512) and his younger brother, Jem, left the Ottomans unable to undertake major campaigns against the west for many years. However, the land route from Constantinople to the Crimea was secured in 1484 with the conquests of Akkerman and Kilia, and the Ottoman-Venetian war of 1499–1502 showed that the Ottomans now were a major naval power.

The last years of Bayezid II's reign, and most of that of his successor Selim I (1512–20), were largely taken up with events in the east: Iran, Egypt and the western fertile crescent. The rise of the Safavids in Iran (after 1501) brought to power a state both militarily strong and ideologically hostile to the Ottomans. Shi'ism, the form of Islam favoured by the Safavids, was also attractive to dissident forces and groupings within the Ottoman state, who rallied to support the new dynasty in Iran. A series of Shia-inspired risings among the Turcoman tribes of eastern Anatolia in the last years of Bayezid II's reign was a prelude to the war which broke out in the reigns of Selim and Shah Isma'il (1501–24), culminating in the defeat of the Safavids at the battle of Çaldiran in 1514. For a time, eastern Anatolia was secured and the threat of religious separatism removed.

Selim's annexation of the emirate of Dhu'l-Qadr in 1515 brought the Ottomans into direct contact with the Mamluke empire for the first time. Over the next two years Selim destroyed the Mamlukes politically and militarily, conquering Aleppo and Damascus in 1516, and taking Cairo in 1517. As well as bringing Syria and Egypt under Ottoman control, this campaign also added the holy places of Christendom and Islam to the empire, thus increasing the prestige and authority of Selim and his successors. At Selim's death in 1520 the Empire stretched from the Red Sea to the Crimea, and from Kurdistan to Bosnia, and had become a major participant and contender in the international power politics of the day. Furthermore, substantial Turkish Muslim migration to the Balkans had begun to make permanent changes in the demographic and ethnic structure of that area.

The siege of Rhodes 1522 (below) The elite of the Ottoman army is depicted storming the walls of the city, defended by knights of St John. The elite was formed by the Janissaries, the famous infantry corps founded early in the Ottoman state's history, and the *sipahis*, the Muslim feudal cavalry. The Janissaries, seen here with firearms, were raised by the *Devshirme*, a compulsory levy of Christian boys begun late in the 14th century and which soon became a fundamental institution of the Empire. They were regarded in Christian Europe as the most formidable component of the Ottoman army.

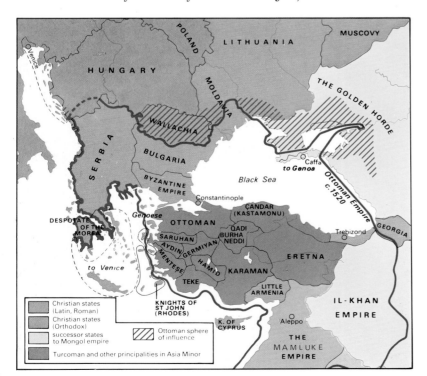

2/Before the Ottomans (left) Invasion and war between Latins, Byzantines, Muslims and Mongols had destroyed the last shred of the former Byzantine and Muslim empires in the Middle East. The Balkans and Anatolia, entirely fragmented by the early 14th century, were to become, under the Ottomans, the provinces of a single empire.

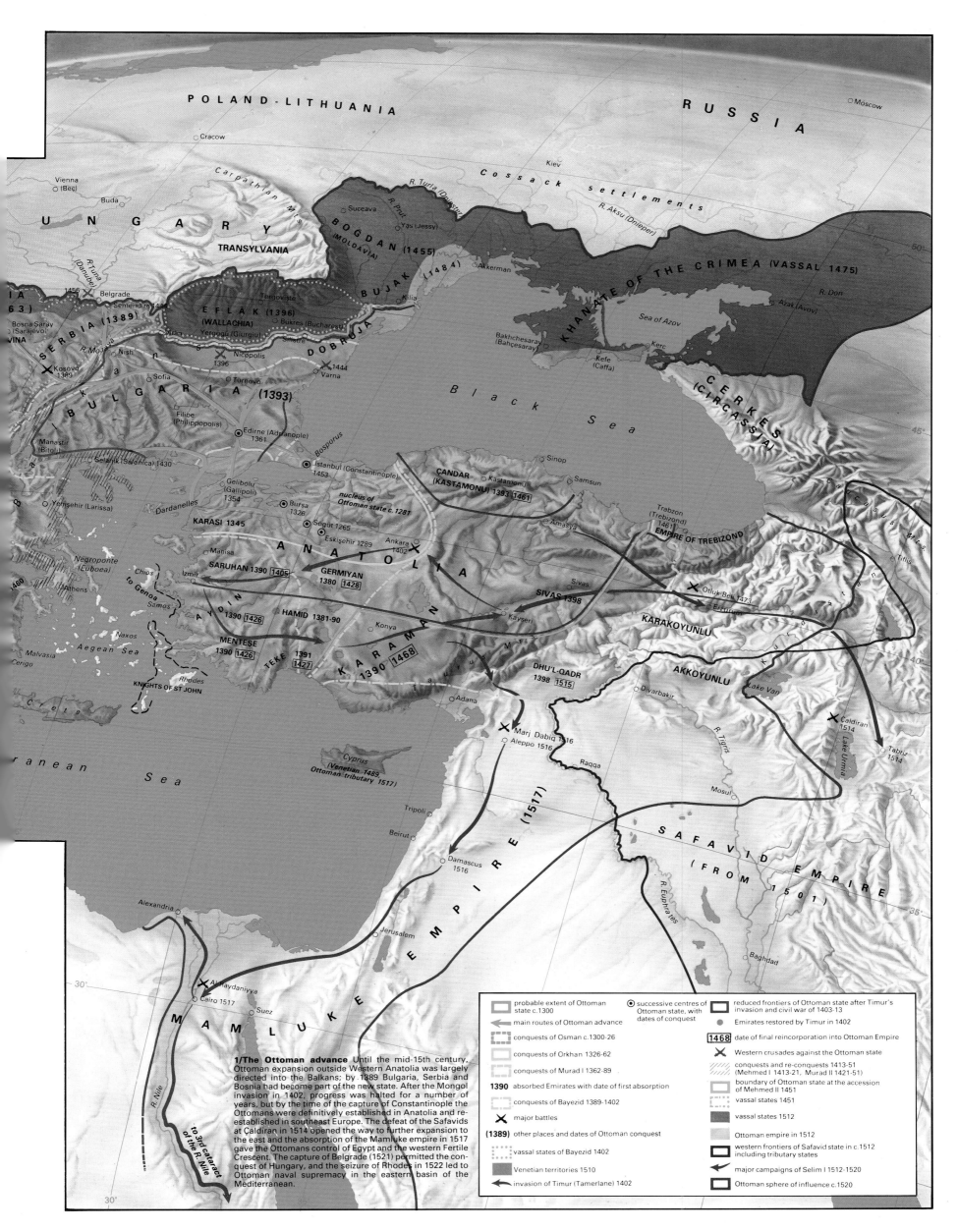

POLAND-LITHUANIA

RUSSIA

o Moscow

o Cracow

Kiev o

C o s s a c k   s e t t l e m e n t s

Vienna
(Beç)

Buda o

C a r p a t h i a n   M t s

R. Aksu (Dnieper)

50

TRANSYLVANIA

Suceava o

R. Prut (Dniester)

BOGDAN
(MOLDAVIA)
(1455)

Yás (Jessy) o

Akkerman o

KHANATE OF THE CRIMEA (VASSAL 1475)

R. Don

1456
Belgrade
Semendire 14 R. Danube

Tergoviste o

(1484)
BUJAK

Bakhchesaray
(Bahçesaray)

Sea of Azov

Azak (Azov) o

IA
(63)

Bosna Saray
(Sarajevo)

SERBIA (1389)

EFLAK
(WALLACHIA)

Bukres (Bucharest) o

Silistre o

DOBROJA

Kerc o

Kefe
(Caffa)

ÇERKES
(CIRCASSIA)

VINA

R. Morava

Nish o

Yeroğu (Giurgiu)

N i c o p o l i s

Tornovo o

1444
Varna o

B l a c k   S e a

45

Kosovo
1389

Sofia o

1396

BULGARIA   (1393)

Filibe
(Philippopolis) o

Manastir
(Bitoli)

Edirne (Adrianople)
1361

Bosporus

Sinop o

Samsun o

Selanik (Salonica) 1430

Istanbul (Constantinople)
1453

ÇANDAR
(KASTAMONU) 1393 1461

Kastamonu o

Trabzon
(Trebizond)
1461

CAUCASUS

Tiflis o

Gelibolu
(Gallipoli)
1354

nucleus of
Ottoman state c.1281

Amasya o

EMPIRE OF TREBIZOND

Yenişehir (Larissa) o

Dardanelles

Bursa
1326

Sögüt 1265

Eskisehir 1289

Ankara
1402

Negroponte
(Euboea)

Manisa o

SARUHAN 1390 1405

ANATOLIA

GERMIYAN
1380 1428

Sivas o

Otluk Beli 1473

Erzerum

1460

Athens o

Izmir

to Genoa

Chios

AYDIN 1390 1426

HAMID 1381-90

Konya o

Kayseri o

SIVAS 1398

KARAKOYUNLU

Samos

Aegean Sea

Naxos o

MENTEŞE
1390 1426

TEKE 1391 1427

KARAMAN 1390 1468

AKKOYUNLU

Lake Van

Çaldiran
1514

Malvasia o

Cerigo

Rhodes

KNIGHTS OF ST JOHN

T a u r u s

DHU'L-QADR
1398 1515

Diyarbakir o

Tabriz
1514

40

Crete

Adana o

Marj Dabiq 1516

Aleppo 1516

R. Tigris

Lake
Urmia
1514

ranean   Sea

Cyprus
(Venetian 1489,
Ottoman tributary 1517)

Raqqa o

Mosul o

SAFAVID

Tripoli o

M a m l u k e   E m p i r e   (1517)

Beirut o

E M P I R E

Damascus
1516

R. Euphrates

(FROM 1501)

35

Alexandria o

Jerusalem o

Baghdad o

30

Al-Haydaniyya

Cairo 1517

Suez o

MAMLUKE

R. Nile

to 3rd cataract
of the R. Nile

1/The Ottoman advance Until the mid-15th century,
Ottoman expansion outside Western Anatolia was largely
directed into the Balkans; by 1389 Bulgaria, Serbia and
Bosnia had become part of the new state. After the Mongol
invasion in 1402, progress was halted for a number of
years, but by the time of the capture of Constantinople the
Ottomans were definitively established in Anatolia and re-
established in southeast Europe. The defeat of the Safavids
at Çaldiran in 1514 opened the way to further expansion to
the east and the absorption of the Mamluke empire in 1517
gave the Ottomans control of Egypt and the western Fertile
Crescent. The capture of Belgrade (1521) permitted the conquest of Hungary, and the seizure of Rhodes in 1522 led to
Ottoman naval supremacy in the eastern basin of the
Mediterranean.

probable extent of Ottoman state c.1300

main routes of Ottoman advance

conquests of Osman c.1300-26

conquests of Orkhan 1326-62

conquests of Murad I 1362-89

1390 absorbed Emirates with date of first absorption

conquests of Bayezid 1389-1402

major battles

(1389) other places and dates of Ottoman conquest

vassal states of Bayezid 1402

Venetian territories 1510

invasion of Timur (Tamerlane) 1402

successive centres of Ottoman state, with dates of conquest

Emirates restored by Timur in 1402

1468 date of final reincorporation into Ottoman Empire

Western crusades against the Ottoman state

conquests and re-conquests 1413-51 (Mehmed I 1413-21, Murad II 1421-51)

boundary of Ottoman state at the accession of Mehmed II 1451

vassal states 1451

vassal states 1512

Ottoman empire in 1512

western frontiers of Safavid state in c.1512 including tributary states

major campaigns of Selim I 1512-1520

Ottoman sphere of influence c.1520

reduced frontiers of Ottoman state after Timur's invasion and civil war of 1403-13

Eastern Europe in the 14th century

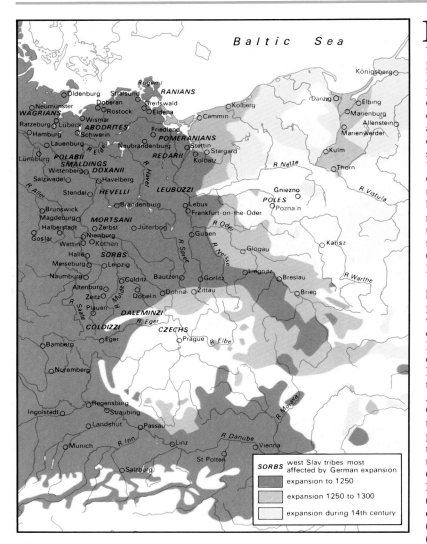

2/German eastward colonization *(above)* For two centuries after 1125 peasants, soldiers and merchants moved in a steady stream into the rich, welcoming land between the rivers Elbe and Oder, swamping the local Slav tribes, developing the land and opening up the Baltic to new, profitable international trade. Monasteries, particularly the Cistercians, undertook large-scale land-drainage schemes, for which they called in peasants from the Netherlands.

3/The conquest of Prussia by the Teutonic Knights *(below)* In 1231 Hermann Balke, provincial master of the Teutonic Order, crossed the river Vistula with a crusading army, swiftly founding new fortified cities such as Königsberg (1255). Systematic subjection of the pagan Prussian tribes gave way, after 1309, to 100 years of prosperity. In 1202, another military order, the Brethren of the Sword, was founded in Latvia by the bishop of Riga, but in 1237 it amalgamated with the Teutonic Knights.

DURING the 14th century Europe's political centre of gravity shifted eastwards. Whereas the onset of economic depression, the prolonged and devastating wars between England and France (see page 140), and the political dislocation of Germany after the death of Frederick II in 1250 (see page 118), all resulted in a period of instability, weak government and unrest in the west, in the east the same period saw the rise and consolidation of powerful states with relatively modern institutions. Under Charles IV of Bohemia (1346–78), Casimir the Great of Poland (1333–70) and Louis the Great of Hungary (1342–82), the lands between the Baltic and the Balkans entered the mainstream of European history for the first time. Their cultural integration is symbolized by the foundation of universities at Prague (1348), Cracow (1364), Vienna (1365), and (briefly) at Pécs (1367).

Earlier states established in eastern Europe had proved unstable. Like Kievan Russia (see page 114), they split in the 12th century into warring principalities, and the Mongol invasions caused a further setback, particularly in Hungary. After 1250, however, a new phase of concentration began. First in the field was Bohemia under Ottocar II (1253–78), who set out to build a great territorial state including Austria and extending to the Adriatic. But Ottocar's ambitions provoked the opposition of the Bohemian nobility and of the German princes, and his defeat and death in 1278 left the way open for the Habsburgs to establish their power in Austria. Confusion and conflict in Germany, the bitter struggle between Ludwig IV of Bavaria (1314–47) and Pope John XXII (1316–34) over the imperial succession, and the extinction of the Přemyslid dynasty in Bohemia (1306) and the Árpád dynasty in Hungary (1301), all helped in the process. By the time of Rudolf IV (1356–65), the Habsburgs had consolidated their position and Austria, Poland, Hungary and Bohemia were major territorial powers. At the same time, in southeast Europe, Stefan Dushan (1331–55) assumed the title of 'Tsar of the Serbs and Greeks' and created a great Serbian empire which reached from the Mediterranean coast opposite Corfu to Salonika and controlled the whole of the Bulgarian hinterland.

The half-century between 1330 and 1380 thus saw a remarkable flowering of government and civilization in east and east-central Europe. In the case of Serbia, the foundations soon proved extremely fragile – after Dushan's death his empire was torn by separatism and faction, and

succumbed to the Ottoman Turks at the important battle of Kosovo in 1389 – but the foundations on which the Polish, Bohemian and Hungarian rulers built were more solid. Bohemia's financial strength and early prominence owed much to the opening of the silver mines of Kutná Hora (Kuttenberg) in the 13th century, and to Prague's strategic position on the trade routes from east to west. Poland profited from the opening of the Baltic sea-route by German merchants, becoming a major exporter of timber and grain. Using their new-found economic power, the rulers of the period set about building centralized states on the western model. Their object was to curb the nobility, encourage new, independent social groupings, codify the law, and set up royal tribunals to which all classes – particularly the nobility – would be subject. The *Statutes of Casimir the Great* (1347–64) and a grandiose but abortive attempt to introduce similar legislation in Bohemia, the so-called *Majestas Carolina*, are monuments to their efforts; Stefan Dushan also promulgated a code of laws, the *Dušanov Zakonik*, in 1349.

The decisive factor in the transformation of eastern Europe, however, was the influx of German and Netherlandish settlers, who cleared forest and waste land, drained swamps, founded villages, and created vast reserves of arable land capable of sustaining a rapidly growing population. German eastern colonization, checked by the great Slav revolt of 983 (see page 116), began again around 1125 as a result of population pressure, and quickly submerged the west Slav peoples (Wagrians, Abodrites, Sorbs, Lusatians) inhabiting the country between the Elbe and the Oder. Military and predatory at first, and with missionary ambitions, the expansion soon developed into a vast movement of peasants, often called in by Slav princes who, anxious to develop their territories, granted the settlers the privilege of living under German law. A second thrust came by sea: the conquest of Wagria opened the Baltic to the Germans, and after the foundation of Lübeck (1143) a string of German cities (Wismar, Rostock, Stralsund, Greifswald, Stettin, Cammin, Kolberg) sprang up along the Baltic coast. From these later emerged the Hanseatic League, established in 1358. The immediate consequence was a series of expeditions, beginning in 1186, and intended to extend German sway as far as the Gulf of Finland. But although Livonia was formally subdued (1207), no appreciable German colonization occurred except in the cities (Riga, Dorpat, Reval), where German merchants played a prominent role in the Russian trade. Nevertheless, German enclaves remained an important element along the eastern Baltic littoral and in parts of Hungary right down to the 20th century.

Colonization reached its peak in the half-century after 1220. By 1300 it was slowing down, except in the territories of the Teutonic Knights, who had been called in as auxiliaries in 1226 by Konrad, Duke of Masovia, against the heathen Prussians. That same year East Prussia was granted by the Emperor Frederick II to the Master of the Teutonic Order, who was also made an imperial prince. The conquest of Prussia, unlike German colonization elsewhere beyond the Oder, was a ruthless military operation, followed by systematic settlement. Some 1400 villages and 93 towns were founded between 1280 and 1410. Under Winrich of Kniprode (1351–82), the greatest Grand Master of the Order, the Teutonic Knights reached the zenith of their power. But their efforts to link up their territory in Prussia with Pomerania in the west and with Livonia in the northeast inevitably provoked hostile reactions. Poland, in particular, saw itself threatened and, further east, Lithuania, the largest territorial state of 14th-

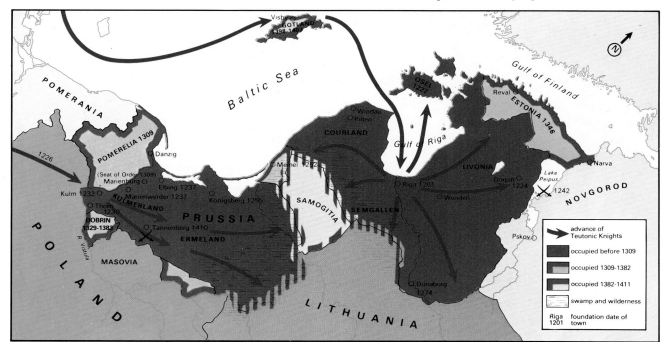

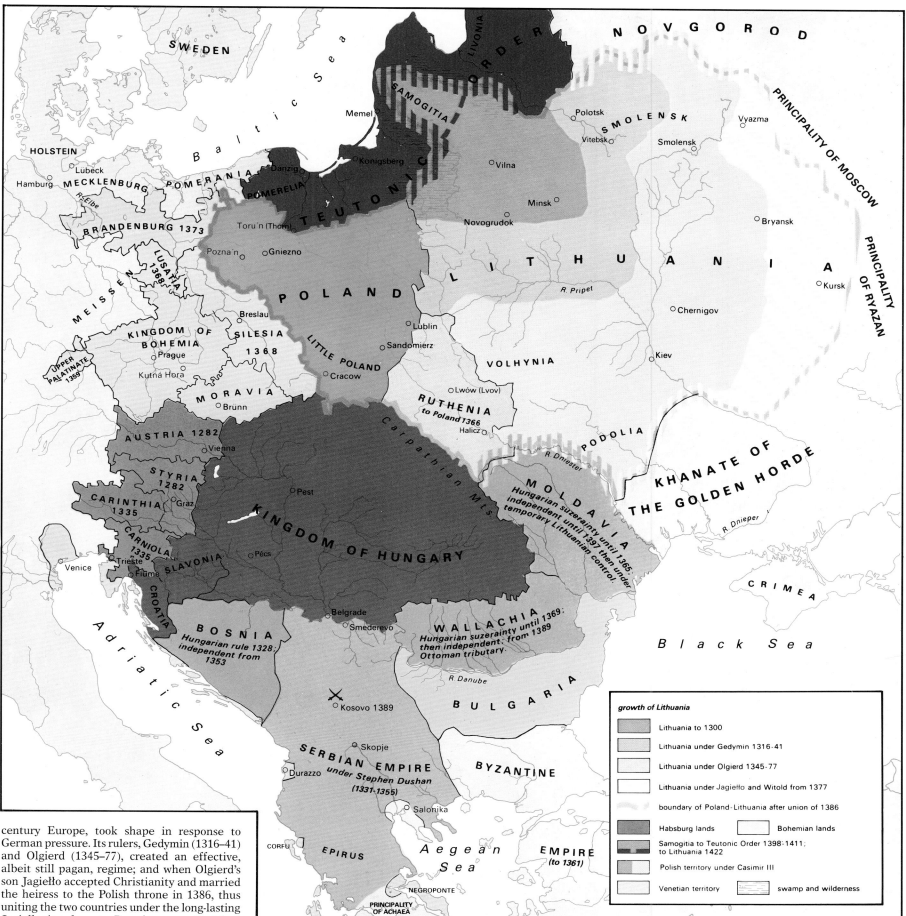

Map labels:

SWEDEN

Baltic Sea

HOLSTEIN
Lübeck
Hamburg
R. Elbe
MECKLENBURG
POMERANIA
POMERELIA
Danzig
Memel
Königsberg
Vilna
Polotsk
Vitebsk
SMOLENSK
Smolensk
Vyazma

ORDER
LIVONIA
SAMOGITIA
TEUTONIC

NOVGOROD

PRINCIPALITY OF MOSCOW

Minsk
Novogrudok
Bryansk

BRANDENBURG 1373
LUSATIA 1368
MEISSEN
Toruń (Thorn)
Poznań
Gniezno

POLAND

LITHUANIA

PRINCIPALITY OF RYAZAN

Kursk

UPPER PALATINATE 1359
KINGDOM OF BOHEMIA
Prague
SILESIA 1368
Breslau
Kutná Hora
LITTLE POLAND
Cracow
Lublin
Sandomierz
R. Pripet
Chernigov
Kiev

MORAVIA
Brünn

VOLHYNIA
RUTHENIA to Poland 1366
Lwów (Lvov)
Halicz

AUSTRIA 1282
Vienna
STYRIA 1282
CARINTHIA 1335
Graz
CARNIOLA 1335
SLAVONIA
Trieste
Fiume
CROATIA
Venice

Pest

KINGDOM OF HUNGARY

Pécs

PODOLIA
R. Dniester
MOLDAVIA
Hungarian suzerainty until 1365; independent until 1391; then under temporary Lithuanian control.

KHANATE OF THE GOLDEN HORDE

R. Dnieper

CRIMEA

Adriatic Sea

BOSNIA
Hungarian rule 1328; independent from 1353

Belgrade
Smederevo

WALLACHIA
Hungarian suzerainty until 1369; then independent; from 1389 Ottoman tributary.

Black Sea

Carpathian Mts

R. Danube

BULGARIA

Kosovo 1389

SERBIAN EMPIRE under Stephen Dushan (1331-1355)

Skopje
Durazzo

BYZANTINE

EMPIRE (to 1361)

CORFU
EPIRUS

Salonika

Aegean Sea

NEGROPONTE

PRINCIPALITY OF ACHAEA

Legend:

growth of Lithuania

- Lithuania to 1300
- Lithuania under Gedymin 1316-41
- Lithuania under Olgierd 1345-77
- Lithuania under Jagiełło and Witold from 1377
- boundary of Poland-Lithuania after union of 1386
- Habsburg lands
- Bohemian lands
- Samogitia to Teutonic Order 1398-1411; to Lithuania 1422
- Polish territory under Casimir III
- Venetian territory
- swamp and wilderness

---

century Europe, took shape in response to German pressure. Its rulers, Gedymin (1316–41) and Olgierd (1345–77), created an effective, albeit still pagan, regime; and when Olgierd's son Jagiełło accepted Christianity and married the heiress to the Polish throne in 1386, thus uniting the two countries under the long-lasting Jagiellonian dynasty, Prussia was outmatched and its crusading pretensions lost their force. Defeated by the Poles at Tannenberg (1410), it entered a period of decline which culminated in the Peace of Toruń (1466) whereby Pomerelia, Danzig and other parts of the Order's former lands passed under Polish rule.

The long conflict with Prussia also adversely affected Poland. To gain support in the wars, the Jagiellonian rulers were forced to make concessions to the gentry (*szlachta*). Furthermore, the union between Poland (predominantly Catholic) and Lithuania (predominantly Orthodox) was far from untroubled. With the rise of Muscovy under Ivan III (1462–1505) and the inception of the policy of the 'reassembly of the Russian land' (see page 158), Poland came under pressure from the east, particularly since Casimir the Great, checked by the Prussian Knights on the Baltic, had expanded in the southeast and annexed Galicia (Halicz) and Ruthenia (Rus). Hungary, meanwhile, was exposed to Ottoman attacks (see page 136); and, in Bohemia, social

and religious unrest beginning under Charles IV's son, Wenceslaus (1378–1419), undermined the power of the crown. After the condemnation and burning of Jan Hus, the Bohemian reformer, at the Council of Constance (1415), the long Hussite wars (see page 140) quickly took on nationalist, anti-German overtones and divided and ruined the country, preparing the way for the eventual rise of the Austrian Habsburgs (see page 182) to the leading position in east-central Europe.

Nevertheless the changes of the 14th century were of lasting importance. Just as the centre of political power in Germany had moved east from the Rhine to the Elbe and from the Elbe to the Oder, so the rise of Poland, Lithuania, Hungary and Bohemia introduced a new political constellation, which lasted until the beginning of the 17th century, when Moscow, Vienna, Sweden and Istanbul began to struggle for mastery of the region.

1/Eastern Europe in 1386 (*above*) The marriage in 1386 of Queen Jadwiga of Poland (1382-99) to Jagiełło of Lithuania, who henceforth styled himself Władysław II, brought about the 'personal union' of these two already powerful kingdoms, creating a formidable new political force and threatening the Teutonic Knights.

Prague (*below*) Under Charles IV (1346-78), Prague became an important capital and a symbol of the new eastern Europe. The Cathedral of St Vitus and the famous royal residence, the Hradschin, were embellished and extended, the Charles University founded (1348) and lavish efforts made to attract merchants and trade.

PRAGA

The crisis of the 14th century in Western Europe

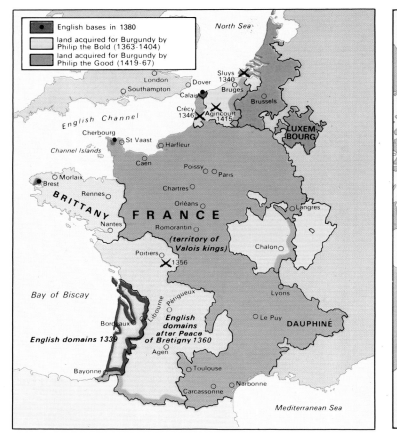

4/The Hundred Years' War (above) England's attempt to conquer France began in 1337, and came close to success with the great victories of Crécy (1346) and Poitiers (1356). France recovered after 1360 (Peace of Brétigny), but Henry V's invasion in 1415 again gave England control of northern France (see page 146). All remaining English garrisons except Calais were expelled in 1453.

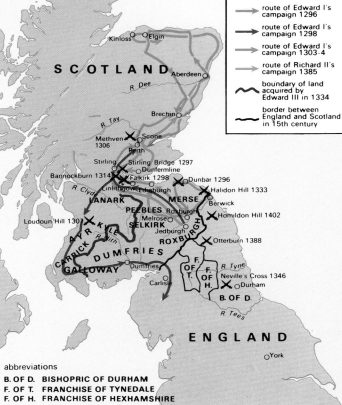

route of Edward I's campaign 1296
route of Edward I's campaign 1298
route of Edward I's campaign 1303-4
route of Richard II's campaign 1385
boundary of land acquired by Edward III in 1334
border between England and Scotland in 15th century

abbreviations
B. OF D. BISHOPRIC OF DURHAM
F. OF T. FRANCHISE OF TYNEDALE
F. OF H. FRANCHISE OF HEXHAMSHIRE

2/The Anglo-Scottish Wars (above) The effort of Edward I of England (1272-1307) to subjugate Scotland culminated in Edward II's disastrous defeat at Bannockburn in 1314. Throughout the century and beyond, the Scots, often fighting in alliance with France, were a threat to England's security.

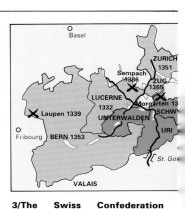

3/The Swiss Confederation (above) Characteristic of the disintegration of the 14th century was the success of the Swiss mountain cantons in throwing off Habsburg rule. The three cantons which formed the original Confederation in 1291 were joined by five others before the end of the 14th century, after the decisive defeat of Austria at the battle of Morgarten (1315).

The Black Death (below) In 1347, plague of Asiatic origin spread from the southeast across the European continent, wiping out perhaps a third of the western population in about two years. Until the early 18th century scarcely a decade went by without a recurrent outbreak. Unlike famine, the pestilence affected every social rank and class, and the psychological impact was profound. The disease, spread by infected fleas carried by rats, was particularly virulent, and few who caught it ever recovered. This illustration from the Czechoslovakian Stiny Codex shows death strangling a plague victim.

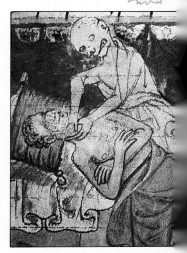

THE monarchies of western Europe were confronted in the 14th century by an aristocracy eager to reassert position and privilege though not to dismember the state. Fragmentation was, nonetheless, a threat everywhere, conspicuously so in France after 1337, where the Hundred Years' War exacerbated particularist dissension. French expansion to the east (Dauphiné, 1353) was checked by a royal fief, the Duchy of Burgundy, swollen by acquisition of the imperial County of Burgundy (1363) and Flanders (1384). In England, war with the Scots was an ever-present threat and a frequent reality; and while military successes in France under Edward III (1327–77) and Henry V (1413–22) eased English aristocratic restlessness, in the long run the French wars only sharpened tensions of which Edward II (1307–27) and Richard II (1377–99) were victims. Both were deposed and murdered. In Germany, the Golden Bull of 1356 defined the pattern for a century of political strife: a king without real power and princes incapable of preserving peace in their separate domains. The Wittelsbachs, Habsburgs and Luxembourgs, who contested for the crown, were more concerned to strengthen their own patrimonies than to stabilize the German monarchy. Papal intervention further intensified monarchical weakness. A web of leagues and confederations, of which the Swiss Confederation (after 1291) was the most successful and enduring, emerged to fill the political vacuum.

By 1400 five Italian states were predominant: Florence, Venice, the Papal States, Naples and Milan. Milan, under its Visconti lords, was the most powerful and threatened the security of the rest; the papacy, weakened by its transfer to Avignon (1305–77) and the Great Schism (1378–1417), enjoyed the lowest prestige (though Avignonese popes were no mere puppets of French kings). At the same time, failure to check corruption and incompetence in the Latin Church inspired reformers who advanced from complaints about abuses to assaults on hierarchical authority and even on orthodox doctrine. Religious and political objectives mingled in England and Bohemia among followers of John Wyclif and Jan Hus.

Spain, like Italy, was a theatre of operation for bands of mercenaries employed by every side in dynastic wars. Aristocratic reaction to Castilian royal authority triumphed in the Trastámara usurpation (1369). Regionalism surfaced after the death of Martin IV of Aragon in 1410, but the settlement of 1412 acknowledged the importance of monarchy to all component sections. Iberian boundaries in fact remained essentially unchanged despite intermittent warfare including a Trastámara threat to overwhelm Portugal, decisively terminated at Aljubarrota (1385). In Denmark, Norway and Sweden the crisis for monarchy loomed not as a prospect of domination by special interests but as a threat to the existence of more than a titular kingship. By 1400 what power remained to the three crowns had fallen to one ruler, Margaret of Norway (Union of Kalmar, 1397). Yet the northern kingdoms were not united and the supremacy of the aristocracy remained undiminished.

Though growth in population and productivity was steady until the later 13th century, both began to decline prior to the Great Famine of 1315–17. Textile manufacture in Flemish and Italian cities and maritime trade fell off sharply before 1330. Banking failures, beginning with the Buonsignori of Siena (1298), culminated in the collapse of the great Florentine banking houses of Bardi and Peruzzi in the 1340s. Mineral production slumped; in many regions reclamation and colonization virtually ceased while land went out of cultivation and timber supplies were exhausted. Resources and wealth were redistributed as established commercial and industrial centres passed their peak and new rivals prospered: for example English producers gained a substantial share of a diminishing cloth industry, while Portuguese and Castilian shipping burgeoned in 1400. Farmland was converted to pasturage for sheep in England and Castile and for cattle in the Netherlands and northern Germany. Monopolistic restrictions designed to secure established positions in a waning market adversely affected the volume of trade and enabled some large towns to prosper at the expense of neighbouring villages. At the same time, the putting-out system deprived townsmen of work in the cloth trades.

Pestilence, beginning with the Black Death (1346–53), and popular insurrection exacerbated social and economic tensions. Erosion of the manorial system progressed unevenly, but throughout western Europe the servile tenant was transformed in a steadily increasing ratio into freeholder, leaseholder, sharecropper or wage-worker. In any of these capacities, or indeed if they remained serfs, the survivors prospered from depopulation after mid-century. Meanwhile, urban labourers organized to bargain for economic improvement and political power, and revolts erupted in both cities and countryside. Most, apparently, were spontaneous; many were brutally repressed, and few accomplished enduring results. The Sicilian Vespers (1282), spreading from Palermo, drove the Angevins from Sicily. Hostility to the French also mingled with bitter antagonism toward burgher oligarchies and landlords in Flemish uprisings such as the Matins of Bruges (1302) and the ensuing battle of Courtrai. Non-violent takeovers of power by Jacob van Artevelde (Ghent, 1337), Cola di Rienzi (Rome, 1347), and Etienne Marcel (Paris, 1357) were bourgeois movements with popular support in which the leaders were ultimately victims of mob violence. Underlying religious sentiment and anti-clericalism permeated much popular protest. In the Great Revolt of 1381 in England, it was radically reformist; in the popular frenzy against the Jews in Spain (1390–92), it combined outrage over social inequity with orthodox bigotry. Although these outbursts were assaults on privilege and exploitation – whether feudal and manorial vestiges, clerical abuse, royal taxation or guild monopoly – many demands were either visionary or unrelated to actual causes of complaint. Foreigners (French, Hanseatic merchants, Jews, Flemings) were often the victims and state power was inevitably the loser.

extent of spread of the Black Death

	1346
	1347
	mid-1348
	end 1348
	mid-1349
	end 1349
	1350
	c.1351
	c.1353
	little or no plague mortality

political change

- union of Kalmar 1397
- Milanese territory under Giangaleazzo Visconti 1378-1402
- territory under Florentine control, end 14th century
- Luxembourg lands c.1400
- Wittelsbach lands
- Habsburg lands

social unrest

- areas of disturbance during Peasants' Revolt in England, 1381
- ● centre of urban revolt
- rural uprisings

religious unrest

- spread of Lollardry in England to death of Richard II, 1399
- area of Hussite influence

- ⊗ defeat in battle of lower class
- ✕ battle
- □ Hussite centre

the Western Schism 1378-1417 *(inset map right)*

- areas giving allegiance to Pope in Rome
- areas giving allegiance to Pope in Avignon
- allegiance officially to Rome but shifting local allegiances

Swiss confederation *(inset map left)*

- original cantons 1291-1315
- ✕ battles for independence
- cantons added to 1389
- main roads

the Great Schism 1378-1417

Avignon
Rome

THURGAU
Näfels 1388 ✕
GLARUS 1388
GRISONS
...hard Pass

SCOTLAND
Shetlands
Orkneys
Hebrides
Edinburgh
Carlisle
Newcastle
Armagh
IRELAND
Wexford
WALES
Chester
York
Lincoln
ENGLAND
Norwich
Bristol
Bury St Edmunds
London
Winchester

NORWAY
Bergen
Oslo
SWEDEN
Uppsala
Stockholm
Visby
DENMARK
Copenhagen
Baltic Sea

North Sea

RUSSIAN STATES
Novgorod
Riga
Königsberg
Danzig
Smolensk
PRINCIPALITY OF MOSCOW

TEUTONIC ORDER
POMERANIA
Hamburg
Bremen
Lübeck
FRIESLAND
Amsterdam
HOLLAND
BRANDENBURG
Magdeburg
SAXONY
Brunswick
SILESIA
Warsaw
POLAND
LITHUANIA
Kiev
R Dnieper
Cracow
R Oder
R Elbe

Roosebeke 1382
Bruges
Antwerp
FLANDERS
Ypres
Ghent
Aachen
Liège
Cologne
HOLY
ROMAN
Mainz
Frankfurt
BOHEMIA
Prague
MORAVIA
Tabor
Trier
UKRAINE
R Dniester

Agincourt
Crécy
Amiens
Rouen
Mello 1358
Rheims
Meaux 1358
Paris
Chartres
Troyes
Orléans
FRANCONIA
Strasbourg
Regensburg
EMPIRE
Augsburg
BAVARIA
Passau
Munich
Vienna
AUSTRIA
Salzburg
Buda
Pest
HUNGARY
R Danube
WALLACHIA
Bucharest
Belgrade
Black Sea

BRITTANY
FRANCE
BURGUNDY
Poitiers
R Loire
SWABIA
Basle
Constance
SWISS CONFED.
Lausanne
Geneva
SAVOY
Lyons
R Rhône
Alps
Milan
CARINTHIA
Trieste
Venice
REPUBLIC OF VENICE
Bay of Biscay
Bordeaux
ENGLISH GASCONY
AQUITAINE
R Dordogne
Cahors
Massif Central
Toulouse
Montpellier
Narbonne
DAUPHINÉ
Turin
Genoa
Ravenna
PROVENCE
Avignon
Marseilles
Pisa
Florence
Ancona
BOSNIA
SERBIAN PRINCES
Ragusa
BULGARIA
Adrianople
Constantinople
PRINCIPALITY OF ALBANIA

NAVARRE
ARAGON
Saragossa
Barcelona
Valencia
Balearic Islands
Corsica
Sardinia
Siena
PAPAL STATES
Rome
KINGDOM OF NAPLES
Naples
Amalfi
Adriatic Sea
Salonica
DUCHY OF ATHENS
ACHAEA
OTTOMAN TURKS

Palermo
Messina
KINGDOM OF SICILY
Mediterranean Sea
Rhodes
Crete

1/Famine, plague and popular unrest Inadequately financed and weakened by war and internal dissension, western European monarchy underwent severe strains throughout the 14th century. Recession, compounded by famine and pestilence, led to conflicts in all countries between the autocracy and the urban oligarchies on the one hand, and the peasants and urban proletariat on the other. The Western Church was also rent with schism.

141

Merchants and finance in Europe c.1500

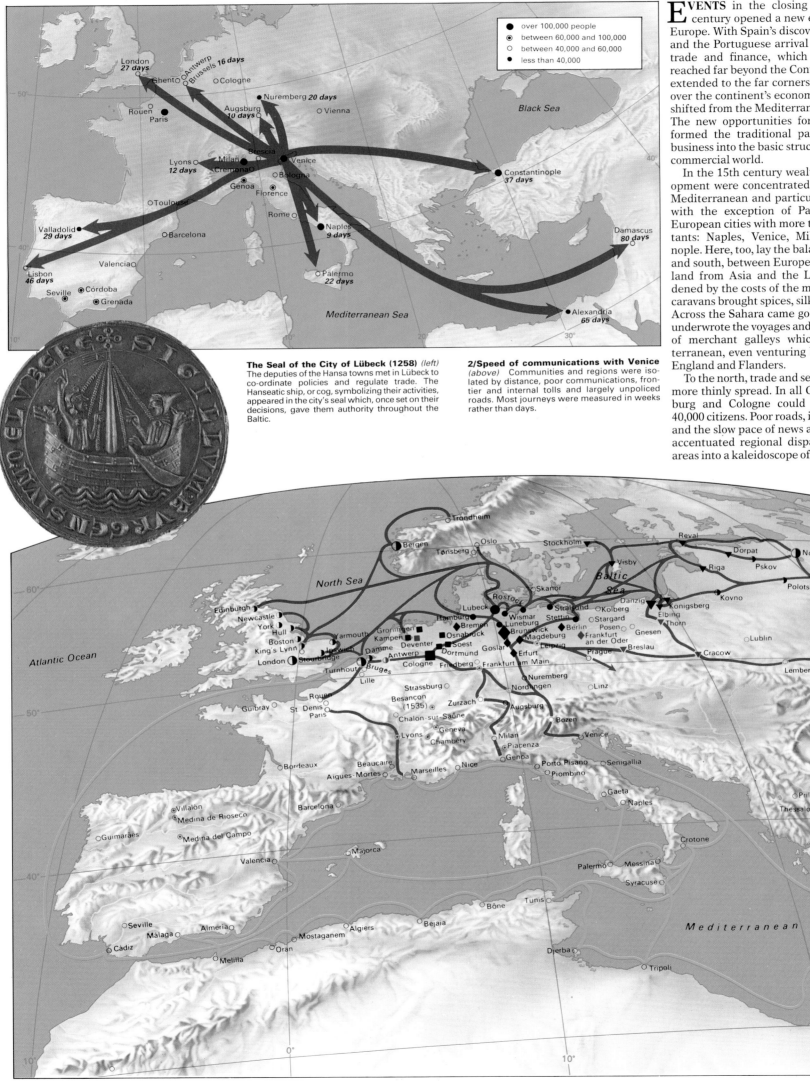

Legend:
- ● over 100,000 people
- ◉ between 60,000 and 100,000
- ○ between 40,000 and 60,000
- • less than 40,000

The Seal of the City of Lübeck (1258) *(left)*
The deputies of the Hansa towns met in Lübeck to co-ordinate policies and regulate trade. The Hanseatic ship, or cog, symbolizing their activities, appeared in the city's seal which, once set on their decisions, gave them authority throughout the Baltic.

2/Speed of communications with Venice *(above)* Communities and regions were isolated by distance, poor communications, frontier and internal tolls and largely unpoliced roads. Most journeys were measured in weeks rather than days.

EVENTS in the closing years of the 15th century opened a new economic future for Europe. With Spain's discovery of the Americas and the Portuguese arrival in India, European trade and finance, which before had rarely reached far beyond the Continent itself, rapidly extended to the far corners of the globe. Moreover the continent's economic centre of gravity shifted from the Mediterranean to the Atlantic. The new opportunities for profit soon transformed the traditional patterns of medieval business into the basic structures of the modern commercial world.

In the 15th century wealth and urban development were concentrated largely around the Mediterranean and particularly in Italy. Here, with the exception of Paris, were the only European cities with more than 100,000 inhabitants: Naples, Venice, Milan and Constantinople. Here, too, lay the balance, between north and south, between Europe and the East. Overland from Asia and the Levant, heavily burdened by the costs of the middlemen, the Arab caravans brought spices, silks, cotton and drugs. Across the Sahara came gold and ivory. Venice underwrote the voyages and organized the fleets of merchant galleys which plied the Mediterranean, even venturing beyond Gibraltar to England and Flanders.

To the north, trade and settlement were much more thinly spread. In all Germany, only Augsburg and Cologne could muster more than 40,000 citizens. Poor roads, indifferent transport and the slow pace of news and communications accentuated regional disparities and isolated areas into a kaleidoscope of local markets. From

Venice, an important centre for Europe, the average journey took 9 days to Naples, 27 to London, 46 to Lisbon and 65 to Alexandria. Despite the difficulties, however, Italian connections reached far and wide. The Medici of Florence, following the example of the Bardi and Peruzzi a century and a half earlier, controlled substantial banking agencies in the principal transalpine capitals.

Northern Europe itself specialized in the products of sea, farm, mine and forest, many of them monopolized by the merchants of the Hanseatic League (the Hansa). This association of cities, led by Lübeck in the Baltic, promoted trading monopolies and successfully sought exclusive privileges for itself in Scandinavia, the Low Countries, Russia, Germany and England. Its activities were principally based on a network of towns in Germany and four great trading posts, or *kontore*: the Tyskebrugge in Bergen (timber and fish); the Peterhof in Novgorod (furs); the Steelyard in London (wool and cloth); and the Assemblies in Bruges (cloth). Until its harbour silted up in the late 15th century, Bruges was the main *entrepôt* market where Mediterranean produce and commercial interests met those of the Baltic and the North Sea.

Meanwhile, the substantial payment and credit requirements needed to facilitate the physical movement of goods were still mainly met by the great periodic fairs, which had emerged in the Middle Ages (see page 120), and by a 14th century invention, the bill of exchange (a written promise to pay money in another town to a named individual). After the brief prosperity of Geneva, the most famous fairs of the 15th century convened at Lyons, strategically placed on the great trade route through the Rhône valley. There the merchants of Florence, Lucca, Genoa and Germany met four times a year, free from certain taxes and tolls, to settle accounts and clear bills of exchange from the principal markets of Europe.

But as the economy expanded the traditional mercantile structure proved progressively less adequate. It could no longer cope fully with the opportunities presented by the new Atlantic markets, the rapid increase in domestic demand, and the commercial exploits of the merchants of Portugal and Spain (see page 154). By the 1550s, these two great colonial powers had not only opened up the world, but also created huge demands for investment in new methods and institutions. A more advanced technology was required to discover the most profitable sea routes, and train seamen to cope with winds and currents different from those of the Mediterranean. New market structures emerged to cater for changing needs and demands. The intermittent fairs gradually gave place to more permanent markets and bourses, open each weekday throughout the year. With the eclipse of Bruges, the merchant community moved to Antwerp on the Scheldt, with its access to the Rhine and the cloth towns of southern Flanders. Its population grew from 47,000 in 1496 to 100,000 in 1560, making it the largest city in northern Europe, and its multi-national merchant community used negotiable cheques as well as discounted and endorsed bills of exchange. For the first time, credit replaced cash as the principle medium of exchange and interest rates in the city fell from 25 per cent around 1500 to 9 per cent in the 1550s.

The expansion and diversification of trade spawned a fresh generation of rich merchants and bankers. In part this was due to consolidation: the number of banks in Florence declined from 33 in 1460 to 8 in 1516, while several cities created public banks whose credit was guaranteed by the government. However, whether public or private, most of the new banks were far richer than their predecessors: whereas the Peruzzi of Florence in the 1340s had capital assets worth 147 kg of silver, and the Medici of the same city a century later possessed assets worth 1750 kg, the Fugger of Augsburg in 1546 boasted assets 13,000 kg. When the Habsburg Charles V secured his election as Holy Roman Emperor in 1519 by bribery, creating a monarchy that included not only Germany and Austria but also Spain, the Low Countries, and most of the New World (see page 182), the operation was largely financed by the Fugger. Starting as peasant weavers and expanding into silver, copper and mercury mining, this German family grew immensely rich and powerful as moneylenders to the Court and its aristocracy. As security, they normally demanded monopoly rights over various forms of mining trade and revenue collection. They controlled the Spanish customs, and gradually extended their influence throughout the Habsburg empire and its colonies overseas. Their operations stretched from Danzig to Lisbon, from Budapest to Rome and from Moscow to Chile. In 1552 a well-timed loan to Charles V at Villach, when he was abandoned by all his other allies, saved the Imperial cause from certain defeat.

The private financiers of great states ran great risks, however. Both the Fugger, before their descendants turned from banking to land ownership, and their thrusting Genoese competitors suffered heavy losses when the Spanish government repudiated its debts, which happened on six separate occasions between 1557 and 1627. Accordingly after the bankruptcy of 1575, the Fugger increasingly withdrew from such business. The merchant bankers of Genoa, who took their place, had been forced to seek new commercial channels in the 1520s, when their city chose the Emperor's side against France and they were barred from the Lyons fairs. Charles V compensated them for a while with the fairs of Besançon, which were later moved to the north Italian town of Piacenza, where some 200 merchants (representing perhaps 100 commercial firms and 50 merchant banks) met four times a year to settle accounts worth around 15 million gold crowns for the Spanish government and the merchant community alike. Thanks to the new instruments of credit, less than one per cent of these sums changed hands in cash. But such periodic meetings, as elsewhere, could no longer cater for the growing volume of business. Nevertheless, their enterprise paved the way to modern finance in the Atlantic markets of Amsterdam and London.

(see page 154)

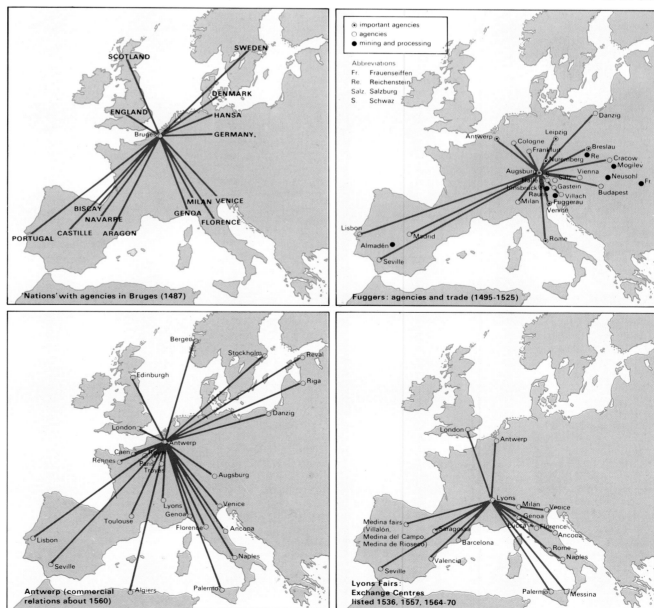

3/The four major networks of trade (below) Commercial fairs, which brought together merchants from different areas to exchange goods and settle accounts, originated in Champagne in the 12th century. In time similar fairs appeared elsewhere – at Lyons in France, at Bruges and Antwerp in the Low Countries, at Piacenza in Italy, at Medina del Campo in Spain – as the volume of European trade expanded. Each catered for slightly different geographical regions, although the major centres, some of them very large, featured in each system. By 1500 the fairs at Medina, held for 50 days twice a year, brought together some 2500 merchants. Moreover some individual commercial firms, such as the Fugger of Augsburg, possessed extensive networks of their own. Nevertheless, these traditional financial institutions proved inadequate in the course of the 16th century for, quite apart from the new markets carved out in America, Asia and Africa, the wealth and population of Europe itself burgeoned. In Italy, in the Low Countries and (somewhat later) in England, permanent bourses, central clearing banks and financial institutions guaranteed by the state were founded to bridge the gap.

1/Two trading empires Venice and the Hansa provided sea-links between the Mediterranean and northern Europe in the later Middle Ages. Venetian galleys brought spices, silks, wines and fruit; Hanseatic counting houses (kontore) held ready stocks of metals, fish, textiles and Russian furs. Their meetings in Flanders joined two huge zones of commercial activity and the resulting trade-flows brought great profit to Italy's merchant-financiers. Genoa, like Venice, had a long history of trade in the Mediterranean and across Europe. In the early 16th century Genoese merchants were firmly established in numerous commercial centres, above all Seville, and were ready to take a leading part in providing the less developed Iberian powers with the tools of economic control.

site of important fair
site of lesser fair
routes of Venetian merchant galleys
Hanseatic trade routes

The Hanseatic League

● Wendish and Pomeranian circle
♦ Saxony, Thuringia, Brandenburg circle
▼ Prussia, Livonia, Sweden circle
■ Rhine, Westphalia, Netherlands circle
● ♦ ▼ ■ chief city
● ♦ ▼ ■ associated city
◐ kontore   ◑ subsidiary kontore
◑ other important city

Note: Places that are important fairs as well as Hanseatic cities have red symbols

'Nations' with agencies in Bruges (1487)

Fuggers: agencies and trade (1495-1525)
● important agencies
○ agencies
● mining and processing
Abbreviations
Fr. Frauenseiffen
Re. Reichenstein
Salz. Salzburg
S. Schwaz

Antwerp (commercial relations about 1560)

Lyons Fairs:
Exchange Centres listed 1536, 1557, 1564-70

The Americas on the eve of European conquest

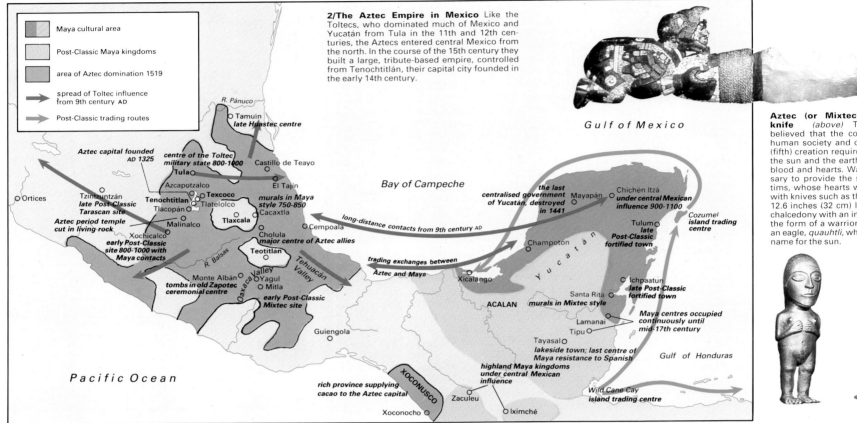

2/The Aztec Empire in Mexico Like the Toltecs, who dominated much of Mexico and Yucatán from Tula in the 11th and 12th centuries, the Aztecs entered central Mexico from the north. In the course of the 15th century they built a large, tribute-based empire, controlled from Tenochtitlán, their capital city founded in the early 14th century.

Aztec (or Mixtec) sacrificial knife *(above)* The Aztecs believed that the continuation of human society and of the present (fifth) creation required nourishing the sun and the earth with human blood and hearts. War was necessary to provide the sacrificial victims, whose hearts were removed with knives such as this one, about 12.6 inches (32 cm) long, made of chalcedony with an inlaid handle in the form of a warrior costumed as an eagle, *quauhtli*, which was also a name for the sun.

Hollow figurines *(above)* of gold and silver, a little under 5 inches (16 cm) high, used by the Incas as offerings at sacred sites. Some have been found dressed in miniature woven garments. These typical examples, now in the American Museum of Natural History, are from an island in Lake Titicaca.

E**VEN** before the arrival of European colonialism, the western hemisphere was a crucible of imperial experiment.

The term 'Aztecs' is conventionally applied to the dominant group in the Valley of Mexico at the time of European discovery. Their true origins are hard to disentangle from the evidence of their own self-contradictory myths, but at least one group seems likely to have been nomads who settled among the agrarian city-states of the Lake Texcoco region in the early 14th century. Their lake-bound city of Tenochtitlán gradually acquired the alliance or submission of neighbouring communities until, as the dominant partner in a lakeland confederacy, it became the principal beneficiary of a complex network of tributary relationships throughout the entire region.

Around 1500, Aztec armies extended the reach of their predatory system of tribute-exaction as far as the River Pánuco in the north and Xoconusco in the south. Borne by trade, their cultural influence reached further still, across the northern deserts into what are now the southern United States, over the Caribbean to the Taino of Haiti, who adopted their ritual ball-games and stone courts, and southeast beyond Xicalango, where the remotest Aztec garrison was stationed, into Yucatán, where many communities acquired Nahua-speaking elites from central Mexico.

Tribute was the source of this empire's strength and weakness alike. The densely concentrated population of Tenochtitlán could not survive on locally raised resources. Huge quantities of food, clothing and ritual goods had to be levied from far afield: a surviving tribute-list, which may not be complete, lists over 225,000 bushels (8181 m³) of maize and 123,400 cotton mantles, with corresponding quantities of beans, sage, purslane, chillies, cacao, incense, lime, salt and precious exotica due every year. Other Aztec cities had comparable rates of consumption. The market of Tlatelolco, Tenochtitlán's neighbour, was said to be frequented by 50,000 people. According to an early colonial source, the ruler's household in Texcoco, Tenochtitlán's ally, received 40,000 tortillas a year.

In addition, the Aztecs sustained a prodigious material culture, featuring monumental stone building, vital sculpture, sumptuous goldwork and extravagant featherwork, all demanding intensive labour and expensive ingredients. Finally, their religion exacted a heavy toll in human sacrifices – those offered at the dedication of the main temple of Tenochtitlán, for instance, in 1487, are variously estimated in early colonial sources at between 10,000 and 80,000 – almost all of them captured in war or procured by ritual exchanges of victims with independent or partially subjected communities.

The voracious appetite of the Aztec system obliged its consumers to be masters of warfare. It also made them vulnerable to a concerted withdrawal of tribute by suppliers. Isolated by the diplomacy of the Spanish invaders after 1519, the Aztec 'capital' was effectively starved into surrender.

The Andean environment made the Inca empire very different. For this was a territorial state, organizing and enforcing collaboration between producers of complementary goods at different micro-climatic levels. The effect was enhanced by the empire's long, thin shape, which gave it responsibility not only over every habitable environment above sea level but also over a vast climatic swathe from north to south, encompassing more than 30 degrees of latitude. The Incas were capable of re-locating large populations in the interests of maximizing production or increasing security. In the early 16th century, the Inca ruler Huayna Capac was said to have re-settled in Cochabamba 14,000 people from areas as far apart as Cuzco and northern Chile. The most conspicuous evidence of the essential unity of the empire was its road system, more than 12,500 miles (20,000 km) long.

Despite its different character, however, the Inca world also exhibited some of the structural weaknesses of the Aztecs. It, too, was the creation of a small group of people of obscure origins whose rapid expansion from their base in Cuzco did not begin before the second quarter of the 15th century. Again, religion strained resources (though the tally of human sacrifice was less extravagant) because of the vast households maintained for the cults of dead rulers: the costs this entailed may have contributed to division among the elite which developed into the devastating civil war that raged at the time of the Spanish conquest. Many subject peoples found the burden of Inca rule oppressive and were willing to collaborate with an invader.

In the extent of their sway and in the scale of their material achievements, the Aztec and Inca polities were unique in pre-colonial America; but cultures almost as impressive in their various ways developed in many parts of the hemisphere. In the agriculturally limited environment of the Amazon rain forest, a fragile civilization was created in densely populated riverside settlements, sustained by fish and turtle-farming and by cultivation of bitter manioc. Without forging empires or building in stone, peoples in regions adjoining the Inca and Aztec worlds produced enviable concentrations of wealth and created marvellous works of art: the Mixtecs, for example, most of whom were tributaries of the Aztecs in what are now the Mexican states of Oaxaca and Guerrero, were hamlet-dwellers who have left masterpieces of goldwork and painting on hides; among the Chibcha-speaking peoples of the Valley of Bogotá, the Muisca were textile exporters who acquired vast amounts of gold from neighbours. In what are now New Mexico and Arizona, complex irrigation systems were in place, one of them covering 247,000 acres (100,000 ha) in the Salido Valley.

Though North America was for the most part sparsely populated, some areas showed potential for demographic success and political sophistication by the time they fell victim to European expansion – especially among the Iroquois, whose fortified proto-urban communities came to be embraced in a powerful 'confederacy', and in the Carolinas, where the first Europeans reported fabulous surplus wealth, signs of long-range trade and high standards of craftsmanship. Even in the Great Plains, agricultural techniques had been introduced from the south and northeast, and it was only in the remotest extremities and deepest recesses of the hemisphere that the rigours of the environment limited man's potential to hunting and gathering.

Sacred maize plant *(above)* Maize, beans and squash were the domesticated plants on which settled life depended over much of the Americas. Maize, especially, is a sacred plant, as is illustrated by this 'corn person' from a 20th-century Navaho blanket.

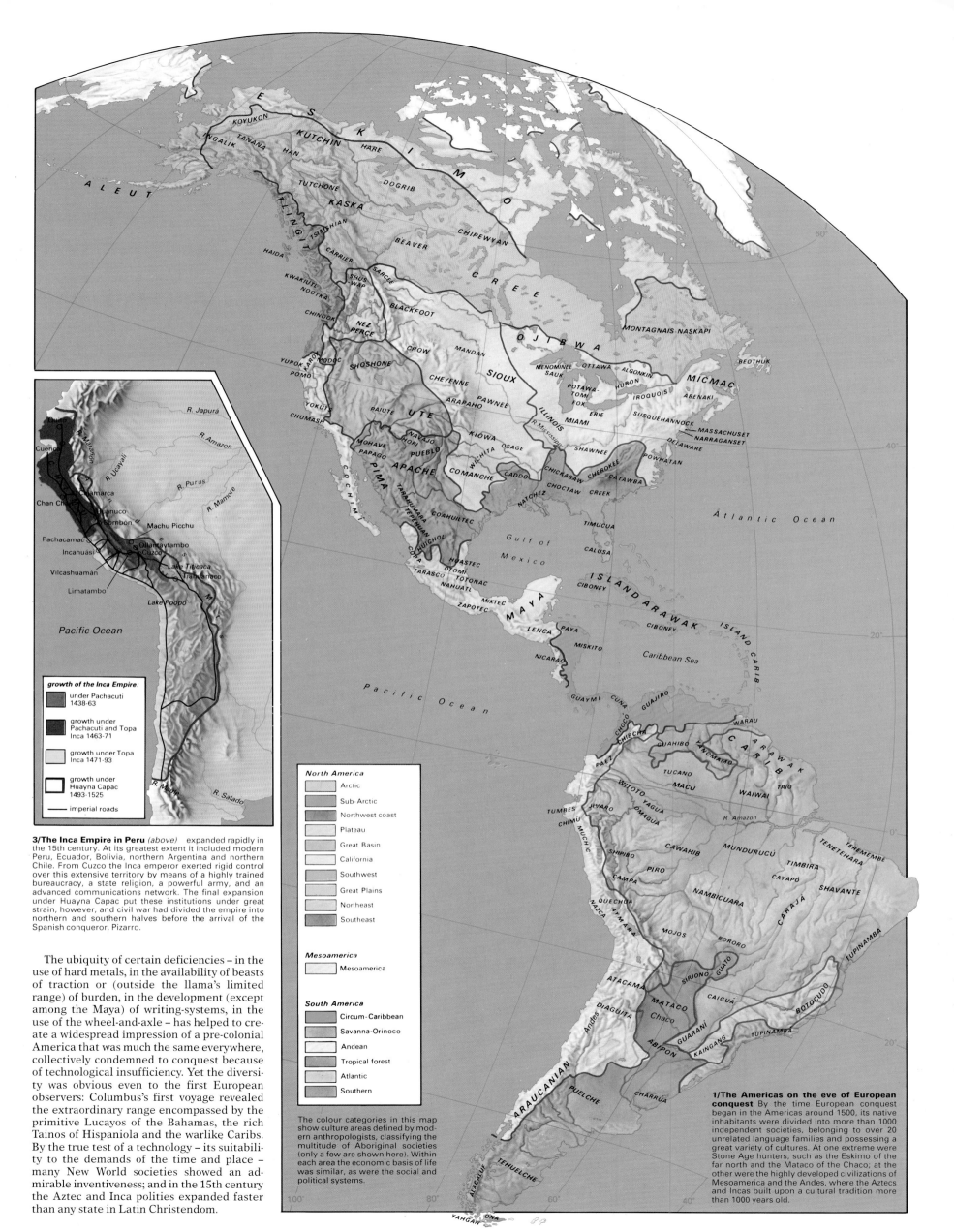

growth of the Inca Empire:

◼ under Pachacuti 1438-63

◼ growth under Pachacuti and Topa Inca 1463-71

◻ growth under Topa Inca 1471-93

◻ growth under Huayna Capac 1493-1525

— imperial roads

3/The Inca Empire in Peru *(above)* expanded rapidly in the 15th century. At its greatest extent it included modern Peru, Ecuador, Bolivia, northern Argentina and northern Chile. From Cuzco the Inca emperor exerted rigid control over this extensive territory by means of a highly trained bureaucracy, a state religion, a powerful army, and an advanced communications network. The final expansion under Huayna Capac put these institutions under great strain, however, and civil war had divided the empire into northern and southern halves before the arrival of the Spanish conqueror, Pizarro.

The ubiquity of certain deficiencies – in the use of hard metals, in the availability of beasts of traction or (outside the llama's limited range) of burden, in the development (except among the Maya) of writing-systems, in the use of the wheel-and-axle – has helped to create a widespread impression of a pre-colonial America that was much the same everywhere, collectively condemned to conquest because of technological insufficiency. Yet the diversity was obvious even to the first European observers: Columbus's first voyage revealed the extraordinary range encompassed by the primitive Lucayos of the Bahamas, the rich Tainos of Hispaniola and the warlike Caribs. By the true test of a technology – its suitability to the demands of the time and place – many New World societies showed an admirable inventiveness; and in the 15th century the Aztec and Inca polities expanded faster than any state in Latin Christendom.

North America
- Arctic
- Sub-Arctic
- Northwest coast
- Plateau
- Great Basin
- California
- Southwest
- Great Plains
- Northeast
- Southeast

Mesoamerica
- Mesoamerica

South America
- Circum-Caribbean
- Savanna-Orinoco
- Andean
- Tropical forest
- Atlantic
- Southern

The colour categories in this map show culture areas defined by modern anthropologists, classifying the multitude of Aboriginal societies (only a few are shown here). Within each area the economic basis of life was similar, as were the social and political systems.

1/The Americas on the eve of European conquest By the time European conquest began in the Americas around 1500, its native inhabitants were divided into more than 1000 independent societies, belonging to over 20 unrelated language families and possessing a great variety of cultures. At one extreme were Stone Age hunters, such as the Eskimo of the far north and the Mataco of the Chaco; at the other were the highly developed civilizations of Mesoamerica and the Andes, where the Aztecs and Incas built upon a cultural tradition more than 1000 years old.

145

The new monarchies: Europe at the close of the 15th century

AS A RESULT of the economic and political setbacks of the 14th century (see page 140), by about 1400 no dominant state existed in Europe. Germany and Italy were already fragmented, and in neither was there any clear preponderance. In the east, the powerful states of the 14th century (see page 138) crumbled and new empires, such as those of Casimir IV of Poland (1447–92) or Matthias Corvinus of Hungary (1458–90), proved ephemeral. In the west, the Iberian peninsula was a prey to civil war, while France was torn apart by the feud between Burgundians and Armagnacs, a situation made far worse when Henry V of England (1413–22), the ally of Burgundy, invaded Normandy in 1415 and extended English control to the Loire.

This unstable situation changed after 1450. The Muscovites and the Ottoman Turks rapidly subjugated large areas of eastern Europe (see map 1, and pages 136 and 158). In the west, Burgundy, the rising star of the 15th century, which seemed destined to become a major power between France and Germany, was partitioned after Charles the Bold was killed in battle in 1477 (see map 2), and the English were expelled from French soil (except from Calais) by 1453. In Spain, the warring kingdoms of Castile and Aragon were united in 1479, and in 1492 their combined forces completed the reconquest of the last Islamic strongholds in Spain. In England, failure in France and the loss of Normandy (1453) provoked civil war ('The Wars of the Roses'), but after 1485 a new dynasty, the Tudors, succeeded in restoring

order and extended royal control in the turbulent outlying regions through the Council of the North and the Council of the Marches of Wales. In Germany, a series of dynastic alliances united the Habsburg lands with those of Luxembourg (1437) and Burgundy (1477). All these possessions, and later those of the Spanish royal family, came to the Emperor Charles V (1519–58), making him the greatest Christian ruler since Charlemagne (see pages 182-3).

The states which achieved these territorial successes were very different from the 'feudal monarchies' of the 12th and 13th centuries (see page 122). New conceptions of statecraft, exemplified for later generations by Machiavelli's famous treatise, *The Prince*, were in the air, and new institutions were created to enhance the king's authority. New courts, such as the English Star Chamber, were set up to impose law and order; new taxes (such as the French *taille*, 1439), and new machinery to collect them, were introduced; and permanent ambassadors were sent abroad to monitor the actions and intentions of neighbouring states.

There was also a marked expansion of armies and navies. In France, permanent military formations, the beginning of the standing army, were maintained after 1445, and Louis XI (1461–83) could rely, in his struggles with foreign enemies and overmighty vassals, on the best train of artillery in Europe. Parallel military expansion also occurred elsewhere. The armed forces of the king of Spain, for example, numbered about 30,000 in the 1470s. Some 60 years later, they stood at 150,000.

The philosophy of the new monarchs was expressed by Matthias Corvinus when he told a Silesian assembly in 1474 that he was 'lord and king' and that 'what he with his councillors held to be best, it was for them as dutiful subjects to perform'. The inhabitants of many countries, particularly the commercial classes, were prepared to tolerate this form of royal absolutism in return for security and the suppression of civil strife. The economic recovery visible from c.1450 also helped by providing more taxes. Civil war and economic setbacks had weakened the old nobility, and the church also was brought increasingly under royal control. In 'concordats' with Austria (1448), France (1516) and Spain (1523), the papacy was forced to concede far-reaching rights over the national churches, and in a number of Protestant countries the ruler openly assumed control of spiritual affairs. Henry VIII of England, for example, declared himself 'Supreme Head' of the church in England in 1534.

Nevertheless the institutional armature of the 'new monarchies' was more fragile than it seemed, their apparent modernity often superficial. The new exalted sense of the prince's authority might point to the future, but rulers like Charles the Bold of Burgundy and Maximilian I of Austria still clung to the ideals of the age of chivalry which was passing. The secular state, in which politics are divorced from religion and organized around an impersonal, centralized and unifying system of government, was still two centuries away (see page 178). The 'new monarchies' were at best its forerunner.

1/The new monarchies (below)
In 1500 the strong states of Europe lay at the extreme east and the extreme west of the continent. The Muscovites and the Ottomans were poised to turn the weaker states of east central Europe into their satellites, while France and the Habsburg Netherlands were poised to make inroads into Germany, and Spain was already in the process of absorbing half the Italian peninsula. The German states (and there were almost 1000 of them) were mostly small and lacked the revenues, resources and military strength necessary to resist. Although some of the Italian states were rich and populous, they proved incapable of co-operating for long, and the political scene was complicated by the presence of over 100 small independent units.

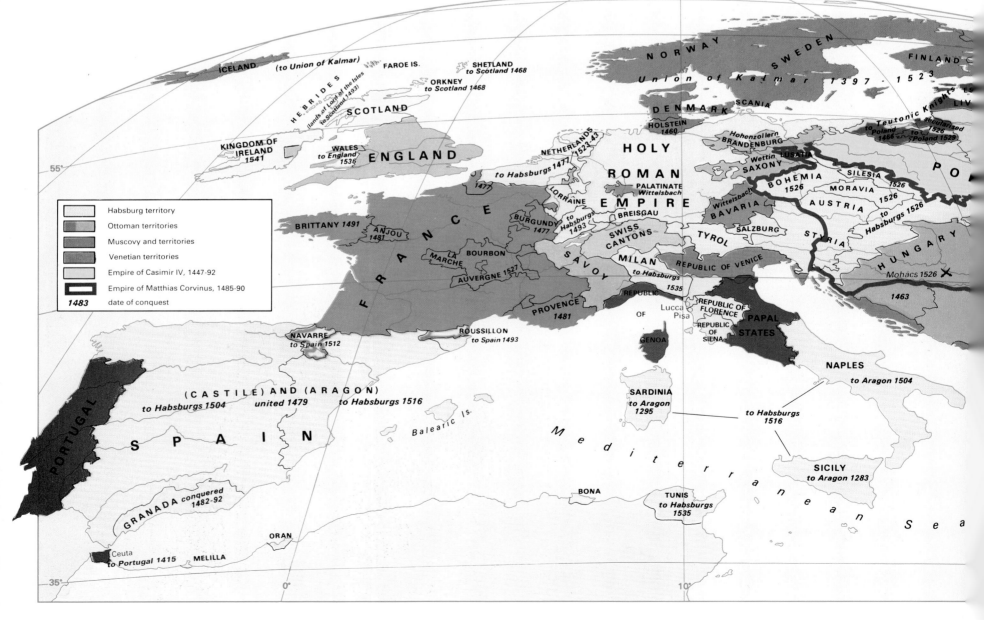

1 **Friesland**: acquired by purchase 1523-4

2 **Groningen**: acquired by negotiation 1536

3 **Overijssel**: acquired by negotiation 1536

4 **Gelderland**: conquered 1473, lost 1477; conquered 1481, lost 1492; conquered again 1543

5 **Utrecht**: acquired by negotiation 1536

6 **Holland**: acquired by treaty 1433

7 **Zeeland**: acquired by treaty 1433

8 **Brabant**: inherited 1404

9 **Limburg**: acquired by gift 1396

10 **Flanders**: acquired by marriage 1384

11 **Boulonnais**: ceded by treaty 1435, lost 1477

12 **Artois**: acquired by marriage 1384, lost 1477; regained 1493

13 **Hainaut**: acquired by treaty 1433

14 **Cambrai**: conquered 1543

15 **Namur**: acquired by purchase 1429

16 **Luxembourg**: inherited 1451

17 **Ponthieu**: ceded by treaty 1435, lost 1477

18 **Amiens**: ceded by treaty 1435, lost 1463; regained 1465, lost 1477

19 **Vermandois**: ceded by treaty 1435, lost 1463; regained 1465, lost 1477

20 **Bar**: conquered 1475, lost 1476

21 **Lorraine**: conquered 1475, lost 1476

22 **Burgundy**: inherited 1363, lost 1477

23 **Franche-Comté**: acquired by marriage 1384, lost 1477; regained 1493

24 **Alsace**: partially conquered 1469, lost 1477

25 **Tournai**: conquered 1521

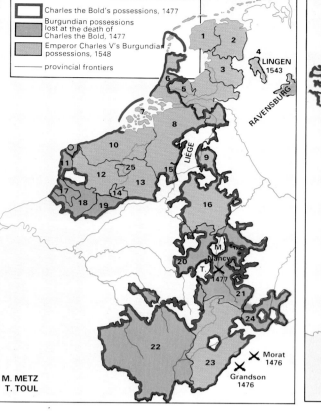

M. METZ
T. TOUL

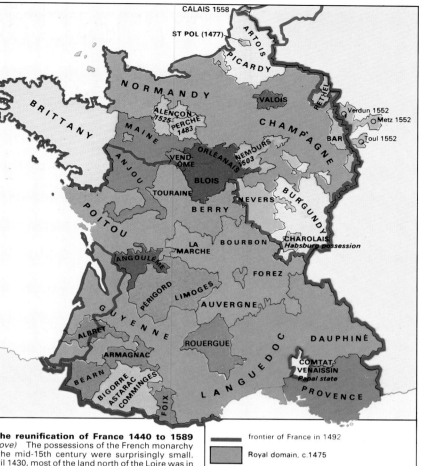

2/State-building in the Low Countries (above)

In the late 14th and 15th centuries, by a combination of force, inheritance, purchase and negotiation, the Valois dukes of Burgundy succeeded in building up a chain of territories along the northern and eastern borders of France. Their domains included some of the most prosperous areas in Europe – above all Flanders and Brabant, with their rich commercial and industrial centres – which enabled the dukes both to patronize a cultural Renaissance and to intervene decisively in international affairs. However, Duke Charles the Bold (1467-77) overreached himself and met defeat at Morat and Grandson (1476) and death at Nancy (1477), whereupon his French fiefs (Burgundy and Picardy) were confiscated by Louis XI. However, the rest of the Burgundian inheritance passed to Maximilian of Austria, husband of Charles's heiress, and thence to their grandson, the Emperor Charles V, who added further territories in the Netherlands. In 1548 Charles united his 17 territories in the Low Countries, both inherited and acquired, into a single political federation, but barely 20 years later rebellion tore the new state asunder (see page 180).

3/The reunification of France 1440 to 1589 (above)

The possessions of the French monarchy in the mid-15th century were surprisingly small. Until 1430, most of the land north of the Loire was in the hands of English and Burgundian forces, and even to the south the actual domain covered less than half the total territory. The reconquest in the 1440s of Normandy, Gascony and the other lands held by the English doubled both the territory obeying Charles VII and the royal domain. But the area under the crown's direct control was still relatively small until a series of confiscations and deaths added the lands of the dukes of Burgundy (1477), Anjou (1481), Brittany (1491) and Bourbon (1527). This left only a handful of semi-independent fiefs (of which many came to the crown when Henry of Navarre became King Henry IV in 1589).

	frontier of France in 1492
	Royal domain, c.1475
	lands annexed from Burgundy, 1477
	lands of René of Anjou, annexed 1481
	lands of Duke of Brittany, annexed 1491
	lands brought to the crown by Louis XII, 1498
	lands brought to the crown by Francis I, 1515
	lands of Duke of Bourbon, annexed 1527
	lands brought to the crown by Henry IV, 1589
	other fiefs annexed, with date
	fiefs still independent at the end of the sixteenth century
	lands recognizing English suzerainty, 1429

The Renaissance (below)

The 'new monarchs' of Europe left lasting monuments to their wealth and power. Patronage on an unprecedented scale produced the rich cultural harvest known as the Renaissance. The movement began in two areas at the end of the 14th century: in the Netherlands, at the court of the Dukes of Burgundy and in the great commercial centres such as Bruges and Antwerp; and in the major city-states of Italy – Florence, Milan, Venice, Naples and Rome. From these centres new styles in art, architecture, literature and music soon spread over the whole continent as far as Moscow. Italian architects had been employed by Ivan III since the 1470s. The purest Renaissance building in Moscow is the Cathedral of the Annunciation (below) in the Kremlin. The external decoration is distinctly Italianate, although the main structure was Russian in inspiration.

For most of the 16th century Italians continued to dominate architecture as Netherlanders dominated music, and both were prominent in art; but the Renaissance brought a flowering of vernacular literature in every country, from Spain to Sweden. Thanks to the spread of printing after 1455, the new cultural advances could be shared and improved upon by others.

THE Indian historian K. M. Panikkar described the period from 1498 to 1947, from Vasco da Gama's discovery of the sea route to India to the declaration of Indian independence, as the European age in history. Other historians have pointed out the element of exaggeration in this definition. If the Europeans had withdrawn from their isolated settlements around the coasts of Asia and Africa in 1750, they would have left behind relatively few traces. Nevertheless, around 1500 the balance, which hitherto had weighed heavily on the side of Asia, began to change, and after 1750 the change was momentous.

Before 1500 civilization had been essentially land-centred, and contacts by sea remained relatively unimportant. If the year 1500 marks a new period in world history, it is because henceforward direct sea contact linked the different continents. This resulted not only in the integration in a global system of regions which hitherto had gone their way in isolation, but also in a challenge to the age-old land-centred balance between the Eurasian civilizations. Only Australia and the smaller islands of the Pacific remained immune; but even they began to fall into European clutches before the end of the 18th century.

Even so, the speed of European expansion should not be exaggerated. The 16th century saw a remarkable resurgence of Muslim power in the Ottoman Empire, Safavid Persia and Mughal India. China and Japan closed their doors to the West. As late as the days of Voltaire, Turkey and China were the exemplars of civilized living, to which Europe could only look with envy and respect. The advent of the Industrial Revolution put Europe ahead; but the fruits of that process – some of them poisonous fruits – were only garnered in the 19th century. The period from 1500 to 1815 was a transitional period in world history, and European society, for all its thrusting novelty, was still essentially an agricultural society of lords and peasants, closer to its agrarian past than to its industrial future.

5 The world of

The main façade of the Palace at Versailles

the emerging West

The world on the eve of European expansion

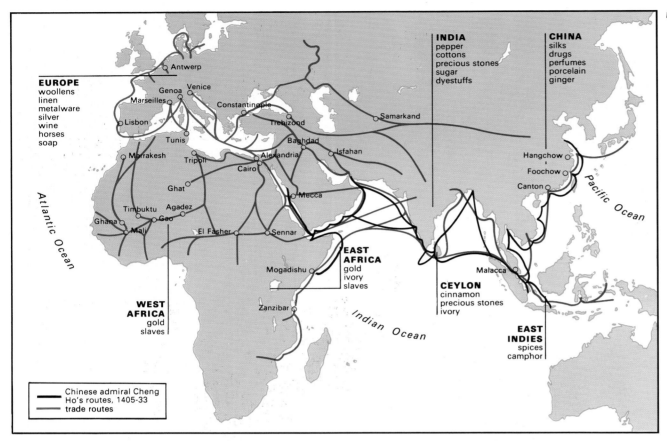

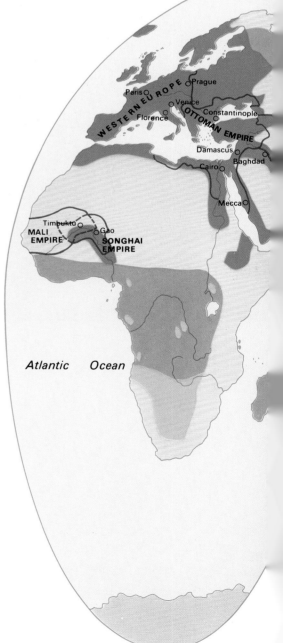

THE central feature of world history between 1500 and 1815 was the expansion of Europe and the spread of European civilization throughout the globe. Down to 1500 the world had, on the whole, pressed in on Europe; after 1500 Europe pressed out into the world. By 1775 a new global balance was in existence.

In the early 16th century Europe still stood on the periphery of the civilized world, overshadowed by the Ming Empire of China, the most powerful and advanced state of the period, and by the rising Ottoman and Safavid empires of the Middle East. Both in wealth and in population China, with over 100 million inhabitants (more than the whole of Europe), loomed far ahead. Islam was still actively making converts in Central and Southeast Asia and among the peoples of sub-Saharan Africa.

The area occupied by the major civilizations, roughly equivalent to the area of plough cultivation, was nevertheless still relatively small in 1500. Over three-quarters of the world's surface was inhabited either by food gatherers or herdsmen – as in Australia and most of Siberia, North America and Africa – or by hand cultivators, especially in Southeast Asia, Africa and Central and South America. But the plough cultivators were far more productive, and it is probable that between two-thirds and three-quarters of the

2/Trade on the eve of Portuguese expansion *(left)* When Vasco da Gama set out for India, the world's richest trade routes ran from east to west. They made fortunes for the Muslim kingdoms of the Near East and for ports handling the western end.

3/Distribution of races in 1500 *(left)* **and subsequent diffusion** *(below)* Before 1500 there existed, in effect, worldwide racial segregation. The Negroids were concentrated in sub-Saharan Africa and a few Pacific islands; the Mongoloids in central Asia, Siberia, and the Americas; the Caucasoids in Europe, North Africa, the Middle East and India; and the Australoids in Australia and India. By 1775 this pattern had fundamentally altered as the result of six principal intercontinental migrations: from Europe to North, Central and South America; from northern European countries to Africa (and later Australia); from Africa to the Americas; from Russia across the Urals into Siberia; from India to East Africa, South Africa and the Caribbean; and from China into Southeast Asia. By far the greatest change occurred in the Americas, where the native population declined in some areas by up to 90 per cent within a century, to be replaced by Europeans, Blacks and, in parts of Latin America, a mixed race of *mestizos*.

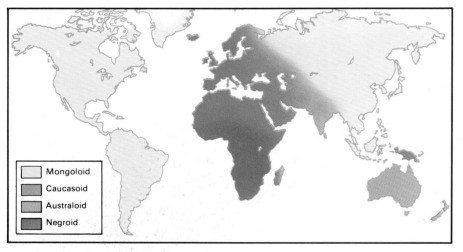

	Mongoloid
	Caucasoid
	Australoid
	Negroid

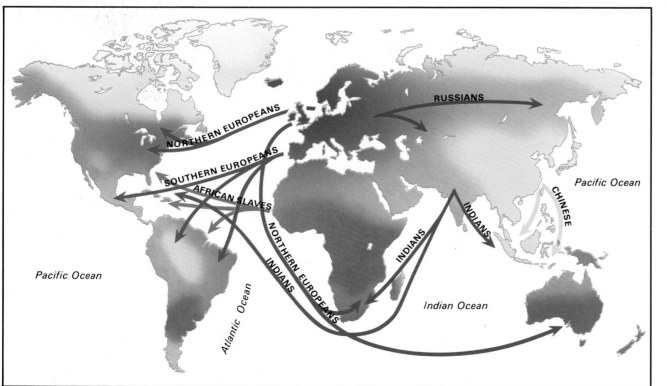

total population was concentrated in the relatively small area which had been brought under the plough.

This concentration of both people and wealth closely matches the location of the major Eurasian civilizations. The comparative fragility of the Aztec and Inca civilizations in the Americas, and of the African kingdoms immediately south of the Sahara, which were outstanding in many respects, may be partly explained, first, by their geographic isolation and lack of external stimulus and, second, by their dependence on hand cultivation. After 1500, when the expansion of Europe brought all continents for the first time into direct contact with each other, these non-Eurasian civilizations sometimes found themselves unable to put up more than a feeble resistance to outside aggression.

It is nevertheless important not to exaggerate the tempo of change. Although in America the Aztec and Inca empires were destroyed by 1521 and 1535 respectively, elsewhere the political impact of Europe was extremely limited before the second half of the 18th century. China and Japan remained intact, and in India the Europeans were kept at arm's length for 250 years following the arrival of Vasco da Gama in 1498. There, as in West Africa and Southeast Asia, the European presence was largely confined to trading stations along the coast. The cultural influence of Europe was even more negligible, and Christianity made little headway, except where it was imposed by the conquerors in the Philippines and America, until it was backed by the resources of western technology in the 19th century.

On the other hand, the European discoveries opened the way to a global redistribution of resources: migrations of peoples, diffusion of animals and plants, release of mineral wealth,

expansion of cultivation and re-alignment of trade. The spread of food plants – almost all domesticated by prehistoric man in various parts of the world – had proceeded slowly until 1500; they thereafter became common to every continent. In addition, the American Indians pioneered two major cash crops: tobacco and cotton (derived largely in its commercial form from varieties they had domesticated, though other species were known and used in the Orient before 1500). Cane sugar, introduced by Europeans into Brazil and the West Indies from the late 16th century, also quickly became a staple of foreign trade.

This interchange of plants produced an enormous surge in food supplies, which made possible the unprecedented growth of human populations in modern times. It also initiated a corresponding increase in intercontinental trade. Before 1500, this trade was limited to Eurasia and Africa, and involved mostly luxury goods; after 1500, the combination of regional economic specialization and improved sea transport made possible the gradual transformation of the limited medieval luxury trade into the modern mass trade of new bulky necessities – hence the flourishing 'triangular trade' of rum, cloth, guns and other metal products from Europe to Africa, slaves from Africa to the New World, and sugar, tobacco and bullion from the New World to Europe.

It was not until the 19th century, with the opening of the Suez and Panama canals and the construction of transcontinental railways in Canada, the United States, Siberia and Africa, that areas and lines of commerce which had previously been separate finally blended into a single economy on a world scale; but the first stages of global integration were completed in just over two centuries beginning in 1500.

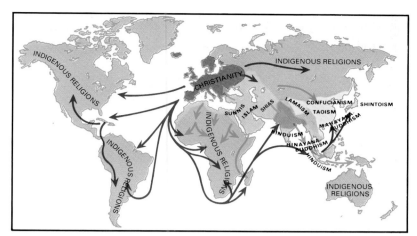

4/The diffusion of world religions (16th-19th centuries) *(above)* In 1500 Christianity remained almost entirely a European religion, but the great Catholic powers, Spain and Portugal, imposed it wherever their vessels touched land and the Orthodox and Protestants soon followed suit.

5/The diffusion of plants (16th-19th centuries) *(below)* Wheat, originating in the Near East, had spread across Africa and Eurasia; now it spanned the globe, and was soon joined by bananas, yams, rice and the sugar cane, all from Asia, and by maize, and both sweet and ordinary potatoes, from the Americas.

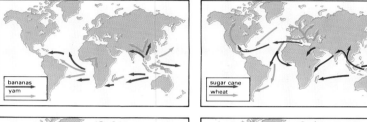

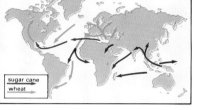

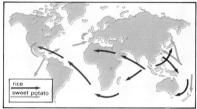

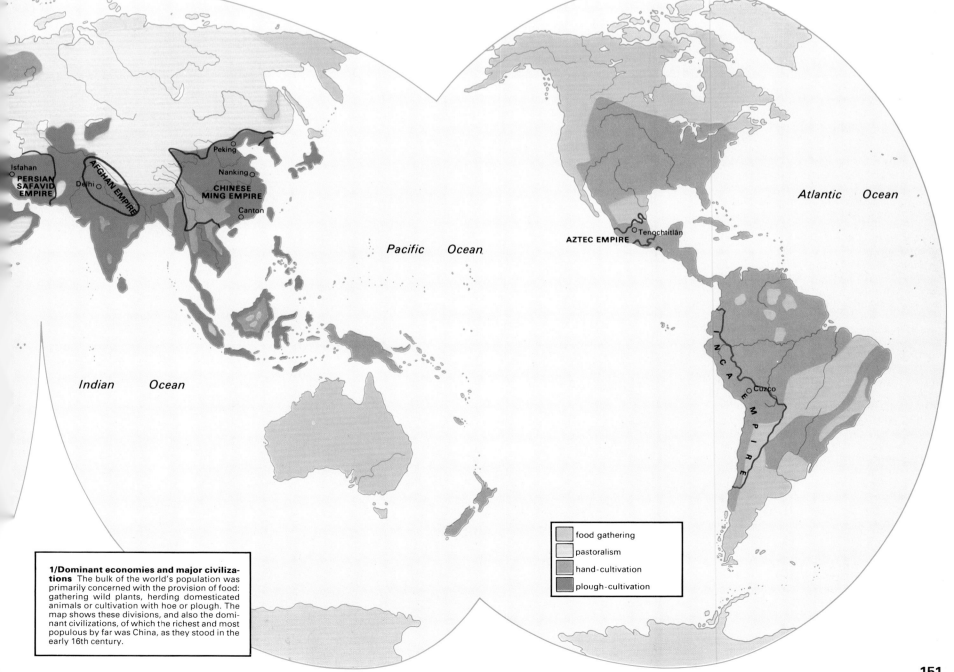

1/Dominant economies and major civilizations The bulk of the world's population was primarily concerned with the provision of food: gathering wild plants, herding domesticated animals or cultivation with hoe or plough. The map shows these divisions, and also the dominant civilizations, of which the richest and most populous by far was China, as they stood in the early 16th century.

food gathering
pastoralism
hand-cultivation
plough-cultivation

European voyages of discovery 1487 to 1780

IN 1480 the principal seafaring peoples of the world were separated not only by great expanses of uncharted sea but also by continental landmasses whose extent and shape were unknown. Regular European shipping was still mainly confined to the North Atlantic, the Mediterranean and the Baltic. The West African coast had been explored cursorily, and only very recently, by Europeans, but the coast from the Gaboon to Mozambique was unknown to any regular, long-range shipping. In the Americas, limited raft and canoe-borne navigation took place on the Pacific coasts of Ecuador and Peru and in the Caribbean, but no communication with Europe nor – so far as is known – with other parts of the Pacific. In the East several seafaring peoples overlapped. Indian, Persian and Arab ships plied the northern Indian Ocean. Chinese shipping, which in the past had sailed intermittently to East Africa, by 1480 usually went no farther west than Malacca, but shared the shallow seas of the Malay archipelago with local shipping, chiefly Javanese. No shipping used the southern Indian Ocean: Javanese contacts with Madagascar had long ceased. Chinese shipping, dense in the China Seas and the archipelago, went no further east than the Philippines. The great areas of the central Pacific were crossed only occasionally and perilously by Polynesian canoes. In the north Pacific, except in Japanese and Korean coastal waters, there was no shipping at all.

In the course of three centuries, approximately between 1480 and 1780, European seaborne explorers linked together these separate areas of maritime communication, and opened all seas, except in the regions of circumpolar ice, to European ships. In this long process of discovery, several distinct stages can be distinguished. Initially, in the late 15th century, two series of voyages searched for a sea passage to southern Asia in the hope of opening direct trade for spices. One series, based on Portugal, sailing by a southeast route, and employing local navigators in the East, eventually reached their declared destinations: the entrance to the Indian Ocean (1488), Malabar (1498), Malacca (1511), and the Moluccas (1512). The other series, based on Spain and sailing west or southwest, was less successful in its immediate purpose but more fruitful in incidental discovery: the Spaniards hit upon the West Indies (1492) and the Spanish Main (1498). Eventually they reached Southeast Asia (1521), but by a route too long and arduous for commercial use. In the process of search they proved the Pacific to be a great ocean and not, as some respected authorities had supposed, a mere arm of the Indian Ocean. To reach the Pacific they had to circumvent an immense landmass, which they believed initially to be a peninsula of Asia, but which by the 1520s they accepted as a new world; though its complete separation from Asia was not proved until the 18th century. They immediately began to settle the area, and for more than 100 years kept it effectively an Iberian preserve.

The combined effect of Spanish and Portuguese discovery was to show that all the oceans of the world, at least in the southern hemisphere, were connected. For about a century Spain and Portugal, by the use and threat of force, prevented other Europeans from using the connecting passages, except for occasional raids. The third great series of voyages, therefore, mostly English, French or Dutch in inception, looked for corresponding passages to Asia in the northern hemisphere, in the west, northwest or northeast. Unsuccessful in their primary purpose, they revealed another continental landmass with a continuous coast from the Caribbean to the Arctic, and opened the way for the exploration and settlement of eastern North America by northern Europeans.

After 1632 the search for the northern pas-

sages was abandoned. By that time influential groups in England and the Netherlands had defied the Iberian monopoly and opened trade with Asia by the southeast route. The last three-quarters of the 17th century and the first quarter of the 18th century was a period of settlement and of commercial consolidation rather than of new discovery; the encouragement which the Dutch East India Company gave to Tasman's exploration of the Australian coast in 1633–53 was exceptional and was openly regretted by the directors of the Company. A series of circumnavigations by buccaneers or privateers, around the turn of the century, was similarly barren of practical results.

A second age of discovery began in the 18th century, inspired as much by scientific curiosity as by hope of commercial advantage. The voyages were organized by governments rather than by private investors and were made by warships commanded by naval officers, often accompanied by scientists and painters. The objects were, in general, the exploration of the Pacific (in particular the location of a Great South Land believed, on the authority of Ptolemy, Ortelius and others, to extend north of the Tropic of Capricorn in the South Pacific), and the discovery of a strait between northeast Asia and northwest America leading to the Arctic Ocean and thence, possibly, round to the Atlantic – the old Northwest Passage from the opposite side. The results, in part at least, were negative: there is no habitable southern continent, other than Australia; the passage to the Arctic, though it exists, is choked with ice. On the other hand, many unknown island groups were discovered: New Zealand was determined to consist of two main islands and its coasts were charted; the attractive and habitable east coast of Australia was explored, and shortly afterwards settled; the general configuration of the American and Asian coasts of the north Pacific was revealed; and the old problem of keeping men alive and healthy on long ocean voyages was, in large measure, solved. By 1780, as the French explorer La Pérouse complained, few of the world's coastlines remained to be explored.

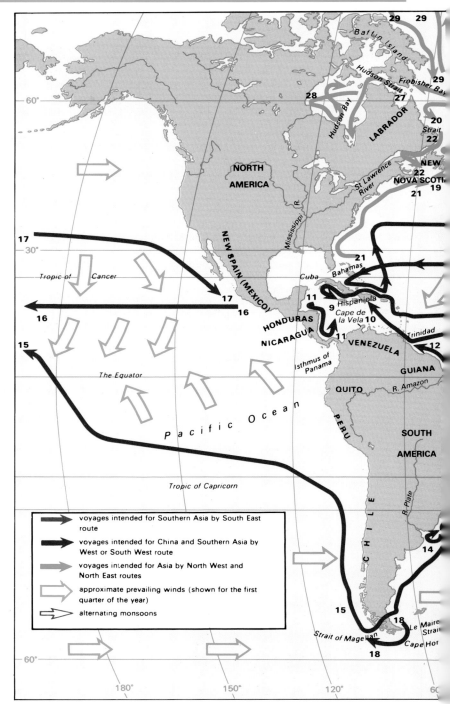

	voyages intended for Southern Asia by South East route
	voyages intended for China and Southern Asia by West or South West route
	voyages intended for Asia by North West and North East routes
	approximate prevailing winds (shown for the first quarter of the year)
	alternating monsoons

Voyages in the Caribbean:
30/Bastidas and La Cosa 1501-2 explored coast from Gulf of Maracaibo to Gulf of Urabá.
31/Pinzón and Solís 1508 sent from Spain to find strait to Asia, perhaps followed E. coast of Yucatán.
32/Ponce de León 1512-3 sailed from Puerto Rico, explored coast of Florida from N. of Cape Canaveral to (possibly) Pensacola. May have sighted Yucatán on return. First explorer to note force of Gulf Stream.
33/Hernández de Córdoba 1517 sailed from Cuba, explored N. and W. coasts of Yucatán. First report of Maya cities.

34/Grijalva 1518 followed S. and W. coasts of Gulf of Mexico as far as River Pánuco.
35/Pineda 1519 explored N. and W. coasts of Gulf of Mexico from Florida to River Pánuco. Finally ended hope of strait to Pacific in that region.

2/Voyages in the Caribbean, 1493 to 1519
(below) Spanish expeditions explored the Caribbean searching for a seaway to China, India and the Golden Chersonese. They found it landlocked on the west; took to slaving, pearling and plunder; encountered settled, city-building peoples; and founded a European empire.

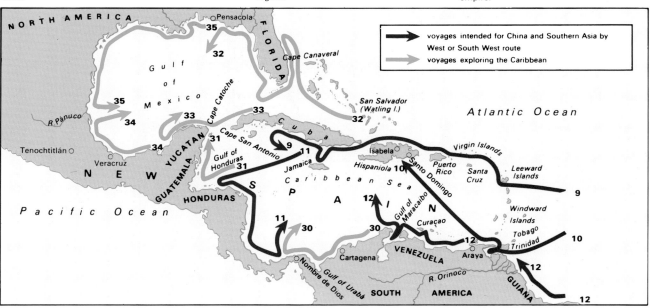

| | voyages intended for China and Southern Asia by West or South West route |
| | voyages exploring the Caribbean |

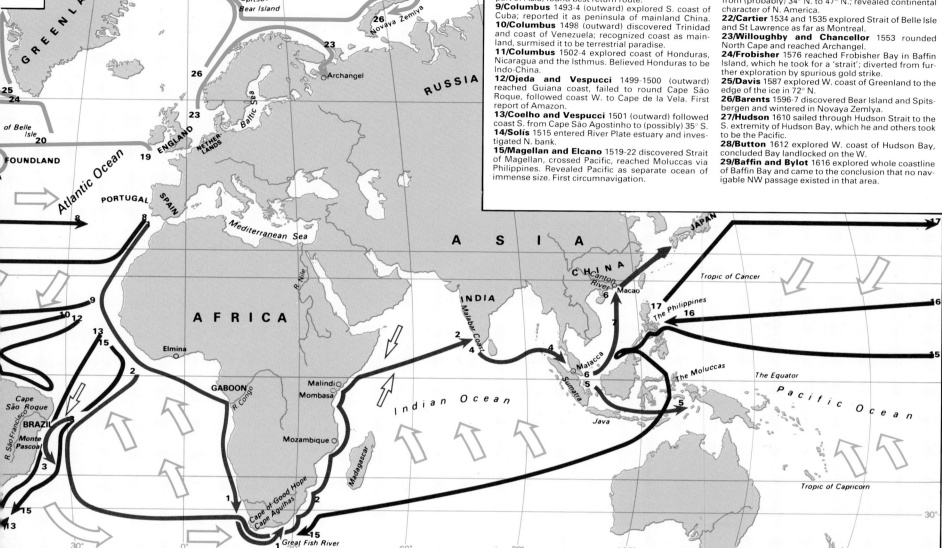

1/Major European voyages of discovery from about 1480 to 1630 (below) Explorers seeking sea routes to Asia found, in addition, a continent hitherto unknown to Europe, and an ocean of unsuspected extent. They proved that all the oceans were connected, and that the world was much bigger than accepted authorities had taught.

Voyages intended for S. Asia by SE route:
1/Dias 1487-8 (outward) discovered open water S. of Cape Agulhas; entered Indian Ocean; reached Great Fish River.
2/Vasco da Gama 1497-8 (outward) made best use of Atlantic winds on way to Cape of Good Hope; reached India, guided by local pilot.

3/Cabral 1500 (outward) the second Portuguese voyage to India, landed in Brazil, probably accidentally.
4/First Portuguese voyage to Malacca, 1509.
5/Abreu 1512-3 visited Moluccas.
6/First Portuguese visits to Canton River, 1516.
Voyages intended for China and S. Asia by W. or SW route:
7/Da Mota, Zeimoto and Peixoto 1542-3 Portuguese discovery of Japan.
8/Columbus 1492-3 (outward and homeward) discovered islands in Bahama group, explored N. coasts of Cuba and Hispaniola; interpreted discoveries as part of Asia; found best return route.
9/Columbus 1493-4 (outward) explored S. coast of Cuba; reported it as peninsula of mainland China.
10/Columbus 1498 (outward) discovered Trinidad and coast of Venezuela; recognized coast as mainland, surmised it to be terrestrial paradise.
11/Columbus 1502-4 (outward) explored coast of Honduras, Nicaragua and the Isthmus. Believed Honduras to be Indo-China.
12/Ojeda and Vespucci 1499-1500 (outward) reached Guiana coast, failed to round Cape São Roque, followed coast W. to Cape de la Vela. First report of Amazon.
13/Coelho and Vespucci 1501 (outward) followed coast S. from Cape Agostinho to (possibly) 35° S.
14/Solís 1515 entered River Plate estuary and investigated N. bank.
15/Magellan and Elcano 1519-22 discovered Strait of Magellan, crossed Pacific, reached Moluccas via Philippines. Revealed Pacific as separate ocean of immense size. First circumnavigation.

16/Saavedra 1527 discovered route from coast of Mexico across Pacific to Moluccas.
17/Urdaneta 1565 found feasible return route Philippines to Mexico in 42° N. using W. winds.
18/Schouten and Le Maire 1616 discovered route into Pacific via Le Maire Strait and Cape Horn.
Voyages intended for Asia by northern route:
19/Cabot 1497 (outward) rediscovered Newfoundland, first sighted by Norsemen in 11th century; believed it NE extremity of Asia.
20/Corte-Real 1500 rediscovered Greenland.
21/Verazzano 1524 traced E. coast of N. America from (probably) 34° N. to 47° N.; revealed continental character of N. America.
22/Cartier 1534 and 1535 explored Strait of Belle Isle and St Lawrence as far as Montreal.
23/Willoughby and Chancellor 1553 rounded North Cape and reached Archangel.
24/Frobisher 1576 reached Frobisher Bay in Baffin Island, which he took for a 'strait'; diverted from further exploration by spurious gold strike.
25/Davis 1587 explored W. coast of Greenland to the edge of the ice in 72° N.
26/Barents 1596-7 discovered Bear Island and Spitsbergen and wintered in Novaya Zemlya.
27/Hudson 1610 sailed through Hudson Strait to the S. extremity of Hudson Bay, which he and others took to be the Pacific.
28/Button 1612 explored W. coast of Hudson Bay, concluded Bay landlocked on the W.
29/Baffin and Bylot 1616 explored whole coastline of Baffin Bay and came to the conclusion that no navigable NW passage existed in that area.

A pepper harvest in Malabar (below) Pepper accounted for over 70 per cent by volume of the world spice trade in the 16th century. The most valuable variety, *piper nigrum*, shown here, was native to India and hard to transplant successfully. Demand from Europe and China spread it to selective parts of the East, but Portuguese efforts to introduce it in Africa and America in the 17th century met with little success.

3/European exploration of the Pacific, 1720 to 1780 (right) Most 18th-century voyages of discovery were searches for a habitable southern continent or for a usable northern strait. Both proved imaginary. The expeditions revealed instead the islands of New Zealand, a habitable eastern Australia, many attractive islands and a valuable whale fishery.

Voyages in the Pacific:
36/Roggeveen 1722 discovered Easter Island and some of the Samoan group. Circumnavigation.
37/Bering 1728 sailed from Kamchatka, discovered strait separating NE Asia and NW America.
38/Wallis 1766-8 discovered Society Islands (Tahiti), encouraged hope of habitable southern continent. Circumnavigation.
39/Cook 1768-71 charted coasts of New Zealand, explored E. coast of Australia, confirmed existence of Torres Strait. Circumnavigation.
40/Cook 1772-5 made circuit of southern oceans in high latitude, discovered New Hebrides, discovered many islands, ended hope of habitable southern continent. Circumnavigation.
41/Cook and Clerke 1776-80 discovered Sandwich Islands (Hawaii), explored NW coast of N. America from Vancouver Island to Unimak Pass, sailed through Bering Strait to edge of pack ice, ended hope of navigable passage through Arctic to Atlantic.

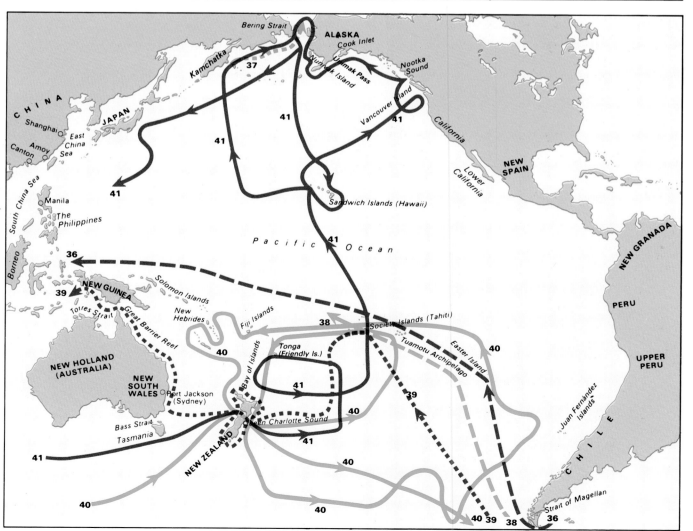

European expansion overseas: Spain and Portugal 1500 to 1600

By 1500 Portuguese possessions outside Europe included several island groups in the Atlantic and the Gulf of Guinea, and a few trading stations on the west coast of Africa (above all the fortress-factory of Elmina). Cloth and hardware were bartered for slaves and gold dust, a dozen or so ships making the voyage between Portugal and Guinea every year.

After the discovery of the sea route to India, the Portuguese endeavoured to become suppliers of spices to Europe by capturing or leasing trading posts and fortified bases on the east coast of Africa, around the northern shores of the Indian Ocean, and in the Malay archipelago. By the mid-16th century they maintained more than 50 forts and factories in a tenuous string from Sofala to Nagasaki. Strategically the most important bases were Mozambique (1507); Goa (1510), the headquarters of the Portuguese governor-general in the East; Ormuz (1515) at the mouth of the Persian Gulf, a major port of trans-shipment in the international spice trade; and Malacca (1511), also a major spice market, on the strait connecting the Indian Ocean with the South China Sea. All these were outright Portuguese possessions. East of Malacca, the position of the Portuguese was precarious and their activity purely commercial. Their settlement at Macao was first occupied in 1557, through the connivance or indifference of Chinese officials. From there they traded to Nagasaki, where they were welcomed as carriers of Chinese goods, since the Chinese government forbade its own subjects to trade directly with Japan. At Ternate they maintained a fortified warehouse, built to collect cloves produced in the Moluccas (and nowhere else at the time) but a league of

Muslim princes expelled them and restored the site to the local ruler in 1575.

All these Far-Eastern enterprises, together with the gold of the Zambezi basin through Sofala, paid for the pepper and other spices shipped annually from Goa to Lisbon for distribution to western Europe. The Portuguese never achieved anything like a monopoly: large quantities of pepper crossed the Indian Ocean in Arab, Persian and Indian ships, to reach Europe via the Red Sea, Cairo and Alexandria, and Portuguese attempts to control this route, by seizing Aden as a base, proved unsuccessful. Nevertheless, Portuguese power was sufficient to channel much of the Indian Ocean trade through harbours under their control and to extort tolls or duties from local shipping by threat of sinking or plundering those who refused to pay. If they could not fully control this trade, they successfully preyed upon it, and for 100 years had no European rivals.

The Spaniards, like the Portuguese, moved quickly to exploit their late 15th-century discoveries. The settlement of Hispaniola began in 1493, partly in the hope of finding gold, partly with the intention of developing a base for trade

1/Iberian trade, establishments and settlements by c.1600 (*below right*) In the East, the Portuguese 'empire' consisted of fortified bases and trading posts, few of them bigger than a single city and its hinterland, some of them mere warehouse compounds; by 1600 there were more than 50 such establishments. In the West, however, because of the considerable numbers of Spanish and Portuguese who emigrated to the Americas during the 16th century, the Iberians had by 1600 occupied all the areas of dense native population, had built impressive cities and towns, and had created an elaborate territorial administration controlled from Europe.

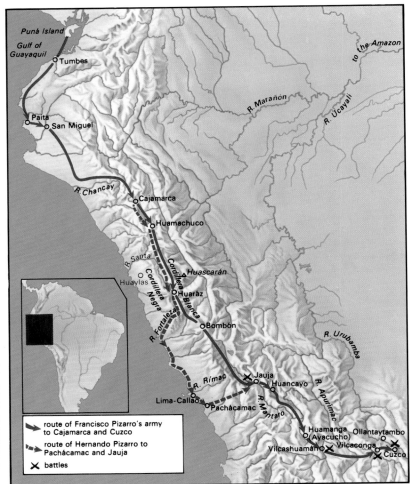

route of Francisco Pizarro's army to Cajamarca and Cuzco

route of Hernando Pizarro to Pachácamac and Jauja

✕ battles

3/The Spanish invasion of Peru 1531-3 (*above*) showing Tumbes, where Pizarro landed; Cajamarca, where Atahuallpa was seized at his first meeting with Pizarro; Jauja, the site of the first serious battle; Vilcaconga, where Soto was ambushed; and Cuzco, the Inca highland capital.

Acapulco Small, unhealthy harbour town, sheltered anchorage. Terminus of annual Manila Galleon voyages.
Aden Major harbour at entrance to Red Sea; successfully resisted an attack by Portuguese fleet 1513.
Arequipa Principal Spanish city of southern Peru, founded in 1540 by Pizarro.
Arica The port for Arequipa and Potosí.
Asunción Capital of province of Paraguay; the earliest surviving Spanish settlement in Plate River basin, founded in 1541.
Bahia Capital of Bahia province and of viceroyalty of Brazil; founded in 1549.
Buenos Aires Founded 1580 by Juan de Garay, governor of Paraguay, to provide access to the sea.
Calicut First town in Malabar visited by Portuguese 1498.
Callao Port for Lima.
Cartagena Harbour and naval base. Founded 1533 by Pedro de Heredía, later strongly fortified.
Cochin Portuguese *feitoria*, occupied 1502, fortified 1503. Early allied with Portuguese against Calicut.
Colombo Portuguese *feitoria*, occupied 1517, fortified 1520. Principal centre for collection of cinnamon. 1600 Portuguese controlled most of Ceylon coast.
Cuzco Inca capital of Peru, captured and occupied by Spaniards 1533.
Diu Island. Portuguese *feitoria* and major base, heavily fortified; acquired 1535 by treaty with ruler of Gujerat.
Elmina Principal Portuguese settlement on Gulf of Guinea, founded and fortified 1481. Centre for collection and shipment of Ashanti gold. By 1600 important as slave depot.
Goa Administrative, commercial and spiritual headquarters of Portuguese in east, captured 1510.
Guadalajara Capital of New Galicia, Spanish foundation 1531.
Guatemala Founded 1542 by Pedro de Alvarado.
Guayaquil Harbour for Quito region; principal ship-building centre on Pacific coast.
Havana Assembly point for combined annual convoys for return to Spain. Good, almost land-locked harbour, heavily fortified.
Hooghly (Ugolim) Founded 1599 by Portuguese traders – seemingly without fort. Silk and cotton collection centre.
Lima (Cuidad de los Reyes) Capital of viceroyalty of Peru; Spanish city, founded 1535 by Francisco Pizarro.
Luanda Principal centre for export of slaves from Angola to Brazil, founded 1575.
Macao Portuguese town and *feitoria*, estab-

lished c.1557 with tacit permission of local Chinese authorities. Unfortified. Collection centre for Chinese silk.
Malacca Portuguese *feitoria*; captured and occupied 1511; fortified; principal centre of spice trade.
Malindi First Swahili town to welcome Portuguese in 1498.
Manila Spanish town and fortress in Luzon, Philippines. Founded 1571; by 1600 a major commercial harbour and administrative centre. Connected by annual sailings with Mexico and China, with silver westbound, silk eastbound.
Mérida Spanish capital of province of Yucatán, founded 1542 by Francisco de Montejo on site of antecedent Maya town.
Mexico City Capital of vice-royalty of New Spain. Large Spanish and Indian city, formerly Tenochtitlán, Aztec capital, captured 1521.
Mombasa Portuguese *feitoria* occupied 1505; before and after occupation a major trading centre; persistently resisted Portuguese, sacked 1505, 1529, 1587. Major fortress (Fort Jesus) constructed 1593-5.
Mozambique Major Portuguese base, occupied 1507; port of call for outbound fleets of *Carreira da India*.
Nagasaki Only Japanese port where Portuguese had permission to trade (until 1639).
Nombre de Dios Shanty town on north coast of Isthmus of Panama, important as terminus of convoys from Spain and as starting point of portage to Panama.
Olinda Capital of Pernambuco province, founded c.1535. Recife, the port for Olinda, was already in 1600 a larger town.
Ormuz Portuguese *feitoria*, and major strategic base, occupied 1515. A major market and port of trans-shipment in spice trade.
Potosí Principal silver mining centre of viceroyalty of Peru; silver discovered 1545; in 1600 probably the biggest concentration of Europeans in the Americas.
Puebla Prosperous Spanish city, founded 1532, by 1600 important for provisioning convoys returning from Veracruz to Seville.
Quito Indian city occupied by Benalcázar 1533; Spanish city incorporated 1541.
Saltillo Capital of province of Nuevo León; Spanish foundation 1586; cattle town.
San Agostín Small, isolated fortress on south-east coast of Florida, founded 1565 to cover passage of convoys through Straits.
San Juan de Puerto Rico Windward defence of Spanish Caribbean and of trans-Atlantic convoys. Immense fortifications begun 1591.
Santa Fé de Bogotá Provincial capital New Granada; founded 1538.
Santa Marta Prosperous port and base for

hinterland expeditions. Founded 1525.
Santiago Capital of captaincy-general of Chile. Founded 1541 by Pedro de Valdivia.
Santo Domingo Founded 1496 by Bartholomew Columbus; capital of Hispaniola, administrative centre for Spanish Caribbean.
São Tomé Portuguese island plantation; important source of sugar and of provisions.
Sofala Portuguese *feitoria*, occupied 1505; port of outlet for gold of Zambezi basin (Monomatapa) mostly shipped to Mozambique, thence to Goa.
Spice Islands (Moluccas) Portuguese *feitoria* with light fortification in Ternate (1513), Tidore (1529), Amboina and the Banda Islands; collection centres for cloves, nutmeg and mace; all still occupied with local permission in 1600, except Ternate from which the Portuguese were expelled in 1575.
Timor Portuguese *feitoria*, in 1600 administrative centre, and collection centre for sandalwood destined for sale in China.
Veracruz Most important harbour on Gulf of Mexico. Terminus of annual convoys from Spain; founded by Cortés 1519.
Zacatecas Principal silver mining centre, Spanish foundation 1546.

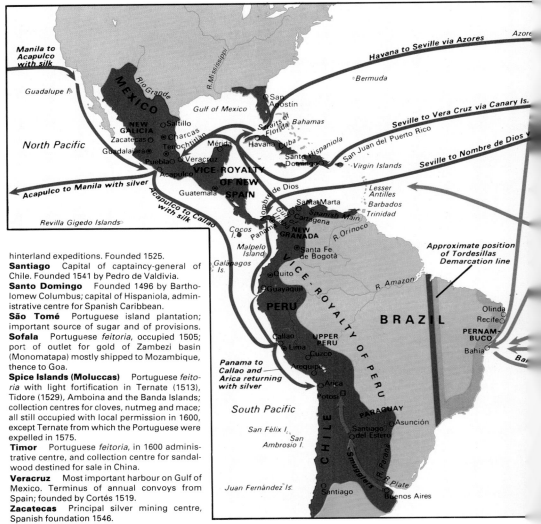

with China, supposedly nearby. The discovery of the continental coast opened alternative opportunities – for slaving and for acquiring pearls and gold trinkets by trade or plunder. Mainland settlement began in 1509-10, on both shores of the Gulf of Urabá and along the Isthmus coast. Panama, the first Pacific settlement, was established in 1519. But during the next two decades the nature of the Spanish enterprise in America was transformed by the conquest of two fabulously rich and highly exploitable lands: the area of the Aztec hegemony in Mesoamerica and the empire of the Incas in the Andean region.

In both areas, relatively small Spanish task forces exploited existing divisions in the victim-societies. In Mexico, for example, tributary peoples of the dominant communities around Lake Texcoco joined the Spaniards in a huge confederacy: accounts from Tlaxcala – headquarters of the Aztecs' bitterest foes – represent the war as an indigenous conflict, with a little Spanish help. In Inca Peru, divisions between dominant and subordinate groups were complicated by hostilities between the Inca elite based in the southern heartland of Cuzco and those in the northern outpost of Quito. By collaborating with local and regional rulers, the Spaniards were able to replace the outgoing dominant groups without arousing much new opposition. Yet neither conquest was easy: Cortés's force only just escaped destruction at an early stage of hostilities and Inca resistance continued until 1572.

In the 1520s news of the conquest of central Mexico, and descriptions of the elaborate culture and dense population encountered there, attracted a rush of emigrants to Mexico both from Spain and from the islands. A similar rush followed the conquest in Inca Peru in the early 1530s, though Peru was less accessible than Mexico and could be reached only by trans-shipment and a troublesome portage across the Isthmus of Panama. Hispaniola had been the base for the settlement of Central America, Cuba for that of Mexico, Panama for that of Peru; each in turn was to some extent depopulated by emigration to the new conquests. Now Mexico and Peru became the focus of Spanish settlement in the New World, initially because they were the chief centres of settled, organized native population before the Spanish arrived, and subsequently because they were the main sources of precious metals. No other major conquest – Guatemala (1523–42), New Granada

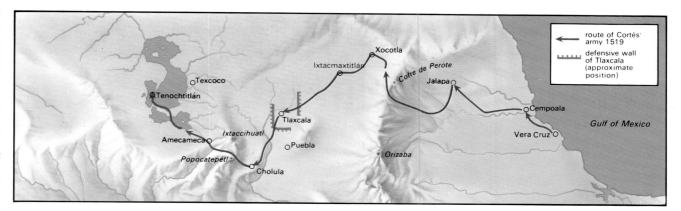

(1536–9) or central Chile (1540–58) – compared with them in either respect, and their pre-eminence was recognized when a vice-regal administration was formally established in Mexico in 1535. Administrative organization in Peru was delayed by faction struggles among the conquerors, but there too vice-regal government was firmly established by 1550.

Spanish population in the New World was largely concentrated in towns and initially wholly parasitic upon Indian society; but Spaniards soon developed characteristic economic activities, chiefly ranching and mining, employing Indian labour. Immensely productive silver mines were discovered, both in Mexico and in Peru, in the 1540s. Potosí in Upper Peru became the biggest single source of silver in the world and remained so for 100 years. By the 1560s silver had become the chief export to Spain, with cochineal, hides, tallow and sugar far behind. After 1564 these immensely valuable shipments necessitated a rigid system of trans-Atlantic convoys escorted by warships, and later in the century heavy fortification of principal harbours and strategic points: Cartagena, Veracruz, Havana, San Juan del Puerto Rico. In the 1570s Spaniards also established themselves in Cebu and Luzon in the Philippines, and large quantities of silver began to be shipped annually from Mexico to Manila, chiefly to purchase Chinese silk, some for use in Mexico, some for re-export to Peru, and some, after portage across Mexico, destined for Spain.

The line of demarcation established by the Treaty of Tordesillas in 1494, though its precise position could not be determined, clearly excluded Spaniards from much of eastern South America. However, the Portuguese only settled Brazil in the 1530s, impelled to it by fear of being forestalled by the French. Bahia was founded as an administrative capital in 1549; the first slave-worked sugar plantations and mills appeared shortly afterwards, on a pattern already familiar in São Tomé in the Gulf of Guinea. Between 1575 and 1600 coastal Brazil became the foremost sugar-producing territory in the western world, and attracted many land-hungry emigrants from Portugal and the Azores. The Brazilian demand for slave labour gave new importance to the Portuguese trading stations in West Africa, where the gold trade had dwindled as the gold became exhausted, and caused the Portuguese slavers to extend their operations from Guinea south to Angola. The Portuguese town and slave depot of Luanda was founded in 1575 and slave ships shuttled directly between Angola and Brazil, with the slaves paid for in low-grade tobacco grown in Brazil. Any surplus could easily be disposed of in Spanish America because, on the one hand, the Spaniards had no direct access to the source of slaves but could pay in silver and, on the other, because from 1580 until 1640 Spain and Portugal were united under a common crown.

Thus Iberia ruled not one overseas empire, but three: the silver empire of Spanish America, the spice empire of the Indian Ocean, and the sugar empire of the South Atlantic. At the end of the 16th century the whole vast, cumbersome structure was at the height of its power and prosperity. French, English and, latterly, Dutch raids harassed its harbours, its shipping and its colonial outposts; but none succeeded in causing major damage.

2/The Spanish invasion of Mexico 1519-20 (above) showing old Vera Cruz, the first Spanish city; Cempoala, whose ruler was encouraged by Cortés in revolt against the Mexica; Tlaxcala, home of Cortés's principal allies; and Tenochtitlán, capital of the Aztecs, on its island in Lake Texcoco.

Aztec ceremonial shield (above) with feather design on a woven fibre backing. Such mosaics, often incorporating thousands of feathers, were cherished works of art in ancient Mexico. Few now survive. This example was sent, with other loot, to Charles V by Cortés in 1520. The coyote was the personal emblem of the war chief Ahuitzotl, Moctezuma's predecessor. The shield is now in the Museum für Völkerkunde, Vienna.

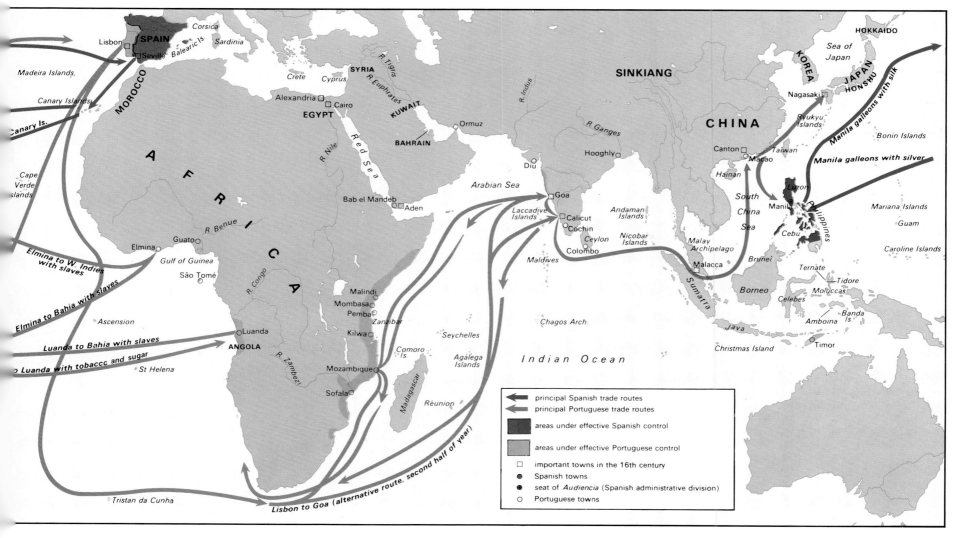

European expansion overseas: Holland, Britain and France 1600 to 1713

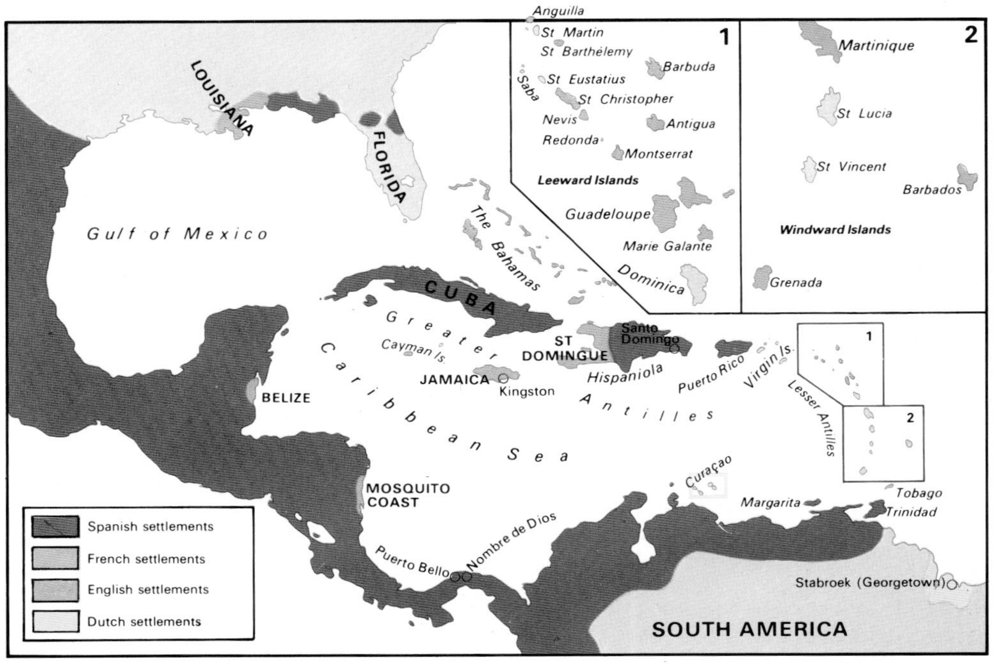

3/European settlement in the West Indies *(above)* Sugar was the most profitable of all the exotic products imported into Europe in early modern times. From the middle of the 17th century until after the end of the 18th, sugar-producing islands in the West Indies were considered by Europeans the most desirable of all overseas possessions.

Bahamas English from 1670 (Treaty of Madrid).
Belize Acknowledged as Spanish territory, but occupied c.1660 by English logwood cutters.
Curaçao Captured from Spaniards by Dutch, 1634, formally ceded 1648 (Treaty of Münster).
Jamaica Captured from Spain by English 1655. Formally ceded 1670 (Treaty of Madrid).
Leeward Islands Barbuda (1628), Nevis (1628), Antigua (1632) and Anguilla (1650) were continuously English from first settlement. Monserrat (1632), taken by French in 1664, restored in 1668. St Christopher, shared by English and French settlers, 1625-1713, wholly English in Treaty of Utrecht. St Barthélemy, Guadeloupe and Marie Galante, French from first settlement (1648, 1635, 1648). St Eustatius (1632), Saba (1640) and St Martin (1648) confirmed to the Netherlands in 1648 (Treaty of Münster), though subsequently changed hands several times. Dominica, claimed by both England and France, inhabited only by Caribs in 1713.
Mosquito Coast English alliance with local Indians; a few English settlers; claimed by Spain.
Saint-Domingue Evacuated by Spaniards c.1605; occupied by French buccaneers; formally ceded to France 1697 (Treaty of Rijswijk).
Tobago French from 1677.
Virgin Islands Tortola English from 1666; St Thomas Danish from 1671.
Windward Islands Martinique continuously French since first settlement (1635); Grenada claimed by France 1650, in 1713 had a few French settlers; St Lucia and St Vincent, disputed between England and France, inhabited in 1713 only by Caribs.

IN THE early 17th century northern Europeans, already experienced in Caribbean smuggling, in raids on Spanish shipping and minor harbours, and in attempts (occasionally successful) on returning Portuguese Indiamen, began to establish permanent colonies in the Americas and to develop eastern trades on their own account. In competing with the traditional Iberian enemy in these fields of activity, they possessed important advantages: fewer political commitments and less dispersed interests in Europe; easier access to sources of ship-building material, especially in the Baltic, producing cheaper ships and (increasingly as the century progressed) more and better ships; a more vigorous commercial attitude towards overseas endeavour; and more sophisticated devices for concentrating investment capital and spreading financial risk. The organization which they used most commonly for distant trade or settlement, or both combined, was the chartered joint-stock company, a device earlier developed on a limited scale in northern Italy, but virtually unknown in Spain and Portugal. The companies might be empowered to trade, settle, conquer, administer and defend.

In the East, the most formidable European group throughout the 17th century was the Dutch East India Company, first formally incorporated in 1602. In 1619 this huge concern, the biggest trading corporation in Europe, established its eastern headquarters at Batavia, well to windward of Malacca and Goa, so acquiring a permanent strategic advantage. Its captains pioneered a direct route to Batavia, provisioning (after 1652) at the new Dutch settlement at the Cape, then running east before the 'roaring forties', and entering the archipelago by way of the Sunda Strait. The company never became in the 17th century – nor did its directors wish it to become – a major territorial power; but by acquiring bases in strategic locations, by bringing pressure on local rulers, and by squeezing other Europeans out, it established a monopoly of the more valuable trades of the archipelago. Elsewhere in the East it traded, as all Europeans did, in competition with other merchants, native and European, on terms laid down by Asian rulers; but throughout the 17th century it held its own against all European rivals.

The English East India Company, incorporated in 1600, was a somewhat smaller concern rarely able to resist Dutch pressure in the archipelago, and principally engaged in trade in cotton goods and pepper from India, first at the Mughal port of Surat, subsequently at stations of its own at Madras, Bombay and Calcutta. In 1685 it began a modest trade to China, purchasing tea and porcelain at Amoy, and later at Canton, where from 1698 its factors found themselves in competition with the French *Compagnie de Chine.*

As a result of the commercial competition and naval aggression of these corporations, which continued irrespective of formal war or peace in Europe, the Portuguese *Estado da Índia* shrank both in territorial extent and in commercial profit; and many native trades, by sea or by land caravan, which the Portuguese had hardly touched – or had touched only to the extent of levying tolls – also began to dry up. The Red Sea and the Persian Gulf both became commercial backwaters as the companies gathered more and more of the trade between Europe and Asia into their own capacious, well-armed ships.

In America the Portuguese fared better. The Dutch West India Company – less well entrenched than its eastern counterpart, but formidable nonetheless – conquered Pernambuco in 1630 and in the next few years seized the Portuguese slaving stations in west Africa, without which the Brazilian plantations were unworkable; but in the 1640s the Portuguese, having made themselves independent of Spain, recovered the Angola barracoons, and in 1654 they drove the Dutch from Brazil. The West India Company turned to the Caribbean, though much Brazilian sugar (handled by Dutch private merchants) continued to flow through Amsterdam. Brazil, however, was not wholly dependent on sugar; in the 1690s a series of gold strikes in Minas Gerais made it a principal supplier of gold as well.

For Spaniards the 17th century was a period of industrial, commercial and financial debility, of faltering government and of repeated military defeat. The weight of misfortune fell much more heavily on Spain itself than upon the Spanish Indies, which remained relatively prosperous and – outside the Caribbean sea lanes – relatively peaceful. In the 1620s and 1630s a powerful offensive by the Dutch West India Company in the Caribbean interrupted the flow of silver to Spain and permitted the creation of English and French settlements in unoccupied islands in the Lesser Antilles. These settlements in a few decades became prosperous sugar plantations, using Brazilian methods, employing African slave labour, and initially selling their crop to Dutch carriers. In the second half of the century, buccaneering raids, often undertaken with the connivance of French and English colonial governors, caused much damage to minor Spanish harbours, and some islands actually in Spanish possession changed hands. By the end of the century, a long string of modest but growing colonies, English, French and Dutch, stretched intermittently along the American seaboard from Barbados to Quebec. Many of them, the sugar islands especially, had themselves become objects of contention between the metropolitan governments.

Every major European war was reflected by fighting in the Americas. The treaties of Münster (1648), Breda (1667), Nijmegen (1678), Rijswijk (1697) and Utrecht (1713) all included cessions of American territory. Mainland colonies were less esteemed by governments and by

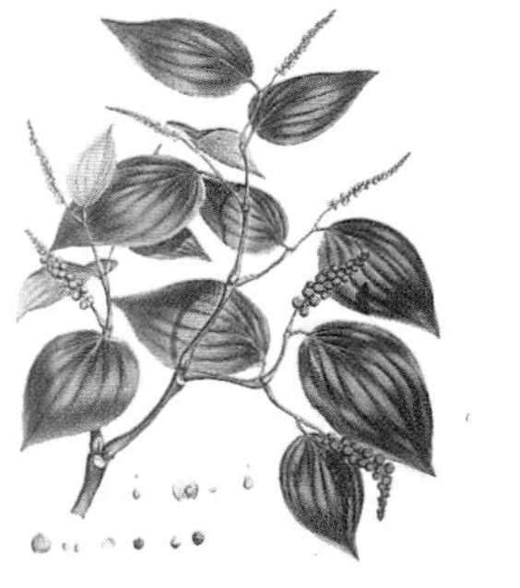

The importance of spices In northern Europe, before the development of winter feed for cattle in the late 17th century, many beasts had to be slaughtered every autumn and the meat preserved for winter eating. Hence the eager demand for spices, both as condiments and as preservatives, and the large profits to be made by importing them to Europe. Of the most important spices, pepper *(above)* grew in many places in southern Asia; cinnamon was virtually confined to Ceylon, cloves to the Moluccas and nutmeg *(below)* to Amboina and the Banda Islands. In the 16th century, the Indian Ocean trade in these commodities had been shared between Malayan, Indian, Persian, Arabian and Portuguese merchants. In the course of the 17th century the Dutch East India Company, by a combination of force and diplomacy, seized control of the sources of the most valuable spices and established a virtual monopoly of their shipment to Europe.

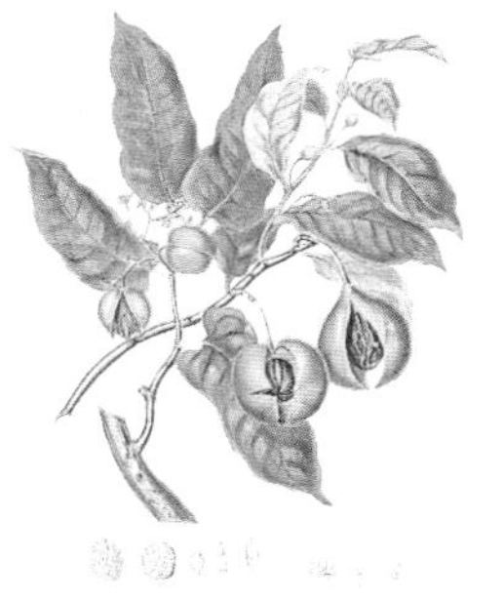

1/Commercial expansion to the East *(below right)* During the 17th century northern European commercial companies – Dutch, French, English and others – established trading stations throughout the East. The Portuguese lost much of their former trade and some territory; and the overland caravan trade between Europe and Asia dwindled.

Achin (Atjeh) Early visited by Europeans (Dutch 1577, English 1602, French 1623) but resisted European penetration. Important commercial harbour and source of gold, but decayed by 1713.
Amoy First Chinese port visited by English traders, 1685.
Bassein (Baçaim) Economic capital of Portuguese Province of the North. Still prosperous in 1713.
Bandar Abbas (Gombroon) Successor to Persian trade of Ormuz. Dutch and English East India Companies maintained factories there.
Bantam Dutch factory established 1598, English 1602; Dutch expelled English 1682, reduced sultan to vassalage 1683.
Batavia Eastern headquarters of Dutch East India Company, established 1619 on site of small town of Jakarta, acquired by conquest from Bantam, and fortified.
Bombay Principal English station in western India, acquired by treaty from Portuguese 1660. Fortified.
Calcutta Principal English station in Bengal, founded 1690 on uninhabited site, after English withdrawal from Hooghly; fortified.
Canton Principal Chinese harbour in which (after 1684) Europeans were allowed to trade. All the East India Companies maintained factories there.
Cape of Good Hope Settlement begun by Dutch East India Company 1652; victualling station for its ships.
Chandernagore Principal French station in Bengal; acquired 1688; in 1713 still very small.
Chinsura Principal Dutch station in Bengal, acquired 1656 after Dutch withdrawal from Hooghly.
Cochin Principal harbour of Malabar. Taken by Dutch from Portuguese 1663.
Colombo Principal harbour of Ceylon. Taken by Dutch from Portuguese 1656.
Macao Portuguese settlement. After loss of Malacca to Dutch, Macao merchants altered business, becoming chief suppliers of silk to Manila for export in the galleons.
Macassar Taken by Dutch fleet 1669; sultan remained as Dutch vassal.
Madras Principal English station on Coromandel coast; occupied 1640 by treaty with local ruler; successor to Masulipatam (occupied 1611); fortified.
Malacca (Melaka) Taken from Portuguese by Dutch with Achinese help, 1641.
Manila Only significant Spanish harbour in the East, terminus of Acapulco-Manila galleons and administrative centre of Spanish Philippines.
Mocha Harbour for Beit el Fakih, marketing centre for Arabian coffee.
Mombasa Major harbour; Portuguese defeated and expelled by forces of Imam of Oman, 1698 (see page 154).
Mozambique Portuguese town and factory; repelled Dutch attempts at conquest in early 17th century.
Nagasaki Only Japanese port in which Europeans were allowed to trade; privilege restricted to Dutch East India Co. from 1639.
Negapatam Principal Dutch station on Coromandel coast, taken from Portuguese by Dutch 1659.
Ormuz Portuguese expelled by Shah Abbas with help of English fleet, 1622. In 1713 almost deserted.
Pondicherry Principal French station in India, occupied 1683 by treaty with local ruler.
Spice Islands (Moluccas, Amboina, Banda Islands) Dutch East India Co. held some islands, having expelled Portuguese early in 17th century, and monopolized spice trade in all.
Surat Major harbour of Mughal Empire. All East India Companies had factories there.
Tellicherry Principal English station on Malabar coast; small fortified factory, outside native town, built 1683, centre for collection of pepper.
Tenasserim Disputed territory between Ayutthaya (Siam) and Pegu (Burma), with several good harbours and busy trade.
Zanzibar Portuguese island, town and factory.
Zeelandia Dutch factory in Formosa, operated from 1624 to 1662, when island occupied by Ming forces and Dutch expelled.

orthodox economists in France and England than were the islands. Colbert was almost alone among leading statesmen in actively encouraging North American settlement, by making seigneuries conditional on occupation, by granting land, on the St Lawrence River and elsewhere, to demobilized soldiers, by assisting passages and providing tools, seed and stock. As a result of his efforts the population of New France, though never more than a tenth of that of the English colonies, became militarily very formidable. Nova Scotia (Acadia) in French hands was considered a serious threat to New England; it was the object of repeated attack and counter-attack, especially during King William's War and the War of the Spanish Succession; even after its annexation in 1713 the English hold on it remained precarious. The chain of French trade forts on the Great Lakes and in the Ohio-Mississippi valleys, because it threatened to block westward expansion, alarmed the English colonists and their metropolitan government. The emergence of French explorers on the shore of the Gulf of Mexico in 1682 caused grave concern in Spain.

The major Spanish colonies, however, despite widespread foreign smuggling and occasional interruption of communications, were never seriously threatened. They owed their safety partly to their inaccessibility, partly to their own capacity for resistance and partly to increasing fear of French domination which towards the end of the century caused both the English and the Dutch to seek insurance by some form of accommodation with Spain.

In 1700, the childless Carlos II of Spain died and the Spanish Habsburg dynasty died with him. As feared by England, Holland and Austria, he bequeathed his crown and empire to France (see page 188). Unwilling to tolerate the huge colonial empire and agglomeration of power which would result from a union of the two countries and their possessions, the three countries allied to fight in a succession war which lasted for a dozen years and ended in a French promise that the new Bourbon king of Spain would never wear the crown of France. It also resulted in a number of colonial gains and commercial concessions for England.

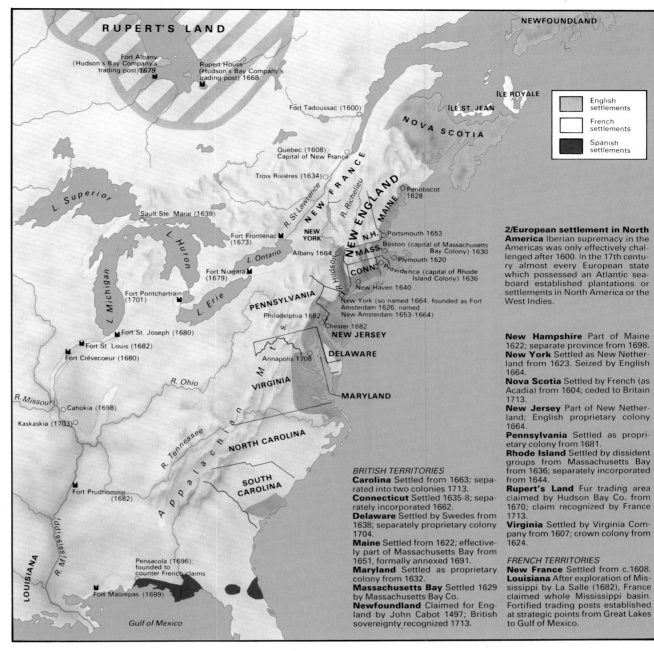

2/European settlement in North America Iberian supremacy in the Americas was only effectively challenged after 1600. In the 17th century almost every European state which possessed an Atlantic seaboard established plantations or settlements in North America or the West Indies.

New Hampshire Part of Maine 1622; separate province from 1698.
New York Settled as New Netherland from 1623. Seized by English 1664.
Nova Scotia Settled by French (as Acadia) from 1604; ceded to Britain 1713.
New Jersey Part of New Netherland; English proprietary colony 1664.
Pennsylvania Settled as proprietary colony from 1664.
Rhode Island Settled by dissident groups from Massachusetts Bay from 1636; separately incorporated from 1644.
Rupert's Land Fur trading area claimed by Hudson Bay Co. from 1670; claim recognized by France 1713.
Virginia Settled by Virginia Company from 1607; crown colony from 1624.

FRENCH TERRITORIES
New France Settled from c.1608.
Louisiana After exploration of Mississippi by La Salle (1682), France claimed whole Mississippi basin. Fortified trading posts established at strategic points from Great Lakes to Gulf of Mexico.

BRITISH TERRITORIES
Carolina Settled from 1663; separated into two colonies 1713.
Connecticut Settled 1635-8; separately incorporated 1662.
Delaware Settled by Swedes from 1638; separately proprietary colony 1704.
Maine Settled from 1622; effectively part of Massachusetts Bay from 1651, formally annexed 1691.
Maryland Settled as proprietary colony from 1632.
Massachusetts Bay Settled 1629 by Massachusetts Bay Co.
Newfoundland Claimed for England by John Cabot 1497; British sovereignty recognized 1713.

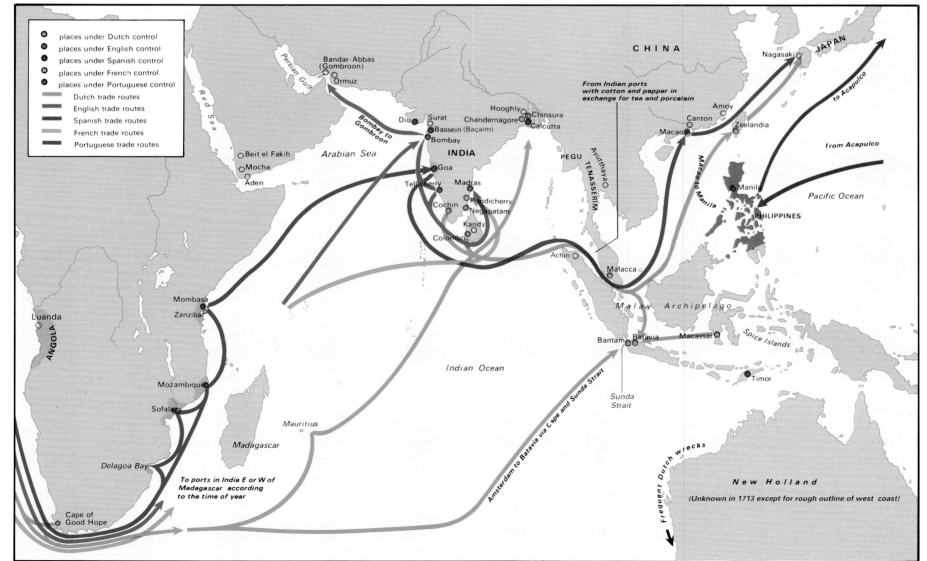

Russian expansion in Europe and Asia 1462 to 1815

2/Economic activity in 1600, 1725, 1815 (above) By 1600 industry had concentrated in and around Moscow, consisting mainly of the processing of animal and vegetable products. By 1725, thanks to Peter the Great's initiative, the extensive smelting of copper and iron was established in the Urals. By 1815 a third industrial area had arisen around St Petersburg.

Russian woodcut (below) showing a procession of envoys followed by merchants carrying furs at the court of the Holy Roman Emperor c.1570. By the early 17th century the demand for luxury furs became the motive for economic expansion eastwards into Siberia to tap its seemingly inexhaustible supply.

THE state created by the Grand Princes of Moscow in the northeast part of the Russian territory known as Muscovy expanded for 350 years at the expense of Sweden, Poland and Lithuania in the north and west, of the Tartars and the Ottoman Empire in the south, and of the nomadic tribes of inner Asia in the east.

After the Mongol invasion of the 13th century, the Russian lands which had formed part of Kievan Rus were split. The east became subject to Mongol overlordship, under the shadow of which the principality of Moscow rose to dominate its neighbours and eventually to throw off the Tartar yoke. The west was absorbed by the neighbouring Lithuanian principality, and was eventually joined to Poland.

Muscovy in 1462 was virtually isolated: it was cut off from almost all contact with the western world by the hostility of its neighbours, and was unable to share in the scientific and cultural advance of Europe, experiencing neither the Renaissance nor the Reformation, though some artistic and intellectual influences did penetrate the Church and the Court. Muscovite isolation was increased by the growth of the religious schism between the Eastern and Western Christian churches. Since 1054 the Russian Orthodox Church had deeply distrusted Roman catholicism and, in 1448, by electing its own metropolitan, declared its independence from Constantinople, soon to fall to the Ottoman Turks.

The growing power of Muscovy was manifested in the ruthless annexation of the great city-republic of Novgorod by Ivan III in 1478, followed by the proclamation of independence from the Tartars in 1480. In the 16th century the republic of Pskov was annexed, and Muscovy began its great advance eastwards, the conquest of the khanates of Kazan in 1552 and Astrakhan in 1556 conferring control of the Volga down to the Caspian Sea. Although Muscovy was still not safe from the Crimean Tartars who sacked Moscow in 1571, and although it failed to extend its hold on the Baltic Sea in the long and debilitating Livonian wars conducted by Ivan IV ('the Terrible'), notable successes occurred elsewhere. On the one hand, from the 1580s, the lucrative fur trade lured enterprising Russians deeper and deeper into Siberia until the Pacific coast was reached in 1639, and a number of forts were erected (Tobol'sk, Eniseisk, Yakutsk,

Nerchinsk), which established Russian control over northern Asia and opened the way for silk trade with China (a commerce which also developed along the Volga with Persia). On the other, during the late 16th century and throughout the 17th, Russian colonization also spread southwards across the Oka River, and Ukrainians migrated eastwards from Poland into the forest-steppe zone. Many frontier posts were established which subsequently developed into towns, such as Orel in 1564, and Kursk and Voronezh in 1586.

In 1613, after the 'Time of Troubles' (1598–1613) which followed the extinction of the old Muscovite ruling house, Michael, the first of the Romanov dynasty was elected tsar. During the rest of the 17th century Muscovites turned their attention to the conquest of the lands lost earlier to Lithuania, Sweden and Poland, and in spite of a number of setbacks, made substantial territorial gains between 1640 and 1686. In 1648 the Cossacks of the Ukraine rose against Poland and transferred their allegiance to the tsar, thus inaugurating a long and confused period of warfare in which Poland, Russia, Sweden and the Ottomans took part, lasting until 1686, when the treaty between Russia and Poland was signed, confirming the cession of Kiev and the lands of the middle Dnieper to Russia.

Isolation remained Russia's major problem. There was great potential foreign demand for the products of the Russian forests, but Muscovy could not benefit from this because hostile Swedes, Poles and Turks blocked sea and land communications with Europe. British merchants had opened up the White Sea route to Archangel (founded by Ivan IV in 1584), but, owing to an unfavourable climate, it was navigable only in the brief summer season.

Having failed to advance to the Black Sea, Peter I (the 'Great') concentrated after 1700 on achieving his 'window on the west', and in a long war, marked by the great victory of Poltava in 1709, he finally wrested Estonia and Livonia from Sweden at the Treaty of Nystad in 1721, acquired the ancient port of Riga, and founded the new one of St Petersburg (1703). Russia's new status was proclaimed to Europe when the title of tsar was formally changed to that of emperor in 1721.

Peter's successors reverted to his policy of expansion on the Black Sea, which was carried to a successful conclusion by Catherine II (the 'Great') in her first (1768–74) and second (1787–92) Turkish wars. The Tartar khanate of the Crimea was annexed, and Russia now controlled the northern shore of the Black Sea from the Dniester to the Caucasus. Odessa, founded in 1794, rapidly became the principal port for Russian exports to the Mediterranean.

The period from 1772 to 1815 saw the Russian land frontier advanced 600 miles (970 km) at the expense of Poland. By the partitions of 1772, 1793 and 1795 Russia obtained much of the former Polish-Lithuanian Commonwealth and, after the interlude of Napoleon's Grand Duchy of Warsaw, the Congress of Vienna agreed to the tsar becoming king of a reconstituted Polish kingdom.

The 18th century wars required a large armaments industry and a correspondingly productive metallurgical base. This was established by Peter I, mainly in the Urals, which abounded in iron and copper ores and were clad in extensive forests suitable for charcoal-making. Peter I founded factories, gave investment incentives, encouraged new management, and established a form of industrial serfdom.

The population of the empire grew both by territorial acquisition and by natural increase, from some 10 million in 1600, to 15.6 million in 1725. The census of 1811–12 gave the enlarged Russian empire a population of 42.75 million.

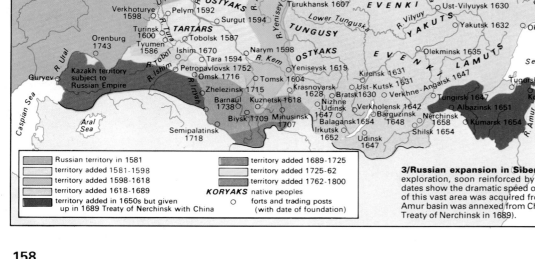

3/Russian expansion in Siberia Rivers facilitated rapid exploration, soon reinforced by strategic forts. Foundation dates show the dramatic speed of expansion. Although most of this vast area was acquired from indigenous peoples, the Amur basin was annexed from China (though returned by the Treaty of Nerchinsk in 1689).

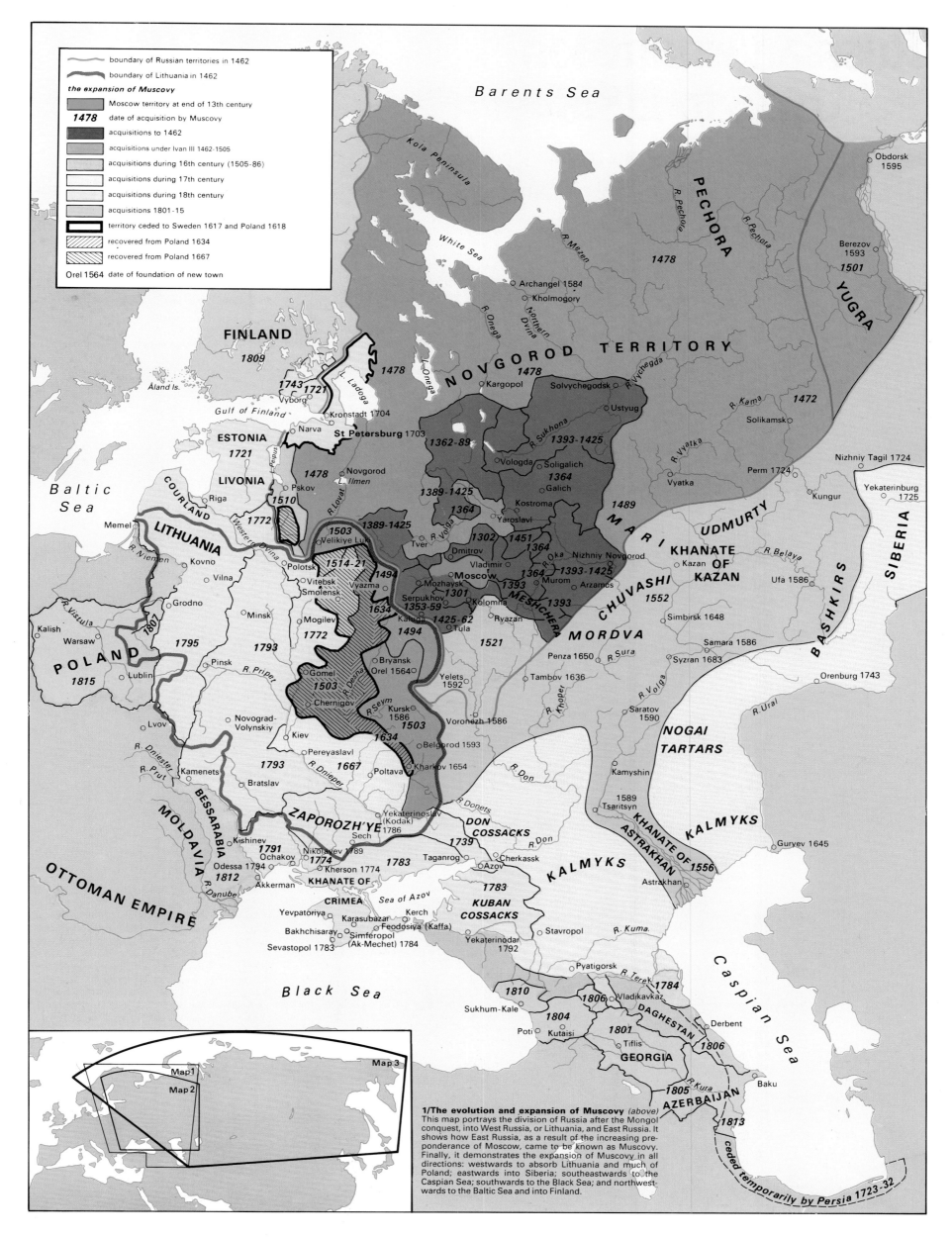

Legend

the expansion of Muscovy
- boundary of Russian territories in 1462
- boundary of Lithuania in 1462
- Moscow territory at end of 13th century
- *1478* date of acquisition by Muscovy
- acquisitions to 1462
- acquisitions under Ivan III 1462-1505
- acquisitions during 16th century (1505-86)
- acquisitions during 17th century
- acquisitions during 18th century
- acquisitions 1801-15
- territory ceded to Sweden 1617 and Poland 1618
- recovered from Poland 1634
- recovered from Poland 1667
- Orel 1564 date of foundation of new town

Barents Sea

Kola Peninsula
R. Pechora
R. Pechora
Obdorsk 1595
1478
PECHORA
R. Mezen
White Sea
R. Onega
Archangel 1584
Kholmogory
Northern Dvina
R. Vychegda
Berezov 1593
YUGRA
1501
FINLAND
1809
1478
1743 *1721*
Vyborg
L. Ladoga
Kargopol
Solvychegodsk
Ustyug
R. Sukhona
NOVGOROD TERRITORY
R. Kama
1472
Gulf of Finland
Kronstadt 1704
St Petersburg 1703
Narva
1362-89
Vologda
Solikamsk
ESTONIA
1721
1478
Novgorod
L. Ilmen
1393-1425
Soligalich
1364
Galich
Perm 1724
Nizhniy Tagil 1724
Baltic Sea
LIVONIA
Pskov
Riga
1478
1364
Yaroslavl
Kostroma
1489
MARI
Vyatka
R. Vyatka
Kungur
Yekaterinburg 1725
COURLAND
1510
1389-1425
R. Loyat
1364
R. Volga
1302
1451
1364
Nizhniy Novgorod
KHANATE OF KAZAN
Kazan
Ufa 1586
R. Belaya
SIBERIA
Memel
LITHUANIA
1772
Western Dvina
Velikiye Luki
1503
1389-1425
Tver
Dmitrov
1364
R. Oka
Murom
1393-1425
Arzamas
CHUVASHI
1552
BASHKIRS
R. Niemen
Kovno
Polotsk
1514-21
1494
Vyazma
Smolensk
Vladimir
Moscow
1393
MESHCHERA
1393
Simbirsk 1648
Vilna
Vitebsk
1301
Mozhaysk
Serpukhov
1301
Kaluga
1425-62
Tula
MORDVA
Samara 1586
Syzran 1683
Grodno
Minsk
Mogilev
1772
1634
1353-59
1494
1521
Penza 1650
R. Sura
POLAND
1807
1795
Pinsk
R. Pripet
1793
Bryansk
Orel 1564
Yelets 1592
Tambov 1636
R. Khoper
R. Volga
Orenburg 1743
Kalish
Warsaw
1815
Lublin
Lvov
Novograd-Volynskiy
1503
Gomel
Chernigov
R. Desna
1503
Kursk 1586
1503
Voronezh 1586
Saratov 1590
NOGAI TARTARS
R. Ural
R. Vistula
1793
Kiev
Pereyaslavl
R. Seym
1634
Belgorod 1593
R. Don
Kamyshin
KALMYKS
R. Dniester
Kamenets
Bratslav
1793
R. Dnieper
1667
Poltava
Kharkov 1654
R. Donets
1589
Tsaritsyn
KHANATE OF ASTRAKHAN 1556
R. Prut
MOLDAVIA
BESSARABIA
ZAPOROZH'YE
Yekaterinoslav (Kodak) 1786
Sech
1739
DON COSSACKS
R. Don
Cherkassk
Guryev 1645
OTTOMAN EMPIRE
Kishinev
1791
Nikolaev 1789
1774
Ochakov
Kherson 1774
Taganrog
Azov
1783
KUBAN COSSACKS
KALMYKS
Astrakhan
Odessa 1794
R. Danube
1812
Akkerman
KHANATE OF CRIMEA
Sea of Azov
Yekaterinodar 1792
Stavropol
R. Kuma
Caspian Sea
Yevpatoriya
Karasubazar
Kerch
Feodosiya (Kaffa)
Bakhchisaray
Simferopol (Ak-Mechet) 1784
Sevastopol 1783
Black Sea
1810
Pyatigorsk
R. Terek
1784
Vladikavkaz
Derbent
DAGHESTAN
Sukhum-Kale
1804
1806
1801
1806
Poti
Kutaisi
Tiflis
GEORGIA
Baku
R. Kura
1805
AZERBAIJAN
1813
ceded temporarily by Persia 1723-32

1/The evolution and expansion of Muscovy *(above)*
This map portrays the division of Russia after the Mongol conquest, into West Russia, or Lithuania, and East Russia. It shows how East Russia, as a result of the increasing preponderance of Moscow, came to be known as Muscovy. Finally, it demonstrates the expansion of Muscovy in all directions: westwards to absorb Lithuania and much of Poland; eastwards into Siberia; southeastwards to the Caspian Sea; southwards to the Black Sea; and northwestwards to the Baltic Sea and into Finland.

Colonial America
1535 to 1783

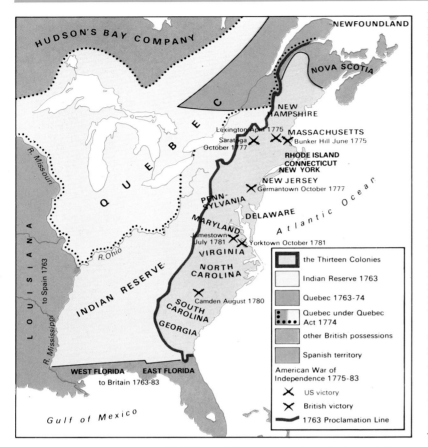

3/British North America *(above)* and the American War of Independence. Fighting began in April 1775. In June the colonies' Continental Congress created a regular army under George Washington. Despite several defeats and the loss of New York in September 1776, Washington hung on and at Christmas 1776, after successfully crossing the Delaware, enjoyed a series of victories, culminating in Saratoga (1777). Final triumph was only assured, however, with the signing of a Franco-American alliance in 1778 (joined by Spain in 1779). Reinforced by French troops and naval support, Washington compelled the main British field army to surrender at Yorktown on 19 October 1781. The resulting Treaty of Versailles in 1783 recognized the Great Lakes in the north and the Mississippi in the west as the frontiers of the nascent United States.

A rich inhabitant *(below)* of Bahia, the capital of colonial Brazil until the mid-18th century, being carried in a litter by Black slaves.

THE traditions taken to America by early European settlers were modified by interaction with the indigenous peoples, and by the impact of the hemisphere's array of environments.

The dominant mainland colonies of the 16th century developed far from the original explorers' bases, in Mexico and Peru, where densely concentrated native populations provided a labour force, and where great silver mines were exploited from the 1540s onwards. Spanish rule gradually extended into the ranching zones of pampas and prairies, while missionaries pushed the frontier into regions of sparse population and modest economic prospects, especially in central and southern South America and, by the 18th century, into what is now the southwest United States. Except for the Caribbean, the area around the River Plate, and the approaches to the Strait of Magellan and Cape Horn – all areas of strategic importance for guarding long-range routes – Spain left the unpromising Atlantic seaboard to others.

In partial consequence, the hemisphere came to be occupied by a variety of colonial societies. Whereas South America, with its long coast and transcontinental river systems, was penetrated and exploited extensively, the area north of Spanish control, where the accessible coasts are short in relation to North America's great bulk, had to be colonized by the laborious development of overland routes from east to west, a process barely begun even by the late 18th century. Despite decimation by incoming diseases, the native populations remained relatively large and concentrated in most Spanish colonies, where traditional means of production and patterns of settlement survived and where a *mestizo* elite formed. The warm-climate Atlantic colonies of Spaniards, English, Dutch, French and Portuguese relied on imported Black labour and plantation crops, such as indigenous cotton and tobacco or implanted sugar. North of Virginia, settlers huddled in civic utopias or spread trapping or trading outposts into the northern forests. Where they could not be exploited, indigenous peoples tended to be expelled or exterminated, despite protection in Spanish areas by crown and church. Evangelization was taken seriously only in Spanish and French areas.

Almost everywhere, the 'pioneering spirit' of the colonists and the vast distances separating them from their homelands prevented effective metropolitian control. Spain's American empire was a 'modern' state – bureaucratic and rigorously purged of 'feudal' influences from the Old World, but the practical power of the crown was hardly greater than in the less systematic regimes established by colonists from other countries. Around the middle of the 18th century, however, the home powers began to rationalize methods of administration and maximize the fiscal yield of colonies which were becoming unacceptably costly to defend.

In North America, Spain adopted a more vigorous policy. As her miners, soldiers and priests moved further into the semi-desert lands of the American southwest, new military governments were organized: in Texas (1718), Sinaloa (1734), New Santander (1746) and California (1767). By then Spanish authority extended eastwards to the Mississippi, and northwards to Monterrey and San Francisco, halting only where it encountered the Russians, now probing south from Alaska along the Pacific coast.

Meanwhile, the French, whose first explorers, like Cartier, had already penetrated far up the St Lawrence River by 1535, extended their North American territories in a vast sweep from the northern shores of Acadia (later Nova Scotia) beyond the Great Lakes and down the eastern banks of the Mississippi to the Gulf of Mexico and the settlement of New Orleans (founded in 1718). New France's trappers, soldiers and missionaries thrust far into the forests, founding future cities (Quebec, 1608; Ville-Marie, later Montreal, 1642; Detroit, 1701).

The French, like the Spaniards, were few and widely dispersed. The highly profitable fur trade not only discouraged formal colonization but inevitably brought conflict: first with the Dutch and their Indian allies, the Iroquois; then, after the fall of New Amsterdam (later New York) to the English in 1664, with the far more numerous Anglo-Saxon colonists of the eastern seaboard. After a false start in the 1580s, serious development began there with the founding of Jamestown, Virginia (1607), and the Mayflower landing in Massachusetts Bay (1620). By the end of the 17th century the 12 'continental colonies' (Georgia joined in 1733) already boasted a prosperous agricultural, commercial and fishing economy, with the beginnings of a manufacturing industry and a population of some 250,000.

Anglo-French hostility deepened as England, starting in 1670, built up her own formidable fur-trading empire based on the rich hunting grounds around Hudson Bay; and each major European war of the period had its parallel across the Atlantic. The Peace of Utrecht in 1713 gave Britain Nova Scotia, Newfoundland and a clear field for the Hudson's Bay Company; but the French and Indian War 1754–60, pre-dating and then forming part of the near-global Seven Years' War (1756–63: see page 190), finally extinguished France's American ambitions. With the Treaty of Paris (1763) all Canada and the land east of the Mississippi were ceded to Britain, while Louisiana went to Spain in compensation for France's earlier transfer, to England, of the once-Spanish area of Florida.

In South America, although English, French and Dutch interlopers were confined to the Guyanas, Spanish-Portuguese rivalry became intense. During the period of union of the Spanish and Portuguese crowns (1580–1640), Portuguese slavers, prospectors, raiders and frontiersmen pushed along the Amazon and its tributaries into regions reserved by treaty for Spain. In consequence, Portugal profited from the new finds of gold and diamonds of Brazil in the 18th century and proved able to seize frontier areas developed by the Spanish Jesuit missionaries. Meanwhile, despite often intense pressure, Spain retained most of her island

2/Population and settlement *(below)* Three main strands have created the ethnic pattern of the Americas: the settlers, primarily western European; the Black slaves, from west and east Africa; and the indigenous peoples. The map shows the frontier between European settlement and Indian land. The colours on the colonies are explained in the key to map 1 *(right)*.

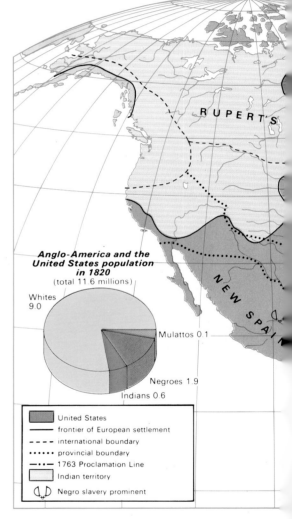

empire in the Caribbean: except for Jamaica, only unfavoured islands of the outer Antilles were permanently abandoned to interlopers.

Intervention from metropolitan governments tended not only to provoke international conflicts but also to alienate the colonists. In 1763, the British Crown, imitating Spain's tradition of defence of the Indians against colonial depredations, established the so-called Proclamation Line, near the crest of the Allegheny Mountains, and declared all land to the west to be an Indian Reserve. But the line, lacking geographical reality, scarcely stemmed the westward surge of settlers and land speculators: it merely irritated the independent-minded colonists, thus compounding their increasing resistance to British tax demands and trade controls. By 1768 the line had been revised to open up large new areas, but this still did not satisfy demand; in 1774 the Quebec Act, re-expanding the boundaries of the new Canadian colony to the Mississippi and Ohio rivers, was interpreted as damaging to the interests of Virginia and Pennsylvania. Coinciding with the bitterly resented Coercive Acts, this move helped light the fuse for the American War of Independence (1775–83).

Legend:
- French territory
- Spanish territory
- Portuguese territory
- Dutch territory
- Russian territory
- British by 1763
- ceded by France to Britain 1763
- ceded by France to Spain 1763
- United States 1783
- --- international boundary
- ⋯ provincial boundary
- → *major exports*
- colonization routes
  - Spanish
  - Portuguese
  - British
  - Russian
  - French

Arctic Ocean

GREENLAND

RUPERT'S LAND
(Hudson's Bay Company)

Hudson Bay

Unexplored

Disputed

by Russia

and Spain

San Francisco

LOUISIANA

furs

NEWFOUNDLAND
ceded to Britain 1763

QUEBEC
R St Lawrence
Quebec
Montreal

NOVA SCOTIA
whale products, fish

Detroit
R. Ohio

UNITED
STATES
OF
AMERICA
1783

Boston
New York
Philadelphia

*naval stores,
furs, fish, grain*

Los Angeles (1780)

Interior Provinces

Rio Grande

R Mississippi

THE THIRTEEN COLONIES

Jamestown

*tobacco,
grain*

WEST FLORIDA

skins New Orleans

EAST
FLORIDA (Br.1763-83)

North

N E W

S P A I N

silver

Mexico

Gulf of Mexico

silver

Belize (Br. 1683)

BAHAMA
ISLANDS
(Br.1783)

CUBA

A t l a n t i c

sugar, tobacco

WEST INDIES *Ocean*

SANTO DOMINGO

JAMAICA
(Br. 1655)

SAINT
DOMINGUE

GUADELOUPE (Fr.)

MARTINIQUE (Fr.)

Central
America

*cochineal,
gold*

C a r i b b e a n   S e a

CURAÇAO
(Dutch 1634)

tobacco

*tobacco
cocoa beans, hides*

Caracas

GUIANA

Paramaribo

Cayenne

gold

Venezuela
R Orinoco

Panama

Santa Fè de Bogotá

NEW GRANADA
1739

*drugs,
rare plants*

Pacific Ocean

Quito

*gold,
naval stores*

R Amazon

B R A Z I L

Treaty of Tordesillas 1494

*dyewoods,
sugar,
tobacco,
cotton*

R São Francisco

Bahia

*silver,
drugs*

Lima

P E R U

Cuzco

UPPER
PERU

Potosi

R Paraguay

R Paraná

*gold,
diamonds*

Rio de Janeiro

*copper,
grain*

C H I L E

RIO DE LA PLATA
1776

R Paraná

beef

*hides,
silver*

Buenos Aires

frontier

(Indian)

FALKLAND Is.

South Atlantic Ocean

Inset map (left):

LAND

QUEBEC

US

slave
trade
from
Africa

Venezuela

NEW GRANADA

P E R U

B R A Z I L

P E R U

C H I L E

RIO DE
LA PLATA

**Spanish American
population in 1800**
(total 16.9 millions)

Whites 3.3

Indians 7.5

Negroes 0.8

Mestizos 5.3

1/Colonial America *(above)* Two great
empires and three relatively smaller ones flourished in the western hemisphere in the 16th to
18th centuries. Richest by far were the Spanish
conquests, whose bullion directly or indirectly
(through contraband trade and piracy) enriched
much of western Europe.

Trade and empire in Africa 1500 to 1800

THREE main processes dominate the history of Africa from 1500 to 1800, of which the first was the growth of large political units in much of Black Africa. During these three centuries independent African political and cultural states reached their apogee, and across the Sudanic belt of west Africa replaced empires established much earlier, such as Ghana and Mali (see page 134). In 1464 one of Africa's most renowned kings and military heroes, Sunni Ali, became ruler of the Songhay people who lived along the eastern part of the Niger bend, around the city of Gao.

Sunni Ali's conquests built up a huge Songhay Empire, but his son was deposed as ruler by an even greater leader, Askia the Great, who reigned from 1493 to 1528. Trade flourished – especially across the Sahara – and the Songhay Empire incorporated a number of great commercial cities, including Timbuktu, Jenne and Gao, which became centres of learning and Muslim piety.

Trading communities from the rich Hausa city states and others of the Dyola, a Mande people from Mali and Songhay, gave rise to a series of states (the Mossi-Dagomba and the Akan-Asante) in the savannah and forest country to the south of the Niger. By 1500 Oyo and Benin, two of the great states of present-day Nigeria, had emerged in the woodlands to the west of the Niger delta where supreme examples of the plastic arts of Africa were to be produced, among them the Ife and Benin terracottas and bronzes.

Elsewhere in Black Africa similar processes were at work, producing powerful kingdoms from societies of iron-working agriculturalists and cattle-keepers. In favourable environments, the number of people (and their cattle) increased and their economies diversified, giving rise to trade in iron and copper goods and other wares, all of which provided the basis for stronger political control over a larger area. When the Portuguese arrived off the coast south of the estuary of the Congo (Zaire) River in 1484, they came upon the brilliant Kongo kingdom just inland. South of the Congo basin lay a string of Bantu-speaking African states including the Luba and Lunda kingdoms, while in the fertile lands between the lakes of east Africa a whole series of states evolved, the most prominent of which were Rwanda and Buganda.

Another prosperous region was the plateau of present-day Rhodesia, with kingdoms based upon Zimbabwe; while the Mwenemutapa empire, well known to the Portuguese and other early Europeans, centred on the area to the northeast of modern Harare. Numerous other peoples between the great kingdoms and over much of southern Africa slowly developed smaller, less flamboyant states.

The first occupation of Zimbabwe can be traced back to early Iron Age farmers around the 4th century AD. It was occupied for a second time in the 10th century by people who traded in copper and gold and 200 years later stone was worked for buildings at the site. However fire later destroyed Zimbabwe, leading to rebuilding from about the middle of the 14th century and today's impressive ruins: a huge palace in the valley sports a girdle wall more than 30 feet (10 m) high, constructed of dressed stone, while the hill overlooking the palace is crowned by a massive temple or acropolis. At the peak of its greatness, Zimbabwe was the political and religious centre of a considerable trading state with connections as far distant as China.

The second dominant historical process was the continual expansion of Islam. Not only was northern Africa fully Islamized, but during the period 1500 to 1800 Islam consolidated its position in the Sudanic lands, and spread even further south and along the coast of east Africa. In the Horn of Africa initial trading rivalry between Christian Ethiopia and the Muslim coastal states, especially Adal, became a long, bitter religious and political conflict: Sultan Ahmad Gran of Adal launched a fierce attack in the 1520s, and Muslim armies pushed into the heartlands of Ethiopia. Pagan Oromo (Galla) from the south and east then invaded and settled the exhausted Christian empire as well as Adal itself.

Meanwhile, in 1517, the Ottomans conquered the Mamlukes in Egypt, and subsequently extended Ottoman control over Tripoli and Tunis; Algiers was ruled by corsair princes, who owed allegiance to the Ottomans. Only Morocco remained independent, governed for much of this period by factions of the Sharifian dynasty.

In the 16th century much of coastal north Africa was the scene of a prolonged religious and economic conflict between the Christian powers, especially Spain and Portugal, and the Ottoman Empire and Morocco. In 1590, at the height of its power, Morocco invaded the Songhay Empire and set up a client state in the Sudan; this invasion disrupted the economic life of the whole region but at the beginning of the 18th century the politics and commerce of Muslim west Africa grew again in a burst of Islamic proselytizing which reached its zenith with the great Holy Wars of the 1790s (see page 234).

The third process saw the increasing involvement of Europeans in the destiny of Africa as they sought gold, ivory, woods and, above all, slaves to work the mines and plantations of the Americas. Although, even by 1800 the number of European territorial possessions was small, their domination of the oceanic trading systems had considerable direct and indirect effects on a great many Africans, including those in the far interior. At the southern tip of Africa, Dutch and French Huguenot settlers arrived after 1652 and by 1800 had killed or conquered the Khoisan peoples but encountered much more serious resistance from the Bantu of the southeast.

The slave trade was inaugurated by the Portuguese who were soon joined by the Dutch, French and British in setting up 'factories' along the coast where slaves were bought. From 1450 to 1870, at least 11.5 million Africans were captured for the trade, of whom perhaps 10 million survived the horrors of the 'middle passage' to reach the Americas. Most came from west Africa, though by 1800 east Africa was contributing to this Atlantic system as well as sending slaves to India and the Muslim world. Nor did the traditional trans-Saharan trade decline.

The precise effects of the slave trade are hotly debated, especially in relation to population size and to the emergence of states such as Dahomey or Ashanti which supplied slaves. Overall, Europeans definitely gained and Africa's own economic development was probably inhibited. By 1800, Africans had made great progress in evolving distinctive social and political forms but their independence was already seriously compromised. But debates on gains and losses should not obscure the cruelty and indignity suffered by the slaves themselves, a fact that continues to cast a shadow over modern race relations.

1/Developments in trade and empire (right) During the 300 years from 1500 to 1800, the course of African history developed along both well-established lines and in new ways. The interaction between Mediterranean and Sudanic Africa, which had begun in pre-Roman times, continued, with Islam making deeper inroads into tropical Africa. African states and cultures, generally deep in the interior of the continent, also continued their mainly slow and steady – though sometimes most dynamic – growth. However, many parts of Africa came increasingly under the economic influence of western European states, with profound political and economic effects on coastal peoples.

Bronze plaque from Benin (below) Within the rich artistic traditions of West Africa, the bronzes produced in Benin (modern Nigeria) by the lost-wax process from the 15th century onwards are outstanding. In court art destined for the *oba* (king), naturalism gave way to stylized designs emphasizing power and generally, as here, celebrating a conquest or victory. This form of sculpture may have drawn its inspiration from woodcuts in books shown to the artists by early Portuguese visitors.

2/The Portuguese exploration of Africa (below) Under the patronage of Prince Henry the Navigator (1394-1460), Portuguese explorers steadily penetrated southwards in search of gold, spices and slaves. In 1488 one Portuguese expedition reached the Cape of Good Hope, while another reconnoitred east Africa, preparing the way for Vasco da Gama's first direct seaborne journey to India in 1497.

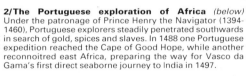

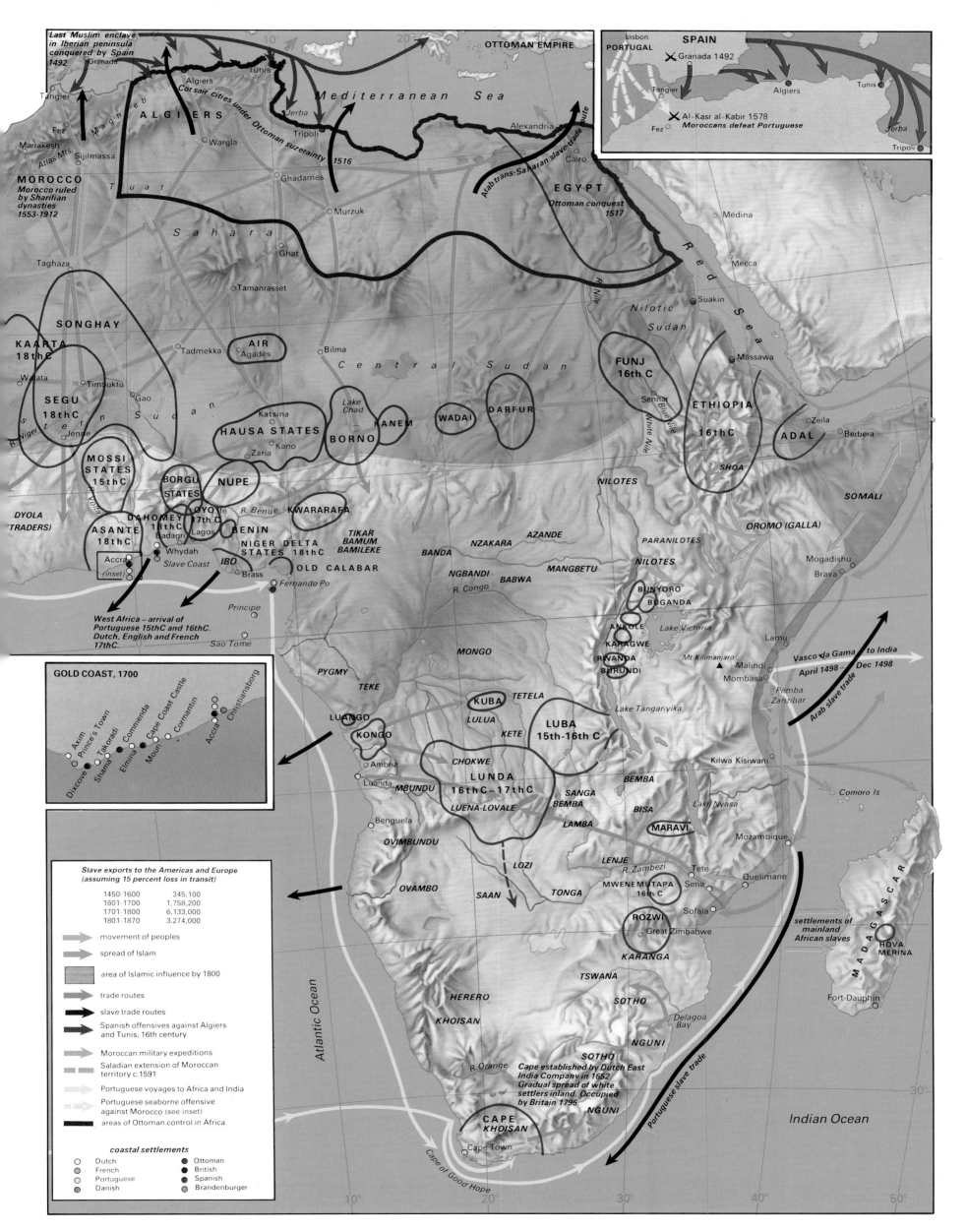

East Asia at the time of the Ming dynasty 1368 to 1644

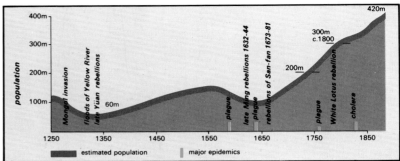

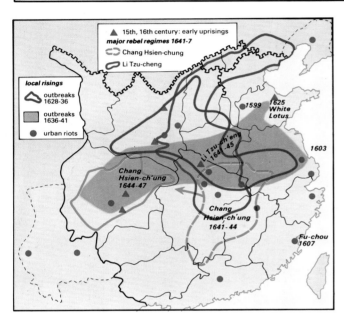

4/Japan's century of civil war, 1467 to 1590 *(above)* The powerful centralized regime established by the Kamakura shoguns was destroyed in the 1330s, to be replaced by the Ashikaga, a new dominant military family, until 1400, when their power declined. The Onin War (1467-77) began a century of strife between the feudal lords. The map shows the political fragmentation of the country in about 1560; Oda Nobunaga and Toyotomi Hideyoshi gradually reunified Japan by 1590, preparing the way for the powerful state of the Tokugawa, set up in 1603.

3/Rebellions under the Ming *(left)* Rural distress produced a number of rebellions during the 15th century, mostly in central and south-eastern China. In the early 17th century taxation and economic pressures produced urban risings in the great cities, and from the 1620s great numbers of peasant rebellions in central and northern China. In the 1640s two rebels, Li Tzu-ch'eng and Chang Hsien-chung, became contenders to found a new dynasty.

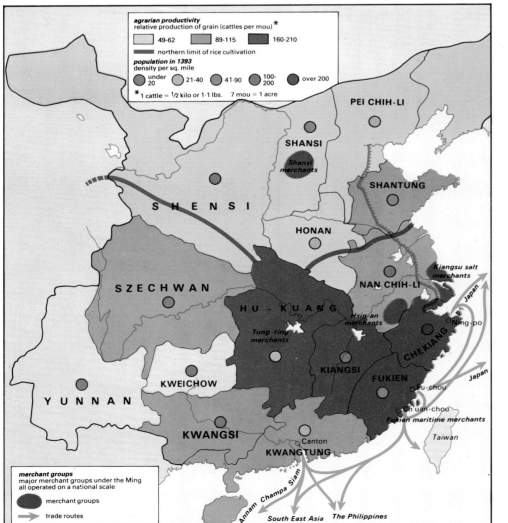

THE Mongols caused immense destruction in China, especially during the conquest of the north before 1241: much of the land went out of cultivation; cities and industries were largely destroyed; countless people died and many more became slaves. In the south Mongol rule was less harsh after 1279, but under the Mongol (Yüan) dynasty (1280–1367) the Chinese were ruthlessly exploited, productivity fell and commerce was badly disrupted. Popular resentment erupted in a wave of popular risings from 1335 onwards. In 1354–9 disastrous floods in the eastern plain caused further distress, and major rebellions flared up in Chekiang, the Yangtze valley, Shantung and Honan. Ultimately, however, one of the rebel leaders, Chu Yan-chang, overcame his rivals and established a new dynasty, the Ming, in Nanking in 1368. By 1387 Chu had conquered all of China, and in 1388 dealt the Mongols their final defeat.

Until the end of the 14th century the Ming were preoccupied with the restoration of normal life. Their first priority was to revive agriculture: irrigation and drainage works were rebuilt in great numbers, reforestation carried out on a grand scale, and vast numbers of people moved to repopulate the devastated north. At the same time, attempts were made to break the power of the large landowners and encourage small peasants for, unlike the Sung, who had depended heavily on trade and merchants as sources of revenue, the Ming wished to revert to the ancient system of reliance on agriculture for revenues. To facilitate the movement of products and people they built a new canal system to link the Yangtze valley with Peking which became the capital in 1421. The Ming also attempted to revive the concept of a self-sufficient army, and established a class of hereditary military families settled in 'military colonies' on the frontiers and at other strategic locations.

In 1393 the Chinese population was just over 60 million, 40 per cent fewer than under the late Sung, but peace and internal stability allowed it to increase again until by 1580 it probably numbered about 130 million, although major plagues caused a drastic reduction in the late 16th century and again in the 1640s. However, improved agricultural techniques now enabled China to feed its growing population. New crops were introduced, while cotton, which had become common under the Mongols, was widely grown in the Yangtze valley and the north of Kiangsu. In the dry west and northwest sorghum became a common grain crop, and in the 16th and 17th centuries Spanish and Portuguese maritime traders introduced further imports, such as the sweet potato, maize, peanuts, Irish potato and tobacco, which could be grown on soils unsuited to traditional produce.

The Ming government took a negative attitude towards trade. It abandoned the use of paper money which the Mongols had misused, seriously damaging the economy. Despite a government monopoly in some important areas,

2/The Ming economy *(left)* Chinese silk and cotton textiles and ceramics were exchanged in Manila for Spanish silver from the New World; and from the early 17th century tea was exported to Europe via Dutch traders. China imported silver, spices, sulphur, sandalwood, and copper from Japan.

Ming naval power *(above)* As this detail from a painting of the defence of Korea illustrates, the Ming were a considerable naval power, even in the 1590s, capable of intervening in the affairs of distant nations.

Population fluctuations *(left)* At the beginning of the Ming, China still suffered from the effects of Mongol rule: population had fallen drastically, especially in the north. With extensive reconstruction, population rose steadily, and agriculture became more productive. Outbreaks of plague in the 1500s and the 1640s, however, again reduced the population in many areas.

industry boomed and the great cities of the Yangtze delta, Nanking, Suchou, Wu-hsi, Sung-chiang and Hang-chou, became major industrial centres, particularly for textiles. They were supplied with grain and raw cotton by the grand canal from the north, and by the Yangtze from Hunan and Hupeh. Large movements of goods were also needed to supply Peking and the garrisons on the northern borders – the system of self-sufficient military colonies soon decayed – and several powerful groups of merchants arose (see map 2) to handle this huge volume of trade. In the late 16th century commerce was also stimulated by the inflow of silver from the New World, used to pay for Chinese exports of tea, silk and ceramics.

The Ming state reverted to the institutions of T'ang times, abandoning many Sung innovations. Government was simple: control over the vast population was effected largely through the 'gentry' (*shen-shih*), degree-holders who had been through the examination system and shared the values of the bureaucracy without actually holding office. But the new system discouraged innovation and was overcentralized, and abolition of the post of chief minister made all decisions dependent upon the emperor.

At first the Ming engaged in an aggressive foreign policy. Campaigns against the Mongols in the far north, the restoration of Korea to vassal status in 1392, the occupation of Annam from 1407 to 1427 and immense seaborne expeditions extended Chinese power to new limits. These ventures proved costly, however, and after an attempted invasion of Mongolia in 1449 ended in the emperor's capture, the Ming reverted to a defensive strategy. In the 16th century they came under constant pressure from revived Mongol power under Altan Khan (1550–73) and from attacks from the sea. Japanese-based pirates constantly harassed the coasts, and after 1550 invaded coastal districts in force, sailed up the Yangtze, and attacked major cities. The Portuguese, by comparison a minor irritant, first appeared in 1514 and from 1557 were permanently established in Macao.

The pirate threat did not diminish until 1590, when Japan was reunified after over a century of civil war and political disunion. But Japanese unity brought new dangers: in 1592 forces under Hideyoshi invaded Korea and the Chinese had to send huge armies to aid their vassals. Another expedition against Korea in 1597-8 again caused terrible destruction and again required Chinese involvement.

These major threats coincided with a decline in Ming government. After 1582 the emperors refused to conduct court business or even to see their ministers. Power passed into the hands of eunuchs who, with their own army and secret police, were able to terrorize officials and populace alike, and to extort heavy taxes. Reformist officials attempted to counter them but this only led to purges and factional discord.

The Ming had suffered rebellions before: an uprising in Fukien and Chekiang in 1448-9 led to 1 million deaths. After 1627, however, a wave of rebel movements broke out after repeated crop failures in the northwest, and by 1636 much of central, northern and northwest China was in rebellion. The main contenders for power were Chang Hsien-cheng, who ravaged the eastern plain and the Yangtze valley before setting up a kingdom in Szechwan, and Li Tzu-ch'eng in Shan-hsi, Hupeh and Honan. When Li took Peking in 1644, the last Ming emperor committed suicide. But Li's ambition to found a dynasty was thwarted by the irresistible intervention of the Manchus, who in the previous quarter century had established a powerful state in the northeast (see page 170).

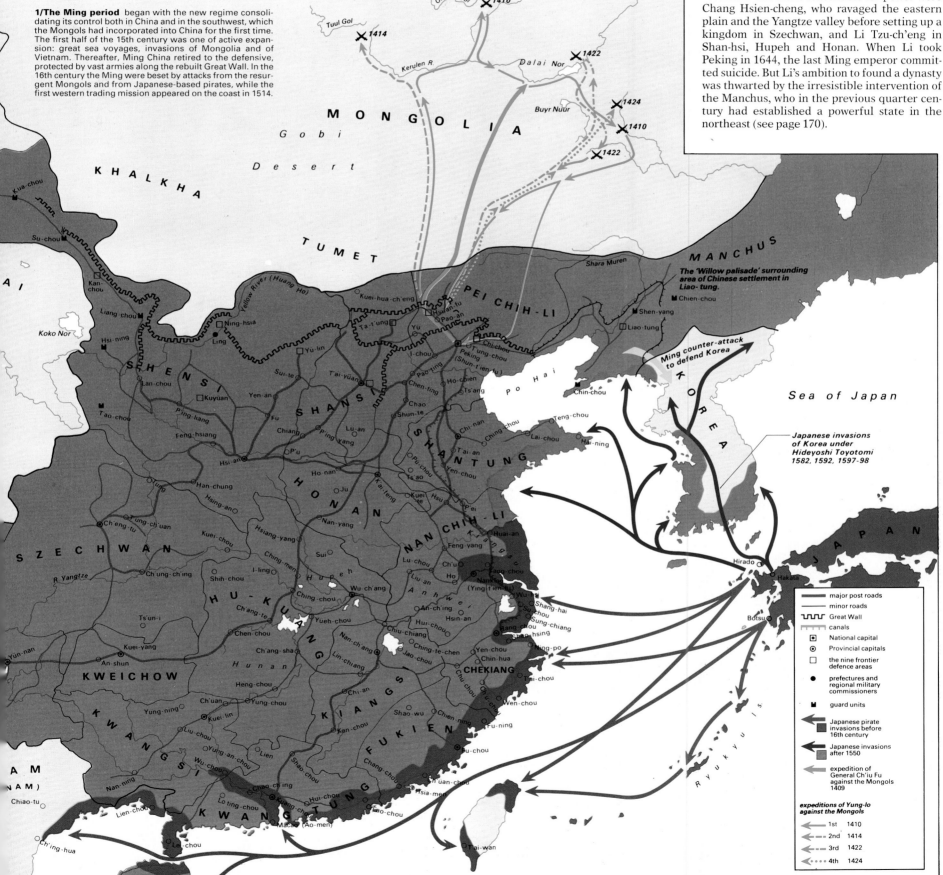

1/The Ming period began with the new regime consolidating its control both in China and in the southwest, which the Mongols had incorporated into China for the first time. The first half of the 15th century was one of active expansion: great sea voyages, invasions of Mongolia and of Vietnam. Thereafter, Ming China retired to the defensive, protected by vast armies along the rebuilt Great Wall. In the 16th century the Ming were beset by attacks from the resurgent Mongols and from Japanese-based pirates, while the first western trading mission appeared on the coast in 1514.

major post roads
minor roads
Great Wall
canals
National capital
Provincial capitals
the nine frontier defence areas
prefectures and regional military commissioners
guard units
Japanese pirate invasions before 16th century
Japanese invasions after 1550
expedition of General Ch'iu Fu against the Mongols 1409

expeditions of Yung-lo against the Mongols
1st 1410
2nd 1414
3rd 1422
4th 1424

The resurgence of Muslim power 1520 to 1639

1/The Ottoman, Safavid and Mughal empires *(right)* The great Muslim victories of Mohács on the Danube and Panipat in the Ganges basin took place in the same year, 1526. Subsequently, the Ottoman frontier advanced still further into Europe, and the Mughals in India extended their domains southwards until the end of the 17th century. The Ottoman triumph was less enduring; weakened by internal revolts, and challenged by the Habsburgs in Europe, Muscovy in southern Russia and the Safavids in Persia, they gradually retreated from Hungary, the Caucasus and Iraq; by the end of the 17th century many of the gains realised in the reign of Suleiman the Magnificent (1520-66) had been lost.

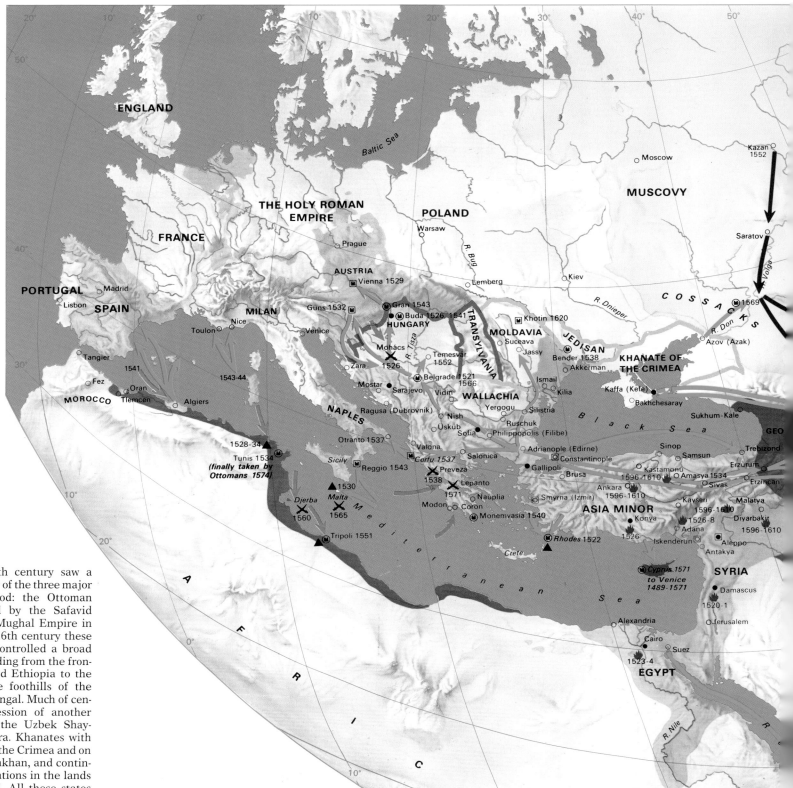

THE first half of the 16th century saw a great advance in the power of the three major Muslim states of the period: the Ottoman Empire, the state founded by the Safavid dynasty in Persia, and the Mughal Empire in India. In the middle of the 16th century these three polities occupied or controlled a broad belt of lands and seas, extending from the frontiers of Morocco, Austria and Ethiopia to the fringes of central Asia, the foothills of the Himalayas, and the Bay of Bengal. Much of central Asia was in the possession of another dynasty of Turkish origin, the Uzbek Shaybanids, who ruled in Bukhara. Khanates with Muslim rulers still existed in the Crimea and on the Volga at Kazan and Astrakhan, and continued to do so for many generations in the lands along the ancient Silk Road. All these states were the creation of Turkish-speaking Muslim dynasties of a strongly military character. All, with the exception of the Safavids, affirmed their adherence to orthodox (Sunni) Islam; the Safavids, however, followed Shi'ism, a fact which encouraged bitter rivalry and intermittent warfare between them and their Ottoman and Uzbek neighbours throughout the 16th and early 17th centuries.

By the death of Mehmed II (1481) the Ottomans had conquered Constantinople and overrun the Balkans. Shortly afterwards the sudden revival of Persia under Ismail I (1500–24) drew them back to Asia. Ismail was defeated in 1514, Syria and Egypt conquered in 1516–17. With the accession of Suleiman I (1520–66) the assault on Europe was renewed. After the battle of Mohács (1526), Hungary was overrun and Vienna besieged (1529); but Persia still remained independent. Nevertheless the Ottoman Empire, buttressed by wealth acquired from the conquest of Egypt, was indisputably the greatest

Muslim power of the age. In the early years of Suleiman's reign, the subjects of the Sultan numbered perhaps 14 million (compare this with Spain which at this time had 5 million inhabitants whilst England had 2.5 million). The population of Constantinople itself, which at the time of the Ottoman conquest had been no more than 40,000, increased tenfold, and Ottoman and European writers alike testified to the splendour of its public works, the impressiveness of the imperial mosques and the outstanding quality of administrative, charitable and educational institutions. To European observers, such as the Habsburg Emperor's ambassador Busbecq, the magnificence of the Ottoman state, and the strength and discipline of the Ottoman army, were matters for admiration – and concern.

Persia, also, under the new dynasty enjoyed a remarkable revival of art, architecture and trade, which reached its culmination in the reign of Abbas I (1587–1629), while in India Babur, an

Suleiman I at Mohács *(right)* The military might, order and discipline of the Ottoman army in the first half of the 16th century are vigorously depicted in this miniature. Suleiman I is shown surrounded by his vezirs, sipahis and janissaries.

adventurer from central Asia who had seized power in Afghanistan in 1504, swept aside the effete sultanate of Delhi and founded the Mughal Empire in 1526. Here again (see page 168) there was a great efflorescence of culture, which reached its peak during the reign of Akbar (1556–1605). But the vast extension of Muslim power and influence concealed a number of flaws. The most serious problem was the continuing clash between Sunni Turkey and Shia Persia, which drove a wedge into the Muslim world. Just as the Ottomans allied with

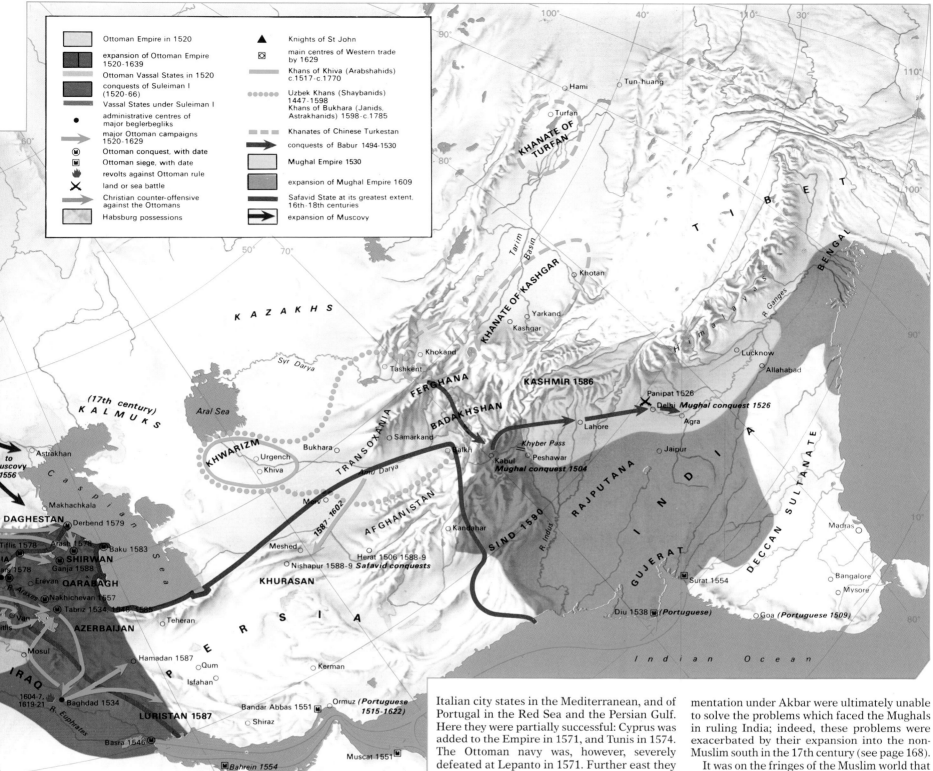

Map labels:
KHANATE OF TURFAN, Hami, Tun-huang, Turfan, T I B E T, KHANATE OF KASHGAR, Khotan, Yarkand, Kashgar, Tarim Basin, B E N G A L, R. Ganges, Lucknow, Allahabad, KASHMIR 1586, FERGHANA, Khokand, Tashkent, Panipat 1526, Delhi *Mughal conquest 1526*, Agra, Lahore, *Khyber Pass*, Kabul *Mughal conquest 1504*, Peshawar, Jaipur, BADAKHSHAN, TRANSOXANIA, Samarkand, Bukhara, Balkh, Syr Darya, Aral Sea, KAZAKHS, RAJPUTANA, I N D I A, SIND 1530, KHWARIZM, Urgench, Khiva, Anu Darya, Merv, 1587-1602, AFGHANISTAN, Kandahar, R. Indus, DECCAN SULTANATE, GUJERAT, Madras, Surat 1554, Bangalore, Mysore, (17th century) KALMUKS, Astrakhan, to Muscovy 1556, Caspian Sea, Makhachkala, DAGHESTAN, Derbend 1579, Meshed, Herat 1506 1588-9 *Safavid conquests*, Nishapur 1588-9, KHURASAN, Diu 1538 *(Portuguese)*, Goa *(Portuguese 1509)*, Indian Ocean, Tiflis 1578, Arash 1578, Baku 1583, GIA, SHIRWAN, Ganja 1588, Kars 1578, QARABAGH, Erevan, R. Araxes, Nakhichevan 1657, Tabriz 1534, 1548-1585, Van, Bitlis, AZERBAIJAN, Teheran, P E R S I A, Mosul, Hamadan 1587, Qum, Isfahan, Kerman, IRAQ, 1604-7 1619-21, Baghdad 1534, R. Euphrates, LURISTAN 1587, Basra 1546, Bandar Abbas 1551, Ormuz *(Portuguese 1515-1622)*, Shiraz, Bahrein 1554, Muscat 1551, A R A B I A, Medina, Jidda, Mecca, Red Sea, Sana, Socotra *(Portuguese 1507)*, YEMEN, Zabid, Aden 1538, to Malindi (1584)

Italian city states in the Mediterranean, and of Portugal in the Red Sea and the Persian Gulf. Here they were partially successful: Cyprus was added to the Empire in 1571, and Tunis in 1574. The Ottoman navy was, however, severely defeated at Lepanto in 1571. Further east they proved unable to prevent the capture of Socotra (1507) and Ormuz (1515) by the Portuguese, still less the establishment of a Portuguese presence in India itself.

For the Ottomans, the year 1538, when the armies and fleets of the Sultan in one season reduced Moldavia to vassal status, defeated a poorly led Christian armada at Preveza, and appeared against the Portuguese under the walls of Diu, was certainly an *annus mirabilis*. However, the conflicts on the Hungarian and Persian frontiers both began to lose their momentum in the last two decades of Suleiman's reign. In the second half of the 16th century, the wars against the Safavids (1578–90 and 1603–19) and against the Habsburgs (1593–1606) ended in the loss of the Caucasus territories and in the Habsburgs' last payment of tribute for Hungary. Furthermore, during these wars the lifeblood of the Empire, its (traditionally recruited) ruling class and its army, was drained away. The changing conditions of war, the effects of inflation after 1584, and the insoluble problem of a rising population, a shrinking economy, and a static frontier, had by the early decades of the 17th century produced a crisis in the Ottoman state.

In Persia the political weakness of the Safavids in the latter part of the 16th century was redressed by Abbas I, but after his death in 1629 the Safavid dynasty, too, entered a period of weakness, leading to ultimate demise. Following a similar pattern, in India the administrative reorganization and religious experi-

mentation under Akbar were ultimately unable to solve the problems which faced the Mughals in ruling India; indeed, these problems were exacerbated by their expansion into the non-Muslim south in the 17th century (see page 168).

It was on the fringes of the Muslim world that the changes in this period were the most ominous. At sea, the Portuguese circumnavigation of Africa and their attempt to put a stranglehold on the indigenous trade of the Indian Ocean had not gone unnoticed by the Ottomans; as successors to the Mamlukes they were able at least to hold the Portuguese at bay during the 16th century. However, the arrival of the English, and later the Dutch, brought into the region powers economically stronger and politically more ruthless than the Portuguese. Their effect was increasingly felt during the remainder of the 17th century. Meanwhile, to the north, the Muslim successor states of the Mongol Empire had by the middle of the 16th century for the most part entered on the last stages of decline and decay. The khanates of Kazan and Astrakhan were annexed by Muscovy in 1552 and 1556. This brought Russian forces to the mouth of the Volga, thus driving a wedge between the Ottomans and the Uzbeks. On the other hand, the khanate of the Crimea, another successor state of the Golden Horde, continued in existence and was at times a useful military auxiliary of the Ottomans as well as a barrier closing off the Black Sea from hostile Christian states to the north. By the 1620s, however, Cossack raiders were appearing on the Black Sea and ravaging its shores. In less than a century the Islamic world had passed from the offensive to the defensive, and the great Islamic empires, which had seemed so formidable in the 16th and 17th centuries, failed to match the transformations taking place in the West.

France against the Habsburgs, so the Safavids allied with Austria against the Turks. Secondly, the Mughal and Safavid empires were essentially based on land, and when the Portuguese appeared in the Indian Ocean, hitherto a Muslim lake, the empires found themselves at a disadvantage. After their conquest of Egypt, the Ottomans assumed the defence of their territories against the seapower of Spain and the

The Mughal Empire and the growth of British power in India

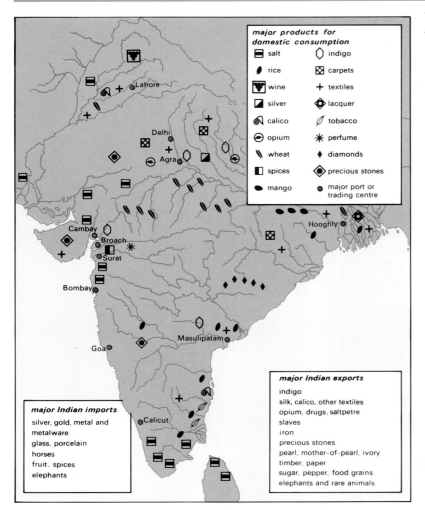

2/Mughal India: economic products and trade *(above)* Textiles from Bengal, Gujerat and Coromandel were India's main export; also sugar to Japan and Persia, and pepper and saltpetre to Europe. The main imports were gold and silver.

major products for domestic consumption
- salt
- rice
- wine
- silver
- calico
- opium
- wheat
- spices
- mango
- indigo
- carpets
- textiles
- lacquer
- tobacco
- perfume
- diamonds
- precious stones
- major port or trading centre

major Indian imports
silver, gold, metal and metalware
glass, porcelain
horses
fruit, spices
elephants

major Indian exports
indigo
silk, calico, other textiles
opium, drugs, saltpetre
slaves
iron
precious stones
pearl, mother-of-pearl, ivory
timber, paper
sugar, pepper, food grains
elephants and rare animals

3/The growth of British power to 1805 *(below)* and principal Maratha states in 1795 *(below right)*. After Tipu's death at Seringapatam (1799), the Marathas represented the only major obstacle to British supremacy, largely achieved by 1805.

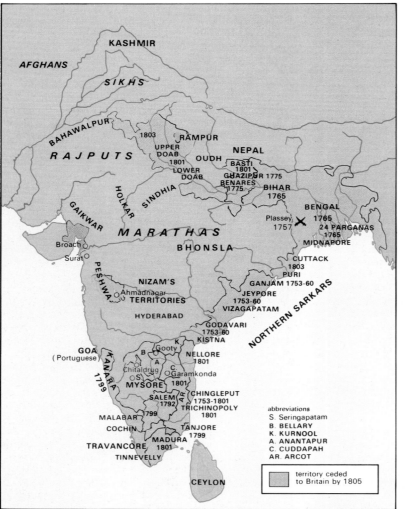

abbreviations
S. Seringapatam
B. Bellary
K. Kurnool
A. Anantapur
C. Cuddapah
AR. Arcot

territory ceded to Britain by 1805

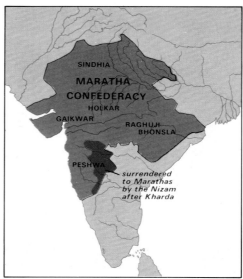

MARATHA CONFEDERACY
SINDHIA
HOLKAR
GAIKWAR
RAGHUJI BHONSLA
PESHWA
surrendered to Marathas by the Nizam after Kharda

BABUR, fifth in line from Tamerlane entered India in the 1520s from Afghanistan. With his victory at Panipat in 1526 he established the Mughal Empire, but died before he could make the foundations firm. His son, Humayun, was expelled by the Afghans of South Bihar, under their leader Sher Shah, and it took a full-scale new invasion, brilliantly consolidated by Babur's grandson, Akbar (1556–1605), to restore Mughal rule. This now extended to Bengal in the east and the river Godavari in the south, as well as Kashmir, Baluchistan, Sind and Gujerat. Most of the Rajput princes became tributary allies, and the empire, divided into *subahs* (provinces), was administered by a new class of bureaucrats, the *mansabdars*, ranked in a military hierarchical system which has no exact parallel outside India. A standardized tax system and tolerance towards the non-Muslim majority helped to foster one of the great flowerings of Indian civilization, particularly in painting, architecture and poetry. The reign of Akbar is considered one of the golden ages in India's past. Unlike his descendants, who, thanks to his policy of marriage alliances with the Rajput princely families, were half Indian, Akbar was entirely a foreigner in India. Yet his sense of identification with the life and culture of the country he reconquered was remarkable, resulting in an unprecedented degree of synthesis between Indian and Persian cultural forms. The Mughal school of miniature painting, which combined the traditions of the Persian and Rajput schools, flourished under his patronage. His red sandstone capital at Fatehpur Sikri similarly expressed a striking synthesis of Hindu and Islamic traditions of architecture. The new style reached its climax in the days of his grandson, Shahjahan, the builder of the Taj Mahal.

Akbar's political inheritance included a ceaseless thrust towards territorial expansion, especially towards the south. New territories were added under Shahjahan (1627–56) and the Mughal domains reached their furthest extent under Aurangzeb (1656–1707), who seized the throne after a fratricidal war. Bijapur and Golconda were annexed, Assam briefly occupied, and Chittagong wrested from Arakan. But the southern conquests led to confrontation with a new Hindu power, the Marathas, who under Sivaji (1627–80) had established an independent kingdom in the western Ghats, with outposts in Coromandel and Mysore. The execution of Sivaji's son in 1689 failed to check the Maratha inroads, for by 1700 they were ravaging the Deccan and had reached Bengal. Meanwhile, the former Rajput allies were at war, and Sikhs, Jats and Satnamis were in revolt near the capital. Underlying these signs of open disaffection

was a failure to pay sufficient attention to the economic and administrative structure of the empire, so that disintegration of Mughal control accelerated during the first half of the 18th century. Aurangzeb's personal adherence to the Islamic *shari'at* (law) has led to some condemnation of policies which seemed to ignore, or hurt, powerful non-Muslim interests, but recent scholarship tends to highlight the structural causes for decline.

Shortly after Aurangzeb's death, Oudh, the Deccan and Bengal became effectively independent, owing only nominal allegiance to Delhi. The Peshwas, officially the chief ministers of Sivaji's house, presided over a confederacy of Maratha chiefs, the Sindhias, Gaikwars, Holkars and Bhonslas. Their territories stretched deep into north, west, central and eastern India, while in the south, the Muslim state of Mysore grew into a formidable power under Haidar Ali and his son, Tipu Sultan. By the late 18th century, the Mughal emperor had become a Maratha protégé. Indeed the Marathas seemed destined to succeed the Mughals. Such hopes were effectively destroyed at the Third Battle of Panipat (1761), when an Afghan chief, Ahmad Shah Abdali, defeated the Peshwas' forces; but Abdali's immediate withdrawal to Afghanistan left a power vacuum in north India.

Meanwhile European influence in India grew rapidly after the death of Aurangzeb. The War of the Austrian Succession (1740–8) saw the French and English trading companies in armed conflict along the Carnatic coast. With the death of the local ruler, the Nizam of Hyderabad, this developed into open war (1744–63), ending in British victory and the eclipse of France's Indian ambitions. Robert Clive's triumph at Plassey in 1757 brought effective control over the lands and revenues of Bihar, Orissa and Bengal (where the East India Company had established its new trading centre of Calcutta in 1690). Thanks to these resources, the Company could sustain a permanent army of over 100,000 men: by 1768 the Northern Sarkars were secured from the Nizam, while Benares and Ghazipur were wrested from Oudh in 1775. But British supremacy was only assured after a series of battles with the Marathas and Mysore, of which the outcome was frequently uncertain. Nevertheless the company's possessions steadily expanded – particularly with the destruction of Mysore in the 1790s – until by the turn of the century they formed a continuous block from Malabar to Coromandel. In the north, however, no attempt was made to move into the old Mughal heartlands.

In Britain, the Regulating Act of 1773 and the Younger Pitt's India Act of 1784, had placed these new Indian acquisitions firmly under British parliamentary control (and also led to the impeachment of Warren Hastings, the first Governor-General of Bengal). Now they were to be consolidated into the beginnings of an imperial realm.

Thanks to France's preoccupation with Europe (see page 202), the British swiftly defeated Tipu, the most effective of the Indian leaders, and embarked on the Second Maratha War. Both these produced large accretions of territory, alongside important but subsidiary annexations in Gooty, Garamkonda, Surat, Tanjore, the Carnatic, and large parts of Oudh and Chitaldrug. The Maratha defeats delivered the Upper Doab, Rajputana, Broach, Ahmadnagar and the southwest Deccan, while subsidiary alliances, another important policy instrument, won recognition of British suzerainty from nearly all the major Indian rulers. In 1803, the Mughal emperor himself accepted British protection: British supremacy was now an acknowledged fact.

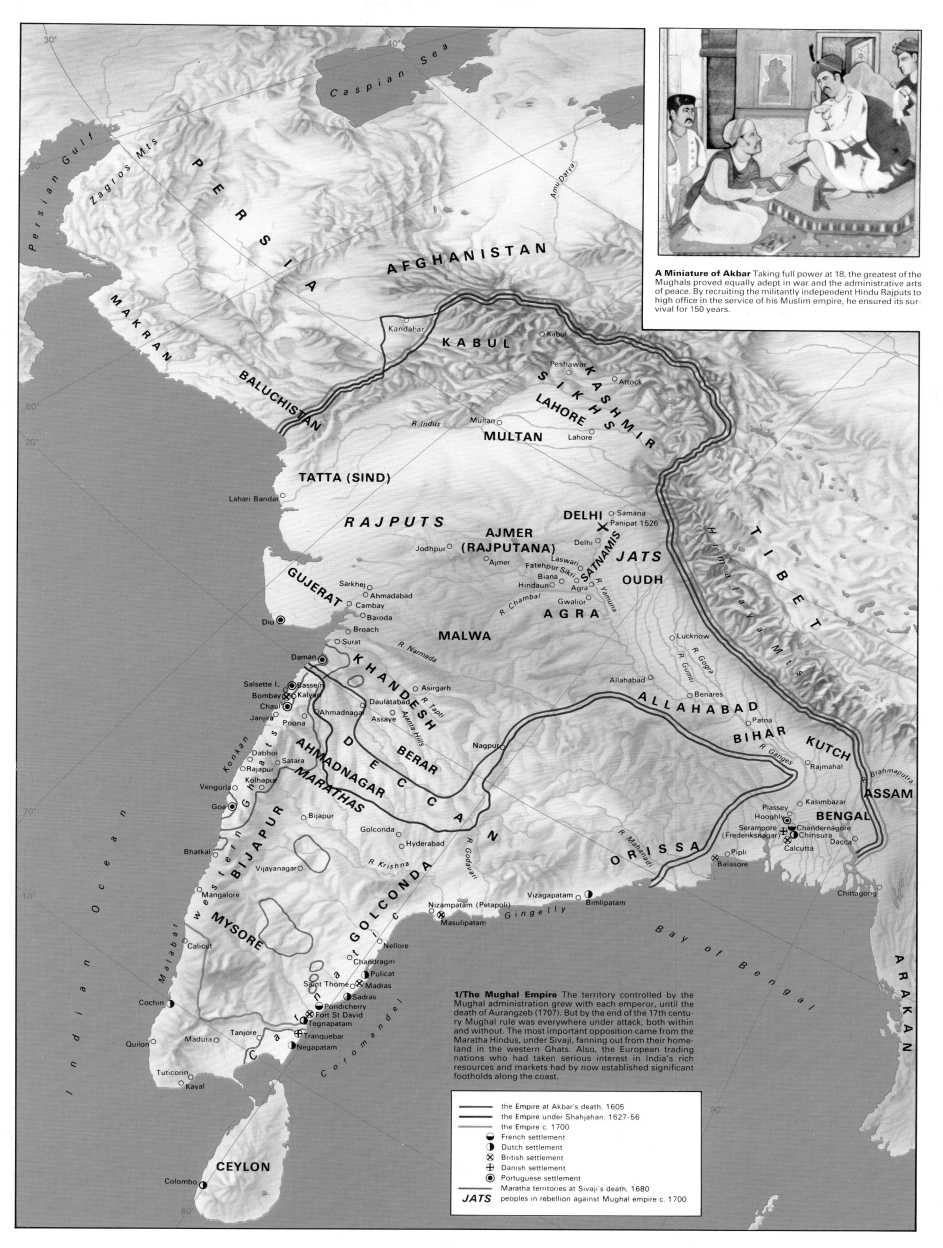

A Miniature of Akbar Taking full power at 18, the greatest of the Mughals proved equally adept in war and the administrative arts of peace. By recruiting the militantly independent Hindu Rajputs to high office in the service of his Muslim empire, he ensured its survival for 150 years.

1/The Mughal Empire The territory controlled by the Mughal administration grew with each emperor, until the death of Aurangzeb (1707). But by the end of the 17th century Mughal rule was everywhere under attack, both within and without. The most important opposition came from the Maratha Hindus, under Sivaji, fanning out from their homeland in the western Ghats. Also, the European trading nations who had taken serious interest in India's rich resources and markets had by now established significant footholds along the coast.

the Empire at Akbar's death, 1605
the Empire under Shahjahan, 1627-56
the Empire c. 1700
◖ French settlement
◑ Dutch settlement
⊗ British settlement
✛ Danish settlement
◉ Portuguese settlement
Maratha territories at Sivaji's death, 1680
JATS peoples in rebellion against Mughal empire c. 1700

East Asia at the time of the Ch'ing Dynasty

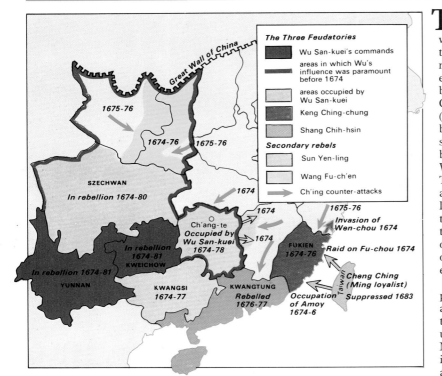

2/Rebellion of the Three Feudatories *(above)* The southern provinces, where resistance to the Ch'ing continued, were allowed to become the personal domains of various generals. Most important of these was Wu San-kuei, governor of Yunnan and Kweichow, who exercised great power over all the western provinces. In 1674 the Ch'ing government attempted to reassert control over Kwangtung.

As a result the governors of all the southern and western provinces rose in a rebellion which lasted until 1681. For a time most of southern and western China was in rebel hands, but by 1677 only the southwest remained. After Wu San-kuei's death in 1678 the government slowly reduced the surviving rebels, and in 1683 occupied Taiwan, whose Ming loyalist leader Cheng Ching had supported the rebels.

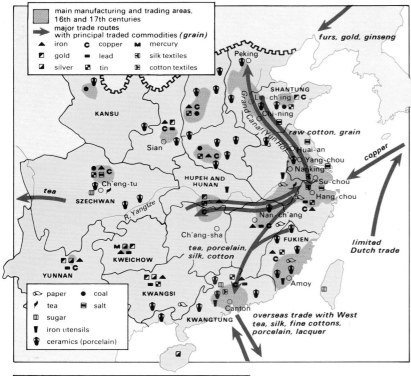

3/The Ch'ing economy *(above)* By the 17th century China had developed considerable regional specialization and a nation-wide marketing system. Some cities in the lower Yangtze sustained large and varied handicraft industries. These industries drew their raw materials and food for their populations from great distances by the Yangtze and by the Grand Canal, which also supplied food and manufactured goods to Peking.

The Chinese economy in the 19th century *(left)* Chinese exports of tea increased by over 50 per cent in the period shown. Silk exports grew fourfold. But everexpanding imports of opium converted a net inflow of silver into a net outflow from the mid-1820s, with serious effects on the Chinese internal economy.

THE Ch'ing dynasty (1644–1911) was established by a non-Chinese people, the Manchus, who gradually expanded in the first decades of the 17th century from their homeland in the mountains of southeast Manchuria into the modern provinces of Liaoning and Kirin. Supported by many Chinese, they established a stable Chinese-style state with its capital at Mukden (modern Shenyang) from 1625 to 1644; from this base they invaded Korea, reducing it to vassal status in 1637, and Inner Mongolia which became a Manchu dependency in 1629–35. When the Ming were toppled by the rebel Li Tzu-ch'eng in 1644, the Manchus invaded China and proclaimed a new dynasty. In spite of Ming loyalist resistance in the south, most of the country was under Manchu control by 1652 but resistance continued in the southwest until 1659, and on the southeast coast Ming loyalists in 1662 occupied Taiwan (never previously under Chinese control), where they remained until 1683.

After the collapse of Ming resistance and suppression of the rebellion of the Three Feudatories (see map 2), the Ch'ing enjoyed more than a century of internal peace and prosperity under a succession of very able rulers. The Manchus maintained their predominant place in government, and above all in the military, but also established a good working relationship with their Chinese officials. However at the end of the 18th century, deeply influenced by Chinese education and culture, the Manchus began to lose their sharp identity and a number of risings of minority peoples, harshly exploited by Chinese and Manchus alike, took place: in Yunnan in 1726–9; among the Chinese Muslim minority in Kansu in 1781–4; among the Yao people of Kwangsi in 1790; and among the Miao people of Kweichow in 1795–7 and again in 1829. But the massive Chin-ch'uan tribal rebellions in western Szechwan were the most serious. These first broke out in 1746–9 and after simmering for years were renewed in 1771–6, when order was finally restored after ruinously expensive military operations. A further rising occurred in the newly occupied territory of Taiwan in 1787–8, but for all their ferocity these events occurred in peripheral areas and posed no major threat to the dynasty.

At the end of the 18th century, rebellion took on a new form. By this time, although China remained immensely powerful, productive and populous, a major economic crisis loomed ahead. The area available for agriculture, which had been expanded by the introduction of new crops (maize, sweet potato, groundnuts, tobacco) in the 16th and 17th centuries, was now almost totally occupied. The only vacant area suitable for Chinese-style agriculture was Manchuria which was deliberately preserved as a Manchu homeland and Chinese settlement in it banned. Meanwhile, held in check by the epidemics of the late 16th and the 17th centuries and by the rebellions and hostilities of the late Ming and early Ch'ing, the population trebled between 1650 and 1800, from 100 million to 300 million and continued to increase at a headlong pace, reaching 420 million by 1850. This constantly growing population had to be fed by ever more intensive cultivation of a limited area, and by the end of the 18th century population pressure was beginning to generate widespread hardship and impoverishment.

This hardship began to produce risings and rebel movements, usually inspired by secret societies, among the Chinese population. The first major outbreak was known as the White Lotus rebellion which erupted in the mountainous borderlands of Szechwan, Shensi and Hupeh in 1795–1804, and again on a lesser scale some years later. In Shantung a rebellion of the Eight Trigrams sect broke out in 1786–8, and in 1811 a large-scale rising of the Heavenly Principle sect took place in Honan, Hopeh (Chihli) and Shan-

tung, accompanied by an attempted coup in Peking, before its final suppression in 1814. More risings occurred among the border peoples: the Tibetans near Koko Nor in 1807, the Yaos in Kweichow in 1833, and in Sinkiang where the oases of Yarkand and Kashgar were in open rebellion from 1825 to 1828.

The basic economic problems of the country were exacerbated by government policies of external expansion, which placed a great strain on the empire's very inefficient financial administration. Another contributory factor was foreign trade: during the 17th and 18th centuries extensive export trades, mostly in tea, silk, porcelain and handicraft goods, grew up under government licence at Canton and with the Russians at Kyakhta. Since the Chinese economy was largely self-sufficient, these exports were paid for mostly in silver, the standard medium of currency in China. Late in the 18th century, however, the foreign powers began to import opium into China from India and the Middle East to pay for their exports. By the 1830s opium imports had outstripped Chinese exports of tea and silk, and a drain of silver out of China began, which had increasingly serious effects upon the economy and further impoverished the state finances.

Moreover, the quality of Ch'ing government began a sharp decline. In the late 18th century corruption became rife at every level of government from the court downwards, affecting both the civil administration and the Manchu armies whose demoralization, lack of supplies and equipment were highlighted by the White Lotus rising. Again, the administration did not increase to keep pace with the vast growth of population and by the early 19th century the bureaucracy was grossly understaffed, and government came to delegate more and more power to members of the local gentry who acted as their unpaid agents.

By the 1820s, Manchu China was the world's largest and most populous empire, directly controlling vast territories in inner Asia and treating as tributary states still larger areas: Korea, Indochina, Siam, Burma, Nepal. But within this huge empire, effective Ch'ing administrative and military control was gradually declining, while inexorable economic pressures increased which could be cured only by large-scale technological innovation and radical reorganization. Neither was imminent and in the meantime China faced new pressures from the expansionist Western powers.

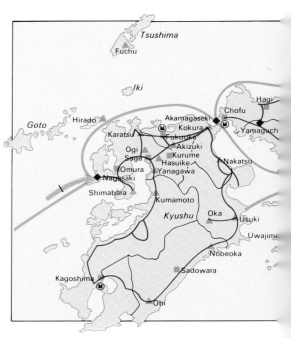

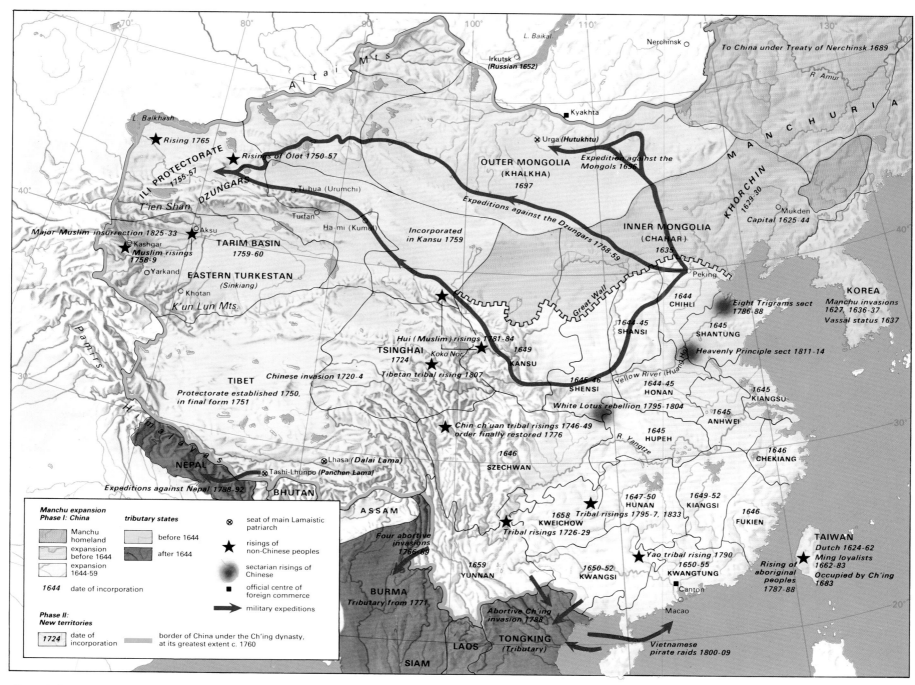

Map 1 labels (Chinese imperial expansion)

L. Baikal.
Nerchinsk
To China under Treaty of Nerchinsk 1689
R. Amur
Irkutsk (Russian 1652)
Altai Mts
Kyakhta
Rising 1765
Risings of Ölöt 1750-57
Urga (Hutukhtu)
OUTER MONGOLIA (KHALKHA) 1697
Expedition against the Mongols 1696
MANCHURIA
ILI PROTECTORATE 1755-57
T'ien Shan DZUNGARS
Tu-hua (Urumchi)
Expeditions against the Dzungars 1758-59
INNER MONGOLIA (CHAHAR) 1635
KHORCHIN 1629-30
Mukden
Capital 1625-44
Major Muslim insurrection 1825-33
Aksu
TARIM BASIN 1759-60
Turfan
Ha-mi (Kumul)
Incorporated in Kansu 1759
Peking
Kashgar
Muslim risings 1758-9
EASTERN TURKESTAN (Sinkiang)
Yarkand
Khotan
K'un Lun Mts
Great Wall
1644 CHIHLI
Eight Trigrams sect 1786-88
KOREA Manchu invasions 1627, 1636-37 Vassal status 1637
1643-45 SHANSI
1645 SHANTUNG
Heavenly Principle sect 1811-14
Pamirs
Hui (Muslim) risings 1781-84
TSINGHAI 1724
Koko Nor
1649 KANSU
1645-46 SHENSI
Yellow River (Huang Ho)
1644-45 HONAN
1645 KIANGSU
TIBET
Chinese invasion 1720-4
Protectorate established 1750, in final form 1751
Tibetan tribal rising 1807
White Lotus rebellion 1795-1804
1645 ANHWEI
Chin-ch'uan tribal risings 1746-49 order finally restored 1776
R. Yangtze
1645 HUPEH
Lhasa (Dalai Lama)
1646 SZECHWAN
1646 CHEKIANG
Tashi-Lhunpo (Panchen Lama)
NEPAL
BHUTAN
Expeditions against Nepal 1788-92
Himalayas
ASSAM
1647-50 HUNAN
1649-52 KIANGSI
1646 FUKIEN
Four abortive invasions 1766-69
1658 KWEICHOW
Tribal risings 1726-29
Tribal risings 1795-7, 1833
TAIWAN Dutch 1624-62 Ming loyalists 1662-83 Occupied by Ch'ing 1683
1659 YUNNAN
1650-52 KWANGSI
1650-55 KWANGTUNG
Yao tribal rising 1790
Rising of aboriginal peoples 1787-88
Canton
Macao
BURMA Tributary from 1771
Abortive Ch'ing invasion 1788
TONGKING (Tributary)
Vietnamese pirate raids 1800-09
LAOS
SIAM

Legend (Map 1)

Manchu expansion Phase I: China
Manchu homeland
expansion before 1644
expansion 1644-59
1644 date of incorporation

tributary states
before 1644
after 1644

⊗ seat of main Lamaistic patriarch
★ risings of non-Chinese peoples
sectarian risings of Chinese
■ official centre of foreign commerce
→ military expeditions

Phase II: New territories
1724 date of incorporation
border of China under the Ch'ing dynasty, at its greatest extent c. 1760

4/Japan in isolation (below) In 1603 Tokugawa Ieyasu, who had established military dominance over the Japanese state reunified in 1590 by Hideyoshi, was made Shogun (Military Leader) by the powerless imperial court. The shogunate he founded lasted until 1868 and gave Japan a much-needed period of political stability. A complex government emerged in which the many fiefs (han) of feudal lords (daimyo) – some 250 in number – were dominated and regulated by the Shogun's government (Bakufu) in Edo. Society was organized in a hierarchy of classes, and a legal code enacted. The Christian missionaries active in the late 16th century were banned after 1612, and Christians systematically persecuted in the 1630s. Japanese were forbidden to travel abroad, and foreign contacts were limited to the Dutch, who maintained a post at Nagasaki, the Chinese and Koreans. Despite this isolation, Tokugawa Japan was extremely prosperous. Trade and cities grew rapidly. The population rose from about 20 million in 1600 to about 30 million in the 18th century. By the 19th century Japan was prosperous, well governed, had a high standard of literacy, and was far better prepared than China to meet the challenge of Western expansion.

1/Chinese imperial expansion (above) Throughout the late 17th and the 18th centuries the Manchus pursued an expansionist policy which left them in control of the Amur region in the northeast, Mongolia, Dzungaria, the Tarim basin, the Ili region east of Lake Balkhash, and Tibet. Only a small part of these vast regions was incorporated under Chinese administration, and apart from military garrisons few Chinese or Manchus settled there. But these campaigns of conquest, triggered off in part by the fear of Russian expansion into Siberia and of British and French expansion into India, were immensely expensive. Chinese military expeditions went still further: four attacks on Burma in 1766-69, an expedition into Nepal in 1788-92, and a large-scale invasion of Tongking in 1788. All ended in failure. A series of widespread peasant rebellions occurred in the late 18th and early 19th centuries, usually inspired by millenarian sects. In almost every case they broke out in areas severely affected by the economic problems caused by population pressure.

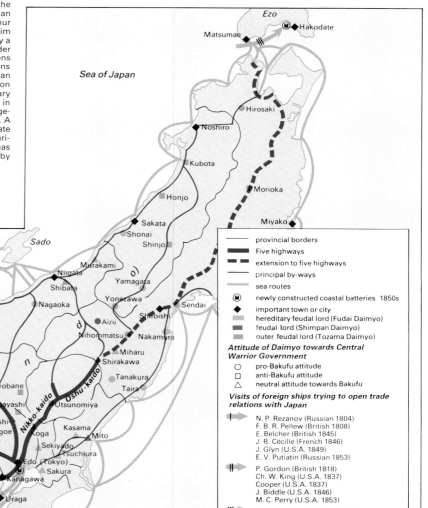

Map 2 labels (Japan)

Ezo
Matsumae
Hakodate
Sea of Japan
Hirosaki
Noshiro
Kubota
Morioka
Miyako
Honjo
Sado
Sakata
Shonai
Shinjo
Murakami
Oki
Niigata
Shibata
Yamagata
Yonezawa
Sendai
Nagaoka
Matsue
Tottori
Matsushiro
Takada
Toyama
Kanazawa
Aizu
Shiroishi
Tsuyama
Maruoka
Daishoji
Matsumoto
Nihommatsu
Nakamura
Hiroshima
Fukui
Sabae
Ueda
Miharu
Tanakura
Taira
Matsuyama
Obama
Takasaki
Shirakawa
Okayama
Sasayama
Miyazu
Kurobane
Fukuyama
Tatsuno
Himeji
Kameyama
Hikone
Kyoto
Nakasendo
Tateyashi
Kasama
Mito
Matsuyama
Marugame
Akashi
Hyogo
Fushimi
Yodo
Ise
Koshu-kaido
Oshi
Koga
Sekiyado
Tsuchiura
Shikoku
Kochi
Tokushima
Kishiwada
Osaka
Kameyama
Koriyama
Nagoya
Kuwana
Kawagoe
Oshu-kaido
Nikko-kaido
Ozu
Tsu
Nishio
Okazaki
Edo (Tokyo)
Sakura
Yoshida
Hamamatsu
Tokaido
Kanagawa
Hisai
Sumpu
Numazu
Odawara
Uraga
Kakegawa
Shimoda
Oshima

Legend (Map 2)

— provincial borders
━ Five highways
▪▪▪ extension to five highways
— principal by-ways
sea routes
Ⓜ newly constructed coastal batteries 1850s
◆ important town or city
hereditary feudal lord (Fudai Daimyo)
feudal lord (Shimpan Daimyo)
outer feudal lord (Tozama Daimyo)

Attitude of Daimyo towards Central Warrior Government
○ pro-Bakufu attitude
□ anti-Bakufu attitude
△ neutral attitude towards Bakufu

Visits of foreign ships trying to open trade relations with Japan
→ N. P. Rezanov (Russian 1804)
F. B. R. Pellew (British 1808)
E. Belcher (British 1845)
J. B. Cécille (French 1846)
J. Glyn (U.S.A. 1849)
E. V. Putiatin (Russian 1853)
⇒ P. Gordon (British 1818)
Ch. W. King (U.S.A. 1837)
Cooper (U.S.A. 1837)
J. Biddle (U.S.A. 1846)
M. C. Perry (U.S.A. 1853)
⇛ A. K. Laxmann (Russian 1793)

Southeast Asia and the European powers 1511 to 1826

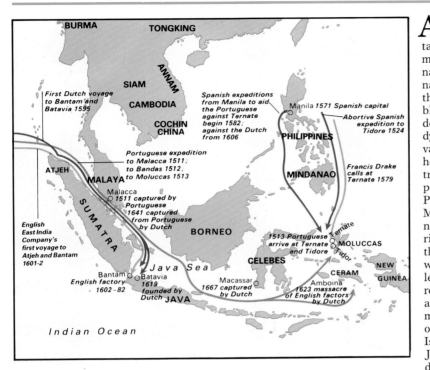

2/The spice routes (*above*) The Portuguese first appeared in the Moluccas and Bandas in 1512-13 and Francis Drake visited Ternate in 1579. The Dutch began to trade with them in 1599 and though the Anglo-Dutch treaty of 1619 provided for joint trading, the Dutch forced their partners out. The Spaniards in Manila came to the aid of the Portuguese in the Moluccas, and a long struggle ensued before the Dutch gained full control.

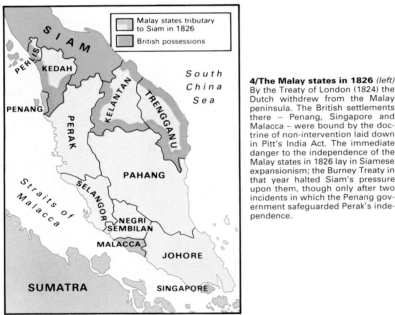

4/The Malay states in 1826 (*left*) By the Treaty of London (1824) the Dutch withdrew from the Malay peninsula. The British settlements there – Penang, Singapore and Malacca – were bound by the doctrine of non-intervention laid down in Pitt's India Act. The immediate danger to the independence of the Malay states in 1826 lay in Siamese expansionism; the Burney Treaty in that year halted Siam's pressure upon them, though only after two incidents in which the Penang government safeguarded Perak's independence.

3/Dutch expansion in Java (*below*) Dutch territorial expansion in Java began through Sultan Agung of Mataram's attempts to capture Batavia. After his death in 1646 the Dutch East India Company, by intervening in succession disputes, gradually became the strongest polit-ical force in the island, with the ruling houses coming under its control and paying their debts by cessions of territory. The maintenance of its trade monopoly played a vital part in this expansion.

AT THE beginning of the 16th century Burma consisted of four monarchies: Arakan (capital Myohaung), Burmese Ava, dominating the main Irrawaddy valley, Burmese Toungoo, dominating the Sittang valley, and Mon Pegu, dominating the Irrawaddy delta and Tenasserim. To the north and east of Ava a number of formidable Shan states threatened Burmese independence, but half a century later the Toungoo dynasty conquered both Shans and Mons. In the valley of the Chao Phraya the ruler of Ayutthaya headed a powerful Thai kingdom which controlled much of the eastern coast of the Malay peninsula, while the Laotian kingdom of Luang Prabang stretched along the upper and middle Mekong. The Vietnamese of Tongking and northern Annam had in 1471 annexed Cham territories down to Qui Nhon and later absorbed the remaining Cham lands to the south before wresting the Mekong delta from Cambodia, leaving Phnom Penh the capital of the much reduced Khmer kingdom. In the Malay archipelago the Javanese empire of Majapahit was little more than a memory, having split into hundreds of small states with little cohesion. However Islamization was spreading through Sumatra, Java and Borneo, chiefly from Malacca which dominated the Malay states of the peninsula and Sumatra's east coast.

In 1511, in the name of the king of Portugal, Alfonso de Albuquerque conquered the great emporium of Malacca but, its ruling family escaped and established the Sultanate of Johore inland, with much the same territorial sway as Malacca had exercised over the mainland Malay states and those of the Sumatran coast opposite. The Portuguese objective was to dominate the spice trade through a chain of forts linked by naval power and, had they united, the Malay states might have driven out the invaders; but Atjeh in Sumatra strove against Johore for the leadership of the Malay world, and it was left to the Dutch East India Company, formed in 1602, to conquer the Portuguese settlements.

Meanwhile the Spaniards established themselves in the Philippines, capturing Manila in 1571 and making it their capital. At the time of the Spanish occupation, the Philippines had no political organization except for the Muslim states on Mindanao and these, in alliance with the sultans of the Sulu archipelago, maintained their independence until the 19th century. From their centre at Batavia in western Java the Dutch controlled the Moluccas and Banda islands, the 'Spice Islands', reducing the local rulers to retainer status. In 1641 they took Malacca from the Portuguese but their attempts to wrest Manila from the Spanish all failed.

Like the Portuguese, the Dutch empire began as one of fortified trading posts based upon sea power. But Sultan Agung of Mataram (1613–46), campaigning for supremacy over Java, failed

twice to conquer Batavia and from the 1670s his successors became dependent upon Dutch aid in their constant succession struggles, paying for it by cessions of territory. The Sultanate of Bantam, with its immensely valuable pepper trade, came under Dutch control in the same way in 1684. The staff of their weaker rival, the English East India Company, were expelled from its factory there and the settlement transferred to the pepper port of Benkulen on the west coast of Sumatra. After the 'Massacre of Amboina' in 1623 the Company abandoned direct trade to the Spice Islands and relied upon obtaining spices indirectly through Macassar in the Celebes (Sulawesi) but in 1667 that source too dried up with the Dutch conquest of the port.

The mainland monarchies of Arakan, Burma, Siam, Cambodia, Luang Prabang and Annam had little interest in European trade. They employed Portuguese adventurers as mercenaries in the 16th century, but the attempts of the latter to seize power in Lower Burma and Cambodia at the end of the century caused strong xenophobia. This increased in the next century as a result of the behaviour of the Portuguese freebooters (*feringhi*) and the attempts of the Dutch to monopolize Siam's foreign trade. To check the Dutch, King Narai (1661–88) and his Greek adviser, Constant Phaulkon, made the mistake of invoking French aid. Louis XIV's takeover bid, involving the planting of French garrisons at Bangkok and Mergui, stirred up strong popular reaction which led both to a change of dynasty at Ayutthaya and to the expulsion of the French, with heavy loss of life.

Burma became the scene of dramatic events when the Mons rebelled in 1740 and set up a king of their own at Pegu. Their capture of the Burmese capital, Ava, in 1752 brought a new Burmese leader, Alaungpaya, to the fore. Joseph Dupleix at Pondicherry intervened on the side of the Mons and the English East India Company at Madras responded by seizing the island of Negrais at the mouth of the Bassein river as a naval base. Alaungpaya defeated the Mons and their French allies, founding Rangoon in 1755 as the southern port of a reunited Burma, and in 1759 captured Negrais from the British who subsequently left Burma altogether.

By that time the English East India Company's expanding trade with China had encouraged it to look for a more southerly site for a naval station, and in 1786 it acquired Penang for this purpose from the Sultan of Kedah. The conquest of the Dutch Republic in 1795 by French revolutionary armies provoked the British to occupy Malacca and a number of Dutch settlements in the archipelago. In 1811 Java was conquered but after the fall of Napoleon in 1815, the British restored their gains in Southeast Asia to the Dutch. New tensions arose, however, when Raffles acquired Singapore for the British, and the conflict only ended with the Anglo-Dutch treaty of 1824 which drew a dividing line through the Straits of Malacca. As a result the British abandoned their west Sumatran settlements and the Dutch handed over Malacca and recognized British possession of Singapore. Borneo, omitted from the treaty, became the subject of further disagreement between the two parties when, in the 1840s, James Brooke assumed the title Rajah of Sarawak.

After failing to make good its conquest of Siam in 1767, the aggressive dynasty founded by the Burmese leader Alaungpaya switched its efforts westwards to Arakan, Manipur and Assam, which it conquered and from which it threatened Bengal. The first Anglo-Burmese war of 1824–6 which resulted led to the annexation of Assam, Arakan and Tenasserim by British India and measures to stabilize India's northeast frontier. Arakan's once-famous rice industry revived through contact with India but the great development of Burma's rice production and the

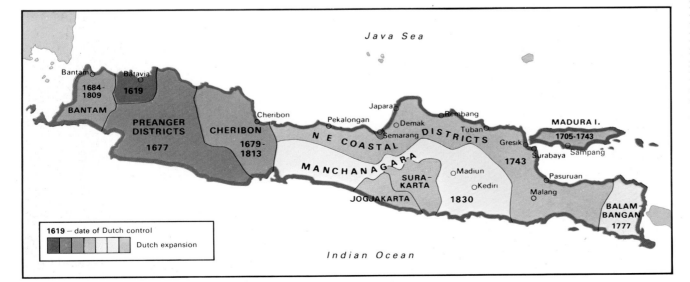

1619 – date of Dutch control
Dutch expansion

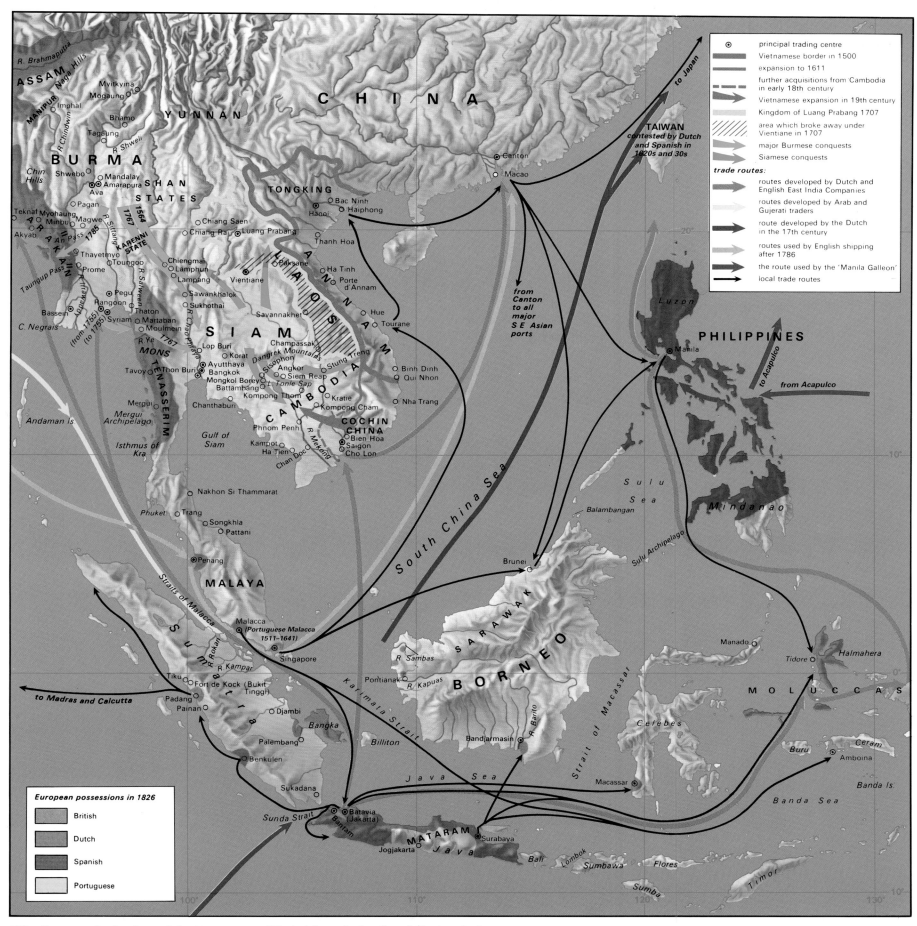

trade routes: (legend)

- ⊙ principal trading centre
- Vietnamese border in 1500
- expansion to 1611
- further acquisitions from Cambodia in early 18th century
- Vietnamese expansion in 19th century
- Kingdom of Luang Prabang 1707
- area which broke away under Vientiane in 1707
- major Burmese conquests
- Siamese conquests

trade routes:
- routes developed by Dutch and English East India Companies
- routes developed by Arab and Gujerati traders
- route developed by the Dutch in the 17th century
- routes used by English shipping after 1786
- the route used by the 'Manila Galleon'
- local trade routes

European possessions in 1826
- British
- Dutch
- Spanish
- Portuguese

1/The Europeans in Southeast Asia *(above)* The increasing European demand for spices and pepper led the maritime powers to seek direct trade with the islands producing them, thereby opening new fields for the missionary and the adventurer. The Dutch drove all their rivals out of the spice trade; Spain took over the Philippines. European activities made little impact upon the mainland monarchies, but in the 18th century brought coffee, China tea and *chinoiserie* into European social life.

systematic exploitation of its teak forests only began after the British occupation of the Irrawaddy delta region in the wake of the second Anglo-Burmese war of 1852.

European activities seldom impinged upon the economies of the Southeast Asian states before the 19th century, when the Industrial Revolution created an increasing demand for raw materials, markets and openings for capital investment. Great Britain's impact was minimal until the foundation of Singapore in 1819 as a free trade port. Earlier, the Spaniards had sought to keep the Philippines incommunicado, but the Manila Galleon, trading with Acapulco

(Mexico), brought the silver dollar into the international trade of the western Pacific. After the British occupation of 1762–4 temporarily opened Manila to world commerce, the Spaniards began to foster the cultivation of tobacco, sugar, hemp and other commercial products, some of which became important in world markets, though Manila itself was not officially opened to foreign traders until 1834.

At an earlier stage the Portuguese and the Dutch had forced their way into the long-established spice and pepper trades and their counterpart, the import of Indian textiles into Southeast Asia. In the 18th century the Dutch introduced coffee cultivation into the parts of Java they directly controlled, but their policy of 'buy cheap, sell dear' bore heavily upon the peasantry. Nevertheless the principle of free peasant cultivation was maintained until 1830 when, with the introduction of the so-called 'Culture System', the Javanese were compelled to devote one-fifth of their land to export crops designated by the government.

Guns and fortresses played an essential role in defending European trade overseas. The fortifications of Manila, Batavia and Malacca rivalled those of Europe in size and strength; while even smaller but well-defended forts at outposts such as Macao *(right)* sufficed to protect Western merchants and assure favourable terms of trade.

173

The European economy: agriculture and agricultural society 1500 to 1815

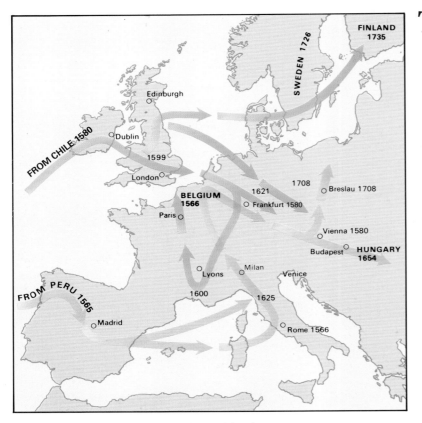

2/The introduction of the potato to Europe *(above)* Yielding four times as much carbohydrate per acre as wheat, this South American import spread rapidly after its arrival in 1565 – first in gardens and small farms, then as a key field crop after 1700.

3/Land Reclamation in the Netherlands *(left)* Between 1540 and 1715 the people of Friesland, Zealand and Holland wrested 364,565 acres from the sea, mainly around the river estuaries, and another 84,638 acres (34,278 ha) from the edges of the inland lakes. Their capital-intensive methods, based on widespread use of windmills and pumps, were adapted, with great success, to draining the English fenlands, and, to a lesser extent, in France, Italy and North Germany.

THE agricultural economy of early modern Europe as a whole improved only slowly, mainly in response to the needs of the steadily rising population which grew from about 70 to 190 million between 1500 and 1800. But there were sharp regional contrasts. Whereas the majority of European farmers were subsistence peasants on smallholdings of from 5 to 25 acres (2 to 10 ha), the situation in northwest Europe, especially in Britain and the Low Countries, was quite different. There an agricultural revolution beginning in the 16th century had produced a highly efficient, commercialized farming system by 1800. Most farms elsewhere, however, still consisted of many small parcels of ground distributed throughout the village lands. Each farm usually had a small adjacent enclosed paddock and sometimes an orchard. Techniques and levels of productivity had hardly changed since Roman times and most peasants probably produced only about 20 per cent more each year than they needed to feed their families and their livestock, and to provide the next year's seed. Consequently, in most countries, about 80 per cent of the people worked on the land. In Britain and the Low Countries, however, the proportion fell rapidly during the later 18th century – down to 33 percent in Britain by 1811 – as improved agriculture provided the food requirements of the growing industrial towns and cities.

Except in Britain and the Netherlands, most improvements in this period came from the introduction of new, more productive crops, mainly from America. Thus the potato became a basic staple in western Europe, starting in Spain and Italy. In Ireland it allowed such a massive increase in population (from 2.5 to 8 million) that disaster struck when the crop failed in 1846. American maize, like the potato, gave a far higher yield than the established cereals – bar-

ley, millet and sorghum – and was widely adopted in southern Europe.

Buckwheat, useful on poor soils, entered northern Europe from Russia while, in the Mediterranean, sugar cane, rice and citrus fruits had arrived from Asia before 1500. Sugar production declined after 1550, however, in the face of competition from Madeira, the Canaries and, after 1600, the West Indies and Brazil.

These slow crop changes contrasted strongly with the rapidly developing northwest. The Dutch began the process by pouring capital into reclaiming land from the sea. Naturally wishing to avoid leaving land fallow every third year (as under the traditional system), they discovered that fertility could be maintained by simple crop rotation involving the alternation of arable with artificial grasses and industrial crops such as rapeseed, flax and dyestuffs (especially madder). Turnips, on which sheep could be grazed in winter producing manure as well as mutton and wool, were especially important, as were peas, beans and clovers, all of which restored nitrogen to the soil. English farmers, often encouraged by progressive landlords, copied and developed these innovations. Irrigation, massive drainage schemes and woodland clearance increased the productive acreage, while land enclosure and soil treatments (especially marling and liming) encouraged improved husbandry. By the 1740s, grain exports accounted for one-tenth of England's total export earnings, and the old fear of starvation had been banished.

Such techniques gradually spread as the growth of towns encouraged more specialization in food production. Holland concentrated on dairy products and was exporting 90 per cent of her cheese by 1700. The Danes were sending

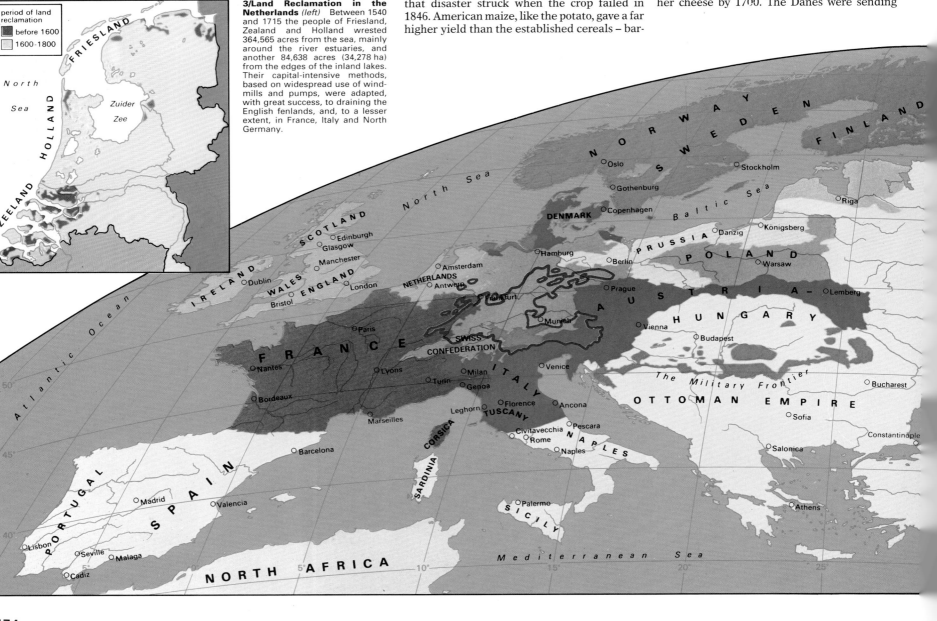

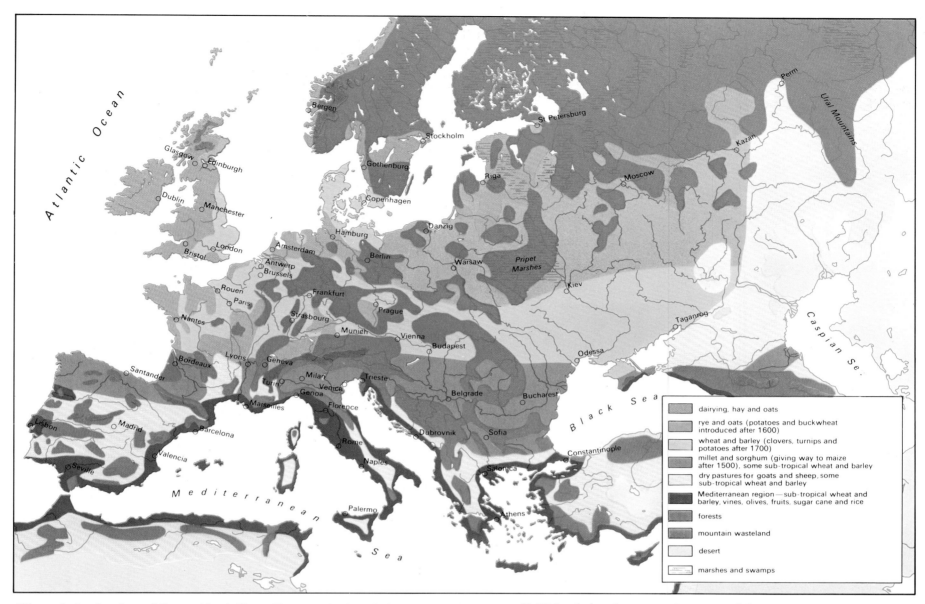

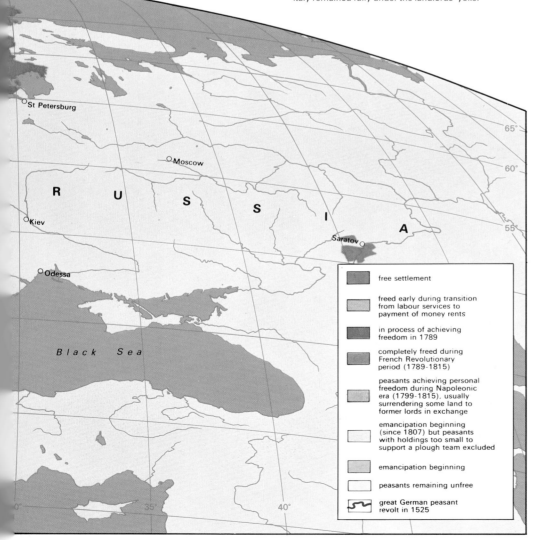

4/The agricultural regions of Europe *(above)* The main areas are shown as they were in 1600, distinguished by predominant activity or crops. Boundaries are only approximate. Potatoes gradually took over from cereals in many parts of northern and central Europe, while maize in the south replaced millet and sorghum.

Map legend:

- dairying, hay and oats
- rye and oats (potatoes and buckwheat introduced after 1600)
- wheat and barley (clovers, turnips and potatoes after 1700)
- millet and sorghum (giving way to maize after 1500), some sub-tropical wheat and barley
- dry pastures for goats and sheep, some sub-tropical wheat and barley
- Mediterranean region—sub-tropical wheat and barley, vines, olives, fruits, sugar cane and rice
- forests
- mountain wasteland
- desert
- marshes and swamps

1/The emancipation of the peasantry *(below)* By 1812, the peasants of Britain, Scandinavia and the Netherlands had long been free. Those of Denmark and the Habsburg's Austrian Empire, were encouraged in their efforts by the revolution of 1789, which unshackled the French peasantry and revivified emancipation movements in Poland and Germany, scene of the most famous peasant revolt (1525). Only Russia, Spain, Portugal and Southern Italy remained fully under the landlords' yoke.

Map legend:

- free settlement
- freed early during transition from labour services to payment of money rents
- in process of achieving freedom in 1789
- completely freed during French Revolutionary period (1789-1815)
- peasants achieving personal freedom during Napoleonic era (1799-1815), usually surrendering some land to former lords in exchange
- emancipation beginning (since 1807) but peasants with holdings too small to support a plough team excluded
- emancipation beginning
- peasants remaining unfree
- great German peasant revolt in 1525

80,000 head of cattle a year to Germany, and the Dutch, German and Italian cloth industries were sustained by massive imports of Spanish wool. The exchange of northern Europe's cereals and timber for the fruits, wines and oils of the Mediterranean lands grew apace, with Danzig and Leghorn as the leading *entrepôts*.

All improvements in productivity depended on breaking the old feudal relationships which oppressed the peasants, however, and here there was a sharp east-west cleavage. Prior to 1500 feudalism had been stronger in the older settled areas of western Europe than in the sparsely peopled lands of eastern Europe and Russia. After 1500 this changed completely: peasants in northwest Europe exchanged the traditional labour services on their lords' land for a money rent (especially in England and the Netherlands) or, in France and farther south, for share-cropping tenancies (*métayage*). They also gradually freed themselves from burdensome personal services and dues, though this required revolutionary action, inspired by France in 1789, before it was complete.

In total contrast, feudal power grew and spread in eastern Europe until it became almost slavery. Feudal lords increased their power, halting migration to empty lands farther east (as in Russia) and increasing grain-export profits (as in eastern Germany and Poland-Lithuania). Free peasants only survived in newly conquered lands if they agreed to perform military service instead of paying rent. Notable examples were the Volga Cossacks around Saratov and the settlers on the 'military frontier' in Hungary after it was freed from the Turks in the early part of the 18th century.

The peasants of western Germany occupied a middle position. They had tried to win complete freedom in a great revolt in 1525, and for a short time they controlled most of southern Germany before their revolt was savagely crushed. Yet the worst east European excesses were averted, and the peasants gradually moved towards greater freedom between 1600 and 1800. Their slow emancipation was, however, an important reason why the German industrial revolution came so late.

Jethro Tull's Seed Drill *(above)* Described in Tull's *Horse Hoeing Husbandry* (1733) this machine gradually ousted wasteful hand-scattering.

Developments in Animal Breeding 1 *(above)* Robert Bakewell's New Leicester long-wool sheep had a decisive influence on animal husbandry.

Developments in Animal Breeding 2 *(above)* The Colling brothers' short-horn cattle helped start a new world industry.

The European economy: trade and industry 1550 to 1775

Baling press *(above)* from a German textile mill, used to prepare cloth for transportation. Even before 1700 expanding woollen and linen industries in Saxony and Bohemia began to encroach on traditional English and Flemish markets.

3/Atlantic trade in the 18th century *(left)* Slaves and tropical produce from the new colonial empires made fortunes for all the main west European ports from Cádiz to Glasgow, shown here according to the size of their trade.

EUROPE'S population expanded fast in the 16th century, was retarded by famine, plague and large-scale war in the 17th, and did not register rapid growth until the middle of the 18th century. The total population nearly doubled during this period, and towns and cities grew even faster. In 1500 only five cities – Constantinople (by far the largest), Paris, Milan, Naples and Venice – had more than 100,000 inhabitants. By 1700 this number had almost trebled, and London, Paris and Constantinople had passed the half-million mark.

The increased complexity of government, a marked acceleration of trade and finance, a growing taste for organized pleasure and conspicuous consumption, and a feeling that survival was better assured in the cities, all helped to hasten this trend. The resulting problems, particularly the need to guarantee large and reliable urban food supplies, also created new opportunities. Most notably, until the mid-17th century, they generated a massive demand for eastern Europe's wheat and rye, great quantities of which went to western Europe, reaching even as far as Portugal, Spain and Italy. This trade fed the burgeoning economic strength of Holland, now nearly monopolizing the Baltic carrying trade.

The Netherlands, whose shipbuilders, merchants and manufacturers consistently maintained a leading position in this period, formed the hinge for a gradual but decisive shift in commercial power. In 1500 industry remained largely concentrated in the narrow corridor running from Antwerp and Bruges, through Ulm and Augsburg, to Florence and Milan (see pages 142–3). Although English woollens, French linens and Spanish iron all possessed international reputations and markets, the main non-agricultural activity, whether it was in textiles and weapons, or in newer developments like paper, glass, printing and cloth-making, all lay along this north-south line. By 1700 this axis had swung through almost 90 degrees. At one end stood Britain and the Dutch Republic, home of the greatest textile producers, the largest merchant fleets, the most active traders, and the most advanced ship and metalwares manufacturers in Europe; eastward the line extended through the metal and woollen districts of the lower Rhine to the great industrial concentrations in the hills of Saxony, Bohemia and Silesia. By contrast the great trading cities of northern Italy and the southern Netherlands, dominant two centuries earlier, were mostly stagnant after a severe decline.

The advance of technology was patchy and intermittent. The power-driven silk mills of the Po valley were the mechanical wonders of the 17th century, but were seldom imitated elsewhere. The spread of watch-making in the early 18th century created a repository of precision

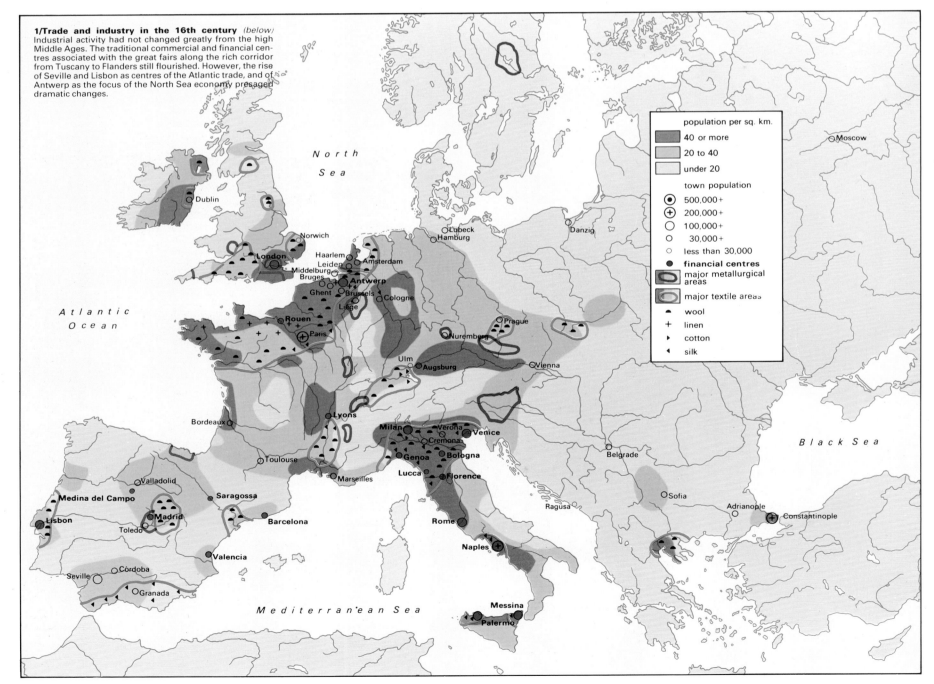

1/Trade and industry in the 16th century *(below)* Industrial activity had not changed greatly from the high Middle Ages. The traditional commercial and financial centres associated with the great fairs along the rich corridor from Tuscany to Flanders still flourished. However, the rise of Seville and Lisbon as centres of the Atlantic trade, and of Antwerp as the focus of the North Sea economy presaged dramatic changes.

population per sq. km.
- 40 or more
- 20 to 40
- under 20

town population
- 500,000+
- 200,000+
- 100,000+
- 30,000+
- less than 30,000
- **financial centres**
- major metallurgical areas
- major textile areas
- wool
- linen
- cotton
- silk

skills, and Newcomen's mine pump opened the way to the advance of the steam engine. But the crucial breakthrough to the age of steam, James Watt's separate condenser (1769), made its industrial impact only in the last years of the century. Industrial expansion was achieved by increasing the number of workers while still using the old methods. Even this, however, helped improve industrial organization, by splitting up production processes, developing production in rural areas free of urban restriction, and drawing on the cheap part-time labour of peasant families. Wool, linen and much metal manufacture was controlled by traders who organized a scattered cottage labour force. By the 18th century this had become the typical form of all but local and luxury industry.

More impressive than the slow and erratic spread of industry was the striking increase in international trade. No longer confined to Europe, the maritime powers, with their colonies and trading ports established all over Asia and the Americas, attracted a fast-growing stream of new exotic tropical products: tea, coffee, sugar, chocolate, tobacco. They were purchased with European manufactures – the British linen and metalware industries particularly thrived on the expanding colonial markets – and with the shipping, insurance and merchandising services that built up the wealth of the western ports, all the way from Bordeaux up to London, Glasgow and Hamburg. All these became the seats of wealthy merchant firms and great shipping interests.

Governments assisted those sectors of economic activity that they favoured. Holland and England waged wars to protect and expand their shipping and trading interests, but did not consistently aid industry. The governments of France and the central European states, by contrast, established new industries and gave pro-

tection and subsidies to old ones. Increasingly costly wars, however, had an influence even more powerful than explicit economic policies. They called for heavy taxation, with the burdens falling largely on the producing classes, and large borrowings that undermined the precarious stability of Europe's gradually evolving monetary systems. The wars were ruinous to Spain and damaging to France and many smaller states; only Britain and the Dutch Republic kept their military commitments within realistic financial bounds.

Trade and war also generated an unprecedented demand for money. After being in desperately short supply, gold and silver were amply provided from Spanish Mexico and Peru after 1550, supported from the 1690s by Brazilian gold. This bullion was redistributed all over Europe by merchants and by Spanish government transactions, much of it going to finance Europe's large trade deficits with the East Indies and the Levant. The money supply was also supplemented by the growth of banking in western Europe: breaking away from the older banking methods of Italy and the German towns, which were heavily engaged in government lending, Dutch and English banks served private interests with giro and foreign exchange facilities and short-term credits. For a century, almost from its opening in 1609, the Amsterdam Exchange Bank, with links in every important commercial centre, was the undisputed focus of continental trade; Britain could compete with it only when, after 1694, the Bank of England provided a focus for older private banking firms.

With low interest rates, free capital movement, secure international payments and an assured savings flow, the foundations of modern finance were now firmly laid in Britain and the Dutch Republic.

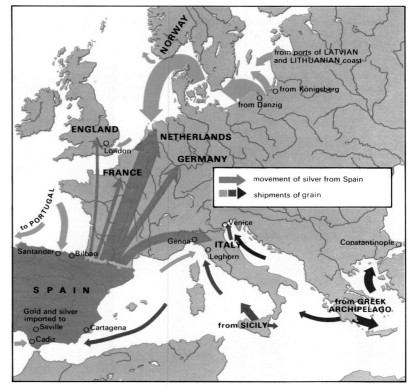

4/Grain trade and silver flows within Europe 1550-1650 *(above)* The bullion-bearing galleons from the Indies brought a flood of liquid funds to the Spanish treasury. But it flowed out as fast as it arrived, both to finance Habsburg imperialism and to pay for the Baltic grain now needed to victual a Mediterranean no longer able to feed itself.

2/Trade and industry in the 18th century *(below)* Dramatic changes occurred even before the Industrial Revolution. Italy and Spain lost ground, while England (with major metal-working and mining interests), Holland (building ships for the whole of Europe), France (behind a high protective wall), and Sweden (exploiting her mineral resources), all forged ahead fast.

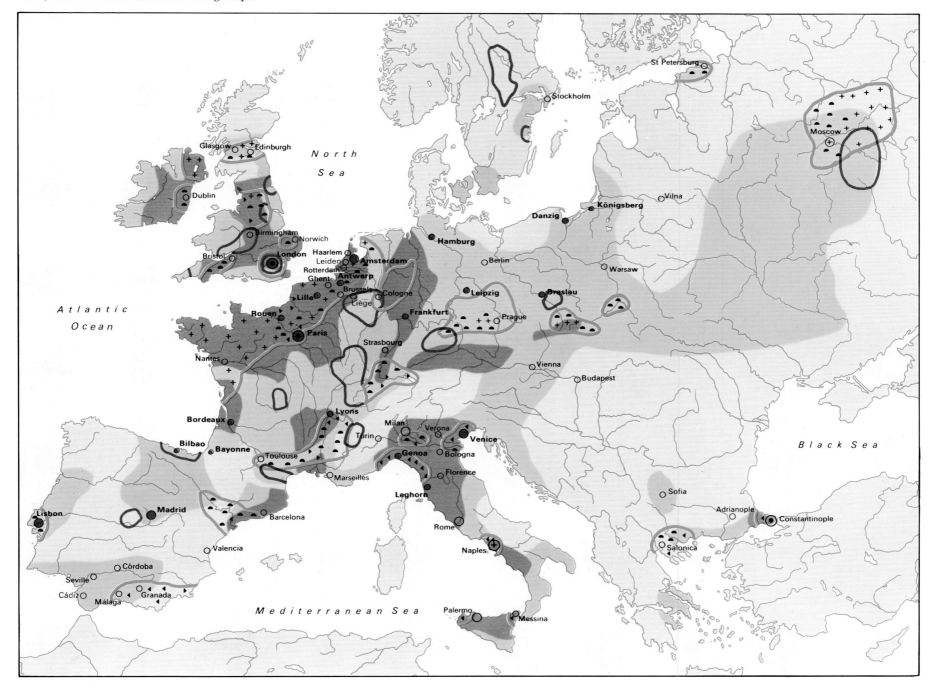

Reformation and counter-reformation: the wars of religion in Europe 1517 to 1648

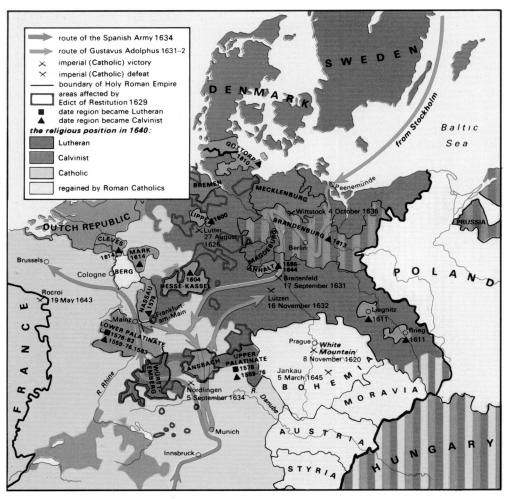

2/**Religious wars crippled France** (below) between 1562 and 1598 and again between 1621 and 1629. By 1562 French Protestants (known as 'Huguenots') numbered over one million – perhaps five per cent of the total population – with strong bases in Paris, the northwest and the south of the kingdom. Catholic military pressure, coupled with popular hostility (most notably the Massacre of St Bartholomew in 1572), virtually eradicated Protestantism north of the Loire, but by 1598 the movement still retained sufficient strength to secure from the crown the right to garrison numerous towns and a number of special courts to guarantee toleration (the Edict of Nantes). These concessions were withdrawn in 1629, after another war, but toleration continued until 1685 when the government unilaterally revoked the Edict of Nantes.

3/**The Thirty Years' War, 1618-48** (above) redrew the religious and political map of central Europe. In the first phase (1618-29), the Habsburgs and their Catholic supporters extirpated Protestantism in Bohemia, Moravia, Austria and Styria, and reclaimed church lands in Germany secularized by Protestant rulers (the Edict of Restitution). This provoked an invasion by Gustavus Adolphus of Sweden, supported by French subsidies and several North German princes (1631-2). Only the intervention of a powerful Spanish army in 1634 checked the Protestant revival. After fourteen more years of ferocious fighting the participants agreed, by the Peace of Westphalia, to concede perpetual toleration to Lutheran and Calvinist worship wherever it was embraced by secular rulers and to allow the German states political and religious autonomy.

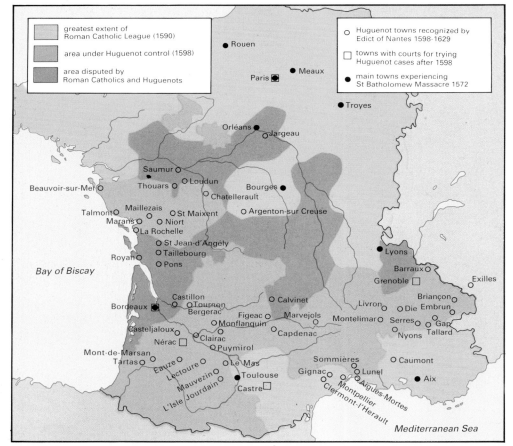

RELIGION held a central place in the lives of the people of early modern Europe. It elevated and dignified every major action in their lives, from birth and baptism to death and burial, and it held out the hope of salvation. The need for reassurance about the after-life appears to have been particularly acute in the years around 1500.

At first this spiritual revival was contained within the existing churches: Roman Catholic in the west and Greek Orthodox in the east, with the frontier running through Poland-Lithuania (two-fifths Orthodox) and the eastern and southern fringes of Hungary to reach the Adriatic just south of Ragusa. The only important groups outside these two monolithic communities were the Jews, the Lollards (a small and fragmented group of English dissenters), the Muslims in southern Spain, and the Hussites (including over half the population of Bohemia and Moravia). 'Heresy' was thus virtually dead in 1500 and, faced by no substantial rivals, the Roman Catholic church became complacent and failed to deploy its wealth adequately to satisfy the 'spiritual hunger' of the early 16th century. Clerical absenteeism, for example, increased and numerous ignorant and immoral priests discredited the Church in the eyes of many laymen. It was the conjuncture of a spiritually bankrupt yet materially acquisitive church at a time of heightened religious awareness which explains why a religious revolution occurred in the 16th century.

Within only 50 years, almost 40 per cent of the inhabitants of Europe accepted a 'Reformed' theology. The first reformers came from Germany and German-speaking Switzerland, led by Martin Luther (1483–1546) in north Germany, and Huldreich Zwingli (1484–1531) in Zurich (the first state to renounce allegiance to Rome, in 1520) and the surrounding areas. By 1570, out of every 10 subjects of the Holy Roman Emperor, 7 were Protestants. The Protestants already held Scandinavia, Baltic Europe and England. There was a limited penetration of France, Spain, Italy and the Netherlands, and of the German settlements in eastern Europe.

Then came a new wave of Protestantism, the work of John Calvin (1509–64), a Frenchman, who implemented his ideas from 1541 in the city-state of Geneva. Calvinism made swift progress: in France there were over 100 Calvinist churches by 1559 and perhaps 700 by 1562; in the Netherlands, there were perhaps 20 Calvinist churches by 1559 and over 150 by 1566; in Germany, several Lutheran states (most notably the Palatinate and Brandenburg) changed their official religion to Calvinism; and in Scotland a complete reformed polity was established by act of Parliament in 1560. Calvin's church also achieved some striking successes in eastern Europe, especially in Poland and Transylvania, two countries which also tolerated the existence of other minority groups in some numbers: Unitarians, Bohemian Brethren, Anabaptists and Jews. In Hungary and in other areas under Ottoman control, Catholic worship was prohibited and Calvinism received official protection. Calvinism also won more adherents among the Slavs, both noble and middle class, than Lutheranism.

Religious toleration was often fragile, however. In many countries, including the Holy Roman Empire, it was the product of weakness rather than strength, and it only occurred in countries where the state was not strong enough to impose the religious uniformity which in early modern times was considered essential to political survival. It was inevitable that the 'states without stakes' would disappear as soon as their governments became powerful enough to enforce a single faith on all their subjects. Less predictable was that the chosen faith after 1570 should so often have been Catholicism.

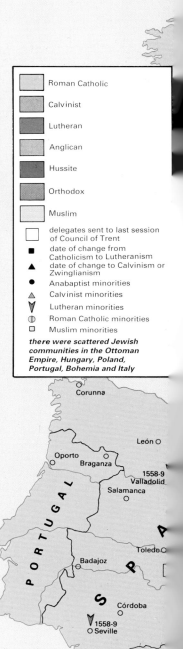

Not everyone who wished to reform the Church in the earlier 16th century rejected the authority of the Pope. Ignatius Loyola (1491–1556), founder of the Jesuit order, was just one of the many who decided that the best way to achieve salvation was to remain obedient to Rome and to persuade others to do the same. Eventually even the Papacy began to accept the need for some reforms, and delegates from all over Europe attended the General Council of the Church held at Trent, on the border between Italy and Germany. There were three sessions (1545–7, 1551–2 and 1562–3) which achieved three things: condemnation of the worst clerical abuses; definition of the precise doctrine of the Church (the *professio fidei tridentina*); and the creation of an efficient system of ecclesiastical supervision, to maintain clerical standards. In addition, an educational offensive was mounted to promote orthodoxy among the laity.

With the aid of this revitalized organization, the Catholic Church began to regain some of its losses. The Protestant 'share' of the European continent fell from 40 to 20 per cent between 1570 and 1650. In Poland, the largest country of eastern Europe, a succession of kings actively favoured Catholicism, and the number of Protestant churches in the country fell from around 560 in 1572 to only 240 in 1650.

Much the same happened in the Habsburg lands further south: the Protestants were expelled from Austria (1597) and from Styria (1600). In France, the crown and the militant Catholic League waged war for decades in order to contain the Protestant challenge. Although there were perhaps 1.25 million Protestants in France in 1562, by 1685, when the remainder were forced to choose between conversion to Catholicism or expulsion, scarcely 500,000 remained.

The decisive phase of the struggle between Protestants and Catholics took place in the Holy Roman Empire. It began in 1618–21 when Emperor Ferdinand II, with the aid of troops and treasure from Spain, the German Catholics and the Papacy, defeated the Bohemian Protestants. Catholicism soon became the only permitted religion in Bohemia and Moravia.

Encouraged by this success, the Emperor tried to reduce the power of the Protestant princes in Germany. Despite the aid sent to the princes by England, Denmark and the Dutch Republic, in 1629 the Emperor's forces were victorious and an 'Edict of Restitution' was issued which reclaimed large areas of Church land held by the Protestants. The German Protestants were only saved from collapse by the arrival of substantial military aid from King Gustavus Adolphus of Sweden: the Emperor's forces were defeated at Breitenfeld (1631) and badly mauled at Lützen (1632). But Spain intervened in 1634 to help the Emperor, and France in 1636 to help his enemies, turning the war into a free-for-all with fighting spreading to almost the whole continent. The political as well as the religious rivalries of over a century were settled at the great battles of Nördlingen (1634), Wittstock (1636), Rocroi (1643) and Jankau (1645), and at the Peace of Westphalia which followed (see page 186). The religious and political frontiers of central Europe which were then agreed lasted unchanged for 100 years.

Spreading the word of God (above) Of the 250,000 or so works printed in Europe between 1447 (the date of the earliest surviving printed book) and 1600, about three-quarters were written about religion. The Reformation would have been impossible without printing-presses like this one, which graced the cover of a book printed in Paris in 1511.

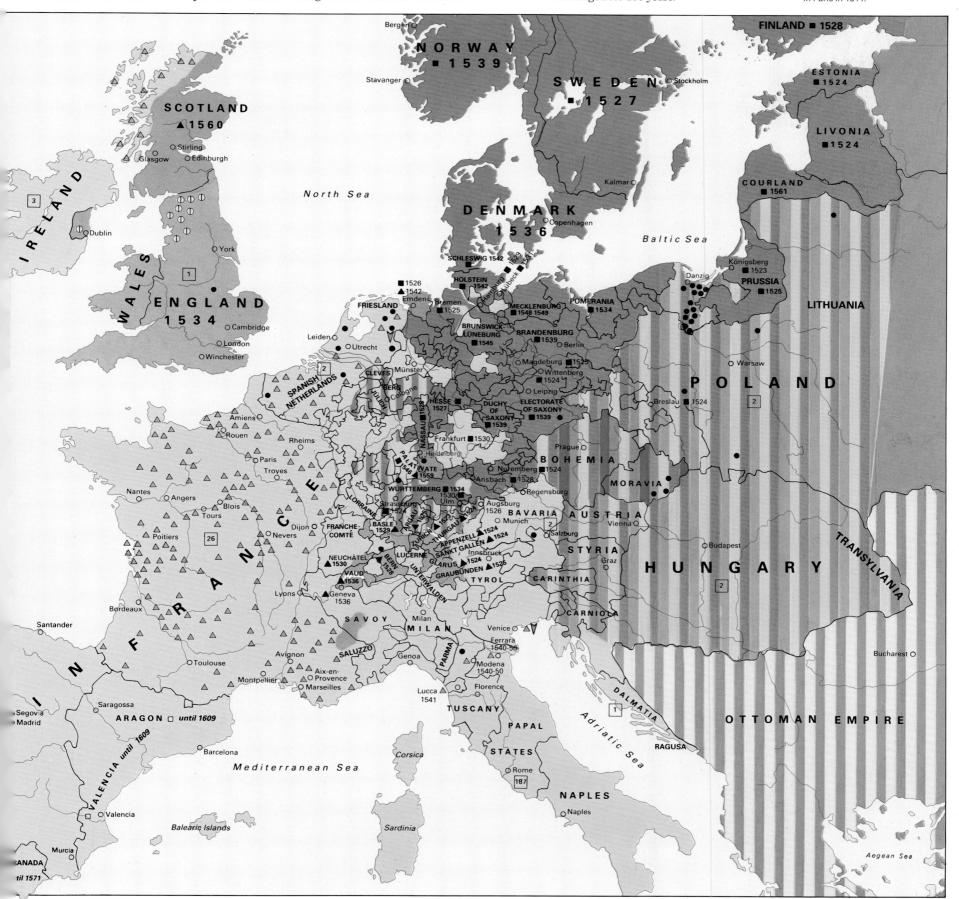

The rise of the modern state in northwest Europe 1500 to 1688

The Universal Soldier (above)
This cartoon, first printed in the 1640s as propaganda against the English Parliamentary army in Ireland, reflects the civilians' hatred of the ill-fed soldier who enforced government policies while taking everything he needed from the local people – down to the sausages of his shoe buckles!

DESPITE their apparent strength, until 1660 the 'new monarchies' of Europe (see page 146) never entirely escaped from the framework of government which they had inherited. The wealth, bureaucracies, control of religion and standing armies were not sufficient to break the patterns of personal dependence which had characterized monarchy in the feudal period (see page 122). The state still relied on the goodwill of its nobles for the enforcement of its policies (in England, for example, the Tudors depended upon unpaid Justices of the Peace, always local landowners, to apply their laws), and failure to retain the support of the landed classes could provoke major revolts. The French aristocracy staged several rebellions against the crown, culminating in the Fronde (1648–53); a section of the English aristocracy rebelled against Elizabeth I in 1569–70 (the 'Northern Rising') and many English peers supported Parliament's stand against Charles I after 1640; nobles of the Netherlands opposed their 'natural prince', Philip II of Spain, in 1566, 1572 and 1576.

The Fronde, the English Civil War and the Dutch Revolt were only the most important of the rebellions which threatened the 'new monarchies' of northwest Europe: uprisings against the state were a continuing fact of life throughout the 16th and 17th centuries. Some revolts arose from attacks on the privileges of the 'estates'; others were caused by economic hardship – from taxes imposed at a time of high prices and widespread unemployment, as was the case in most French popular revolts, or from the enclosing of common land, which caused the revolts of 1549 and 1607 in England. Other uprisings (the Pilgrimage of Grace of England in 1536 and the Covenanting Movement in Scotland in 1638) were triggered by unpopular religious policies. In all cases the revolts were a response to attempts at innovation. Governments everywhere were endeavouring to create, in the words of James VI of Scotland soon after he became King of England in 1603: 'one worship to God, one kingdom entirely governed, one uniformity of laws'. The problem, however, was one of means, not ends. Neither James nor any of his fellow sovereigns had the resources to enforce such ambitious new policies. They lacked the revenues and the officials required. Even in France, which had the largest civil service in Europe, most of the 40,000 royal officials either bought their offices or acquired them by hereditary succession and could thus pursue a course independent of the crown. They became a distinct aristocratic caste – the *noblesse de robe*.

The barriers to centralization in early modern times were formidable. Many subjects did not speak the same language as their government (Breton and Provençal in France, Cornish and Welsh in England, Frisian in the Netherlands); there were many 'dark corners of the land' which were too inaccessible to be effectively governed; certain 'corporations', notably the Church, possessed privileges which protected them against state interference; and provinces recently annexed by the crown (see page 146) were protected by charters guaranteeing their traditional way of life. The most serious political upheavals occurred when the state tried to erode or remove these privileges: the Dutch rebelled in 1566, 1572 and 1576 largely because they believed that the central government, controlled from Spain, threatened their traditional liberties; and they continued their armed opposition until 1609, when Spain, in effect, recognised the independence of the seven provinces still in rebellion. The Dutch Rebellion was born

(see map 1). In England, Parliament began a civil war against Charles I in 1642 because it believed that he intended to destroy the established rights of 'free-born Englishmen'; they too maintained their armed resistance, with the help of the Scots, until the power of the king was shattered in battle, and Charles himself was tried and executed in 1649 (see map 2). The English Republic, which survived for 11 years, immediately set about reducing the independence of Scotland and Ireland, and created for the first time a unified government for the British Isles. Although Charles' son was restored in 1660 with full powers and even a small standing army, another revolt in 1688, supported by the Dutch, drove James II into exile and ensured that the power of the crown in England would never again be absolute. Although opposition in France did not go to such lengths, the absolutist policies and fiscal exactions of Cardinal Mazarin (1602–61), chief minister of Louis XIV, so alienated the crown's officials, the nobles and the people of Paris that in 1649 they drove the king from his capital and forced him to make major concessions. Royal control was not fully restored until 1655.

In all three countries, however, the structure of the state survived. None of the rebels seriously questioned the need for strong government, only the location of that strength. 'The question was never whether we should be governed by arbitrary power, but in whose hands it should be', wrote an English republican in 1653, and in England the 'great rebelion' gave rise to a strikingly modern state. After 1660, and even more after 1688, power was shared between Parliament, representing merchants and landowners, and the crown; but the power was absolute, even after 1707, when Scotland was incorporated to form Great Britain. In France, the failure of the Fronde cleared the way for the absolutism of Louis XIV (see page 188). In both France and England the last major effort to resist the rise of the central power and defend local autonomy had failed; there was to be no further 'great rebellion' for over a century. The Dutch Revolt, however, did protect local independence against central encroachment. Despite the preponderance of Holland within the Republic, the other six provinces retained a large measure of autonomy. But this decentralized system, reminiscent of the 15th century, seriously weakened the Dutch, particularly in commercial competition with France and Britain. The Dutch were at a permanent disadvantage in a world which permitted no profit without power and no security without war. No sooner had they broken free of Spain (the independence asserted in 1609 was formally recognized in 1648) than they were attacked on land by France (1672–8 and 1689–1713), and at sea by England (1652–3, 1665–7 and 1672–4). The strain and expense of these wars proved too much, and Dutch strength declined. The 18th century and its profits – particularly in the colonial world – would belong to the newly unified modern states, France and Great Britain.

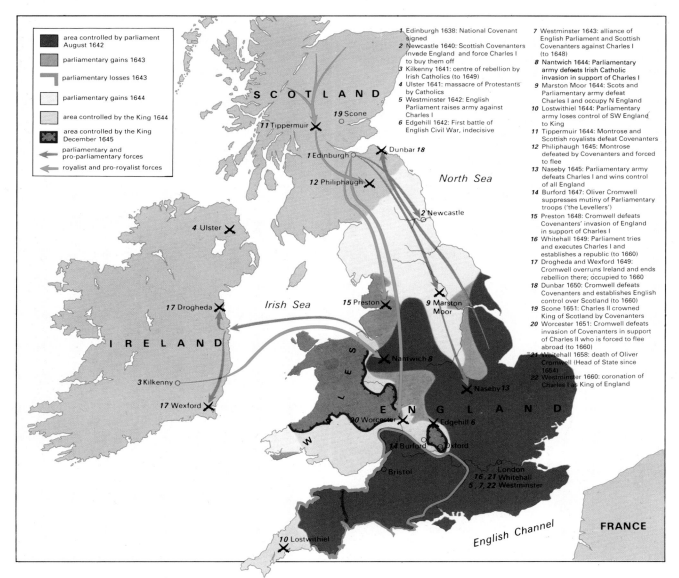

1 Edinburgh 1638: National Covenant signed
2 Newcastle 1640: Scottish Covenanters invade England and force Charles I to buy them off
3 Kilkenny 1641: centre of rebellion by Irish Catholics (to 1649)
4 Ulster 1641: massacre of Protestants by Catholics
5 Westminster 1642: English Parliament raises army against Charles I
6 Edgehill 1642: First battle of English Civil War, indecisive
7 Westminster 1643: alliance of English Parliament and Scottish Covenanters against Charles I (to 1648)
8 Nantwich 1644: Parliamentary army defeats Irish Catholic invasion in support of Charles I
9 Marston Moor 1644: Scots and Parliamentary army defeat Charles I and occupy N England
10 Lostwithiel 1644: Parliamentary army loses control of SW England to King
11 Tippermuir 1644: Montrose and Scottish royalists defeat Covenanters
12 Philiphaugh 1645: Montrose defeated by Covenanters and forced to flee
13 Naseby 1645: Parliamentary army defeats Charles I and wins control of all England
14 Burford 1647: Oliver Cromwell suppresses mutiny of Parliamentary troops ('the Levellers')
15 Preston 1648: Cromwell defeats Covenanters' invasion of England in support of Charles I
16 Whitehall 1649: Parliament tries and executes Charles I and establishes a republic (to 1660)
17 Drogheda and Wexford 1649: Cromwell overruns Ireland and ends rebellion there; occupied to 1660
18 Dunbar 1650: Cromwell defeats Covenanters and establishes English control over Scotland (to 1660)
19 Scone 1651: Charles II crowned King of Scotland by Covenanters
20 Worcester 1651: Cromwell defeats invasion of Covenanters in support of Charles II who is forced to flee abroad (to 1660)
21 Whitehall 1658: death of Oliver Cromwell (Head of State since 1654)
22 Westminster 1660: coronation of Charles II as King of England

Key:
- area controlled by parliament August 1642
- parliamentary gains 1643
- parliamentary losses 1643
- parliamentary gains 1644
- area controlled by the King 1644
- area controlled by the King December 1645
- parliamentary and pro-parliamentary forces
- royalist and pro-royalist forces

2/Civil War in the British Isles, 1642-60 (left) At first, most of north and west England rallied to Charles I, while most of the east and south supported Parliament; Ireland was paralyzed by a bitter civil war of its own; and Scotland stayed neutral. The campaigns of 1642 brought small Parliamentary gains in the northwest but heavy losses in the southwest, and the king seemed likely to win until 1643, when Parliament secured the support of the Scottish Covenanters (who had signed the National Covenent in 1638 against Charles I's attempt to impose the English liturgy). In 1645 Charles was decisively defeated at Naseby and his Scottish lieutenant, Montrose, was routed at Philiphaugh, but the king managed to ally with the Covenanters against Parliament. In 1647 the Parliamentary army was weakened by mutinies in favour of a more democratic government (the 'Levellers' movement), but the troubles were suppressed swiftly and the army moved on to defeat the Covenanters at Preston (1648), Dunbar (1650) and Worcester (1651) and to subjugate Ireland (1649). Charles I was tried and executed (1649) and a republic was created which extended English control over the entire British Isles until 1660, when monarchy was restored.

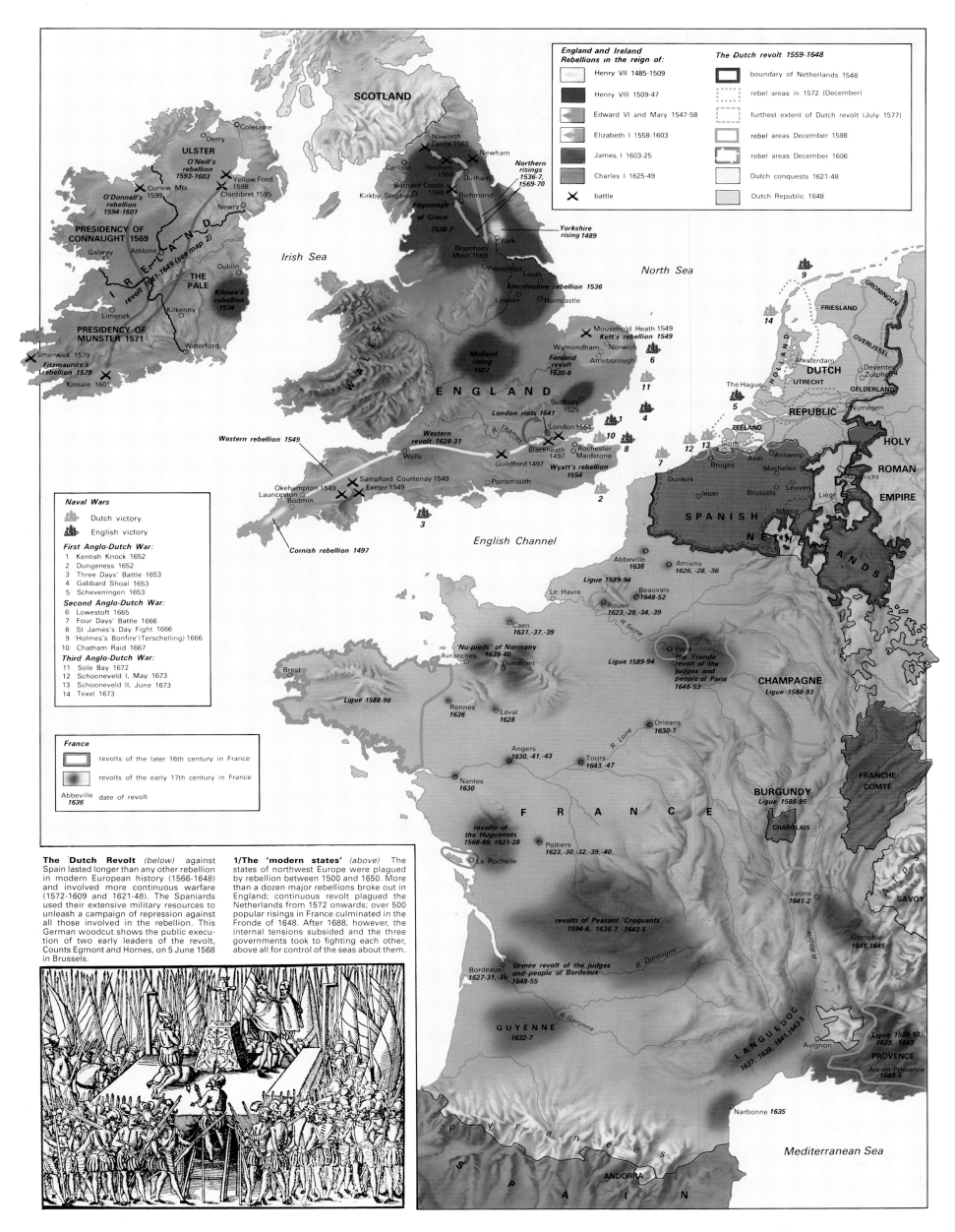

England and Ireland
Rebellions in the reign of:
- Henry VII 1485-1509
- Henry VIII 1509-47
- Edward VI and Mary 1547-58
- Elizabeth I 1558-1603
- James, I 1603-25
- Charles I 1625-49
- ✕ battle

The Dutch revolt 1559-1648
- boundary of Netherlands 1548
- rebel areas in 1572 (December)
- furthest extent of Dutch revolt (July 1577)
- rebel areas December 1588
- rebel areas December 1606
- Dutch conquests 1621-48
- Dutch Republic 1648

Naval Wars
- Dutch victory
- English victory

First Anglo-Dutch War:
1 Kentish Knock 1652
2 Dungeness 1652
3 Three Days' Battle 1653
4 Gabbard Shoal 1653
5 Scheveningen 1653

Second Anglo-Dutch War:
6 Lowestoft 1665
7 Four Days' Battle 1666
8 St James's Day Fight 1666
9 'Holmes's Bonfire' (Terschelling) 1666
10 Chatham Raid 1667

Third Anglo-Dutch War:
11 Sole Bay 1672
12 Schooneveld I, May 1673
13 Schooneveld II, June 1673
14 Texel 1673

France
- revolts of the later 16th century in France
- revolts of the early 17th century in France
- Abbeville *1636* date of revolt

The Dutch Revolt (below) against Spain lasted longer than any other rebellion in modern European history (1566-1648) and involved more continuous warfare (1572-1609 and 1621-48). The Spaniards used their extensive military resources to unleash a campaign of repression against all those involved in the rebellion. This German woodcut shows the public execution of two early leaders of the revolt, Counts Egmont and Hornes, on 5 June 1568 in Brussels.

1/The 'modern states' (above) The states of northwest Europe were plagued by rebellion between 1500 and 1650. More than a dozen major rebellions broke out in England; continuous revolt plagued the Netherlands from 1572 onwards; over 500 popular risings in France culminated in the Fronde of 1648. After 1688, however, the internal tensions subsided and the three governments took to fighting each other, above all for control of the seas about them.

The Mediterranean world 1494 to 1797

IN THE three centuries from 1494 to 1797 the Mediterranean world underwent two dramatic changes. First the primacy of the Italian cities was lost as the sea became the theatre of a power-struggle between two multi-national empires whose interests were only partly Mediterranean: the Spanish Habsburgs and the Ottoman Turks. Second, in the 17th century the whole area lost significance as initiative and sea-power, even in the Mediterranean, passed to the Atlantic nations.

The loss of Italian primacy was precipitated by the creation of the Habsburg Empire. Charles V, elected Holy Roman Emperor in 1519, ruled not only the Habsburg lands in Austria, South Germany and the Netherlands, but also the realms bequeathed by his maternal grandparents, Ferdinand and Isabella, in Spain, Italy and North Africa

Each inheritance was soon significantly expanded. In 1526 his brother and close ally Ferdinand succeeded to the crowns of Bohemia (which included Moravia, Silesia and Lusatia) and Hungary, creating a huge Habsburg power block running from the Adriatic almost to the Baltic. In 1535 Charles himself acquired both Lombardy and Tunisia, and throughout his reign the dynasty's holdings in the Netherlands grew (see page 146, map 2). Above all, in America, his Castilian subjects toppled first the Aztec and then the Inca state (see page 154).

Although Charles V's empire was divided at his death in 1558, with the central European lands passing to Ferdinand, Charles's son Philip II still ruled a formidable inheritance. He, too, was able to extend it. From 1571 the Philippines were added by conquest; between 1580–3 Portugal and her overseas possessions by inheritance. In the process, the first empire in history on which the sun never set was created.

This state-building had serious consequences for Italy. Spanish viceroys ruled Naples, Sicily and Sardinia, with a Spanish governor in Lombardy, while Spanish naval bases controlled the seas around Tuscany and Liguria. Throughout the 16th century, successive French attempts to gain a foothold in the peninsula all met with defeat.

Even the largest independent states of Italy lacked room for manoeuvre in the face of Spain's overwhelming strength. Genoa, with its colony of Corsica, was economically reliant on Spain, since 80 per cent of its seaborne trade was transacted with the territories of Philip II. Papal attempts to oppose the Habsburgs ended in catastrophe: the sack of Rome itself in 1527 and a humiliating invasion in 1556-7. Even Venice was threatened by Habsburg territories on all sides: Lombardy and Croatia by land and Brindisi by sea. Admittedly Spanish troops, treasure and galleys provided an effective defence for Italy against the Turks, ensuring that no part of the peninsula fell under Muslim control, as Otranto had done in 1480–1, and coming to the rescue of any beleaguered outpost, as at Malta in 1565. But the political costs of protection were high.

While Habsburg influence pushed along the northern coast of the Mediterranean to the Strait of Otranto, the Turks reached along the southern coast towards the Strait of Gibraltar. One by one, the North African outposts mostly established by Spain after the reconquest of the last Muslim kingdom in Spain, the kingdom of Granada, in 1492 came under Ottoman domination – Algiers (1529), Tripoli (1551), Bougie (1555) – while major expeditionary forces were wiped out at Mostagenem (1558) and Djerba (1560). In 1565 the Turks besieged Malta, to which the Knights Hospitallers of St John had been driven back from Rhodes in 1522. Though Malta was relieved, and despite the great naval victory by a combined Spanish-Papal-Venetian fleet at Lepanto (1571), the Ottoman tide was

not stemmed. The victory at Lepanto could not save the Venetian island of Cyprus from Turkish conquest, and the Sultan's fleet was soon rebuilt. As the Turkish Grand Vizir told a Venetian envoy: 'You have shaved our beard, but it will soon grow again; we have cut off your arm and you cannot grow another.'

Accordingly, in 1573 the Republic made a separate peace and the following year the Turks took Tunis from its Spanish defenders. Only the Ottoman decision to attack Persia saved Philip II, heavily committed to a war in the Netherlands, from further losses (see pages 166 and 180). In 1577 Spain gratefully concluded a truce with the Sultan.

The reduction of Turkish pressure in the western Mediterranean was now doubly necessary because Anglo-Dutch sea-power in the Atlantic had made the traditional route from Spain to the Netherlands too dangerous. The 'Spanish Road' connecting the Habsburg heartland, Spain and Italy, with Brussels and Vienna, became the lifeline of the Spanish Empire in Europe, carrying troops and bullion to sustain the Habsburg's wars in northern Europe.

Meanwhile commercial interest was bringing other powers into the Mediterranean. France maintained an informal alliance with the Turks after 1526 and Marseilles thrived on the eastern trade; the English Levant Company established itself in Constantinople in 1581; and from 1590 Dutch fleets brought Baltic corn, Norwegian timber and colonial wares into the Mediterranean.

To profit from this trade, the Grand Duke of Tuscany declared Leghorn (Livorno) a free port in 1593. To prey on it, northern pirates invaded the sea and joined the 'Barbary corsairs' who made Algiers into a great pirate city, the Croatian Uskoks of the Adriatic, and the Turkish corsairs of Albania, the Morea and Anatolia. In time of war, local rulers also invested in privateering and increased the need of trading nations for political stability on the seas.

In general, they achieved it. On the one hand, though the Turks acquired Crete from Venice after a long war (1645–69), they stayed out of the western Mediterranean; on the other, though Spanish control of Italy was challenged by France throughout the 17th century, the effective changes were dynastic, not territorial. Even when Louis XIV's grandson was established on the Spanish throne in 1713 (see page 188), the Mediterranean balance of power was preserved.

(see page 146, map 2)

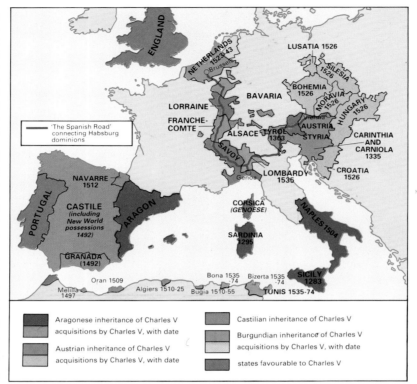

(see page 146, map 2)

2/The Habsburg Empire in Europe (left) Emperor Charles V was heir to four separate inheritances, one from each of his grandparents. From Ferdinand of Aragon he acquired Sicily, Naples, Sardinia and Aragon, adding Milan and Tunis in 1535. The legacy of Ferdinand's wife Isabella included Castile, Granada and the West Indies; Charles added Mexico (1519) and Peru (1533). Mary of Burgundy provided most of the Netherlands, and the Ottomans adding a number of provinces (see page 146, map 2). Her husband Maximilian of Habsburg bequeathed him Austria, Tyrol, Carinthia, Alsace and the title of Holy Roman Emperor; while Charles's brother Ferdinand added Bohemia, Moravia, Silesia and parts of Hungary in 1526.

3/Italy divided (right) From the collapse of Imperial power in the 13th century, down to the 18th century, northern Italy was divided into about 300 separate states. Although all were still technically 'imperial fiefs', whose rulers had to perform homage to the Holy Roman Emperor, they were effectively independent. A few (most notably Venice and Genoa) were republics; the rest were principalities controlled by members of some 60 aristocratic families. As long as this fragmentation lasted, foreign domination of the peninsula prevailed.

1/The struggle for power in the 16th century (below) The expanding power of Spain in the west and of the Ottoman Empire in the east frequently clashed in the Mediterranean. Spain was enriched by its new Atlantic acquisitions in the Americas, and the Ottomans by their Middle Eastern and Balkan gains. The turning point came in 1577-8, when Philip II and the Ottoman Sultan, both preoccupied with imperial concerns elsewhere, concluded an uneasy but lasting peace. Spain turned her attention northwards, to the Netherlands and Germany, while the Turks attacked Persia.

Aragonese inheritance of Charles V acquisitions by Charles V, with date	Castilian inheritance of Charles V
Austrian inheritance of Charles V acquisitions by Charles V, with date	Burgundian inheritance of Charles V acquisitions by Charles V, with date
	states favourable to Charles V

The Venetian Republic controlled extensive territories in the eastern Mediterranean and the Lion of Venice stood guard on coastal fortresses in Greece and the Balkans, as well as in Crete and (above) Cyprus. The lion stands on land as well as water, symbolizing the Republic's dominance of its hinterland as well as the Adriatic.

The Austrian Habsburgs secured Milan; after some exchanges, a branch of the Spanish Bourbons received Naples and Sicily; Sardinia was neutralized in the hands of Savoy; and Tuscany fell in 1737 to a junior branch of the Habsburgs.

Lesser principalities were similarly shared out. Only the republics of Venice, Genoa and Lucca remained relatively undisturbed. Genoa preserved its rule over Corsica, though challenged by a long revolt from 1755 to 1768; and Venice managed to cling to its possessions at the mouth of the Adriatic – Cattaro, Corfu, Levkas, Cephalonia, Zante – until the extinction of the Republic by Napoleon in 1797.

The principal guardian of this relative stability was Great Britain. British fleets had first entered the Mediterranean in force under Cromwell during the 1650s, to pursue royalist vessels and to chastise the Barbary pirates: Admiral Robert Blake bombarded Tunis and menaced the Bey of Algiers in 1655. From 1662 to 1683 Britain held Tangier, guarding the entrance to the Mediterranean; in 1704 it took Gibraltar from Spain and kept it. In addition Sardinia served as a British base from 1708 to 1714, and Minorca from 1708 to 1783.

But generally the British preferred diplomacy to direct control, until Napoleon's invasion of Italy and annexation of Egypt and Malta at the end of the 18th century convulsed the eastern and western Mediterranean alike and brought British naval power to dominate both.

	Venetian fortified centres
	Spanish Habsburg territory
	Austrian Habsburg territory
	Spanish client states
	Venetian territory
	Ottoman Empire and protectorates

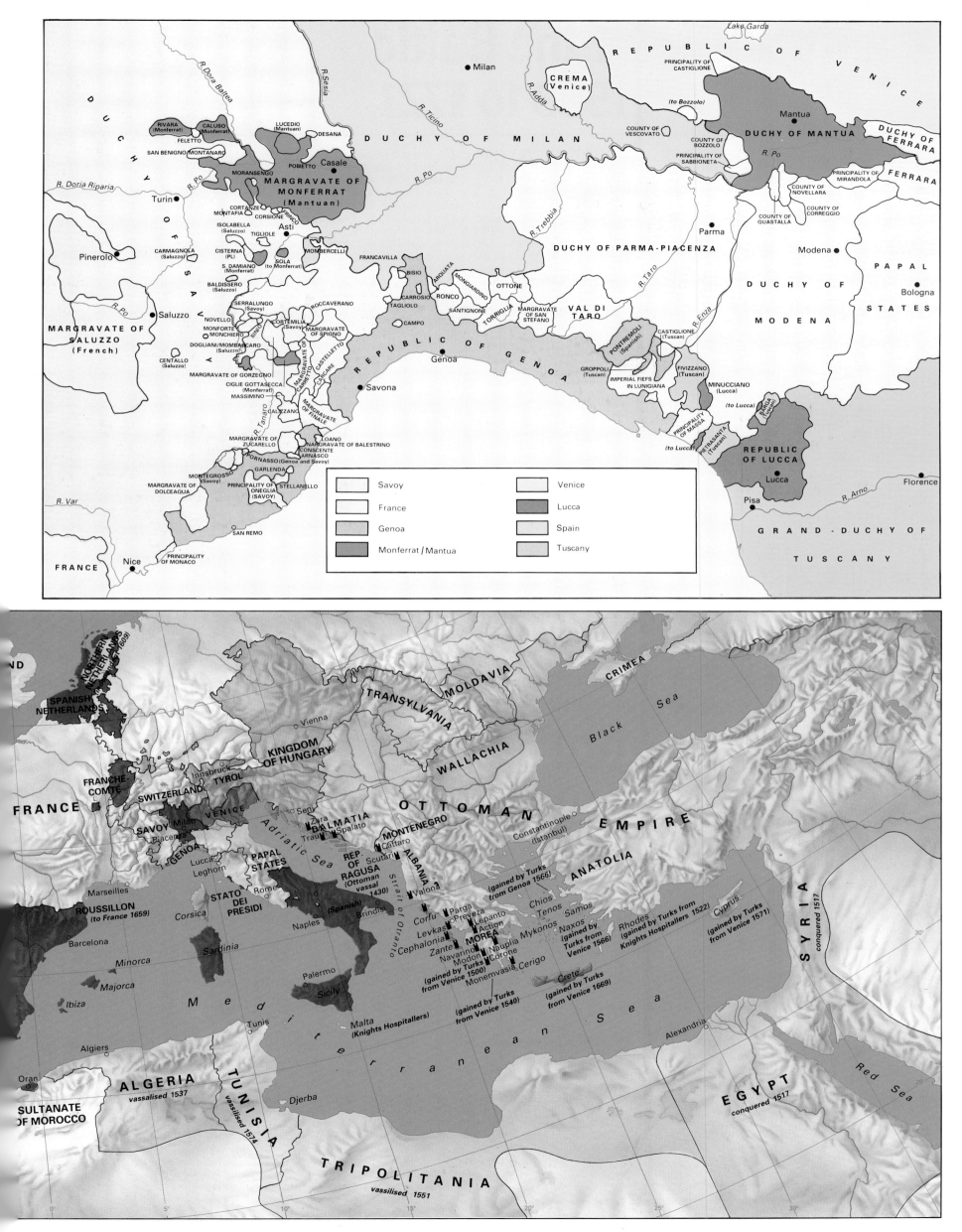

The struggle for the Baltic 1523 to 1721

1561 Reval, an independent Hanseatic port, threatened by the commercial rivalry of Viborg and Narva and the ambitions of Poland and Denmark to control Livonia, put itself under Swedish protection.

1595 Peace of Teusina added Narva and effectively the whole of Estonia, turned the Gulf of Finland into a Swedish waterway and pushed the northern borders across the Arctic Circle.

1617 Peace of Stolbovo confirmed possession of Estonia, added Ingermanland, Karelia and the river Neva, and cut off Russia, including its great trading city of Novgorod (sacked 1616), from all access to the Baltic.

1645 All Livonia became Swedish through the Armistice of Altmark (1629); the Peace of Brömsebro transferred Ösel, Gotland, Jämtland, Härjedalen and a 30-year control over Halland from Denmark-Norway.

1648 With the Peace of Westphalia ending the Thirty Years' War, Sweden gained West Pomerania, including the important ports of Stettin and Wismar, and the bishoprics of Bremen and Verden.

1658 Peace of Roskilde brought Scania, Blekinge, Bohuslän, Trondheim and Bornholm; but additional Swedish demands created a Danish-Dutch alliance, renewed war, rebellion in Scania and defeat at Funen (1660).

1660 After the death of Charles X, fighting ceased. The treaty of Copenhagen returned Trondheim and the island of Bornholm to Denmark, and formally abandoned Sweden's earlier attempts to close the Baltic to foreign warships.

1721 The treaties ending the Great Northern War (1700-21) marked the effective break-up of the Swedish Empire. In the east, Karelia and the Baltic provinces were lost, and in Germany, Bremen-Verden and most of West Pomerania.

THE Baltic is an almost land-locked, frequently ice-bound area of water covering over 166,000 square miles (430,000 km²). In early modern times it provided the great bulk of the timber, tar, pitch, hemp and flax for the ships with which England, Holland, France, Spain and Portugal built their world trading empires, as well as much of the grain needed to ensure the rest of the Continent against poor harvests, and the copper for its everyday money. The Sound Tolls, imposed on most of the commerce passing between the Baltic and the North Sea, gave Denmark (which usually controlled the narrow passages) a formidable source of wealth and power but created bitter rivalry with her neighbours. The resulting struggles, with their threats to security of supply, constantly interlocked with wider European affairs – the maritime jealousies of Britain, France and the Netherlands, the dynastic confrontation of Bourbon and Habsburg, the religious conflicts between Catholic and Protestant. There was thus much more than parochial significance in the complex Baltic power shifts of these 200 years, which saw the final decline of the Hanseatic League, Sweden's dramatic rise and eclipse, the waning of Denmark's power, the virtual elimination of Poland and the advance of Russia and Brandenburg-Prussia.

From 1397 to 1523, Denmark, Norway and Sweden were united in the Union of Kalmar but early in the 16th century Sweden finally broke away and re-established its independence under Gustavus Vasa (1523–60). Gustavus broke with Rome, adopted Lutheranism, and set about improving the country's economic, naval and military strength. Its initial position was extremely fragile: the only ice-free outlet to the North Sea consisted of an 11-mile (18-km) strip of coast between the Danish province of Halland and the Norwegian province of Bohuslän. Although defended by the fortress of Älvsborg, it fell several times to invading Danish forces. Denmark also controlled the southern shores adjoining The Sound, and a string of strategic islands, while the Hanseatic port of Lübeck, in return for its help in the wars of independence, was given a near-monopoly of Swedish foreign trade. This was broken, by a temporary alliance of Sweden and Denmark, as early as 1525, but the possibility of economic strangulation remained. In the east, too, the rising power of Muscovy openly coveted both Finland, under Swedish control since the 14th century, and the rapidly disintegrating territories of the Teutonic Knights south of the Gulf of Finland, which represented a major trading outlet for Gustavus Vasa's new port of Helsingfors. Gradually rising tensions under Gustavus's sons, Eric XIV (1560–8) and John III (1568–92), finally erupted in the Seven Years' War of the North (1563–70). On balance Sweden held her own in this struggle, although she had to pay a crippling ransom to Denmark for the return of Älvsborg, and by 1581 she was becoming a significant force even beyond the Baltic region.

Her role was complicated by dynastic and religious considerations: John III had married a Polish (and Roman Catholic) princess, and his son ascended the Polish throne in 1587 as Sigismund III. A major constitutional crisis followed when he also became king of Sweden on his father's death in 1592, but he was deposed in 1599, and his Lutheran uncle ultimately took the crown as Charles IX. Poland and Sweden, already deeply at odds over their opposing interests in Livonia, remained open enemies for 50 years. Indeed, at the accession in 1611 of Charles's 17-year-old son, Gustavus Adolphus, Sweden was ringed by hostile states, and her constitutional and financial weaknesses appeared to make a mockery of her long-held aim to turn the Baltic into a Swedish lake. Amazingly, by 1660 the dream had almost

become reality.

Gustavus's reign started with a serious setback. At the Peace of Knäred (1613) Sweden had to make further sacrifices to regain her fort of Älvsborg, lost to Denmark again two years before. However, the years from the Peace of Stolbovo to the Peace of Westphalia (1617–48) brought large new territories (see maps on left). Although Gustavus was killed in 1632, Sweden was now an international power.

Even before Westphalia, fear of Sweden's growing might had again brought war to Scandinavia: in 1643–5 Sweden fought Denmark, and in the resulting Peace of Brömsebro, Denmark lost Gotland, Ösel and Halland. Norway, too, had to part with substantial lands. Renewed Danish attacks while the Swedes under Charles X were embroiled with Russia, Brandenburg and Poland led to further Danish

The victory of Gustavus Adolphus at the Battle of Breitenfeld in 1631 *(above)* almost instantly made Sweden a Great Power. Although the king died the following year, Swedish forces retained many of the German territories occupied after Breitenfeld, as well as Livonia and other Baltic lands wrested from Poland and Russia.

humiliation. Attacking from the south, Charles occupied Jutland, led his troops across the frozen waters of the Great Belt in the winter of 1658 and threatened Copenhagen. At the Peace of Roskilde, Sweden was granted Scania, Blekinge, Bornholm, Bohuslän and Halland.

This was the climax. Henceforth Sweden's foes allied increasingly effectively against her. When Denmark invaded Scania and started the Scanian War (1676–9), Sweden was saved from territorial loss only by her French ally Louis XIV. After the cautious reign of Charles XI (1660–97), the tide turned. The old king was succeeded by his brilliant, impetuous 15-year-old son, Charles XII, and three years later the Great Northern War broke out, which in 20 years was to lay the foundations for the greatness of Russia and to erase Sweden and Poland from the ranks of the major powers.

The war started with the crushing victory of Narva, when Charles' troops decisively defeated a Russian army five times its size. But events in Poland (see page 192) side-tracked the Swedish forces. Peter the Great recaptured Narva (1704), annihilated the Swedes at Poltava (1709), and in the final peace treaties (1719–21) gained Livonia, Estonia, all of Ingermanland, Karelia and southeast Finland. With minor exceptions, former Swedish areas of Germany were divided between Hanover and the newly emergent state of Brandenburg-Prussia. Other naval powers, for whom a prime objective had always been to prevent the Baltic becoming a 'closed sea', regarded the decay of the Swedish Empire with relief.

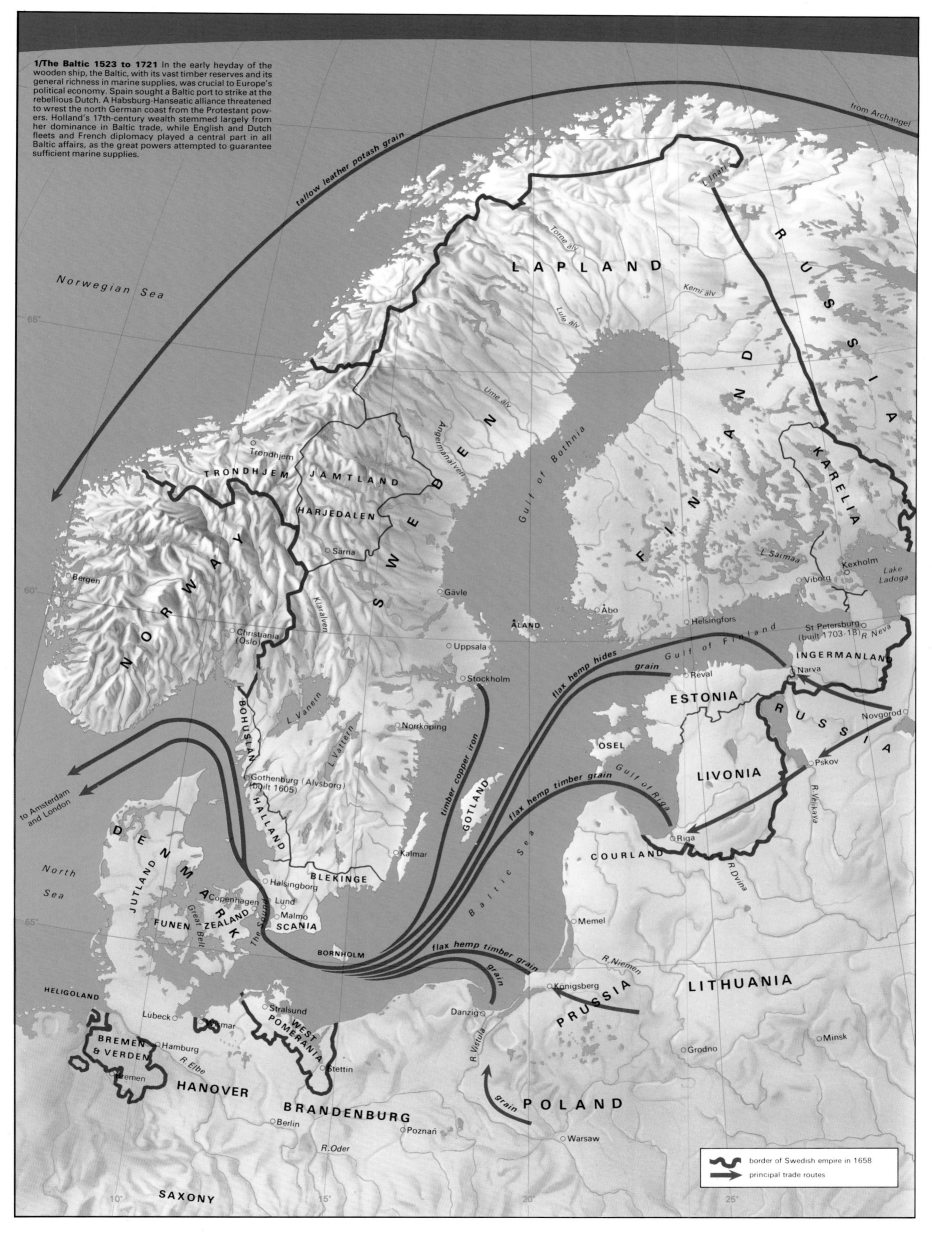

1/The Baltic 1523 to 1721 In the early heyday of the wooden ship, the Baltic, with its vast timber reserves and its general richness in marine supplies, was crucial to Europe's political economy. Spain sought a Baltic port to strike at the rebellious Dutch. A Habsburg-Hanseatic alliance threatened to wrest the north German coast from the Protestant powers. Holland's 17th-century wealth stemmed largely from her dominance in Baltic trade, while English and Dutch fleets and French diplomacy played a central part in all Baltic affairs, as the great powers attempted to guarantee sufficient marine supplies.

Norwegian Sea

from Archangel

tallow leather potash grain

LAPLAND

Torne älv

Kemi älv

R U S S I A

Lule älv

65°

Ume älv

Angermanälven

S W E D E N

Gulf of Bothnia

F I N L A N D

L. Inari

K A R E L I A

Trondhjem

TRONDHJEM   JÄMTLAND

HÄRJEDALEN

Klarälven

Sarna

L. Saimaa

Kexholm

Lake Ladoga

Viborg

60°

Bergen

N O R W A Y

Christiania (Oslo)

Gävle

Åbo

Helsingfors

St Petersburg (built 1703-18) *R Neva*

Uppsala

ÅLAND

INGERMANLAND

BOHUSLÄN

L. Vänern

Stockholm

flax hemp hides

grain

Gulf of Finland

Reval

Narva

Novgorod

HALLAND

L. Vättern

Norrköping

ESTONIA

R U S S I A

Gothenburg (Alvsborg) (built 1605)

timber copper iron

G O T L A N D

ÖSEL

LIVONIA

Pskov

R. Velikaya

flax hemp timber grain

Gulf of Riga

Kalmar

R. Dvina

Riga

North Sea

D E N M A R K

JUTLAND

Halsingborg

BLEKINGE

COURLAND

Copenhagen

Great Belt

FUNEN   ZEALAND

Lund

Malmö

SCANIA

The Sound

Baltic Sea

Memel

55°

BORNHOLM

flax hemp timber grain

grain

R. Niemen

LITHUANIA

to Amsterdam and London

HELIGOLAND

Königsberg

PRUSSIA

Lübeck

Stralsund

WEST POMERANIA

Danzig

grain

Minsk

BREMEN & VERDEN

Kalmar

Hamburg

R Elbe

Stettin

R. Vistula

grain

Grodno

Bremen

HANOVER

BRANDENBURG

POLAND

Berlin

Poznań

Warsaw

R. Oder

SAXONY

10°   15°   20°   25°

```
~~~>  border of Swedish empire in 1658
───>  principal trade routes
```

185

Germany disunited 1648 to 1806

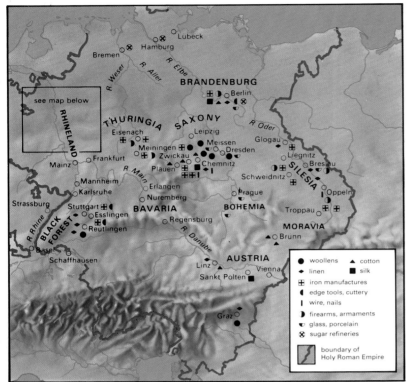

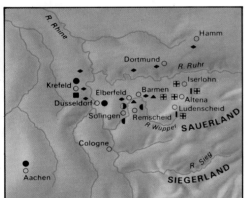

2/Industrial growth in the 18th century *(above)* Urban development centred on Vienna, Berlin, Hamburg and Bremen; textiles and iron enriched Saxony, Silesia and the lower Rhineland.

Meissen Harlequin and Columbine *(above)* The first Meissen factory opened near Dresden in 1710, after Böttger, an alchemist employed by the Elector of Saxony, succeeded in reproducing the translucency of Chinese porcelain with local clay. This piece dates from 1743.

THE Peace of Westphalia, signed in 1648, finally ended the religious and political differences that had caused the Thirty Years' War (see page 178). The Habsburg emperors lost most of their authority over the rulers of Germany, recognized the secularization of all church lands effected between 1555 and 1624, and granted full toleration to Calvinist as well as Lutheran secular rulers. Religion never again led to war within the Empire. However these achievements had a high price: on the one hand, Germany was ravaged and impoverished by 30 years of war; on the other, it was now divided into hundreds of separate states, some large but most small, with each ruler, Catholic or Protestant, lay or ecclesiastical, rich or poor, formally accorded a measure of sovereignty. The Reich still had common institutions, including a diet, or *Reichstag*, which sat permanently at Regensburg (where the most important delegate was probably the French ambassador) but their effectiveness was limited.

Among the mosaic of small, petty and 'duodecimo' states, only Austria represented a major force. Her preponderance was, however, increasingly based on the extent of the ruling Habsburgs' possessions outside Germany: in Hungary, Italy, and later the Netherlands. The few other princes of any importance likewise tended to derive their strength – and often their titles – from outside the Empire. The Elector of Brandenburg, raised to royal dignity in 1701, took his title from Prussia (outside the imperial boundary, and under Polish overlordship from 1461 to 1657). The Elector of Hanover became King of England in 1714, and the Elector of Saxony, King of Poland in 1697. Sweden ruled over Bremen and West Pomerania, and Denmark over Holstein, while France, always alert to extending her territories at German expense, annexed Franche Comté (1678), Strassburg (1681), the rest of Alsace (1697), and Bar and Lorraine (1766). Only the jealous vigilance of England, the Dutch Republic, Sweden and Russia prevented her from seizing much more.

The population of Germany, between 20 and 25 million on the eve of the 30-year struggle, was savagely reduced. The loss of life, which varied greatly from place to place but reached 70 per cent in some areas, was not made good until well

1/Germany in 1648 Germany was divided into 234 distinct territorial units, 51 free cities and a large number of estates of imperial knights. It was kept weak by religious division and dynastic rivalry. The map shows this extraordinary fragmentation in the west and the contrasting situation in the east, where large principalities had grown up as a result of medieval colonization and state-building outside the Empire. The eastern provinces of Prussia and Austria were to play the preponderant role in eventually unifying Germany.

	Austrian Habsburg
	Spanish Habsburg
	Wettin (Albertina)
	Wettin (Ernestina)
	Hohenzollern
	Franconian line
	Brandenburg line
	Wittelsbach
	Bavarian line
	Palatinate line
	Oldenburg lands
	ecclesiastical lands
	imperial cities
	Holy Roman Empire, 1648
	Swedish from 1648

into the 18th century. War also accelerated the economic decline which had set in around 1600. The great south-German commercial cities of Nuremberg and Augsburg (where the Fugger went bankrupt in 1627) suffered, like Venice, from the shift in trade from the Mediterranean to the Atlantic. The Hanseatic ports, once dominant in the Baltic and the North Sea (see page 142), failed to stem the growing power of the Dutch, and dissolved their League in 1669.

The rise of Prussia, begun under the Great Elector (1640–88) and continued by Frederick William I (1713–40) and his son Frederick the Great (1740–86), disguised the fragility of the Prussian state – quickly shown by its collapse in 1806. Certainly its rulers evolved a significant armoury of administrative and military institutions, as well as a highly characteristic set of social attitudes in the course of imposing order on their widely scattered territories. However, down to 1700, Brandenburg-Prussia was outstripped by Bavaria, and until the middle of the 18th century by Saxony, in wealth and population. It was only with the acquisition of Silesia (1742) and the successful conclusion of the wars which had been fought over that province with Austria (1763), that Prussia really began to affect the balance of power within the Empire. Not until the partitions of Poland was it possible to create a continuous Prussian territory extending from Memel to Magdeburg (see map 3).

Frederick the Great's forced industrialization programme, largely based on Silesia's iron and

3/The rise of Prussia The 1648 Peace, the weakening of Poland, inheritance, the northern wars (1655-60, 1700-21), and the War of the Austrian Succession (1740-8) enabled her Hohenzollern rulers to extend and consolidate the territories of Brandenburg-Prussia.

	Brandenburg in 1648
	Prussian acquisitions 1648-1707
	acquisitions 1715, 1720
	acquisitions 1742, 1744, 1772

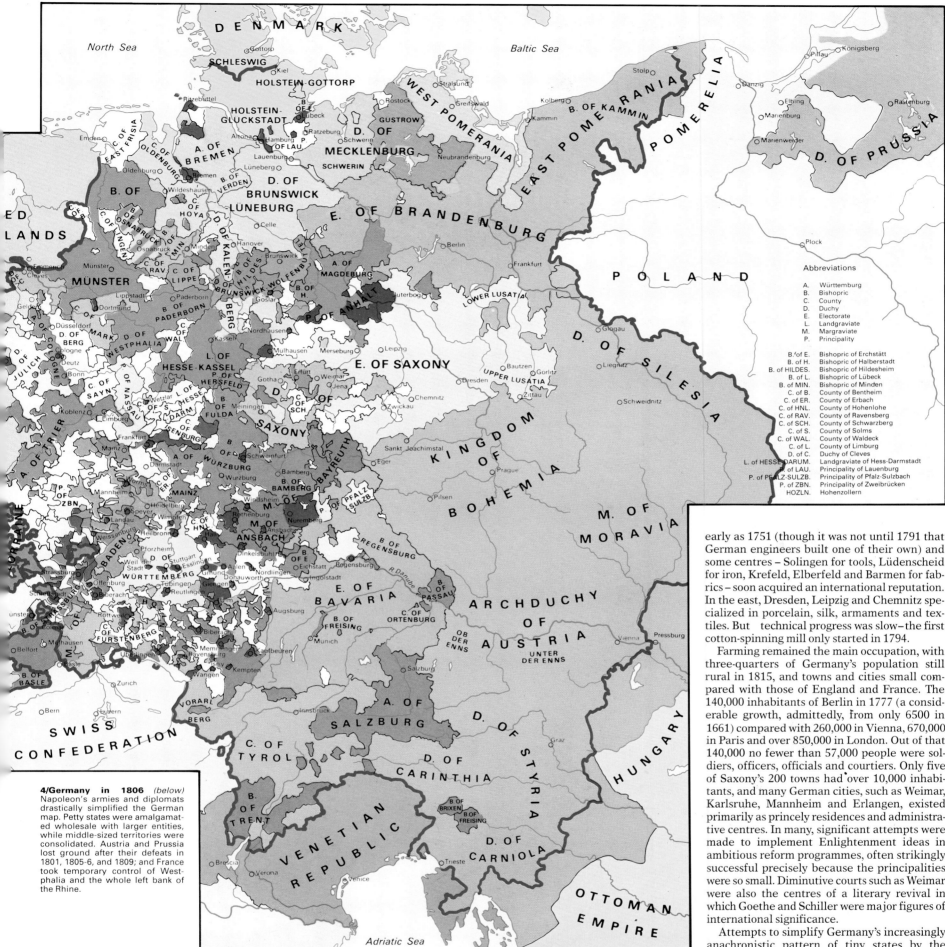

4/Germany in 1806 (below)
Napoleon's armies and diplomats drastically simplified the German map. Petty states were amalgamated wholesale with larger entities, while middle-sized territories were consolidated. Austria and Prussia lost ground after their defeats in 1801, 1805-6, and 1809; and France took temporary control of Westphalia and the whole left bank of the Rhine.

early as 1751 (though it was not until 1791 that German engineers built one of their own) and some centres – Solingen for tools, Lüdenscheid for iron, Krefeld, Elberfeld and Barmen for fabrics – soon acquired an international reputation. In the east, Dresden, Leipzig and Chemnitz specialized in porcelain, silk, armaments and textiles. But technical progress was slow–the first cotton-spinning mill only started in 1794.

Farming remained the main occupation, with three-quarters of Germany's population still rural in 1815, and towns and cities small compared with those of England and France. The 140,000 inhabitants of Berlin in 1777 (a considerable growth, admittedly, from only 6500 in 1661) compared with 260,000 in Vienna, 670,000 in Paris and over 850,000 in London. Out of that 140,000 no fewer than 57,000 people were soldiers, officers, officials and courtiers. Only five of Saxony's 200 towns had over 10,000 inhabitants, and many German cities, such as Weimar, Karlsruhe, Mannheim and Erlangen, existed primarily as princely residences and administrative centres. In many, significant attempts were made to implement Enlightenment ideas in ambitious reform programmes, often strikingly successful precisely because the principalities were so small. Diminutive courts such as Weimar were also the centres of a literary revival in which Goethe and Schiller were major figures of international significance.

Attempts to simplify Germany's increasingly anachronistic pattern of tiny states by the Austrian Emperor, Joseph II (1780–90) were frustrated by Prussia, now powerful enough to block anyone else's unificatory moves but not to initiate any of her own. Redrawing the political map only began in earnest under the impact of France's post-revolutionary wars. The 64 ecclesiastical principalities were secularized in 1803; 45 of the 51 free cities, the remaining imperial knights, and other small territories were absorbed into larger units. After 1806 Napoleon and his lieutenants simplified matters even more (see map 4).

These changes marked the end of the old Reich, providing a springboard for the developments of the 19th century. Their significance was formally recognized in 1806, when Francis II of Austria (1792–1806) finally abdicated his sonorous, though now almost meaningless title. He was the last Holy Roman Emperor, in a line that had lasted 850 years.

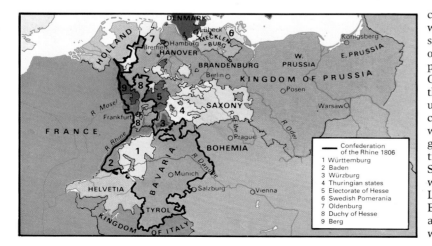

coal, was only a modest success. Although they were widely admired and emulated, many of his state-sponsored enterprises failed even in his own lifetime, and few survived the French occupation of 1806. Nevertheless, 18th-century Germany was not an economic backwater. While the older cities stagnated, new industries sprang up in rural districts where they could escape the crippling guild restrictions. Apart from Silesia, where the major landowners combined with government to invest in mining, iron and textiles, the main areas were the Sauerland and Siegerland massifs in the lower Rhineland, where water power was available from the rivers Lahn, Sieg and Wupper, and Saxony, with its Erzgebirge, which was probably the most advanced of all. Germany's first steam engine was installed in a lead mine near Düsseldorf as

Abbreviations

A.	Württemburg
B.	Bishopric
C.	County
D.	Duchy
E.	Electorate
L.	Landgraviate
M.	Margraviate
P.	Principality

B. of E.	Bishopric of Erchstätt
B. of H.	Bishopric of Halberstadt
B. of HILDES.	Bishopric of Hildesheim
B. of L.	Bishopric of Lübeck
B. of MIN.	Bishopric of Minden
C. of B.	County of Bentheim
C. of ER.	County of Erbach
C. of HNL.	County of Hohenlohe
C. of RAV.	County of Ravensberg
C. of SCH.	County of Schwarzberg
C. of S.	County of Solms
C. of WAL.	County of Waldeck
C. of L.	County of Limburg
D. of C.	Duchy of Cleves
L. of HESSE DARUM.	Landgraviate of Hess-Darmstadt
D. of LAU.	Duchy of Lauenburg
P. of PFALZ SULZB.	Principality of Pfalz-Sulzbach
P. of ZBN.	Principality of Zweibrücken
HOZLN.	Hohenzollern

Confederation of the Rhine 1806
1 Württemburg
2 Baden
3 Würzburg
4 Thuringian states
5 Electorate of Hesse
6 Swedish Pomerania
7 Oldenburg
8 Duchy of Hesse
9 Berg

The ascendancy of France 1648 to 1715

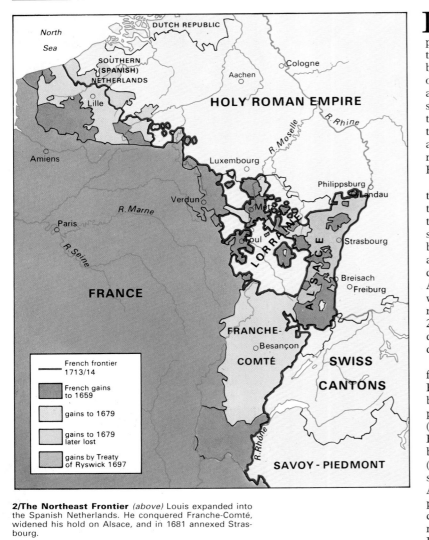

2/The Northeast Frontier (*above*) Louis expanded into the Spanish Netherlands. He conquered Franche-Comté, widened his hold on Alsace, and in 1681 annexed Strasbourg.

3/War of the Spanish Succession 1701/2, 1713/14 Carlos II – ruler of Spain, Spanish America, the south Netherlands and half of Italy – died childless in November 1700 and bequeathed his entire empire to Philip, younger grandson of Louis XIV of France. This sudden concentration of territory in the hands of the Bourbon dynasty overturned the balance of power in Europe and provoked war with Britain, the Dutch Republic, the Holy Roman Emperor, Portugal and Savoy. The struggle raged in the Netherlands, Italy and Germany, as well as in Spain, with initial Bourbon victories followed by a string of defeats (1704-9). Eventually, by the compromise peaces of Utrecht (1713) and Rastatt (1714), Philip retained Spain and Spanish America, while Savoy and the Austrian Habsburgs partitioned the rest.

DURING the reign of Louis XIV France became so influential in Europe that other powers feared her ascendancy, regarding her – to use a contemporary expression – as an 'exorbitant' state, dangerous to the balance of power on the Continent and threatening the religious as well as the political freedom of individual states and princes. Louis was suspected of plans to oust the Austrian Habsburgs from their traditional position as elected Holy Roman Emperor, and of spearheading a second Catholic counter-reformation. He was generally held to aim at French hegemony over Europe.

Such fears rested upon solid ground. Although war, civil and international, had for more than a century impeded progress in manufactures, in trade, in overseas expansion, and in ship-building, the relatively peaceful years between 1659 and 1672 gave Louis XIV and his able ministers and administrators a chance to catch up with France's rivals in all three fields. At the same time the French army and navy were greatly expanded. The richness of French resources, including a population estimated at 20 million, played a significant part in these developments, but so did conscious effort and directives from the centre.

Louis' military objectives, however, were at first limited and concerned the security of France's northern and eastern frontiers. Habsburg encirclement, forged by the family compacts of the Austrian and Spanish Habsburgs (see page 182), was still felt to be pressing round France though the Peace of Westphalia (1648) brought sovereignty over Metz, Toul and Verdun (occupied by the French since 1552) and possession of the landgravates of Upper and Lower Alsace, while the Peace of the Pyrenees (1659) plugged the gap in the southern frontier: Spain ceded Roussillon and northern Cerdagne. Yet many *portes* (gates) remained through which France could be invaded, from the Spanish

Netherlands in the north, through Lorraine and the Belfort Gap, right down to the Barcelonette valley from Italy. Spain still held Franche-Comté on the eastern border, and Louis' hold over Alsace was weakened by imperial suzerainty over its ten principal towns. The near-certainty, after 1665, that the Spanish king Carlos II would die without fathering heirs and consequently leave his possessions to the Austrian Habsburgs raised the spectre of a resurrection of the empire of Charles V. This helps to explain the two aggressive wars of Louis' reign: the War of Devolution, fought to lay claim to part of the Spanish Netherlands in 1667–8, and the attack on the Dutch Republic in 1672. The latter, much to Louis' discomfiture, escalated into a European-wide war and was not settled until 1678–9.

Louis tried to avoid large-scale war after 1679 by resort to arbitration and multi-lateral treaties to settle European problems, but the memories of his early wars and the enormous power of France made the rest of Europe suspicious. Indeed, he preferred brief campaigns or the diplomatic isolation of those who opposed him by the use of subsidies to rulers and presents to influential ministers. His conquest of Spanish Netherlands territory (1668) and of Franche-Comté (1678) might be forgiven, but his 'reunion' policy to expand his control of German border areas was vigorously opposed; and he lost the sympathy of all Protestant powers once his anti-Huguenot measures in France began to bite. The deleterious economic effects of the exodus of over 200,000 French Huguenots in the 1670s and 1680s have been greatly exaggerated, but the international consequences of Louis' revocation of the Edict of Nantes (1685) were far-reaching, and contributed both to the outbreak of both the Nine Years' War (1689–97) and the War of the Spanish Succession (1701–14).

The defensive element in Louis' foreign policy is still disputed among historians, but can be demonstrated in various ways: by the construction of a *barrière de fer* of fortresses around the whole of France, thickest on the ground in the north and east; by the decision, put into effect by 1696, to quit Italy (thus abandoning a cornerstone of the policies of Richelieu and Mazarin) to permit concentration of resources on the defensive *barrière*; and by the clauses in the second partition treaty of 1700 which – while giving Spain, the Spanish Netherlands and Spanish holdings overseas to an Austrian archduke – ceded the Spanish possessions in Italy to France, but with specific provisions and plans for 'exchanges' to strengthen the eastern frontier: the Duchy of Milan was to be exchanged for Lorraine, and Naples and Sicily, it was hoped, for Savoy and Piedmont.

Parallel to this preoccupation with the northern and eastern frontiers went an intense concern to catch up with the Maritime Powers (England and the Dutch Republic) in overseas settlements and commerce, and especially to have a share in the illicit trade with Spanish America. Here Louis aroused such resentment and fear that the English and the Dutch would only contemplate one of Louis' younger grandsons inheriting the Spanish throne if they themselves were given territories and strongpoints in the West Indies, on the Spanish Main, in Spanish North Africa, on Spain's Balearic Islands and in Spain itself. The Maritime Powers knew full well that no union of the two dynasties, that of Spain and that of France, was intended; but unless they received compensation of the kind mentioned above they feared that French ascendancy in overseas trade would become a corollary of French ascendancy in Europe. They could no more free themselves from such fears than could Louis from his conviction that the Austrian Habsburgs, who between 1683 and 1699 made such vast reconquests from the Turks in Hungary, would sooner or later turn west to

regain, as they loudly proclaimed, everything lost to France by their dynasty between 1552 and 1678.

French ascendancy between 1648 and 1715 was not, it should be remembered, only apparent in the political fields which can be illustrated in an historical atlas. Indeed, in the perspective of cultural and intellectual history, Louis' work for French literature, architecture, learning, and for science and the arts in general, and his pensions paid to a great number of European poets, artists and scholars, whether they studied in France or not, may seem more important than his wars. His Versailles building programme and his support for academies became models for other princes; French became the language of the educated classes all over Europe and helped to create the cosmopolitan civilization of the late 17th and the early 18th centuries. France also made progress during his reign in the number of colleges and hospitals (a combination of hospitals, workhouses and houses of correction); in codification of laws; in administrative procedures and efficiency; and in a range of practical improvements from the street lighting and policing of Paris to the digging of the Languedoc canal (completed by 1684) which provided cheap and efficient communication between the Atlantic and the Mediterranean.

Taken as a whole, the reign fixed the French frontiers in Europe (though colonial cessions had to be made to Great Britain) and foreshadowed the exchange which in 1738 brought the certainty of Lorraine's incorporation with France (achieved by 1766); while, in the history of French civilization, the reign is deservedly honoured with the title *Le Grand Siècle*.

frontiers and administration

～ frontier of France 1713-14

administrative units of Louis XIV's reign, the *généralités* (generalities)

⊙ seat of intendants, Louis XIV's royal commissioners

⊕ *parlement* (law courts)

defence

▟ fortifications (the so-called *barrière* or *frontière de fer*)

▟ fortifications built by Vauban but ceded during reign of Louis XIV

➜ fortification gap, possible invasion route (*porte*)

⚓ galley port

⚓ naval port

economic

‡ commercial harbours

major manufactures

▯ brandy
🐚 cloth
▢ glass
⊞ iron
◖ madder dye
▭ paper
♟ pottery
▣ printing
▤ salt
▨ silk
◉ soap
⊠ tapestry and carpets
🍇 wine

1/Administrative units and defensive fortification system This map indicates those provinces of France which had *parlements* (law courts) and delineates the administrative units of the reign, the 'generalities'. It shows the towns where the intendants, the royal commissioners appointed by the king 'at his pleasure' (and thus not able to buy or sell their offices), resided. The fortresses in the iron belt round France, built or improved by Vauban from 1679 onwards, are indicative of the increasingly defensive stance of the monarchy.

The struggle for empire
1713 to 1815

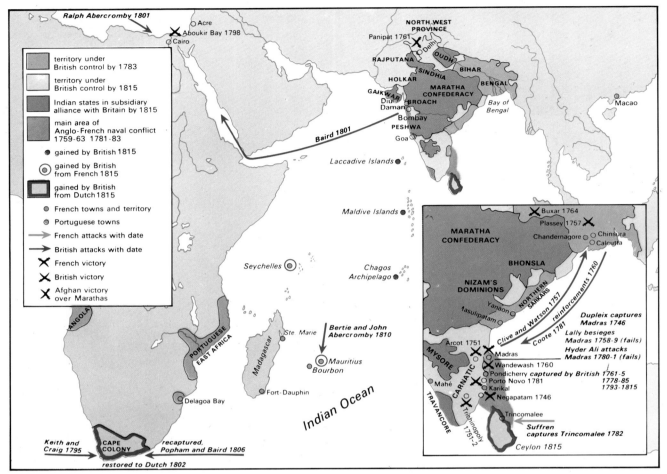

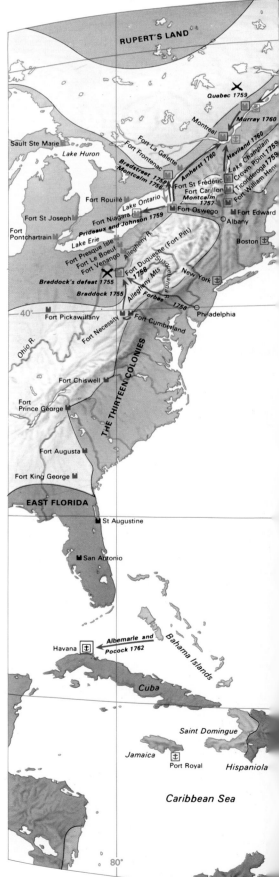

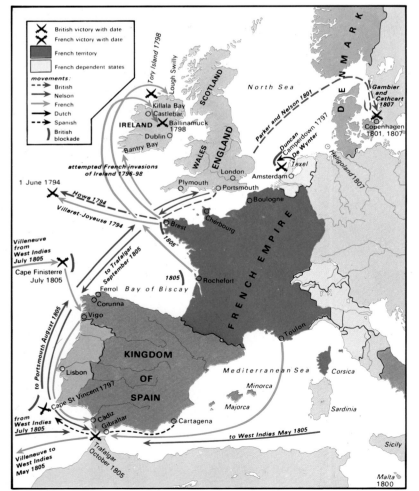

2/The Franco-British struggle for India (*above*) The capture of Madras by Dupleix in 1746 began the struggle for India. As in America, British sea power proved decisive: Dupleix was checked at Trichinopoly in 1752, and after the capture of Bengal in 1757 the British could reinforce the Carnatic at will. The capture of Pondicherry in 1761 destroyed French power, and with local resources and control of the sea the British were able to hold off all subsequent challenges.

3/The British triumph in home waters, 1794-1805 (*below*) In the final confrontation between Great Britain and France the decisive battles were fought in European waters. Weakened by the French Revolution, the French fleet was no match for the British, and as successive invasion attempts foundered against British superiority at sea, Britain occupied its rival's possessions. By 1815 British possession of the key strategic colonies left it the supreme imperial power.

BY leaving the Spanish empire and its trading monopolies substantially intact, the Treaty of Utrecht (1713) sought to establish a stable state system in Europe and overseas based upon the balance of power. Instead, it perpetuated the principal causes of colonial conflict. Territorial expansion continued throughout the 18th century and led to serious clashes between Portugal and Spain in the Banda Oriental (Uruguay), between Spain and Great Britain in Georgia, and between Great Britain and France in North America. Trading monopolies proved an even greater source of friction. Illegal trade with the Spanish empire flourished, and Spanish attempts to suppress British and Dutch smugglers from Jamaica, St Eustatius and Curaçao reduced the Caribbean to a state of undeclared war. Further north, British efforts to enforce similar restrictions upon its American colonists provoked resistance and finally open revolt.

But although dissension originated in the unsettled situation overseas, the outcome depended upon the actions of the European states. During 1739–40 the fragile peace collapsed as Great Britain and Spain went to war in defence of their trading rights, and Frederick the Great's invasion of Silesia began the mid-century struggle for supremacy in eastern Europe (see page 192). The outbreak of hostilities between Great Britain and France in 1744 brought the war for Caribbean trade and the war for Silesia together into a single global conflict that extended from North America to India, and from the West Indies to Russia. This struggle, which lasted intermittently until 1815, rapidly became a duel between Great Britain and France for global supremacy. European states, American settlers, North American Indian chiefs and Indian princes all fought as subsidized and dependent allies of these two great powers. Local factors determined the nature of local struggles, but all were subordinated to the larger conflict.

The Treaty of Aix-la-Chapelle (1748) settled none of the outstanding questions, and fighting began again in North America in 1754. By 1756 France had achieved local military superiority, its strategically sited forts preventing further British expansion. But the key to colonial victory was control of the lines of communication, and thus sea power. The outbreak of the Seven Years' War in Europe transformed the local struggle; in the wider conflict of 1756–63, while France was handicapped by its continental commitments, Great Britain took control of the Atlantic and isolated the French forces in North America. Cut off from reinforcements, Louisbourg fell in 1758, Quebec in 1759. The capture of Montreal in 1760, following British naval victories at Quiberon Bay and Lagos, completed the fall of French Canada. In the West Indies, by 1763 the British were in control of Spanish

Havana and all the French islands except St Domingue. These were restored at the Treaty of Paris (1763), but Great Britain retained the North American mainland east of the Mississippi, including Florida which was ceded by Spain.

The British triumph was short-lived. Between 1763 and the American War of Independence (1776–83: see page 164), France rebuilt both its navy and its alliances in pursuit of revenge. By 1781, confronted in home waters by a hostile coalition of France, Spain and the Dutch Republic, threatened by the 'armed neutrality' of the Baltic powers, and overstrained by the need to defend an empire stretching from Canada to India, Great Britain was forced to surrender control of North American waters. The French blockade of Yorktown forced a major British army to surrender, and although Rodney's victory off the group of islands known as The Saints in 1782 saved British possessions in the West Indies, Great Britain was obliged to recognize American independence at the Treaty of Versailles (1783). Nevertheless, the triumph of 1763 ensured that the new United States

developed as an English-speaking nation. Trading contacts quickly revived, and despite occasional differences, the cultural link between the two countries exercised a profound influence on subsequent history..

During these same years the British found a new empire in India. The emergence of independent princes from the ruins of the Mughal Empire in the early 18th century gave the British and the French East India companies opportunities to intervene in local politics. Here again sea power was decisive. Thus, after early French successes, Great Britain's ability to reinforce its position by sea enabled it to check Dupleix's ambitious designs in the Carnatic. But the real foundation of the British empire in India followed Clive's victory at Plassey (1757) which gave the British control of the rich province of Bengal (see page 168). During the Seven Years' War reinforcements from Bengal enabled the British to eliminate French influence in the Carnatic. Henceforth, despite a French challenge in 1781-83, Great Britain was the predominant European power in India.

The French Revolution of 1789 shattered the

Nelson's Victory (left) A British ship of the line carrying 102 guns and 850 men, HMS *Victory* became famous as the flag ship of Admiral Horatio Nelson. Ships such as the *Victory* were used throughout the 18th century. Nelson was the supreme tactician of the age of sail, and his victory over the combined French and Spanish fleets at Trafalgar in 1805 finally ensured British triumph in the long struggle for empire.

French navy and, despite a partial recovery after 1794, France never regained the position as a competitive naval power. This alone ruined Napoleon's plans for the invasion of Great Britain. By 1815, the French, Spanish, Dutch and Danish fleets were defeated, their colonies mostly in British hands. With the acquisition of the Cape, Ceylon and Mauritius, Great Britain secured the route to India and the East, and laid the foundations for the second British empire. It occupied a position of unrivalled power throughout large areas of the world, and its influence was to be a decisive factor in their evolution.

1/The struggle in the North Atlantic and North America, 1754-63 (below) After 1748 France built up its forces in North America to encircle the British colonies from the west, but its position there and in the West Indies depended upon constant reinforcement from Europe. Isolated by the British blockade in European waters, that position deteriorated rapidly after 1758 and the French overseas empire collapsed before determined British attacks. The sugar islands of the Caribbean were returned in 1763, but the fall of Montreal ended French power in North America.

191

The Ottoman Empire, Austria and Russia: Eastern Europe from 1648 to 1795

1/Territorial gains and losses in eastern Europe 1648-1795 (above) During this period the western powers began to realize that the Ottoman Empire, once the terror of Europe, was no longer an invincible force and had indeed become dangerously weak. As Austria and Russia sought advantage from Turkish disintegration, Prussia expanded, while France and Sweden tried to maintain the traditional balance. With France increasingly paralysed, and Britain's attention concentrated beyond Europe, the eastern powers were able to contrive the Partitions of Poland (see map 5).

Legend:
- Russian conquests from Poland 1667-1795
- Russian conquests from Sweden 1700-43
- Russian conquests from Turkey 1768-92
- Prussian conquests from Austria 1740-41
- Prussian conquests from Sweden 1721
- Prussian conquests from Poland 1772-95
- Habsburg conquests from Turkey 1683-1775
- Habsburg conquests from Poland 1772-95
- Turkish conquests from Venice 1669-1718

4/The Silesian Wars (below) The intensive struggle began when the Prussians first won Silesia, at Mollwitz (1745). Hohenfriedberg (1745) ended the first Austrian attempt at reconquest. In the Seven Years' War, the Prussians occupied Saxony and Bohemia as far as Prague (1757) and, although the Austrian victory at Kolin freed Bohemia, recovery of Silesia was foiled by Frederick's brilliant success at Leuthen. The Russians briefly occupied Berlin after Kunersdorf (1759) but they failed to inflict a decisive defeat on Frederick II's highly mobile forces. Russia's withdrawal from the struggle after Peter III's accession (1762) forced Austria to renounce Silesia for good.

Legend:
- X battles between Austria and Prussia
- X battle between Saxony and Prussia
- X battles between Russia and Prussia
- X battle between Austria with Russia and Prussia

SULTAN Mehmed IV, in whose reign the Ottoman Empire launched its last major military onslaught on the West, came to the throne in 1648, just as the Treaty of Westphalia ended the Thirty Years' War. Between then and the final partition of Poland in 1795, an almost continuous series of wars, frontier changes, alliances and population movements profoundly altered the balance of power in Eastern Europe.

During this period the Ottoman menace to Europe first dwindled and then disappeared. There were attempts, notably under the capable dynasty of grand viziers recruited from the Köprülü family, to revive the fortunes of the Empire but it was by now lagging behind the various military innovations of its European rivals and the battle of St Gotthard in 1664 displayed the military superiority of the Austrians. The Ottoman failure at the second siege of Vienna in 1683, thanks to the efforts of a coalition led by the Polish king, John III Sobieski (1674–96), dramatically demonstrated Turkish weakness.

However the Ottoman Empire by no means plunged headlong into collapse. There was success against Venice with Köprülü Mehmed Paşa's re-taking of Tenedos and Lemnos in 1657 and the important capture of Crete in 1669; and although they lost some ground in Hungary, in 1690 Grand Vizir Fazil Mustafa Paşa retook Niş and Belgrade. Serbia, lost earlier to Austria, was regained in the encounters of 1737–9. There was even a period in the 18th century (1748–68) when the empire was at peace.

Nevertheless Ottoman failures far outnumbered their successes for they lost heavily both to the Habsburgs and to Russia, suffering a series of major defeats such as those administered by Prince Eugene of Savoy at Zenta in 1697, when Turkish corpses formed islands in the river Tisza, and at Peterwardein in 1716, after which Eugene took Temesvar and, the following year, Belgrade. After the peace settlements of Carlowitz (1699), the Prut (1711), Passarowitz (1718), Belgrade (1739), Küçük Kaynarca (1774) and Jassy (1798), the Ottomans found themselves shorn of Hungary, the Banat, Transylvania and Bukovina. To Russia, similarly, they had lost the north coast of the Black Sea from the Dniester to the Caucasus. Russian claims that the Treaty of Küçük Kaynarca granted the Tsar the right to defend Orthodox interests in Ottoman lands presaged future humiliation, culminating in the Eastern Crisis of 1853 and the Crimean War (1854–6) (see page 224).

The reconquest of Hungary, together with the acquisitions that followed the War of the Spanish Succession, promoted the Austrian Habsburgs to great-power status. But territory alone did not signify strength. Resistance by the Hungarian nobility to the extension of absolutist control hampered the full development of the country's resources. Large areas had been devastated and depopulated during the Turkish wars, and the main economic achievement of this period was the recolonization of this land by hard-working immigrants, many from southwest Germany. Though the first settlements were unsuccessful, almost 50,000 immigrants arrived in the 1760s and 1770s, with a further 25,000 in the 1780s. Their skills and crafts made possible a more intensive and diversified agriculture.

The real weakness of the Habsburgs was revealed when the male line died out in 1740. This was the signal for Frederick II of Prussia to occupy Austria's highly-industrialized province of Silesia. He crushed the Austrian forces sent against him at Mollwitz (1741), and although after the peace of Aix-la-Chapelle, in 1748, Maria Theresa vigorously reformed her army and administration, encouraged economic development and entered into alliances with France and Russia, the bitterly fought Seven Years' War (1756–63), failed to win her back the

lost territory. Prussia had emerged as a rival, challenging the traditional pre-eminence of the Habsburg dynasty in Germany.

John Sobieski's successful participation in the alliance against the Turks had temporarily masked the growing disintegration of Poland, but in fact this process continued almost throughout the 17th and 18th centuries. The disastrous reign of John II Casimir Vasa (1648–68) saw the rebellion of the Ukrainian Cossacks, who accepted Russian suzerainty in 1654, and a Russian–Cossack invasion which detached most of eastern Poland. The Swedes, under Charles X Gustav, then occupied northern Poland and Lithuania (1655), until their brutality inspired a successful counter-attack. The Russians were also expelled (although they retained Smolensk and the eastern Ukraine), until 1687, when peace was signed with Russia, but even John Sobieski's successes did more to help the emergence of Austria and Russia than to strengthen his own country.

At Sobieski's death in 1696, 18 candidates sought the votes of the nobles who had the right to elect a monarch for the 'Polish-Lithuanian Commonwealth'. The winner was Augustus 'the Strong' of Saxony, who as Augustus II reigned until 1733. His ambition to conquer Livonia from Sweden sparked off the Great Northern War in 1700 in alliance with Peter the Great of Russia. The Swedes under Charles XII again devastated Poland, destroying a third of its cities, and forcing Augustus's temporary abdication. Ultimately the real victor was Peter I who restored Augustus to the throne, but seized Livonia for himself. A marsh was drained to found St Petersburg as a warm-water port, and the new city became Russia's capital in 1715.

In 1733 a French-supported candidate was elected king of Poland, but Russian and Saxon troops placed Augustus's son on the throne as Augustus III. Poland now ceased to count as a military power in Eastern Europe. With Frederick II's seizure of Silesia, Prussia now controlled her trade outlets to western Europe, though Poland still had direct access to the Baltic through Danzig.

The decline of Poland was balanced by the rise of Russia which freely based her armies in Polish territory and made use of Polish ports in the Seven Years' War. On the death of Augustus III in 1763, Catherine II of Russia procured the election of Stanislas Poniatowski as king (1764–95), but her intervention in Polish religious divisions provoked civil war in Poland and encouraged the Ottoman Porte to declare war in 1768 in order to stem the imminent Russian advance. This war was to reveal the full extent of Russia's military power. Russia's armies advanced through the Danubian principalities; her navy, making its first appearance in the Mediterranean, destroyed the Turkish fleet at Chesmé (1770) and the total collapse of the Ottoman Empire appeared a distinct possibility. From then on 'the eastern question' became a central issue in European affairs, as each great power tried to ensure that the Ottoman realms should not fall intact into one of the other's hands.

The presence of Russian forces near the mouth of the Danube in 1770 aroused the determined opposition of Austria, which tried to involve Prussia in an anti-Russian block. Frederick II, with much to lose and little to gain from a Balkan conflict, proposed the first Polish partition, thus shifting the great-power conflict to an area where he had most to gain. Hence Poland paid the price for Russia's initial moderation in relation to Turkey. Further losses soon followed. After the annexation of the Crimea in 1783, the exodus of the Crimean Tartars, who preferred to live under Turkish rule, opened up all their vast, fertile lands to Russian coloniza-

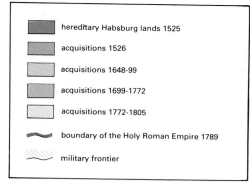

	hereditary Habsburg lands 1525
	acquisitions 1526
	acquisitions 1648–99
	acquisitions 1699–1772
	acquisitions 1772–1805
	boundary of the Holy Roman Empire 1789
	military frontier

3/Growth of the Habsburg Empire (right) The Austrian branch of the Habsburg dynasty was founded by Charles V's brother Ferdinand, who took advantage of a marriage tie to have himself elected king of Bohemia and Hungary in 1526. But for nearly two centuries he and his successors had to dispute possession of Hungarian territory with the Ottomans. After the Turkish collapse following the siege of Vienna (map 2), the Habsburgs were able to expand rapidly down the Danube. Their gains were consolidated at the treaties of Carlowitz (1699) and Passarowitz (1718), though some land was lost again by the treaty of Belgrade (1739). Another consequence of the contest with the Turks was the establishment from the 16th century of a frontier area under the direct control of military authorities in Vienna which survived until the 1870s. Austria's largest 18th-century acquisitions resulted from the First and Third Partitions of Poland (map 5), but her gains from the latter proved short-lived.

tion. Russia's next offensive against Turkey (1787–92) for the first time provoked British opposition. But at the peace of Jassy in 1792, Russia acquired the coast between the Bug and the Dniester, and control of trade in the Dniester basin.

The outbreak of the French Revolution in 1789 reduced French influence in Eastern Europe and when Poland promulgated the Constitution of 3 May 1791, she had no defence against Russia and Prussia which organized a second partition in 1793. After the Polish rising of 1794, Russia and Prussia completed the extinction of Poland in 1795 together this time with Austria.

2/Siege of Vienna (below) The Turks, advancing from the east, laid siege to the city in July 1683. The garrison and citizens held out long enough for the slow-moving German and Polish relief forces to cross the Danube and traverse the hilly country to the north and west. They finally swept down the slopes of the Wienerwald on 12 September and destroyed the Turks, who failed to fortify their siege camp. The relief of Vienna marked the beginning of the Habsburg Empire's rise to great-power status.

5/The Partitions of Poland (left) In the First Partition (1772), Russia made relatively modest gains, Prussia annexed the territory dividing Pomerania from East Prussia except for Danzig, and Austria annexed a large area to the north of Hungary including Lemberg (Lwów). In the Second Partition (1793), Russia annexed the entire eastern territory inhabited by Ukrainians and White Russians, while Prussia gained Danzig, Thorn and Posen, and pushed her frontier eastwards close to Warsaw. In the final Partition (1795) Prussia annexed Warsaw itself, Austria West Galicia, including Cracow, and Russia the remaining Polish territory, including modern Lithuania.

	Poland before the partitions
	Russian, Prussian and Austrian acquisitions in the First Partition, 1772
	Russian and Prussian acquisitions in the Second Partition, 1793
	Russian, Prussian and Austrian acquisitions in the Third Partition, 1795

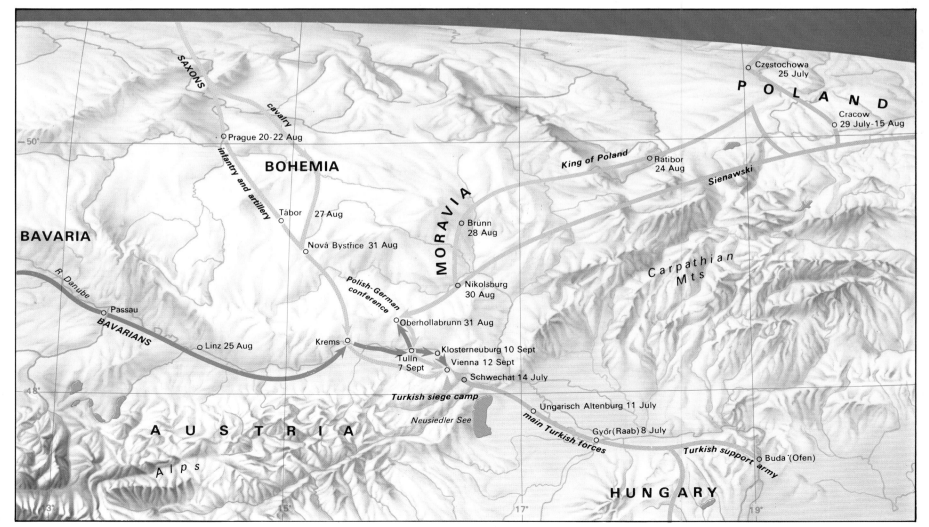

The emerging global economy c.1775

B**Y THE** late 18th century, on the eve of industrialization, European economic dominance was already extensive, if very uneven. Some parts of the world, most notably the areas of European conquest and settlement in the Americas were closely integrated into the economy of western Europe. By contrast, although the volume of European trade in some regions of Africa and Asia was growing rapidly, its overall effect on the mass of the population of both continents remained limited.

Even in 1775 the Spanish colonies of Central and South America still ranked as the most valuable European possessions overseas. In the highlands of Mexico and the Andes the Spaniards had conquered huge indigenous populations whose labour, in spite of catastrophic mortality from new diseases, supported agriculture, some manufacturing and great silver mining operations. American silver and the now declining gold of Brazil provided Europe with its main supply of bullion, and continued to do so at a high level until well into the 19th century. Legal shipments of Spanish-American silver were only permitted to Spain itself, but much silver also flowed out through the Caribbean and via the River Plate to Europe or across the Pacific to the Philippines. The legal export of manufactured goods to Spanish America likewise passed through Spain, even if most of the goods were made elsewhere, especially in France. This legal trade was also supplemented by a substantial illegal traffic, most notably by the British in the Caribbean, into the Spanish colonies.

Along the Atlantic coast from Brazil in the south to the Chesapeake in the north, but above all in the islands of the Caribbean, plantation societies had developed to meet the demand for

tropical agricultural produce: cacao, tobacco, indigo, cotton and, most valued of all, sugar. European consumption of such produce rose very rapidly in the late 18th century. Since most plantations depended on African slaves, this increased consumption meant increased shipments of slaves from Africa, both to extend the areas under cultivation and to maintain the level of existing slave populations in conditions where, with the exception of the North American mainland, deaths considerably exceeded births.

Along the northeast coast of North America, some 2 million white British subjects in the Thirteen Colonies and 100,000 or so French in recently conquered Canada were mostly engaged in agriculture. Where plantation crops for direct export to Europe – tobacco, indigo or rice – could not be grown, North American farming was heavily dependent on the prosperity of the West Indies as an outlet for huge surpluses of grain, flour, meat, timber and fish.

A closely integrated Atlantic economy had thus emerged. By 1775 the mainland colonies throughout the Americas were generally self-sufficient in food and limited manufacturing took place in some of them. But their white populations consumed very large quantities of imported European manufactured goods and the prosperity of almost all depended on their ability to export to Europe. The northern colonies were also linked to the West Indies, their exports of timber and foodstuffs enabling the islands to concentrate on sending even larger consignments of tropical crops across the Atlantic. Forced migration from West Africa and more or less voluntary migration from Europe provided much of America with its labour. Even the native American peoples of the north, living far beyond the colonial frontiers, were drawn into the Atlantic economy by the fur trade. In return for furs they received European goods, such as firearms or alcohol, which fundamentally reshaped their way of life.

Historians now doubt that the prosperity of western Europe derived from intercontinental trade, but transatlantic commerce certainly made a very important contribution to the economic development of at least France and Britain. By 1775 France had become Europe's major supplier of sugar and the value of French colonial trade as a whole grew six-fold from 1730 to 1776. Britain dominated the import of tobacco, while by 1775 almost 40 per cent of British exports were destined for America. The prosperity of many western European ports – Seville, Cádiz, Lisbon, Bordeaux, Nantes, Bristol, Liverpool and Glasgow – largely depended on Atlantic trade, shipping out migrants and manufactured goods and redistributing throughout Europe the great inflows of American produce.

In Asia, although the volume of trade also greatly increased during the 18th century and its composition changed in important respects, in essentials Europeans traded in 1775 much as they had done since the 16th century. They mostly operated from Asian ports or from small coastal enclaves to which Asian merchants delivered goods. The great monopoly East India companies of the British and the Dutch, founded in the 17th century, still dominated trade between Europe and Asia beyond the Levant (as the Middle East was then generally called). The main business of the companies continued to be the shipment to Europe of exotic Asian crops or of goods manufactured with skills that Europe could not yet match. The old spice and pepper trades had by the 18th century been eclipsed by a boom in textiles, cotton cloth and silk from India, and in new drinks for European consumers: Chinese tea and Javan coffee. In contrast to the Americas, few European manufactured goods could as yet be sold in Asia, except in the Mediterranean ports of the Ottoman empire: European exports were not yet competitive in markets around the Indian Ocean or the China Sea. So increased imports of Asian goods generally depended on shipments of American silver, either re-exported from Europe or carried across the Pacific to Manila in the Philippines, and thence to China.

European trade of course had important economic consequences for much of maritime Asia in stimulating the demand for export commodities, such as the cotton cloth produced by Indian weavers, and in injecting large quantities of silver into India and China. But most of Asia's economic life remained relatively unaffected by contact with the West and much long-distance trade continued to be conducted by Asian merchants using their own ships, or caravans of pack animals on overland routes. For instance the buoyant European demand for tea in the late 18th century probably absorbed less than 15 per cent of the available output through the port of Canton, the only point of access for European shipping allowed by the Chinese. China's principal trade arteries were the Grand Canal, the river systems and the junks that plied between Japan and Southeast Asia.

In two areas of great economic importance for Asian trade, however, conditions were changing radically by 1775. In Bengal the British had conquered a huge Indian province following the battle of Plassey in 1757, placing the province's economy under direct European control in a fashion unprecedented in Asia. Instead of paying for goods with imported silver, the British could now collect the taxes previously levied from their subjects by Indian rulers. Dutch political power in Java was less effective but they, too, could impose economic controls and receive commodities, above all coffee, as tribute. Trade through the Mediterranean between Europe and the Levant lay much closer to the Atlantic pattern. Europeans exported manufactured goods, especially cloth, in return for raw materials, such as wool, cotton and silk.

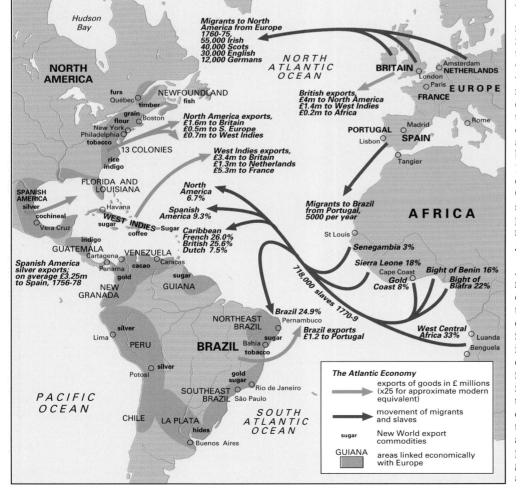

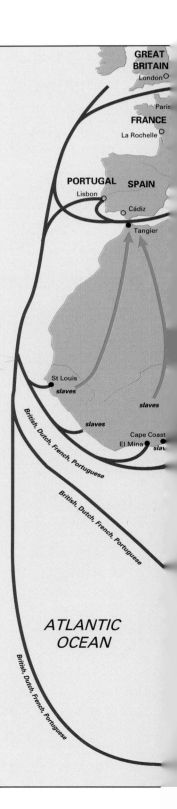

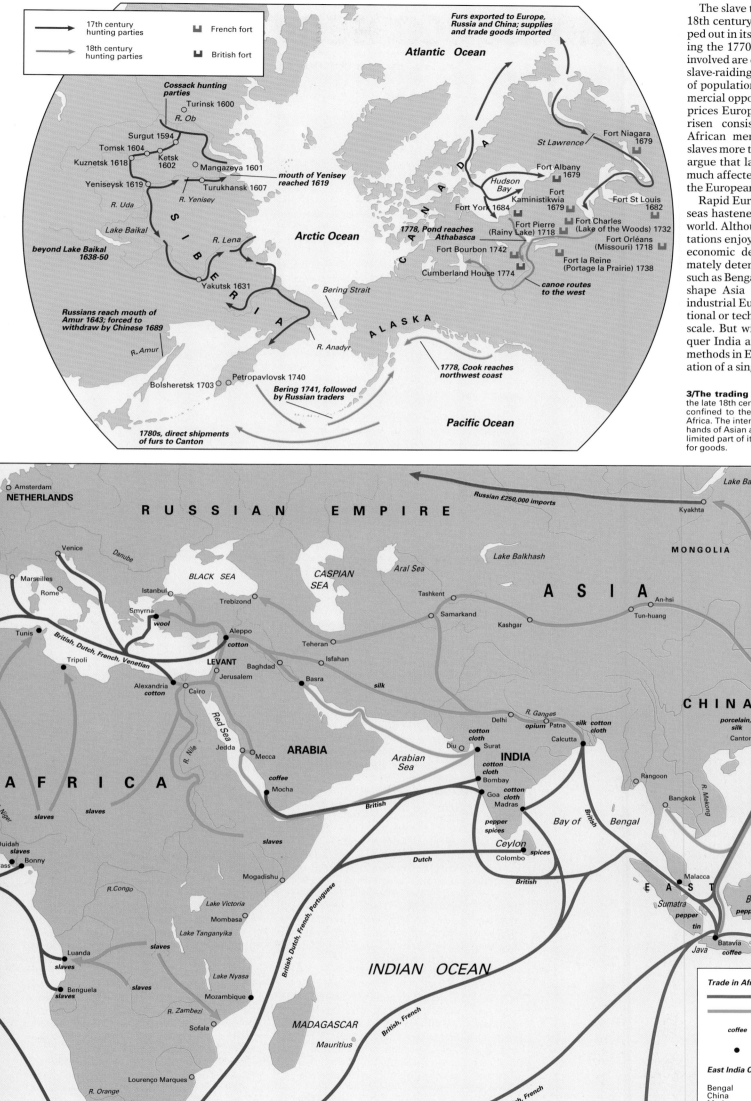

The slave trade reached its apogee in the late 18th century, with some 2,300,000 people shipped out in its last 30 years – 70,000 annually during the 1770s. The consequences for the areas involved are disputed. Disruption from wars and slave-raiding and the adverse economic effects of population loss must be set against the commercial opportunities created by the trade. The prices Europeans paid for slaves seem to have risen consistently, which implies that the African merchants and rulers who dealt in slaves more than held their own. However, many argue that large parts of West Africa were not much affected, either for better or for worse, by the European demand for slaves.

Rapid European commercial expansion overseas hastened the economic integration of the world. Although the Americas outside the plantations enjoyed a degree of self-sufficiency, the economic development of America was ultimately determined by Europe. Except in cases such as Bengal and Java, Europe could not as yet shape Asia or Africa: a still essentially preindustrial Europe could not deploy its organizational or technological advantages on a decisive scale. But with the British now poised to conquer India and with the rise of new industrial methods in Europe, the stage was set for the creation of a single global economy.

3/The trading worlds of Asia and Africa (below) In the late 18th century direct European trade was still largely confined to the rim of the great land mass of Asia and Africa. The internal trade of the continents remained in the hands of Asian and African merchants and only a relatively limited part of it was linked to satisfying Europe's demand for goods.

Map 1 legend:

→	17th century hunting parties
→	18th century hunting parties
⊔	French fort
⊔	British fort

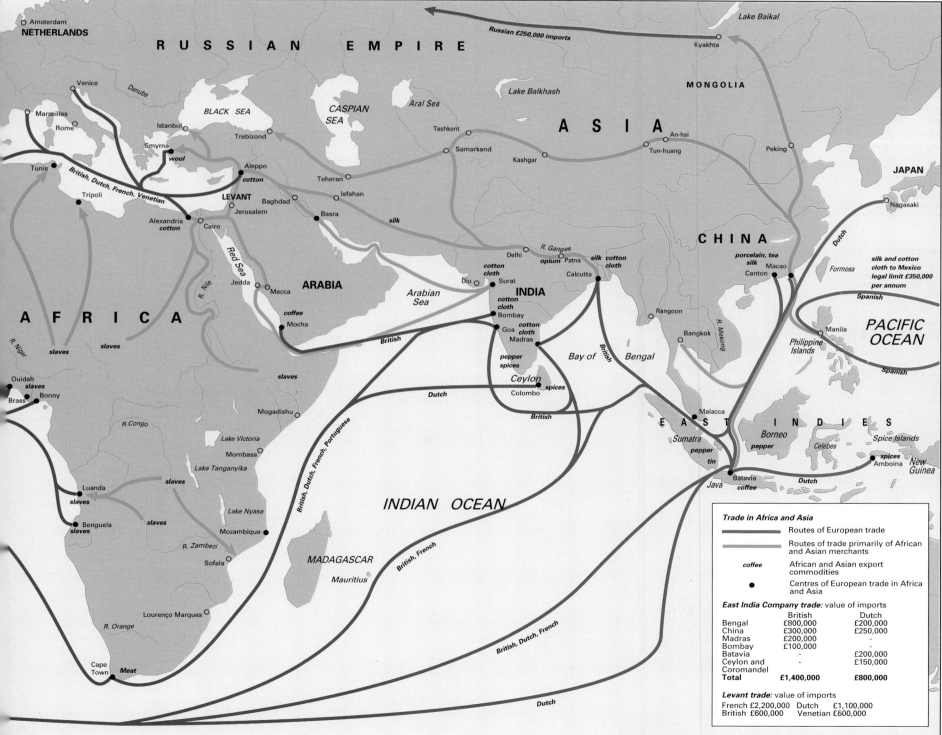

Map 2 legend:

Trade in Africa and Asia

— Routes of European trade

— Routes of trade primarily of African and Asian merchants

coffee — African and Asian export commodities

● — Centres of European trade in Africa and Asia

East India Company trade: value of imports

	British	Dutch
Bengal	£800,000	£200,000
China	£300,000	£250,000
Madras	£200,000	-
Bombay	£100,000	-
Batavia	-	£200,000
Ceylon and Coromandel	-	£150,000
Total	**£1,400,000**	**£800,000**

Levant trade: value of imports

French	£2,200,000	Dutch	£1,100,000
British	£600,000	Venetian	£600,000

The Industrial Revolution begins: Great Britain 1760 to 1820

Falkirk
Carron ironworks (engineering)

Glasgow
Tennent (chemicals)
Monteith (cotton)
Napier (shipbuilding)

Prestonpans
Roebuck & Garbett (chemicals)

New Lanark
Robert Owen (cotton)

Newcastle upon Tyne
Robert Stephenson (locomotives)

Darlington
Kendrew & Porterhouse (linen)

Leeds
Gott (woollens)
Marshall (linen)

Todmorden
Fielden (cotton)

Blackburn
Peel family (cotton)

Bury
Peel family (cotton)

Bolton
Crompton (cotton)

Manchester
McConnel & Kennedy (cotton)
A. & G. Murray (cotton)
Sharp Roberts (engineering)
Nasmyth (engineering)

Birkenhead
Laird (shipbuilding)

Newton le Willows
Robert Stephenson & Tayleur
(Vulcan Foundry)

Stockport
Oldknow (cotton)
Horrocks (cotton)
Marsland (cotton)

Sheffield
Huntsman (steel)
Walker (steel)

Bersham (Wrexham)
J. Wilkinson (iron)

Cromford
Arkwright & Strutt (cotton)

Stoke
Wedgwood (pottery)

Coalbrookdale
Darby family (iron)

Broseley
J. Wilkinson (iron)

Bilston
J. Wilkinson (iron)

Tipton
Aaron Manby (engineering & shipbuilding)
James Keir (chemicals)

Birmingham
Roebuck & Garbett (chemicals)
Boulton & Watt (steam engines)

Penydarran
Homfray (iron)

Dowlais
Guest (iron & engineering)

Cyfarthfa
Crawshay (iron & engineering)

London
Bramah (engineering)
Maudslay, Field & Co (engineering)
London (Millwall)
Fairbairn (shipbuilding)

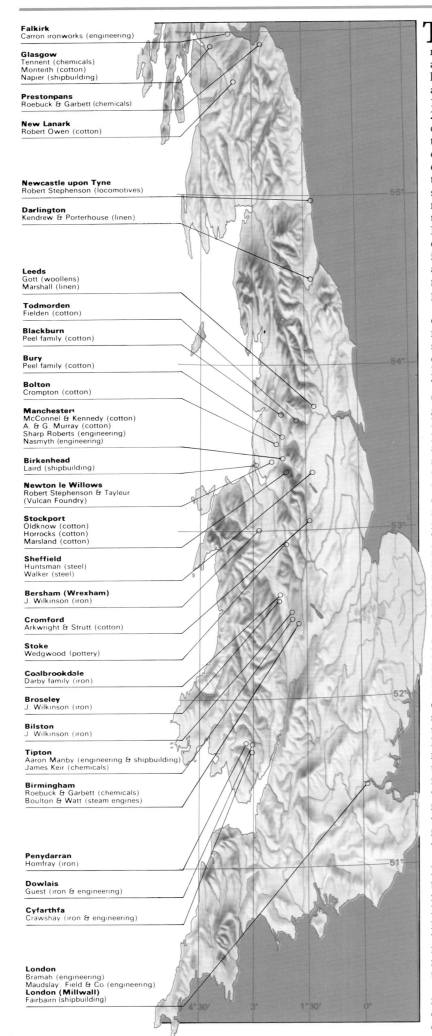

3/Pioneer entrepreneurs *(above)* In the manufacturing regions that developed after 1750 certain men stood out: some like Huntsman, Crompton, Arkwright and Stephenson, as inventors; others (McConnel and Kennedy, Gott, Marshall) as founders of great firms. The large pioneer enterprises shown on the map played a significant role in the Industrial Revolution; but in some industries – textiles and cutlery, for example – the firms remained mostly small.

THE Industrial Revolution – the transition from a predominantly agrarian to a predominantly industrial economy – marked the start of a new period in world history. Even in Europe, however, its impact remained limited until 1820, and in many countries until the middle of the 19th century; while in the wider world (see page 214) its revolutionary consequences were felt only much later. The process began in 18th-century Britain. By 1750, that country already boasted a prosperous and expanding economy: the changes to its structure which occurred during the reign of George III (1760–1820) were substantial, but they represented a continuing accumulative process of modernization which can be traced back to the 16th century at least. Even in Britain, rapid growth rates in total industrial output did not take place before 1800. However, in the half-century or so before this, striking acceleration occurred in certain sectors of manufacturing, notably cotton textiles, coal and pig iron.

The first revolution of its kind in the world occurred in Great Britain, and not on the continent of Europe, for many reasons. Britain possessed valuable resources, such as coal, iron, tin, copper, stone and salt; her agriculture was highly efficient and already highly commercialized. The transport facilities – navigable rivers (Clyde, Thames, Severn, Trent, Ouse, Humber), good harbours (London, Bristol, Liverpool, Newcastle upon Tyne), and the sea – were supplemented by networks of new canals, toll roads and colliery railways. It was much cheaper to send goods, particularly bulky goods, by water than by land, and England's economic growth in the second half of the 18th century was stimulated by the heavy traffic on her inland waterways and along her coasts. A striking example was the movement of large quantities of coal from the Tyne and Wear to London. Again, Lancashire had a climate which proved particularly suitable for the manufacture of cotton cloth, and this constituted the great growth industry in England at the time of the Industrial Revolution. The remarkable growth of London provided an expanding market for manufactured goods.

While continental Europe was plagued by one conflict after another in the 18th century, Great Britain fought her wars abroad and was free from internal strife except for two brief Jacobite revolts in 1715 and in 1745. The Wars against the French (see page 190) enabled the British to extend their empire – and to expand their overseas markets – in Canada and India. The loss of the American colonies did not, for many years, lessen the importance of the United States as a market for British manufactured goods. Again, the temporary loss of continental markets suffered during the revolutionary and Napoleonic wars was counterbalanced by the opening up of new trading opportunities across the Atlantic, while the stimulus of war helped the iron, engineering, shipbuilding and textile industries which supplied the armed forces.

At a time when commerce in continental Europe was strangled by customs barriers, river tolls and local taxes, men and goods moved freely all over Great Britain after the union of England and Scotland in 1707. The government played its part in maintaining law and order, providing a stable currency, protecting industry from foreign competition, and taking special measures to foster shipping, overseas trade and the woollen industry.

With a few important exceptions – such as mining and shipbuilding – only a modest initial capital was required to set up a new industrial enterprise. In the cotton industry, a small workshop and relatively inexpensive machines were all that the pioneer entrepreneur needed. Robert Owen had to borrow only £200 to get started. An industrialist could often expand his undertaking by ploughing back some of his prof-

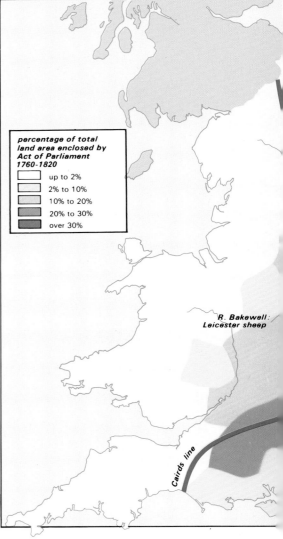

percentage of total land area enclosed by Act of Parliament 1760-1820
- up to 2%
- 2% to 10%
- 10% to 20%
- 20% to 30%
- over 30%

R. Bakewell: Leicester sheep

Caird's line

2/The agrarian revolution *(above)* Industrial growth generally follows an agrarian revolution; in England after 1750 the completion of enclosure of old commons and open fields, together with scientific farming, increased the output of food for a growing population and of raw materials for expanding industries. Increased prosperity enabled the agricultural community to buy more manufactured goods and to invest in new industries and public works. 'Caird's Line' indicates the division between grazing and dairy lands (to the west) and the chief grain districts (to the east).

its into the business. Although the family business or partnership which financed its own expansion was very common, enterprises were also established with capital derived from land or from commerce. Short-term loans were often available from the country (provincial) banks at low rates of interest.

A series of inventions and innovations in the second half of the 18th century greatly increased the output of consumer and capital goods. They included new spinning machines and looms, coke-smelting, puddling, and the introduction of crucible cast steel. Above all, the steam engine provided industry with a new source of power and made possible the replacement of small workshops by large factories. However this process was gradual and the factory did not become the characteristic unit of industrial organization until after 1830.

Social conditions, too, favoured economic progress. The class structure in England was less rigid than in continental Europe. No social stigma prevented the landed gentry from engaging in industry or trade; no legal impediments prevented an artisan from rising in the social scale. However, the bulk of early industrialists were drawn from the wide middle ranks of British society. In spite of some sporadic violent opposition to the new order – machine-breaking and rick-burning – a labour force grew which eventually accepted factory discipline.

Down the coalmine (left) This sketch of small boys dragging a trolley in a coalmine illustrates one aspect of the human suffering involved during the Industrial Revolution. The employment of women and children under ground was prohibited in 1842.

1/The pattern of industrial expansion (below) Rapid industrial expansion took place in regions where minerals, particularly coal and iron ore, could be exploited. Many of these natural resources were conveniently situated near ports. Thus coal from Durham and Northumberland could be shipped to London from ports on the Tyne and Wear. The manufacturing regions were linked by a network of toll roads, by navigable rivers, and by canals. The Industrial Revolution was associated with a movement of population to the coalfields, ports and new manufacturing districts.

Watt's rotative beam steam engine (above) In 1765 James Watt invented his first steam engine, which was used almost exclusively to work pumps. In 1781 he invented the rotative engine, which could turn a shaft and so drive machinery. Whilst the engines were under patent the firm of Boulton & Watt built about 200 steam pumps and over 300 rotative engines.

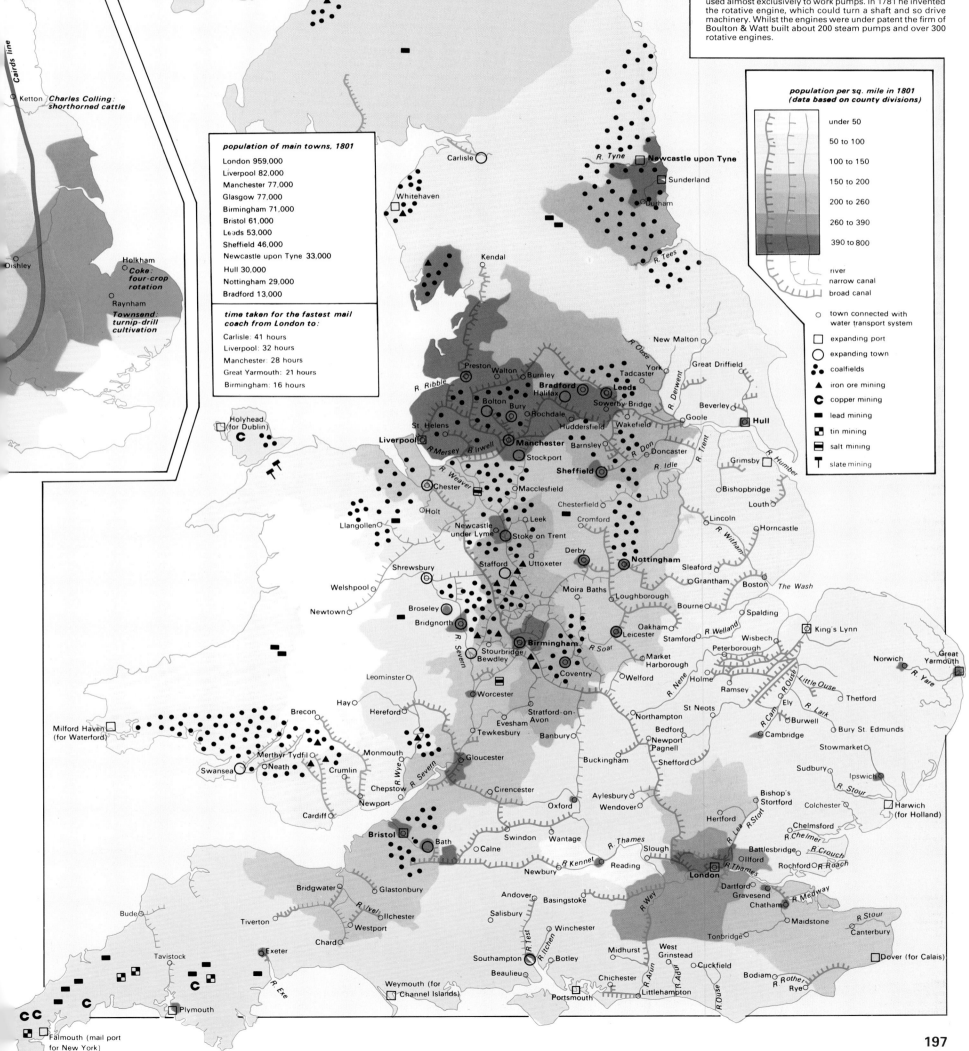

population of main towns, 1801

London 959,000
Liverpool 82,000
Manchester 77,000
Glasgow 77,000
Birmingham 71,000
Bristol 61,000
Leeds 53,000
Sheffield 46,000
Newcastle upon Tyne 33,000
Hull 30,000
Nottingham 29,000
Bradford 13,000

time taken for the fastest mail coach from London to:

Carlisle: 41 hours
Liverpool: 32 hours
Manchester: 28 hours
Great Yarmouth: 21 hours
Birmingham: 16 hours

population per sq. mile in 1801
(data based on county divisions)

under 50
50 to 100
100 to 150
150 to 200
200 to 260
260 to 390
390 to 800

river
narrow canal
broad canal
○ town connected with water transport system
□ expanding port
◯ expanding town
•: coalfields
▲ iron ore mining
C copper mining
■ lead mining
⊡ tin mining
⊟ salt mining
T slate mining

The age of revolt 1773 to 1814

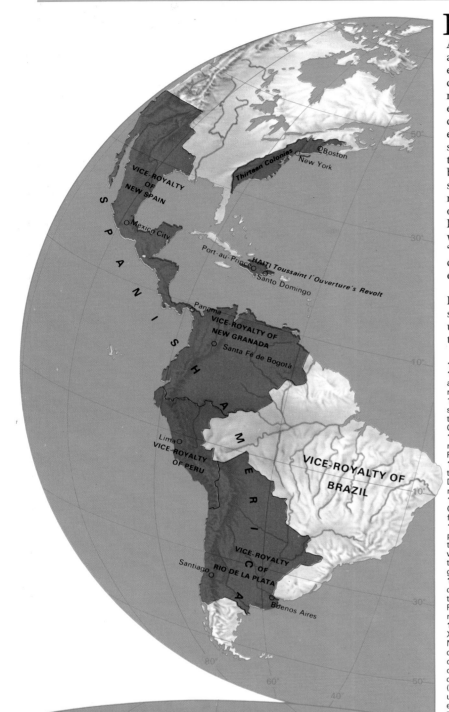

BY THE late 18th century, complex economic and cultural processes had produced in the Americas societies that were more advanced and more complex than the regimes that governed them. In eastern and central Europe, by contrast, enlightened rulers strove to impose more centralized, bureaucratic systems of government on societies still basically feudal in character. Broadly speaking, conditions in western Europe and the New World produced a series of revolutions which created political systems based on open, accountable government, based on written constitutions and elected, if seldom truly democratic, assemblies; elsewhere, rulers such as Joseph II and Catherine the Great of Russia saw reforms crumble in the face of local particularism, noble power and an almost wholly agrarian, feudal economic structure. The 'age of revolution' was in fact limited geographically and served to widen the gap between eastern and western Europe.

The two major states of western Europe in the late 18th century, Britain and France, both had sophisticated economies based on growing populations – and expanding domestic markets for their industries – and burgeoning overseas

trade. They were also the centres of the Enlightenment, whose leading thinkers, although seldom overtly political, often pointed to the gap between the needs of society and the ability of governments to meet them; none envisaged reform by revolution.

Britain possessed the more advanced political system, based on a single national parliament which afforded a degree of representative government and an efficient system of taxation that allowed the state to tap the expanding wealth of the society it ruled. By contrast, France was a modern society and economy ruled by a government dependent on a medieval system of taxation. The last quarter of the century saw several attempts by the French monarchy to reform the fiscal system but they failed through a mixture of vested interests centred on the nobility and the wealthy tax-farmers, and fears that a monarchy made financially secure would soon become despotic. By the late 1780s, it was obvious that 'reform from above' had failed.

Although Britain avoided a crisis of this kind at home, its attempts to reform the administration of its 13 North American colonies produced a series of confrontations which culminated in

1/The age of revolt (left and below)
1755, 1793 Corsica Local clans led by Paoli rebelled against Genoese rule and established independent democratic government. France bought the island from Genoa in 1768 and crushed the revolt. A second attempt by Paoli to secure independence from (revolutionary) France, 1793, led to brief British occupation; the rise of Bonaparte, himself a Corsican, put an end to separatist movement.
1768 Geneva Middle-class citizens of small city-state rebelled against domination by few patrician families; with French support the latter reasserted predominance 1782.
1773 Southeast Russia Cossacks, peasants and Asiatic tribes rebelled in Volga and Ural region under Pugachev, a Don Cossack. After fierce fighting, Russian army put down rebellion in autumn 1774 (see page 158).
1775 America Prolonged resistance by the Thirteen Colonies to Britain's financial policies resulted in open warfare and Declaration of Independence, 1776 (see page 160).
1785 Dutch Netherlands Three-cornered struggle for power between *Stadholder*, patrician families who controlled Estates General, and middle-class Patriot party which aimed to democratize government. In 1787 Prussian troops defeated Patriot army and restored *Stadholder* with greater powers.
1787 Austrian Netherlands (Belgium) Revolt against centralizing policy of Emperor Joseph II, led to proclamation of the Republic of the United Belgian Provinces (1790). Faction fights broke out between noble and middle-class rebels; Austrian Emperor retook area end 1790.
1789 France The Estates-General, summoned by Louis XVI to solve his financial difficulties, turned itself into a National Assembly, proclaimed Rights of Man, and issued constitution (1791). Risings by peasantry and Parisians overthrew feudal social and political order; Louis XVI's opposition, and attempted flight, led to abolition of monarchy (1792). King and Queen were guillotined as traitors (1793). Threat of invasion by a coalition under Austria led under the Jacobins to 'reign of terror', ended by fall and execution of Robespierre (1794). Following weak rule of Directory (1795-99) power passed to Napoleon Bonaparte.

1789 Liège Middle-class citizens supported by workers and peasants expelled prince-bishop and abolished feudalism. Bishop restored by Austrian troops, 1790.
1790 Hungary Magyar nobles rejected edicts of Austrian emperor and demanded greater independence for Hungary within Habsburg Empire; later, frightened by peasant disturbances, accepted compromise with the monarchy.
1791 Poland King, supported by patriotic nobles, adopted constitution to modernize and strengthen government. Catherine II of Russia organized counter-revolution with support of some of greater nobles to restore old regime, invaded Poland and divided large areas with Prussia. Attempt by Kosciuzko and patriotic nobles to rise against invaders crushed, Poland partitioned between Russia, Austria and Prussia and ceased to exist as independent state.
1791 Haiti Slave rising in western (French) part of island (Saint Domingue) resulted in rise of Black leader, Toussaint l'Ouverture; by 1801 had conquered rest of island from Spaniards and secured virtual independence. Island then seized by the French, rising suppressed, and independence not fully secured until 1825.
1793 Sardinia In return for expelling French revolutionary invaders, islanders demanded autonomy within combined kingdom of Piedmont-Sardinia. King re-asserted his authority when French threat subsided in 1796.
1798 Ireland Rebellion of United Irishmen seeking independence from England, put down by British army. Leading conspirator, Wolfe Tone, committed suicide.
1804 Serbia Revolt against Ottoman atrocities led to demands for autonomy within the Ottoman Empire and later for independence. Rebels under Kara George fought until the Ottoman reoccupation of Serbia in 1813.
1808 Spain After Napoleon placed his brother, Joseph, on the throne a national rising against the French provided an opening for an expeditionary force under Wellington. Liberal constitution proclaimed by Cortes of Cádiz in 1812, but it did not survive restoration of Bourbon king in 1814.
1809 Tyrol After Austria renewed war against Napoleon, the peasants of Tyrol, whose territory had been taken from Austria by Napoleon in 1805 and given to Bavaria, rebelled against new rulers. In spite of brave stand under Andreas Hofer, an innkeeper, revolt was crushed by Bavarian and French troops.
1810 Spanish America Discontent against mother country increased after 1808, when colonists faced prospect of new imperialist policies from either Napoleon or Spanish liberals; beginning of revolutionary movement which secured independence of entire sub-continent during following two decades (see page 222).

boundaries at 1789

areas affected by revolt

the American Revolution (1775–81), and independence for the colonists (see page 160). These events took place on what was still the fringe of the developed world and had little direct impact on contemporary events in Europe. Believing themselves forced into rebellion by a state bent on despotism, the colonists created their own political structures and fashioned a new state for themselves; they turned to the political thinkers of the Enlightenment, and to Montesquieu in particular, because of his preference for a system of checks and balances in government, which they felt would protect their rights as individuals. By drawing up a formal, written constitution, with a government composed wholly of elected officials, the American revolutionaries consciously advanced western political culture from the world of closed, absolutist government, to one of open, accountable public life.

An abortive revolution in the Netherlands in 1787–8 closely paralleled events in America. The loose, federal structure of the Dutch Republic seemed threatened by reforms proposed by its head, the Stadholder, to strengthen the army. Fears of despotism led to provincial revolts and the emergence of a 'patriot movement', demanding increased municipal independence and wider participation in politics. The revolt was quickly crushed, but it represents the same mix of traditional sources of resistance to reform and the new concerns already evident in America. The growing financial crisis precipitated similar, but more convulsed events in France in 1789. Louis XVI, faced by determined opposition to his plans for tax reform, summoned the Estates General, a body of elected representatives of the whole realm which had not met since 1614. Effectively, this brought a new group of men into the centre of French political life. Louis's indecision in the face of a bad harvest, peasant revolts, imminent bankruptcy and, above all, the bitter conflict between the noble and non-noble deputies, created a power vacuum into which the Estates General stepped, now the self-proclaimed National Assembly. It quickly seized the initiative, abolishing all fiscal privileges – an act which greatly reduced the political power of the nobility, the Church and many towns and provinces – and creating a uniform system of administration which destroyed the old provinces and their local representative assemblies. By 1791, a centralized state had been created, almost at a stroke, with a new constitution based on a limited monarchy in partnership with an assembly elected on a narrow franchise based on wealth. This was where unity among the revolutionaries ended, however. The course of the Revolution from 1791 until 1799 was marked by a series of violent splits within the ranks of the new political class over how democratic the constitution should be, over the continued need for a monarchy and, at root, over whether the Revolution should be halted. Whereas in America similar divisions evolved in a generally peaceful climate, three important factors pushed events in France into violence: Louis XVI attempted to regain the initiative at several points and emerged as the centre of opposition to the constitution he was meant to protect; many of the reforms – particularly those touching the Church – were deeply unpopular with the vast mass of the peasantry; above all, the other European powers soon intervened to try and halt the Revolution and take advantage of a France weakened by internal divisions. All these things destroyed the settlement of 1791. By 1792, France was at war with Austria and Prussia and, by 1793, with Britain. In the same year, Louis – and the constitution built around him – gave way to a Republic with a war government centred on a new National Convention, elected by universal male suffrage. Divisions within its ranks leading to a civil war among the revolutionaries leading – via several purges of the government and the abandonment of the democratic constitution of 1793 – to a consensus based on fear that allowed Napoleon to take power in 1799 as a military dictator pledged to protect the new political classes from the wrath of their enemies, while depriving them of power.

Deep-seated hatred towards the new regime provoked counter-revolutionary revolts, most successfully in the Vendée, in western France, but resistance to conscription and dislike of many other reforms engendered a bitter if fragmented guerrilla war against the Revolution all over France. As French armies occupied most of western Europe, this process was repeated on a wider scale, reaching its height in the Spanish resistance to Napoleon's invasion (1808–1813). In Italy, western Germany, Spain and the Netherlands, the 'sister republics' set up by the French along revolutionary lines rested solely on military force and were swept aside after the defeat of Napoleon in 1814.

It was very different in Latin America, where the Spanish colonies won their independence in a series of revolutionary wars and created republics with institutions, laws and constitutions modelled directly on French and North American examples. The European settlers retained too tight a grip on the Indian masses for dangerous popular resistance to their rule to develop. However, following independence the new political classes of Spanish America soon descended into bitter factionalism which continued well into the 19th century. Only the Portuguese colony of Brazil took a peaceful path to independence. Nevertheless, the influence of the French revolution proved much more direct and permanent in Latin America than in many parts of eastern and central Europe, where the old order resisted its advance as successfully as it had the reforms of the Enlightened Despots.

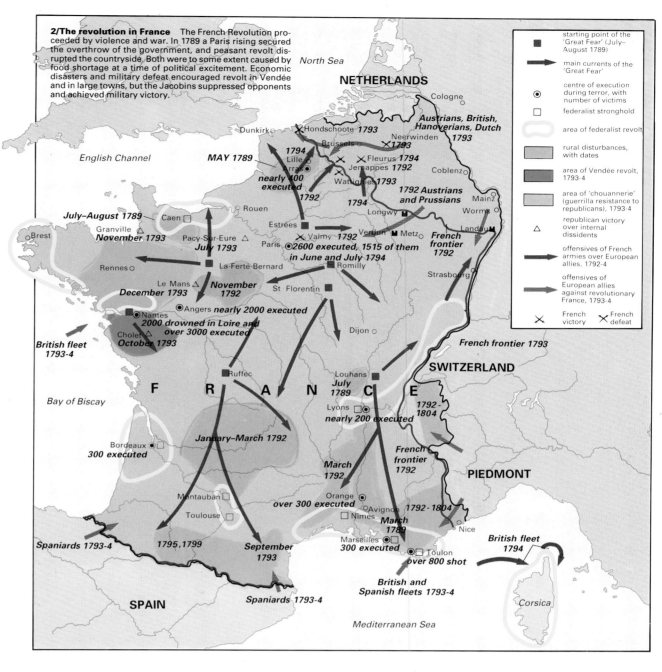

2/The revolution in France The French Revolution proceeded by violence and war. In 1789 a Paris rising secured the overthrow of the government, and peasant revolt disrupted the countryside. Both were to some extent caused by food shortage at a time of political excitement. Economic disasters and military defeat encouraged revolt in Vendée and in large towns, but the Jacobins suppressed opponents and achieved military victory.

- starting point of the 'Great Fear' (July–August 1789)
- main currents of the 'Great Fear'
- centre of execution during terror, with number of victims
- federalist stronghold
- area of federalist revolt
- rural disturbances, with dates
- area of Vendée revolt, 1793-4
- area of 'chouannerie' (guerrilla resistance to republicans), 1793-4
- republican victory over internal dissidents
- offensives of French armies over European allies, 1792-4
- offensives of European allies against revolutionary France, 1793-4
- French victory × French defeat ×

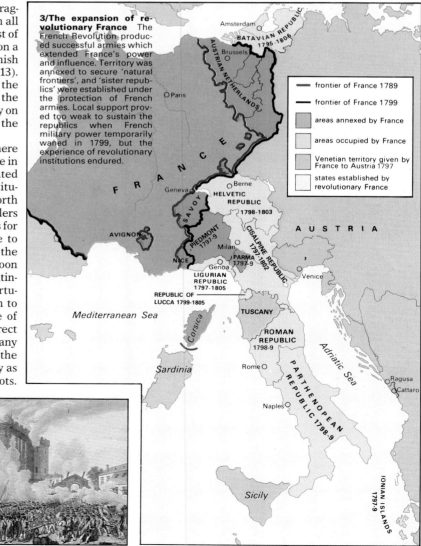

3/The expansion of revolutionary France The French Revolution produced successful armies which extended France's power and influence. Territory was annexed to secure 'natural frontiers', and 'sister republics' were established under the protection of French armies. Local support proved too weak to sustain the republics when French military power temporarily waned in 1799, but the experience of revolutionary institutions endured.

- frontier of France 1789
- frontier of France 1799
- areas annexed by France
- areas occupied by France
- Venetian territory given by France to Austria 1797
- states established by revolutionary France

The storming of the Bastille on 14 July 1789 (right) began the French Revolution because the government's failure to prevent the release of the few political prisoners held there demonstrated the collapse of its authority.

Napoleon and the reshaping of Europe

2/Napoleonic institutions *(above)*, designed to create a society based on wealth and merit rather than on prescription and privilege, were established to some degree over the whole of western Europe. Their effect varied according to the type of control Napoleon exercised (see map 1) and the length of time they operated. Spain officially received Napoleonic institutions in a modified form for about five years, but their effectiveness varied with the fortunes of war.

Map legend:
areas which experienced Napoleonic institutions in full:
- for more than 10 years
- for less than 5 years

areas which experienced modified forms of Napoleonic institutions:
- for more than 8 years
- for less than 5 years

The Legion of Honour *(above)* was created in 1802 to reward both soldiers and civilians for outstanding service to the state. The distinction was accompanied by a pension. Critics complained that revolutionary equality had given way to elitism, but the Legion became popular throughout the French Empire. One of the recipients of the honour was Goethe.

NAPOLEON Bonaparte's most important contribution to the history of modern Europe lay not in his dazzling military career but, rather, in the creation of an empire in western Europe ruled in accordance with the basic reforms of the French Revolution. Its administrative and ideological coherence made it very different from existing empires, most notably those of the Habsburgs or the Ottoman Empire, and brought a new, often traumatic experience of life under a modern state to the peoples of France, Italy, Germany, Spain and the Low Countries.

Napoleon was barely 30 years old when he became First Consul and head of the French Republic in November, 1799. His rise through the ranks of the revolutionary army to the rank of general at the age of 28 had been facilitated by the chaos wrought by continuous war between France and the coalition of anti-revolutionary powers led by Britain, Austria and Russia. However, he then displayed great audacity and skill as a diplomat and politician in exploiting his military victories in northern Italy in 1796–7. Having effectively pursued his own diplomatic policy, negotiating peace with the defeated Austrians on his own terms, he created a new state in northern Italy, the Cisalpine Republic, which foreshadowed much of his future agenda for conquered territories. Relying on a thin stratum of pro-French Italian patriots and, where he could, the wealthier landowners, Napoleon's new state was closely modelled on republican France. From the outset of his political career, the essence of Napoleon's approach to territorial expansion was to impose French institutions on the areas under his control.

Napoleon came to power in France through a coup organized by several leading politicians in order to strengthen, rather than destroy, the moderate republican regime which had ruled France since 1795: the Directory. Four years later the military tide had turned against France and republican politicians feared that the regime would not survive another serious military defeat or a resurgence of counter-revolution within France. Faced with the alternatives of a revival of extreme republicanism and a renewal of the Terror, or a stronger executive centred on the army, the political elite created by the Revolution chose the second: by 1799, the 'French Revolution' had come to mean less the concept of parliamentary government, than the defence of a highly centralized, aggressively anti-royalist, anti-clerical state. By executing Louis XVI and nationalizing Church lands, the men of the Directory bound themselves less to the Revolution than to the struggle against counter-revolution; and when, in 1800, Napoleon's new constitution emasculated the legislature at the expense of his own office, it was seen as a small price to pay for his more basic guarantees of security to the revolutionaries.

In his subsequent reforms, Napoleon did not destroy the Revolution, so much as reinterpret it in the light of new priorities imposed by the lack of widespread support. To compensate for this, Napoleon pursued the existing policy of bureaucratic centralization to its logical conclusion. The executive was progressively strengthened, first by Napoleon's appointment as Consul for life in 1802 and then by the creation of an hereditary Empire (1804). At a more basic level the main unit of local government, the *département*, was now headed by a prefect appointed from the centre, rather than by an elected council. To most revolutionaries, these changes were acceptable as a means of preserving their domination of public life; Napoleon's reforms may have weakened them in relation to the central executive, but at least most of them survived in office. The *Code Napoléon* consolidated the majority of the major legal reforms of the Revolution. Feudal privilege remained abolished and although Napoleon soon created his own titles and honours, none of them carried legal or fiscal distinctions; equality before the law was reaffirmed, as was the essentially secular nature of the state. When Napoleon negotiated the Concordat with Pope Pius VII in 1802, he did so from a position of strength that ensured no alienated Church properties were returned and that the clergy remained under strict state control.

The strength which enabled him to carry

1/The Empire of Napoleon *(right)* By 1812 Napoleon controlled the greater part of western Europe, exacting men and money for his armies but bringing greater opportunities for men of talent. Only Spain, supported by Britain, was in rebellion against him. In 1812, however, his invasion of Russia met with disaster. Driven back into France, he was obliged to abdicate (1814). His Empire was destroyed, but many of his ideas lived on.

through these reforms rested upon two foundations: success in restoring law and order within France and a series of stunning military victories against the allies. Early in his rule, Napoleon created the *Gendarmerie*, a para-military police force drawn from the ranks of the army, which specialized in policing the countryside and was solidly loyal to the regime. Through it, banditry and counter-revolutionary guerrillas were gradually defeated and this internal reconquest of France gratified the propertied classes, in general, as well as the revolutionary politicians, and opened the way for reintegration of the nobility into state service. It also paved the way for the more efficient enforcement of mass conscription, instituted in 1792 and regularized the following year.

The spectacular military victories of 1800–7 were founded not only on the military genius of one man, but on the creation of a modern administrative machine capable of sustaining prolonged war. Napoleon's own campaign of 1800 in Italy, together with those of his subordinates on the Rhine, re-established French hegemony in the areas temporarily lost in 1799, but the most momentous victories came against Austria and Russia at Austerlitz in December, 1805, then over Prussia at Jena in 1806 and, finally, over Russia at Eylau in 1807. These campaigns, ending with an uneasy alliance with Russia (the Peace of Tilsit, 1807), advanced French domination into central Europe. 'Satellite kingdoms'

The crossing of the Berezina River *(above)* between 25 and 29 November 1812 was one of the most harrowing and heroic moments of Napoleon's retreat from Moscow. Napoleon drew off the Russians by a clever decoy: while his engineers worked day and night in icy water to create pontoon-bridges, his forces escaped, although thousands of wounded were left behind. This picture is thought to have been painted by an officer present at the scene.

taneously – in the small German states loyal to Napoleon: Bavaria, Baden, Württemberg, Nassau and Saxony. Above all, the conscription of people of these regions – usually for the first time – gave them a painful introduction to the practical realities of the modern state.

By 1807, only the conflict with Britain remained unresolved and it was the attempt to defeat her that led directly to the next, ultimately disastrous phase of Imperial expansion. In order to enforce his plan of economic warfare against Britain – the Continental System – Napoleon was driven into further annexations between 1808 and 1811, first along the North Sea coast as far as Hamburg, and in central Italy (Tuscany and the Papal States). The demands of the blockade also led him to intervene directly in Spain, where a new satellite kingdom was created in 1808 under Joseph (Murat, Napoleon's brother-in-law, took Naples). These annexations did not follow the smooth path of the earlier ones; they constituted an 'outer empire', where French institutions never became a reality and where resistance to their reforms proved ferocious. In Spain, the vastness of the country, together with the presence of a British army in Portugal, rendered military occupation difficult and armed popular resistance widespread; in the Papal States, the deposition of the Pope not only led to Napoleon's excommunication, but to mass passive resistance to most aspects of French rule; all along the North Sea coast smuggling reached staggering proportions, fostered by the Royal Navy. Resistance to conscription spawned banditry almost everywhere. In 1809 the French client state of Bavaria faced a popular revolt of its own in the Tyrol, provoked by the introduction of a series of reforms on the French model, while widespread but unco-ordinated revolts broke out in central Italy and the countryside around Venice.

Those areas longest under French rule, such

were created in these areas – the Grand Duchy of Berg, ruled by Napoleon himself; the Kingdom of Westphalia under his brother, Jerome; and the Grand Duchy of Warsaw, a limited restoration of Poland – while in Italy, the Kingdom of Naples came under his eldest brother, Joseph, and Napoleon himself became ruler of the Kingdom of Italy in the north. Another Bonaparte brother, Louis, became King of Holland, replacing the oldest 'satellite state', the Batavian Republic.

All these polities saw attempts to introduce the most important aspects of the French system of government. In practice, this meant an assault on the feudal privileges of the nobility, on the place of the Church in society, and on deep-rooted particularist traditions. French-style reforms were also adopted – usually spon-

as the Rhineland, northwestern Italy (the former states of Genoa and Piedmont-Savoy) experienced many of the beneficial aspects of French rule, as did the Grand Duchy of Warsaw, the only part of the Empire where Napoleon could draw on a developed sense of national identity. Elsewhere, Imperial rule provoked the same popular resistance faced by the revolutionary governments in France in the 1790s.

By the time Napoleon launched his disastrous invasion of Russia in 1812 – motivated by the Tsar's failure to support the anti-British blockade – French hegemony was seriously compromised in all but the inner core of the Empire – France itself, the Rhineland and northwest Italy – and even France, exhausted financially and ruined by the blockade, turned against Napoleon in 1814. His brief, audacious return to power in 1815 – the '100 Days' – ended in a crushing defeat by the allies at Waterloo (although it also showed that his unpopularity in France had been largely transitory).

The rapid collapse of the Napoleonic state system between 1812 and 1814 should not be allowed to disguise the fundamental influence of French rule on the evolution of modern Europe. In western Europe, even many of those most hostile to French imperialism embraced the principles behind their reforms and admired the efficiency of the Napoleonic state, none more so than the Spanish liberals who, while resisting a French siege in the port of Cádiz, drew up a constitution along French lines. Throughout the early 19th century, Spanish, German and Italian reformers envisaged the modern state in essentially Napoleonic terms. Conversely, the European masses learnt to distrust exactly this same model, identifying it with conscription, atheism and oppression. The years 1799–1814 saw the creation of a subtle set of attitudes which would not be erased by the Congress of Vienna.

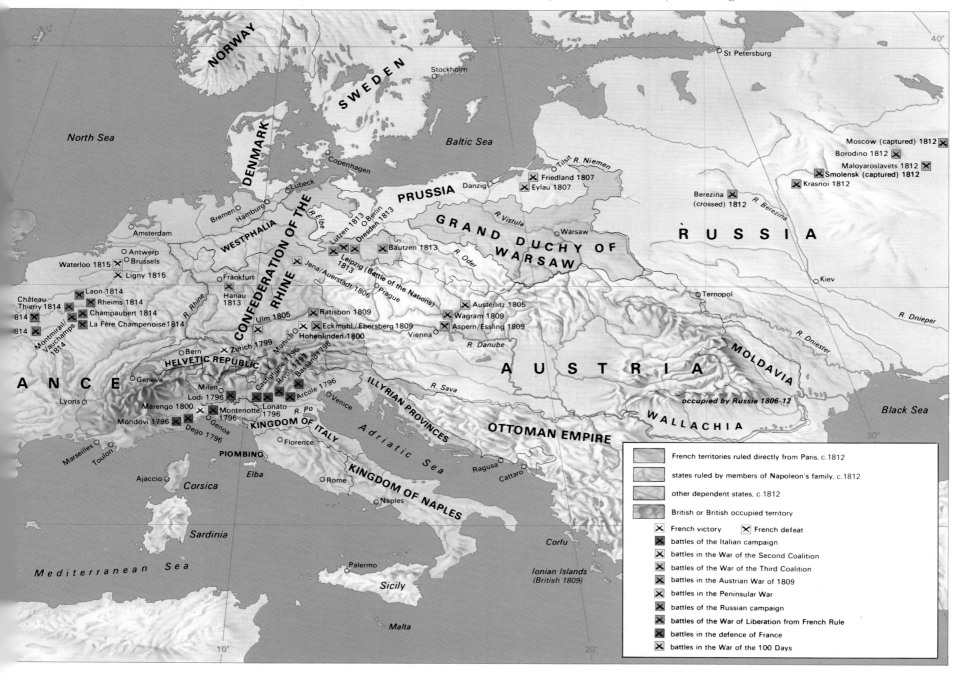

French territories ruled directly from Paris, c.1812

states ruled by members of Napoleon's family, c.1812

other dependent states, c.1812

British or British occupied territory

☒ French victory   ☒ French defeat

☒ battles of the Italian campaign

☒ battles in the War of the Second Coalition

☒ battles of the War of the Third Coalition

☒ battles in the Austrian War of 1809

☒ battles in the Peninsular War

☒ battles of the Russian campaign

☒ battles of the War of Liberation from French Rule

☒ battles in the defence of France

☒ battles in the War of the 100 Days

ETWEEN 1815 and 1914 Europe thrust out into the world, impelled by the force of its own industrialization. Millions of Europeans poured overseas and into Asiatic Russia, seeking and finding new opportunities in the wider world. Between 1880 and 1900 Africa, a continent four times the size of Europe, was parcelled out among the European powers. And when in 1898 the United States of America, following Europe's lead, annexed Puerto Rico, the Philippines and other islands of the Pacific, and asserted a controlling voice in Latin American affairs, it seemed as though Western expansion had secured the domination of the white race over the non-white majority. But expansion carried with it the seeds of its own destruction. Even before European rivalries plunged the continent into the war of 1914-18, the beginnings of anti-European reaction were visible in Asia and Africa, and no sooner had the United States occupied the Philippines than they were met by a nationalist uprising.

Today, in retrospect, we can see that the age of expansive imperialism was a transient phase of history; nevertheless, it left a lasting European imprint. The world in 1914 was utterly different from the world in 1815, the tempo of change during the preceding century greater than previously during whole millennia. Though industry in 1914 was only beginning to spread beyond Europe and North America, and life in Asia and Africa was still regulated by age-old traditions, the 19th century inaugurated the process of transformation which dethroned agricultural society as it had existed for thousands of years, and replaced it with the urban, industrialized, technocratic society which is spreading – for good or for ill – like wildfire through the world today.

6

The age of

The Eiffel Tower, Paris, built in 1889 for the Centennial Exposition

European dominance

Population growth and movements
1815 to 1914

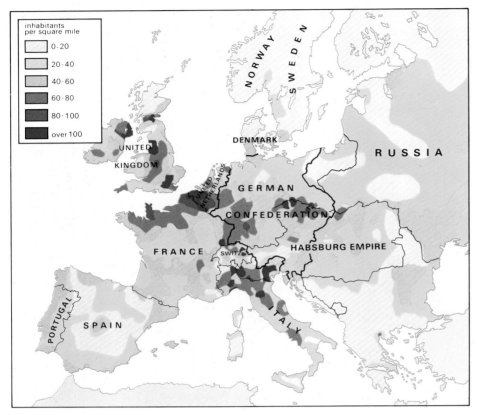

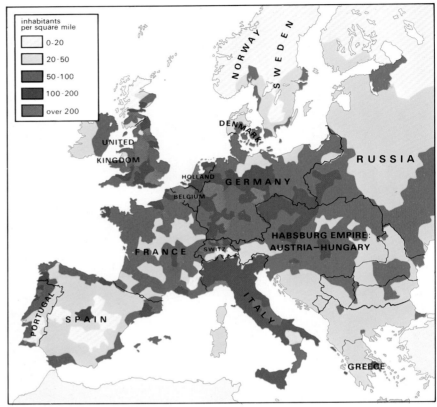

3/Europe's population in 1820 (above) The major centres were the industrialized regions of the United Kingdom and a few major cities and ports (London, Paris, St Petersburg, Liverpool, Bordeaux, Hamburg, Marseilles).

4/Europe's population by c.1900 (above) was concentrated in the main industrial British centres: the Midlands, Yorkshire, Lancashire, south Wales, Tyneside, Clydeside; in Belgium, France and Germany (the Ruhr, Rhineland, Upper Silesia).

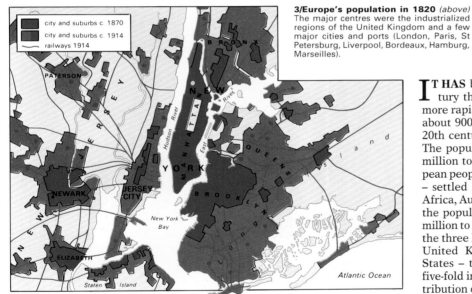

New York (above) By 1810 New York had outstripped its rivals to become the most dynamic urban centre in the New World. In 1810 its population was only 100,000, but passed 1 million by 1871.

Immigration (below) During the 19th century more than two-thirds of all immigrants to the United States passed through the port of New York where the Statue of Liberty symbolized their hopes.

IT HAS been estimated that in the 19th century the population of the world expanded more rapidly than in any previous period, from about 900 million to 1600 million. (During the 20th century it was to grow four times faster.) The population of Europe increased from 190 million to 423 million; at the same time, European peoples – emigrants and their descendants – settled in North and South America, South Africa, Australia, New Zealand and Siberia, and the population of these regions grew from 5.7 million to 200 million between 1810 and 1910. In the three leading industrial states in 1914 – the United Kingdom, Germany and the United States – the population had increased nearly five-fold in the previous hundred years. The distribution of the world's population at the beginning of the 20th century was estimated to be as follows (again in millions): Europe 423, Asia 937, Africa 120, North and South America 144, and Australia 6. There were, however, exceptions to the general growth in population. Ireland, for example, had a declining population: it fell from 8.2 million in 1841 to 4.4 million in 1911.

Various factors promoted the overall growth of the population during the 19th century. In Europe, in the United States, and in the colonies and spheres of influence of European states, the greatly improved methods of industrial and agricultural production, coupled with more efficient communications, provided work and food for expanding populations. The colonial powers established mines and plantations in their overseas territories which supplied manufacturing countries with increased quantities of raw materials and foodstuffs. Advanced industrial regions were free from the food shortages which were all too common in backward countries. There was no parallel in Britain, France or Germany to the famines that afflicted Ireland in 1847, India in 1866 and 1877, China in 1878 and Russia in 1891. Advances in medicine, improved sanitation and higher standards of personal hygiene resulted in a dramatic reduction in mortality from cholera, tuberculosis, smallpox, typhus and typhoid.

Population growth was not spread evenly over urban and rural districts. The expansion of old cities and the founding of new towns were characteristic features of the industrial age. The population of some cities with a history going back to medieval times – London, Cologne, Lyons, Moscow and many others – increased rapidly in the 19th century. Towns which had been mere villages, or had not even existed, in the previous century sprang to life as great centres of industry, commerce or mining. Middlesbrough and Barrow in England; Gelsenkirchen, Oberhausen and Königshütte in Germany; Łódź in Poland; and a host of towns in the United States and in the English colonies were examples of this type of mushroom urban growth. In industrial countries more and more people worked and lived in towns while fewer lived in the country.

Populations not only grew more rapidly in the 19th century than ever before but also migrated on a considerable scale. Millions of people moved from Europe to the United States or to British colonies in North America, South Africa, Australia and New Zealand, building up new communities of white settlers which produced foodstuffs and raw materials for the countries they had left behind. The 'Europeanization' of vast territories overseas was a significant factor in increasing the political influence of the major European states throughout the world. Migrations within states or regions included movements of workers from one district to another, seeking employment either on the land during the harvest, or in towns, where job opportunities existed in factories and mines or in public works such as railway building. Irishmen sought work in Liverpool, Manchester and Glasgow; Poles moved to the coal mines in the Ruhr. Some migration was temporary in character. Irishmen who went to England or Scotland to dig potatoes generally returned home when the harvest was over. From Italy, seasonal labourers went to work in France, Germany and Switzerland – and even in the Argentine – and it has been estimated that in 1914 there were no fewer than 3 million of these migrant workers. In Russia some peasants secured jobs in urban factories for the winter and then returned to work in their villages during the summer. However, emigration from one country to another – especially when long distances were involved – usually tended to be more permanent.

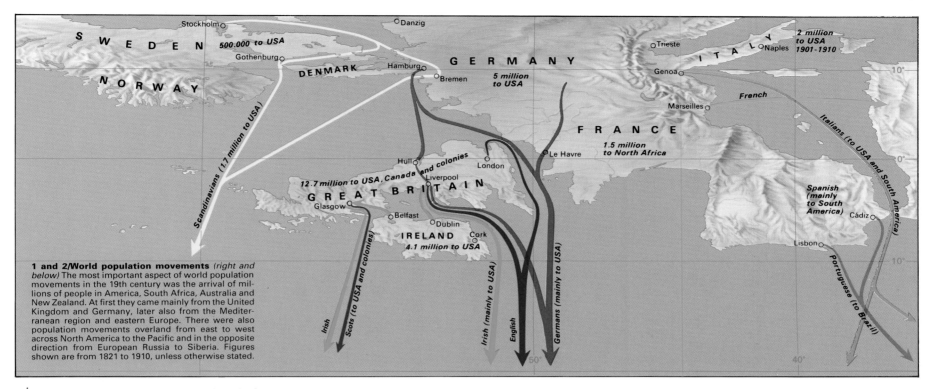

1 and 2/World population movements (right and below) The most important aspect of world population movements in the 19th century was the arrival of millions of people in America, South Africa, Australia and New Zealand. At first they came mainly from the United Kingdom and Germany, later also from the Mediterranean region and eastern Europe. There were also population movements overland from east to west across North America to the Pacific and in the opposite direction from European Russia to Siberia. Figures shown are from 1821 to 1910, unless otherwise stated.

Some of those who left their native land had no choice in the matter. The convicts transported from England to Australia up to 1867, or from France to Devil's Island, did not go of their own accord. Nor were Russian political prisoners exiled to Siberia, or the Negro slaves shipped from West Africa to the Americas or from Zanzibar to Arabia, willing migrants. The Atlantic slave trade, though prohibited by international agreements shortly after the Napoleonic wars, survived (albeit on a much reduced scale) until after the middle of the 19th century; and not until the 1890s was the Arab slave trade on the east coast of Africa at last stamped out.

Two factors influenced the timing of emigration and the destination of the migrants. One was the fact that conditions at home were unsatisfactory, the other that the United States, Canada, Australia and New Zealand had much to offer new settlers. Some emigrated because they were persecuted on account of their religious or political beliefs. German liberals who were harassed by Metternich's police, or Russian Jews who feared for their lives, found sanctuary in the United States. But most emigrants from Europe sought a new home. And in the first half of the 19th century they braved great dangers and hardships to cross the Atlantic to North America. The Irish who emigrated at the time of the great famine of 1847, and the German peasants who gave up their smallholdings in Baden and Württemberg a year or two later because they could no longer make ends meet, had nothing to lose and everything to gain by leaving home. Whenever there was a trade slump in the industrial regions of Europe some of the unemployed emigrated. Cheap – even free – land for farmers, good prospects for employment in mines and factories and democratic institutions made the United States a promised land for those who crossed the Atlantic. The hope of making a fortune quickly brought tens of thousands of immigrants to America and Australia during the gold rushes in California (1849) and Victoria (1851).

In the first half of the 19th century the bulk of the European emigrants came from the United Kingdom (2.4 million) and Germany (1.1 million). In the second half of the century those from the United Kingdom (9.5 million) and Germany (5 million) were joined by others from Italy (5 million), the Scandinavian countries (1 million), Belgium, Spain and the Balkans. The British settled mainly in the United States and the British colonies, while the Germans went to the United States (above all Pennsylvania and the mid-West) and to South America (especially Rio Grande do Sul in Brazil). French emigrants settled in Algeria, Italians in Tunis and Argentina, and Russians in Siberia. (It has been estimated that the white element in world population grew from 22 per cent in 1800 to 35 per cent in 1930.)

There were also considerable population movements in Asia and across the Indian Ocean and the Pacific. From China – particularly from the southern provinces – there was a continuous flow of settlers to Siam, Java and the Malay peninsula. Chinese also emigrated to California, British Columbia and New South Wales. From India emigrants crossed the Indian Ocean to Natal and East Africa. In British East Africa they eventually surpassed the white settlers in numbers and probably in aggregate wealth. However, some of the Chinese and Indian emigrants were coolies who were engaged by contractors for a fixed term to work on plantations, in mines, and on public works. This system of indentured labour was open to grave abuses which were only gradually eradicated.

emigration from Europe
emigration from Japan
emigration from China
emigration from India
migration from European Russia

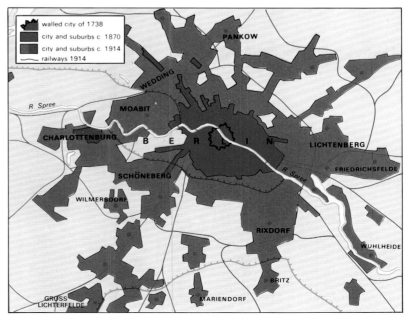

walled city of 1738
city and suburbs c. 1870
city and suburbs c. 1914
railways 1914

Urban growth: Berlin (right) A typical example of the expansion of a European city brought about by the construction of railways and the development of consumer industries. The court, the administration, the army and the university also contributed to population growth.

The Industrial Revolution in Europe 1815 to 1870

IN THE first half of the 19th century the United Kingdom was the leading manufacturing country in the world although modern factories, with machines driven by steam, also functioned in some regions on the continent of Europe. As early as 1809 a visitor to the valleys of the Ruhr and the Wupper described them as a 'miniature England'. On the Continent, as in Britain, the coalfields were the most important centres of industrial growth. The largest coal fields were situated in the Nord *département* of France, the valleys of the Sambre and the Meuse in Belgium, and the Ruhr valley in Germany. Here modern industries developed in the first half of the 19th century.

Elsewhere on the Continent progress towards industrialization was largely confined to capital cities (Paris, Berlin), to centres of communications (Lyons, Cologne, Frankfurt-am-Main, Cracow, Warsaw), to major ports (Hamburg, Bremen, Rotterdam, Le Havre, Marseilles) and to particular districts such as the textile regions of Lille, Roubaix, Mulhouse, Barmen-Elberfeld (Wuppertal), Chemnitz, Lodz and Moscow, and to the iron and engineering districts of the Loire basin, the Saar, and Upper Silesia.

Although in certain important respects the Industrial Revolution on the Continent followed a somewhat similar pattern to that in Britain, there were also significant differences. In the early 19th century the continental countries could benefit from earlier English experience. British blueprints, machinery and steam engines were installed in continental factories, and some British skilled artisans also migrated to Europe. Moreover, British entrepreneurs and financiers helped to found new industrial enterprises on the Continent. In France, Aaron Manby and Daniel Wilson founded the Charenton ironworks, Humphrey Edwards became a partner in the Chaillot engineering plant, Richard Roberts planned the layout of a cotton mill for André Koechlin at Mulhouse, while Thomas Brassey and W. and E. Mackenzie built many French railways.

In time, however, continental countries ceased to rely upon Britain for new machines. In France, for example, several important inventions were made, such as the Jacquard loom, the Séguin multi-tubular boiler, and the Heilmann mechanical comb, while native entrepreneurs, such as Alfred Krupp of Essen, showed that they had the initiative and skill to build up large enterprises without assistance from abroad. Krupp eventually became one of the largest manufacturers of armaments in Europe – a reminder that wars and preparations for war were a significant factor in the expansion of the iron and steel industries. By the 1850s and 1860s the economies of both France and the German states were capable of sustaining an autonomous industrialization, drawing upon indigenous supplies of management, skill and capital.

While in Britain private investors were generally able to raise the capital to found new business undertakings and public works without government assistance, pioneer entrepreneurs on the Continent frequently had difficulty in securing the funds to build factories and to buy modern machines. Consequently the state played a more important role than it did in Britain in fostering industrial expansion. In Prussia, for example, the Overseas Trading Corporation (*Seehandlung*), a nationalized undertaking, engaged in wholesale trade, operated steamships on the Brandenburg waterways, and owned or controlled textile mills, engineering plants, paper factories and chemical works. In Belgium and in some German states (Hanover, Brunswick, Baden) railways were built and operated by the state, while in France most lines were constructed jointly by the state and by private companies. However, private investment banks – institutional innovations absent in Britain –

also proved valuable in funding and promoting early industrialization.

In central Europe many tariff barriers, which had long hampered economic progress, fell between 1815 and 1870. Within the German states the customs union (*Zollverein*), established in 1834, gradually expanded so that by 1870 only Hamburg and Bremen retained their tariff independence. In the Habsburg dominions the customs frontier between Austria and Hungary was abolished in 1850. In Russia the customs frontier with Congress Poland was abolished in 1851, while Italy achieved both political and economic unity in the 1860s.

Improved communications also promoted economic expansion on the Continent. Navigation on the great rivers – the Seine, Loire, Rhine, Elbe, Oder, Vistula and Danube – was improved and numerous tolls were either reduced or abolished. Transport by inland waterways was of particular significance in the Low Countries, Brandenburg, and the basin of the Seine. In France the reign of Louis Philippe (1830–48) saw the construction of several canals, while in the German states the Main-Danube and the Saar

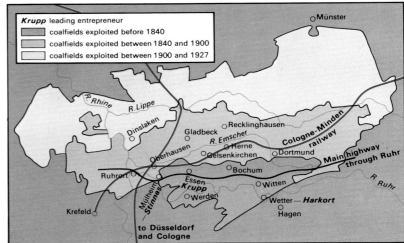

3/The expansion of the Ruhr (above) The exploitation of the Ruhr coalfield began in the valley of the River Ruhr. During the 19th century deeper seams to the north of the Ruhr were gradually opened up. The establishment of the Ruhrort as a coal port and the construction of the Cologne-Minden railway stimulated expansion. Mulvany established new collieries (Shamrock at Herne and Hibernia at Gelsenkirchen) while Krupp of Essen became the leading ironmaster in the district.

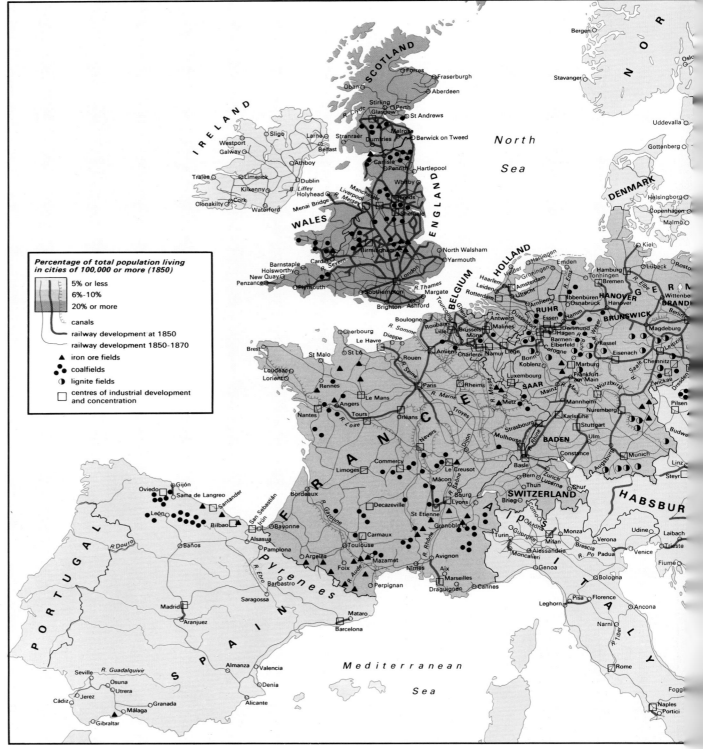

canals proved important undertakings.

But it was the railways which really propelled the Continent into the industrial age. By 1850 the Belgian railway network was virtually complete, and within the German states most of the main lines had been built except for one linking Berlin and Danzig. In France, however, many main lines remained only in the planning stage, though Paris was connected by rail with Lille, Le Havre and Orléans. Substantial acceleration in French railroad construction occurred only in the 1850s and 1860s under the encouragement of Napoleon III's authoritarian government.

1/Industrialization of Europe to 1850 (below) The early industrial areas in Europe were mainly regions with deposits of coal or iron ore, such as Lancashire, Yorkshire, the Ruhr, and France's Nord *département*. Relatively isolated coalfields or ironfields, such as Upper Silesia and the Donets basin, could be developed only when railways had been built. Urbanization and industrialization went hand in hand: except for some capital cities and ports all the large towns lay in manufacturing regions.

2/Customs unions in Europe in the 19th century (right) In the 18th century, trade in Europe had been hampered by tariffs. France abolished internal tariffs in 1790; German states in the early 19th century. The German customs union, founded in 1834, linked independent states and preceded political unification (1871) (see page 213).

George Stephenson's six-wheel locomotive of 1833 (above) the so-called 'Patentee', was widely used both in Britain and on the Continent. His first locomotive ran at Killingworth Colliery in 1814. He was responsible for the construction of the Stockton and Darlington, and the Liverpool and Manchester railways.

The Industrial Revolution in Europe 1870 to 1914

Krupp's gun at the Paris exhibition of 1867 (above)
In his search for new outlets for steel, Alfred Krupp of Essen began to experiment with armaments in the 1840s and showed a six-pounder cannon with a cast steel barrel at the Great Exhibition in the Crystal Palace, London, in 1851. It was not until 1859 that he received an order from the Prussian military authorities for 300 steel barrels. In 1863 Krupp obtained a large contract for steel guns from the Russian government and at the Paris Exhibition of 1867 Krupp, now established as a leading manufacturer of armaments, showed a 50-ton steel cannon which was subsequently presented to the King of Prussia.

soda made from ammonia (a coal by-product) while the textile industries employed synthetic (aniline) dyes made from coal tar. Nitrates from natural sources and 'synthetic' nitrogen and phosphates formed the raw materials for the production of explosives and fertilizers. Other branches of the chemical industries included the production of drugs, insecticides, perfumes, cosmetics, and photographic accessories. From the early 20th century, plastics (manufactured from resins prepared from coal tar acids), were used to create a wide variety of products, while synthetic textiles, such as artificial silk, also became popular.

Germany played a leading part in the development of electricity and chemicals. In the electrical industry two large cartels were formed, the Siemens-Schuckert group and the *Allgemeine Elektrizitäts Gesellschaft*, headed by the two pioneers who dominated the industry: Werner Siemens and Emil Rathenau. The expansion of the chemical industry owed much to the invention of synthetic dyes and new drugs in the laboratories of great German firms, and here as well two cartels developed which

1/The industrialization of Europe 1870-1914 (below) Industrial regions, such as Lancashire, Yorkshire, south Wales, Clydeside, the Ruhr, the Saar, the Nord *département*, and the Sambre-Meuse region in Belgium, which developed in the first half of the 19th century continued to expand after 1870, joined by further regions, such as the Donets basin, which opened up with the development of the rail network. The construction of the Berlin-Baghdad railway as far as Ras el-'Ain, and the completion of the Trans-Siberian railway, extended Europe's economic links with the Near East and the Far East, while the opening of the Kiel Canal stimulated the trade of the Baltic region. After 1870 new branches of manufacture, such as the chemical and electrical industries, joined the old established industries of coal, iron and textiles.

BETWEEN 1870 and 1914 Europe and the United States experienced a second industrial revolution. By 1850 Great Britain was the leading industrial nation in the world, transformed from a predominantly agrarian into a predominantly manufacturing country. During the second industrial revolution Britain remained one of the leading manufacturing states but Germany, united in 1871, now set the pace in the race for industrial supremacy. In addition to expanding its established industries – coal, iron, textiles – it took the lead in the development of new economic activities such as chemicals and electricity. At the same time Germany's exports of manufactured products and services (banking, insurance, shipping) expanded prodigiously. The world economy experienced a 'great depression' in the 1870s and 1880s, which affected most European economies to some extent: Germany suffered in the 1870s, France until 1900 and Britain perhaps until 1914. In most economies, however, including important new entrants such as Sweden, Italy and Russia, industrial growth was particularly pronounced in the period 1896–1914.

In the second – as in the first – industrial revolution Britain produced important new machines and processes: Perkin's synthetic mauve dye (the first aniline dye), the Bessemer steel converter, the Gilchrist-Thomas basic steel process, and Parsons' steam turbine. But the invention and development of the internal combustion engine, the diesel engine, the automobile, the electric dynamo and electric traction largely occurred in Germany, while the ring frame, the sewing machine, the typewriter, the filament lamp and the telephone all originated in the United States.

The first industrial revolution was a 'revolution of coal and iron', the second a 'revolution of steel and electricity'. In the first half of the 19th century steel became almost a semi-precious metal, costing between £50 and £60 a ton, compared with £3 to £4 a ton for pig iron. Initially, steel was made by the cementation process, or by Huntsman's crucible method, but in the second half of the 19th century the new Bessemer and Siemens-Martin processes – improved by Gilchrist and Thomas – greatly increased steel production. World output rose from a mere 540,000 tons (550,800 t) in 1870 to 14,600,000 (14,892,000 t) in 1895 – accompanied by a dramatic fall in prices.

The electrical industry provided the world with a new source of energy to supplement steam power: with the appearance of efficient dynamos in the 1860s, electricity could be used

to drive machinery and trams and to light streets, factories and homes. Water power found a new application in hydro-electric power stations. Italy, in particular, with no national coal resources, turned increasingly to hydro-electric power after 1905. Another new form of energy in the second half of the 19th century came from the internal combustion engine, with petrol as its fuel. A nascent petroleum industry which exploited and refined the oil resources of the United States, Russia and the Middle East enabled stationary gas engines, motor vehicles and ships to be driven by petrol or diesel oil.

The expansion of new chemical industries formed another significant aspect of the development of manufactures after 1870. For centuries chemicals had derived from natural substances – alkalis from vegetable ashes and dyes from madder root, indigo and so forth. Now more and more chemical substances were obtained from coal by-products, nitrogen and phosphates. The soap and glass industries used

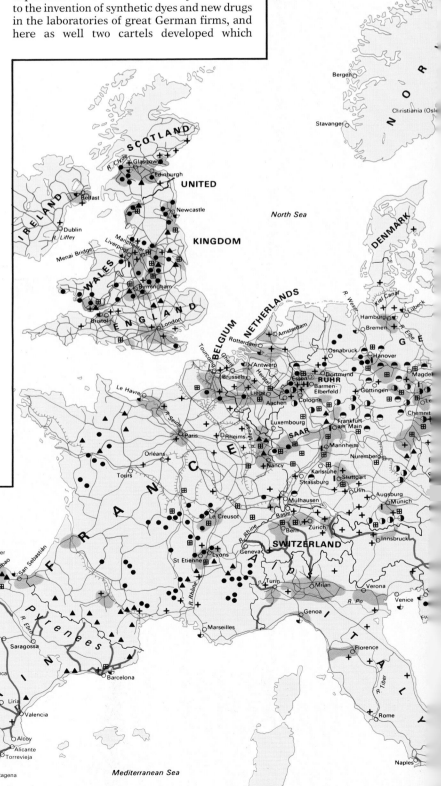

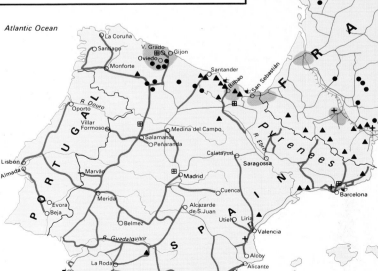

areas of industrial concentration 1870-1914

✛ centres of textile industry

╎ centres of chemical industry

centres of shipbuilding industry

coalfields

⊞ centres of engineering, armaments and metal industries

▲ iron ore fields

◗ lignite fields

potash fields

centres of petroleum industry

European railway network 1870 (largely complete)

railway development 1870-1914

canals

merged, in two stages, in 1916 and 1925, to form the German Dye Trust (*I.G. Farben*). Germany's production of coal, iron and steel also expanded until by 1914 it produced twice as much steel and nearly as much coal as Britain. At the same time Germany's shipbuilding industry and mercantile marine both expanded dramatically: by the outbreak of the First World War Germany's shipyards could build 400,000 tons (408,000 t) of merchant ships a year in addition to warships and river craft, while its mercantile marine of 2,400,000 tons (2,448,000 t) included some of the finest trans-Atlantic liners.

In Russia, too, striking industrial progress occurred between 1870 and 1914. At the end of this period the cotton industries had 745 mills employing 388,000 operatives and turning out products valued at 589 million roubles. The linen industry expanded rapidly in the last quarter of the 19th century with the aid of foreign capital. At the same time the woollen industry, with major centres at Moscow, St Petersburg and Lodz, had 700,000 spindles, 4500 looms and 150,000 operatives. Moreover, an important new industrial region, based on coal and iron ore resources, developed in the basin of the Donets, with great iron and steel works. The opening of the railway to Krivoy Rog in 1886 enabled high-grade iron ore to be sent from there to the ironworks in the Donets basin. Meanwhile the exploitation of Russia's oil wells at Baku and Grozny also stimulated Russia's economic development after 1880. The Nobel brothers from Sweden were the pioneer entrepreneurs of this new industry, building refineries at Baku and launching the world's first oil tanker on the Caspian in 1878 to ply between Baku and Astrakhan.

Again, the construction of the Trans-Siberian and Trans-Caucasian railways enabled Russia to tap some of the vast natural resources of its territories in Asia. The main acceleration in growth resulted from a state-sponsored programme of industrialization directed by the Finance Minister, Count S.I. Witte, during the 1890s. By 1914, the Russian industrial sector ranked among the four or five largest in the world. But unlike the industrial states of western Europe, Russia also had a very large number of small domestic workshops which survived side by side with modern plants and factories.

Nevertheless, at the end of the 19th century even in highly industrialized countries in Europe a high proportion of the population remained engaged in agriculture. In Germany, for example, the agricultural population in 1895 amounted to 18.5 million – just over one-third (35.5 per cent) of the total population. Most of eastern Europe (Poland, Romania, Bulgaria) and much of southern Europe (Spain, Greece, southern Italy) was still, by modern standards, under-developed. In France, industry at the end of the century was generally small in scale; in countries such as Poland and Spain industrialization remained confined to a few enclaves (Lodz; Bilbao, Barcelona) and the way of life of the bulk of the population had virtually been untouched by the great upsurge of industry elsewhere between 1870 and 1914.

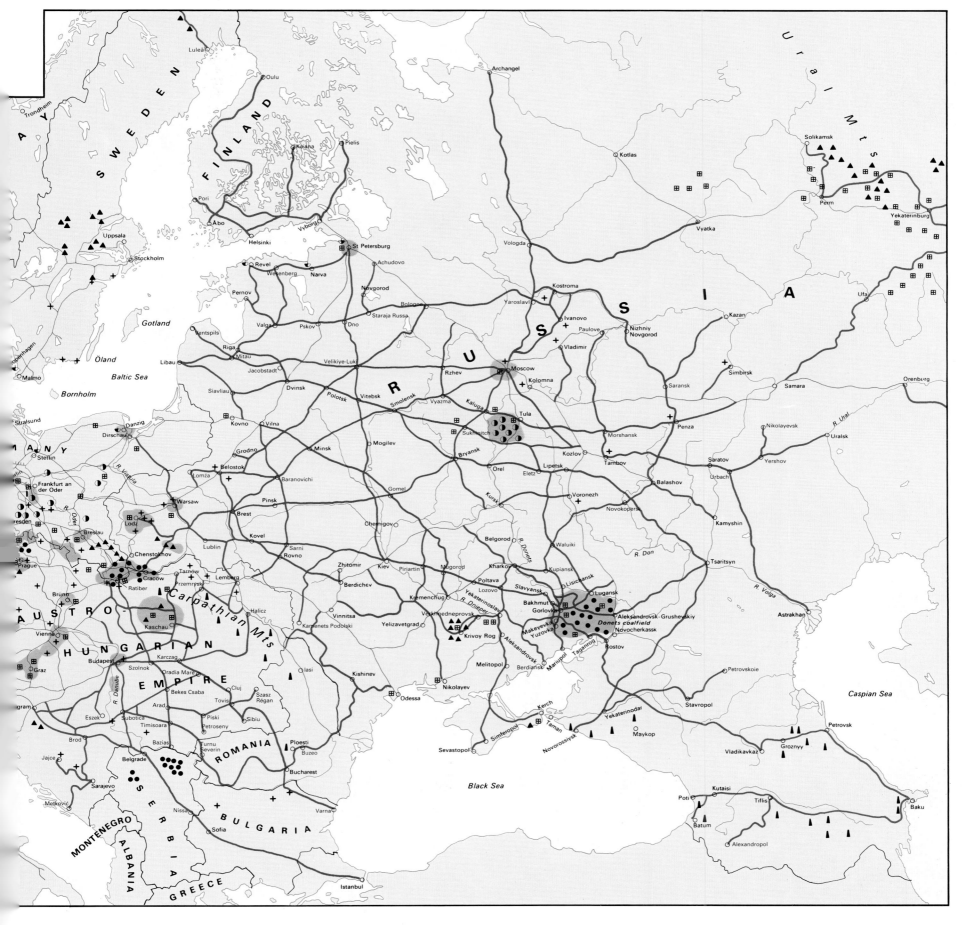

The rise of nationalism in Europe 1800 to 1914

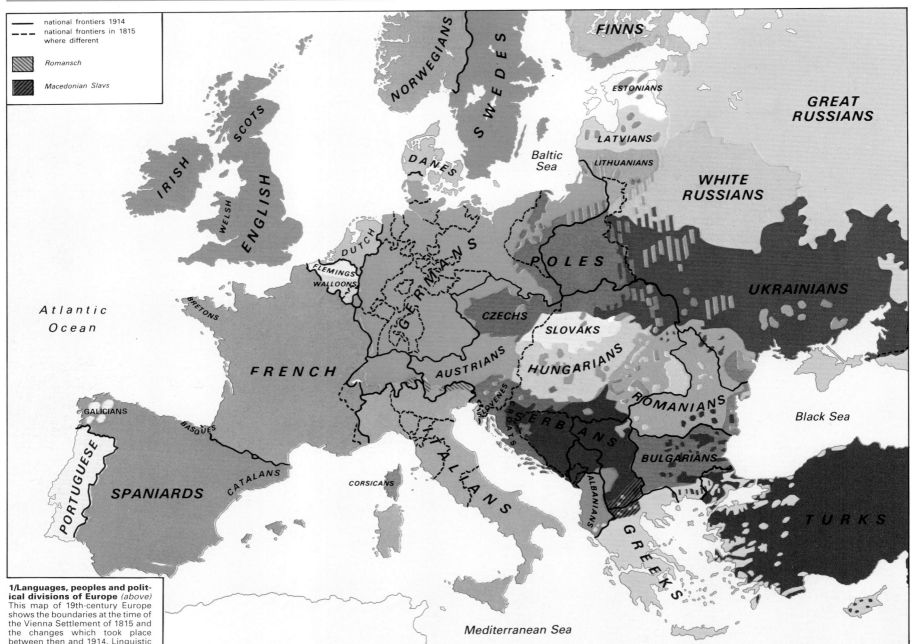

Legend:
— national frontiers 1914
- - - national frontiers in 1815
where different

Romansch

Macedonian Slavs

1/Languages, peoples and political divisions of Europe (above)
This map of 19th-century Europe shows the boundaries at the time of the Vienna Settlement of 1815 and the changes which took place between then and 1914. Linguistic boundaries were rarely precise and political frontiers often left linguistic minorities, and even majorities, under alien rule. The map shows the major languages, but some are too scattered to be included: Sorb (or Wendish, Lusatian) in Prussia and Saxony; Masurian in East Prussia; Vlach in Macedonia, Epirus and Transylvania; Gallego, a dialect of Portuguese in Galicia, Spain; and Yiddish: there were some five million Jews, many living in the large European towns, but most in the Pale of Settlement (Lithuania, Russia, Poland, the Ukraine, Bessarabia and the Crimea).

The Great Powers (below)
Russia, Great Britain, Germany, France and Austro-Hungary try to keep the lid on the Balkan conflict in this cartoon from a 1912 issue of the London magazine *Punch*. They succeeded on this occasion, but in 1914 they failed.

THE French Revolution, by destroying the old regime, was the great catalyst of change in Europe. The revolutionary armies carried with them not only the slogan of 'liberty, equality and fraternity' but also the ideas of liberalism, self-government and nationalism, which proved to be the central themes of 19th-century European history. Already before 1789, in reaction against the rational spirit of the Enlightenment, writers such as Herder (1744–1803) had emphasized the sense of national identity. The state continued to be regarded as a dynastic-patrimony, however: an estate to which owners of lesser estates owed allegiance and service. This conception was challenged by the French revolutionary governments, which called upon oppressed peoples to rise against their landlords and rulers. But French oppression under Napoleon produced nationalist reactions in Spain, in Russia, in the Tyrol, eventually (after 1807) in Germany. This was one source of the nationalism of the later 19th century.

Nevertheless, the strength of nationalism in the earlier 19th century can easily be exaggerated. Down to 1866 most Germans and Italians were more attached to their provincial cultures (Bavarian, Hessian, Tuscan, Emilian) than to the ideal of national unity. Only where there was alien rule were there loud protests, chiefly from the middle classes (lawyers, teachers, businessmen): in Italy against Austria, in Ireland against England, in Belgium against Holland, in Greece against Turkey, in Poland against Russia, in

Norway against Sweden. Rarely did they affect the peasant masses, the bulk of the European population at this time. Even in the Ottoman Empire, in spite of the corrupt, oppressive and increasingly incompetent Turkish government and the resentment of Christians against Muslim overlordship, little active national opposition existed, except in the region which during the 1820s became the core of modern Greece. In the far-flung Austrian Empire, ruling over a score of nationalities, only the Czechs and the Hungarians, both peoples with proud memories of an independent past, were restive, though they sought autonomy within the Empire, not national independence.

Furthermore, after the defeat of Napoleon in 1815, the victorious powers were hostile to nationalist aspirations which they saw, correctly, as associated with liberalism and therefore a threat to constituted authority. At the Congress of Vienna, under the influence of Talleyrand and Metternich, the powers adopted the principle of 'legitimacy' as a basis for redrawing the map of Europe. Metternich believed that any concessions to nationalism would be fatal to Austria, and he resisted them on all fronts down to 1848. In this period only Greece and Belgium (1830) achieved independence, and in both cases special factors – notably the rivalry of the Great Powers – were involved. Elsewhere, in Poland (1831, 1846), Germany (1848), Italy (1848) and Hungary (1849), owing to internal dissensions and the solidarity of the conserva-

tive powers, nationalist risings failed. The Poles, dispersed within three empires, remained a subject people until 1918-19. The Hungarians, however, exploiting Austrian weakness in its war with Prussia, managed to win equal status with the German-speaking population by the *Ausgleich* (Compromise) of 1867.

In Italy and Germany provincialism and apathy were overcome by the expansionist policies of Piedmont and Prussia (see page 212). After 1848 a new generation of European statesmen no longer upheld the old order, and industrial and commercial expansion gave a new impetus to the desire for national unity. Nationalism was now seen as a stabilizing force; that is to say, it was thought that unified national states would have no further ambitions, and apostles of nationalism such as Mazzini (1805–72) predicted a new age when satisfied national states would co-operate peacefully in a democratic federation of peoples. After 1870 it quickly became clear that this was an illusion. Though it is true that the Czechs of Bohemia never aspired, before 1918, to more than autonomy within the Habsburg Empire, and the Slavs of Bosnia and Herzegovina were content to exchange Turkish for Austrian rule, nationalist ideas spread rapidly, particularly among the Balkan peoples. Though the standard criterion of nationality was language, linguistic groups were so mixed that a division on the basis of language was impracticable, particularly in the Balkan peninsula. Moreover, language was not always recognized

GERMAN EMPIRE

RUSSIAN EMPIRE

AUSTRO-HUNGARIAN EMPIRE

Vienna

Budapest

BESSARABIA

MOLDAVIA
semi-independent 1829

Jassy

BOSNIA
administered by Austria-Hungary 1878
annexed 1908

Banja Luka

ROMANIA

Galatz

HERZEGOVINA

Sarajevo

Belgrade   Požarevac

Craiova

Braila

Mostar

SERBIA
principality 1817; independent 1878

WALLACHIA
semi-independent 1829

Ploiesti

Bucharest

united 1859; independent 1878;
Kingdom 1881

MONTENEGRO

SANJAK OF
NOVIBAZAR

Nish

Vidin

principality 1878

Turtukaia Silistria

Kotor (Cattaro)

Podgorica

Ipek (Peć)

Mitrovica

Pirot

BULGARIA

Plevna

independent 1908

R. Danube   DOBRUJA

Roschuk

Constantsa

Cetinje

to Serbia 1878

Sofia

Trnovo

Balchik

L. Scutari

Prizren

to Serbia 1913

Küstendil

EASTERN RUMELIA

Shumla

Scutari

Uskub (Skoplje)

Kumanovo

Kočani

to Bulgaria
1913

Philippopolis

to Bulgaria 1885

Varna

Tirana

ALBANIA
principality 1913

L. Ochrida

R. Vardar

Strumitsa

R. Maritsa

to Bulgaria 1913

Burgas

Black
Sea

Saseno I.

L. Prespa

Monastir

MACEDONIA

Valona

Koritsa

Argyrokastron

Cape Stylos

to Greece
1913

EPIRUS

R. Aliakmon

Salonica

Kavalla

to Bulgaria 1913

Adrianople

THRACE

Dede-Agach

San Stefano

Bosporus

Constantinople

Corfu

Yanina

Arta

Preveza

THESSALY
to Greece 1881

Larissa

Volos

Aegean
Sea

Lemnos

Thasos
Samothrace

Imbros

Dardanelles

Tenedos

Ionian
Sea

IONIAN ISLANDS

Patras

KINGDOM OF GREECE

Athens
Piraeus

Lesbos

Chios

OTTOMAN
EMPIRE

Tripolis

Nauplia

independent 1830

Samos

Nikaria

to Greece 1864

Dodecanese
(occupied by Italy 1912;
ceded by Turkey 1920)

Rhodes

Canea   Suda Bay

CRETE

Candia

independent 1898

to Greece 1913

- - - frontier of Ottoman empire 1800

——— proposed Bulgaria under Treaty of
San Stefano 1878

━━━ national frontiers after the Balkan
wars 1912 - 13

——— railway

by those wishing to redeem their long lost brothers as the sole criterion of nationality. In Macedonia, Greeks, Serbians and Bulgarians made conflicting nationalistic claims and, like nationalists within the Habsburg Empire, expressed them in terms of folklore, literature, and national history as well as those of linguistic and racial theory. As a result of their endeavours, by 1913 the Turks had lost almost all their possessions in Europe. Nor was nationalist unrest confined to the Turkish and Habsburg Empires. Great Britain was faced with troubles in Ireland, and Norway demanded separation from Sweden.

Serbian nationalist activities in Bosnia and the resolve of Austria-Hungary to resist them became the immediate cause of war in 1914. This war led to the disruption of the Habsburg, German and Russian Empires and the formation of Czechoslovakia, Poland, Yugoslavia, Hungary, Estonia, Latvia and Lithuania. Although established in recognition of the principle of 'national self-determination', two of these states, Czechoslovakia and Poland, contained

large German minorities, the redemption of which later became an aim of German policy.

2/The Balkans *(above)* From the later 18th century onwards the Russians encouraged uprisings in the Turkish Balkan provinces. The Great Powers, fearing Russian domination of the Near East and wishing to preserve the Ottoman Empire as a viable power, endeavoured to pacify the Balkans by extracting concessions to the Slavs, Greeks and Romanians. Following the Crimean War, in 1856 they imposed a settlement on Russia and Turkey and in 1878 at the Congress of Berlin they recognized the complete independence of Serbia, Montenegro and Romania, but reduced the territory which the Pan Slav Treaty of San Stefano had allocated to the new Principality of Bulgaria.

This upheaval made the Powers aware of the complexity of the rivalries between the races inhabiting the Balkan peninsula, and of the dangerous incompatibility of their own ambitions there. For the next 30 years, despite growing racial and religious strife in Macedonia and a Greco-Turkish war in 1897, the Powers clung stubbornly to the territorial status quo, seeking to pacify the Balkan Christians by a programme of administrative reforms under Austro-Russian supervision. But the Austro-Hungarian annexation of Bosnia (1908) revived the fires of nationalism and destroyed the unity of the Powers. In 1912 the Balkan states formed a league to expel the Turks from Macedonia; but after their victory the old rivalries over the spoils re-emerged. The Second Balkan War left Serbia and Greece in possession of most of Macedonia and parts of Albania.

3/Scandinavia *(right)* The Treaty of Nystad (1721) marked the decline of Sweden as a great Northern and Baltic power (see page 188).

In 1809 Sweden had ceded Finland to Russia. In 1815 her new dynasty received Norway, formerly a Danish possession, under an arrangement ensuring considerable autonomy and a separate government. During the 19th century, the pan-Scandinavian movement, which aimed at a close union between Denmark, Sweden and Norway, came to nothing and in 1905 Norway became completely independent with its own dynasty.

NORWAY

SWEDEN

FINLAND

Part of Sweden 1154-1809

Russian 1809–1917

independent 1917

Trondheim

United 1814-1905

Tammerfors (Tampere)

Åbo (Turku)

Helsingfors (Helsinki)

KARELIA

Bergen

Christiania

Uppsala

St Petersburg

Stavanger

Stockholm

United 1397-1814

RUSSIA

DENMARK

Copenhagen

Malmo

SCHLESWIG
HOLSTEIN
1866 to Prussia

Kiel

SWEDISH
POMERANIA
to Prussia 1815

Stettin

Germany and Italy: the struggles for unification 1815 to 1871

The Bismarck tower *(above)* Towering sculptures of Bismarck, the chief architect of German unity, were erected in Germany during the 1890s. Their medieval style recalls the period of the Teutonic Knights and the heyday of German expansion in the Middle Ages.

EVEN before the defeat of Napoleon and the Congress of Vienna (1815), demands for national unity stirred in Germany and Italy, but they remained largely confined to literary and academic circles. Only Stein in Prussia aspired to translate them into a political programme and he was swept aside in 1808: after 1815 Metternich, the Austrian chancellor, and his allies, had no difficulty in restoring the traditional rulers. Although during the period of the 'Restoration' (1815–48) some unrest surfaced, fomented chiefly by ex-military personnel and officials formerly employed in the Napoleonic administration, the revolts of 1820 and 1821 (in Naples and Piedmont) and those of 1830–1 (in Parma, Modena and Romagna) had no national aims, while the liberals in Hanover, Brunswick, Hesse-Kassel and Saxony were satisfied with moderate constitutional changes. Not until 1848 did the national question, both in Germany and in Italy, come to the fore, and then only to reveal cross-purposes within nationalist ranks. In Italy, uprisings in Venice, Rome, Messina, Palermo, Reggio and Milan ended in failure, while in July 1848 Charles Albert of Piedmont was decisively beaten by the Austrians at Custoza.

In 1848 revolts took place in all major German states and in May a 'National Assembly' of deputies elected from all over the *Deutscher Bund* (including both German and non-German parts of the Austrian Monarchy) met at Frankfurt to embark on the self-appointed task of drawing up a constitution for Germany which they hoped to unite by consent. However they soon became divided between *Grossdeutsche* (those who wanted a federal Germany, including Austria and extending from the Baltic to the Adriatic) and *Kleindeutsche* (those who wanted a smaller Germany, excluding Austria, under Prussian leadership). The Prussian liberals denounced the provisional government of United Germany, with the Austrian Archduke John as its Regent, and demanded instead a Prussian constitution. By a small majority the Frankfurt Assembly offered the German crown to the king of Prussia, who rejected it with contempt.

After the failure of the revolutions of 1848–9 Germany reverted to a joint Austro-Prussian hegemony while Italy remained divided. However, after the appointment of Cavour as prime minister of Sardinia-Piedmont (1852) and of Bismarck as chief minister in Prussia (1862), liberal nationalists in Italy and Germany showed some readiness to support the expansionist aims of Piedmont and Prussia. The policies of Napoleon III, a 'revisionist' with nationalist inclinations, gave encouragement to these aims, as did the weakening of Austria, which lost the support of Russia after the Crimean War (1854–6: see page 226). Napoleon III now favoured a strong Prussia in northern Germany and a relatively powerful Sardinia-Piedmont in northern Italy within an Italian federation (including Tuscany, the Kingdom of Naples and the Papal States) under the presidency of the Pope. Both powers, he anticipated, would be the natural allies of France. He hoped, moreover, to create a Rhineland kingdom as a client state of France.

Prussia had long been an expansionist power. Despite losses during the Napoleonic Wars, in 1815 she received a part of Saxony and territory in western Germany with the intention of raising a bulwark against France and of buttressing Holland. Thereafter her policy was to weld together her eastern and western territories and to this end, from 1828, she formed a series of customs unions (*Zollvereine*). In 1834 a single German Zollverein was created, which expanded

3/The unification of Germany *(below)* The political unification of Germany involved wars against Denmark in 1864, against Austria in 1866 and against France in 1870. Austria was excluded from the North German Confederation of 1867, which comprised the German states north of the River Main. Austria's remaining influence in Germany finally perished in 1871, when the states of Southern Germany decided to join the German Empire.

Prussia in 1815	● Free city
acquired by Prussia 1815-66	
boundary of German Confederation of 1815	
boundary of North German Confederation of 1866	
Imperial territory of Alsace-Lorraine 1871	
boundary of German Empire 1871	
Austro-Prussian forces attack Denmark 1864	
Prussian armies in the war with Austria 1866	
German armies in the Franco-Prussian war 1870-71	

under the impact of the development of German railways and industrialization. By the 1850s Prussia had gained an economic preponderance over Austria but not until Bismarck came to power did she challenge Austria's political leadership. The trouble began with the Schleswig and Holstein question. In 1864 Austria and Prussia, acting on behalf of the German Confederation, went to war with Denmark, defeated her, and took over the administration of the two duchies (Convention of Gastein, 1865). When Austria attempted to follow a separate policy in Holstein and to deprive Prussia of her rights under the traditional dualistic arrangements, Bismarck made war on Austria, defeated her at Sadowa (1866), excluded her from Germany, and formed the North German Confederation (1867) under Prussian control. Following Prussia's defeat of France at Sedan (1870) and her annexation of Alsace and Lorraine, the German states south of the Main, through sheer economic necessity, joined the new German Reich.

In Italy, Cavour, realizing that Piedmont's expansion depended on foreign support, allied with France (the Plombières agreement, 1858) against Austria, and in June 1859 the two allies won decisive victories at Magenta and Solferino. However, fearing the formation of a hostile European combination and the creation of an overmighty Piedmont, Napoleon III hastily concluded a preliminary settlement at Villafranca. At the definitive Peace of Zurich (November 1859) most of Lombardy went to Piedmont but, on being offered compensation in Nice and Savoy, Napoleon agreed to plebiscites in Tuscany, Parma and Modena, where spontaneous revolutions had broken out. These plebiscites favoured union with Piedmont which thus doubled in size. In June 1860 the patriot Garibaldi

and his 'thousand' volunteers took Sicily and, in September, Naples. Cavour, fearing that the final stages of unification might weaken the influence of Piedmont, sent troops to the Papal States and brought Garibaldi to heel. Plebiscites were held which resulted in the union of Sicily, Naples, Umbria, Romagna and the Marches with Piedmont-Sardinia. In 1861, an Italian parliament met in Turin and proclaimed Victor Emmanuel II king of united Italy. In April 1866 Cavour's successors made a treaty with Prussia and, following Austria's defeat at Sadowa in the Austro-Prussian war, Italy acquired Venetia from Austria. In 1870 it obtained Rome, the French having been obliged to withdraw their occupation forces as a result of the Franco-Prussian war.

The making of modern Italy and the creation of the German Empire not only changed the European balance of power but fostered a spirit of *realpolitik* and militarism. Neither state felt fully satisfied with its achievements: Italy retained hopes of obtaining the Alto Adige, Trieste and Fiume; and the new Reich, despite Bismarck's claim that Germany was 'satiated', pursued expansionist policies in both Posen and Elsass-Lothringen (the former Alsace-Lorraine). In the period 1871–1914, however, both powers were compelled to devote attention to internal problems, to improve and expand their armed forces and to seek markets and raw materials outside Europe in competition with the other powers. Moreover, while Italy remained tied to Germany and Austria by the treaty of triple alliance, she was debarred from her irredenta; and so long as Germany remained allied with the Austrian-Hungarian monarchy any hopes of a Greater Germany had to be abandoned.

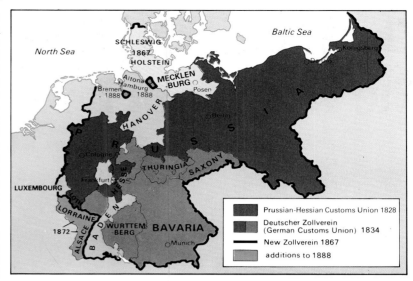

1/The economic unification of Germany (above) Well before the diplomatic skill of Bismarck and the military genius of Moltke came into play, the officials responsible for the creation of the German *Zollvereine*, the developers of German roads, railways and canals, the pioneers in industry, shipping and banking had prepared for the political unification of Germany.

Garibaldi (left) and his 'thousand' played an important role in the unification of Italy, conquering Sicily and Naples in 1860. However his attempts in 1862 and 1867 to wrest Rome from papal rule both failed.

2/The unification of Italy (below) The rapid expansion of Piedmont-Sardinia, which began with the acquisition of Lombardy in 1859, led, at the expense of the loss of Nice and Savoy, to the creation of the United Italy of 1861. The new kingdom acquired Venetia in 1866 and in 1870 Rome, which became the capital.

The Industrial Revolution in the wider world 1850 to 1929

AFTER the middle of the 19th century the Industrial Revolution, which had spread from Great Britain to northwest Europe and the eastern seaboard of the United States, expanded further afield in ever-widening circles. However it did so at very different rates, depending largely on the economic, social and cultural conditions in the recipient lands.

Societies modelled on the West and formed or dominated by Europeans adopted industrialization with the same ease as the home country, with the Anglo-Saxon areas of settlement (as in Europe) well ahead of those of the Spanish and Portuguese. In most non-colonial societies, however, industrialization was a foreign transplant rather than an indigenous growth, and economic as well as political control tended to pass to

Europeans, effectively limiting industrialization to certain enclaves and hardly touching the lives of the majority of inhabitants.

As late as 1930, India and China exhibited all the features of such enclave industrialism. In India, 69 per cent of all cotton workers in 1919 were employed in Bombay Province, two-thirds of them in Bombay City, while much of the country's steel was manufactured by a single firm, Tata Iron and Steel Co. at Tatanagar in Bihar, which in 1926–7 produced 650,000 tons (663,000 t) of pig iron and 600,000 tons (612,000 t) of steel. Chinese industry grew in the late 19th century but mainly along the lines of the railway concessions granted to foreign groups, capitalists who had no interest in the development of the country. Between 1895 and

Cheap and abundant labour *(above)* attracted British capital to India, financing factories to manufacture locally produced materials, above all cotton and (in mills such as the one pictured near Calcutta in 1929) jute.

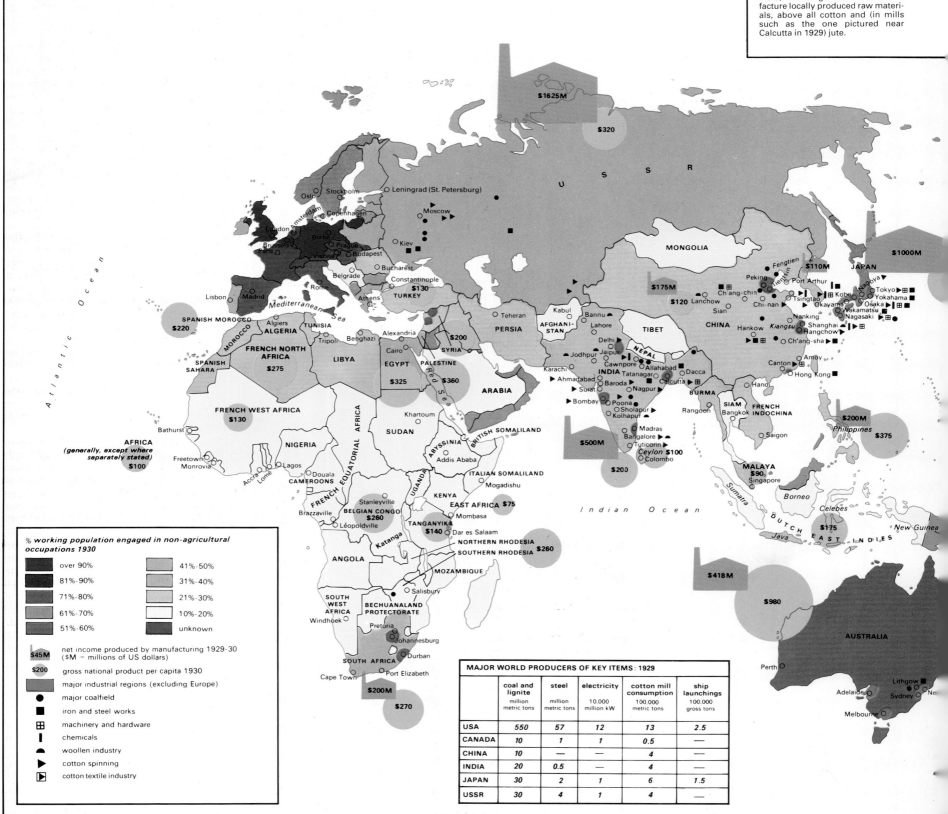

% working population engaged in non-agricultural occupations 1930

- over 90%
- 81%-90%
- 71%-80%
- 61%-70%
- 51%-60%
- 41%-50%
- 31%-40%
- 21%-30%
- 10%-20%
- unknown

$45M — net income produced by manufacturing 1929-30 ($M = millions of US dollars)

$200 — gross national product per capita 1930

- major industrial regions (excluding Europe)
- major coalfield
- iron and steel works
- machinery and hardware
- chemicals
- woollen industry
- cotton spinning
- cotton textile industry

	coal and lignite million metric tons	steel million metric tons	electricity 10,000 million kW	cotton mill consumption 100,000 metric tons	ship launchings 100,000 gross tons
USA	550	57	12	13	2.5
CANADA	10	1	1	0.5	—
CHINA	10	—	—	4	—
INDIA	20	0.5	—	4	—
JAPAN	30	2	1	6	1.5
USSR	30	4	1	4	—

MAJOR WORLD PRODUCERS OF KEY ITEMS: 1929

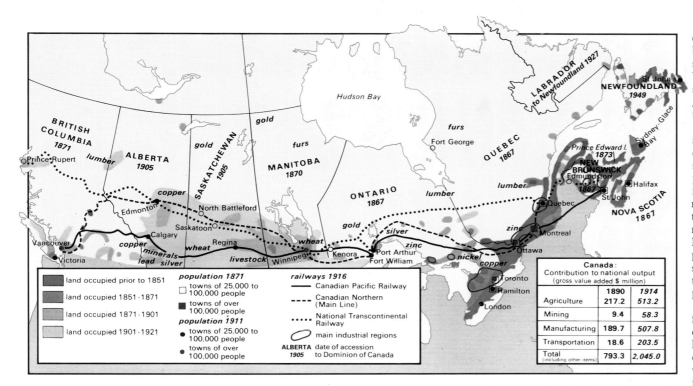

Canada: Contribution to national output (gross value added $ million)	1890	1914
Agriculture	217.2	513.2
Mining	9.4	58.3
Manufacturing	189.7	507.8
Transportation	18.6	203.5
Total (including other items)	793.3	2,045.0

2/Canada in 1915 (above) after a quarter of a century of rapid economic development. An influx of people and capital followed hard on the heels of expanding exports of wheat and timber after 1890. Mining was well under way by 1914 and manufacturing grew mainly after that date.

overlapping stages, the first normally directed by westerners to exploit some valuable product such as metallic ores, agricultural produce or oil. Virtually the whole world had reached that stage by 1930 with the major exception of Japan, where the initiative came entirely from the Government and from native entrepreneurs.

The second stage developed from the need to service and repair the major plants focussed on export production. Businesses also sprang up to supply the needs of an increasingly demanding population, but since these firms often merely replaced and destroyed existing traditional native handicraft industries, the proportion of the population engaged in manufacture did not necessarily grow and may even have declined. For this reason, rather than registering the proportion engaged in manufactures, the main map shows the comparative non-agricultural population. Latin America, North Africa and many parts of Asia had reached this stage by 1930.

Such growth could sometimes be extremely fast. In Canada, which became the classic 'wheat economy' once all the land in the United States had been occupied in the early years of the 20th century, 73 million acres (29.6 million ha) of land were occupied in 1900–16 and $400 million of foreign investment a year were attracted, together with streams of immigrants. The mining of coal, gold, lead, zinc, nickel and copper followed, taking the country well along the road to industrialization.

In South Africa, gold was discovered in 1886; by 1900, the gold fields employed 100,000 workers and Johannesburg, with fewer than 100 inhabitants in 1885, had 237,000 in 1911. Katanga, where copper deposits were first discovered in 1900, by 1914 produced 10,550 tons (10,760 t) of copper and by 1930 its output, together with that of Northern Rhodesia, had risen to 305,000 tons (311,000 t) from an industry that employed 30,000 African miners.

In Malaya, tin production was first encouraged on a large scale by the abolition of British import duties on the metal in 1853 and by 1900 Malaya was responsible for nearly half the world's tin exports. Most tin, however, was produced neither by European nor by native enterprise but by Chinese settlers and, apart from the port of Singapore, the effects of the large new industries were limited and localized. Rubber was another burgeoning industry in Malaya at this time; rubber trees were first grown there in 1894 and by 1905 plantations occupied 50,000 acres (20,250 ha) increasing to 300,000 acres (121,500 ha) in 1910.

In China pig-iron production rose from 477,000 tons (486,500 t) in 1928 to 5.9 million tons (6.02 million t) in 1937, steel from 30,000 tons (30,600 t) to 5.3 million tons (5.4 million t) and coal from 25 million tons (25.5 million t) to 124 million tons (126.5 million t) in the same period; but, as in Malaya, the benefit to the local economy was minimal.

The third stage was the development of industries which competed with manufactured goods on world markets. Iron and steel, textiles and machinery always form the most important of such commodities, and have therefore been emphasized in the main map which shows that Australia, New Zealand, Japan and some very limited areas in China and Manchuria, India, Latin America, and around the Mediterranean had reached this stage by 1929. Again, Japan stands out as the only wholly independent non-European society to have successfully embraced western industrialism before the Depression of 1929. Indeed her industrial economy had been growing strongly since 1885 and she had established many large-scale modern industries such as ship-building, machine-building and steel-making even before 1914.

1917, 60 percent of the foreign-owned firms in China held 40 per cent of the capital and were located in only two provinces, Kiangsu and Fengtien.

Industrial development outside Europe and the United States generally occurred in three

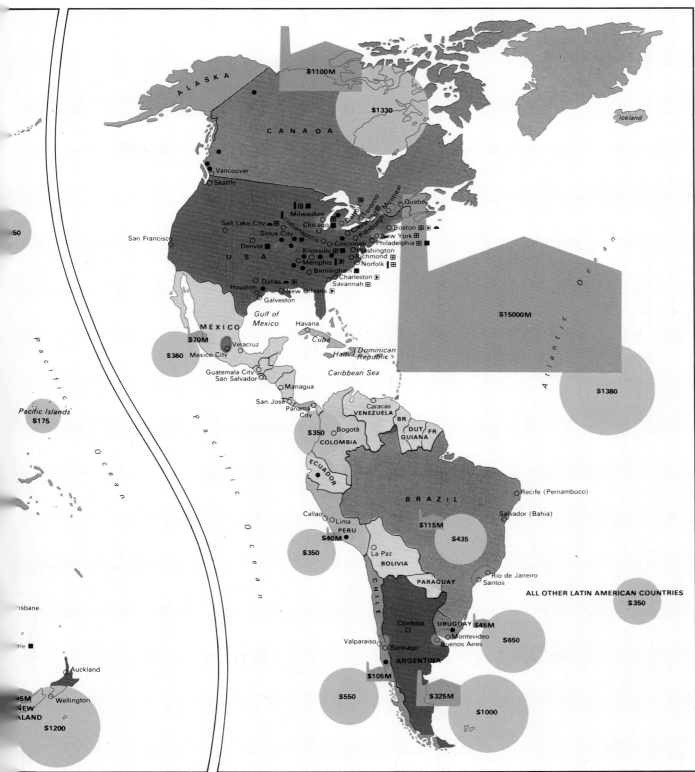

1/Industrialization outside Europe and North America (left) remained the exception rather than the rule in 1929. Even after the 'opening' of Africa in the 1880s and 1890s, the amount of European capital which flowed into the colonial world was relatively small and, except in India, colonial governments were disinclined to invest in the infrastructure of ports, roads and railways. Even by the end of the period such transport and industry as did exist focussed on the ports trading with Europe and/or were worked by European settler communities.

The making of the United States: westward expansion 1783 to 1890

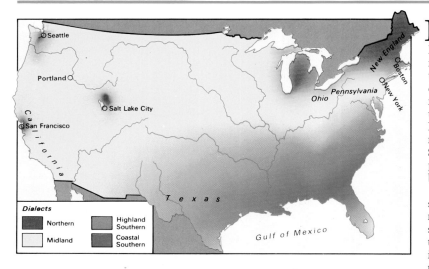

Dialects
- Northern
- Midland
- Highland Southern
- Coastal Southern

2/Migration and settlement (above) The American population flowed west in several distinct migration streams. The best guide to their location is the study of linguistic geography, which still preserves the history of the westward movement in the different spatial patterns of American speech. One migration stream led westward from New England to New York, Ohio and the northern plains. Another went by sea from Boston and New York to San Francisco and Seattle. Still a third went overland from Vermont and western New York to Salt Lake City. The largest migration stream rose in Pennsylvania and spread westward through the middle of the continent to California. Two southern streams flowed side by side, one southwest through the mountains, the other along the coast. They met and merged in Texas.

1/Westward expansion (below) There were several separate frontiers in American history: the frontier of the explorer, the fur trader, the miner, the cattleman and sheep-herder, and finally the domestic frontier with which the Wild West ended. Each of those westward movements had its own special rhythm, its own settlements and its own routes.

IN 1783 the American republic was small and weak: its population was just over 3 million people; half its territory was held by hostile neighbours; its colonial economy was still tributary to the mother country; and its polity was dangerously disordered. In under 100 years, the new nation had become a giant: by 1890 its population had grown larger than that of any European nation except Russia, and its economy was the most productive in the world. United States territory had grown to continental proportions, while its republican government had become strong, centralized, and highly stable.

The expansion of the American republic was sustained by its vast abundance of physical resources. As the great powers of Europe pursued their imperial dreams in Africa and Asia, the United States enjoyed the luxury of a built-in empire. The westward movement may be understood as a type of domestic imperialism, with many of the same motives as European imperialism but with profoundly different results. The native culture of North America was not merely conquered but destroyed; an integrated capitalist democracy developed in its place.

In 1783, when its independence was officially recognized, the United States occupied an area of about 800,000 square miles (2,072,000 km²), much of it rich arable land. That immense territory was soon enlarged by other tracts, even larger and more fertile. The Louisiana Purchase of 827,000 square miles (2,142,000 km²) was a

mighty windfall for President Thomas Jefferson in 1803. West Florida was taken by force during James Madison's administration and East Florida (60,000 square miles, 155,400 km²) by purchase, backed by the threat of force, during the presidency of James Monroe.

A second set of acquisitions between 1845 and 1853 completed the contiguous area of the continental United States. Protracted negotiations for the territory of Oregon (285,000 square miles, 738,150 km²) finally ended with a compromise in 1846. The Texas republic (390,000 square miles, 1,010,000 km²) was annexed in 1845, and the vast Mexican cession (529,000 square miles, 1,370,110 km²) was a spoil of war in 1848. Finally came the Gadsden Purchase in 1853, bought from Mexico to control a promising

3/Land cessions and density of settlement (below) In 1783 the new nation extended from the Atlantic coast to the Mississippi river. Its territory was enlarged in just two great spates of expansion. During the first (1803-19), three Virginian presidents acquired Louisiana and the Floridas. During the second, the heyday of 'manifest destiny' (1845-53), Texas, Oregon, California and the remainder of the southwest were added, thereby completing the area occupied by the 48 contiguous states of today.

expansion of white settlement by:
- 1750
- 1790
- 1850
- 1890
- largely unsettled by 1890

Oregon Country 1846 • 1818 • Louisiana Purchase from France 1803 • Mexican Cession 1848 • USA 1783 • Texas annexed 1845 • Gadsden Purchase 1853 • West Florida annexed 1812 • East Florida annexed 1819

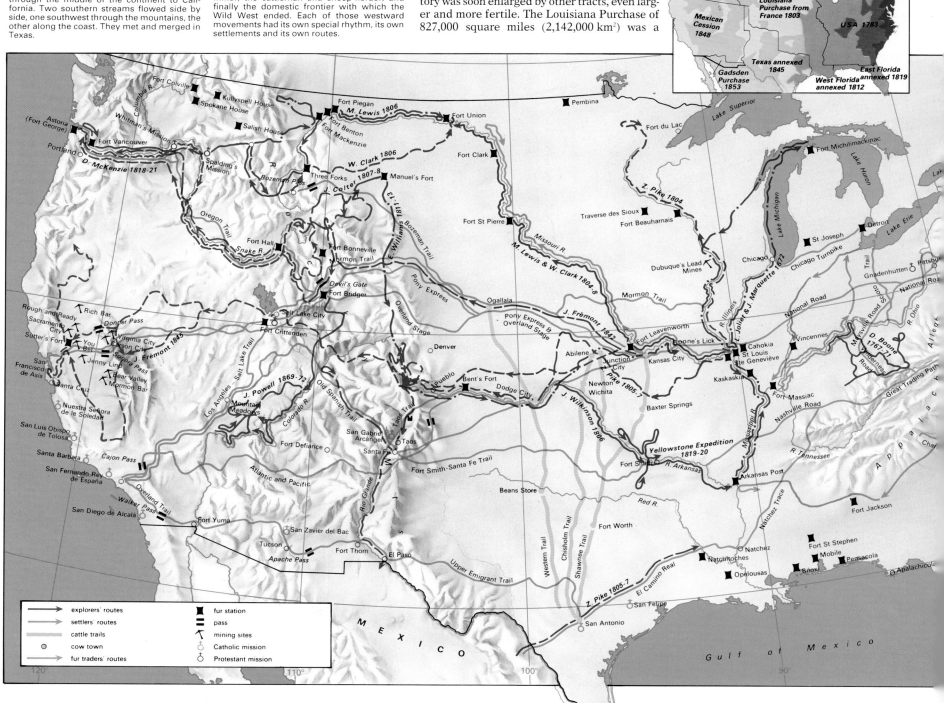

explorers' routes
settlers' routes
cattle trails
cow town
fur traders' routes
fur station
pass
mining sites
Catholic mission
Protestant mission

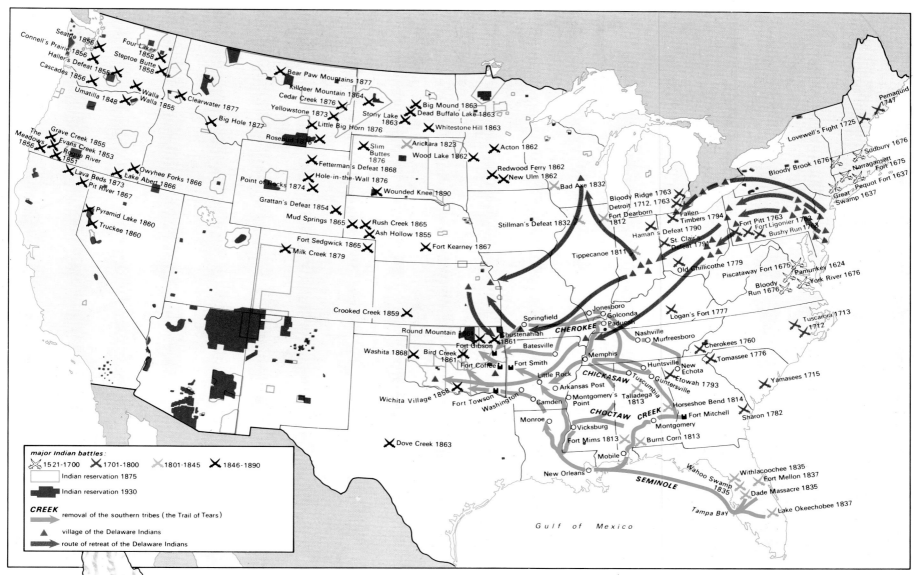

major Indian battles:
✕ 1521-1700   ✕ 1701-1800   ✕ 1801-1845   ✕ 1846-1890
▢ Indian reservation 1875
■ Indian reservation 1930
CREEK → removal of the southern tribes (the Trail of Tears)
▲ village of the Delaware Indians
➤ route of retreat of the Delaware Indians

Gulf of Mexico

railroad route. Compared with other acquisitions, it was trivial in size – a mere 30,000 square miles (77,700 km²: about the same size as England).

This enormous landmass was occupied almost as swiftly as it was acquired. Before 1776 the Americans were slow to settle the interior, which they called the 'back-country'. After 1800 the 'back-country' became 'frontier' in American parlance, and the line of settlement advanced westward with astonishing speed. By its conventional *American* definition, 'frontier' is understood to mean the outer edge of the area with a population density of at least two persons per square mile. Before 1783 that line was still largely east of the Appalachian mountains, except for a small settlement in Kentucky. Just 30 years later, however, the great centre of the continent was occupied. By 1820 the frontier had crossed the Mississippi and by the 1840s had reached the 100th meridian that bisects North Dakota and runs through central Texas. Beyond this line, rainfall was inadequate (under 20 inches/508 mm) to support traditional humid-zone mixed farming. Aridity thus distinguished the West (except the Pacific northwest) from the rest of the nation, and expansion faltered until settlers acquired the means to continue an advance transformed through wheat and cattle ranching. The Great Plains were only subdued after 1865 with the aid of new technology – the railroads, the steel plough, the six-shooter, the barbed-wire fence and modern steel windmills. The superintendent of the 1890 census observed that for the first time in American history, a single frontier-line no longer appeared on his map. In a sense, the frontier had come to an end.

Westward migration (*right*) by covered wagon started at the end of the 18th century and gathered pace after the breaching of the Allegheny mountains and the entry of immigrants to the mid-west by way of the Great Lakes and the Mississippi. This idealized portrait, complete with peaceful Indians, shows a wagon train emerging unopposed from the Rocky Mountains. In reality, the immigrants were resisted by Indian tribes driven westward by the ever increasing pressure.

4/The fate of the Indians (*above*) Colonization was largely a negative experience from the perspective of the indigenous peoples: expansion became contraction, democracy became tyranny, prosperity became poverty, and liberty became confinement. Before 1600 perhaps 10 million Indians lived north of the Rio Grande, speaking more than 2000 languages and subsisting in small villages or nomadic bands on maize, game, fish and the fruits of the forest. The arrival of the Europeans brought fundamental changes. From them, the Sioux obtained their horses, the Navajo their sheep and the Iroquois their guns. But the impact was mostly disadvantageous: the New England tribes, devastated by disease, were broken in the Pequot War (1636) and King Philip's War (1675-6); in the middle colonies, the Delaware nation was defeated by the Dutch in the Esopus Wars (1660-63). The southern tribes, despite having adopted 'civilized' habits, fared no better. Planters, led by President Andrew Jackson, obtained a law for their 'removal' and, though the Supreme Court opposed it, some 50,000 Cherokee were rounded up and sent on a winter trek to arid Oklahoma in 1838. Many died en route. The Choctaw, Creek and Chickasaw suffered a similar fate. Even the Seminole, isolated in the Florida swamps, were only able to resist for a decade or so.

5/The buffalo (*right*) On the Great Plains, the economic and spiritual base of Indian culture was destroyed when the buffalo herd was cut in two by the first transcontinental railroad (1869) and then slaughtered in a deliberate campaign to starve out the Sioux. By the 1890s, the buffalo, like the Indians, survived only on reservations.

6/Indian culture after the conquest (*below right*) As the material base of Indian culture crumbled, its spiritual structure was replaced by many new systems of belief. The Ghost Dance was a religion of resistance, first developed in non-violent form c.1890 by the Paiute prophet Wovoke. The Sioux made it a warrior's faith, which led inevitably to the battle of Wounded Knee (1890). The Peyote drug cult, on the other hand, was a religion of accommodation, drawing its doctrines from Indian and European sources and serving as a spiritual bridge from one culture to another.

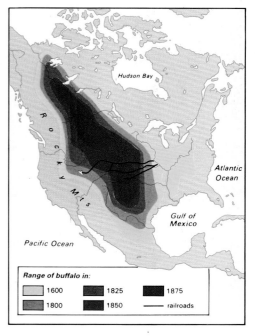

Range of buffalo in:
▢ 1600   ▣ 1800   ■ 1825   ▣ 1850   ■ 1875   — railroads

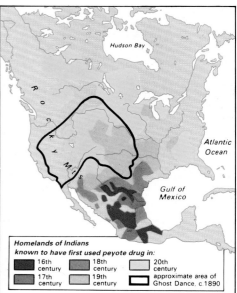

Homelands of Indians known to have first used peyote drug in:
■ 16th century   ▣ 17th century   ▣ 18th century   ▢ 19th century   ▢ 20th century   ▭ approximate area of Ghost Dance c.1890

The making of the United States: civil war and economic growth

railroads in operation in 1840
railroads in operation in 1870
railroads in operation in 1920

New York

San Francisco

Kansas City

New Orleans

2/Westward expansion *(above)* The vast extent of the United States (five times greater than Great Britain, France, Germany and Japan combined) made improved transport essential to economic growth. The railways lowered overland freight rates 500 per cent and travel time 900 per cent in their first 20 years of operation. The westward movement of population and transport brought in their wake corresponding extensions of agricultural production.

leading cotton-growing states in 1840
leading cotton-growing states in 1926
principal wheat and corn (maize) states in 1859
principal wheat and corn (maize) states in 1919

THE Civil War was the bloodiest conflict in American history. It cost the lives of more Americans than all the nation's other wars combined, and the consequences equalled the scale and cost – 4 million black slaves were emancipated, central power was established beyond question, and the hegemony of the northern states and capitalism was confirmed.

After the territorial gains of the 1840s, the issue of extending slavery into the unsettled west dominated US politics. Abraham Lincoln opposed extension but insisted that the federal government lacked the authority to interfere where slavery existed. Nevertheless, South Carolina quit the Union soon after Lincoln's election, followed by six lower southern states which formed the Confederate States of America in February 1861. When South Carolinians fired the first shots at Fort Sumter in April, Virginia, North Carolina, Tennessee and Arkansas joined the secessionists. For Lincoln the fundamental issue was whether a constitutional republic could preserve itself and its territorial integrity against internal subversion; he recognized no constitutional right of secession. By 1863 pressure from radical Republicans and military expediency added a second war aim: the commitment to restore the Union: freeing the slaves in the rebel states.

The volunteer armies on both sides were virtually armed mobs in 1861: serious military operations began in spring, 1862. Northern strategy sought to deny the South vital resources by a naval blockade, to control key river routes and forts in the west, and to capture the Confederate capital of Richmond. Despite overwhelming superiority in manpower and resources, however, the Union victory took four years. There were two main reasons: first, the South had superior generalship during the first two years of war; second, the North's goals required occupation of the South and destruction of its armies, whereas the southern goal of independence required a primarily defensive strategy. In the east, General Robert E. Lee thwarted two invasions of Virginia in 1862 and carried the war into the North, only to be stopped at Antietam, Maryland, in September 1862 and decisively defeated at Gettysburg, Pennsylvania, in July 1863. By then, in the west, the Union had gained control

of the Mississippi and Tennessee rivers and opened the way for invasion of the lower South. By 1864 the Union blockade was effective and General Ulysses S. Grant began his invasion of Virginia which, combined with General Philip T. Sherman's march through Georgia and South Carolina, destroyed the South's armies by the spring of 1865.

Changing war fortunes highlighted the importance of railroads: the Northern network was more extensive, linking food-producing regions to urban consumers, whereas the more limited southern system was designed primarily to deliver plantation goods to ports. Food shortages were common and Confederate efforts to procure supplies at submarket prices were fiercely resisted by civilians. By contrast, the North's economy met the needs of total war without overly inconveniencing its civilians. Yet desertion and war-weariness affected both sides. The growing reluctance of non-slaveholders (most southerners) to support the 'slaveocracy' was matched by northern unwillingness, after emancipation in January 1863, to 'fight for the niggers'.

The true victor in the war was northern big business. The rise of a corporate economy accompanied the economic modernization ultimately responsible for northern success. Although many of the criteria for modernization – per capita increase of agricultural and industrial output, technological innovation, urbanization, expansion of education – were in place before the war, they had remained largely restricted to the North which now exploited its wartime dominance in Congress to impose its economic system on the entire nation through protective tariffs for manufactures, the Homestead Act (embodying the free-soil ideology), a uniform currency and federal support for railroad construction, all measures opposed by the antebellum South. Northern business also took advantage of the new markets created by government procurement to consolidate and expand. Corporate America was born.

Economic growth in 19th-century America was the fastest in world history. Between 1825 and 1910 output grew at an average annual rate

of 1.6 per cent per capita, while the population, through natural increase and immigration, doubled every 27 years. The nation's rapid recovery from the Civil War offered striking testimony to the momentum of expansion: settlers moving west to occupy untilled soils accelerated mechanization, the use of fertilizers and the introduction of new strains. The US soon became the world's leading agricultural producer.

But railroads constituted the single most significant element in the nation's economic surge, lowering costs, opening up new production areas and markets, and, not least, unifying a far-flung, disparate nation. The need to integrate trunk lines even led to the standardization of times zones in 1883. By 1890 the US rail network was bigger than the entire European system. Other factors contributing to growth included abundant natural resources, a literate population, a managerial and organizational revolution, political stability, large-scale foreign capital investment and a pervasive entrepreneurial ethic. Between 1877 and 1892 factory output trebled, making the United States also the world's leading industrial power.

3/Union states and Confederate states *(below)* Geography largely determined the allegiance of the various slave-plantation and free-labour economies at the outbreak of the Civil War. The five most northerly slave states remained in the Union, though part of their population supported the Confederacy.

MISSOURI

Bentonville
19 Mar 65

Confederates under General A.S. Johnston attack Union army under Grant at Shiloh on April 6th but are defeated and driven back to Corinth after bloodiest battle in the war's first year.

ARKANSAS

Grant and Porter

Nov 1862-July 1863 After several failures to capture Vicksburg, Grant crosses Mississippi below the Fort, defeats General Johnston's forces at Jackson, and forces Vicksburg to surrender after 6 weeks' siege. Port Hudson falls 5 days later, giving Union complete control of the Mississippi and splitting Confederacy in two.

Vicksburg 4 July 63
Champions Hill 16 May 63

MISSIS

Port Hudson 9 July 63
Baton Rouge 12 May 62

LOUISIANA

Mississippi R.

The Iron Horse The railways were ess economic growth but also to the transpor tion and supplies in the Civil War – the firs which railways played a vital role.

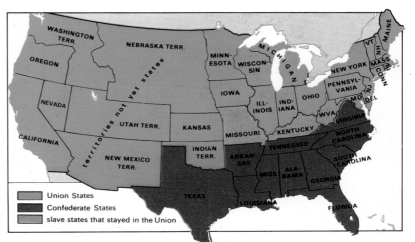

WASHINGTON TERR.
NEBRASKA TERR.
OREGON
MINN-ESOTA
WISCONSIN
MICHIGAN
NEW YORK
VT
MAINE
MASS
NEVADA
IOWA
PENNSYL-VANIA
CALIFORNIA
UTAH TERR.
KANSAS
MISSOURI
ILL-INOIS
IND-IANA
OHIO
WVA
KENTUCKY
MD
DEL
VIRGINIA
NORTH CAROLINA
NEW MEXICO TERR.
INDIAN TERR.
ARKAN-SAS
TENNESSEE
MISS
ALA-BAMA
SOUTH CAROLINA
GEORGIA
TEXAS
LOUISIANA
FLORIDA

Union States
Confederate States
slave states that stayed in the Union

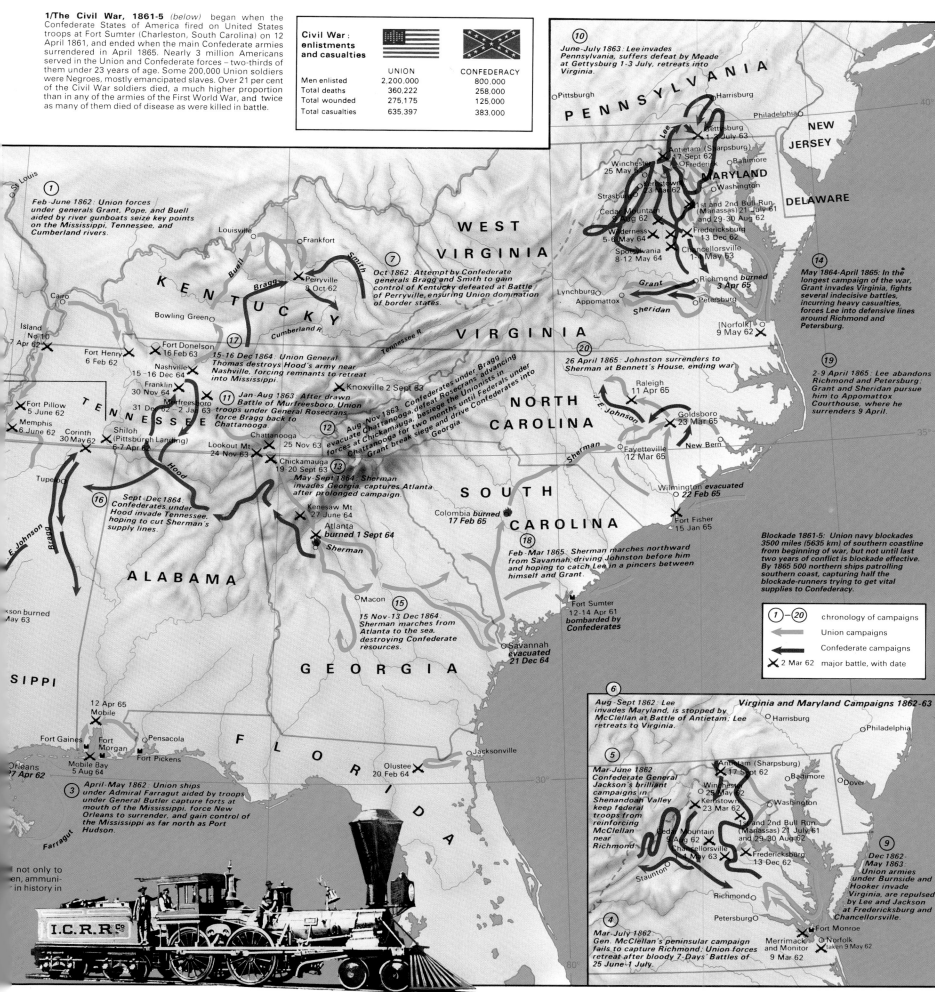

1/The Civil War, 1861-5 (below) began when the Confederate States of America fired on United States troops at Fort Sumter (Charleston, South Carolina) on 12 April 1861, and ended when the main Confederate armies surrendered in April 1865. Nearly 3 million Americans served in the Union and Confederate forces – two-thirds of them under 23 years of age. Some 200,000 Union soldiers were Negroes, mostly emancipated slaves. Over 21 per cent of the Civil War soldiers died, a much higher proportion than in any of the armies of the First World War, and twice as many of them died of disease as were killed in battle.

Civil War: enlistments and casualties

	UNION	CONFEDERACY
Men enlisted	2,200,000	800,000
Total deaths	360,222	258,000
Total wounded	275,175	125,000
Total casualties	635,397	383,000

10 June-July 1863: Lee invades Pennsylvania, suffers defeat by Meade at Gettysburg 1-3 July, retreats into Virginia.

1 Feb-June 1862: Union forces under generals Grant, Pope, and Buell aided by river gunboats seize key points on the Mississippi, Tennessee, and Cumberland rivers.

7 Oct 1862: Attempt by Confederate generals Bragg and Smith to gain control of Kentucky defeated at Battle of Perryville, ensuring Union domination of border states.

14 May 1864-April 1865: In the longest campaign of the war, Grant invades Virginia, fights several indecisive battles, incurring heavy casualties, forces Lee into defensive lines around Richmond and Petersburg.

17 15-16 Dec 1864: Union General Thomas destroys Hood's army near Nashville, forcing remnants to retreat into Mississippi.

20 26 April 1865: Johnston surrenders to Sherman at Bennett's House, ending war.

19 2-9 April 1865: Lee abandons Richmond and Petersburg; Grant and Sheridan pursue him to Appomattox Courthouse, where he surrenders 9 April.

11 Jan-Aug 1863: After drawn Battle of Murfreesboro, Union troops under General Rosecrans force Bragg back to Chattanooga.

12 Aug 1863: Confederates under Bragg evacuate Chattanooga, defeat Rosecrans advancing forces at Chickamauga, besiege Unionists in Chattanooga for two months until Federals under Grant break siege and drive Confederates into Georgia.

16 Sept-Dec 1864: Confederates under Hood invade Tennessee, hoping to cut Sherman's supply lines.

13 May-Sept 1864: Sherman invades Georgia, captures Atlanta after prolonged campaign.

18 Feb-Mar 1865: Sherman marches northward from Savannah, driving Johnston before him and hoping to catch Lee in a pincers between himself and Grant.

15 15 Nov-13 Dec 1864: Sherman marches from Atlanta to the sea, destroying Confederate resources.

Blockade 1861-5: Union navy blockades 3500 miles (5635 km) of southern coastline from beginning of war, but not until last two years of conflict is blockade effective. By 1865 500 northern ships patrolling southern coast, capturing half the blockade-runners trying to get vital supplies to Confederacy.

3 April-May 1862: Union ships under Admiral Farragut aided by troops under General Butler capture forts at mouth of the Mississippi, force New Orleans to surrender, and gain control of the Mississippi as far north as Port Hudson.

①—⑳	chronology of campaigns
←	Union campaigns
←	Confederate campaigns
✕ 2 Mar 62	major battle, with date

6 Aug-Sept 1862: Lee invades Maryland, is stopped by McClellan at Battle of Antietam; Lee retreats to Virginia.

Virginia and Maryland Campaigns 1862-63

5 Mar-June 1862: Confederate General Jackson's brilliant campaigns in Shenandoah Valley keep federal troops from reinforcing McClellan near Richmond.

9 Dec 1862-May 1863: Union armies under Burnside and Hooker invade Virginia, are repulsed by Lee and Jackson at Fredericksburg and Chancellorsville.

4 Mar-July 1862: Gen. McClellan's peninsular campaign fails to capture Richmond; Union forces retreat after bloody 7-Days' Battles of 25 June-1 July.

not only to ... en, ammuni-... in history in

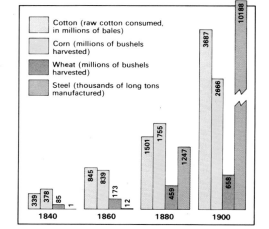

I.C.R.R. Co.

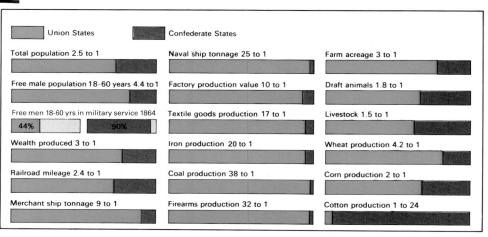

Economic growth, 1840-1900 (left) The growth of American agriculture and industry reflected in this graph resulted from technological innovations (especially reapers and threshing machines, and the Bessemer and open-hearth steel-making processes) as well as population growth and the settlement of new land.

Comparative resources, Union and Confederate states, 1861 (right) Because the South lacked the North's industrial capacity, the Confederacy was obliged to import or capture most of its arms. As the Union blockade tightened and the Confederate transport system broke down through inability to replace equipment, the agricultural South experienced difficulty even in feeding itself.

Cotton (raw cotton consumed, in millions of bales)
Corn (millions of bushels harvested)
Wheat (millions of bushels harvested)
Steel (thousands of long tons manufactured)

Union States / Confederate States

Total population 2.5 to 1
Free male population 18-60 years 4.4 to 1
Free men 18-60 yrs in military service 1864 — 44% / 90%
Wealth produced 3 to 1
Railroad mileage 2.4 to 1
Merchant ship tonnage 9 to 1

Naval ship tonnage 25 to 1
Factory production value 10 to 1
Textile goods production 17 to 1
Iron production 20 to 1
Coal production 38 to 1
Firearms production 32 to 1

Farm acreage 3 to 1
Draft animals 1.8 to 1
Livestock 1.5 to 1
Wheat production 4.2 to 1
Corn production 2 to 1
Cotton production 1 to 24

The making of the United States: politics and society 1776 to 1930

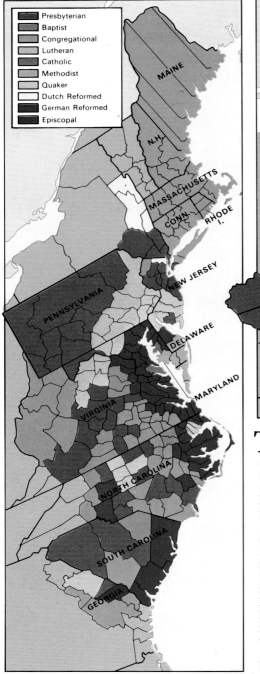

1/The election of 1800 *(above and above right)* In the election of 1800, power passed from the ruling Federalist party to its Jeffersonian challengers. That peaceful revolution provided a foundation for stable republicanism in North America. Voting patterns reflected the distribution of ethnic and religious groups.

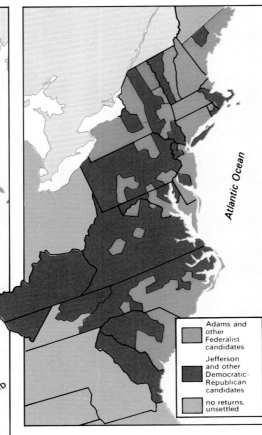

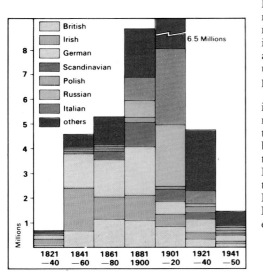

Immigration in the 19th and early 20th century *(above)* Economic change, population surplus, and famine sent millions of Europeans to North America, where scarcity of labour and virgin agricultural land provided economic opportunity. In the 1890s there was a fundamental shift in the sources of immigrants from northwest to southern and eastern Europe. Russian Jews and subject nationalities of the Austro-Hungarian Empire as well as Poles and Italians now constituted the majority of immigrants.

power was greatly facilitated by the complexity of those electoral patterns.

By 1828 the Federalist party had disappeared and the Jeffersonians had divided into the National-Republicans, headed by John Quincy Adams, and the Democratic-Republicans led by Andrew Jackson (the election that year prefigured the evolution of the Whig and Democratic parties). Jackson ran strongly among the common people of northern cities and the southern countryside; his opponents in 1828 and later were strongest in rural New England and the old northwest, and among the commerical and planter elites of both north and south. National Republicans/Whigs found their greatest support among Unitaritans, Congregationalists, Presbyterians and Episcopalians; Jacksonians were strongest among Baptists and Catholics; Methodists and Lutherans were divided.

Although many of these patterns persisted in 1860, the divisive sectional issue of slavery overshadowed them. The Democratic party, which had traditionally united different ethnic and economic groups across sectional lines, broke into two parties, one southern, one northern, which ran John C. Breckinridge and Stephen A. Douglas respectively for the presidency. Battered remnants of the Whigs formed the Constitutional Union party, with John Bell as its candidate, to try to unite conservatives in both sections, but Bell ran well only in the border states. The anti-slavery Republicans, entirely a northern party, nominated Abraham Lincoln on a platform of slavery containment. Carrying every county in New England and most of the counties in the other free states (but only two counties in all the south), Lincoln won the presidency with only 39 per cent of the popular vote. His election precipitated the secession of 11 slave states, and brought on the Civil War.

For a generation after the war, ethnic, religious and sectional patterns dominated American elections. As the party of union, emancipation, and reform, the Republicans won the votes of most evangelical Protestants in the north and of Blacks in the south, while the Democrats enjoyed the support of most whites in the south and many non-evangelical Protestants in the north. Class was only a minor factor in determining party allegiance, but since an increasing percentage of unskilled working men in the north were immigrants and Catholics, there appeared to be a relation between class and party in some northern states.

In the election of 1896, economic issues jolted old ethnic and religious patterns. William Jennings Bryan and the Democrats, campaigning for an inflationary policy of expanded silver coinage, carried all but three counties in the silver states of the west, as well as the farm states of Kansas and Nebraska, and the south. However, fearing the impact of inflation on real wages, and attracted by McKinley's repudiation of traditional Republican anti-Catholicism, northern working men of Catholic as well as Protestant faiths joined native-born middle-class Protestants in voting Republican. The Democratic party, in power during the Panic of 1893, became stigmatized as the party of depression. The sectional and rural/urban divisions in this election were striking: McKinley carried every county in New England (despite the region's large Catholic population), all but one county in New York, and all but two in New Jersey. He was the only Republican candidate in the 19th century to carry New York City. For 20 years before 1896 the two major parties had been evenly balanced in national elections; McKinley's success in winning many immigrant and urban votes while losing only the farmers and miners of thinly-populated western states moved the Republican party in a more urban, cosmopolitan and progressive direction and ensured its domination until the 1930s.

THE United States represents a paradox in political history: a republic of imperial dimensions which drew its unity from its multitude of differences, any one of which – ethnic, regional, economic or religious – might have destroyed it. Instead, the multiplicity of conflicts in America prevented any one of them from tearing it apart.

In 1776 most Americans were of British descent and Protestant faith. During the next 150 years, however, nearly 40 million people migrated to the United States, with the result that the map of the nation became a mosaic of many different religions. Roman Catholics, Methodists, Baptists and Lutherans became the largest denominations, with scores of smaller rivals. The ethnic map of American society likewise became infinitely more complex.

As the country expanded, its regions also became more diverse. The difference between north and south – between a system of wage labour and bond labour – became the most dangerous difference, as it was at once economic, political and racial. Before 1860 more than 90 per cent of the Black population lived below the Mason-Dixon line, making race a regional problem: not until the First World War did significant numbers of Blacks move north. But as the economy developed the distribution of wealth became increasingly unequal between both individuals and regions: rich and poor concentrated in urban areas, while the middle classes remained predominantly rural.

American presidential elections reflected the interplay of these patterns of ethnicity, religion, region and class. The 1800 campaign, in which the Republican candidate Thomas Jefferson beat the Federalists' John Adams, saw a coalition of New England Congregational elites, Dutch burghers in New York and free Blacks in the middle states lining up against the northern Baptist yeomen, Virginia Episcopalian planters, Irish immigrants in the cities and German farmers in Pennsylvania. The peaceful transfer of

2/The election of 1860 *(right)* In 1860 the American Union was split by the issue of slavery. The Republican candidate, Abraham Lincoln, promised to contain the westward expansion of slavery. He carried every county in New England, most of New York, and much of the northwest. John C. Breckinridge ran strongly throughout the south, but ironically the counties where slavery was strongest voted heavily for a compromise candidate, John Bell. The nominee of the northern Democrats, Stephen A. Douglas, did well in the popular vote, but carried few counties.

3/The election of 1896 *(below)* The main issue of this election was the monetary system. The Republican candidate, William McKinley, stood for preservation of the gold standard, while the Democrat William Jennings Bryan crusaded, for a bimetallic silver and gold standard, whose expected inflationary impact would benefit farmers of the south and west. This issue, plus Bryan's fundamentalist Protestantism and McKinley's religious pluralism, help to explain the sectional pattern of the voting, with the urbanized northeast and north central states solidly Republican and the south and west equally solidly Democrat.

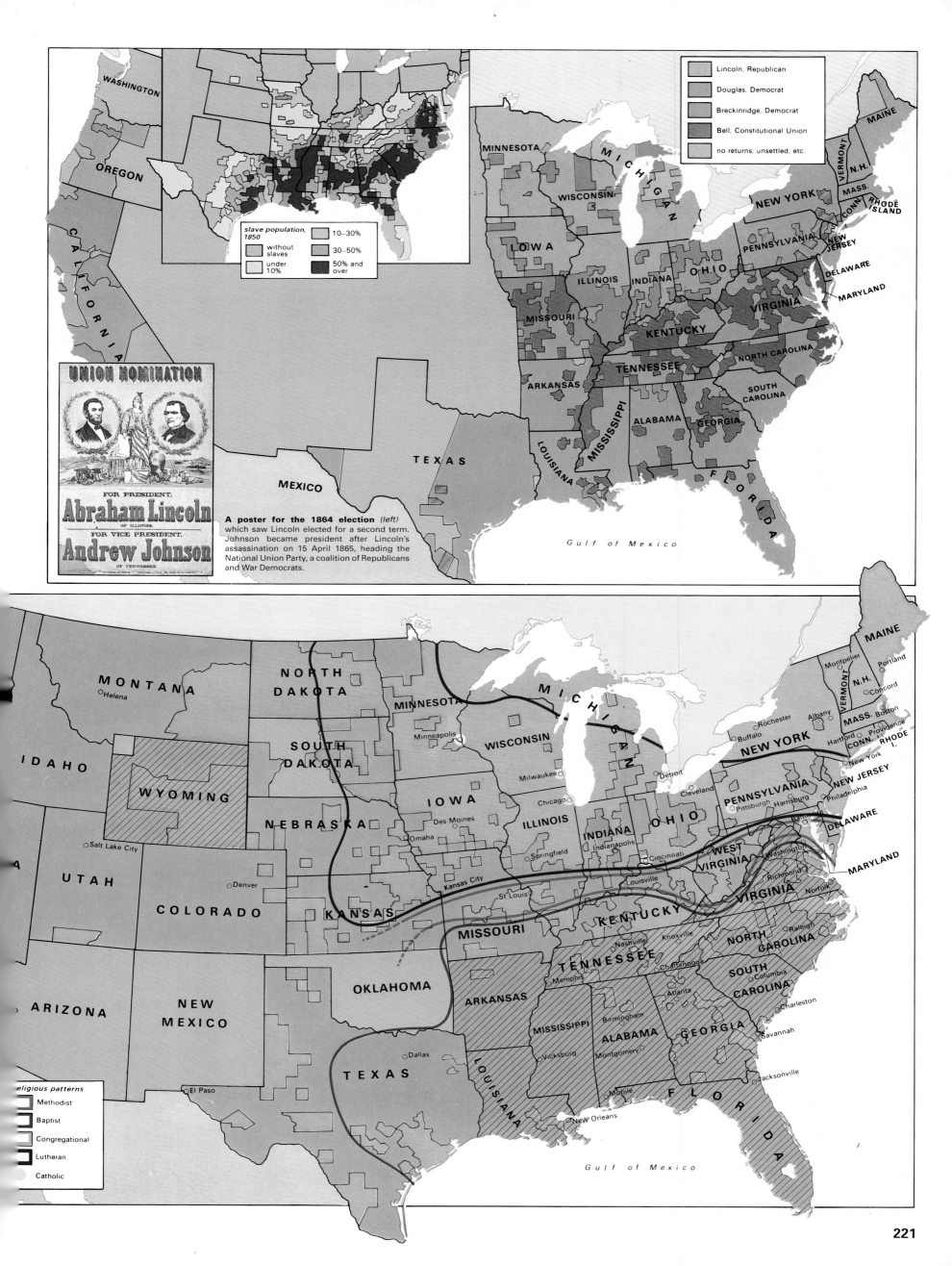

slave population, 1850

without slaves · under 10% · 10–30% · 30–50% · 50% and over

Lincoln, Republican
Douglas, Democrat
Breckinridge, Democrat
Bell, Constitutional Union
no returns, unsettled, etc.

UNION NOMINATION

FOR PRESIDENT.
Abraham Lincoln
OF ILLINOIS.

FOR VICE PRESIDENT.
Andrew Johnson
OF TENNESSEE.

A poster for the 1864 election (left) which saw Lincoln elected for a second term. Johnson became president after Lincoln's assassination on 15 April 1865, heading the National Union Party, a coalition of Republicans and War Democrats.

WASHINGTON · OREGON · CALIFORNIA · MEXICO · TEXAS · LOUISIANA · MISSISSIPPI · ALABAMA · GEORGIA · FLORIDA · SOUTH CAROLINA · NORTH CAROLINA · ARKANSAS · TENNESSEE · KENTUCKY · VIRGINIA · MARYLAND · DELAWARE · MISSOURI · ILLINOIS · INDIANA · OHIO · PENNSYLVANIA · NEW JERSEY · NEW YORK · IOWA · WISCONSIN · MINNESOTA · MICHIGAN · MAINE · VERMONT · N.H. · MASS. · CONN. · RHODE ISLAND

Gulf of Mexico

religious patterns

Methodist
Baptist
Congregational
Lutheran
Catholic

MONTANA · Helena · NORTH DAKOTA · SOUTH DAKOTA · MINNESOTA · Minneapolis · WISCONSIN · Milwaukee · MICHIGAN · Detroit · NEW YORK · Rochester · Albany · Buffalo · Hartford · Providence · CONN. · RHODE I. · MASS. · Boston · VERMONT · Montpelier · N.H. · Concord · MAINE · Portland

IDAHO · WYOMING · UTAH · Salt Lake City · NEBRASKA · Omaha · IOWA · Des Moines · ILLINOIS · Chicago · Springfield · INDIANA · Indianapolis · OHIO · Cleveland · PENNSYLVANIA · Pittsburgh · Harrisburg · Philadelphia · NEW JERSEY · New York · DELAWARE

COLORADO · Denver · KANSAS · Kansas City · MISSOURI · St Louis · KENTUCKY · Louisville · Cincinnati · WEST VIRGINIA · VIRGINIA · Washington · Richmond · Norfolk · MARYLAND · Baltimore

ARIZONA · NEW MEXICO · OKLAHOMA · Dallas · El Paso · TEXAS · ARKANSAS · Memphis · TENNESSEE · Nashville · Knoxville · Chattanooga · NORTH CAROLINA · Raleigh · SOUTH CAROLINA · Columbia · Charleston · GEORGIA · Atlanta · Savannah · MISSISSIPPI · Vicksburg · ALABAMA · Birmingham · Montgomery · Mobile · LOUISIANA · New Orleans · FLORIDA · Jacksonville

Gulf of Mexico

221

Latin America: independence and national growth 1810 to 1910

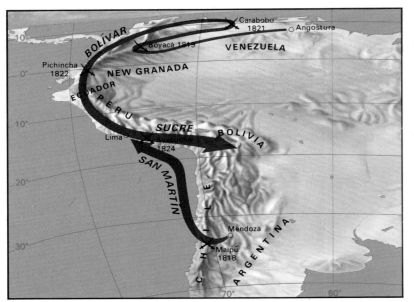

2/Independence campaigns 1810 to 1826 (above)
Latin America's main wars of liberation, against Spain, lasted until 1826. They involved two major forces: one, led by the Venezuelans, Bolívar and Sucre, converging on Peru, the central Spanish bastion; the other, the Army of the Andes, with San Martín's Argentines and Bernardo O'Higgins' Chileans, attacking the Peruvian capital, Lima.

3/Export economies and foreign investment (below) The new nations of Latin America were classic export economies, exploiting cheap land and labour to produce raw materials for a world market. Foreign competition and small, subsistence-level domestic markets held back development of national industries; characteristic economic institutions were the plantation, the ranch and the mine. From the 1880s, a massive immigration of foreign manpower and capital, reinforced by railways and improved ocean transport, accelerated economic growth.

E MANCIPATION between 1808 and 1826 was precipitated by the Napoleonic invasion of Spain and Portugal (see page 200). This released a long dormant nationalism, now able to express itself in demands for political freedom, administrative autonomy and economic self-determination. Having fled from Lisbon to Rio de Janeiro, which then became the centre of the empire, the Portuguese royal family presided over the relatively peaceful transition of Brazil from colony to independent nation. Assuming the title Emperor and renouncing his claims to the Portuguese throne, Peter I declared the independence of Brazil after his father had returned to Portugal. This, and fears of slave revolt which inhibited factionalism amongst the planter elite, made for greater institutional continuity and minimal social change. Spain, on the other hand, sought to crush its colonies' pretensions. Spanish American independence then swept across the sub-continent in two violent movements: the southern revolution was carried by San Martín's Army of the Andes from Buenos

Aires to Chile and beyond; the northern revolution, more vigorously harassed by Spain, was led by Bolívar from Venezuela to the mountainous battlefield of Boyacá in Colombia (then called New Granada). Both converged on Peru, the fortress of Spain in America. In the north, Mexican insurgency followed a course of its own – first frustrated social revolution, then prolonged counter-revolution and finally a successful power-seizure by the conservative commander Iturbide, enthroned as Emperor Agustín I. Everywhere independence was essentially a political movement, involving a transfer of authority but little social and economic change.

The wars of independence caused substantial loss of life and property which, although less destructive in absolute terms than European conflicts of the period, provoked insecurity and a flight of capital and labour. In much of Spanish America the struggles for independence assumed the character of a civil war rather than a clear-cut conflict between American insurgents and royalist forces from the peninsula, and civil disorder continued after the final defeat of

General José de San Martín (above) and his army crossed the Andes from Argentina in 1817 to liberate Chile from royalist forces. After a long siege of Lima, his forces declared Peru's independence in July 1821. The following year at Guayaquil, Ecuador, San Martín ceded control of his army to Simón Bolívar and retired to Europe where he died in 1850.

Spanish arms, inhibiting national reorganization and economic recovery. The first decades of freedom were occupied with violent political debate – between centre and regions, between agriculturists, mine-owners and industrialists, and between supporters of cheap imports and defenders of national production. Feuds between anti-clerical 'liberals' and 'conservatives' characterized Colombian and Mexican political history for much of the period. On the whole, policies of primary export and cheap imports prevailed. British (and later French and North American) merchants, bankers and shippers were ready and eager to fill the entrepreneurial vacuum left by Spain.

Prospects of national economic development were really defeated by the social structure of the new states. Impoverished rural populations offered little support for local industry. The old colonial division between a privileged minority, monopolizing land and office, and a mass of peasants and workers survived independence and grew even sharper. The new power base was the *hacienda*, the great landed estate. A social rather than an economic investment, it depended on cheap, servile labour. While slavery was formally abolished in much of Spanish America, it survived in attenuated form in some areas until the 1840s. In Brazil (and also Cuba which remained a Spanish colony) slavery was regarded as a vital component of plantation agriculture and continued until the 1880s. Indeed, the trans-Atlantic slave trade flourished until the early 1850s, despite strong opposition from the European powers. Even after abolition, blacks, like the majority of *mulattos* and *mestizos*, remained at the foot of the economic ladder. After the wars, new rulers sought to reduce ten-

4/Population and immigration (below) Latin America inherited a complex racial structure. Spanish American societies were composed in varying proportions of a great mass of Indians, a lesser number of *mestizos*, and a minority of whites. The Indian base of this pyramid was extensive in Peru, Mexico and Guatemala, less so in the Rio de la Plata and Chile. The slave trade from Africa had also added the Negro, from whom were descended *mulattos* and other mixed groups. Brazil was a slave society until 1888, with blacks and mixed bloods occupying the lower end of the social scale. Both Argentina and Brazil received massive immigration from Europe in the late 19th century.

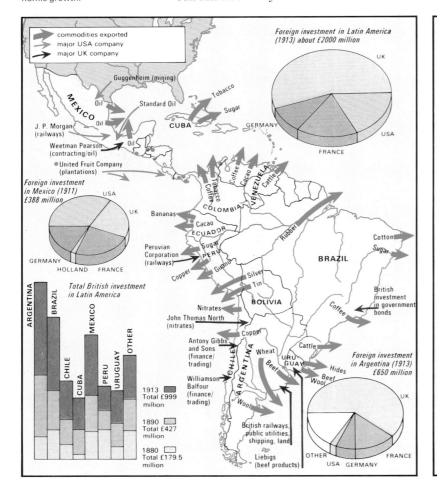

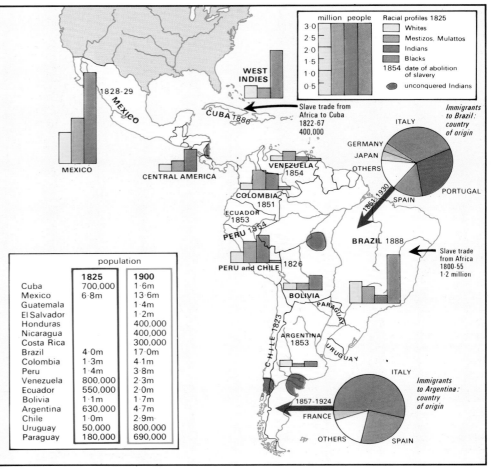

population		
	1825	**1900**
Cuba	700,000	1·6m
Mexico	6·8m	13·6m
Guatemala		1·4m
El Salvador		1·2m
Honduras		400,000
Nicaragua		400,000
Costa Rica		300,000
Brazil	4·0m	17·0m
Colombia	1·3m	4·1m
Peru	1·4m	3·8m
Venezuela	800,000	2·3m
Ecuador	550,000	2·0m
Bolivia	1·1m	1·7m
Argentina	630,000	4·7m
Chile	1·0m	2·9m
Uruguay	50,000	800,000
Paraguay	180,000	690,000

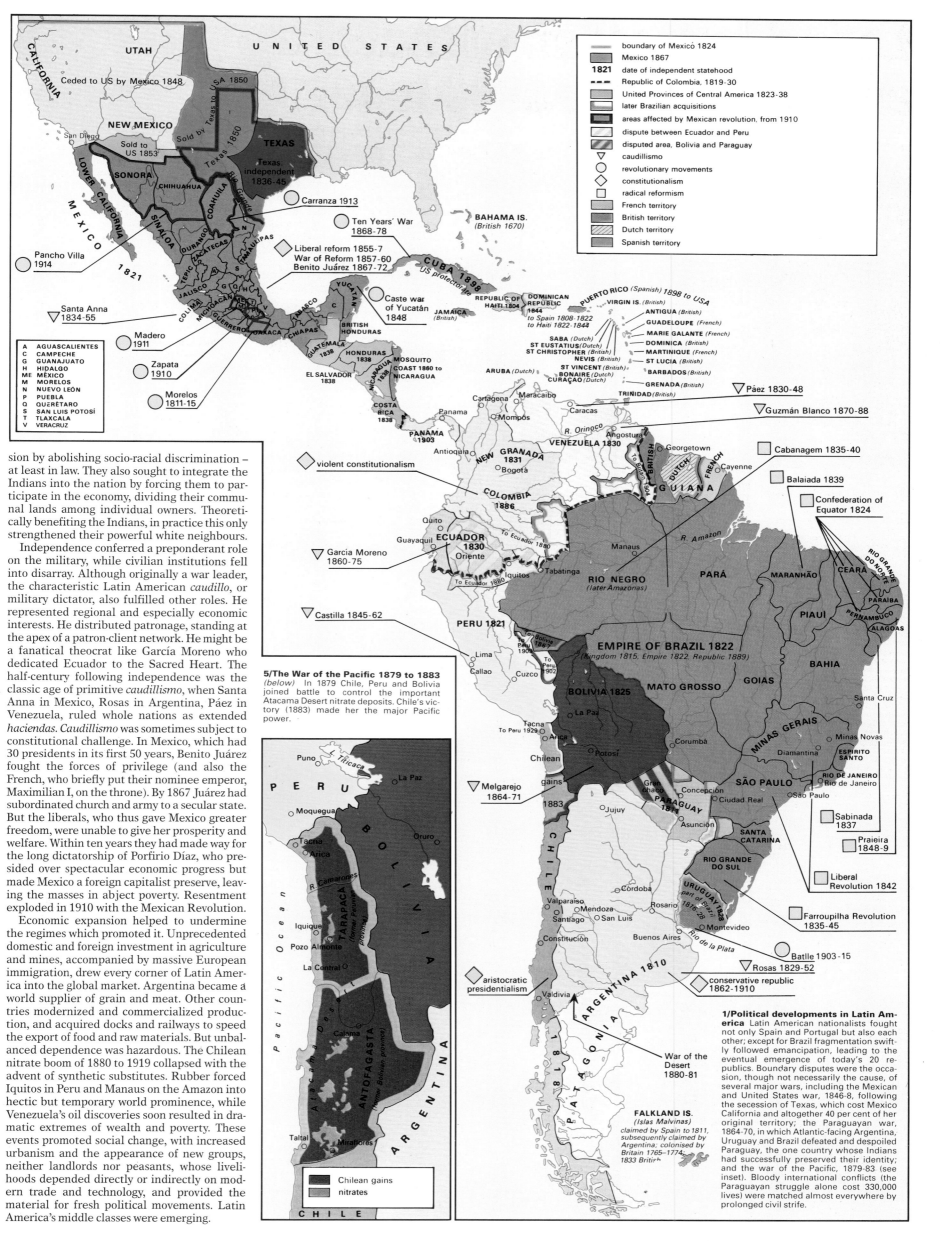

sion by abolishing socio-racial discrimination – at least in law. They also sought to integrate the Indians into the nation by forcing them to participate in the economy, dividing their communal lands among individual owners. Theoretically benefiting the Indians, in practice this only strengthened their powerful white neighbours.

Independence conferred a preponderant role on the military, while civilian institutions fell into disarray. Although originally a war leader, the characteristic Latin American *caudillo*, or military dictator, also fulfilled other roles. He represented regional and especially economic interests. He distributed patronage, standing at the apex of a patron-client network. He might be a fanatical theocrat like García Moreno who dedicated Ecuador to the Sacred Heart. The half-century following independence was the classic age of primitive *caudillismo*, when Santa Anna in Mexico, Rosas in Argentina, Páez in Venezuela, ruled whole nations as extended *haciendas*. *Caudillismo* was sometimes subject to constitutional challenge. In Mexico, which had 30 presidents in its first 50 years, Benito Juárez fought the forces of privilege (and also the French, who briefly put their nominee emperor, Maximilian I, on the throne). By 1867 Juárez had subordinated church and army to a secular state. But the liberals, who thus gave Mexico greater freedom, were unable to give her prosperity and welfare. Within ten years they had made way for the long dictatorship of Porfirio Díaz, who presided over spectacular economic progress but made Mexico a foreign capitalist preserve, leaving the masses in abject poverty. Resentment exploded in 1910 with the Mexican Revolution.

Economic expansion helped to undermine the regimes which promoted it. Unprecedented domestic and foreign investment in agriculture and mines, accompanied by massive European immigration, drew every corner of Latin America into the global market. Argentina became a world supplier of grain and meat. Other countries modernized and commercialized production, and acquired docks and railways to speed the export of food and raw materials. But unbalanced dependence was hazardous. The Chilean nitrate boom of 1880 to 1919 collapsed with the advent of synthetic substitutes. Rubber forced Iquitos in Peru and Manaus on the Amazon into hectic but temporary world prominence, while Venezuela's oil discoveries soon resulted in dramatic extremes of wealth and poverty. These events promoted social change, with increased urbanism and the appearance of new groups, neither landlords nor peasants, whose livelihoods depended directly or indirectly on modern trade and technology, and provided the material for fresh political movements. Latin America's middle classes were emerging.

5/The War of the Pacific 1879 to 1883
(below) In 1879 Chile, Peru and Bolivia joined battle to control the important Atacama Desert nitrate deposits. Chile's victory (1883) made her the major Pacific power.

1/Political developments in Latin America Latin American nationalists fought not only Spain and Portugal but also each other; except for Brazil fragmentation swiftly followed emancipation, leading to the eventual emergence of today's 20 republics. Boundary disputes were the occasion, though not necessarily the cause, of several major wars, including the Mexican and United States war, 1846-8, following the secession of Texas, which cost Mexico California and altogether 40 per cent of her original territory; the Paraguayan war, 1864-70, in which Atlantic-facing Argentina, Uruguay and Brazil defeated and despoiled Paraguay, the one country whose Indians had successfully preserved their identity; and the war of the Pacific, 1879-83 (see inset). Bloody international conflicts (the Paraguayan struggle alone cost 330,000 lives) were matched almost everywhere by prolonged civil strife.

The disintegration of the Ottoman Empire 1800 to 1923

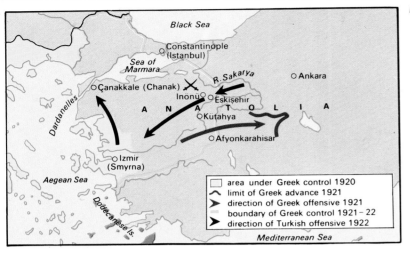

THE period 1800 to 1923 saw the disintegration and final collapse of the Ottoman Empire. Plagued by wars and the revolts of subject peoples demanding national independence, the Empire lost territory steadily. Faced with gradual dismemberment, wars and financial collapse, the sultans attempted to reform the unwieldy state. At the same time opposition to their rule developed, culminating in the Young Turk Revolution of 1908–9. By then, however, the Sultan's hands were tied because the fate of the Empire was largely decided by the wishes of the Great Powers who preferred the survival of a weakened Ottoman state to the dangerous power vacuum in southeast Europe which would follow an Ottoman collapse.

In 1798 Napoleon invaded Egypt, only to be defeated by the British. Peace was arranged in 1802 and three years later Muhammed Ali was appointed governor by the Sultan. Under his rule and that of his son Ibrahim, Egypt was *de facto* independent of the Porte, Ibrahim even invading Syria and Anatolia and defeating the Ottoman army at the battle of Nezib in 1839. In 1841 the Sultan recognized Mohammed Ali as hereditary viceroy of Egypt and Ibrahim as Governor of Crete. In 1881 the French annexed Tunisia; the following year the British occupied Egypt. There were also wars with Russia, rebellions in the Arab provinces and almost constant revolts in the Balkans (starting with the Greek

War of Independence in 1821, which resulted in the recognition of the sovereign Greek Kingdom in 1830). By 1882 the Ottomans had lost 40 per cent of their Empire, and they lost more at the beginning of the 20th century. The Balkan Wars ended in 1913 with the Ottomans surrendering Crete, most of the Aegean islands, Thrace, Macedonia and Albania. In North Africa, Libya fell to the Italians in 1912. In all, between 1908 and 1913 the Ottoman government ceded 30 per cent of its remaining possessions.

Throughout this period the Great Powers constantly interfered in Ottoman affairs, either united in enforcing settlements on the government or in opposition to each other over influence within the Empire. The London Protocol of 1830 established the sovereign kingdom of Greece, guaranteed by Britain, Russia and France. Hereditary rule for Mohammed Ali in Egypt was set out under the terms of the Treaty of London, concluded between Russia, Austria, Prussia, Great Britain and the Ottoman government in 1840. Foreign intervention precipitated the Crimean War (1853–6) and the Lebanese crisis of 1860–1, while Russian and Austrian pres-

3/The Greco-Turkish War, 1920-22 *(above)* After the First World War, the Allies proposed to dismember Turkey under the Treaty of Sèvres (1920). Nationalist opposition crystallized around the country's only unbeaten general, Mustapha Kemal, and erupted after the Greek occupation of Smyrna (1920). Turkish resistance, centred on Ankara, was at first unable to counter the Greek advance towards central Anatolia, but the Turks rallied and drove the Greeks back after two major battles at Inönü (1921). The tide gradually turned in the Nationalists' favour: they concluded a border agreement with the Soviet Union (1921), and made separate pacts with France and Italy, who withdrew from the Turkish mainland. In 1922, Turkish forces reoccupied Smyrna, massacring many of the Greek population. Advancing towards the Dardanelles, they met a British detachment at Çanakkale, and confrontation appeared inevitable. Eventually, however, Turkish demands were met and the Treaty of Lausanne (1923) recognized Turkish sovereignty.

Turkey's flag provides a link with the Byzantine and Ottoman Empires. After the light of the crescent moon reputedly saved Byzantium from Philip of Macedon, the device was adopted by the Byzantines and the Ottoman conquerors.

1/The Middle East and North Africa 1798-1923 *(right)* The Ottoman Empire and the regions adjoining it broke up into a large number of political units in the course of the 19th and early 20th centuries:

Albania Ottoman province until independence secured late 1912 after fierce fighting.

Armenia Western part in Ottoman Empire, eastern in Persia; east part occupied by Russia 1804; briefly a united independent republic 1918-20; autonomy promised but not given due to non-ratification of Treaty of Sèvres (1920); subsequently absorbed by Turkey and USSR.

Azerbaijan Mainly under Persian rule until early 19th century; partly occupied by Russia 1803-28; briefly independent 1918-20, thereafter incorporated into USSR; Azeri Turkish speakers roughly equally divided between USSR and Persia.

Bahrain Independent skeikhdom under al-Khalifa family since 1783; British protection from 1820, formalized in agreements in 1880 and 1892.

Bessarabia Ceded to Russia by Ottomans under Treaty of Bucharest (1812); southern part returned to (Ottoman) Moldavia under terms of settlement after Crimean War (1856); recovered by Russia 1878. Incorporated into Romania 1918.

Bosnia-Herzegovina Ottoman; Austrian administration from 1878; incorporated into Austro-Hungarian Empire, 1908; part of Yugoslavia after 1918.

Bulgaria Ottoman province since 14th century; unsuccessful national rising 1875-6; given autonomy but partitioned 1878; united with Eastern Rumelia 1885; independent kingdom 1908; gained Macedonia and Western Thrace 1913; present (1993) boundaries from 1919.

Crete Ottoman province since 1669; autonomous 1898; incorporated in Greece 1913.

Georgia Independent kingdom under intermittent Persian control; incorporated into Russia 1801; briefly independent 1918-20; thereafter incorporated into USSR.

Greece Ottoman rule since 14th century; independent state after revolts of 1821, 1833; enlarged by additions of Crete (1913) and Macedonia (1913).

Iraq Formed out of three former Ottoman provinces of Basra, Baghdad and Mosul, 1920; unified as kingdom under Hashemite monarchy, 1921-58; under British mandate, 1920-32.

Kars and Ardahan Fortress of Kars occupied by Russia, 1828; returned to Ottomans after Crimea, 1856; to Russia after San Stefano, 1878; incorporated in Armenian Republic, 1918-20; re-occupied by Turkey after 1920.

Kuwait Autonomous sheikhdom under as-Sabah family since c.1756; treaty of protection with Britain, 1899-1961.

Lebanon Ottoman conquest, 1516-7; Mount Lebanon ruled by Ma'n princes (12th century 1697), then Shihab princes (1697-1840), both generally independent of Istanbul; 'double qaimaqamate' established after re-assertion of Ottoman control, 1840-61; given privileged status after civil war of 1860-1 under Christian governors, 1861-1914; French occupation 1918-20; enlarged and given republican status under French mandate, 1920-46.

Macedonia Ottoman province; divided between Greece, Serbia and Bulgaria 1913.

Montenegro Autonomous region within Ottoman Empire (prince-bishops until 1851, then princes); independent 1878; kingdom 1910; incorporated into Yugoslavia after 1918.

Palestine Ottoman conquest, 1516-7; ruled by provincial governors and/or local dynasts until 1917; British conquest 1917-8, assigned to Britain as mandate (1920-47) with British obligation to facilitate creation of Jewish national home.

Persia Independent kingdom under Qajar Shahs 1779-1924; Constitutional Revolution, 1905-11; British and Russian agreement on partition into spheres of influence, 1907.

Qatar Autonomous sheikhdom under al-Thani family since late 18th century; treaty of friendship and protection with Britain, 1916-71.

Romania Ottoman provinces of Moldavia and Wallachia under local rulers until united in 1861; independent kingdom, 1878, enlarged by the addition of Bessarabia, 1918.

Serbia Ottoman province; autonomous from c.1817; independent kingdom, 1878; incorporated after 1918 into what later became Yugoslavia.

Syria [Name formerly applied to whole area of modern Syria, Israel-Palestine, Lebanon, Jordan] Ottoman conquest 1516-7; British conquest/occupation 1918; independent Arab state 1918-20; French occupation 1920, French mandate within present geographical boundaries (Sanjak of Alexandretta ceded to Turkey, 1939) 1920-46.

Transjordan Formerly part of Ottoman province of Damascus; princedom (Hashemite family) under British mandate for Palestine 1921-3; separate administration created 1923.

Trucial Oman Small sheikhdoms under British protection, 1820s-1971.

Tunisia Ottoman conquest, 1574; virtually independent under Husainid dynasty, 1705 to French occupation in 1881; French protectorate, 1881-1956.

Yemen Local rulers belonging to Za'idi (Shia) sect; nominally incorporated into Ottoman Empire, 1517; Aden occupied by Britain 1839; declaration of independence, 1918.

sure helped secure the independence of Bulgaria, Montenegro, Serbia and Romania by 1878. In 1876 the Bulgarian situation resulted in Britain's call for an international conference to be held at Istanbul. The Sultan disapproved but proved powerless to prevent it taking place. He did, however, reject every proposal the conference made, resulting in its failure and breakup in 1877 and giving rise to the London Protocol of 1877. Inspired by Russia, this protocol called for the demobilization of Balkan, Russian and Ottoman armies and introduction of reforms under Great Power supervision. These proposals, too, were rejected by the Sultan. Russian gains under the Treaty of San Stefano in 1878 so alarmed the other powers, however, that a settlement less favourable to Russia was worked out at the Congress of Berlin later that same year.

The finances of the Empire rapidly deteriorated until in 1875 the state became virtually bankrupt and Sultan Abdulaziz suspended payment of the interest due on the Ottoman debt. From now on the Empire's survival became dependent on foreign governments. At the end of 1881 the Sultan agreed to supervision of the Ottoman finances by European bankers and the Ottoman Public Debt Commission was set up by the Muharrem Decree.

Throughout the 19th century the sultans made various attempts to modernize their empire. Military reforms were introduced, but not always successfully: Selim III, who aimed to create a modern army, was deposed in 1807

when his troops mutinied against attempted reforms. The Janissaries rebelled in 1826 against reforms under Mahmud II, but this provoked their abolition. Two edicts, in 1839 and 1856, stressed the subjects' rights to security of life and property, equitable taxation and limited military service, and emphasized complete equality between Muslim and Christian subjects in the Empire. Here, as in other spheres, the gap between the ideal and the reality was apparent, and opposition to the reforms soon developed. In 1865 the Society of New Ottomans was formed, calling for constitutional government and resulting in the promulgation of a Constitution in 1876. Parliament opened in 1877 but disbanded after one year, to remain in abeyance until recalled 30 years later. Opposition to the Sultan continued with the formation in 1889 of the Ottoman Society for Union and Progress which finally forced the restitution of the Constitution in 1908 and the abdication of the Sultan in the following year. However the Society did not stay loyal to the ideas of the Constitution and by 1913 had come to dominate the administration.

After the First World War, which Turkey entered on the side of the Germans in 1914, the Middle East came firmly under British and French colonial control. The Sultan collaborated with Great Britain, only to see the Sultanate abolished in 1920 by Mustafa Kemal, the leader of the opposition, two years after Turkey signed the unfavourable Treaty of Sèvres. In 1923, a new settlement was formulated and the Treaty of Lausanne signed, building the new state of Turkey out of the rubble of the Ottoman empire.

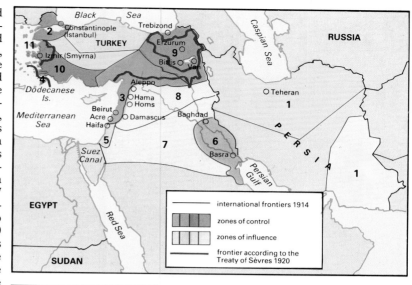

	international frontiers 1914
	zones of control
	zones of influence
	frontier according to the Treaty of Sèvres 1920

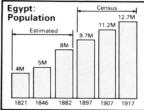

Egypt: Population

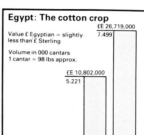

Egypt: The cotton crop

Value £ Egyptian = slightly less than £ Sterling
Volume in 000 cantars
1 cantar = 98 lbs approx.

2/Secret agreements among the Powers (above) In 1907, Britain and Russia divided Persia into spheres of influence (**1**). During the First World War, Britain, France, Italy and Russia made a series of agreements to divide the Ottoman Empire in the event of an Allied victory. In 1915, the Anglo-Franco-Russian Agreement gave Constantinople, the Straits and the Dardanelles to Russia (**2**), (in return for commercial freedom for British shipping and a promise to reconsider Persia in Britain's favour), and the creation of a French sphere of influence in Syria and Cilicia (**3**). The Treaty of London (1915: Britain, France, Italy) promised Italy part of southwest Turkey and confirmed her in possession of the Dodecanese Islands (**4**). The Sykes-Picot Agreement (1916: Britain, France, Russia) internationalized Palestine (**5**), gave Britain control of Mesopotamia (**6**), and the ports of Haifa and Acre, and a sphere of influence (**7**) linking the two areas. France was to control Cilicia and the Syrian coast, including Lebanon, and have a sphere of influence including most of the Ottoman province of Mosul (**8**). Russia gained northwest Anatolia and large parts of Armenia and Kurdistan (**9**). By the Treaty of Saint-Jean de Maurienne (1917), the Italians were promised the Ottoman provinces of Antalya, Aydin, Konya and Izmir (**10**). At the same time the British were negotiating with Sharif Husain of Mecca to gain Arab support against the Ottomans. In Oct. 1915 Husain was promised an independent Arab state in the Arab provinces of the Ottoman Empire, except Baghdad and Basra, the districts of Mersina and Alexandretta, and portions of Syria to the west of Damascus, Homs, Hama and Aleppo. Finally, the Balfour Declaration (Nov. 1917) stated that the British Government favoured 'the establishment in Palestine of a National Home for the Jewish people'. After the war, the Treaty of Sèvres (never ratified) proposed the internationalization of Constantinople and the Straits, the cession of Smyrna and its hinterland to Greece (**11**), and the creation of independent states in Armenia and Kurdistan. After the success of the Turkish national movement, the Treaty of Lausanne (1923) gave Turkey most of her modern territory; the Arab provinces were partitioned between Britain and France; Italy secured only the Dodecanese, while the 'independent Arab state' in Damascus fell to the French in July 1920.

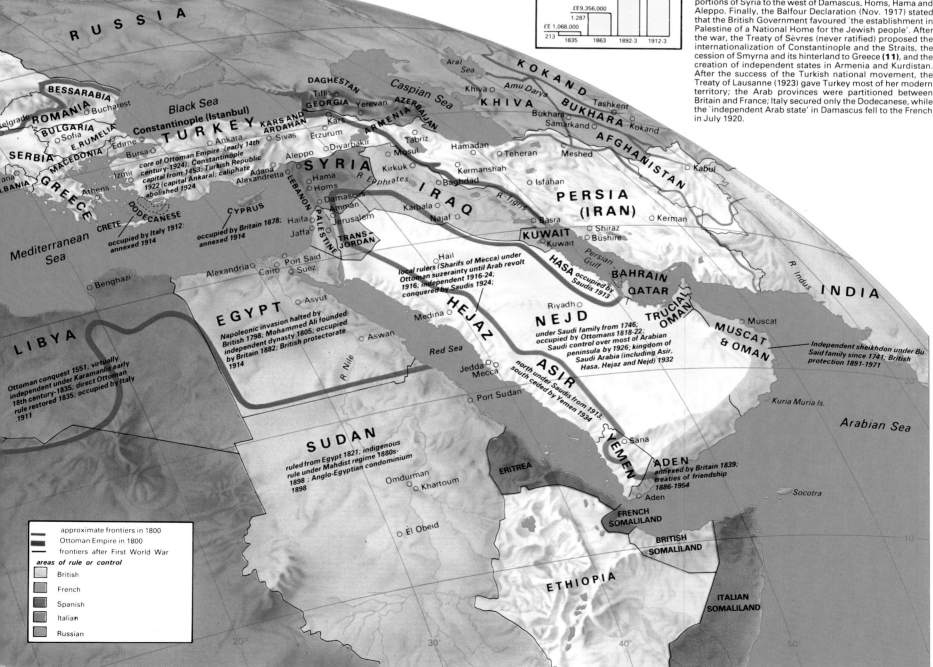

	approximate frontiers in 1800
	Ottoman Empire in 1800
	frontiers after First World War

areas of rule or control

	British
	French
	Spanish
	Italian
	Russian

225

The Russian Empire: expansion and modernization 1815 to 1917

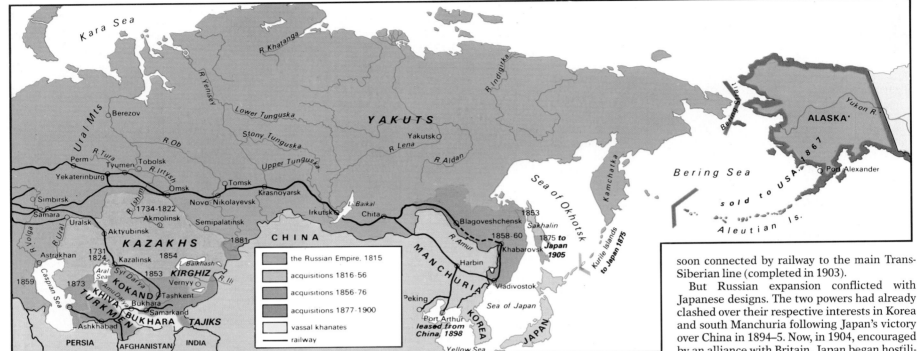

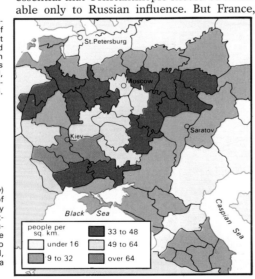

2/Russia in Asia (*above*) During the 19th century, Russian authority extended southwards across the deserts of central Asia inhabited by nomadic Kazakhs, Turkmen and others, to embrace the irrigated areas at the foot of the central Asian mountains. In the Far East, acquisition of the Amur territory and Sakhalin was followed by penetration of Manchuria and Korea, but the war with Japan (1904-5) ended Russian influence in these provinces, and southern Sakhalin was abandoned.

3/Rural population (*right*) Despite emigration to the steppes of the southern Ukraine, to southeast Russia, the Volga lands and beyond into Siberia, the rich black-earth lands of the south-central provinces became increasingly overcrowded, resulting in the subdivision of holdings and severe soil exhaustion.

4/The Crimean War (*below*) resulted from the determination of Britain and France, abetted by Austria, to prevent Russia benefitting from the impending dissolution of the Ottoman Empire. The war centred on the Allied attempt to take the naval base of Sevastopol, which fell in September 1855 after a year-long siege.

For 40 years after the Congress of Vienna, Russia remained the strongest military power in Europe and, in concert with Austria and Prussia, she used her strength to maintain the order established in 1815. Britain and France, however, drifted away from the principles which had inspired the Congress. British public opinion abhorred the absolutism and repression of the Russian system, while France emanated revolutionary impulses that threatened established monarchies everywhere.

Russian interests in the West after 1815 focussed on the Balkans and on the straits connecting the Black Sea with the Mediterranean. Since Turkey's Balkan subjects were mostly Orthodox Slavs, Russia considered herself their natural protector; because Turkey lay athwart Russia's link with the Mediterranean it seemed essential that Constantinople should be amenable only to Russian influence. But France, Austria and Prussia also had imperial ambitions in these areas, while Britain opposed any further Russian aggrandizement. In 1841 an international Straits Convention closed the Bosporus to Russian warships, but in 1853 the Russians invaded Turkey's Danubian provinces and also gained control of the Black Sea by sinking the Turkish fleet. In 1854, therefore, Britain and France declared war and invaded the Crimea. Meanwhile Austria insisted on the withdrawal of Russian troops from the Balkans, substituting her own. Unable to dislodge the invaders, Russia in 1856 accepted the humiliating terms of the Peace of Paris: no navy would be kept on the Black Sea nor bases kept on its shores.

The revolts of the Balkan Slavs and their repression by the Turks provoked another Russian invasion of the Balkans in 1877 but, faced with the united opposition of the great powers, Russia again had to give way. At the Congress of Berlin (1878), having at great cost liberated fellow Slavs and believers from oppression, Russia had to stand by while the fruits of victory were either transferred to Austria or handed back to Turkey.

Although Russia's policies and actions in the West thus failed, success crowned her expansion in the East. Military domination over the Kazakh nomads east of the Caspian was secured by forts, beginning with Akmolinsk in 1830 and ending with Vernyy (now Alma-Ata) in 1854. Mountain campaigns between 1857 and 1864 completed Russian control of the Caucasus, and the victorious armies then subdued the peoples of central Asia: the Uzbek khanates of Kokand, Bukhara and Khiva, the Turkmen nomads and the Tadzhik and Kirgiz mountaineers. Russia thus completed the acquisition of the whole of northern Asia as far as – and sometimes into – the great mountain chains which separate it from Persia, Afghanistan, India and China. Even colonization of North America continued into the early 19th century and forts were built as far south as California (Fort Ross, 1812). This penetration was short-lived, but Alaska was held until 1867, when it was sold to the United States. In the Far East the Treaties of Aigun (1858) and Peking (1860) brought the Russian frontier south to the Amur River and, on the Pacific coast, to south of Vladivostok (founded in 1860), while the southern part of Sakhalin was acquired from Japan in exchange for the Kuril Islands (1875). In 1891 the Trans-Siberian railway was begun and in 1898 China leased Port Arthur on the Yellow Sea, giving Russia a warm-water port unimpeded by winter ice. This was soon connected by railway to the main Trans-Siberian line (completed in 1903).

But Russian expansion conflicted with Japanese designs. The two powers had already clashed over their respective interests in Korea and south Manchuria following Japan's victory over China in 1894–5. Now, in 1904, encouraged by an alliance with Britain, Japan began hostilities with a Russia handicapped by the need to fight far from her main centres of industry and population. The Treaty of Portsmouth (1905) compelled her to give up the concessions she had won, to leave Manchuria, and to return southern Sakhalin to Japan. This defeat in the East was to add fuel to the flames of revolution at home. There, Alexander II (1855–81) had initiated a number of reforms in the 1860s to remedy the backwardness exposed by the Crimean War: new local government organizations (*zemstva*); educational reforms; and radical changes in the legal system. Central to all these measures was the emancipation of the serfs in 1861. And yet, still compelled to remain in their village communities, peasants felt aggrieved that they now had to acquire by purchase (often) less land than they had earlier worked. With rural population on the increase, the peasants' desire for more land became widespread.

To improve defence and bolster Russia's position in Europe, as well as to transport people and goods, the government from the late 19th century embarked on an industrialization programme with railways at its centre. Much railway building aimed at facilitating the movement of troops to frontier areas, but it made possible not only migration from overcrowded central Russia to western Siberia but also the movement of peasants to urban areas in Russia, creating an industrial proletariat to man the growing number of factories. St Petersburg and Moscow became textile and metal-working centres, while metallurgical industries developed in the Ukraine. The urban population increased – from 6 to 18.6 million – between 1863 and 1914.

Such rapid economic transformation in a backward country was bound to produce social and political discontent. Peasant dissatisfaction continued over land, increased taxes and the pressure of increasing commercialization, while workers protested over low wages and appalling conditions. Revolutionary parties were quick to exploit these new hardships and grievances, while the new professional classes pressed for political reform. In the wake of defeat in the Russo–Japanese War, all this unease culminated in the revolution of 1905. Tsar Nicholas II (1894–1917) was forced to create a parliament (*duma*), while Prime Minister Stolypin set in motion a number of reforms, above all in agriculture. By 1914 Russia had been drawn into the First World War, and within three years political and military ineptitude, together with a severely overstrained economy, brought about the downfall of the Romanov dynasty (see page 254).

Legend

- ● urban population increase, 1861-1914 the circle is proportionate to the size of growth
- ■ economic activity to 1861
- ▨ economic activity 1861-1914
- ⊞ metallurgical and metalworking industry
- ◆ coal mining
- ▲ iron ore mining
- ⊕ textile industry
- Ɩ sugar refining
- ⬥ oil industry
- ═ railway

The Trans-Siberian Railway (*above*) was begun in 1891 and completed in 1903, facilitating the movement of peoples and goods between European Russia and Siberia, and linking Russia to Manchuria, China, Korea and, indirectly, Japan.

1/European Russia 1815-1917 Little economic growth occurred in Russia before the 1860s, when a number of reforms, including the emancipation of the serfs (1861), and a spate of railway building stimulated industrial development, although all-out industrialization and urbanization had to await state intervention from the mid-1880s. Concentrations of poverty-stricken workers in the towns created the proletariat among whom revolutionary ideas flourished.

The collapse of the Chinese Empire 1842 to 1911

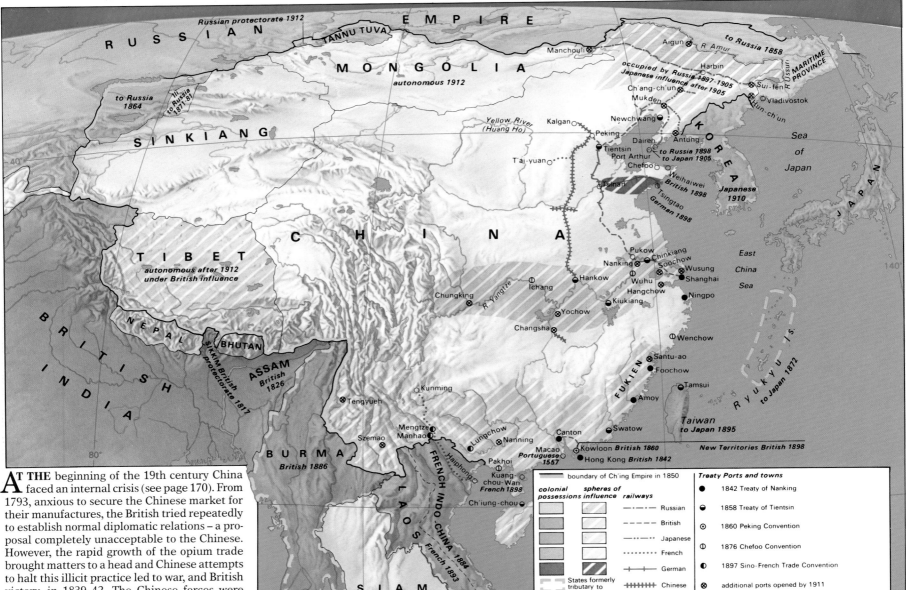

AT THE beginning of the 19th century China faced an internal crisis (see page 170). From 1793, anxious to secure the Chinese market for their manufactures, the British tried repeatedly to establish normal diplomatic relations – a proposal completely unacceptable to the Chinese. However, the rapid growth of the opium trade brought matters to a head and Chinese attempts to halt this illicit practice led to war, and British victory, in 1839–42. The Chinese forces were decisively defeated. China was forced to cede Hong Kong and open five Treaty Ports in which foreign residents were permitted to trade and were freed of Chinese jurisdiction. French and American treaties followed and Shanghai soon replaced Canton as the centre of foreign trade and influence. Exports of tea and silk flourished, and the opium trade continued to expand.

Nonetheless, the Chinese failed to understand the new challenge the western powers presented. Until the 17th century China had remained superior to the West in many ways, and during the 18th century the Ch'ing empire reached the peak of its prosperity and stability, while its armies conquered a vast new empire in inner Asia. But the rapid growth of Europe overtook China at precisely this time and although the empire remained self-sufficient it was now forced to deal with the expansionist Western powers which enjoyed technological superiority, wealth and a capacity for organization engendered by the Industrial Revolution. As the 19th century progressed the empire's ruling class, nurtured in a tradition of unquestioned Chinese cultural supremacy, proved unable either to understand the new challenge or to modernize the country. As a result, China fell further and further behind.

Even if the Ch'ing government had responded to this new situation and accepted the need to modernize the empire it could have done little, for internal developments now involved it in a desperate struggle for survival. Defeat in the Opium War weakened imperial authority, and switching the export trade from Canton to Shanghai exacerbated the economic problems of the south. In 1850 a rebellion broke out in

Kwangsi which rapidly grew into a full-scale dynastic revolt: the T'ai-p'ing T'ien-kuo (Heavenly Kingdom of Great Peace). Moving north to the Yangtze valley the rebels took Nanking in 1853 and established control over much of central China until final defeat in 1864.

The T'ai-p'ing T'ien-kuo was only the most serious of the many insurrections that erupted in the 1850s and 1860s, affecting a large part of the empire before the last of them was finally quelled in 1878. The Ch'ing armies and government proved inadequate to deal with these internal threats, too, and the suppression of the rebellion was largely the work of a small number of far-sighted provincial governors who established modern armies and arsenals, and trained their own experts in Western technology. They remained a minority, however. Most of the court and the bureaucracy were intent on the restoration of the traditional institutions rather than on change.

The fighting devastated China – the wealthy region around Nanking did not recover for decades – with the T'ai-p'ing and Nien rebellions alone leaving 25 million dead, and the Muslim risings (1863–73) depopulating vast tracts of Yunnan and the northwest. To make matters worse, a terrible famine in the north in 1877–9 led to the death of at least 10 million people from starvation.

These grave disorders favoured the foreign powers, which still lacked normal diplomatic relations with China. In 1856, after the failure of their attempts at negotiation, the British and French began another war which ended with the

occupation of Peking. The ensuing peace settlement finally secured diplomatic representation at the Imperial Court, opened more treaty ports and allowed foreign missionaries freedom of movement throughout China.

Meanwhile, the Russians took advantage of the situation to occupy the Amur River region in 1858 and the Maritime Province in 1860. In 1871 they occupied the Ili valley in Turkestan, only withdrawing in 1881 when China paid an indemnity. A further Chinese defeat came in a war with France over Indo-China in 1884–5, followed by humiliation at the hands of Japan which, faced with the same challenge, had begun to transform itself into a modern industrialized power. The Japanese had already intervened in Taiwan, in the Ryukyu Islands and in Korea. Finally, in 1894–5 Japan overwhelmed the Chinese forces in a full-scale war before annexing Taiwan.

This defeat at last convinced many Chinese that radical changes were inevitable: in 1898 Emperor Kuang Hsu and a group of radicals attempted a sweeping reform programme, but the conservative Manchus, led by Dowager Empress Tzu Hsi, carried out a coup to prevent its implementation. Meanwhile, the foreign powers, believing China to be on the point of final collapse, joined in a scramble for further rights and concessions, carving out spheres of influence and leasing territories as bases. This produced a wave of xenophobia which inspired the Boxer Rising in northeast China, where the rebels first attacked missionaries, and then the foreign legations in Tientsin and Peking. The

2/The dismemberment of the Ch'ing Empire (above) During the 19th century China was forced to cede Hong Kong to Great Britain and to open to foreign trade ever more regions in which foreigners enjoyed extra-territorial rights. At the same time she lost extensive territories in the north and northeast to the expansionist Russian empire, and was challenged in peripheral states such as Nepal, Burma, Laos, Tongking, the Ryukyus and Korea, which had been her vassals. With the collapse of the Ch'ing Empire in 1911 China also lost control of Tibet and Mongolia.

Japan defeats China (above) In the Sino-Japanese war of 1894-5 the carefully modernized western-style Japanese army disastrously routed the ill-led Chinese forces.

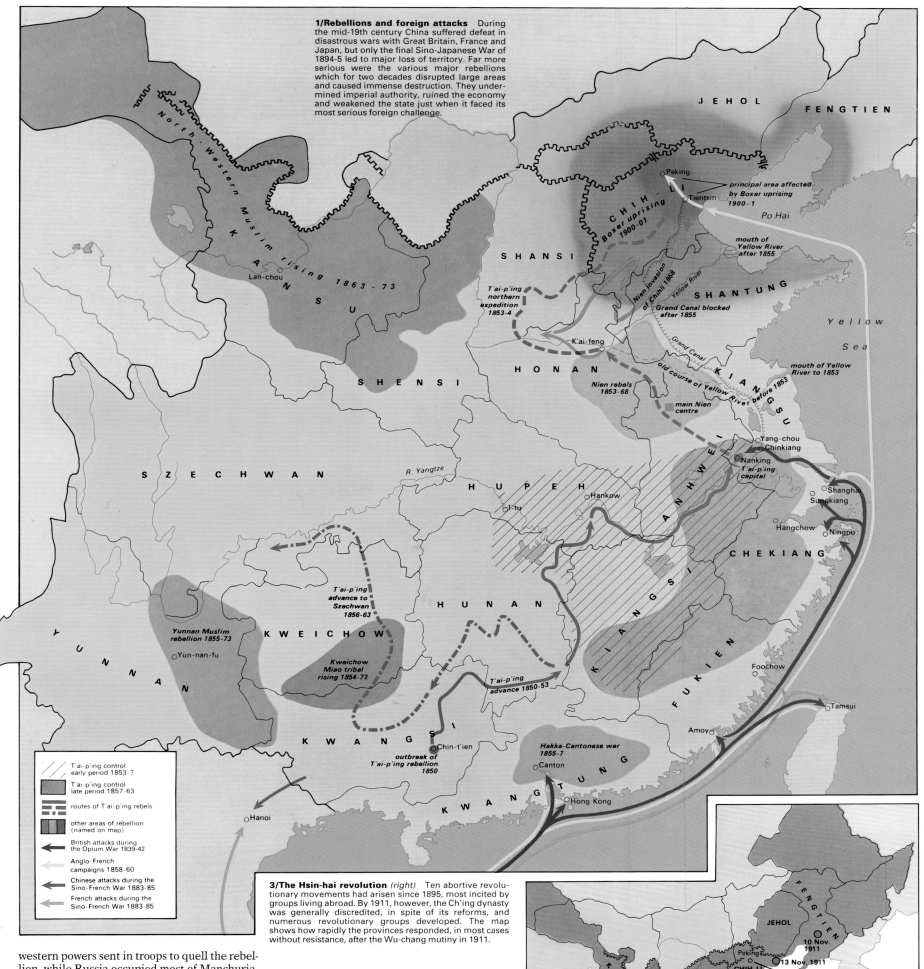

1/Rebellions and foreign attacks During the mid-19th century China suffered defeat in disastrous wars with Great Britain, France and Japan, but only the final Sino-Japanese War of 1894-5 led to major loss of territory. Far more serious were the various major rebellions which for two decades disrupted large areas and caused immense destruction. They undermined imperial authority, ruined the economy and weakened the state just when it faced its most serious foreign challenge.

Map labels:

JEHOL — FENGTIEN

North-western Muslim rising 1863-73

K A N S U

Lan-chou

Peking

Tientsin

principal area affected by Boxer uprising 1900-1

Po Hai

CHIH-LI — Boxer uprising 1900-01

SHANSI

mouth of Yellow River after 1855

Nien invasion of Chihli 1868

SHANTUNG

Yellow River

Grand Canal blocked after 1855

T'ai-p'ing northern expedition 1853-4

S H E N S I

K'ai-feng

HONAN

Grand Canal — old course of Yellow River before 1853

KIANGSU

mouth of Yellow River to 1853

Yellow Sea

Nien rebels 1853-68

main Nien centre

Yang-chou — Chinkiang

S Z E C H W A N

R. Yangtze

H U P E H

Hankow

I-tu

ANHWEI

Nanking — T'ai-p'ing capital

Shanghai — Sungkiang

Hangchow — Ningpo

CHEKIANG

T'ai-p'ing advance to Szechwan 1856-63

H U N A N

K I A N G S I

Yunnan Muslim rebellion 1855-73

KWEICHOW

Yün-nan-fu

Kweichow Miao tribal rising 1854-72

FUKIEN

Foochow

Y U N N A N

T'ai-p'ing advance 1850-53

K W A N G S I

Chin-t'ien — outbreak of T'ai-p'ing rebellion 1850

Hakka-Cantonese war 1855-7

Canton

K W A N G T U N G

Amoy

Tamsui

Hanoi

Hong Kong

Legend:

T'ai-p'ing control: early period 1853-7

T'ai-p'ing control: late period 1857-63

routes of T'ai-p'ing rebels

other areas of rebellion (named on map)

British attacks during the Opium War 1839-42

Anglo-French campaigns 1858-60

Chinese attacks during the Sino-French War 1883-85

French attacks during the Sino-French War 1883-85

western powers sent in troops to quell the rebellion, while Russia occupied most of Manchuria. The final settlement wrung yet more concessions from the Chinese, and also imposed a huge indemnity upon them.

After 1901 it was at last accepted that change was imperative and a remarkable series of reforms was pressed through: a modernized state structure, elected assemblies, modern armies, a modern law code, educational reform and the abolition of the civil service examinations largely responsible for the ultra-conservative attitudes of the bureaucracy. Equally striking economic changes took place. Railways, mining, banking and industry all grew rapidly. However, modernization was concentrated in the Treaty Ports where a modern press, modern publishing industry and modern schools could flourish, free from government interference, thus enabling revolutionary and reformist parties to develop.

From the 1890s ever-increasing numbers of young men studied abroad, especially in Japan, before returning converted to western political ideas and by 1910 many of them were active in government, business, teaching and the army. It became clear, however, that the conservative Manchus were determined to cling to power in spite of the reforms. Among the populace revolutionary ideas and widespread disillusion with imperial authority replaced policies of reform. Over a two-month period in 1911, after a small-scale army mutiny broke out in Wu-ch'ang and obliged the Manchu governor to flee, almost every province declared its independence unopposed and the T'ung-men-hui (Revolutionary Alliance) party set up a provisional government at Nanking, where its leader, Sun Yat-sen, was proclaimed president on 1 January 1912.

3/The Hsin-hai revolution (right) Ten abortive revolutionary movements had arisen since 1895, most incited by groups living abroad. By 1911, however, the Ch'ing dynasty was generally discredited, in spite of its reforms, and numerous revolutionary groups developed. The map shows how rapidly the provinces responded, in most cases without resistance, after the Wu-chang mutiny in 1911.

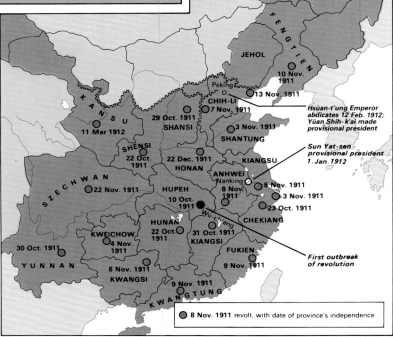

Map labels:

FENGTIEN

JEHOL — 10 Nov. 1911

Peking — 13 Nov. 1911

CHIH-LI — 7 Nov. 1911

KANSU — 11 Mar 1912

SHANSI — 29 Oct. 1911

SHANTUNG — 3 Nov. 1911

SHENSI — 22 Oct. 1911

HONAN — 22 Dec. 1911

KIANGSU

Hsüan-t'ung Emperor abdicates 12 Feb. 1912; Yüan Shih-k'ai made provisional president

Sun Yat-sen provisional president 1. Jan 1912

SZECHWAN — 22 Nov. 1911

ANHWEI — 8 Nov. 1911 — Nanking — 5 Nov. 1911

3 Nov. 1911

23 Oct. 1911

HUPEH — 10 Oct. 1911 — Wu-ch'ang

First outbreak of revolution

HUNAN — 22 Oct 1911

KIANGSI — 31 Oct. 1911

CHEKIANG

KWEICHOW — 4 Nov. 1911

FUKIEN — 9 Nov. 1911

YUNNAN — 30 Oct. 1911 / 6 Nov. 1911

KWANGSI — 9 Nov. 1911

KWANGTUNG

8 Nov. 1911 revolt, with date of province's independence

India under British rule 1805 to 1935

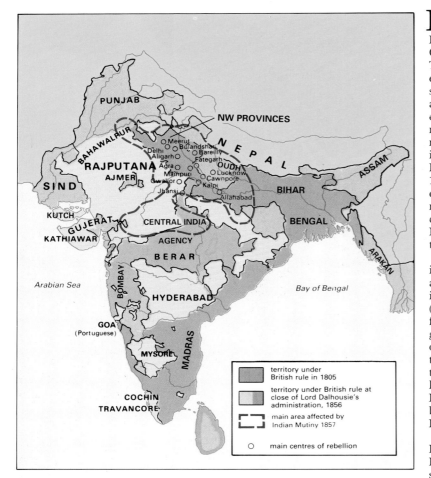

1/India in 1857 *(above)* The Mutiny began at Meerut on 10 May and spread swiftly to other parts of northern India, involving Hindus and Muslims. Sikh loyalty in the Punjab, and passivity in the Deccan and south, turned the tide in favour of the British.

2/The acquisition of Burma *(below)* Part of Britain's Indian dominion until 1935, Burma was annexed, along with her dependencies of Arakan, Manipur and Assam, as a result of three wars fought in 1826, 1852 and 1885. The Shan States were acquired in 1890.

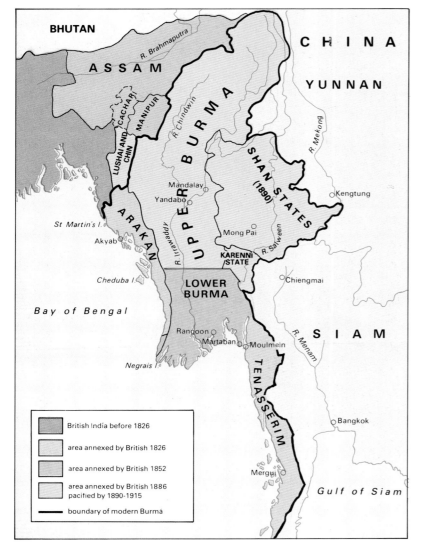

Legend:
- British India before 1826
- area annexed by British 1826
- area annexed by British 1852
- area annexed by British 1886 pacified by 1890-1915
- boundary of modern Burma

BY 1805 the English East India Company's hegemony was an established fact in the Indian sub-continent. In another 50 years the Company emerged as the paramount power. The Third Anglo-Maratha War (1813–23) marked the end of the most serious threat to the Company's supremacy. With the conquest of Sind (1843) and the Sikh kingdom of the Punjab (1849), the empire became coterminous with the country's natural frontiers in the northwest, while in the north the wars with Nepal (1814–6) extended it into the Himalayan foothills. To the east, the British clashed with the Burmese empire and, by 1885, had annexed all its territories. Within the empire, Dalhousie's Doctrine of Lapse (1848–56) resulted in the absorption of autonomous but dependent states, such as Oudh and several Maratha kingdoms, into the directly administered territories.

The hostility of dispossessed rulers and agrarian classes, as well as suspicions of intended assaults on India's traditional faiths – aroused by innovations including the prohibition of *suttee* (cremation of a Hindu widow on her husband's funeral pyre) and the introduction of cartridges greased with the fat of taboo animals for the use of native Indian soldiers (sepoys) – erupted in the rebellion of 1857–8. Beginning as a mutiny of the Company's sepoys, it soon involved princes, landlords and peasants in northern and central India and was only crushed after 14 months of bitter fighting. The direct administration of India was now taken over by the British Crown.

India soon acquired a pivotal position in the British imperial system and became involved in European rivalries, particularly after the Russian advance in central Asia (see page 226). The attempt to stabilize Afghanistan as a buffer state under friendly Amirs generated a series of wars which were fought with Indian armies and which increased India's debts. The background to the third Anglo-Burmese War (1885) was the growing rivalry with France in Southeast Asia. Security of the Indian empire was also a major concern in Great Britain's involvement in the partition of Africa (see page 236). From Abyssinia to Hong Kong, the Indian army was freely deployed to protect British interests.

India was absorbed into the world economy as a dependency of Great Britain. The Company's monopoly over the Indian market was lost by 1833 (except for opium and salt) through persistent pressure from British commercial and business interests, which also demanded the development of modern transport in India to facilitate the import of British manufactures and export of raw materials. By 1853, India had lost its world-wide market for textiles and was importing the products of Lancashire. The Lancashire cotton famine, generated by the American Civil War, led to a cotton boom in the

Deccan and thus to regional specialization in cropping patterns in India. Railway development, financed by British capital, and the opening of the Suez canal in 1869, contributed to a sevenfold increase in India's foreign trade between 1869 and 1929. Despite severe British competition, some modern industries developed under Indian entrepreneurs; but in most areas neither the character of the economy nor traditional agriculture experienced any basic change. The gross national product increased very slowly, but with sustained population growth from 1921 onwards, per capita income declined. In short, India developed the typical characteristics of an under-developed economy while contributing substantially to Britain's favourable balance of payments.

Administrative developments also contributed to India's absorption into a world order dominated by Europe. English civil servants inspired by Benthamite ideas abandoned earlier hesitations to interfere with the indigenous social order. Tenurial systems guaranteeing property rights in land, a network of modern irrigation in parts of the country, prohibition of social customs abhorrent to humanistic ideas, and the development of a modern judiciary and civil service were among the chief expressions of the new spirit. The net results of such policies are still a matter of debate. Probably the rural propertied classes benefitted, but often at the cost of the mass of producers. Periodic famines continued to take heavy tolls of life, while commercial agriculture flourished. Professional groups, employees of the colonial administration, and landed proprietors created by the new tenurial systems constituted the new elite of colonial India. Western-style education – officially supported only from 1835 – is traceable to the material and cultural aspirations of these new social groups. Knowledge of the West generated social and literary movements influenced by western models but looking back, selectively, to India's past traditions. The Brahmo Samaj founded by Rammohan Roy (1828), aiming at restoring Hindu monotheism, and the frankly revivalist Arya Samaj, represent the two most important examples of this new consciousness.

Awareness of an Indian identity, reinforced by overt British racism, soon acquired a political dimension first expressed through local political associations and public agitation over specific issues. The Indian National Congress, the first all-Indian political organization, was founded in 1885 with official blessing. Beginning as a tame annual gathering of affluent public men, it soon developed an extremist wing which questioned the foreigner's right to rule India. In 1905, the first mass agitation – anticipating Gandhi's non-violent non-cooperation and propagating *swaraj* (self-rule) – was launched to resist the decision

4 and 5/Population: social and economic change *(below)* Between 1881 and 1931 population rose from 253.9 million to 352.8 million, with a slight acceleration at the beginning of the 1920s. Over the same period the proportion of literates grew only from 35 to 80 per thousand; a mere 101 people in every 10,000 were able to read and write in English. Nevertheless, the beginnings of a modern economy were emerging.

inhabitants per sq. km.
- over 250
- 150 to 250
- 100 to 150
- 50 to 100
- 25 to 50
- under 25

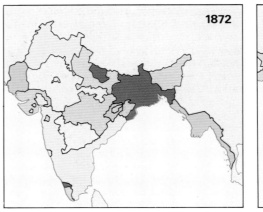

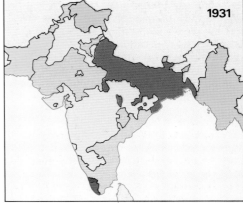

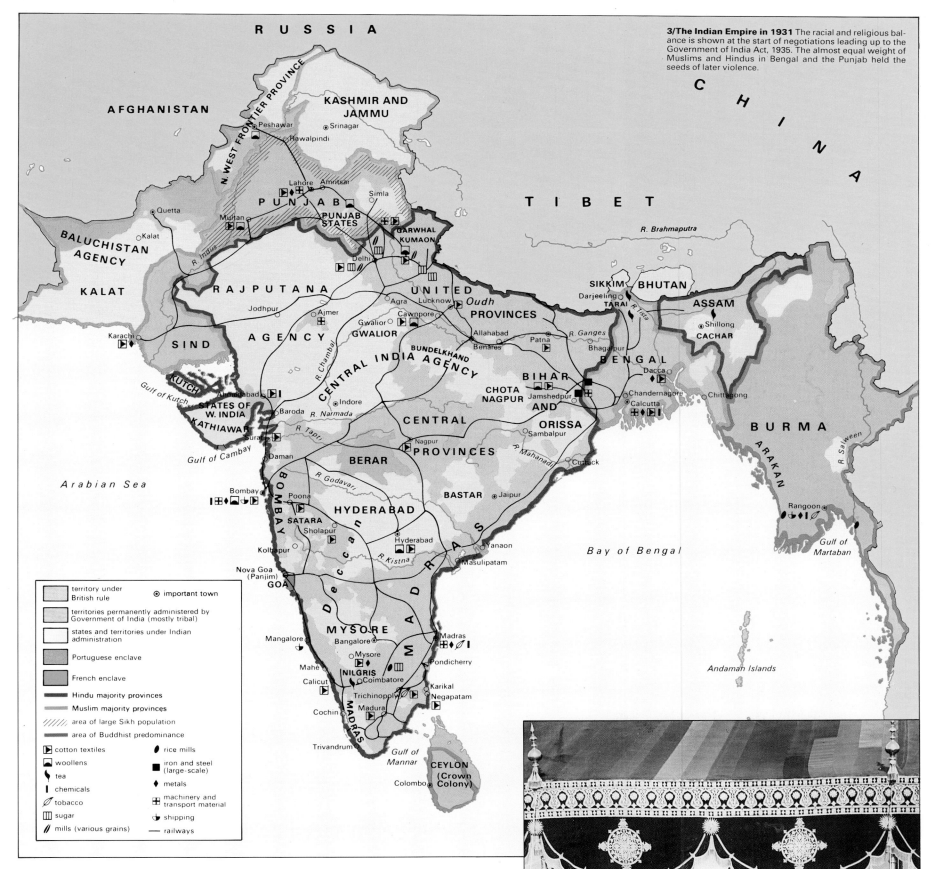

to partition the province of Bengal, while revolutionary groups adopted terror to attain the same goal (see page 244). Political awareness and expectations were quickened by the First World War and a Ministerial Proclamation (1917) declaring the realization of responsible government to be the goal of British rule in India. The Indian Councils Act of 1909 had already established a provincial legislature, and the Montagu-Chelmsford reforms (1919) extended the provincial councils. But repressive legislation enacted in 1919 authorizing detention without trial seemed to conflict with this goal. Against it, Gandhi deployed his weapon of *satyagraha*, or non-violent mass action, first developed in his fight against racist laws in South Africa. The response included the Amritsar massacre, provoking intense racial bitterness. Indian Muslims, many of whom had refused to join Congress, were incensed by the Allies' treatment of the Turkish sultan, their spiritual head. The Non-Cooperation Movement (1920–2), aimed at redressing the Khalifat and Punjab 'wrongs' and winning *swaraj*, was the first all-Indian mass movement to involve the peasantry. But the Hindu-Muslim unity achieved did not long survive its suspension. Elections to the expanded

provincial councils with their communal electorates further soured relations.

While communal riots undermined national unity in the mid-1920s, a radical wing within Congress under the leadership of the young Jawaharlal Nehru and Subhas Chandra Bose pressed for renewed militant action against the British, and induced Congress to adopt complete independence (*purna swaraj*) as its goal (1929). When in 1930 Gandhi launched the Civil Disobedience Movement (1930–4) for the attainment of that independence, he and some 60,000 of his followers were arrested. Nevertheless the movement was a watershed. Suspended in 1931 as a result of an agreement with Viceroy Irwin, it was resumed when Gandhi returned from the abortive constitutional discussions at the Round Table Conference in London. Negotiation had failed, and the policy of confrontation espoused by the younger leaders was reinforced. Nevertheless, the Government of India Act of 1935 seemed to presage further rapid constitutional steps towards independence (see page 256).

The 1911 Durbar (right) King George V was crowned King Emperor of India at a durbar, or assembly of notables, in Delhi in 1911. A decision to annul the unpopular partition of Bengal was announced at this durbar.

The development of Australia and New Zealand

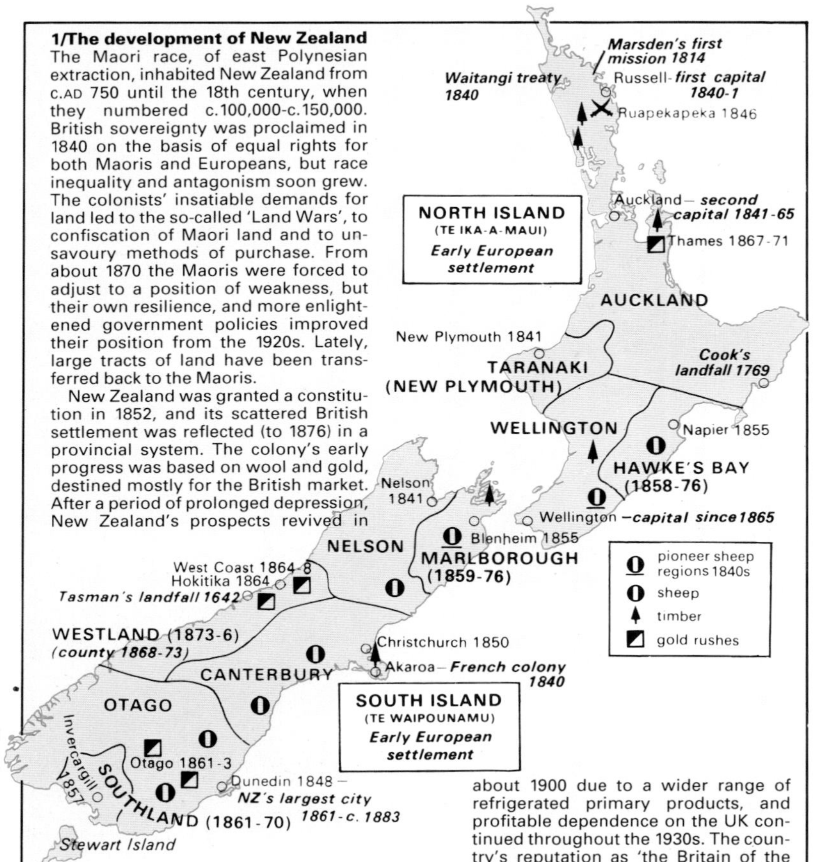

Marsden's first mission 1814
Waitangi treaty 1840
Russell - first capital 1840-1
Ruapekapeka 1846
NORTH ISLAND
(TE IKA-A-MAUI)
Early European settlement
Auckland - second capital 1841-65
Thames 1867-71
AUCKLAND
New Plymouth 1841
TARANAKI
(NEW PLYMOUTH)
Cook's landfall 1769
WELLINGTON
Napier 1855
HAWKE'S BAY
(1858-76)
Nelson 1841
Wellington - capital since 1865
NELSON
Blenheim 1855
MARLBOROUGH
(1859-76)
West Coast 1864-8
Hokitika 1864
Tasman's landfall 1642
WESTLAND (1873-6)
(county 1868-73)
Christchurch 1850
Akaroa - French colony 1840
CANTERBURY
OTAGO
SOUTH ISLAND
(TE WAIPOUNAMU)
Early European settlement
Invercargill 1857
Otago 1861-3
Dunedin 1848 - NZ's largest city 1861-c. 1883
SOUTHLAND (1861-70)
Stewart Island
pioneer sheep regions 1840s
sheep
timber
gold rushes

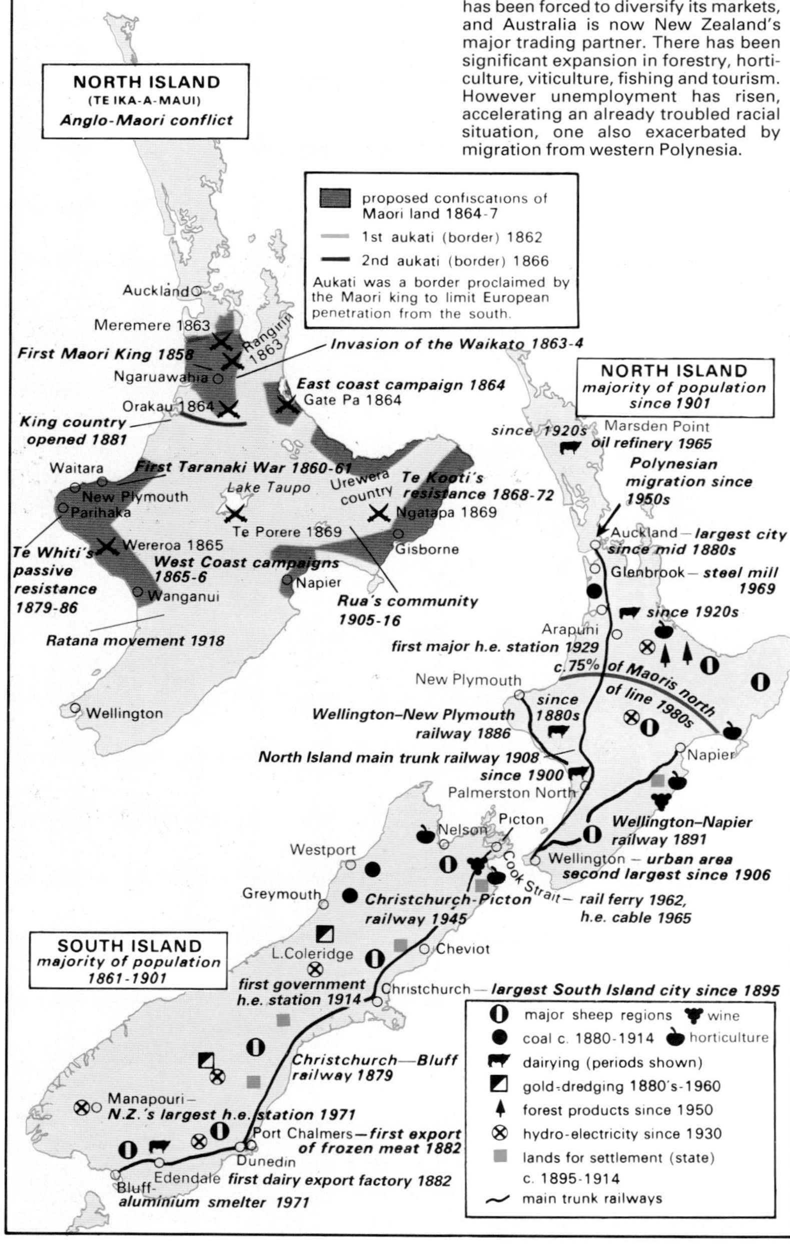

NORTH ISLAND
(TE IKA-A-MAUI)
Anglo-Maori conflict
proposed confiscations of Maori land 1864-7
1st aukati (border) 1862
2nd aukati (border) 1866
Aukati was a border proclaimed by the Maori king to limit European penetration from the south.
Auckland
Meremere 1863
Rangiriri 1863
Invasion of the Waikato 1863-4
First Maori King 1858
Ngaruawahia
Orakau 1864
East coast campaign 1864
Gate Pa 1864
King country opened 1881
Waitara
First Taranaki War 1860-61
Lake Taupo
Urewera country
Te Kooti's resistance 1868-72
New Plymouth
Parihaka
Ngatapa 1869
Te Porere 1869
Te Whiti's passive resistance 1879-86
Wereroa 1865
West Coast campaigns 1865-6
Gisborne
Wanganui
Napier
Rua's community 1905-16
Ratana movement 1918
Wellington
NORTH ISLAND
majority of population since 1901
since 1920s
Marsden Point oil refinery 1965
Polynesian migration since 1950s
Auckland - largest city since mid 1880s
Glenbrook - steel mill 1969
since 1920s
Arapuni
first major h.e. station 1929
c.75% of Maoris north of line 1980s
New Plymouth
since 1880s
Wellington-New Plymouth railway 1886
North Island main trunk railway 1908
since 1900
Napier
Palmerston North
Nelson
Picton
Wellington-Napier railway 1891
Westport
Wellington - urban area second largest since 1906
Cook Strait - rail ferry 1962, h.e. cable 1965
Greymouth
Christchurch-Picton railway 1945
SOUTH ISLAND
majority of population 1861-1901
L.Coleridge
first government h.e. station 1914
Cheviot
Christchurch - largest South Island city since 1895
Christchurch-Bluff railway 1879
Manapouri - N.Z.'s largest h.e. station 1971
Port Chalmers - first export of frozen meat 1882
Dunedin
Edendale first dairy export factory 1882
Bluff - aluminium smelter 1971
major sheep regions
wine
coal c. 1880-1914
horticulture
dairying (periods shown)
gold-dredging 1880's-1960
forest products since 1950
hydro-electricity since 1930
lands for settlement (state) c. 1895-1914
main trunk railways

1/The development of New Zealand The Maori race, of east Polynesian extraction, inhabited New Zealand from c.AD 750 until the 18th century, when they numbered c.100,000-c.150,000. British sovereignty was proclaimed in 1840 on the basis of equal rights for both Maoris and Europeans, but race inequality and antagonism soon grew. The colonists' insatiable demands for land led to the so-called 'Land Wars', to confiscation of Maori land and to unsavoury methods of purchase. From about 1870 the Maoris were forced to adjust to a position of weakness, but their own resilience, and more enlightened government policies improved their position from the 1920s. Lately, large tracts of land have been transferred back to the Maoris.

New Zealand was granted a constitution in 1852, and its scattered British settlement was reflected (to 1876) in a provincial system. The colony's early progress was based on wool and gold, destined mostly for the British market. After a period of prolonged depression, New Zealand's prospects revived in about 1900 due to a wider range of refrigerated primary products, and profitable dependence on the UK continued throughout the 1930s. The country's reputation as 'the Britain of the south' was reflected in its support of the UK in two world wars. Since Britain entered the EEC in 1973, New Zealand has been forced to diversify its markets, and Australia is now New Zealand's major trading partner. There has been significant expansion in forestry, horticulture, viticulture, fishing and tourism. However unemployment has risen, accelerating an already troubled racial situation, one also exacerbated by migration from western Polynesia.

AUSTRALIA and New Zealand long remained isolated from the rest of the world. Although the Portuguese may have reached the Australian continent in the 1520s, the first definite European landfalls were those of the Dutch from 1606 onwards, deliberately in the north, and accidentally in the west and south as a consequence of sailing with the westerlies too far to the east of the Cape of Good Hope. In 1642–3, Tasman discovered Van Diemen's Land (Tasmania) and the western coasts of New Zealand, and in 1644 extensively surveyed Australia's northern and western coasts. However these places held no attractions to a European nation 'not interested in science, only in money'.

During his 1768–71 circumnavigation of the world, James Cook sailed around New Zealand, establishing that it consisted of two large islands, and charted the previously unexplored eastern coast of Australia. The voyage yielded extensive collections of Antipodean species, but in 1786 the pursuit of imperial ambitions decided the British Government to establish a penal colony in New South Wales. Arthur Phillip founded the first European settlement at Sydney in 1788 and the need to secure the sea-routes against the French (who were also active in Pacific exploration), and for places of secondary punishment, led to settlements at Norfolk Island (1788–1814, 1825–55), Newcastle (1801), Hobart (1803–4), Launceston (1804), Brisbane (1824), and Albany (1826).

In 1829 Britain annexed the whole of Australia but British settlement was effectively confined to the small Cumberland Plain behind Sydney until the 1820s, when westward exploration and a change of government policy led to the occupation of extensive inland pastoral regions. By the 1850s both substantial free migration and demand in Europe for fine wool saw the continent's southeast become a vast sheep farm. Private colonizations began at Perth (1829), Melbourne (1835) and Adelaide (1836). Convict transportation to eastern Australia ceased in 1840, but in the 1850s gold discoveries produced another surge of free migration. In the second half of the 19th century, pastoralists both expanded sheep-farming and turned to raising beef cattle in the immense northern regions. Wheat was grown on the inland plains, and sugar and dairy production took place on the coastal plains and hinterlands. By the 1890s most of the continent had been explored, and much of it nominally settled by Europeans. However, not all settlements proved viable, as experience showed the hazards of attempting agriculture and pastoralism on intrinsically poor lands in low-rainfall belts. Even in the 20th century, despite extensive water conservation and irrigation schemes, large areas of the continent remain marginal to European life.

Roving bands of European and American timber-getters, sealers and whalers frequented the harbours of New Zealand from the 1790s onwards, with the Bay of Islands becoming a centre of activity in the 1810s and 1820s. In 1840, Britain negotiated with the Maori for North Island, and simply annexed South Island. Thereafter, the European occupation of New Zealand paralleled that of Australia, with pastoralism, agriculture, gold discoveries and free migration.

The Australian colonies of New South Wales, Victoria, South Australia, Western Australia, Tasmania and Queensland gained responsible government between 1855 and 1890. Despite some rivalry, regional differences never prevented a sense of common destiny, and the colonies joined to form the Commonwealth of Australia in 1901. New Zealand, at first divided into six provinces for purposes of administration and colonization, gained responsible government in 1856. As the power of the central administration grew, that of the provinces declined, to be abolished in 1876. Both countries achieved sovereign status with the Statute of Westminster in 1931.

Like other 'new Europes', from the mid-19th until the mid-20th century, Australia and New Zealand distinguished themselves by large excess production of wool, meat, grain and dairy products. In Australia, the gold rushes of the 1850s and 1880s brought extra wealth, and for a time encouraged the growth of inland populations. However as centralizing systems of communication and transportation developed (coastal and interior shipping, roads, railways, telegraph), the dominance of the coastal cities increased, especially that of Sydney and Melbourne. By the 1890s two-thirds of Australians lived in urban areas along the coasts, a trend that has steadily increased through the 20th century. The New Zealand situation is similar.

Some manufacturing did develop in urban centres, but with limited investment, high labour costs, low productivity and small markets, industries usually succeeded only thanks to protective tariffs. Since 1950, spectacular discoveries have been made of minerals, coal, and oil and gas in and about Australia; but again, most of these materials have been directly exported. In the 20th century, political and economic change abroad as well as social change at home have obliged Australia and New Zealand to develop trade with countries outside the former British Commonwealth. The emergence of the EC and the resultant loss of traditional markets, and the view that the countries of the Pacific Rim will become the economic hub of the world in the 21st century, have been powerful influences in furthering economic independence from Britain.

The influence of the indigenous on the emergent culture has been much greater in New Zealand than in Australia, and this fact for long bolstered a more tolerant society. In the late-19th century xenophobia swept across Australia, partly because of its cultural isolation and partly because of union agitation. From the 1890s until the 1960s the White Australia Policy limited entry to Europeans but failed to prevent the steady diversification of the society, particularly given the migration of large numbers of southern Europeans after 1945. In the 1970s and 1980s a wave of Asian immigration furthered this process. Until very recently migration to New Zealand was not so various but the growth of significant non-Maori Polynesian populations has again brought old violence to the fore.

The fates of the indigenous peoples in each country have diverged. In Australia, violence, disease and dispossession decimated the Aborigines in the 19th century. Traditional culture survives best in the north, west and centre, but even there inevitable adaptations to new realities have occurred. Aborigines had to wait until the second half of the 20th century before their status in law became unambiguous, and they were accorded land rights. In the 1970s and 1980s, Australian governments spent large amounts of money in efforts to improve the circumstances of the Aborigines, though without marked success. In New Zealand, on the other hand, the Treaty of Waitangi and more successful resistance have meant a more nearly, though not entirely, equal co-existence for Maori and European. In both countries a new consciousness of separate identity has recently emerged among the indigenous peoples, accompanied by political activity reflecting this consciousness.

5/Settlement and development *(right)* After 1820 settlement spread inland from scattered coastal towns, but vast arid areas of the continent remained sparsely populated and the total population did not reach 5 million until 1918. Exports of wool, wheat and minerals enabled Australians to enjoy the highest per capita income in the world by 1900, a position not maintained despite recent extensive mineral discoveries. Most Australians depend on urban employment: according to the 1991 census, 62 per cent of the population (16-17 million) lived in or near 12 major cities, including 3.5 million in Sydney and 3 million in Melbourne. Canberra, federal capital since 1927 and the largest inland city, has a population of 278,894.

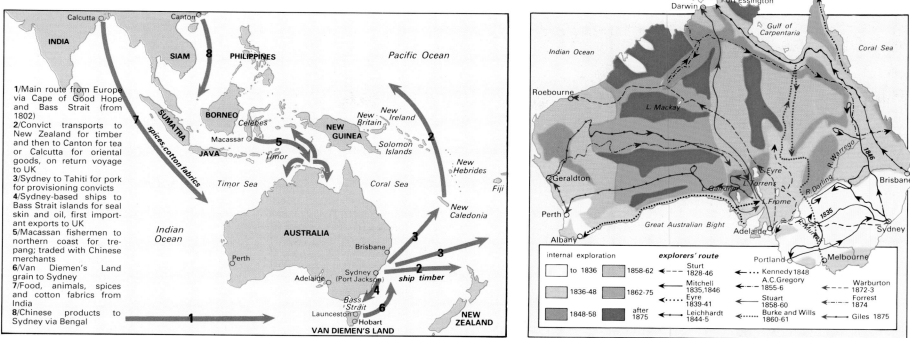

(see map 5)

1/Main route from Europe via Cape of Good Hope and Bass Strait (from 1802)

2/Convict transports to New Zealand for timber and then to Canton for tea or Calcutta for oriental goods, on return voyage to UK

3/Sydney to Tahiti for pork for provisioning convicts

4/Sydney-based ships to Bass Strait islands for seal skin and oil, first important exports to UK

5/Macassan fishermen to northern coast for trepang; traded with Chinese merchants

6/Van Diemen's Land grain to Sydney

7/Food, animals, spices and cotton fabrics from India

8/Chinese products to Sydney via Bengal

internal exploration

to 1836
1836-48
1848-58
1858-62
1862-75
after 1875

explorers' route

Sturt 1828-46
Mitchell 1835, 1846
Eyre 1839-41
Leichhardt 1844-5
Kennedy 1848
A.C. Gregory 1855-6
Stuart 1858-60
Burke and Wills 1860-61
Warburton 1872-3
Forrest 1874
Giles 1875

4/Early trade *(above)* While the British colony in New South Wales did struggle briefly to establish itself, imperial land and trade policies rather than unwelcoming environment impeded its progress at first. Showing a remarkable energy in circumventing restrictions, by 1800 Sydney residents had pioneered trade in seal skins and seal oil, timber and coal, and some Pacific items. Following commissioner T.J. Bigge's 1823 recommendation that New South Wales and Van Diemen's Land be allowed to develop as free colonies, the colonists quickly turned to the raising of fine-wooled sheep. In 1828, Australia exported 2,000,000 lbs of wool to Britain. However it was not until the mid-1830s that the value of wool exported exceeded that of the products of the shores and seas.

2/The discovery of Australia *(right)* Although the north, west and south coasts were discovered in the 17th century and the east coast in the 18th, detailed charting by Matthew Flinders, Thomas-Nicolas Baudin and Philip Parker King came in the early 19th century.

3/ Exploration *(above)* Because the navigators failed to discover river mouths, inland explorers searched first for an inland sea, then made attempts to reach the centre of the continent and to cross it from south to north, and finally traversed the western part between the coast and the Overland Telegraph Line (built 1870-72, see map 5).

Dutch discoveries to 1644
coasts charted by 1802

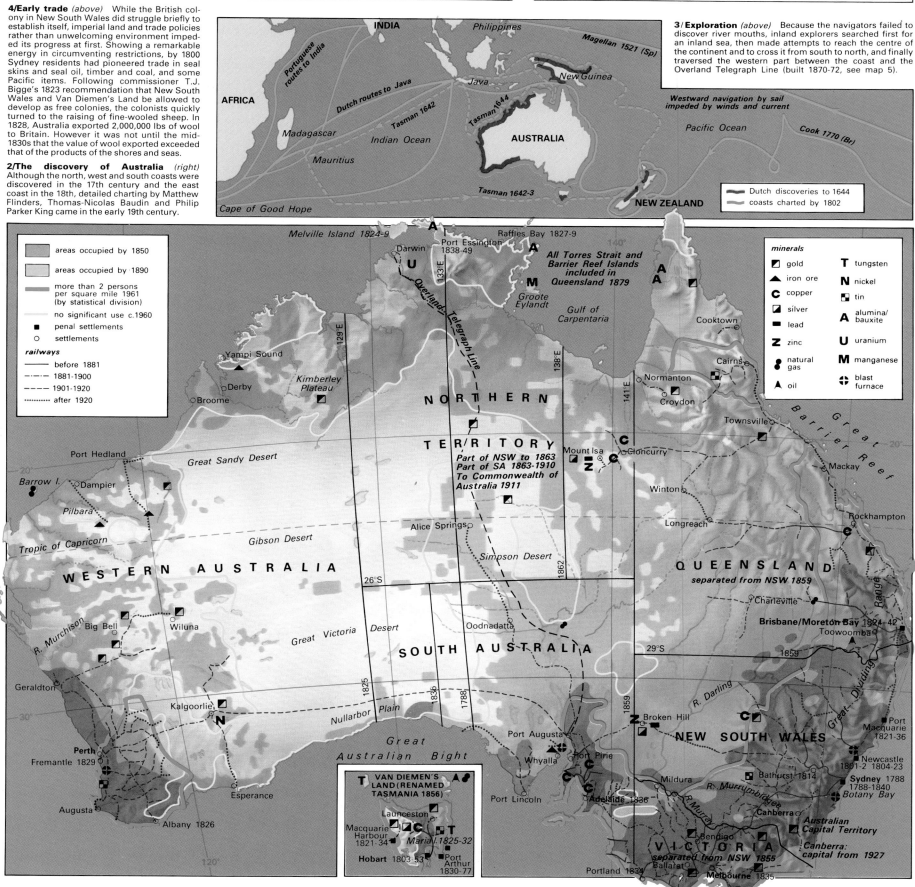

areas occupied by 1850
areas occupied by 1890
more than 2 persons per square mile 1961 (by statistical division)
no significant use c.1960
penal settlements
settlements

railways
before 1881
1881-1900
1901-1920
after 1920

minerals
gold
iron ore
copper
silver
lead
zinc
natural gas
oil
T tungsten
N nickel
tin
alumina/bauxite
U uranium
M manganese
blast furnace

All Torres Strait and Barrier Reef Islands included in Queensland 1879

NORTHERN TERRITORY
Part of NSW to 1863
Part of SA 1863-1910
To Commonwealth of Australia 1911

WESTERN AUSTRALIA

QUEENSLAND
separated from NSW 1859

SOUTH AUSTRALIA

NEW SOUTH WALES

VICTORIA
separated from NSW 1855

VAN DIEMEN'S LAND (RENAMED TASMANIA 1856)

Canberra: capital from 1927

Africa before partition by the European powers 1800 to 1880

DURING the 80 years prior to the European partition of the continent, much of west Africa was profoundly affected by an Islamic religious revival which took the form of holy wars (*jihads*) waged mainly against backsliding Muslim (or partly Muslimized) communities. The great warriors of the *jihad* were the Fulani cattle-keepers, widely scattered among the agricultural communities of the Sudanic region. Though the Fulani were largely pagan, a section of them became Muslims, fervent in the faith of the newly converted. In the 18th century they set up theocracies in the far west – Futa Toro and Futa Jallon – and at Masina, in the former Mali and Songhay empires on the upper Niger. It was the Muslim Fulani in Hausaland, however, who set up the largest Islamic state of the 19th century. In 1804 a Fulani religious leader, Uthman dan Fodio, was proclaimed Commander of the Faithful (*Amir al-Mu'minin*), and declared a *jihad* against the infidel. Within a few years his formidable army of horsemen (many of them drawn from the pagan Fulani) conquered all the Hausa city states, and struck east into Adamawa and southwest into Nupe and Yorubaland. Uthman dan Fodio's son became the Sultan of Sokoto, an empire still in existence when the British invaded Nigeria in the 1890s.

An even fiercer *jihad* was conducted by another holy man, al-Hajj Umar from Futa Jallon, whence he conquered the Bambara kingdoms and Masina, and was only prevented from reaching the Atlantic by the French presence on the Sénégal River. In fact Islam increasingly became a counterforce as Europeans advanced, especially in the case of the Mandingo Muslim leader Samori, who carved out another empire south of the Niger; he was finally defeated by the French only in 1898.

South of the area of the *jihads*, the slave trade flourished for many years (see page 162) but the British in particular began to try and replace it with 'legitimate trade' accompanied by the introduction of the Gospel. The explorers Park, Clapperton and Lander had discovered the course of the Niger and in 1841-2 the British government sent an official expedition inland by water to establish 'Christianity, commerce and civilization'. This failed; but the new demands of Europeans for palm oil, groundnuts and other products forced African states to adapt and change, a process which involved considerable instability among the 'forest states'.

East and west central Africa formed another huge area where new trading patterns caused disruption and change. The western world evinced an almost insatiable appetite for ivory in the 19th century (for billiard balls and piano keys), and the hunting of elephants and trading of their tusks became a major economic activity in much of this part of the continent. Many states and peoples grew rich on the proceeds – the Chokwe and King Msiri in central Africa, for instance, and Buganda and the Nyamwezi in East Africa. In central Africa the foreign traders were often Portuguese from settlements in Angola and Mozambique, while in East Africa, Swahili-Arabs from Zanzibar made contact with the states in the interior, in many instances bringing their Islamic religion with them. Some peoples – particularly around lakes Nyasa and Tanganyika – suffered severely from the Arab slave trade, which often went hand in hand with that in ivory.

In northeast Africa the territorial expansion of Egypt, ruled after Napoleon's invasion at the beginning of the century by Mohammed Ali, nominally viceroy of the Ottoman Sultan, brought a foretaste of the later European partition. Mohammed Ali's armies conquered the northern Nilotic Sudan, founding Khartoum as the capital of the province in 1821. Mohammed Ali had refused to sanction the Suez Canal, but after his death in 1849 construction went ahead. His grandson, the Khedive Ismail, consolidated Egyptian control over much of the littoral of the Red Sea and Horn of Africa. He also pushed south up the Nile towards the Great Lakes in an attempt to create a major African empire. Partly in response to this Egyptian activity, Ethiopian political power revived under the emperors Theodorus and Johannes.

Only two areas of Africa were colonized by European powers before the partition: in 1830 the French invaded Algeria (nominally part of the Ottoman Empire), and in the course of a long and bitter struggle, conquered and settled the territory; at the other end of the continent, the British took over the Cape from the Dutch during the Napoleonic Wars and extended the area of settlement. Coincidentally in time, but unrelated in cause, a major political and demographic revolution occurred among the peoples of the interior of southern Africa, initiated by the formation of the Zulu kingdom by Shaka in 1818. Large numbers of Nguni and Sotho-speaking peoples moved away from the troubled area (the period is known as the *Mfecane*, or Time of Troubles), the Ndebele (Matabele) into present-day Zimbabwe, the Nguni as far north as Zambia, Malawi and Tanzania, where their presence created even more disruption, and the Sotho (Kololo) into Barotseland (Zambia). These African wars and migrations were enormously complicated by the presence of increasing numbers of Europeans, including the Boers – white pastoralist farmers who left Cape Colony to avoid British rule, many of them at the time of the 'Great Trek' of 1836. In the 1850s Britain recognized the republics of Orange Free State and Transvaal which the Boers founded; but the desire to keep order and the lure of wealth, notable after the discovery of diamonds near the Orange Free State, soon brought the British back into contention with the Boers.

1/Africa 1800-1880 This period saw rapid change in Africa as societies adapted to militant Islam, increased trade, European explorers, Christian missionaries, and rulers who were acquiring firearms. The blend of internal and external forces created tensions and instabilities which seemed to become more acute in the 1870s, providing both a reason and an excuse for European takeover in the next decade.

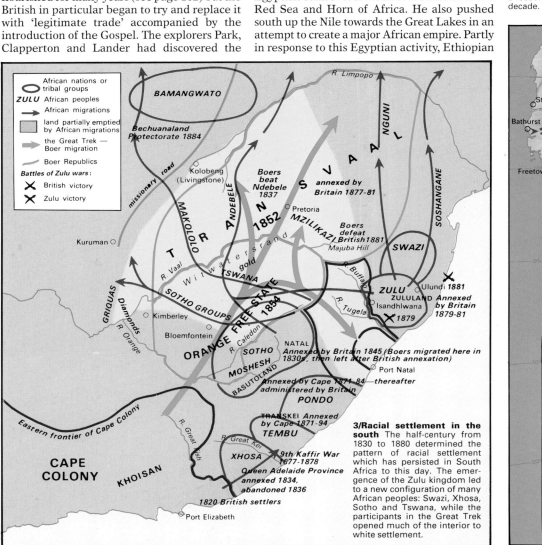

3/Racial settlement in the south The half-century from 1830 to 1880 determined the pattern of racial settlement which has persisted in South Africa to this day. The emergence of the Zulu kingdom led to a new configuration of many African peoples: Swazi, Xhosa, Sotho and Tswana, while the participants in the Great Trek opened much of the interior to white settlement.

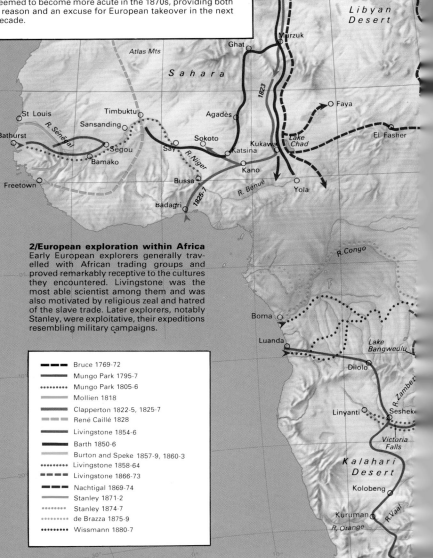

2/European exploration within Africa Early European explorers generally travelled with African trading groups and proved remarkably receptive to the cultures they encountered. Livingstone was the most able scientist among them and was also motivated by religious zeal and hatred of the slave trade. Later explorers, notably Stanley, were exploitative, their expeditions resembling military campaigns.

Bruce 1769-72
Mungo Park 1795-7
Mungo Park 1805-6
Mollien 1818
Clapperton 1822-5, 1825-7
René Caillé 1828
Livingstone 1854-6
Barth 1850-6
Burton and Speke 1857-9, 1860-3
Livingstone 1858-64
Livingstone 1866-73
Nachtigal 1869-74
Stanley 1871-2
Stanley 1874-7
de Brazza 1875-9
Wissmann 1880-7

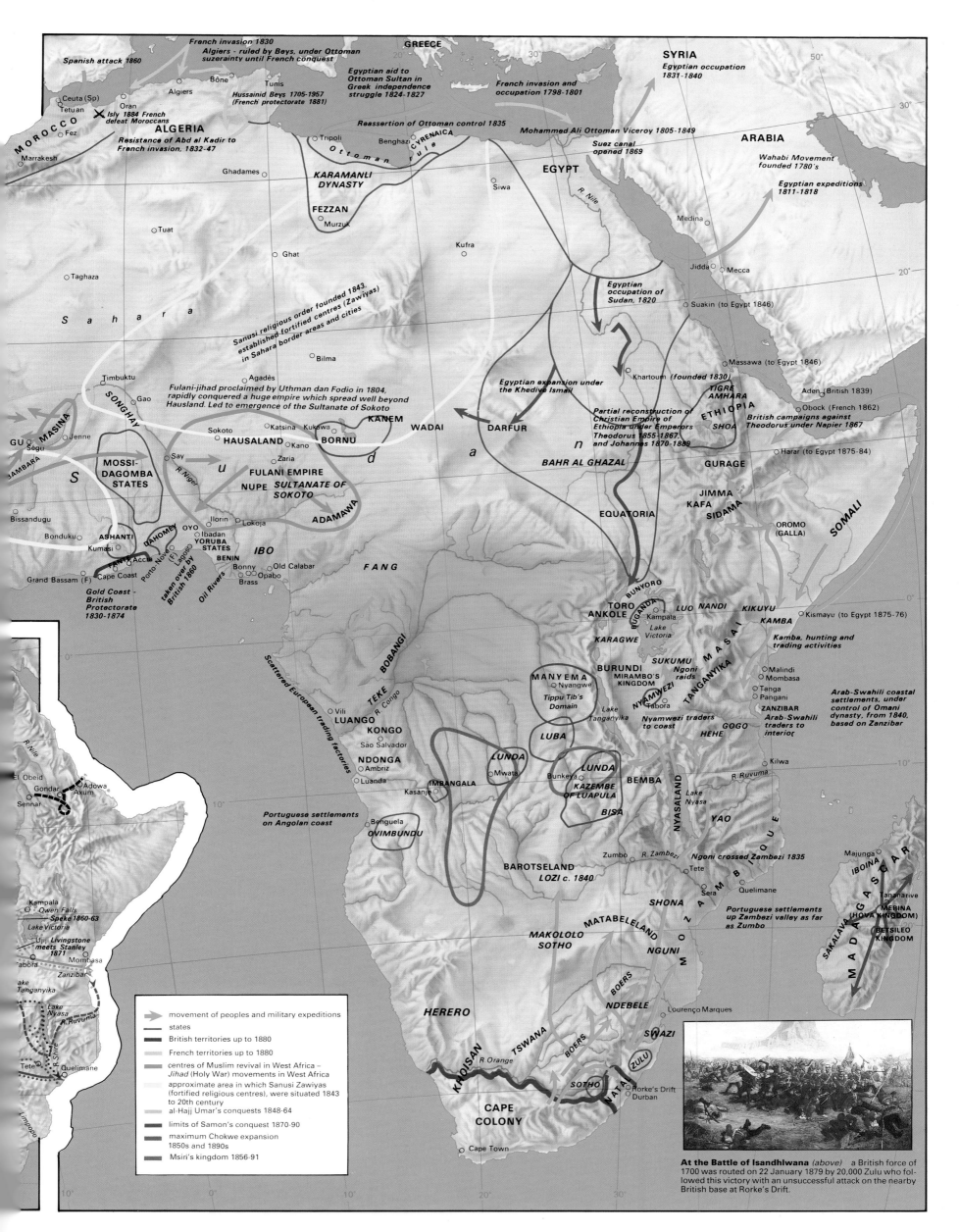

GREECE

Spanish attack 1860

French invasion 1830
Algiers - ruled by Beys, under Ottoman suzerainty until French conquest

Egyptian aid to Ottoman Sultan in Greek independence struggle 1824-1827

French invasion and occupation 1798-1801

SYRIA
Egyptian occupation 1831-1840

Bône
Tunis
Algiers
Hussainid Beys 1705-1957 (French protectorate 1881)

Ceuta (Sp)
Tetuan
Oran
Isly 1884 French defeat Moroccans

MOROCCO
Fez

Marrakesh

ALGERIA
Resistance of Abd al Kadir to French invasion, 1832-47

Reassertion of Ottoman control 1835

Mohammed Ali Ottoman Viceroy 1805-1849

Suez canal opened 1869

ARABIA

Wahabi Movement founded 1780's

Tripoli
Benghazi
CYRENAICA
Ottoman rule

Ghadames

EGYPT

Medina

Egyptian expeditions 1811-1818

KARAMANLI DYNASTY

Siwa
R. Nile

Jidda
Mecca

Tuat

FEZZAN

Murzuk

Kufra

Sahara

Taghaza

Ghat

Egyptian occupation of Sudan, 1820

Suakin (to Egypt 1846)

Bilma

Sanusi religious order founded 1843, established fortified centres (Zawiyas) in Sahara border areas and cities

Massawa (to Egypt 1846)

Timbuktu
Agadès

Fulani-jihad proclaimed by Uthman dan Fodio in 1804, rapidly conquered a huge empire which spread well beyond Hausland. Led to the emergence of the Sultanate of Sokoto

Khartoum (founded 1830)

TIGRE
AMHARA

Aden (British 1839)

Obock (French 1862)

Gao

Egyptian expansion under the Khedive Ismail

ETHIOPIA
SHOA

British campaigns against Theodorus under Napier 1867

GU
MASINA
SONGHAY

Jenne
Ségu

Katsina
Kukawa

KANEM
WADAI

DARFUR

Partial reconstruction of Christian Empire of Ethiopia under Emperors Theodorus 1855-1867, and Johannes 1870-1889

Harar (to Egypt 1875-84)

S
MOSSI-DAGOMBA STATES

Sokoto
HAUSALAND
Kano
Zaria

BORNU

GURAGE

BAHR AL GHAZAL

Say
R. Niger

FULANI EMPIRE

u

n
a

JIMMA
KAFA
SIDAMA

Bissandugu

Bonduku

NUPE
SULTANATE OF SOKOTO

Ilorin
Lokoja

EQUATORIA

OROMO (GALLA)

SOMALI

ASHANTI
Kumasi

DAHOMEY
OYO
Ibadan
YORUBA STATES

ADAMAWA

BENIN

IBO

Kismayu (to Egypt 1875-76)

Grand Bassam (F)
Cape Coast
Accra
Porto Novo (F)
Lagos
taken over by British 1860

Bonny
Opobo
Brass
Old Calabar

FANG

BUNYORO

TORO
ANKOLE
BUGANDA
Kampala
Lake Victoria

LUO NANDI
KIKUYU
KAMBA

Gold Coast - British Protectorate 1830-1874

Oil Rivers

KARAGWE

Kamba, hunting and trading activities

Malindi
Mombasa

Scattered European trading factories

BOBANGI

SUKUMU
BURUNDI
MIRAMBO'S KINGDOM
Ngoni raids

MASAI
TANGANYIKA

Tanga
Pangani

TEKE
R. Congo

MANYEMA
Nyangwe

NYAMWEZI
Tabora

ZANZIBAR
Arab-Swahili traders to interior

Arab-Swahili coastal settlements, under control of Omani dynasty, from 1840, based on Zanzibar

Vili

LUANGO

Tippu Tib's Domain

Lake Tanganyika

HEHE
GOGO

Nyamwezi traders to coast

KONGO
São Salvador

LUBA

LUNDA

Kilwa

NDONGA
Ambriz

Mwata

Bunkeya
LUNDA
KAZEMBE OF LUAPULA

BEMBA

R. Ruvuma

Luanda

IMBANGALA

NYASALAND
Lake Nyasa

YAO

Kasanje

BISA

Benguela

OVIMBUNDU

BAROTSELAND
LOZI c. 1840

Zumbo
R. Zambezi
Tete

Ngoni crossed Zambezi 1835

Sera
Quelimane

Portuguese settlements on Angolan coast

SHONA

Portuguese settlements up Zambezi valley as far as Zumbo

Majunga
IBOINA

Tananarive

MERINA (HOVA KINGDOM)

MATABELELAND

MAKOLOLO
SOTHO

NGUNI

M
O
Z
A
M
B
I
Q
U
E

SAKALAVA
BETSILEO KINGDOM

MADAGASCAR

HERERO

NDEBELE

Lourenço Marques

Portuguese settlements

KHOISAN
TSWANA
BOERS

SWAZI
ZULU

CAPE COLONY

R. Orange
BOERS
R. Limpopo

SOTHO
NATAL

Rorke's Drift
Durban

Cape Town

Legend

→ movement of peoples and military expeditions
— states
▬ British territories up to 1880
▬ French territories up to 1880
▬ centres of Muslim revival in West Africa – Jihad (Holy War) movements in West Africa
▬ approximate area in which Sanusi Zawiyas (fortified religious centres), were situated 1843 to 20th century
▬ al-Hajj Umar's conquests 1848-64
▬ limits of Samori's conquest 1870-90
▬ maximum Chokwe expansion 1850s and 1890s
▬ Msiri's kingdom 1856-91

At the Battle of Isandhlwana (above) a British force of 1700 was routed on 22 January 1879 by 20,000 Zulu who followed this victory with an unsuccessful attack on the nearby British base at Rorke's Drift.

Inset map (left)

R. Nile
El Obeid
Gondar
Adowa
Axum
Sennar

Kampala
Owen Falls
Speke 1860-63
Lake Victoria

Ujiji Livingstone meets Stanley 1871

Tabora
Mombasa

Zanzibar

Lake Tanganyika

Lake Nyasa
R. Ruvuma

Tete
R. Shire
Quelimane

Limpopo

The partition of Africa 1880 to 1913

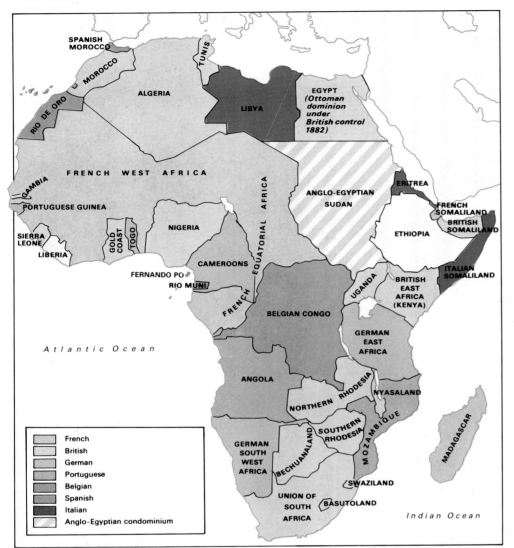

2/Alien rule in Africa in 1913 (above) Once the partition of Africa among the European powers got under way, the whole continent was carved up in a remarkably short period: the major arrangements were made within 15 years.

Legend:
- French
- British
- German
- Portuguese
- Belgian
- Spanish
- Italian
- Anglo-Egyptian condominium

BY 1879 European influence in Africa was already considerable, so the sudden and rapid imposition of *political* control was in a sense a culmination of processes already underway. There were, however, some new forces at work.

Comparatively few areas of Africa were directly ruled by Europeans in 1880: in the north, the French had been engaged in conquering Algeria since the 1830s; small French and British colonies existed in West Africa (Senegal, Sierra Leone, the Gold Coast, Lagos and Gabon); and old-established but moribund Portuguese settlements in Angola and up the Zambezi valley in Mozambique. Only in the south, where the British colonists of the Cape were already locked in rivalry with the Afrikaners of the Transvaal and the Orange Free State, did political control extend to the interior. Yet within two decades the entire continent had been seized, fought over and partitioned. Of the 40 political units into which it had been divided by 1913 – on some occasions with little more than a ruler and pencil wielded in London, Paris or Berlin – direct European control extended to 36. Only Ethiopia, which had fought off the Italians, and Liberia, with its financial links to the United States, claimed real independence. France, the largest beneficiary, controlled nearly one third of Africa's 11.7 million square miles (30.3 million km²).

Many ingredients contributed to this imperialistic explosion. The progress of industrialization in Europe created a demand for new sources of raw materials, new markets and new fields for investment, which meant more demands on Africans and so more tensions which Europeans might overcome by the imposition of political control. Industrialization created tensions in Europe, too, for which some politicians such as Joseph Chamberlain of Great Britain saw colonization as an outlet. The rivalries between the European states were transferred to the extra-European world, and to Africa in particular. This meant that often trivial incidents between competing European traders in Africa achieved the status of major international crises, and that initiatives undertaken locally by European agents, occurring in rapid succession, set in motion the undignified scramble for possession of the continent. Chronologically, tensions rose between c.1876 and 1884. The powers met at the Berlin West Africa Conference in November 1884 with the object of averting partition and maintaining access for all. They failed. In fact annexations increased despite government hesitations before something of a pause set in from 1885 until 1889. Then existing, largely coastal, acquisitions were extended into the hinterlands, now with much more government enthusiasm.

In West Africa, French army officers, denied the chance of avenging the defeat of 1870 in Europe (see page 246), sought glory advancing inland from Senegal in the late 1870s. This brought them into conflict with the British in Gambia and Sierra Leone, and with African states such as the empires of Samory and al-Hajj Umar (see page 234). Along the West African coast intense Anglo-French rivalry grew in the regions of the Gold Coast, Togo, Dahomey and Yorubaland. French attitudes towards Great Britain hardened after the unilateral British invasion and occupation of Egypt in 1882, but the intervention of other European powers spread these squabbles all over the continent.

After the explorer Stanley's epic journey down the Congo River in 1877, the ambitious King Leopold of the Belgians took him into his personal service. Having already shown a strong desire to become involved in Africa at his Brussels Geographical Conference of 1876, Leopold was both a key player and a catalyst in the Scramble. In 1879 Stanley returned to the lower Congo and laid the foundations of the huge private domain the king later carved out for himself in the Congo basin. Stanley's activities stimulated others in the same area. The French naval officer de Brazza concluded some vital treaties with African chiefs, and on his return to Europe, France readily took up his claims. The action of France brought an immediate British and Portuguese response, though this came to nothing because of pressure exercised by Bismarck. Bismarck bought off French thoughts of revenge over the loss of Alsace-Lorraine by allowing France a free hand in Africa: this he was able to do by blackmailing Great Britain over Egypt. Then Germany itself entered the race by grabbing territory in four widely separated regions: Togoland, the Cameroons, South-West Africa and East Africa. French and German initiatives in West Africa led Great Britain to intervene actively, especially in securing the lands which became Nigeria. The far interior was left to the French, who by 1900 had swept right across the western Sudan region.

The German presence in southern Africa revived Portuguese ambitions, and the threat of Afrikaner expansion led to British thrusts into the interior of central Africa, into what later became Rhodesia, Zambia and Malawi. The initiative for these drives came largely from the Cape industrialist and politician Cecil Rhodes. Likewise, German colonization in East Africa (Tanganyika) produced its British counterpart when the prime minister, Lord Salisbury, laid claim to the region of the Great Lakes (Uganda) and the intervening territory down to the coast, which later became Kenya. The British were also drawn from their position in Egypt to intervene in the affairs of the Sudan, which had rebelled against Egypt in 1881 under an Islamic religious leader, the Mahdi. At the same time, French successes in the west – the occupation of Gabon in the western Congo, the conquest of the ancient kingdom of Dahomey (1893) and a three-pronged drive towards Lake Chad – caused Great Britain to mobilize the resources of the Royal Niger Company, to seize the emirates of Nupe and Ilorin, and to embark on a series of armed clashes with the African states within its trading sphere. The tension reached its height in 1898, when France's Commandant Marchand, after a two-year march from Gabon, faced British troops at Fashoda on the White Nile, and the two countries only just averted open war.

Partition, which had begun as a fairly peaceful process, now caused increasing bloodshed. Ethiopia inflicted a heavy defeat on the Italians at Adowa in 1896. Some 120,000 Sudanese died during the British suppression of the Mahdist state. Rhodes' settler forces engaged in bitter battles with the Matabele and Mashona as they moved north, and the white colonists everywhere came to rely increasingly on the repeating rifle and the Maxim gun. Conflict reached its climax with the Boer War (1899–1902) in which the British, with great difficulty, won control of the Transvaal gold mines (discovered on the Witwatersrand in 1886) and absorbed the Afrikaner republics.

The black Africans elsewhere in Africa, though they bitterly opposed the 'forward moves' of the European powers (see page 244), never offered concerted resistance, and were fairly easily dealt with piecemeal. Of the handful of African states still precariously independent in 1902, Libya was invaded by Italy in 1911, and Morocco survived until 1912 before being divided between France and Spain.

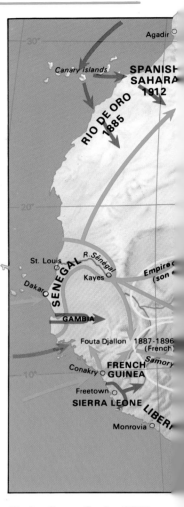

Charles George Gordon (1833-85) (top right) sent to the Sudan in 1884 to protect British bases, ignored orders to retreat and confronted the Islamic leader, the Mahdi, and his followers who besieged Khartoum for ten months. On 26 January 1885 Gordon and the entire garrison were massacred.

1/The partition of Africa (right) Despite the rapidity and apparent ease of the partition, nearly everywhere Europeans encountered resistance to their invasion of Africa. Much of this was local, and could be dealt with piecemeal, often using other African groups as allies. Some resistance was sustained, such as that of Samori to the French in West Africa in the 1880s. In all cases, European policy was to divide and rule. By the 1890s the white man had an overwhelming superiority of military hardware and the machine gun became the handmaiden of partition.

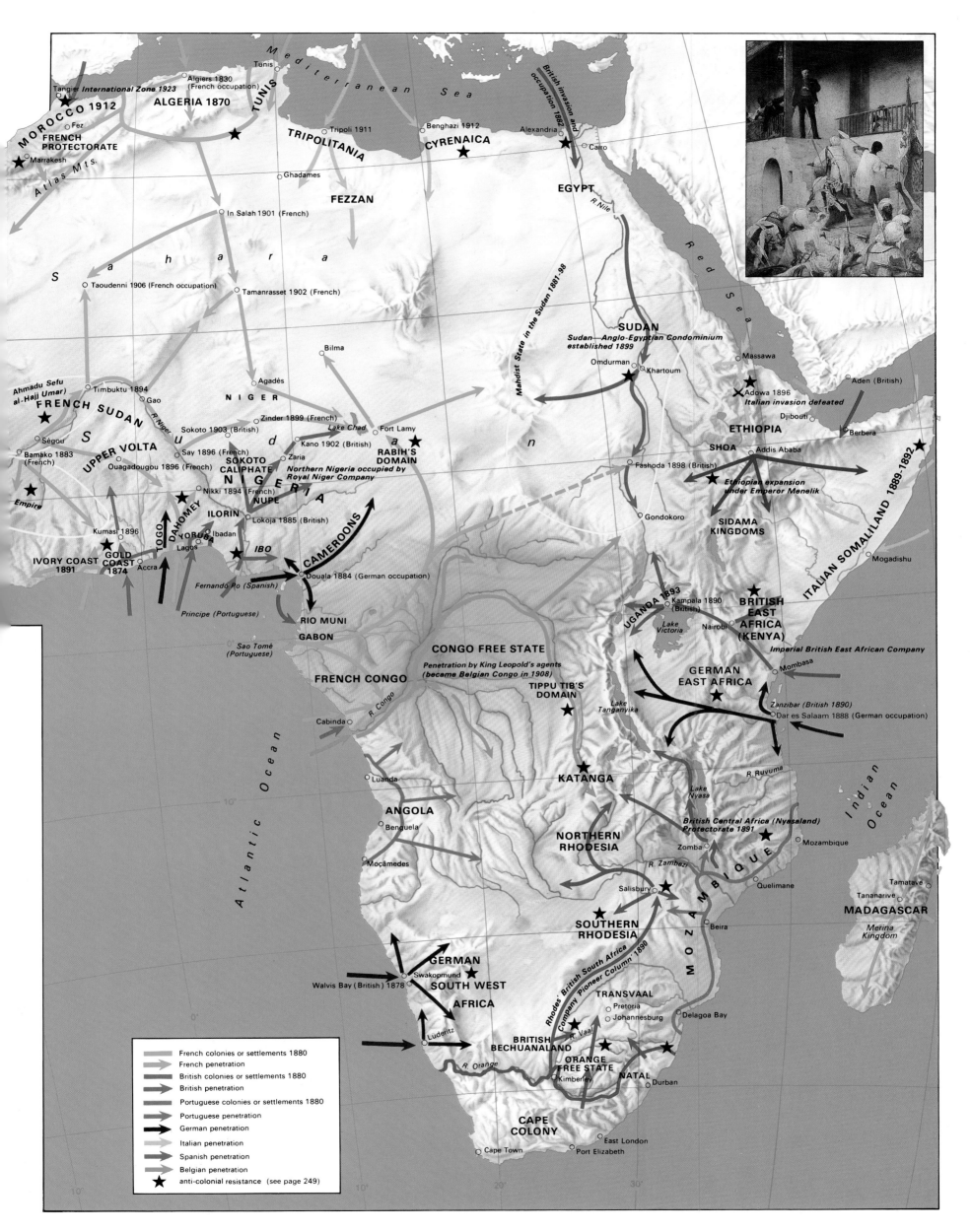

Mediterranean Sea

Tangier *International Zone 1923*
MOROCCO 1912
Fez
FRENCH PROTECTORATE
Marrakesh
Atlas Mts.

Algiers 1830 (French occupation)
Tunis
ALGERIA 1870
TUNIS
TRIPOLITANIA
Tripoli 1911
Benghazi 1912
CYRENAICA
Alexandria
Cairo

Ghadames
FEZZAN
In Salah 1901 (French)

S   a   h   a   r   a

Taoudenni 1906 (French occupation)
Tamanrasset 1902 (French)

EGYPT
R. Nile

Bilma
Agadès

British invasion and occupation 1882

Mahdist State in the Sudan 1881-98

SUDAN
Sudan—Anglo-Egyptian Condominium established 1899
Omdurman
Khartoum

Massawa
Aden (British)

Ahmadu Sefu al-Hajj Umar)
FRENCH SUDAN
Timbuktu 1894
Gao
NIGER

Adowa 1896
Italian invasion defeated
ETHIOPIA
SHOA
Addis Ababa
Djibouti
Berbera

Ségou
Bamako 1883 (French)
UPPER VOLTA
R. Niger
Sokoto 1903 (British)
Say 1896 (French)
Zinder 1899 (French)
Lake Chad
Fort Lamy
Kano 1902 (British)
RABIH'S DOMAIN

Fashoda 1898 (British)
Ethiopian expansion under Emperor Menelik
SIDAMA KINGDOMS

Empire
Ouagadougou 1896 (French)
SOKOTO CALIPHATE
Zaria
NIGERIA
Northern Nigeria occupied by Royal Niger Company
Nikki 1894 (French)
NUPE
Gondokoro

ITALIAN SOMALILAND 1889-1892

Kumasi 1896
DAHOMEY
ILORIN
YORUBA
Ibadan
IBO
Lokoja 1885 (British)
CAMEROONS

IVORY COAST 1891
GOLD COAST 1874
Accra
Lagos
Fernando Po (Spanish)
Douala 1884 (German occupation)

UGANDA 1893
Kampala 1890 (British)
BRITISH EAST AFRICA (KENYA)
Lake Victoria
Nairobi
Imperial British East African Company
Mombasa

Principe (Portuguese)
RIO MUNI
GABON

Sao Tomé (Portuguese)

FRENCH CONGO

CONGO FREE STATE
Penetration by King Leopold's agents (became Belgian Congo in 1908)
TIPPU TIB'S DOMAIN

R. Congo
Cabinda

Lake Tanganyika

GERMAN EAST AFRICA
Zanzibar (British 1890)
Dar es Salaam 1888 (German occupation)

Luanda

KATANGA

R. Ruvuma

ANGOLA
Benguela
Moçâmedes

NORTHERN RHODESIA

Lake Nyasa
British Central Africa (Nyasaland) Protectorate 1891
Zomba
Mozambique

Indian Ocean

MADAGASCAR
Merina Kingdom

R. Zambezi
Salisbury
SOUTHERN RHODESIA
Beira
Quelimane
Tamatave
Tananarive

GERMAN SOUTH WEST AFRICA
Swakopmund
Walvis Bay (British) 1878
Lüderitz

Rhodes' British South Africa Company 'Pioneer Column' 1890

TRANSVAAL
Pretoria
Johannesburg
Delagoa Bay
R. Vaal

BRITISH BECHUANALAND
ORANGE FREE STATE
Kimberley
NATAL
Durban
R. Orange

CAPE COLONY
Cape Town
East London
Port Elizabeth

Atlantic Ocean

	French colonies or settlements 1880
	French penetration
	British colonies or settlements 1880
	British penetration
	Portuguese colonies or settlements 1880
	Portuguese penetration
	German penetration
	Italian penetration
	Spanish penetration
	Belgian penetration
★	anti-colonial resistance (see page 249)

The expansion and modernization of Japan 1868 to 1918

3/The Russo-Japanese War (above) After surprising Tsarist ships at Port Arthur (8 February 1904), Japan's forces achieved a series of victories, culminating in the capture of Port Arthur (January 1905), the Battle of Mukden (February-March), and the destruction of Russia's Baltic Fleet in the Tsushima Straits (May).

Adults and children (left) study together in a typical Meiji-period classroom scene.

1/Industrial Japan (below) By 1918 the country's first major phase of modern economic growth was completed. Urban population had substantially increased, port cities and installations had expanded to meet changes in the scale and structure of foreign trade, and a main railway network, nationalized in 1906, connected all major centres. The First World War diverted the energies of all significant competitors and opened large new markets for manufactured exports. Japanese shipping now operated worldwide.

JAPAN avoided excessive interference by expansionist Western powers during the latter half of the 19th century by implementing successful policies for rapid modernization and economic development. The very countries that had threatened her independence became models for her own development and hence fuelled her imperialist ambitions. The process began in the 1850s and by 1920 the Japanese empire was firmly established.

Two centuries of semi-isolation, during which feudalism gradually disappeared, ended when the Western powers, led by the United States, demanded access to Japanese ports for trade. The 'unequal treaties' concluded under threat in 1858 contributed to the overthrow of the ruling Tokugawa house in January 1868. Direct imperial rule was then nominally restored in the name of the Meiji emperor (1867–1912).

The new leaders implemented widespread reforms in the belief that a modern economy and military would ensure Japan's international independence and equality. They abolished the feudal domains (1871) and replaced them with a system of prefectures controlled by a powerful central bureaucracy staffed by graduates of Japan's new universities. A Western-style peerage (1884), cabinet government (1885) and bicameral legislature (1889) provided a foundation for political unity and stability. Samurai privilege was abolished, a conscript army created (1873), and a navy founded and equipped with modern ships. A national education system, instituted in 1872, provided teaching for 90 per cent of school-age children by 1900. Legal codes, largely based on French and German models (except in traditional areas such as the family system) were introduced, beginning in 1882.

Economic modernization did not come easily, even though Japan started with greater advantages than most Asian countries. By 1868 she already had an extensive network of domestic commerce and credit and, despite a shortage of arable land, intensive agriculture supported a population of 30 million. For several centuries a major copper producer, Japan also had adequate coal deposits, some already in use, and enough accessible ore to supply a burgeoning iron industry. Japanese scholars began to study and experiment with Western science and technology, learning at first from books imported by the Dutch, but after 1858 directly from foreigners or in foreign countries. By 1869 a Western-style ship built in Japan crossed the Pacific with a Japanese crew. From then on many students went abroad, either for short training visits to Europe and America, or for longer stays at Western universities. This provided knowledge not only of technical skills, but also of political and economic affairs. Later development depended heavily on Japan adopting institutions such as the joint stock company and banks, as well as the government's success in providing a stable social and financial environment and in undertaking important economic reforms and industrialization policies.

The land tax reform of 1873, which replaced feudal dues with cash payments based on the value of land, led to agrarian unrest and consolidation of land holdings. However it also ensured a secure source of revenue for the government, with land tax accounting for over half of total government revenue before 1900. Up to one-third of state expenditure went on the development of commerce and industry while, to encourage the transfer of technology and stimulate private investment, the government built model factories in strategic and import-saving industries, such as steel and textiles, and became directly involved in the development of transport and communications. It also provided indirect encouragement in the form of subsidies, tax privileges for the shipbuilding and shipping industries, the quality control of export goods (such as silk), and technical training schemes. Following a period of rapid inflation and foreign exchange crisis, financial stability was introduced in the mid-1880s with a short period of severe deflation and the establishment of a sound banking system.

Within this framework, capitalism made rapid headway – in textiles by the 1880s and in heavy industry after 1895 – quickly making Japan the outstanding example of large-scale industrialization in the non-Western world. Further impetus came from Japan's increasing penetration of foreign markets during the First World War. Foreign trade rose sharply from the 1890s, as Japan exploited major outlets in China and the United States, and her trade structure changed strikingly as she became a large-scale importer of raw materials and exporter of finished goods.

These developments paralleled considerable changes in the Japanese way of life. Population rose from 35 million in 1873 to 55 million in 1918 when, although half the population was still engaged in agriculture, nearly one-third lived in towns of 10,000 or more inhabitants, especially in the major industrial areas of Honshu and northern Kyushu, and along the coastal belt between them. Moreover, these areas were

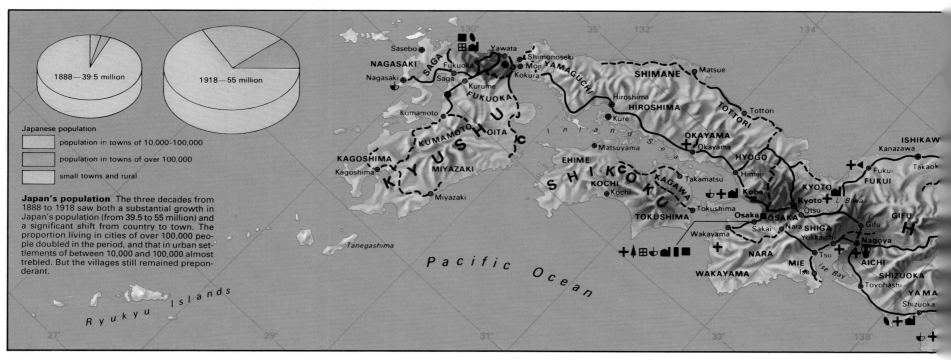

1888 — 39.5 million	1918 — 55 million	

Japanese population
- population in towns of 10,000-100,000
- population in towns of over 100,000
- small towns and rural

Japan's population The three decades from 1888 to 1918 saw both a substantial growth in Japan's population (from 39.5 to 55 million) and a significant shift from country to town. The proportion living in cities of over 100,000 people doubled in the period, and that in urban settlements of between 10,000 and 100,000 almost trebled. But the villages still remained preponderant.

linked to most parts of the country by a railway system totalling 6200 miles (10,000 km) of government trunk routes (nationalized 1906) connecting a network of privately owned local lines.

National strength brought expansion overseas and, although foreign policy initially concentrated upon problems of defence, economic considerations also played a role: in many of the new colonies Japan successfully introduced similar policies to her own for improving agriculture and industry. Japan and Russia had partitioned the Kurils by treaty in 1855, but Japan relinquished a claim to part of Sakhalin in return for the entire Kuril chain in 1875. Britain and the United States agreed to Japan's takeover of the Bonin (Ogasawara) islands in 1873, while the islands of the Ryukyu archipelago (claimed in 1872) became a Japanese prefecture in 1879 despite Chinese protests.

As Japan's strength and confidence grew, so did nationalist and imperialist ambitions. The 'unequal treaties' were revised in 1894, though the revisions did not come into effect until 1911. In 1894–5 a victorious war against China, arising from disputes in Korea, led to the Treaty of Shimonoseki in 1895, which granted Formosa (Taiwan) to Japan. From then on, Japan and Russia clashed over their respective interests in Korea and South Manchuria, culminating in Japanese victory in the war of 1904–5. She gained land victories in Manchuria, notably at Port Arthur and Mukden, and defeated the Russian fleet in the Tsushima Straits in May 1905. The Treaty of Portsmouth (1905) gave her a lease of Liaotung in China (Kwantung Leased Territory), plus extensive rights in South Manchuria and a colony in southern Sakhalin (Karafuto). Korea was made a protectorate and later annexed (1910). Finally the outbreak of war in Europe in 1914 allowed Japan to extend her rights on the Chinese mainland, this time in

the former German sphere in Shantung, as well as in Manchuria and Fukien. In the Twenty-one Demands she made sweeping claims in these areas most of which were incorporated in treaties with China in 1915. Despite bitter Chinese resentment, Japan's allies nevertheless acquiesced with a series of separate agreements which also recognized her claims to captured German islands in the northern Pacific. The Versailles Conference confirmed most of these gains in 1919 and Japan emerged as a major power with a permanent seat on the Council of the League of Nations.

However, there was another side to the story: the era of reform on which Japan's international success was founded also helped to destroy the basis of stability at home. The deaths and retirement of the Meiji generation of leaders opened the way for a power struggle between fresh contenders. By 1918 the army already indicated a willingness to act independently of civil control in operations against Russia in Siberia. Party politicians appealing to Western parliamentary ideas sought power through the support of businessmen. Finally some rejected the whole trend of Japan's modern history: traditionalists, offended by the sacrifice of Japanese to Western-style habits and institutions, and representatives of the tenant farmer and the factory labourer, who resented the capitalist structure. After the end of the war in 1918 Japan suffered a wave of strikes in major industrial centres, followed by widespread rural unrest, and in 1921 Hara Kei, prime minister and party leader, was assassinated by a young right-wing fanatic. In these events lay the seeds of future disruption that presaged a new phase of conflict.

2/Growth overseas *(right)* 1868 brought an explosion of Japanese interest in the West and in her neighbours. By 1876, Japan had asserted rights in several islands. By 1918 her holdings included a mainland empire.

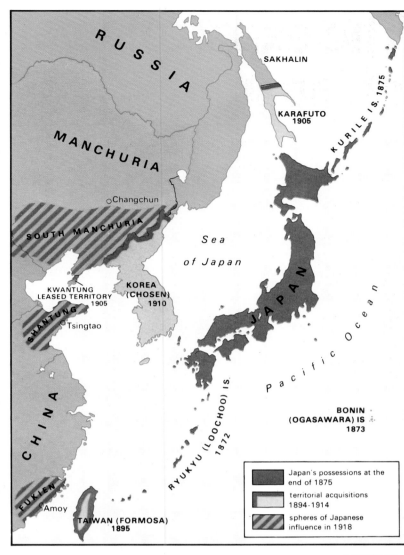

Japan's possessions at the end of 1875

territorial acquisitions 1894-1914

spheres of Japanese influence in 1918

Japan's trading partners *(right)* The United States had already become Japan's major trading partner by 1918-22, with imports and exports roughly in balance. China was more important as a customer than as a supplier, and India the reverse. Western dominance of the China trade was not duplicated in Japan.

Japan's trading partners 1918-1922

exports   imports

The dramatic growth of Japanese trade *(below right)* The growth of imports and exports is shown in yen. The yen was first issued in 1871 at parity with the dollar but declined steadily until 1894, when the exchange rate stabilized at 2 yen to the dollar, where it remained, with small variations, until 1931.

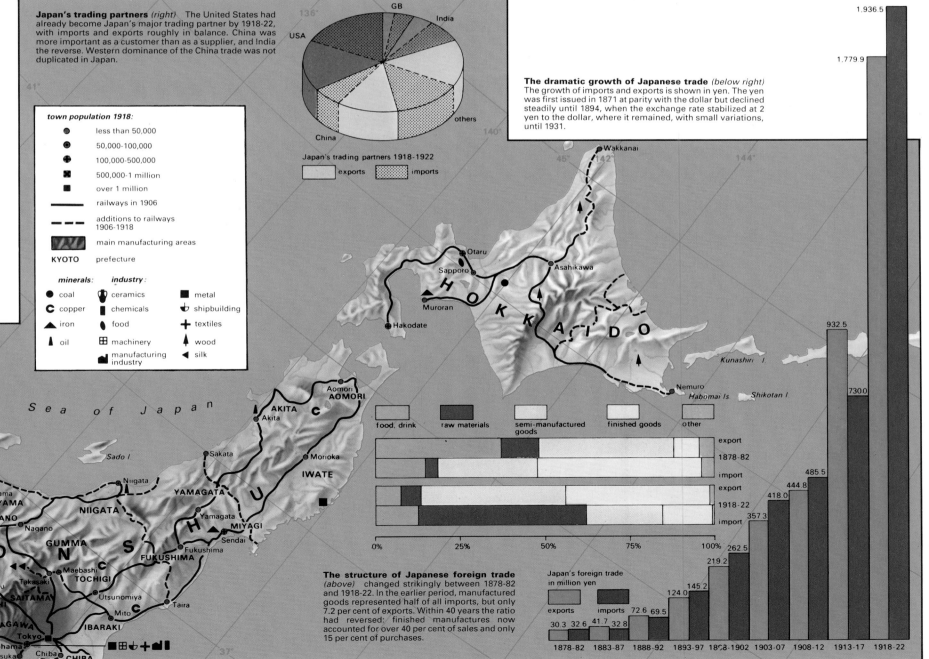

town population 1918:
- less than 50,000
- 50,000-100,000
- 100,000-500,000
- 500,000-1 million
- over 1 million

railways in 1906

additions to railways 1906-1918

main manufacturing areas

KYOTO prefecture

minerals:
- coal
- C copper
- iron
- oil

industry:
- ceramics
- chemicals
- food
- machinery
- manufacturing industry
- metal
- shipbuilding
- textiles
- wood
- silk

The structure of Japanese foreign trade *(above)* changed strikingly between 1878-82 and 1918-22. In the earlier period, manufactured goods represented half of all imports, but only 7.2 per cent of exports. Within 40 years the ratio had reversed: finished manufactures now accounted for over 40 per cent of sales and only 15 per cent of purchases.

food, drink   raw materials   semi-manufactured goods   finished goods   other

export 1878-82
import 1878-82
export 1918-22
import 1918-22

0% 25% 50% 75% 100%

Japan's foreign trade in million yen

exports   imports

	1878-82	1883-87	1888-92	1893-97	1898-1902	1903-07	1908-12	1913-17	1918-22
exports	30.3	41.7	72.6	124.0	219.2	357.3	418.0	730.0	1,936.5
imports	32.6	32.8	69.5	145.2	262.5	444.8	485.5	932.5	1,779.9

European colonial empires 1815 to 1914

THE 19th century is often seen as the great age of European expansion or 'imperialism', and one of the main themes of 20th-century history has been the anti-colonialist reaction it has provoked among the peoples of Asia and Africa. In fact the creation of large new empires occupied only the last half of the century. As late as 1871, apart from the possessions of Great Britain in India and South Africa, of Russia in Siberia and central Asia, and of France in Algeria and Indo-China, the European stake in Asia and Africa was confined to trading stations and strategic posts. Colonial struggles had played an important part in European politics in the 18th century (see page 190), but by the mid-19th century empire-building seemed to have lost its attractions. On a theoretical level, its mercantilist justification had been demolished by Adam Smith and the 'Manchester School' of economists. More practically, Great Britain's flourishing trade with both the United States and South America appeared to show that political control was not necessary for commercial success. The

future British prime minister, Benjamin Disraeli, expressed the prevailing orthodoxy when he said, in 1852, 'the colonies are millstones round our neck'.

Nevertheless, the European powers were in no hurry to abandon their overseas possessions. Spain and Portugal lost their empires in the western hemisphere as they became weaker at home. By 1830 their former colonies in South and Central America were all but independent (see page 222). Russia too surrendered her North American territories, selling Alaska to the United States in 1867. But France, which had lost most of its first empire by 1815, gradually built a new one, conquering Algeria in the 1830s and 1840s, expanding its colony of Senegal in the 1850s, taking various Pacific islands (Tahiti, the Marquesas) in the 1840s, and annexing Saigon in 1859. Great Britain was also steadily acquiring new territories. By the peace settlements of 1815 she retained the Cape of Good Hope and the maritime provinces of Ceylon from the Dutch, Malta from the Knights

of St John, Mauritius and the Seychelles from France and some West Indian islands from France and Spain. Fearing a French challenge, she extended her claim to sovereignty over the whole of Australia in the 1830s and over New Zealand in 1840. Her power continued to expand in India (see page 230), and by 1858 the boundaries of British India and of the Princely States under British tutelage were roughly as they would remain until independence in 1947. Elsewhere she acquired Singapore in 1819, Malacca in 1824, Hong Kong in 1842, Natal in 1843, Labuan in 1846, Lower Burma in 1852, Lagos in 1861 and Sarawak in 1888. Many of these acquisitions were strategic points, commanding sea routes. Great Britain was particularly sensitive about the route to India, her most valuable overseas possession. This apparent paradox between theory and practice is explained by the fact that the British felt that their prosperity and survival depended on trade and, although they preferred to safeguard this by 'influence', they never ruled out direct political

1/The closing of the world system (*below*) At the time of Napoleon's final defeat (1815), vast areas of the globe were still unknown to Europeans and millions of people lived untouched by European influence. A century later, European explorers had penetrated the most remote regions. After them had come missionaries, traders, bankers, soldiers and administrators. Africans and Asians were rarely able to repulse the superior technological forces of Europe; many had passed under European political control. The map shows how widespread and complete this movement was. The small inset map shows the situation by 1870; the larger map, from 1870 to 1914.

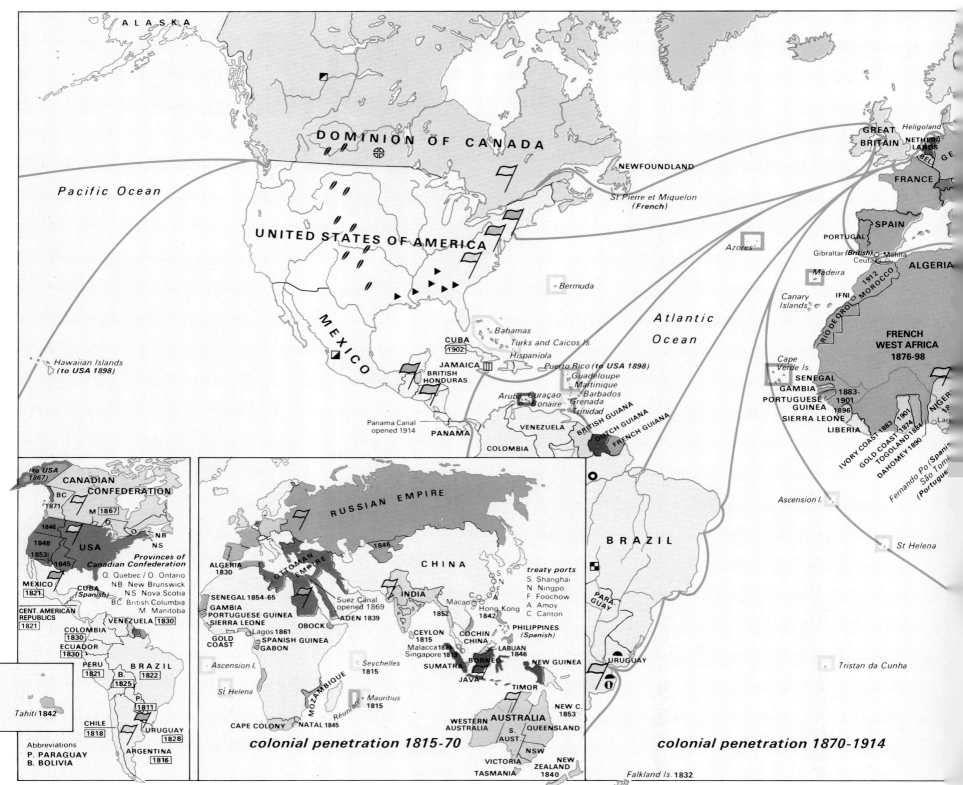

colonial penetration 1815-70

colonial penetration 1870-1914

or military intervention.

The late 19th century saw a new imperial outburst of an intensely competitive kind. In the scramble for territory, resources, markets and outlets for capital investment, an immense part of the world's total land area passed under European control. But many desirable areas were already pre-empted: the Monroe Doctrine discouraged further European involvement in the western hemisphere; latecomers such as Germany and Italy had to look to Africa, the Pacific or China. Great Britain, France and even Portugal re-entered the lists. The United States seized former Spanish territory in the war of 1898. Japan, emerging as a great Pacific power, began to covet Korea, Formosa and even mainland China. Of the great trading nations, the Netherlands almost alone remained content with their existing (and prosperous) possessions in the East Indies.

Between 1871 and 1914 the French empire grew by nearly 4 million square miles (10.4 million km²) and nearly 47 million people, mainly in north and west Africa and Indo-China, where Laos and Tongking were added to Cambodia and Cochin China, but she also secured Madagascar and some Pacific territories. Germany acquired an empire of 1 million square miles (2.6 million km²) and 14 million colonial subjects in South-West Africa, Togoland, the Cameroons, Tanganyika and the Pacific islands. Italy obtained Libya, Eritrea and Italian Somaliland but failed to secure Abyssinia. Leopold II

of the Belgians got international recognition for his Congo State (later the Belgian Congo). Portugal extended her territory in Angola and Mozambique. Great Britain made the greatest gains of all in Africa, controlling inter alia Nigeria, Kenya, Uganda, Northern and Southern Rhodesia, Egypt and the Sudan, and in the Pacific, where she took Fiji, parts of Borneo and New Guinea, and other islands. She added 88 million subjects to her empire and, by 1914, exercised authority over a fifth of the world's land surface and a quarter of its peoples.

Africa was completely partitioned (see page 236) and China seemed likely to share the same fate. Russia joined the other European powers in competing for influence here. Her land empire in central Asia and Siberia had grown enormously since the 1860s and over 7 million Russians had emigrated from European to Asiatic Russia between 1801 and 1914. In China, the late 19th century saw the 'battle of the concessions', when the leading contenders manoeuvred for commercial advantage and financial and railway concessions. But the Chinese state, although debilitated, was stronger and more centralized than the divided polities of Africa. The Chinese held the West at bay until the First World War which was a watershed. Although the British empire actually grew in size after the war, with the addition of the former German colonies, indiscriminate land-grabbing was no longer considered acceptable conduct in a world supposedly ruled by the League of Nations.

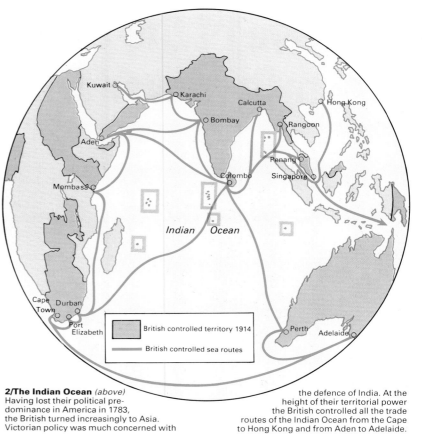

2/The Indian Ocean (above)
Having lost their political predominance in America in 1783, the British turned increasingly to Asia. Victorian policy was much concerned with the defence of India. At the height of their territorial power the British controlled all the trade routes of the Indian Ocean from the Cape to Hong Kong and from Aden to Adelaide.

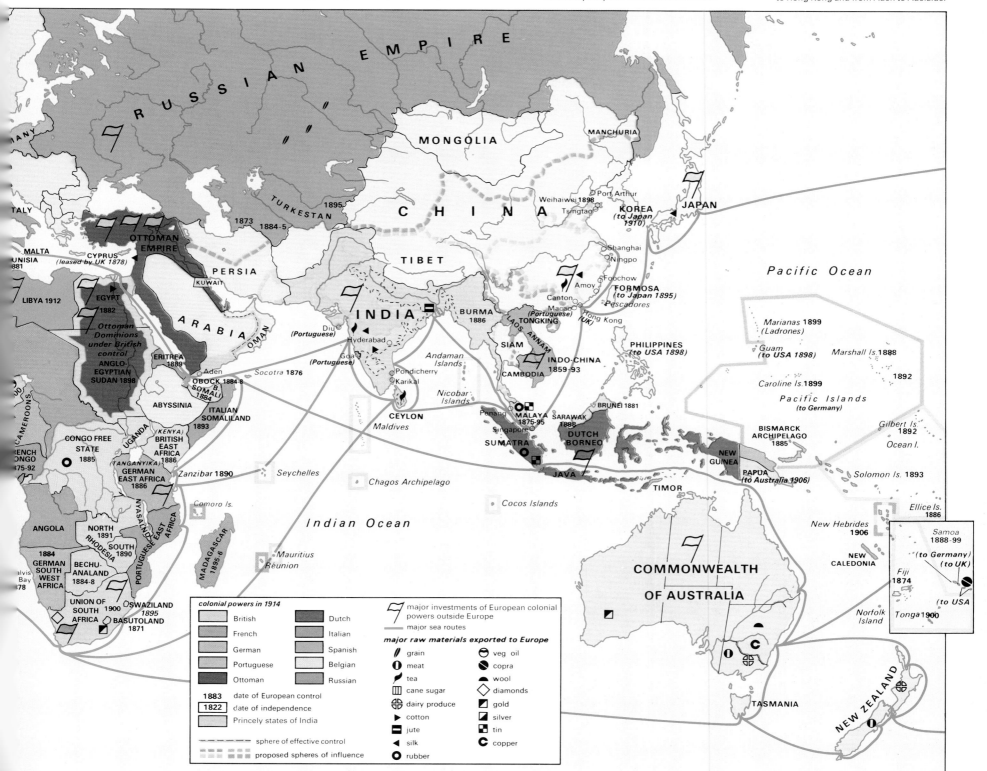

The rise of the United States to world power 1867 to 1917

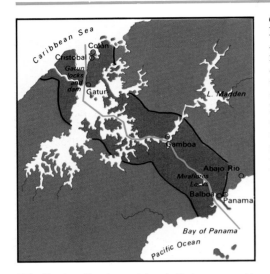

2/The Panama Canal zone (above) Under a treaty with Panama (1903) the US leased the zone in perpetuity, but also took possession of it as 'if it were sovereign'. However, under two treaties ratified in 1978, the Canal zone was handed over to Panama, with the canal itself due to be relinquished by the US by the end of 1999.

THE United States emerged onto the world stage in 1867, followed by Germany in 1870. Between them these two imperial powers exerted a decisive influence in transforming the modern world. In 1917, by entering the war on the side of Great Britain and France, the US brought about a decisive German defeat and thereby made itself the world's greatest power.

The preceding half-century, from 1867 to 1917, was a period of intense international rivalries, of which the United States took full advantage. American ambitions had manifested themselves since the 18th century, but dissension between the northern and southern states, culminating in the Civil War of 1861 to 1865, slowed expansion to a halt. When the forward movement was resumed, industrialism and later finance capitalism appeared as potent forces superimposed upon the earliest type of empire-building which had stressed commerce and territory. This new imperialism vented itself in war against Spain in 1898, a watershed year when the US plunged into world politics; meanwhile, it had been strengthening its navy and occupying strategic outposts before claiming supremacy in the Caribbean and the Pacific.

The first step in the resumption of this new forward movement was the acquisition of Alaska in 1867 as the result of a deal with Russia. To Americans, Alaska was both the back

3/The Alaska border dispute (below) The rush to the Klondike gold fields in 1897 brought this dispute near the boiling stage. Canada feared the loss of the northwest, but a politically oriented tribunal, with a British judge holding the casting vote, allowed the boundary demanded by the US (1903).

land claimed by US
land claimed by Canada
boundary agreed 1903

door to Canada and a 'finger pointed at Asia'. Many Americans believed that British North Ameria, encircled in this way, would be forced into the Union, thus fulfilling the dream of a contintent-wide empire. But the Canadians frustrated these hopes, first by federation (1867), then by the purchase of Rupert's Land from the Hudson's Bay Company (1869). Finally, they attracted Manitoba (1870) and British Columbia (1871) into the new Dominion, thus blunting the northward thrusts of the United States. Tensions with Britain stemming from the American Civil War were eased by the Treaty of Washington (1871).

With the Aleutian island chain stretching out toward Japan, Alaska was the natural bridge to northeast Asia. Since the mid-19th century, however, Hawaii had been the main entrepôt to the Orient. A three-power rivalry involving Britain and France had kept American relations with this native kingdom in an unsettled state, but by annexing Midway Island (1867) the United States moved ahead of the other two powers. A commerical treaty in 1875 made Hawaii a virtual American protectorate, and in 1887 the United States obtained Pearl Harbor as a coaling station and future naval base. Annexation entered its final stage in 1893, when a group of sugar planters and Honolulu businessmen, aided by American residents, overthrew the native monarchy and established a republic. The outbreak of war with Spain in 1898 furnished the impetus for formal annexation. Wake Island followed in 1899. In 1878, the Americans had established a base at Pago Pago in the Samoan group, where the British and Germans also aspired to acquire territory. Friction resulted in a treaty (1899) partitioning the group, but the Germans lost their share to New Zealand during the First World War.

In the Pacific the United States aimed to secure the 'Open Door', a term coined by Secretary of State John Hay in 1899 to convey the vision of a new imperialist system, granting open ports and free trade to the major trading powers. The Americans were determined to outpace the Europeans in this scramble for markets. The chief fruits of the Spanish-American war in the Pacific were the Philippines and the island of Guam, formally ceded by Spain in the peace treaty of 1898.

The United States now had its 'stepping stones' to China, already the focus of international rivalry as a field for capital investment (see page 228). Backed by the government, American bankers and entrepreneurs expected to reap their full share of the unlimited opportunities China was supposed to offer. Their attention was concentrated particularly on Manchuria which promoters conceived of as America's 'new West', to be gridironed by railways owned and managed from the United States. These designs were finally thwarted when Russia and Japan divided Manchuria between themselves by treaty in 1907 and 1910.

American expansion was far more successful in the Caribbean and Mexico. From the latter the United States had wrested the provinces of Texas, New Mexico and California between 1846 and 1848. Land, mining and oil companies, competing with European interests, penetrated the country after 1880 but were checked by the 1911 revolution, which foreshadowed a far-reaching programme of nationalization. President Wilson reacted with two armed interventions: an occupation force to Veracruz in 1914, and a punitive expedition across the Rio Grande in 1916 both of which met vigorous Mexican resistance. In the Caribbean, the war on Spain had led to the conquest of Puerto Rico and the conversion of Cuba into a protectorate (1903). Britain, the other power chiefly interested in the Caribbean, recognized the changed situation and gave the United States a free hand with the Hay-

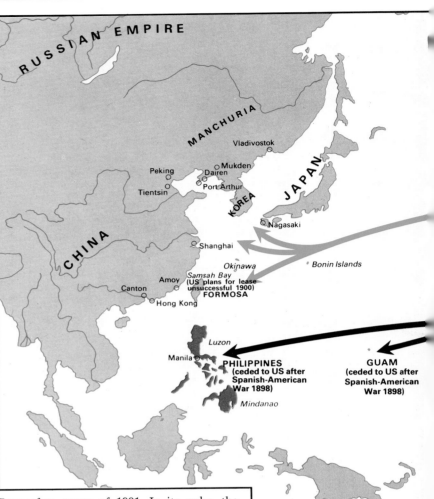

Pauncefote treaty of 1901. In its wake, the Americans built and controlled the Panama Canal (opened in 1914).

The ideological basis for this hegemony was the Monroe Doctrine which, even when first set forth in 1823, implied an intention to treat Latin America as a United States sphere of influence. Although expansionist ambitions were temporarily dropped with the outbreak of the Civil War (1861), the Monroe Doctrine was by no means forgotten. The French attempt to erect a puppet empire in Mexico (1862–7) offered it a fresh challenge, and in actually beginning work on a canal across Panama the French engineer, Ferdinand de Lesseps, builder of the Suez Canal, caused further objections. As President Hayes put it, any such canal must be regarded as 'virtually a part of the coastline of the United States' (1879).

Interfering in a British dispute with Venezuela over a boundary question, the United States in 1895 declared itself 'practically sovereign on this continent', and the British acquiesced. Obstinacy on the part of Colombia in failing to bow to American demands for canal rights across Panama led to an insurrection accompanied by the forcible detachment of that country from Colombia. The United States then guaranteed the 'independence' of Panama but under terms that made it a protectorate.

This period of dominance in the Caribbean survived under difficulties until about 1945. Mexican resistance stiffened into open defiance (1934–8), tactics had to be altered to appease the larger South American countries, and intense diplomacy was undertaken to offset the activities of Nazi Germany. Interventions that occurred from time to time in the affairs of the Caribbean republics were covert or indirect; on the surface the Monroe Doctrine was transformed into the 'Good Neighbour' policy, and every effort was made to convince Latin America of US good intentions. But obviously new forces were at work, and the Monroe Doctrine continued to recede farther into the background.

An American view (above) of the relative importance of Uncle Sam and John Bull, from The New York Journal in 1898. The Times of London predicted, after America's crushing victory over Spain, that the US would henceforth play a prominent role in world affairs.

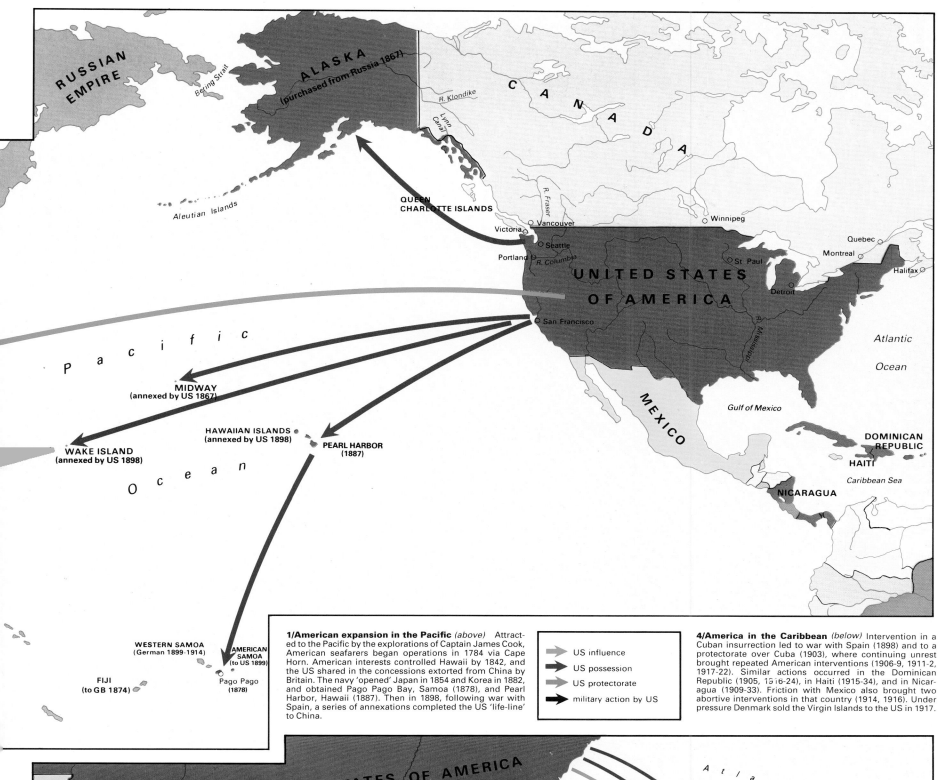

1/American expansion in the Pacific (above) Attracted to the Pacific by the explorations of Captain James Cook, American seafarers began operations in 1784 via Cape Horn. American interests controlled Hawaii by 1842, and the US shared in the concessions extorted from China by Britain. The navy 'opened' Japan in 1854 and Korea in 1882, and obtained Pago Pago Bay, Samoa (1878), and Pearl Harbor, Hawaii (1887). Then in 1898, following war with Spain, a series of annexations completed the US 'life-line' to China.

US influence
US possession
US protectorate
military action by US

4/America in the Caribbean (below) Intervention in a Cuban insurrection led to war with Spain (1898) and to a protectorate over Cuba (1903), where continuing unrest brought repeated American interventions (1906-9, 1911-2, 1917-22). Similar actions occurred in the Dominican Republic (1905, 1916-24), in Haiti (1915-34), and in Nicaragua (1909-33). Friction with Mexico also brought two abortive interventions in that country (1914, 1916). Under pressure Denmark sold the Virgin Islands to the US in 1917.

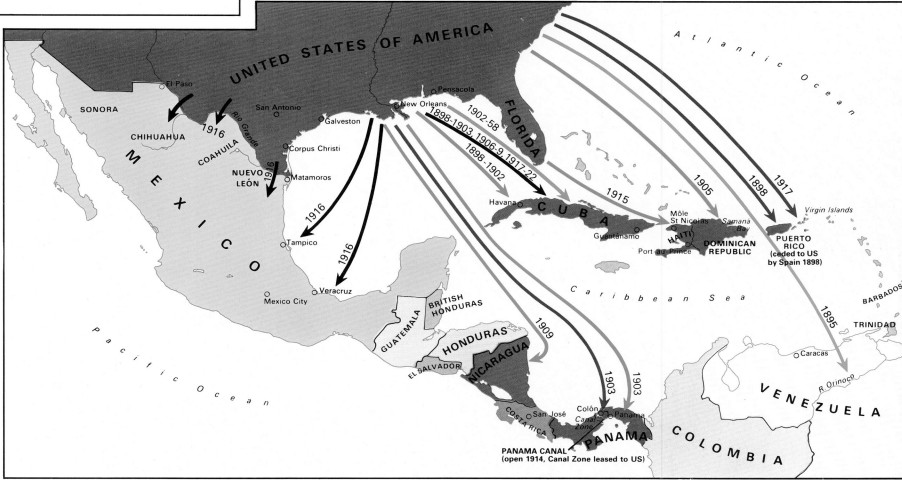

The anti-colonial reaction 1881 to 1917

Shooting the Pig and Decapitating the Sheep (above) This detail from a popular Chinese woodcut of the 1890s illustrates graphically the intensity of anti-western feeling in the colonial and semi-colonial world. The pig is Christ, the sheep are the Christians. This was the sentiment behind the Boxer rising of 1900, but it was duplicated in many other parts of the world.

THE 'new imperialism', beginning with French occupation of Tunis in 1881 and British occupation of Egypt in 1882, unleashed an anti-colonial reaction throughout Asia and Africa, the extent, intensity and significance of which have rarely been fully appreciated. In Tunisia French intervention provoked a large-scale Islamic rising, followed by spasmodic warfare in the south; in Egypt the British faced a national revolt under Arabi Pasha. Independence was not passively surrendered either in Africa or in Asia. In Annam the emperor, Ham Nghi, took to the mountains in 1883 and resisted French occupation until 1888. The British suffered repeated setbacks in the Sudan at the hands of the Mahdi and his successor, the Khalifa, including the annihilation of the garrison of Khartoum under General Gordon in 1885. Russia, desperately opposed in the Caucasus from 1834 to 1859 by Shamil, 'ruler of the righteous and destroyer of the unbeliever', encountered further Muslim resistance when it invaded central Asia. The Italians were decisively defeated by the Abyssinians at Adowa in 1896; and when the United States occupied the Philippines in 1898, the Americans also found themselves involved in a costly war with nationalist forces under Emilio Aguinaldo, which cost them some 7000 casualties and dragged on until 1902.

Even after occupation, the European powers had to face almost continuous unrest. Aguinaldo was captured, but the Islamic population of Mindanao carried on resistance in the Philippines. In Indo-China the 'Black Flags' took up the struggle when Emperor Ham Nghi was captured in 1888, and after 1895 a new leader appeared in the person of De Tham, who resisted the French until 1913. In Africa the British met equally determined resistance from the Ashanti, Matabele, Zulu and other African peoples, and oppressive German rule provoked the great Herero and Maji-Maji revolts in South-West Africa and Tanganyika in 1904 and 1905.

Much of this resistance was a negative explosion of resentment, xenophobia and despair. But it was also conservative and backward-looking, with a strong traditionalist and religious character. In Egypt and North Africa nationalists such as Afghani and Mohammed Abduh called for an Islamic revival to expel the infidel, and the Mahdiyya, which effectively controlled the Sudan from 1881 to 1898, was a Muslim revivalist movement, directed at once against Egyptians and Europeans. Hinduism played a similar role in fomenting resistance in India, as did Confucianism in China. But this conservative, traditionalist reaction to European imperialism, which had little prospect of success in view of the immense military preponderance of the colonial powers, was accompanied elsewhere by a more positive response, particularly in countries such as Turkey, Egypt, China and India

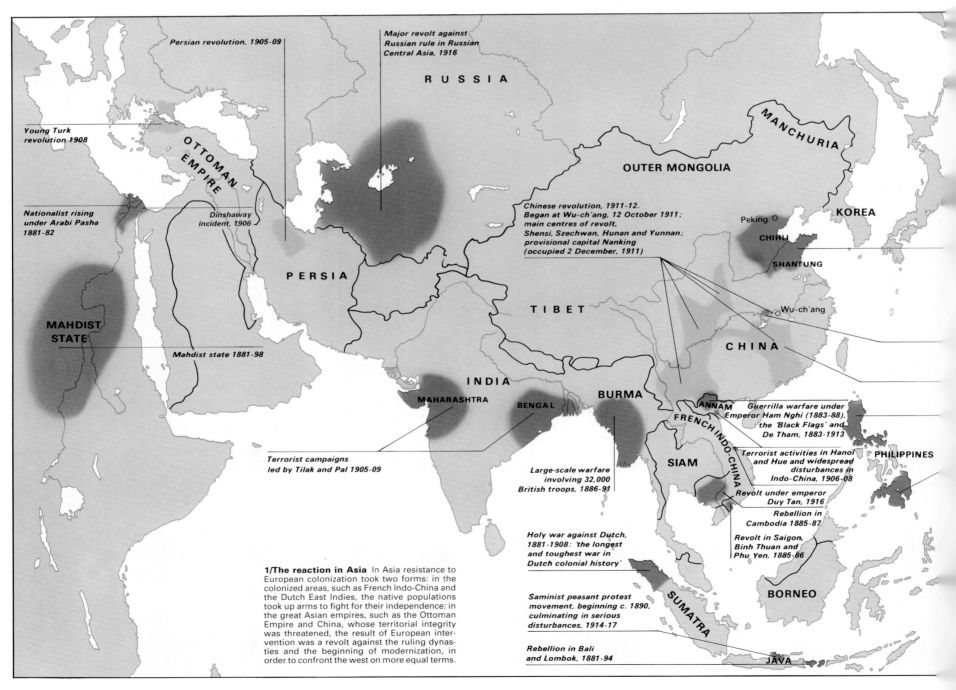

Persian revolution, 1905-09

Major revolt against Russian rule in Russian Central Asia, 1916

RUSSIA

Young Turk revolution 1908

OTTOMAN EMPIRE

MANCHURIA

OUTER MONGOLIA

Nationalist rising under Arabi Pasha 1881-82

Dinshaway incident, 1906

Chinese revolution, 1911-12. Began at Wu-ch'ang, 12 October 1911; main centres of revolt, Shensi, Szechwan, Hunan and Yunnan; provisional capital Nanking (occupied 2 December, 1911)

Peking ○

KOREA

CHIHLI

SHANTUNG

PERSIA

TIBET

Wu-ch'ang

MAHDIST STATE

CHINA

Mahdist state 1881-98

INDIA

MAHARASHTRA

BENGAL

BURMA

ANNAM

Guerrilla warfare under Emperor Ham Nghi (1883-88), the 'Black Flags' and De Tham, 1883-1913

FRENCH INDO-CHINA

Terrorist activities in Hanoi and Hue and widespread disturbances in Indo-China, 1906-08

Terrorist campaigns led by Tilak and Pal 1905-09

Large-scale warfare involving 32,000 British troops, 1886-91

SIAM

PHILIPPINES

Revolt under emperor Duy Tan, 1916

Rebellion in Cambodia 1885-87

Revolt in Saigon, Binh Thuan and Phu Yen, 1885-86

Holy war against Dutch, 1881-1908: 'the longest and toughest war in Dutch colonial history'

1/The reaction in Asia In Asia resistance to European colonization took two forms: in the colonized areas, such as French Indo-China and the Dutch East Indies, the native populations took up arms to fight for their independence; in the great Asian empires, such as the Ottoman Empire and China, whose territorial integrity was threatened, the result of European intervention was a revolt against the ruling dynasties and the beginning of modernization, in order to confront the west on more equal terms.

Saminist peasant protest movement, beginning c. 1890, culminating in serious disturbances, 1914-17

BORNEO

SUMATRA

Rebellion in Bali and Lombok, 1881-94

JAVA

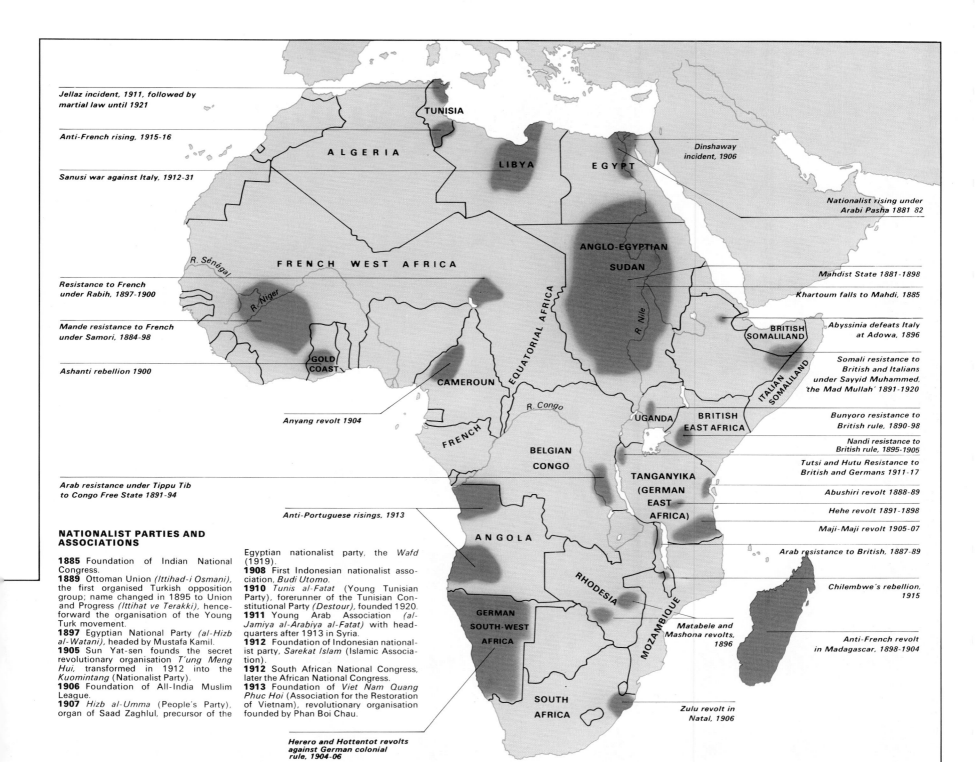

Jellaz incident, 1911, followed by martial law until 1921

Anti-French rising, 1915-16

Sanusi war against Italy, 1912-31

Resistance to French under Rabih, 1897-1900

Mande resistance to French under Samori, 1884-98

Ashanti rebellion 1900

Arab resistance under Tippu Tib to Congo Free State 1891-94

Anti-Portuguese risings, 1913

TUNISIA

ALGERIA

LIBYA

EGYPT

FRENCH WEST AFRICA

R. Sénégal

R. Niger

GOLD COAST

CAMEROUN

FRENCH EQUATORIAL AFRICA

R. Congo

BELGIAN CONGO

ANGOLA

GERMAN SOUTH-WEST AFRICA

SOUTH AFRICA

RHODESIA

MOZAMBIQUE

ANGLO-EGYPTIAN SUDAN

R. Nile

UGANDA

BRITISH EAST AFRICA

BRITISH SOMALILAND

ITALIAN SOMALILAND

TANGANYIKA (GERMAN EAST AFRICA)

Anyang revolt 1904

Dinshaway incident, 1906

Nationalist rising under Arabi Pasha 1881 82

Mahdist State 1881-1898

Khartoum falls to Mahdi, 1885

Abyssinia defeats Italy at Adowa, 1896

Somali resistance to British and Italians under Sayyid Muhammed, 'the Mad Mullah' 1891-1920

Bunyoro resistance to British rule, 1890-98

Nandi resistance to British rule, 1895-1905

Tutsi and Hutu Resistance to British and Germans 1911-17

Abushiri revolt 1888-89

Hehe revolt 1891-1898

Maji-Maji revolt 1905-07

Arab resistance to British, 1887-89

Chilembwe's rebellion, 1915

Anti-French revolt in Madagascar, 1898-1904

Matabele and Mashona revolts, 1896

Zulu revolt in Natal, 1906

Herero and Hottentot revolts against German colonial rule, 1904-06

NATIONALIST PARTIES AND ASSOCIATIONS

1885 Foundation of Indian National Congress.
1889 Ottoman Union (*Ittihad-i Osmani*), the first organised Turkish opposition group; name changed in 1895 to Union and Progress (*Ittihat ve Terakki*), henceforward the organisation of the Young Turk movement.
1897 Egyptian National Party (*al-Hizb al-Watani*), headed by Mustafa Kamil.
1905 Sun Yat-sen founds the secret revolutionary organisation *T'ung Meng Hui*, transformed in 1912 into the *Kuomintang* (Nationalist Party).
1906 Foundation of All-India Muslim League.
1907 *Hizb al-Umma* (People's Party), organ of Saad Zaghlul, precursor of the Egyptian nationalist party, the *Wafd* (1919).
1908 First Indonesian nationalist association, *Budi Utomo*.
1910 *Tunis al-Fatat* (Young Tunisian Party), forerunner of the Tunisian Constitutional Party (*Destour*), founded 1920.
1911 Young Arab Association (*al-Jamiya al-Arabiya al-Fatat*) with headquarters after 1913 in Syria.
1912 Foundation of Indonesian nationalist party, *Sarekat Islam* (Islamic Association).
1912 South African National Congress, later the African National Congress.
1913 Foundation of *Viet Nam Quang Phuc Hoi* (Association for the Restoration of Vietnam), revolutionary organisation founded by Phan Boi Chau.

Boxer uprising 1899-1900 - Shantung and Chihli

Anti-western riots, 1891

large-scale republican rising, 1906-07 - Hunan, Kiangsi, Kwangtung

Nationalist revolt under Aguinaldo 1898-1902

Continuing resistance of Moros, 1898-1913

where western interference had already undermined the old order. The bankruptcy of Turkey in 1875 and of Egypt in 1879 drove home the lesson that the only hope of halting western encroachment was to get rid of archaic institutions and decadent, semi-feudal dynasties and carry through a programme of modernization and reform. In Turkey the Russian assault in 1877 and the dismemberment of the Ottoman Empire by the European powers at the Congress of Berlin in 1878 fanned the patriotism of the Young Turks, who were to rise in revolution in 1908. In China the disastrous war with Japan in 1894–5, and the threat of partition which was its immediate consequence, led to the abortive Hundred Days' Reform of 1898 and, after its failure, to the bitterly anti-foreign Boxer rising. In Egypt the revolt of Arabi Pasha, directed first against the khedive Tewfik, a pliant tool of European interests, turned against the foreigners after the British occupation in 1882. In India the National Congress, founded in 1885, which pursued a moderate policy of constitutional reform, was joined after 1905 by a militant, Hindu-inspired, terrorist movement led by the Maharashtrian Brahmin, Bal Gangadhar Tilak.

All these movements were 'proto-nationalist' rather than nationalist in character: the disparate elements they brought together lacked unity and clearly defined objectives, and none achieved lasting results. In the Ottoman Empire the Young Turks deposed Sultan Abdul Hamid II in 1908, but their attempts at reform floundered. In China the republic proclaimed in 1912 gave way a year later to the dictatorship of Yüan Shih-k'ai. In Persia strikes and riots in 1906 forced the Shah to convoke a national assembly, the *majlis*, which drew up a liberal constitution, and when his successor attempted to revoke it, he was deposed in 1909; but the Shah was restored two years later and the *majlis* suppressed. In spite of these and other setbacks the movement of protest and resistance should not be written off as a failure. Though xenophobic and anti-foreign in origin, already before 1914 it was being transformed into a modern nationalist movement. The clearest evidence of this change is the appearance of nationalist associations and political parties. Many of these were small groups of the disaffected intelligentsia; but a few already had a mass following. The membership of Sarekat Islam, the first politically based Indonesian nationalist organization, founded in 1912, was 360,000 in 1916 but over 2 million by the end of the First World War.

That war gave new impetus to the incipient nationalism stirring in Asia and Africa before 1914. Even earlier the flame of resistance had been fanned by the Japanese victory in the Russo-Japanese war of 1904–5, which showed that the European powers were not invincible. Chinese nationalists, Sun Yat-sen later recalled, 'regarded the Russian defeat by Japan as the defeat of the West by the East', and the repercussions were felt throughout Asia from Persia to Indo-China, where it sparked off the Chieu conspiracy against France in 1906. By diverting the imperialist powers' attention from their colonies, the outbreak of war in Europe in 1914 created new opportunities. When in 1914 the

2/The reaction in Africa (*above*) The partition of Africa among the European powers, inaugurated at the Berlin Conference of 1884, provoked a movement of resistance among the African peoples which was never quelled, in spite of harsh repression. The map shows the extent and continuity of rebellion throughout the whole period from 1887 to 1917.

British proclaimed a protectorate over Egypt, they united Egyptian opposition and gave the final impetus to anti-British sentiment, already inflamed by public executions carried out at Dinshawai in 1906. In Russia a major revolt broke out among the Muslim peoples of central Asia in 1916. In North Africa there were risings against the French in Tunisia in 1915–6, supported by the Sanusi tribesmen of the Sahara who had been waging war against the Italians ever since the Italian occupation of Tripolitania and Cyrenaica in 1911 and 1912. France also had to face disaffection in Annam in 1916, and in Nyasaland the withdrawal of regular troops to fight the Germans on the northern frontier made it possible for John Chilembwe to stage a revolt against the British settlers in 1915. The persistence of opposition in spite of disheartening setbacks and harsh repression is most remarkable. None of the powers which had launched the scramble for colonies in 1884 was secure in its possessions; nowhere was the finality of European rule accepted. The tangible achievements of nationalists in this period were negligible; but by keeping the flame of resistance alive, they inaugurated the process which led, a generation later, to the collapse of the European empires and the emancipation of the colonial peoples.

European rivalries and alliances 1878 to 1914

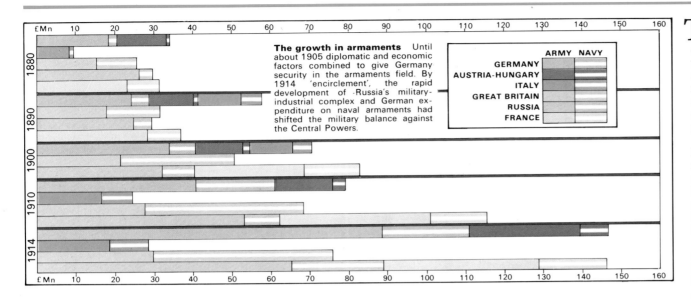

The growth in armaments Until about 1905 diplomatic and economic factors combined to give Germany security in the armaments field. By 1914 'encirclement', the rapid development of Russia's military-industrial complex and German expenditure on naval armaments had shifted the military balance against the Central Powers.

	ARMY	NAVY
GERMANY		
AUSTRIA-HUNGARY		
ITALY		
GREAT BRITAIN		
RUSSIA		
FRANCE		

THE years 1871 to 1914 saw the apogee of the European state system. The Great Powers established their control of the non-European world to an extent never witnessed before or since; within Europe they sought security in a multi-faceted system of diplomatic alignments and alliances. Although always implying threats of war, as long as it remained flexible the system permitted the peaceful adjustment of rivalries.

Four wars in a dozen years had solved the Italian and German questions and revised the map of Europe from Denmark to Sicily; for four decades after 1871 no more wars broke out between the Great Powers, and although irredentist and nationalist grievances continued to fester, territorial questions ceased to be an issue for most governments.

Of the Great Powers, only France proved unable to reconcile itself to the rise of the new German Empire which had robbed it of primacy in Europe; this, rather than the cession of Alsace-Lorraine in 1871, constituted the basic cause of Franco-German estrangement and the one fixed point in the shifting alignments of the Great Powers during the armed peace of 1871 to 1914. In itself, however, this did not pose a threat to peace: France was in no position to challenge a Germany which had developed by the end of the century into the strongest military-industrial power in the world; nor for the first half of the period could it find an ally to provide even a diplomatic counterweight to German power.

The other five major states of Europe all accepted the changed balance of power set up in 1871. Neither Austria-Hungary nor Russia felt inclined to support France because all the three eastern empires shared a common conservative ideology of co-operation against the threat of proletarian revolution which they discerned in the Paris commune of 1871, the activities of the Second International after 1889, and the progress of social democracy consequent upon the progress of industrialization. In 1882 even the Italian government joined the conservative camp and clamped down firmly on irredentist propaganda about Italians still languishing under Habsburg rule. Nor could France find support elsewhere. By the 1880s a variety of economic, social, political and strategic factors drove the European powers (except Austria) to intensify their 'imperialist' activities outside Europe; and disputes over Tunis (1881) and Egypt (1882) ensured that France's relations not only with Italy but also with Britain became as cool as her relations with Germany. Finally, dynastic links between the Hohenzollerns and the Romanovs and a community of interest in suppressing Polish nationalism, still counted for much in Russo-German relations. Altogether, Germany succeeded for some 20 years after 1871 in convincing most of Europe of her conservative and pacific intentions, and France remained isolated.

Less intractable than the Franco-German estrangement, but equally permanent and sometimes threatening to combine with it, was the potential clash of Austro-Hungarian and Russian interests in southeast Europe, where a combination of misgovernment and insurgent nationalism threatened to destroy the Ottoman Empire (see page 210). Russia considered it essential to ensure that no other power achieved a position from which it could control the Straits

1a/The Dual Alliance: October 1879 *(below)* recognized the fact that Germany could never afford to let Austria-Hungary succumb to a Russian attack, but Germany, as a conservative empire with an interest in keeping Poland down still had much in common with Russia. Bismarck sympathized with Russia's efforts to consolidate its position in Bulgaria, and even exploited Germany's new role as an ally to force Austria-Hungary into line, pouring scorn on its attempts to enlist the support of Britain, Italy and Germany against Russia.

1b/Bismarck's system at its zenith: 1883 *(below)* Austria-Hungary, rebuffed by Gladstone, fell back on co-operation with Germany and Russia in the Three Emperors' Alliance (1881). But the Dual Monarchy still reinsured itself with the Triple Alliance (1882), which guaranteed Italy's neutrality in a war with Russia; while its alliances with Serbia and Romania lessened the risk of Russia exploiting Serbian and Romanian irredentism against it. The Triple Alliance was worth more to Germany, providing for Italy's assistance in the event of a French attack.

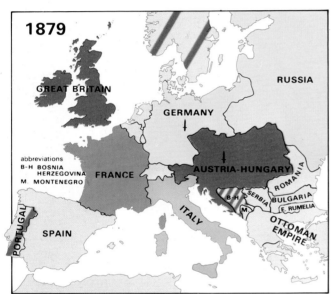

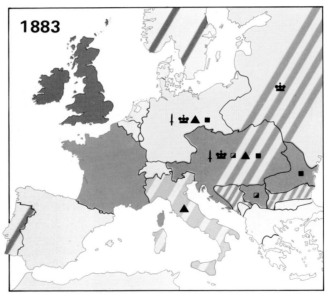

1c/The 'Mediterranean' Entente: 1887 *(below)* The Three Emperors' Alliance survived the crisis over the union of Bulgaria and E. Rumelia in 1885, but the Austro-Russian contest for control of Bulgaria (1886-7) destroyed it. Bismarck had promised the Russians his continued support in the Reinsurance Treaty, but the 'Mediterranean' agreements of Feb.-Mar. and Dec. 1887 between Britain, Italy and Austria-Hungary (Spain acceding in May), to resist supposed French and Russian designs in the Mediterranean and at the Straits, annihilated Russian influence in Bulgaria.

1d/The 'New Course' in Germany: 1891 *(below)* Italy acceded to the Austro-German-Romanian alliance in 1888, and between 1889 and 1894 Germany, with a new emperor and chancellor, swung into line behind the Mediterranean Entente. Already, before the Reinsurance Treaty was dropped after Bismarck's fall in 1890, Russo-German relations had deteriorated sharply as a result of disputes over tariffs and loans after 1887. France drew steadily closer to Russia; the first of a series of loans was concluded in 1888 and a military convention was signed in 1892.

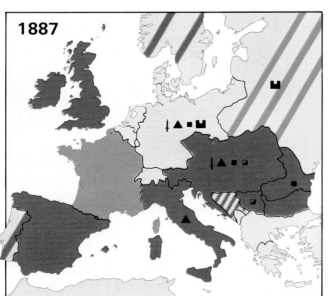

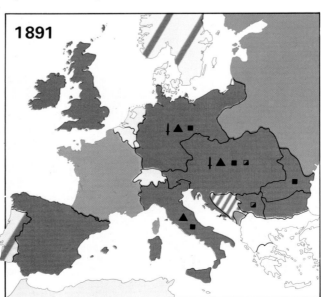

↓	Austro-German alliance 1879-1918
♛	three Emperors' alliance 1881-7
☑	Austro-Serbian alliance 1881-95
▲	triple alliance 1882-1915
■	Austro-German-Romanian alliance 1883-1916
⊔	reinsurance treaty 1887-90
○	Franco-Russian alliance 1894-1917
◆	Russo-Bulgarian military convention 1902-13

Stripes, similar and identical colours indicate an entente or community of interests.

at Constantinople, through which passed much of the grain export trade on which Russia's economy and Great Power status depended. Russia's fundamental aim was therefore defensive; but its tactics varied from trying to bolster up and influence the Ottoman government, to assisting its Christian subjects to resist in the hope of replacing the empire by a string of submissive satellites.

To Austria-Hungary, Russia's efforts to achieve security by extending its influence in the Ottoman Empire seemed dangerous and offensive, either as threatening Austria-Hungary's 'colonial' markets in the Balkans, or as portending the encirclement of the Habsburg monarchy by a crowd of irredentist states under Russian protection. Nevertheless, for most of the period the Austrians were able to achieve a conservative understanding with the Tsarist government against revolutionary nationalism in both Russia and the Ottoman Empire. But when these agreements broke down (1878, 1886, 1908) Austria-Hungary sought salvation in trying to establish its own economic and diplomatic control of the Balkan states; and in building up international coalitions to oppose Russia.

In this policy Austria-Hungary could usually count on support from the United Kingdom where many regarded Russia's interest in the Ottoman Empire as a threat to the overland and Suez routes to India, already threatened (in their view) by Russian expansion towards Persia and Afghanistan. Until the Anglo-Russian agreement of 1907 removed these fears, rivalry between the two powers in the Near East, in central Asia and, in the 1890s, in China, was perhaps the chief determinant of diplomatic relations between the island empire and the continental Powers. The Anglo-Italo-Austrian entente of 1887-97 against Russia (and France) was, as Salisbury told Queen Victoria, 'as close an alliance as the Parliamentary character of our institutions will permit'.

In the early 1890s even Germany lent her support to this combination. Already in 1887 Bismarck had increased the tariffs against Russian grain exports in order to protect the economic interests of Prussian landowners; now he ended Russia's practice of borrowing on the Berlin stock exchange the money to finance potentially threatening armaments and strategic railways. When France made the Paris bourse available instead, the foundations were laid for the Franco-Russian alliance of 1894. Germany's attempts to parry this by co-operating with Russia in the Far East after 1895 proved only partially successful; but Russia's concentration at this period on its Far Eastern interests at least allowed the Austrians to re-establish the conservative entente in 1897. By the end of the 1890s, therefore, three groups of Powers co-existed in Europe: the British Empire; its chief opponent, the Franco-Russian alliance; and the Triple Alliance (Germany, Austria-Hungary, Italy) – an unstable equilibrium which allowed for endless diplomatic manoeuvring and therefore probably favoured peace.

The dangerous simplification of alignments into a bi-polar system started with the development of German *Weltpolitik*, a challenge to all three established imperial powers, and one which convinced Great Britain in particular that Germany was out to dominate the European continent. By 1907 Great Britain had made up its differences with France and Russia, and joined with them in a Triple Entente to contain – or in Berlin's view to 'encircle' – Germany. By 1914 the Germans and their Austrian allies were deeply concerned about this 'encirclement', particularly in the Balkans, the most unstable area of Europe. The breakdown of the Austro-Russian entente when Austria-Hungary annexed Bosnia and Herzegovina in 1908, and the Balkan wars of 1912 and 1913 which replaced Turkey-in-Europe by a complex of dissatisfied and mutually antagonistic Balkan states, created a highly volatile situation, and when, in 1914, it looked as though Serbian ambitions were reopening the issue, Vienna decided that it was now or never. When Berlin, impelled by the fear of 'encirclement', decided to support Vienna far beyond the terms of the defensive alliance of 1879, the fuse was lit which exploded in the First World War.

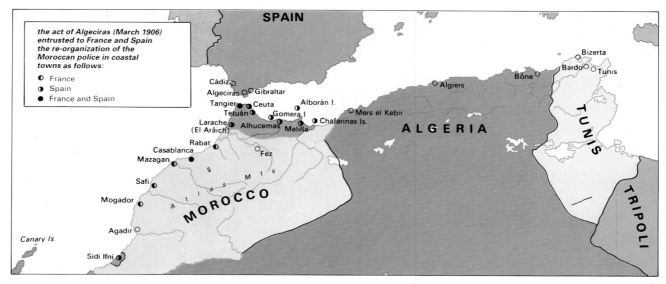

2/The balance of power in Morocco (above) By agreements with Italy, Great Britain and Spain (1902-4), France prepared to extend its influence in Morocco. German objections to French encroachments between 1905 and 1912 were important in encouraging the British government to strengthen its ties with France to prevent Germany overthrowing the European balance of power.

the act of Algeciras (March 1906) entrusted to France and Spain the re-organization of the Moroccan police in coastal towns as follows:
◐ France
◑ Spain
● France and Spain

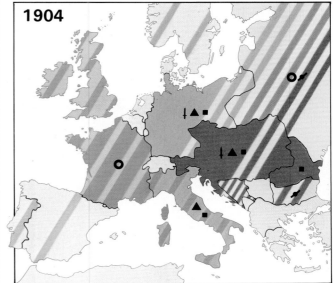

The Dreadnought battleships of the Royal Navy (right) in review off Portsmouth in 1911, guaranteed Britain from invasion at home and defended access to her empire abroad. The British government aimed at a 'two-power standard': a total naval strength equal to that of her two closest rivals.

1e/The Austro-Russian Entente: 1897 (below) The Germans now abandoned the 'New Course', ceasing to underwrite Austria-Hungary in the Balkans and co-operating in the Far East with Russia and France. Britain, after the Armenian massacres, refused to promise to fight for the Sultan. Austria-Hungary, torn by domestic strife, and with its Balkan alliances in decay, settled for an entente with Russia to put Balkan problems 'on ice' (1897). Russia still improved its position in Bulgaria, signing a military convention (1902); and in Serbia, after a coup by nationalist army officers in 1903.

1f/The Anglo-French Entente: 1904 (below) By 1902 France – partly to weaken the Triple Alliance – had settled the 20-year dispute with Italy; in 1904 it reached agreements about Egypt and Morocco with Britain. Meanwhile, Russia and Austria-Hungary extended their entente. Germany's clumsy efforts to exploit Russia's embarrassments over Japan in order to renew formal ties with St Petersburg and to browbeat France out of recent agreements with Britain failed; the Anglo-French link was even strengthened when Russia settled its own extra-European disputes with Britain in 1907.

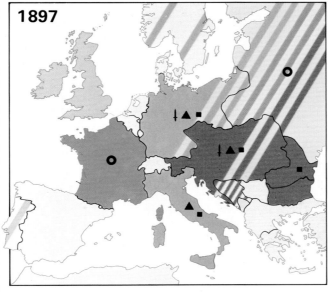

1897

1g/Europe after the Bosnian crisis: 1909 (below) Between the Moroccan crises of 1905-6 and 1911, Anglo-German relations, complicated by the naval issue, reached their nadir. Friction between Russia and Austria-Hungary over the Austro-Serbian 'Pig War' (1906-11), the Sanjak railway project and the annexation of Bosnia and Herzegovina put an end to the entente of 1897 and severely strained Russo-German relations (although the Potsdam agreement over Persia and the Baghdad railway in Nov. 1910 showed that the German 'wire to St Petersburg' had not been broken).

1h/Europe on the eve of war: 1914 (below) Between 1911 and 1914 the fronts between Triple Alliance and Triple Entente hardened, the grudging attitude of the latter towards Italy's ambitions in Tripoli and Albania helping restore links between Italy and her allies. In 1912-13 Austria-Hungary watched in alarm while a Russian-sponsored Balkan League expelled the Turks from Europe. The Austro-Romanian alliance was a dead letter. Although there were signs of Anglo-German co-operation on Balkan and colonial issues, Russo-German relations deteriorated sharply.

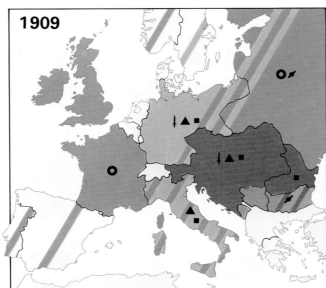

1909

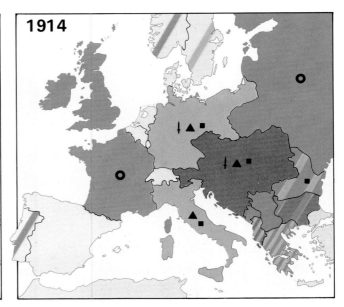

1914

The First World War 1914 to 1918

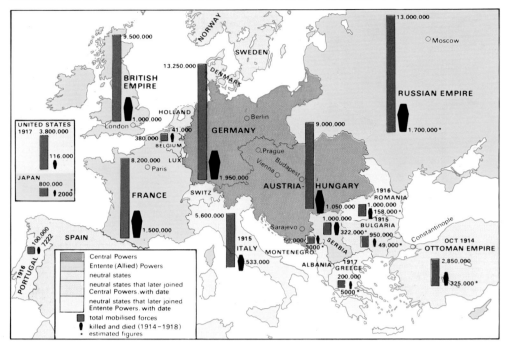

1/The line-up of the Powers *(above)* By 1914 the European powers were already divided into two rival camps (see page 247). After the outbreak of war both groups sought allies. Germany and Austria-Hungary were joined by Turkey and Bulgaria. Russia, France and Great Britain sought and gained the support of Japan, Italy, Romania and, after a long struggle, Greece. By far the most important adherent to the Allied cause was the United States, which declared war on Germany on 6 April 1917. In Europe, the price in terms of human life and material destruction changed people's conception of war; it is estimated that over 8 million combatants were killed.

2/The German attack in the west and the battle of the Marne *(left)* 1 Germans invaded Belgium, successfully taking Liège on 16 August; the French offensive in Alsace was defeated with heavy loss. 2 A further French offensive towards the Ardennes was defeated, and the British and one French army were forced to retreat from the Mons area to avoid encirclement. 3 The Germans were too weak to go west of Paris as they planned and passed northeast of the city to cross the Marne. 4 The exposed German army north of Paris was attacked by the French army on 5 September, and in manoeuvring to oppose the French attack left a gap on its own eastern flank. 5 British and French forces advanced into the gap. 6 The German army retired to the Aisne to regroup.

THE war which began in August 1914 – to contemporaries the 'Great War' – marked the end of one period of history and the beginning of another. Starting as a European war, it turned in 1917 into a world war, and thus can be seen as a bridge between the age of European predominance and the age of global politics. The spark that triggered it off was the assassination of the Austrian heir-presumptive, Archduke Franz Ferdinand, by Bosnian terrorists at Sarajevo on 28 June 1914. In the ensuing crisis, since none of the powers was prepared to accept diplomatic defeat, war replaced diplomatic manoeuvre.

Many expected a short war, over by Christmas 1914. The Germans knew that their chances in a long war on two fronts were slender. Their war plan, drawn up by Schlieffen in 1905, was to trap and annihilate the French army by a great encircling movement through Belgium, before the Russians had time to mobilize. But the Russians mobilized unexpectedly quickly, invaded East Prussia, defeated the German 8th Army at Gumbinnen (20 August), and drew off German reserves from the west. The Germans managed to defeat the Russian invasion at Tannenberg (26–29 August), but were not strong enough to exploit their victory. In the west the Allies outmanoeuvred the Germans in the Battle of the Marne (see map 2), 5–8 September. The Schlieffen Plan was always a gamble; when it failed the Germans had no alternative strategy. On 8–12 September the Russians won a crushing victory over Austria at Lemberg. A last, mutual, attempt by the German and Allied armies to outflank each other in Flanders failed in November, and both sides dug in on a line 400 miles (644 km) long from the Channel to the

At the Krupp munitions factory in Essen *(below)* women took over tasks traditionally performed by men, such as filling shells with shrapnel.

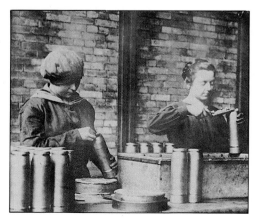

Swiss frontier. In the east, mobile warfare was still possible because of the far lower density of men and guns – a possibility brilliantly exploited by the Germans at Gorlice-Tarnow in 1915, and by the Russian general Brusilov in 1916.

In the west, from the beginning of 1915 the dominant factors became trenches, barbed wire, artillery, machine-guns and mud. The war of mobility gave way to a war of attrition. One entrenched man with a machine-gun was more than a match for 100 advancing across open country. Railways could bring up defenders faster than slowly moving troops could advance into the front-line gaps which they had created at such high human cost.

Yet the German occupation of Belgium and northern France made it inevitable that the Allies should seek to expel them. This meant repeated French offensives in Artois and Champagne in 1915, assisted by small British offensives at Neuve Chapelle and Loos. For 1916 the Allies planned a joint offensive on the Somme, but the Germans struck first, at Verdun, with the intention of bleeding the French army to death. Casualties ran to over 700,000. On 1 July 1916, the British launched their first mass offensive of the war, on the Somme. The fighting lasted until November and casualties reached at least 1 million. It failed to break the stalemate.

By now the conflict was becoming a total war demanding mobilization of industry, carried out in Germany by Rathenau and in Britain by Lloyd George. Answers to the trench stalemate were sought in technology: poison gas was first used by the Germans at Bolinów in January 1915; the British invented the tank and fielded 36 of them in the Somme battle but due to manufacturing difficulties it was only in November 1917, at Cambrai, that the first mass tank attack took place – also proving indecisive.

The struggle spread to the skies, where the handful of reconnaissance aircraft of 1914 gave place to fighters, bombers and artillery-spotters. With the Zeppelin airship and the Gotha long-range bomber the Germans introduced strategic bombing of enemy towns. Using naval blockades the Allies sought to starve the industries and

peoples of the Central Powers; Germany riposted by U-boat attacks on British shipping.

Confronted by failure in the west, the Allies sought successes on other fronts: the Dardanelles (April 1915 – January 1916); an offensive in Mesopotamia against the Turks; a landing at Salonika to help the Serbs. All ended in failure or stalemate. Italy, which entered the war on the Allied side on 23 May 1915, likewise failed to break the Austrian front on the Isonzo.

The Eastern Front, too, produced no decision, despite the German–Austrian offensive at Gorlice-Tarnow in 1915 and a far-reaching Russian advance under Brusilov in 1916. Serbian resistance was crushed, but the Germans were now embedded in the prolonged two-front war they had dreaded. By the end of 1916 all the combatants recognized that victory was far off. There were peace feelers, but annexationist demands and secret treaties ruled out a compromise peace. The war went on under new and ruthless leaders: the soldiers Hindenburg and Ludendorff in Germany, the civilians Lloyd George in Britain and later Clemenceau in France. On 1 February 1917 Germany declared unrestricted U-boat warfare, in the hope of bringing Britain to her knees. This was narrowly averted by the introduction of the convoy system in May 1917. But the U-boat offensive brought the United States into the war on 6 April 1917 – a potentially decisive help to the Allies.

In March, revolution broke out in Russia, sparked by heavy losses, war-weariness and economic dislocation. On 15 March 1917 the Tsar abdicated: the future of Russia as an ally lay in doubt. By May France was in deep trouble too. An offensive by the new Commander-in-Chief, Nivelle, failed to achieve his promised object of a breakthrough leading to peace. Mutinies swept the French army with parallel civilian

The naval war *(below)* After the Battle of Jutland (1916) both sides used naval means to cut the other's supply lines. In reply to a British instituted open blockade of the Central Powers, the Germans resorted to unrestricted submarine warfare in February 1917 and one out of every four ships leaving British ports was sunk.

Allied shipping losses 1914-18 (tons)

Britain 7.800.000
France 900.000
Italy 872.000
U.S. (while neutral) 56.000
(while belligerent) 397.000
Greece 346.000
Russia 183.000

Key to maps 2 and 3

→ major Central Powers offensives
➤ major Allied offensives
✴ battles
✴ battles costing over 250.000 killed
⚓ naval mutinies
army mutinies
▼ food riots
⚓ naval bases
major naval battles
German raids on English coast

All battles, offensives, mutinies, etc., coloured according to year

1914	1917
1915	1918
1916	

farthest German advance in West, 1914
the trench line, November 1914
farthest Russian advance in east, 1914-15
Russian front, November 1915
territory held by Central Powers, December 1917 (close in the west to the 'Hindenburg Line')
front line at time of Brest Litovsk armistice between Germany and Russia, December 1917
German penetration of Russia, March 1918
armistice line in West, November 1918
railways

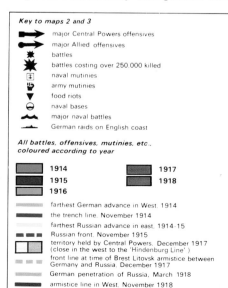

unrest on the home front. The British planned an offensive at Ypres as the best means of keeping German pressure off the French and encouraging Russia. The 'Passchendaele' offensive, dogged by bad weather, failed to break the German front; each side suffered some 250,000 casualties.

In November 1917 the Bolsheviks seized power in Russia (see page 254) and in December sued for peace at Brest-Litovsk. At last the Germans could concentrate the bulk of their strength on the Western Front. On 21 March 1918 Hindenburg and Ludendorff launched a series of offensives aimed at victory in the west before the Americans could arrive in strength. They failed, despite impressive initial success. On 18 July the new Allied *generalissimo*, Foch, launched a French counterstroke. On 8 August Haig followed with a brilliant success near Amiens. From then on the Allies hammered the enemy without respite, breaking the Hindenburg Line on 27–30 September. Meanwhile Germany's allies, Austria, Turkey and Bulgaria were beginning to collapse under Allied offensives. On 29 September Ludendorff acknowledged defeat and urged his government to ask for an immediate armistice. In October the German fleet mutinied; revolution and abdication of the Kaiser followed, and the new German government accepted the Allies' armistice

terms. Fighting ceased on 11 November 1918. The material and human cost of the war had been immense; the political and social consequences were enormous, including the dismantlement of the Ottoman and Hapsburg empires and civil war in Russia. The Europe of 1914 had vanished.

4/The war in the Middle East *(right)* The war was not confined to Europe. In order to protect the Persian wells an Anglo-Indian force occupied Basra (22 Nov. 1914), and marched on Baghdad (Oct. 1915); they were forced to retreat and surrendered to the Turks at Kut (April 1916). Meanwhile, the British had repelled a Turkish attempt to cross the Suez Canal (1915), and a counter-offensive force entered Palestine in 1916. Here they were assisted by the British-sponsored Arab revolt against Ottoman rule, which broke out in June 1916 under Sherif Hussein of Mecca, but they were checked by the Turks at Gaza in 1917. To the north, the Russians occupied Turkish Armenia (July 1916), and held it until the Russian revolution restored initiative to the Ottomans. In autumn 1917, British forces under General Allenby rallied, and pushed through Gaza to Jerusalem (11 Dec.). In Mesopotamia Kut was retaken, and Baghdad was finally captured (10 March 1917); Mosul was occupied shortly after the Anglo-Turkish Armistice (20 Oct. 1918), while Damascus had fallen to British and Arab troops at the beginning of the same month.

The war spilled over into Africa and the Far East where Germany quickly lost its colonial possessions (see page 240). The South Africans conquered German South-West Africa in July 1915; the British and French took the Cameroons and Togoland. In German East Africa the British had a far more difficult task because of the determined German defence under General von Lettow-Vorbeck. In the Pacific, Australian, New Zealand and Japanese troops captured the German colonies within four months of the outbreak of war, and the concessions in China also fell to Japanese and British forces.

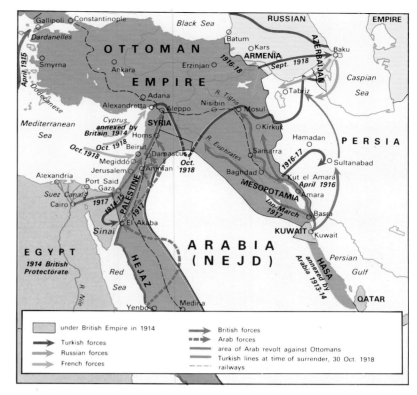

3/The Great War in Europe *(below)* On the Western Front only the opening and closing stages (see map 2) saw a war of movement. From late 1914 to spring 1918 the superiority of defence based on trench-systems and machine-guns over slow-moving offensives by infantry, preceded by the fire of immense concentrations of artillery, imposed a stalemate. Only when armies had been weakened by years of attrition did sweeping advances again become possible. In Eastern Europe and the Balkans, with a lower density of manpower and weaker defences, the war was more mobile. However the Italian front along the River Isonzo saw another stalemate, despite 11 Italian offensives against the Austrians, until, the German-Austrian victory at Caporetto in October 1917 and the Italian victory at Vittorio Veneto a year later.

THE date at which the European age gave way to the age of global civilization is a matter of debate. Some historians have picked out 1917 as a year of destiny. Others have seen 1947, the year of Indian independence, and 1949, the year of the Chinese revolution, as decisive turning points. The United States' declaration of war in 1917 turned a European conflict into a world war while the Bolshevik revolution in Russia, challenging the existing social and political order, split the world into two conflicting ideological camps; the independence of India and the revolution in China symbolized the resurgence of Asia and the gathering revolt against the West. All were important historical events; but a single world economy existed even earlier, and the rise of the United States to world power between 1867 and 1917 was an omen of things to come.

Today it is obvious that we live in a post-European age. By making the whole world one, the European powers stirred up forces which spelled their own eclipse. The world wars between 1914 and 1945 whittled away the resources of the European powers, and only the healing of the wounds, symbolized by the formation of the European Economic Community in 1957, restored their fortunes. Europe's exhaustion after 1945 benefitted the Soviet Union and the United States, the two superpowers on the eastern and western flanks, whose rivalry produced an age of bipolarity. But bipolarity too proved to be a temporary phenomenon. The recovery of Europe, the emancipation of Asia and Africa, the rise of Japan, and finally the collapse of the Soviet empire brought a new constellation into being, and with it the threat of a confrontation between rich nations and poor nations, and of the exhaustion of global resources through overpopulation. No one can foretell the shape of things to come. All this section can do is to show, in historical perspective, how the world changed during the past 60 years, and to chart the emergence of significant new factors.

7 The age of

The Statue of Liberty and World Trade Center, New York

global civilization

The formation of a world economy 1870 to 1914

Ο NE of the main developments of the period between 1870 and 1914 was the integration of the world's economy into a single interdependent whole, to an extent inconceivable in earlier ages. The focus of this process was Europe, with the United States as a subsidiary centre, and it was from there that the impulses went out which opened up the remaining landmasses of the globe to European exploration and penetration, as well as linking the continents, settled and unsettled, colonial and independent, with the industrial and commercial capitalism which had already conquered most of Europe and North America.

Three closely interrelated aspects of this process are illustrated here. One was the development of means of communication, with railways and shipping predominating, but canals, river navigation and roads also playing a significant part in some areas of the globe. The basic technical problems of railways had been solved well before 1870, though improvements in speed, capacity, safety, reliability and comfort were continuously implemented afterwards. Yet at that date they were limited almost wholly to Europe and the United States, and even there complete networks existed only in northwest Europe and in the eastern states of the USA: the first United States 'transcontinental' link between the Pacific and Atlantic oceans had been forged only in 1869, though others were to follow in 1881, 1883 and 1893. In 1870, Europe had 60,400 miles (97,250 km) of track open, the United States and Canada 56,300 miles (90,643 km), and the rest of the world 9100 miles (14,650 km) – most of it built by European or North American engineers. By 1911 the world's network of tracks had increased to 657,000 miles (1.06 million km), the areas outside Europe, the United States and Canada now accounting for 175,000 miles (281,750 km). Among the most striking achievements were the completion of transcontinental lines in Canada (1886), in Russia to the Pacific coast at Vladivostok (1904) and in South America, across the Andes, in 1910. Railways also breached many other mountain barriers which had hitherto inhibited traffic flows between adjacent countries: the main lines and tunnels across the Alps are illustrated in map 2. Yet despite relatively rapid growth, the rest of the world's railways still largely consisted of single trunk lines instead of the dense network of the industrial countries. This reflected the differing role of the railways in regions outside Europe and North America, where they were often built primarily as strategic lines, or as a means of tapping certain exportable primary products, rather than as an integral part of an industrialized community.

The expansion of world shipping was equally striking. It was in fact greater than the statistics indicate, as in 1870 most of the world's tonnage, apart from the British, still consisted of sailing vessels, whereas by 1913 it was composed mostly of steamers. Because of the higher speed and greater regularity obtainable in powered ships, one steam ton was generally reckoned to be the equivalent of four sailing tons, while steamers themselves greatly increased in speed and efficiency. For passengers, comfort and safety also improved. The diagram (far right) contrasts the conditions and amenities available in an earlier passenger liner with those in one of the finest vessels of the immediate pre-war years. Such developments largely removed the hardships of the crossing, which once held back emigration except among the poor and desperate, for the millions who now flocked to North and South America, while for first-class passengers crossings on regular liners became indulgences of luxury. Again, the main shipping traffic was to be found among the advanced countries and the white dominions, or between them and their producers of raw materials. The traffic among

the latter had grown very little.

Canals were also built in this period, particularly in Europe. The most significant for world trade were the ship canals that broke through important land barriers: the Suez Canal, completed in 1869, carried 437,000 net register tons in 1870 and 20,034,000 net tons in 1913; the Panama Canal, opened in August 1914, carried 4,900,000 tons (5,000,000 t) of cargo in its first year. The savings in distance achieved by these two canals were especially great for the journeys from Europe to India, and for the routes between the east and west coasts of the United States.

Developments in transport reflected the concurrent developments in trade. Foreign trade, as a proportion of world output, increased from 3 per cent to 33 per cent between 1800 and 1913. It tripled in volume between 1870 and 1914, and again was concentrated on the links among the industrialized countries, or between them and their suppliers of primary materials, and the varied markets now opening up for their manufactures: only 11 per cent of the world's trade was carried on among the primary producers themselves in 1913. Among industrial nations, trade permitted specialization, with some advantages to consumers' choice and a very considerable contribution to furthering large-scale production. But trade between them and the primary producers was of a different nature. While in a sense it opened up the latter to western influences, it was not in any way directed by them, nor did it reflect their needs, except accidentally. The initiative came from entrepreneurs in the West, looking for markets, food and raw materials.

The operation of a single multi-national system of world trade, pivoting on London, was facilitated by the adoption of a gold standard for the currencies of the chief European nations between 1863 and 1874. It was also intimately connected with the third type of international

SUEZ CANAL

London	via Cape 10,667 nautical miles / via Suez 6,274 nautical miles	41% saved	Bombay
London	via Cape 11,900 nautical miles / via Suez 8,083 nautical miles	32% saved	Calcutta
London	via Cape 11,740 nautical miles / via Suez 8,362 nautical miles	29% saved	Singapore
London	via Cape 13,180 nautical miles / via Suez 9,799 nautical miles	26% saved	Hong Kong

PANAMA CANAL

Liverpool	via Magellan 13,502 nautical miles / via Panama 7,836 nautical miles	42% saved	San Francisco
New York	via Magellan 13,135 nautical miles / via Panama 5,262 nt mls	60% saved	San Francisco
Liverpool	via Magellan 8,747 nautical miles / via Panama 7,207 nautical miles	18% saved	Valparaiso
New York	via Magellan 8,385 nautical miles / via Panama 4,633 nautical miles	45% saved	Valparaiso
New York	via Magellan 16,579 nautical miles / via Panama 11,530 nautical miles	30% saved	Hong Kong
New York	via Magellan 13,000 nautical miles / via Panama 9,332 nautical miles	29% saved	Sydney

Suez and Panama (*above*) Not until the advent of the commercial aeroplane was the world again so significantly shrunk as by the opening of these two great canals.

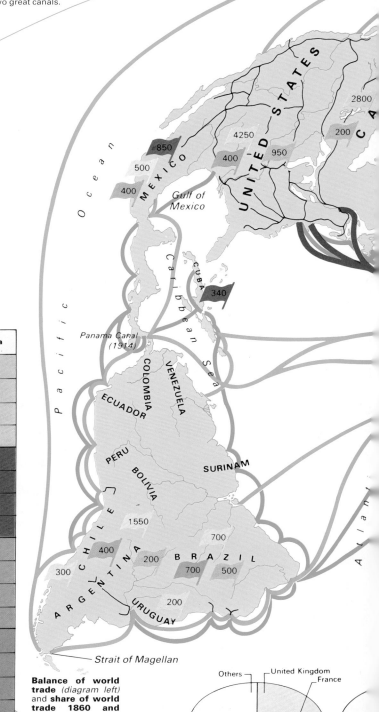

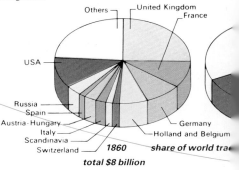

Balance of world trade (*diagram left*) **and share of world trade 1860 and 1913** (*diagram right*) Great Britain was the world's biggest trading nation in 1860 but by 1913 Germany had twice the exports to Europe, and America was catching up just as fast. British, Dutch and French networks were still predominant in the wider world.

		Europe	N. America	S. America	Asia	Africa
UNITED KINGDOM	imports 1860	419	252	96	143	80
	exports 1860	358	132	74	139	36
	imports 1913	1548	848	393	458	220
	exports 1913	917	265	272	620	248
USA	imports 1860	217	—	80	29	—
	exports 1860	249	—	46	11	—
	imports 1913	893	199	381	298	26
	exports 1913	1479	469	294	140	29
FRANCE	imports 1860	234	47	41	16	34
	exports 1860	293	49	53	3	45
	imports 1913	880	187	183	192	148
	exports 1913	937	89	94	36	181
HOLLAND	imports 1860	92	5	3	32	—
	exports 1860	87	2	1	14	—
	imports 1913	624	190	87	274	14
	exports 1913	1131	57	9	73	14
GERMANY	imports 1913	1402	423	290	250	118
	exports 1913	1828	184	183	130	50
RUSSIA	imports 1913	556	—	—	—	—
	exports 1913	719	—	—	—	—

figures in million dollars US

linkage shown here: foreign investment. Normally flowing from more advanced to poorer regions, the transfer of capital had earlier in the 19th century been largely a European and North American phenomenon, and much of it remained so until 1914. In this setting, the process undoubtedly assisted and speeded economic advancement, especially when devoted to building up the costly infrastructure, such as railways and other public works, for developing nations which could then ultimately repay their international debts. But increasingly, as these investments flowed into non-industrial regions of Europe such as Russia, the Balkan countries and the Ottoman Empire, and then to overseas territories which lacked both the knowledge and the power to direct the capital flow, it did not help to develop them, but rather to colonize them, often destroying existing native industry. Loans made to governments, or to enterprises guaranteed by government, as many inevitably were, raised serious questions of political control; and as

rival European powers fought for concessions and controls in overseas areas, the rivalries and conflicts engendered thereby became part of the drive to imperialism and to war.

Britain was the largest source of foreign investment, and London a highly important centre of banking. British overseas assets in 1914 totalled nearly £4000 million. France and Germany were the other chief lenders, but the total foreign investments of France, Germany, Belgium, Holland and the United States put together amounted to less than £5500 million. The United States and Russia were still, in fact, net borrowers of foreign capital.

Closely associated with the movement of capital was the large-scale migration of labour illustrated on page 204.

2/Alpine tunnels and railways *(right)* Only two rail routes pierced the Alps in 1870, but in the next 41 years they were joined by another ten, many of them involving feats of tunnel-building and civil engineering on an unprecedented scale.

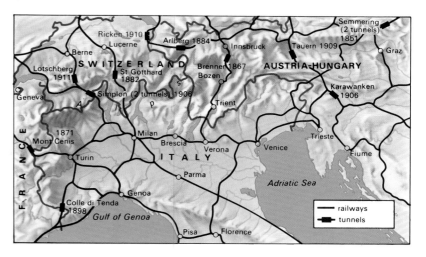

1/The development of the world economy *(below)* Between 1870 and 1914 the whole world became closely connected by an intricate web of transport routes, communication channels, trading relationships and financial flows. The major benefits, however, remained concentrated where the network was at its most dense – among the industrial nations of Europe and North America.

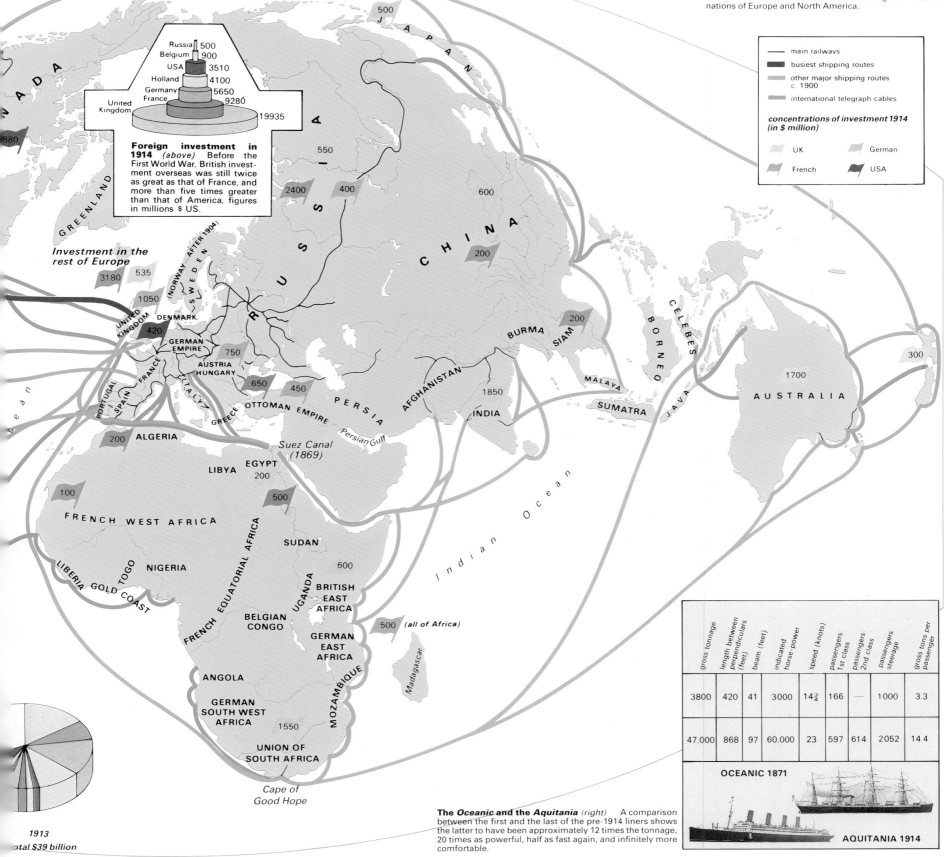

Foreign investment in 1914 *(above)* Before the First World War, British investment overseas was still twice as great as that of France, and more than five times greater than that of America, figures in millions $ US.

| main railways |
| busiest shipping routes |
| other major shipping routes c 1900 |
| international telegraph cables |

concentrations of investment 1914 (in $ million)

| UK | German |
| French | USA |

Investment in the rest of Europe

	gross tonnage	length between perpendiculars (feet)	beam (feet)	indicated horse-power	speed (knots)	passengers, 1st class	passengers, 2nd class	passengers, steerage	gross tons per passenger
OCEANIC 1871	3800	420	41	3000	14¾	166	—	1000	3.3
AQUITANIA 1914	47,000	868	97	60,000	23	597	614	2052	14.4

The *Oceanic* and the *Aquitania* *(right)* A comparison between the first and the last of the pre-1914 liners shows the latter to have been approximately 12 times the tonnage, 20 times as powerful, half as fast again, and infinitely more comfortable.

1913 Total $39 billion

The Russian Revolution
1917 to 1929

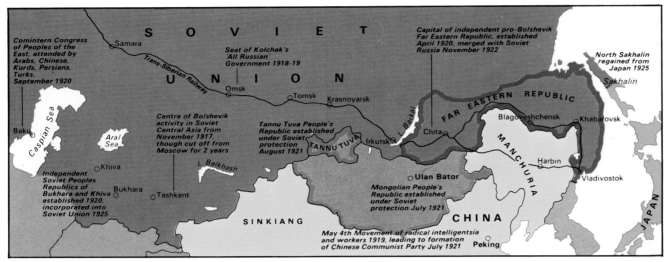

3/Red Star over Asia (left) '... the east has been definitely drawn into the revolutionary movement ... In the last analysis, the outcome of the struggle will be determined by the fact that Russia, India, China, etc. account for the overwhelming majority of the population of the globe.' (from Lenin's last article, March 1923). As the prospects of revolution dimmed in the west, Lenin looked eastwards to the countries colonized by the great powers. Here the struggle for national independence might be combined with the fight for socialism. Victory, though perhaps far off, would fatally weaken the capitalist world.

Architect of revolution (*left*) From its foundation in 1903, Lenin dominated the Bolshevik party. His combination of theoretical originality, political decisiveness and passionate dedication to the socialist cause made him the greatest revolutionary leader of modern times. Trotsky (*bottom right of picture*), the only other Bolshevik whose stature approached Lenin's during the revolution and civil war, himself acknowledged that without Lenin the Bolshevik revolution would have been impossible.

2/Red Star over Europe (*below*) 'If we come out now, we shall have all proletarian Europe on our side.' (Lenin, October 1917). The Bolsheviks seized power firmly convinced that socialist revolution was imminent in advanced western countries. These, they believed, would come to the aid of backward Russia. At first events in central and eastern Europe seemed to justify their optimism. By 1921, however, revolution was on the retreat, and Soviet Russia isolated.

NO SINGLE event has had such decisive impact upon the modern world as the Russian Revolution of 1917. It opened a new epoch in Russia's history, transforming an underdeveloped country into an industrial and military superpower, and fundamentally altering the pattern of international relations. Above all, it inaugurated the age of modern revolutions. By showing that Marxists could gain power and begin the construction of a socialist society, the Bolsheviks inspired revolutionaries everywhere.

By February 1917 the strain of war had fatally weakened the Tsarist government. Liberals, socialists, businessmen, generals, nobles – all were plotting its overthrow. Yet the disturbances in Petrograd (formerly St Petersburg) which, in four days destroyed the regime, owed little to organized opposition. Sheer hunger turned wage demands into a general strike and bread queues into anti-government demonstrations. Ordered to disperse the crowds, the garrison mutinied. Nicholas II set out for the capital from his military headquarters at Mogilev, but was prevented from arriving by railway workers. On 15 March at Pskov he abdicated. Authority now passed to a provisional government established by prominent *duma* (parliament) politicians. But its power was limited by the existence of the Petrograd Soviet (or Council) of Workers' and Soldiers' Deputies. The latter, to whom the Soviets throughout Russia looked for leadership, constituted an alternative government. At first, however, the instability of 'dual power' was not apparent. The Soviet's moderate Menshevik and Socialist–Revolutionary leaders supported the government, and in May entered it. Even the Bolsheviks initially gave their qualified support.

Their policy was dramatically reversed in April when Lenin returned to Petrograd. All Europe, he declared, was on the brink of socialist revolution. Marxists should therefore destroy the Provisional Government and transfer all power to the Soviets. The government, struggling to maintain order, was faced with outright opposition. As the war dragged on, the desire for peace spread and desertions from the army escalated. Impatient with official procrastination over agrarian reform, the peasants began to seize land. Urban workers became increasingly militant. A popular uprising (the 'July Days') followed the army's disastrous June offensive. Ordinary people were looking for alternative solutions and support grew for the Bolsheviks, with their promise of 'peace, bread and land'. In September they won control of the Petrograd and Moscow Soviets, and in October gained a majority at the Second All-Russian Congress of Soviets. Yet a threat also came from the Right. In September the Commander-in-Chief, General Kornilov, marched on the capital determined to restore order, only to be abandoned by his troops. Two months later, on 25 October (7 November by the new calendar introduced in

early 1918), the Bolsheviks struck. They seized strategic points in Petrograd, arrested the Provisional Government and assumed power. Few thought they could retain it. Even the Bolsheviks believed only revolution in western Europe could guarantee survival. When Germany demanded humiliating territorial concessions in return for peace, a majority wanted to fight on, however hopelessly. Nevertheless, Lenin's determination to gain time prevailed, and the Treaty of Brest-Litovsk was signed in March 1918. Almost immediately, White Russian armies, assisted by foreign powers, attacked the young Soviet republic. After three years of brutal civil war, the Bolsheviks emerged victorious – but at enormous cost. Some 13 million people perished in the war and subsequent famine; the economy was shattered; money lost significance and was replaced by barter which, combined with an attempt at state direction of the economy, was dignified (after the event) by the title 'War Communism'. In the battle with counter-revolution, democracy vanished, the dictatorial power of the Communist Party replaced rule by Soviets in all but name. As the civil war ended, strikes and riots broke out, culminating in mutiny at the Kronstadt naval base in February 1921. The regime ruthlessly suppressed rebellion. Economic concessions, however, were granted. In March 1921, Lenin announced the New Economic Policy (NEP). Food requisitioning was replaced by a tax in kind, with peasants allowed to sell surplus produce on the free market. Private firms were freed from government control and retail trade largely returned to private hands. Yet the state retained control of the economy's 'commanding heights': heavy industry, banking and finance, and foreign trade.

By the mid-1920s, under the NEP, pre-war levels of agricultural and industrial production were all but regained. The more relaxed atmosphere domestically was accompanied by the resumption of relations with the outside world. A trade agreement with Britain in 1921 was followed by the Rapallo Treaty of 1922 with Germany and by diplomatic recognition in 1924 (the year which saw the creation of the USSR) from Britain and France among others.

This temporary stability was soon under threat, however. Was the NEP a pause before the renewal of the socialist offensive, or a long-term programme for acquiring the economic preconditions for socialism? Lenin provided no answer before his death in January 1924. During the struggle for the succession, two distinct lines emerged: Trotsky's policy of encouraging revolution abroad and industrializing rapidly at home, and Stalin's strategy of gradual economic growth plus recognition of capitalism's temporary stabilization – 'permanent revolution' versus 'socialism in one country'. Labelled an extremist, Trotsky had, by 1925, been edged out of high government office. Within a few years Stalin (who had become General Secretary in 1922) gained absolute control.

The failure of the government to procure adequate supplies of food from the peasantry threatened the towns with famine as well as jeopardizing Bolshevik power and the socialist revolution. By exploiting the image of isolation at home and abroad, in 1929 Stalin embarked on forced collectivization of agriculture and rapid industrialization, and thus initiated a new era in the Soviet revolution.

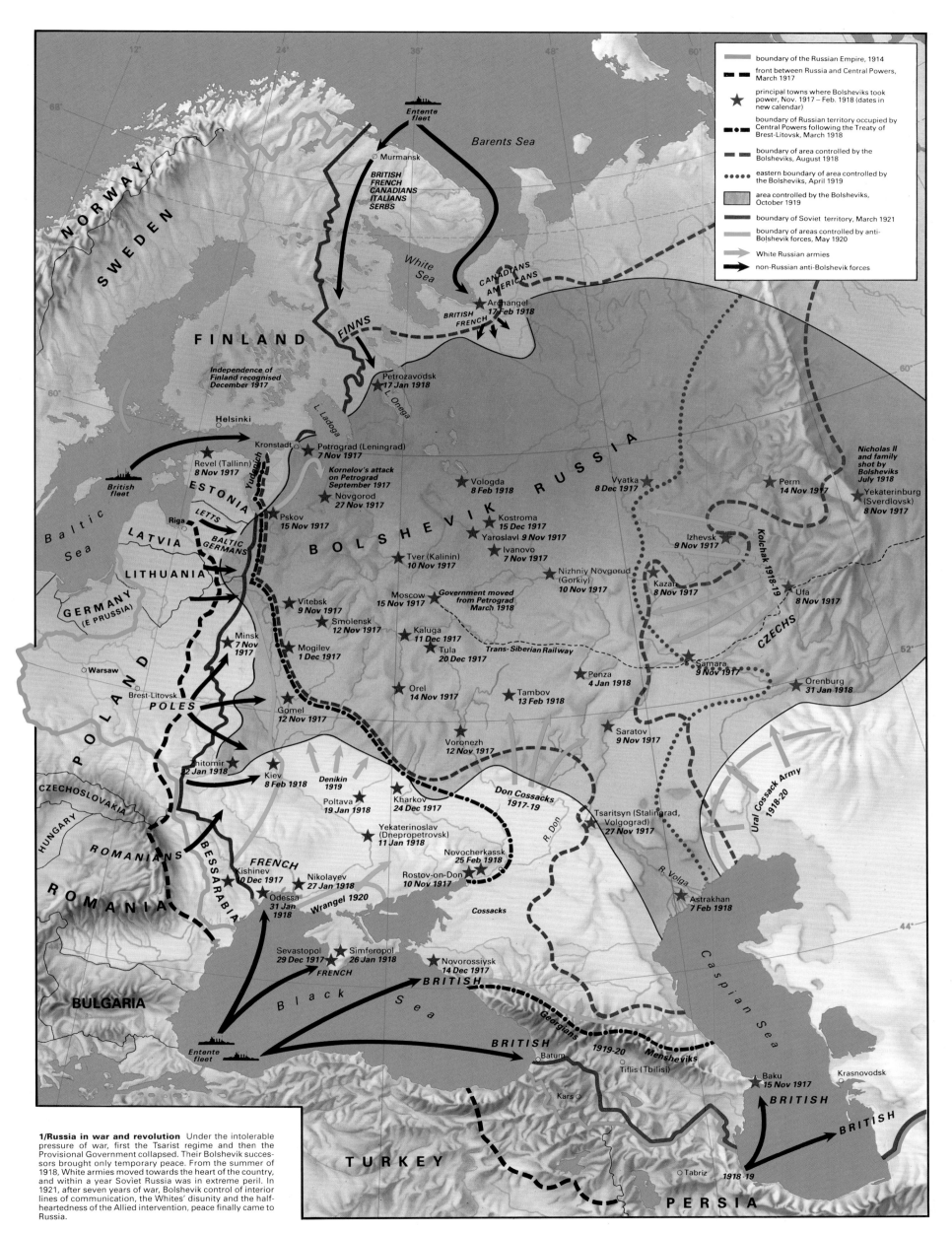

Legend:

- boundary of the Russian Empire, 1914
- front between Russia and Central Powers, March 1917
- ★ principal towns where Bolsheviks took power, Nov. 1917 – Feb. 1918 (dates in new calendar)
- boundary of Russian territory occupied by Central Powers following the Treaty of Brest-Litovsk, March 1918
- boundary of area controlled by the Bolsheviks, August 1918
- eastern boundary of area controlled by the Bolsheviks, April 1919
- area controlled by the Bolsheviks, October 1919
- boundary of Soviet territory, March 1921
- boundary of areas controlled by anti-Bolshevik forces, May 1920
- → White Russian armies
- ➜ non-Russian anti-Bolshevik forces

Map labels:

NORWAY · SWEDEN · FINLAND · Barents Sea · White Sea · Entente fleet · Murmansk

BRITISH FRENCH CANADIANS ITALIANS SERBS

CANADIANS AMERICANS · Archangel 17 Feb 1918 · BRITISH FRENCH

FINNS · Independence of Finland recognised December 1917 · Petrozavodsk 17 Jan 1918 · L. Ladoga · L. Onega

Helsinki · Kronstadt · Petrograd (Leningrad) 7 Nov 1917 · Kornelov's attack on Petrograd September 1917 · Vologda 8 Feb 1918 · Vyatka 8 Dec 1917 · Perm 14 Nov 1917

Nicholas II and family shot by Bolsheviks July 1918 · Yekaterinburg (Sverdlovsk) 8 Nov 1917

British fleet · Revel (Tallinn) 8 Nov 1917 · ESTONIA · Novgorod 27 Nov 1917 · Kostroma 15 Dec 1917 · Yaroslavl 9 Nov 1917 · Izhevsk 9 Nov 1917 · Kolchak 1918-19

BOLSHEVIK RUSSIA

Baltic Sea · Riga · LETTS · LATVIA · Pskov 15 Nov 1917 · BALTIC GERMANS · Yudenich · Tver (Kalinin) 10 Nov 1917 · Ivanovo 7 Nov 1917 · Nizhniy Novgorod (Gorkiy) 10 Nov 1917 · Kazan 8 Nov 1917 · Ufa 8 Nov 1917 · CZECHS

LITHUANIA · Vitebsk 9 Nov 1917 · Moscow 15 Nov 1917 · Government moved from Petrograd March 1918 · Smolensk 12 Nov 1917 · Samara 9 Nov 1917

GERMANY (E PRUSSIA) · Minsk 7 Nov 1917 · Mogilev 1 Dec 1917 · Kaluga 11 Dec 1917 · Tula 20 Dec 1917 · Trans-Siberian Railway · Penza 4 Jan 1918 · Orenburg 31 Jan 1918

Warsaw · POLAND · Brest-Litovsk · POLES · Gomel 12 Nov 1917 · Orel 14 Nov 1917 · Tambov 13 Feb 1918 · Saratov 9 Nov 1917

CZECHOSLOVAKIA · Zhitomir 12 Jan 1918 · Kiev 8 Feb 1918 · Denikin 1919 · Voronezh 12 Nov 1917 · Ural Cossack Army 1918-20

HUNGARY · Poltava 19 Jan 1918 · Kharkov 24 Dec 1917 · Don Cossacks 1917-19 · Tsaritsyn (Stalingrad, Volgograd) 27 Nov 1917

ROMANIANS · BESSARABIA · Yekaterinoslav (Dnepropetrovsk) 11 Jan 1918 · R. Don · R. Volga

ROMANIA · Kishinev 10 Dec 1917 · FRENCH · Nikolayev 27 Jan 1918 · Novocherkassk 25 Feb 1918 · Rostov-on-Don 10 Nov 1917 · Astrakhan 7 Feb 1918

Odessa 31 Jan 1918 · Wrangel 1920 · Cossacks · Caspian Sea

Sevastopol 29 Dec 1917 · Simferopol 26 Jan 1918 · Novorossiysk 14 Dec 1917 · FRENCH

BULGARIA · Black Sea · BRITISH · BRITISH

Entente fleet · Batum · Georgians 1919-20 · Mensheviks · Baku 15 Nov 1917 · Krasnovodsk

Tiflis (Tbilisi) · BRITISH · BRITISH

Kars · TURKEY · Tabriz 1918-19 · PERSIA

1/Russia in war and revolution Under the intolerable pressure of war, first the Tsarist regime and then the Provisional Government collapsed. Their Bolshevik successors brought only temporary peace. From the summer of 1918, White armies moved towards the heart of the country, and within a year Soviet Russia was in extreme peril. In 1921, after seven years of war, Bolshevik control of interior lines of communication, the Whites' disunity and the half-heartedness of the Allied intervention, peace finally came to Russia.

Imperialism and nationalism 1919 to 1941

BY THE 1920s the European empires in Asia and North Africa had reached their greatest extent. At the end of the First World War, France gained control of Syria and Lebanon. Iraq, Palestine and Transjordan were assigned to Britain, whose area of control already included Egypt, the Sudan, the southern and eastern fringes of Arabia, India, Burma, Ceylon and the Malay states. The Dutch remained in the East Indies, the Spaniards consolidated their control over the northern zone of Morocco, and the Italians retained Libya. After this, the only important addition was Ethiopia, conquered by Italy in 1936. Turkey, Persia, Saudi Arabia, Yemen, Afghanistan and Siam stayed independent, but only within limits: the military power of Europe and the domination of world markets by the industrial states of the West were facts which even independent countries had to take into account. Moreover, this situation began to assume a new dimension with the increasing demand for oil for armies and industry, and the discovery and exploitation of large oil resources in the Middle East, especially in Persia and Iraq.

The position of the imperial powers was weaker than it seemed, however. The exhaustion of the victors in the First World War; the growth of a new conception of imperial rule as something temporary and limited, expressed both in the British idea of progress towards 'dominion status' and in the mandate system of the League of Nations; criticism and challenges voiced by the United States, the USSR and later by Nazi Germany: all these limited the freedom of action of Great Britain and France. The countries of Asia and North Africa were for the most part also countries of ancient literate civilization, with a tradition of independence or participation in their own government; in some of them, several generations of modern education had produced an elite which played some part in colonial administration and wished to obtain greater autonomy as a step towards independence.

Thus the colonial powers were faced with increasing opposition in Asia and North Africa, though not yet in sub-Saharan Africa. They reacted with a mixture of repression and concession. Opposition was of two kinds: either led by traditional rulers or by elites making use of indigenous social forces. Thus in Morocco first Spanish and then French rule was threatened by a revolt in the Rif Mountains, led by Abd el-Krim and only suppressed with difficulty (1921–6); and in Cyrenaica, the Italian conquest met with prolonged resistance from the Sanusi tribesmen. The ruler of Afghanistan, long dependent on British India in foreign affairs, threatened the British position on the troubled Northwest Frontier in 1919, and secured his independence by treaty in 1921.

In other places, the new educated elite espoused the idea that each nation (whether defined in territorial or in ethnic terms) should have its own independent state. But in this period nationalist movements could only present a serious challenge in countries where they were able to mobilize wider support. This occurred first in Turkey, where the nationalists, led by Mustafa Kemal (Atatürk), proved able to defeat Anglo-French plans for the partition of the Ottoman Empire, to abolish their own traditional system of government, and to create an independent Turkish republic in 1923.

In the former Arab regions of the Ottoman Empire similar attempts to secure independence had less success. In Syria, a nation-wide revolt beginning in the Jebel Druze was eventually suppressed (1925–7), and the French made only minor concessions before the end of the Second World War. In Iraq, a revolt in 1920 helped to persuade the British to create an autonomous government under an Arab king, Faisal, of the Hashemite dynasty of the Hejaz, which some nationalists were willing to accept as a first step; by 1932, Iraq had secured formal independence and membership of the League of Nations, but a British military presence continued under the new treaty. In Palestine, the conflict resulting from Britain's support for the creation of a Jewish national home led to distur-

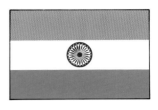

The Indian national flag (above), adopted by the Congress Party in 1930, showed a spinning wheel, the symbol of Gandhi's appeal to Indians to revive their traditional way of life and win economic independence. It was first hoisted by Nehru as President of Congress on 1 January 1930 to launch the civil disobedience campaign.

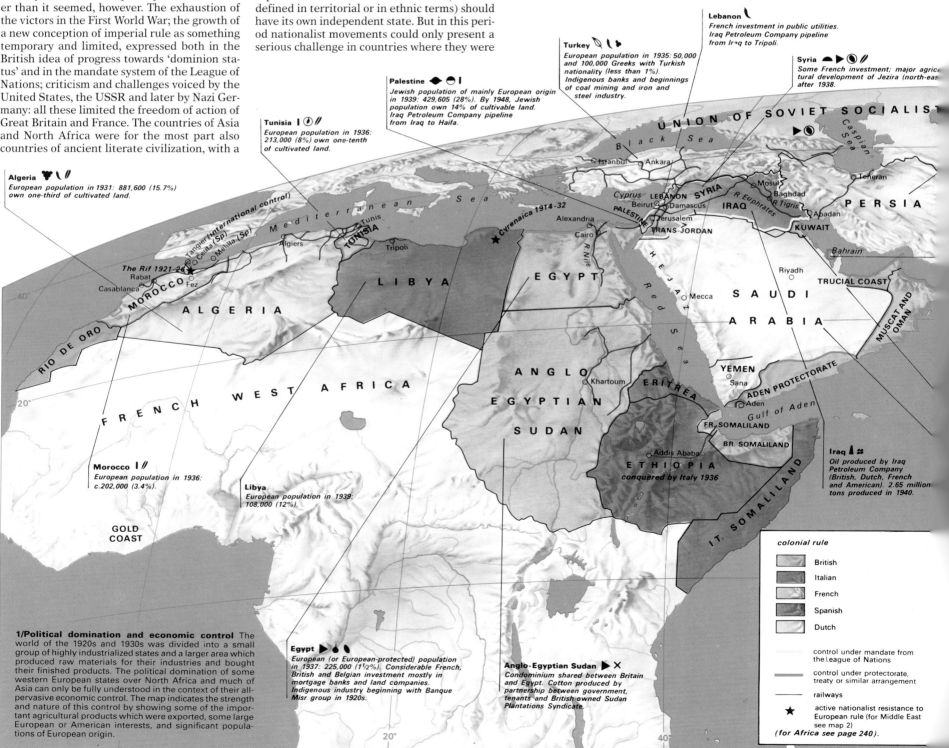

Lebanon
French investment in public utilities. Iraq Petroleum Company pipeline from Iraq to Tripoli.

Turkey
European population in 1935: 50,000 and 100,000 Greeks with Turkish nationality (less than 1%). Indigenous banks and beginnings of coal mining and iron and steel industry.

Syria
Some French investment; major agricultural development of Jezira (north-east) after 1938.

Palestine
Jewish population of mainly European origin in 1939: 429,605 (28%). By 1948, Jewish population own 14% of cultivable land. Iraq Petroleum Company pipeline from Iraq to Haifa.

Tunisia
European population in 1936: 213,000 (8%) own one-tenth of cultivated land.

Algeria
European population in 1931: 881,600 (15.7%) own one-third of cultivated land.

Morocco
European population in 1936: c.202,000 (3.4%).

Libya
European population in 1939: 108,000 (12%).

Iraq
Oil produced by Iraq Petroleum Company (British, Dutch, French and American). 2.65 million tons produced in 1940.

1/Political domination and economic control The world of the 1920s and 1930s was divided into a small group of highly industrialized states and a larger area which produced raw materials for their industries and bought their finished products. The political domination of some western European states over North Africa and much of Asia can only be fully understood in the context of their all-pervasive economic control. The map indicates the strength and nature of this control by showing some of the important agricultural products which were exported, some large European or American interests, and significant populations of European origin.

Egypt
European (or European-protected) population in 1937: 225,000 (1½%). Considerable French, British and Belgian investment mostly in mortgage banks and land companies. Indigenous industry beginning with Banque Misr group in 1920s.

Anglo-Egyptian Sudan
Condominium shared between Britain and Egypt. Cotton produced by partnership between government, tenants and British-owned Sudan Plantations Syndicate.

colonial rule

- British
- Italian
- French
- Spanish
- Dutch

— control under mandate from the League of Nations

— control under protectorate, treaty or similar arrangement

— railways

★ active nationalist resistance to European rule (for Middle East see map 2)

(for Africa see page 240)

bances in the 1920s, while opposition to the rise in Jewish immigration after Hitler's seizure of power in Germany in 1933 led to a widespread Arab revolt between 1935 and 1939. In Egypt, the main nationalist party, the Wafd under Saad Zaghlul, succeeded in mobilizing considerable popular support. A national revolt in 1919 ultimately led Britain to concede independence in 1922, although a number of important matters were 'absolutely reserved to the discretion of His Majesty's Government'. In 1936 an Anglo-Egyptian treaty gave Egyptians wider control over their affairs, but military control and the management of the Suez Canal remained in European hands. Further west, in the European colonies of North Africa, nationalist feeling was less developed: the Moroccan and Algerian movements only began in the 1930s, and pressures exerted on the French by the Néo-Destour in Tunisia failed to change basic policies.

In India, too, the main nationalist party, the Indian National Congress, gathered wide popular support, thanks largely to the leadership of Mohendas K. Gandhi. By linking the idea of nationalism with traditional Hindu thought and action, Gandhi propelled India into the age of mass politics. His first civil disobedience campaign in 1920 misfired, and was followed by a period of repression. But in 1930, profiting from the unrest caused by unemployment and the world economic depression, he launched a second campaign which went on for some years and played a part in inducing the British to introduce the Government of India Act in 1935. This provided a framework of participation, in central and still more in provincial governments, which the more conservative elements in Congress were able to accept (although it appealed less to more radical nationalists such as Jawaharlal Nehru); in 1937 Congress controlled the majority of the 14 provincial governments. This phase, however, came to an end with the Second World War: Congress decided not to participate in the war effort, and its ministers resigned. By this time, moreover, the leaders of the Muslim population were developing their own movements; in 1940 their most powerful group, the Muslim League, which sought special status for the Muslim parts of India, passed a resolution calling for an autonomous Pakistan.

In other areas of the colonial world the distress of the 1930s provided nationalist leaders with the popular support hitherto mostly lacking. Thus in the Gold Coast, cocoa farmers, hit by falling world prices, were stirred into action; while throughout the West Indies, beginning in St Kitts in 1935, riots and strikes broke out. In some cases, the result was concessions which created a temporary balance of forces, as in Ceylon, where a new constitution came into force from 1931, and in Burma, which was separated from India and given a limited kind of responsible government in 1935. In the Dutch East Indies a phase of revolutionary movements, beginning with the Communist revolt of 1926, was suppressed with only limited changes in provincial government, and the Dutch proved able to ride out the storm until the arrival of the Japanese in 1941–2. In Indo-China the French made no concessions, and the preservation of firm French control led to unrest in the 1930s and the creation of the Viet Minh by Ho Chi Minh in 1941. The period as a whole saw the rise of new, more radical nationalist leaders – Azikiwe in West Africa, Ho Chi Minh in Vietnam, Nehru in India, Sukarno in Indonesia, Bourguiba in Tunisia – who understood better than their predecessors how to manipulate popular forces and who would make their mark after the end of the Second World War.

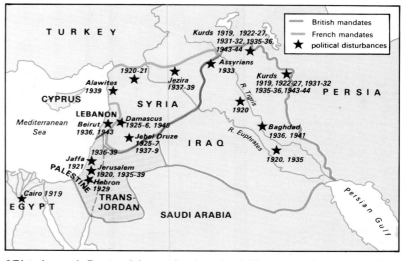

2/Disturbances in Egypt and the mandated territories of the Middle East, 1919 to 1945 *(above)* These included instances of opposition to British and French imperialism and also attempts by rural or minority populations to resist the newly-created central governments.

Egypt 1919 Nation-wide revolt, organized by the Wafd Party, against British refusal to consider an Egyptian request for independence and the end of the British protectorate.

Palestine 1920, 1921, 1929, 1935-9 Riots and disturbances, followed by Arab Revolt (1935-9): expressions of opposition by indigenous Arab population to Jewish immigration, land purchase and exclusivist labour policy. Nation-wide strikes and rural rising 1936-9. Jewish agitation for increased immigration.

Syria/Lebanon 1920-1, 1925-7, 1936-9, 1943-5 Local rebellions (Aleppo 1920-1, Jebel Druze 1925-7) against French administration; national risings against the mandate (1925-7); further revolt against French failure to grant independence (1943-5). Local revolts against centralized government in Jebel Druze (1937-9), Jezira (1937-9) and Alawite area (1939). Local disturbance in Beirut in 1936 between anti-French Muslims and pro-French Armenian Christians.

Iraq 1920, 1933, 1936, 1941 Rural revolt against British military rule (1920); massacre of Assyrian Christians (community closely associated with British rule) (1933); major rising in the Euphrates basin against centralized government (1935); military coup (1936); attempted seizure of power by pro-Axis politico-military group (Baghdad 1941).

Iraqi Kurdistan 1919, 1922-7, 1931-2, 1935-6, 1943-4 Kurds promised (and subsequently denied) autonomy under unratified Treaty of Sèvres (1920); revolts in northern Iraq led by Sheikh Mahmud Barzinji, later by Mulla Mustafa Barzani.

Anti-colonial uprisings *(below)*
Afghanistan 1919 Anglo-Afghan war May-June 1919 precipitated by King Amanullah's declaration of Afghan independence, following recognition by Soviet Russia; British acquiescence, August 1919.

The Rif 1921-6 Attempt by Berber tribesmen under Abd el-Krim to establish state independence of Spanish, and later French, rule.

Cyrenaica 1914-32 Protracted attempt by Arabs of Cyrenaica, within the framework of the Sanusi religious brotherhood, to resist Italian occupation.

India 1919-41 Most populous and complex society to be wholly colonized, its nationalist movement was the most articulate and highly organized. General disturbances, characterized by Gandhi's civil disobedience campaigns: first in 1920, called off in 1922 after violence and bloodshed; second in 1930, inaugurated by famous 'march to the sea', called off in 1934. Important disturbances took place in Amritsar (1919) when British troops dispersed urban demonstration with considerable loss of life, and in Bengal (1923-32) which had a long period of intermittent terrorist activity.

Dutch East Indies 1926 Attempted rebellion by the Communist party in support of nationalist demand for self-rule.

Indo-China 1930 Urban strikes and rural rebellion, aiming at national independence and mainly organized by the Communist Party led by Ho Chi Minh.

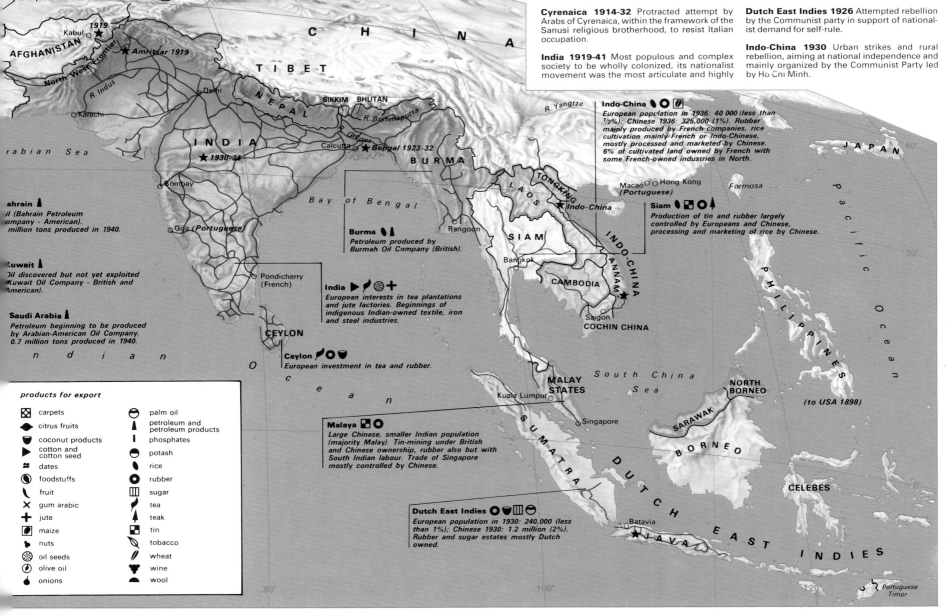

products for export

carpets		palm oil	
citrus fruits		petroleum and petroleum products	
coconut products		phosphates	
cotton and cotton seed		potash	
dates		rice	
foodstuffs		rubber	
fruit		sugar	
gum arabic		tea	
jute		teak	
maize		tin	
nuts		tobacco	
oil seeds		wheat	
olive oil		wine	
onions		wool	

Persia
Oil (Anglo-Iranian Oil Company; British control) forms two-thirds of all exports. 8.62 million tons produced in 1940.

Bahrain
Oil (Bahrain Petroleum Company - American). million tons produced in 1940.

Kuwait
Oil discovered but not yet exploited (Kuwait Oil Company - British and American).

Saudi Arabia
Petroleum beginning to be produced by Arabian-American Oil Company. 0.7 million tons produced in 1940.

Indo-China
European population in 1936: 40 000 (less than ½%); Chinese 1936: 325,000 (1%). Rubber mainly produced by French companies, rice cultivation mainly French or Indo-Chinese, mostly processed and marketed by Chinese. 6% of cultivated land owned by French with some French-owned industries in North.

Siam
Production of tin and rubber largely controlled by Europeans and Chinese, processing and marketing of rice by Chinese.

Burma
Petroleum produced by Burmah Oil Company (British).

India
European interests in tea plantations and jute factories. Beginnings of indigenous Indian-owned textile, iron and steel industries.

Ceylon
European investment in tea and rubber.

Malaya
Large Chinese, smaller Indian population (majority Malay). Tin-mining under British and Chinese ownership, rubber also but with South Indian labour. Trade of Singapore mostly controlled by Chinese.

Dutch East Indies
European population in 1930: 240,000 (less than 1%); Chinese 1930: 1.2 million (2%). Rubber and sugar estates mostly Dutch owned.

The Chinese Revolution
1912 to 1949

1/The Northern Expedition 1926-7 In 1926 the Kuomintang and their Communist allies launched a major expedition to unify the country. Their government was moved to Wuhan, which became the centre of the Left. In April 1927 Chiang Kai-shek carried out a purge of the Communists and transferred the capital to Nanking. Subsequent operations against the Feng-tien faction in the north were joined by Yen Hsi-shan, warlord of Shansi, and Feng Yü-hsiang leader of the Kuo-min-chün faction. Although the Kuomintang now claimed to control China, many areas remained outside their effective control.

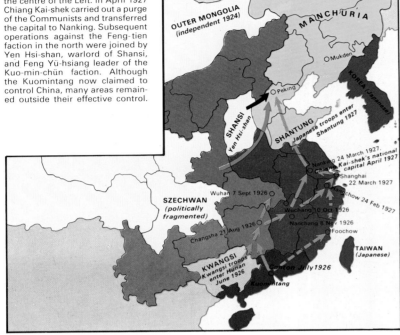

warlord groups	the Northern expedition
area controlled by Feng-tien faction (Chang Tso-lin)	area controlled by Kuomintang
area controlled by Kuo-min-chün (Feng Yü-hsiang)	
area controlled by Chihli faction (Sun Ch'uan-fang)	main Kuomintang forces
area controlled by Chihli faction (Wu P'ei-fu)	minor Kuomintang forces
T'ang Chi-yao, warlord of Yunnan and Kweichow	Yen Hsi-shan (warlord of Shansi 1912 onwards)
Kwangsi clique (group of warlords)	Kuo-min-chün

2/The Nationalist (Kuomintang) regime (1928-37) only controlled part of China. The northeast was occupied by Japan from 1931 and the Japanese constantly attempted to gain complete control of northern China. Warlords ruled supreme in many provinces, while other areas fell into anarchy. Large tracts of Kiangsi were under a Communist regime from 1931 to 1934, and by 1936 the Communists possessed a new base in the northwest at Yenan.

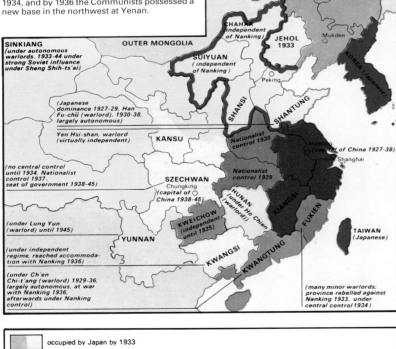

	occupied by Japan by 1933
	area in which Japan attempted to establish a puppet North China state 1935
	area under effective control of Chiang Kai-shek's Nationalist government at Nanking 1928
	brought under Nanking control 1929-34
	brought under Nanking control 1935-37
	brought under Nanking influence 1935-37

THE foundation of the Republic in 1912 failed to produce a lasting solution to China's problems. Within weeks Sun Yat-sen, the revolutionary who had been elected China's first president, was replaced by Yuan Shih-k'ai, China's most powerful military figure under the old order. Yuan soon became involved in bitter political struggles with the revolutionary leaders, suppressed a 'Second Revolution' that broke out in the provinces in 1913, and by 1914 was a virtual dictator.

These events left China seriously weakened. The government was forced to borrow huge sums abroad to offset the lack of a modern revenue system, with all customs receipts passing into foreign hands. Tibet and Mongolia broke away, becoming autonomous (albeit under British and Russian dominance respectively), and in 1924 Mongolia finally became independent. More serious were the expansionist plans of Japan. When the outbreak of the First World War diverted the attention of the Western powers from Asia, Japan seized the German leased territory and sphere of influence in Shantung, and then presented China with a set of demands which would have reduced her to a Japanese dependency. Yuan resisted the more extreme demands, but in 1915 a treaty was signed establishing Japanese dominance in Shantung, Manchuria and Inner Mongolia, and provoking a massive upsurge of nationalist feeling.

Yuan died in 1916, after attempting unsuccessfully to have himself made emperor. His regime left China with a weak and unstable central government, while real authority in the provinces passed increasingly into the hands of the generals. For the next decade, although the government in Peking claimed to rule China, it remained the puppet of one group of generals or another, and the country was divided among rival warlords, some of whom, as in Shansi, Kwangsi and Manchuria, established relatively stable regimes, occasionally instituting reformist programmes. In other areas, such as Szechwan, anarchy prevailed, with a host of petty commanders living off the countryside. Even some of the most powerful warlord leaders, such as Feng Yü-hsiang, failed to establish a permanent territorial base. In the 1920s a series of devastating wars between the major warlord coalitions not only destroyed orderly civil government but also caused millions of casualties and untold physical damage and disruption. Only the Treaty Ports remained secure under foreign protection.

The early 1920s saw an upsurge of revolutionary activity. Both the revolutionaries and the nascent Communist party benefitted from widespread popular reaction against foreign interference, the grossly unfair terms of the Paris Peace Conference, which reinforced Japan's position in Shantung, and economic exploitation. In 1919 this upsurge of nationalism erupted in the 4 May Movement, in which a new generation of Western-oriented students and intellectuals, joined by urban workers, first became a force in politics, preventing the government from signing the Treaty of Versailles.

Sun Yat-sen's revolutionary party established a regional regime in Canton, and from 1923 Sun reorganized the Nationalist (Kuomintang) Party and its army, with aid and advice from the Comintern, and entered into an alliance with the still minuscule Communist Party. Sun died suddenly in 1925, a year in which anti-foreign feeling reached a new peak with widespread strikes and boycotts involving both organized labour and the merchant class. Communist influence rapidly gained ground in the industrial cities. In 1926 Chiang Kai-shek, the principal general of the Kuomintang army, led a 'Northern Expedition' aimed at eliminating the warlords and unifying the nation. At the end of the year the Nationalist government moved to Wuhan, while its armies marched into the lower Yangtze, taking Nanking and Shanghai in April 1927. Chiang Kai-shek now instigated a purge of his Communist allies, and set up a regime of his own in Nanking. Communist troops rose against Chiang in Nanchang in August 1927, but were easily put down, as was a peasant rising in Hunan. In 1928 Chiang's armies again turned north and took Peking.

Although the Nationalists now dominated China, and were recognized as the national government, the warlords still flourished. Even after the most powerful of them, Yen Hsi-shan and Feng Yü-hsiang, were defeated in a major war in 1929–30, many provinces retained a great degree of autonomy and warfare with provincial armies repeatedly broke out. Chiang's government held firm centralized control only over the rich provinces of the lower Yangtze, where they modernized the administration and the army, built a road system and railways, and established new industry in spite of world depression and constant Japanese pressure. But much of this development was concentrated in the cities, particularly in Shanghai and Nanking.

In addition to continued warlord power, Chiang had to face the far more serious threat of Japanese expansion, for the Japanese constantly interfered in warlord politics, especially in the northeast. In 1931 they occupied Manchuria, in 1933 establishing the puppet state of Manchukuo under the last Manchu emperor, P'u Yi. They then occupied the neighbouring province of Jehol, and in 1935 unsuccessfully attempted to establish a puppet regime controlling all of northern China. In Manchuria they rapidly built up the basis of a modern economy, with a dense railway network and a variety of heavy and light industries on a scale unmatched anywhere else in China.

A second threat to Chiang's position came from the Communists. After the purges of 1927 and a series of abortive insurrections, the power of the Communist Party in the cities was systematically broken, and the Communist leaders retreated to remote mountain areas where they established local regimes. Most important of these was the Kiangsi soviet, based at Jui-chin, where from 1929–34 the Communist Party controlled several million people and developed reform programmes as a peasant-based party rather than as a party of the urban proletariat, based on the Russian model. Chiang's armies repeatedly attacked Kiangsi, and in 1934 the Communist leaders decided to abandon the area. The ensuing Long March led them to the northwest, where another minor Communist base had existed since 1930 in Pao-an. At the Tsunyi conference held during the Long March, the party's peasant-based wing finally took charge under Mao Tse-tung, whose policies were put into practice in the new Communist base area centred on Yenan.

Even now, Chiang's first priority was to crush the Communists and his provincial rivals, rather than resist the Japanese, but in 1936 he was forced to form a united front against the common enemy. The Japanese responded by invading in force, and by the end of 1938 they occupied most of north and central China, the main coastal ports and all the centres of modern industry. The Nationalists retreated into the impregnable mountains of Szechwan and the southwest, and the fighting subsided until the Japanese offensives of 1944, which brought further areas into their hands.

Although they occupied a large part of China, the Japanese controlled only the major cities and the lines of communication. The occupied zones contained many centres of Chinese resistance, often dominated by Communists who gained widespread credibility as the party actively pursuing guerrilla warfare, and won the sympathy of the peasant farmers by the reform

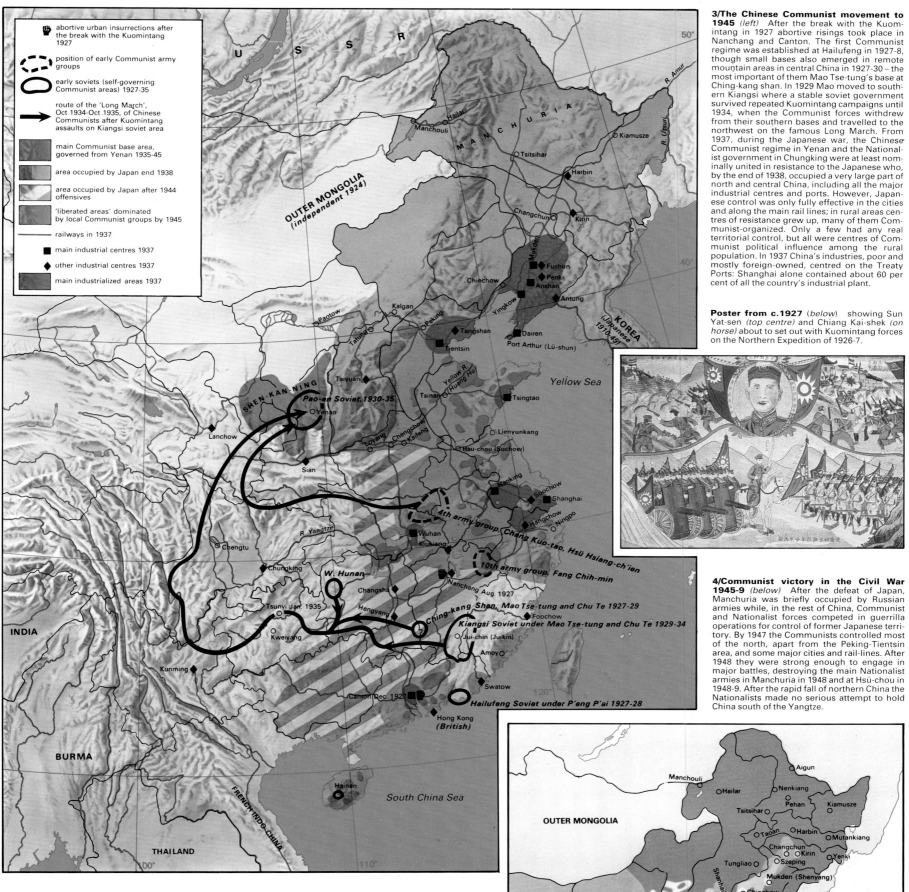

Legend (main map):

- abortive urban insurrections after the break with the Kuomintang 1927
- position of early Communist army groups
- early soviets (self-governing Communist areas) 1927-35
- route of the 'Long March', Oct.1934-Oct.1935, of Chinese Communists after Kuomintang assaults on Kiangsi soviet area
- main Communist base area, governed from Yenan 1935-45
- area occupied by Japan end 1938
- area occupied by Japan after 1944 offensives
- 'liberated areas' dominated by local Communist groups by 1945
- railways in 1937
- main industrial centres 1937
- other industrial centres 1937
- main industrialized areas 1937

3/The Chinese Communist movement to 1945 (*left*) After the break with the Kuomintang in 1927 abortive risings took place in Nanchang and Canton. The first Communist regime was established at Hailufeng in 1927-8, though small bases also emerged in remote mountain areas in central China in 1927-30 – the most important of them Mao Tse-tung's base at Ching-kang shan. In 1929 Mao moved to southern Kiangsi where a stable soviet government survived repeated Kuomintang campaigns until 1934, when the Communist forces withdrew from their southern bases and travelled to the northwest on the famous Long March. From 1937, during the Japanese war, the Chinese Communist regime in Yenan and the Nationalist government in Chungking were at least nominally united in resistance to the Japanese who, by the end of 1938, occupied a very large part of north and central China, including all the major industrial centres and ports. However, Japanese control was only fully effective in the cities and along the main rail lines; in rural areas centres of resistance grew up, many of them Communist-organized. Only a few had any real territorial control, but all were centres of Communist political influence among the rural population. In 1937 China's industries, poor and mostly foreign-owned, centred on the Treaty Ports: Shanghai alone contained about 60 per cent of all the country's industrial plant.

Poster from c.1927 (*below*) showing Sun Yat-sen (*top centre*) and Chiang Kai-shek (*on horse*) about to set out with Kuomintang forces on the Northern Expedition of 1926-7.

4/Communist victory in the Civil War 1945-9 (*below*) After the defeat of Japan, Manchuria was briefly occupied by Russian armies while, in the rest of China, Communist and Nationalist forces competed in guerrilla operations for control of former Japanese territory. By 1947 the Communists controlled most of the north, apart from the Peking-Tientsin area, and some major cities and rail-lines. After 1948 they were strong enough to engage in major battles, destroying the main Nationalist armies in Manchuria in 1948 and at Hsü-chou in 1948-9. After the rapid fall of northern China the Nationalists made no serious attempt to hold China south of the Yangtze.

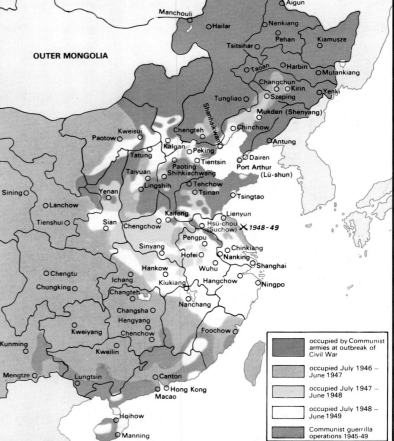

Legend (Civil War map):

- occupied by Communist armies at outbreak of Civil War
- occupied July 1946 – June 1947
- occupied July 1947 – June 1948
- occupied July 1948 – June 1949
- Communist guerrilla operations 1945-49

programmes practised in their base area around Yenan. By 1945 the Communists claimed to control numerous 'liberated areas', but only enjoyed real power in a few of them.

When the Second World War ended in 1945 the Nationalist government returned to Nanking. During the war years it had become increasingly dependent upon American aid and finance, and increasingly reactionary and corrupt. By 1945 it was widely discredited, its armies were demoralized and inflation was rampant. However, after the Japanese surrender, the Nationalist and Communist forces raced to take possession of former Japanese-held territory, the Communists gaining control of much of the north and most of Manchuria which the Russians had briefly occupied. For some time negotiations continued in an attempt to reach a political settlement and to create a national government, but hostilities persisted between Nationalist and Communist forces, and in 1947 developed into open civil war. In 1948 the initiative passed to the Communists, who defeated the crack Nationalist armies in Manchuria and entered Tientsin and Peking in January 1949. Further south a major battle around Hsü-chou raged from November 1948 to January 1949 with half a million troops engaged on each side. The Nationalists were defeated: Nanking fell in April, Shanghai in May, Canton in October 1949. On 1 October 1949 the People's Republic of China was founded and by May 1950 the Nationalist government had fled to Taiwan.

The civil war completed the destruction that had taken place during the warlord period and the Japanese occupation. In 1949 most of the Chinese industrial plant was in ruins; the Japanese industrial base in Manchuria had been looted by the Russians; and much of the rail system was inoperative. Years of hyperinflation had destroyed the currency, the banking system and urban business. But for the first time since 1911 a strong regime controlled all Chinese territory, with plans, already tested in limited areas, for the regeneration of the economy and the transformation of the country.

European political problems 1919 to 1934

THE collapse of the Central Powers in the autumn of 1918 and the subsequent peace treaties of Versailles (28 June 1919) between the Allies and Germany, of St Germain (10 September 1919) with Austria, of Neuilly (27 November 1919) with Bulgaria, and of Trianon (4 June 1920) with Hungary, brought about major frontier changes, the emergence of a number of new states and the enlargement of others fortunate enough to be on the victorious side. New states included Finland, Estonia, Latvia and Lithuania (all now independent of their former Russian overlords); Poland (reconstituted from the three empires which had shared in its partition at the end of the 18th century); Czechoslovakia, comprising the old Habsburg 'crown lands' of Bohemia, Moravia and Lower Silesia, together with Slovakia and Carpathian Ruthenia from former Hungarian territory; and Yugoslavia, comprising the territories of the former independent kingdoms of Serbia and Montenegro, the former Habsburg crown land of Croatia, the former Turkish provinces of Bosnia and Herzegovina, and the Habsburg provinces in Slovenia and Dalmatia. Romania enlarged itself greatly, taking Transylvania from Hungary, Bukovina from Austria, Bessarabia from Russia and southern Dobruja from Bulgaria. Italy took the South Tyrol (Alto Adige) and the Triestino, the former Habsburg province of Istria. France recovered Alsace-Lorraine, and Belgium took the small frontier areas of Eupen and Malmédy. Plebiscites held in the disputed areas of Upper Silesia, Marienwerder, Allenstein and Schleswig resulted in more or less satisfactory solutions on ethnic lines, although the Poles did their best to annex Upper Silesia by force of arms.

The ethnic elements in the other settlements were far from satisfactory and left linguistically identical groups scattered across eastern Europe, except on the boundary between Greece and Turkey, where at the end of the Greco-Turkish war of 1920–2 (see page 224) a wholesale exchange of populations was negotiated. Danzig and the Saarland were administered under League of Nations supervision, the Saarland reverting to Germany by plebiscite in January 1935. Peace with Turkey was delayed until the Treaty of Lausanne (24 July 1923), owing to the inability of the Allies to impose their terms on a renascent Turkish national movement despite their enlisting the help of the Greeks. On Europe's eastern frontiers settlement had to await the victory of the Bolsheviks in the Russian civil war, and the repulse first of the Polish invasion of Russia and then of the Soviet invasion of Poland. The Western Powers proposed a mediated frontier along the Curzon Line (Spa Conference, July 1920), the frontier finally agreed at the Treaty of Riga (October 1920) giving Poland a large minority of White Russians and Ukrainians.

The destruction of the Habsburg Empire, the disarmament of Germany, and the effects of the Russian Revolution and civil war completely altered the balance of power in Europe. In terms of population and industrial strength, Germany was now without counterbalance in central Europe. The only hope of those powers who stood to lose by a revision of the peace treaties was the maintenance of overwhelming military strength in alliance against any revival of German power. France tried to restrain Germany by signing alliances with the new states of Poland and Czechoslovakia, and by using the issue of reparations to hold Germany down. But France's efforts to promote a separatist movement in the Rhineland, and its occupation of the Ruhr to enforce payment of reparations in 1923, proved disastrous. Thereafter Germany and France came much closer together, and the Treaty of Locarno (1925) established a system of guarantees along the Franco-German and Belgian-

German frontiers. Germany joined the League of Nations (1926), but at the same time signed a pact of friendship and non-aggression with the USSR; French and British forces occupying the Rhineland were steadily withdrawn, and the European powers began discussions intended to lead to a world disarmament agreement.

Superficially, Europe in 1929 gave the appearance of a stable system secured against war by the sanctions clauses of the covenant of the League of Nations. But the illusory nature of that security had been shown when Italy's naval action against the Greek island of Corfu in 1923, like Poland's seizure of Vilnius from Lithuania in 1920, went unpunished. Another weakness was the lack of stability in the domestic politics of many European powers, particularly in eastern Europe, and the weakness of the economic underpinning of the international system. The strains of the war of 1914–8 and the defects of the peace settlements, coupled with the major strains of economic adjustment, occasionally accompanied by disastrous inflation, combined to strengthen anti-parliamentary and revolutionary groups, parties and movements of both left and right throughout Europe (see page 254). Moreover the Russian Revolution led to the creation of a new Third Socialist International (the Comintern) which insisted that all affiliated parties and movements should follow its leadership and organizational model. This split the socialist parties of Europe into rival parliamentary socialist and revolutionary Communist sections,

and made their defeat by the right inevitable.

Some of the new regimes and movements were organized on nationalist totalitarian lines on the model of Italian Fascism, which achieved power in 1922. Others (Poland, Yugoslavia, Greece) were simply military-bureaucratic tyrannies. In Germany armed risings and major breakdowns of public order created an atmosphere of incipient civil war until the economic recovery of 1924. Great Britain experienced a series of strikes, culminating in the General Strike of 1926; and in Ireland from 1919 to 1922 violent guerrilla-style warfare raged between the forces of the Irish nationalists, who set up their own underground government in 1919, and the British. The settlement of 1921 preserved the Protestant stronghold of Ulster under British rule and made the rest of Ireland a dominion of the Empire, but led to a bitter conflict within the new Irish Free State between radicals and moderates, settled only in 1923.

The stabilization of 1925–9 was thus more apparent than real, and with the onset of the Depression (see page 262), financial and economic chaos returned to Europe. Unemployment mounted drastically, especially in Germany and Great Britain. In Germany after 1930 the anti-parliamentary movements of right and left, Nazis and Communists, increased their strength enormously. In Great Britain a 'national' government, with a huge majority in the 1931 general election, maintained parliamentary control. In Germany, after the failure of Brüning,

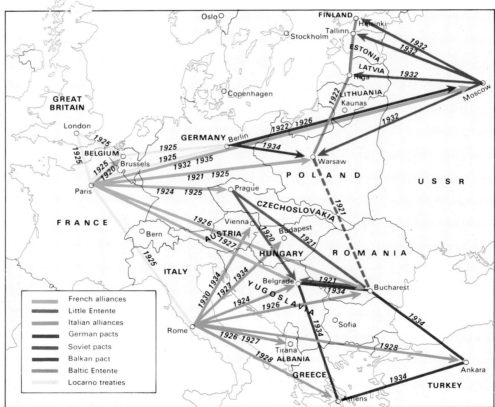

	French alliances
	Little Entente
	Italian alliances
	German pacts
	Soviet pacts
	Balkan pact
	Baltic Entente
	Locarno treaties

1920 Franco-Belgian military convention.
1920 Czechoslovak-Yugoslav defensive alliance (against Hungarian revisionism), converted **1921** into 'Little Entente' by alliances between Czechoslovakia and Romania and between Romania and Yugoslavia. The system further cemented by Franco-Polish alliance (19 February 1921) and alliance between Poland and Romania (against USSR), later by treaties between France and Czechoslovakia (1924), France and Romania (1926), and France and Yugoslavia (1927).
1922 Baltic Entente between Poland, Estonia, Latvia and Finland (defensive alignment against USSR).
1922 Rapallo Treaty between Germany and Soviet Union, consolidated by Treaty of Berlin (1926).
1924 Adriatic Treaty (Italy and Yugoslavia) confirming status quo in Adriatic.
1925 Locarno treaties: Germany, France, Belgium, Great Britain, Italy guarantee frontiers in West. Treaties of mutual assistance in event of German aggression between France and Poland and France and Czechoslovakia.

1926 Pact between Italy and Albania, converted into alliance (1927).
1926 Treaty of Friendship between Italy and Romania.
1927 Italian-Hungarian treaty (putting Italy on side of revisionist powers).
1928 Treaties between Italy and Turkey and Italy and Greece.
1930 Treaty of Friendship between Italy and Austria.
1932 Non-aggression pact between France and USSR, leading to Franco-Russian Mutual Assistance Treaty (1935). Further non-aggression treaties concluded between USSR and Finland, Estonia, Latvia and Poland (to protect Russia's western frontier).
1934 Balkan Pact (Yugoslavia, Romania, Turkey, Greece) to forestall German and Russian revisionist pressures.
1934 Rome Protocols (Italy, Austria, Hungary) to strengthen Italy's position in Danubian region in face of National Socialist Germany.
1934 German-Polish Non-Aggression Treaty (beginning of collapse of French security system in Eastern Europe).
1936 Germany denounces Locarno treaties.

2/The European Security System, 1921-34 (left) The peace settlements of 1919 were supported by a series of pacts and alliances with three main purposes: to prevent Germany from seeking to reverse the verdict of the First World War; to build up a *cordon sanitaire* against Bolshevik Russia; to maintain the territorial settlement in Eastern Europe and forestall treaty revision, particularly on the part of Hungary. The map shows clearly the key position of France, in alliance with Poland, as the main support of the Little Entente, and the comparative isolation of the two 'outsiders', Germany (which only recovered freedom of manoeuvre after 1934) and the Soviet Union. It also shows the ambition of Italy under Mussolini to play a major role in the Mediterranean and in the Danubian basin. Nevertheless, the French security system operated effectively until the onset of the Depression (see page 262), which weakened France and after 1936, if not before, undercut its alliances in Eastern Europe. The decisive change came with the German-Polish Neutrality Pact (1934), which knocked the lynch-pin out of France's defensive system. After 1936, when Germany repudiated the Locarno treaties of 1925, a new period began, leading to the outbreak of war in 1939 (see page 264).

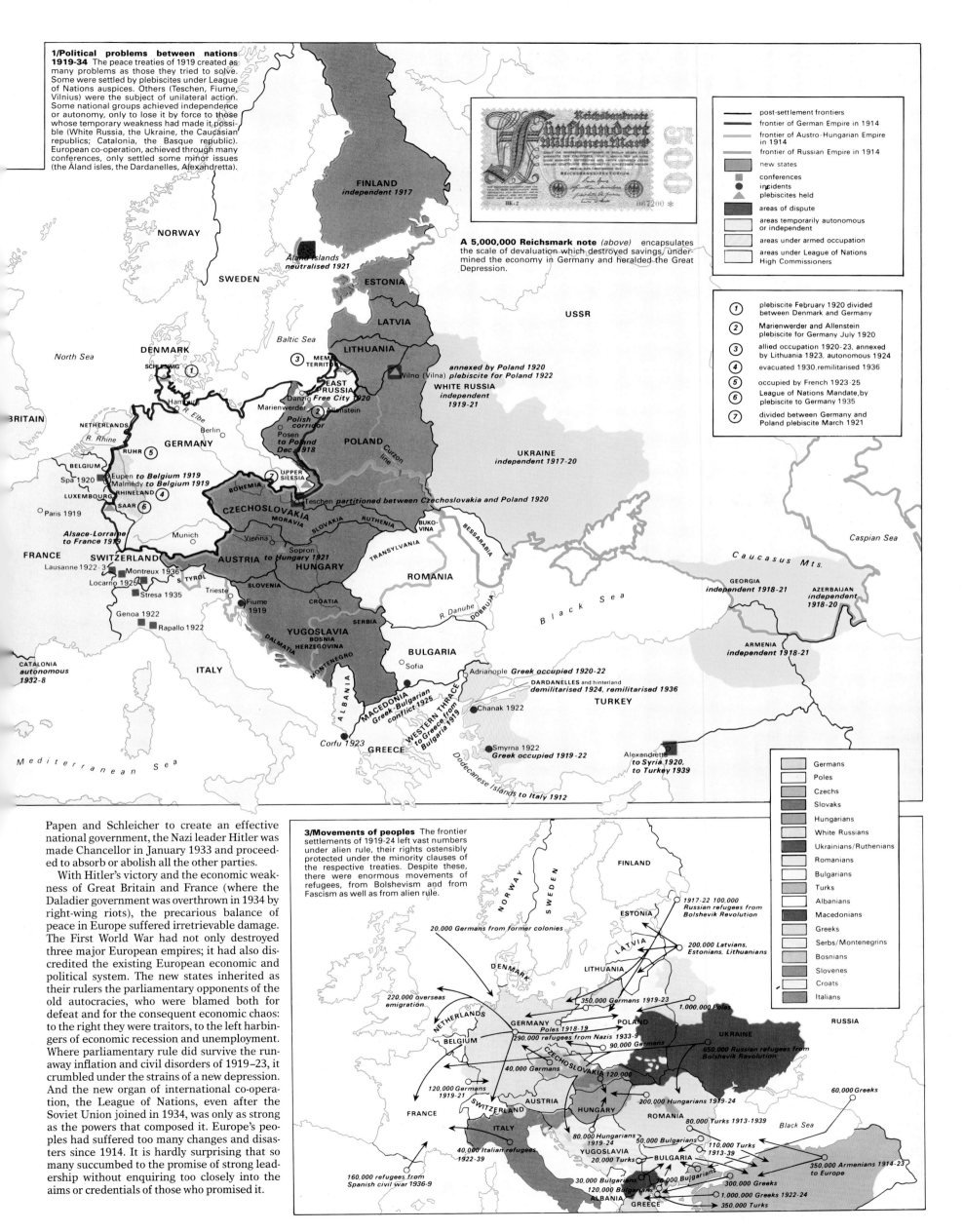

1/Political problems between nations 1919-34 The peace treaties of 1919 created as many problems as those they tried to solve. Some were settled by plebiscites under League of Nations auspices. Others (Teschen, Fiume, Vilnius) were the subject of unilateral action. Some national groups achieved independence or autonomy, only to lose it by force to those whose temporary weakness had made it possible (White Russia, the Ukraine, the Caucasian republics; Catalonia, the Basque republic). European co-operation, achieved through many conferences, only settled some minor issues (the Åland isles, the Dardanelles, Alexandretta).

A 5,000,000 Reichsmark note (above) encapsulates the scale of devaluation which destroyed savings, undermined the economy in Germany and heralded the Great Depression.

post-settlement frontiers
frontier of German Empire in 1914
frontier of Austro-Hungarian Empire in 1914
frontier of Russian Empire in 1914
new states
conferences
incidents
plebiscites held
areas of dispute
areas temporarily autonomous or independent
areas under armed occupation
areas under League of Nations High Commissioners

1. plebiscite February 1920 divided between Denmark and Germany
2. Marienwerder and Allenstein plebiscite for Germany July 1920
3. allied occupation 1920-23, annexed by Lithuania 1923, autonomous 1924
4. evacuated 1930, remilitarised 1936
5. occupied by French 1923-25
6. League of Nations Mandate, by plebiscite to Germany 1935
7. divided between Germany and Poland plebiscite March 1921

3/Movements of peoples The frontier settlements of 1919-24 left vast numbers under alien rule, their rights ostensibly protected under the minority clauses of the respective treaties. Despite these, there were enormous movements of refugees, from Bolshevism and from Fascism as well as from alien rule.

Germans
Poles
Czechs
Slovaks
Hungarians
White Russians
Ukrainians/Ruthenians
Romanians
Bulgarians
Turks
Albanians
Macedonians
Greeks
Serbs/Montenegrins
Bosnians
Slovenes
Croats
Italians

Papen and Schleicher to create an effective national government, the Nazi leader Hitler was made Chancellor in January 1933 and proceeded to absorb or abolish all the other parties.

With Hitler's victory and the economic weakness of Great Britain and France (where the Daladier government was overthrown in 1934 by right-wing riots), the precarious balance of peace in Europe suffered irretrievable damage. The First World War had not only destroyed three major European empires; it had also discredited the existing European economic and political system. The new states inherited as their rulers the parliamentary opponents of the old autocracies, who were blamed both for defeat and for the consequent economic chaos: to the right they were traitors, to the left harbingers of economic recession and unemployment. Where parliamentary rule did survive the runaway inflation and civil disorders of 1919–23, it crumbled under the strains of a new depression. And the new organ of international co-operation, the League of Nations, even after the Soviet Union joined in 1934, was only as strong as the powers that composed it. Europe's peoples had suffered too many changes and disasters since 1914. It is hardly surprising that so many succumbed to the promise of strong leadership without enquiring too closely into the aims or credentials of those who promised it.

The Great Depression 1929 to 1939

THE chronology of the 'Slump' is well known, but its causes are still debated. It is, however, certain that the stock market crash of 1929 and the ensuing world-wide financial collapse were only the manifestation of deeper weaknesses in the world economy. The instability arose from several sources. The First World War caused a dramatic increase in productive capacity, especially outside Europe, but without a corresponding increase in continuing demand. Above all, a world-wide imbalance existed between agriculture and industry: the rewards of growth accrued disproportionately to the industrialized countries and, within them, to their industrial and financial sectors. Increased production allowed food and raw material prices to decline throughout the 1920s, worsening the terms of trade for countries dependent on the export of such commodities, and decreasing their ability to buy the industrial products of Europe and the United States. Within the latter, wages lagged behind profits, impairing the development of domestic markets and limiting the potential of new industries, such as automobiles, to replace declining ones, such as textiles. International finance never fully recovered from the dislocations of the First World War. The pre-war system of fixed exchange rates and free convertibility (see page 252) was replaced by a compromise – the Gold Exchange Standard – which never achieved the stability necessary to rebuild world trade.

The slump was touched off by financial crisis. The great Bull Market of the late 1920s – itself a sign of weakness and shrinking opportunities for investment – gave way to a precipitous fall in stock prices in October 1929. In the ensuing scramble for liquidity, funds flowed back from Europe to America and the shaky European prosperity collapsed. In May 1931, the Austrian Credit–Anstalt Bank defaulted. When England left the Gold Standard, allowing sterling to depreciate in September 1931, virtually the entire world was affected. In many industrial countries, over a quarter of the labour force was thrown out of work. Prices and wages plummeted, industrial production fell to 53 per cent of its 1929 level in Germany and the United States, and world trade sank to 35 per cent of its 1929

value. For many the Depression seemed endless: as late as 1939, average world unemployment was over 11 per cent. But the impact of the slump was uneven, with some economies rebounding relatively quickly and others languishing throughout the decade.

In retrospect, it is evident that considerable structural changes took place in the 1930s: new industries continued to progress; consumption patterns shifted; peripheral areas increased their output of industrial goods; and real wages rose. A new economic world order, anchored on Wall Street and Detroit, struggled to be born. But even by 1939 the lynchpin of this new system had not yet regained the level of industrial output of 1929, and it ultimately required a second world war to pull the United States out of economic depression.

At first, governments usually responded to the Depression with futile efforts to preserve the gold value of their currencies and to balance budgets through less spending. Soon, however, the dire consequences led one government after another to attempt to stimulate the domestic economy by reflation (e.g. public works), devaluation (in the hope of increasing exports), farm subsidies, regulated cartelization, protective and preferential tariff arrangements (e.g. the Ottawa Agreements, 1932), or some combination of these policies.

These measures achieved mixed results. Success hinged on applying consistent and firm stimulants and, more importantly, on the speed and extent of rearmament. Germany and the United Kingdom rearmed early, stimulating their own economies and those of the Commonwealth, Scandinavia and eastern Europe. France and the United States rearmed late, and suffered much more severely in the recession of 1937-8. Internationally, government policies led to a decrease and redirection of trade. By 1935, much of the world had divided into five currency blocs: the sterling and dollar areas, the gold and yen blocs, and the German-dominated exchange control area. Though plagued by instability, these groupings corresponded roughly to the new patterns of trade and influence.

The revival of economic nationalism was paralleled by a new intensity in international poli-

tics. The Japanese export offensive had its political reflex in military aggression against China. Hitler, Mussolini and the Japanese exploited the disarray which the economic collapse had brought about, and gradually the world polarized into two armed camps: the Axis (Germany, Italy and Japan) and the 'democracies' (led by the United Kingdom, France and the United States). In between stood the Soviet Union, the one country which, isolated from the world market, had managed to sustain economic growth throughout the 1930s, and which both sides tried, alternately, to ally with or to isolate.

Few countries emerged from the Depression without undergoing some dramatic domestic transformation. In Africa, Asia and Latin America, nationalist and revolutionary movements gained new bases of support, as the crisis radicalized urban workers, poor peasants and agricultural labourers. The developed world followed one of two patterns. The first was liberal and democratic, typified by Roosevelt's New Deal in the United States, and by the Popular Front government in France. In both countries, the election of left- or liberal-minded administrations unleashed enormous waves of strikes and trade union organization, and stimulated numerous efforts at reform. Much more common was the path to the right. The resignation of the Hamaguchi Cabinet in 1931 marked the effective end of Japan's weak experiment in constitutional democracy. With the coming of the Depression, fascist movements spread throughout Europe, carrying Hitler to power in Germany in January 1933, followed two months later by Dollfuss in Austria. Most of eastern Europe quickly followed suit. Even in France, the United Kingdom and the USA, fascist movements arose, pressurizing governments from the right and harassing reform movements.

In summary, the Great Depression brought the collapse not only of economic liberalism, but also of liberal political institutions. Yet the triumph of the authoritarian regimes was short-lived. They too proved incapable of restoring the old order, or of establishing a stable new one, and ultimately perished in the course of the Second World War.

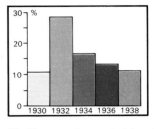

World unemployment (*above*) In the early 1930s unemployment reached record levels in almost all industrialized countries and many workers remained jobless throughout the decade. Unemployment fuelled labour militancy and mass protest, as in this demonstration in New York (*below*), and destabilized governments and the lives of workers alike.

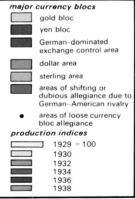

Gains for Washington Commonwealth Federation, 1934-6

WASHINGTON

OREGON

CALIFORNIA

NEVADA

Farm workers begin organising 1933

San Francisco general strike, May-July 1934

Dr Townsend founds Townsend Clubs Jan. 1934 under slogan '$200 a month at sixty

1934 Upton Sinclair, leader of End Poverty in California, wins Democratic primary for governor but loses election.

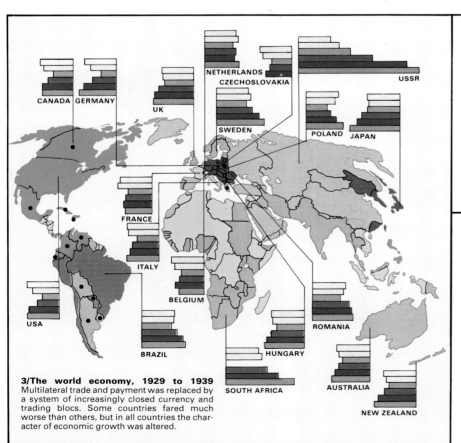

3/The world economy, 1929 to 1939 Multilateral trade and payment was replaced by a system of increasingly closed currency and trading blocs. Some countries fared much worse than others, but in all countries the character of economic growth was altered.

major currency blocs
- gold bloc
- yen bloc
- German-dominated exchange control area
- dollar area
- sterling area
- areas of shifting or dubious allegiance due to German–American rivalry
- • areas of loose currency bloc allegiance

production indices
- 1929 = 100
- 1930
- 1932
- 1934
- 1936
- 1938

US statistics (*below*) These statistics, especially for the years 1937-8, show both the extreme depth of the Depression in the United States and the country's weak, slow and halting recovery.

Commodity production 1926 to 1938 (*above*) The movement of commodity prices, stocks and production, especially in the drastic price decline, caused severe hardship and dislocation in many countries, particularly those dependent upon agricultural and raw materials exports.

	unemployment (no. in 000's)	Federal budget surplus + or deficit − (millions of $)	days lost through strikes (000's)	no. of union members (000's)
1930	4340	+737	3320	3632
1932	12060	−2,735	10500	3226
1934	11340	−3,689	19600	3249
1936	9030	−4,424	13900	4164
1938	10390	−1,176	9150	8265

1/The depression in the US
1929 Oct. Wall Street Crash.
1930 Hawley-Smoot Tariff passed.
1931 Hoover declares moratorium on war debts.
1932 Jan. Reconstruction Finance Corporation established, with power to use $2 billion to underwrite banks and businesses. **July** Federal Home Loan Bank Act provided $125 million to prevent foreclosures. **Nov.** Roosevelt elected president promising 'New Deal'.
1933 4 Mar. Roosevelt inaugurated. **9 Mar.** to **16 June** 'Hundred Days' of reform:
Bank Holiday. Glass-Steagall Act (reform of banking). Federal Securities Act. US goes off gold. Agricultural Adjustment Admin-

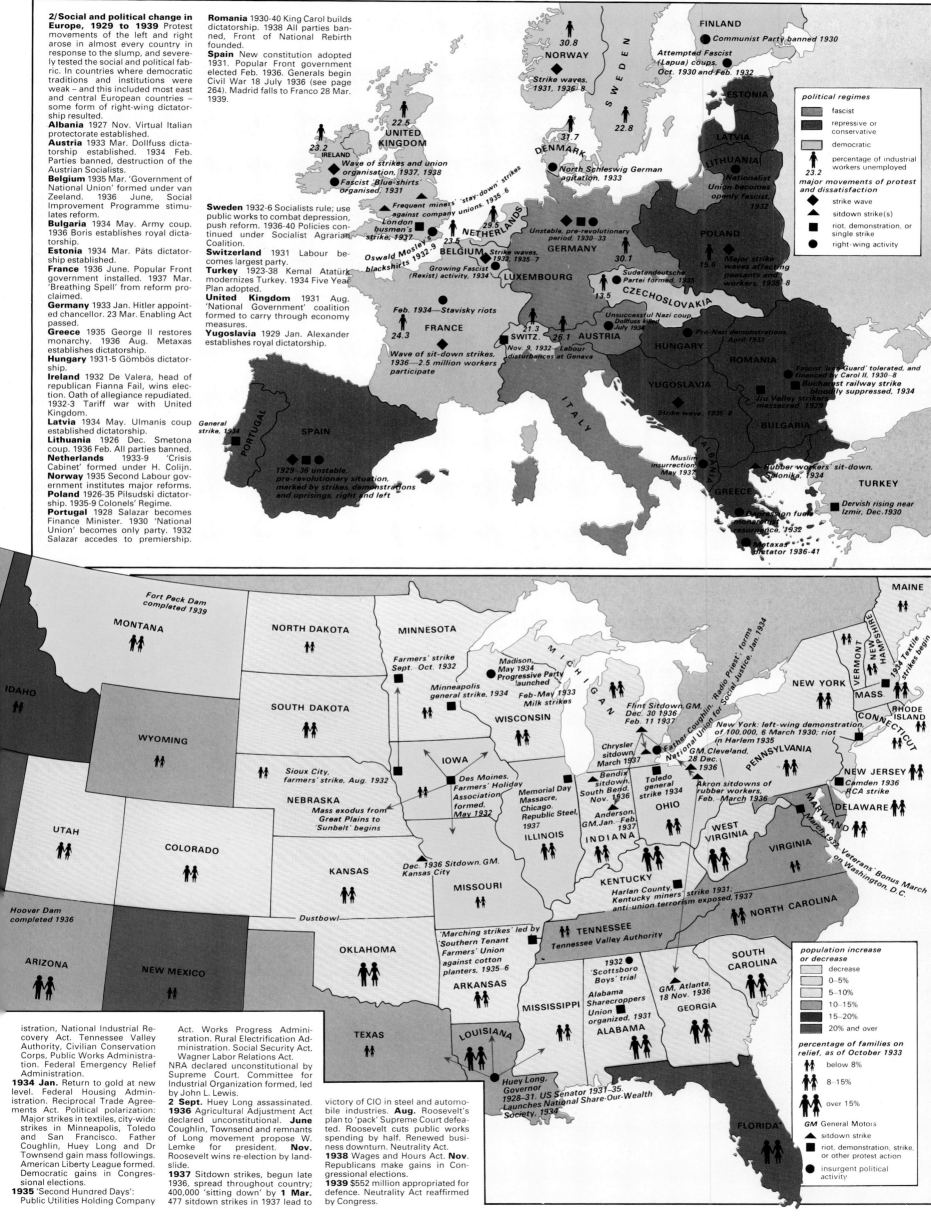

2/Social and political change in Europe, 1929 to 1939 Protest movements of the left and right arose in almost every country in response to the slump, and severely tested the social and political fabric. In countries where democratic traditions and institutions were weak – and this included most east and central European countries – some form of right-wing dictatorship resulted.

Albania 1927 Nov. Virtual Italian protectorate established.

Austria 1933 Mar. Dollfuss dictatorship established. 1934 Feb. Parties banned, destruction of the Austrian Socialists.

Belgium 1935 Mar. 'Government of National Union' formed under van Zeeland. 1936 June. Social Improvement Programme stimulates reform.

Bulgaria 1934 May. Army coup. 1936 Boris establishes royal dictatorship.

Estonia 1934 Mar. Päts dictatorship established.

France 1936 June. Popular Front government installed. 1937 Mar. 'Breathing Spell' from reform proclaimed.

Germany 1933 Jan. Hitler appointed chancellor. 23 Mar. Enabling Act passed.

Greece 1935 George II restores monarchy. 1936 Aug. Metaxas establishes dictatorship.

Hungary 1931-5 Gömbös dictatorship.

Ireland 1932 De Valera, head of republican Fianna Fáil, wins election. Oath of allegiance repudiated. 1932-3 Tariff war with United Kingdom.

Latvia 1934 May. Ulmanis coup established dictatorship.

Lithuania 1926 Dec. Smetona coup. 1936 Feb. All parties banned.

Netherlands 1933-9 'Crisis Cabinet' formed under H. Colijn.

Norway 1935 Second Labour government institutes major reforms.

Poland 1926-35 Pilsudski dictatorship. 1935-9 Colonels' Regime.

Portugal 1928 Salazar becomes Finance Minister. 1930 'National Union' becomes only party. 1932 Salazar accedes to premiership.

Romania 1930-40 King Carol builds dictatorship. 1938 All parties banned, Front of National Rebirth founded.

Spain New constitution adopted 1931. Popular Front government elected Feb. 1936. Generals begin Civil War 18 July 1936 (see page 264). Madrid falls to Franco 28 Mar. 1939.

Sweden 1932-6 Socialists rule; use public works to combat depression, push reform. 1936-40 Policies continued under Socialist Agrarian Coalition.

Switzerland 1931 Labour becomes largest party.

Turkey 1923-38 Kemal Atatürk modernizes Turkey. 1934 Five Year Plan adopted.

United Kingdom 1931 Aug. 'National Government' coalition formed to carry through economy measures.

Yugoslavia 1929 Jan. Alexander establishes royal dictatorship.

political regimes
- fascist
- repressive or conservative
- democratic

percentage of industrial workers unemployed 23.2

major movements of protest and dissatisfaction
- strike wave
- sitdown strike(s)
- riot, demonstration, or single strike
- right-wing activity

istration, National Industrial Recovery Act. Tennessee Valley Authority, Civilian Conservation Corps, Public Works Administration. Federal Emergency Relief Administration.

1934 Jan. Return to gold at new level. Federal Housing Administration. Reciprocal Trade Agreements Act. Political polarization: Major strikes in textiles, city-wide strikes in Minneapolis, Toledo and San Francisco. Father Coughlin, Huey Long and Dr Townsend gain mass followings. American Liberty League formed. Democratic gains in Congressional elections.

1935 'Second Hundred Days': Public Utilities Holding Company Act. Works Progress Administration. Rural Electrification Administration. Social Security Act. Wagner Labor Relations Act. NRA declared unconstitutional by Supreme Court. Committee for Industrial Organization formed, led by John L. Lewis.

2 Sept. Huey Long assassinated.

1936 Agricultural Adjustment Act declared unconstitutional. **June** Coughlin, Townsend and remnants of Long movement propose W. Lemke for president. **Nov.** Roosevelt wins re-election by landslide.

1937 Sitdown strikes, begun late 1936, spread throughout country; 400,000 'sitting down' by **1 Mar.** 477 sitdown strikes in 1937 lead to victory of CIO in steel and automobile industries. **Aug.** Roosevelt's plan to 'pack' Supreme Court defeated. Roosevelt cuts public works spending by half. Renewed business downturn. Neutrality Act.

1938 Wages and Hours Act. **Nov.** Republicans make gains in Congressional elections.

1939 $552 million appropriated for defence. Neutrality Act reaffirmed by Congress.

population increase or decrease
- decrease
- 0-5%
- 5-10%
- 10-15%
- 15-20%
- 20% and over

percentage of families on relief, as of October 1933
- below 8%
- 8-15%
- over 15%

GM General Motors
- sitdown strike
- riot, demonstration, strike, or other protest action
- insurgent political activity

The approach of the Second World War 1931 to 1941

1934-35
German-Polish non-aggression pact 1934
Rome protocols March 1934
Franco-Soviet/Soviet-Czech pact May 1935 (see also 1936-37)

1936-37
Axis November 1936 and May 1939
declaration of neutrality 1936
Anglo-Egyptian treaty 1936

1938-39
British and French guarantees for Poland, Greece, Turkey and Romania 1939
★ Anglo-Franco-Polish and Anglo-Franco-Turkish alliances September 1939
Copenhagen declaration of neutrality July 1938
Anglo-French staff talks April 1936 and May 1938, March – June 1939
German-Soviet non-aggression pact 1939

1/European alliances and alignments (above) France and Great Britain sought associates to deter German or Italian aggression. Hitler tried either to isolate or, as with the Axis and the Anti-Comintern Pact, to distract potential opponents. Mussolini hoped to control Hitler's rate of expansion to match Italy's capabilities. Other countries concluded non-aggression pacts with Hitler or joined in the 'neutralist' Declaration of Copenhagen, hoping to contract out of war.

2/The expansion of Japan, 1931-41 (below) Japanese expansion in Manchuria and northern China before 1936 was designed to control China's potentialities and eliminate British, American and Soviet influence. From 1937 to 1940 Japan sought victory in China both by direct conquest and by isolating China from external aid. American economic counter-pressure led in 1941 to the decision to conquer and hold 'Greater East Asia', seen as a self-sufficient, defensible empire.

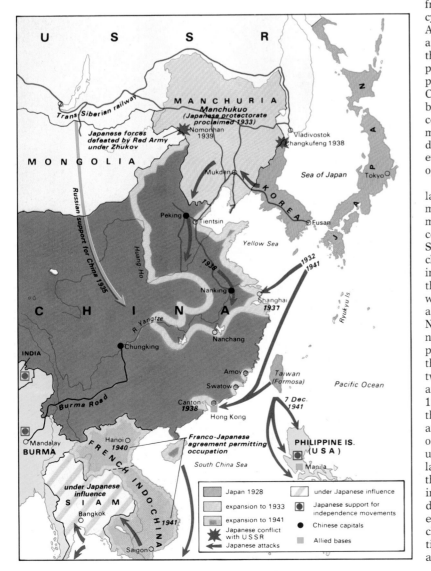

Japan 1928
expansion to 1933
expansion to 1941
under Japanese influence
Japanese support for independence movements
★ Japanese conflict with U S S R
Japanese attacks
Chinese capitals
Allied bases

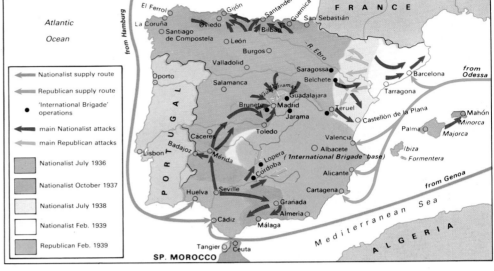

Nationalist supply route
Republican supply route
● 'International Brigade' operations
main Nationalist attacks
main Republican attacks

Nationalist July 1936
Nationalist October 1937
Nationalist July 1938
Nationalist Feb. 1939
Republican Feb. 1939

THE settlements that ended the First World War, and specifically the German treaty concluded at Versailles, have attracted little sympathetic treatment from historians – at best condemned as flawed, at worst castigated as containing the origins of a second conflict. It is as well, therefore, to note three matters: that the Depression was at least as important in the unfolding of inter-war events as an imperfect peace settlement; that the revision of the Versailles settlement in the 1930s to the point where its provisions were effectively set aside still could not prevent the outbreak of war; and that the first challenge to the Versailles order came not in Europe but in the Far East and for reasons largely divorced from Versailles arrangements.

Japanese expansionism in the 1930s arose from a desire to achieve economic self-sufficiency, military security and leadership of eastern Asia. Under the impact of the Depression, Japan after September 1931 overran Manchuria and then set about the reduction of its neighbouring provinces – by 1936 Jehol had been added to the puppet state of Manchukuo in Manchuria and Chinese authority in the border provinces had been compromised. This process gave Japan control of an economy that in effect underwrote much of her subsequent expansion and trading deficits of the later 1930s, while the unfolding of events both led and reflected European developments in two critically important ways.

First, Japan's expansion on the Asian mainland was largely the product of an increasingly militant nationalism and was accompanied by a militarization of society that accounted for the collapse of democratic government in Japan. Second, her conquest of Manchuria directly challenged the Versailles settlement's most important goals: the international authority of the League of Nations and the preservation of world peace through collective security against aggression. From the outset the League of Nations had been plagued by two basic weaknesses: confusion over whether it was to ensure peace by the maintenance or by the revision of the Versailles settlement; and the absence of two of the most important powers, Soviet Russia and the United States. Nevertheless, in the 1920s a number of further treaties – notably those concluded at Washington and Locarno – and a general desire for peace ushered in a period of optimism that was closely tied to the values of liberal democracy, though in truth the latter was a somewhat delicate bloom. Indeed, this optimism and democratic practice were the immediate casualties of the Depression: by 1939 democracy had been extinguished in most of eastern and central Europe, and the forces of change then underway had assumed a revolutionary impetus that found expression in national rather than social terms.

3/The Spanish Civil War, 1936-9 (above) The Civil War grouped the military, the political right and the Roman Catholic Church (with German and Italian 'volunteers' and military aid) against the 'Popular Front' government, republicans, anti-clericals, anarchists, socialists and Communists, and Basque and Catalan autonomists (with Soviet military aid). Against widespread criticism, Great Britain and France initiated an international non-intervention agreement to prevent escalation into a Mediterranean conflict with Italy.

Before the Depression, with Soviet Russia preoccupied with her domestic problems, the only real challenge to the post-war order was provided by fascist Italy. But Italy, the least of the great powers, was marginalized: France's primacy within Europe meant that there was no balance of power that Italy could seek to manipulate to her advantage. With the onset of the Depression, however, the balance began to be restored with the re-emergence of Germany as potentially the strongest power in Europe. Under Hitler after 1933, Germany was bent upon reversing the verdict of 1918 and was conscious, given the failure of the League of Nations to oppose Japan over Manchuria, of the weakness of Britain and France. In the event, Hitler's challenge to the post-war order did not emerge until 1936, when Italy's attempt to add Abyssinia to her empire had already strained her relations with Britain and France. Thereafter, crisis followed crisis in rapid succession. Germany reoccupied the Rhineland in March 1936, yet France failed to respond to an action that struck at the heart of the alliance system with which she had surrounded Germany. July 1936 brought an attempt by the Spanish army to overthrow the democratically elected Republican government. The failure of this attempt led to a civil war that lasted until March 1939 and diverted French and British attention from events elsewhere. In November 1936 Germany, Italy and Japan formed the Anti-Comintern Pact, specifically intended to neutralize the Soviet Union but in effect serving notice to the democracies of these three states' ever-closer association in challenging the existing order.

Meanwhile in December 1936, China made serious attempts to end her seemingly interminable civil wars in order to present a united front to future Japanese encroachment. Since Japan's position in and designs upon China depended upon Chinese division and weakness, in July 1937 the Japanese military used an otherwise insignificant incident to begin the full-scale invasion of northern and central China. By October 1938 most of China north of the Yangtze had been overrun by Japanese forces, but despite sponsoring a number of puppet regimes in her area of conquest, Japan found she could not end her China venture either by force or negotiation.

In Europe by October 1938 the scene had been transformed by two crises: the German

annexation of Austria and the Franco-British initiative to dismember Czechoslovakia in an attempt to preserve the general European peace through the appeasement of Germany. In reality Germany could not be appeased: her occupation of the rump Czech state and of Memel in March 1939 forced Britain and Fränce to recognize the paradox that peace could only be secured by war or the threat of war. To make the latter credible, however, Britain and France needed to associate themselves with the Soviet Union and this, in the summer of 1939, they failed to do. The result in September 1939 was the gradual start of war in Europe, with Germany concentrating in turn upon states that individually were smaller or less powerful than herself until, by spring 1941, German domination of the European mainland could only be contested by the Soviet Union.

4/German and Italian expansion 1934-9 (left) Hitler first eliminated the restrictions of Versailles (the recovery of the Saarland by plebiscite, remilitarization of the Rhineland, annexation of Austria). Then, pretending to advocate self-determination for German minorities, he turned on France's allies, Czechoslovakia and Poland. Czechoslovakia's multi-racial composition facilitated, with British and French acquiescence at Munich, its progressive partition. Polish resistance to German claims (Danzig, the 'Corridor') led to war with Great Britain and France earlier than planned despite Hitler's agreement with the USSR to divide Poland and the Baltic states.

① Plebiscite to join Germany 1935
② Czech territory given to Germany by Munich agreement 1938 (Sudetenland)
③ Czech territory taken by Poland Sept. 1938
④ Slovak territory to Hungary Nov. 1938
⑤ Annexed by Germany 1938 (Anschluss)
⑥ Occupied by Hungary March 1939
⑦ Annexation of Memel March 1939
⑧ Occupied by Italy April 1939

← Italian campaigns 1935-36

5/The campaigns in Europe 1939-41 (right) In September 1939 Hitler overran Poland; in 1940 Denmark, Norway, the Low Countries and the defeat of France followed. Great Britain, its army in France evacuated from Dunkirk, rejected Hitler's peace offers and defeated his *Luftwaffe*. Mussolini's abortive attack on Greece, British intervention and an anti-Axis coup in Yugoslavia led to German occupation of Yugoslavia, Greece and Crete (May 1941). In June 1941 Hitler attacked the Soviet Union.

Propaganda Following the rise of National Socialism, propaganda took on new dimensions. *Above*: protest against bombing of Madrid, 1937, during Spanish Civil War; *below*: exhortation to vote for Hitler in 1938 plebiscite.

■ Axis territory 1 September 1939
■ Axis satellites   ■ Axis occupied
→ German advances   ⚑ airborne landings
→ Italian advances
→ Soviet forces
→ Allied forces   ⇢ retreat and withdrawal
🔥 cities severely damaged by bombing
■ Soviet occupied territory 1939-40
■ British Empire   □ neutral powers

The war in Asia and the Pacific 1941 to 1945

REASSURED by the Russo–Japanese non-aggression pact of 1941 (see page 264) and with no possibility of a military victory or political solution to her war in China, Japan turned her attention increasingly to the European colonial empires in Southeast Asia. There she hoped to find the raw materials and markets that would ensure economic independence from an increasingly unfriendly United States. Racial antipathy and a belief in the inevitability of conflict had long clouded relations between Japan and the United States but after the outbreak of war in Europe and the collapse of the democracies, the United States, whose interests in the Far East seemed threatened by Japan's aggrandizement, slowly moved to centre stage in opposing Japan's growing hegemony in eastern Asia.

In June 1941 Japan took advantage of the invasion of the USSR by her Axis ally, Germany, in order to occupy Indo-China, leading the United States to impose an economic blockade. Japan responded by attacking the US Pacific Fleet at Pearl Harbor on 7 December. After ten years of sacrifice in building up her armed forces and four years of war on the Asian mainland, Japan was faced with a 'now or never' choice. She chose to go to war in an attempt to forestall American military preparation and thus buy the time needed to secure and develop the resources of Southeast Asia.

By challenging the United States, Japan sought to fight the world's greatest industrialized power to a stalemate and bring about a negotiated peace that would recognize her primacy in eastern Asia. The dangers implicit in such a course of action, and the narrowness of the margins on which Japan would have to conduct such a war, were only dimly perceived by the Japanese high command, but within six months of the start of the Pacific war Japanese forces had overrun American, British and Dutch possessions throughout Southeast Asia: Hong Kong surrendered on Christmas Day 1941; Singapore on 15 February; the Netherlands East Indies in March; and the last American base in the Philippines, Corregidor, on 7 May.

In the process of eliminating the Western presence throughout the western Pacific and Southeast Asia, Japanese forces carried the war to the borders of India (and even Madagascar), to coastal Australia and into the southwest Pacific. Yet in these same months, at the flood tide of their success, Japanese forces failed to inflict a naval defeat on the United States sufficient to impair American military capacity and morale. Instead, a reverse in the Coral Sea in May 1942 was followed in June by the devastation of the Imperial Navy's front-line carrier force off Midway Island. Reverting to a defensive strategy that required it to support outlying bases subjected to American assault, the Imperial Navy incurred unacceptable losses in the first American counter-offensive of the war, during the Guadalcanal campaign of August 1942 – February 1943.

Thereafter, without the means to end the war that she had initiated, Japan slowly lost her strategic mobility as she became obliged to fight defensively on widely separated fronts and against multiple enemies. Foremost among them was the United States whose increasing strength enabled her to prosecute four main major efforts in addition to the support she afforded to the British in India and to the Chinese. From the outset of the Pacific war, particularly after autumn 1943, the United States conducted a devastatingly successful (mainly submarine) campaign against Japanese shipping: towards the end of the war Japan faced physical starvation and industrial collapse for want of the shipping and imports needed to sustain her society and the war effort.

From autumn 1943 the United States also employed an increasingly effective island-hopping strategy using amphibious forces that bypassed the major centres of Japanese resistance, with American advances across the Pacific relying on an ultimately overwhelming carrier offensive that was to take the war to the Japanese home islands. The carrier force enabled the US Navy to fight and win the battles of the Philippine Sea and Leyte Gulf in 1944, to fight for and secure air supremacy over the western Pacific and the Japanese home islands, and to impose a close blockade of Japan in the last weeks of the war. Moreover, it was the carriers that ensured the capture by amphibious forces of the Mariana Islands with bases close enough to launch the strategic air offensive that shattered Japanese urban areas in the last six months of the war. By spring 1945 American advances across the Pacific had all but severed Japan from Southeast Asia and the resources for which she had gone to war. Indeed, her outer zone was in the process of disintegration, with the British reconquest of Burma and the Allied offensive into the East Indies.

At Cairo in 1943, the Allies had announced that they would fight until Japan's unconditional surrender, stripping it of all territories acquired after 1895. Even though Japan showed no signs of giving up, post-war policy planners in the US Department of State believed that Japan might stop its fanatical resistance if it knew what the Allies really meant by 'unconditional surrender', and prepared a policy statement defining unconditional surrender in specific terms. Simultaneously, the secret work on a nuclear weapon, which Churchill and Roosevelt had sanctioned in 1942, was nearing completion. In July 1945 a special commission recommended to President Truman that the bomb be used against Japan. The American Secretary of War, Henry Stimson, argued instead that Japan should be given a chance to surrender before the bomb was used. But at Potsdam that month, the Allied leaders approved the Potsdam Declaration appealing to Japan to surrender or face destruction, confirmed the territorial limits set at Cairo, called for an Allied occupation of Japan, the elimination of its armed forces and the establishment of a peacefully inclined and responsible government. When Japan failed to reply positively to this offer, President Truman ordered the first atomic bomb to be dropped on Hiroshima on 6 August 1945. Three days later a second bomb was dropped, on Nagasaki, and Russia entered the war against Japan.

By the time the attacks upon Hiroshima and Nagasaki and the Soviet offensive in Manchuria

1/The Japanese advance 1941-2 (*below*) In the first six months of the war in Asia and the Pacific, Japan, by virtue of holding the initiative, careful preparation and local air and naval superiority, inflicted a series of humiliating defeats on the western powers. The Philippines, the East Indies, Burma, Hong Kong, Malaya and Singapore were overrun by Japanese forces at minimal cost and often with contemptuous ease. But in the great expanse of the Pacific, the victory that Japan needed in order to neutralize American power eluded her. She sought not to conquer the United States but to destroy both the American capacity to dispute her gains in Southeast Asia and American morale. However, the pre-emptive attack on Pearl Harbor only temporarily crippled the US Pacific Fleet, and the immunity of American industry to disruption ensured that the Americans were able to recover their strength and to fight in the Pacific the war of attrition they were certain to win.

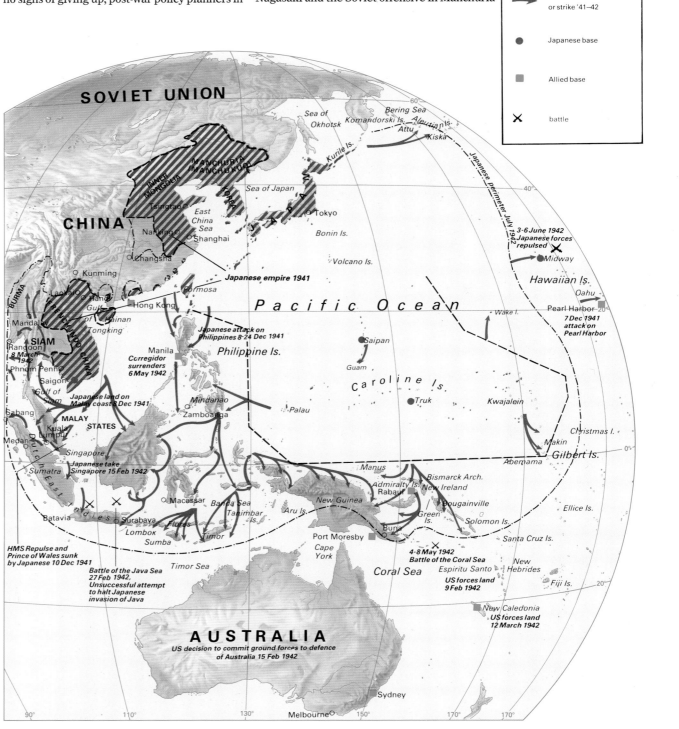

Japanese advance or strike '41–42

● Japanese base

■ Allied base

✕ battle

SOVIET UNION

CHINA

MANCHURIA / MANCHUKUO
INNER MONGOLIA

Tsingtao
Nanking
Shanghai
Changsha
Kunming

Sea of Okhotsk
Komandorski Is.
Kurile Is.
Sea of Japan
East China Sea
Tokyo
Bonin Is.

Bering Sea
Aleutian Is.
Attu
Kiska

Japanese Perimeter July 1942

3-6 June 1942 Japanese forces repulsed ✕
● Midway

Volcano Is.

Hawaiian Is.
Oahu
Pearl Harbor
7 Dec 1941 attack on Pearl Harbor

BURMA
Mandalay
Rangoon
8 March 1942
SIAM
Phnom Penh
Saigon
Gulf of Siam
Sabang
MALAY STATES
Medan
Kuala Lumpur
Singapore
Sumatra
Batavia
Surabaya
Lombok
Sumba

Japanese empire 1941
Formosa
Hong Kong
Hainan
Gulf of Tongking

Japanese attack on Philippines 8-24 Dec 1941
Manila
Corregidor surrenders 6 May 1942
Japanese land on Malay coast 8 Dec 1941
Mindanao
Zamboanga
Palau
Japanese take Singapore 15 Feb 1942

Philippine Is.
Saipan
Guam
Truk
Caroline Is.
Kwajalein

Wake I.

Christmas I.
Makin
Abemama
Gilbert Is.

Macassar
Banda Sea
Tanimbar Is.
Timor
Aru Is.
Flores
Timor Sea

New Guinea
Manus
Admiralty Is.
Rabaul
New Ireland
Bismarck Arch.
Green Is.
Bougainville
Buna
Port Moresby
Cape York
Solomon Is.

Ellice Is.

Santa Cruz Is.

HMS Repulse and Prince of Wales sunk by Japanese 10 Dec 1941

Battle of the Java Sea 27 Feb 1942, Unsuccessful attempt to halt Japanese invasion of Java

4-8 May 1942 Battle of the Coral Sea
Coral Sea
Espiritu Santo
US forces land 9 Feb 1942
New Hebrides
Fiji Is.

New Caledonia
US forces land 12 March 1942

AUSTRALIA
US decision to commit ground forces to defence of Australia 15 Feb 1942

Sydney
Melbourne

heralded her surrender on 15 August 1945, Japan was utterly exhausted and comprehensively defeated. On 2 September 1945, on board USS *Missouri* in Tokyo Bay, General MacArthur, the Allied Supreme Commander, accepted Japan's surrender.

However, the end of hostilities brought neither peace nor stability to the Far East. The European defeat in 1941 and subsequent Japanese occupation had combined to fan nationalist and Communist sentiments that were to change the map of East and Southeast Asia over the next three decades as the attempted restoration, after Japan's defeat, of the colonial empires gave rise to a generation of conflicts throughout the area.

The atomic bomb (*right*) The picture shows the devastation inflicted by the first atomic bomb, dropped on Hiroshima on 6 August 1945. Nagasaki suffered the same fate three days later and the combined death toll was over 150,000. The world had entered the nuclear age.

2/The Allied counter-offensive (*below*) The stages of Japanese defeat divided into two phases, the first a difficult and protracted struggle in the southwest Pacific, and then the sudden and dramatic collapse of Japanese air and naval power throughout the western Pacific. Allied gains in the southwest Pacific between July 1942 and November 1943, after the Japanese defeat off Midway in June 1942, decisively weakened Japan as she faced Allied offensives across the central as well as the southwest Pacific. In addition, the Allies successfully mounted an unrestricted submarine campaign against Japanese shipping. By November 1944, when American bombers, operating from the Marianas, first raided the Japanese home islands, the merchant fleet was all but destroyed. Allied occupation of the Philippines (late 1944) and Okinawa (April 1945) effectively severed Japan's lines of communication with Southeast Asia. By mid-August, after two atomic bombings, Japan capitulated.

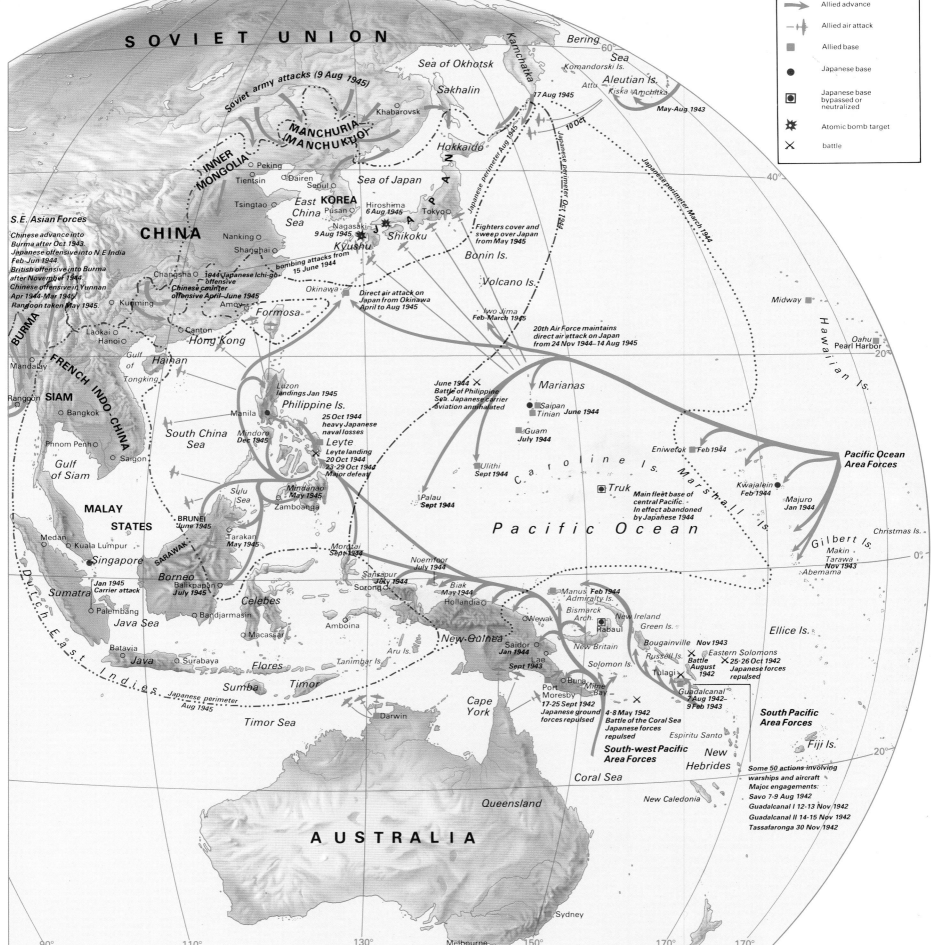

The European War 1941 to 1945

DEFEAT in total war is necessarily comprehensive. Between September 1939 and May 1941 Germany established a mastery of the European mainland that appeared unchallengeable precisely because she avoided total war; but in the course of 1941 her actions resulted in the escalation of the scale and intensity of the war to levels which she could not sustain. In that year the Soviet Union and United States, both powers individually at least the equal of an expanded Germany drawing upon the resources of a conquered continent, were brought into the war against the European Axis powers with the result that for the first time Europe's fate was to be decided by external, non-European states.

Germany's failure to rout the Soviet Union in a single campaign need not have proved fatal; but combined with her declaration of war on the United States in December 1941, following Japan's attack on Pearl Harbor, it in effect determined the outcome of the European war. Between them the US and the USSR possessed sufficient resources to ensure Germany's defeat in a protracted struggle. American financial and industrial power underpinned the Allied cause and American air power played the leading role in the German defeat in the air, whereas Germany's military defeat in the field was primarily achieved by the Soviet Union in the course of a struggle on the Eastern Front that was fought with a barbarism unknown in Europe since the wars of religion. In one sense this was appropriate: ideology was the touchstone of

faith in the Nazi–Soviet conflict, and if Nazism had provided German forces with their cutting edge in the years of victory, so Nazism was self-defeating in that it prevented Germany's consolidation of that success and ultimately turned almost every European hand against her. Other than slavery and death, Nazism had nothing to offer the conquered peoples of Europe, even those peoples and states that associated themselves with Germany; and therefore Germany, which could hold only by conquest, was unable to tap the full political and economic resources of the continent and thus free herself of commitments that she found increasingly difficult to maintain as the tide of war turned against her.

Although her armies reached the outskirts of Leningrad and Moscow and secured Kiev, Kharkov and Rostov in the south, Germany in 1942 had either to secure the victory that had eluded her in 1941 or face the certainty of defeat in the face of the resources marshalled by her enemies. In the course of 1942, however, Germany incurred two reverses. Militarily, her offensive on the Eastern Front miscarried when a series of spectacular victories and territorial gains led to her disastrous defeat at Stalingrad. Additionally, the British victory in Egypt and the Anglo-American landings in French North Africa imposed upon Germany a commitment in southern Europe that she could ill afford. In the course of 1943 this commitment increased with the defection of Italy, the wavering loyalty of Germany's other associates and the amphibious threat posed by the Western Allies. Likewise, 1943 saw Germany's growing need to commit forces to the defence of her own skies as the Anglo-American strategic bombing offensive began to assume momentum, whilst that same year brought two further telling German defeats. In the course of 1943 the U-boat offensive

in the Atlantic first faltered and then was curbed, while in July German forces on the Eastern Front were routed around Kursk in a battle that ensured that the initiative finally and irrevocably passed to their enemies.

Thereafter the Allied powers closed in around Germany. In 1944 the Soviets undertook a series of massive offensives that all but cleared their territory and took the war deep into Poland and the Balkans, while the western Allies, having won air superiority over Germany by spring, landed in occupied France and by the end of the year had taken the war to Germany's western border, in addition to having cleared southern and central Italy. With her factories using their last stocks of raw material, the labour force reduced for military service and cities laid waste by bombing, Germany by the end of the year could not avoid defeat so long as her enemies continued to co-operate. Their individual self-interest, their need for unity while Japan remained undefeated, and the evidence provided when the first concentration and death camps were overrun preserved that unity of purpose even as the approaching end of the war gave proof that allies are not necessarily friends and the weakening of the common enemy brought to the fore conflicting interests hitherto held in check by common need.

The last weeks of the war in Europe saw Allied armies break into the German heartland with the Soviets securing Berlin's surrender on 2 May. Hitler committed suicide on 30 April, and Germany's unconditional surrender (effective 9 May) brought an end to the most destructive war in Europe's history. One-hundred million men and women were mobilized to fight. The dead have been estimated at 15 million military and 35 million civilians (20 million of these being Soviet citizens, six million Jews, four-and-a-half

The Russian flag hoisted on the ruins of the Reichstag *(right)* Russian forces took Berlin in May 1945. The Soviet Union bore the lion's share of all land fighting from 1941 to 1944, suffering 7.5 million military deaths alone and untold devastation.

3/The defeat of Germany *(right)* Hitler's failure to defeat Great Britain in the Blitz and the Atlantic and to overthrow Stalin's regime in the Soviet Union made his own defeat inevitable, as irreconcilable ideologies ruled out a compromise peace. The German armies were defeated in detail on the eastern front, and the British and Americans knocked out Italy and invaded France, making German collapse, under attack from east, west and south, only a question of time.

6/The Normandy landings *(inset right)* On 6 June 1944 American, British and Canadian armies landed in Normandy, breaching the German fortifications ('Atlantic Wall'). Allied air strikes on German communications prevented German counter-attack. Artificial 'Mulberry' harbours turned the beaches into ports adequate for all necessary supplies.

1/Hitler's 'New Order' in Europe *(below)* Hitler divided Europe into four: pure Aryan areas annexed to or occupied by Germany and integrated into the German economy; occupied 'non-incorporated' areas; puppet and satellite states; and the occupied and despoiled Slavic east, earmarked for German colonization, whose native population would become illiterate helots.

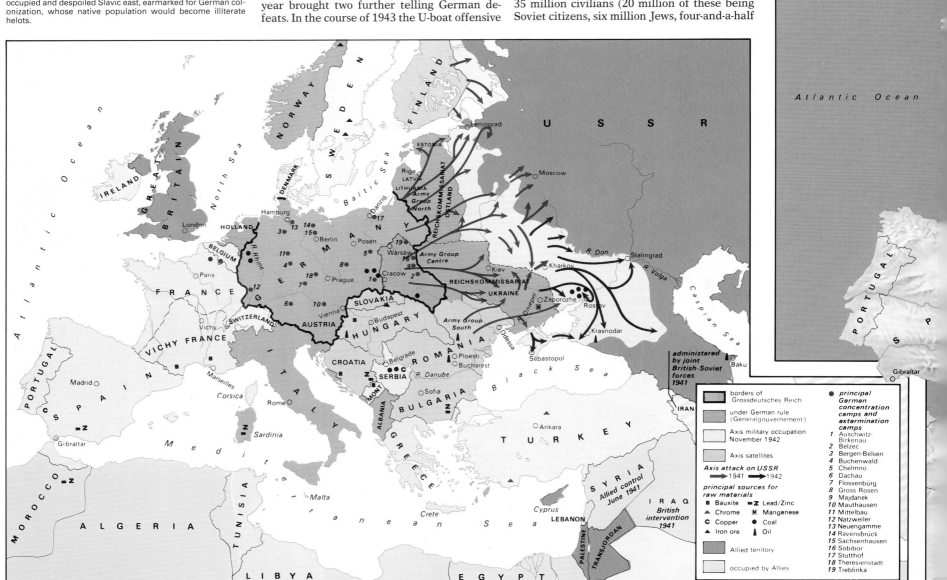

million Poles). There are no reliable estimates of the wounded. In addition, over 10 million Germans were expelled from Eastern Europe or fled the Russian advance. Germany rounded up Europe's Jewish and Gipsy minorities for slaughter in the death-camps. Stalin deported sixteen minority peoples from the Crimea and Caucasus for alleged collaboration with the Germans. When the war ended, Europe was bankrupt and European Russia was in ruins. Only the United States, whose money and industries had, through 'lend-lease', sustained and augmented the war economies of her allies, seemed the real and immediate victor.

2/The Battle of the Atlantic *(right)* The German campaign against British shipping began in the western approaches to Britain, moving in April 1941 to the mid-Atlantic 'gap', then beyond the range of British air-cover. The entry of the United States into the war opened further killing-grounds in US waters and the Caribbean to the new German long-range U-boats. After May 1943, patrolling of the 'gap' by very long range aircraft, with airborne radar acting on deciphered U-boat radio traffic, destroyed the existing U-boats' effectiveness.

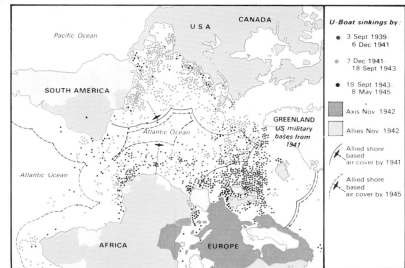

4/The Battle of Stalingrad *(inset below)* In November 1942 the Russians encircled the German Sixth Army near Stalingrad, broke a rescue attempt and rolled the German front back to the Kharkov-Taganrog line.

5/The Battle of Kursk *(inset bottom)* In July 1943 Hitler launched his last major offensive on the eastern front. It failed because of his own hesitation, superior Russian firepower and well-founded fears of an Italian collapse following the Allied invasion of Sicily.

Europe
1945 to 1973

THE war left Europe in 1945 politically disorganized and economically prostrate, a situation greatly exacerbated by large-scale population movements (see map 1). The outlook was bleak, with political uncertainty, fostered by the antagonism between the USA and the USSR, hampering recovery.

Meanwhile, the dismantling of the German New Order and the political reconstruction of Europe were taking place under the shadow of the US–Soviet conflict. The political frontiers of Europe were established at the Yalta and Potsdam conferences between the Soviet Union, the United Kingdom and the United States in February and July–August of 1945 respectively. Germany and Austria (the *Anschluss* of 1938 nullified) were divided into occupation zones and placed under four-power control. It was not until 1955 that Austria re-emerged as an independent, though permanently neutralized, state or that sovereignty was fully restored to West Germany. There was also an inter-Allied Control Council in Berlin, which, though within the Soviet zone, was itself divided into zones (see map 1). This created problems for the Western powers during the 'airlift' crisis of 1948–9 and 1958–61, when the Soviets sought to incorporate the Western sectors of Berlin into a demilitarized Free City. The latter crisis climaxed with the building of the Berlin Wall by the East Germans in 1961.

The two new German states were formed in 1949 (see map 2). West Germany, the Federal Republic (BRD), joined the European Coal and Steel Community (ECSC) in 1952 and the North Atlantic Treaty Organization (NATO) in 1955. Communist East Germany, the German Democratic Republic (DDR), joined the Warsaw Pact Treaty Organization, which was also established in 1955. The Western Powers refused to recog-

nize the DDR for many years, until in 1972 West Germany reversed its policy and accorded recognition. (The other Western Powers followed suit in 1975.)

The two halves of Europe developed strikingly differently: in the West, democracy and unprecedented consumer prosperity, with its attendant problems; in the East, oppression, privation and shabbiness. Indeed from 1947, when the United States launched the Marshall Plan for the economic recovery of the continent, Western Europe experienced an economic miracle. Led largely by West Germany, which had been forced to rebuild its war-devastated industries almost from stratch, increased integration of markets, mobility of labour and flexible responses to technology saw year after year of rapidly rising prosperity.

The six countries of the European Coal and Steel Community, formed in 1952, joined to form the European Economic Community (EEC) in 1957. These in turn became the Euro-

pean Community (EC) and were joined in 1973 by the United Kingdom, Ireland and Denmark. The EEC underpinned the economic revival of Western Europe. Between 1958 and 1962 trade between member states grew by 130 per cent. In just seven years, Italian industrial production grew by 103 per cent, for example. However, the benefits were largely restricted to the core countries. Areas on the periphery, such as Greece, as well as non-EEC Western countries such as. Spain and Portugal, both still ruled by pre-war fascist dictatorships, remained backward. Elsewhere there were pockets of persistent depression. Northern Ireland, prosperous in the immediate post-war years, suffered a sharp setback after 1969 as terrorism escalated. In France, there was unrest in Brittany, where average incomes were only 60 per cent of those in Paris, as well as in Corsica. However, the surge of growth was seriously checked in 1973, when the cheap oil that had underpinned much of the West's prosperity underwent a 250-per cent

1/Post-war population movements *(below)* The collapse of Hitler's Third Reich in 1945 released millions of prisoners of war and slave-workers incarcerated in Germany during the war. Furthermore, some 5 million Russian prisoners, refugees and servicemen were forcibly repatriated. A more lasting shift of population was the expulsion of Germans from some of their pre-war territories, especially in Eastern Europe, and from the lands they had annexed in the late 1930s. A further movement at the end of the war was the result of the westward expansion of the Soviet Union, especially the annexation of the Baltic states: Estonia, Latvia and Lithuania.

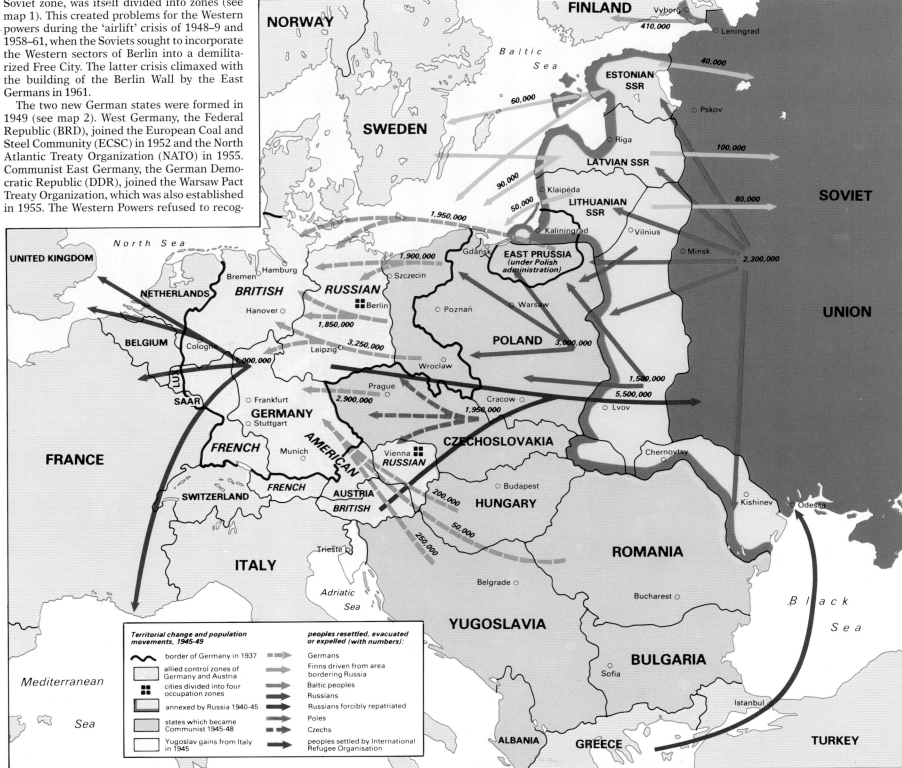

Territorial change and population movements, 1945-49

- 〜〜〜 border of Germany in 1937
- allied control zones of Germany and Austria
- cities divided into four occupation zones
- annexed by Russia 1940-45
- states which became Communist 1945-48
- Yugoslav gains from Italy in 1945

peoples resettled, evacuated or expelled (with numbers):

- Germans
- Finns driven from area bordering Russia
- Baltic peoples
- Russians
- Russians forcibly repatriated
- Poles
- Czechs
- peoples settled by International Refugee Organisation

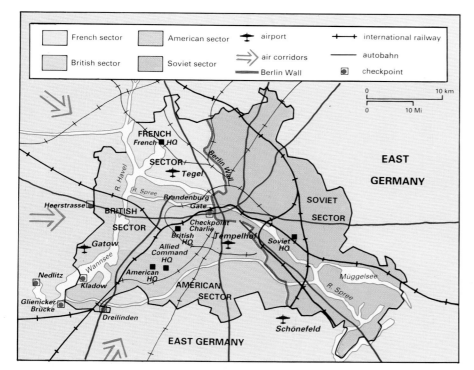

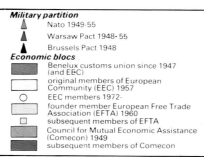

price rise imposed almost overnight by the Organization of Petroleum Exporting Countries (OPEC).

Despite the handicaps of its centralized economies, communist Europe also experienced strong growth rates. But these were not accompanied by the consumption booms that occurred in the West, while pollution from heavy industries became a serious problem across much of the region. In addition, there was persistent agitation against the East's communist rulers and the Soviet presence. This led to violent revolts in East Germany in 1953, in Poland and (the most violent and bloodily supressed) Hungary in 1956, in Czechoslovakia in 1967–8 and again in Poland in 1970. These were crushed either by Soviet force or by the local police and army.

Though still divided into three blocs – Western, communist and neutral (see map 3) – politically, by 1970 Europe had successfully settled on a new course. The old tensions were largely removed and a new era of peaceful co-operation was inaugurated.

4/Changes in economic structure 1960-81 (below)
There was a sharp decline in the numbers employed in agriculture. Even where it was the principal source of employment in the early 1950s, it was almost universally later overtaken by the industrial and service sectors. Though the Eastern bloc and other previously predominantly agricultural countries increased numbers employed in industry, most of Western Europe suffered an industrial depression with increasing numbers employed in the service sector. Even where the service sector was not the main source of employment, it saw marked growth after the war.

2/Post-war Germany (above right), as well as losing territory to Poland and the Soviet Union in 1945, was divided into British, American, Soviet and French zones, Berlin being subdivided into four sectors (above), each governed by one of the occupying powers. The victors intended to treat the country as a single unit, but by 1948 co-operation between them had broken down. Britain and the United States had already amalgamated their zones in 1947 and in conjunction with France they began to prepare for the formation of the West German government, The Soviet Union retaliated by trying to drive the Western Powers from Berlin by means of a blockade, but an airlift of supplies to West Berlin (1948-9) broke it. In 1958 they tried again. The crisis peaked in August 1961 with the building of the Berlin Wall.

3/Military and economic blocs (right)
The Western defence group NATO (1949) is shown confronting the Warsaw Treaty Organization (1955). Their economic counterparts were the EEC, formed in 1957, and COMECON, formed in 1949.

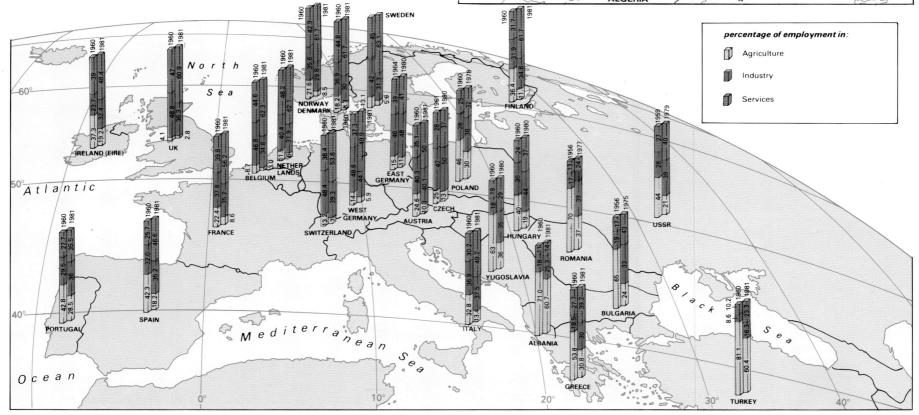

Retreat from empire from 1939

IN 1939 seven European powers held colonial possessions: Great Britain, France, the Netherlands, Italy, Belgium, Spain and Portugal. The first three were, to varying degrees, committed to the evolution of their colonial territories towards self-government, and this commitment was reinforced, in the case of Great Britain and France, by the terms under which they had been granted mandates by the League of Nations over territories formerly part of the German and Ottoman empires. Great Britain alone conceived the ultimate goal as going beyond self-government to independence, but with membership of the Commonwealth (as defined by the Statute of Westminster, 1931) a goal already reached in 1939 by Canada, South Africa, Australia and New Zealand, and towards which India was considered to be moving slowly. The continental powers thought more in terms of evolution towards a common citizenship, and saw their colonies largely as overseas parts of the metropolitan territory. These commitments were, however, complicated both by the resistance of sizeable minorities of European settlers, with consequent inter-racial tensions, and by clashes between the European ideal of evolution along Western lines (e.g. in education and in economic development) and the powerful Islamic, Hindu, Buddhist and Confucian cultures of their colonial subjects.

The need to raise Western-educated elites from the colonial peoples to man at least the lower ranks of colonial administrations had already contributed to the growth of important local nationalist movements, some of which also benefitted from Soviet, Chinese or Japanese influence. The reluctance of metropolitan legislatures or electorates to fully finance European administrations also encouraged the colonial powers to rely on indigenous local authorities wherever these were powerful enough to be used by the European governments.

The events of the Second World War had revolutionary effects on the slow processes of development within the main colonial empires. In Europe, Belgium, France and the Netherlands were overrun by Germany (see page 264). The governments of Belgium and the Netherlands took refuge in England; that of France accepted defeat and compromise with Germany and Italy so completely that in part of the overseas territories an anti-capitulation movement, the Free French, sprang up, while the British and Americans felt obliged to take over Vichy-held territories in the Middle East and North Africa. Italy's African colonies passed under British occupation. In Southeast Asia, Germany's Japanese ally expelled the colonial powers from Malaya, the Dutch East Indies and Burma, and established governments based on local nationalist movements in Burma in 1942 and the Dutch East Indies and Indo-China in 1945. After the surrender of Japan these governments won much popular backing and were strong enough to force the colonial power – in the case of Burma with only minimal violence, in the Dutch East Indies and Indo-China after prolonged conflict – to recognize their independence.

In India the war years aborted the brief experiment in partial self-government begun in 1937, and in 1942, Gandhi (see page 230) and the Congress leadership were arrested and the mass uprising of 'Quit India' was suppressed with great firmness. The radical leader, Subhas Chandra Bose, escaped and organized an Indian National Army under Japanese auspices. At the end of the war, the newly-elected Labour government in London decided to move rapidly towards full self-government for India. But the British were now too weak to impose a political settlement of their choice: neither they nor Congress could prevent the Muslim demand for partition of the sub-continent and in 1947 power was transferred to the two states of India and Pakistan (see page 278).

In France, the Fourth Republic replaced the old empire by a new *Union française* consisting of metropolitan France with its overseas *départements* and territories, and a group of associated states, including Laos, Cambodia and a French-inspired Republic of Vietnam. But in Vietnam the French 'satellite' administration was opposed by the forces of the Democratic Republic of Vietnam which were committed to independence, and after the defeat of Dien Bien Phu the French were forced, in 1954, to withdraw (see page 276). In 1957 Great Britain took the first major step towards conferring independence in Africa by granting of independence to Ghana.

Attempts to solve the problem posed by white settler minorities in central Africa by the creation of a Central African Federation broke down in 1963, and Rhodesia, which had enjoyed white settler self-government since 1923, declared its independence, without British agreement, in 1965. France, after the collapse of the Fourth Republic in 1958, replaced the *Union française* with the *Communauté française*, but this was unacceptable to Guinea, which opted for complete independence; 13 others followed its example in 1960, leaving Algeria the only French possession in Africa.

In the French territories of the Middle East and North Africa, the effects of British or American occupation and protection had helped to revitalize the independence movements. Italy's two main colonial possessions, Libya and Somalia, placed under UN mandate in 1945, became independent in 1951 and 1960; Eritrea, was absorbed uneasily into Ethiopia.

At the same time, Great Britain hoped to maintain her links with the Arab world after the ending of the mandates system by encouraging the formation of the Arab League, and later by the Baghdad Pact, a military alliance intended to link the US, Great Britain, Pakistan and various pro-Western Middle Eastern states. However, the creation of the State of Israel in 1948, Nasser's seizure of power in 1952, and the disastrous outcome of the Anglo-French-Israeli invasion of Egypt in 1956 combined to diminish British and French influence and credibility in the region. Bitter conflicts in Cyprus and Aden led Great Britain to withdraw in 1960 and 1967, and a British presence east of Suez was abruptly renounced in January 1968. Many of the smaller Gulf sheikhdoms combined to form the United Arab Emirates in 1971. France realized its inability to sustain prolonged conflict in more than one of its North African territories; Morocco and Tunisia became independent in 1956, while Algeria suffered eight years of war until the French capitulated and withdrew in 1962.

Given the rapidity of political change in many colonial territories and the existence of major ethnic or religious divisions within them, it is not surprising that colonial withdrawal was frequently accompanied – or soon followed – by violence, and the setting up of repressive regimes. In other cases, ethnic or tribal units extended across frontiers: Indonesian claims over all Malay-speaking areas in the 1950s and 1960s led to conflict with Malaysia, and Somalia laid claim to areas of Kenya and Ethiopia. By the mid 1960s only Portugal still held important colonial possessions in Africa. However, prolonged guerrilla war and the collapse of the dictatorship in Lisbon eventually brought independence but not peace to Angola and Mozambique in 1975. Spain continued to occupy a few tiny enclaves in Morocco, but abandoned the Sahara to Morocco and Mauritania in 1976 (Mauritania subsequently gave up its territorial claim). After 13 years of guerrilla warfare, white minority rule ended in Rhodesia, which became Zimbabwe in 1980. Namibia finally became independent in 1990, leaving South Africa the sole survivor of white power on the African continent.

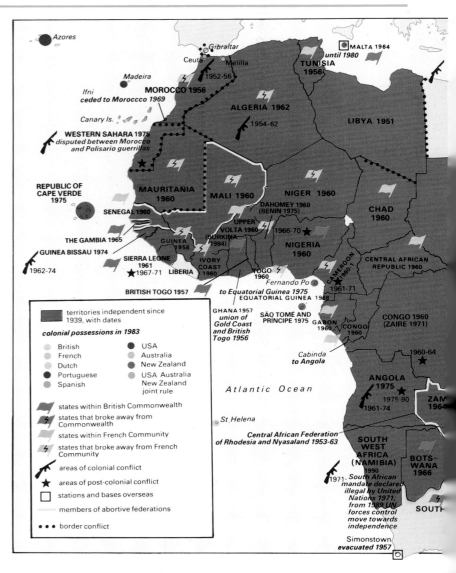

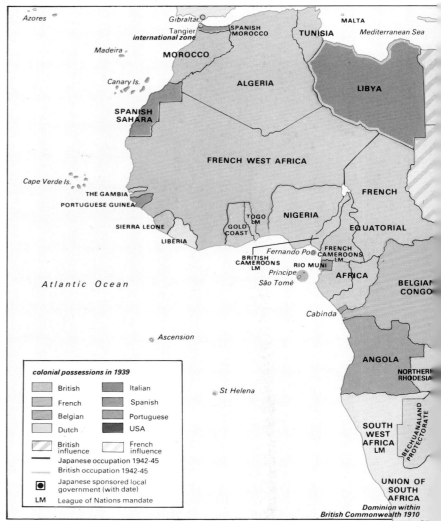

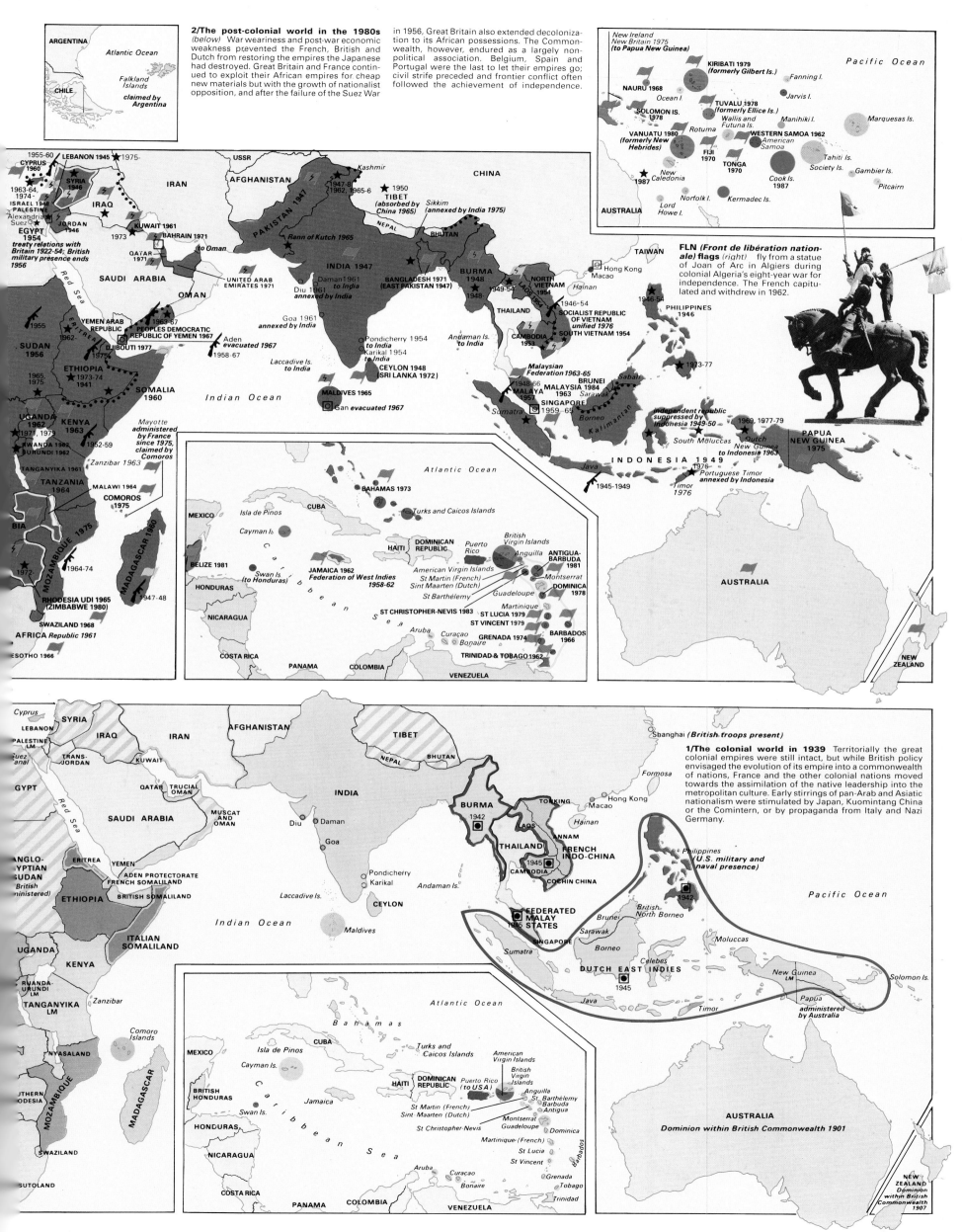

2/The post-colonial world in the 1980s

(below) War weariness and post-war economic weakness prevented the French, British and Dutch from restoring the empires the Japanese had destroyed. Great Britain and France continued to exploit their African empires for cheap new materials but with the growth of nationalist opposition, and after the failure of the Suez War in 1956, Great Britain also extended decolonization to its African possessions. The Commonwealth, however, endured as a largely non-political association. Belgium, Spain and Portugal were the last to let their empires go; civil strife preceded and frontier conflict often followed the achievement of independence.

FLN (*Front de libération nationale*) **flags** (*right*) fly from a statue of Joan of Arc in Algiers during colonial Algeria's eight-year war for independence. The French capitulated and withdrew in 1962.

1/The colonial world in 1939

Territorially the great colonial empires were still intact, but while British policy envisaged the evolution of its empire into a commonwealth of nations, France and the other colonial nations moved towards the assimilation of the native leadership into the metropolitan culture. Early stirrings of pan-Arab and Asiatic nationalism were stimulated by Japan, Kuomintang China or the Comintern, or by propaganda from Italy and Nazi Germany.

East Asia from 1945

JAPAN in August 1945 was at peace but in ruins, its major cities largely reduced to rubble and its economy devastated. Its people, moreover, were completely disoriented – they had not been prepared for defeat, especially not for defeat delivered in a uniquely devastating manner with the dropping of atomic bombs on Hiroshima and Nagasaki, followed by occupation by a foreign power. The occupation of Japan, placed under the authority of the Far Eastern Commission, included representatives of all the countries that had fought Japan. But in effect it was an American undertaking. Under General Douglas MacArthur, the occupation administration sought to demilitarize Japan and create a peaceful, democratic state. At the beginning of 1946, the emperor publicly denied his divinity, while the new constitution of May 1947 stated that sovereignty belonged to the people, made the Diet (the Japanese parliament) the highest political authority and established an independent judiciary. It also contained a renunciation of war as a means of settling international disputes. The American occupation administration also reformed Japan's education system, removing from the syllabus all material which had encouraged military and authoritarian values; instituted a programme of land reform which ended absentee landlordism; and sought, albeit without real success, to break up the great concentrations of corporate power. With the advance of the communists in China and the deterioration in American-Soviet relations after 1948, however, the Americans increasingly saw Japan as a potentially important ally, but one whose value would depend upon the reconstruction of its economic power. With its work effectively complete, the occupation ended formally in September 1951.

For Korea, Japan's defeat ended the harsh Japanese colonial regime imposed in 1910. But it also brought division. During the war it had been agreed that the Soviet Union would accept the surrender of Japanese forces north of the 38th parallel, the United States those to the south. Subsequently, Soviet forces supported the establishment of a communist state in the north under Kim Il-sung, a guerrilla leader who had spent considerable time in the Soviet Union. Kim created a communist party and state on the Soviet model: manufacturing industries (which had mostly been owned by the Japanese) were nationalized; land reform instituted; and a large military force built up. In the south, an American occupation administration was created which, after initial hopes of unification were dashed, worked toward the establishment of representative government. In August 1948, the strongly anti-communist Syngman Rhee became president of the Republic of Korea, ending American military government. Korea was now firmly divided, but both north and south entertained strong ambitions to unite the country under their own rule.

In June 1950 the North Koreans attacked the south, pushing the South Korean and United States forces back toward Pusan. The counter-attack came in September 1950, with an amphibious landing under MacArthur at Inchon, leading to the recapture of Seoul and a further offensive that promised to unify Korea by force. As the Americans advanced to the Yalu River in November 1950, the Chinese committed substantial forces to Korea. These regained control of the north. Further advances south were beyond them, however. Stalemate followed. In April 1951 President Truman dismissed MacArthur from his post, an indication that the United States would not seek to extend the war. Truce talks began in July and an armistice was signed in July 1953.

The establishment of the People's Republic of China in 1949 (see page 258) marked a fundamental turning point in the modern history of

China. After a century of severe internal conflict and disintegration, commonly provoked or exacerbated by external aggressors, China was now strongly governed by leaders who had a decisive vision of the society they wished to create. Whatever the excesses and failures since 1949 – not least the systematic repression of much of the population – that fundamental achievement must be recognized. This also means that China's modern experience should be judged less against the contemporary achievements of its neighbours in East Asia (the striking economic success of Japan, South Korea and Taiwan contrasting with China's frequent paralysis) but against its own past.

A central concern of the new regime was the economy – crucially, the raising of agricultural production and the creation of a heavy industrial base. In the early and mid-1950s, China closely followed the Soviet model of directed economic planning. Although China's first Five-Year Plan achieved some success, by the late 1950s Mao Tse-tung had lost faith in the gradualist approach of planners and technicians and sought instead to mobilize the revolutionary energies of China's vast population. The 'Great Leap Forward' was initiated early in 1958 and involved the creation of huge rural communes and urban associations charged with the organization of production. However, many of the specific projects (such as the construction of backyard furnaces to produce iron and steel) were simply unworkable and the Great Leap Forward was abandoned early in 1961. Four years later, Mao again unleashed the revolutionary energies of the Chinese people with the 'Great Proletarian Cultural Revolution' (1965–69) which sought to prevent the re-establishment of vested interests, careerism and bureaucratic arrogance in the party and state by launching 'permanent revolution'. Once again, ideology triumphed over expertise, producing chaos and misery.

In its external relations, the new communist regime, although denied recognition by the United States and excluded from the United Nations, quickly established itself on the world stage. China played an important role in the Geneva Conference on Indo-China in 1954 and at the Conference of Asian-African states held in Bandung, Indonesia, the following year. China

also maintained close relations with the Soviet Union in this period, accepting numerous Soviet experts and loans and some industrial plant. But that relationship also contained tensions, partly over territory, partly over policy and ideology within the communist world, particularly after the death of Stalin in 1953. When Khrushchev denounced Stalin in 1956 and began to promote the concept of peaceful coexistence with the capitalist bloc, a split became inevitable. It came in 1960. China's own realignment with the West took place only some 10 years later, after the Cultural Revolution, and was marked most dramatically by the official visit to China of US President Nixon in 1972.

Mao Tse-tung died in September 1976. Under the new dominant figure, Deng Xiaoping, a major shift in economic policy took place. Material incentives were re-established and foreign trade and investment encouraged. But the new directions taken by the economy were accompanied by an increasing pressure for

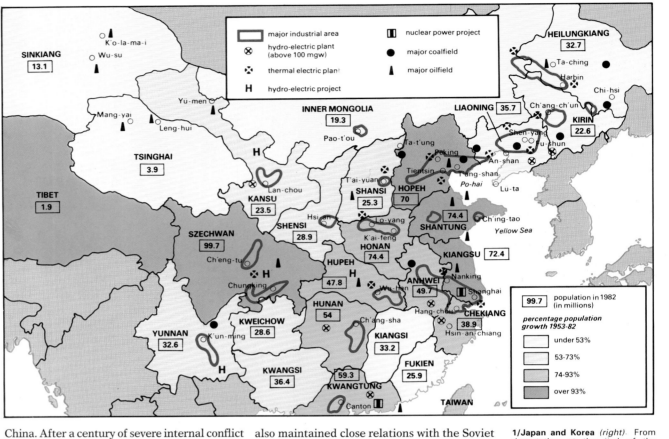

1/Japan and Korea (right) From devastation at the end of the Second World War, Japan emerged as an economic power house, by the 1980s challenging even the United States, its conqueror and, after the war, occupying power. After division into communist north and capitalist south in the civil war of 1950-3 (see map 2), the development of the two Koreas followed contrasting paths. North Korea, locked in its self-imposed communist fastness, remained an economic backwater, handicapped by the weight of the rigid ideology imposed on it by its leader, the ruthlessly authoritarian Kim Il-sung. South Korea, though far from a model democratic state for much of the post-war period, has developed a thriving industrial base. Like Japan in the same period, it has specialized in high-tech industries.

2/The Korean War (left) The Korean War carried the Cold War to the Far East. Occupied in 1945 by Soviet and American forces, the country was already divided de facto by 1948. In 1950, after the withdrawal of the occupying armies, the North Koreans attacked the South. The United States and United Nations immediately intervened. After initial North Korean successes, the Americans under General MacArthur counter-attacked and advanced to the Chinese frontier. This resulted in Chinese intervention and stalemate, ended only by the armistice of Panmunjom and the partition of the country along the 38th parallel.

3/The development of China (left)
The world's most populous nation, China developed rapidly after the civil war and communist takeover in 1949. The People's Republic established an industrial infrastructure, with growing petroleum and nuclear capabilities. But the country's industrial and agricultural expansion was slowed by the Great Leap Forward of the late 1950s and the Cultural Revolution of the mid-60s and her economy remained far below the spectacular growth of its neighbours in the Far East. Its potential for growth nonetheless remains enormous: a huge population, vast natural resources and low-cost base, allied to the latent entrepreneurial spirit of its people, are assets waiting to be tapped.

The economic recovery of Japan (right) As the level of Japanese exports grew after the war so Japanese investment overseas increased, too. By the end of the 1980s the country was a long-established economic super- power. But however impressive Japan's economic performance since 1945, the country has still had to contend with the global economic slow-down of the 1990s.

greater political freedoms. Here the Chinese leadership would not yield: pro-democracy protests in Peking in 1989 were violently crushed.

With the end of the occupation in 1951, Japan began a period of exceptionally high economic growth and within 20 years had become an economic super-power. The 1950s saw strong emphasis on the development of heavy industry: Japan soon became the world's principal ship-builder and the third-largest producer of iron and steel. But from the 1960s, Japanese industry moved into the production of high-technology consumer manufacturing – cars, televisions, cameras and computers – much of it directed toward export markets across the world. Indeed, most of the Japanese industrial and trading giants (Mitsui, Mitsubishi, Toyota) also established production or assembly plants overseas, notably in Southeast Asia but also in Europe and North America. It is for this reason that the volume of Japan's foreign investment rose dramatically from the early 1970s. Japan's phenomenal economic expansion owed much to government intervention and support, largely directed through the powerful Ministry of International Trade and Industry (MITI), and

the distinctive character of employee-company relations, which emphasized extensive consultation and group loyalty. But Japan's status as an economic super-power still left the country's international role unresolved. Whatever its prestige as an economic power, on the world stage the country remained a pygmy.

The Korean peninsula, following the 1953 truce, was divided between two intensely hostile and heavily armed regimes. The north remained under the leadership of Kim il-sung, the focus of an extraordinary personality cult; and although material conditions for the people gradually improved the country virtually excluded the non-communist world. In the south, student revolts ended Syngman Rhee's authoritarian rule in 1960 and a military coup brought Park Chung-hee to power with a presidential administration, backed by the military, from 1963. Following the assassination of Park in 1979, a new military strongman, Chun Doo Hwan, came to power. From the mid-1960s, South Korea embarked on rapid industrialization and emerged as one of the 'little tigers' of the Asian economy. That industrialization was strongly oriented towards the production of consumer manufac-

turing for export markets and depended on low wage costs and, at least initially, heavy foreign investment. Over this period of rapid economic growth, South Korean regimes showed little tolerance of political dissent: open protest, commonly student led, was forcefully crushed.

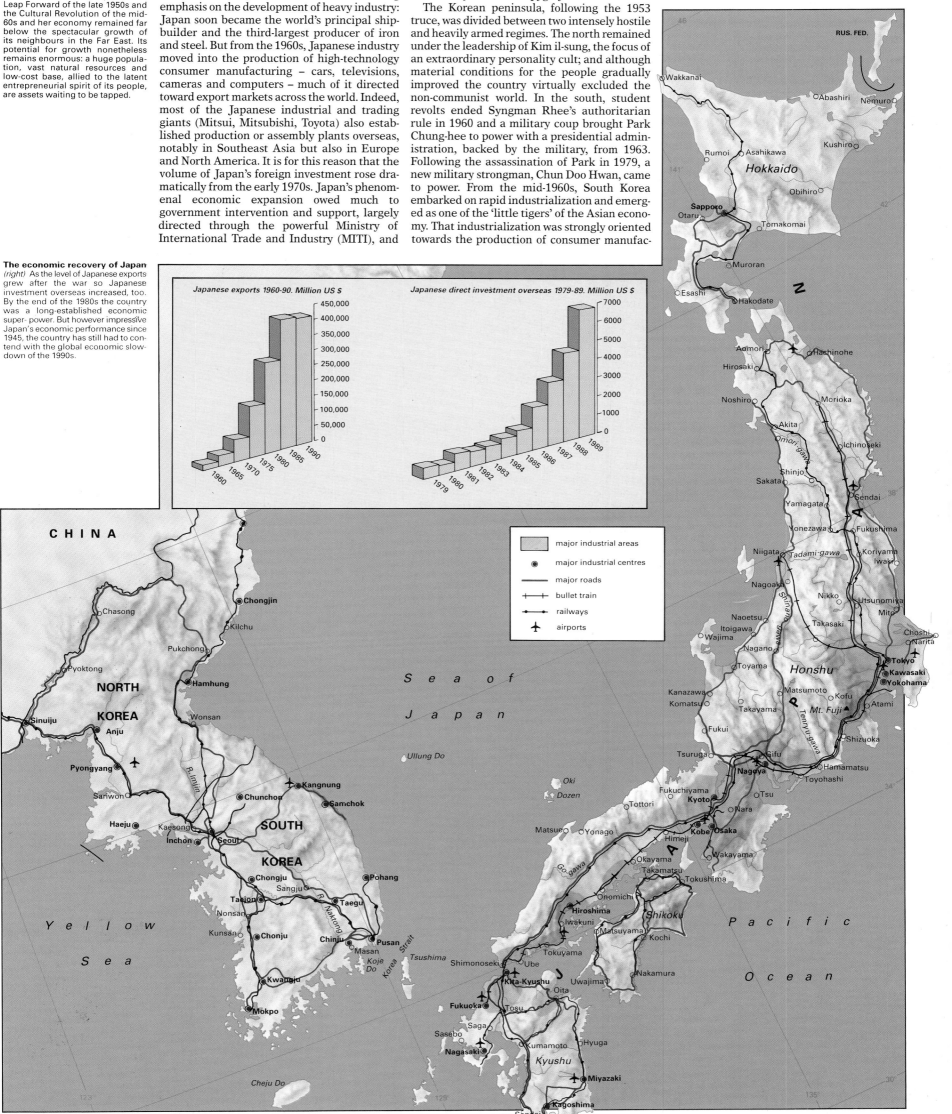

Japanese exports 1960-90. Million US $

Japanese direct investment overseas 1979-89. Million US $

	major industrial areas
	major industrial centres
	major roads
	bullet train
	railways
	airports

Southeast Asia from 1945

THE Japanese military advance into Southeast Asia in 1941–2 expelled western colonial regimes from the region but after Japan's collapse in mid-1945 those same powers sought to return to their pre-war territories, though with widely differing ambitions.

The United States returned to the Philippines where, in the mid-1930s, it had established a time-table for constitutional reform and subsequent political independence. Consequently, many Filipinos fought alongside the Americans in 1941 and again during the liberation of their islands in 1944; and, despite the political turmoil and physical destruction of the war years, the Americans left the Philippines as agreed in July 1946. Political instability, however, led to a weakened Philippine economy in the 1980s: the embezzlement of the national coffers by the Marcos family and its acolytes, growing weight of popular protest against their regime between 1983 and 1986, and the insecurity of the Aquino administration (frequently threatened by coups), brought in severe economic difficulties.

Unlike the US in the Philippines, the British returned to Burma and Malaya committed to re-establish colonial rule but soon had to accept that withdrawal was inevitable. Burma, whose pre-war constitutional evolution had been closely tied to that of India, followed her to political independence in January 1948. The British withdrawal from Malaya began in the early 1950s and the peninsular states achieved political independence in 1957 (in 1963 they were joined by Singapore, Sabah and Sarawak in a wider independent union, the Federation of Malaysia). The process of withdrawal from the Malay peninsula was accompanied by a communist insurrection, the Malayan 'Emergency', which endured from mid-1948 until 1960. Led by the

protracted and became one of the most bitter armed conflicts of the 20th century. After the Japanese collapse in August 1945, Ho Chi Minh established a communist regime in the north while the French, with British help, re-imposed their rule in the south with dreams of recreating their Southeast Asian empire, even without north Vietnam. For over a year Ho Chi Minh sought unsuccessfully to persuade the French to withdraw peacefully, arguing that the south was an integral part of his country, but late in 1946 war broke out between his supporters (the Viet Minh) and the French, only ending with the humiliating French defeat at Dien Bien Phu in spring 1954. However, France's departure did not leave a unified Vietnam: at the Geneva Conference convened immediately after Dien Bien Phu, the Soviet Union and China put pressure on the Viet Minh to accept a 'temporary' partition of Vietnam at the 17th parallel. The Viet Minh assumed that nationwide elections scheduled for 1956 would lead to unification under the communists but the new Vietnamese administration in the south and its American patron refused to sign the Geneva agreement and no elections were held.

In 1959 the north Vietnamese again resorted to arms to achieve unification. The anti-communist regime in the south enjoyed massive American support: ordnance and advisers to begin with, but ground troops and air-strikes after 1965. In the ensuing guerrilla war, the north received supplies from China and the Soviet Union. By the late 1960s, however, it became clear that US intervention could not halt communist 'aggression' towards the south and that US involvement was damaging the American economy and creating wide divisions within American society (divisions further

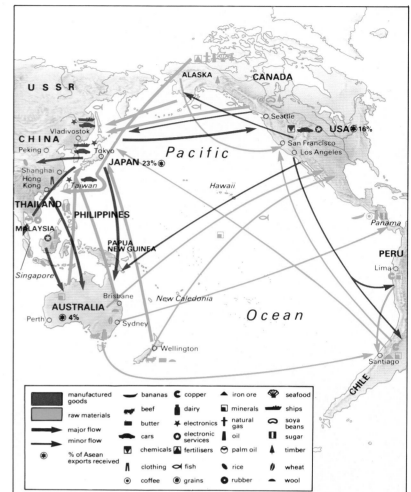

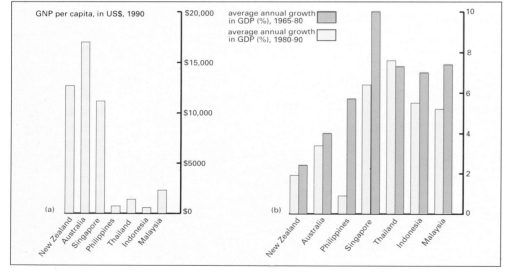

Economic success is reflected (far left) in per capita gross national product figures for 1990. Average annual growth in gross domestic product (left) from 1965-80 and 1980-90 remained high in politically stable economies.

2/Trade flows around the Pacific rim (above) The post-war years saw high economic growth rates in some parts of East and Southeast Asia, encouraged by America. The US-Japanese trade flow consisted primarily of agricultural exports to Japan and electronic and automobile imports to the US; but as many other Asian countries developed their markets in manufactured goods they became increasingly dependent on imported raw materials. The level of US and Japanese investment in Southeast Asia showed the importance of the Pacific rim as an economic sphere of influence and indicated an informal empire of trade and investment centred on Japan, Taiwan, Singapore and the US west coast.

The contrasting faces of Southeast Asia after 1945. The adoption of microchip technology (above) and the export of inexpensive electronic manufactures brought increasing economic prosperity to Malaysia, Singapore, Taiwan and Thailand. However, in countries such as Burma (below) civil unrest in the cities and a devastated countryside extinguished any immediate hope of economic advancement.

ethnic Chinese of the Malayan Communist Party, it was less concerned with expelling the British administration – the British were clearly keen to leave – than with the socio-political structure of the state that would succeed it.

At the other extreme lay the Dutch and French administrations returning to Indonesia and Vietnam, respectively. Both were fiercely determined to re-establish their rule regardless of the political ambitions of the indigenous peoples; and both encountered fierce resistance from populations politicized and, frequently, armed by the Japanese. As a result, the Dutch and the French became enmeshed in lengthy and bloody anti-colonial wars. Helped by division among local leaders, the Dutch in Indonesia came close to defeating the infant republic but world opinion turned against them. Eventually the US forced the Dutch to yield by threatening to cut American reconstruction aid to Europe and, in late December 1949, the Dutch withdrew.

The French struggle in Vietnam proved more

widened in 1970 by the extension of the war into Cambodia). Negotiations between Hanoi and Washington began in late 1968 and under the agreement eventually reached in early 1973 American ground troops withdrew. The US continued to supply the Saigon regime on a massive scale but when the communists launched an orthodox military offensive in spring 1975, the south's army simply collapsed. Vietnam was now unified, under Hanoi.

Three decades of war left the Vietnamese economy in ruins and hopes of rapid economic reconstruction after unification remained unfulfilled. The country's geriatric and ideologically rigid leadership found that building a modern economy demanded political and administrative skills very different from those used to defeat the US. Moreover, real peace remained elusive: Vietnam clashed briefly with China and then found itself drawn into Cambodia, where its troops were instrumental in the overthrow of the Pol Pot regime in late 1978. Vietnamese inter-

GNP per capita, in US$, 1990

average annual growth in GDP (%), 1965-80
average annual growth in GDP (%), 1980-90

(a) New Zealand, Australia, Singapore, Philippines, Thailand, Indonesia, Malaysia

(b) New Zealand, Australia, Philippines, Singapore, Thailand, Indonesia, Malaysia

3/Indo-China *(right)* From 1945 to 1954 Indo-China struggled against French colonial rule. After defeat at Dien Bien Phu (1954) the French withdrew, but the US refused to subscribe to the Geneva agreements and instead established a counter-revolutionary government in Saigon under President Ngo Dinh Diem. The result was the second Indo-Chinese war of 1957-73. In spite of saturation bombing and the commitment of over half a million ground troops, the US failed to break North Vietnamese resistance. A compromise settlement in 1973 led eventually to the collapse of the Saigon government in 1975, when the US finally withdrew.

areas controlled by the NLF

areas controlled by the Saigon government

contested areas

7th US Fleet 1964

vention endured through the 1980s, inflicting additional damage on the country's economic and administrative resources and reinforcing its ostracism by the western, capitalist world. Economic reconstruction was also severely hampered by the withholding of US recognition, thereby denying Vietnam access to the World Bank and the International Bank for Reconstruction and Development. Towards the end of the 1980s, however, with its per-capita income among the lowest in the world, Vietnam began to move towards a market economy and to attract foreign investment and technology.

Political instability after 1945, occasionally allied with ideological rigidity, had damaging economic consequences in other parts of Southeast Asia as well. In Burma economic growth since independence in 1948 remained extremely poor, partly because of ethnic and communist insurrections but mainly because Burma's political leadership inflexibly pursued a policy of economic self-sufficiency. In Indonesia earlier political divisions were exacerbated by efforts to create a cohesive national political and economic structure across a vast archipelago which had been disunited under the Dutch. Regional rebel-

lions against the centre, notably the West Sumatra rebellion in 1958, became a prominent feature of the 1950s and 1960s. However Indonesia resisted fragmentation largely because of the political skills and driving oratory of President Achmed Sukarno who launched numerous campaigns – for the nationalization of Dutch businesses in the 1950s; for Indonesian sovereignty in West Irian; against the formation of the Malaysian federation in 1963 – in order to sustain the spirit of the revolution. Sukarno's dramatic politics and their damaging economic consequences ended in September 1965, when he was replaced as President by Raden Suharto.

These histories of economic instability contrasted dramatically with the rates of growth achieved by Malaysia, Singapore, Thailand and even Indonesia from the late 1960s. Despite the world recession of the 1980s, each experienced an average annual growth rate well in excess of 5 percent – thanks primarily to the creation of a substantial industrial base oriented towards export markets throughout Asia, Europe and North America. Industrial production and exports concentrated on textiles and electronic goods, and Malaysia, in partnership with a Japanese multinational, even began production of a car (the Proton) which found a substantial market in Europe.

Numerous factors contributed to this rapid industrial growth: all these economies, with the exception of Singapore, possessed large pools of cheap labour; while labour legislation ensured that workers remained quiescent – an added attraction for multinationals seeking a low-paid, docile workforce. In addition, local governments sought to attract substantial foreign investment through tax incentives and infrastructural development. A major part of that investment came from Japan which emerged as the principal economic partner for many of the countries of Southeast Asia. Political stability, too, played a key role in underpinning the economic strategy of industrial development and the attraction of foreign investment: Suharto in Indonesia, Lee in Singapore and Mahathir in Malaysia all ruled firmly and suppressed internal opposition.

1/Revolt and war *(below)* dominated Southeast Asia after 1945. The voluntary or forced withdrawal of colonial administrations seldom resulted in peace or economic stability as political, religious and ethnic rivalries flared into national or international conflicts.

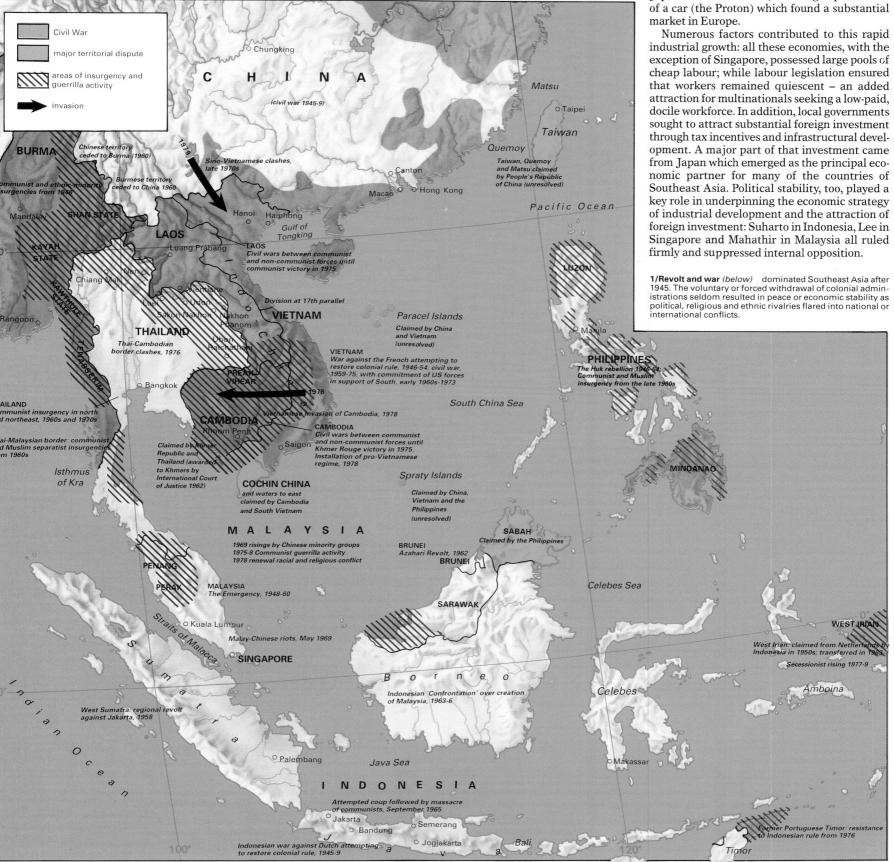

Civil War

major territorial dispute

areas of insurgency and guerrilla activity

invasion

CHINA *(civil war 1945-9)*

Chinese territory ceded to Burma (1960)

Sino-Vietnamese clashes, late 1970s

Burmese territory ceded to China 1960

Taiwan, Quemoy and Matsu claimed by People's Republic of China (unresolved)

BURMA

Communist and ethnic minority insurgencies from 1948

LAOS
Civil wars between communist and non-communist forces until communist victory in 1975

Division at 17th parallel

THAILAND
Thai-Cambodian border clashes, 1976

Paracel Islands
Claimed by China and Vietnam (unresolved)

VIETNAM
War against the French attempting to restore colonial rule, 1946-54; civil war, 1959-75, with commitment of US forces in support of South, early 1960s-1973

THAILAND
Communist insurgency in north and northeast, 1960s and 1970s

Thai-Malaysian border: communist and Muslim separatist insurgencies from 1960s

PREAH VIHEAR

CAMBODIA
Civil wars between communist and non-communist forces until Khmer Rouge victory in 1975. Installation of pro-Vietnamese regime, 1978

Vietnamese invasion of Cambodia, 1978

South China Sea

PHILIPPINES
The Huk rebellion 1946-54; Communist and Muslim insurgency from the late 1960s

Claimed by Khmer Republic and Thailand (awarded to Khmers by International Court of Justice 1962)

COCHIN CHINA
and waters to east claimed by Cambodia and South Vietnam

Spraty Islands

Claimed by China, Vietnam and the Philippines (unresolved)

MINDANAO

MALAYSIA
1969 risings by Chinese minority groups
1975-8 Communist guerrilla activity
1978 renewal racial and religious conflict

SABAH
Claimed by the Philippines

BRUNEI
Azahari Revolt, 1962

Isthmus of Kra

Celebes Sea

PENANG

PERAK

SARAWAK

WEST IRIAN

West Irian: claimed from Netherlands by Indonesia in 1950s; transferred in 1969

Secessionist rising 1977-9

MALAYSIA
The Emergency, 1948-60

Malay-Chinese riots, May 1969

SINGAPORE

B o r n e o

Celebes

Amboina

Indonesian 'Confrontation' over creation of Malaysia, 1963-6

West Sumatra: regional revolt against Jakarta, 1958

Java Sea

INDONESIA

Former Portuguese Timor: resistance to Indonesian rule from 1976

Attempted coup followed by massacre of communists, September 1965

Indonesian war against Dutch attempting to restore colonial rule, 1945-9

South Asia since independence

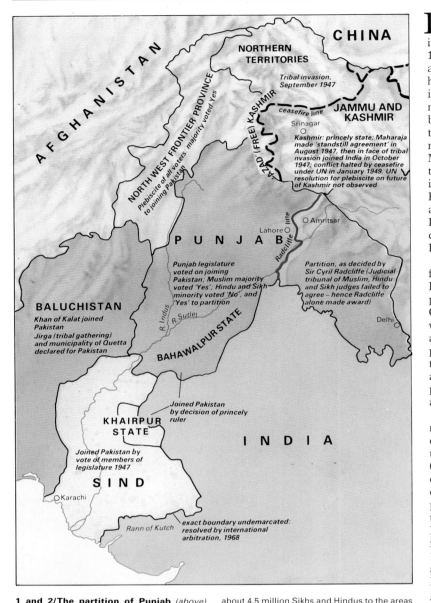

1 and 2/The partition of Punjab (above) **and Bengal** (below) The division of the Indian sub-continent in 1947 particularly affected Punjab and Bengal. The result of partition was a great exodus. Some 6 million Muslims migrated from Punjab to the new Pakistan and about 4.5 million Sikhs and Hindus to the areas between Amritsar and Delhi. In Bengal over 2 million Hindus left the eastern sector (now Bangladesh); thousands of Muslims from Bihar, Calcutta and elsewhere sought shelter in East Bengal.

INDEPENDENCE from British rule came to India and Pakistan in August 1947, to Burma in January 1948, and to Ceylon in February 1948, but was fraught with difficulties for India and Pakistan. The Indian National Conference had favoured a strong central government to implement economic development and promote national integration but the Muslim League, led by Mohammed Ali Jinnah, rejected this. Thus the price of independence for the Hindu-dominated Congress was the creation of a separate Muslim state of Pakistan, and the partition of the provinces of Punjab in the west and Bengal in the east. Hindu-Muslim rioting and the British desire for a rapid departure from India after the Second World War forced the Viceroy, Lord Mountbatten, to hasten plans for independence and on 15 August 1947 the new states of India and Pakistan came into being.

The delimitation of new frontiers led to conflict, particularly in Punjab and Bengal. In Punjab, the boundary cut through rich farmland populated by Sikhs, Muslims and Hindus. Communal riots raged, and an exodus began, with Muslims moving westwards into Pakistan and Sikhs and Hindus eastwards into India. The partition of Bengal produced similar results, though, unlike West Pakistan, the east retained a sizeable Hindu minority. As many as 500,000 people may have lost their lives during partition, and 14 million fled across the new boundaries.

The resettlement of so many refugees was a major burden on the new states and conflict has continued between immigrant and resident populations. Independence also left the fate of the 600 princely states of the sub-continent undecided: rulers could either join India or Pakistan, or opt for their own independence. The latter proved impractical and most promptly acceded to either India or Pakistan, but when the Muslim Nizam of Hyderabad resisted, his state was forcibly absorbed after Indian 'police action' in 1948. Kashmir's Hindu ruler also hesitated, but an invasion of tribesmen from the Northwest Frontier, backed by Pakistan, persuaded him to join his Muslim-majority state to India, though with the promise of a plebiscite on the issue. A United Nations ceasefire line was agreed in 1949, but Kashmir remained a major cause of contention between India and Pakistan.

All states of south Asia have been troubled by demands from religious, ethnic and linguistic minorities. The Government of India's attempt to promote Hindi as a national language was strenuously resisted in the Dravidian south, especially in Madras province (now Tamil Nadu). In 1956, the government of Jawaharlal Nehru reluctantly agreed to reorganize the states along linguistic lines, but conflict over state boundaries and demands for new states or greater regional autonomy has remained. In the northeast, tribal groups led by the Nagas and Mizos, have sought either independence or statehood. Conflict has been exacerbated by migration across linguistic frontiers, for instance by Tamils to Bombay, or even international boundaries, as in the case of Bangladeshi migration from East Pakistan into Assam and Tripura. Nor was conflict between Hindus and Muslims resolved by partition which left India with a large Muslim minority. Communal tension grew, particularly over religious sites such as the disputed Babri mosque at Ayodhya.

Ethnic and regional conflicts in Pakistan have periodically erupted into violence, particularly in Sind, where the local population has clashed with Muhajir refugees from India. In 1971 these differences led to the breakup of Pakistan after only 24 years. East Pakistan, some 1000 miles (1600 km) from its western partner, deeply resented its economic and political subordination. Pakistan's military leader, Yahya Khan, tried to repress demands for autonomy in the East, but the Government of India intervened in support of local guerrillas, the Pakistan army was defeated and the new state of Bangladesh emerged under Sheikh Majibur Rahman.

For its part, Ceylon experienced an untroubled transfer of power in 1948 and for 30 years had a relatively stable political system. During this time, however, the Buddhist, Sinhala-speaking majority sought to consolidate its political dominance. Some 800,000 Tamil workers on the tea estates, descended from labourers brought in by British planters, were disenfranchised after independence and rendered stateless. Many were eventually repatriated to India; only about 100,000 acquired citizenship in 1986. The pursuit of a pro-Buddhist, Sinhala-only policy in Ceylon, renamed Sri Lanka in 1972, increased fears of exclusion from employment and political decision-making among the Hindu Tamil minority. A campaign began for autonomy within a loose federal state or, failing that, for a separate Tamil state ('Eelam'), and by 1986 the rebels, led by 'Tamil Tiger' guerrillas, had virtually driven government forces from the Jaffna peninsula. Continuing conflict drew the Government of India into stationing an Indian 'peace-keeping force' in the area from 1987 to 1990.

Thus internal conflicts in south Asia have often had important regional as well as domestic ramifications and, along with the legacies of colonial rule and the quest for political security, have resulted in a series of international clashes. Although the French departed peacefully from their coastal enclaves (principally Pondicherry) in 1956, the Portuguese were only expelled by force from Goa in 1961. A dispute over India's Himalayan frontiers, only partly delineated under British rule, plunged India into war with China in 1962. Despite China's unilateral decision to withdraw from much of the territory taken, the war left India feeling insecure and led to a massive military presence along the contested border, the incorporation of Sikkim into India in 1975, and attempts to establish a wider Indian hegemony over the region. In 1965 Pakistan sought to resolve the dispute over Kashmir by military means: in the ensuing fighting India made some territorial gains, but a subsequent agreement at Tashkent restored the status quo.

All the main states of south Asia have tried parliamentary government, though Nepal and Bhutan retained their monarchies. But democracy has had little success in the face of military coups and political assassinations. Following a period of parliamentary instability, Pakistan first came under martial law in 1958 with General Ayub Khan. He and his successor, General Yahya Khan, retained military control of Pakistan until 1971. Six years of civilian rule failed to break the pattern and in 1977 the military returned under General Zia ul Huq. His death in 1988 brought only a precarious restoration of civilian government. Bangladesh's brief experiment with democracy likewise ended with the murder of Majibur Rahman in 1975 and a series of military coups.

India has kept the military at bay, but between 1975 and 1977 prime minister Indira Gandhi declared a state of emergency until, with misplaced confidence, she called a general election and was heavily defeated. Re-elected in 1980, she faced growing unrest in Punjab, where Sikh extremists demanded the creation of an independent state of Khalistan. In 1985 Mrs Gandhi was assassinated by her Sikh bodyguard and her son Rajiv became prime minister. Despite his initial popularity, Rajiv Gandhi experienced continuing difficulties over Punjab, Sri Lanka and other regional issues. After falling from power he, too, was killed in 1991, further emphasizing the bloody path of assassination and political strife in south Asia since partition.

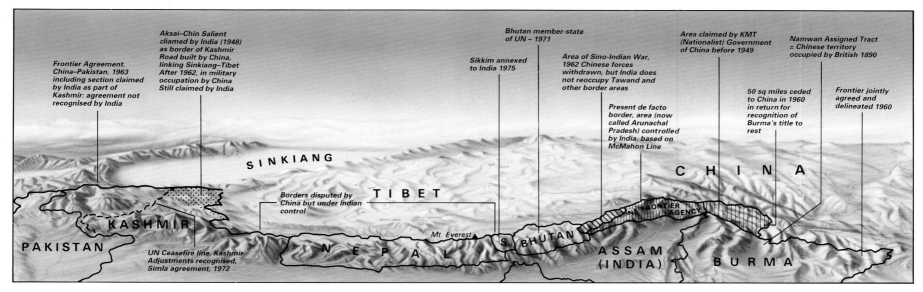

Frontier Agreement. China–Pakistan, 1963 including section claimed by India as part of Kashmir: agreement not recognised by India

Aksai-Chin Salient claimed by India (1948) as border of Kashmir Road built by China, linking Sinkiang–Tibet After 1962, in military occupation by China Still claimed by India

Bhutan member-state of UN – 1971

Sikkim annexed to India 1975

Area of Sino-Indian War, 1962 Chinese forces withdrawn, but India does not reoccupy Tawang and other border areas

Area claimed by KMT (Nationalist) Government of China before 1949

Namwan Assigned Tract = Chinese territory occupied by British 1890

Present de facto border, area (now called Arunachal Pradesh) controlled by India, based on McMahon Line

50 sq miles ceded to China in 1960 in return for recognition of Burma's title to rest

Frontier jointly agreed and delineated 1960

SINKIANG

TIBET

CHINA

Borders disputed by China but under Indian control

KASHMIR

PAKISTAN

Mt. Everest

NEPAL

BHUTAN

FRONTIER AGENCY

ASSAM (INDIA)

BURMA

UN Ceasefire line, Kashmir Adjustments recognised, Simla agreement, 1972

3/Ethnic and Political Conflict (below) Since independence the countries of south Asia have suffered from internal conflicts as well as major confrontations between states. There have been three wars between India and Pakistan and one between India and China. Both Pakistan and Sri Lanka have endured civil war, and key areas of India have spent long periods under martial law or president's rule. Boundaries inherited from colonial rule have been one factor in international disputes, but domestic and regional conflict has also arisen from migration, demands for greater autonomy from centralizing states, and from attempts by religious, linguistic and ethnic minorities to assert their own identities or resist incorporation into larger political and cultural units.

4/Boundary disputes (above) When China lost control over Tibet the British unilaterally fixed the boundaries of India along the McMahon Line (1914). In 1959 Communist China reoccupied Tibet and began to assert rights to territories also claimed by India. In 1962 China invaded the Northeast Frontier Agency, defeated the Indian Army and imposed its own boundary lines, still disputed by India.

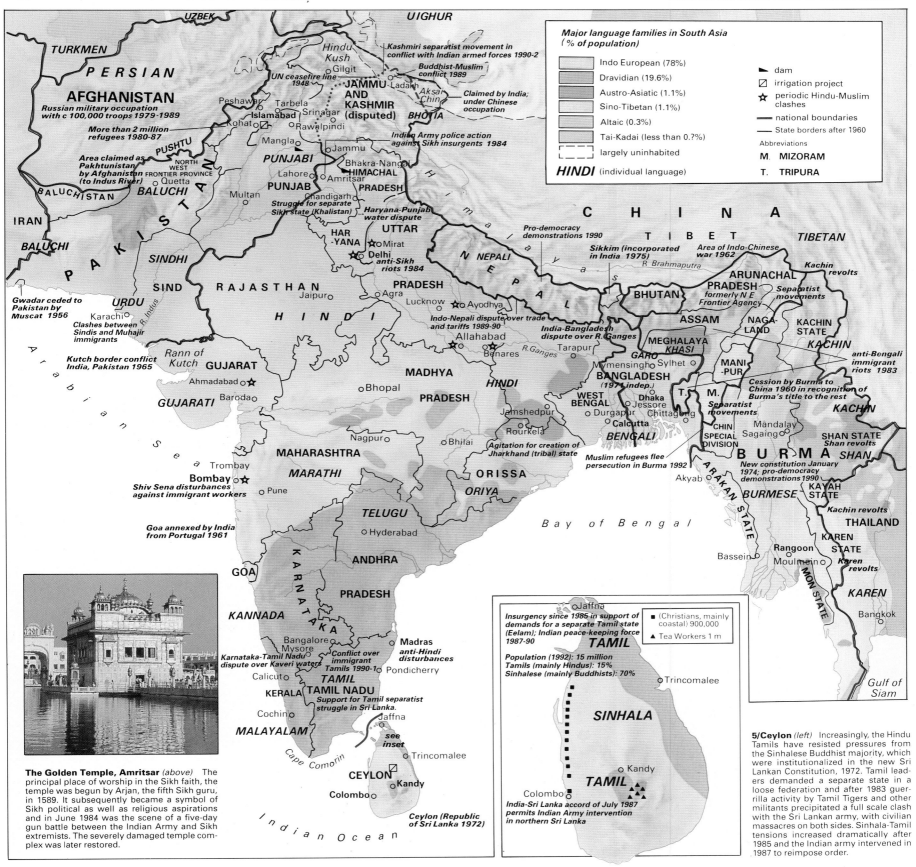

Major language families in South Asia (% of population)
- Indo European (78%)
- Dravidian (19.6%)
- Austro-Asiatic (1.1%)
- Sino-Tibetan (1.1%)
- Altaic (0.3%)
- Tai-Kadai (less than 0.7%)
- largely uninhabited

HINDI (individual language)

- dam
- irrigation project
- periodic Hindu-Muslim clashes
- national boundaries
- State borders after 1960

Abbreviations
M. MIZORAM
T. TRIPURA

The Golden Temple, Amritsar (above) The principal place of worship in the Sikh faith, the temple was begun by Arjan, the fifth Sikh guru, in 1589. It subsequently became a symbol of Sikh political as well as religious aspirations and in June 1984 was the scene of a five-day gun battle between the Indian Army and Sikh extremists. The severely damaged temple complex was later restored.

5/Ceylon (left) Increasingly, the Hindu Tamils have resisted pressures from the Sinhalese Buddhist majority, which were institutionalized in the new Sri Lankan Constitution, 1972. Tamil leaders demanded a separate state in a loose federation and after 1983 guerrilla activity by Tamil Tigers and other militants precipitated a full scale clash with the Sri Lankan army, with civilian massacres on both sides. Sinhala-Tamil tensions increased dramatically after 1985 and the Indian army intervened in 1987 to reimpose order.

Insurgency since 1985 in support of demands for a separate Tamil state (Eelam); Indian peace-keeping force 1987-90

(Christians, mainly coastal) 900,000
Tea Workers 1m

Population (1992): 15 million
Tamils (mainly Hindus): 15%
Sinhalese (mainly Buddhists): 70%

India-Sri Lanka accord of July 1987 permits Indian Army intervention in northern Sri Lanka

The emancipation of Africa from 1946

IN 1939 control over most of the African continent appeared secure, but within 40 years white control was confined to a South African *laager*. However, the Second World War and the consequent social changes, often accompanied by heightened political consciousness, strengthened the hands of African leaders committed to the social and political advancement of their nations.

Equally important were changes taking place outside Africa. Allied victory greatly increased the prestige of the USSR, while the USA emerged determined to prevent the colonial powers from impeding the extension of American influence. In France and Britain, liberals and socialists sympathetic to African claims initiated programmes of social improvement and political reform (though these ran into difficulties in territories where they threatened the interests of white settler populations). But even reformers appreciated that colonial empire might assist Britain and France to recover some of their economic strength and political influence. From about 1947 the onset of the Cold War and the continuing dollar famine pointed towards a certain reassertion of colonial control; France's fierce repression of rebellion in Madagascar was only the most striking demonstration of this.

Some nationalist movements nevertheless effectively challenged these policies. In 1948 riots in Accra and other Gold Coast towns constrained the British government to initiate constitutional reforms which three years later enabled the Convention Peoples' Party of Kwame Nkrumah to achieve a striking electoral success. Meanwhile disturbances in the Ivory Coast led the French government to seek reconciliation with the *Rassemblement Democratique Africain*, which had been hitherto distrusted because of Communist influence. By 1960 both British and French governments had begun to transfer responsibility to elected governments in their West African colonies.

Muslim North Africa longer-established nationalist movements received great stimulus from the overthrow of the Egyptian monarchy in 1952, and the subsequent rise of Gamal Abdel Nasser. In 1953-4 Britain agreed to withdraw her troops from the Suez Canal zone and to accelerate the independence of Sudan; in 1956 France accepted the independence of the protectorates of Tunisia and Morocco. But in Algeria, which was considered part of metropolitan France,

French determination to maintain control had been clear since their repression of a popular rising in 1945; in November 1954 the *Front de Libération Nationale* began a war which continued with increasing ferocity until 1962 (see map 3) when independence was granted. In 1956 Britain and France (in concert with Israel) attempted to protect their interests in the Suez Canal and reassert their power in the region by invading the Suez Canal zone; but strong opposition from the USA, the USSR and the UN showed that such methods were no longer practicable.

In the south and east, the crucial event of the post-war years was the election of a Nationalist government in South Africa under D.F. Malan, dedicated to the establishment of an Afrikaner Republic and policies of racial apartheid. Settlers in Kenya, though numbering only about 40,000, at one time hoped for ascendancy in an East African dominion; but these hopes perished after 1952, when the British government assumed responsibility for combatting the Mau Mau insurrection directed against the settlers.

In Central Africa the British in 1953 enacted the federation of Nyasaland and Northern and Southern Rhodesia, with Rhodesian whites in a dominant position; but after 1960 this too collapsed under the force of what the British Prime Minister Harold Macmillan called the 'wind of change'. Ghanaian independence provided a great stimulus to African nationalists; Dr Hastings Banda returned from a pan-African conference in Accra in 1958 to lead the anti-Federation movement in Nyasaland (Malawi), while Patrice Lumumba's enthusiasm accelerated the drive to independence in the Belgian Congo, now Zaire (see map 2). With the achievement of independence in Nigeria and most of the former French colonies, 1960 appeared to be Africa's year.

During the 1960s, however, this state of euphoria largely evaporated. The African economy proved fragile, and the ethnic rivalries and political disorders of Zaire were reproduced in other states; military coups and takeovers became more common, and in Nigeria led in 1967 to a destructive civil war. While the Algerian revolutionaries achieved independence in 1962 after a bitter eight-year war, the Portuguese government failed to learn its lesson: nationalists were driven into revolutionary warfare in Angola, Mozambique and Guinea-Bissau. In 1965 Ian Smith illegally declared the independence of white-dominated Rhodesia; the British govern-

ment failed to repress this rebellion, and during the 1970s African nationalists resorted to armed rebellion here also. Behind these surviving colonial regimes stood the growing economic and military power of South Africa, since 1961 a republic outside the Commonwealth and committed to repressive measures against militant African nationalists.

In 1974 the overthrow of the Portuguese dictatorship opened the way to independence for her African colonies. By 1980 the armed struggle of nationalist guerrillas, the support of the Organization of African Unity (united on this as on nothing else), and international pressures through the British government, interacted to replace the rebel regime in Rhodesia by the Republic of Zimbabwe. South Africa sought to protect itself by tightening its illegal control of Namibia, by military incursions into neighbouring states, and by conceding to the impoverished labour reserves known as 'Bantustans' a spurious independence. By the later 1980s, however, it was clear that the apartheid system could not survive. The key event here was the decision to release Nelson Mandela in February 1990 and open negotiations with the African National Congress to achieve a new political settlement.

For the new states, immediate economic prospects remained poor. For some, the exploitation of petroleum and other minerals offered short-term relief, though often at the cost of diverting resources from producing food for rapidly growing populations. Increasingly, elected governments proved unable to control problems of poverty, corruption and ethnic rivalry and were replaced by military dictatorships or single-party regimes. In the 1980s and early 1990s, civil war, famine, drought and an appalling refugee problem became dominant themes in West, East and southern Africa.

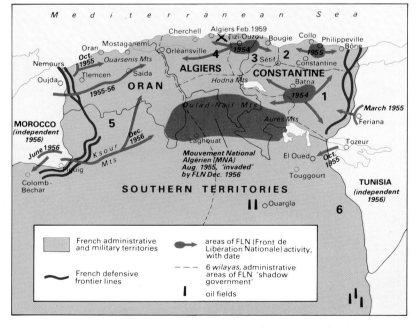

2/The Congo crisis, 1960-5 (*left*)
Tribal and regional factions in the Congo (independent 20 June 1960) led to demands for a federal constitution. However, the federalist leader, Kasavubu, of the Bakongo tribal party (ABAKO) was opposed by Lumumba's centralist *Mouvement National Congolais* (MNC). After a compromise a central government was formed, but the army, left under Belgian officers, mutinied on 4 July. Belgium flew in troops to protect her civilians and interests. On 11 July the mineral-rich province of Katanga seceded under Moise Tshombe. Lumumba and Kasavubu, convinced that Belgium wished to regain control, called in the UN. Following the dismissal of Lumumba, and his murder in Katanga, the UN intervened with US support, but attempts to reach a compromise with Katanga were abandoned. By 1963 Katanga was overrun by the UN. Tshombe, who had withdrawn to Angola, was recalled as President in 1964 and, with Belgian and US aid, suppressed a new revolt backed by the OAU. But both he and Kasavubu were overthrown by the army under Mobutu in November 1965.

3/The Algerian Civil War, 1954-62 (*above*)
In 1945 France assumed Algeria would be reincorporated into the Fourth Republic. However, this assumption was challenged by nationalist demonstrations which were followed by violent repression. Subsequent reforms did not satisfy the more nationalist Algerians; in 1954 they formed the *Front de Libération Nationale* (FLN) and launched attacks on 1 November on French positions throughout Algeria. France was committed to protecting oil and gas resources, but faced a formidable underground army – a revolutionary movement of socialist inspiration, capable of eliminating its rival the *Mouvement Nationaliste Algérien* (MNA). In 1958 the threat of a military coup by the frustrated French army brought de Gaulle to power in France. Holding Algeria was only possible at an unacceptable price since the FLN could not be broken, refusing offers to negotiate peace without independence. In the Evian agreements of March 1962 de Gaulle finally recognized Algerian sovereignty, though with provision to safeguard continuing French interests.

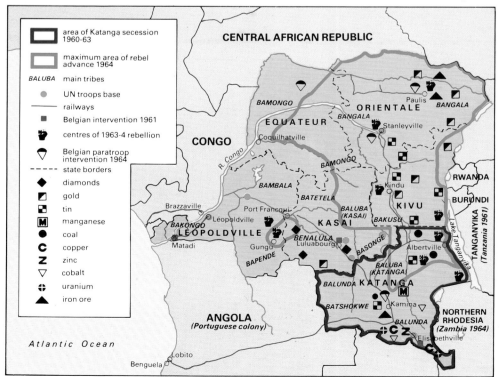

▭	area of Katanga secession 1960-63
▭	maximum area of rebel advance 1964
BALUBA	main tribes
●	UN troops base
	railways
■	Belgian intervention 1961
✊	centres of 1963-4 rebellion
▽	Belgian paratroop intervention 1964
---	state borders
◆	diamonds
◪	gold
■	tin
M	manganese
●	coal
C	copper
Z	zinc
▽	cobalt
⊕	uranium
▲	iron ore

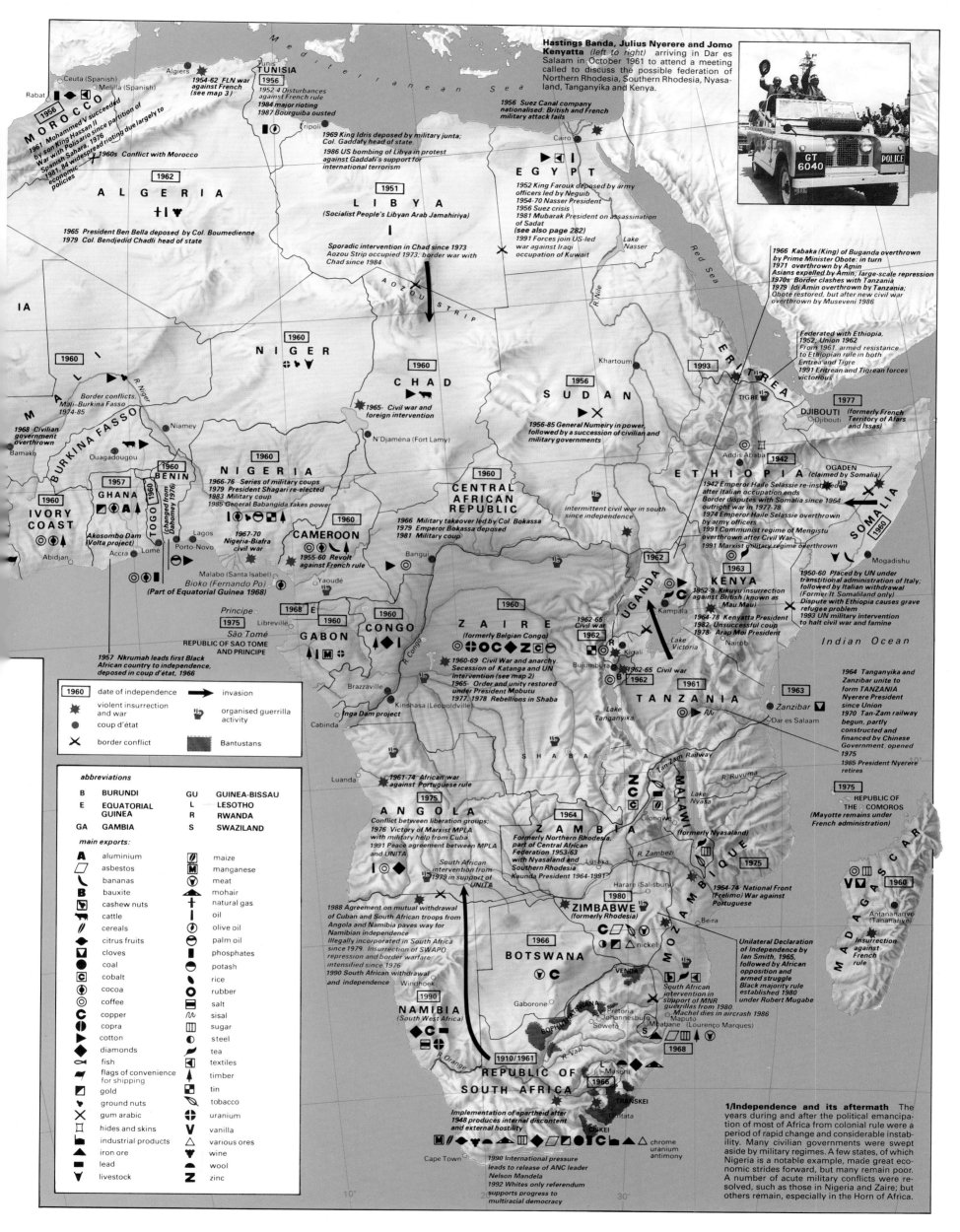

Hastings Banda, Julius Nyerere and Jomo Kenyatta (left to right) arriving in Dar es Salaam in October 1961 to attend a meeting called to discuss the possible federation of Northern Rhodesia, Southern Rhodesia, Nyasaland, Tanganyika and Kenya.

MOROCCO
1956
1961 Mohammed V succeeded by son King Hassan II. War with Polisario since partition of Spanish Sahara, 1976
1981, 84 widespread rioting due largely to economic policies

Ceuta (Spanish)
Melilla (Spanish)
Rabat
Algiers
Tunis
TUNISIA 1956
1954-62 FLN war against French (see map 3)
1952-4 Disturbances against French rule
1984 major rioting
1987 Bourguiba ousted

ALGERIA 1962
1965 President Ben Bella deposed by Col. Boumedienne
1979 Col. Bendjedid Chadli head of state

Tripoli
1969 King Idris deposed by military junta; Col. Gaddafy head of state
1986 US bombing of Libya in protest against Gaddafi's support for international terrorism

LIBYA 1951
(Socialist People's Libyan Arab Jamahiriya)

1956 Suez Canal company nationalised: British and French military attack fails

Cairo
EGYPT
1952 King Farouk deposed by army officers led by Negub
1954-70 Nasser President
1956 Suez crisis
1981 Mubarak President on assassination of Sadat (see also page 282)
1991 Forces join US-led war against Iraqi occupation of Kuwait

Lake Nasser
Red Sea

Sporadic intervention in Chad since 1973
Aozou Strip occupied 1973; border war with Chad since 1984
AOZOU STRIP

NIGER 1960

MALI 1960
Border conflicts, Mali–Burkina Fasso 1974-85
Niamey

BURKINA FASSO 1960
1968 Civilian government overthrown
Bamako
Ouagadougou

CHAD 1960
1965- Civil war and foreign intervention
N'Djaména (Fort Lamy)

SUDAN 1956
Khartoum
1956-85 General Numeiry in power, followed by a succession of civilian and military governments

ERITREA 1993
Federated with Ethiopia, 1952, Union 1962. From 1961, armed resistance to Ethiopian rule in both Eritrea and Tigre
1991 Eritrean and Tigrean forces victorious
TIGRE 1977
DJIBOUTI (formerly French Territory of Afars and Issas)
Djibouti

1966 Kabaka (King) of Buganda overthrown by Prime Minister Obote: in turn 1971 overthrown by Amin. Asians expelled by Amin; large-scale repression
1970s Border clashes with Tanzania
1979 Idi Amin overthrown by Tanzania; Obote restored, but after new civil war overthrown by Museveni 1986

NIGERIA 1960
1966-76 Series of military coups
1979 President Shagari re-elected
1983 Military coup
1985 General Babangida takes power
Lagos

GHANA 1957
Akosombo Dam (Volta project)
Accra

IVORY COAST 1960
Abidjan

BENIN 1960 (Changed from Dahomey 1976)
TOGO 1960
Porto-Novo
Lomé

1957 Nkrumah leads first Black African country to independence, deposed in coup d'état, 1966

CAMEROON 1960
1955-60 Revolt against French rule
Yaoundé
Malabo (Santa Isabel)
Bioko (Fernando Po) (Part of Equatorial Guinea 1968)

1967-70 Nigeria-Biafra civil war

Principe
São Tomé
Libreville
REPUBLIC OF SAO TOME AND PRINCIPE 1975
GABON 1960
CONGO 1960
Brazzaville
Kinshasa (Leopoldville)
Inga Dam project
Cabinda

CENTRAL AFRICAN REPUBLIC 1960
1966 Military takeover led by Col. Bokassa
1979 Emperor Bokassa deposed
1981 Military coup
Bangui

intermittent civil war in south since independence

ETHIOPIA 1942
Addis Ababa
1942 Emperor Haile Selassie re-instated after Italian occupation ends
Border disputes with Somalia since 1964: outright war in 1977-78
1974 Emperor Haile Selassie overthrown by army officers
1991 Communist regime of Mengistu overthrown after Civil War
1991 Marxist military regime overthrown
OGADEN (claimed by Somalia)

ZAIRE (formerly Belgian Congo) 1960
1960-69 Civil War and anarchy. Secession of Katanga and UN intervention (see map 2)
1965- Order and unity restored under President Mobutu
1977, 1978 Rebellions in Shaba
R. Congo

UGANDA 1962
Kampala
RWANDA 1962 1962-65 Civil war
Kigali
BURUNDI 1962 1962-65 Civil war
Bujumbura
Lake Victoria
Nairobi

KENYA 1963
1952-9 Kikuyu insurrection against British (known as Mau Mau)
1964-78 Kenyatta President
1982 Unsuccessful coup
1978- Arap Moi President

SOMALIA 1960
Mogadishu
1950-60 Placed by UN under transitional administration of Italy; followed by Italian withdrawal (Former It. Somaliland only)
Dispute with Ethiopia causes grave refugee problem
1993 UN military intervention to halt civil war and famine

Indian Ocean

TANZANIA 1961
Zanzibar
Lake Tanganyika
Dar es Salaam
1964 Tanganyika and Zanzibar unite to form TANZANIA. Nyerere President since Union
1970 Tan-Zam railway begun, partly constructed and financed by Chinese Government, opened 1975
1985 President Nyerere retires

Tan-Zam Railway
SHABA
Luanda

1961-74 African war against Portuguese rule

ANGOLA 1975
Conflict between liberation groups: 1976 Victory of Marxist MPLA with military help from Cuba
1991 Peace agreement between MPLA and UNITA

South African intervention from 1979 in support of UNITA

1988 Agreement on mutual withdrawal of Cuban and South African troops from Angola and Namibia paves way for Namibian independence
Illegally incorporated in South Africa since 1979. Insurrection of SWAPO repression and border warfare intensified since 1976
1990 South African withdrawal and independence

ZAMBIA 1964
Formerly Northern Rhodesia, part of Central African Federation 1953-63 with Nyasaland and Southern Rhodesia. Kaunda President 1964-1991
Lusaka
R. Zambezi

MALAWI 1964 (formerly Nyasaland)
Lilongwe
Lake Nyasa
R. Ruvuma

REPUBLIC OF THE COMOROS 1975 (Mayotte remains under French administration)

MADAGASCAR 1960
Antananarivo (Tananarive)
Insurrection against French rule

MOZAMBIQUE 1975
1964-74 National Front (Frelimo) War against Portuguese
Beira
South African intervention in support of MNR guerrillas from 1980
1986 Machel dies in aircraft 1986
Maputo (Lourenço Marques)

ZIMBABWE (formerly Rhodesia)
Harare (Salisbury)
Unilateral Declaration of Independence by Ian Smith, 1965, followed by African opposition and armed struggle. Black majority rule established 1980 under Robert Mugabe

BOTSWANA 1966
Gaborone

NAMIBIA (South West Africa) 1990
Windhoek
R. Orange

REPUBLIC OF SOUTH AFRICA 1910/1961
BOPHUTHATSWANA
Pretoria
Johannesburg
Soweto
Mbabane
VENDA 1979
SWAZILAND 1968
LESOTHO 1966
Maseri
TRANSKEI 1976
CISKEI
Cape Town

Implementation of apartheid after 1948 produces internal discontent and external hostility
1990 International pressure leads to release of ANC leader Nelson Mandela
1992 Whites only referendum supports progress towards multiracial democracy

---

Legend:

1960 date of independence
→ invasion
✸ violent insurrection and war
✊ organised guerrilla activity
● coup d'état
✕ border conflict
▨ Bantustans

abbreviations
B BURUNDI
E EQUATORIAL GUINEA
GA GAMBIA
GU GUINEA-BISSAU
L LESOTHO
R RWANDA
S SWAZILAND

main exports:
A aluminium
⬭ asbestos
bananas
B bauxite
cashew nuts
cattle
cereals
citrus fruits
cloves
coal
C cobalt
cocoa
coffee
copper
copra
cotton
diamonds
fish
flags of convenience for shipping
gold
ground nuts
gum arabic
hides and skins
industrial products
iron ore
lead
livestock
maize
M manganese
meat
mohair
natural gas
oil
olive oil
palm oil
phosphates
potash
rice
rubber
salt
sisal
steel
sugar
tea
textiles
timber
tin
tobacco
uranium
vanilla
various ores
wine
wool
Z zinc
chrome
uranium
antimony

1/Independence and its aftermath The years during and after the political emancipation of most of Africa from colonial rule were a period of rapid change and considerable instability. Many civilian governments were swept aside by military regimes. A few states, of which Nigeria is a notable example, made great economic strides forward, but many remain poor. A number of acute military conflicts were resolved, such as those in Nigeria and Zaire; but others remain, especially in the Horn of Africa.

The Middle East from 1945

THE Middle East has occupied world attention more consistently than any other region since 1945: Israel and its Arab neighbours have engaged in four full-scale wars; Israel has invaded Lebanon twice; two Gulf wars have been fought; military coups have reinforced a regional pattern of internal repression; waves of refugees have been forced to flee, from Cyprus to Afghanistan. In the immediate post-war period, a combination of war weariness, financial pressure and local opposition gradually led Britain and France to abandon formal control over the area, while growing nationalism and increasing Soviet involvement encouraged the US to take a more active interest in the region.

In the 1950s and 1960s, the US was the most powerful external influence in the Middle East, using the fear of Soviet expansion to increase its support for Israel, which, with Saudi Arabia, and Iran until 1979, functioned as the principal surrogates of American interests. The Soviet Union backed Egypt, Iraq and Syria with arms and rhetoric, but while the leaders of these and other local regimes reiterated their passionate commitment to anti-imperialism, Arab unity, the Palestinian cause and revolutionary socialism, the reality was very different. The Arab countries were unable to combine effectively in wars against Israel in 1948, 1956 and 1967, but in 1973, although victory continued to elude them, they at least succeeded in calling into question Israel's previous reputation for invincibility.

In the face of continued Arab opposition, the State of Israel has expanded since its foundation in 1948 well beyond its original borders into the West Bank and Gaza (1967), Sinai (1956, 1967–1982) and the Golan Heights (1967: incorporated unilaterally into Israel in 1981), and has controlled a strategic zone in south Lebanon since 1978. Egyptian president Anwar Sadat's sur-

prise visit to Israel in 1977 and the bilateral treaty between Egypt and Israel which followed did, however, lead to the return of the Sinai peninsula to Egypt in 1982. Egypt remains the only Arab country to have made peace with Israel.

Meanwhile, hundreds of Israeli civilians have been killed in Palestinian guerrilla attacks and thousands of Lebanese and Palestinian civilians have died in the Israeli attacks on Lebanon, notably in the invasion which carried the Israelis to Beirut in 1982.

But while the conflict between Israel and the Arabs has been the most persistent, other Middle East hostilities – including the Lebanese civil war – have proved even more deadly. The war against Iran, launched by Iraq's President Saddam Hussein in 1980, turned into a lethal campaign of attrition reminiscent of First World War trench warfare. The Iraqi leader then took Iraq into arguably the most one-sided war in history by invading Kuwait in August 1990 and defying US-led United Nations pressure to withdraw. Contingents from US and European air forces bombed Iraq for nearly six weeks before a 100-hour land onslaught broke through Iraqi forces in February 1991 and drove them out of Kuwait. Saddam's late effort to invoke the Islamic cause failed and Saudi Arabia became a temporary base for US, British and French forces. Even Egypt and Syria contributed troops to the anti-Saddam coalition.

Arab nationalism in the years immediately after the Second World War was secular, its hero President Nasser of Egypt. Nevertheless, a Muslim revival has been a significant feature of the Middle East in the last quarter of the 20th century: the 1978–9 revolution in non-Arab Iran installed an Islamic theocracy and fundamentalism gained in appeal among both Shia and Sunni Muslims. It became a badge of hostility to

the West in Iran, to the Russians in Afghanistan and elsewhere to the regime in power. In Algeria, the attraction proved so strong that the authorities in 1992 cancelled a second round of elections when it seemed that the fundamentalists would be voted into office. Islamic fervour also took root in the Arab territories occupied by Israel after the 1967 war, although the mainstream political force there continued to be the secular Palestine Liberation Organization (PLO). However, while Israel rejected PLO participation in the Middle East peace talks brokered by the US, which opened at the end of 1991, the outside world understood that the Palestinian representatives were loyal to the PLO. Irrespective of their ultimate chances of success, these talks represented a milestone in Israeli-Arab relations: American pressure and regional changes following the Gulf War had finally brought Israel into negotiations with all its Arab neighbours for the first time since the formation of the state.

In the meantime, national disparities in social conditions throughout the Middle East have arguably increased more than in any other region. With the exception of Iran and Algeria, where it has not proved a panacea for high birth rates, oil wealth and small populations have given Arab Gulf states some of the highest per capita incomes in the world, with development programmes to match, but have turned them (as well as Saudi Arabia and Libya) into magnets for immigrants from Egypt, Jordan, Yemen and the Indian sub-continent. Uncontrolled urban growth in Cairo, for example, with its population of between 12 and 15 million, has seen many Egyptians move to the oil-rich nations to escape appalling living conditions at home. But demographic pressures have been most explosive in the Lebanon, where the rural exodus of Shia Muslims to Beirut, which began in the 1950s, has

1/The Middle East since independence (below) With the exception of the smaller states of the Arabian peninsula (which had all become independent by 1971), most of the nations of the Middle East had obtained formal independence from Britain or France by 1950, although both sought to maintain their influence through military and other alliances. During the 1950s many of the constitutional monarchies and republics established by Britain and France in the 1930s were overthrown by nationalist-inspired military coups, ushering in regimes of varying degrees of permanence and stability. For many in the Arab world, the success of Nasser in Egypt provided a model for their aspirations for true independence, especially after his successful nationalization of the Suez Canal in 1956. However, pan-Arab nationalism and calls for Arab unity have proved largely powerless to resolve any settlement of the outstanding problems in the area: the glaring contrasts between rich and poor, the virtual absence of democracy, and economic dependence on the outside world. Almost all the poorer states (particularly Jordan, Syria and Egypt) suffer from chronic inflation and massive migration from rural areas to cities, and most, even the most fertile, are net importers of food.

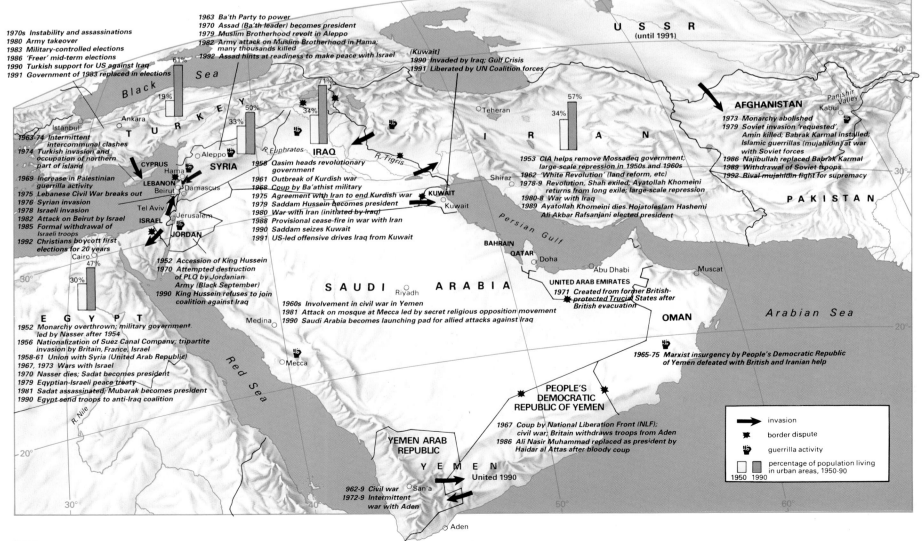

2/Israel and Palestine (*right*) For many centuries Palestine had an Arabic-speaking Muslim majority and Christian and Jewish minorities, but in the late 19th century the proportions began to change as Jews from Eastern Europe began to emigrate, under the pressure of Russian persecution and of the new 'Zionist' ideal of the recreation of a Jewish national state. In 1917, during the First World War, the British government stated that it looked with favour upon the establishment of a Jewish national home in Palestine, provided that the position of the non-Jewish population was not harmed. These two obligations were embodied in the mandate under which Great Britain administered the country, subject to supervision by the League of Nations, but they proved difficult to reconcile, particularly after the rise of Hitler, when Jewish emigration from Europe increased sharply (in 1922, Jews formed 11 per cent of the population; in 1936, 29 per cent; in 1946, 32 per cent). Arab fears led to a serious revolt before the Second World War; after the war and the holocaust of European Jewry, the Jewish demand that the survivors be allowed to immigrate, American pressure in support of it, and Arab fear that such immigration would lead to their subjection or dispossession, caused the British government to declare its intention of withdrawing. A plan to partition Palestine into a Jewish and an Arab state, with Jerusalem under international control, was adopted by the United Nations General Assembly on 29 Nov. 1947, but was rejected by the Arabs. On the day of British withdrawal, 14 May 1948, David Ben Gurion proclaimed the state of Israel and a war ensued between the Jews and the Palestinian Arabs, supported by the neighbouring Arab states, whose Arab armies were defeated. The greater part of Palestine became the Jewish state of Israel, most of the rest was amalgamated with Transjordan to become Jordan. The Gaza Strip was occupied by Egypt. During and

after the fighting, two-thirds of the Palestinian Arabs became refugees in Jordan, Gaza, Syria and Lebanon. After 1948, the wish of the refugees to return to their homes and of the Palestinians in general to have their own state, the refusal of Israel to accept Palestinian claims and of the Arab states to recognize Israel, and the intervention of external forces, led to three further wars: in 1956 the Israelis, following increasing *fedayeen*, or guerrilla, raids, attacked Egypt in secret agreement with Great Britain and France, but were compelled to withdraw under pressure from the United States and the Soviet Union; in June 1967 the Israelis moved to prevent what they saw as a threat to their existence, when the Straits of Tiran were closed to Israeli shipping by President Nasser of Egypt, and occupied the west bank of the Jordan, Sinai and the Golan Heights in Syria; in 1973 an Egyptian and Syrian attack on Israel had a limited military success, and opened a new phase of negotiations. It gradually became clear that President Sadat of Egypt had little desire to continue the struggle and his visit to Jerusalem (Nov. 1977), followed by the Egyptian-Israeli Camp David Accords (1978), confirmed this. However, Begin's Likud government now began to take a harder line on the West Bank (which it claimed as an integral part of biblical Israel) by greatly increasing the settlements begun by its Labour predecessors. The focus of conflict shifted in 1978, when Israel invaded southern Lebanon to counter Palestinian guerrilla (PLO) activity and advanced as far as Beirut in 1982. Israel withdrew from Sinai in 1982 in line with the Camp David agreement. In 1987 a prolonged period of resistance to Israeli rule, known as the *intifada*, began on the West Bank and in Gaza. But by 1991, the emphasis had reverted to diplomacy when, in the aftermath of the Gulf War, the US succeeded in bringing Israel and all its Arab neighbours into extended peace talks.

added a layer of slums to the Palestinian refugee camps and another ingredient to the recipe for civil war.

There appears little prospect that the Western powers will stop trying to exert their influence in the Middle East, whether to safeguard oil supplies, or protect blatantly persecuted peoples such as the Kurds of northern Iraq. The collapse of the Soviet Union may have ended the superpower rivalry which once dominated the area, but the emergence of a new tier of states with predominantly Muslim populations in what was the USSR has not set at rest Western anxieties about a volatile region.

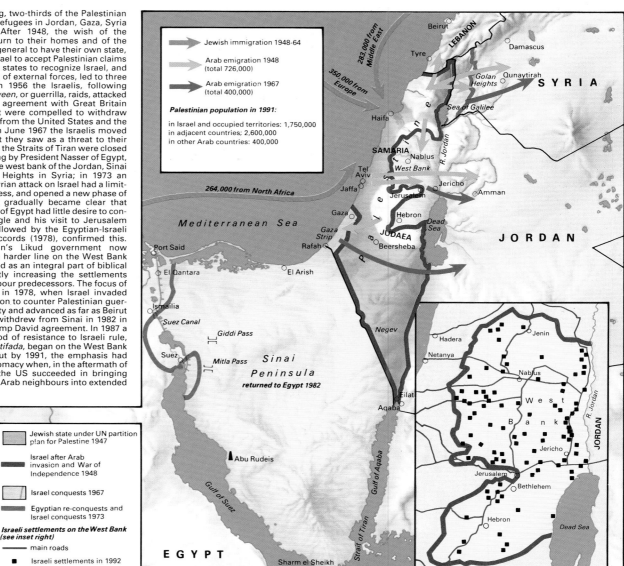

Key:
- Jewish immigration 1948-64
- Arab emigration 1948 (total 726,000)
- Arab emigration 1967 (total 400,000)

Palestinian population in 1991:
in Israel and occupied territories: 1,750,000
in adjacent countries: 2,600,000
in other Arab countries: 400,000

- Jewish state under UN partition plan for Palestine 1947
- Israel after Arab invasion and War of Independence 1948
- Israel conquests 1967
- Egyptian re-conquests and Israel conquests 1973
- *Israeli settlements on the West Bank (see inset right)*
- main roads
- ■ Israeli settlements in 1992

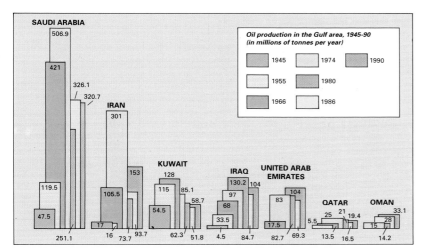

Oil production in the Gulf area, 1945-90 (in millions of tonnes per year)
- 1945
- 1955
- 1966
- 1974
- 1980
- 1986
- 1990

Oil production (*above*) Oil is the region's most valuable natural asset. Production and revenues increased dramatically with the Opec price rise in 1973. However later figures show the impact of the wars between Iran and Iraq. Ironically, oil wealth has contributed to serious inflation in poorer states; also, the lack of indigenous skilled labour has made large-scale immigration and the presence of a high proportion of foreign workers permanent features of the area.

4/The Lebanese Crisis (*right*) The Lebanese political system has been based on the distribution of offices between the various communities (Maronite, Orthodox, Catholic and Armenian Christians, Sunni and Shia Muslims and Druze) in a way which ensured the pre-eminence of the Maronites, although by the 1970s they were no longer the largest single community. Muslim opposition forces joined with the Palestinian (PLO) guerrillas in the mid-1970s in a civil war aimed at changing the balance of power. Syria intervened in 1976 and its troops remained in occupation. Lebanon subsequently became the principal arena of the Arab/Israeli conflict. Israel invaded in 1978 and, more massively, in 1982 when it expelled the PLO from Beirut. After the Israeli withdrawal from all but a southern security zone in 1985, inter-factional fighting continued and became particularly bitter between Christian militias. Elections held in 1992 after an earlier agreement on power-sharing reached at Taif, Saudi Arabia, were boycotted by the Christians, who objected to the continued presence of Syrian troops.

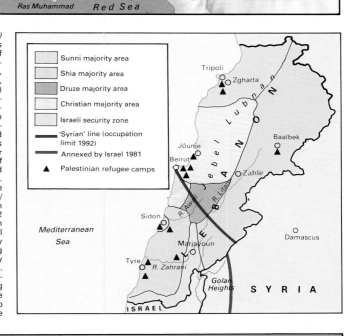

- Sunni majority area
- Shia majority area
- Druze majority area
- Christian majority area
- Israeli security zone
- 'Syrian' line (occupation limit 1992)
- Annexed by Israel 1981
- ▲ Palestinian refugee camps

3/The Persian Gulf remains the world's most heavily exploited region of oil and natural gas. But the area's share of global output had fallen from 41 per cent in 1979 to 26 per cent in 1991. In the 1980s, the war between Iran and Iraq interrupted the export of oil from the Gulf. The immediate effect of the conflict over Kuwait was almost to eliminate production there and in Iraq. But other states, notably Saudi Arabia, increased output enough to bridge the gap.

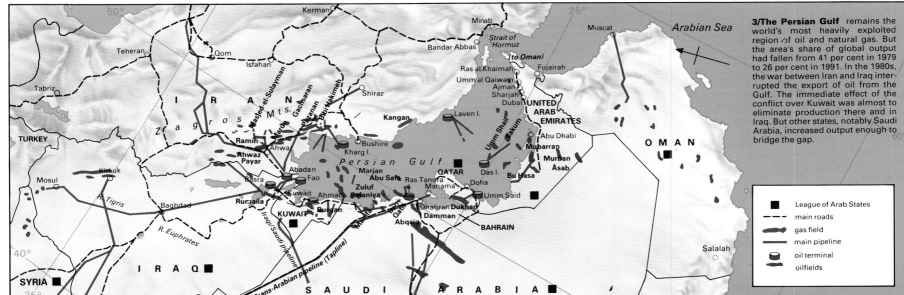

- ■ League of Arab States
- --- main roads
- gas field
- main pipeline
- oil terminal
- oilfields

Latin America: revolution and reaction from 1930

THE Great Depression of 1929 struck Latin America a shattering blow, cutting off supplies of foreign capital and lowering the price of its primary products in the world markets. As a result, many countries, forced to rely upon their own resources, undertook import substitution industrialization programmes. In the short run this caused distress to states that lacked the political power to protect themselves. Urban workers lost faith in middle-class liberal and radical parties which had until then represented their interests and began looking toward populist leaders who offered immediate relief, such as Getúlio Vargas in Brazil and Juan Perón in Argentina, who accelerated the process of industrialization. Backed by organized labour, both dictators appealed directly to the masses, offering in return higher wages, more jobs and the possibility of unionization (albeit state-controlled in the case of Brazil). Yet they were unable to deny or negate the interests of the armed forces or opposition factions. In 1954 Vargas committed suicide as his support collapsed, and the following year Perón was overthrown by a dissatisfied military who thought his power base undermined their own interests.

The prospects of further reform began to grow dim even in Mexico, the homeland of revolution. In the 1930s, it is true, Lázaro Cárdenas increased land distribution to peasants, organized labour's position in government and nationalized the oil industry. However, by the 1940s a new emphasis on industrialization, foreign investment and closer ties with the US undermined the reforms of the previous decade.

In some countries – Uruguay, Mexico, Brazil and Argentina – the initial wave of change produced noticeable results. In the rest, two factors thwarted industrial expansion. First, population growth, especially from the 1950s, outstripped economic development; second, during the Second World War, Latin America was cut off from foreign capital and goods, and forced to industrialize. Large profits accrued, but few reached the working class, widening further the gulf between rich and poor.

If industrialization offered no panacea for economic and social ills, Marxism and the example of the Soviet Union provided an alternative ideological inspiration. Communist parties existed in Latin America from the 1920s, but they exercised little influence until President Árbenz in Guatemala, sympathetic to Marxist principles, undertook a programme of agrarian reform in 1951. His project was short-lived: he was overthrown in 1954 by conservative forces backed by the US. The Guatemalan revolution exemplified the dilemma, present throughout the 1950s, of creating a welfare state without the resources to sustain it: at what point does investment in social welfare hinder rather than promote economic growth? The problem was seen above all after the violent left-wing Bolivian revolution in 1952. The tin mines were nationalized, the Indians enfranchised and agrarian reform promoted. But inflation and declining productivity eroded any gains.

In 1959, the Cuban revolution sought to create social change and economic growth simultaneously. Under the communist leader Fidel Castro, land was collectivized, businesses nationalized and state-organized education and health care provided for all Cubans. Yet any gains were won at the cost of political freedom and rigid centralized control. Furthermore, in spite of efforts to industrialize, sugar remained the island's main export and dependency upon foreign communist aid increased.

Nevertheless, despite causing massive impoverishment the Cuban revolution became the role model for many Latin American urban and rural social movements: in Uruguay, Argentina, Brazil and Bolivia. Che Guevara's rural guerrilla movement in Bolivia enjoyed some support, posing a serious threat to security forces until his death in 1967. Urban guerrillas presented an alternative revolutionary focus, but their political base proved too narrow to accomplish their goals. Meanwhile, left-of-centre parties, including Christian Democrats, sought to prove that reform and freedom need not be incompatible. But in both Venezuela and Chile popular pressure to step up the pace of reform proved irresistible. The election of Salvador Allende in Chile in 1970 saw the return of an avowedly Marxist government, backed by a coalition of leftist parties, though one eager to demonstrate that social change could be introduced by largely constitutional means. However, pressure from the landed oligarchy, the business community and the US resulted in a coup in 1973 and the military dictatorship of General Pinochet, which lasted until 1989.

Meanwhile, the economies of the 20 Latin American nations underwent major structural changes. Investments in manufacturing and commerce expanded dramatically while the traditional export sectors in mining and agriculture lost their dynamism. This economic shift brought other transformations in its wake. New social and political groups replaced the established oligarchy, explosive urbanization occurred, and a further concentration of income intensified social tensions. At the same time, dependence upon imported capital goods, raw materials, technology and foreign capital created enormous foreign debts which neither the traditional export sector nor manufactured exports could meet. Military governments in several countries during the 1970s, combining political conservatism with economic liberalism, found support among the new economic power bases. The more liberal regimes in Mexico and Venezuela briefly presided over economic prosperity thanks to the surge in oil prices after 1973, but falling demand for oil combined with excessive state expenditure eventually cast a shadow over their future development.

Other regimes saw their free market economies challenged by the world-wide recession after 1973. Both the Argentine and Brazilian military governments reacted to economic contraction and political opposition by employing repressive measures which lasted until the 1980s. Argentina's attempt in 1983 to assert its claim to the Falklands (Malvinas) Islands (held by Britain), although meant to rally support for the national cause, failed totally and instead brought about the downfall of the military government. This experience called into question the role of the military in domestic and international politics throughout the subcontinent.

Meanwhile, in Central America, increasing leftist insurgency led to the overthrow of the Somoza regime in Nicaragua in 1979 by the Marxist Sandinista movement and to civil conflict in El Salvador with the assassination of Archbishop Romero in 1980. The US backed the 'contras' in Nicaragua, who sought to overthrow the Sandinista government. In 1989, opposition candidate Violetta Chamorro won the presidency of Nicaragua in free elections. In Guatemala, meanwhile, instability continued to increase.

During the 1980s three problems dominated Latin American. The debt crisis continued to spiral out of control. Inflation, unemployment and population growth threatened to engulf the democratic governments of Brazil, Argentina, Chile and Peru. Finally the apparently insatiable demand of North America and Europe for narcotics created a 'black economy' that increased tensions between the main areas of clandestine production and transit of the drugs: Colombia, Bolivia, Peru, Panama and the United States. In 1989 US troops invaded Panama and removed by force its head of state, Manuel Noriega, to answer drug charges before a US court.

Nevertheless, by 1992 democratic governments prevailed in many states of the subcontinent, although in Brazil President Collor de Mello faced impeachment proceedings for embezzlement while in Peru the extreme left Sendero Luminoso (Shining Path) launched a vicious civil war leading President Fujimori to suspend the constitution in 1992. Mexico's liberal administration, having de-nationalized several key industries, signed a Free Trade Agreement (NAFTA) in 1992 with Canada and the United States, creating the largest integrated trading bloc in the world. Its effects on the economies of the three signatories, however, remained uncertain.

2/Economic development *(below)* Latin America's traditional primary-export economy was modified, though not transformed, by the Great Depression and the Second World War. The search for economic development and independence met with some success in some countries and impetus was given to import substitution. But the area continued to depend upon the developed world for markets for its raw material exports, for imports of industrial capital goods, for technology and for finance.

1/Latin America 1930-1992 *(right)* The political consequences of the great depression varied in each country but there was a trend towards nationalism and a preference for right-wing or populist dictatorships. World ideological conflicts after 1945 were reflected in the Guatemalan, Bolivian and Cuban revolutions. The latter had followers but no successful imitators.

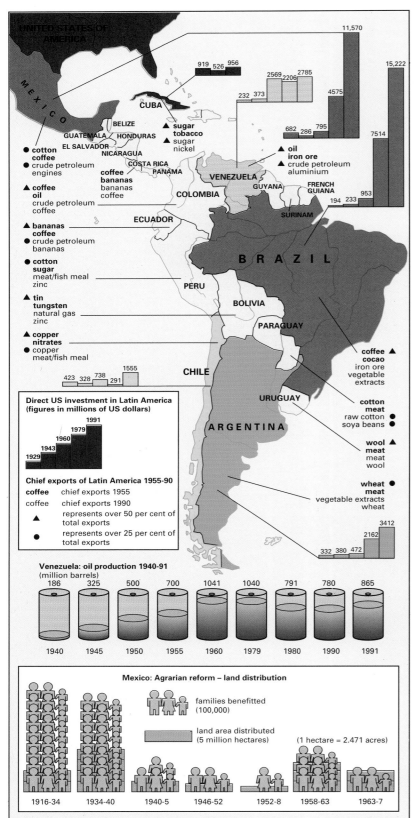

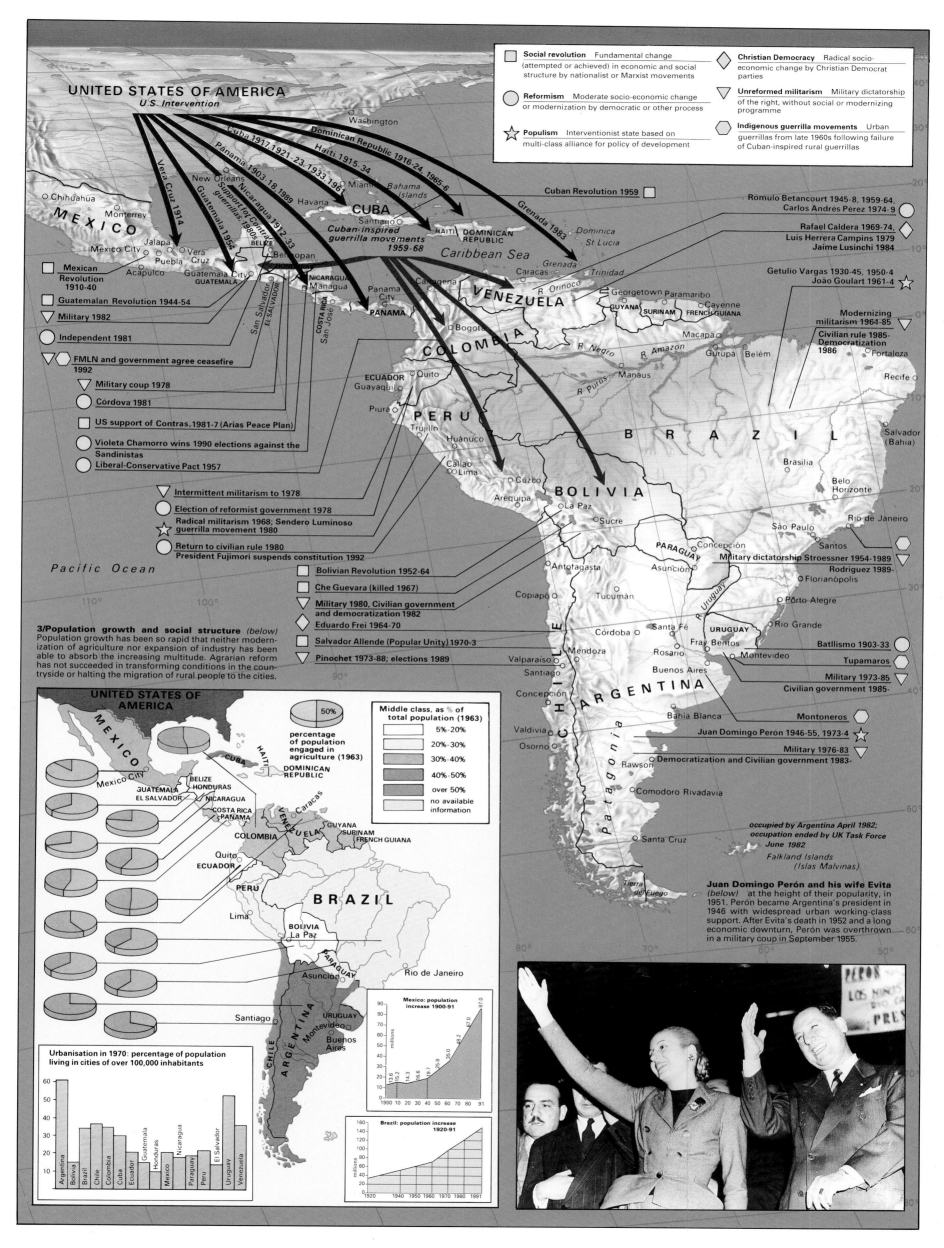

Legend

- ☐ **Social revolution** Fundamental change (attempted or achieved) in economic and social structure by nationalist or Marxist movements
- ○ **Reformism** Moderate socio-economic change or modernization by democratic or other process
- ☆ **Populism** Interventionist state based on multi-class alliance for policy of development
- ◇ **Christian Democracy** Radical socio-economic change by Christian Democrat parties
- ▽ **Unreformed militarism** Military dictatorship of the right, without social or modernizing programme
- ⬡ **Indigenous guerrilla movements** Urban guerrillas from late 1960s following failure of Cuban-inspired rural guerrillas

United States of America
U.S. Intervention

- Cuba 1917,1921-23,1933,1961
- Dominican Republic 1916-24, 1965-6
- Haiti 1915-34
- Panama 1903-18, 1989
- Vera Cruz 1914
- New Orleans
- Nicaragua 1912-33
- Support for Contra guerrillas 1980s
- Guatemala 1954
- Grenada 1983

Cuban Revolution 1959 ☐

Cuba — *Cuban-inspired guerrilla movements 1959-68*

Mexico
- ☐ Mexican Revolution 1910-40
- ☐ Guatemalan Revolution 1944-54
- ▽ Military 1982
- ○ Independent 1981
- ▽ FMLN and government agree ceasefire 1992
- ▽ Military coup 1978
- ○ Córdova 1981
- ☐ US support of Contras,1981-7 (Arias Peace Plan)
- ○ Violeta Chamorro wins 1990 elections against the Sandinistas
- ○ Liberal-Conservative Pact 1957

Peru
- ▽ Intermittent militarism to 1978
- ○ Election of reformist government 1978
- ☆ Radical militarism 1968; Sendero Luminoso guerrilla movement 1980
- ○ Return to civilian rule 1980
  President Fujimori suspends constitution 1992

Bolivia
- ☐ Bolivian Revolution 1952-64
- ☐ Che Guevara (killed 1967)
- ▽ Military 1980, Civilian government and democratization 1982
- ◇ Eduardo Frei 1964-70
- ☐ Salvador Allende (Popular Unity) 1970-3
- ▽ Pinochet 1973-88; elections 1989

Venezuela
- ⬡ Rómulo Betancourt 1945-8, 1959-64, Carlos Andrés Pérez 1974-9
- ◇ Rafael Caldera 1969-74, Luis Herrera Campins 1979 Jaime Lusinchi 1984

Brazil
- ☆ Getulio Vargas 1930-45, 1950-4 João Goulart 1961-4
- ▽ Modernizing militarism 1964-85
  Civilian rule 1985- Democratization 1986

Paraguay
- ▽ Military dictatorship Stroessner 1954-1989
  Rodríguez 1989-

Uruguay
- ⬡ Batllismo 1903-33
- ⬡ Tupamaros
- ▽ Military 1973-85
  Civilian government 1985-

Argentina
- ⬡ Montoneros
- ☆ Juan Domingo Perón 1946-55, 1973-4
- ▽ Military 1976-83
  Democratization and Civilian government 1983-

occupied by Argentina April 1982; occupation ended by UK Task Force June 1982
Falkland Islands (Islas Malvinas)

3/Population growth and social structure *(below)* Population growth has been so rapid that neither modernization of agriculture nor expansion of industry has been able to absorb the increasing multitude. Agrarian reform has not succeeded in transforming conditions in the countryside or halting the migration of rural people to the cities.

Juan Domingo Perón and his wife Evita *(below)* at the height of their popularity, in 1951. Perón became Argentina's president in 1946 with widespread urban working-class support. After Evita's death in 1952 and a long economic downturn, Perón was overthrown in a military coup in September 1955.

Middle class, as % of total population (1963)
- 5%-20%
- 20%-30%
- 30%-40%
- 40%-50%
- over 50%
- no available information

50% percentage of population engaged in agriculture (1963)

Urbanisation in 1970: percentage of population living in cities of over 100,000 inhabitants

(bar chart: Argentina, Bolivia, Brazil, Chile, Colombia, Cuba, Ecuador, Guatemala, Honduras, Mexico, Nicaragua, Paraguay, Peru, El Salvador, Uruguay, Venezuela)

Mexico: population increase 1900-91
13.6, 15.2, 14.3, 16.6, 19.7, 25.8, 35.0, 48.2, 67.0, 87.0

Brazil: population increase 1920-91

The United States 1933 to 1993

THE New Deal administrations of President Franklin Roosevelt, from 1933 to 1940, failed to restore American employment and industrial production to their 1929 levels; but by public investment and wholesale restructuring of the economy, above all by accustoming the people to economic leadership from Washington, they prepared the country for the world role thrust upon it by the Second World War, which brought economic recovery and victory.

The requirements of wartime production solved the unemployment problem at last. Economic output, to meet the needs of the army, the navy and the allies, was gigantic. This performance demonstrated the economic possibilities which, when realized, were to create an epoch of unprecedented prosperity and power.

Peace brought no serious interruption to the upward trend for more than 20 years, and gross national product nearly trebled in real terms between 1950 and 1980, while income per head almost doubled. A number of factors brought this about: population increase; technological advances coupled with the emergence of new consumer goods; the stimulus given to the economy by reconversion from war to peace; the sudden spending of wartime savings between 1945 and 1948; and the rearmament programmes connected with the the Cold War and the Korean War (1948–53). Affluence seemed wholly normal. Business confidence was never less than buoyant. And on this basis of wealth and hope the American people began to transform their entire way of life.

Rising expectations were a genuinely revolutionary force. There was a 'baby boom', a huge stimulus to demand, which started in the Second World War. There was a second great migration to the West. And after 1945 immigration rose steadily. By the 1980s Spanish-speaking immigrants were the dominant population group in many parts of the South and Southwest, and Miami had become a Latin-American city. But perhaps the most noticeable change was the expansion of the suburbs. Easy credit, cheap fuel (for homes and cars), mass production of housing and automobiles and the giant road-building programmes of the federal and state governments were among the factors encouraging Americans in their millions to move off the farms and out of the cities into endless miles of suburbs. So although the population of the central cities grew from 48 million to 64 million between 1950 and 1970, that of their urban fringes grew from 21 million to 55 million. The total population rose from 132 million in 1940 to almost 250 million in 1980.

Underpinning national prosperity were a strong dollar, vast national resources and government investment in research and education. Undermining it were the insatiable appetites of American consumer society; the marked tendency of American capitalists to spend their profits rather than reinvest them and of industrial workers to claim higher wages and easier conditions of work without regard to the effect of such claims (if successful) on prices and on the international competitiveness of the American industrial machine; and the growing inability of this most pampered nation to believe that things could ever be different. This last characteristic bred a recklessness in many policy-makers and citizens which put the whole position of the country at risk. The Vietnam War (1965–73) would in any case have been inflationary but was made more so by the refusal of the Johnson and Nixon administrations to impose any curb on incomes and consumption. The result was the great crisis of 1973, when the cartel of oil-exporting nations (OPEC) first imposed an oil embargo and then took advantage of apparently unquenchable American demand to increase oil prices by nearly 250 per cent. American industry allowed itself to be undersold by more efficient foreign competitors so that exports sank steadily against imports. Defeat in Vietnam and economic uncertainty made the later 1970s a troubling time for Americans. Nationalism, a tax-payers' revolt and a widespread wish to be reassured elected Ronald Reagan to the presidency in 1980. With the cheerful acquiescence of the voters he began to accelerate all the disturbing trends of the previous decade. He cut taxes by a third, thereby releasing a flood of spending power on to the market. He vastly increased expenditure on armaments, so creating the biggest national deficit in history. He did nothing about the structural defects of American industry, so the new purchasing power went overwhelmingly to imports, creating an equally unprecedented trade deficit. At the same time, the Federal Reserve Board's successful attempts to curb inflation meant that foreign capital poured into the United States, financing the deficits and maintaining a boom in national and international trade.

Such 'Reaganomics' contributed significantly to the stock market crash in October 1987 and a run on the dollar. Nonetheless, the presidency of George Bush (1988–92) largely continued the Reagan policies. Despite some spectacular overseas ventures, notably the Gulf War (1991), voters became increasingly worried by these fundamental economic troubles, by the increasing pace of urban decay and by persistent environmental problems. President Bill Clinton, voted into office in November 1992, headed an administration that faced many challenges.

Yet these 60 years brought many notable achievements: victory in the Second World War and the reconstruction of Western Europe through the Marshall Plan (launched in 1947); the space exploration programme; major advances in minority rights with the passage of the Civil Rights Act of 1964 and the Voting Rights Acts of 1965; and the successful resistance to Soviet expansionism without direct war and the ending of the Cold War.

The superior technology (above) and management techniques which helped maintain her as the world's most sophisticated industrial power were shown by the speed with which the US responded to the early Soviet lead in rocketry. Propelled by a Saturn V rocket, American astronauts reached the moon on 20 July 1969.

3 and 4/Urban growth (below and right) Rapid suburban growth has tended to link formerly separate urban areas to create 'super cities', nowhere more dramatically than in the Los Angeles region (map 4). An interstate highway system totalling about 40,000 miles (64,400 km) by 1980 facilitated long-distance movement of people and the rise of complex networks of residence and work (map 3).

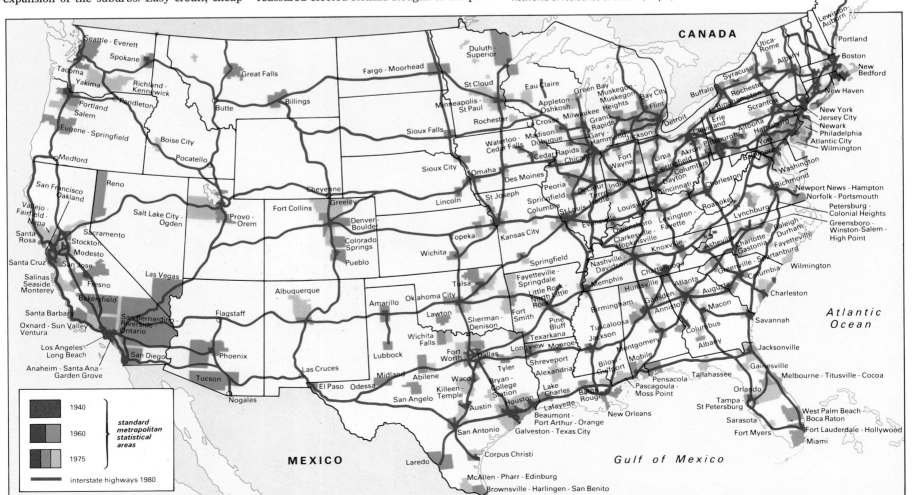

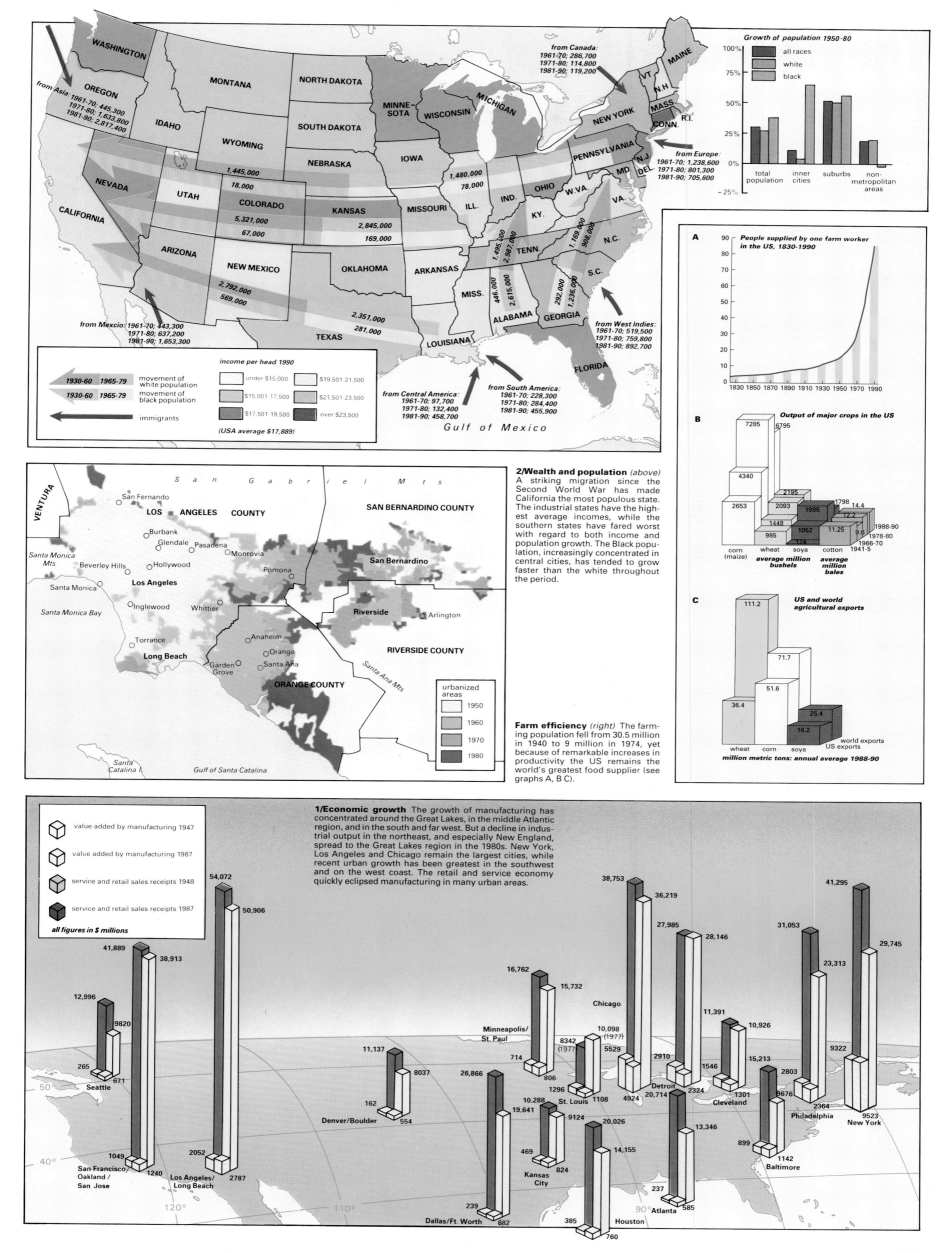

2/Wealth and population (above)
A striking migration since the Second World War has made California the most populous state. The industrial states have the highest average incomes, while the southern states have fared worst with regard to both income and population growth. The Black population, increasingly concentrated in central cities, has tended to grow faster than the white throughout the period.

Farm efficiency (right) The farming population fell from 30.5 million in 1940 to 9 million in 1974, yet because of remarkable increases in productivity the US remains the world's greatest food supplier (see graphs A, B C).

1/Economic growth The growth of manufacturing has concentrated around the Great Lakes, in the middle Atlantic region, and in the south and far west. But a decline in industrial output in the northeast, and especially New England, spread to the Great Lakes region in the 1980s. New York, Los Angeles and Chicago remain the largest cities, while recent urban growth has been greatest in the southwest and on the west coast. The retail and service economy quickly eclipsed manufacturing in many urban areas.

Growth of population 1950-80
- all races
- white
- black

A People supplied by one farm worker in the US, 1830-1990

B Output of major crops in the US
average million bushels / average million bales

C US and world agricultural exports
million metric tons: annual average 1988-90

The development of the Soviet Union after 1929

HAVING introduced the first five-year plan of industrialization in 1928, late in 1929 Stalin embarked on the forced collectivization of agriculture, transforming a mass of small, individual peasant holdings into huge state and collective farms. The results were disastrous. Unable to feed their animals, peasants slaughtered them, while they saw their own seed-corn requisitioned and dumped on the world market to pay for foreign machinery. The collective farms did not function as expected: there was not nearly enough machinery (only 278,000 tractors in use in 1934) and the peasants were badly paid and demoralized – it was 1951 before yields returned to their 1928 levels. The result was a great famine in 1932–3 which affected the Ukraine in particular, killing millions.

During the 1930s the rural catastrophe caused 40 million people to move to the towns, where their fresh labour was used mainly for construction, making the growth-rates of the Soviet economy under the first and second five-year plans (1928–32 and 1933–7) startling and unique. But the economy was based on existing industries and skills which had developed under the last Tsar, when Russia was the fourth major economic power in the world, so a crash programme to disseminate new technical skills was quickly implemented. Foreign machinery was acquired in return for grain-exports and such devices as the sale of 40 paintings from the Hermitage Museum to American millionaires. In the 1930s the Germans and the Americans proved relatively generous with credits and these stimulated considerable growth in the iron, coal and steel industries. By 1940, the iron industry founded in 1928 in the Ukraine and central Urals had been expanded and modernized. Two new large iron and steel bases were established: one near a massive iron ore deposit at the new town of Magnitogorsk in the southern Urals, and the other on the Kuzbass coalfield at Stalinsk (Novokuznetsk).

Such rapid growth depended on coercion of the workforce, however. Yezhov, head of the NKVD (People's Commissariat of Internal Affairs), launched 'the Great Terror' in 1936, which sent millions to labour-camps or execu-tion, killed off two-thirds of the Soviet officer-corps and seriously weakened the Red Army before its great war with Hitler. Thus, when Germany attacked in 1941, the USSR seemed likely to fall within a few weeks.

However, much of the industrialization of the early five-year plans had occurred in eastern regions that remained beyond the reach of the Germans – a vital factor in Soviet survival. During the Second World War the industrialization of these strategically safe regions greatly accelerated, while the western parts of the country suffered devastation. The already fragile agricultural sector now endured the destruction of its farm buildings and equipment.

Nevertheless, remarkable economic reconstruction occurred after the war. The output of heavy industry grew in the 1950s and light industry, neglected under Stalin, also progressed. Siberian reserves of oil, gas and mineral ores were discovered and exploited, and powerful hydro-electric and coal-fired generating stations appeared in eastern Siberia and Kazakhstan. The Soviet economy was linked to those of her eastern European satellites, where high-quality engineering products were of immense value to the USSR's technological progress.

After Stalin's death in 1953, however, his successors were forced to recognize the immensity of the agricultural problem: a growing population expected the oft-promised increase in their standard of living yet agriculture remained scarcely more productive than before the Revolution. Not until the premiership of Khrushchev did grain production increase and it was Brezhnev who, in 1965, introduced a range of measures designed to improve the collective farmer's lot.

By the 1960s the Soviet Union, like the United States, was recognized as a 'superpower', with a comparable degree of military strength. Although Soviet gross national product still fell well short of its rival's, the USSR overtook the USA in the production of iron ore, cement, steel and oil, and rapidly developed the world's largest reserves of natural gas. Nevertheless, the Soviet economy began to enter a crisis in the late 1970s. Increasingly, the USSR found the arms-race more costly than did the USA, and financial alarm-bells rang when the USA threatened to introduce its 'Star Wars' anti-missile defence system. In 1985 a new Soviet leader, Gorbachev, came to power with a programme of reform designed to achieve a 'revolution within the revolution'.

From 1985 to 1990 Gorbachev successfully improved relations with China and the West in order to provide peaceful external conditions for reconstruction. He introduced *glasnost* in the media to encourage open criticism of glaring deficiencies in the economy and society, and then established limited political democracy in the hope that, even though the Communist Party was difficult to reform, he could outflank conservative forces and introduce change through popular support. But price-rises and shortages occurred in the cities; dependence on the West for food and technical assistance increased. Gorbachev reduced the role of the Communist Party, became Executive President and increased presidential powers, but new legislative bodies in the republics increasingly opposed state power, making economic reform even more difficult to implement. In desperation, he withdrew from central and eastern Europe, hoping to reduce costs and improve the situation at home. However, the resurgence of nationalism in many constituent republics threatened the entire Union.

All these measures antagonized the party's old guard and opposition to Gorbachev crystalized from 1989. In August 1991 a coalition of conservatives from within his own government attempted a coup d'etat. But it was Gorbachev's

2/Changes in republican status until 1991 (*below, top*) Autonomous Soviet Socialist Republics (ASSRs) were created for important nationalities within Union Republics (SSRs): the Karelo-Finnish Republic became an ASSR, and the Crimean ASSR was incorporated in the Ukrainian SSR, while the Volga-German ASSR was dissolved. Although these maps cover only the western part of the country, all the Union republics (SSRs) are shown. The eastern regions not included on the maps were wholly within the Russian Soviet Federated Republic (RSFSR), but contained two Autonomous Republics: the Buryat-Mongolian ASSR (capital Ulan Ude) and the Yakutian ASSR (capital Yakutsk).

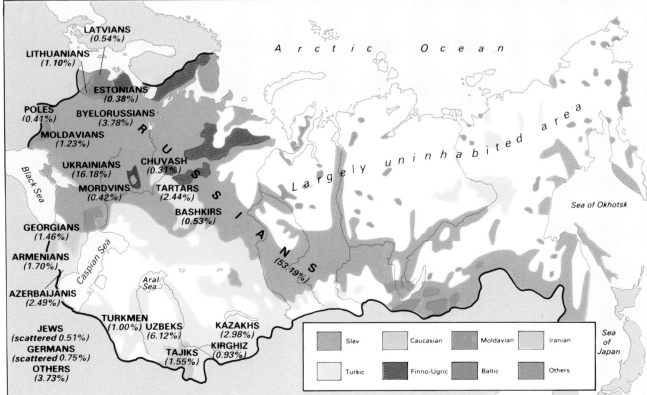

3/The movement of population
(right) From 1929 to 1939 major population growth occurred in Moscow and Leningrad, where early Soviet industrial expansion was concentrated. The second period (1939-59) included the war, and reflected the eastward movement of industry and urban population away from the war zones. More urban growth took place in the west between 1959 and 1970.

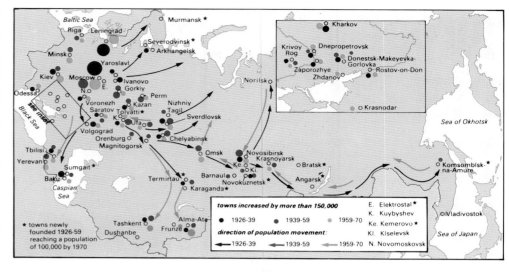

rival from the radical camp, Boris Yeltsin, who succeeded in challenging the plotters and liberated the beleaguered President. An attempted counter-revolution thus precipitated a new revolution, much as it had done in 1917. By the end of 1991 this new anti-Communist revolution saw not only Yeltsin's accession to power but also the dissolution of the Soviet Union itself. Yeltsin's new administration pressed on with the business of economic reform, while also attempting to salvage from the Union as much political and economic integration as possible; yet the resulting Commonwealth of Independent States (CIS) seemed merely a faint shadow of its predecessor, the Russian republic itself fell prey to open conflict between rival nationalities, and the prospects for the success of the economic reform programme – and with it the very existence of democratic forms of government – remained extremely uncertain.

In 1942, with the Germans occupying vast areas of the USSR, propagandists sought to appeal to the people's deep-seated love for their homeland. This poster *(above)* by Alexei Kokorekin urges, 'Follow this worker's example. Produce more for the front.'

1/The Soviet Union after 1929
(right) In this period Russia was transformed from a backward peasant economy into a highly industrialized, militarily powerful state, second only to the USA, but at the cost of immense human suffering, intensified by the German invasion.

4/The different nationalities in the USSR 1989 *(left)* The Soviet Union comprised many different ethnic groups, languages, religions and cultures. The majority of the population were of Slavic origin, including the Russians and Ukrainians who constituted the first and second largest national groups. Russian served as the official language throughout the USSR and most people were bi- or even trilingual as they attempted to retain their ethnic origins. Some groups, such as the Azerbaijanis, the Armenians and the Baltic states, were keen not only to retain their national origins but also to establish their independence from the Soviet Union.

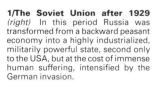

Europe from 1973

PRE-WAR fascist regimes survived into the 1970s in two European countries: Portugal and Spain. Democracy was restored to both countries within the space of a year: in 1974 in Portugal, the result of the failure of colonial wars in Africa; in 1975 in Spain following the death of General Franco. The process was smoother in Spain, where, despite an attempted right-wing coup in 1981, King Juan Carlos exercised a restraining hand. Spain joined NATO in 1982; in 1986 both countries joined the European Community. 1974 also saw the restoration of democracy in Greece, where a right-wing junta had seized power in 1967. Greece, too, joined the European Community, in 1981.

But these changes in southern Europe paled in comparison with events in Eastern Europe in the late 1980s. These involved nothing less than the disintegration of the Soviet Union and the collapse of communism in every one of its satellite states as well as in Yugoslavia and Albania. As remarkable as the sudden collapse of this apparently permanent system was the creation, in its wake, of 15 new countries.

The reasons for this startling transformation were as much economic as political. Throughout the 1970s and 1980s the economies of the communist bloc had declined rapidly. Zero growth rates and immense external debts combined in the end to bankrupt the region. Unable any longer to guarantee the survival of its client states, the Soviet Union effectively abandoned them. In Prague in April 1987, Soviet leader Mikhail Gorbachev asserted that the "entire system of political relations between the socialist countries can and should be built unswervingly on a foundation of equality and mutual responsibility. No one has the right to claim a special position in the socialist world. The independence of each party, its responsibility to its

people, the right to resolve questions of the country's development in a sovereign way – for us these are indisputable principles." There could be no clearer hint to Eastern Europe's leaders – and their peoples – that they were on their own. The 'Brezhnev Doctrine', formulated after the Soviet invasion of Czechoslovakia in 1968 and under which the Soviet Union claimed the right to intervene in the affairs of its satellites if any threatened to leave the Soviet camp, had been decisively repudiated.

The specific chain of events which led to the fall of communism began in August 1988 with strikes and demonstrations in Poland calling for the recognition of the trade union Solidarity. By 1991, free elections had been held in every country in the region, including the Soviet Union, and the two Germanies had been reunited. Except in Romania, the transformation had been relatively peaceful, even if the attempted hardline coup in the Soviet Union in August 1991 threatened for a moment to unleash a civil war. But it was inevitable that such rapid and far-reaching changes should bring their own problems: political instability, as former communists sought to reassert their authority; ethnic conflicts, as age-old nationalisms reasserted themselve; and economic dislocations, as the new governments attempted to switch their moribund economies from communism to capitalism.

The fall-out from these sudden events was most extreme in Yugoslavia, which in 1991 simply disintegrated under pressure from the long-suppressed rivalries of its ethnic groups. When in June that year the republics of Slovenia and Croatia declared their independence, a bloody seven-month civil war followed between the Croats and the Serbs. In January 1992 further fighting broke out between Serbs, Croats and Muslims in Bosnia-Herzegovina. In the face of

such vicious fighting – and of clear evidence of 'ethnic cleansing', a new name for an old problem: the systematic removal and, in some cases, extermination of rival ethnic groups – the United Nations imposed sanctions on Serbia and dispatched humanitarian aid under guard by UN troops. Attempts at political settlement foundered, however. In Czechoslovakia, meanwhile, the general election of June 1992 revealed the tensions between Czechs and Slovaks and at the end of the year the country became two, the Czech Republic and Slovakia. Even in former East Germany, buttressed by massive subsidies from its western partner and where the fall of the Berlin Wall had generated a surge of enthusiasm for the future, the return to democracy proved far from painless. Despite the genuine desire to see democracy and market-led economic reforms succeed, the problems of restructuring societies impoverished by communism remained acute.

In the long term, the former communist world set membership of the European Community as its goal. The EC had continued to expand throughout the 1970s and 1980s. The first direct elections to the European Parliament were held in June 1979. In 1985, in an attempt to guarantee future prosperity, the EC agreed an agenda and timetable for the creation of a single European market under which the EC would become a single free-trade zone. Some wanted to proceed even further down the road to integration and in 1989 proposals for European monetary union and a charter of fundamental social rights were brought forward. Despite fears that national sovereignty would be replaced by an unaccountable bureaucracy which, however well intentioned, would choke the international competitiveness of the EC in a web of misdirected regulations, at Maastricht in

2/Northern Ireland (right)
Terrorism has plagued parts of Europe intermittently since 1973. Nowhere has it proved so intractable as in Northern Ireland. Deeply entrenched attitudes on the part both of nationalists, principally the IRA, who demand union with the Republic of Ireland, and loyalists, who remain determined to maintain the Province's links with Great Britain, have contributed to persistent sectarian violence that has resisted all attempts at political settlement. Where other terrorist organizations in Europe have all been dismantled, those in Northern Ireland have embedded themselves in the fabric of life in the Province.

3/The fall of communism (below)
The speed with which communism disintegrated across Eastern Europe and its birthplace, the Soviet Union, after 1988 was remarkable. What almost all observers took for the system's permanence proved an illusion. With the formal dissolution of the Soviet Union in December 1991, Lenin's great experiment was over. Equally noteworthy were the number of new states formed and the ethnic conflict, above all in former Yugoslavia, that surfaced when long-suppressed ancient identities were given free rein again. The reconstruction of the region has also been hampered by the severe economic shortcomings of every former communist country, the fragility of their new democratic institutions and the vigorous efforts of many former communists to regain their lost authority. The struggle for control of the USSR's huge nuclear and conventional arsenals has added to the instability.

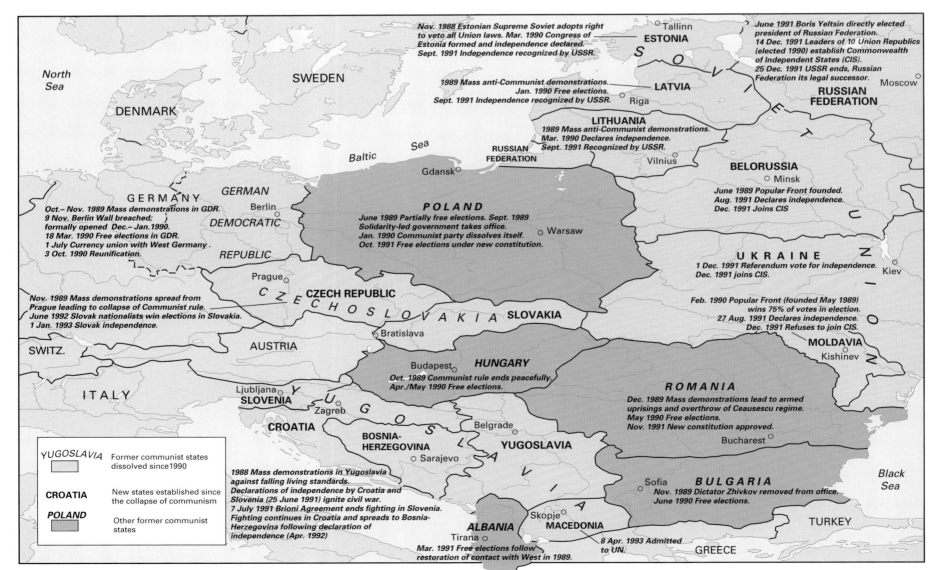

Nov. 1988 Estonian Supreme Soviet adopts right to veto all Union laws. Mar. 1990 Congress of Estonia formed and independence declared. Sept. 1991 Independence recognized by USSR.

June 1991 Boris Yeltsin directly elected president of Russian Federation. 14 Dec. 1991 Leaders of 10 Union Republics (elected 1990) establish Commonwealth of Independent States (CIS). 25 Dec. 1991 USSR ends, Russian Federation its legal successor.

1989 Mass anti-Communist demonstrations. Jan. 1990 Free elections. Sept. 1991 Independence recognized by USSR.

1989 Mass anti-Communist demonstrations. Mar. 1990 Declares independence. Sept. 1991 Recognized by USSR.

June 1989 Popular Front founded. Aug. 1991 Declares independence. Dec. 1991 Joins CIS.

Oct.– Nov. 1989 Mass demonstrations in GDR. 9 Nov. Berlin Wall breached; formally opened Dec.– Jan.1990. 18 Mar. 1990 Free elections in GDR. 1 July Currency union with West Germany. 3 Oct. 1990 Reunification.

June 1989 Partially free elections. Sept. 1989 Solidarity-led government takes office. Jan. 1990 Communist party dissolves itself. Oct. 1991 Free elections under new constitution.

1 Dec. 1991 Referendum vote for independence. Dec. 1991 joins CIS.

Nov. 1989 Mass demonstrations spread from Prague leading to collapse of Communist rule. June 1992 Slovak nationalists win elections in Slovakia. 1 Jan. 1993 Slovak independence.

Feb. 1990 Popular Front (founded May 1989) wins 75% of votes in election. 27 Aug. 1991 Declares independence. Dec. 1991 Refuses to join CIS.

Oct. 1989 Communist rule ends peacefully. Apr./May 1990 Free elections.

Dec. 1989 Mass demonstrations lead to armed uprisings and overthrow of Ceausescu regime. May 1990 Free elections. Nov. 1991 New constitution approved.

1988 Mass demonstrations in Yugoslavia against falling living standards. Declarations of independence by Croatia and Slovenia (25 June 1991) ignite civil war. 7 July 1991 Brioni Agreement ends fighting in Slovenia. Fighting continues in Croatia and spreads to Bosnia-Herzegovina following declaration of independence (Apr. 1992)

Nov. 1989 Dictator Zhivkov removed from office. June 1990 Free elections.

Mar. 1991 Free elections follow restoration of contact with West in 1989.

8 Apr. 1993 Admitted to UN.

YUGOSLAVIA	Former communist states dissolved since1990
CROATIA	New states established since the collapse of communism
POLAND	Other former communist states

December 1991 the EC agreed in principle to work towards eventual economic and monetary union and the formation of a common European foreign and security policy. In effect, the blueprint for a European superstate was agreed. Despite rejection by the Danes in a referendum in the spring of 1992 (who reversed their decision in a second referendum a year later) and increasing scepticism among some of its hither-to most enthusiastic supporters, the EC remained committed to this ambitious goal. However, its problems were greatly compounded by the clear difficulties of achieving the necessary economic 'convergence' among member countries when the Exchange Rate Mechanism (ERM), which tied EC currencies at agreed exchange rates, an essential step to a common currency, nearly collapsed following the forced withdrawals of Italy and Britain from the system in the autumn of 1992. Similarly, attempts to formulate a common foreign policy – for example towards the civil war in former Yugoslavia – were conspicuous for their lack of success. The euphoria of the months following the fall of the Berlin Wall had given way to uncertainty and fear as recession, ethnic strife and civil war reappeared on the European stage.

1/The European Community Applications for membership of the EC underline its dominant economic position within Europe. The EFTA countries, minus Switzerland and Iceland, have applied for membership in 1994/5. Poland, the Czech Republic, Slovakia, Hungary, Bulgaria and Romania also have all applied for membership. Existing trade agreements with Turkey, Malta and Cyprus may also lead to membership. The Ukraine is the only former Soviet state to have applied, though others have made informal approaches.

The Cold War 1949 to 1990

THE term 'Cold War' was coined by the American statesman Bernard Baruch in April 1947 to describe the increasing state of tension between the United States and the Soviet Union. But the roots of that tension went back much farther than the immediate aftermath of the Second World War

America and Russia first came into conflict towards the end of the 19th century over their policies in China, and after the Bolshevik revolution of 1917 an ideological strand was added to the existing geopolitical rivalry between the two powers. As well as being an imperial rival in East Asia, the new Soviet state espoused a doctrine (communism) which threatened the entire world capitalist system, of which the United States was taking over the leadership.

Two factors prevented the conflict from becoming acute during the period between the world wars. Firstly, the United States and the Soviet Union were preoccupied with internal problems. Secondly, more immediate foreign dangers faced both countries: Nazi Germany and Imperial Japan. Indeed, during the Second World War, Russia and America became allies against these common enemies, although the Soviet Union did not enter the war against Japan until the final month.

Looked at against this background of mutual suspicion and hostility, the breakdown of their alliance after 1945 is less surprising, especially since all the other world powers, including Britain, had been so weakened by the war that the United States and the Soviet Union found themselves in the position of two 'superpowers' – another expression invented in the United States, by the author William Fox in 1943 – whose interests and in some cases armed forces confronted each other around the world.

The conflict which developed came about because each side regarded the other as irreconcilably hostile. It differed from previous international conflicts because it was truly global in scope and because, with the advent of nuclear weapons, a genuine possibility existed that it could lead to the end of most life on the planet.

The global nature of the Cold War emerged very early on, with a struggle for influence in China, the Middle East and Europe. It later extended to the rest of Asia, Latin America and Africa. The situation in Europe stabilized relatively quickly (see page 270), but elsewhere things proved much more fluid. Many of the newly independent states of the Third World, for example, led by India, deliberately sought to avoid committing themselves to either side in the conflict and pursued a policy of neutrality. It seemed that the Soviet camp had gained an enormous advantage with the Communist victory in the Chinese civil war (1949), but by 1963 the Russians and the Chinese were openly quarrelling over territory and ideology, and thenceforth China, which became a nuclear power in 1964, could no longer be counted an ally of the Soviet Union. The American-led alliances in Southeast Asia (SEATO) and the Middle East (CENTO), founded in 1954 and 1959 respectively, both broke up in the 1970s as a result of the withdrawal of various members. NATO (North Atlantic Treaty Organization) survived the end of the Cold War in 1990.

Initial Soviet weakness followed by the nuclear 'balance of terror' helped restrain the two superpowers from engaging in open or 'hot' war with each other. The closest they came was in October 1962, when the Soviet Union attempted to instal intermediate range nuclear missiles on the island of Cuba in order to redress the balance, but agreed to withdraw them after an American naval blockade and a promise to remove some NATO missile sites from Turkey. However, they both either exploited or entered a number of local conflicts in which they armed, equipped and trained the opposing sides. On three major occasions they fought against those they regarded as each other's proxies: the United States against the Chinese and the North Koreans in the Korean War (1950–3); the United States against the North Vietnamese in the second Indochina war (1961–75); and the Soviet Union against the rebels in the Afghan civil war (1979–89). In addition they both intervened on a large scale to influence and, if need be, to subvert the political processes of other countries by means of their principal foreign intelligence agencies, the CIA (US) and the KGB (USSR).

The United States's decision to drop two atomic bombs on Japan in August 1945 inaugurated a new era in the history of warfare. For four years the Americans maintained a monopoly of nuclear weapons but the Soviet Union exploded its first nuclear bomb at the end of August 1949. The first American test of the much more powerful thermonuclear or hydrogen bomb took place in November 1952. It was approximately 770 times as powerful as the atomic bomb dropped on Hiroshima. The Russians exploded their first thermonuclear device in August 1953.

To begin with these weapons could only be dropped from aircraft which gave the United States an enormous advantage because of its access to bases within relatively close range of the Soviet Union. Later however both powers developed ballistic missiles which carried nuclear warheads. The long-range inter-continental ballistic missile (ICBM) and the submarine-launched ballistic missile (SLBM) both first deployed in the early 1960s enabled the Soviet Union to even up the odds. By the mid-1980s the nuclear arsenals of the two superpowers were further enhanced by the development of multiple independently targeted warheads equal to about 9 billion tons of TNT. (By comparison, the explosive power of the two atomic bombs dropped on Japan in 1945 was the equivalent of about 35 thousand tons.)

A desire to limit the spread of nuclear weapons led to the conclusion of a partial test ban treaty in 1963 and a nuclear non-proliferation treaty in 1968, but not all nuclear powers or potential nuclear powers signed these agreements (e.g. France, China, India) while others later reneged on their commitment (e.g. Iraq).

Despite false dawns after the death of Stalin in 1953 and the strategic arms limitation and Helsinki agreements of 1972 and 1975, the Cold War continued. Its end was undoubtedly precipitated by the economic and political difficulties

In order to assess the threat from both nuclear and conventional attack, the two superpowers needed good intelligence, a resource that may be divided into a number of categories. HUMINT (human intelligence) is information gathered on the ground by spies; COMINT (communications intelligence) involves the interception of communications of all kinds; SIGINT (signals intelligence) the interception and decoding of encrypted messages; ELINT (electronic intelligence) the interception and analysis of all kinds of electro-magnetic emissions (radar, missile control links, for example); and IMINT (imagery intelligence) the photography of enemy activities. This photograph (above) is an example of IMINT taken from a US spy satellite over a nuclear aircraft carrier under construction at Nikolayev in Ukraine.

1/The age of 'bipolarity' (right) By dividing the world into two armed camps, the Cold War introduced the age of 'bipolarity'. The USSR feared that the US would attempt to restore a liberal economic and political system in eastern Europe, while the United States feared that the USSR would overrun western Europe. Both sought to defend themselves by building up alliances. The US also sought to 'contain' Russia by creating a series of military bases (particularly bases for its nuclear bombers) around the Soviet perimeter. But developments in guidance and delivery systems for nuclear warheads made the policies obsolescent, and at the same time the rigid monolithic blocs began to loosen, particularly after 1958 when France, under General de Gaulle, refused to accept American political leadership, and in 1960 when the Sino-Soviet dispute came into the open.

of the Soviet Union, which Mikhail Gorbachev, its leader between 1985 and 1991, felt could only be resolved by reducing the crushing burden of military expenditure (see page 288). Finally, in 1990, after the collapse of Communist power in eastern Europe, NATO and the Warsaw Pact declared that the other was no longer an enemy. Further agreements on the reduction of nuclear and conventional forces soon followed.

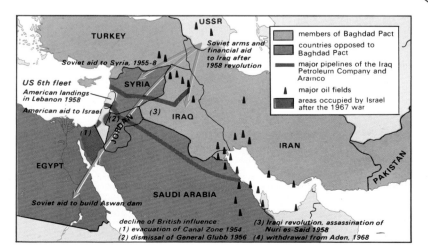

decline of British influence:
(1) evacuation of Canal Zone 1954
(2) dismissal of General Glubb 1956
(3) Iraqi revolution, assassination of Nuri es-Said 1958
(4) withdrawal from Aden, 1968

- members of Baghdad Pact
- countries opposed to Baghdad Pact
- major pipelines of the Iraq Petroleum Company and Aramco
- ▲ major oil fields
- areas occupied by Israel after the 1967 war

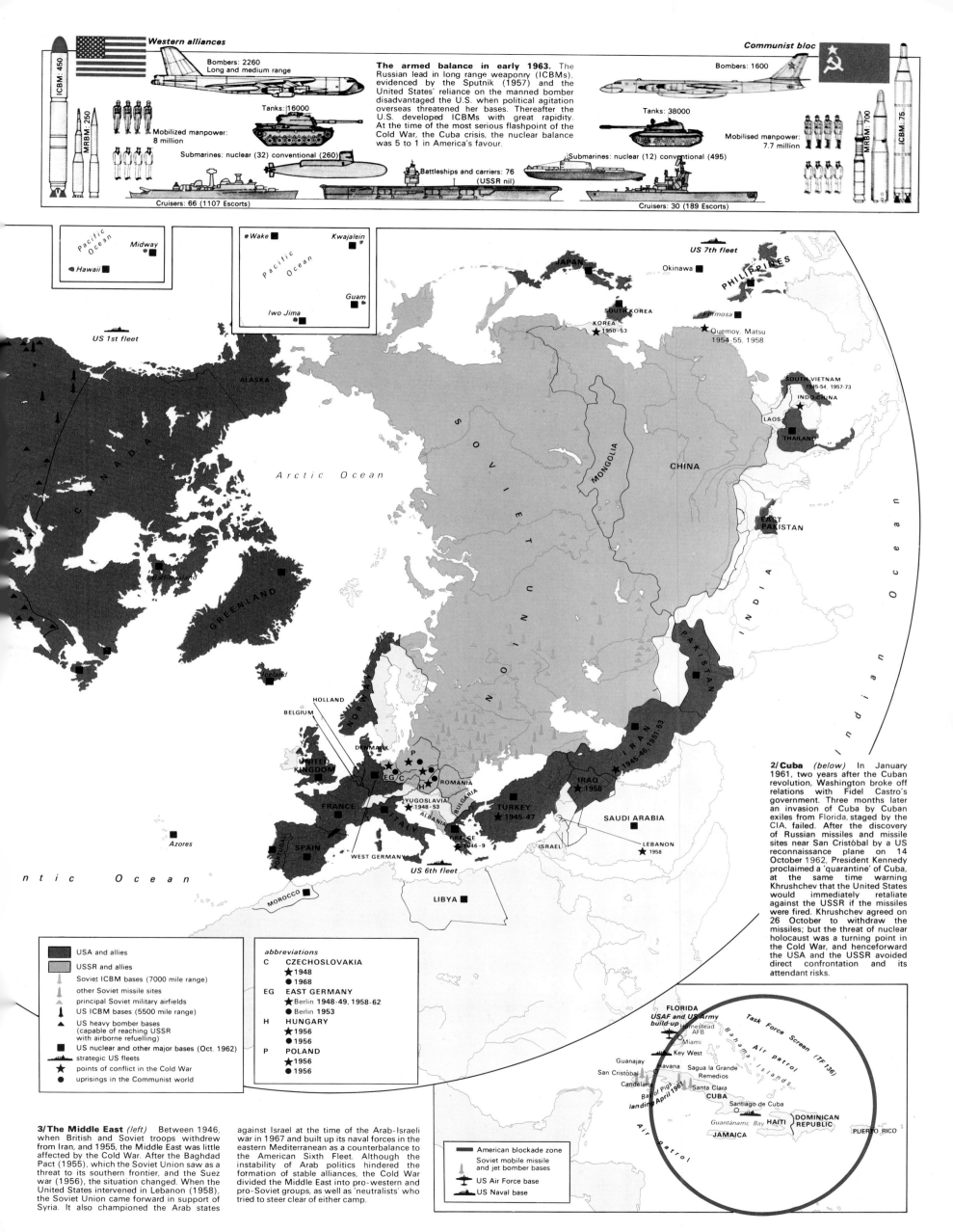

Western alliances

ICBM: 450
MRBM: 250

The armed balance in early 1963. The Russian lead in long range weaponry (ICBMs), evidenced by the Sputnik (1957) and the United States' reliance on the manned bomber disadvantaged the U.S. when political agitation overseas threatened her bases. Thereafter the U.S. developed ICBMs with great rapidity. At the time of the most serious flashpoint of the Cold War, the Cuba crisis, the nuclear balance was 5 to 1 in America's favour.

Bombers: 2260 Long and medium range

Mobilized manpower: 8 million

Tanks: 16000

Submarines: nuclear (32) conventional (260)

Battleships and carriers: 76 (USSR nil)

Cruisers: 66 (1107 Escorts)

Communist bloc

Bombers: 1600

Tanks: 38000

Mobilised manpower: 7.7 million

MRBM: 700
ICBM: 75

Submarines: nuclear (12) conventional (495)

Cruisers: 30 (189 Escorts)

US 7th fleet

US 1st fleet

US 6th fleet

2/Cuba (below) In January 1961, two years after the Cuban revolution, Washington broke off relations with Fidel Castro's government. Three months later an invasion of Cuba by Cuban exiles from Florida, staged by the CIA, failed. After the discovery of Russian missiles and missile sites near San Cristóbal by a US reconnaissance plane on 14 October 1962, President Kennedy proclaimed a 'quarantine' of Cuba, at the same time warning Khrushchev that the United States would immediately retaliate against the USSR if the missiles were fired. Khrushchev agreed on 26 October to withdraw the missiles; but the threat of nuclear holocaust was a turning point in the Cold War, and henceforward the USA and the USSR avoided direct confrontation and its attendant risks.

3/The Middle East (left) Between 1946, when British and Soviet troops withdrew from Iran, and 1955, the Middle East was little affected by the Cold War. After the Baghdad Pact (1955), which the Soviet Union saw as a threat to its southern frontier, and the Suez war (1956), the situation changed. When the United States intervened in Lebanon (1958), the Soviet Union came forward in support of Syria. It also championed the Arab states against Israel at the time of the Arab-Israeli war in 1967 and built up its naval forces in the eastern Mediterranean as a counterbalance to the American Sixth Fleet. Although the instability of Arab politics hindered the formation of stable alliances, the Cold War divided the Middle East into pro-western and pro-Soviet groups, as well as 'neutralists' who tried to steer clear of either camp.

abbreviations

C CZECHOSLOVAKIA
  ★ 1948
  ● 1968
EG EAST GERMANY
  ★ Berlin 1948-49, 1958-62
  ● Berlin 1953
H HUNGARY
  ★ 1956
  ● 1956
P POLAND
  ★ 1956
  ● 1956

Legend:
- USA and allies
- USSR and allies
- Soviet ICBM bases (7000 mile range)
- other Soviet missile sites
- principal Soviet military airfields
- US ICBM bases (5500 mile range)
- US heavy bomber bases (capable of reaching USSR with airborne refuelling)
- US nuclear and other major bases (Oct. 1962)
- strategic US fleets
- ★ points of conflict in the Cold War
- ● uprisings in the Communist world

- American blockade zone
- Soviet mobile missile and jet bomber bases
- US Air Force base
- US Naval base

293

The world in the 1990s

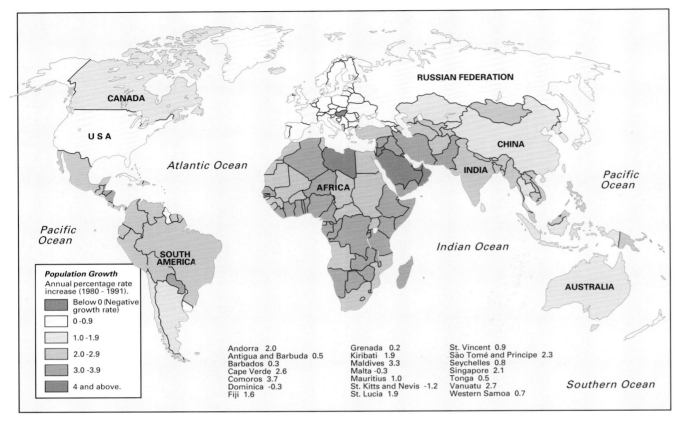

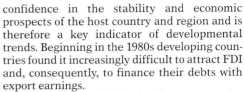

Population Growth
Annual percentage rate
increase (1980 - 1991).

- Below 0 (Negative growth rate)
- 0 - 0.9
- 1.0 - 1.9
- 2.0 - 2.9
- 3.0 - 3.9
- 4 and above.

Andorra 2.0	Grenada 0.2	St. Vincent 0.9
Antigua and Barbuda 0.5	Kiribati 1.9	São Tomé and Principe 2.3
Barbados 0.3	Maldives 3.3	Seychelles 0.8
Cape Verde 2.6	Malta -0.3	Singapore 2.1
Comoros 3.7	Mauritius 1.0	Tonga 0.5
Dominica -0.3	St. Kitts and Nevis -1.2	Vanuatu 2.7
Fiji 1.6	St. Lucia 1.9	Western Samoa 0.7

confidence in the stability and economic prospects of the host country and region and is therefore a key indicator of developmental trends. Beginning in the 1980s developing countries found it increasingly difficult to attract FDI and, consequently, to finance their debts with export earnings.

In the 1960s and 1970s developing countries had attracted large amounts of FDI, drawn mainly by low labour costs. With the pace of innovation shortening product cycles and placing a premium on skills necessary to operate computer-assisted machinery, however, low labour costs lost some of their capital pull. Coupled with multinational positioning for access to markets in the triad economies, FDI in the developing world grew at reduced levels. In the earlier 1980s the world share of FDI in developing countries totalled 25 per cent; between 1985 and 1990 it shrank to a mere 17 per cent. Moreover, as regional economic integration took place in and among the triad countries external economic barriers restricted access to world

2/Population growth, 1985-90 *(left)* Populations have increased, except for a few advanced countries and very small states with negative or zero growth. Developing countries have the highest annual growth rates and are least able to cope with them: since 1972 the world population has grown by 1.7 billion, of which 1.5 billion live in the developing world. By contrast, in the same period world GDP increased by $2000 billion with only 15 per cent accruing to the developing world.

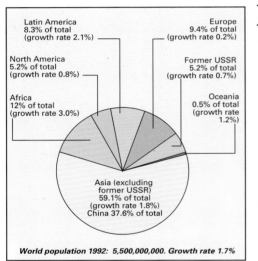

Latin America 8.3% of total (growth rate 2.1%)

North America 5.2% of total (growth rate 0.8%)

Africa 12% of total (growth rate 3.0%)

Europe 9.4% of total (growth rate 0.2%)

Former USSR 5.2% of total (growth rate 0.7%)

Oceania 0.5% of total (growth rate 1.2%)

Asia (excluding former USSR) 59.1% of total (growth rate 1.8%) China 37.6% of total

World population 1992: 5,500,000,000. Growth rate 1.7%

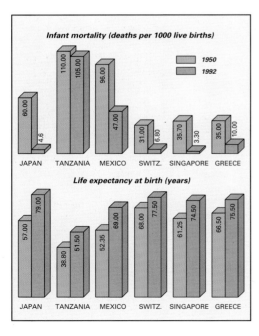

Infant mortality (deaths per 1000 live births)

	JAPAN	TANZANIA	MEXICO	SWITZ.	SINGAPORE	GREECE
1950	60.00	110.00	96.00	31.00	35.70	35.00
1992	4.6	105.00	47.00	6.80	3.30	10.00

Life expectancy at birth (years)

	JAPAN	TANZANIA	MEXICO	SWITZ.	SINGAPORE	GREECE
1950	57.00	38.80	52.35	68.00	61.25	66.50
1992	79.00	51.50	69.00	77.50	74.50	75.50

The gap between nations *(above)* The graphs illustrate the discrepancies between developed and developing countries in infant mortality and life expectancy. Tanzania is among those states in Africa where famine and disease, including AIDS (acquired immune deficiency syndrome), have reached critical levels.

B\Y THE early 1990s profound structural change had transformed the international political system and was reshaping the global economy. The most dramatic development was the end of the Cold War with the collapse in 1989 of the Soviet Empire, followed in 1991 by the disintegration of the Soviet Union itself. America no longer dominated the world economy, increasingly 'globalized' owing to the reduction of regulatory barriers to the free flow of capital and the boost given to large-scale distribution and production by the revolution in communications and computer technologies. However, a contradictory trend of regionalism had produced an incipient 'triad' of economic trading blocs centring on North America, Europe (in the form of the European Community) and Japan. Worldwide inequalities in the distribution of wealth persisted, even worsening as the growing importance of advanced technologies marginalized the economies of developing countries, many of which were still paralysed by the debt crisis of the 1980s.

Despite unprecedented growth in prosperity after the Second World War, between 1960 and 1992 the economic gap separating the richest and poorest fifths of the world doubled. In part, the meagre economic performance of developing countries stemmed from rapid population growth unaccompanied by adequate increases in national income. The world population explosion slowed in the late 1980s but long-term demographic increase remained a serious problem. Improvements in health care reduced infant mortality rates and extended lifespans, but in areas with food shortages, such as sub-Saharan Africa, famine remained rife into the 1990s.

The processes unleashed by globalization harmed much of the developing world. Above all, the focus of economic competition shifted in the late 1980s from trade to capital. Between 1984 and 1989 the flow of foreign direct investment (FDI) rose at an annual rate of 29 per cent – three times faster than trade – to reach a total of $1500 billion. Growth in world trade in goods, on the other hand, declined from 8.5 per cent in 1988 to 3 per cent in 1991, the lowest figure since 1983.

Direct investment – the purchase of tangible assets in a foreign country – implies long-term

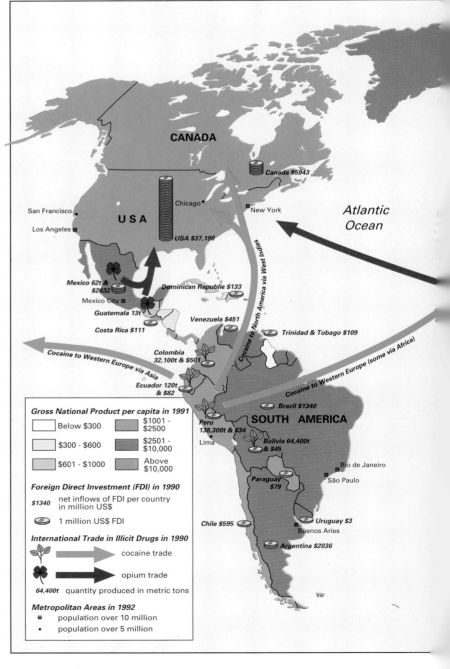

Gross National Product per capita in 1991

- Below $300
- $300 - $600
- $601 - $1000
- $1001 - $2500
- $2501 - $10,000
- Above $10,000

Foreign Direct Investment (FDI) in 1990

$1340 net inflows of FDI per country in million US$

○ 1 million US$ FDI

International Trade in Illicit Drugs in 1990

→ cocaine trade

➤ opium trade

64,400t quantity produced in metric tons

Metropolitan Areas in 1992

■ population over 10 million

• population over 5 million

markets, costing developing countries $500 billion a year in lost earnings.

Developing countries did possess a clear competitive advantage in the production and distribution of illicit drugs, identified by the United Nations in 1992 as a $500-billion-a-year business, second only to the world trade in arms. The illegal drugs trade thrived in the increasingly integrated world economy, with financial deregulation facilitating money laundering, and regional integration contributing to increasingly porous borders. In 1988 an estimated $85 billion worth of drug money was laundered in the United States and Europe; by 1992 this had risen to $250 billion.

Drug production offered a vital source of hard currency and employment. Approximately 400,000 of Bolivia's 6.5 million population worked directly in the drug trade, for example. Though it was organized crime that profited most, individuals gained too. Latin American farmers cultivated no more lucrative cash crop than coca. Similarly, in 1990 Peruvian coca farmers earned an average of $1500-2000 a year, their gross income per acre exceeding that of a coffee farmer tenfold, and of a rice farmer twentyfold. In 1991 Colombia exported an estimated 200 tons of cocaine to Europe. Europe-wide cocaine seizures soared, rising from 1.5 tons in 1986 to 16 tons in 1991, but still accounted for only a fraction of the illegal drug trade.

The post-communist transition to market economies and the loosening of border controls risked stimulating drugs production in eastern Europe and Russia while providing new conduits for existing suppliers. In 1992 farmers in the former Soviet Union cultivated an estimated 3 million acres of marijuana and a growing number of poppies – in the Ukraine impoverished farmers even grew them in the 'forbidden zone' surrounding the Chernobyl nuclear reactor, site of a toxic explosion in 1986. Nor did all post-com-

3/Ozone depletion (below) No event more effectively illustrates the potentially dramatic consequences of environmental degradation than depletion of the ozone layer, here depicted as it occurs each spring over the Antarctic. Essential to the protection of the earth's surface from damaging ultra-violet rays, ozone is destroyed by chlorofluorocarbons (CFCs). In 1975 the concentration of chlorine in the Earth's atmosphere was 1.4 parts per billion. By 1992 it had almost reached 3 parts per billion, a sufficient increase to open this hole in the ozone layer 12-19 miles (20-30 km) above the Antarctic.

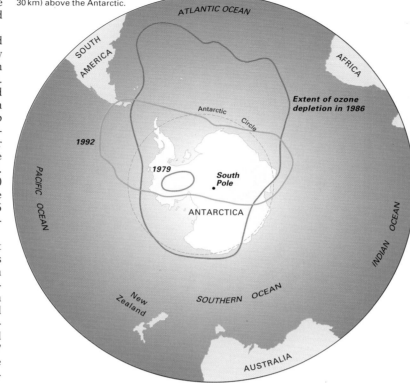

munist governments ratify the 1988 Vienna convention criminalizing money laundering and declaring the 1990s the UN decade against drug abuse.

The UN also played a prominent role in addressing public concern about environmental degradation. The UN Conference on the Environment and Development held in Rio de Janeiro in June 1992 constituted a watershed. More governments (185) participated and more heads of state (131) attended the 'Earth Summit' than any previous international gathering. Achievements of the conference were mixed, but widespread concern about global pollution and climate change placed sustainable development firmly on the international agenda.

The emission of pollution and 'greenhouse gases', the result principally of continuing dependence on fossil fuels as sources of cheap energy, risked a potentially disastrous warming of the Earth's climate. The economies of industrialized countries, which produced much of the existing contamination, were better able to adapt to new, less-damaging technologies. However, developing countries, responsible for a growing proportion of the contamination, feared yet another expensive obstacle to their economic growth. In the absence of compensation from their wealthier neighbours many of them proved reluctant to alter development strategies. In fact the wealthy states of the northern hemisphere gave approximately $55 billion in aid to the developing world, amounting to approximately 0.45 per cent of their income. Nonetheless, the UN proposed setting a target of $125 billion (or 0.7 per cent of income) to foster sustainable development, a move that generally found little support in the North.

Economic stagnation and political repression in some regions led to an increase in the scale and frequency of cross-border migrations and internal displacement. Most occurred in the developing world, where in 1992 an estimated 30 million people remained unsettled after fleeing their countries or homes. By contrast, in the developed world refugees and displaced persons numbered approximately 8 million.

Two events in particular focused international attention on refugees – the 1989 flood of East Germans into West Germany following the easing of east European border restrictions; and the flight of Kurds from Iraq to escape government repression in the wake of Iraq's defeat at the hands of the US-led UN coalition forces in the Gulf War of 1991. The first precipitated Germany's reunification; the second threatened the stability of the Middle East, where Kurds form the fourth-largest ethnic group but remain dispersed among four countries all of which are opposed to the formation of an independent Kurdish state. The gravity of the Kurdish exodus to Turkey, where 400,000 Kurds starved and froze to death in mountainous terrain, prompted the international community to intervene in Iraq's internal affairs and thus to acknowledge that the division between the internal and external policies of a state are not absolute.

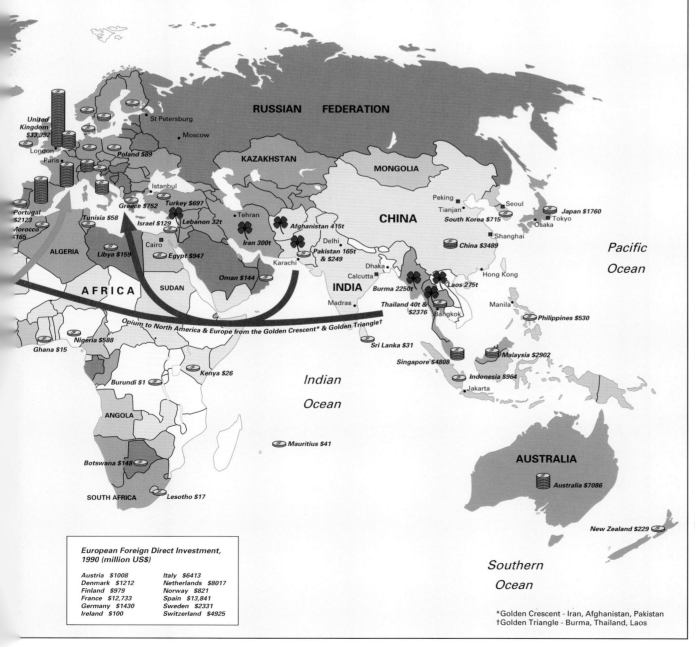

*Golden Crescent - Iran, Afghanistan, Pakistan
†Golden Triangle - Burma, Thailand, Laos

European Foreign Direct Investment, 1990 (million US$)

Austria $1008	Italy $6413
Denmark $1212	Netherlands $8017
Finland $979	Norway $821
France $12,733	Spain $13,841
Germany $1430	Sweden $2331
Ireland $100	Switzerland $4925

4/Foreign Direct Investment (below) In 1990 the 'triad' of developed trading blocs (North America, Europe and Japan) attracted more than four-fifths of worldwide foreign direct investment.

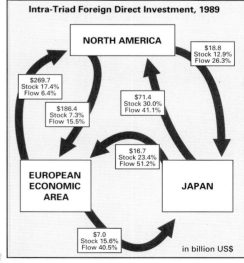

1/Drugs and investment (left) Flows of FDI reveal that 'globalization' of the world economy has largely been limited to the wealthiest countries organized increasingly as a triad of economic blocs. Fully 70 per cent of triad FDI has flowed to other triad countries, reflecting low confidence in long-term prospects for sustained economic growth elsewhere. Comparing flows of drugs and FDI suggests that eradication of drug trafficking will be difficult without reducing the demand in wealthy countries which makes the trade so lucrative, particularly for those countries least able to attract legitimate long-term investment.

Acknowledgements

Acknowledgements and Bibliography: Maps

We have pleasure in acknowledging the following: Map 4, page 55, is based, with kind permission, on a map on page 51 in W H McNeill, M R Buske, A W Roehm, *The World...its History in Maps*, Chicago 1969 © Denoyer-Geppert.

Map 3, page 274, is based with permission on material reproduced from *Population Change in China* by Paul White, page 3, *The Geographical Magazine*, London, January 1984.

Map 3, page 278, is based with permission on material reproduced from *A Historical Atlas of South Asia*, by Joseph E Schwartzberg (ed.), Chicago 1978.

Map 4, page 287, is based with permission on *The Slowing of Urbanization* in the US by Larry Long and Diana DeAre, page 35, *Scientific American*, July 1983.

Among the large number of works consulted by contributors, the following contain valuable maps and other data that have been particularly useful:

I. History Atlases

Atlas zur Geschichte 2 vols. Leipzig 1976
Bazilevsky, K V, Golubtsov, A, Zinoviev, M A *Atlas Istorii SSR*, Moscow 1952
Beckingham, C F *Atlas of the Arab World and the Middle East*, London 1960
Bertin, J (et al) *Atlas of Food Crops*, Paris 1971
Bjørklund, O, Holmboe, H, Røhr, A *Historical Atlas of the World*, Edinburgh 1970
Cappon, L (et al) *Atlas of Early American History*, Chicago 1976
Darby, H C, Fullard, H (eds.) *The New Cambridge Modern History* vol. XIV: Atlas, Cambridge 1970
Davies, C C *An Historical Atlas of the Indian Peninsula*, London 1959
Engel, J (ed.) *Grosser Historischer Weltatlas*, 3 vols., Munich 1953-70
Fage, J D *An Atlas of African History*, London 1958
Gilbert, M *Russian History Atlas*, London 1972
Gilbert, M *Recent History Atlas 1860-1960*, London 1966
Gilbert, M *First World War Atlas*, London 1970
Gilbert, M *Jewish History Atlas*, London 1969
Hazard, H W *Atlas of Islamic History*, Princeton 1952
Herrmann, A *Historical and Commercial Atlas of China*, Harvard 1935
Herrmann, A *An Historical Atlas of China*, Edinburgh 1966
Jedin, H, Latourette, K S, Martin, J *Atlas zur Kirchengeschichte*, Freiburg 1970
Kinder, H, Hilgermann, W DTV *Atlas zur Weltgeschichte* 2 vols. Stuttgart 1964 (published in English as *The Penguin Atlas of World History*, London 1974 & 1978)
Matsui and Mori *Ajiarekishi chizu*, Tokyo 1965
May, H G (ed.) *Oxford Bible Atlas*, Oxford 1974
McNeill, WH., Buske, M R, Roehm, A W *The World...its History in Maps*, Chicago 1969
Nelson's Atlas of the Early Christian World, London 1959
Nelson's Atlas of the Classical World, London 1959
Nelson's Atlas of World History, London 1965
Nihon rekishi jiten Atlas vol., Tokyo 1959
Palmer, R R (ed.) *Atlas of World History*, Chicago 1965
Paullin, C O *Atlas of the Historical Geography of the United States*, Washington 1932
Ragi al Faruqi, I (ed.) *Historical Atlas of the Religions of the World*, New York 1974
Roolvink, R *Historical Atlas of the Muslim Peoples*, London 1957
Schwartzberg, J E (ed.) *A Historical Atlas of South Asia*, Chicago 1978
Shepherd, W R *Historical Atlas*, New York 1964
Toynbee, A J, Mers, E D *A Study of History, Historical Atlas and Gazetteer*, Oxford 1959
Treharne, R F, Fullard, H (eds.) *Muir's Historical Atlas*, London 1966
Van der Heyden, A M, Scullard, H H *Atlas of the Classical World*, London 1959
Wesley, E B *Our United States...its History in Maps*, Chicago 1977
Westermann *Grosser Atlas zur Weltgeschichte*, Brunswick 1976
Whitehouse, D & R *Archaeological Atlas of the World*, London 1975
Wilgus, A C *Latin America in Maps*, New York 1943

II. General Works

Abu-Lughod, J L *Before European Hegemony: The World System AD1250-1350*, Oxford 1991
Ajayi, J F A, Crowder, M *History of West Africa*, 2 vols., 3rd ed., 1985-
Allchin, B & R *The Birth of Indian Civilization*, London 1968
Australia, Commonwealth of, Department of National Development, *Atlas of Australian Resources*, 3rd series, 1980
Barraclough, G *Medieval Germany*, Oxford 1938 & 1967
Basham, A L *The Wonder That Was India*, 2 vols., 3rd revised, London 1987
Beresford, M *New Towns of the Middle Ages*, London 1967
Bolton, G (ed.) *Oxford History of Australia*, Oxford 1986
Braudel, F *The Mediterranean and the Mediterranean World in the Age of Philip II*, 2 vols., London 1972-3
Boardman, J (ed.) *The Oxford History of the Classical World*, Oxford 1989
Bury, J B, Cook, S A, Adcock, F E (eds.) *The Cambridge Ancient History*, Cambridge 1923-; 2nd ed. 1982
Bury, J B, Gwatkin, H M, Whitney, J P (eds.) *The Cambridge Medieval History*, Cambridge, 1911-
Chang, K C *The Archaeology of Ancient China*, 4th ed., New Haven 1986
Chaudhuri, K N *Trade and Civilization in the Indian Ocean: An Economic History From the Rise of Islam to 1750*, Cambridge 1985
Chaudhuri, K N *Asia Before Europe: Economy and Civilization of the Indian Ocean from the Rise of Islam to 1750*, Cambridge 1991
Coedès, G *Les Etats Hindouisés de l'Indochine et d'Indonésie*, Paris 1964
Cook, M A (ed.) *A History of the Ottoman Empire to 1730*, Cambridge 1976
Crowder, M *West Africa Under Colonial Rule*, London 1968
Curtin, P D *The Atlantic Slave Trade*, Madison, 1972
Curtin, P D *Cross-cultural Trade in World History*, Cambridge 1984
Dalton, B J *War and Politics in New Zealand, 1855-1870*, Sydney 1967
Darby, H C (ed.) *An Historical Geography of England Before AD 1800*, Cambridge 1936 & 1960
Davis, R W *The Industrialization of Soviet Russia*, 3 vols., Cambridge 1989
Despois, J, Raynal, R *Géographie de l'Afrique du Nord*, Paris 1967
East, W G *The Geography Behind History*, London 1965
East, W G *An Historical Geography of Europe*, 5th ed., London 1967
Edwardes, M *A History of India*, London 1961
Evans, B L *Agricultural and Pastoral Statistics of New Zealand*, 1861-1954, Wellington 1956
Fage, J D, Oliver, R (eds.) *Cambridge History of Africa*, Cambridge 1975-
Ferguson, J *The Heritage of Hellenism*, London 1973
Fisher, C A *South-East Asia*, London 1964
Fletcher, A *Tudor Rebellions*, 3rd ed., London 1983
Fowler, K *The Age of Plantagenet and Valois*, New York 1967
Fourquin, G *Histoire Economique de l'Occident Médiéval*, Paris 1969
Ganshof, F L *Etude sur le Développement des Villes entre Loire et Rhin au Moyen Age*, Paris-Brussels 1943
Geelan, P J M, Twitchett, D C (eds.) *The Times Atlas of China*, London 1974
Gernet, J *Le Monde Chinois*, Paris 1969; English translation 1982
Graff, E, Hammond, H E *Southeast Asia: History, Culture, People*, 5th revised ed., Cambridge 1980
Grousset, R *The Empire of the Steppes: A History of Central Asia*, New Brunswick N J 1970
Guillermaz, J *Histoire du Parti Communiste Chinois*, Paris 1968; English translation 1972
Hall, D G E *A History of South-East Asia*, 4th ed., London 1981
Harlan, J R "The Plants and Animals that Nourish Man", *Scientific American* 1976
Harlan, J R, Zohary, D "The Distribution of Wild Wheats and Barleys", *Science* 1966
Harley, J B, Woodward, D *The History of Cartography*, 2 vols., Chicago 1987-
Hatton, R M *Europe in the Age of Louis XIV*, London 1969
Hawke, G R *The Making of New Zealand: An Economic History*, Cambridge 1985
Henderson, W O *Britain and Industrial Europe, 1750-1870*, Liverpool 1965
Hopkins, A G *Economic History of West Africa*, London 1973
Hourani, A *A History of the Arab People*, Harvard 1991
Inalcik, H *The Ottoman Empire: The Classical Age, 1300-1600*, reprint, London 1989
Inikori, J E, Engerman, S L *The Atlantic Slave Trade: Effects on Economy, Society, and Population in Africa, America, and Europe*, Durham, NC 1992
Jeans, D N *An Historical Geography of New South Wales to 1901*, Sydney 1972
Jennings, J D *Prehistory of North America*, 3rd ed., Mountain View, Calif. 1989
Johnson, G (ed.) *New Cambridge History of India*, Cambridge 1989-
Kahan, A *Russian Economic History*, Chicago 1991
Kennedy, J *A History of Malaya, 1400-1959*, London 1967
Kjölstad, T, Rystad, G *5000 år: Epoker och utvecklingslinjer*, Lund 1973
Koeningsberger, H G, Mosse, G L, Bowler, G Q *Europe in the Sixteenth Century*, 2nd ed., London 1989
Laird, C E *Language in America*, New York 1970
Langer, W L (ed.) *An Encyclopedia of World History*, revised ed., London 1987
Lapidus, I M *A History of Islamic Societies*, Cambridge 1988
Lattimore, O *Inner Asian Frontiers of China*, New York 1951
Lyashchenko, P I *History of the National Economy of Russia to the 1917 Revolution*, New York 1949
Majumdar, R C *The Vedic Age*, Bombay 1951
Majumdar, R C *History and Culture of the Indian People, Age of Imperial Unity*, Bombay 1954
Macmillan's Atlas of South-East Asia, London 1988
Mantran, R *Histoire de l'Empire Ottoman*, Paris 1989
McNeill, W H *The Rise of the West: A History of the Human Community*, Chicago 1991
McNeill, W H *Plagues and Peoples*, New York 1992
Meining, D W *On the Margins of the Good Earth*, New York 1962, London 1963
Mellaart, J *The Neolithic of the Near East*, London 1975
Miquel, A *L'Islam et Sa Civilisation*, Paris 1968
Morrell, W P, Hall, D O W *A History of New Zealand Life*, Christchurch 1962
Moss, H St L B, *The Birth of the Middle Ages*, Oxford 1935
Mulvaney, D J *The Prehistory of Australia*, London 1975
Musset, L *Les Invasions: Les Vagues Germaniques*, Paris 1965
Musset, L *Les Invasions: Le Second Assaut contre l'Europe Chrétienne*, Paris 1971
The National Atlas of the United States of America, Washington DC 1970
Neatby, H *Quebec, The Revolutionary Age 1760-1791*, London 1966
Ogot, B A (ed.) *Zamani, A Survey of West African History*, London 1974-1976
Oliver, R, Fagan, B *Africa in the Iron Age c. 500 BC-1400 AD*, Cambridge 1975
Oliver, R, Atmore, A *Africa Since 1800*, 3rd ed., Cambridge 1981
Oliver, W H, Williams, R R *Oxford History of New Zealand*, Oxford 1981
Osbourne, M E *Southeast Asia: An Introductory History*, 2nd ed., Sydney 1983
Ostrogorsky, G *History of the Byzantine State*, Oxford 1969
Parker, W H *An Historical Geography of Russia*, London 1968
Phillips, J R S *The Medieval Expansion of Europe*, Oxford 1988
Piggott, S *Prehistoric India to 1000 BC*, London 1962
Pitcher, D E *An Historical Geography of the Ottoman Empire*, Leiden 1973
Postan, M M *Medieval Trade and Finance*, Cambridge 1973
Powell, J M *An Historial Geography of Modern Australia: the Restive Fringe*, Cambridge 1988
Ragozin, Z A *History of Vedic India*, Delhi 1980
Rizvi, A A *The Wonder That Was India: 1200-1700*, 2 vols., London 1987
Roberts, J M *The Hutchinson History of the World*, revised ed., London 1987
Sanders, W T, Marino, J *New World Prehistory: Archaeology of the American Indian*, Englewood Cliffs, N J 1970
Saum, L O *The Fur Trader and the Indian*, London 1965
Seltzer, L E (ed.) *The Columbia Lippincott Gazetteer of the World*, New York 1952
Simkin, C F *The Traditional Trade of Asia*, Oxford 1968
Smith, C T *An Historical Geography of Western Europe before 1800*, revised ed. London & New York 1978
Smith, W S *The Art and Architecture of Ancient Egypt*, revised ed., London 1981
Snow, D *The American Indians: Their Archaeology and Prehistory*, London 1976
Stravrianos, L S *The World Since 1500: A Global History*, 6th ed., Englewood Cliffs, N J 1991
Stavrianos, L S *The World to 1500: A Global History*, 5th ed., Englewood Cliffs, N J 1991
Stein, Sir Aurel *Travels in Central Asia*, London 1935
Stoye, J *The Siege of Vienna*, London 1964
Tate, D J M *The Making of South-East Asia*, Kuala Lumpur 1971
Thapar, R *A History of India*, London 1967
The Times Atlas of the World, 9th Comprehensive Edition, London 1992
Toynbee, A J *Cities of Destiny*, London 1967
Toynbee, A J *Mankind and Mother Earth*, Oxford 1976
Twitchett, D, Loewe, M (eds.) *The Cambridge History of China*, Cambridge 1979-
U S Strategic Bombing Survey, Summary Report (Pacific War), Washington 1946
Van Alstyne, R W *The Rising American Empire*, reprint, Oxford 1974
Van Heekeren, H R *The Stone Age of Indonesia*, 2nd revised ed., The Hague 1972
Wadham, S, Wilson, R K, Wood, J *Land Utilization in Australia*, Melbourne 1964
Watters, R F *Land and Society in New Zealand*, Wellington 1965
Wheatley, P *The Golden Khersonese*, Kuala Lumpur 1966
Wheeler, M *Early India and Pakistan to Ashoka*, London 1968
Wickins, P L *An Economic History of Africa From Earliest Times to Partition*, New York 1981
Willey, G *An Introduction to American Archaeology*, vols. 1 & 2, Englewood Cliffs, N J 1970
Williams, M *The Making of the South Australian Landscape*, London 1974
Wilson, M, Thompson, L *Oxford History of South Africa*, vols. 1 & 2, Oxford, 1969, 1971

Acknowledgements: Pictures and Illustrations

Unless stated to the contrary all the illustrations used in this book are the work of the following artists: Peter Sullivan, David Case, John Grimwade, Tom Stimpson, Chris Fen, Chee Chai, Chris Burke, Ken Tan.

The publishers wish to thank the following museums, publishers and picture agencies for permission to base illustrations upon their photographs or to reproduce them. Where there is no such acknowledgement we have been unable to trace the source, or the illustration is a composition by our illustrators and contributors.

Archiv der Hansestadt, Lübeck **142**
Associated Press **292**
The Chester Beatty Library and Gallery of Oriental Art, Dublin **169**
The Bridgeman Art Library **175**
British Library **91, 106, 129, 132**
British Museum **34, 90, 144**
Cambridge University Museum of Archaeology & Anthropology **34**
Jean-Loup Charmet, Paris **200**
Church Missionary Society **244**
James Davis Travel Photography **173**
C M Dixon **32, 60, 66, 75, 88, 92, 98, 100, 104**
E T Archive **35, 40, 156, 175, 186, 189, 199, 210, 219, 261, 262, 267**. Also from E T Archive: National Museum, Karachi **65**; Musée Guimet, Paris **71**; University Museum, Cuzco **144**; Bibliothèque Nationale, Paris **153**; V&A Museum **156**; National Maritime Museum, Greenwich **191**; Cavalry Museum, Pinerolo **213**; National Army Museum **235**; The Gordon Boy's School, Woking **237**; British Library **259**
Giraudon, Paris **228**
Susan Griggs **30-1, 250-1**
Sonia Halliday Photographs **136, 166, 182**
Robert Harding Picture Library **50-1, 53, 58, 59, 81, 96-7, 147, 148-9, 202-3**
Historiographical Institute, Tokyo **246**
Michael Holford **55, 56, 63, 82, 130, 158**
Hulton Deutsch Collection Limited **179, 197, 227, 242, 285**
Imperial War Museum **288**
Institute of Agricultural History & Museum of Rural Life, University of Reading **175**
Japan Information Centre **276**
The Billie Love Historical Collection **214**
Photo Hubert Josse **134, 201**
A F Kersting **121**
Larousse, Paris **181**
Magnum **273**
Magyar Nemzeti Museum **42**
Tony Morrison South American Pictures **222**
Musee de l'Affiche, Paris **265**
Museo Civicio Luigi Bailo, Sake Collection, Treviso, Italy **265**
Museum für Völkerunde **155**
National Maritime Museum, Greenwich **247, 253**
National Museum of Ireland **127**
Natural History Museum **32, 37**
Peter Newark's Western Americana **217, 221**
Novosti Press Agency **268**
The Photographer's Library **68-9**
Axel Poignant Archive **48**
Popperfoto **231, 248, 254, 279, 281**
Reed Consumer Books/Musée de l'oeuvre, Notre Dame, Strasbourg **184**
Scala (Museo Pio-Clementino, Vaticano **86**); **102**
Chris Scarre **44**
Science Museum **197, 207**
Science Photo Library/NASA **286**
Skyscan Balloon Photography **84, 123**
Spectrum Colour Library **72**
Frank Spooner Pictures **276**
Werner Forman Archive **94, 109, 116, 124, 140, 144, 162**. Also from Werner Forman Archive: Museum of Anthropology, Mexico **47**; Viking Ship Museum, Bygdoy **111**

Glossary

This glossary is intended to provide supplementary information about some of the individuals, peoples, events, treaties, etc. which, because of lack of space, received only brief mention on the maps or in the accompanying texts. It is not a general encyclopedia: only names mentioned in the atlas proper are included. Names printed in **bold** type have their own glossary entries.

ABBAS I, THE GREAT (c.1557-1629) Shah of Persia. Attaining the throne in 1587, he reorganized and centralized the **Safavid** state. His reign was marked by cultural efflorescence and territorial expansion. Having crushed the rebellious **Uzbeks** (1597) he drove the **Ottomans** from their possessions in western Iran, Iraq and the eastern Caucasus (1603-7), and extended Safavid territories (temporarily) from the Tigris to the Indus. He moved the capital to Isfahan.

ABBASIDS Second major dynasty in Islam, displacing the **Umayyads** in 750. It founded a new capital, Baghdad, in 762, but its political control over the Islamic world, almost complete in the 9th and early 10th centuries, gradually decayed. Its rulers frequently became figureheads for other regimes: the last true caliph was killed by Mongols in 1258 and later Abbasid caliphs, nominally restored in 1260, were merely court functionaries to Egypt's **Mamluke** sultans.

ABD AL KADIR (1808-83) (also known as Abd el-Kader and Abdal-Qadir). Algerian independence leader. He was elected in 1832 to succeed his father as leader of a religious sect; as emir, he took control of the Oran region, successfully fought the French, and in 1837 concluded the Treaty of Tafna; he extended his authority to the Moroccan frontier; renewed hostilities (1840-7) ended with his defeat and imprisonment, though he was freed in 1852.

ABD ALLAH (1846-99) Khalifa, or religious and political leader, in the Sudan after the death of the Mahdi in 1885. In 1880 he became a disciple of the **Mahdi, Mohammed Ahmed**, whom he succeeded. As leader of the Mahdist movement he launched attacks on Egypt and Ethiopia; he consolidated power within the Sudan, building up an effective centralized state, until invaded by Anglo-Egyptian forces under Kitchener. He lost the battle of Omdurman in 1898, and was killed the following year while resisting Anglo-Egyptian troops.

ABD EL-KRIM (1882-1963) Founded Republic of the Rif (1921-6), the North African precursor of many 20th-century independence movements. His forces defeated major French and Spanish armies until overwhelmed, in May 1926, by 250,000 Franco-Spanish troops. He was exiled to Réunion, but escaped to Egypt where he was given political asylum in 1947.

ABDÜL HAMID II (1842-1918) Last important Ottoman sultan, 1876-1909. He carried further some lines of modernization already begun, and used Islamic sentiment to resist European encroachments. The revolt by **Young Turks** in 1908 against his autocratic rule led to his deposition, 1909; he was imprisoned at Salonika, 1910, and died in Istanbul eight years later.

ABRAHAM First of three patriarchs of the **Jews** (Abraham, his son Isaac, Isaac's son Jacob). Born in Ur, he migrated via Harran in Syria to Canaan (Palestine), the land promised by God to his descendants. Abraham, Isaac and Jacob have been dated to the early or middle 2nd millennium BC. According to much later tradition, he was considered to be the progenitor of the Arabs through his other son, Ishmael.

ABREU, ANTONIO DE 16th-century Portuguese navigator, who in 1512 discovered the Banda Islands, Indonesia, during an exploratory voyage to the Moluccas.

ABU BAKR (c.573-634) Close friend and adviser to **Mohammed**, and said to have been the first male convert to Islam. He became Mohammed's father-in-law, and accompanied him on the historic journey to Medina in 622. Accepted after Mohammed's death as caliph – 'successor of the Prophet of God'; under his two-year rule central Arabia accepted Islam and the Arab conquests began, with expansion into Iraq and Syria.

ABUSHIRI REVOLT An insurrection in 1888-9 by the Arab population of those areas of the East African coast which were granted by the sultan of Zanzibar to Germany in 1888. It was eventually suppressed by an Anglo-German blockade of the coast.

ACHAEMENIDS Ancient Persian dynasty of Fars province. **Cyrus II the Great**, a prince of the line, defeated the **Medes** and founded the Achaemenid Empire, 550-330 BC. Descended traditionally from Achaemenes (7th century BC), the senior line of his successors included Cyrus I, Cambyses I, Cyrus II and **Cambyses II**, after whose death in 522 BC the junior line came to the throne with **Darius I**. The dynasty was extinguished with the death of Darius III in 330 BC after defeat by **Alexander the Great** (331 BC).

ACHESON, DEAN (1893-1971) US Secretary of State, 1949-53. He was responsible for many important policy initiatives under President **Truman**, including the implementation of the **Marshall Plan**, the **North Atlantic Treaty Organization**, non-recognition of Communist China and the rearming of West Germany.

ADAMS, JOHN (1735-1826) Second President of the United States, 1797-1801. A leading advocate of resistance to British rule before the American War of Independence, in 1776 he seconded the Declaration of Independence. He was American envoy to Britain, 1785-8, and author of *Thoughts on Government* (1776).

ADAMS, JOHN QUINCY (1767-1848) Sixth President of the United States, 1825-9. The son of **John Adams** he was Secretary of State, 1817-25; in this post he contributed to the shaping of the **Monroe Doctrine**. In 1843 he led the opposition to the annexation of Texas.

ADENAUER, KONRAD (1876-1967) German statesman. He studied law and served in the Provincial Diet of the Rhineland (1920-33) until dismissed from office (1933). He suffered constant harassment by the **Nazis** until 1945 when he became active in the newly formed Christian Democratic Union. He became chancellor of the Federal Republic of Germany from 1949 until his retirement in 1963. Known affectionately as 'der Alte' (the Old Man), he remained deeply committed to close ties with the democratic Christian west.

AESCHYLUS (525/4-456 BC) Athenian dramatist, who also fought at the **Battle of Marathon**, 490 BC. He wrote at least 80 plays, mostly tragedies, of which seven survive in full: *The Persians, The Seven against Thebes, The Suppliants, The Oresteia* trilogy and *Prometheus Bound*. He was the creator of tragic drama.

ÆTHELRED II (d.1016) King of Wessex, England, from 978. His reign was marked by a steady increase in Danish influence; in 1013 he fled to Normandy and the English recognized the Danish king, **Sven Forkbeard**, as their ruler.

AFGHANI, JAMAL AD-DIN AL- (1838-97) Muslim agitator, reformer and journalist. Born in Persia, he was politically active in Afghanistan, Istanbul and Cairo. Exiled from Egypt in 1879 for political reasons, he published (1884) *The Firmest Bond*, a periodical attacking British imperialism and advocating Islamic reform. Exiled from Persia in 1892, he spent his remaining years in Istanbul; he instigated the assassination of the Shah in 1896.

AGHLABIDS Muslim Arab dynasty, ruling much of North Africa from 800 to 909. They controlled Tunisia and eastern Algeria, conquered Sicily in 827 and invaded southern Italy. They were finally defeated and replaced by the **Fatimids**.

AGIS IV (c.262-239 BC) King of Sparta who, in 243 BC, attempted to introduce a 'communist' programme of land redistribution and debt cancellation. Tricked by an unscrupulous uncle and unable to complete his reforms quickly enough, he was forced to leave the country for war with the Aetolians in 241; in his absence a counter-revolution put his enemies in power, and after a mock trial he was executed.

AGUINALDO, EMILIO (1869-1964) President of the short-lived Philippine Republic (1898-1901). Of mixed Chinese and Tagalog ancestry, he fought Spanish rule as leader of the revolutionary Katipunan Society. Exiled in 1897, he returned, first to cooperate with US forces, and then to lead a three-year insurrection. He was captured and deposed in 1901. In 1945 he was briefly imprisoned for supporting Japanese occupation. He became a member of the Philippine Council of State in 1950.

AGUNG, SULTAN Third ruler of Mataram, the Muslim kingdom which, in the 17th century, dominated central and much of eastern Java. He sought an alliance against Bantam and, when this was refused, attacked Batavia (now Jakarta), founded in 1619 by the **Dutch East India Company**. Defeated there in 1629, he undertook the Islamization of eastern Java by force; but failed in all attempts to conquer Bali, which remained loyal to traditional Hindu-Buddhist culture.

AGUSTÍN I Emperor of Mexico: *see* **Iturbide**.

AHMADU SEFU (1835-97) Son and successor of **al-Hajj Umar** (d.1864), a Tukolor chief whose kingdom was on the Upper Niger. He came to power some years after his father's death, but his kingdom was eventually destroyed by the French in the 1890s.

AHMED GRAN (c.1506-42) Muslim conqueror in 16th-century Ethiopia. He gained control of the Somali Muslim state, Adal, and declared a *jihad* (holy war) against Christian Ethiopia. By 1535, with help from Turkish troops and firearms, he had seized three-quarters of the country, and in 1541 defeated a Portuguese relief force. He was killed in battle against the new Ethiopian leader, Galawdewos.

AHMOSE *see* **Amosis I**.

AIDAN, ST (d.651) Born in Ireland, he trained as a monk at Iona, off the Isle of Mull, West Scotland. He was consecrated bishop of the newly-converted Northumbrians in 635; he established his church and monastery on Lindisfarne, off the northeast coast of England, from where evangelists set out to convert large areas of northern England, under the protection of kings Oswald and Oswin of Northumbria.

AIGUN, TREATY OF Agreement reached in 1858 by which China ceded the north bank of the Amur river to Russia. Together with further gains under the **Treaty of Peking** (1860), this gave Russia access to ice-free Pacific waters; the port of Vladivostok was founded in 1860.

AIX-LA-CHAPELLE, TREATY OF Agreement reached in 1748 which concluded the War of the Austrian Succession; Austria ceded Silesia to Prussia, Spain made gains in Italy, and **Maria Theresa** was confirmed in possession of the rest of the Austrian lands.

AKBAR (1542-1605) Greatest of India's **Mughal** emperors. Born in Umarkot, Sind, he succeeded his father, Humayun, in 1556. During his reign he consolidated Mughal rule throughout the sub-continent, winning the loyalty of both Muslims and Hindus; at his death he left superb administrative and artistic achievements, including the fortress-palace at Agra and the magnificent but now deserted city of Fatehpur Sikri.

AKHENATEN XVIIIth Dynasty Egyptian pharaoh, reigning 1379-62 BC; the son of Amenhotep III, he took the throne as Amenhotep IV. He promoted the monotheistic cult of Aten, the god in the sun disc; changed his name c.1373 BC and transferred the capital from Thebes to the new city of Akhetaten (El-Amarna). With his wife, Nefertiti, and six daughters, he devoted the rest of his reign largely to the cult of Aten, dangerously neglecting practical affairs.

AKKADIANS Name given to a wave of Semitic-speaking immigrants from the west, of increasing prominence in Mesopotamia from the first third of the 3rd millennium. **Sargon** of Agade was of Akkadian origin.

AK KOYUNLU Turcoman tribal federation, ruling eastern Anatolia, Azerbaijan and northern Iraq from c.1378 to 1508. The dynasty, whose name means 'white sheep', was founded by Kara Yüllük Osman (ruled 1378-1435), who was granted control over the Diyarbakir region of Iraq by **Timur** in 1402. Under Uzun Hasan (1453-78) they expanded at the expense of the **Kara Koyunlu** ('black sheep') but were defeated by the Ottomans in 1473. They finally succumbed to internal strife and to pressure from the **Safavids**.

AL- For all Arabic names prefixed by al-, see under following element.

ALANS Ancient people, first noted in Roman writings of the 1st century AD as warlike, nomadic horse-breeders in the steppes north of the Caucasus Mountains. Overwhelmed by the **Huns** in 370, many Alans fled west, reaching Gaul with the **Vandals** and **Suebi** in 406 and crossing into Africa with the Vandals in 429.

ALARIC I (c.370-410) **Visigothic** chief and leader of the army that captured Rome in AD 410. Born in Dacia, he migrated south with fellow-tribesmen to Moesia, and briefly commanded a Gothic troop in the Roman army. Elected chieftain in 395, he first ravaged the Balkans and then, in 401, invaded Italy; the 'sack' of Rome, following a decade of intermittent fighting, negotiation and siege, was in fact relatively humane and bloodless, as Alaric's main aim was to win land for the settlement of his people.

ALARIC II (d.507) King of the **Visigoths**. From his accession in AD 484 he ruled Gaul south of the Loire and all Spain except Galicia. He issued a code of laws known as the Breviary of Alaric. He died after defeat by **Clovis**, king of the Franks, at the Battle of Vouillé, near Poitiers.

ALAUDDIN KHALJI (d.1316) Sultan of Delhi who usurped the throne in 1296 from the sons of Jalaluddin. He unified much of northern India, thanks to heavy taxes and a standing army, and began the Muslim penetration of the south. He repelled a series of Mongol invasions between 1297 and 1306.

ALAUNGPAYA (d. 1760) King of Burma and founder of the Konbaung dynasty which ruled until the British annexation of 1886. He rose from the position of village headman to lead resistance against invading Mons of Lower Burma; recaptured the Burmese capital, Ava, in 1753, finally seizing Pegu, the Mon capital, in 1757; and massacred staff of the **English East India Company**'s trading settlement on the island of Negrais, 1759. He was mortally wounded during the siege of the Siamese capital, Ayutthaya.

ALBIGENSIANS (Albigenses) Members of a heretical Christian sect, following the **Manichaean** or **Cathar** teaching that all matter is evil. Strongly entrenched in southern France around the city of Albi in the 12th century, they were subjected to violent attack by northern French nobles in the Albigensian Crusade after 1209.

ALBUQUERQUE, AFONSO DE (1453-1515) Portuguese empire-builder. Appointed Governor-General of Portuguese India in 1509, he seized Goa and several Malabar ports, 1510; Malacca and the coast of Ceylon, 1511.

ALEMANNI Germanic tribe which in the 5th century AD occupied areas now known as Alsace and Baden; defeated in 496 by the Franks under **Clovis**.

ALEXANDER THE GREAT (356-323 BC) Most famous conqueror of the ancient world. The son of **Philip II of Macedon**, he was taught by **Aristotle**. Succeeding his father in 336, he reaffirmed Macedonian dominance in Greece and between 334 and 323 BC led his armies all but 'through to the ends of the earth'. He was only 32 when he died in Babylon. His victories, though never consolidated into a world empire, spread Greek thought and culture throughout Egypt, northern India, central Asia and the eastern Mediterranean. His body, sealed in a glass coffin and encased in gold, was preserved in Alexandria, the city he founded as his own memorial, but the tomb has never been located.

ALEXANDER I (1888-1934) King (1921-34) of the Serbo-Croat-Slovene state whose name he changed to Yugoslavia in 1929. Prince Regent of Serbia, 1914-21. Enthroned in 1921, he established a royal dictatorship in 1929. He was assassinated.

ALEXANDER II (1818-81) Tsar of Russia. The son of Nicholas I, he succeeded in 1855. He emancipated the serfs in 1861, and introduced legal, military, educational and local government reforms; he extended the Russian frontiers into the Caucasus (1859) and Central Asia (1865-8), and defeated Turkey in the last of the Russo-Turkish wars (1877-8). He was assassinated.

ALEXANDER II (1198-1249) King of Scotland, son of William I the Lion. He succeeded to the throne in 1214, and sided with the rebel English barons against **King John** in the following year. He paid homage to Henry III in 1217, and in 1221 married his sister Joan. Under the Peace of York, which he concluded in 1237, Scotland abandoned English land claims and the border was fixed in more or less its present position.

ALEXANDER III (d.1181) Pope 1159-81. Distinguished canon lawyer, at one time professor at the University of Bologna. As pope, he opposed secular authority over the Church, allying successfully with the cities of Lombardy against Emperor **Frederick I Barbarossa**, and imposed a penance on **Henry II** of England for the murder of Thomas Becket, Archbishop of Canterbury.

ALEXIUS I COMNENUS (1048-1118) Byzantine emperor who seized the imperial throne in 1081. He was victorious over the Normans of Italy and the **Pecheneg** nomads; revived the Byzantine economy; founded the Comnene dynasty; and reluctantly accepted the arrival of the First **Crusade** in the East (1096-7).

ALFONSO X, THE WISE (1221-84) King of Castile and León, succeeding to the throne in 1252. He promulgated the *Siete Partidas*, Spain's great medieval code of laws; captured Cádiz and the Algarve from the Moors.

ALFRED THE GREAT (849-99) King of Wessex, England, succeeding his brother, Æthelred I, in 871. The early part of his reign was spent in hard struggle against Danish (Viking) invaders, in which he was gradually successful; Wessex itself was freed by 878, London retaken in 885, and the country divided on the line London-Chester. A notable lawgiver, he encouraged learning, vernacular translations of Latin classics and the compilation of an historic record, the Anglo-Saxon Chronicle; he also created many fortifications, a fast, mobile army and the beginnings of a fleet.

ALI (c.600-61) Mohammed's cousin, second convert and son-in-law (married to the Prophet's daughter, **Fatima**), who became fourth caliph after the murder of Othman in 656. His accession led to civil war; he was murdered by a dissident supporter, Ibn Muljam. His descendants' claim to be imams, heirs of the Prophet as leaders of the community, still divides Islam (see **Shi'ism**).

ALLENBY, EDMUND HENRY HYNMAN (1861-1936) 1st Viscount; British field marshal. After service in France he commanded British forces in Palestine, 1917-18; he conducted a successful campaign against the Ottoman Turks culminating in the capture of Jerusalem (9 December 1917), victory at Megiddo (September 1918), and the capture of Damascus.

ALLENDE GOSSENS, SALVADOR (1908-73) Chilean statesman, elected president, 1970, becoming the world's first democratically-chosen Marxist head of state. He instituted a major programme of political, economic and social change, but ran into increasing opposition both at home and abroad, and was killed during the successful right-wing military *coup d'état* which brought to power General **Pinochet**.

ALMOHADS Berber dynasty ruling North Africa and Spain, 1130-1269, inspired by the religious teachings of Ibn Tumart. It defeated the **Almoravids**, 1147, and established its capital at Marrakesh; captured Seville, 1172. Its control over Islamic Spain was largely destroyed by the Christian victory of Las Navas de Tolosa in 1212.

ALMORAVIDS Saharan Berbers who built a religious and military empire in northwest Africa and Spain in the 11th and 12th centuries, after halting the advance of Castilian Christians near Badajoz, 1086; they ruled all Muslim Spain except El Cid's Christian Kingdom of Valencia. Their sober, puritanical style of art and architecture replaced the exuberant work of the **Umayyads** whose Córdoba government collapsed in 1031.

ALTAN KHAN (1507-82) Mongol chieftain who terrorized China during the 16th century. He became leader of the Eastern Mongols in 1543; in 1550 he crossed the Great Wall into northern China, and established his capital, Kuku-khoto (Blue City), just beyond the Wall; he concluded a peace treaty with China in 1570. In 1580 he converted the Mongols to the *Dge-bugs-pa* (Yellow Hat) sect of Lamaism, a mystical Buddhist doctrine originating in Tibet, and gave the head of the sect the title of Dalai ('all-embracing') Lama.

ALTMARK, ARMISTICE OF Truce concluded in May 1629 ending the war (since 1621) between Sweden and Poland. Sweden won the right to levy tolls along the Prussian coast, but renounced this when the agreement was renewed for 26 years in 1635.

AMBROSE, ST (c.339-97) He served as governor of Aemilia-Liguria, in northern Italy, c.370-4; appointed Bishop of Milan in 374, he was frequently in conflict with imperial authority. His writings laid the foundation for medieval thinking on the relationship between Church and state.

AMHARIC The most widely spoken language of Ethiopia, of Semitic origin, derived from Geez, a southern Arabian tongue related to Arabic and Hebrew, and still used in the liturgy of the Ethiopian Orthodox Church. It displaced and partially absorbed the indigenous Cushitic languages of the western highlands.

AMIN DADA, IDI (1925-) President of Uganda. He joined the British army in 1946, and was promoted to commander of the Ugandan army in 1965. He seized power in 1971 during the absence of President Milton Obote, and subsequently expelled all Asians (1972) and most Britons (1973). Having survived revolts against his repressive regime, he was overthrown in 1979 when Ugandan exiles seized power and (1980) restored Dr Obote.

AMORITES Immigrants from Syria into Mesopotamia, where they took over political supremacy from the **Sumerians** and **Akkadians** at the beginning of the 2nd millennium BC. Babylon's first dynasty was Amorite; to this belonged Hammurabi (1792-1750 BC). In the Bible, the term 'Amorite' is used to describe the pre-Israelite inhabitants of Palestine.

AMOSIS I Founder of Egypt's XVIIIth Dynasty. He completed the expulsion of **Hyksos** after the death of his brother, **Kamose**. Reigned c.1570-1546 BC; with the aid of his mother, Queen Ahhotep, who may have acted as co-regent early in his reign, he extended Egyptian control into Palestine and Nubia, and reopened trade with Syria. He died leaving the country prosperous and reunited.

AMSTERDAM EXCHANGE BANK Important early financial institution founded in 1609 with an official monopoly of foreign currency dealings in the city. It played a key part in the development of monetary instruments and commercial credit in western Europe.

ANAXAGORAS (c.500-c.428 BC) Greek philosopher. He taught a theory of cosmology based on the idea that the universe was formed by Mind; his particulate theory of matter opened the way to atomic theory. He was exiled as part of a political attack on his friend **Pericles**, perhaps c.450 BC, after suggesting that the sun was an incandescent stone.

ANGEVINS Dynasty of English kings, often known as the Plantagenets, beginning with **Henry II** (reigned 1154-89). Descended from Geoffrey, Count of Anjou, and Matilda, daughter of Henry I; the direct line ended with **Richard II** (reigned 1377-99).

ANGLO-SAXONS Term originally coined to distinguish the Germanic tribes ruling England from 5th to 11th centuries AD, from the Saxons of continental Europe, the Angles and the Saxons being the most prominent of the invaders; later extended to mean 'the English' and their descendants all over the world.

AN LU-SHAN (703-57) Rebel Chinese general. Of Sogdian and Turkish descent, in 742 he became military governor of the northeast frontier districts. After the death of his patron, the emperor's chief minister Li Lin-fu, in 752, great rivalry developed between him and the courtier Yang Kuo-chung; in 755 he turned his 160,000-strong army inwards and marched on the eastern capital, Lo-yang, proclaiming himself emperor of the Great Yen dynasty in 756 and capturing the western capital, Ch'ang-an. He was murdered the next year. The rebellion petered out by 763, but resulted in the serious weakening of the authority of the **T'ang** dynasty.

ANSKAR or Ansgar (801-65) Frankish saint, known as 'the Apostle of the North', who conducted missions to the Danes (826) and Swedes (829); first archbishop of Hamburg, 834.

ANTI-COMINTERN PACT Joint declaration by Germany and Japan, issued on 25 November 1936, that they would consult and collaborate in opposing the **Comintern** or Communist International. It was acceded to by Italy in 1937, and later became the instrument by which Germany secured the loyalty of its Romanian, Hungarian and Bulgarian satellites and attempted to bind Yugoslavia.

ANTIGONUS III DOSON (c.263-221 BC) King of Macedonia from 227 BC, who created and led the Hellenic League (founded 224 BC) which defeated **Cleomenes III** of Sparta.

ANTIOCHUS III (242-187 BC) **Seleucid** king of Syria, who succeeded his brother, Seleucus III, in 223. After an inconclusive war with Egypt, he conquered Parthia, northern India, Pergamum and southern Syria, and invaded Greece (192), but was decisively driven back by the Romans at Thermopylae and defeated at Magnesia in Asia Minor (190). By his death the empire had been reduced to Syria, Mesopotamia and western Persia.

ANTONY (c.82-31 BC) Marcus Antonius, best known as Mark Antony. A member of a prominent Roman family, he became joint consul with **Julius Caesar** in 44 BC; after Antony's defeat of Caesar's assassins, Brutus and Cassius, at Philippi, he controlled the armies of the Eastern Empire; started liaison with **Cleopatra**; war broke out between him and Octavian, 32 BC. He committed suicide after naval defeat at Actium.

APACHE Indian hunters and farmers, located in the North American southwest. They probably originated in Canada, reaching their main hunting grounds, west of the Rio Grande, some time after the year 1000. The main groupings were the Western Apache, including the Mescalero and Kiowa tribes, and the Eastern Apache, including the Northern and Southern Tonto. In the colonial period they proved an effective barrier to Spanish settlement, and under such leaders as Cochise, Geronimo and Victorio in the 19th century, figured largely in the frontier battles fought in the American advance westward. After Geronimo's surrender in 1886, the remaining survivors became prisoners of war in Florida and Oklahoma; after 1913 they were allowed to move to reservations in Oklahoma and New Mexico.

APAMEA, PEACE OF Agreement ending the Syrian War between Rome and Seleucia; signed in 188 BC after the battle of Magnesia (190 BC). The Seleucid king, **Antiochus III**, paid an indemnity of 15,000 talents, surrendered his elephants and ships, and ceded all Asia Minor west of the Taurus Mountains.

APOLLONIUS (c.295-c.230 BC) Poet and director of the library at Alexandria in the 3rd century BC; known as 'Rhodius' because he chose to retire to the island of Rhodes. His four-book epic, the *Argonautica*, tells the story of Jason's quest for the Golden Fleece.

ARABIAN AMERICAN OIL COMPANY (ARAMCO) Joint venture, set up in 1936 by **Standard Oil** of California and Texaco to exploit petroleum concessions in Saudi Arabia. It is now among the most powerful oil groups in the world, with additional partners Exxon and Mobil. In 1974 the Saudi Arabian government acquired a 60 per cent stake in the company and in 1979 took complete control. The services of the four US companies were retained to operate the production facilities on behalf of the government.

ARABI PASHA (1839-1911) Egyptian military leader. After service in the Egyptian-Ethiopian War, 1875-6, he was made a colonel; he joined the officers' mutiny, 1879, against **Ismail** Pasha, and in 1881 led the movement to oust Turks and Circassians from high army posts. Minister of War, 1882, he quickly became a national hero with his slogan *Misr lil Misriyin* ('Egypt for the Egyptians'); he was commander-in-chief, 1882, when the British navy bombarded Alexandria, and was defeated on 13 September at Tell-el-Kebir by British troops under Sir Garnet Wolseley. He was captured and sentenced to death, but instead was exiled to Ceylon.

ARAB LEAGUE Association of Arab states, with its headquarters in Cairo. Founded in 1945 by Iraq, Trans-Jordan, Lebanon, Saudi Arabia, Egypt, Syria and Yemen, it was later joined by other states as they became independent: Algeria, Bahrain, Djibouti, Kuwait, Libya, Mauritania, Morocco, Oman, Qatar, Somalia, Sudan, Tunisia, United Arab Emirates. The PLO has been a full member since 1976. Egypt was expelled between 1978 and 1989.

ARAUCANIANS (sometimes known as the Mapuche). A warlike Indian tribe in southern Chile which successfully resisted many Inca and Spanish incursions. The first native group to adopt the Spaniards' horses, they became brilliant cavalry fighters, and in 1598 three hundred mounted Araucanians wiped out a major Spanish punitive expedition. They retained effective independence, despite numerous Spanish and Chilean attempts to subdue them, until the late 19th century.

ARBENZ GUZMÁN, JACOBO (1913-71) Guatemalan political leader of Swiss immigrant parentage. He rose to the rank of colonel in the Guatemalan army; played a leading role in the democratic revolution of 1944, becoming Minister of Defence, 1945, and President of Guatemala, 1951; he inaugurated a radical left-wing land reform programme. He was overthrown in a United States-backed military coup in 1954.

ARCHILOCHUS Greek satirical poet, writing about 700 BC; many fragments of his work survive.

ARCHIMEDES (c.287-212 BC) Greek mathematician and scientist. Born in Syracuse, he studied in Alexandria. He calculated the upper and lower limits for the value of π; devised a formula for calculating the volume of a sphere; invented, among many other things, Archimedes' Screw, for raising large quantities of water to a higher level, and also Archimedes' Principle, which enabled him to discover, with a cry of 'Eureka!', the impurity in King Hiero's crown by weighing it in and out of water in comparison with pure gold and pure silver. He returned to Sicily to design weapons and defence strategies for King Hiero, and was killed during the Roman siege of his native city.

ARDASHIR I (d.241) Founder of the Sasanian Empire of Persia; born in the late 2nd century AD. Ardashir took the crown of Persis in 208. He rapidly extended his territory, defeating his Parthian overlords at Hormizdagan in 224, and occupying their capital, Ctesiphon. He made Zoroastrianism the state religion.

ARIANISM *see* **Arius**

ARISTOPHANES (c.450-c.380 BC) Athenian comic dramatist. Eleven of some 40 plays survive, including *The Frogs*, *The Birds* and *Lysistrata*; they are highly political, brilliant in language and verse, dramatic situation, parody, satire, wit and farce, sparing neither men nor gods.

ARISTOTLE (384-322 BC) Greek philosopher and scientist. Born in Thrace, he studied in Athens under Plato. He taught the young **Alexander the Great**, then established his Lyceum in Athens, 335, and founded the Peripatetic school of philosophy. He was an outstanding biologist. His voluminous works, covering almost every aspect of knowledge, survive mainly in the form of lecture notes, edited in the 1st century AD.

ARIUS (c.AD 250-336) Originator of the Christian doctrine known as Arianism, later condemned as the Arian heresy. A pupil of Lucian of Antioch, he taught that the son of God was a creature, not consubstantial or coeternal with the Father. He was excommunicated for these views by the provincial synod of Alexandria in 321, unsuccessfully defended his belief in 325 before the **Council of Nicaea** and was banished. He died on the point of being reinstated by the Emperor **Constantine**. His controversial teachings divided the Church for many centuries.

ARKWRIGHT, SIR RICHARD (1732-92) English inventor and pioneer of the factory system, who invented the water-frame (1769) and other mechanized spinning processes.

ARMENIANS Indo-European people occupying, in ancient times, the area now comprising northeast Turkey and modern Armenia. They were converted to Christianity in the late 3rd century. Armenians boast a highly distinctive culture, which flowered particularly during periods of independence and reached peaks in the 10th and 14th centuries. During the First World War the Ottoman government deported most Armenians in Asia Minor (about 1,750,000 people) to the Syrian and Mesopotamian provinces. Armenians claim that over 1 million deportees were systematically killed at this time in a policy of genocide.

ARMINIUS (c.18 BC-AD 21) German tribal chief and early national hero, known also as Hermann. He became leader of the Cherusci after service and honour with Roman forces; in AD 9 he defeated and massacred three Roman legions at the Battle of Teutoburg Forest; held off Roman attacks, AD 16-17, but was murdered by his own people during a war with the Marcomanni, another German tribe. Described by Tacitus as *liberator haud dubie Germaniae* ('undoubtedly the liberator of Germany').

ARNOLD OF BRESCIA (c.1100-55) Radical theologian and religious reformer who studied under Peter Abelard and was condemned with him at the Council of Sens in 1140. He later moved to Italy where, in alliance with the citizens of Rome, he strongly attacked Pope

Eugenius III and forced him to leave the city. He was captured and executed at the pope's request by **Frederick Barbarossa**. His leading anti-clerical argument was that spiritual persons should not possess temporal goods.

ÁRPÁD Magyar dynasty, ruling Hungary from late 9th century to 1301; named after Árpád, who was chosen in 889 to lead seven Magyar tribes westward from their homeland on the river Don. Under Béla III (1172-96), Hungary was established as a major central European power, but was later weakened by the Mongol invasion (1241-2); the dynasty died out with Andrew III (1290-1301), who left no heir.

ARTAXERXES II MNEMON (c.436-358 BC) King of Persia, son of Darius II (reigned 423-404); he changed name from Arsaces on his accession in 404. He was challenged by his brother, Cyrus the Younger (c.430-401), but defeated and killed him at Cunaxa, near Babylon, 401.

ARTEVELDE, JACOB VAN (c.1295-1345) Flemish leader during the early phases of the **Hundred Years' War**. In 1338 he emerged as one of five 'captains' governing the town of Ghent; formed an alliance with the English king, **Edward III**, against France and the Count of Flanders; ruled as chief captain until killed in a riot.

ARYAN Contentious term used at various times to describe a member of the Caucasian race from which the Indo-European peoples supposedly sprang; in **Hitler**'s Germany, a member of the so-called 'master' or 'Nordic' race. Correctly applied to the Indo-Iranian branch of the eastern Indo-European group of languages, and at one time to the hypothetical parent language of that group.

ARYA SAMAJ Hindu reform movement; its followers reject all idolatrous and polytheistic worship and insist on the sole authority of the **Vedas**.

ASHANTI (Asante) One of several states of Akan-speaking peoples of southern Ghana, Togo and Ivory Coast. Also an independent kingdom in southern Ghana in the 18th and 19th centuries, taking an active part in the Atlantic slave trade. Ultimately failing to resist British penetration, it was annexed in 1901, and is now an administrative region of Ghana.

ASHANTI WARS Engagements fought in 1824-7, 1873-4, 1893-4 and 1895-6 between the west African kingdom of Ashanti, which originated in the 17th century, and the British, at first to prevent Ashanti expansion into the British (coastal) colony of the Gold Coast and subsequently as resistance by the Ashanti to the attempted imposition of British rule over them. Final annexation of Ashanti came in 1901; it is now a province of independent Ghana.

ASHKENAZIM From the Hebrew word *Ashkenaz*, meaning Germany. It refers to the Jews of the Germanic lands, many of whom emigrated eastward in the Middle Ages. Today it represents most of the Jews of Europe, the British Commonwealth, the United States, the USSR, South America and approximately half the Jewish population of Israel. The word is used in distinction to **Sephardim**, who have slightly different customs and rites.

ASHOKA *see* Asoka

ASHURNASIRPAL II (d.858 BC) King of Assyria, 884-858 BC, who began the 1st millennium expansion of the Assyrian Empire to the Mediterranean. Monuments and inscriptions describe with great frankness the harsh treatment of conquered peoples in ancient warfare. He created Calah (Nimrud) as his new capital.

ASIENTO Monopoly granted to an individual or company for the exclusive supply of Negro slaves to the Spanish colonies in America. The first asiento was signed by the Spanish court with Genoese entrepreneurs in 1517, later it passed mainly to the Portuguese until 1640, and then in succession to the French Royal Guinea Company and to the British South Sea Company (until 1750). It was finally extinguished in 1793, when all Spanish colonial trade was freed from central control.

ASKIA THE GREAT (d.1538) Founder of the Askia dynasty, rulers of the Songhay Empire, centred round the capital of Gao in present day Mali, from 1492-1591. He rose to power in 1493, reigning as Mohammed I Askia; he promoted the spread of Islam in his domains and made a pilgrimage to Mecca in 1495-7. He was deposed in 1528 by his sons, led by Askia Musa.

ASOKA (Ashoka) (d.232 BC) Greatest of the Mauryan emperors of early India, succeeding his father, **Bindusara**, in 272 BC. In 260 BC he inflicted a crushing defeat on Kalinga (modern Orissa), the last major independent Indian state. He was converted to **Buddhism** and from then developed a policy of toleration and non-violence, renouncing conquest.

ASSASSINS European name given to the Nizari branch of the Ismailis, organized by the leader of the 'new preaching', Hadan-i Sabbah (d.1124). They ruled parts of northern Persia and coastal Syria from strongholds of which Alamut in Persia was the most important, and played a part in the general history of Persia and Syria, partly because of their practice of killing opponents (hence 'assassination'). The leader of the Syrian group was known to Crusaders as the 'Old Man of the Mountains'. Their political power was ended by the Mongols in Persia, and by the **Mamlukes** in Egypt.

ASSYRIANS Warlike people of northern Mesopotamia, remarkable for fighting prowess, administrative efficiency (after 745 BC) – which made possible the control of an empire of unprecedented size – and for the magnificent bas-reliefs in their palaces. They formed an independent state in the 14th century BC, and under the Neo-Assyrian Empire dominated much of the Near East until destroyed by a Chaldaean-Mede coalition in 612 BC. In modern times the term is applied to an ancient Christian sect, found chiefly in Turkey, Iraq and Iran, whose members claim to be descended from the ancient Assyrians.

ASTURIAS, KINGDOM OF Founded in 718 in the extreme north of Spain by a group of Visigothic nobles after the Muslim invasions. Expanded and established on a firm basis under Alfonso I (739-57), it included northwest Spain and northern Portugal. For almost two hundred years it remained the sole independent Christian bastion in Iberia; it survived many attacks and, particularly under Alfonso III (866-910), began to push its frontier further south. After 910 it continued as the kingdom of León.

ATAHUALLPA (c.1502-33) Last independent ruler of the **Inca** Empire in Peru. He was given the subsidiary kingdom of Quito on the death of his father, **Huayna Capac**; he fought a war with his brother **Huascar**, and deposed him in 1532, just before the Spaniards invaded the Inca realms. Taken prisoner by **Francisco Pizarro**, he was accused of complicity in his brother's murder and executed.

ATATÜRK (1881-1938) Founder and first President of the republic of Turkey. Originally named Mustafa Kemal, he was born in Salonika; he graduated from Istanbul Military Academy, in 1902. He resigned from the army in 1919 to support the Turkish independence movement, and in the same year was elected president of the National Congress. After British and Greek occupation (1920), he opened the first Grand National Assembly, was elected first President and Prime Minister, and directed operations in the Greco-Turkish War of 1920-2. After the peace treaty of 1923 he abolished the Ottoman caliphate and began a far-reaching reform and modernization programme. He took the name Atatürk, 'Father of the Turks', in 1934.

ATHANASIUS (c.296-373) Theologian, statesman and saint, born in Alexandria (Egypt). He attended the **Council of Nicaea**, 325, and was appointed bishop of Alexandria in 328. He became both Egyptian national leader and the chief defender of orthodox Christianity against the heresy of Arianism. His major writings include a *Life of St Antony*, a short treatise *On the Incarnation of the Word*, and *Four Orations against the Arians*.

ATTALUS III (d.133 BC) Last independent king of Pergamum, reigning 138-133 BC. On his deathbed he bequeathed his kingdom to Rome, which then (129) organized it into the province of Asia.

ATTILA (c.406-453) Sole ruler of the vast **Hun** empire after the murder of his brother Bleda c.445. He overran much of the Roman Empire, reaching Orléans in Gaul, 451, and the river Mincio in Italy, 452; his empire collapsed after his death.

ATTLEE, CLEMENT (1883-1967) British Prime Minister. Educated at Oxford University, he briefly practised law, then spent 1907-22 (apart from war service) working among the poor in London's East End. He became Mayor of Stepney, 1919, and a Member of Parliament, 1922; a junior minister in the Labour governments of 1924 and 1929-31; and was a member of **Churchill**'s War Cabinet. As Prime Minister, 1945-51, he presided over the establishment of the Welfare State in Britain and the granting of independence to India, Pakistan, Burma and Ceylon; he relinquished British control of Egypt and Palestine. He was created Earl Attlee in 1955.

AUGUSTINE OF HIPPO, ST (354-430) Leading thinker of the early Christian Church. After a restless youth, recorded in his *Confessions*, he was converted in 386, baptized by **St Ambrose** the following year, and in 396 appointed Bishop of Hippo, in North Africa. His greatest work, *The City of God*, was written between 413 and 426 as a philosophic meditation on the sack of Rome by the **Visigoths** in 410.

AUGUSTUS (63 BC-AD 14) First Emperor of Rome, born Gaius Julius Caesar Octavianus; great-nephew, adopted son and heir of **Julius Caesar**. With **Antony** and Lepidus he emerged victorious in the civil war against Brutus and Cassius, after Caesar's murder. He broke with Antony and defeated him at Actium in 31 BC; offered sole command in Rome, he brought peace and prosperity to the empire, over which he effectively ruled from 27 BC until his death.

AURANGZEB (1618-1707) Last of India's great Mughal emperors. Son of the emperor **Shahjahan**; he succeeded in 1658 after a struggle with his brothers. Up to 1680 he successfully consolidated power over Hindu and Muslim subjects, but later his empire began to disintegrate through rebellions, wars with the **Rajputs** (erstwhile allies) and the **Marathas**; his reversal of the traditional policy of tolerance towards the Hindus contributed to his difficulties.

AUSTRO-SERBIAN 'PIG WAR' Tariff conflict in 1906-11 between Austria-Hungary and Serbia, which also exacerbated anti-Habsburg agitation in Bosnia (occupied by Austria in 1878, annexed in 1908).

AVVOCATI (or Avogadro) Prominent family of medieval Vercelli, Italy. Supporters of the **Guelph** (anti-imperial) party, they engaged in a semi-permanent feud with their Ghibelline (pro-imperial) rivals until in 1335 the city came under the control of the **Visconti** of Milan.

AXUM Ancient city and kingdom of northern Ethiopia, an offshoot of one of the Semitic states of southern Arabia in the last millennium BC. By the start of the Christian era it was the greatest ivory market of northeast Africa. Converted to **Christianity** in the 4th century AD, it was gradually transformed, after the Muslim conquest of the Red Sea littoral in the 10th century, into the modern Amhara state of Ethiopia.

AYLWIN, PATRICIO (1919-) Chilean lawyer and politician. He served as president of the Christian Democratic Party (PDC) in 1973 and 1987-91. He led the opposition coalition formed to reject General Pinochet in a national plebiscite in October 1988 and was elected President of Chile in March 1990.

AYYUBIDS Sunni Muslim dynasty, founded by **Saladin**. It ruled Egypt, Upper Iraq, most of Syria and Yemen from Saladin's death in 1193 until the **Mamluke** rise to power (1250).

BABUR (1483-1530) Founder of the **Mughal** dynasty of Indian emperors. Son of the ruler of Ferghana, central Asia, he lost this territory while seeking to conquer Samarkand (1501-4). He captured Kandahar, strategic point on the northern road to India, 1522; occupied Delhi, 1526, and established himself on the imperial throne. He wrote poetry and his memoirs.

BACSONIAN AND HOABINHIAN Stone Age cultures of Southeast Asia, characterized by the fact that their typical implements and artefacts are worked on one side only. They were named after two provinces of northern Vietnam, Bac Son and Hoa Binh, where the largest concentration of examples have been found.

BAFFIN, WILLIAM (c.1584-1622) English navigator; sailed (1612) with Captain James Hall's expedition in search of the Northwest Passage; in 1615 and 1616, with Captain **Robert Bylot**, he penetrated the waters between Canada and Baffin Island, and deep into Baffin Bay, both named after him. Working for the **English East India Company** he surveyed the Red Sea and the Persian Gulf.

BAGHDAD PACT *see* **Central Treaty Organization**.

BAIBARS (1223-77) Mamluke sultan, ruling Egypt and Syria, 1260-77. Born among the **Kipchak** Turks north of the Black Sea, he was sold as a slave to an Egyptian soldier. He fought and defeated both Crusaders and Mongols before seizing the throne.

BAKEWELL, ROBERT (1725-95) English animal-breeder who revolutionized the development of meat-bearing strains in sheep and cattle. His successes included the Leicester Longhorn cow (now superseded by the Shorthorn) and the heavy, barrel-shaped, Leicester sheep. He was the first man to commercialize large-scale stud-farming.

BALAIADA Revolutionary uprising, 1838-41, in Maranhão province, Brazil; it was finally suppressed by the imperial general, Duque de Caxias.

BALBAN (1207-87) Sultan of Delhi, originally a junior member of the Forty, made up from personal slaves of Itutmish, who divided the kingdom after his death. He acted as deputy to Sultan Nasiruddin Mahmud (reigned 1246-66), whom he succeeded; he ably consolidated Muslim power, despite continual war with **Rajputs**, Mongols and Hindu states.

BALFOUR DECLARATION Letter from Britain's Foreign Secretary, Arthur Balfour, dated 2 November 1917, to Lord Rothschild, a leader of British Jewry, stating British support for the establishment in Palestine of a national home for the Jewish people, provided that the rights of the non-Jewish communities be respected. Approved at the San Remo Conference in 1920, it was incorporated into the mandate over Palestine granted to Britain by the **League of Nations** in 1922.

BALKAN LEAGUE The outcome of bilateral agreements made by Bulgaria with Serbia, Greece and Montenegro, leading to the Balkan Wars against Turkey, 1912-13. It collapsed completely in June 1913 when Bulgaria attacked Greece and Serbia in the hope of preventing them from acquiring the bulk of Macedonia.

BALKAN WAR, FIRST War that largely expelled the Ottomans from Europe. Montenegro, Bulgaria, Greece and Serbia attacked the Ottoman Empire in October 1912; by December only the fortresses of Adrianople (Edirne), Scutari (Shkodër) and Yannina (Ioannina) remained in Turkish hands, and they too were lost to Turkey by the Treaty of London (May 1913) which also, at Austrian insistence, created the Albanian state to keep Serbia from the Adriatic.

BALKAN WAR, SECOND War among the victors of the First Balkan War over the division of Macedonia, June-August 1913. Romania intervened on the side of Greece and Serbia against Bulgaria, which suffered heavy defeat reflected in the Treaty of Bucharest (10 August 1913); meanwhile, the Turks took the opportunity of regaining Adrianople (Edirne) from Bulgaria.

BALKE, HERMANN (d.1239) Provincial master of the **Teutonic Order**, who began the conquest of the pagan Prussians in 1231, at the head of a crusading army.

BAMBARA Also known as Banmana. West African people from the Upper Niger region of the Republic of Mali. Their spoken language is derived from the **Mande** group, but their method of writing is distinctive, as is its associated cosmological system. The Bambara states, Segu (founded c.1600) between the Senegal River and the Niger, and Kaarta (c.1753) on the Middle Niger, flourished until the mid-19th century.

BANDARANAIKE, SOLOMON (1899-1959) Prime Minister of Ceylon, 1956-9. He resigned from the Western-orientated United National Party in 1951 to form the nationalist Sri Lanka Freedom Party; in 1956 his People's United Front, an alliance of four nationalist-socialist groups, won a sweeping electoral victory. As Prime Minister he replaced English with Sinhala as the official language, fostered **Buddhism**, and established diplomatic relations with Communist states. He was assassinated and succeeded by his widow.

BANK OF ENGLAND Central financial institution of Great Britain. It was founded in 1694 with the initial object of lending King William III £1,200,000 at 8 per cent. Originally a private, profit-making institution, its public responsibilities were extended and defined by Bank Charter Acts of 1833 and 1844; it was finally transferred to public ownership in 1946.

BANTU A large group of closely related languages, spoken by the majority of the black inhabitants in Africa south of the Equator. By association, the term is sometimes applied to the people themselves, especially in South Africa.

BAPTISTS Members of a Christian Protestant movement dating from the 16th century. They are now represented by many churches and groups of churches throughout the world, organized in independent congregations. Many follow the practice of baptism by total immersion, and insist that the rite should take place only when the initiate is old enough to appreciate its significance.

BARAKZAI Tribal group from which emerged Afghanistan's ruling dynasty, from 1837 to 1973. The brothers who founded the dynasty seized control of the country in 1826 and divided it between them; Dost Mohammed Khan consolidated and unified the family rule, c.1837, and his direct descendants held the throne until 1929 when, after the abdication of the reigning monarch, succession passed to a cousin's line; the military coup of 1973 overthrew the monarchy and a republic was declared.

BARBAROSSA Name of two Greek brothers, famous as Algerian Muslim pirates. Barbarossa I (c.1473-1518) was killed by the Spaniards after a series of raids on the Spanish coast; Barbarossa II, also known as Khair ed-Din (c.1466-1546), took over command on his brother's death and in 1519 became a vassal of the Ottoman sultan, for whom he repulsed an invasion by the emperor **Charles V** in 1541.

BARDI Important Florentine family, established there in the 11th century, which flourished in trade and finance, especially from the mid-13th to the mid-14th century. It became the greatest merchant and banking company in Europe at that time, and exercised considerable political influence. Defaults on debt payments by **Edward III** of England and by Florence finally led to bankruptcy and collapse in 1345.

BARENTS, WILLEM (c.1550-97) Dutch explorer of the Arctic, who in 1594 and 1595 rounded northern Europe to reach the Novaya Zemlya archipelago. He is remembered particularly for his charting of northern waters; the Barents Sea is named after him.

BARTH, HEINRICH (1821-65) German geographer and explorer. After travels in Tunisia and Libya (1845-7), he set off on a British-sponsored expedition across the Sahara. Returning after 10,000 miles, he wrote *Travels and Discoveries in North and Central Africa* (1857-8), still one of the richest sources of information on the area. He became Professor of Geography at Berlin in 1863.

BASIL I (d.886) Byzantine emperor. Of peasant stock, he was the founder of the Macedonian dynasty, so called from his place of origin. He rose to be co-emperor with Michael III in 866, but murdered Michael in 867. He began formulating the legal code (completed by his son, **Leo VI**) known as the Basilica.

BASIL II (958-1025) Most powerful of Byzantium's Macedonian emperors. He was crowned co-emperor with his brother Constantine in 960; claimed sole authority, 985; extended Byzantine rule to the Balkans, Mesopotamia, Georgia and Armenia. His conquest of the Bulgarian Empire earned him the nickname 'Bulgar Slayer'.

BASTIDAS, RODRIGO (1460-1526) Spanish explorer who discovered the mouths of the Magdalena river in modern Colombia, and founded the Colombian city of Santa Marta.

BATLLE Y ORDÓÑEZ, JOSE (1856-1929) President of Uruguay. He founded a newspaper, *El Dia*, 1886; elected President in 1903, by a narrow margin, he emerged victorious from the ensuing civil war (1904-5), and was re-elected, 1905-7, and again, after freely stepping down, 1911-15. He inaugurated a wide-ranging programme of social and economic reform. Defeated over constitutional reform in 1918, he went on to serve as president of the national executive council in 1920 and 1926.

BATU KHAN (d.1255) Leader of the **Golden Horde**. The grandson of **Genghis Khan**, in 1235 he was elected western commander-in-chief for the Mongol Empire, and entrusted with the invasion of Europe. By 1240 he had conquered all Russia; by 1241, after defeating Henry II, Duke of Silesia, and the Hungarians, he was poised to advance further west. However, on hearing of the death of **Ogedei** (December 1241) he withdrew his forces to take part in the choice of successor. He later established the Kipchak khanate, or the Golden Horde, in southern Russia.

BAYEZID I, YILDIRIM (c.1360-1403) Known as 'the Thunderbolt'. Ottoman ruler. Succeeding to the throne in 1389, he claimed the title of sultan and attempted to establish a strong centralized state based on Turkish and Muslim institutions. He conquered large areas of the Balkans and Anatolia; blockaded Constantinople, 1391-8; invaded Hungary, 1395, and crushed at Nicopolis in 1396 the Crusaders sent to repel him. He was defeated by **Timur**'s Mongol armies at Ankara in 1402, and died in captivity, with his empire partitioned between his sons and the restored Anatolian principalities.

BAYEZID II (c.1447-1512) Ottoman sultan, succeeding to the throne in 1481. His reign marked a reaction from the policies of his father, **Mehmed II**. The conquest of Kilia and Akkerman (1484-5) gave the Ottomans control over the mouth of the Danube and the land route from Constantinople to the Crimea; the later years of Bayezid's reign were taken up by war with Venice (1496-1503), by growing social unrest in Anatolia connected with the rise of the **Safavids** under their leader Ismail, and by the struggle among the sons of Bayezid for the succession to the Ottoman throne.

BEAUMANOIR, PHILIPPE DE RÉMI, SIRE DE (c.1246-96) French administrator and jurist; wrote *Coutumes de Beauvoisis* (c.1280-3), one of the earliest codifications of French law.

BELGAE Ancient Germanic and Celtic people, inhabiting northern Gaul; some emigrated to southern Britain in the 1st century BC. Gallic Belgae were conquered by **Julius Caesar** in 57 BC and the British in 55-54 BC.

BELGRADE, TREATY OF Peace agreement of 1739 ending the Turkish-Austrian War of 1737-9. Austria surrendered most of its gains under the **Treaty of Passarowitz** (1718), and thus re-established the line of the rivers Danube and Save as the frontier between the two empires.

BELISARIUS (c.494-565) Byzantine general. Under Emperor Justinian I he swept the **Vandals** out of North Africa and **Ostrogoths** out of Italy (533-40); repulsed Persian assaults (541-2).

BELL, JOHN (1797-1869) Nominee for President of the United States on the eve of the American Civil War. He entered Congress, 1827; became Secretary for War, 1841, and a US senator, 1847-59. He opposed the extension of slave-holding, though a large owner himself; nominated on a Constitutional Union ticket, 1860, he at first opposed secession, then supported it.

BENEDICT OF NURSIA, ST (c.480-c.540) Founder of a Christian monastic order. He became a hermit, but c.529 decided to form a monastic community, which he established at Monte Cassino in Italy, and for which, in the 530s, he composed the Benedictine Rule (a relatively short document of 73 chapters) which has served as the basis of Christian monastic organization.

BEN-GURION, DAVID (1886-1973) Israeli labour leader, politician and statesman; born in Poland. He became active in **Zionist** affairs, emigrated to Palestine in 1906 and became secretary-general of the labour movement in 1921. In the struggle to found an independent Jewish state, he cooperated with the British during the Second World War but led the political and military struggle against them, 1947-8. He was the first Prime Minister (and also Minister of Defence) of the new state of Israel, 1948-53, and again 1955-63. He continued to exert an influence as its founding father and elder statesman in retirement from the Negev Kibbutz of Sede Boker until his death.

BENTHAMITE Follower of the English utilitarian philosopher Jeremy Bentham (1748-1832). Benthamite thinking, summed up in the concept of the Pleasure Principle ('men seek pleasure and avoid pain') and the belief that institutions should be judged by their ability to promote 'the greatest happiness of the greatest number', influenced many later legal and political reforms.

BERBERS Original peoples of North Africa, who were colonized by Rome. Invaded by the Arabs in the 7th century AD, they were converted to Islam after some resistance. Those in or near cities were gradually absorbed into Arabic culture, but Berber languages continue to be spoken, particularly in mountain and pastoral regions of Morocco and Algeria.

BERING, VITUS JONASSEN (1681-1741) Danish navigator and discoverer of Alaska. After a voyage to the East Indies, he joined the Russian navy of **Peter the Great**; in 1724 he was appointed by the tsar to establish whether Asia was joined to North America, and in 1728 sailed through the strait which now bears his name, into the Arctic Ocean. He died when his ship was wrecked on Bering Island, east of the Kamchatka peninsula.

BERLIN, CONGRESS OF Meeting of European statesmen in June-July 1878 under the presidency of **Bismarck** to revise the Treaty of **San Stefano** (1878), concluded by Russia and Turkey. Bulgaria, greatly reduced in extent, became an autonomous principality. The independence of Romania, Serbia and Montenegro was confirmed. Austria-Hungary was given the right to occupy Bosnia and Herzegovina, and Russia was confirmed in its possession of Ardahan, Kars and Batum.

BERNARD, ST (c.1090-1153) He entered the Cistercian Order in 1113, only 15 years after the foundation of the monastery of Cîteaux, and soon became its leading light. Two years later, he founded the monastery of Clairvaux, also in southeast France, and remained its abbot for the rest of his life. Through personal influence, teaching and voluminous writings, he dominated the theological and to a large extent also the political life of his times, particularly by securing the recognition of Innocent II as Pope in 1130, by advice to his former pupil **Eugenius III** (Pope 1145-53), and by preaching the second **Crusade** in 1147.

BESANT, ANNIE (1847-1933) Theosophist, social reformer and Indian independence pioneer. She was a Fabian Socialist, with George Bernard Shaw, in the late 1880s, and was converted to the theosophic ideas of Helen Blavatsky, 1889-91. She spent much of her remaining life in India, jointly founding the Indian Home Rule League in 1916.

BESSEMER, SIR HENRY (1813-98) British inventor of the Bessemer steel-making process. He developed various mechanical devices, including a movable date stamp, and in the Crimean War the first rotary shell. In 1856 he announced a process for purifying molten iron with a blast of air; with contributions from other inventors, his work made possible the Bessemer converter and the mass production of cheap steel.

BETANCOURT, RÓMULO (1908-81) Venezuelan political leader. Imprisoned while a student, and exiled to Colombia, he returned in 1936 to lead the anti-Communist left-wing underground movement; again exiled, 1939-41, in 1941 he organized Acción Democrática (AD), and became president of the revolutionary governing junta after the overthrow of President Medina Angarita, 1945. Forced yet again into exile by the Pérez Jiménez regime, 1948-58, he became President of Venezuela, 1959-64.

BHONSLAS Dynasty of **Maratha** rulers in western India, founded by the family of King **Sivaji**. They were leaders in the 18th-century Maratha confederacy formed to resist the British; later they became British clients (1816-53).

BINDUSARA (d.272 BC) Early Indian emperor, succeeding his father, **Chandragupta Maurya**, in 279 BC. He campaigned in the Deccan, as far south as Mysore, and brought most of the subcontinent under Mauryan control.

BISMARCK, PRINCE OTTO VON (1815-98) German statesman, known as 'the Iron Chancellor'. He was appointed Minister-President of Prussia, 1862; after wars against Denmark (1864) and Austria (1866), he formed the North German Confederation (1867), and after the **Franco-Prussian War** (1870-1) inaugurated the German Empire (1871-1918). As German Chancellor (1871-90) he instituted important social, economic and imperial policies and played a leading role in the European alliance systems of the 1870s and 1880s.

BLACK FLAGS Chinese bandits and mercenary groups active in Annam and Tongking, 1873-5, led by Liu Yung-fu, a former T'ai-p'ing rebel. Called on by the mandarins of Hanoi to oppose the French (1873), they were responsible for the defeat and death of several French commanders during a decade of bitter guerrilla war.

BLACKFOOT INDIANS A group of Indian tribes of Algonquin stock. They were one of the strongest Indian confederations in the early 19th century but were gradually defeated and subdued by the US settlers. Their name derived from the colour of their moccasins.

BLAKE, ROBERT (1599-1657) English admiral; he commanded **Cromwell**'s navy in the English Interregnum, and defeated the Dutch, the Spaniards, and the Barbary corsairs.

BLIGH, WILLIAM (1754-1817) British vice-admiral. He served on Captain **James Cook**'s last voyage; he was commanding the *Bounty* when the crew mutinied in 1789 in the South Seas and set him adrift in an open boat. On his voyage of exploration of 1791 he made discoveries in Tasmania, Fiji and the Torres Straits. He fought at Gibraltar (1782), Camperdown (1797) and Copenhagen (1801). He was Governor-General of New South Wales, 1805-8, from which post he was deposed by force and imprisoned until 1810.

BLITZ Second World War term for a sudden attack, particularly from the air; derived from the German word *Blitzkrieg*, or lightning war.

BOETHIUS (c.480-524) Late classical scholar and statesman, born in Rome. He was appointed consul under **Theodoric** the Ostrogoth in 510. He translated **Aristotle**'s *Organon* and helped to preserve many classical texts; he wrote on music, mathematics and astronomy. His **Christianity**, clear from some short treatises, is not mentioned in his larger works. After falling from favour with Theodoric, he wrote his *De consolatione philosophiae* in prison. He was executed on charges of treason.

BOGOMILS Balkan religious sect, flourishing from the 10th to the 15th century. It inherited **Manichaean** doctrines from the **Paulicians**; believed the visible world was created by the devil; rejected baptism, the Eucharist, the Cross, miracles, churches, priests and all orthodox Christianity. Its leader, Basil, was publicly burned in Constantinople c.1100. Adopted by the ruling class in Bosnia, it also directly influenced the **Cathars** in Italy and **Albigensians** in France; it died out after the Ottoman conquest of southeast Europe because many of its adherents converted to Islam.

BOLESŁAW I CHROBRY, 'THE BRAVE' (966-1025) First fully-accepted king of Poland, son of **Mieszko I**. He inherited the principality of Greater Poland, 992; reached the Baltic, 996, and seized control of Cracow and Little Poland. Crowned by Emperor **Otto III**, 1000, he was embroiled in wars, 1002-18, with Emperor Henry II over lands seized in Lusatia, Meissen and Bohemia. He defeated Grand Prince Yaroslav I of Kiev (1018), and placed his son-in-law on the Kievan throne.

BOLÍVAR, SIMON (1783-1830) Venezuelan soldier-statesman who freed six South American countries from Spanish rule. He participated in Venezuela's declaration of independence in 1811, fleeing to Haiti after the Spanish counter-revolution; liberated New Granada (Colombia) in 1819; Venezuela, 1821; Ecuador, 1822; Peru, 1824; and Upper Peru, renamed Bolivia, in 1825. A liberal political thinker but an autocratic ruler, he failed in his real ambition to establish a union of Spanish-American peoples: most of the nations he had helped to create were in turmoil or conflict when he died.

BOLSHEVIKS Named from *Bolsheviki*, Russian for 'those of the majority', the name adopted by **Lenin**'s supporters in the Russian Social-Democratic Workers' Party at the 1903 Congress when, advocating restriction of membership to professional revolutionaries, they won a temporary majority on the central committee. From 1912 they constituted a separate party. Seizing control of Russia in October 1917, in March 1918 they adopted the name 'Communists'.

BONAPARTE *see* **Napoleon I**

BONIFACE VIII (c.1235-1303) Pope, 1294-1303. He reasserted papal claims to superiority over temporal powers; his Bull *Clericis laicos* (1296) led to conflict with **Edward I** of England, and particularly with **Philip IV** of France, over taxation of the clergy, but the dispute soon widened to cover the whole relationship of Church and state. He was briefly kidnapped at Anagni by the French, 1303, but soon released; to escape repetition of such treatment, the papacy took up residence at Avignon – the so-called 'Avignon Captivity'.

BONIFACE, ST (c.675-754) Often called the Apostle of Germany; born in Nursling, Wessex. He was ordained priest c.705 under his original name of Wynfrith. He left England in 716 to evangelize the Saxons. He was sent first into Hesse and Thuringia by Pope Gregory II (722-35), and then into Bavaria by Gregory III. He became Archbishop of Mainz, 751; organized German and reformed Frankish churches. He was martyred by pagan **Frisians**.

BOONE, DANIEL (1734-1820) American frontiersman, explorer and fighter in Kentucky and Missouri. He created the wilderness road, northwest of the Appalachians.

BOSE, SUBHAS CHANDRA (1897-1945) Indian nationalist leader; educated Calcutta and Cambridge, England. He was imprisoned (1924-7) for his part in **Gandhi's** non-cooperation movement. On his release he was elected president of Bengal's provincial congress. He spent most of the next decade in prison or exile, until 1938 when he became president of the Indian National Congress; under house arrest (1940), he escaped to Germany. He formed an Indian volunteer force to attack the Western allies and in 1943, with Japanese support, invaded India from Rangoon. He died two years after his defeat, in an air crash in Taiwan.

BOURBONS European ruling family. Descended from Louis I, duke of Bourbon (1279-1341), grandson of King **Louis IX** of France (reigned 1226-70), the Bourbons held the thrones of France (1589-1791 and again 1814-48), Spain (more or less from 1700 to 1931), and Naples and Sicily (1735-1860). The Spanish line was restored after the death of **Franco** in 19755.

BOURGUIBA, HABIB (1903-) Tunisian politician. He became a journalist in 1930 on a paper which advocated self-government for Tunisia. He founded his own Neo-Déstour party in 1934 to achieve independence from France, but was imprisoned 1934-6, 1938-45 and 1952-4, and in exile 1945-9. He became first Prime Minister of independent Tunisia in 1956-7, its first President 1957-87, and 'President for Life' 1975-87.

BOXER REBELLION Chinese popular uprising in 1900, aiming to drive out all foreign traders, diplomats and particularly missionaries. The name is derived from a secret society, the I-ho-ch'üan (Right and Harmonious Fists), which had earlier violently opposed the ruling **Ch'ing** (Manchu) dynasty, but in 1899 began to attack westerners. On 18 June 1900, as hostilities grew, the Empress Dowager ordered the execution of all foreigners; hundreds were besieged in the Peking legation quarter until relieved on 14 August by an international expeditionary force, which then looted the capital. Peace and reparations were finally agreed in September 1901.

BRACTON, HENRY DE (d. c.1268) Medieval English jurist, judge of King's Court under Henry III (1247-57). Author of *De legibus et consuetudinibus Angliae* ('On the laws and customs of England'), one of the oldest and most influential treatises on common law.

BRADDOCK, EDWARD (1695-1755) English general who in 1754 was appointed to command all British land forces in North America; he was ambushed (with his army) and killed by mixed French and Indian forces while leading an expedition against Fort Duquesne.

BRAHMA Hindu creator of the universe who, with **Vishnu** and **Shiva**, forms the leading trinity of Hindu gods.

BRAHMO SAMAJ Hindu theistic society, founded in 1828 by the religious reformer, **Rammohan Roy**. It split into two in 1865, when the philosopher Keshub Chunder Sen (author of *The Brahmo Samaj Vindicated*) founded a separate branch known as 'Brahmo Samaj of India'. It was the earliest modern reform movement in India.

BRASSEY, THOMAS (1805-70) English railway contractor, trained as a surveyor, in 1835 he built the Grand Junction line, and later helped to finish the London-Southampton link. Starting with the Paris-Rouen line (1841-3), he went on to build railway systems all over the world, including the 1100 mile (17700 km) Grand Trunk in Canada (1854-9).

BRAZZA, PIERRE SAVORGNAN DE (1852-1905) Piedmontese explorer and colonizer who made pioneering journeys through equatorial Africa, 1873-7. He negotiated treaties with African chiefs which were then taken up by the French, whose service Brazza subsequently entered, governing the region north of the Congo for France, 1887-97.

BRECKINRIDGE, JOHN CABELL (1821-75) Unsuccessful Southern Democrat candidate for the United States presidency on the eve of the American Civil War (1861-5). Born in Kentucky, he entered the US Congress in 1851; Vice-President to James Buchanan, 1857-61; US Senator, 1861; expelled after joining the Confederate army. He served as brigadier, major-general and later Secretary for War in the Confederacy; fleeing to England at the end of hostilities, he returned in 1868.

BREDA, TREATY OF Inconclusive agreement, signed 31 July 1667, ending the Second Anglo-Dutch War (1665-7). France, which had supported the Dutch, gave up Antigua, Montserrat and St Kitts, in the West Indies, to Britain, but recovered Acadia (now Canada's Maritime Provinces); England acquired New York and New Jersey from the Dutch; Holland won valuable sea-trading concessions.

BREST-LITOVSK, TREATY OF Peace agreement, signed March 1918, between Russia and the Central Powers. Russia recognized the independence of Poland, Finland, Georgia, the Baltic States and the Ukraine, and agreed to pay a large indemnity. The treaty was declared void under the general armistice of 1918.

BREZHNEV, LEONID ILICH (1906-82) Soviet leader. He joined the Communist Party, 1931; became Red Army political commissar, major-general, 1943; a member of the Communist Party Central Committee, 1952. He succeeded **Khrushchev** as First Secretary of the Party, 1964; enunciated the Brezhnev Doctrine to justify invasion of Czechoslovakia, 1968, by Warsaw Pact forces; replaced Podgorny as President of the USSR, 1977-82.

BRIAN BORU (c.941-1014) High King of Ireland. He succeeded as ruler of a small Irish kingdom, Dal Cais, in 972, and also of Munster. Brian defeated Ivar, the Norse king, in Inis, Cathaig in 977; attacked Osraige (982); was recognized as ruler of southern Ireland (997) and by 1005 claimed his position as king of all Ireland. He was killed after the battle of Clontarf.

BRITAIN, BATTLE OF Series of aerial encounters between the German Luftwaffe and the British Royal Air Force, mainly over southern England, fought between July and October 1940. As a result of her failure to win air mastery, Germany abandoned plans for a seaborne invasion of Britain.

BRONZE AGE In the Old World, the first period of metal-use, based on copper and its alloys. Beginning in the Near East in the 3rd millennium BC, and in Europe after 2000 BC, and independently in Southeast Asia at the same time, this technology spread among both peasant and urban societies – Bronze Age civilizations included Sumer, Egypt, the Indus and Shang China.

BROOKE, SIR JAMES (1803-68) Founder of a dynasty of 'white rajahs' in Sarawak, northwest Borneo. He served with the **English East India Company**'s army in the Burma War 1824-6; assisted the Rajah of Brunei in suppressing various rebellions, and in 1843 was made Rajah of Sarawak.

BRUCE *see* **Robert I of Scotland**

BRUNHILDE (c.545-613) Twice regent of Austrasia and for a period the most powerful ruler in **Merovingian** France. The daughter of Athanagild, Visigothic king in Spain, she married Sigebert, son of Lothar, king of the Franks. The murder of her sister, Galswintha, precipitated a 40-year feud in Gaul. The deaths of her husband and her son, **Childebert II**, placed her at the head of affairs until 599 when palace officials drove her out. In 613 she was executed by being tied to a wild horse.

BRÜNING, HEINRICH (1885-1970) German statesman. He became leader of the Catholic Centre Party, 1929, and formed a conservative government in 1930 without a Reichstag majority. After parliamentary rejection of his major economic plans, he began to rule by presidential emergency decree. He resigned the chancellorship in May 1932 after the failure of both his foreign and his domestic policies.

BRUSATI Prominent family of medieval Novara, Italy. Supporters of the **Guelph** (anti-imperial) party, they enjoyed a brief supremacy in the city 1305-15, but were overcome by their Ghibelline (pro-imperial) rivals, supported by the **Visconti** family in neighbouring Milan.

BRUSILOV, ALEKSEY ALEKSEYEVICH (1853-1926) Russian general who led the Russian offensive against Austria-Hungary in June-August 1916; he became the supreme Russian commander in 1917. Under the **Bolsheviks** he directed the war against Poland, 1920; he retired in 1924 as inspector of cavalry.

BRUSSELS PACT Defensive alliance of 1948 providing for military, economic and social co-operation, signed by France, Great Britain and the Benelux countries.

BRYAN, WILLIAM JENNINGS (1860-1925) Three times unsuccessful candidate for the presidency of the United States. Entering politics in 1888, he quickly won a reputation as a Populist orator; he was elected to Congress in 1890. He won his first presidential nomination in 1896, at the age of 36; defeated then, and again in 1900 and 1908, he remained a leading political figure and was appointed Secretary of State by **Woodrow Wilson** in 1913. As a pacifist, he resigned in 1915 when the US protested to Germany over the sinking of the *Lusitania*.

BUDDHA, GAUTAMA (c.563-483 BC) Founder of the world religion known as **Buddhism**. Born on the modern border between India and Nepal, the son of a nobleman of the Hindu Kshatriya caste, traditionally he was inspired to change his life at the age of 29 by the sight of an old man, a sick man, a corpse and an itinerant ascetic. In the Great Renunciation he gave up his privileges and for six years practised extreme asceticism, then abandoned it in favour of deep meditation, receiving enlightenment as he sat under a tree. The remainder of his life was spent teaching and serving the order of beggars which he founded.

BUDDHISM Religious and philosophic system based on the teachings of Gautama, the **Buddha**, who rejected important features of his native **Hinduism** in the 6th century BC. In his first sermon at Benares he preached the Four Noble Truths and the abandonment of desire and sorrow by systematic pursuit of the Noble Eightfold Path, the ultimate end of which is Nirvana, the elimination of all desire and anguish. This remains the basis for the Dharma or Teaching, carried out through the Samgha or monastic Order. Since the Buddha's death the religion has developed along two distinct and sometimes conflicting lines: Theravada (or Hinayana), in Southeast Asia, stressing monasticism and avoiding any taint of theism or belief in a god; and Mahayana, in China, Japan, Tibet and Korea, which embraces more personal cults.

BUGANDA Former kingdom and later administrative region, occupying 17,311 square miles (44,835 km²) of present-day Uganda, inhabited largely by the Baganda tribe. It was an important independent power from the 17th to the 19th century, becoming a British protectorate in 1894; limited self-government, under British rule, was granted in 1900.

BUKHARIN, NIKOLAI IVANOVICH (1888-1938) Bolshevik economist and theoretician. He lived in exile in New York until the Revolution, when he returned to Russia (May 1917) and became leader of the Communist Party's Right faction, which advocated cautionary progress to full socialism through the continuation of the New Economic Policy (NEP). A member of the Politburo, 1918-29, and head of the Third International, 1926-9, he was expelled from the Politburo in 1929 because of his association with Trotskyist opposition to **Stalin**. Restored in 1934, when he became editor of *Izvestia*, he was again expelled in 1938 and was executed after the last of the Great Purge Trials.

BUNYORO One of the earliest East African kingdoms, founded in the 16th century and occupying territory now part of Uganda. It prospered until the 19th century, when it lost ground and power to neighbouring **Buganda**. Its last ruler, Kabarega, was deposed by the British in 1894, and his kingdom absorbed into the British protectorate in 1896.

BUONACOLSI Prominent family of medieval Mantua, Italy. They rose to dominance in the late 13th century; confirmed as lords of the city by Emperor Henry VII in 1311, they were overthrown in a coup by their rivals the Gonzaga family in 1328.

BUONSIGNORI Italian banking house, founded in Siena in 1209, which became the foremost company in Europe. It began to collapse in 1298 and finally closed its doors in 1309.

BURGUNDIANS Germanic people, originally from the Baltic island of Bornholm (Burgundaholm), 1st century AD. In the 5th century they established a powerful kingdom in the Saône and Rhône valleys, extending to the Rhine; they were defeated and absorbed by the **Franks** in 534.

BURKE, EDMUND (1729-97) British statesman, orator and political theorist. He entered Parliament in 1765, and made a reputation with eloquent speeches and writings on the American question and on the arbitrary government of George III. He sought abolition of the slave trade; in his *Thoughts on the revolution in France* (1790) he bitterly condemned the outbreak of revolution and predicted increasing violence.

BURTON, SIR RICHARD FRANCIS (1821-90) Explorer and English translator of *The Thousand and One Nights*. He visited Mecca in 1853 and was the first European to reach Harar, Ethiopia, in 1854; with **Speke** he discovered Lake Tanganyika in 1858.

BUSH, GEORGE HERBERT WALKER (1924-) US political leader and 41st President. From a wealthy Connecticut family, active in the navy during World War II, he graduated from Yale (1948). After two terms in the House of Representatives from Texas (1967-71), he was ambassador to the **United Nations**, chairman of the Republican National Committee and Director of the Central Intelligence Agency during the 1970s. He served as **Ronald Reagan**'s Vice President (1981-9) and as President (1989-93).

BUSHMEN *see* **San**

BUTTON, SIR THOMAS (d.1634) English navigator, and the first to reach the western shores of Hudson Bay (1612-13). He also discovered the Nelson River, which rises in Manitoba and runs into Hudson Bay.

BUWAYHIDS (Buyids) Dynasty originating in northern Persia. They occupied Baghdad, capital of the **Abbasid caliphate**, in 945; though **Shias**, they ruled the central lands of the caliphate in the name of the Abbasid caliph. Their power was ended by the occupation of Baghdad in 1055 by the **Seljuks**.

BYLOT, ROBERT English navigator and discoverer of Baffin Bay (1615); because he was suspected of disloyalty the bay was named after his lieutenant, **William Baffin**.

BYNG, JOHN (1704-57) English admiral, remembered mainly for an epigram by the French writer Voltaire who said that he was court-martialled and shot *'pour encourager les autres'* after failing to relieve Minorca.

CABANAGEM Revolutionary uprising, 1835-40, in the Paré region of Brazil. The term was coined from *cabana* or cabin, perhaps an allusion to the lowly origins of the insurgents.

CABOT, JOHN (c.1450-c.1499) Italian explorer (real name Giovanni Caboto). Precise details of his travels are much in dispute, but around 1484 he moved from Italy to London, and in 1496 was given authority by **Henry VII** to search for unknown lands; after one abortive attempt, he left Bristol in 1497 in a small vessel, the *Mathew*, and made landfall, probably in the region of Cape Breton, Nova Scotia. The fate of his second, larger expedition in 1498 remains unknown.

CABOT, SEBASTIAN (1476-1557) Explorer, cartographer and navigator. Before 1512 he worked for **Henry VIII** of England; seconded to assist Spain against the French, he was appointed in 1518 as pilot-major to the Spanish *Casa de la Contratación*; in 1526 he led an expedition intended for the Moluccas via the Magellan Straits, but diverted it to the Río de la Plata and spent three years exploring Paraná and Paraguay. He published a celebrated but unreliable world map 1544, and organized an expedition to seek the Northeast Passage.

CABRAL, PEDRO ALVARES (1467/8-1520) Reputed discoverer of Brazil, commissioned by the Portuguese king, Manuel I, to sail to India; he sighted and claimed Brazil for Portugal, 1500, before continuing the voyage in which he lost 9 out of his 13 ships in storms; he bombarded Calicut, established a Portuguese factory at Cochin and returned to Portugal with his four remaining ships loaded with pepper. He was not subsequently employed at sea.

CAINOZOIC Geological era, starting c.65 million years ago, during which all surviving forms of mammal life (including Man) first evolved, and the earth's surface assumed its present form.

CALDERA RODRIGUEZ, DR RAFAEL (1916-) Venezuelan political leader. He was secretary of the Venezuelan Catholic youth organization, 1932-4, and in 1936 founded the country's national union of students. In 1946 he founded the Committee of Independent Political Electoral Organizations (COPEI); an unsuccessful presidential candidate in 1947, 1958 and 1963, he finally became President, as the candidate of COPEI, in 1969, holding the post until 1974, in which year he was appointed senator for life.

CALIPHATE The office of caliph, regarded by **Sunnis** as successor to the Prophet **Mohammed** in his capacity as leader of the Islamic community. The first four caliphs ('patriarchal', 'rightguided' or 'orthodox' caliphs) ruled from Medina; they were succeeded first by **Umayyads** ruling from Damascus, 661-750; then by the **Abbasids** of Baghdad, whose dynasty continued until 1258, although effective power was held by various dynasties of sultans – **Buwayhids**, **Seljuks**. In the 10th century two other dynasties took the title of caliph: a branch of the Umayyads in Spain, and the **Fatimids** in Cairo. The last Abbasid caliph was killed by the Mongol conquerors of Baghdad in 1258, and the caliphate virtually came to an end. The title was revived by the Ottoman sultans in the 19th century, but abolished by the Turkish Republican government in 1924.

CALLIMACHUS (c.305-c.240 BC) Poet from Cyrene who worked in Alexandria, compiling a 120-volume critical catalogue of the great Library; only fragments of his 800 recorded works survive, but his *Aetia* ('*Origins*') and his shorter poems had a profound influence on Roman authors, including Catullus and Propertius. He refused to write long epics, saying that 'a large book is a great evil'.

CALVIN, JOHN (1509-64) French theologian who established strict Presbyterian government in Geneva. He wrote *Institutes of the Christian Religion* (1536-59), setting out his teachings - that the state should support the Church, that biblical authority should override Church tradition, and that the sacraments, though valuable, are not essential to true religion. He strongly influenced the Huguenots in France, the Protestant churches in Scotland and the Netherlands, and the Puritan movement in England and North America.

CAMBYSES II (d.522 BC) Second Achaemenid Persian emperor, the eldest son of **Cyrus**, whom he represented in Babylon, 538-530 BC; he succeeded on Cyrus' death in 530. He invaded Egypt, taking Memphis in 525 and was returning home when he heard of the usurpation by his brother **Smerdis**, and died soon afterwards.

CAMINO, DA Medieval Italian family, prominent in the affairs of the city of Treviso. It first gained power through Gherado (c.1240-1306), a noted soldier of fortune. His sons wavered between the rival **Guelph** and Ghibelline factions in Italian politics, resulting in the murder of one and the expulsion of the other from Treviso in 1312.

CANUTE *see* **Cnut the Great**

CÃO, DIOGO 15th century Portuguese navigator who explored much of the west coast of Africa. He was the first European to reach the mouth of the Congo (1482).

CAPETIANS Ruling dynasty of France, 987-1328. It was founded by Hugh Capet, elected king in 987 to replace the previous **Carolingian** line; gradually he and his successors extended their control, initially limited to the area around Paris, to cover the larger part of present-day France; they also began to develop many of the country's main political institutions, such as the *Parlements* (royal law courts) and the States General (representative assemblies). Notable Capetian kings included **Philip II Augustus** (reigned 1180-1223), (St) **Louis IX** (1226-70), and **Philip IV** the Fair (1285-1314).

CARACALLA (188-217) Roman emperor, born Marcus Aurelius Antoninus at Lugdunum (modern Lyons), son of Emperor Septimius Severus. He gained the imperial throne in 211 and in the following year extended Roman citizenship to virtually all inhabitants of the Empire. He murdered his wife, Fulvia Plautilla, and younger brother, Geta. He was assassinated at Carrhae, Mesopotamia, while preparing his second campaign against Parthia.

CARDENAS, LAZARO (1895-1970) Mexican soldier and radical leader. Governor of home state of Michoacán, 1928-32; Minister of the Interior, 1931; President of Mexico, 1934-40. During his term of office he launched a Six-Year Plan, a land redistribution programme, the expropriation of foreign-owned oil companies (1938) and a renewed attack on the Catholic Church; he was Minister of Defence, 1942-5.

CARLOWITZ, TREATY OF A truce agreement, signed on 26 January 1699, ending hostilities (1683-99) between the Ottoman Empire and the Holy League (Austria, Poland, Venice and Russia). Under its terms Transylvania and much of Hungary was transferred from Turkish control to Austrian, making Austria the dominant power in eastern Europe. In 1700 the armistice was confirmed by the Treaty of Constantinople.

CARNOT, LAZARE NICOLAS MARGUERITE (1753-1823) French military engineer and statesman who directed the early successes of the French revolutionary armies (1793-5); he was a member of the Directory, the five-man group ruling France, 1795-9. Although opposed to **Napoleon**'s rise to power Carnot later rallied to the emperor in resisting the invasion of France, 1814, and was Minister of the Interior during the **Hundred Days**, 1815; he died in exile.

CAROL II (1893-1953) King of Romania who supplanted his son Michael as legitimate ruler in 1930 and created a royal dictatorship. He was deposed in 1940.

CAROLINGIANS Royal dynasty descended from Pepin of Landen (d.AD 640), chief minister of the **Merovingian** king, Chlothar II. Pepin's illegitimate grandson was **Charles Martel**, after whom the dynasty was named. His great-great grandson was the emperor **Charlemagne**. The dynasty continued to rule in East Francia (Germany) until 911, and in West Francia (France) until 987.

CARRACK Large round sailing ship developed in the Middle Ages for both trade and naval warfare, particularly by the Genoese and Portuguese. Deep-keeled and high in the water, the vessel had two or three masts, castles fore and aft, and was usually well armed with cannon. Larger versions were used by the Portuguese in trade to the East Indies and Brazil in the 16th century.

CARRANZA, VENUSTIANO (1859-1920) President of Mexico. The son of a landowner, he was active in politics from 1877; as governor of Coahuila, in 1910, he supported **Madero**, and in 1913 led the opposition to Madero's successor, Victoriano Huerta. He set up a provisional government, defeated the armies of **Pancho Villa**, and was installed as first President of the Mexican Republic (1917). He fled during an armed uprising in 1920, and was betrayed and murdered in the mountains near Vera Cruz.

CARREIRA DA INDIA The round voyage between Portugal and India, inaugurated with **Vasco da Gama**'s pioneering expedition of 1497-8 and continuing until the age of steam. Under sail the journey averaged 18 months, including the stay at Goa.

CARRON Pioneer Scottish ironworks, established by John Roebuck. Founded with capital of £12,000 in 1760, it was the first to use a cast-iron blowing-cylinder to increase airblast. Technicians trained there started ironmaking in Russia and Silesia.

CARTIER, JACQUES (1492-1557) Explorer of Canada, commissioned by **Francis I** of France to sail in search of gold, spices and a new route to Asia; he entered the Gulf of St Lawrence in 1534, and on subsequent expeditions established a base at Quebec and reached Montreal.

CASIMIR I, THE RESTORER (1016-58) King of Poland. He ascended the throne in 1039; he recovered the former Polish provinces of Silesia, Masovia and Pomerania, lost by his father **Mieszko II**; he restored central government and revived the Catholic Church, but failed to throw off German suzerainty.

CASIMIR III, THE GREAT (1310-70) King of Poland. He succeeded to the throne in 1333. He concluded a favourable peace with the **Teutonic Order** in 1343, and annexed the province of Lwów from Lithuania during the 1340s. The last ruler of the **Piast** dynasty, he agreed in 1339 to the union of Poland and Hungary after his death. At home he unified the government, codified laws and founded new towns and the first university in eastern Europe at Cracow in 1364.

CASIMIR IV (1427-92) King of Poland. A member of the **Jagiellonian** dynasty, he succeeded to the Grand Duchy of Lithuania in 1440 and to the throne of Poland in 1447. He defeated the Teutonic Knights and recovered West Prussia for Poland by the Treaty of Torún, 1466. Thereafter he sought to create a Polish empire stretching from the Baltic to the Black Sea but was checked by the Turks and, at the time of his death, by **Ivan III** of Russia.

CASTILLA, RAMÓN (1797-1867) President of Peru. Born in Chile, he fought for the Spaniards until captured by Chilean patriots; changing sides, he fought in Peru with **Bolívar** and **San Martín**. The first elected President, 1845-51 and again 1855-62, he built up Peru's economic strength by the exploitation of newly-discovered guano and sodium nitrate deposits.

CASTRO, FIDEL (1926-) Prime Minister of Cuba. Law graduate, 1950; after failure to win power by a coup, 1953, he led the guerrilla group '26th of July Movement'; invaded Cuba in 1956 but failed to raise a revolt and fled to the mountains; regrouped, and finally displaced the Batista regime in 1959. He was boycotted by the United States after his **Marxist** aims became apparent; survived the Bay of Pigs invasion of 1961, and the Cuban missile crisis, 1962; with Soviet aid (to 1990) he promoted a programme of land and economic reform. In 1976 he sent troops to Angola (withdrawn 1991), and embarked on an increasingly active African and Central American policy.

CATEAU-CAMBRÉSIS, TREATY OF Agreement signed in 1559 to end the war between France, Spain and England. Spain's claims in Italy were recognized by France, making the former the dominant power in southern Europe; France gained the bishoprics of Toul, Metz and Verdun; England finally surrendered Calais.

CATHARS (CATHARISM) A doctrinal heresy descended from the **Manichaeism** of the early Christian Church but with some non-Christian roots, which from the mid-11th century spread rapidly in western Europe, throughout northern Italy and southern France (where the Cathars were known as **Albigensians**). Their chief tenet was the dualism of good and evil, which was contrary to Catholic belief although in some respects resembling it. They also devoted themselves to poverty and evangelism, in these respects resembling both the **Humiliati** and the monastic orders. **Innocent III** launched the Albigensian Crusade against them in 1209 and his successors combated them with the **Inquisition**.

CATHERINE II, THE GREAT (1729-96) Born a princess of the German principality of Anhalt-Zerbst, she married in 1744 Peter of Holstein-Gottorp who in 1762 became Tsar **Peter III**. Six months later she usurped his throne with the aid of her lover, G. Orlov. She advanced Russia's status as a great power, conquering the north shore of the Black Sea from Turkey, and with Prussia and Austria completed the partition of Poland in 1795. She carried out a number of domestic reforms, none of which improved the status of the serfs. She published her *Instruction for the drafting of a new code of laws* in 1767 and wrote many plays and historical works.

CATHOLIC LEAGUE Union of German Catholic princes, formed in 1609 in opposition to the Protestant Union of 1608, and headed by Maximilian I of Bavaria. Its armies, under Tilly (1559-1632), played an important part in the early stages of the Thirty Years' War (1618-48), in which they conquered Bohemia, 1619-22, and defeated Denmark, 1624-9.

CAVALCABO Prominent family of medieval Cremona, Italy. Supporters of the **Guelph** (anti-imperial) party, they gained control of the city in the second half of the 13th century, retaining power until 1312 when they were driven out by Emperor Henry VII. In 1314 they returned, but were driven out permanently by the **Visconti** of Milan in 1344.

CAVOUR, COUNT CAMILLO BENSO (1810-61) Italian statesman. He abandoned court and an army career, visited England and then embarked on a career in finance, agriculture, industry and radical politics. In 1848 he founded the newspaper, *Il Risorgimento*, to champion monarchical and liberal aims, and promote democratic reforms. He entered the Piedmontese cabinet in 1850, and was given control of government, 1852, by the new king, **Victor Emmanuel II**. He was primarily responsible for creating the United Kingdom of Italy of 1861.

CEAUCESCU, NICOLAE (1918-1989) Romanian political leader. Active in the illegal Communist party, he was imprisoned for eight years, before and during World War II. Minister of agriculture (1950-4); deputy armed forces minister (1950-4); Politburo member and president of Romania (1967-89). He enforced rigid domestic policies, suppressed political opposition ruthlessly, and concentrated on economic development along strict **Marxist**-Leninist lines. He was executed in 1989 after the overthrow of his government in a bloody revolution.

CELTS Ancient people of western Europe called by the Greeks *Keltoi* and by the Romans *Celtae*. Now more generally used of speakers of languages descended from these, notably Breton in France, Welsh, Cornish, Gaelic (Scots and Irish), and Manx in the British Isles. Archaeologically often used as synonymous with **La Tène** style.

CENOZOIC *see* **Cainozoic**

CENTRAL TREATY ORGANIZATION (CENTO) Defence alliance, originally known as the Baghdad Pact, between Iran, Iraq, Pakistan, Turkey and the United Kingdom, signed in 1955. The headquarters were moved from Baghdad to Ankara in 1958, and the name changed with the withdrawal of Iraq in 1959. The Pact was weakened from the first by the refusal of the United States, which had sponsored it, to become a full member. It aroused the hostility of **Nasser**, and an ill-judged attempt to recruit Jordan led to riots which nearly caused the fall of King Hussein. Dissolved in 1979.

CHALCEDON, COUNCIL OF Fourth ecumenical council of the Christian Church, called in 451 to pronounce on the nature of Christ; it condemned **Monophysitism** as a heresy.

CHALDEANS A group of Semitic tribes, related to the Aramaeans, who settled in the marsh areas of southern Babylonia c.1000 BC. They eventually spread up the Euphrates, infiltrating into territories of many of the major cities of Babylonia, almost to Babylon. By the late 8th century BC, Chaldean chieftains, notably Ukin-zer and Marduk-apal-iddina (Merodach-baladan of the Bible), sought the kingship of Babylonia, producing endemic disturbance. A Chaldean dynasty, whose best-known ruler was Nebuchadnezzar, succeeded to the kingship from 625 to 539 BC. In the Hellenistic and Roman period the term 'Chaldeans' was used to describe Babylonian astrologers generally, without any ethnic basis.

CHAMBERLAIN, JOSEPH (1836-1914) British political leader. Mayor of Birmingham, 1873-6, and a pioneer of radical local government, he became a Member of Parliament in 1876. He was Colonial Secretary in the Conservative government, 1895-1903, during the last, and for Great Britain vital, stages of the partition of Africa; he was responsible for sending Kitchener to the Sudan, for declaring a protectorate over Uganda, and – most important – for the Anglo-Boer War of 1899-1902. He resigned to campaign for Imperial Preference (*see* **Ottawa Agreement**) and tariff protection for British industry.

CHAMORRO, VIOLETA BARRIOS DE (1939-) Nicaraguan politician and widow of the Nicaraguan journalist and writer Pedro Joaquin Chamorro, assassinated in 1978 because of his bitter opposition to the Somoza political regime. The National Opposition Union candidate for President in 1989-90, she was elected to the Presidency in April 1990. She has sought a balance between **Sandinista** and opposition forces in governmental programs.

CHAMPA Ancient kingdom of Indo-China, originally occupying most of the central coastal region of modern Vietnam, and inhabited by the Chams, a people of Malay affinity. Founded c.AD 192, according to Chinese sources, it had close tributary relations with China down to the 16th century, but avoided a Chinese attempt at conquest in 1285. Frequent wars against the Vietnamese led to piecemeal loss of territory, and then to annexation of the main part of Champa by 1471; the kingdom disappeared completely c.1700, apart from Cham communities surviving near Phan Thiet and Phan Rang. Its Hindu temples survive at various places, indicating Indian cultural influence.

CHANAK INCIDENT (1922) Landing of British troops at Çanakkale (Chanak) on the Dardanelles to oppose a Turkish takeover of the straits. **Lloyd George**, the British Prime Minister, was accused of recklessness and his government fell.

CHANCA Andean tribe occupying land in Andahuaylas, Peru. In 1440 they attacked but were heavily defeated by the neighbouring, previously insignificant, **Incas**.

CHANCELLOR, SIR RICHARD (d.1556) Navigator and pioneer of Anglo-Russian trade. In 1553 he was appointed pilot-general to Sir Humphrey Willoughby's expedition seeking a northeast passage to China. Separated from them by bad weather, he continued into the White Sea and overland to Moscow, where he was warmly received by Tsar **Ivan IV**. He returned to England in 1554 after negotiating the formation of the Muscovy Company.

CHANDELLAS Rajput warrior clan, ruling Bundelkhand, northern India, from the 9th to the 11th century. Defeated in 1001 by Muslim armies of **Mahmud of Ghazni** and expelled from their great fortress of Kalinjar (1023), they were reduced to vassalage by Prithviraja of Ajmer in 1082.

CHANDRAGUPTA II Indian king of the Gupta dynasty, reigning c.375-415, son of Samudragupta. Traditionally renowned for his valour and chivalry, he fought a long campaign against the Sakas (388-409). He extended Gupta power, by war in northern India and by marriage in the Deccan, and took the title *Vikramaditya*, Sun of Prowess.

CHANDRAGUPTA MAURYA Founder of the first Indian empire, he usurped the throne of the Ganges Valley kingdom of Magadha, 321 BC. He exploited the power vacuum left by the retreat of **Alexander the Great** from northwest India, defeated the forces of **Seleucus I Nicator**, 305-303 BC and acquired Trans-Indus province (now part of Afghanistan). He is said to have been converted to **Jainism** at the end of his life, abdicating in 297 in favour of his son **Bindusara**, and dying, as a monk, by deliberate starvation.

CHANG CH'IEN (d.114 BC) Chinese diplomat and explorer, sent in 138 BC by the Han emperor **Wu-ti** to establish contact with the **Yüeh-chih** tribes, and the first man to bring back to China reliable reports of central Asia. He was captured and held for 10 years by the **Hsiung-nu** tribes but still completed his mission, returning after 13 years. He made many other journeys, his travels taking him as far as the Tarim Basin, Ferghana, Bactria, Sogdiana and the Hellenic outpost-states established by **Alexander the Great**. Besides information, his efforts gave China its first access to such valuable products as large, fast horses, grapes and alfalfa grass.

CHANG HSIEN-CHUNG (c.1605-47) Chinese rebel leader in the last days of the **Ming** dynasty. Trained as a soldier, he was dismissed from the imperial army and started bandit raids in northern Shensi, 1628. He moved into Honan and Hupeh in 1635. Forced to surrender in 1638, he was nevertheless allowed to retain his forces, and rebelled again in 1639. In 1643 he failed to set up administrations in Wuchang and Changsha. He retreated into Szechwan, but captured Cheng-tu in 1644 and took the title of King of the Great Western Kingdom. His government disintegrated in a reign of terror in 1646, and he was killed the following year.

CHANG KUO-T'AO (1897-1979) A founder of the Chinese Communist Party (CCP). After playing a minor role in the May 4 Movement, he represented Peking Marxists at the first CCP Congress at Shanghai in 1921. He helped to found the CCP-sponsored Labour movement and developed close ties with the **Comintern**. From 1929 he played a major role in Communist base areas on the borders of Honan, Anhwei and Hupeh, and led his forces through Szechwan on an important leg of the Long March. From 1935 he engaged in bitter debates with **Mao Tse-tung**; attempting to set up an independent base in the far northwest, his troops were disastrously defeated in Kansu. After 1938 he defected to the Nationalists and lived in semi-retirement, moving to Hong Kong in 1949, and writing his autobiography.

CHANG TSO-LIN (1873-1928) Chinese warlord known as 'the Old Marshal'. Originally an officer in a Manchurian army, he built up control of southern Manchuria, and from 1917 increasingly dominated Manchuria and much of northern China until 1928. After 1921 he controlled Inner Mongolia. Attempts to control the Peking government led to war with **Wu P'ei-fu** in 1922, in which Chang was initially defeated. In 1924 he concluded a pact with the Soviet Union, which recognized his regime in Manchuria as independent. Later that year he invaded northern China, seriously defeating Wu P'ei-fu and driving south almost to Shanghai. His power was backed by the tacit support of the Japanese, who supported him in Manchuria as a buffer against Soviet influence, and to whom he granted major concessions in Manchuria. Unable to counter the growing power of the **Kuomintang** (Nationalist Party) armies under **Chiang Kai-shek**, which invaded his territories in 1927, he abandoned Peking to them. He was killed when Japanese extremists blew up his private train.

CHARLEMAGNE (742-814) Emperor of the **Franks**, son of **Pepin the Short**. Succeeded as joint king, 768; sole ruler from 771. He conquered most of the Christian territory in western Europe, defeating the Lombards and converting the pagan Saxons, and he allied with the papacy to counter the dominance of Byzantium. On Christmas Day 800 in St Peter's, Rome, he was crowned and anointed by the Pope and became the first emperor of non-Roman origins and the first of the German emperors of the Middle Ages.

CHARLES I, OF ANJOU (1226-85) Angevin king of Naples and Sicily, younger brother of **Louis IX** of France. He acquired the county of Provence, 1246; defeated the last **Hohenstaufen** in 1266 and 1268 to conquer Naples and Sicily, and in 1277 became heir to the kingdom of Jerusalem. Transferring his capital from Palermo to Naples, he set off the revolt of the Sicilian Vespers, 1282, and was defeated by the alliance of the Sicilians and Peter III of Aragon in the Bay of Naples, 1284.

CHARLES I (1600-49) King of England, Scotland and Ireland, son of **James VI (and I)**. Succeeding in 1625, he came increasingly into conflict with his English Parliament over religion, foreign policy and taxation. After being forced to sign the Petition of Right (1628), he ruled without Parliament until 1640; rebellion broke out in Scotland in 1638, in Ireland in 1641 and in England in 1642. Defeated in the civil wars that followed, he was captured in 1647 by the English army under **Cromwell**, tried and beheaded.

CHARLES IV (1316-78) King of Bohemia, 1346-78, and ruler of the German Empire from 1355, son of John of Luxembourg and Elizabeth, sister of last native Bohemian king. He reformed the finances and legal system, and built up the power of the monarchy in Bohemia, but left Germany largely to the princes; in 1356 he issued the **Golden Bull**, laying down a permanent constitution for the Empire.

CHARLES V (1500-58) Holy Roman Emperor. He was the son of Philip I (died 1506), heir to the Burgundian states, and of Joanna (declared insane in 1506), heiress to Castile and Aragon, to which he succeeded in 1516. Elected emperor in 1519, he annexed Lombardy (1535), and several Netherlands provinces, but was eventually defeated (1551-5) by an alliance of Turks, French and German Lutherans. He abdicated in 1556, leaving his German possessions to his brother Ferdinand (elected emperor in 1558), and the rest to his son **Philip II**. He retired to a monastery in 1557.

CHARLES IX (1550-1611) Effective ruler of Sweden from 1599, and king 1604-11. The third son of **Gustavus I Vasa**; in 1568 he helped his brother, then crowned as **John III**, to depose their half-brother **Eric XIV**. A strong Lutheran, he first broke with John over religion and then, after the accession of John's Catholic son, **Sigismund III**, called the Convention of Uppsala, 1593, to demand the acceptance of **Lutheranism** as the state religion. Appointed regent in Sigismund's absence, he precipitated a civil war and deposed the king, 1599. He died after strengthening Sweden's metal-based economy and provoking the Kalmar War with Denmark, 1611-13.

CHARLES X GUSTAV (1622-60) King of Sweden, son of John Casimir, Count Palatine of Zweibrücken, and Catherine, eldest daughter of **Charles IX**. He fought with the Swedish armies in Germany, 1642-5. His cousin, Queen Christina of Sweden, appointed him commander of the Swedish forces in Germany and also her official successor. He was crowned in 1654, invaded Poland in 1655 and Denmark in 1657-8, and won an advantageous peace.

CHARLES XI (1655-97) King of Sweden, succeeding his father, **Charles X Gustav**, in 1660. He was kept in tutelage by aristocratic regents until Sweden's defeat by Brandenburg at Fehrbellin in 1675; he then established absolute rule, expanding the royal estates to cover 30 per cent of Sweden and Finland and rebuilding the armed forces to match those of Denmark. In 1693, the Swedish Diet granted him unrestricted powers to ensure his reforms.

CHARLES XII (1682-1718) Warrior king of Sweden, eldest son of **Charles XI**, succeeding to the throne in 1697. Brilliantly defeated the anti-Swedish coalition (formed in 1699 to crush Sweden's Baltic hegemony) of Denmark, Russia, Poland and Saxony, invading each in turn (1700-6). He invaded Russia again with Cossack help in 1708 but was routed at Poltava, 1709, taking refuge in Turkey which he succeeded in turning against Russia. Forced to leave Turkey in 1714, he was killed while fighting in Norway.

CHARLES ALBERT (1798-1849) King of Sardinia-Piedmont. Son of the Prince of Carignano, he was exiled from Italy and brought up in revolutionary Paris and Geneva, succeeding his father in 1800. He was involved in an abortive plot to displace his cousin as king of Piedmont in 1821. He ascended the throne on his cousin's death in 1831. He sought to lead the unification of Italy, granting representative government and declaring war on Austria in 1848. Defeats at Custoza, 1848, and Novara, 1849, forced his abdication. He died in Portugal.

CHARLES THE BOLD (1433-77) Duke of Burgundy, son of **Philip the Good**, inheriting the title in 1467. He attempted to conquer the lands dividing his territories of Luxembourg, Burgundy, the Low Countries and Franche-Comté; but was defeated and killed in battle. Soon after this, in the year 1483, Burgundy passed to the French crown, and Charles' other domains became part of the **Habsburg dominions**.

CHARLES MARTEL (c.688-741) Reunifier of the **Franks**. The illegitimate son of Pepin of Herstal, mayor of the Palace of Austrasia, he emerged, after a five-year struggle, as his father's successor and as effective ruler of all the Franks, 719. He defeated the Muslims, advancing north from Spain, near Poitiers, 732; subdued Burgundy, 733, the **Frisians**, 734, and the Aquitainians 735. He retired in 741, and died the same year.

CHEOPS (Khufu) Second king of Egypt's IVth Dynasty (early 26th century BC), succeeding his father, Snefru. He built the Great Pyramid of Giza and three subsidiary pyramids for his principal wives.

CHEPHREN (Khafre) Fourth king of Egypt's IVth Dynasty (late 26th century BC). The son of **Cheops**, he succeeded his brother, Djedefre. He built the second of the three pyramids of Giza and the granite valley temple linked to it by a causeway.

CH'I Large and powerful Chinese state in the period 771-221 BC, located on the eastern edge of the North China Plain (modern Shantung and Hopeh). In the 7th and 6th centuries BC Ch'i began to expand, absorbing its smaller neighbours; during this period it was also the most technologically advanced state in China. Under the semi-legendary Duke Huan it gained short-lived hegemony over all Chinese territories in 651. In the 3rd century BC a new ruling house again attempted to impose sole dominance on China, but it failed, and in 221 Ch'i was absorbed by Ch'in.

CHIANG KAI-SHEK (1887-1975) Chinese general and political leader. He took control of the **Kuomintang** in 1926 and established a stable republican government in Nanking, 1928-37. He fought warlords, Japanese invaders and the Chinese Communist Party (with occasional periods of alliance) until finally defeated in 1949. He withdrew to Taiwan (Formosa) to form the Chinese Nationalist government, of which he remained President until his death.

CHIBCHA (also known as Muisca) South American Indians, at the time of the Spanish conquest occupying the high valleys near today's Bogotá and Tunja, Colombia. Their tightly centralized political structure, based on intensive agriculture, was crushed in the 16th century, and since the 18th century (when their language ceased to be spoken) they have been fully assimilated with the population of Colombia.

CHICHIMECS Barbarian and semi-civilized Indian groups who invaded central Mexico from the north in the 12th and 13th centuries and ended the rule of the **Toltecs**; the Aztecs originated as one of the Chichimec tribes.

CHILDEBERT II (570-95) King of Austrasia, son of **Sigebert** and **Brunhilde**. After the murder of his father he became the pawn of various aristocratic factions in Austrasia, who favoured alliance with one or other of his two uncles, Chilperic or Guntram. He led an expedition to Italy in 584; ousted the supporters of Chilperic in 585 and allied with Guntram; and after Guntram's death in 593 controlled almost all of Gaul.

CHILDERIC (d.481) Chieftain of the Salian Franks, occupying territory between the rivers Meuse and Somme. He helped the Romans to defeat the **Visigoths**, near Orléans in 463, and again in 469; and cleared the Saxon pirates from the area of Angers. He died in Tournai, where his richly equipped tomb was discovered in 1653, and was succeeded by his son **Clovis**.

CHILEMBWE, JOHN (1860-1915) Nyasaland missionary and rebel leader, now regarded as one of the spiritual forebears of modern Malawi. He worked closely with the European fundamentalist Joseph Booth, 1892-5. In 1897 he received a degree from the United States Negro theological college. On his return to Nyasaland in 1900 he founded the Providence Industrial Mission with Negro Baptist finance. He protested in 1914 against economic oppression and the use of Nyasa troops in the First World War. He was shot after leading a suicidal revolt against British rule.

CHIMÚ South American Indians, famous for their goldware and pottery, whose rule immediately preceded that of the **Inca** in Peru. Their comparable, though small-scale, civilization, centred at Chanchán in the Moche Valley about 300 miles north of Lima, was conquered by **Pachacuti** in 1465-70.

CHIN Dynasty ruling northern China from 1122 to 1234. Rising from the nomadic Jurchen tribes of northern Manchuria who destroyed their overlords, the **Khitan** dynasty of the Liao, in 1125, it went on to defeat the Sung and to establish control of the territory north of the Huai River. It was destroyed, in turn, by the Mongols in 1234.

CH'IN First great Chinese imperial dynasty: founded by **Shih Huang-ti**; *see pages 80-81*.

CHIN-CH'UAN RISINGS Series of risings of the aboriginal peoples of western and northwest Szechwan in 1745-9, flaring up intermittently again until 1776. The risings tied down large Manchu armies in difficult mountain terrain, and their suppression was extremely costly.

CHIN FU (1633-92) Chinese official responsible for major water improvements under the early Ch'ing dynasty. From 1677 he dredged and banked up the frequently flooding Yellow River (Huang Ho), and made large-scale repairs to the Grand Canal.

CH'ING Last imperial dynasty in China. See *pages 170-1, 228-9*.

CHOKWE (Bajokwe) People occupying the southern region of Zaire, northeast Angola and northwest Zambia, formed by a mixture of aboriginal groups and **Lunda** invaders; they were famous ivory-hunters in the 19th century.

CHOU Chinese dynasty, c.1122-221 BC. The Western Chou (c.1122-771 BC) were originally semi-nomadic barbarians from west of the North China Plain. They conquered the lands ruled by the previous Shang dynasty and extended them. Their territory was organized in a 'feudal' system of virtually independent fiefs; in 771 central authority finally broke down. During the Eastern Chou (771-221 BC), China became one of the world's most advanced regions; its greatest philosophers, **Confucius** and **Lao-tzu**, lived at this time, and from this period date many of its most characteristic innovations.

CHREMONIDES' WAR The last flicker of Athenian aggression. In 267 BC a citizen called Chremonides called for a Greek league of liberation with the support of Egypt against the Macedonian king, Antigonus Gonatus; few others joined, and after an intermittent siege Gonatus captured the city in 262. Athens never again sought political leadership in classical times.

CHRISTIANITY Religion of those who have faith in **Jesus**. In the central traditions of Christianity the single God is nonetheless a Trinity – the Father, the Son (incarnate in the human life of Jesus of Nazareth) and the Holy Spirit. Christianity spread despite persecution, and in the 4th century was adopted by the Roman ruling class. Despite divisions it has remained one of the great world religions, sending its missionaries all over the world.

CH'U One of the Chinese states which, with Ch'i, Ch'in and, later, Chin, contended between 771-221 BC for the domination of China. Based on present-day Hupeh, in the fertile Yangtze Valley of southern China, Ch'u had a completely distinctive culture of its own. It expanded very rapidly into Anhwei and Hunan, and eventually controlled all central China. In 223 BC it was finally absorbed by Ch'in, but 15 years later, when Ch'in collapsed, a Ch'u aristocrat, Hsiang Yü, briefly became emperor of China; but his reign only lasted a few months before the advent of the **Han** dynasty.

CHURCHILL, SIR WINSTON LEONARD SPENCER (1874-1965) British statesman and author. The son of Lord Randolph Churchill, he served as a soldier and journalist in Cuba, India, the Sudan and South Africa before becoming a Conservative Member of Parliament in 1900. He was a minister in both the Tory and Liberal governments between 1908 and 1929, serving as First Lord of the Admiralty, 1911 to 1915. During the 1930s he warned of the growing threat from **Nazi** Germany, and later directed Britain's war effort as First Lord of the Admiralty in 1939-40, then as premier and Minister of Defence, 1940-5. He was Prime Minister again in 1951-5. His works, written while out of office, include *The World Crisis, 1916-18* (1923-9), *The Second World War* (1948-53) and *A History of the English-speaking Peoples* (1956-8); he won the Nobel Prize for literature in 1953.

CHU TE (1886-1976) 'Father' of the Chinese Red Army. Originally a military officer in Yunnan and Szechwan, he went to Shanghai in 1921 and joined the Chinese Communist Party in 1922. After studying in Germany (1922-6) he took part in the abortive rising in Nanch'ang in 1927. With **Mao Tse-tung** he built a famous fighting unit in the Kiangsi Soviet, took part in the Long March, commanded Communist forces in the Sino-Japanese War and became commander-in-chief during the civil war with the Nationalists. During the 1930s and 1940s he played a major role in developing Communist policies in rural areas, and in strategic planning. In 1949 he became vice-chairman of the central people's government and by 1958 was looked on as natural successor to Mao as head of state. However, in 1959 he was passed over in favour of Liu Shao-ch'i, and had little real power after that time.

CHU YÜAN-CHANG (1328-98) Chinese emperor, founder of the **Ming** dynasty. Born in Anhwei province, he joined a monastery, but between 1356 and 1364 led insurgent forces, gradually gaining control of the region north of the Yangtze, being proclaimed Prince of Wu in 1364. Driving out the Mongols in 1368, he established the Ming dynasty with its capital at Nanking and reigned for 30 years under the title Hung Wu.

CIMMERIANS Indo-European people driven from their homelands in southern Russia, north of the Caucasus and the Sea of Azov, by the closely-related **Scythians** in the 8th century BC. They were turned aside into Anatolia where they conquered Phrygia, 696-95. After their rout by Alyattes of Lydia, c.626, they were absorbed by surrounding groups.

CISTERCIAN Religious Order founded at Cîteaux, in southeast France, in 1098. It rose to great prominence under the influence of **St Bernard**; by the end of the 12th century it had more than 500 monasteries all over Europe. The motive of the foundation was the re-establishment of the primitive rigour of the Rule of St Benedict, which had lately been neglected.

CLAPPERTON, HUGH (1788-1827) Scottish explorer of West Africa. He joined an expedition journeying south from Tripoli across the Sahara; in 1823 he reached Lake Chad, and travelled in what is now northern Nigeria. He made a second expedition to southern Nigeria; he died near Sokoto after crossing the Niger.

CLARK, WILLIAM (1770-1838) American explorer. With Meriwether Lewis he led a momentous expedition (1804-8) up the Missouri River and over the Rocky Mountains to the Pacific, opening vast territories to westward expansion.

CLAUDIUS I (10 BC-AD 54) Fourth Roman emperor, born Tiberius Claudius Drusus Nero Germanicus, nephew of the emperor **Tiberius**. He achieved power unexpectedly in AD 41, after the murder of his elder brother's son, **Caligula**; annexed Mauretania, North Africa, 41-2; invaded Britain, 43, and extended the Empire in the East. He had his third wife, Messalina, killed on suspicion of conspiracy, and was almost certainly poisoned by his fourth, his niece Agrippina.

CLAUSWITZ, CARL von (1780-1831) Prussian general and philosopher of war. He played a prominent part in the military reform movement after the disastrous defeat by **Napoleon** at Jena in 1806. He served as a staff officer with the Russian Army, 1812-13, but returned to Prussian service in 1814-15. After the defeat of Napoleon he was appointed director of the War Academy, a purely administrative post which gave him ample time for historical and theoretical writings. His most famous and still influential book, *On War*, was published posthumously.

CLEMENT OF ALEXANDRIA (c.AD 150-c.213) Saint, and principal reconciler of early Christian beliefs with the mainstream of Graeco-Roman cultural tradition. Born in Athens, he settled in Egypt, and became head of the Catechetical School, Alexandria. He taught many future theologians (e.g. Origen) and church leaders (Alexander, Bishop of Jerusalem), and wrote important ethical and theological works.

CLEMENT OF ROME Saint, first Apostolic Father of the Christian Church and Bishop of Rome at the end of the 1st century AD. Author of the *Letter to the Church of Corinth*, an important source for the Church history of the period.

CLEMENT IV (d.1268) Pope 1265-8. A Frenchman who had been in the service of **Louis IX**, his pontificate signified the growth of French influence in the Church which predominated during the next hundred years. He allied with **Charles of Anjou** to drive the **Hohenstaufen** out of Italy.

CLEOMENES III (d.219 BC) King of Sparta, succeeding his father, Leonidas, in 235 BC. He successfully fought the Achaean League, 228-26; usurped the constitutionally jointly-held Spartan throne to establish virtual autocracy, 227; reintroduced many of the 'communist' ideas of **Agis IV**. His predominance in the Peloponnese was challenged by the Macedonian, **Antigonus Doson**; defeated by Doson at Sellasia in 222, he escaped to Egypt and was interned by Ptolemy IV. He committed suicide after an abortive attempt at revolution in Alexandria.

CLEOPATRA (c.70-31 BC) Last Ptolemaic ruler of Egypt, the daughter of King Ptolemy Auletes. Joint heir with her brother, she was made queen by **Julius Caesar** in 48 BC. She went to Rome as his mistress, but transferred her affections to **Antony**, who then left for four years, but returned after breaking with Octavian. She committed suicide after the Egyptian fleet was defeated at Actium and the troops of her ally, Antony, refused to fight.

CLINTON, BILL (1946-) US politician and 42nd President. He studied international affairs at Georgetown (1968) and as a Rhodes Scholar at Oxford (1968-70), then received his law degree from Yale (1973). He served as Attorney General of Arkansas (1977-9); Governor of Arkansas (1979-81; 1983-92) and as the national Democratic candidate, in 1993 defeated George Bush to become US President.

CLIVE, ROBERT (1725-74) Conqueror of Bengal and founder of British power in India. He arrived in India in 1743 as a clerk in the **English East India Company**. He fought French, and later (1757) Indian, forces to establish British control in Bengal, where he was twice Governor (1757-60 and 1765-7). His rule was marred by corruption scandals; despite successful Parliamentary defence in 1773, he committed suicide the following year.

CLOVIS I (c.466-511) Founder of the kingdom of the **Franks**, succeeding his father, **Childeric**, as ruler of the Salian Franks in 481, and gradually uniting all other Frankish groups under his rule. He defeated the last Roman authority in northern Gaul in 486, defeated the **Burgundians** and the Alemans, and drove the **Visigoths** from Aquitaine in 507. Sometime before 508 he converted to Catholic Christianity, and was baptized at Rheims; he issued the Salic law for his people, and established his capital at Paris. His descendants, the **Merovingians**, ruled the Frankish kingdom until 751.

CLUNIAC The monastery of Cluny (near Mâcon, Burgundy) was founded in 910 by the Duke of Aquitaine, and wielded a tremendous influence on the life of the Church for the next two centuries. The respect in which the Cluniacs were held through their many foundations all over western Europe, the statesmanlike activity of their leaders and the hierarchical organization of the Order under the abbot of Cluny, combined to make it one of the foundation stones of the general reform of the Church led by Pope **Gregory VII**.

CNUT THE GREAT (c.995-1035) King of England (where he is remembered as Canute), Denmark and Norway. The son of **Sven Forkbeard**, he went to England with his father in 1013; he divided the country with Edmund II in 1016, assuming rule over all the country on Edmund's death in the same year. He succeeded to the Danish throne in 1019 and invaded Scotland in 1027.

COELHO, DUARTE (c.1485-1554) Portuguese soldier. He was granted the captaincy of Pernambuco in 1534, and developed it into the most flourishing colony in Brazil.

COLBERT, JEAN BAPTISTE (1619-83) Minister of Finance to **Louis XIV** of France. Personal assistant to Cardinal **Mazarin**, he became a dominant member of Louis' Council of Finance, and in 1665 was made Controller-General. He reformed taxes, founded state manufactures, created the French merchant fleet and laid the basis for France's economic dominance in late 17th century Europe.

COLIJN, HENDRIKUS (1869-1944) Dutch statesman. Fought in Sumatra where he was later colonial administrator. He entered the Dutch parliament in 1909; became war minister, 1911-13; finance minister, 1923-5; Prime Minister, 1925-6 and 1933-9. In his second term as premier he instituted successful anti-depression policies. He was forced to resign in 1939. Arrested by the Germans in 1941, he died three years later in a concentration camp.

COLLA People of the high Andes who in pre-Columbian times occupied the area south of Lake Titicaca. They were conquered by the **Incas** in the early 15th century.

COLLING BROTHERS English 18th-century stockbreeders, farming near Darlington, who developed the shorthorn cow, c.1780, into an animal equally good for milk and meat.

COLTER, JOHN (c.1775-1813) United States trapper and explorer, who in 1807 discovered the area now known as Yellowstone National Park. He was also a member of the Lewis and **Clark** expedition.

COLUMBA (521-579) Irish saint, famous as the missionary who carried Christianity to **Picts** in Caledonia (Scotland). He founded the monastery at Iona, 563, the mother house of numerous monasteries on the Scottish mainland.

COLUMBUS, CHRISTOPHER (1451-1506) Genoese navigator, discoverer of America and founder of the Spanish empire in the Americas. In 1492 he obtained finance from the Spanish court to seek the east by sailing west. His three ships, the *Pinta*, *Niña* and *Santa María*, sighted San Salvador on 12 October 1492. During his second voyage, in 1493, he founded Isabela, the first European city (now deserted) in the New World, in the Dominican Republic. His third journey, 1498-1500, revealed the mainland of South America. He was embittered when administrative disasters and lack of political sense made the king of Spain reluctant to trust his governor-

ship. His last voyage, 1502-4, coasted Honduras, Nicaragua and the isthmus of Panama, and ended with his ships beached off Jamaica.

COMINTERN The Third Socialist International, set up in 1919 to replace the **Second International** by those who condemned it for its failure to prevent the First World War. Captured immediately by the leadership of Bolshevik Russia, it split the world socialist movement between evolutionary and revolutionary parties, fomenting a number of uprisings in Europe and in European colonies in Southeast Asia in the 1920s. Extensively purged by **Stalin**'s secret police in the 1930s, it was formally dissolved in 1943.

COMNENES Byzantine dynasty holding the imperial throne, 1081-1185. Isaac I, son of Manuel Comnenus, a Paphlagonian general, became emperor briefly from 1057 to 1059, but his nephew, **Alexius I** (reigned 1081-1118), consolidated the family's power. The elder line died out in 1185, but after the sack of Constantinople by Crusaders (1204) relatives founded the Empire of Trebizond, lasting until 1461, when David Comnenus was deposed.

CONFEDERATION OF THE RHINE Created by **Napoleon I** in 1806 after the dissolution of the Holy Roman Empire, to gather his client states into a federation of which he was 'protector'. Excluding Austria and Prussia, it formalized French domination over German territory, and lasted until Napoleon's defeat.

CONFLANS, TREATY OF Agreement concluded in 1465 between **Louis XI** of France and the League of the Public Weal, under which Louis agreed to return land captured on the Somme to the League's leader, **Charles the Bold**, duke of Burgundy, and promised him the hand of his daughter, Anne of France, with the territory of Champagne as dowry.

CONFUCIUS Chinese philosopher. He served as a public administrator, c.532-c.517 BC, then spent the rest of his life teaching and editing the ancient Chinese classics. His sayings, collected after his death as *The Analects*, formed the basis for Chinese education and social organization until the 20th century. His philosophy was conservative: he advocated submission to one's parents and of wives to husbands, loyalty of subjects to ruler, and conformity to established social forms. He advocated the supremacy of ethical standards and rule by 'humanity' and moral persuasion rather than brute force, and laid great stress on ritual observance. Confucianism has been deeply influential in Japan, Korea and Vietnam as well as in China.

CONGREGATIONALIST Member of one of the independent Protestant churches established in the 16th and 17th centuries in the belief that each congregation should decide its own affairs. Among its famous followers were John Winthrop, founder of the Massachusetts Bay Colony in 1629, and **Oliver Cromwell**, Lord Protector of England, 1649-60. Congregationalism became the established religion in 17th century New England; many such churches still survive in North America and in Great Britain.

CONSTANTINE I (c.287-337) Roman emperor, known as 'the Great'. Born in Naissus, now Niš, Serbia, he was brought up at the court of **Diocletian**, and became Western emperor in 312 and sole emperor in 324. Committed to Christianity, he issued the Edict of Milan, 313, extending toleration to all faiths; addressed the Council of Nicaea, 325, called to resolve some of its crucial theological disputes; founded many churches and was baptized shortly before his death. He built Constantinople as a new Rome on the site of Byzantium, 324, as his permanent capital, and was largely responsible for the evolution of the empire into a Christian state.

CONSTANTINOPLE, COUNCILS OF The first council, an ecumenical gathering of the Christian Church held in AD 381, reaffirmed the teaching of the **Council of Nicaea** and defined the doctrine of the Holy Trinity. The second, in 553, rejected the Nestorian version of Christianity and defined the unity of the person of Christ in his two natures, human and divine. This was reasserted in the third council in 680-1. The fourth, summoned in 869-70, excommunicated Photius, Patriarch of Constantinople (he was reinstated ten years later) and forbade lay interference in the election of bishops.

CONTRAS A counter-revolutionary insurgent force formed by the **Reagan** administration (1981-9) to fight against the **Sandinista** government in Nicaragua (1979-89). They included former supporters of the Somoza regime, members of the National Guard and disaffected opposition

leaders. With substantial US military training and aid, they carried out military operations from Honduras, but proved unable to topple the Sandinistas and were demobilized in exchange for free elections in 1989.

COOK, JAMES (1728-79) Explorer of the Pacific Ocean. Appointed 1768 to take members of the British Royal Society to Tahiti and locate *Terra Australis Incognita*, or Unknown Southern Continent, he instead charted the coasts of New Zealand and established its insular character, explored the east coast of Australia, navigated the Great Barrier Reef (1770); on his second voyage of circumnavigation, 1772-5, he finally disposed of the notion of an inhabited southern continent; on the third voyage, 1776-80, he discovered the Sandwich (Hawaiian) Islands and proved that no navigable passage connected the north Pacific and north Atlantic. He was famous for his radical dietary methods, which protected all his men from the previously unavoidable scourge of scurvy. He was killed in Hawaii.

COPT Member of the Coptic Church, an ancient **Monophysite** branch of **Christianity**, founded in Egypt in the 5th century. Persecuted by Byzantines for theological reasons, but relatively secure after the Muslim comquest of Egypt, the Church, with its strong monastic tradition, survived. Its 3 to 4 million followers today still use the Coptic language, derived from ancient Egyptian, for their version of the Greek liturgy.

CORFU INCIDENT Italian bombardment and temporary occupation of the island in September 1923, in retaliation for killing of Italian officers in Greece.

CORNISH REBELLION English uprising in 1497 against the heavy taxes levied by **Henry VII** to pay for his Scottish wars. The rebels killed a tax collector at Taunton (Devon) and marched on London, but they were attacked and defeated in their camp at Blackheath by government troops; 2000 rebels died and the leaders were hanged.

CORREGGIO, DA Italian family, prominent in the affairs of the Emilian city of Correggio from the 11th century until 1634, and of Parma in the 14th century. Its territories were sold to the House of **Este** in 1634. The dynasty finally died out in 1711.

CORSAIRS Pirates, particularly on the Maghreb ('Barbary') Coast of North Africa.

CORTE-REAL, GASPAR and MIGUEL Portuguese explorer brothers who made a series of voyages in the late 15th and early 16th centuries under royal commission to discover lands in the northwest Atlantic within the Portuguese domain. Gaspar travelled along the coast of southeast Greenland and crossed the Davis Strait to Labrador; Miguel visited Newfoundland and possibly the Gulf of St Lawrence in 1502. Both were lost at sea.

CORTÉS, HERNÁN (1485-1547) Conqueror of Mexico. At the age of 19 he settled in Hispaniola and in 1511 sailed with Diego de Velásquez to conquer Cuba; from there, in 1518, he headed an expedition to colonize the Mexican mainland, and achieved a complete and remarkable victory over the Aztec empire. In 1524 he led an arduous and profitless expedition to Honduras. The rest of his life was spent fighting political enemies and intriguers both in New Spain and at home in Spain.

COSA, JUAN DE LA (c.1460-1510) Spanish geographer and traveller. He owned **Columbus**' flagship, the *Santa Maria*, and served as his pilot. He compiled a celebrated map, dated 1500, showing Columbus' discoveries, **Cabral**'s landfall in Brazil, **Cabot**'s voyage to Canada, and **da Gama**'s journey to India. Sailed with **Bastidas** in 1500; explored Darien, 1504. He died during an expedition to central America and Colombia.

COSSACKS Bands of warlike adventurers recruited mainly from Ukrainian, Polish, Russian and Tartar fugitives and runaway serfs. Renowned for their horsemanship, courage and ruthlessness, they were active on the borders of the Ottoman Empire with Poland and Russia from the 15th century. One of their bands in the service of the Stroganov family, under Yermak, conquered the Siberian Khanate for **Ivan IV**. The Cossacks' principal settlement was at Zaporozhye on the Dnieper, and from here they rebelled against Poland in 1648. The settlement was destroyed after the Peace of Kücük Kaynarca in 1774, but other Cossack hosts entered Russian service as cavalry regiments (e.g. Don Cossacks). They survived as semi-autonomous societies into the Soviet period, when they set up short-lived anti-Bolshevik governments.

COUGHLIN, FATHER CHARLES EDWARD (1891-1979) Populist and anti-semitic Catholic priest; born in Canada. From 1930 he broadcast weekly to large audiences in the United States, at first supporting President **F.D. Roosevelt**, but then dropping him in 1936. He edited an increasingly right-wing journal, *Social Justice*, until publication ceased in 1942 after the magazine was banned from the mails for infringing the Espionage Act.

COVENANTERS Those who signed the Scottish National Covenant in 1638, pledging to defend Presbyterianism against all comers. Covenanting armies entered England in 1640, 1644 and 1651; they were defeated by **Cromwell** at Dunbar (1650) and Worcester (1651). The Westminster Confession (1643), drawn up after agreeing the Solemn League and Covenant with the English Parliamentarians, defined the worship, doctrines and organization of the Church of Scotland. The movement faded away after 1690, when the official Scottish religion became Episcopalianism.

COVILHÃ, PERO DE 15th century Portuguese explorer sent by the crown in 1487 to see whether the Indian Ocean connected with the Atlantic. His reports from Ethiopia, which he reached after travels in India and Arabia, were important in the Portuguese decision to send the fleet of **Vasco da Gama** to India in 1497-8. Covilhã reached the court of the emperor of Ethiopia, whom he thought was a descendant of **Prester John**.

CRASSUS, MARCUS LICINIUS (c.112-53 BC) Wealthy Roman, third member of the First Triumvirate with **Julius Caesar** and **Pompey**. He sought power and prestige to equal his political colleagues; invaded Mesopotamia. He was ignominiously defeated and killed by Parthians at the Battle of Carrhae.

CRIPPS, SIR STAFFORD (1889-1952) British lawyer and politician. He became a member of the Labour Party in 1929, and served in the Cabinet 1930-1. A leading left-wing MP during the 1930s, he was ambassador to Moscow, 1940-2, and headed missions sent to India with plans for self-government in 1942-3 and 1946 (both plans were rejected by the Indian leaders). He held Cabinet office 1942-50, including the post of Chancellor of the Exchequer, 1947-50.

CROATS East European people who migrated in the 6th century from White Croatia, now in the Ukraine, to the Balkans. Their conversion to Roman Catholicism in the 7th century has continued to divide them from their Orthodox neighbours, the **Serbs**. The first Croatian kingdom, formed in the 10th century, was united by marriage with the crown of Hungary in 1091. In 1918 an independent Croatia was proclaimed, but it immediately entered the union of Slav states known as Yugoslavia; a Fascist-led independent state of Croatia, under Ante Pavelič, lasted from 1941 to 1945 before reunification with Yugoslavia under the Communist partisans. Independent again from 1991.

CROMPTON, SAMUEL (1753-1827) British inventor who pioneered the automatic spinning mule, 1779, so called because it combined the principles of the jenny and the water frame.

CROMWELL, OLIVER (1599-1658) Head of republican Britain. Elected to the English Parliament in 1640; he led the 'New Model' army to victory in the Civil War, and supported the execution of **Charles I** in 1649. He crushed uprisings by the **Levellers**, 1649, and by opponents in Ireland and Scotland, 1649-51, unifying the British Isles for the first time in a single state. He was appointed Lord Protector (effectively dictator) by army council in 1653. He declined the offer of the monarchy in 1657.

CROQUANTS Peasants who rose in large-scale and well-organized revolts in the Saintonge, Angoumois and Périgord regions of France in 1593-5, 1636-7 and 1643-5. The colloquial meaning of the name is 'clodhopper' or 'nonentity'.

CRUSADES The First Crusade, a holy war waged from 1096 until 1099 by Christian armies from western Europe against Islam in Palestine and Asia Minor, was inspired by a sermon of Pope **Urban II** in 1095. Its leaders included Robert of Normandy, Godfrey of Bouillon, Baldwin and Robert II of Flanders. Nicaea and Antioch were successfully besieged, Jerusalem stormed in 1099, and the Christian kingdom of Jerusalem established by Godfrey of Bouillon.

The Second Crusade, 1147-9, was inspired by **St Bernard**. It was led by the emperor, Conrad III, and by **Louis VII** of France, but foundered on quarrels between its leaders and the barons of the kingdom of Jerusalem, who were in alliance with Muslim Damascus, which the newly-arrived Crusaders wished to attack. The Crusade petered out fruitlessly, and the Latin kingdom was soon weaker than ever.

The Third Crusade, 1189-92, was led by Emperor **Frederick I Barbarossa** (who died before reaching Palestine), King Richard I of England and King **Philip II Augustus** of France. It aimed to regain Jerusalem, which had been captured by the Muslim leader **Saladin** in 1187. It failed to do so, but the coast between Tyre and Jaffa was ceded to Christians and pilgrimage to Jerusalem was allowed.

The Fourth Crusade (1202-4) was originally intended to attack Egypt, centre of Muslim power in the late 12th century. The crusading armies, heirs to a long hostility towards Byzantium, were diverted by Venice, which provided the transport first to Zara on the Adriatic, and then to Constantinople, which fell on 13 April 1204 and was subjected to three days of massacre and pillage. A horrified Pope **Innocent III**, who had called the crusade, was unable to re-establish control, and his legate absolved the Crusaders from their vow to proceed to the Holy Land.

CULTURE SYSTEM A system of land cultivation introduced in the 19th century by the governor-general of the Dutch East Indies , van den Bosch. Under the system each cultivator set aside an agreed portion of his land for the cultivation of certain cash crops – primarily coffee, tea, sugar, indigo and cinnamon – to be delivered at fixed prices to the government in lieu of land rent. It was such a success that all the safeguards against exploitation of labour gradually broke down; Javanese agriculture benefited in various ways, but at the price of oppression and, in places, famine. The system was strongly attacked by the Dutch Liberals, who came to power in 1848, and abolition began in the 1860s. Coffee, the most profitable item in the system, was removed from it only in 1917.

CURZON LINE Ethnically-defined frontier between the former USSR and Poland, proposed in 1919 by the British Foreign Secretary Lord Curzon (1859-1925). At the time it was not accepted by either party; after victory in the Russo-Polish war of 1919-20, Poland, as a result of the **Treaty of Riga**, 1921, retained over 50,000 square miles (129,500 km^2) east of the line. The Russo-Polish frontier as settled in 1945 in some respects conforms to the Curzon recommendations.

CUSHITIC Group of languages, related to Egyptian and Berber, spoken originally in the western highlands of Ethiopia; many elements are now partially absorbed into **Amharic**, the official national language. The most widely used Cushitic dialects today include Galla, Somali and the much-divided Sidamo group.

CYNICS Followers of the way of life of Diogenes of Sinope (c.400-325 BC), nicknamed the Dog (hence Cynic, i.e. doglike), who pursued non-attachment or self-sufficiency by a drastic attack on convention, and by renouncing possessions, nation and social obligations, and choosing self-discipline and a simple life. Cynicism returned to prominence in the early Roman Empire.

CYNOSCEPHALAE, BATTLE OF First decisive Roman victory over a major Greek army, fought in Thessaly in 197 BC against **Philip V of Macedon**, who commanded 25,000 troops.

CYPRIAN, ST (c.200-58) Early Christian theologian. He practised law in Carthage, and was converted to **Christianity** c.246. Elected Bishop of Carthage, c.248, in 250 he fled from Roman persecution, but regained his authority on his return the following year. He was exiled in 257 in a new persecution under Emperor **Valerian**. After attempting to return, he was tried and executed – Africa's first martyr-bishop.

CYRIL (826-69) and METHODIUS (816-85) Brother saints, known as 'the apostles of the Slavs'. They worked to convert the **Khazars**, northeast of the Black Sea; sent by Byzantine Emperor Michael III into Greater Moravia, 863. They translated the scriptures into the language later known as Old Church Slavonic, or Old Bulgarian. The 'Cyrillic' alphabet, used today in most Slavonic countries, is named after St Cyril.

CYRUS II, THE GREAT (d.529 BC) Known as 'the Elder' or 'Cyrus the King' in the Old Testament. Founder of the Persian **Achaemenid** Empire. Originally a vassal king to the **Medes** in Anshan (Fars province), 559 BC, he rebelled. After capturing the Median capital Ecbatana in 550, he conquered and in most cases liberated Babylonia, Assyria, Lydia, Syria and Palestine. He ordered the rebuilding of the Temple in Jerusalem.

DALHOUSIE, JAMES ANDREW BROUN-RAMSEY, 1st Marquis (1812-60) British colonial administrator. He was appointed the youngest-ever Governor-General of India in 1847; during his nine-year term he annexed vast territories, including the Punjab and Lower Burma, built railways, roads and bridges, installed a telegraph and postal system, opened the Ganges Canal, acted against thuggee (murder and robbery), dacoity (armed robbery) and the slave trade, and opened the Indian Civil Service to native Indians.

DANEGELD Tax levied in Anglo-Saxon England by King **Æthelred II** (978-1016) to finance the buying-off of Danish invaders; it was preserved as a revenue-raising device by the Anglo-Norman kings who last made use of it in 1162. The name itself is Norman, replacing the earlier, Old English *gafol* (tribute).

DANELAW Region of eastern England, north and east of a line from the Dee to the Tees rivers, governed in the 9th and 10th centuries under the Danish legal code. Some of its legal and social elements survived the **Norman Conquest**, gradually dying out in the course of the 12th century.

DANTE ALIGHIERI (1265-1321) Italian poet, born in Florence. He was sentenced to death in 1301 on political charges, but escaped; the remainder of his life was spent in exile. His greatest work, the *Commedia* (written c.1308-20, known since the 16th century as the *Divina Commedia*), is the earliest masterpiece written in Italian. It traces an imaginary journey through Hell, Purgatory and Heaven, and symbolically describes the progress of the soul from sin to purification.

DANTON, GEORGES-JACQUES (1759-94) French revolutionary who helped to found the Cordeliers Club, 1790; as Minister of Justice, 1792, he organized the defence of France against the Prussians. He was a member of the Committee of Public Safety 1793, but was overthrown by his rival, **Robespierre**, and guillotined.

DARBY Family of English iron-masters whose enterprise helped to create the Industrial Revolution. Abraham Darby I (c.1678-1717) was the first man to smelt iron ore successfully with coke instead of charcoal. His son, Abraham II, built over a hundred cylinders for the **Newcomen** steam engine. His grandson Abraham III built the world's first iron bridge, over the Severn at Coalbrookedale, 1779, and the first railway locomotive with a high-pressure boiler (for Richard Trevithick, 1802). The new smelting process had a slow start, but in the second half of the 18th century developed rapidly, leading to a great increase in the output of pig-iron and of cast-iron goods.

DARIUS I (c.550-486 BC) King of ancient Persia (reigned 522-486 BC). Son of Hystaspes, satrap of Parthia and Hyrcania; he extended Persian control in Egypt and western India; invaded Scythia across the Bosporus, 513. His attack on Greece was defeated at **Marathon**, 490; he died while preparing a second Greek expedition.

DAVID (died c.972) King of the Israelites, son of Jesse. Reared as a shepherd boy, he slew the giant Goliath, champion of the Philistines. He was disaffected from Saul, king of Israel, but was accepted as king after Saul's death; he established his capital at Jerusalem. Traditionally believed to have composed many of the Biblical Psalms. Christian tradition claims that **Jesus** was among his descendants, as a member of the House of David, from which, according to Jewish belief, the Messiah must spring.

DAVIS, JOHN (c.1550-1605) English explorer, who in 1585 made the first of three unsuccessful attempts to find a Northwest Passage through the Canadian Arctic; detailed in his later treatise, *The World's Hydrographical Description*, 1595. He fought against Spanish Armada, 1588; discovered the Falkland Islands, 1592; sailed with Walter Raleigh to Cádiz and the Azores, 1596-7. He was killed by Japanese pirates on the last of three voyages to the East Indies.

DELIAN LEAGUE Confederation of ancient Greek states, with its headquarters on the sacred island of Delos, originally created under the leadership of Athens in 478 BC to oppose **Achaemenid** Persia. Initially successful; however, freedom to secede was not permitted. In 454 BC the treasury was transferred to Athens, and the League became effectively an Athenian empire.

DEMOSTHENES (384-322 BC) Ancient Greek statesman and orator. He led the democratic faction in Athens; engaged in bitter political rivalry with his fellow-orator Aeschines; roused the Athenians to oppose both **Philip of Macedon** and **Alexander the Great**. He died by self-administered poison.

DENG XIAOPING (1904-) Chinese statesman. In 1924 he joined the Chinese Communist Party. Following the split between nationalists and communists (1927) he worked for the central committee in Shanghai. He participated in the 'long march' led by **Mao Tse Tung** (1934-5), served in the Red Army against the Japanese and nationalists and was elected to the central committee after the establishment of the People's Republic of China (1949). Falling from power during the Cultural Revolution (1966-9), he was reinstated as vice-premier (1973), only to be removed again in 1976. In 1977 he returned as the dominant political figure, introducing free market policies in agricultural and industrial sectors and promoting cultural and scientific exchanges with Western powers.

DENIKIN, ANTON IVANOVICH (1872-1947) Russian general. After the revolution in 1917 he joined the anti-Bolshevik armies in south Russia. Promoted to commander in 1918, he led an unsuccessful advance on Moscow in 1919 and in 1920 resigned and went into exile.

DE THAM (c.1860-1913) Vietnamese freedom fighter. He joined a local pirate band and started organizing formidable attacks on the French colonists. As 'the tiger of Yen Tri' he built up a large guerrilla army; the great-uncle of Ho Chi Minh was a member. He attacked the French railway, 1894, and temporarily ran Yen Tri district as an autonomous empire. In 1906-07 he linked with the other main anti-French group under **Phan Boi Chau**. Implicated in the abortive 'Hanoi Poison Plot' in 1908, he was later assassinated.

DIARMAT, MAC MAEL (1010-71) King of Leinster, Ireland, between 1040 and 1071. He extended his authority over much of the Scandinavian kingdom of Dublin (1071) and planned to make himself High King, but death intervened and Ireland disintegrated into warring sub-kingdoms until the Norman invasion of 1170.

DÍAZ, PORFIRIO (1830-1915) Dictatorial President of Mexico. He joined the army fighting against the United States (1846-8), in the War of the Reform (1857-60), and in opposition to the French (1862-7). Involved in unsuccessful revolts in 1871 and 1876, he returned later in 1876 from the US and defeated the government at the battle of Tecoac. Elected President in 1877, he gradually consolidated power; he was re-elected in 1884 and effectively ruled the country until 1910, modernizing its economy at great social cost. The military supporters of **Madero** forced him to resign in 1911. He died in exile in Paris.

DIESEL, RUDOLF (1858-1913) Inventor of the heavy oil internal combustion engine bearing his name. Trained at Technische Hochschule, Munich; worked two years at the Swiss Sulzer Machine Works, and then in Paris at Linde Refrigeration Enterprises. He started work on his engine in 1885, making his first working model in 1893.

DENSHAWAI INCIDENT Anti-British incident in Egypt in 1906. British officers shooting pigeons near a village in the Delta became involved in a fight with peasants who owned the pigeons; one officer died of sunstroke. Savage punishment of villagers provoked strong demonstrations against the British.

DIOCLETIAN (245-316) Roman emperor, born Aurelius Valerius Diocletianus, in Dalmatia. Acclaimed by his soldiers as emperor in 284, at a time of deep economic, political and military trouble, he took sole control of affairs in 285 and forced through an immense programme of legal, fiscal and administrative reform, restoring much of Rome's former strength. He abdicated in 305.

DIODOTUS I Founder of the ancient Greek kingdom of Bactria, originally subject to the **Seleucid** kings, Antiochus I and II. He rebelled and made himself king (250-230); he was succeeded by his son, Diodotus II Soter.

DISRAELI, BENJAMIN (1804-81) 1st Earl of Beaconsfield, statesman, novelist and twice British Prime Minister; born of a Jewish family but baptized as a Christian. He first stood for Parliament as a radical, but was elected as Conservative MP in 1837. Quarrelled with Sir Robert **Peel** over the repeal of the Corn Laws, 1846, and emerged as a leader of the rump of the Conservative Party. He succeeded Lord Derby as Prime Minister for a few months in 1868 and became Prime Minister again, 1874-80. He incorporated concern for the Empire into the Conservative programme in his Crystal Palace speech of 1872 and saw a link between imperialism and social reform at home; his real concern was for India and the route to India. Represented Britain at the **Congress of Berlin** in 1878; his ministry was associated with a forward policy in Afghanistan and South Africa.

DOENITZ, KARL (1891-1981) German naval commander and briefly head of state. In the First World War he served as a submarine officer. After the succession of **Hitler** he supervized the clandestine construction of a new U-boat fleet; he was appointed commander of submarine forces in 1936, head of the German navy in 1943 and head of the northern military and civil command in 1945. Named in Hitler's political testament as the next President of the Reich, he assumed control of the government for a few days after Hitler's suicide on 2 May 1945. Sentenced to ten years' imprisonment as a Nazi war criminal in 1946, he was released in 1956.

DOLLFUSS, ENGELBERT (1892-1934) Chancellor of Austria, 1932-4, who effectively made himself dictator until he was assassinated by Austrian Nazis.

DOMINICANS *see* **Friars**

DOMITIAN (AD 51-96) Roman emperor, born Titus Flavius Domitianus, son of Emperor **Vespasian**; succeeded his brother, **Titus**, in AD 81. He is remembered for his financial rapacity and the reign of terror (particularly 93-6) waged against his critics in the Senate; he was murdered by conspirators, including his wife, Domitia Longina.

DONATUS (d. c.355) Leader of the Donatists, a North African Christian group named after him, who broke with the Catholic Church in 312 after a controversy over the election of Caecilian as Bishop of Carthage; Donatus, appealing against the appointment, was over-ruled by a council of bishops, 313, by another at Arles, 314, and finally by Emperor **Constantine**, 316. The dissidents were persecuted, 317-21, then reluctantly tolerated; they continued to gain strength (perhaps through African nationalist feeling). In 347 Donatus was exiled to Gaul, where he died. The movement continued but, thanks to the teachings of St Augustine, and to state persecution, it had disappeared by c.700.

DORIANS Last of the Hellenic invaders to press into Greece from the north, c.1100 BC, perhaps from Epirus and southwest Macedonia, traditionally via Doria in central Greece. They recognized three 'tribes', the Hylleis, perhaps coming down the east, the Dymanes down the west, and the Pamphyloi covering minor groupings. They spread through the Peloponnese and to the islands of Cythera, Melos, Thera, Crete, Rhodes, Cos and into southern Anatolia. Many unresolved questions about them continue to challenge archaeologists.

DOUGLAS, STEPHEN ARNOLD (1813-61) United States Senator. He was elected to Congress in 1843 and to the Senate in 1846. He strongly supported 'popular sovereignty' (local option) on the question of slavery. In 1858 he engaged in a series of highly-publicized debates with **Abraham Lincoln**, to whom he lost in the presidential election. He condemned secession on the outbreak of the Civil War.

DRAKE, SIR FRANCIS (c.1540-96) English seaman who led buccaneering expeditions to west Africa and the Spanish West Indies, 1566-75, 1585-6 and 1595-6. He circumnavigated the globe in his ship the *Golden Hind*, 1577-80; raided the Spanish fleet in Cádiz, 1587, and fought against the Spanish Armada, 1588.

DRAVIDIAN Group of seven major and many minor languages, including Tamil, Telugu, Kanarese, Malayalam, Gondi and Tulu, spoken mainly by some 110 million people in southern India (also known collectively as Dravidians); characteristically these are darker, stockier, longer-headed and flatter-faced than the Indic or Aryan races of northern India.

DRUID Member of a pre-Christian religious order in Celtic areas of Britain, Ireland and Gaul. It has been retained as a name for officers in the modern Welsh Gorsedd.

DUAL MONARCHY OF AUSTRIA-HUNGARY Political system, 1867-1918, established by the Compromise of 1867 which granted a large measure of autonomy to the Hungarian lands of the former Austrian Empire.

DULLES, JOHN FOSTER (1888-1959) US lawyer and statesman. He began legal practice in 1911; became counsel to the US commission to negotiate peace after the First World War, 1918-19, and to other government bodies. He was special adviser to the Secretary of State, 1945-51, and filled that post himself, 1953-9. He was associated with a vigorously anti-Communist US foreign policy.

DUMA Lower house of the Russian parliament, established by Tsar **Nicholas II** in 1905; on the collapse of tsarism in February 1917 leading Duma politicians formed the Provisional Government.

DUPLEIX, JOSEPH FRANÇOIS (1697-1763) French administrator, Governor-General of Chandernagore 1731-41, and of Pondicherry 1741-54. His expansionist ambitions in southern India were checked by **Robert Clive**, 1751-2; he was recalled in 1754.

DUTCH EAST INDIA COMPANY (Vereenigde Oostindische Compagnie, VOC) Powerful trading concern set up in 1602 to protect Dutch merchants in the Indian Ocean and to help finance the war of independence with Spain. Under able governors-general, such as Jan Pieterszoon Coen, 1618-23, and Anthony van Diemen, 1636-45, the company effectively drove both British and Portuguese out of the East Indies, and established Batavia (now Jakarta) as its base for conquering the islands. Growing corruption and debt led to the company's dissolution in 1799.

DUY TAN (1888-1945) Emperor of Annam, the son of Emperor Thanh Thai, whom he succeeded in 1907. His reign was a period of revolt against the French colonial power; after one revolt, which sought to make him a real emperor, he was deposed and exiled to Réunion in 1916. Later he served with the Free French forces in the Second World War; he died in an air crash.

EADGAR (c.943-75) English king; younger son of Edmund I. He became king of Mercia and Danelaw, 957, on the deposition of his brother Eadwig, and in 959 succeeded to the throne of West Saxons and effectively all England. He reformed the Church in England.

EAM (Initials in Greek for National Liberation Front). One of the Greek resistance movements, formed in 1941 to fight the German and Italian armies of occupation. By 1944, when the Germans evacuated, it controlled two-thirds of the country. It rejected Allied orders to disarm in December 1944, but accepted the Varkiza Peace Agreement, 1945; it participated in large-scale civil war, 1946-9.

EAST INDIA COMPANY *see* **English East India Company** and **Dutch East India Company**.

EC Founded in 1957 with the Treaty of Rome, which was signed by six nations and called originally the European Economic Community, the European Community was formed to promote economic and political co-operation as part of the process of post-war reconstruction. From 1986 it had 12 member nations. Despite undoubted benefits (between 1958 and 1962 trade between member states increased by 130 per cent) economic co-operation brought many problems – for example, the Common Agricultural Policy, developed to ensure a fair standard for farmers, led to massive over-production and higher prices. In 1992 Europe became in theory a single market, and the removal of physical, technical and financial barriers began. The **Maastricht Treaty** (1991) called for closer political union among EC member states.

EDEN, Anthony, 1st Earl of Avon (1897-1977) British statesman and Foreign Secretary, 1935-8, 1940-5 and 1951-5. He supported the **League of Nations** in the 1930s and was **Churchill**'s deputy for a decade before succeeding him as prime minister (1955-7). Eden's determination to confront President **Nasser** of Egypt resulted in the **Suez** Crisis of 1956 which, added to poor health, led to his resignation.

EDEN TREATY Trade agreement between Britain and France, negotiated in 1786-7 by William Eden, 1st Baron Auckland (1744-1814), which gave the British free access to French markets. By encouraging the export of French corn to Britain, the treaty contributed to popular tension during the food crisis preceding the French Revolution.

EDWARD THE CONFESSOR (c.1003-65) King of England, son of **Æthelred II** the Unready. Exiled after Æthelred's death (1016) when the Danes again seized power in England, he returned from Normandy, 1041, and succeeded to the throne of his half-brother, Harthacnut, 1042; however, the main power in the kingdom remained first with Godwin, Earl of the West Saxons, then with his son, Harold, named as king on Edward's death. Claims that Edward had previously promised the throne to Duke William of Normandy led to the **Norman Conquest** (1066).

EDWARD I (1239-1307) King of England; the son of Henry III. He led the royal troops to victory in the Barons' War (1264-6); succeeded to the throne, 1272; conquered Wales (1277-83); established suzerainty over Scotland and defeated the Scottish revolt under **William Wallace**, 1298. His consistent utilization of Parliament in wide-ranging legislation consolidated its institutional position. He died on an expedition to suppress the revolt of **Robert Bruce** of Scotland.

EDWARD II (1284-1327) King of England, son of **Edward I**, whom he succeeded in 1307. He ruled, weakly and incompetently, through favourites such as Piers Gaveston (murdered 1312) and the Despensers (executed 1326). He was heavily defeated by the Scots at Bannockburn, 1314, and strongly opposed by the English barons, who in 1311 tried to subject him to control by a committee of 'lords ordainers'. He was deposed and put to death when his queen, Isabella, invaded from France with her ally, Roger Mortimer.

EDWARD III (1312-77) King of England, son of **Edward II**, succeeding in 1327. By 1330 he had freed himself from subjection to his mother, Isabella, and her ally, Roger Mortimer. Defeated the Scots, 1333 and 1346; at the start of the **Hundred Years' War** he defeated the French fleet at Sluys, 1340, and invaded France. His notable victories at Crécy, 1346, and Calais, 1347, with that of his son at Poitiers, 1356, were consolidated by the Peace of Brétigny in 1360. He resumed war in 1369, and by 1375 had lost all his previous gains except Calais, Bordeaux, Bayonne and Brest.

EIGHT TRIGRAMS Secret north Chinese sect, part-religious, part-political. It flourished, particularly in Chihli, Shantung and Honan, in the 19th century, and was involved in the palace revolution in Peking in 1814.

EISENHOWER, DWIGHT DAVID (1890-1969) 34th President of the United States, 1953-61. He was commander of the American forces in Europe, and of the Allies in North Africa, 1942; directed the invasions of Sicily and Italy, 1943; became Supreme Allied Commander, 1943-5, and Commander, NATO land forces, 1950-2. Under his presidency, the Korean War was ended, 1953, **SEATO** formed, and federal troops were ordered (1957) to enforce racial desegregation of US schools at Little Rock, Arkansas.

EISNER, KURT (1867-1919) German socialist leader. In 1914 he opposed German aid to Austria-Hungary, and became leader of the pacifist Independent Social Democratic Party in 1917; he was arrested as a strike-leader the following year. After his release he organized the overthrow of the Bavarian monarchy and proclaimed an independent Bavarian republic. He was assassinated by a right-wing student.

ELCANO, JUAN SEBASTIÁN DE (d.1526) First captain to make a complete circumnavigation of the earth. A Basque navigator, he sailed in 1519 as master of the *Concepción* under **Magellan**; after Magellan's death he took command of the three remaining ships and returned to Spain, 1522, with one ship, the *Victoria*. Henceforth his family coat-of-arms carried a globe and the motto *Primus circumdedisti me* ('You were the first to circle me').

ELECTOR Historically, one of the small group of princes who, by right of heredity or office, were qualified to elect the Holy Roman Emperor. Originally, in the 13th century, there were six; from 1356 to 1623 there were seven - the archbishops of Mainz, Trier and Cologne, the King of Bohemia, the Count Palatine of the Rhine, the dukes of Saxony and the Margrave of Brandenburg. By 1806, when the Empire ended, there were ten.

ELIZABETH I (1533-1603) Queen of England. The daughter of **Henry VIII** and Anne Boleyn, she succeeded to the throne in 1558. Her re-establishment of a Church of England independent of Rome, 1559, led to her excommunication by Pope Pius V in 1571. She survived a Spanish attempt to put the sentence into effect (Spanish Armada, 1588). She made English authority effective in Ireland (1601).

ELLMAN, JOHN English 18th century sheep-breeder, farming at Glynde, Surrey, who in about 1780 began developing short wool varieties, a process which eventually transformed the Southdown sheep from a light, long-legged animal into one solid, compact and equally good for mutton and for wool.

ENCYCLOPEDISTS Group of French writers, scientists and philosophers connected with the influential *Encyclopédie ou dictionnaire raisonné des sciences, des arts et des métiers*, edited 1751-72 by Denis Diderot (1713-84) assisted by d'Alembert (1717-83); the work and its contributors powerfully expressed the new spirit of 18th century rationalism.

ENGLISH EAST INDIA COMPANY Founded in 1600 to trade with the East Indies, but excluded by the Dutch after the Amboina Massacre in 1623. The company negotiated concessions in Mughal India and won control of Bengal in 1757, but its political activities were curtailed by the Regulating Act of 1773 and the India Act of 1784. Its commercial monopoly with India was broken in 1813, and that with China in 1833. It ceased to be the British government's Indian agency after the Mutiny in 1857; its legal existence ended in 1873.

ENTREPÔT Commercial centre, specializing in the handling, storage, transfer and dispatch of goods.

EON OF STEILA (d.1148) Christian heretic. He preached opposition to the wealth and organization of the Roman Catholic Church, gaining followers in Brittany and Gascony before being imprisoned by Pope **Eugenius III** at the Synod of Rheims. He died in prison; his followers, such as the **Henricians** and **Petrobrusians**, faded away.

EPICUREANS Followers of the Greek philosopher Epicurus (341-271 BC). To Epicurus happiness ('pleasure') was all; it consisted in freedom from disturbance. So the wise men free themselves from fear, through scientific understanding, and from desire, by 'doing without'. The structure of the universe is atomic; death is annihilation; gods exist but do not intervene in human affairs. The Epicureans fostered friendship and discouraged ambition. The system was expounded by the Roman poet Lucretius (c.94-55 BC).

EPIRUS, DESPOTATE OF Byzantine principality in southern Albania and northwest Greece, organized as a rival principality during the Western occupation of Constantinople after the Fourth Crusade. Founded in 1204 by Michael Angelus Ducas, it was continually attacked by Nicaea, Bulgaria and later, after the restoration of Michael VIII Palaeologus, by Byzantium itself. In the 13th century it was a pre-Renaissance centre for classical studies; it was re-annexed to Byzantium in 1337.

EPISCOPALIAN Member of the Protestant Episcopal Church of Scotland and the United States, a believer in the principle that supreme authority in the Church lies with the bishops assembled in council, rather than with a single head.

ERATOSTHENES (c.276-c.194 BC) The first systematic geographer. He directed the Library at Alexandria, c.255 BC; wrote on astronomy, ethics and the theatre; compiled a calendar, showing leap years, and a chronology of events since the Siege of Troy; calculated the earth's circumference with remarkable accuracy. He was known as Beta, because he was good without being supreme in so many fields. He is said to have starved himself to death after going blind.

ERIC XIV (1533-77) King of Sweden, 1560-8, the son of **Gustavus I Vasa**. He seized strategic territory in Estonia, prompting Denmark and Norway to initiate the Seven Years' War of the North. He was accused of insanity and deposed by his half-brothers, 1568, after failing to win the war and after defying the Swedish nobility in order to make his commoner mistress, Karin Mansdotter, queen. He died in prison.

ERIK BLOODAXE (d.954) King of Norway and of York in the 10th century, named to commemorate his murder of seven of his eight brothers. The son of **Harald Finehair**, he was expelled from Norway, 934; by 948 he was king of York and ruled there until expelled in 954. He was killed at Stainmore.

ESKIMOS People of the western Arctic region, thinly spread in small settlements across the northern coasts of North America, from Alaska to Greenland. Of closely related physical type, language and culture, these groups, totalling some 50,000 people, share a common adaptation to the harsh living and hunting conditions of the Arctic tundra.

ESSENE Member of an ancient Jewish sect founded between the 2nd century BC and 2nd century AD. It was characterized by stern asceticism, withdrawal, communistic life, ceremonial purity, a rigorous novitiate lasting three years, identification of Yahweh with the Sun, and a mystic belief in immortality. The Dead Sea Scrolls, found in the Qumran (1947-1956), probably belonged to an Essene community; attempts to link **Jesus** to them are implausible.

ESTE Italian family which presided over an unusually brilliant court, ruling as princes in

Ferrara from the 13th century until 1598, and as dukes in Reggio and Modena from 1288 until the mid-19th century. The dynasty was founded by the margrave Albert Azzo II (d.1097); their connection with Ferrara ended when Clement VIII imposed direct papal rule.

ETRUSCANS A people in Italy inhabiting Etruria, the land between the rivers Tiber and Arno, west and south of the Apennine hills. Their origins are unknown, but they possibly came from Asia Minor. From 800 BC to their decline in the 5th century BC they developed an elaborate urban civilization, particularly notable for its tombs; they were ultimately absorbed by Rome. The Etruscan language is still largely undeciphered.

EUGENIUS III (d.1153) The first Cistercian Pope (1145-53), a pupil of **St Bernard**, whose *De Consideratione* presented his views on how the Pope should lead the Church. Forced to leave Rome because of conflict with the city and with **Arnold of Brescia**, he was finally re-established by the Treaty of Constance (1153) with **Frederick I Barbarossa**.

EURIPIDES (480-406 BC) Last of the three great Athenian tragic dramatists; 19 of his 92 plays survive, distinguished by their concentration on real human problems expressed in contemporary language. He left Athens in 408, moved to Thessaly and then Macedon, where he wrote *The Bacchae*; he died at the court of King Archelaus.

EUROPEAN COMMUNITY *see* **EC**

EUSEBIUS (c.265-340) Bishop of Caesarea. His *History of the Church* is the first scholarly work on the early institutions of Christianity.

EXARCHATE Under the Byzantine and the Holy Roman Empires, it referred to the governorship of a distant province; in the eastern Catholic Church, to the area of responsibility of certain high-ranking ecclesiastics known as exarchs (approximate equivalents of patriarchs or archbishops).

FAIRBAIRN, SIR WILLIAM (1789-1874) Victorian authority on factory design who wrote the classic treatise, *Mills and Millwork*. A builder of ships and bridges, he constructed many iron ships at Millwall, London, between 1835 and 1849, and also invented the rectangular tube used on **Robert Stephenson**'s Menai Bridge.

FANG CHIH-MIN (1900-1935) Early leader of the Chinese Communist Party. He became prominent in Communist and **Kuomintang** affairs in Kiangsi during the 1920s; helped to found the Communist base in northeast Kiangsi, which developed into the Fukien-Chekiang-Kiangsi Soviet in the early 1930s. He led the 10th Army Corps when encircled by the Nationalist Army in mid-1934, and the following year was captured and executed by the Nationalists.

FAROUK I (1920-65) King of Egypt. The son of Fuad I, he succeeded to the throne in 1936. He was involved in the long struggle for power with the nationalist party, the **Wafd**; during the Second World War Britain, then in occupation of Egypt, forced him to appoint a Wafdist government. He was deposed and exiled after the military *coup d'état* organized by **Neguib** and **Nasser**.

FARROUPILHA REVOLUTION Provincial uprising in Rio Grande do Sul, southern Brazil; it flared intermittently, 1835-45, until finally suppressed by the armies of Pedro II under the Duque de Caxias. The name means 'rags', alluding to the rebels' lack of uniforms.

FASCISM Originally the anti-democratic and anti-parliamentarian ideology adopted by the Italian counter-revolutionary movement led by **Mussolini**; characterized by advocacy of the corporate, one-party state, to which all aspects of life are subordinated. It was later extended to describe any extreme right-wing political creed that combines absolute obedience to the leader with a willingness to use brute force to gain power and suppress opposition.

FATIMA (c.616-33) Mohammed's daughter, and first wife of **Ali**. The imams recognized by the **Shias** are her descendants, and Shias have a special reverence for her; her descendants led a moderate wing of the Shias, the second major division of Islam, and some of those claiming descent from her founded the **Fatimid** dynasty.

FATIMIDS North African dynasty claiming descent from **Fatima**, **Mohammed**'s daughter, founded in 908 in Tunisia by the imam, Ubaidallah. Muizz, the fourth Fatimid caliph, conquered Egypt and founded Cairo, 969. In the 11th century, they supplanted the **Abbasids** as the most powerful rulers in Islam, but were finally abolished by **Saladin** (1171).

FEDERALISTS Name, first used in 1787, to denote the supporters of the newly-written United States' Constitution; and later for a conservative party which was hostile to the Revolution in France, favourable to an alliance with Great Britain and generally supportive of central authority in America. From 1791 to 1801 Federalists controlled the national government, organized the new nation's administrative and tax machinery, and formulated a policy of neutrality in foreign affairs. In 1801 they were displaced by an opposition group led by **Thomas Jefferson**, and never again held national office.

FEITORIA Fortified factory or trading post, established by the Portuguese during their period of maritime dominance.

FENG YÜ-HSIANG (1882-1948) Chinese warlord, nicknamed 'the Christian general'. At first an officer in the Hwai army under **Yüan Shih-k'ai**, he served in the Peiyang army after the 1911 revolution. From 1918 he created a private army, controlling a large part of northwest China, 1912-20; he was involved in a series of *coups d'état* and civil wars, 1920-8, but never acquired a permanent territorial base. To relieve chronic financial pressures he sought the help of Russia, but in 1929 was forced to relinquish control of his troops to **Chiang Kai-shek**. His army, joined by **Yen Hsi-shan**, attempted to form a northern coalition against Chiang, and in 1929-30 they fought a bitter war. When it ended he joined the Nationalist government, but never again had any real power.

FENLAND REVOLT Prolonged local opposition, 1632-8, to government-sponsored measures to drain and enrich the fens of eastern England, thus depriving the local population of common rights. **Oliver Cromwell** was one of the leaders of the revolt.

FERDINAND III (c.1199-1252) Saint and king of Castile (1217-52) and León (1230-52). He united the crowns of Castile and León, and completed the conquest of all Moorish dominions in Spain except **Granada**.

FERDINAND OF ARAGON (1452-1516) The son of John II of Aragon. His marriage in 1469 to Isabella of Castile united the two principal kingdoms in the Iberian peninsula. The kingdom of Granada was annexed by Castile in 1492, while in 1504 Ferdinand conquered Naples which remained under Spanish control until 1713. In 1512 he acquired Navarre. It was during the joint rule of Ferdinand and Isabella that the **Inquisition** was established in Castile in 1478, **Columbus's** first voyage to the new world was supported, and the **Jews** were expelled from Castile in 1492.

FEUDALISM Political system of medieval Europe, based on the mutual obligations of vassal and superior, linked by the granting of land (the feud, or fee) in return for certain services. The feudal lord normally had rights of jurisdiction over his tenants, and held a feudal court. Similar systems (sometimes also termed 'feudal' by analogy) are found in other parts of the world (e.g. early China and Japan) at a similar stage of development.

FIANNA FÁIL Irish political party; founded in 1926 by **de Valera** to espouse republican nationalism and erase all English influence from Irish public life.

FIELDEN, JOSHUA (d.1811) Cotton industry pioneer. In 1780 he was still a peasant farmer, operating two or three weaving looms; by 1800 he owned a five-storey cotton mill in Todmorden, Yorkshire. After his death his sons developed the business – Fielden Brothers, Waterside Mills – into one of the largest cotton mills in Britain.

FIGUERES FERRER, JOSÉ (1906-90) Costa Rican political leader. He worked as a coffee planter and rope-maker; exiled to Mexico 1942-4, he became Junta President of the Republic, 1948, but resigned in 1949; he was President of Costa Rica 1953-8 and 1970-4.

FISSIRAGA Prominent family of medieval Lodi, Italy. Supporters of the **Guelph** (anti-imperial) party, they rose to prominence in the 1280s; in 1311 their leader, Antonio Fissiraga, was captured by the **Visconti** of Milan and died in prison (1327).

FIUME INCIDENT Unsuccessful attempt to seize the Adriatic sea port in September 1919, by a private Italian army, led by the poet Gabriele d'Annunzio, to forestall its award to Yugoslavia at the Paris Peace Conference.

FIXED EXCHANGE RATES Regime under which the value of one currency bears a constant relationship to that of another: e.g. the pound sterling in the period 1949-67, when it was always worth US $2.80. Such relations linked most major currencies in the period 1947-71, under the so-called Bretton Woods System, but that then gave place to a period of mainly 'floating' rates.

FLAMININUS (c.227-174 BC) Principal Roman general and statesman during the period when Greece became a Roman protectorate. He defeated **Philip V of Macedon** at **Cynoscephalae** in 197 BC; declared that all Greeks should be free and governed by their own laws in 196; and supported Greek autonomy in Asia Minor during Rome's wars with the **Seleucids**.

FLAVIANS Dynasty ruling the Roman Empire from AD 69 to 96. It was founded by **Vespasian** (69-79) and continued by his sons, **Titus** (79-81) and **Domitian** (81-96).

FLINDERS, MATTHEW (1774-1814) Maritime explorer of Australia, born in Lincolnshire, England. He entered the Royal Navy in 1789, from 1795 to 1799 he charted much of Australia's east coast between Fraser Island and Bass Strait, and circumnavigated Tasmania; in 1801-2, as commander of the *Investigator*, he surveyed the whole southern coast, and in 1802-3 circled the entire continent. He was interned by the French in Mauritius, 1803-10; his *Voyage to Terra Australis* was finally published about the time of his death.

FOCH, FERDINAND (1851-1929) French soldier, Marshal of France, a teacher of military history and author of many standard works. Appointed a general in 1907, he won distinction during the First World War in the first battle of the Marne, 1914, the first battle of Ypres, 1915, and the battle of the Somme, 1916. He was appointed as commander-in-chief of the French armies in 1917, and after the onset of the German offensive in spring 1918 was appointed to command all French, British and American forces.

FORREST, JOHN (1847-1918) 1st Baron Forrest, Australian explorer and statesman. He led several expeditions across Western Australia from 1869; became Surveyor-General of Western Australia, 1883-90 and its first premier, 1890-1901. He held Cabinet office in several ministries in the federal government of the new Commonwealth of Australia between 1901 and 1918.

FOURTEEN POINTS Programme put forward by United States President **Woodrow Wilson** in 1918 for a peace settlement following the First World War. Several of the Points related to the right of self-determination of peoples; although statesmen at the Peace Conference were thinking of the rights of the successor states of the Austro-Hungarian and Ottoman empires, the principle was noted by colonial peoples in Asia and Africa. The final proposal for a 'general association' to guarantee integrity of 'great and small states alike' led to the setting up of the **League of Nations**.

FRANCIS I (1494-1547) King of France; he succeeded his cousin, **Louis XII**, in 1515. In 1520 he attempted unsuccessfully to win the support of the English king, **Henry VIII**, for his struggles with the **Habsburgs**; he pursued his rivalry alone in a series of Italian wars (1521-5, 1527-9, 1536-7, 1542-4), but finally abandoned Italian claims in 1544. He was a noted patron of Renaissance art.

FRANCIS II (1768-1835) The last Holy Roman Emperor. The son of Leopold II, he succeeded to the imperial title in 1792 and held it until dissolution of the Empire by **Napoleon** in 1806. He continued to reign as the first Emperor of Austria, under the title Francis I; through his chancellor, **Metternich**, he confirmed Austria's position as a leading European power.

FRANCISCANS *see* **Friars**

FRANCO, FRANCISCO (1892-1975) Spanish dictator. A general in the Spanish army, he organized the revolt in Morocco in 1936 which precipitated the Spanish Civil War of 1936-9, from which he emerged as head of state ('El Caudillo'). He was named regent for life in 1947. In 1969 he proposed that Prince Juan Carlos of Bourbon should ultimately take the throne, as indeed he did at Franco's death.

FRANCO-PRUSSIAN WAR Struggle provoked by rivalry between France and the growing power of Prussia, reaching a head over the candidacy of Leopold of Hohenzollern for the throne of Spain. Prussian armies under von Moltke invaded France and quickly won victories at Wörth, Gravelotte, Strasbourg, Sedan and Metz between August and October 1870. **Napoleon III** abdicated, and the Third French Republic was declared on 4 September 1870; Paris, under siege for four months, surrendered on 28 January 1871. Under the Treaty of Frankfurt (May 1871) France ceded Alsace and East Lorraine to the newly-established German Empire, and agreed to pay an indemnity of 5 billion francs.

FRANKS Germanic peoples who dominated the area of present-day France and western Germany after the collapse of the West Roman Empire. Under **Clovis** (481-511) and his **Merovingian** and **Carolingian** successors they established the most powerful Christian kingdom in western Europe. Since the disintegration of their empire in the 9th century the name has survived in France and Franconia. In the Middle East, the Crusaders were generally referred to as Franks, and the word came into several oriental languages to mean 'European'.

FRANZ FERDINAND (1863-1914) Archduke of Austria, nephew of, and from 1896 heir to, the Emperor Franz Joseph I (1830-1916). He was assassinated on 28 June 1914 at Sarajevo, an incident which provoked the Austrian ultimatum to Serbia that led directly to the outbreak of the First World War.

FREDERICK THE GREAT (1712-86) King of Prussia, son of **Frederick William I**, whom he succeeded, as Frederick II, in 1740. He entered the War of the Austrian Succession, won the battle of Mollwitz, 1741, and acquired the economically valuable province of Silesia, which he retained through the **Seven Years' War** (1756-63). He annexed West Prussia in the First Partition of Poland, 1772; formed the Fürstenbund (League of German Princes), 1785. He patronized writers and artists, including Voltaire; wrote *L'Antimachiavel*, 1740, and *History of the House of Brandenburg*, 1751.

FREDERICK I BARBAROSSA (c.1123-90) King of Germany, 1152, emperor 1155; second of the **Hohenstaufen** dynasty. In 1154 he launched a campaign to restore royal rights in Italy; captured Milan, 1162, and Rome, 1166; supported the anti-pope against the powerful Pope **Alexander III**, but was defeated by the **Lombard League** (Legnano 1176): reached a *modus vivendi* with the papacy and Italian cities at the Peace of Venice (1177) and Peace of Constance (1183). He was drowned in Syria while leading the Third **Crusade**.

FREDERICK II (1194-1250) Last great **Hohenstaufen** ruler. He was elected German king in 1212, after civil war and disorder in Germany, Italy and Sicily following the early death of his father, **Henry VI**, in 1197. He left Germany for Italy in 1220 to concentrate his energies on restoring royal authority in Sicily (Constitution of Malfi, 1231); he was crowned emperor by Pope Honorius III in 1220, and led the Fifth Crusade, 1228-9, but his Italian ambitions brought him into conflict with Honorius' successors, Gregory IX and **Innocent IV**. He was excommunicated and deposed at the Council of Lyons (1245), and forced to make lasting concessions to German princes to win their support against the papacy and the Lombard cities. The conflict was continuing at the time of his death, and was only resolved when **Charles of Anjou** defeated Frederick's son and grandson at Benevento (1266) and Tagliacozzo (1268).

FREDERICK II OF PRUSSIA *see* **Frederick the Great**

FREDERICK AUGUSTUS I (1670-1733) Elector of Saxony (1694-1733) and, as Augustus II, King of Poland, 1697-1733. He succeeded as Elector of Lutheran Saxony in 1694, then became a Catholic in order to be elected king of Poland in 1697; elected by a minority of Polish nobles, he used his Saxon army to secure his coronation. He entered the **Great Northern War** and was defeated by **Charles XII** of Sweden (1702). Deposed in 1706 and his kingdom occupied until 1709 by Stanisław Leszczyński, a rival Polish king, he was restored at the Treaty of Stockholm, 1719. He was succeeded by **Frederick Augustus II**, his son (Augustus III of Poland).

FREDERICK AUGUSTUS II (1696-1763) Elector of Saxony (1733-63) and, as Augustus III, King of Poland (1735-63). The only legitimate son of **Frederick Augustus I** of Saxony. He married Maria Josepha, daughter of the Emperor Joseph I, in 1719. In 1733 he succeeded as Elector of Saxony, and in the same year drove his rival Stanisław I Leszczyński into exile and was elected King of Poland (as Augustus III) by a minority vote. He supported Austria against Prussia in the War of the Austrian Succession (1740-8) in 1742, and again in 1756 in the **Seven Years' War**. He failed to counter the growing influence of the Czartoryski and Poniatowski families.

FREDERICK WILLIAM (1620-88) Elector of Brandenburg, known as the Great Elector. He succeeded in 1640 and successfully reconstructed his domain after the ravages of the Thirty Years War; created a standing army after agreement with the Estates; fought France and Sweden, 1674; defeated the Swedes at Fehrbellin, 1675, and concluded the **Peace of Nijmegen**.

FREDERICK WILLIAM I (1688-1740) King of Prussia, son of Frederick I, and father of **Frederick the Great**. After succeeding to the throne in 1713, he reorganized the administration and economy to sustain an army of 83,000 men, and won most of western Pomerania from Sweden under the Treaty of Stockholm, 1720.

FREI, EDUARDO (1911-82) Chilean political leader, and a founder member, in 1935, of the National Falange, later renamed the Christian Democrat Party. He edited a daily newspaper, *El Tarapacá*, 1935-7. He held office as Minister of Public Works, and was President of Chile from 1964 until 1970, when the Christian Democrats were defeated by **Allende** in the presidential election.

FRÉMONT, JOHN CHARLES (1813-90) United States' explorer and mapmaker who headed expeditions to survey the Des Moines River (1841), the route west to Wyoming (1842), the mouth of the Columbia River (1843), and California (1845). He was the Republican Party's nominee for President of the United States, 1856; he was Governor of Arizona, 1878-83.

FRIARS During the first decade of the 13th century St Francis (1181-1226) and St Dominic (1170-1221) were independently moved to raise the standard of religious life in Europe by instructing the populace (particularly in the towns) through preaching and example, in order to counteract the growing menace of heresy. The Franciscans (Order of Friars Minor, or Grey Friars) were informally recognized by Pope **Innocent III** in 1209 and formally established in 1223; the Dominicans (Order of Preachers, or Black Friars) were formally established in 1216. The Franciscan St Bonaventura (1221-74) and the Dominican St Thomas Aquinas (1226-74) were among their most prominent early members. Friars took the monastic vows of poverty, chastity and obedience, but differed from monks in two main respects: their convents were bases for preaching tours, not places of permanent residence like monasteries, and they sought education at the newly-founded universities. Other 13th-century Orders of friars were the Austin Friars and the Carmelites.

FRISIANS Germanic people. They first entered the coastal provinces of western Germany and the Netherlands in prehistoric times, ousting the resident Celts; after the collapse of Rome, the territory was infiltrated by Angles and **Jutes** on their way to England. The Frisians were conquered and converted to Christianity by **Charlemagne**.

FROBISHER, SIR MARTIN (c.1535-94) Explorer of Canada's northeast coasts, who sailed in 1576 with three ships in search of a Northwest Passage to Asia; he reached Labrador and Baffin Island, but failed to find gold or establish a colony. He became vice-admiral to **Drake** in the West Indies, 1585, was prominent in fighting the Spanish Armada, and was mortally wounded fighting Spanish ships off the coast of France.

FRONDE Complex series of uprisings against the French government under **Mazarin** during the minority of **Louis XIV**. Leaders of the Paris *parlement* were imprisoned in 1648 after violent protests against taxation. They were freed by popular revolt in Paris, supported by a separate rebellion of the nobility in alliance with Spain, which escalated into open warfare. The Fronde disintegrated soon after the victory of the royal armies at Faubourg-St Antoine in 1652.

GADSDEN PURCHASE Sale to the United States of some 30,000 square miles (78,000 km²) of land along the Mexico-Arizona border, required by the US to provide a low pass through mountains for railway construction. The purchase was negotiated by US minister to Mexico James Gadsden in 1853 at a cost of $10 million.

GAIKWARS Powerful **Maratha** family which made its headquarters in the Baroda district of Gujarat, west-central India, from 1734 to 1947. In 1802 the British established a residency in Baroda to conduct relations between the **East India Company** and the Gaikwar princes.

GAISERIC (428-77) King of the **Vandals**, also known as Genseric. He transported his whole people, said to number 80,000, from Spain to North Africa in 429; sacked Carthage, 439, after defeating the joint armies of Rome's Eastern and

Western Empires, and declared independence. By sea he attacked, captured and looted Rome, 455; and fought off two major Roman expeditions (460 and 468).

GALLA Large ethnic group in Ethiopia. Cushitic-speaking camel nomads, in a series of invasions from their homelands in the southeast of the country they migrated north and east, and by the end of the 16th century had reached almost to Eritrea. Since then they have largely been assimilated into, and dominated by, the rival Amharic and Tigrean cultures.

GALLEON Powerful sailing ship developed in the 15th and 16th centuries for Mediterranean and ocean navigation. Larger than the galley, with a ratio of beam to length of 1 to 4 or 5, usually with two decks and four masts (two square-rigged and two lateen), it was heavily armed and used in particular by Spain in fleets across the Atlantic and in the annual voyage from Acapulco to Manila.

GALLIC WARS The military campaigns in which the Roman general, **Julius Caesar**, won control of Gaul. As described in his account, *De Bello Gallico*, the conquest took eight years, from 58 to 50 BC; in the first phase, 57-54 BC, Roman authority was fairly easily established, but suppression of a large-scale revolt in 53 BC, led by the Gallic chieftain, Vercingetorix, required all Caesar's skills.

GAMA, VASCO DA (1462-1524) First discoverer of a continuous sea route from Europe to India via the Cape of Good Hope. In 1497-9 he led a Portuguese expedition round Africa to India; a second voyage in 1502 established Portugal as controller of the Indian Ocean and a world power. He died shortly after his arrival to take up an appointment as the Portuguese viceroy in India.

GANDHI, INDIRA (1917-86) Indian Prime Minister and head of state, 1966-77 and 1980-6. The daughter of **Nehru**, she was elected to the premiership in 1966, and won national elections in 1967 and 1971; she led India in war against Pakistan, 1971. She declared a national emergency in 1975, after an adverse legal decision on her own election. Defeated in the elections of 1977, she was returned to office in 1980 as leader of the Congress I party. She was assassinated in 1986 by Sikh extremists.

GANDHI, MOHENDAS K (1869-1948) Indian independence leader. Born in a strict Hindu community, he studied law in England 1889-92, then worked in South Africa as a lawyer and subsequently as a leader of the civil rights movement of Indian settlers, 1893-1914. Entering politics in India in 1919, he turned the previously ineffectual Indian National Congress into a potent mass organization. He perfected the disruptive techniques of mass disobedience and non-violent non-cooperation; during protest against the Salt Tax (1930) 60,000 followers were imprisoned. Three major campaigns, in 1920-2, 1930-4 and 1940-2, played a major part in accelerating India's progress to Dominion status in 1947. He bitterly opposed partition, and worked incessantly to end the Hindu-Muslim riots and massacres accompanying the emergence of independent India and Pakistan. He was assassinated by a Hindu fanatic.

GARCÍA MORENO, GABRIEL (1821-75) Theocratic president of Ecuador, 1860-75. He based his regime on ruthless personal rule and forcible encouragement of the Roman Catholic Church. All education, welfare and much state policy were turned over to clerics; political opposition and alternative religions were suppressed. He encouraged agricultural and economic reform, and Ecuadorian nationalism. He was assassinated.

GARIBALDI, GIUSEPPE (1807-82) Italian patriot and member of **Mazzini**'s Young Italy movement. He was a guerrilla leader in South America, and a founder of independent Uruguay in her war against Argentina. He established himself as a national hero in 1849 as the defender of the Roman Republic against the French. In 1860 he led the expedition of 'The Thousand' in Sicily, and occupied Naples, thus ensuring the unification of Italy. He had led a victorious force against the Austrians in 1859, and repeated the operation in 1866, but was defeated by the French in his attack on Rome in 1867.

GAUGAMELA Battlefield near the River Tigris, scene of **Alexander the Great**'s most notable victory, in 331 BC, when, greatly outnumbered, his Macedonian cavalry and Thracian javelin-throwers routed the Persian armies of Darius III by brilliant tactics, and opened the way to Babylon and Susa for him.

GAULLE, CHARLES DE (1890-1970) French soldier and statesman. He escaped to London after the French surrender to Germany, 1940; organized the Free French forces and led the French government-in-exile from Algiers, 1943-4. He was first head of the post-war provisional government, 1944-6. In 1953 he withdrew from public life, but returned in 1958 to resolve the political crisis created by the civil war in Algeria; hostilities ceased in 1962. He established the Fifth Republic, becoming its first President, 1959 and presided over France's spectacular economic and political recovery. Resigned in 1969 after an adverse referendum vote on constitutional reform.

GEDYMIN (c.1275-1341) (or Giedymin) Grand Duke of Lithuania, ancestor of the **Jagiełło** dynasty. Came to power in 1316, ruling a vast pagan principality based on Vilna. He built the strongest army in eastern Europe to hold his empire in the east and south, while repelling the advances of the Knights of the **Teutonic Order** against the Prussians, who were one of his Lithuanian tribes.

GENERAL MOTORS America's largest industrial manufacturing corporation; in 1988 General Motors' worldwide sales of cars and trucks totalled 8.1 million units.

GENERAL PRIVILEGE Legal document, compiled in 1293, setting out limits of royal power in Aragon and Valencia. Approved, under protest, by King **Peter III** of Aragon, it was a source of acrimony between king and subjects until abolished in 1348 by Peter IV, the Ceremonious, after defeating his nobles at the battle of Epila.

GENGHIS KHAN (c.1162-1227) Mongol conqueror. According to the anonymous *Secret History of the Mongols* Temujin (his personal name) first became leader of an impoverished Central Asian clan. He overcame all rivals, gathering a fighting force of 20,000 men, and by 1206 was acknowledged as Genghis Khan by all the people of the Mongol and Tartar steppes. He invaded northern China, capturing Peking in 1215, and destroyed the Muslim empire of Khwarizm, which covered part of central Asia and Persia, between 1216 and 1223.

GEORGE II (1890-1947) King of Greece, 1922-3, but exiled on the formation of the republic in 1923. Restored in 1935, he was again exiled during the Second World War. He returned to Greece in 1947.

GERMAN CONFEDERATION A grouping of 38 independent German states under the presidency of Austria, set up at the **Congress of Vienna** (1815). Superseded by the Frankfurt Parliament in 1848, it was re-established in 1851, and then dissolved by Prussia after the Seven Weeks' War of 1866.

GHAZNAVIDS Afghan dynasty, founded by Sebuktigin, father of **Mahmud of Ghazni**, in 977. At its greatest extent the empire stretched from the Oxus River in central Asia to the Indus River and the Indian Ocean. Under Mahmud's son, Masud (reigned 1037-41), much northern territory was lost to the **Seljuks**; the last Indian possessions were conquered by **Muizzudin Muhammad** in 1186.

GHURIDS Dynasty ruling northwest Afghanistan from the mid-12th to the early 13th century. Under **Muizzudin Muhammad** the empire was extended into northern India, helping the establishment of Muslim rule in the sub-continent.

GIRONDINS Members of a moderate republican party during the French Revolution, so named because the leaders came from the Gironde area. Many were guillotined, 31 October 1793, after the group had been overthrown by the rival **Jacobins** the previous June.

GLADSTONE, WILLIAM EWART (1809-98) British Prime Minister. Entered Parliament in 1832 as a Tory; President of the Board of Trade, 1843-5, and Colonial Secretary, 1845-6. He resigned after the repeal of the Corn Laws; later became Chancellor of the Exchequer, 1853-5 and 1859-66. He led the newly-formed Liberal party to victory, 1868, and was four times Prime Minister, 1868-74, 1880-5, 1886 and 1892-4. He was responsible for many military, educational and civil service reforms, and for the Reform Act of 1884; he was repeatedly defeated over attempts to bring about Irish home rule.

GODUNOV, BORIS FYODOROVICH (c.1551-1605) Tsar of Muscovy. He rose in power and favour at the court of **Ivan IV**, the Terrible, and was appointed guardian of Fyodor, the Tsar's retarded son, when Fyodor succeeded in 1584. Godunov banished his enemies and became effective ruler, and was himself elected tsar

when Fyodor died without heirs in 1598. Plagued by war, pestilence, famine and constant opposition from the boyars (the old Russian nobility), he was unable to fulfil his desired programme of social, legal, diplomatic and military reforms. His sudden death during civil war with a pretender known as 'the false Dmitri' precipitated Russia into a devastating 'time of troubles'.

GOEBBELS, PAUL JOSEPH (1897-1945) Hitler's Minister of Propaganda. He entered journalism in 1921, and in 1926 was appointed by Hitler as district administrator of the National Socialist German Workers' Party (NSDAP), becoming its head of propaganda in 1928. On Hitler's accession to power (1933) he was appointed Minister for Public Enlightenment and Propaganda, controlling the press, radio, films, publishing, theatre, music and the visual arts. He committed suicide, with his wife and six children, in Hitler's besieged Berlin bunker.

GOETHE, JOHANN WOLFGANG VON (1749-1832) Most famous of all German poets, novelists and playwrights. Minister of State to the Duke of Saxe-Weimar, 1775, and one of the outstanding figures of European literature. His early novel, *The Sorrows of Young Werther*, 1774, expressed the reaction against the Enlightenment, the sensation of 'emotion running riot' and the conflict between the artist and society. He returned to classicism after a visit to Italy, 1786-8, which affected his whole life and work; from this period onwards his work (*Faust*, part I and part II, 1808, 1832, *Wilhelm Meister*, 1791-1817, *Tasso*, 1789) has a philosophical content which lifts it out of time and place and gives it a universal quality.

GOKHALE, GOPAL KRISHNA (1866-1915) Indian independence leader. He resigned in 1902 from a professorship of history and political economy at Ferguson College, Poona, to enter politics; advocated moderate protest and constitutional reform. He was President of the Indian National Congress, 1905, and founder of the Servants of India Society, dedicated to the alleviation of poverty and service to the underprivileged.

GOLDEN BULL OF 1356 Constitution of the Holy Roman Empire, promulgated by the Emperor **Charles IV**; confirmed, *inter alia*, that succession to the German throne would continue to be determined by seven electors, convened by the Archbishop of Mainz, but that henceforth the electoral lands and powers would be indivisible, and inheritable only by the eldest son, thus removing confusion over the right to vote; it sanctioned the primacy of the territorial princes under loose imperial suzerainty. It also rejected traditional papal claims to rule during periods when the throne was vacant.

GOLDEN HORDE Western portion of the Mongol Empire, also known as the Kipchak khanate. Founded by **Batu** c.1242, it dominated southern Russia to the end of the 14th century. It was finally broken up by **Timur** to form three Tartar khanates: Kazan, Astrakhan and the Crimea.

GOLD EXCHANGE STANDARD Device evolved at the Genoa monetary conference, 1922, after the collapse of the **Gold Standard** during the First World War, to maintain the stability of currency exchange rates. Under this system central banks redeemed their currency not in gold, as before, but in a currency that is convertible into gold. The system collapsed 1931-3, but was revived after the Second World War, and during the period 1958-71 most European treasuries adopted this approach, treating the US dollar as the main unit in which they accumulated reserves.

GOLD STANDARD Monetary system in which the value of currency in issue is legally tied to a certain quantity of gold. During the last quarter of the 19th century virtually all major trading nations adopted this policy and most attempted to return to it after the break caused by the First World War; this attempt was abandoned in the slump of the 1930s. The US dollar finally came off gold in 1971.

GÖMBÖS, GYULA (1886-1936) Hungarian Prime Minister. In 1919 he set up a proto-fascist movement and helped organize the overthrow of the Communist government. At first he opposed the conservative premier, István Bethlen (1921-31), but joined his administration in 1929 and in 1932 was swept to power by the 'radical right' movement. He advocated a reactionary, anti-Semitic programme and alliance with Germany and Italy, but was restrained by the head of state, Admiral Horthy.

GOMES, FERNÃO 15th century Portuguese merchant who in 1469 was granted a monopoly to explore the West African coast and keep all trading profits. Gomes and his captains explored as far as the Congo River, and prepared the way for the voyage of **Vasco da Gama** to India in 1497-9.

GOMUŁKA, WŁADYSŁAW (1905-82) Polish Communist leader. A youth organizer for the banned Communist Party, 1926, and a wartime underground fighter, he was stripped of Party membership in 1949 after incurring the displeasure of Stalin, but re-admitted in 1956 to become First Secretary of the Central Committee. Resistance to his regime erupted in riots in 1968; he was deposed and retired in 1970.

GORBACHEV, MIKHAIL (1931-) Soviet statesman. After studying law at Moscow University (1953) he headed the Young Communist League in his native Stavropol. He became agriculture secretary of the central committee of the Soviet Communist Party (1978); a full member of the Politburo (1980); general secretary of the Soviet Communist Party (1985-91) and president of the Soviet Union (1988-91). He promoted economic and social reforms programs known as *glasnost* (openness) and *perestroika* (restructuring), and negotiated two arms limitation treaties (1987, 1990), effectively ending the Cold War. Opposed to the breakup of the Soviet Union, he met with growing opposition which brought about his resignation in 1991.

GORDON, CHARLES GEORGE (1833-85) British general, first distinguished for bravery in the Crimean War (1854-6). He volunteered for service in China, where his exploits in the 'Arrow' war, the T'ai-p'ing Rebellion and the burning of the emperor's Summer Palace earned him the nickname 'Chinese Gordon'. In 1884 he was sent to the Sudan (where he had earlier been Governor-General) to evacuate British troops from Khartoum; he was besieged and killed by Sudanese followers of **Mohammed Ahmed al-Mahdi**.

GORGIAS OF LEONTINI (c.483-c.376 BC) Ancient Greek rhetorician, noted for his poetic language and carefully balanced clauses. In his treatise *On Nature* he argued the essential non-existence, unknowability and incommunicability of Being. He was portrayed with respect by **Plato** in *Gorgias*.

GORM King of Denmark, father of **Harald Bluetooth**; died after 935.

GOTHIC Relating to the art and language of the **Ostrogoths** and **Visigoths**. During the Renaisssance, the word was used to typify the barbarism of the Middle Ages; it still refers to the style of church architecture, with characteristic pointed arches, predominant from the 12th to the 15th century, and to the painting and sculpture associated with it.

GOTT, BENJAMIN (1762-1840) English manufacturer of woollen cloth and philanthropist. In 1793 he established a woollen mill in Leeds, introducing an improved mechanical cloth-cutting device in spite of much hostility.

GOTTFRIED VON STRASSBURG German medieval poet, author of *Tristan*, the classic version of the story of Tristan and Isolde. He lived and worked in the late 12th and early 13th centuries.

GOULART, DR JOÃO (1918-76) Brazilian political leader. He joined the Brazilian labour party, Partido Trabalhista, in 1945 and became national party director in 1951, Minister of Labour and Commerce, 1953-4, Vice-President of Brazil, 1956, was re-elected in 1961 and became president that year. He was deposed in a military *coup d'état*, 1964.

GOVERNMENT OF INDIA ACT British Act of Parliament of 1935 embodying a number of constitutional reforms, including 'provincial autonomy' and a federal structure at the centre. Only the provisions relating to the provinces were implemented, the proposals for federation being rejected by the Indian political parties.

GRANADA, KINGDOM OF Last foothold of the Muslims in Spain. Ruled by the **Nasrid** dynasty, 1238-1492, it prospered by welcoming Moorish refugees from Seville, Valencia and Murcia; it built one of Islam's most famous architectural achievements, the Alhambra (Red Fortress). The kingdom was finally conquered by Christian forces in 1492.

GRANT, ULYSSES SIMPSON (1822-85) 18th President of the United States, 1869-77. He was commander-in-chief of the Union armies during the American Civil War. His administration (Republican) was marked by corruption and bitter partisanship between the political parties.

GREAT ELECTOR *see* **Frederick William, Elector of Brandenburg**

GREAT FEAR Series of rural panics, spreading through the French countryside between 20 July and 6 August 1789, at the onset of the French Revolution. Following a series of peasant disorders, during which stores of grain were looted and châteaux burned, rumours of invasion by armed brigands spread in five main currents covering the greater part of the country, which stimulated further disorders that petered out as suddenly as they had begun.

GREAT NORTHERN WAR Struggle between Sweden and Russia, 1700-21, mainly for control of the Baltic. **Charles XII** of Sweden at first defeated an alliance of Russia, Denmark, Poland and Saxony (1700-6), but was heavily defeated at Poltava by **Peter the Great** of Russia in 1709. This advantage was lost when Turkey declared war on Russia in 1710, and fighting continued in Poland and Scandinavia until Charles' death in 1718. In the final settlement Sweden lost Livonia and Karelia to Russia (which gained permanent access to the Baltic Sea), and abandoned its claims to be a great power.

GREAT SCHISM A political split in the Catholic Church, lasting from 1378 to 1417, during which rival popes – one in Rome, the other in Avignon – attempted to exert authority. The result of a serious split among cardinals and high churchmen on ecclesiastical reform, and the political influence of the French monarchy, the Schism was resolved by the Council of Constance, 1414-17.

GREGORY I 'THE GREAT' (c.540-604) Pope, saint and one of the Fathers of the Christian Church. During his papacy (590-604), he strengthened and reorganized Church administration, reformed the liturgy, promoted monasticism, asserted the temporal power of the papacy, extended Rome's influence in the West and sent St Augustine of Canterbury on his mission to convert the English.

GREGORY VII (c.1020-85) Pope and saint, born in north Italy and given the name Hildebrand. He served under Pope Gregory VI during the Pope's exile in Germany after deposition by the Emperor **Henry III**. He was recalled to Rome by Pope **Leo IX**, and thereafter was often the power behind the papal throne. He was made a cardinal by **Alexander II** (1061-73), and elected by acclaim as his successor. From 1075 he was engaged in the contest over **lay investiture** with Emperor **Henry IV**, whom he excommunicated in 1076; after absolving him at Canossa in 1077, he re-excommunicated him after fresh attacks. Gregory was driven from Rome in 1084. He was canonized in 1606.

GRIJALVA, JUAN DE (c.1489-1527) Spanish explorer. Sailing along the coast of Mexico, where he discovered the River Grijalva (named after him) in 1518, he was probably the first of the *conquistadores* to hear of the rich Aztec civilization of the interior.

GRUFFYDD AP LLEWELYN (d.1063) Briefly king of all Wales. He challenged the authority of existing dynasties holding power over Welsh kingdoms; seized control in Gwynedd in the northwest, Deheubarth in the southwest, and for a short period the whole country; he devastated the borderland with England.

GUELPH and GHIBELLINE The two great rival political factions of medieval Italy, reflecting the rivalry of Guelph dukes of Saxony and Bavaria and the **Hohenstaufen**. The names Guelph and Ghibelline came to designate support for the papal (Guelph) side against the imperial (Ghibelline) side in the struggle between the **papacy** and the **Holy Roman Empire**.

GUEST, SIR JOSIAH (1785-1852) British industrialist. He created an improved smelting process at the family ironworks at Dowlais (near Merthyr Tydfil, Wales) and raised its annual iron production to 75,000 tons, mostly in the form of rails for the new railways.

GUEVARA, ERNESTO 'CHE' (1928-67) South American revolutionary leader, born in Argentina. He qualified as a doctor of medicine, 1953; became chief aide to **Fidel Castro** in his successful Cuban revolution, 1959; wrote *Guerrilla Warfare*, 1960 and *Episodes of the Revolutionary War*, 1963. He was killed in Bolivia, trying to establish a guerrilla base there.

GUGGENHEIM, MEYER (1828-1905) Founder of modern American metal-mining industry; born in Switzerland, he emigrated to the United States in 1847. In the early 1880s he bought control of two Colorado copper mines, and quickly built up a worldwide network of mines, exploration companies, smelters and refineries. With his son Daniel (1856-1930) he merged all the family interests in 1901 into the American Smelting & Refining Company.

GUPTA Imperial dynasty, ruling in northern India from the 4th to the 6th centuries AD. It first rose to prominence under Chandragupta I, ruling over Magadha and parts of Uttar Pradesh, c.319-35. Its power was extended and reinforced under **Samudragupta** (reigned c.335-75), **Chandragupta II** (c.375-415) and Kumaragupta (c.415-54). The dynasty was later weakened by domestic unrest and **Hun** invasion, and effectively eliminated as a major political force by 510.

GURJARAS Central Asian tribe, reaching India with the **Hun** invasions of the 4th and 5th centuries AD. They settled in Rajasthan, in western India, and were reputed ancestors of the **Pratiharas**.

GUSTAVUS I VASA (c.1496-1560) King of Sweden (1523-60), founder of the Vasa dynasty. He fought in Sweden's 1517-18 rebellion against Denmark, was interned but returned in 1520 to lead another rebellion against Denmark. He was elected king of Sweden in 1523, thus breaking up the **Union of Kalmar**. He introduced the **Lutheran** Reformation; and in 1544 persuaded the Diet to make the monarchy hereditary in his Vasa family line.

GUSTAVUS II ADOLPHUS (1594-1632) King of Sweden, grandson of **Gustavus I Vasa**. He succeeded to the throne in 1611 and made Sweden a major political and military power. He entered the Thirty Years' War on the side of the Protestants, 1630, and conquered most of Germany. He was killed at the battle of Lützen.

GUTIANS (Guti) Ancient mountain people from the Zagros range, east of Mesopotamia. They destroyed the empire of Akkad, c.2230 BC, and exercised sporadic sovereignty over much of Babylonia for the next century. Traditionally they were eclipsed as a historical force after the defeat of the last king, Tirigan, by Utu-Khegal of Uruk, c.2130 BC. The Gutians were primarily remembered in later tradition as barbarians.

GUZMÁN BLANCO, ANTONIO (1829-99) President of Venezuela. He was appointed special finance commissioner to negotiate loans from Great Britain; seized control of the government in 1870; as head of the Regeneration party was elected constitutional president, 1873; ruled as absolute dictator until 1877, and again 1879-84 and 1886-8, laying the main foundations of modern Venezuela, and accumulating a vast personal fortune. Ousted by a coup d'état during one of his visits to Europe, he died in Paris.

HABSBURGS Major European royal and imperial dynasty from the 15th to the 20th century. The ascendancy of the family began in 13th-century Austria. Frederick V Habsburg was crowned Holy Roman Emperor in 1452, as Frederick III; the title remained a family possession until the Empire was dissolved in 1806. At their peak, under Charles V (Charles I of Spain), Habsburg realms stretched from eastern Europe to the New World; after Charles' death, the house split into the Spanish line, which died out in 1700, and the Austrian line, which remained in power – after 1740 as the House of Habsburg-Lorraine – until 1918.

HADRIAN IV (c.1100-59) Pope 1154-9. Born Nicholas Breakspear, and the only English Pope, he renewed the initiative of the papacy in the spirit of **Gregory VII**, notably in the incident of Besançon, when he claimed that the imperial crown was held from the Pope. He expelled the heretic **Arnold of Brescia** from Rome.

HADRIAN, PUBLIUS AELIUS (AD 76-138) Roman emperor. Adopted by **Trajan** as his son, whom he succeeded in 117. He abandoned the policy of eastern expansion in order to consolidate frontiers and initiated far-reaching military, legal and administrative reforms; his fortifications in Britain and Syria still stand. He travelled widely in the Empire, encouraging the spread of Greco-Roman civilization and culture.

HAFSIDS Dynasty of **Berber** origin, ruling Tunisia and eastern Algeria c.1229-1574. The most famous ruler, Mustansir (1249-77), used the title of caliph; his diplomacy averted danger from the Crusade of **Louis IX** and extended his influence into Morocco and Spain.

HAIDAR ALI (1722-82) Muslim ruler of Mysore, southern India. He created the first Indian army equipped with European firearms and artillery. He deposed the local rajah and seized the throne, c.1761. He defeated the British several times between 1766 and 1780, but finally lost in the three battles of Porto Novo, Pollilu and Sholinghar. Before his death he implored his son **Tipu** to make peace with the invaders.

HAIG, DOUGLAS (1861-1928) 1st Earl Haig. British field marshal, commander-in-chief of the British forces in Flanders and France 1915-18, during the First World War. His strategy of attrition on the Somme (1916) and in Flanders (1917), especially at the third battle of Ypres (or Passchendaele), resulted in enormous British casualties.

HAILE SELASSIE I (1892-1975) Emperor of Ethiopia. A close relative of Emperor **Menelik II** (1889-1913), he was appointed to provincial governorships from 1908, became regent and heir apparent to Menelik's daughter Zauditu in 1916. He took Ethiopia into the **League of Nations** in 1923, and became emperor in 1930, introducing bicameral Parliament the following year. He was driven out by the Italian occupation of 1936-41 but he led the reconquest, with British aid, and began to modernize the country. He survived a coup threat in 1960, but in 1974 news of the famine in the Wollo district and an armed mutiny provoked a revolution which deposed him. He died under house arrest.

HAJJ UMAR, AL- (1794-1864) West African Tukolor warrior-mystic, founder of the Muslim empire based on Masina in the western Sudan (now in the republic of Mali). He became a member of the newly-founded militant religious order, the Tijaniyya. He made a pilgrimage to Mecca in 1826 and returned inspired to propagate Islam in the western Sudan. In 1852 he embarked upon a great and bloody *jihad* (holy war) which resulted in the conquest of much of the western Sudan. The campaign brough him into violent conflict with the French, who were expanding up the Senegal River. He was killed in battle. By the end of the 19th century his empire was finally conquered by the French.

HAKKA North Chinese people who migrated south under the Sung dynasty (1126-1279) to Kwangtung and Fukien where they remained a distinct social group, living in separate communities, usually in poor uplands. They were involved in many bitter communal feuds in the 18th and 19th centuries, culminating in the Hakka-Punti war in the 1850s. Many emigrated after the T'ai-p'ing rebellion, and they are now widely spread throughout East Asia.

HALLSTATT Early Celtic Iron Age culture, flourishing in central Europe c.2700-5002 BC, named after an Austrian village in the Salzkammergut, where an archaeologically important cemetery was found in the 19th century. The culture was notable for elaborate burials, in which the dead person was placed in a four-wheeled chariot, of which examples have been found from the Upper Danube region to Vix in Burgundy.

HAMAGUCHI, OSACHI (1870-1931) Japanese statesman. Official of the finance ministry, 1895-1924, and Finance Minister 1924-6. In 1927 he was elected leader of the new Rikken Minseitō (Constitutional Democratic) Party, and became Japanese Prime Minister in 1929. He decreed drastic deflationary policies, but was assassinated before they could take effect. The army forced his colleagues to resign, thus bringing democratic government to an end.

HAMDANIDS Bedouin dynasty controlling Mosul and Aleppo, 905-1004; renowned warriors and patrons of Arab art and learning.

HAMMADIDS North African Berber dynasty, a branch of the **Zirids**. In the reign of the Zirid leader Badis Ibn al-Mansur (995-1016) they gained control of part of Algeria; in 1067, under attack from the **Fatimids** and their Bedouin allies, they established themselves in the port of Bejaia (Bougie), and developed a successful trading empire until conquered by the **Almohads** in 1152.

HAMMARSKJÖLD, DAG (1905-61) Swedish and international statesman. Son of a Swedish Prime Minister, he entered politics in 1930 and became Deputy Foreign Minister in 1951. Elected as Secretary-General of the **United Nations** in 1953, he greatly extended the influence both of the UN and of its secretary-general, striving to reduce the tensions caused by decolonization in Africa, particularly in the Congo (1960-1), where he was killed in an air crash.

HAMMURABI King of Babylon, reigning 1792-1750 BC. He succeeded his father, Sin-Mabullit, and extended his small kingdom (originally only 80 miles long and 20 miles wide, 129 km x 32 km) to unify all Mesopotamia under Babylonian rule. He published a collection of laws on a basalt stele, 8 feet (2.4m) high, now in the Louvre Museum.

HAM NGHI (1870-c.1940) Emperor of Vietnam. He reached the throne in 1884 after intense intrigue following the death of his uncle, the emperor Tu Duc; at the instigation of his regents, Nguyen Van Tuong and Thou That Thuyet, he led a revolt against the French, 1885; he fled after its failure, was deposed in 1886, captured and exiled to Algeria.

HAN Chinese imperial dynasty, ruling from 206 BC to AD 9 (Former Han), and AD 25-220 (Later Han); *see pages* 80-1.

HAN FU-CHÜ (1890-1938) Military officer who served under **Feng Yü-hsiang**, 1912-28. He was appointed governor of Honan in 1928; defecting from Feng in his confrontation with **Chiang Kai-shek**, in 1929, he controlled Shantung from 1930 to 1938 and brought it under the control of Nanking. In 1937 the Japanese invaded Shantung; he put up only token resistance and was executed for dereliction of duty the following year.

HANNIBAL (247-183 BC) Most famous Carthaginian general, son of another great soldier, Hamilcar Barca. He was commander-in-chief in Spain aged 26; after the outbreak of the Second **Punic War** against Rome (218-201) he led 40,000 troops, with elephants, over the Alps to smash the Roman armies at Lake Trasimene, 217, and Cannae, 216. Forced to abandon Italy in 203 as Rome had attacked Carthage itself, he was finally defeated at Zama in 202 and later driven into exile. He committed suicide.

HANSEATIC LEAGUE Association of medieval German cities and merchant groups which became a powerful economic and political force in northern Europe. With a centre for meetings in the city of Lübeck, the members established an important network of Baltic trade, and a string of commercial bases stretching from Novgorod to London and from Bergen to Bruges. In its heyday during the 14th century the Hansa included well over a hundred towns; its influence gradually faded with the emergence of powerful competitor states, and the last meeting of the Diet was held in Lübeck in 1669.

HARALD BLUETOOTH (d. c.985) King of Denmark from c.940. He accepted the introduction of Christianity into his kingdom, and strengthened its central organization; he successfully defeated German and Norwegian attacks on Denmark, unifying its disparate elements.

HARALD I FINEHAIR (c.860-c.940) First king claiming sovereignty over all Norway, in the second half of the 9th century, the son of Halfdan the Black, ruler of a part of southeast Norway and a member of the ancient Swedish Yngling dynasty, whom he succeeded when very young. His conquests culminated in the Battle of Hafrsfjord, c.900; many defeated chiefs fled to Britain and possibly Iceland. The best account of his exploits is given in Snorri Sturlson's 13th century saga, the *Heimskringla*.

HARALD II GREYCLOAK (d. c.970) Norwegian king, son of **Erik Bloodaxe**. He overthrew his half-brother, Haakon the Good, c.961, ruling oppressively, with his brothers, until c.970. He is credited with establishing the first Christian missions in Norway. He was killed in battle against an alliance of local nobles and his former supporter, **Harald Bluetooth**.

HARA TAKASHI (1856-1921) First 'commoner' (i.e. untitled) Prime Minister of modern Japan. Graduated from Tokyo university into journalism and then entered foreign service in 1882. He became ambassador to Korea in 1897, chief editor of the Osaka *Mainichi* newspaper in 1899. He helped to found the Rikken-Seiyukai (Friends of Constitutional Government) Party, 1900, and built it into an American-style party machine, meanwhile rising to ministerial and finally prime ministerial rank in 1918. He was assassinated by a right-wing fanatic after opposing the use of Japanese troops in Siberia.

HARKORT, FRIEDRICH (FRITZ) (1793-1880) Pioneer entrepreneur in the German engineering industry. In 1819 Harkort and Kamp, in partnership with Thomas (an English engineer), established works producing textile machinery and steam engines at Wetter in the Ruhr district. The plant was later expanded to include the puddling process. Harkort twice visited England to recruit skilled mechanics. He was a pioneer in the construction of steamships on the Weser and the Rhine, and was also a leading advocate of railway building in Germany.

HARSHA (c.590-c.647) Indian ruler, second son of a king in the Punjab. He ultimately exercised loose imperial power over most of northern India. Converted from **Hinduism** to **Buddhism**, he was the first to open diplomatic relations between India and China (c.641); his court, at Kanauj, his early years and his model administration are described in Bana's poem *The Deeds of Harsha*, and the writings of the Chinese pilgrim, Hsüan Tsang.

HARUN AL-RASHID (c.763-806) Fifth caliph of the **Abbasid** dynasty, immortalized in *The Thousand and One Nights*. He inherited the throne in 786, ruling territories from northwest India to the western Mediterranean; his reign saw the beginning of the disintegration of the **caliphate**.

HASHEMITES Direct or collateral descendants of the prophet **Mohammed**, who was himself a member of the house of Hashem, a division of the Quraysh tribe. In the 20th century, Hussein ibn Ali, descendant of a long line of Hashemite *sharifs* or local rulers of Mecca, and King of Hejaz, 1916-24, founded the modern Hashemite dynasty, carried on by his sons, King Feisal of Iraq and King Abdullah of Jordan.

HASSAN II (1929-) King of Morocco, 17th monarch of the Alaouite dynasty. The son of **Mohammed V**, he became commander-in-chief of the Royal Moroccan Army in 1957. Succeeding to the throne in 1961, he held the posts of Prime Minister, 1961-3 and 1965-7, Minister of Defence, 1972-3, and commander-in-chief of the army from 1972. He established strong monarchical government, and was the main force behind the abortive attempt to partition the former Spanish Sahara between Morocco and Mauritania.

HASTINGS, FRANCIS RAWDON-HASTINGS (1754-1826) 1st Marquis. Early Governor-General of Bengal. He landed in India, 1813; defeated the Gurkhas, 1816; conquered the Maratha States and cemented British control east of the Sutlej River. He purchased Singapore, 1819, but resigned under a financial cloud, 1823; he was Governor of Malta 1824.

HASTINGS, WARREN (1732-1818) First Governor-General of British India, 1774-85. He carried out important administrative and legal reforms, but was impeached on corruption charges, 1788; he was finally acquitted, after a long and famous trial, in 1795.

HAUSA West African people, organized from about the 11th century into a loose grouping of states centred to the west of Lake Chad. In the 16th century Kano became the greatest of the Hausa cities, but the Hausaland region only came under unified control after conquest by the Fulani in the early 19th century. They are now one of the largest ethnic groups in Nigeria.

HAVEL, VACLAV (1936-) Czech playwright and politician. Widely regarded as the leading Czech playwright of his generation, he commented on the struggles of contemporary intellectuals in his plays. His works were banned after the Soviet invasion (1968), but remained available abroad. In the 1970s he became spokesman for human rights groups and was imprisoned. After the resignation of the entire politburo, he formally entered politics to become the first president of an independent Czechoslovakia (1989) in the 'Velvet Revolution'. In January 1993 he was elected President of the new Czech Republic.

HAWLEY-SMOOT TARIFF United States tariff, passed in 1930, which set the highest import duties in American history, attracted immediate retaliation from European governments, and is considered to be one of the factors responsible for deepening the Great Depression.

HAY, JOHN (1838-1905) US secretary of state (1898-1905). A skillful diplomat, he is best known for his Open Door Policy in China (1900). He also helped negotiate the end of the Spanish-American war (1898), was active in the decision to retain the Philippines, thus marking the US as a major imperialist power, and completed the second Hay-Pauncefote Treaty (1901), granting the US exclusive rights to build a canal across the Isthmus of Panama. He assisted in diplomatic efforts to assure Panamanian independence and the beginning of canal construction (1903).

HAY-PAUNCEFOTE TREATY Composite name for two Anglo-American agreements, signed in 1900 and 1901, freeing the US from a previous commitment to international control of any projected Central American canal. It freed US hands for the building of the Panama Canal, which was completed in 1914.

HAYES, RUTHERFORD B. (1822-93) 19th President of the United States, and the first chief executive to say openly that an isthmian canal must be American-owned. This pronouncement correlates with the beginning of a programme of naval expansion.

HEAVENLY PRINCIPLE SECT (T'ien-li chiao) Secret sectarian movement connected with the **White Lotus** society, with a large following during the late 18th century in northern China (Hopei, Honan, Shantung), led by Lin Ch'ing and Li Wen-ch'eng, who began a rebellion in Honan in 1813. A small group infiltrated Peking and entered the palace.

HEGIRA (hijra) Arabic word for 'emigration', and the starting date of Muslim era. By order of **Omar I**, the second caliph, in AD 639, Islamic letters, treaties, proclamations and events were to be dated by reference to the day, 16 July 622, on which the Prophet **Mohammed** migrated from Mecca to Medina.

HELLENISM Culture, philosophy and spirit of ancient Greece, spread across Asia and across Europe through the Roman adoption of Greek models; through thought and art, it touched Buddhism, Christianity, Hinduism and Islam. It was revived in the western world in the Renaissance and other renaissances. It is often associated with humanism, rationality and beauty of form.

HELLENISTIC The era from 323 to 30 BC, when the eastern Mediterranean and the Near East were dominated by dynasties and state governments founded by the successors of **Alexander the Great**.

HENRICIANS Followers of Henry of Lausanne, an itinerant preacher of southern France in the 12th century, whose criticisms of the Church followed those of the **Petrobrusians** and were transmitted to the more numerous and better organized **Waldensians**.

HENRY II (1133-89) King of England. Grandson of Henry I, he became Duke of Normandy in 1150 and Count of Anjou in 1151. He married Eleanor of Aquitaine in 1152 after her repudiation by Louis VII of France. He succeeded to the English throne in 1154; in his own right and that of his wife, he ruled over domains extending from Ireland to the Pyrenees and Mediterranean. He was noted for his expansion of the judicial and administrative authority of the English crown; his generally successful reign was marred by quarrels with Thomas Becket, Archbishop of Canterbury, and with his own family.

HENRY II (1333-79) King of Castile, 1369-79. The natural son of Alfonso XI, Henry drove his brother Pedro (1356-69) from the throne with French aid and founded the Trastámara dynasty, which continued until 1504.

HENRY III (1017-56) German king 1039-56, and emperor 1046-56. He brought Church reform to Rome at the Synod of Sutri, 1046, and appointed a succession of Germans – notably **Leo IX** – to the papacy.

HENRY IV (1050-1106) German Emperor, son of **Henry III** and Agnes of Poitou. He succeeded in 1056 under his mother's regency. He broke with Pope **Gregory VII** over the investiture issue in 1075, was excommunicated and declared deposed by him, but restored after performing penance to the Pope at Canossa in 1077; he was excommunicated again in 1080. He appointed Clement III as anti-Pope in 1084, but was outmanoeuvred by Pope **Urban II** and his position was weakened by the revolts of his sons Conrad and the future emperor, **Henry V**. He died after defeating Henry at Visé, near Liège.

HENRY IV (1367-1413) King of England, 1399-1413, son of John of Gaunt and grandson of **Edward III**. He was banished in 1398 by **Richard II**, but returned in 1399 to depose his cousin and seize the throne. He put down baronial rebellions under Owen Glendower and Sir Henry Percy in 1403, and under Thomas de Mowbray in 1405; he was the subject of two plays by Shakespeare.

HENRY IV (1533-1610) King of France, 1589-1610, son of Antoine, King of Navarre. He married Marguerite of Valois, daughter of the French king, **Henry II**, in 1572. He emerged as Protestant leader in the French wars of religion, and was excommunicated, 1585. Reconciled with King Henry III in 1589, he abjured the Protestant faith in 1593 and was crowned king in 1594. He drove the Spaniards out of Paris, and declared war on the Spanish king, Philip II, in 1595. In 1598 he signed the **Edict of Nantes**, granting toleration to French Protestants. He married Marie de' Medici, 1600; authorized **Jesuits** to reopen colleges in Paris, 1603. He was assassinated.

HENRY V (1387-1422) King of England, son of **Henry IV**, whom he succeeded in 1413. In 1415 he reopened the **Hundred Years' War** in support of his claims to the French throne; won the battle of Agincourt, 1415, and conquered Normandy, 1419. Under the Treaty of Troyes he married Catherine of Valois and became heir to the French king, Charles VI. Renewed war, 1421, the year before his death.

HENRY VI (1165-97) Son of **Frederick I Barbarossa**, he was chosen as German king in 1169; married Constance, daughter of **Roger II** of Sicily in 1186, and inherited Roger's kingdom in 1189; crowned emperor in 1191, after Frederick's death on the Third **Crusade**. The ransom of Richard I, whom he held prisoner, 1193-4, enabled him to overcome internal opposition in the Lower Rhineland and Saxony led by **Duke Henry**, and then to finance his conquest of Sicily after the death of the rival claimant, King Tancred, in 1194. He died of malaria while preparing a crusade. Because his son **Frederick II** was then aged only two years, his death caused a succession dispute in the Empire.

HENRY VII (1457-1509) King of England. He became head of the royal House of Lancaster which challenged their cousins, the House of York, for the crown of England; exiled until 1485, when he defeated and killed the Yorkist, Richard III, he then became king and ended the civil war (**Wars of the Roses**). He founded the **Tudor** dynasty, which lasted until 1603, creating a strong central government in England after almost a century of disruption.

HENRY VIII (1491-1547) King of England, son of **Henry VII**, succeeding in 1509. His desire for a male heir caused his search for a means to declare his first marriage, to Catherine of Aragon, invalid; after papal refusal, and non-recognition of his second marriage in 1533 to Anne Boleyn, Parliament passed the Act of Supremacy, 1534, declaring Henry head of the English Church; monasteries were suppressed (1536, 1539). Wales was brought into legal union with England, 1534-6.

HENRY, DUKE OF SAXONY (c.1130-95) Known as 'the Lion'. He spent his early years fighting for his father's duchies. He was granted Saxony in 1142 but had to wait until 1156 for Bavaria; founded Munich in 1157 and Lübeck in 1159. Stripped of his lands after breaking with **Frederick I Barbarossa**, 1179-80, he was twice exiled, 1181-5 and 1189-90, but was reconciled with Emperor **Henry VI** in 1194.

HENRY THE NAVIGATOR (1394-1460) Portuguese prince, third son of John I and Philippa of Lancaster. He helped in the capture of Ceuta, Morocco, in 1415, and at the age of 26 was made Grand Master of Portugal's crusading Order of Christ. Thereafter, he devoted much of his life to the encouragement of maritime trade and discovery, to the organization of voyages to West Africa and to occasional crusading operations in Morocco.

HERACLIAN DYNASTY Byzantine dynasty, ruling from AD 610 to 711, founded by Emperor Heraclius (610-41) and ending with Justinian II (685-95, and again 705-11).

HERACLIUS (c.575-641) Eastern Roman Emperor. The son of a governor of Africa, in 610 he seized the crown from Emperor Phocas; fought and defeated the Persians, 622-8; restored the True Cross to Jerusalem, 630; persecuted the **Jews**, 632. His armies were beaten by Muslim Arabs in 636, and Syria and Palestine (640) and Egypt (642) lost to Islam. In the meantime he restored the administration of the remaining provinces and laid the foundations for the medieval Byzantine state.

HERDER, JOHANN GOTTFRIED VON (1744-1803) German critic, linguist and philosopher who wrote on the origins of language, poetry and aesthetics. He was a leading figure in the literary movement known as *Sturm und Drang*. He made a famous collection of German songs (*Volkslieder*, 1778-9), wrote the *Essay on the Origin of Language* (1772), and at Weimar, where he became superintendent of schools in 1776, *Reflections on the Philosophy of the History of Mankind* (1784-91).

HEREDIA, PEDRO DE (c.1500-54) Spanish soldier who founded Cartagena in modern Colombia in 1533, and several other New World cities. He amassed a vast fortune through his many expeditions to the interior.

HERERO Bantu-speaking peoples of southwest Africa, mostly in central Namibia and Botswana.

HERERO REVOLT A protest which broke out in 1904 against German colonial oppression of the Herero and other peoples of southwest Africa. In 1907, when the risings ended, over 65,000 Hereros out of an original 80,000 had been killed, starved in concentration camps or driven into the Kalahari Desert to die.

HERNÁNDEZ DE CÓRDOBA, FRANCISCO Name of two Spanish soldier-explorers active in the New World at the beginning of the 16th century. The first, born c.1475, went in 1514 to the Isthmus of Panama with Pedro Arias de Ávila, and in 1524 was sent to seize Nicaragua from its rightful discoverer, Gil González de Ávila; after founding the towns of Granada and León and exploring Lake Nicaragua he defected to **Cortés**, and was executed by a rival in 1526. His namesake went to Cuba with Velázquez in 1511 and later commanded the expedition that coasted Yucatán and made the first recorded European contact with **Mayan** civilization; he died in 1517.

HEROD ANTIPAS (21 BC-AD 39) Tetrarch of Galilee during the lifetime of **Jesus**. The son of Herod the Great, he inherited part of his father's kingdom under the Roman suzerainty, c.4 BC. He was goaded into beheading John the Baptist, but later refused to pass judgement on Jesus himself.

HERODOTUS (c.484-c.420 BC) Greek writer, known as 'the father of history'. He travelled widely in Asia, Egypt and eastern Europe; his *Histories*, a history of the Greco-Persian wars and the events preceding them, is one of the world's first major prose works, incorporating many vivid and, to contemporaries, almost incredible travellers' tales; modern research has sometimes shown even the wildest of them to contain an element of truth.

HIDEYOSHI *see* **Toyotomi**

HINDENBURG, PAUL VON (1847-1934) German soldier, President of Germany 1925-34. Recalled from retirement in 1914 to take command in east Prussia after the Russian invasion, he won the victory of Tannenberg, and the first and second battles of the Masurian Lakes (1914-15). Appointed a field-marshal and supreme commander of all German armies, 1916, he became virtual dictator of German domestic policy, too, until the armistice. As President he was persuaded to appoint **Hitler** as Chancellor in 1933.

HINDENBURG LINE Fortified line on the Western Front in the First World War, taken up by German armies following the battle of the Somme in 1916. A formidable defence system, it was eventually pierced in September 1918 by the British and French forces.

HINDUISM Predominant religion of India; all-embracing in its forms, capable of including external observances and their rejection, animal sacrifice and refusal to take any form of life, extreme polytheism and high monotheism.

HIPPOCRATES (c.460-c.377 BC) Ancient Greek physician, traditionally regarded in the West as the father of medicine. He believed in the wholeness of the body as an organism, in the close observation and recording of case-histories, and in the importance of diet and climate. The works making up the Hippocratic Collection, forming the library of the medical school at Cos, where he taught, reflect the continuing effects of his work. The Hippocratic Oath is still used as a guide to conduct by the medical profession.

HIPPODAMUS OF MILETUS Ancient Greek architect who flourished in the 5th century BC. He is best known for the grid system of street planning, developed for the Athenian port of Piraeus, the pan-Hellenic settlement of Thurii and perhaps the new city of Rhodes.

HIROHITO (1901-89) Emperor of Japan, supposedly the 124th direct descendant of Jimmu, Japan's legendary first ruler. An authority on marine biology, and the first Japanese crown prince to travel abroad (1921), he succeeded his father in 1926. He tried, ineffectually, to avert war with the United States, and broke political deadlock in 1945 to sue for peace. He ended centuries of public imperial silence to broadcast Japan's announcement of surrender on 15 August 1945. He became a constitutional monarch, with greatly restricted powers and was succeeded, in 1989, by his son, Akihito.

HITLER, ADOLF (1889-1945) German dictator. Born in Austria, he moved to Munich in 1913, served in the German army, joined the National Socialist German Workers' Party and reorganized it as a quasi-military force. He tried unsuccessfully to seize power in Bavaria, 1923; wrote *Mein Kampf* (*My Struggle*) in prison, elaborating his theories of Jewish conspiracy and **Aryan** superiority. Appointed Chancellor, 1933; in 1936 he remilitarized the Rhineland, in 1938 invaded Austria and Czechoslovakia and in 1939 Poland. His sweeping initial successes in the Second World War were followed by defeats in Russia and North Africa, 1942-3. He survived an assassination plot in 1944, but committed suicide in 1945 as the Russians entered Berlin.

HITTITES A people speaking an Indo-European language who had occupied central Anatolia by the beginning of the 2nd millennium BC, quickly absorbing the older population. The Old Hittite

kingdom, c.1750-1500 BC, later expanded into the Hittite Empire, c.1500-1190, which at its greatest extent controlled all Syria and briefly much of northern Mesopotamia. After the collapse of the empire, various neo-Hittite kingdoms survived in the region for a further 500 years.

HOABINHIAN *see* **Bacsonian**

HOCHE, LOUIS-LAZARE (1768-97) French Revolutionary general. He enlisted in the French Guards, 1784, was appointed corporal, 1789; as commander of the army of the Moselle (1793) he drove Austro-Prussian forces from Alsace. He suppressed the **Vendée** counter-revolution, 1794-6. He commanded an expedition to Ireland to help rebels against England which failed due to storms at sea.

HO CHIEN (1887-1956) Warlord who controlled Hunan province, 1929-37. He played a major role in the campaigns against the Communists, 1930-5, supported by Kwangsi and Kwangtung. On the outbreak of the Japanese war he became a minister in the National government. He resigned in 1945.

HO CHI MINH (1890-1969) President of the Democratic Republic of Vietnam (North Vietnam), 1945-69. He was a founding member of the French Communist Party, 1920; and founded the Indo-Chinese Communist Party, 1930. He escaped to Moscow, 1932, but returned to Vietnam, 1940. Imprisoned in China, 1942-3, he emerged as leader of the **Viet Minh** guerrillas; he declared Vietnam independent, 1945, and played a dominant role in both the first and the second Indo-China wars, 1946-52, and from 1959 until his death.

HOHENSTAUFEN German royal dynasty, ruling Germany and the **Holy Roman Empire**, 1138-1254, and Sicily, 1194-1268. It restored German power and prestige after the setbacks during the Investiture Contest (*see* **Lay Investiture**); it became increasingly embroiled with the papacy for control of Italy following the marriage of **Henry VI** to the Sicilian heiress in 1186. The extirpation of the dynasty by the French allies (**Charles of Anjou**) of Pope **Clement IV** in 1268 continued a period of disunity and territorial fragmentation in Germany and Italy. The Hohenstaufen period marked the high point of German courtly culture, exemplified by the works of Wolfram von Eschenbach, **Gottfried von Strassburg** and Walther von der Vogelweide.

HOHENZOLLERN German dynastic family, ruling in Brandenburg-Prussia, 1415-1918, and as German emperors 1871-1918. They were originally descended from Burchard I, Count of Zollern, in Swabia (d.1061); a subsidiary branch, the Hohenzollern-Sigmaringens, held the throne of Romania from 1866 to 1947.

HOLKARS Ruling dynasty of Indore, southern India, founded by Malhar Rao Holkar, a Maratha soldier who, at his death in 1766, had become virtual king in the region of Malwa. Power crystallized during the long reign of his son's widow, Ahalyabai (1767-95); family forces were defeated by the British in 1804, and princely power ended with Indian independence in 1947.

HOLY ROMAN EMPIRE Name first bestowed in 1254 to denote the European lands ruled by successive dynasties of German kings. It was used retrospectively to include the empire of **Charlemagne**, on whom Pope Leo III conferred the title of Roman Emperor in 800; and also applied to the domains held by **Otto II** (d.983) and his successors. At its fullest extent the Empire included modern Germany, Austria, Bohemia, Moravia, Switzerland, eastern France, the Netherlands and much of Italy. The title lapsed with the renunciation of imperial dignity by Francis II in 1806.

HOMER Putative author of the two great Greek national epic poems, *The Iliad* (or *The Wrath of Achilles*) and *The Odyssey*. The poems stand in a bardic tradition, using verse formulas, but each suggests composition by a single mind. Homer may have composed *The Iliad* in the 8th century BC in the eastern Aegean; the date of *The Odyssey* is less certain.

HOMFRAY family British industrialists. They built an ironworks at Penydarren, near Merthyr Tydfil, Wales, and built the first true railway from there to the sea; in 1804 Richard Trevithick made the first journey in a locomotive engine there, pulling truckloads of iron.

HOMINID Man, considered from the point of view of zoology; a member of the mammalian family *Hominidae*, which includes only one living species, *Homo sapiens*.

HOMINOID Animal resembling man, or with the form of a man.

HOMO SAPIENS Biological genus and species incorporating all modern human beings. It is characterized by a two-legged stance, high forehead, small teeth and jaw, and large cranial capacity; it dates back some 350,000 years.

HONORIUS (384-423) Roman emperor, son of **Theodosius I**. He succeeded to the western half of the Empire when it was divided after his father's death in 395.

HOOVER, HERBERT CLARK (1874-1964) 31st President of the United States. He organized American relief to Europe after the First World War; he was elected Republican President, 1929-33, but bitterly criticized for his failure to combat the Depression. He opposed **Roosevelt's New Deal**; he sat as Chairman of the Hoover Commission, 1947-9 and 1953-5, on simplification of government administration.

HORROCKS, JOHN (1768-1804) Cotton manufacturer. In 1786 he erected a cotton mill at Preston, Lancashire. He was appointed by the **English East India Company** to be the sole supplier of cotton goods to India.

HOTTENTOTS *see* **KHOI**

HOUPHOUËT-BOIGNY, FÉLIX (1905-93) President of the Ivory Coast. A planter and doctor, in 1945 he formed his own political party and was elected to represent the Ivory Coast in the French National Assembly, 1945-58. He entered the French Cabinet, 1956-9, working closely after 1958 with **General de Gaulle** to achieve peaceful decolonization. He became the first Prime Minister of the Ivory Coast in 1959, was elected its first President after independence in 1960, and was re-elected President in October 1990.

HOWE, WILLIAM (1729-1814) 5th Viscount Howe. British general who, after a distinguished career in the **Seven Years' War** (1756-63), commanded British forces during the American War of Independence (1775-8).

HOYSALAS Central Indian dynasty, ruling territory centred on Dorasamudra, near modern Mysore. It was founded by Vishnuvardhana in the first half of the 12th century, consolidated under his grandson, Ballala II, who won control of the southern Deccan, but overthrown in the 14th century by the Turkish sultans of Delhi.

HSIEN-PI Group of tribes, probably of Turkic origin but according to some scholars of mixed Tungusic and Mongolian race. They first emerged as one of the Eastern Hu peoples in southern Manchuria, becoming vassals of the **Hsiung-nu** after 206 BC. From the late 1st century AD they developed into a powerful tribal federation which dominated south Manchuria and Inner Mongolia. The final collapse of Chinese power in the early 4th century enabled them to invade north China repeatedly. Individual Hsien-pi tribes established several short-lived dynasties during the 4th century, and from that time Hsien-pi royal families ruled the dynasties Northern (Toba) Wei, Western Wei, Northern Chou, Eastern Wei and Northern Ch'i, which unified and controlled all of north China.

HSIUNG-NU Chinese name for the vast alliance of nomad tribes that dominated much of central Asia from the late 3rd century BC to the 4th century AD. They were first identified in the 5th century BC, when their constant raids prompted construction of the fortifications which later became the Great Wall of China. Their power was largely broken by the emperor **Wu-ti**; around 51 BC the tribes split into two great groups: the eastern horde, more or less submitting to Chinese control, and the western, which migrated to the steppes. Later, after the collapse of the **Han** dynasty, Hsiung-nu generals, hired as mercenaries, founded the short-lived Earlier Chao and Later Chao dynasties in northern China, c.AD 316-30. No reference to them after the 5th century is extant; the theories linking them with the European **Huns** or the early Turkish empire of central Asia remain unsubstantiated.

HSÜAN-T'UNG (1906-67) Last Emperor of China, succeeding at the age of three on the death of his uncle. He reigned under a regency for three years before being forced to abdicate in 1912 in response to the success of the 1911 revolution. He continued to live in the palace at Peking under the name of Henry Pu-yi until 1924, when he left secretly for a Japanese concession in Tientsin. He ruled as puppet emperor of Manchukuo, 1936-45, was tried as a war criminal in 1950 and pardoned in 1959, when he went to work as a gardener.

HSÜ HSIANG-CH'IEN (1902-91) Commander in Chinese Communist Army, a subordinate of **Chang Kuo-t'ao**, during the Long March, and commander of the Eighth Route Army troops in

the early part of the Sino-Japanese War. He was a leading general in Shansi in the late 1940s during the civil war with the Nationalists, and a member of the Communist Party Central Committee in 1945. He re-emerged as a leading figure in the Cultural Revolution of 1966, and became a member of the CCP Politburo the following year.

HUARI Early Andean civilization (c.AD 600-1000), named after its most characteristic archaeological site, in the highlands of present-day Peru. Its distinctive motif, the 'doorway god' with its rectangular face and rayed headdress, is also found among the vast ruins of Tiahuanaco, on the southern shore of Lake Titicaca, with which it appears to have been linked in its period of imperial expansion.

HUASCAR (d.1533) Son of **Huayna Capac**, on whose death (probably in 1525) he succeeded to the southern half of the Inca Empire, based on Cuzco. He was soon involved in a succession war with his half-brother **Atahuallpa**, who had inherited the northern half of the empire and ruled from Quito. Huascar fled from Cuzco after a series of defeats, but he was captured and forced to watch his family and supporters being murdered. He was himself assassinated by Atahuallpa on the arrival of the Spanish invaders under **Pizarro**, for fear they would restore him to power.

HUAYNA CAPAC (d. c.1525) Inca emperor, youngest son of the principal wife (and sister) of the Inca **Topa**, whom he succeeded in 1493. He reigned most peacefully after an initial succession struggle. He conquered Chachapoyas, in northwest Peru, and later northern Ecuador, returning home on hearing that an epidemic (probably measles or smallpox, brought by Spanish settlers at La Plata) was sweeping his capital, Cuzco; he died after contracting the disease. (Scholars now suggest that his death may have occurred as late as 1530, but that the earlier date was given by the Cuzco Incas in an effort to 'legitimize' **Huascar**'s rule.)

HUDSON, HENRY (c.1550-1611) English seaman, after whom Hudson River, Hudson Strait and Hudson Bay are all named. He explored the islands north of Norway, 1607-8, in search of a Northeast Passage to Asia; in 1609, commissioned by the **Dutch East India Company** to find a Northwest Passage, he sailed up the Hudson River. In 1610, working again for the English, he passed through Hudson Strait and Hudson Bay, but died the following year after being abandoned by his mutinous crew.

HUDSON'S BAY COMPANY Incorporated in England, 1670, to seek a Northwest Passage to the Pacific, to occupy land around Hudson Bay, and to engage in profitable activities. The Company concentrated on fur-trading for two centuries; armed clashes with competitors led to a new Charter, 1821. It lost its monopoly, 1869, as territories were transferred to the Canadian government but is still one of the world's major fur-dealing and general retailing organizations.

HUGUENOTS French followers of the Swiss religious reformer, **John Calvin**. Huguenot rivalry with the Catholics erupted in the French Wars of Religion, 1562-98; under the **Edict of Nantes**, 1598, the two creeds were able to co-exist, despite another religious war 1621-9, but when this edict was revoked by **Louis XIV** in 1685 many Huguenots preferred to flee the country; they settled, to the great benefit of the host states, in Great Britain, the United Provinces, north Germany and in those colonies overseas in which Protestants were tolerated.

HÜLEGÜ (c.1217-65) Mongol leader, grandson of **Genghis Khan** and younger brother of **Möngke**, who led the epic campaign from East Asia to capture Baghdad in 1258; on the disruption of the Mongol Empire after the death of Möngke, he remained to found the Il-Khan state, dominating Persia and the Middle East.

HUMILIATI A society of penitents in 12th century Europe who followed a life of poverty and evangelism. This brought them into conflict with the hierarchy of the Church, and they were condemned as heretics by Pope Lucius III in 1184. They were in some respects similar to the **Cathars**, but unlike the latter did not originally hold doctrines at variance with the Catholic faith. They were finally suppressed in the late 16th century.

HUNDRED DAYS, WAR OF THE Napoleon's attempt, after being defeated and exiled in 1814, to re-establish his rule in France. It began with his return to Paris from Elba in 1815 and ended with his defeat by Great Britain and Prussia at the battle of Waterloo.

HUNDRED YEARS' WAR Prolonged struggle of England and France, beginning in 1337 and ending in 1453. English forces twice came close to gaining control of France: once under **Edward III** (victories at Crécy, 1346, and Poitiers, 1356; Treaty of Brétigny, 1360), and again under **Henry V** (victory at Agincourt, 1415; Henry was recognized as heir to the French throne, 1420). England's resources were insufficient to consolidate these gains, however, and by 1453 the only remaining English possession in France was Calais, which was lost in 1558.

HUNS Mounted nomad archers who invaded southeast Europe across the Volga c.370, and dominated lands north of the Roman frontier until the defeat of their most famous leader, **Attila**, in Gaul at the battle of the Catalaunian Fields in 451. Their empire broke up and disappeared from history, c.455. The Huna who attacked Iran and India in the 5th and 6th centuries, and the **Hsiung-nu** of central Asia, may have been related to the Huns, but this is unproven.

HUNTSMAN, BENJAMIN (1704-50) English steelmaker who invented the crucible process for making high-quality cast steel, c.1750.

HURRIANS Near Eastern people, possibly from the region of Armenia, who briefly controlled most of northern Syria and northern Iraq in the 15th century BC. The principal Hurrian political unit was the kingdom called Mitanni, centred on the Khabur.

HUS, JAN (1372/3-1415) Czech religious reformer, born in Husinec, Bohemia. In 1409 he was appointed rector of the University of Prague; he was fatally involved in the struggles of the **Great Schism**: tricked by a promise of safe conduct into attending the Council of Constance, he was tried and burned for heresy. His death sparked off a Czech national revolt against the Catholic Church and its German supporters, particularly the Emperor Sigismund. *See also* **Hussites**.

HUSSEIN (d.1931) Hashemite sharif of the Hejaz, western Arabia. In 1915 he agreed to join the war of Great Britain against his Ottoman overlords. He proclaimed himself king of the Arabs in 1916 and began the war, aided by T. E. Lawrence, a British agent (Lawrence of Arabia), but his title was challenged by **Ibn Saud**, sultan of Nejd, after 1919. Hussein was forced to abdicate in 1924 and by 1926 Ibn Saud had conquered all of Arabia, although Hussein's sons ruled in Iraq and Transjordan.

HUSSEIN-McMAHON CORRESPONDENCE Letters exchanged in 1915 between Sir Henry McMahon, British High Commissioner in Cairo, and Hussein, sharif of Mecca and later king of Hejaz, setting out the area and terms in which Great Britain would recognize Arab independence after the First World War. Unpublished for decades, they remained a potent source of controversy and tension in the Middle East, especially in their ambiguous references to the future of Palestine.

HUSSEIN, SADDAM (1937-) Iraqi political leader. Active in the Ba'ath Socialist party since 1957, he brought his party to power through a bloodless coup (1968). He served as deputy chairman of the Revolutionary Command Council (1969-79) and as President of Iraq (1979-). He declared war on Iran (1980) but the war ended in stalemate in 1988. After invading Kuwait in 1990, he faced war with the US-led forces in 1991. Despite overwhelming defeat, he maintained himself in power.

HUSSITES Followers of **Jan Hus**. They broke with the papacy, used the Czech liturgy, and made many converts in Bohemia. From 1420 they repelled numerous attacks by Catholic neighbours, retaining freedom of worship until the battle of the White Mountain in 1620 restored Roman Catholicism and forced the Hussites (and others) into exile.

HYKSOS Asiatic invaders, sometimes known as the Shepherd Kings, who overran northern Egypt c.1674 BC, and established the XVth Dynasty. Their capital, Avaris, was located in the eastern delta of the Nile. They were said to have introduced the horse and chariot into Egypt. Their rule collapsed c.1570 BC.

HYWEL DDA (d.950) Also known as Hywel the Good, and to chroniclers as 'King of all Wales'. On the death of his father, Cadell, c.910, he succeeded as joint ruler of Seisyllwg (roughly, modern Cardiganshire and the Towy valley) and from 920 ruled alone following the death of his brother Clydog; he acquired Dyfed (southwest Wales) and Gwynedd (northwest Wales) by marriage and inheritance. His reign was noted for its peacefulness – internally and with England. Hywel's name is associated with the earliest written Welsh law-code.

IBALPIEL II An Amorite dynast, King of Eshnunna (modern Tell Asmar) in the Diyala region of ancient Iraq. He reigned from 1790 to 1761 BC, when he was overthrown by **Hammurabi** of Babylon.

IBO (now Igbo) People (and language) of southeast Nigeria; they were associated with the attempt to secede from Nigeria and set up the state of Biafra in the 1960s.

IBN SAUD (c.1880-1953) Founder of Saudi Arabia; born at Riyadh, now the Saudi Arabian capital. A member of an exiled ruling family, he recaptured Riyadh in 1902 and began the conquest of central Arabia. He established close relations with Britain in the First World War, occupied Hejaz in 1926 and formally established the kingdom of Saudi Arabia in 1932. He signed the first oil-exploration treaty in 1933.

ICONOCLASM The policy of banning, and often destroying, religious images, officially imposed in 8th and 9th century Byzantium. Veneration of icons, previously encouraged, was first prohibited by **Leo III** in 730; the resulting persecutions reached their peak in 741-75. The policy was reversed, 787-814, but then reimposed until the death of Emperor Theophilus, 842; the final restoration of icon veneration, promulgated in 843, is still celebrated as the Feast of Orthodoxy in the Eastern Church.

ICTINUS Ancient Greek architect working in the 5th century BC. He was largely responsible for the Parthenon at Athens, the Temple of the Mysteries at Eleusis and the Temple of Apollo Epicurius at Bassae; he was joint author of a lost treatise.

IDRIS (1890-1983) Former king of Libya. Leader of the Sanusi Order, 1916; he was proclaimed king of Libya at independence in 1950. He was deposed in a coup by the army in 1969, fled the country for exile in Egypt and in 1971 was sentenced to death *in absentia*.

IDRISI, ABU ABD ALLAH MUHAMMAD AL- (1100-c.1166) Medieval geographer. After travel in Spain and North Africa, he entered the service of **Roger II** of Sicily in about 1145; he became a leading mapmaker and scientific consultant to the court of Palermo. He constructed a silver planisphere showing the world, a 70-part world map and a great descriptive work completed in 1154, *The Pleasure Excursion of One Who is Eager to Traverse the Regions of the World*.

IDRISIDS Islamic dynasty, ruling a kingdom occupying the northern part of what is now Morocco from 789 to 926. It was founded by Idris I, a descendant of the Prophet **Mohammed's** son-in-law, **Ali**; after his death in 791 his son, Idris II, reigned until 828, when the kingdom split into a number of principalities. The Idrisids founded the important city of Fez.

IEYASU *see* **Tokugawa**

IGNATIUS OF LOYOLA, ST (1491-1556) Founder of the order of Jesuits. A page and soldier of **Ferdinand of Aragon**, he made a barefoot pilgrimage to Jerusalem, 1523-4; studied at Alcalá, Salamanca and Paris, where in 1534 he planned a new religious order, the Society (or Company) of Jesus, devoted to converting the infidel and counteracting the Protestant Reformation. His Society was approved by the Pope in 1540, and he was appointed its first Superior, or general, in 1541. He was canonized in 1622.

IGOR SVYATOSLAVICH (1151-1202) Russian warrior who succeeded to the title of Prince of Novgorod-Seversk in 1178, and that of Prince of Chernigov in 1198. He led an ambitious but unsuccessful campaign against the Kuman or **Polovtsy** nomads, ending in total defeat in 1185; escaping from captivity in 1186, he returned to resume his rule.

ILIAD Ancient Greek epic poem in 24 books, better called *The Wrath of Achilles*, describing an episode in the Trojan War; attributed to **Homer**.

ILKHANIDS Mongol rulers of Iran, 1256-1353. The dynasty was founded by **Hülegü** after he seized Persia with an army of 13,000 men; captured Baghdad by 1258. They lost contact with the Chinese Mongols after the conversion of **Mahmud of Ghazni** (1255-1304) to Sunni Islam; the dynasty was later weakened by divisions between **Sunni** and **Shias**.

ILTUTMISH Founder of the Delhi Sultanate, son-in-law and successor of **Qutbuddin Aibak** as ruler of the Muslim conquests in India. During his reign, 1211-36, Delhi established itself as the largest, strongest state in northern India.

IMHOTEP Chief minister of **Zoser**, second king of Egypt's IIIrd Dynasty (27th century BC); later worshipped as the god of medicine in Egypt. He was architect of the world's oldest hewn-stone monument, the step pyramid at Saqqara, the necropolis of Memphis.

INCA Name for the Indian group which dominated the central Andes region in the 15th and 16th centuries; also for their emperor and any member of the royal dynasty. From the capital, Cuzco in Peru, they controlled in the 16th century a region extending from Ecuador to north Chile; although lacking either knowledge of the wheel or any form of writing, their society reached a high level of civilization before being destroyed by the Spaniards in 1533. Occasional Inca uprisings occurred until the 19th century.

INDULF King of Alba (Scotland), 954-62. He captured Edinburgh from the Angles of Northumbria before being killed in battle by the Danes.

INNOCENT III (1160-1216) Pope, 1198-1216. In conflicts with the Empire, France and England he asserted superiority of spiritual over temporal power as **Gregory VII**, **Urban II** and **Alexander III** had done, but more widely and more successfully. With him the medieval papacy reached its highest point of influence over European life. He claimed to dispose of the imperial crown, and excommunicated **King John** of England. His methods were mainly but not entirely political; he reconciled some heretics as well as launching the Albigensian Crusade against them, showed favour to St Francis at the beginning of his mission, and in the Fourth **Lateran Council** (1215) imposed spiritual regulations on the whole Church. The Fourth **Crusade** was the major blemish on his career as Pope.

INNOCENT IV (c.1190-1254) Pope, 1243-54. Continued the struggle of previous Popes to establish superiority of spiritual over temporal power in bitter conflicts with the Emperor **Frederick II**.

INÖNÜ, ISMET (1884-1973) Turkish soldier and statesman, succeeding **Atatürk** as President of the Turkish Republic (1938-50). He commanded the fourth Army in Syria, 1916, became Under-Secretary for War in 1918, joined the independence movement and in 1921 led the Turks to victory in the two battles of Inönü (1921), from which he took his name. He successfully negotiated the **Treaty of Lausanne** and was the first Republican Prime Minister, 1923-38. He advocated one-party rule, 1939-46, but later, in opposition, ardently advocated democratic reform.

INQUISITION Established by Pope Gregory IX in 1233 as a supreme Church court to repress heresy following the Albigensian Crusade, it brought about a considerable reduction in the number of heretics. Torture was permitted in 1252, though used less in the 13th century than later. The Inquisition was reorganized as the 'Sacred Congregation of the Roman and Universal Inquisition or Holy Office' in 1542, again as the 'Congregation of the Holy Office', 1908, and as the 'Sacred Congregation for the Doctrine of the Faith', 1965. The Spanish Inquisition was established in 1478, abolished in 1820, and played an important part in imposing religious and civil obedience.

INVESTITURE CONTEST *see* **Lay Investiture**

IRAQ PETROLEUM COMPANY International consortium, set up to exploit oil concessions in Iraq under an agreement signed in 1925. In 1952 a 50-50 share agreement was reached with the government; in 1961, 99 per cent of the group's undeveloped concessions were nationalized, including the rich North Rumaila field. Under the arrangement finally agreed in 1975, IPC paid £141 million in a tax settlement, receiving 15 million tons of crude oil and the right to continue operating in South Rumaila.

IRON AGE The final period among archaeological periods of the prehistoric and early historic Old World, it takes in the barbarian tribes which were contemporaries of the classical civilizations of the Mediterranean, and much of Africa down to colonial times. Iron began increasingly to replace bronze after 1000 BC, and can still be considered one of the world's most important materials.

IROQUOIS American Indians living round the lower Great Lakes. The Iroquois League, founded between 1570 and 1600, united five tribes – the Mohawk, Oneida, Onondaga, Cayuga and Seneca – as 'the People of the Long House', playing a key part in early American history. After defeating their native enemies, they turned on the French; when joined by the Tuscarora in 1722, they became the 'Six Nations'; split during the American Revolution, the League disbanded under the Second Treaty of Fort Stanwix, 1784.

ISAIAH Old Testament prophet, son of Amoz, who stood alongside the kings of Judah in the last part of the 8th century BC. The book that bears his name falls into two parts; there is glorious poetry and profound insight in all, and many passages are taken by Christians to presage the coming of Christ.

ISAURIAN emperors Dynasty of Byzantine (East Roman) emperors, 717-802.

ISMAIL (1830-95) Khedive, or viceroy, of Egypt under Ottoman sovereignty, grandson of **Mohammed Ali**. He studied in Paris, and became viceroy in 1863; in 1867 he persuaded the Ottoman sultan to grant him the title of khedive. He opened the Suez Canal in 1869 and expanded Egyptian rule in the Sudan. He carried further the process of economic and educational change begun by Mohammed Ali, but in doing so incurred a large foreign debt (£100 million by 1876) which ultimately led to British occupation in 1882. He was deposed in 1879 by the Ottoman sultan, in favour of his son.

ISMAIL I (c.1487-1524) Shah of Persia (1501-24) and founder of the **Safavid** dynasty. In 1501 he established what some historians have regarded as the first truly Iranian dynasty since the Arab conquests, although the dynasty was Turkish-speaking and religious affiliation to **Shia** Islam provided the prime focus of loyalty to it. The strength of the state, resting on the Kizilbash (Turcoman tribes owing allegiance to the shah) enabled it to hold off serious threats from the Ottomans and the **Uzbeks** in 1510, and to stabilize its power on the Iranian plateau.

ISMAILIS Branch of the **Shia** division of Islam, which split from other branches over the question of succession to the sixth imam, and gradually developed theological doctrines of its own. Some Ismaili groups were politically active from the 9th to the 13th centuries establishing local rule in Bahrain and eastern Arabia then, on a larger scale, in Tunisia and Egypt (**Fatimid** caliphate); from there a further group, the 'new preaching' led by Hasan-i Sabbah, established itself in northern Persia (*see* **Assassins**). Ismailis of different groups still exist in Syria, Iran, Yemen, Pakistan and India, where the Aga Khan is head of the most important group.

ISMET *see* **Inönü**

ISOCRATES (436-338 BC) Athenian orator and pamphleteer. Too nervous to speak, he nevertheless composed eloquently for others. He preached in favour of enlightened monarchy and Greek unity in face of the threat from Persia.

ITURBIDE, AGUSTÍN (1783-1824) First emperor of independent Mexico. An officer in the Spanish colonial army, 1797; in 1810 he rejected an invitation to join anti-Spanish revolutionaries, and successfully defended Valladolid for the royalists. After 1820, he led a conservative independence movement. He crowned himself Emperor Agustín I in 1822, but in 1823 abdicated in the face of mounting opposition. Returning from Europe, unaware of the death sentence passed in his absence, he was captured and shot.

IVAN III (1440-1505) Grand Duke of Moscow, succeeding his father, Vasily II, in 1462. By conquering Novgorod in 1478 he made Moscow supreme among the principalities of west Russia, known henceforth as Muscovy. He declared Muscovite independence of the Mongols and stopped tribute payments to the **Golden Horde**.

IVAN IV VASILIEVICH 'THE TERRIBLE' (1530-84) Grand Duke of Moscow, 1533-84, and from 1547 Tsar of Russia. He conquered Kazan in 1552, Astrakhan in 1554, destroyed the free city of Novgorod in 1570, and annexed much of Siberia, to create a unified Russian state. Notoriously cruel, he killed his elder son in anger in 1581. His reign of terror was renowned for the establishment of the *oprichnina*, the forerunner of the political police.

JACKSON, ANDREW (1767-1845) Seventh President of the United States, 1829-37. A lawyer, planter and general, he defeated the British attack at New Orleans in 1815. He was elected as the champion of individual freedom and the common man in 1828. In 1832 he vetoed a bill for establishing a national bank, but otherwise supported strong federal government. He is credited – unjustly – with the introduction of the 'spoils system', the dispensing of official jobs as rewards for political support, into American public life.

JACKSON, THOMAS JONATHAN 'STONEWALL' (1824-63) Confederate general in the American Civil War, best known for his mobile tactics in the Virginia theatre, 1861-3.

JACOBINS Members of a French Revolutionary club, founded in May 1789 among the deputies at Versailles. It was named from the former Dominican monastery where early meetings were held. Under the leadership of **Robespierre** the group became increasingly extreme, overthrowing the moderate **Girondins** in 1793 and instituting the Terror. The movement was eliminated after the *coup d'état* of July 1794.

JACQUARD, JOSEPH-MARIE (1752-1834) French textile-machinery inventor. He started work on the Jacquard loom in 1790, broke off to fight in the French Revolution, and completed his designs in 1801. The machine, working on a punch-card system, was capable of duplicating all traditional weaving motions: it replaced all previous methods of figured silk-weaving. In 1806 his invention was declared public property, winning him a pension and a royalty on all sales. At first his looms were burned and he himself attacked by the handweavers of Lyons, fearing loss of employment, but by 1811, 11,000 looms were installed in France.

JACQUERIE Popular uprising in northeast France in 1358, named from the contemporary nobles' habit of referring to all members of the lower classes as 'Jacques'. Unrest began near Compiègne and quickly spread; peasant armies destroyed numerous castles and killed their inmates. Under their leader, Guillaume Cale (or Carle) the peasants joined forces with the Parisian rebels under **Étienne Marcel**, Cale's forces were crushingly defeated at Clermont-en-Beauvaisis on 10 June, and a general massacre followed.

JADWIGA (1371-99) Queen of Poland in her own right. Her marriage to **Władysław II Jagiełło** linked the thrones of Poland and Lithuania (1386).

JAGIEŁŁO, GRAND DUKE OF LITHUANIA *see* **Władysław II Jagiełło**

JAGIELLONIAN dynasty East European ruling family, prominent from the 14th to the 16th century. Founded by Jagiełło, Grand Duke of Lithuania, grandson of **Gedymin**, who married Queen **Jadwiga** of Poland in 1386, thus uniting the two crowns, it later also ruled Bohemia and Hungary.

JAINISM Early Indian religion, emphasizing non-violence, frugality, and the purification of the soul; it regards the existence of God as irrelevant. Shaped and organized in the 6th century BC by the prophet Mahavira, its basic doctrines, at first transmitted orally, were finally codified in the 5th century AD. Much practised among merchants, traders and money lenders.it is followed today by several million people in western and northern India and around Mysore.

JAMES I OF ARAGON (1208-76) Known as 'the Conqueror'. Born in France, he was acknowledged as king of Aragon and Catalonia in 1214, taking full power in 1227. He conquered the Balearic Islands, and in 1233 began a successful campaign to recover Valencia from the Moors. He renounced his French territories in 1258. He formulated an important code of maritime law, and established the Cortes as a parliamentary assembly.

JAMES VI and I (1566-1625) King of Scotland, Ireland and England. The son of Mary Queen of Scots, he succeeded to the throne of Scotland, as James VI, on his mother's enforced abdication in 1567, and to that of England and Ireland, as James I, in 1603 on the death of **Elizabeth I**. In Scotland he created a strong government for the first time, but in England his absolutist policies, extravagant court spending and High Church and pro-Spanish attitudes made him unpopular.

JAMESON RAID Abortive attack launched from Bechuanaland into the South African Republic (Transvaal) in 1895-6, led by Dr (later Sir) Leander Starr Jameson, a colleague of **Cecil Rhodes**. It was intended to overthrow the Afrikaner government of Paul Kruger (1825-1904), but it resulted in the resignation of Rhodes, the worsening of Anglo-Boer relations and Jameson's imprisonment. Jameson, however, returned to public life as Prime Minister of Cape Colony 1904-8.

JARUZELSKI, WOJCIECH (1923-) Polish military and political leader. Working his way up the ranks of the military and the Communist party he became chief of the general staff (1965-8), defence minister (1968-83), and party Politburo member (1971-90). As prime minister (1981-5) he proved unable either to reach a compromise agreement with the powerful independent union, Solidarity, or solve the country's economic problems. He became president in 1985 but resigned in 1990.

JASSY, TREATY OF Pact signed on 9 January 1792 to end the Russo-Ottoman war of 1787-92. It confirmed the **Treaty of Küçük Kaynarca** (or Kuchuk Kainarji), advanced the Russian frontier to the Dniester River, and reinforced Russian naval power in the Black Sea.

JATAKA A popular tale, relating one of the former lives of **Buddha**. The largest collection, the Sinhalese *Jatakatthavannana*, contains 547 stories; other versions are preserved in all branches of Buddhism, and some reappear in non-Buddhist literature, such as *Aesop's Fables*.

JEFFERSON, THOMAS (1743-1826) Third President of the United States, 1801-9. He trained as a lawyer; opposed British colonial rule; became a member of the Continental Congress (1775-6), and chairman of the committee which drafted the Declaration of Independence. He was minister to France, 1785-9; Secretary of State in Washington's administration, 1790-3; Vice-President, 1797-1801. As President he defended the rights of states and completed the **Louisiana Purchase**. In his old age he founded the University of Virginia.

JEM (d.1495) Claimant to the Ottoman sultanate, the younger son of **Mehmed II**. On his father's death in 1481 he attempted to seize the succession, but was pre-empted by his elder brother **Bayezid II**. He declared himself sultan but was defeated at Yenishehir (1481); after a further vain assault on Konya in 1482 he fled, first to Rhodes, then to France. In 1489 he came under the control of Pope Innocent VIII, who received a pension from Bayezid for keeping him safe. For 14 years he was the centre of European intrigues and schemes to invade the Ottoman realms. Charles VIII of France was making plans to use him in a **Crusade** when he died.

JEROME, ST (c.342-419/20) Born at Stridon, now in Yugoslavia, and educated at Rome, he was baptized c.366. He retired for two years as a desert hermit in 375, was ordained priest in Syria in 378 and in 382 returned to Rome as secretary to Pope Damasus. In 385 he left for Palestine, and established a monastery at Bethlehem. He wrote voluminously, including his influential Latin translation of the Bible and numerous controversial polemics.

JESUIT Member of the Society of Jesus, a Roman Catholic order founded in 1534 by St **Ignatius of Loyola**. Organized to support the papacy, to fight heresy and to conduct overseas missionary activity, it quickly established a dominant influence in the Church. Though suppressed, 1773, by Pope Clement XIV and expelled by many European countries in the 18th century, it was restored by Pope Pius VII in 1814, and is now widely entrenched, particularly in education, with schools and universities all over the world.

JESUS OF NAZARETH (8/4 BC-c.AD 29) Jewish teacher whose preaching, personal example and sacrificial death provide the foundations for the religion of Christianity. The name is the Greek form of Joshua, Hebrew for 'Jehovah is salvation'; to this is often added Christ, from the Greek *Christos*, the Hebrew *Messiah*, or anointed one. Born near the end of the reign of Herod the Great, his ministry and Passion are recounted in the four Gospels of the New Testament. He was crucified, but is believed by his followers to have risen from the dead and ascended to heaven as the Son of God.

JEW Originally a member of the tribe of Judah, the fourth son of Jacob, one of the 12 tribes of Israel which took possession of the Biblical Promised Land of Palestine; later a member of the kingdom of Judah, as opposed to the more northerly kingdom of Israel. After the Assyrian conquest in 721 BC, it applied to all surviving adherents of **Judaism**. In modern times it refers to an adherent of the Jewish religion whether by birth or by conversion, or to the child of a Jewish mother.

JEWISH UPRISING First of two major revolts, AD 66-73, against Roman rule in Judaea. The Romans were expelled from Jerusalem, 66, and the country rose in revolt; a revolutionary government was set up. Jewish forces finally succumbed to the Roman armies of **Vespasian** and **Titus**; Jerusalem was stormed, the Temple burned and Jewish statehood ended in 70, and the Jews' last outpost, Masada, fell in 73. A second revolt, in 132-5, in the days of Emperor **Hadrian**, was suppressed with difficulty by the Romans after three years.

JINNAH, MOHAMMED ALI (1876-1948) Hailed as *Qaid-i-Azam*, 'Great Leader', by Indian Muslims, he was founder and first Governor-General of Pakistan. Born in Karachi, he became a highly successful barrister, and in 1906 entered the Indian National Congress. He supported Hindu-Muslim unity until the rise of **Gandhi**. As President of the Muslim League, which he transformed into a mass movement, he adopted the demand for separate Muslim states in 1940, and headed the Muslims in their independence negotiations, 1946-7, securing the partition of India.

JOHANNES IV (d.1889) Christian emperor of Ethiopia. Originally a *ras*, or prince, of Tigre in northern Ethiopia, his strong, militaristic policies were largely thwarted by external threats – from Egypt, Italy and the Mahdist Sudan – and by the internal rivalry of Menelik, ruler of Shoa. Successful against Egypt, 1856-7, and Italy, 1887, Johannes was finally killed at the battle of Matama in a retaliatory invasion against the khalifa **Abd Allah** of the Sudan.

JOHN (1167-1216) King of England, youngest son of **Henry II**. He tried to seize the throne in 1193 while his brother Richard I was away on **Crusade**. He succeeded in 1199 on Richard's death; lost Normandy and other English possessions to the French; was excommunicated, 1209, in a quarrel with Pope **Innocent III**. In 1215, after six years of strife with his barons, he was forced to accept **Magna Carta**, a charter confirming feudal rights and limiting abuses of royal power. He died during renewed civil war.

JOHN II (1455-95) King of Portugal, nicknamed 'the Perfect Prince'; succeeded his father, Alfonso V, in 1481. He broke the power of the richest family in Portugal, the Braganzas; organized expeditions to explore west and central Africa.

JOHN II CASIMIR VASA (1609-72) King of Poland, son of **Sigismund III**. He fought with the **Habsburgs** in the Thirty Years' War and was imprisoned by the French 1638-40. Created a cardinal in 1647, he was elected King of Poland in 1648 on the death of his brother Władysław IV; he fled in the face of the Swedish invasion of 1655. He lost large areas of Polish territory to Sweden at the Peace of Oliva (1660) and to Russia at the Treaty of Andrusovo (1667). He abdicated in 1668, retiring to France as titular abbot of St-Germain-des-Prés.

JOHN II COMNENUS (1088-1143) Byzantine emperor, 1118-43. He fought unsuccessfully to end Venetian trading privileges, 1122; defeated **Pecheneg**, Hungarian, Serbian and Norman threats to the Empire; attempted to confirm Byzantine suzerainty over the Norman kingdom of Antioch.

JOHN III (1537-92) King of Sweden, 1568-92. The elder son, by his second marriage, of **Gustavus I Vasa**, he overthrew his half-brother, **Eric XIV** in 1568 to seize the throne. A learned theologian, he hoped to reconcile the beliefs of Lutheranism and Roman Catholicism, and fought hard but unsuccessfully to impose his own liturgy, known as *The Red Book*, on the Protestant Swedes. He died bitter and frustrated, leaving an impoverished and divided kingdom to his son **Sigismund III**.

JOHN III SOBIESKI (1624-96) King of Poland and Grand Duke of Lithuania. In 1655-60 he fought in the Swedish war. He became commander-in-chief of the Polish army in 1668 and won victories over **Tartars**, Turks and **Cossacks**. He was elected king in 1674. In 1683 he led the army which drove the Turks back from the gates of Vienna, but failed in a long campaign (1684-91) to extend Poland's influence to the Black Sea.

JOHN XXII (1249-1334) Second Avignon Pope, elected 1316. A lawyer and administrator, he was accused of financial extortion and involvement in politics and lowering the reputation of the papacy as a religious force. He contested the election of Louis of Bavaria as German emperor (1324); declared a heretic by Louis and by the Spiritual Franciscans, whom he had criticized, in return he excommunicated and imprisoned Louis' candidate, the anti-Pope, Nicholas V (1328).

JOHN OF AUSTRIA (1545-78) Spanish military commander, often known as Don John, the illegitimate son of Emperor **Charles V**. He commanded a Christian fleet against the Turks in the Mediterranean, 1570-6, winning the battle of Lepanto in 1571. He was commander of the Spanish army against the Dutch Revolt until his death.

JOHN CHRYSOSTOM, ST (c.347-407) Father of the Christian Church. He became a hermit-monk, and was ordained priest in 386. A renowned preacher, he was appointed Archbishop of Constantinople in 398. In 403 he was indicted on 29 theological and political charges, was deposed and banished.

JOHNSON, LYNDON BAINES (1908-73) 36th President of the United States, 1963-9. Elected to Congress, 1937; Senator for Texas, 1949; majority Senate leader, 1955-61. He was largely instrumental in passing civil rights bills of 1957 and 1960. He was elected Vice-President in 1960, and succeeded after **John F. Kennedy's** assassination in 1963. He inaugurated the Great Society programme, but came under increasing criticism over the US involvement in the Vietnam War; he refused renomination in 1968.

JOHNSTON, ALBERT SIDNEY (1803-62) Confederate general in the American Civil War. He was appointed a second-ranking Confederate commander in 1861, and in the following year was mortally wounded leading a surprise attack at the battle of Shiloh.

JOINT-STOCK System of business finance in which the capital is contributed jointly by a number of individuals, who then become shareholders in the enterprise in proportion to their stake. It is usually, but not necessarily, combined with the principle of limited liability, under which the shareholders cannot be legally held responsible for any debts in excess of their share-capital.

JOLLIET, LOUIS (1645-1700) French Canadian explorer and cartographer. He led French parties of exploration from Lake Huron to Lake Erie, 1669, and down the Mississippi, 1672. This latter expedition reached the junction of the Mississippi and Arkansas rivers, but all Jolliet's maps and journals were lost when his canoe overturned; only the diary of the expedition's chaplain, **Jacques Marquette**, survived. He explored the coast of Labrador, 1694, and in 1697 was appointed Royal Hydrographer for New France.

JOSEPH II (1741-90) Holy Roman Emperor. Son of **Maria Theresa** and the Emperor Francis I, he succeeded to the Empire in 1765, and to **Habsburg** lands in 1780. He continued his mother's attempts to reform and modernize the Habsburg dominions; introduced a new code of criminal law, 1787; suppressed the Catholic contemplative orders; agreed to the first partition of Poland. He was harassed by disaffection in Hungary and the Austrian Netherlands which compelled him to revoke some reforms.

JUAN-JUAN (also called Avars). Central Asian nomad people, controlling the northwest border areas of China from the early 5th to the mid-6th century and spreading to Europe, where they were finally destroyed by **Charlemagne** at the end of the 8th century.

JUÁREZ, BENITO (1806-72) National hero of Mexico. Of Indian parentage, he studied law and entered politics in 1831. Exiled to the United States in 1853, he returned in 1858 and fought in the civil war. After his election as Mexico's first Indian President in 1861, he instituted large-scale reforms, led opposition to the French-imposed Emperor **Maximilian** and defeated him in 1867. He was re-elected President in 1867 and again in 1871.

JUDAH Hebrew patriarch, fourth son of Jacob; also the Israelite tribe to which he was ancestor, and the kingdom established by this tribe in southern Palestine, c.932-586 BC.

JUDAH HA-NASI (c.135-c.220) Jewish sage, known as 'the rabbi' or 'our saintly teacher', son of Simeon ben Gamaliel II. He succeeded his father as patriarch (head) of the Jewish community in Palestine. He codified the Jewish Oral Law (supplementing the Written Law, found in the Pentateuch of Moses), and set down his findings in the **Mishnah** (Teaching), which includes regulations for all aspects of Jewish life.

JUDAH MACCABEE (d.160 BC) Third son of the priest Mattathias the Hasmonean, who initiated the revolt against the **Seleucid** king, Antiochus IV, and his decrees against **Judaism**. He succeeded his father and recaptured most of Jerusalem, re-dedicating the temple in 164 BC; he was killed in battle. Eventually, under his brother Simon, an independent Judaea emerged in 140 BC.

JUDAISM Religion of the Jewish people, distinguished by its pure monotheism, its ethical system and its ritual practices, based on the Pentateuch as interpreted by the rabbis of the Talmudic period (first five centuries AD) and their successors up to the present.

JULIAN (c.331-63) Roman emperor, known as 'the Apostate'. He was educated as a Christian but reverted to paganism and tried to make the Empire pagan again after his election as emperor in 360.

JULIUS CAESAR (c.100-44 BC) Dictator of Rome. He was a patrician, general, statesman, orator, historian – one of the greatest leaders produced by the Roman Republic. He wrote vivid accounts of his conquest of Gaul and his civil war with **Pompey**. He was murdered by Brutus and other conspirators.

JUPITER *see* **Zeus**

JUSTINIAN I (483-565) Byzantine emperor, born at Tauresium in the Balkans, Flavius Anicius Justinianus. He went to Constantinople, where his uncle was the Emperor Justin I, becaming co-emperor and then emperor in 527. He was most successful as a legal reformer (Codex Justinianus, 534) and a great builder (the Santa Sophia). His foreign policy, directed at defending and re-extending the imperial frontiers, achieved the reconquest of North Africa, Italy, southern Spain and western Yugoslavia, but the victories proved fragile.

JUTES Germanic people inhabiting Jutland; with the Angles and Saxons they invaded Britain in the 5th century AD, settling mainly in Kent, Hampshire and the Isle of Wight.

KABIR (1440-1518) Indian mystic, who attempted to combine what he regarded as the best elements in **Hinduism** and Islam, a project completed by his disciple **Nanak**. Kabir's thinking, much of it incorporated into the *Adi Granth*, the sacred book of the **Sikhs**, also contributed to the development of several Hindu cults, notably the Kabirpanth, with its total rejection of caste.

KACHINS Rice-farming tribesmen in northern Burma. They total some 500,000 people, with their own Kachin state, capital Myitkyina.

KÁDÁR, JANOS (1912-89) Hungarian statesman. He became a member of the then illegal Communist Party in 1932, was elected to the Central Committee in 1942 and to the Politburo in 1945. Post-war Minister of the Interior; he was expelled in 1950. Rehabilitated in 1954 he joined Imre Nagy's government, forming a new administration after the suppression of the Hungarian Revolution in 1956. Premier 1956-8 and 1961-5, and later First Secretary of the Hungarian Socialist Workers Party.

KALMAR, UNION OF An agreement, concluded in 1397, under which Norway, Sweden and Denmark shared a single monarch. It broke down in 1523 with the rebellion of Sweden led by **Gustavus I Vasa**.

KALMYKS Buddhist Mongolian nomads, now mainly occupying the Kalmyk Autonomous Soviet Socialist Republic which is located in the steppes around the delta of the Volga.

KAMOSE Last king of Egypt's XVIIth Dynasty (c.1650-1567 BC). He ruled the southern part of the country after the death of his father, Seqenenre II; he began the expulsion of the **Hyksos** from the northern part. He was succeeded by his brother, **Amosis I**, founder of the XVIIIth Dynasty.

KARA KHANIDS Turkic dynasty ruling the central Asian territory of Transoxania from 992 to 1211. In 992 they occupied Bukhara, capital of the then disintegrating Samanid dynasty. Split by internal rivalries, the land fell under the domination of the **Seljuks** in the late 11th century and then under the Kara Khitai. After a brief resurgence under Uthman (ruled 1204-11) the dynasty was extinguished in battle with the **Khwarizm**-shah.

KARA KOYUNLU (Black Sheep) Turcoman tribal confederation, ruling Azerbaijan and Iraq c.1375-1467. They seized independent power in Tabriz under Kara Yusuf (ruled 1390-1400 and 1406-20); were routed by **Timur** in 1400; captured Baghdad, 1410; annexed much of eastern Arabia and western Persia under Jihan Shah (ruled 1437-66). They were finally defeated in 1466 and absorbed by the rival **Ak Koyunlu** (ruler Uzun Hasan).

KARENS Agricultural tribesmen occupying a mountainous area in southeast Burma.

KASAVUBU, JOSEPH (c.1910-69) First President of independent Congo. He entered the Belgian Congo civil service, 1942; he became an early leader of the Congo independence movement, and in 1955 president of Abako (Alliance des Ba-Kongo). Joined with **Lumumba** in an uneasy alliance to share government power in 1960. He dismissed Lumumba in September 1960; he was deposed by **Mobutu** in 1965.

KAUNDA, KENNETH (1924-) First President of independent Zambia. A school headmaster from 1944-7, he became in 1953 secretary-general of the North Rhodesia branch of the African National Congress, and in 1958 broke away to form the Zambia African National Congress. He became Prime Minister of Northern Rhodesia, and President of Zambia in 1964, but was defeated in the presidential election in October 1991.

KAZAKHS Traditionally pastoral nomads occupying a semi-arid steppe region in former Soviet central Asia to the east of the Ural River and extending into China. Their territory was incorporated into the Russian Empire between 1830 and 1854. Russian colonization encroached on their best grazing land before the Revolution, and during the 1930s they were settled on collective farms. There are now over 5 million Kazakhs in the former USSR, most of whom live in Kazakhstan.

KEIR, JAMES (1735-1820) Scottish chemist. A retired army officer, he opened a glass factory in Stourbridge in 1775. Three years later he was placed in charge of the Boulton & Watt engineering works at Soho (Birmingham). In 1779 he patented an alloy capable of being forged or wrought when red hot or cold. In partnership with Alexander Blair he set up a chemical plant to make alkali products and soap.

KEMAL, MUSTAPHA *see* **Atatürk**

KENG, CHING-CHUNG (d.1682) Chinese general, son of Keng Chi-mao (d.1671) who became provincial governor of Fukien after 1660. On Chi-mao's death he succeeded him and in 1674 joined in the rebellion of the **Three Feudatories** to prevent losing control over the province. After initial success in southern Chekiang, he was attacked by superior forces and surrendered in 1676. For a time restored to his province, he was later taken to Peking and was executed.

KENNEDY, JOHN FITZGERALD (1917-63) 35th President of the United States, 1961-3. Member of the House of Representatives 1947-53, Senator for Massachusetts 1953-61. He was the youngest candidate and the first Roman Catholic to be elected to the White House. He confronted the USSR in 1962 and successfully insisted that Russian missiles be withdrawn from Cuba. During his administration, the US launched its first manned space flights. He was assassinated on 22 November 1963 in Dallas, Texas.

KENYATTA, JOMO (1891-1978) First President of independent Kenya. He returned from studying in London, 1946, and became president of the Kenya African Union the following year. Convicted and imprisoned for allegedly running the Mau Mau revolt in 1953, he was released in 1959 under restriction. He was leader of the Kenyan delegation to the London constitutional conference of 1962. He became Prime Minister, 1963-4, and President 1964.

KEPPEL, AUGUSTUS (1725-86) British admiral and politician. He served in the British navy from the age of ten. During the **Seven Years War** (1756-63) he captured Belle Isle in 1761; he participated with **Pocock** and his brother Albemarle in the capture of Havana; he commanded the Channel fleet in 1776. He was court martialled after an indecisive battle with the French off Ushant, 1778, during the American War of Independence. A Member of Parliament from 1761, he became First Lord of the Admiralty, 1782-3.

KETT'S REBELLION English uprising in protest against the enclosure of common land. It was named after Robert Kett, a Norfolk smallholder who led the revolt and stormed Norwich in 1549. He was soon defeated by government forces and executed.

KHALIFA *see* **Abd Allah**

KHANATE State, region or district governed by a khan; the title 'khan' or 'kaghan' was first assumed by the chiefs of a tribe - perhaps of Mongol speech and origin - inhabiting the pastures north of the Gobi desert in the 5th century AD, and known to the Chinese as **Juan-Juan**. The title was destined later to adorn half the thrones of Asia.

KHAZARS Turkic and Iranian tribes from the Caucasus, who founded a major trading empire in southern Russia in the 6th century AD. In 737 they moved the capital north to Itil, near the mouth of the Volga, adopted the Jewish religion, and started massive westward expansion. At their peak in the late 8th century they ruled a huge area, from Hungary and beyond Kiev almost to Moscow. Two Byzantine emperors, Justinian II (in 704) and Constantine V (in 732) took Khazar wives. The Khazars were crushed by **Svyatoslav** in 965.

KHITAN Nomadic tribes who, under the Liao dynasty (947-1125), controlled most of present-day Manchuria, Mongolia and part of northeast China. During the Five Dynasties, when China was weak and divided, they destroyed the Po-hai state in Manchuria and invaded northeast China before establishing a Chinese-style dynasty in 947 and adopting many Chinese administrative techniques. They carried on a border war with the Sung dynasty for control of northern China until 1004 when the Sung agreed to pay an annual tribute. The dynasty was destroyed in 1125 by one of its subsidiary peoples, the Jurchen (*see* **Chin**).

KHMER The predominant people of Cambodia; there are also communities of them in eastern Thailand and the Mekong Delta region of Vietnam. Their ancient civilization is exemplified by the remarkable, mainly Hindu temple complex of the Angkor area, dating from the 9th to the 13th century. After the 14th century most lowland Khmers became Theravada Buddhists; the conflicts with the neighbouring Thai and Vietnamese led to wars in the 17th and 19th centuries, and have re-emerged during and since the Cambodian war of 1970-5 (*see also* **Khmer Rouge**).

KHMER ROUGE Communist regime in Cambodia between 1975 and 1979. Originally organized to oppose the right-wing government of **Lon Nol**, President 1970-5. After defeating him and depopulating the capital, Phnom Penh, it subjected the country to a continuing reign of terror until its overthrow in 1979 by the Vietnamese. In 1991 the movement gained two of the twelve seats on the Cambodian Supreme National Council (composed of representatives of the country's warring factions).

KHOI (HOTTENTOTS) A nomadic pastoral people, and their click language, from Namibia, Botswana and the Northern Cape. Probably related to the **San**.

KHOISAN Relating to the Stone Age Bushmen (**San**) and Hottentot (**Khoi**) inhabitants of southern Africa.

KHOSRAU I ANOHSHIRVAN (d.579) Known as 'the Just', shahinshah of **Sasanian** Persia 531-79. He succeeded his father Kavadh, whom he helped to suppress the Mazdakite heretics. He also reorganized the bureaucracy and religious establishment, fought back against Byzantium, and restored the dynasty's flagging fortunes. He patronized both Greek and Sanskrit learning, and is reputed to have brought the game of chess to the West from India.

KHOSRAU II 'THE VICTORIOUS' (d.628) (also known as Chosroes) The last great **Sasanian** king of Persia. He made a bid for power on the assassination of his father, Hormizd IV, in 590, but was expelled. He fled to Byzantine territory, and after being provided with forces by the Emperor Maurice (582-602) gained the Persian throne in the following year. When Maurice was murdered by the usurper Phocas in 601, Khosrau pledged vengeance against the whole Byzantine people, and invaded the empire with vast forces. Eventually he captured Antioch, Jerusalem and Alexandria, camping repeatedly along the Bosporus opposite Constantinople, but for lack of ships was never able to cross. **Heraclius**, a capable general, overthrew Phocas and, after numerous brilliant campaigns in Asia Minor, finally threatened the Sasanian capital at Ctesiphon. By this time both empires were exhausted, and social unrest at Ctesiphon forced Khosrau's son Shiruya (Siroes) to acquiesce in the killing of his father, and the ending of the war, in 628.

KHRUSHCHEV, NIKITA (1894-1971) Soviet statesman, first secretary of the Soviet Communist Party (1953-64) and prime minister (1958-64). A close associate of **Stalin**, he emerged as leader after his death. He promoted a policy of 'peaceful coexistence' with other foreign powers, but the Cuban missile crisis with the US (1962) and a dispute with China over borders and economic aid brought about his downfall in 1964.

KHWARIZM Ancient central Asian territory along the Amu Darya (River Oxus) in Turkestan; part of **Achaemenid** Persia, 6th to 4th centuries BC. Conquered for Islam in the 7th century AD; it was ruled by an independent dynasty, the Khwarizm-shahs, from the late 11th to the early 13th century; successively conquered by Mongols, Timurids and **Shaybanids**, in the early 16th century it became centre of the khanate of Khiva, under the **Uzbeks**. After repelling many invasions, it was absorbed as a Russian protectorate in 1873. As a result of the 1917 Revolution it became the short-lived Khorezm Peoples' Soviet Republic (1920-4). From 1924-91 the region was split into the Turkmen and Uzbeck SSRs, which became the independent states of Turkmenistan and Uzbeckistan respectively in 1991, following the collapse of the Soviet Union.

KIKUYU Bantu-speaking people of Kenya and their language; they were associated with the Mau Mau revolt against the British in the 1950s.

KILLIAN, ST (d.697) Irish bishop, known as the Apostle of Franconia; he was martyred at Würzburg.

KIM IL-SUNG (1912-) North Korean leader. Involved in guerrilla resistance to Japanese occupation (1930s), he fought in World War II in the Soviet Red Army, returning to Korea in 1945. Head of the Democratic People's Republic of Korea (1948-), he also became the nation's premier (1948-72) and President from 1972. His lengthy rule has been characterized by rigid adherence to communist orthodoxy, economic backwardness and suppression of political opposition.

KING, PHILIP PARKER (1791-1856) British naval officer, explorer of Australia and South America. He conducted surveys of Australia's tropical and western coasts from 1818 to 1822, and of the coasts of Peru, Chile and Patagonia from 1826 to 1830.

KING PHILIP'S WAR Savage conflict between Indians and English settlers in New England, 1675-6. King Philip (Indian name, Metacom) was chief of the Wampanoag tribe; during the fighting 600 white men died and entire Indian villages were destroyed.

KING WILLIAM'S WAR North American extension of the War of the Grand Alliance (1689-97) between William III of England, supported by the **League of Augsburg**, and **Louis XIV**'s France. The British captured parts of eastern Canada but failed to take Quebec; France penetrated into present-day New England but failed to seize Boston. The *status quo* was restored under the **Treaty of Ryswyck**. *See also* **Nine Years' War**.

KIPCHAKS *see* **Polovtsy**

KIPCHAK KHANATE *see* **Golden Horde**

KIRGHIZ Turkic-speaking people of central Asia. They were widely dispossessed of their traditional nomad grazing lands during Russia's 19th-century expansion. Their protest revolt in 1916 was bloodily suppressed, with more than a third of the Kirghiz survivors fleeing to China. The remainder now live mostly in Kirghizia.

KLONDIKE Tributary of the Yukon River, Canada. It became world-famous in 1896, when gold was found in Bonanza Creek; 30,000 prospectors swarmed in from all over the world. By 1910 the main deposits had been worked out and the population reduced to 1000; all mining ceased in 1966.

KNÄRED, PEACE OF Treaty concluding the Kalmar war of 1611-13, fought between Denmark and Sweden over the control of north Norway. It was provoked by Sweden's king, **Charles IX**, claiming sovereignty over the region. The Danes took the Swedish ports of Kalmar (1611) and Älvsborg's vital western harbour (1612). The ignominious peace, including the payment of a massive ransom for the return of Älvsborg, was signed by Charles' son and successor, **Gustavus II Adolphus**.

KNIGHTS HOSPITALLERS OF ST JOHN Members of a military and religious order, the Hospital of St John of Jerusalem, founded in the 11th century to help poor and sick pilgrims to the Holy Land. The Order was recognized by the papacy in 1113; it became active in the **Crusades** but was driven from Palestine in 1291. It conquered Rhodes in 1310, and as the Knights of Rhodes grew in wealth and power until expelled by the Turks in 1522. The Order was moved by **Charles V** to Tripoli (to 1551), and thereafter to Malta until it was deposed by **Napoleon** in 1798, after which it took refuge in Russia. Reformed in 1879 as the charitable order of St John, its English branch is now widely known for its ambulance and first aid work.

KOLCHAK, ALEXANDER VASILYEVICH (1874-1920) Russian counter-revolutionary admiral. He led a *coup d'état* within the **White** (Provisional) government in Siberia in 1918, and was recognized as ruler of Russia by the Western allies; but he was betrayed to the **Bolsheviks** and shot.

KONIEV, IVAN STEPANOVICH (1897-1973) Marshal of the Soviet Union. He was a front commander, 1941-3; senior commander in the liberation of the Ukraine, the Soviet drive into Poland

(1944), and the attack on Berlin and liberation of Prague, 1945. Between 1956 and 1960 he was commander-in-chief of the **Warsaw Pact** forces.

KÖPRÜLÜ (also spelled Kuprili) Family of pashas and generals of Albanian origin, who held high office in the Ottoman state in the second half of the 17th century. The founder of the family's fortunes, Köprülü Mehmed Pasha, was called to the grand vizierate in 1656 by **Mehmed IV** at the age of 80, being succeeded as grand vizier by his son Fazil Ahmed Pasha in 1661, and by his son-in-law Kara Mustafa Pasha (1676-83). The last significant member of the family was Köprülüzade Mustafa Pasha, grand vizier 1689-91. Their military and administrative reforms did much to arrest the decline of the Ottoman house (final reduction of Crete, 1669; conquest of Podolia, 1672), but the over-confident policies of Kara Mustafa Pasha, culminating in his failure before Vienna in 1683, severely damaged the fabric of the state and sowed the seeds of future defeat.

KORAN Holy book of Islam, believed by Muslims to be the word of God communicated to the Prophet, **Mohammed**. The text is said to have been definitely fixed by order of the third caliph, **Othman**; containing 114 chapters of different lengths and content, it serves as a basis of law and social morality as well as of doctrine and devotion.

KORNILOV, LAVR GEORGIYEVICH (1870-1918) Russian general. An intelligence officer during the Russo-Japanese war of 1904-05, and military attaché in Peking 1907-11, he was captured by the Austrians in 1915, escaping the following year. He was placed in charge of Petrograd military district after the February Revolution, 1917; he was appointed commander-in-chief by Kerensky. Accused of attempting a military *coup d'état* he was imprisoned, but escaped and took command of the anti-Bolshevik ('White') army in the Don region. He was killed at the battle for Yekaterinodar.

KOŚCIUSZKO, TADEUSZ (1746-1817) Polish general and patriot. After military training in Warsaw, he went to America to join the 'struggle for liberty' there (1777-80). He fought Russia and then Prussia in 1792-3 in an unsuccessful attempt to save Poland from a second partition. He led a national uprising against Russia and Prussia in 1794 which failed, and precipitated the final partition of Poland the following year. He spent much of the rest of his life in exile, attempting to enlist foreign support for the recreation of a Polish state.

KRUM (d.814) Khan of the Bulgars, 802-14. After **Charlemagne's** defeat of the Avars in 796, he greatly extended the power and territory of the Pannonian Bulgars. His early forays against Byzantium were repulsed, but he decisively defeated Emperor Nicephorus I in 811, and besieged Constantinople in 813, though he died during a second siege the following year.

KRUPP, ALFRED (1812-87) German industrialist and arms manufacturer. He was the son of Friedrich Krupp (1787-1826), founder of the family's cast-steel factory at Essen in 1811. Alfred perfected techniques to produce first railway track and locomotive wheels, then armaments. The Franco-Prussian War (1870-1) was won largely with Krupp field-guns, and the firm became the largest weapon manufacturer in the world, at one time supplying the armies of 46 nations.

KUBLAI KHAN (1215-94) Mongol emperor of China, founder of the Yüan dynasty. Grandson of **Genghis Khan**, he was proclaimed Great Khan in 1260 in succession to his brother **Möngke**. He reunited China, divided since the eclipse of the T'ang dynasty. His court was first described to the West by the Venetian, **Marco Polo**.

KÜÇÜK KAYNARCA, TREATY OF (also known as Kuchuk Kainarji) A pact signed on 21 July 1774 to end the Russo-Ottoman war of 1768-74. Under its terms the Ottomans renounced their previously undisputed control of the Black Sea and allowed Russia the privilege of representing the interests of the Orthodox Christians in Moldavia, Wallachia and the Aegean Islands; this provided the basis much later for Russian interference in the affairs of the Ottoman Empire.

KU KLUX KLAN American anti-Negro secret society, founded in 1866 to assert white supremacy and oppose the rule of the 'carpetbaggers' in the Southern states. It was declared illegal in 1871, but was relaunched in 1915, and broadened to attack not only Negroes but also Jews, Roman Catholics and foreigners. Violently active during the early 1920s in the mid-West and South, and again in the South in the 1960s, it

came under increasing attack as a result of Federal enforcement of the Civil Rights Acts of 1964 and 1965.

KUMANS *see* **Polovtsy**

KUN, BELA (1886-?1937) Hungarian revolutionary leader. He led the Communist insurgents who overthrew the Karolyi regime in 1918. On becoming premier in 1919, he attempted to reorganize the country on Soviet principles, but was forced into exile four months later.

KUO-MIN CHÜN (People's Army) Group of warlord armies led by **Feng Yü-hsiang**, 1924-8.

KUOMINTANG (also known as Chinese Nationalist Party) Political Party, ruling mainland China from 1928 to 1949, and since then (from Taiwan) claiming to be the only legitimate Chinese government. It evolved from a revolutionary group formed after the Chinese Republican Revolution of 1911 and was outlawed in 1913. Three short-lived governments were established under **Sun Yat-sen**, between 1917 and 1923 when the party allied with the Chinese Communists. Jointly they conquered most of the country, but split, 1927-8; co-operation was renegotiated in face of a Japanese invasion, 1937. Civil war was resumed in 1946, ending with Communist victory in 1949.

KURDS A Muslim people, speaking an Indo-European language, numbering up to 19 million, mostly in the mountains where Iran, Iraq and Turkey meet. Hopes of an autonomous Kurdistan emerging from a defeated **Ottoman** Empire, raised by the 1920 **Treaty of Sèvres**, were stillborn: Atatürk suppressed the Kurds. The Soviet Union, whose forces occupied part of Iran in the Second World War, encouraged the proclamation of a Kurdish republic but this collapsed after the Russians withdrew. In Iraq, fighting broke out with government troops in 1961. Nine years later, Baghdad offered the Kurds limited autonomy but the war restarted in 1974. Iranian support for the Kurds was withdrawn following an Iraqi-Iranian agreement in 1975. The Iraqis gassed Kurds at Halabja in 1988. The US-led coalition, which drove Iraq from Kuwait in 1991, encouraged an unsuccessful rising against Baghdad and created a safe haven for Kurds inside northern Iraq.

KUSHANS Imperial dynasty, ruling in central Asia and northern India from the late 1st to the mid-3rd century AD, and traditionally founded by Kanishka, who succeeded to the throne of a kingdom extending from Benares in the east to Sanchi in the south, some time between AD 78 and 144. The Kushan Empire lasted about 150 years, until its kings in Taxila and Peshawar were reduced to vassals of the Persian **Sasanians**.

KYANZITTHA (1084-1112) One of the first great kings of Burma, responsible for the expansion of **Buddhism**.

LA For all personal names prefixed by la, le, etc., see under following element.

LAIRD, MACGREGOR (1808-61) Scottish explorer, shipbuilder and trader. He designed the first ocean-going iron ship, the 55-ton paddle-steamer *Alburkah*, and in it accompanied in 1832 an expedition to the Niger delta. He ascended the river's principal tributary, the Benue, developed West African commerce in an attempt to undermine the slave trade, and pioneered transatlantic shipping routes. He promoted a second major expedition, penetrating 150 miles further up the Niger than any previous European, in 1854.

LAMAISM Form of **Buddhism** established in Tibet c.750. It is derived from Mahayana beliefs, combined with elements of erotic Tantrism and animistic Shamanism. In 1641 the Mongols inaugurated the appointment of the Dalai Lama, to rule Tibet from Lhasa, while the Panchen Lama from the Tashi Lhunpo monastery near Shigatse became spiritual head of the religion. The last Dalai Lama, fourteenth in a line claiming descent from Bodhisattva Avalokiteshvara, ancestor of the Tibetans, accepted exile in India in 1959. Lamaism temporarily lost its hold in Tibet, but again now has widespread support.

LANGOSCO Prominent family of medieval Pavia, Italy. Supporters of the **Guelph** (anti-imperial) party, they gained control of Pavia in 1300-15 and 1357-9, but lost it to their rivals, the **Visconti** of Milan.

LAO-TZU Originator of the Chinese Taoist philosophy. Little definite is known of his life, though he is traditionally said to have met Confucius during the 6th century BC. His authorship of the *Tao-te Ching*, one of the central Taoist texts, is unproven, and it certainly dates from a later period (probably 3rd century BC). Since his

death he has been venerated as a philosopher by Confucians, as a saint or god by many Chinese, and as an imperial ancestor during the **T'ang** dynasty (AD 618-907).

LAPPS Inhabitants of northern Scandinavia and the Kola Peninsula of Russia. The origin of these people is obscure, but their history goes back at least 2000 years. The best known, but smallest, group are nomadic reindeer herders; their forest and coastal cousins rely on a semi-nomadic hunting and fishing economy.

LA TÈNE Celtic Iron Age culture, flourishing in central Europe from c.500 BC until the arrival of the Romans, and in remote areas such as Ireland and northern Britain until the 1st century AD. It was named after an archaeological site excavated near Lake Neuchâtel, Switzerland. Most surviving Celtic art – weapons, jewellery, tableware, horse and chariot decoration – is characteristically La Tène in motif and design.

LATERAN COUNCILS Four Church Councils were held at the Lateran Palace in Rome during the Middle Ages. The first (1123) confirmed the **Concordat of Worms** which ended the Investiture Contest; the second (1139) reformed the Church after the schism at Innocent II's election; the third (1179) marked the end of the conflict with **Frederick I Barbarossa** and introduced a two-thirds majority rule for papal elections; the fourth (1215), the high water mark of **Innocent III's** pontificate, inaugurated large-scale reform to deal with the recent widespread dissatisfaction with the Church, and proclaimed a **Crusade**.

LATIN EMPIRE OF CONSTANTINOPLE From 1204 to 1261 the Byzantine capital, Constantinople, was ruled by a succession of western European crusaders after its capture by the Venetian-backed armies of the Fourth **Crusade**; its wealth was systematically pillaged before it was captured by Michael VIII Palaeologus, the Greek Emperor of Nicaea, in 1261.

LAUSANNE, TREATY OF Agreement signed on 24 July 1923 by First World War Allies with Turkish nationalists. It recognized the territory and independence of the New Turkish Republic which had replaced the Ottoman Empire. Turkey abandoned claims to its former Arab provinces, recognized British and Italian rights in Cyprus and the Dodecanese Islands, and opened the Turkish straits (Dardanelles) linking the Aegean and the Black Sea to all shipping.

LAY INVESTITURE The right claimed by many medieval rulers to appoint and install their own bishops. The denial of this right by the papacy gave rise to the Investiture Contest (1075-1122); a form of settlement was reached at the **Concordat of Worms**.

LEAGUE OF NATIONS Organization set up by the Allies for international co-operation at the Paris Peace Conference in 1919 following the end of the First World War. Weakened by the non-membership of the United States, it failed to halt German, Japanese and Italian aggression in the 1930s. Moribund by 1939, it was replaced in 1946 by the **United Nations**.

LEE, KWAN YEW (1923-) Political leader of the Republic of Singapore. An outstanding law student at Cambridge, he worked for labour unions before entering politics (1954). He founded the People's Action Party in 1955. When Singapore became a self-governing state he was elected prime minister, holding office for over 25 years (1965-90). He promoted economic development, regional co-operation and a policy of non-alignment. A conservative politican of authoritarian temperament, he was also a major spokesman of the Association of Southeast Asian Nations (ASEAN).

LEE, ROBERT E (1807-70) Commander-in-chief of the Confederate (Southern) army in the American Civil War, 1861-5. He graduated top cadet from West Point military academy, 1829; fought in the Mexican War of 1846-8. In 1861 he resigned his commission to lead the Virginian forces; he was military adviser to Jefferson Davis, commander of the Army of Northern Virginia, and General-in-Chief of the Confederate Armies. He surrendered at Appomattox Court House on 9 April 1865. After the war he served as President of Washington College (later Washington and Lee University), Virginia.

LEGALISM Ancient school of Chinese thought, advocating institutional rather than ethical solutions in politics, and teaching that governments should rule by rigid and harshly enforced laws, irrespective of the views of their subjects. It was first adopted as a state ideology by the **Ch'in** dynasty (221-206 BC) and regularly revived since, particularly during periods of national crisis.

LENIN (1870-1924) Architect of the Russian Revolution; born Vladimir Ilych Ulyanov. Converted to Marxism while training to be a lawyer, he was exiled to Siberia, 1897-1900. He led the Bolshevik wing of the Social Democratic Party from 1903. He returned from Switzerland in 1917 at the outbreak of revolution and in October overthrew Kerensky's government to become first head of the Soviet government, 1917-24. His influential writings include *What Is To Be Done?*, *Imperialism, the Highest Stage of Capitalism*, *The State and Revolution* and *The Development of Communism*.

LEO I, THE GREAT (d.461) He succeeded to the papacy in 440, and was the founder of papal primacy. As a theologian he defined Catholic doctrine, and secured the condemnation of the **Monophysites** at the **Council of Chalcedon** (451). He asserted the primacy of the Roman see against Constantinople. In 452 he saved Rome from the **Huns**.

LEO III (675-741) Byzantine emperor, founder of the Isaurian, or Syrian, dynasty. He seized the throne in 717, defeated the Arab attack on Constantinople, and went on to drive them from Anatolia. He launched the policy of **iconoclasm**, which opened deep religious conflict in the Empire.

LEO VI (866-912) Byzantine emperor, known as 'the Wise' or 'the Philosopher'. Son of Basil I the Macedonian, he became co-emperor in 870, and attained full power in 886. He issued a set of imperial laws, the **Basilica**, which became the accepted legal code of Byzantium.

LEO IX (Bruno of Egisheim) (1002-54) Pope and saint. He became Bishop of Toul in 1026, and in 1048 was appointed Pope by **Henry III** of Germany, a relation. He showed his reforming spirit by demanding also to be elected by the clergy of Rome; and also by condemning simony and clerical marriage, and by travelling widely in order to spread reforming ideas. He was defeated and briefly held captive by the Normans of southern Italy. His assertion of papal supremacy led to the great schism of 1054 between the Eastern and Western churches.

LEOPOLD II (1835-1909) King of the Belgians. The son of Leopold I, he succeeded in 1865. He was instrumental in founding the Congo Free State, 1879, over which he secured personal control in 1885. Under his guidance, Belgium became a significant industrial and colonial power. He handed over sovereignty in the Congo to his country in 1908.

LETTOW-VORBECK, PAUL VON (1870-1964) German general. He served in the Southwest Colonial Forces, helping to suppress the Herero and Hottentot rebellions; as commander of the (German) East African Colonial Forces he repelled a British landing in Tanganyika, in 1914, and with less than 17,000 troops pinned down British, Portuguese and Belgian forces of over 300,000 in East Africa, 1914-18. He led the right-wing occupation of Hamburg, 1919. He became a member of the Reichstag, 1929-30 and tried without success to organize conservative opposition to **Hitler**.

LEVELLERS Members of a radical movement both in the Parliamentary army and in London during the English Civil War. It advocated total religious and social equality among 'freeborn Englishmen', and sought an extreme form of republican government based on the pamphlet *The Agreement of the People* (1648) written by its leader, John Lilburne (c.1614-57). It was suppressed by **Oliver Cromwell** at Burford, Oxfordshire in 1649.

LEWIS, JOHN LLEWELLYN (1880-1969) United States labour leader. In 1905 he became legal representative to the United Mine Workers of America, and its president from 1920 to 1960. With the American Federation of Labour (AFofL), he encouraged the organization of mass production workers into industrial unions. Expelled from the AFofL, these unions then set themselves up in 1935 as the Congress of Industrial Organizations (CIO), with Lewis as president. He himself resigned from CIO in 1940, and withdrew the mineworkers in 1942.

LEWIS, MERIWETHER (1774-1809) American explorer; *see under* **Clark, William**

LIBERATION FROM FRENCH RULE, WAR OF Penultimate struggle of the Napoleonic Wars, when the French armies, after their retreat from Russia in 1812, suffered a series of setbacks against a new coalition of Britain, Prussia, Sweden and Austria, culminating in defeat at the battle of the Nations (1813). The allies then advanced to Paris, Napoleon abdicated, peace was made with France and the **Congress of**

Vienna was called (1814) to make a settlement for the rest of Europe.

LIGUE *see* **Catholic League**

LILIUOKALANI (1838-1917) Queen of Hawaii, 1891-5; born in Honolulu. She opposed the renewal of the Reciprocity Treaty, 1887, under which her brother, King Kalakaua, granted the US commercial rights and Pearl Harbor; she supported Oni Pa's party, whose motto was 'Hawaii for the Hawaiians'. Deposed by the US-inspired provisional government in 1893, she abdicated in 1895 after a loyalist revolt. In 1898 she composed the famous Hawaiian song *Aloha Oe*.

LINCOLN, ABRAHAM (1809-65) Sixteenth President of the United States, 1861-5. Raised in the backwoods of Indiana, he was a self-taught lawyer. He entered Congress in 1847, eventually being elected President, on an anti-slavery platform. He fought the Civil War (1861-5) to preserve national unity; proclaimed the emancipation of slaves in 1863, and was assassinated in 1865 by John Wilkes Booth, a fanatical Southerner.

LI TZU-CH'ENG (c.1605-45) Chinese rebel leader, born in Shensi. He was a bandit chieftain, 1631-45, during the final disturbed years of the **Ming** dynasty. After first operating in Shensi, he overran parts of Honan and Hupeh in 1639, and captured Kaifeng (1642) and all of Shensi (1642-4). In 1644 he also invaded Shansi, and in April seized Peking and proclaimed himself emperor. He was defeated by the combined tribes of General **Wu San-kuei** and the **Manchus**, and was driven from Peking, retreating first to Sian and then into Hupeh.

LIVINGSTONE, DAVID (1813-73) Scottish missionary and explorer. He started his mission career in the Botswana region in 1841. He crossed the Kalahari Desert; reached the Zambezi, 1851; and Luanda, 1853; discovered the Victoria Falls, 1855; and explored the basin of Lake Nyasa and the Upper Congo. He was feared lost in early 1870, but was found by **Stanley** near Lake Tanganyika in 1871.

LIVONIAN ORDER Society of German crusading knights, also known as Brothers of the Sword, or Knights of the Sword. They conquered and Christianized Livonia (covering most of modern Latvia and Estonia) between 1202 and 1237, but were reprimanded by both pope and emperor for their brutal approach to conversion. They were destroyed by pagan armies at the battle of Saule in 1236, and the following year were disbanded and reorganized as a branch of the **Teutonic Order**. After secularization (1525) the last Grand Master of the Order became Grand Duke of Courland, a fief of the Polish crown.

LLOYD GEORGE, DAVID (1863-1945) British statesman. Born into a poor Welsh family, he was elected a Liberal Member of Parliament in 1890, and entered the Cabinet as President of the Board of Trade (1905-08) and Chancellor of the Exchequer (1908-15), introducing an ambitious welfare and pension programme. When a coalition Cabinet was formed during the First World War, he became Minister of Munitions (1915-16), and Minister of War (1916), replacing the Liberal Party leader, H.H. Asquith, as Prime Minister later the same year. In 1918 the coalition won a General Election and Lloyd George represented Great Britain at the **Paris Peace Conference**, where he exercised a moderating influence on his allies. In 1922 the Conservative Party withdrew its support from the coalition and the Liberals, divided between Asquith and Lloyd George, were heavily defeated in a new General Election. Although Lloyd George became party leader, 1926-31, and remained in Parliament almost until his death, he became an increasingly isolated political figure, and the Liberal Party steadily declined as a political force.

LOCARNO PACT A treaty, signed 1 December 1925, between Great Britain, France, Germany, Italy and Belgium. Under its terms Britain and Italy agreed to guarantee the frontiers of Germany with Belgium and France and the continued demilitarization of the Rhineland. **Hitler** repudiated it on 7 March 1936, stationing troops on both sides of the Rhine and re-fortifying it.

LOCKE, JOHN (1632-1704) English philosopher. His most important political work, the second *Treatise of Civil Government* (1690) provided the theoretical justification for government with only limited and revocable powers; his main philosophical work, *An Essay concerning Human Understanding* (1690) was the basis for most 18th century European thought on the function of reason and the importance of environment in life.

LOESS Fine, yellowish, often very fertile soil, carried by the wind; large deposits are found in Europe, Asia and North America.

LOLLARDS Members of a reforming religious movement, influential in the 14th and 15th centuries in Europe, especially in England under **John Wyclif**. It was widely popular for its attacks on Church corruption and its emphasis on individual interpretation of the Bible as the basis for a holy life, but was repressed under the English King Henry IV.

LOMBARDS German people ruling northern Italy, 568-774. Originally one of the tribes forming the **Suebi**, they migrated south from northwest Germany in the 4th century. By the end of the 5th century they occupied approximately the area of modern Austria north of the Danube, and in 568 crossed the Alps into Italy. The Lombard kingdom of Italy was conquered by the **Franks** in 774.

LOMBARD LEAGUE Association of north Italian cities, established in the 12th and 13th centuries to resist the authority of the **Holy Roman Empire**. The League was originally founded in 1167, with 16 members and the blessing of Pope **Alexander III** to defy **Frederick I Barbarossa**, hostilities ending in 1177 with the Peace of Venice and in 1183 with the Peace of Constance. In 1226 the League was revived and strengthened to avert new imperial ambitions by **Frederick II** but was dissolved after Frederick's death in 1250.

LONDON RIOTS Popular demonstrations in 1641 by Londoners outside the Houses of Parliament and **Charles I**'s palace at Whitehall, demanding that the king's chief minister, Strafford, should be sentenced to death. He was.

LONG, HUEY PIERCE (1893-1935) United States Senator and Governor of Louisiana. He was elected governor in 1928 after a noisy demagogic campaign for the redistribution of wealth, and became a senator in 1932. He was assassinated.

LON NOL (1914-85) President of Cambodia, 1970-5. He became a general in the army, then Prime Minister, 1966-7, and again in 1969. He seized power from Prince **Sihanouk** in a right-wing coup in 1970, but was ousted and fled to Bali in 1975 when the Communist **Khmer Rouge** overran the country.

LOUIS I, THE GREAT (1326-82) King of Hungary, 1342-82. He succeeded his father, Charles Robert, a member of the Neapolitan dynasty of Anjou, who was invested with the kingdom after the extinction of the Árpád dynasty in 1301. Louis fought wars against Naples and Venice; in 1370 he acquired the Polish crown, but with little power, and won most of Dalmatia in 1381. One of his daughters, Maria, became Queen of Hungary; the other, **Jadwiga**, Queen of Poland.

LOUIS THE PIOUS (778-840) Emperor of the Franks, son of **Charlemagne**. He was crowned co-emperor in 813, was twice deposed by his four sons and twice restored (830 and 834); his death preceded the break-up of the empire.

LOUIS VI (1081-1137) King of France, also known as Louis the Fat. Son of Philip I, he was designated his successor in 1098, and crowned in 1108. He made substantial progress in extending French royal power and fought major wars against Henry I of England (1104-13 and 1116-20). He arranged an important dynastic marriage between his son, **Louis VII**, and Eleanor, heiress of Aquitaine.

LOUIS VII (c.1120-80) Known as *Le Jeune* (the Young). King of France, succeeding his father, **Louis VI**, in 1137, after marrying Eleanor, heiress to the dukedom of Aquitaine, and thus effectively extending his lands to the Pyrenees. He repudiated Eleanor for misconduct in 1152, upon which she married his great rival, **Henry II** of England, who took over the claim to Aquitaine. The later years of his reign were marked by continual conflict with the English.

LOUIS IX (1214-70) Capetian king of France, canonized as St Louis. He was crowned at the age of 13. In 1228 he founded the Abbey of Royaumont, and in 1248 led the Sixth **Crusade** to the Holy Land. He sought peace with England by recognizing Henry III as Duke of Aquitaine. He died on a second Crusade, to Tunisia.

LOUIS XI (1423-83) King of France, son of Charles VII. He succeeded in 1461; in 1477 he defeated a rebellion of nobles, led by **Charles the Bold**, Duke of Burgundy. By 1483 he had united most of France with the exception of Brittany.

LOUIS XII (1462-1515) King of France. Son of Charles, Duke of Orléans, he succeeded his cousin, Charles VIII, in 1498. He embarked on fruitless Italian wars (1499-1504, 1508-13), and was finally driven out by the Holy League – an alliance of England, Spain, the Pope and the Holy Roman Empire – in 1513.

LOUIS XIV (1638-1715) The Sun King (*Le Roi Soleil*), ruler of France without a First Minister, 1661-1715, hence looked upon as the archetype of an absolute monarch. The son of Louis XIII and Anne of Austria, he succeeded in 1643 but remained under **Mazarin**'s tutelage until the cardinal's death. He extended and strengthened France's frontiers, built the palace of Versailles and set a European-wide pattern for courtly life. He founded or refashioned academies, supported artists and craftsmen, writers, musicians, playwrights and scholars, French and non-French. He was hated by Protestants for his revocation of the **Edict of Nantes**; and opposed by the maritime powers and the Austrian Habsburgs who feared that he aimed at European hegemony.

LOUIS XVI (1754-93) King of France, grandson of Louis XV. He married the Austrian Archduchess Marie-Antoinette in 1770, and succeeded to the throne, 1774. The early years of his reign saw France in a state of progressive financial and political collapse; with the outbreak of the French Revolution in 1789 the royal family became virtual prisoners of the Paris mob. Their attempted flight in 1791 led to deposition, trial for treason and execution by guillotine in 1793.

LOUIS-PHILIPPE (1773-1850) King of France, son of Louis-Philippe Joseph, Duke of Orléans. Exiled, 1793-1815, during the French Revolution and the Napoleonic period, he succeeded to the throne in 1830 after the reactionary regime of Charles X had been ended by the July Revolution. His reign was characterized by financial speculation, the ostentatious affluence of the emerging middle class, and growing failure in foreign policy. He abdicated in 1848 after renewed revolutionary outbreaks, and fled to England.

LOUISIANA PURCHASE The western half of the Mississippi Basin, bought from Napoleon in 1803 by President **Thomas Jefferson** for under 3 cents an acre. It added 828,000 square miles (2,144,520 km^2) to the United States, at the time doubling its area, and opened up the West.

LUBA Also known as Baluba. Bantu-speaking peoples, widespread in southeast Zaire. The main present-day groups all trace their history back to the Luba empires which flourished, but finally broke down, in the 16th and 17th centuries. With the **Lunda** they established a series of satellite states, trading with and buying firearms from the Portuguese in Angola until colonized by the Belgians in the late 19th century.

LUDDITE Machine-smasher, originally a member of one of the bands of workers who systematically broke looms, textile plant and machine tools in Lancashire, Yorkshire and the east Midlands of England during the early Industrial Revolution (1811-16). Traditionally named after Ned Ludd, a possibly mythical leader of the rioters.

LUDENDORFF, ERICH VON (1865-1938) German soldier. Chief of staff to **Hindenburg** throughout the First World War, he was increasingly influential in German military and (after 1916) domestic policies. After the failure of the offensives on the Western Front of March 1918 he insisted upon an immediate armistice. He fled to Sweden at the end of the war, but returned in 1919 to take part in the Kapp Putsch (1920) and Munich Beer-Hall Putsch (1923). An early supporter of **Hitler**, he sat as a Nazi deputy in the Reichstag, 1924-8.

LUMUMBA, PATRICE (1925-61) First Prime Minister of Congo (later Zaire). He was educated at a Protestant mission school; became local president of the Congolese trade union, 1955; founded the Mouvement National Congolais, 1958, to work for independence from Belgium. Imprisoned in 1959, he was asked to form the first independent government in 1960. He was removed from office after opposing the Belgian-backed secession of Katanga province. He was murdered.

LUNDA Bantu people, originating in the Katanga-Shaba district of the former Congo (the central Lunda kingdom) and now spread widely over southeast Zaire, eastern Angola, northwest Zambia and the Luapula valley. The Lunda of Kazembe were famous throughout central Africa as ivory and slave traders, especially with the Portuguese.

LUNG YÜN (1888-1962) Chinese warlord. A member of the Lolo minority peoples, he trained as a military officer and joined the staff of **T'ang Chih-yao** in Yunnan. In 1915 he joined the rebellion of Yunnan against **Yüan Shih-k'ai**, which left T'ang in control of the province. In 1927 Lung Yün ousted T'ang, and ruled the Yunnan region as an independent satrapy until 1945. He fostered the cultivation of the opium poppy and inflicted savage taxes on the population. He collaborated unwillingly with **Chiang Kai-shek** during the Japanese War 1937-45, but in 1944 joined a group opposed to the Nationalist government. In 1945 Chiang organized a coup which deposed him, but Lung was given a government post and Yunnan placed under his close relative Lu Han. In 1950 Lung went to Peking as a member of the Communist government, and served until he was purged in 1957.

LUPACA Andean people in the Lake Titicaca region of South America. In alliance with the Incas in the early 15th century they defeated their neighbouring rivals, the **Colla**, but were in turn overthrown and absorbed by the Incas in the 1470s.

LUTHER, MARTIN (1483-1546) German theologian and initiator of the Protestant Reformation. He was ordained priest in 1507, and taught at the University of Wittenberg, 1508-46. His attacks on papal abuses provoked excommunication in 1520, but Luther advanced an alternative theology which was adopted by many states of northern Europe (the Lutheran Reformation).

LUTHERANISM A system of theology, orignated by **Martin Luther** (1483-1546) and expressed in *The Book of Concord* (1580), which incorporated the three traditional Creeds, the Augsburg Confession, Luther's two Catechisms and the Formula of Concord (1577). The main tenets of Lutheranism are that justification is by faith alone and that the scriptures are the sole rule of faith. The Lutherans have traditionally made a sharp distinction between the kingdom of God and the kingdom of the world, so that the state has sometimes seemed autonomous in its own field.

LUVIANS (LUWIANS) A people established in southern Anatolia by the beginning of the 2nd millennium BC, speaking a language closely related to that of the **Hittites**. Many inscriptions are extant in the Luvian language, written in hieroglyphs commonly called 'hieroglyphic Luvian'.

LUXEMBOURGS European ruling dynasty. Initial line, founded by Count Conrad (d.1086) held the lordship of Luxembourg but became extinct in 1136; a collateral descendant, Henry II, Count of Luxembourg, founded a second line including four emperors of the **Holy Roman Empire**: Henry VII, **Charles IV**, Wenceslas and Sigismund; on the death of Sigismund in 1438 the family was replaced on the imperial throne by Albert II of Habsburg and his descendants.

LYNN RIOTS Popular revolt at King's Lynn, Norfolk, England in 1597 against the high price of food and the high taxes imposed by the government of **Elizabeth I** to pay for the war against Spain and for the conquest of Ireland.

MAASTRICHT, TREATY OF (1991) The agreement between the 12 European Community leaders to promote monetary and political union, thereby expanding the European Community's powers over matters previously controlled by national governments. The treaty also called for the introduction of a single currency for the **EC** by 1999 and laid the groundwork for a common defence policy.

MACARTHUR, DOUGLAS (1880-1964) American general who commanded the defence of the Philippines, 1941-2. From 1942-5 he was Commander, United States Forces in the Pacific. He headed United Nations forces in the Korean War (1950-1) until dismissed by President **Truman** after a policy disagreement.

McCLELLAN, GEORGE BRINTON (1826-85) American general, commander-in-chief of the Union forces in 1861-2 during the American Civil War.

McCONNEL & KENNEDY Machinery manufacturers for the rapidly expanding English cotton industry in the late 18th and 19th centuries. For many years the firm was virtually the sole supplier of spinning mules to the industry. John Kennedy (1769-1855) made several improvements in the machines used to spin fine yarns.

McKINLEY, WILLIAM (1843-1901) 25th President of the United States. He served in the Civil War under Colonel (later President) **Rutherford Hayes**. He was a member of Congress, 1877-91, and Governor of Ohio in 1891-5. He defeated the Populist candidate, **William Jennings Bryan**, in the presidential election in 1896 without ever leaving his front porch. He led the country into the Spanish-American war, 1898, and in the suppression of the subsequent Filipino revolt (1899-1902). Re-elected in 1900 with a huge majority, he was shot the following year by an anarchist at the Pan-American Exhibition in Buffalo.

MACEDONIAN DYNASTY Family of Byzantine emperors, founded by Basil I (867-86) and ruling, with some interruptions, until the death of Theodora (1056). Originally peasant marauders, murdering their way to power, they presided over almost two centuries of Byzantium's highest military, artistic and political achievements.

MACHIAVELLI, NICCOLÒ (1469-1527) Florentine statesman, historian and political theorist. In response to foreign invasions and the anarchic state of Italy in his time, he wrote his most famous work, *Il Principe (The Prince)* in 1513, advocating the establishment and maintenance of authority by any effective means.

MACMILLAN, HAROLD (1894-1986) British statesman. A Conservative MP 1924-9 and 1931-64, he was noted for progressive social views and for opposition to the policy of appeasement of the dictators, voting against his party on abandonment of sanctions against Italy in 1936. He was British Minister Resident at Allied headquarters in northwest Africa, 1942-5. He entered the Cabinet in 1951 and held various offices before becoming Prime Minister, 1957-63, and presiding over the peaceful decolonization of British Africa.

MADERO, FRANCISCO (1873-1913) President of Mexico 1910-13. He inspired, organized and eventually led the movement to displace the dictator **Porfirio Díaz**. His arrest in 1909 was soon followed by release and escape to Texas. In 1910 he declared himself the legitimate President, and was elected in 1911 after the military successes of his supporters, Pascual Orozco and **Pancho Villa**. He failed to implement democracy or stem corruption. He was arrested and assassinated in 1913 after betrayal by an army commander, Victoriano Huerta, in the course of a military revolt .

MADISON, JAMES (1751-1836) Fourth President of the United States, 1809-17. A member of the Continental Congress, 1780-3 and 1787-8, he played a leading role in framing the US Constitution (1787). He broke with the **Federalists** and helped to found the Democratic-Republican party; served **Thomas Jefferson** as Secretary of State, 1801-9. During his presidency war broke out between America and Great Britain (1812-14).

MADRID, TREATY OF Agreement signed 14 January 1526 between Emperor **Charles V** and the French king, **Francis I**, taken prisoner after the battle of Pavia (1525). To secure his release, Francis promised to cede certain territories, but once he was back in France he refused to ratify the treaty.

MADRID, TREATY OF Agreement, also known as 'Godolphin's Treaty', between England and Spain in 1670 to end piracy in American waters; Spain also confirmed the English possession of Jamaica, captured in 1655.

MAGELLAN, FERDINAND (c.1480-1521) (Portuguese name, Fernão de Magalhães). First European to navigate in the Pacific Ocean. He was prominent in Portuguese naval and military expeditions to Africa, India and the East, 1505-16. In 1518 he was commissioned by Spain to find a southwest route to the Spice Islands; after sailing through the strait later named after him between South America and Tierra del Fuego, he crossed the Pacific and reached Guam in 1521, with three of his five original ships, but their crews in a state of near-starvation. The round-the-world voyage (the first) was completed by **Elcano** with one ship and 18 survivors, of an original 270 men, after Magellan had been killed by local people near Mactan in the Philippines.

MAGGI Prominent family of Brescia, Italy, which gained control of the city in the later 13th century until the siege by Emperor Henry VII in 1311, after which other families replaced them.

MAGNA CARTA The Great Charter issued under duress by King **John** of England in 1215. Though its provisions, promptly repudiated by John, concerned primarily the relationships of a feudal ruler with vassals, subjects and the Church, revisions and reconfirmations in 1216, 1217, 1225 and most notably by **Edward I** in 1297 asserted the supremacy of the laws of England over the king. Thus it came to be regarded as a keystone of British liberties.

MAGNUS OLAFSSON 'THE GOOD' (1024-47) King of Norway and Denmark, illegitimate son of Olaf Haraldsson (St Olaf). He was exiled to Russia, with his father, at the age of four by **Cnut the Great**. Elected as king in 1039 by Norwegian chieftains, he gained sovereignty over Denmark in 1042. He was unsuccessfully challenged by Cnut's nephew, Sweyn. He agreed to share thrones with his uncle, Harald Hardrada, in 1045. He was killed in a Danish battle while planning to claim the English crown.

MAHABHARATA 'The Great Epic of the Bharata Dynasty'. This vast work of early Indian literature, running to 100,000 couplets (seven times as long as *The Odyssey* and *The Iliad* combined) relates the struggle between two families, the Kauravas and the Pandavas, as well as incorporating a mass of other romantic, legendary, philosophic and religious material from the heroic days of early **Hinduism**. Traditionally ascribed to the sage Vyasa, it was more probably the result of 2000 years of constant accretion and reshaping before reaching its present form c.AD 400. Included in it is the *Bhagavadgita (The Lord's Song)*, probably Hinduism's most important single text.

MAHAVIRA Indian religious teacher of the 6th century BC, principal founder of **Jainism**. At the age of 30 he renounced his family and became an ascetic, wandering for 12 years in the Ganges valley seeking enlightenment. He shaped and organized the Jaina sect, named from his honorific title of *Jina*, the Conqueror.

MAHDI Islamic concept of the messianic deliverer, who will one day fill the earth with justice, faith and prosperity. The title has been frequently adopted by social revolutionaries since Islam's upheavals in the 7th and 8th centuries – notably by Ubaidallah, founder of the **Fatimid** dynasty in 908, Mohammed ibn Tumart, leader of the 12th century **Almohad** movement, and in 1881 by **Mohammed Ahmed al-Mahdi** on declaring rebellion against the Egyptian administration in the Sudan.

MAHDI, MOHAMMED AHMED AL- (d.1885) Mystic founder of a vast Muslim state in the Sudan. He gathered a growing band of supporters through his preaching and interpretation of Islam; in 1881 he proclaimed a divine mission to purify Islam under the title of al-Mahdi, the Right-Guided One. He swiftly mastered virtually all territory once occupied by Egypt; captured Khartoum in 1885, and created the theocratic state of the Sudan. He died in that year at his new capital, Omdurman; the theocratic state fell to forces under the British general Kitchener in 1898.

MAHMUD of GHAZNA (971-1030) Muslim warrior and patron of the arts. He was the son of Sebuktigin, a Turkish slave who became ruler of Ghazna (comprising most of modern Afghanistan and northeast Iran). He succeeded to the throne in 998, and from 1001 to 1026 led 17 invading expeditions to India, amassing an empire including the Punjab and most of Persia. His capital, Ghazna, became an Islamic cultural centre rivalling Baghdad.

MAHMUD II (1785-1839) Reforming Ottoman sultan, nephew of Sultan Selim III. He was brought to the throne in 1808 in a coup led by Bayrakdar Mustafa Pasha, later his grand vizier. He was heavily defeated in wars with Russia, Greece, France and Britain, and by **Mohammed Ali's** insurgents in Syria. He destroyed the moribund Janissary corps in 1826, establishing a modern, European-style army in 1831 and a military academy in 1834. He introduced cabinet government, postal services, compulsory education and European dress.

MAIRE, JAKOB LE (1585-1616) Dutch navigator and South Sea explorer. With **Willem Schouten**, in 1615-16 he sailed through Le Maire Strait, rounded Cape Horn for the first time, and discovered some of the Tuamotus, the northernmost islands of the Tonga group, and the Hoorn islands.

MAJAPAHIT Last of the Javanese Hindu-Buddhist empires, founded after the defeat of the Mongol seaborne expedition against Java in 1292. It rose to greatness under Gaja Mada (d.1364), chief minister of King Hayam Wuruk, with whose death in 1389 its decline began. Its size is a matter for dispute; its effective sway was probably limited to east and central Java, Madura, Bali and Lombok, while its powerful fleets ensured the allegiance and tribute of the Spice Islands and the chief commercial ports of southern Sumatra and southern Borneo.

MAJI-MAJI East African revolt against German colonialism which broke out in 1905 and was suppressed in 1907.

MALAN, DANIEL FRANÇOIS (1874-1959) South African politician. Before entering politics, he studied for the Dutch Reformed Church, receiving a doctorate in divinity at the University of Utrecht, Holland (1905). In 1948 he led a 'purified' National party faction to victory, serving as prime minister (1948-54) of the Republic of South Africa's first exclusively Afrikaner government. A right-wing nationalist, Malan is best known for introducing apartheid into South Africa. He retired from public office in 1954.

MALATESTA Italian family, ruling Rimini from the late 13th century until 1500. They first became lords of the city in 1295, when the **Guelph** leader, Malatesta di Verruchio (d.1312) expelled his Ghibelline rivals. Sigismondo Malatesta (1417-68) is often represented as the ideal Renaissance prince – a soldier who also cultivated the arts. In 1461 he was the subject of a **Crusade** launched by Pope Pius II which deprived the family of most of its powers. Sigismondo's son, Roberto il Magnifico (d.1482), recovered Rimini in 1469, but the dynasty was finally driven out by Cesare Borgia in 1500.

MALFANTE, ANTONIO 15th-century Genoese merchant, sometimes known, exaggeratedly, as 'the first explorer of the Sahara'.

MALINKE People of the ancient West African empire of Mali. As the Dyula, or travelling merchants, their traders have remained a potent factor in the economy of the region since the 13th century.

MAMLUKES Generically, military slaves or freedmen, mainly from the Caucasus or central Asia, and employed by many medieval Muslim states. A group of them established a sultanate which ruled Egypt and Syria 1250-1517, until defeated by the Ottomans.

MANBY, AARON (1776-1850) English engineer. In 1821 he patented his design for an oscillating steam engine, widely used for marine propulsion, and in 1822 launched the first practical iron ship, the Aaron Manby, sailing from London to Paris. He also founded an iron works at Charenton (1810) which made France largely independent of English engine-builders, and in 1822 formed the first company to supply gas to Paris. He returned to England in 1840.

MANCHESTER SCHOOL Group of 19th-century British political economists advocating free trade and *laissez-faire*, led by Richard Cobden (1804-65) and John Bright (1811-89).

MANCHUS People of Manchuria (northeast China) who in 1644 founded the imperial dynasty known as the **Ch'ing**.

MANDATE Former colonial territory, assigned by the **League of Nations** to a victorious Allied power after the First World War under supervision of the League, and in some cases with the duty of preparing it for independence. Great Britain thus assumed responsibility for Iraq, Palestine (from the Ottoman Empire) and Tanganyika (from Germany); France for Syria and Lebanon; and Belgium for Ruanda-Urundi. The arrangement was replaced by the **United Nations'** Trusteeship System in 1946, except for southwest Africa (Namibia), where South Africa retained its mandate until 1990.

MANDE A West African language group, the Mande-speaking people, found primarily in the savannah plateaux of the western Sudan, where they developed such complex civilizations as the Solinke state of Ghana, around 900 to 1100, and the empire of Mali which flourished in the 14th and early 15th centuries. Today the most typical Mande groups are the Bambara, the Malinke and the Solinke, speaking characteristic Mande versions of the Niger-Congo group of languages.

MANDELA, NELSON (1918-) Born in Umtata in the Transkei, Mandela moved to Johannesburg and qualified as a lawyer. In 1944 he joined the African National Congress, becoming its deputy national president in 1952. In 1956 he was arrested and charged with treason but was discharged after a five-year trial. After the Sharpeville massacre and the banning of the ANC in 1960, Mandela went underground but was captured and condemned to life imprisonment in 1964. He was released in February 1990, an event marking the real beginning of political change in South Africa, and resumed leadership of the ANC in the search for a negotiated political settlement.

MANDINGO West African people, related to the larger **Mande** language group, occupying parts of Guinea, Guinea-Bissau, Ivory Coast, Mali, Gambia and Senegal. The many independent tribes are dominated by a hereditary nobility, which in one case, the Kangaba, has ruled unin-

terruptedly for 13 centuries: starting as a small state in the 7th century, Kangaba (on the Mali-Senegal boundary) became the focus for the great Malinke empire of Mali, reaching its peak around 1450.

MANICHAEISM Dualist religion founded in Persia in the 3rd century AD by Mani, 'the Apostle of Light', who tried to integrate the messages of **Zoroaster**, **Buddha** and **Jesus** into one universal creed. It is often regarded, wrongly, as a Christian heresy: properly it is a religion in its own right, and has influenced many other sects, Christian and otherwise, in both East and West. It became extinct in the Middle Ages, but some scriptures have been recovered in this century in Egypt and Chinese Turkestan.

MANSA MUSA Most famous of the emperors of ancient Mali, who reigned 1312-37. He pushed the frontiers of the empire out to the edges of the Sahara, the tropical rain forest, the Atlantic and the borders of modern Nigeria. He made a lavish pilgrimage to Mecca and actively promoted Islam among his subjects; he also developed Saharan trade, introduced brick buildings and founded Timbuktu and Jenne as world centres of Muslim learning.

MANSUR, ABU AMIR AL- (c.938-1002) ('Almanzor' in medieval Spanish and Latin texts) Chief minister and effective ruler of the **Umayyad** caliphate in Córdoba, 978-1002. He overthrew and succeeded his vizier in 978, and fought 50 campaigns against the Christians of northern Spain, including an expedition against the great shrine of Santiago de Compostela in 997.

MANSUR, ABU JAFAR AL- (c.710-75) Second caliph of the **Abbasid** dynasty, great-grandson of **Abbas, Mohammed**'s uncle; he succeeded to the caliphate in 754 on the death of his brother as-Saffah. He completed the elimination of the deposed **Umayyad** dynasty, and founded the city of Baghdad, begun in 762.

MANUEL I COMNENUS (1122-80) Emperor of Byzantium, son of **John II Comnenus**, he succeeded in 1143. He tried but ultimately failed to build alliances in the West; was defeated in 1156 at Brindisi and expelled from Italy. He forced Jerusalem to recognize Byzantine sovereignty in 1159. In 1167 he added Dalmatia, Bosnia and Croatia to his empire. He broke ties with Venice in 1171. His armies were destroyed by the **Seljuk** Turks at Myriokephalon in 1176.

MANZIKERT, BATTLE OF Fought near the town in Turkish-held Armenia (today Malazgirt, Turkey) in 1071; the **Seljuks**, under Sultan Alp-Arslan (1063-72) decisively defeated the Byzantine armies under Emperor Romanus IV Diogenes (1068-71). The victory led to Seljuk conquest of almost all Anatolia, and fatal weakening of Byzantine power.

MAORI Member of the aboriginal Polynesian people inhabiting New Zealand at the time of its European discovery.

MAO TSE-TUNG (1893-1976) First Chairman of the People's Republic of China (1949-77). He helped to found the Chinese Communist Party in 1921, and until 1926 organized peasant and industrial unions. After the Communist split with the **Kuomintang** in 1927 he set up Communist bases in Hunan, and later in Kiangsi. In 1934-5 he led the Long March of the Red Army from Kiangsi to Yenan. He became the dominant figure in the Party after 1935, establishing it as a peasant-based party. During the second Sino-Japanese War (1937-45) he worked for national unity, and after a bitter civil war in 1949 expelled Nationalist forces from mainland China. In 1966 he launched the Cultural Revolution.

MARATHAS Hindu people of western India, famous in the 17th and 18th centuries for their warlike resistance to the **Mughal** emperors. Now the term covers the 10 million or so members of the Maratha and Kunbi castes in the region bounded by Bombay, Goa and Nagpur, or more loosely the 40 million speakers of the Marathi language.

MARATHON, BATTLE OF A famous victory in 490 BC won on the coastal plain northeast of Athens by the Greeks, under the Athenian general Miltiades, over an invading army of Persians. It is remembered *inter alia* for the feat of the runner Phidippides, who raced 150 miles in two days to warn the Spartans and to return with the news that their forces would be delayed by a religious festival.

MARCEL, ÉTIENNE (c.1316-58) Provost of merchants of Paris, deputy to the Estates General (the French national assembly). He proposed in 1355-6 that the Estates should control royal revenues and purge crown officials. He led Paris in a revolt against the crown in 1357-8, and supported the **Jacquerie**. He was assassinated in 1358 after the revolt collapsed.

MARCHAND, JEAN-BAPTISTE (1863-1934) French explorer and general who in 1897 led a remarkable 18-month march from Libreville, in Gabon, to the Upper Nile, occupying Fashoda in 1898. He withdrew after a prolonged confrontation with Kitchener which provoked an international diplomatic crisis.

MARCION (c.100-160) Originator of a religious sect challenging Christianity throughout Europe, North Africa and western Asia from the 2nd to the 5th century. Possibly the son of a bishop of Sinope, he went to Rome c.140, formed separate communities and was excommunicated in 144. He preached the existence of two gods: the Old Testament Creator or Demiurge, i.e. the God of Law, and the God of Love revealed by Jesus, who would overthrow the first. He compiled his own version of the New Testament (the *Instrumentum*), largely based on St Luke and St Paul's Epistles. After his death the Marcionite sect survived many persecutions and remained significant, particularly in Syria, until the 10th century.

MARGARET (1353-1412) Queen of Norway. The daughter of Valdemer III of Denmark, she married Haakon VI of Norway (1343-80), and became effective ruler of Norway and Denmark, c.1387, and of Sweden, 1389. She was regent on behalf of her great-nephew, Eric of Pomerania, who was crowned ruler of Sweden, Denmark and Norway at the **Union of Kalmar** in 1397.

MARI (Cheremiss) Finno-Ugrian speaking peoples now living mainly in the Autonomous Republics of Mari, on the middle Volga, and Bashkir.

MARIA THERESA (1717-80) Elder daughter of the Emperor Charles VI, and one of the most capable **Habsburg** rulers. She was Archduchess of Austria and Queen of Hungary and Bohemia in her own right, and always overshadowed her husband, the elected Emperor Francis I (1745-65). She died after 15 years of widowhood and a troublesome co-regency with her son, **Joseph II**.

MARINIDS Berber dynasty, ruling in Morocco and elsewhere in North Africa from the 13th to the 15th centuries, replacing the **Almohads** on the capture of Fez (1248) and Marrakesh (1269). They launched a holy war in Spain which lasted until the mid-14th century. Despite many attempts, they failed to re-establish the old Almohad empire; after a period of internal anarchy, the related Wattasids assumed control of Morocco in 1465, but were finally expelled, by the **Saadi** sharifs, in 1549.

MARQUETTE, JACQUES (1637-75) French Jesuit missionary and explorer, the first Frenchman to sail on the Mississippi (1673); he explored much of its length with **Jolliet**.

MARRANO Insulting Spanish term for a **Jew** who converted to **Christianity** in Spain or Portugal to avoid persecution but secretly continued to practise **Judaism**; also used to designate the descendants of such a person.

MARSHALL PLAN Popular name given to the European recovery programme, proposed in 1947 by US Secretary of State General George C. Marshall (1880-1959), to supply US financial and material aid to war-devastated Europe. Rejected by Eastern European countries under Soviet pressure, it came into force in Western Europe in 1948 and was completed in 1952.

MARSHALL, WILLIAM (1745-1818) Agriculturalist and leading improver, famous for his 12-volume *General Survey, from personal experience, observation and enquiry, of the Rural Economy of England* (1787-98). He proposed setting up a governmental Board of Agriculture, put into effect by Parliament in 1793.

MARTIN IV (c.1210-85) Pope from 1281 to 1285. He supported **Charles I** of Naples and Sicily, and opposed the Aragonese claims after the **War of the Sicilian Vespers**.

MARXIST Follower of the social, political and economic theories developed by Karl Marx (1818-83). Characteristic beliefs include dialectical materialism, the collapse of capitalism through its internal contradictions, the dictatorship of the proletariat and a withering away of the state after the achievement of a classless society.

MASON-DIXON LINE Originally a boundary line between the American states of Pennsylvania and Maryland named after the English surveyors, Charles Mason and Jeremiah Dixon, who first delineated it, 1763-7. It later became a symbolic frontier between slave and free states in the American Union.

MATABELE (also known as Ndebele). Southern African people, who broke away from the **Nguni** of Natal in the early 19th century. Under **Mzilikazi** they migrated to the High Veld area of modern Transvaal, and later the Marico Valley. In 1837, after confrontation with Dutch settlers in the Transvaal, they crossed the River Limpopo into Matabeleland (southern Rhodesia). The resulting state grew powerful under the leadership of Mzilikazi's successor, Lobengula. They were finally defeated by settlers of the British South Africa Company in 1893.

MATACOS South American Indians, forming the largest and most important group of the Chaco Indians in the Gran Chaco region of northwest Argentina. They were first encountered by Europeans in 1628, and resisted Christianity and colonization, suffering large-scale massacre, before being placed on reservations and in Spanish government colonies. They are now gradually being incorporated into the *mestizo* (mixed blood) population of the Chaco.

MATILDA (1046-1115) Countess of Tuscany. She was a strong supporter of Pope Gregory VII. Having acknowledged (c.1080) papal overlordship of her lands, strategically placed across the route of German invasions of Italy, she eventually made Emperor Henry V her heir, thus giving rise to much conflict between the Empire and the Papacy.

MATTHIAS CORVINUS (1440-90) Elected King of Hungary (1458) and claimant to the throne of Bohemia from 1469. He acquired Moravia, Silesia and Lusatia in 1478, Vienna in 1485, and built up the most powerful kingdom in central Europe. He was also a patron of science and of literature.

MAURYAS First Indian dynasty to establish rule over the whole sub-continent. The dynasty was founded in 321 BC by **Chandragupta Maurya**, and steadily extended under his son Bindusara and grandson **Asoka**. Power was gradually eroded under **Asoka**'s successors, finally dying out c.180 BC.

MAXIMILIAN I (1459-1519) Holy Roman Emperor, son of Frederick III. He married Mary of Burgundy in 1477; was crowned king of Germany in 1486 and emperor in 1493. He achieved a partial reform of the imperial administration, but failed in 1499 to subjugate the Swiss cantons. He was succeeded by his grandson **Charles V**.

MAXIMILIAN (1832-67) Emperor of Mexico. Younger brother of the Austrian emperor, Francis Joseph I, in 1863 he accepted the offer of the Mexican throne as an unwitting pawn in the plot by Mexican opponents of **Juárez** and the French emperor, **Napoleon III**. He was installed by French troops and crowned, 1864. His attempts at liberal reform were nullified by local opposition and lack of funds. He was deserted by the French in 1867, surrounded, starved and tricked into surrender by the armies of Juárez, and shot in June that year.

MAYA Indian people of the Yucatán peninsula and the adjoining areas of southern Mexico, Guatemala and Honduras. The Classic period of Maya civilization (marked by fine buildings, magnificent art and an advanced knowledge of mathematics and astronomy) falls between the 3rd and 9th centuries AD. Archaeologically it is best represented at the southern cities of Tikal, Copán, Uaxactún, Quiriguá and Piedras Negras. In the 9th century, for reasons still poorly understood, Classic Maya civilization declined. Mexican (*see* **Toltec**) influence became important, and the main centres of power shifted to Chichén Itzá and Mayapán in northern Yucatán. Although the Spanish conquest destroyed much of the political and religious life, the Maya still exist as a linguistic and cultural unit in their original homelands.

MAYFLOWER Famous ship that carried the 102 pilgrims of the later United States from England to found the first permanent New England colony at Plymouth, Massachusetts, in 1620. Her precise size is not recorded, but she was probably about 180 tons and some 90 ft (27km) long. Originally she set out for Virginia, but was blown north first to Cape Cod and then to Plymouth.

MAZARIN, JULES (1602-61) Italian-born French statesman. He pursued a career in papal service, 1625-36, was brought into the service of Louis XIII by **Richelieu** in 1639 and, on French nomination, was made a cardinal in 1641. He inherited Richelieu's position as Louis XIII's First Minister. The king made him godfather to the future **Louis XIV**, over whose training for kingship he had a good deal of influence. He showed skill both in handling the civil wars of the **Fronde** and in negotiating gains for France under the treaties of **Westphalia** (1648) and the Pyrenees (1659).

MAZZINI, GIUSEPPE (1805-72) Italian revolutionary and patriot. He founded the very influential Young Italy movement and a journal of that name in 1831. Following the failure of the invasion of Savoy in 1834, and banished from Switzerland, he arrived in London in 1837. In 1849 he was First Triumvir, in effect executive ruler, of the Roman Republic, an office filled with tolerance and enlightenment. As a republican, he refused to acknowledge the Italian Kingdom of 1861.

MEADE, GEORGE GORDON (1815-72) Union general in the American Civil War, best remembered for his victory in the battle of Gettysburg (1863).

MEDES The branch of the Iranian invaders settled in the northwest of present-day Iran. Under Cyaxares (c.625 BC) the Medes became a major military power which, once it had settled accounts with the Scythian invaders of northern Iran, made an alliance with Babylon to destroy the hated Assyrian Empire. Under the last king, Astyages, the Medes were defeated by the Persian **Cyrus II the Great** in 550 BC, in whose empire the 'Medes and Persians' were held in equal honour. Thereafter, especially under the Sasanians, the Medes became effectively merged with the other groupings which came to constitute the Iranian nation-state.

MEDICI Most important of the great families of Florence. Their origins are obscure, but they were established in the 13th century in the cloth trade and in finance, and soon exercised considerable political influence. The family developed three lines: that of Chiarissimo II, who failed to gain power in Florence in the 14th century; that of Cosimo the Elder (1389-1464) who became the hereditary, although uncrowned, monarch of Florence; and that of Cosimo, who became Grand Duke of Tuscany in 1569. The line ended with the death of Gian Gastone, 1737. The family provided many rulers and patrons, and three Popes.

MEGALITH (meaning 'great stone') Monument constructed of large undressed stones or boulders, usually as a ritual centre (e.g. a stone circle) or burial monument (e.g. chambered cairn). Of many different kinds, megaliths were erected by simple agricultural communities in many parts of the world, most notably in **Neolithic** Europe during the 3rd millennium BC.

MEHMED I, ÇELEBI (d.1421) Younger son of **Bayezid I** and reunifier of the Ottoman state after the defeat of Ankara (1402), the death of his father and the civil war (1403-13) with his brothers. Mehmed, from a territorial base at Amasya, moved to defeat successively Isa in Brusa, Süleyman in Edirne (1403-11), and Musa in Rumeli (1411-3), while maintaining nominal allegiance to the Timurids, and later overcoming both dangerous social revolts and Byzantine-inspired attempts to place his brother Mustafa on the throne (1415-16). By his death the prestige, if not the full authority, of the sultanate was restored, enabling it to survive the further shocks of the first years of **Murad II**'s reign.

MEHMED II, FATIH ('the Conqueror') (1432-81) **Ottoman** Sultan succeeding in 1451. By the conquest of Constantinople in 1453 Mehmed II obtained for the Ottoman state a fit site for the capital of a would-be universal world empire. His reign is a record of unceasing warfare: against Hungary, Venice, the **Ak Koyunlu** and the Knights of St John. The last vestiges of Greek rule disappeared (in the Morea 1460, in Trebizond 1461); Serbia (1459), Bosnia (1463) and Karaman (1466) were annexed; Moldavia (1455) and the khanate of the Crimea (1475-8) rendered tributary.

MEHMED IV AVCI ('the Hunter') (1642-93) Ottoman sultan, succeeding in 1648. His reign was most notable for the emergence in 1656 of the grand vizierate as the dominating institution of the state under the ministerial family of **Köprülü**. He fought incessant and not altogether unsuccessful wars in the Mediterranean (reduction of Crete, 1644-69, ended by the 13-year siege of Candia); and on the northern frontiers of the empire (invasion of Transylvania 1654, conquest of Podolia 1672). Against the **Habsburgs** he was less successful (St Gotthard campaign 1663, second unsuccessful siege of Vienna 1683). The subsequent loss of Hungary (1684-7) fuelling popular resentment, and exacerbated by the Sultan's withdrawal from matters of state and notorious obsession with hunting, precipitated his deposition in 1687 and detention until his death.

MEIJI Name meaning 'enlightened rule' by which the Japanese emperor, Mutsuhito, was known during his long reign. Mutsuhito (1852-1912) came to the throne in 1867; within a year the 'Meiji Restoration' ended two and a half centuries of semi-isolation in Japan under the **Tokugawa** shogunate. Under his rule, industrialization and modernization began, and a Western democratic constitution was adopted (1889). By the time of his death, Japan was widely accepted as a world power; his role was largely symbolic, new political leaders being more directly responsible for the reshaping of the nation.

MELGAREJO, MARIANO (1818-71) Bolivian dictator. A general in the Bolivian army, he deposed José Maria Achá in 1864 to become President. He conceded to Chile some of Bolivia's claim to the rich nitrate deposits of the Atacama Desert. He was deposed, and assassinated in the same year.

MENELIK II (1844-1913) Emperor of Ethiopia. He was enthroned in 1889, and in 1896 defeated an Italian invasion at Adowa to ensure his country's independence and consolidate its power. He greatly expanded the boundaries of Ethiopia by conquering Galla lands in the southwest and Ogaden in the east.

MENES Traditionally, the first king to unite Upper and Lower Egypt, c.3100 BC; he may also have founded the royal capital of Memphis. He is said by the historian Manetho to have ruled for 62 years and to have been killed by a hippopotamus.

MENSHEVIKS Named from *mensheviki*, Russian for 'the minority'. Moderate faction in the Russian Social Democratic Party, which generally supported the **Bolshevik** regime during the civil war, after which most Mensheviks were either liquidated or absorbed into the Russian Communist Party, or emigrated.

MENTUHOTEP I Governor of the Theban province who, according to tradition, became the first king of the XIth Dynasty and the founder of the Middle Kingdom, c.2120 BC.

MENTUHOTEP II (d. c.2010 BC) King of Egypt's XIth Dynasty. He acceded c.2060 to the throne of Upper Egypt; in 2046 he launched a campaign against the Heracleopolitan kingdom of Lower and Middle Egypt and by c.2040 had reunited the country.

MERCANTILISM Economic theory much favoured in the 16th and 17th centuries, under which a country's prosperity was held to depend on its success in accumulating gold and silver reserves. It favoured a strict limitation of imports and the aggressive promotion of export trade.

MEROVINGIANS Frankish dynasty, ruling much of Gaul from the time of **Clovis** to their replacement by the **Carolingians** in 751.

MESOLITHIC The middle part of the **Stone Age** in Europe, representing hunting and collecting groups in the period of present-day climatic conditions after the end of the last glaciation, 10,000 years ago. It succeeded the reindeer-hunting groups of the **Palaeolithic**, and was gradually displaced by the incoming farmers of the **Neolithic**.

METAXAS, IOANNIS (1871-1941) Greek military leader. After reaching the rank of general he emerged as dictator of Greece in 1936; he defeated the Italians when they invaded the country in 1940.

METHODIST Member of one of the several Protestant denominations which developed after 1730 from the Church of England revival movement led by John and Charles Wesley. It emerged as a separate church in 1791 with supporters in both North America and Great Britain.

METHODIUS, ST *see* **Cyril**

METHUEN TREATY Commercial agreement signed in 1703 between England and Portugal. It was named after John Methuen (c.1650-1706), at that time British ambassador to Lisbon. The treaty gave a preferential tariff on Portuguese wine in exchange for freer import of English woollens, and helped to promote the drinking of port in England.

METTERNICH, PRINCE KLEMENS WENZEL LOTHAR VON (1773-1859) Austrian statesman. He was ambassador to various nations, and Minister of Foreign Affairs, 1809; following a period of collaboration with France, he then joined the victorious alliance against **Napoleon**. He was a leading figure at the **Congress of Vienna**, 1814-15, during which he restored the Habsburg Empire to a leading place in Europe.

He continued to be dominant in the Austrian government until the revolution of 1848.

MEWAR Independent state in northern India, first prominent in the 8th century under the Rajput clan of the Guhilas. Under Hamir in the 14th century it defied the Muslim armies of **Alauddin**; enriched by the discovery of silver and lead, it continued to battle with the Delhi sultanate and their **Mughal** successors. The state was in decline after Rana Sanga's defeat by **Babur** in 1527; **Akbar**'s long war against Rana Pratap was inconclusive, but Pratap's son accepted Mughal suzerainty.

MEZZOGIORNO Name for the region of Italy south of Rome, covering roughly the area of the former kingdom of Naples. Its longstanding backwardness, unemployment and low standard of living (half the per capita income of the north) have made it a perpetual preoccupation of Italian governments and planners.

MIAO Mountain-dwelling people of China, Vietnam, Laos and Thailand. Divided into more than a hundred groups distinguished by dress, dialect and customs, its members all share a heritage of Sino-Tibetan languages. In China they are concentrated in the provinces of Kweichow, Hunan, Szechwan, Kwangsi and Yunnan and Hainan island.

MIDLAND RISING Peasant rebellion in 1607 in several shires of the English east Midlands, caused mainly by the enclosure of common land by landlords which deprived the local population of grazing rights.

MIESZKO I (d.992) First ruler of united Poland, a member of the **Piast** dynasty. He succeeded as Duke of Poland c.963; he expanded his territories into Galicia and Pomerania. In 966 he accepted (Roman) **Christianity** from Bohemia, and placed his country under the protection of the Holy See (mainly in the hope of securing papal protection against the 'crusade' of the Germans against the Slavs).

MIESZKO II (990-1034) King of Poland, succeeding to the throne in 1025. He lost much territory to Bohemia and the **Holy Roman Empire**.

MILAN, EDICT OF Proclamation issued in AD 313, granting permanent religious toleration for people of all faiths throughout the Roman Empire. It was jointly promulgated by the emperors Licinius in the Eastern and **Constantine I** in the Western Empire.

MILNER, ALFRED (1854-1925) 1st Viscount Milner. British statesman and imperialist. As High Commissioner for South Africa, 1897-1905, he was responsible for the reconstruction of the Transvaal and Orange River Colony after the Boer War. He was a member of the War Cabinet, 1916-18, War Secretary, 1918, and Colonial Secretary, 1919-21.

MILITARY FRONTIER The Habsburg frontier (*Militärgrenze*) consisted at the end of the 16th century of a long strip of southern Croatia in which immigrants, holding land in return for military service, manned a line of forts. The system was later extended to Slavonia and subsequently to the Banat of Temesvár and Transylvania, thus covering the whole frontier with the Ottoman Empire. Highly unpopular among the Croats and Hungarians, it was finally abolished in 1872.

MING Chinese imperial dynasty ruling 1368 to 1644; *see page 164*.

MINISTERIALES Originally of servile status, from the 11th century onwards they served as stewards, chamberlains and butlers to kings and other lords in Germany. Gradually, as they assumed military, administrative and political functions, their social status improved until, in the 14th century, their estates and offices became hereditary, and they were accepted as members of the nobility.

MINOS Early king of Crete, referred to by **Homer** and Thucydides. According to legend he was the son of Zeus and Europa, and husband of Pasiphae. Knossos was said to have been his capital and the focus of his vast seapower. The 'Minoan' civilization of Crete (c.3000-1500 BC) was named after him by Sir Arthur Evans, excavator of Knossos.

MISHNAH Compilation of the oral interpretations of legal portions of the Bible by the **Pharisees** and Rabbis; codified by **Judah ha-Nasi**, in Palestine around AD 200, it served as the basis for the **Talmud**.

MITCHELL, SIR THOMAS LIVINGSTONE (1792-1855) Australian explorer. Born in Scotland, he joined the British Army in 1811 and served in the Peninsular War. As surveyor-general of New South Wales (from 1828) he surveyed

the province, constructed roads and (1831-47) led four major expeditions to explore and chart the Australian interior. He produced *Australian Geography* (1850) for use in schools – the first work to place Australia at the centre of the world – and published his expedition journals.

MITHRAISM Worship of Mithra or Mithras, ancient Indian and Persian god of justice and law; in pre-Zoroastrian Persia a supporter of Ahura Mazda, the great god of order and light. In the Roman Empire Mithraism spread as a mystery-cult with Mithras as a divine saviour, underground chapels, initiation rites, a common meal, and the promise of a blessed immortality. The adherents were men only, mostly soldiers, traders and civil servants. In the 4th century it was ousted by **Christianity**.

MITHRIDATES (120-63 BC) King of Pontus, in Asia Minor. He assumed the throne as Mithridates VI, known as 'the Great'. He fought three wars with Rome, finally being defeated by **Pompey**.

MOBUTU SESE SEKO (1930-) President of Zaire (formerly Congo). He enrolled as a clerk in the Belgian Congolese army in 1949. In the mid-1950s he edited a weekly newspaper *Actualités Africaines*. He joined **Lumumba** in 1958 as a member of *Mouvement National Congolais*; and became chief of staff of the Force Publique after Congo gained independence in 1960. He supported **Kasavubu** and then ousted him in a coup in 1965, put down a white mercenary uprising in 1967 and nationalized the Katanga copper mines. In 1977 he defeated an invasion of Shaba province (Katanga) from Angola. By 1992 he found himself challenged by a growing pro-democracy movement.

MOHAMMED (Muhammad) (c.570-632) Prophet and founder of Islam, born in Mecca in western Arabia (now part of Saudi Arabia). When aged about 25 he married Khadija, widow of a wealthy merchant (later he made several other marriages, some for political reasons). In about 610 he received a religious call, regarded by himself and his followers as revelations from God, later written down in the **Koran**. He was forced by opposition in Mecca to emigrate to Medina in 622 at the invitation of some Arab groups there; this emigration, or **Hegira**, is the starting point of the Muslim calendar. In Medina he became first arbitrator, then ruler of a new kind of religious and political community, the Umma. He conquered Mecca in 630 and then unified much of Arabia under his leadership. After his death he was succeeded as leader of the Umma, but not as prophet, by **Abu Bakr**, first of the line of caliphs.

MOHAMMED ABDUH (1849-1905) Islamic religious reformer, born in Egypt. In 1882 he was exiled for his political activity after the British occupation of Egypt. Returning, he was appointed appellate judge in 1891. He suggested many modernizing liberal reforms in Islamic law, education, ritual and social thought.

MOHAMMED ALI (1769-1849) Founder of modern Egypt; born in Macedonia. He was appointed Ottoman viceroy in Egypt, 1805. He took Syria from the Turks in 1831 but was forced to give it up in 1840 after European intervention. In the following year he was compensated by recognition as hereditary ruler of Egypt and the Sudan.

MOHAMMED V (1910-61) King of Morocco. He succeeded his father as sultan of Morocco in 1927, then under French tutelage which he worked to remove. Deposed and exiled by the French, 1953-5, he was first reinstated as sultan and then recognized as sovereign (1956) and first king of Morocco (1957).

MÖNGKE (d.1259) Mongol leader, grandson of Genghis Khan. He played a prominent part in the great Mongol drive into western Asia and Europe. Elected Great Khan in 1251, he planned a world conquest, from China to Egypt.

MONISM Philosophic doctrine that asserts the single nature of phenomena and denies duality or pluralism (i.e. the separateness of mind and matter). Religiously, it is also the doctrine that there is only one Being, not an opposition of good and evil, or a distinction of God from the world.

MONOPHYSITES Those who followed Eutyches and Dioscorus, Patriarch of Alexandria (d.454), who taught that there was only one nature, not two, in the person of **Jesus** Christ. This doctrine was condemned by the **Council of Chalcedon** (451). Modern churches which grew out of Monophysitism are orthodox in belief though they retain some Monophysite terminology, notably the Coptic, Syrian and Armenian variations.

MONROE, JAMES (1758-1831) Fifth President of the United States. He negotiated the **Louisiana Purchase** (1803). During his presidency, 1817-25, he drew up with his Secretary of State, **John Quincy Adams**, the Monroe Doctrine, which has aimed at excluding foreign influence from the Western Hemisphere ever since.

MONTAGNARDS Hill-dwellers in Indo-China. In Vietnam they cultivate rice on burned-out forest land, live in longhouses or huts raised on piles, trace their descent through the female line, and speak a variety of Mon-Khmer and Malayo-Polynesian languages.

MONTANIST Follower of the heretical Christian sect founded in Phrygia by Montanus and by two women, Prisca and Maximilla, in the 2nd century AD. The group was ecstatic and prophetic, restoring belief in the present power of the Spirit; there was mystical identification with the divine and ascetic practice. **Tertullian** was a notable convert, but by the 3rd century the sect was under condemnation; it persisted in Phrygia until the 5th century.

MONTCALM, LOUIS, MARQUIS DE (1712-59) French general who as commander-in-chief of the French Canadian forces defended Canada against the British in the French and Indian War (1756-60). He was killed during the battle for Quebec on the Heights of Abraham.

MONTESQUIEU, BARON DE (1689-1755) French political philosopher. His main works included *Lettres Persanes* (1721), satirizing French life and politics, and *L'Esprit des Lois* (1748), his masterpiece, which first set out many of the key ideas in modern democratic and constitutional thought, characteristic of the Enlightenment and of rationalism.

MONTFORT, SIMON DE (c.1160-1218) Baron of Montfort (near Paris). He became a leader of the Albigensian Crusade and Count of Toulouse after the battle of Muret, 1213; he extended north French and Catholic influence in the south of France. He was the father of Simon de Montfort, Earl of Leicester, the opponent of Henry III of England.

MORDAUNT, SIR JOHN (1697-1780) British general. In 1756 he commanded the army assembled in Dorset to repel an expected French invasion; in 1757 he led an unsuccessful expedition (with Admiral Hawke) to attack the French naval base at Rochefort, and was court-martialled for his failure.

MORELOS, JOSÉ MARíA (1765-1815) Mexican priest and revolutionary. He joined Hidalgo's insurrection against the Spanish colonial government, 1811, and took command in southern Mexico after Hidalgo's death, leading a successful guerrilla army but with too few men to consolidate his victories. In 1813 he called the Congress of Chilpancingo, which declared Mexican independence, but two years later was captured, defrocked and shot as a traitor after directing a heroic rearguard action against the Spaniards.

MORENO, MARIANO GARCíA (1778-1811) Argentine independence leader. He practised as a lawyer in Buenos Aires; in 1809 published his 'Landowners' petition' (*Representación de los hacendados*) attacking restrictive Spanish trade laws, and in 1810 joined the revolutionary junta which replaced the Spanish administration. He became secretary for military and political affairs; founded Argentina's national library and official newspaper, *La Gaceta de Buenos Aires*. He was forced to resign after prematurely advocating complete separation on a diplomatic mission to London.

MORGAN, JOHN PIERPONT (1837-1913) United States financier. In 1871 he joined the New York firm of Drexel, Morgan & Co. (renamed J. P. Morgan & Co. in 1895); under his guidance this became one of the world's greatest financial institutions, deeply involved in US government borrowing, reorganization of the US railways and the formation of such massive industrial groups as US Steel, International Harvester and the General Electric Company. By the time of his death his name was accepted everywhere as a symbol of 'money power'; he had also formed a great art collection.

MOSES Israelite leader, prophet and lawgiver who flourished some time between the 15th and 13th centuries BC. According to the Old Testament, he was born in Egypt; he led the Israelites out of slavery, and travelled forty years in the Sinai desert seeking Canaan, the land promised to the descendants of **Abraham**. He received the Ten Commandments, the basis of Jewish law; he died within sight of the promised land.

MOSLEY, SIR OSWALD (1896-1980) Leader of the British Union of Fascists. He served as a Member of Parliament, successively as a Conservative, Independent and Labour representative. He left the Labour Party in 1930 to found the right-wing 'New Party' and, later, the BUF or Blackshirts. He was imprisoned by the British government during the Second World War, and subsequently lived in France.

MOSSADEQ, MOHAMMED (?1880-1967) Iranian politician. As Prime Minister, 1951-3, he nationalized the Anglo-Iranian oil company. After a struggle for power with the Shah and his supporters, and with Western oil interests, he was overturned by a *coup d'état* in 1953 and imprisoned until 1956.

MOUNTBATTEN, LOUIS, EARL (1900-79) British military commander. A grandson of Queen Victoria, he entered the Royal Navy in 1913. He was Allied Chief of Combined Operations, 1942-3; Supreme Commander Southeast Asia, 1943-6; last Viceroy (1947) and first Governor-General (1947-8) of India; commanded the Mediterranean fleet (1948-9 and 1952-4); became First Sea Lord (1955-9), Chief of UK Defence Staff and Chairman of Chiefs of Staff Committee (1959-65); and personal aide-de-camp to the British sovereign from 1936. He was killed by Irish terrorists in 1979.

MSIRI (d.1891) African king, also known as Ngetengwa and Mwendo. Born near Tabora, now in Tanzania, in 1856 he settled in southern Katanga (Shaba); with a handful of Nyamwezi supporters, he seized large parts of this valuable copper-producing region, and by 1870 had largely displaced the previous Lunda rulers. His rejection of overtures from the British South Africa Company in the 1880s resulted in the Copper Belt being divided between Great Britain (Zambia) and Belgium (Zaire). He was shot while negotiating with emissaries from **Leopold II** of Belgium's Congo Free State.

MUGABE, ROBERT (1924-) Zimbabwean political leader. He worked as a schoolteacher before joining the nationalist movement in 1960. A Marxist, he co-founded the Zimbabwe African National Union (ZANU) in 1963, but was subsequently imprisoned for 11 years. After his release, he joined the Patriotic Front in 1976 and waged a guerrilla war against the white supremacist government of **Ian Smith**. After the ceasefire (1980), he was elected the first prime minister of independent Zimbabwe.

MUGHALS Dynasty of Muslim emperors in India; *see page 168*.

MUHAMMAD IBN TUGHLUQ (c.1290-1351) Indian empire-builder, who succeeded his father in 1325 as ruler of the Delhi sultanate. He extended the frontiers far into southern India, fighting many campaigns to consolidate his gains; he failed, however, to impose coherent control, and saw his domains begin to crumble before he died.

MUIZZUDIN MUHAMMAD (d.1206) Greatest of the **Ghurids**. He helped his brother to seize power in Ghur, northwest Afghanistan, c.1162, expelled Turkish nomads from Ghazni, 1173; invaded northern India, 1175; annexed the **Ghaznavid** principality of Lahore, 1186. He was defeated by a **Rajput** coalition at Tara, 1191, but returned to rout them in 1192. He was assassinated in 1206.

MUJIBUR RAHMAN (1920-75) East Pakistan (now Bangladesh) political leader. He worked for Bengali rights until independence from British rule (1947), founded the Awami League (1949) opposed to the domination of West Pakistan, of which he became general secretary (1953) and president (1966). Tensions resulting from his party's majority victory and demand for autonomy from West Pakistan (1970) resulted in an India-Pakistan war, and an independent Bangladesh (1971). In 1975 he became president with dictatorial powers, but was killed in a coup the same year.

MUKDEN, BATTLE OF Main land engagement of the Russo-Japanese War (1904-05). Mukden (Shen-yang), the industrial centre of Manchuria, became a tsarist stronghold after Russia obtained extensive railway building rights in the region (1896). The battle lasted over two weeks, starting in late February 1905 and ending with Japanese occupation of the city on 10 March.

MULVANY, WILLIAM THOMAS (1806-85) Irish industrialist. An engineer and civil servant 1833-49, he went to the German Ruhr district in 1854 and directed the opening of coalmines and ironworks there. In 1858 he organized an association of Ruhr industrialists (the *Bergbauverein*) which transformed the Ruhr into the largest coalfield and industrial complex on the European continent.

MÜNSTER, TREATY OF An agreement signed in January 1648 as part of the arrangements known collectively as the Peace of Westphalia, which ended the Thirty Years' War. It brought Spanish recognition of the independence of the Dutch Republic and brought to an end the Dutch Revolt.

MURAD I (c.1326-89) Third ruler of the Ottoman state, succeeding **Orkhan** in 1362. He controlled (or profited from) the continuing Turkish expansion in the Balkans which brought Thrace and later Thessaly, the south Serbian principalities and much of Bulgaria under Ottoman control. Byzantium, Bulgaria and Serbia were successively reduced to vassalage after the defeat of hostile coalition forces at Chirmen (Chermanon) in 1371 and Kossovo in 1389; Murad was killed during the latter battle. Ottoman territory was also expanded in Anatolia (acquisition of Ankara, 1354; hostilities with the Karaman in the 1380s).

MURAD II (1404-51) Ottoman sultan, son of **Mehmed I.** Succeeding to the throne in 1421, he spent the early years of his reign overcoming rival claimants backed by Byzantium or Karaman. After a seven-year war with Venice, Murad took Salonika in 1430. The later years of his reign were dominated by the struggle with Hungary for the lands of the lower Danube, Serbia and Wallachia. Murad gained control over Serbia in 1439 but in 1440 failed to take Belgrade; by 1443 the Ottomans were forced on to the defensive at Izladi, and in the following year, having made an unfavourable peace with Hungary and Karaman, Murad abdicated in favour of his 12-year-old son **Mehmed II.** Following the penetration of the Balkans by a Christian army, Murad led the Ottoman forces to a crushing victory at Varna in 1444. Two years later he reassumed the throne; in 1448 he defeated the Hungarians once more at Kossovo.

MUSSOLINI, BENITO (1883-1945) Italian dictator. He practised as a schoolteacher and journalist; having been expelled in 1914 from the Socialist party for advocating support of the Allied powers, in 1919 he organized the Fascist party, advocating nationalism, syndicalism and violent anti-Communism, backed up by a paramilitary organization, the Blackshirts. He organized a march on Rome in 1922. He was appointed Prime Minister and then, as Il Duce (the Leader), established himself as totalitarian dictator. He invaded Ethiopia in 1935, formed the Rome-Berlin Axis with **Hitler** the following year, and in 1940 declared war on the Allies. He was defeated in 1943, installed by Hitler as head of a puppet state (Republic of Salo) in northern Italy and shot by Italian partisans in 1945.

MWENEMUTAPA (later Mashonaland). Kingdom of southeast Africa between the 14th and 18th centuries, with its capital probably at Zimbabwe; famous for its gold deposits, which attracted Portuguese traders, based in Mozambique, from 1505 onwards.

MYCENAEAN Ancient Greek civilization flourishing c.1600-1100 BC, culturally influenced by Minoan Crete. It was centred on the city of Mycenae, in Argolis, where the most famous surviving monuments include the citadel walls with the Lion Gate, and the Treasury of Atreus.

MZILIKAZI (d.1870) Matabele (Ndebele) chief. He fled from Zululand to set up a new kingdom north of the Vaal River, but was defeated by the Boers, 1836; he withdrew across the Limpopo River and established the Matabele kingdom.

NABOPOLASSAR (d.605 BC) King of Babylon and destroyer of Assyria, a notable of one of the Kaldu (Chaldaean) tribes of southern Babylonia. While governor of the Sea-land province, he assumed leadership of an insurrection against the Assyrians in 627 BC. He founded the last native Babylonian dynasty, the Chaldaean, in 626, quickly gaining control of much of Babylonia. He unsuccessfully besieged Ashur, 616, formed an alliance with the **Medes**, 614, and made a joint assault on Nineveh which was completed in 612. He was succeeded by his son, Nebuchadnezzar.

NANAK (1469-1539) Founding guru of the Sikh faith, combining Hindu and Muslim beliefs into a single doctrine. The son of a merchant, he made an extended pilgrimage to Muslim and Hindu shrines throughout India, returning to the Punjab in 1520 and settling in Kartarpur. His teaching, spread by a large following of disciples, advocated intensive meditation on the divine name; many of his hymns still survive.

NANKING TREATY see Opium War

NANTES, EDICT OF Order, issued in 1598 by Henry IV of France, guaranteeing freedom of worship to French Protestants. Its revocation in 1685 by **Louis XIV** forced many non-Catholics to flee the country, weakening the French economy and creating much international friction.

NAPIER, SIR CHARLES JAMES (1782-1853) British general and prolific author. He served under Wellington in the Peninsular War; and led the British conquest of Sind, 1841-3.

NAPOLEON I (NAPOLEON BONAPARTE) (1769-1821) Emperor of the French; see pages 200-1.

NAPOLEON III (CHARLES LOUIS NAPOLEON BONAPARTE) (1808-73) Emperor of the French, son of Louis Bonaparte and nephew of Napoleon I. He was exiled, like his uncle, after 1815. He wrote Les Idées Napoléoniennes in 1839, was involved in two unsuccessful insurrections, in 1836 and 1840, and returned to France after the 1848 revolution, to be elected President by a huge majority, and to become Emperor in 1852. During his highly prosperous reign, central Paris was rebuilt, Cochin China was acquired and the Suez Canal opened. He was defeated by **Bismarck** in the **French-Prussian War** (1870-1), and after the collapse of his regime in 1871 went into exile in England.

NARAI (d.1688) (also Narayana). King of Siam from 1657 until his death. In his struggle to free his country's foreign trade from Dutch control he sought the help of the **English East India Company's** factors at Ayutthaya. Their inability to help caused him to turn to the French, whose cause was espoused by his Greek adviser, **Constant Phaulkoni,** a convert to Catholicism. After an exchange of missions between Versailles and Lopburi, Narai's up-country residence, **Louis XIV** sent a naval expedition which seized the then village of Bangkok and the port of Mergui (now in Burma) with the declared aim of converting Siam to **Christianity**. The resulting national uprising, led by Pra Phetraja, forced the French to withdraw; Pra Phetraja became regent, and on Narai's death a few months later his successor.

NARAM-SIN The last great ruler of Sumer and Akkad, in ancient Mesopotamia, and grandson of **Sargon.** He reigned c.2291-2255 BC, and was a famous warrior whose victories are commemorated in several extant carvings and monuments, including the impressive stele found at Susa, now in the Louvre Museum.

NASRIDS The last Muslim dynasty in Spain, which rose to power under Muhammad I al-Ghalib (died 1272) and ruled Granada from 1238 until its conquest by the Christians in 1492.

NASSER, GAMAL ABDEL- (1918-70) Egyptian politician. As an army officer he became the leading member of the group which overthrew King Farouk in 1952, under the nominal leadership of General Neguib. In 1954, after a power struggle with Neguib, he became Prime Minister, and in 1956 President until his death. His regime was marked by socio-economic changes – reform of land-tenure, building of the Aswan High Dam – and initially by a foreign policy of neutralism between the great powers and leadership of the Arab nationalist movement, which led to the short-lived union with Syria in the United Arab Republic (1958-61), two wars (with Israel, Great Britain and France, 1956, with Israel, 1967), and increasing dependence on the USSR.

NATO see North Atlantic Treaty Organization

NAVAJO North American Indian tribe which probably emigrated from Canada to the region of the southwest United States between 900 and 1200. After a long history of raids against white settlers in New Mexico, 8000 Navajo were captured by a force under Colonel Kit Carson (1863-4) and interned for four years in New Mexico; in 1868 they were released and sent to a reservation. Today some 100,000 Navajo survive, many still occupying the 24,000 square mile (62,160 km²) reservation in New Mexico, Arizona and Utah. They form the largest Indian tribe in the United States.

NAZISM Term formed from the abbreviation for the National Socialist German Workers' Party – leader **Adolf Hitler.** Its creed covered many of the features of **Fascism.** Its special characteristics were a belief in the racial superiority of the 'Aryan race' and of the German people who, as the purest carriers of Aryan blood, constituted a master race destined to dominate the sub-human Slav peoples of eastern Europe and Russia; virulent anti-semitism expressed in the systematic extermination of the Jewish population throughout Europe, the Jews being accused of an insatiable desire to corrupt and destroy Aryan purity and culture; anti-urbanism and anti-intellectualism, the peasant being held to be purified by his contact with the land; the personality and ruthless political leadership of Hitler, who believed himself destined to risk all to lead the German people to the empire which would last for 1000 years.

NAZI-SOVIET PACT (also known as Molotov-Ribbentrop Pact). Mutual non-aggression pact signed on 23 August 1939 between Germany and Soviet Russia, containing secret protocols which divided eastern Europe between the signatories: eastern Poland, Latvia, Estonia, Finland and Bessarabia to Russia; western Poland and Lithuania (later transferred to the Russian sphere) to Germany. The Russians invaded Poland 17 days after the Germans, on 17 September 1939.

NDEBELE see Matabele

NEGUIB, MOHAMMED (1901-84) Egyptian soldier and President. He was second in command of Egyptian troops in Palestine in the first Arab-Israeli war in 1948. Adopted as their titular head by the Egyptian officers who made the revolution of 1952, after the revolution he became Prime Minister and President of the republic, 1953-4. He was deprived of office after a struggle for power with the real leader of the officers, **Nasser.**

NEHRU, JAWAHARLAL (1889-1964) The first Prime Minister of independent India, 1947-64. Educated in England, in 1920 he joined the nationalist movement led by **Gandhi,** and was imprisoned eight times between 1920 and 1927. He was four times President of the Indian National Congress Party: 1929-30, 1936-7, 1946 and 1951-4.

NELSON, HORATIO (1758-1805) 1st Viscount Nelson. British naval hero, who rose to the rank of admiral in 1797 during the French Revolutionary Wars, winning decisive victories at the Nile (1798) and at Copenhagen (1801). He was killed in 1805 during his most famous battle, Trafalgar, which effectively ended the threat of a French invasion of England.

NEOLITHIC The last part of the **Stone Age,** originally defined by the occurrence of polished stone tools, but now seen as more importantly characterized by the practice of agriculture, for which sharp stone axes were essential forest-clearing equipment. Such cultures emerged in the Near East by 8000 BC, and appeared in Europe from 6000 to 3000 BC.

NERCHINSK, TREATY OF Peace agreement signed in 1689 between Russia and China, as a result of which Russia withdrew from lands east of the Stanovoy Mountains and north of the Amur river. The settlement lasted until the treaties of **Aigun** (1858) and **Peking** (1860) brought Russia to its present boundary with China in the Far East.

NERO (AD 37-68) Roman emperor, succeeding to the imperial title in AD 54. He murdered his mother, Agrippina, in 59. After the fire of Rome in 64 he began a systematic persecution of Christians, and in the following year executed many opponents after the discovery of a plot to depose him. He committed suicide when the governors of Gaul, Spain and Africa united in revolt.

NESTORIANS Followers of Nestorius whose Christian teachings, condemned by the councils of Ephesus (431) and Chalcedon (451), stressed the independence of the divine and human natures of Christ. They are represented in modern times by the Syrian Orthodox Church (approximately 100,000 members in Iran, Syria and Iraq) which first accepted this version of **Christianity** in 486.

NEVSKY, ALEXANDER (c.1220-63) Prince of Novgorod. He defeated the Swedes on the River Neva (hence his name) in 1240; and the Teutonic Knights on frozen Lake Peipus, 1242. He thought resistance to the Mongols hopeless and co-operated with them; in return the Khan made him Grand Prince of Vladimir (i.e. ruler of Russia) in 1252.

NEWCOMEN, THOMAS (1663-1729) English inventor of the atmospheric engine. As an ironmonger, he saw the high cost and inefficiency of using horses to drain the Cornish tin mines, and after ten years of experiment produced a steam machine for this purpose. The first known engine was erected near Dudley Castle, Staffordshire, in 1712. He also invented an internal-condensing jet to produce a vacuum in the engine cylinder, and an automatic valve gear.

NEW DEAL Social and economic programme, instituted 1933-9 by President **F. D. Roosevelt** to combat the effects of world depression in the United States. He used the Federal government to promote agricultural and industrial recovery, to provide relief to the unemployed, and to institute moderate economic and social reform.

NE WIN (1911-) Military dictator of Burma. He joined the nationalistic 'We-Burmans Association' in 1936, and in 1941 went to Taiwan (Formosa) for military training with the Japanese. He was chief of staff, Burma National Army, 1943-5, commander-in-chief of the Burmese Army after independence in 1948, and served as Prime Minister in the 1958 'caretaker' government. He stepped down in 1960 on the restoration of parliamentary administration, but in 1962 led a coup d'état, establishing a Revolutionary Council of the Union of Burma and declaring the Burmese Road to Socialism. He broke Chinese and Indian control of the economy and expelled 300,000 foreigners. He resigned in 1988 under pressure from pro-democracy, communist and nationalist forces.

NGO DINH DIEM (1901-63) President of the Republic of Vietnam. Born into one of Vietnam's royal families, he was interior minister of the emperor Bao Dai's government in the 1930s. In 1945 he was captured by **Ho Chi Minh's** Communists, and fled after refusing Ho's invitation to join his independence movement. Returned in 1954 to head the US-backed government in South Vietnam, but took dictatorial powers, and as a Roman Catholic imprisoned and killed hundreds of Buddhists. He was abandoned by the US, and was assassinated during a military coup d'état.

NGUNI One of the two main Bantu-speaking groups of southern African peoples, including the Swazi, Pondo, Thembu, Xhosa, Zulu and Matabele (Ndebele) nations, mainly occupying land east of the Drakensburg mountains, from Natal to Cape Province.

NICAEA, COUNCILS OF The first council, which was also the first ecumenical gathering of the Christian Church, was called in 325 by the Emperor **Constantine;** it condemned the heresy of Arianism and promulgated the Nicene Creed, which affirms the consubstantiality of Christ the Son and God the Father. The second Nicaean (or seventh ecumenical) council took place in 787 as an attempt to resolve the controversy over **iconoclasm;** it agreed that icons deserved reverence and veneration but not adoration, which was reserved for God.

NICAEA, EMPIRE OF Founded in 1204 by the Byzantine leader Theodore I Lascaris after the Western occupation of Constantinople during the Fourth **Crusade.** Crowned emperor in 1208, Theodore gradually extended his territory to include most of western Anatolia. His successors, while fighting off the despots of Epirus and the Mongols, also attempted to retake Constantinople; success came in 1261 when the Nicaean general, Michael Palaeologus, was able to establish himself as Michael VIII and found the last dynasty of Byzantine emperors.

NICEPHORUS II PHOCAS (c.913-69) Byzantine emperor, who fought as a general under Constantine VII and Romanus II and usurped the throne in 963. He defeated Arab, Bulgarian, Italian and Western imperial enemies. He was murdered in 969 by his own general John Tzimisces, who in turn usurped the throne as John I.

NICHOLAS II (1869-1918) Last tsar of Russia, son of Alexander III. He succeeded in 1894; granted, but then largely withdrew liberal reforms after the revolution of 1905. He was forced to abdicate in March 1917, and was shot at Yekaterinburg (Sverdlovsk, now again Yekaterinburg) by the **Bolsheviks** in July 1918.

NIEN REBELLION Insurrection led by peasant bandit confederations in Anhwei, Honan and Shantung, areas which had suffered from the disastrous flooding of the Huang Ho (Yellow River) in the 1850s.

NIJMEGEN, TREATIES OF Agreements signed 1678-9 to end the Dutch War (1672-8) between France, Spain and the Dutch Republic. France returned Maastricht to the United Provinces and suspended her anti-Dutch tariff of 1667; Spain gave up Franche-Comté, Artois and 16 Flemish garrison towns to France, thus losing its 'corridor' from Milan to the Spanish Netherlands (the Spanish Road). In 1679 the German emperor, Leopold I, accepted the terms, slightly strengthening French rights in Alsace, Lorraine and on the Rhine.

NIMITZ, CHESTER WILLIAM (1885-1965) American admiral, commander-in-chief of the Pacific Ocean Area, 1942-5.

NINE YEARS' WAR Conflict between **Louis XIV** of France and his neighbours, 1689-97, led by William III of England and the Netherlands, allied in the **League of Augsburg**. Their aim was to restrain French territorial expansion, mainly at the expense of the Spanish empire, and in this they eventually succeeded. *See also* **King William's War**.

NIVELLE, ROBERT-GEORGES (1856-1924) French general. After two brilliant victories at Verdun, he was appointed commander-in-chief of the French armies on the Western Front in 1916, but was replaced by Pétain in 1917 after the disastrous failure of the spring offensive and widespread mutiny.

NIXON, RICHARD MILHOUS (1913-) 37th President of the United States. Trained as a lawyer, he was elected to the House of Representatives in 1946 and 1948; elected Republican Senator for California, 1950. He was Vice-President to **Dwight D. Eisenhower** (1953-61); defeated for the presidency by **John F. Kennedy**, 1960, and in the contest for California governorship, 1962. He re-entered politics to defeat Humphrey in the presidential election, 1968, and was re-elected in a landslide victory, 1972. He resigned office in 1974 at the climax of the investigation into the 'Watergate scandal' arising out of an attempt to burgle the Democratic election headquarters during the 1972 campaign.

NIZAM Hereditary title of the rulers of the Indian state of Hyderabad; members of the dynasty founded by Asaf Jah, Subadhar of the Deccan, 1713-48.

NKRUMAH, KWAME (1909-72) The first Prime Minister of independent Ghana (formerly the Gold Coast colony). He graduated from Achimota College in 1930. He wrote *Towards Colonial Freedom* in 1947 in opposition to British rule, and in 1949 formed the Convention People's Party, instituting a programme of non-cooperation. After independence (1957) he became first President of the Ghana republic, 1960; in 1964 he declared a one-party state, but was deposed two years later by the army while on a visit to China.

NOBEL, ALFRED BERNHARD (1833-96) Swedish industrialist, chemist and inventor of dynamite. He began the manufacture of nitroglycerine in Sweden in 1860; his first factory blew up, killing his younger brother Emil. He perfected a much safer dynamite, and patented it in 1867-8. He made an immense fortune from this and from his share of the Russian Baku oilfield. When he died he left the bulk of his money in trust to establish the Nobel prizes for peace, literature, physics, chemistry, medicine and, more recently, economics.

NOK One of the Iron Age cultures in West Africa, flourishing on the Benue plateau of Nigeria between 500 BC and AD 200. It is characterized by its distinctive clay figurines depicting both animals and men.

NORIEGA, MANUAL ANTONIO (1938-) Panamanian military and political leader. Educated at the Military Academy in Peru before becoming a lieutenant in the Panamanian National Guard in 1962. In 1970 he became head of Intelligence Services and in 1983 Dictator and President of the Republic of Panama. Courted by the CIA during the 1960s, he was eventually charged with drug trafficking and forcibly deposed and removed by US troops in 1989 to be indicted.

NORMANS Name derived from Nordmanni, or Northmen, to describe the Viking invaders who in the late 9th century established themselves on the lower Seine, in France. In 911, under their leader Hrolfr (Rollo), they obtained from the French king, Charles the Simple, rights to territory in northern Normandy; in 924 and 933 their control was extended, particularly westward, to include the whole area now known as Normandy. In the 11th century, under Robert and Roger Guiscard, and Duke William (**William I, the Conqueror**) respectively, their descendants conquered both Sicily and England.

NORMAN CONQUEST Name given to the successful invasion of England in 1066 by Duke William of Normandy, crowned king as **William I, the Conqueror**. English resistance was broken and the whole country overrun by 1071 stabilization was achieved by expelling the **Anglo-Saxon** landowners and parcelling out the conquered territory among William's followers, as tenants-in-chief and vassals of the king.

NORTH ATLANTIC TREATY ORGANIZATION (NATO) Defensive alliance, signed in 1949 between Belgium, Canada, Denmark, France, Iceland, Italy, Luxembourg, Netherlands, Norway, Portugal, United Kingdom and United States. Greece and Turkey joined in 1951; West Germany in 1954. France ceased to participate fully in 1966. NATO's headquarters are in Brussels; it deployed some 800,000 land troops in Europe.

NORTHERN RISING Attempted rebellion in northern England against **Elizabeth I** in 1569-70. Led by the Catholic earls of Northumberland and Westmorland, its object was to restore Catholicism by placing the imprisoned (Catholic) Mary Queen of Scots on the English throne. Faced by royal armies, the rebels melted away, although 800 of them died in the only direct clash; the leaders fled abroad.

NORTH GERMAN CONFEDERATION Political union of north German states set up under Prussian leadership after the Seven Weeks' War in 1866. It was enlarged in 1871 after the Franco-Prussian War to become the new German Empire.

NOVATIAN (c.200-c.258) Roman theologian, author of *De Trinitate (On the Trinity)*. He at first supported those Christians whose faith lapsed under persecution, but later strongly condemned all apostasy. After 251, when Cornelius became Pope, this led him to break with the Church and set himself up as a rigorist anti-Pope, at the head of the Novatianist Schism. He was excommunicated in 251, and probably martyred c.258 under the Emperor **Valerian**, but the sect continued to spread in East and West and lasted until the 6th century.

NU-PIEDS Peasants who rebelled in protest against high taxes in Normandy, France, in 1639; named after the salt-gatherers of Avranches, who walked barefoot on the sands. They feared that the introduction of a salt tax (*gabelle*) would reduce sales of their product, and took a leading part in the uprising, which was crushed after four months in a pitched battle with government forces outside Rouen.

NURI ES-SAID (1888-1958) Iraqi statesman. An officer in the Ottoman army, in 1916 he joined the revolt of Sharif **Hussein** against the Ottomans, and in 1921 joined Hussein's son Faysal when he became king of Iraq. He held various ministerial posts, including that of Prime Minister. In 1941 he fled Iraq with the regent, Abdullah, during the period of rule by **Rashid Ali**, returned after the British military re-occupation, and dominated Iraqi politics, with intervals, until he was killed during an army coup. He was associated with the strongly pro-Western policy which led to the formation of the Baghdad Pact (**Central Treaty Organization**) in 1955.

NYAMWEZI A Bantu-speaking people of east Africa, occupying a large area between Lake Victoria and Lake Rukwa. In the 19th century they played a major part in the opening up of the east African interior to European trade from the coast.

NYERERE, JULIUS (1922-) President of Tanzania. Founder president of the Tanganyika African National Union in 1954, he was elected to the Tanganyika legislative council in 1958, and became Chief Minister, 1960-1, and Prime Minister, 1961-2. He was President, first of Tanganyika, 1962-4, and then of Tanzania from 1964 to 1985. He remained in power after 1985 as leader of the only legal party, but in 1992 promised to end the one-party system. The author of *Freedom and Unity* (1967) and Swahili translations of Shakespeare, he developed theories of African socialism, and put these and other economic self-sufficiency policies into practice.

NYSTAD, TREATY OF Agreement in 1721 between Russia and Sweden to end the **Great Northern War**. Russia gained Sweden's Baltic provinces (Estonia and Livonia) and thus a 'window on the west', but restored Finland to Sweden.

OCTAVIAN *see* **Augustus**

OFFA (d.796) King of Mercia, central England, in the 8th century. He constructed an earthwork which still survives (Offa's Dyke) between his kingdom and Wales. He claimed the title 'King of the English' after establishing control over most of the country south of the River Humber.

OGEDEI (d.1241) Mongol ruler, third son of **Genghis Khan**. He was given chief command, in preference to his brothers, Jochi and Chagatai, during the latter part of the Khwarizian campaign, 1220-2; elected Great Khan in 1229, in 1235 he completed the conquest of the **Chin** in northern China and declared war on China's Sung dynasty, and in 1236 conquered Korea. He planned the western campaign that finally carried the Mongols from Siberia to the Adriatic.

O'HIGGINS, BERNARDO (1778-1842) Liberator of Chile, and its first head of state. The son of a Spanish officer of Irish origin; he became a member of the Chilean national congress in 1811; and then led Chilean forces in **San Martín's** Army of the Andes, triumphing over the royalists at the battle of Chacabuco in February 1817. In 1823 he was exiled to Peru, where he died.

OJEDA, ALONSO DE (1465-1515) Spanish adventurer, who sailed under, and later quarrelled with, **Columbus**. In 1499, with **Vespucci**, he explored the coasts of Venezuela and Guiana, landing in the area later claimed by Spain (1593) under the name Surinam. He commanded the first mainland settlement in South America, on the Gulf of Urabá, 1509 – a disastrous failure.

OLDENBURGS Danish royal family, of German origin. Christian, Count of Oldenburg, was elected king of Denmark and Norway in 1448; his direct descendants ruled until 1863, when the succession passed to the present Glücksburg branch.

OLGIERD (d.1377) Grand Duke of Lithuania, reigning 1345-77, son of **Gedymin**, father of **Władysław II Jagiełło**. He invaded Mongol-dominated Russia in 1362-3, seizing the principality of Kiev, but failed to take Moscow in 1368-72. He died fighting the **Tartars**.

OLOF SKÖTKONUNG (d.1022) 'The Tax King'. Christian king of the Swedes and the Gantat; son of Erik the Victorious. He joined the Danish king, **Sven Forkbeard**, to defeat Norway in 1000; though he became a Christian he failed to impose the new religion on his subjects.

OMAR IBN AL-KHATTAB (c.591-644) Second Muslim caliph, and the first to assume the title 'Commander of the Faithful'. At first he opposed Islam, but was converted c.617; his daughter Hafsa became **Mohammed**'s third wife. He aided the first caliph, **Abu Bakr**, in his campaigns, succeeding him without opposition in 634, and carried further the conquests he had begun in Palestine, Syria, Iraq, Persia and Egypt. He was assassinated by a slave of Persian origin.

OPEC *see* **Organization of Petroleum Exporting Countries**

OPIUM WAR Fought between Britain and China, 1839-42, over Chinese attempts to prevent the import of opium from British India in payment for British imports of Chinese tea and silk which had previously been paid in silver, the only exchange acceptable to the Chinese. After a series of defeats, under the terms of the Nanking Treaty China ceded Hong Kong Island to Britain, opened five Treaty Ports to British trade, and relaxed many economic restrictions on foreign merchants.

ORGANIZATION OF PETROLEUM EXPORTING COUNTRIES (OPEC) Multinational organization established by Iran, Iraq, Kuwait, Saudi Arabia and Venezuela (1961) to coordinate petroleum policies and provide members with technical and economic aid. In 1973, in support of the Arab war against Israel, OPEC first halted oil production and then increased prices by 250%, triggering a major worldwide economic recession, but increasing both the revenues and the political influence of the member states. By 1982, however, many nations had reduced their consumption of OPEC oil, forcing a decrease in production and a fall in prices.

ORIGEN (c.185-254) Scholar and theologian, deeply influential in the emergence of the early Greek Christian Church. He wrote many important commentaries, treatises and polemics, culminating c.232 in his *Hexapla* which reconciles six different versions of the Old Testament.

ORKHAN (1274/88-1362) Second ruler (*beg*) of the Muslim principality founded by his father, **Osman I**, whom he succeeded in c.1324. He captured Bursa in 1326, Nicaea (Iznik) in 1331 and Nicomedia (Izmit) in 1337 from Byzantium; by annexing the neighbouring emirate of Karasi in 1345 he was able to involve the Ottomans in the civil wars in Byzantium, and secured a bridgehead in Europe (Rumeli). Orkhan's sons seized Tzympe in 1352, Gallipoli in 1354 and Adrianpole (Edirne) in 1361, thus opening the Balkans to Turkish conquest and Ottoman expansion.

ORMÉE REVOLT Part of the **Fronde** rebellion against **Louis XIV** of France, 1648-53. Bordeaux defied authority until reduced by siege; the rebellion took its name from the *ormes* (elm trees) under which the rebels met to discuss policy.

ORTELIUS, ABRAHAM (1527-1606) Publisher of the first modern atlas, *Theatrum orbis terrarum* (Antwerp, 1570). He worked as a cartographer, antiquary and book dealer.

OSMAN (c.1258-c.1324) Founder of the Ottoman dynasty, a leader active among the Turks settled in the northwest Anatolian borderlands with Byzantium in the latter part of the 13th century. He emerges into history c.1301; after a constant struggle he had by his death conquered most of Bithynia from Byzantium.

OSTROGOTHS Germanic people who occupied the Ukraine in the 4th century AD. During the reign of their great hero King Ermanaric (d.372), they extended their empire from the Black Sea to the Baltic, but were dispossessed c.370 by the advancing Huns. The tribe then wandered and fought in eastern and central Europe until the end of Hunnish domination, c.455. Under their king, **Theodoric** (ruled 493-526), they moved into Italy and established themselves as rulers, with their capital at Verona, until finally dispersed by the armies of **Justinian I** in the mid-6th century.

OTHMAN (d.656) Third Muslim caliph after the death of **Mohammed**. Born into the rich and powerful **Umayyad** clan of Mecca, c.615 he became Mohammed's first influential convert, and was elected caliph in 644 after the death of **Omar**. He promulgated the first official version of the **Koran**, and continued the policy of conquest.

OTTAWA AGREEMENTS A series of arrangements, concluded at the Imperial Economics Conference in 1932, under which Great Britain, having reversed its traditional Free Trade policies and imposed tariffs on most foreign food and raw material imports, allowed free or preferential entry to goods from the British Empire. In return, the colonies and dominions agreed to use tariffs against British goods only to protect their own domestic industries. The underlying doctrine, known as Imperial Preference, was substantially modified by the General Agreement on Tariffs and Trade (GATT) in 1947, and finally evaporated on Britain's entry to the European Economic Community (EC) in 1973.

OTTO I, THE GREAT (912-73) German emperor. As king of East Francia he crushed rebellions involving his brothers Thankmar and Henry (938-9) and his son Liudolf (953-4). He defeated the Magyars at the battle of the Lechfeld (955). He received the imperial crown in 962; by marrying his son **Otto II** to the Byzantine Princess Theophana, 972, he achieved recognition of his Western Empire in Constantinople.

OTTO II (955-83) Son of **Otto I**, and German king from 961, he held the imperial throne jointly with his father from 967 and alone from 973. He tried without success to drive the Greeks and Arabs from southern Italy, 982.

OTTO III (980-1002) German emperor, son of **Otto II**. He was German king from 983 under the regency of his mother (until 991) and grandmother (until 994), being crowned emperor in 996.

OTTO OF FREISING (c.1111-58) German bishop, historian and philosopher, half-brother to King Conrad III. He entered the Cistercian monastery at Morimond, Champagne, c.1132, and became bishop of Freising in 1138. He wrote a world history from the beginning to 1146, and also the *Gesta Friderici*, celebrating the deeds of the **Hohenstaufen** dynasty, particularly of his nephew, **Frederick I Barbarossa**.

OTTOCAR II (1230-1278) King of Bohemia, son of Wenceslaus I, reigning 1253-78. He made his kingdom briefly the strongest state in the **Holy Roman Empire**. He led crusades against the heathen Prussians and Lithuanians, and annexed lands from Styria to the Adriatic. Eclipsed after the election of Rudolf of Habsburg as emperor in 1273, he was forced to renounce all territory save Bohemia and Moravia. He was killed at the battle of Dürnkrut, attempting to reconquer Austria.

OTTOMANS Turkish Muslims; *see pages* 136-7, 166-7.

OWEN THE BALD (d.1015) Last king of the Britons of Strathclyde, a state between Scotland and England, centred on Glasgow, which was annexed by Scotland after Owen's death.

OWEN, ROBERT (1771-1858) Early British socialist and social reformer. He was manager of a model cotton mill at New Lanark, 1799, and pioneered shorter working hours, employee housing, education and co-operative stores. He was partly responsible for the Factory Act of 1819; he formed the Grand National Consolidated Trades Union in 1843.

OXFORDSHIRE RISING Popular revolt in 1596 in the English Midlands against the enclosure of common land by landlords, depriving the local population of grazing rights.

PACHACUTI (d.1471) The ninth **Inca** emperor, reigning from 1438 until his death. He led his people's victorious expansion out of the Cuzco valley towards Lake Titicaca; with his son, **Topa** Inca, he conquered the **Chimú**; he founded the great fortress of Sacsahuaman. His mummified body was found by Juan Polo de Ondegardo, Spanish *corregidor* of Cuzco, in 1539.

PÁEZ, JOSÉ ANTONIO (1790-1873) First President of Venezuela. Part-Indian, he joined the revolution against Spain in 1810 and became one of the chief Venezuelan commanders to **Simon Bolívar**. He participated in the defeat of the Spaniards at Carabobo, 1821, and Puerto Cabello, 1823; in 1829 he led the movement to separate Venezuela from the larger state of Gran Colombia, and effectively controlled the new country from his election as President in 1831 until 1846, when he was forced into exile, returning as dictator in 1861. Driven out again in 1863, he retired to New York.

PAHLEVIS Dynasty in Iran, founded by **Reza Shah Pahlevi** in 1925. Overthrown 1979.

PAL, BIPIN CHANDRA (1858-1932) Indian schoolmaster, journalist and propagandist. After a brief visit to the United States in 1900, he became involved in the movement for Indian self-government (*swaraj*) editing newspapers and giving lectures which advocated non-cooperation with the British. In 1908 he was arrested; he lost his influence to **Tilak** and later to **Gandhi**.

PALAEOLITHIC The first part of the **Stone Age**, from the first recognizable stone tools in Africa over 2 million years ago, to the advanced reindeer-hunters who decorated their caves with wall-paintings in France and Spain around 20,000 years ago. It is divided into the Lower Palaeolithic, associated with early types of man, and the Middle and Upper Palaeolithic, associated with anatomically modern man.

PALAS Warrior dynasty of northern India, controlling most of Bengal and Bihar from the 8th to the 10th century. Founded by Gopala, under his son, Dharmapala, it became a dominant power in east India, with alliances from Tibet to Sumatra. It reached Benares in the 10th century but was blocked by the **Chola** king, Rajendra, and was forced back to defend Bengal, under King Mahipala, after whose death the dynasty declined, giving way to the Sena line.

PAN CH'AO Chinese general, explorer and administrator. Born into a famous scholarly family, he preferred a military life, and was dispatched with a small expedition in 73 to repacify the **Hsiung-nu** tribes. He quickly established a highly effective technique for fomenting intertribal tensions. Appointed Protector-General of the Western Regions in 91, during the next ten years he briefly conquered virtually the whole area from the Tarim basin and the Pamirs almost to the shores of the Caspian – the greatest westward expansion China has ever known.

PANTAENUS (d. c.190) Christian teacher, convert from Stoicism. He made a missionary journey to India. The first head of the Christian Catechetical School in Alexandria, he influenced his associate and successor, **Clement of Alexandria**.

PAOLI, PASQUALE (1725-1807) Corsican patriot, elected president by the islanders during the struggle against Genoese rule. He was forced to submit after Genoa sold the island to France in 1768 and went into exile in Britain 1769-90. He returned in 1793 to lead the revolt against the French revolutionary government. He persuaded the British to take control of Corsica, 1794-6.

PAPACY The office or position of the Pope, as head of the Roman Catholic Church. Also the papal system of government, both ecclesiastical and political, particularly during the centuries in which the papacy counted among the major states of Europe.

PAPEN, FRANZ VON (1879-1969) German politician, elected Chancellor in 1932. He played a substantial part in **Hitler**'s rise to power, and helped to prepare the German annexation of Austria in 1938. He was found not guilty of war crimes at the Nuremberg Trials in 1945, but was sentenced to eight years' imprisonment; he was released in 1949.

PARAMARAS Rajput clan, prominent in northern India from the 9th to the 12th century. Mainly based in Malwa, with their capital at Dhar, near Indore, they were defeated by Turks from Afghanistan in 1192.

PARIS COMMUNE Name assumed on 26 March 1871, in emulation of the Jacobin Assembly of 1793, by a Central Committee established by rioters who had refused on 18 March to recognize the Assembly of Bordeaux which had accepted Prussian peace terms: the revolutionary socialist movement was crushed, with thousands of casualties, by government troops between 21 and 28 May.

PARIS, FIRST PEACE OF Signed on 30 May 1814, it consisted of seven separate treaties negotiated between the restored Louis XVIII of France and the principal European allies. The limits of France were fixed at approximately those of 1 January 1792; Britain restored certain colonies to France and acquired Malta. (*See also* Congress of Vienna.)

PARIS PEACE CONFERENCE *see* **Versailles, Treaty of**

PARIS, SECOND PEACE OF Signed on 20 November 1815, following the '**Hundred Days**'. It deprived **Napoleon** of Elba, reduced France to the limits of 1790, provided for an army of occupation, and imposed an indemnity of 700 million francs. (*See also* **Congress of Vienna**.)

PARIS, TREATY OF (1763) Treaty which ended the **Seven Years' War** (known in North America as the French and Indian War). France ceded to Great Britain all her territory east of the Mississippi, including Canada; Spain similarly gave up Florida to Great Britain, but received the Louisiana Territory and New Orleans from France.

PARK, MUNGO (1771-1806) Scottish explorer of Africa, who sought the true course of the River Niger; his account *Travels in the Interior of Africa* (1797) made him famous. He returned in 1805 to head a second expedition, but was drowned during a skirmish.

PARSEES Modern followers of the Iranian prophet **Zoroaster**. The majority of the sect is descended from the Persian Zoroastrians who fled to India in the 7th century to escape Muslim persecution.

PARSONS, SIR CHARLES ALGERNON (1854-1931) Inventor of the steam turbine. He entered Armstrong engineering works, Newcastle upon Tyne, in 1877 and in 1884 patented the steam turbine, at the same time thus producing the first turbo-generator. In 1897 his powered experimental ship, the *Turbinia*, attained the then record speed of 34 knots.

PARTHIAN EMPIRE Founded in 247 BC when Arsaces, a governor under **Diodotus**, king of the Bactrian Greeks, rebelled and fled west to found his own kingdom south of the Caspian Sea. Under **Mithridates** (171-138 BC) Parthia extended its control over the whole Iranian plateau and into the Tigris-Euphrates region. After the famous Parthian victory over the Romans at Carrhae (53 BC) Parthia was almost continuously at war with Rome, and prevented any permanent Roman expansion beyond the Euphrates. The empire was finally eclipsed in AD 224 by the rise of the **Sasanians**.

PASSAROWITZ, TREATY OF Signed on 21 July 1718, it ended the Austro-Turkish and Venetian-Turkish wars of 1716-18, and marked the end of Ottoman expansion into Europe. Under its terms, the Ottoman Empire lost substantial Balkan territories to Austria.

PATHET LAO Left-wing nationalist movement in Laos, founded in 1950. It joined with the **Viet Minh** to oppose French colonial rule in Indo-China. The first Congress of Neo Lao Hak Sat (Lao Patriotic Front) was held in 1956; throughout the 1960s and early 1970s it fought a civil war against the US-supported government in Vientiane. Its control of the northeast provinces of Sam Neua and Phong Saly was recognized in 1954, when Laos gained independence; it won control of the entire country in 1975.

PATRICK, ST (5th century) British cleric who brought Christianity to Ireland in the mid-5th century. Patron saint of Ireland; associated particularly with Armagh. He wrote *Letter to the Soldiers of Coroticus* and *Confessions*, an account of his work.

PÄTS, KONSTANTIN (1874-1956) President of independent Estonia. He founded the nationalist newspaper, *Teataja (The Announcer)* in 1901, and entered politics in 1904. He was sentenced to death by the Russian authorities in 1905 after an abortive rising. Returning from exile in 1910, in 1918 he became head of the provisional government despite his arrest by German occupation forces. He was Prime Minister, 1921-2, 1923-4, 1931-2, 1932-3 and 1933-4, and became dictator after an attempted Fascist coup in 1934. He was deported to the USSR after the Soviet invasion in 1940 and was believed to have died some 16 years later.

PAUL, ST Jewish convert to **Christianity**, who became the leading missionary and theologian of the early Church. He was born a Roman citizen in Tarsus, now in Turkey. Brought up a **Pharisee**, he persecuted the followers of **Jesus** until his conversion by a vision on the road to Damascus. He became the Apostle to the Gentiles, undertaking three great journeys to the cities of Asia Minor and Greece. His letters, maintaining contact with the communities established there, remain fundamental documents of the Christian faith. Paul was arrested in Jerusalem, c.57, taken to Rome in 60, and probably martyred during the reign of the Emperor **Nero**, between 62 and 68.

PAULICIANS Sect of militant Armenian Christians, founded in the mid-7th century. Influenced by earlier dualist thought, notably **Manichaeism**, its members believed that there were two gods: an evil one, who created the world, and a good one responsible for the world to come. It was suppressed by Byzantine military expeditions in the late 7th and early 9th centuries; many followers then moved to Thrace as frontier soldiers, where they helped to form the ideas of the **Bogomils**.

PEASANTS' REVOLT 14th-century uprising in the English countryside and towns of villeins, free labourers, small farmers and artisans. Initially in protest against the Poll Tax of 1381 and stringent labour regulations imposed after the Black Death, it was concentrated mainly in East Anglia and the southeast. Under the leadership of Wat Tyler, a vast mob invaded London, executing royal ministers and destroying the property of supposed enemies of the common people, extracting promises of redress from the young king, Richard II. However, the insurgents were dispersed, Tyler slain, and insurgent action in other areas vigorously suppressed; the reforms and royal pardons were then revoked.

PEASANTS' WAR A series of rural uprisings in 1524-5 in Austria and central Germany, mainly directed against heavy manorial duties and exactions. Despite the accusations of Catholics that the rebellion was provoked by Lutheran theology, there is little evidence for this. **Luther** himself condemned the peasants, and the rebels were cut down, in several bloody battles, by the combined forces of Lutheran and Catholic landlords.

PECHENEGS Turkic nomads, ruling the steppes north of the Black Sea from the 6th to the 12th century. In the 10th century they controlled the land between the rivers Don and Danube; held back with difficulty by Russians and Hungarians, they then attacked Thrace and increasingly threatened the Byzantine Empire until they were finally annihilated, at the gates of Constantinople, by Emperor **Alexius I Comnenus** in 1091.

PEEL family. The first Robert Peel introduced the calico printing industry to Lancashire, England, when he took the initiative in founding the firm of Haworth, Peel & Yates in Blackburn in 1764. His son Robert (1750-1830) greatly expanded the business and by the end of the 18th century employed some 15,000 workers in various mills. He was an enlightened employer, and when he became a Member of Parliament introduced the first Factory Act (1802). He had been created a baronet in 1800. His son Sir Robert Peel (1788-1850) was Prime Minister from 1841 to 1846.

PEKING CONVENTION Series of agreements made in 1860, reaffirming and extending the Tientsin treaties of 1858. Tientsin was opened as a Treaty Port; Britain obtained control of Kowloon, the city on the mainland opposite Hong Kong island; French missionaries were given a free hand to buy and develop land; war vessels and merchant ships were allowed to navigate in the interior; and Russia obtained the Maritime Provinces east of the Ussuri river.

PELAGIUS Christian teacher and monk, whose belief in man's responsibility for his own good and evil deeds led him into bitter controversy with the 4th-century Church fathers. In Rome c.380 he attacked the lax morality he attributed to the doctrines of Augustine. Cleared of heresy charges at Jerusalem in 415, he responded to further attacks from **Augustine** and **Jerome** by writing *De libero arbitrio (On Free Will)*. He was excommunicated by Pope Innocent I in 417, and condemned at Carthage in 418; the date of his death is unknown.

PENINSULAR WAR Struggle, fought in the Iberian peninsula, 1808-14, between France and an alliance of Britain, Spain and Portugal, in the course of the Napoleonic Wars. Initially forced to evacuate from Corunna (1809), the British, under the future **Duke of Wellington**, returned to fight first a defensive engagement at Torres Vedras, then a successful offensive (1812-14) which drove all French troops from the region.

PEPIN THE SHORT (d.768) First **Carolingian** king, son of **Charles Martel** and father of **Charlemagne**. He became effective ruler of the **Franks** in 747. In 751 he deposed the last Merovingian king and was crowned king himself.

PEQUOT WAR Massacre of the Pequot tribe of North American Indians by British colonists in 1636-8, precipitated by the murder of a Boston trader. By the early 20th century hardly any of the tribe remained in their ancestral lands in Connecticut.

PERICLES (c.495-429 BC) Athenian statesman. As a radical democrat he dominated the city-state from c.460 BC until his death. He converted the League of Delos from an equal alliance into an Athenian empire, and led Athens in the Peloponnesian War against Sparta. His famous Funeral Speech, setting out his vision of an ideal Athens, is reported by **Thucydides**.

PERKIN, SIR WILLIAM HENRY (1838-1907) Discoverer of aniline dyes. In 1853 he entered the Royal College of Chemistry, London, and while working as a laboratory assistant attempted the synthesis of quinine, but instead obtained a substance later named aniline purple, or mauve. In 1856 he produced tyrian purple, the first dyestuff to be produced from coal tar. He was knighted in 1896.

PERMIANS Finno-Ugrian-speaking peoples, including the Votyaks and the **Zyrians**, living in the northwest region of Russia.

PERÓN, JUAN DOMINGO (1895-1974) Argentine head of state. He entered the army, 1911, became Minister of War and Secretary for Labour, 1944; Vice-President, 1944-5, and President, with strong backing from the trade union movement, 1946. Removed from office during the 1955 revolution and exiled to Spain, he returned and was elected to the presidency, 1973.

PERRY, MATTHEW (1794-1858) US naval commander who headed the expedition to Japan of 1853-4 which forced that country to end its 200-year isolation and open trade and diplomatic relations with the world. Perry had earlier captained the first US steamship, the *Fulton* (1837-40); his Japanese exploit, taking four warships into the fortified harbour of Uraga, made him world-famous. Later he strongly urged US expansion in the Pacific.

PERSEUS (c.212-165 BC) Last king of classical Macedonia, son of **Philip V**. He succeeded to the throne in 179 after plotting his brother's execution. He tried to dominate Greece, but by his success precipitated the Third Macedonian War (171-168) with Rome; he was finally defeated at Pydna, southern Macedonia, by the armies of Lucius Aemilius Paullus, and died after three years in captivity.

PERUZZI Important family of Florence, prominent in trade and finance in Europe in the late 13th century, and second only to the **Bardi**. During the **Hundred Years' War** the firm made large loans to **Edward III** of England; these were cancelled in 1342. The king of Naples also defaulted and the king of France exiled them and confiscated their goods; bankruptcy and collapse, both financial and political, followed.

PETER, ST (d. c.AD 64) Foremost of **Jesus**' disciples and recognized by the Roman Catholic Church as its first pope. Originally a fisherman called Simon, or Simeon, from Bethsaida, he was named by Jesus 'Cephas', meaning rock (in Greek, *petros*). After Jesus' death he emerged as the first leader of the early Church, preaching and healing. His later career is obscure, but his residence, martyrdom and burial in Rome can be taken as certain.

PETER I, THE GREAT (1672-1725) Tsar of Russia. He succeeded to the throne in 1682, and took full control in 1689. War with the Ottoman Empire, 1695-6, gave Russia access to the Sea of Azov. He made an extensive tour of western Europe, 1697-8, introduced western technology to Russia, and drastically reformed the system of government. With the **Great Northern War** (1700-21) he won through to the Baltic, and founded the city of St Petersburg which he made his capital.

PETER III (1728-62) Tsar of Russia. He succeeded his aunt, the Empress Elizabeth, in 1762, and immediately ordered Russia's withdrawal from the **Seven Years' War**, thereby causing discontent among his army officers, who deposed and killed him after a reign of only six months. He was succeeded by his wife, **Catherine the Great**.

PETROBRUSIANS Followers of Peter de Bruys, leader (1104-25) of a radical opposition in France to the doctrine and organization of the Roman Church. He rejected infant baptism, transubstantiation, the sacrifice of the Mass, and the organization of worship. He claimed scriptural authority for all his teachings, but he was burned in 1125 as a heretic. His ideas were also taken up by the **Henricians**.

PHAN BOI CHAU (1867-1940) First 20th century Vietnamese resistance leader. He trained for the mandarin examinations; in 1903 he wrote *Cau huyet thu le than (Letters Written in Blood)* urging expulsion of the French colonial rulers. He directed, from Japan, the Duy Tan Hoi (Reformation Society) aiming to put Prince Cuong De on the throne; after exile from Japan in 1908 he reorganized in China and planned the assassination of the French governor, Albert Sarraut, in 1912. He was imprisoned until 1917; converted to Marxism; seized in 1925 and taken to Hanoi, but released after immense public protest.

PHARISEES (and Sadducees) Leading, and antagonistic, Jewish religious sects during the second temple period (to AD 70). Emphasizing the interpretation of the Bible, the development of the oral law and adaptation to new conditions, the Pharisees evolved eventually into the Rabbis of the **Mishnah** and the **Talmud**. The Sadducees believed in the literal truth of the Bible and excluded all subsequent interpretations as well as beliefs in immortality, or devils and angels. The Pharisees, with their dislike of violence, survived the destruction of the temple by the Romans (AD 70); the Sadducees did not.

PHAULKON, CONSTANT (1647-88) An innkeeper's son from Cephalonia who ran away to serve as cabin boy on an English trading vessel and was later taken to Siam by a merchant of the **English East India Company**. Entering the service of King **Narai**, he was promoted to superintend foreign trade. After a quarrel with the chief of the English factory at the capital, Ayutthaya, he supported the French cause at court, but his support for **Louis XIV**'s intervention in Siam in 1687 brought about his downfall in the following year when his patron died. Narai's successor had him publicly executed.

PHIDIAS (c.490-?) Ancient Athenian sculptor. Appointed by **Pericles** to oversee all the city's artistic undertakings, he was responsible for the design and composition of the marble sculptures of the Parthenon. None of his most famous works – three monuments to Athena on the Acropolis and a colossal seated Zeus at Olympia – survive in the original. Exiled on political charges some time after 432 BC he went to Elis; his date of death is unknown.

PHILIP 'THE BOLD' (1342-1404) Duke of Burgundy, son of the French king John II. As a boy he distinguished himself at the battle of Poitiers in 1356; succeeding to his title in 1363, he was co-regent (1382-8) to Charles VI and effective ruler of France during much of the rest of his life.

PHILIP 'THE GOOD' (1396-1467) Duke of Burgundy, son of John the Fearless, he succeeded in 1419. He supported the claims of the English king **Henry V** to the French throne but made peace with the rival monarch, Charles VII, in 1435. He also acquired extensive territories in the Netherlands, and founded the Order of the Golden Fleece in 1429.

PHILIP II AUGUSTUS (1165-1223) First great Capetian king of France, son of Louis VII. He succeeded to the throne in 1179; fought a long, mainly successful campaign to win control of English possessions in France; took part in the Third **Crusade**, 1190-1; acquired major territories in the west and north of France, and began the Capetian conquest of Languedoc.

PHILIP IV (1268-1314) Known as 'the Fair'. Capetian king of France, the second son of Philip III, he became heir on the death of his brother Louis in 1276, and succeeded in 1285. He fought major wars against England, 1294-1303, and Flanders, 1302-5. Continually in conflict with the papacy from 1296, he transferred the papal Curia to Avignon during the Pontificate of Pope Clement V (1305-14).

PHILIP II OF MACEDON (c.380-336 BC) Ruler of Macedon from 359 to 336 BC; father of **Alexander the Great**. He made Macedon a major power. He penetrated Greece by war and diplomacy, defeating Athens and Thebes at the battle of Chaeronea, 338, and bringing the warring city-states of Greece into a forced unity through a federal constitution with himself as leader. He was assassinated while planning an invasion of Persia.

PHILIP V (238-179 BC) King of Macedon, succeeding his cousin, **Antigonus Doson**, in 221. He allied with Carthage against Rome in the Second **Punic War**, and ended the resulting First Macedonian War (215-205) on favourable terms, but suffered a decisive defeat in the Second War at **Cynoscephalae** in 197. The resulting peace treaty confined him to Macedonia and imposed severe indemnities. Seven years of co-operation with Rome relaxed these conditions and his last decade was spent in trying to re-establish control in the Balkans.

PHILIP II (1527-98) King of Spain, Spanish America and the Two Sicilies (1556-98), also ruler of the Netherlands and Lombardy (1555-98) and, as Philip I, King of Portugal (1580-98). Son of Emperor **Charles V**, he became King of England, 1554-8, through his marriage to Mary Tudor. Sought unsuccessfully to suppress the revolt of the Netherlands from 1566 onwards; conquered Portugal in 1580; failed to invade England with his Armada in 1588.

PHRYGIANS Ancient Anatolian people, dominating central Asia Minor from the 13th to the 7th centuries BC. Traditionally of Thracian origin, they settled in northwest Anatolia in the 2nd millennium BC, and after the collapse of the **Hittites** founded a new capital, Gordium, in the central highlands. In about 730 BC the eastern territories fell to Assyria; c.700 BC the legendary king Midas was defeated by the Cimmerians, who burned Gordium and transferred the land to the Lydians.

PIAST First ruling dynasty in Poland, traditionally named after the wheelwright whose son, Ziemowit, inherited the estates of the Prince of Gniezno in the late 9th century. The dynastic territories were consolidated under **Mieszko I**; his son **Bolesław I** was the first king of Poland, and established the Polish frontiers in east and west. The last Piast in the main line, **Casimir III the Great**, died in 1370.

PICTS A group of tribes occupying Scotland north of the river Forth in early Christian times. The name, signifying 'painted people', was first mentioned in Latin texts in AD 297. Known for their fierce raiding and their characteristic towers ('brochs') and symbol stones, they successfully blocked Anglian attempts to control them at the battle of Nechtansmere in 685. The connections between the kings of the Picts and the Scots (Irish immigrants in southwest Scotland) grew closer in the 9th century, leading to the creation of the medieval kingdom of Scotland.

PIKE, ZEBULON MONTGOMERY (1779-1813) American explorer. Commissioned in the US army in 1799, he led parties to the headwaters of the Mississippi, 1805-06, and Arkansas and Red rivers, 1806-7. He was promoted to the rank of brigadier-general in 1813, but was killed in the same year in the assault on York (now Toronto, Canada).

PILGRIMAGE OF GRACE Popular uprising in 1536 in the English counties of Yorkshire and Lincolnshire. The participants were mainly protesting against the religious policies of **Henry VIII**, especially the closure of the monasteries. Its leaders were executed in 1537.

PILGRIM FATHERS Group of English puritan refugees, mostly of the Brownist sect, who sailed in the **Mayflower** in 1620 to found Plymouth Colony, New England.

PILSUDSZKI, JOSEF (1867-1935) Polish general and statesman who struggled to liberate Poland from Russian control from 1887. He was imprisoned in Siberia, 1887-92. After the outbreak of the First World War, he commanded Polish legions under Austro-Hungarian sponsorship, 1914-16. After the Russian Revolution he assumed command of all Polish armies and proclaimed himself head of a new independent Polish state. He defeated the Soviet Union in the war of 1919-21 (*see* **Treaty of Riga**). He resigned in 1922, but a right-wing military *coup d'état* in 1926 brought him back to supreme power until his death.

PINEDA, ÁLVAREZ 16th-century Spanish explorer. In 1519 he led an expedition which followed the Caribbean coast from Florida to the Pánuco river, already reached from the south by **Grijalva** in 1517. Pineda's voyage ended all hope of finding a direct sea contact between the Caribbean and the Pacific.

PINOCHET UGARTE, GENERAL AUGUSTO (1915-) Fomer Chilean head of state. He rose to prominence when appointed commander of the Santiago zone by Chile's Marxist President **Allende** in 1972. He succeeded General Carlo Prats as commander of the army, and emerged after a violent coup as head of the ruling military junta, 1973; he assumed sole leadership in 1974, but stood down as head of state in 1989 following a plebiscite in favour of democratic elections. However he remained Army Commander.

PINZÓN, MARTÍN ALONSO (c.1411-93) Part-owner of **Columbus's** two ships, the *Pinta* and the *Niña*, which took part in the discovery of the Americas. Pinzón commanded the *Pinta* under Columbus, but left the expedition after reaching the Bahamas to search independently for gold. After rejoining the main body he broke away again on the homeward voyage, hoping – but failing – to be first with the news.

PINZÓN, VICENTE YAÑEZ (c.1460-1523) Spanish explorer, younger brother of **Martín Alonso Pinzón**. Commanded the caravel *Niña* in **Columbus**' fleet throughout the 1492-3 voyage to the Americas. Later he probably sighted the Amazon estuary and sailed with **Juan Díaz de Solís** along the coast of central America.

PITT, WILLIAM (1759-1806) Known as 'the Younger'. English statesman, second son of the 1st Earl of Chatham (the Elder Pitt). He entered Parliament in 1781, became Chancellor of the Exchequer 1782-3, and Prime Minister 1783-1801 and again 1804-6. He played a leading part in organizing coalitions against France on the outbreak of the Revolutionary Wars (1793-1802); passed the Act of Union with Ireland, 1800; resigned after George III refused to grant Catholic emancipation in 1801 but was recalled to organize new opposition to the French.

PIZARRO, FRANCISCO (c.1478-1541) Conqueror of Peru, illegitimate son of a Spanish soldier. He went to the Caribbean in 1502, and in 1513 was deputy to Vasco Balboa when he discovered the Pacific Ocean. He led a small force of Spanish adventurers to conquer (and, in fact, to destroy) the **Inca** Empire in Peru, 1531-3, and founded the city of Lima in 1535.

PIZARRO, HERNANDO (c.1501-78) Spanish conquistador, the younger half-brother of **Francisco Pizarro**. He accompanied Francisco to Peru in 1531, and in 1534 returned to Spain with the royal share of the Inca **Atahuallpa**'s ransom. He returned to Peru, and in 1537 was seized at Cuzco by the Pizarros' rival, Diego de Almagro. After his release he led an army to defeat and execute his captor, 1538. He was imprisoned in Spain, 1540-60.

PLANTAGENETS *see* **Angevins**

PLATO (c.427-347 BC) Athenian philosopher, an associate of **Socrates** and the teacher of **Aristotle**. He is best known through his 25 surviving Dialogues, his letters, and his *Apology*, in defence of Socrates. The ten books of *The Republic*, later modified by *The Laws*, outline a complete system for the ideal society. His Academy, outside Athens, was founded to train statesmen; it lasted nearly 900 years after his death, being closed finally by Emperor **Justinian** in 529.

PLEISTOCENE Geological era, characterized by a series of major ice advances, starting approximately 2.5 million years ago and ending in about 8000 BC. During this period Man evolved from pre-human origins to his present appearance and bodily form.

PLINY, THE ELDER (AD 23-79) Roman encyclopedist, accepted as the foremost Western authority on scientific matters until medieval times. After a short army career he settled down to accumulate knowledge and to write. His only surviving work (out of seven known titles) is the vast *Historia Naturalis*; its information, though fascinating and far-ranging, varies considerably in accuracy when checked with other sources.

PLO (Palestine Liberation Organization) Formed in 1964 as an umbrella organization to represent the world's estimated 4.5 million Palestinians, dedicated to the creation of a 'democratic and secular' Palestinian state. Its charter also calls for the elimination of Israel. In 1969, Yasir Arafat, moderate leader of the major faction al-Fatah, became chairman. The PLO remains divided over its commitment to international terrorism and whether or not to negotiate a settlement with Israel.

POCOCK, SIR GEORGE (1706-92) British admiral. He commanded a squadron in the Indian Ocean, 1757-9, and in 1762-3 commanded the fleet which carried an expeditionary force under the Earl of Albemarle to Cuba.

POLENTA, DA Italian family dominating the city state of Ravenna from the end of the 13th to the middle of the 15th century. It first rose to power under Guido da Polenta, a leader of the **Guelph**, or pro-papal faction in the city; from 1322 it was rent by violent intra-family rivalries, and in 1441 the city fell under Venetian control.

POLO, MARCO (1254-1324) Medieval traveller from Venice. He went to Asia in 1271 as a merchant and jeweller with his father and uncle, who had already visited the court of the Mongol khan at Karakorum. He stayed for almost 17 years in China and neighbouring territories in the service of **Kublai Khan**. He escorted a Chinese princess to Persia in 1292 and returned to Venice in 1295. Captured at sea by the Genoese, while in prison he began to dictate an account of his travels: the book has been a best-seller ever since, and subsequent investigation has confirmed almost all its observations, although at the time Polo was thought to have invented most of them.

POLOVTSY Russian name for the Kipchak (Turkish) or Kuman (Byzantine) tribes who dominated the Eurasian steppes in the mid-11th century. They controlled a vast area between the Aral and Black Seas; fought Russians, **Pechénegs**, Byzantines and Hungarians. Dispersed in 1237, when the Mongols killed Bachman, the eastern Kipchak leader, some were absorbed into the **Golden Horde**, others (the Kumans) fled to Hungary.

POLYGNOTUS Ancient Greek painter from Thasos, at work in Athens and elsewhere, 475-447 BC, and famous for works such as the Fall of Troy in the Stoa Poikile at Athens and the vast murals in the Hall of the Cnidians at Delphi, now known only from contemporary descriptions. He was noted for his realism (e.g. transparent drapery) and for moralism.

POMPEY THE GREAT (106-48 BC) Roman statesman and general. He campaigned in Spain and Italy against pirates in the Mediterranean, and against **Mithridates** of Pontus. Consul in 70 BC, in 61 he formed the First Triumvirate with **Crassus** and **Julius Caesar**. He raised an army to defend the state when civil war broke out in 49, but was defeated by Caesar at Pharsalus (Greece) in 48 and fled to Egypt, where he was murdered.

PONCE DE LEÓN, JUAN (1460-1521) Discoverer of Florida, in search of the mythical Fountain of Youth. He sailed with **Columbus** in 1493; in 1508-09, as deputy to the governor of Hispaniola, he helped to settle Puerto Rico. In 1513 he reached Florida, without realizing it was part of the North American mainland; he probably sighted the north coast of Yucatán on his return passage to Puerto Rico. He was mortally wounded in 1521 by **Seminole** Indians when on a second expedition to explore his discovery.

PORTSMOUTH, TREATY OF Agreement signed in New Hampshire, USA, to end the Russo-Japanese War of 1904-5. Russia recognized Japan as the dominant power in Korea, and ceded the lease of Port Arthur, railway concessions in the south Manchurian peninsula, and the southern half of Sakhalin Island. Both powers agreed to recognize Chinese sovereignty in Manchuria.

POTASSIUM-ARGON METHOD Technique for dating the original formation of rocks of igneous origin. It involves measuring the ratio of radioactive argon to radioactive potassium in the sample, and depends for its validity on several crucial assumptions about initial purity, steadiness of decay rates, absence of other factors affecting the radioactive decay process, etc.; but in modern, improved forms it has been used to establish geological age as remote as 4500 million years and as recent as 20,000 years.

POTSDAM CONFERENCE Last inter-Allied conference of the Second World War, held from 17 July to 2 August 1945. The main participants were **Truman**, **Churchill** (with **Clement Attlee**, who became Prime Minister during the conference) and **Stalin**; they discussed the continuation of war with Japan and the form of the forthcoming European peace settlement.

POWELL, JOHN W. (1834-1902) United States Professor of Geology who led four expeditions to explore 900 miles of the Green and Colorado rivers, 1869-75; director of the geological survey of the Rocky Mountains, 1875-80, and of the US Geological Survey, 1880-94.

PRAIEIRA Last significant revolutionary uprising in imperial Brazil. The anti-conservative, anti-Portuguese rebellion broke out in Pernambuco in 1848 and was suppressed by

1850. 'Praieira' was the nickname given to liberals whose newspaper was printed in the Rua da Praia in Recife.

PRATIHARAS Warlike people of northern India, reputedly descended from the **Gurjaras**. By the end of the 8th century they ruled a large part of Rajasthan and Ujjain, and controlled the strategic city of Kanauj. Under King Bhoja they successfully held back the Arab advance into northern India, but were eclipsed by various enemies when a Turkish army sacked Kanauj in 1018.

PRAXITELES Ancient Athenian sculptor, working between 370 and 330 BC. Only one of his works survives in the original, the marble *Hermes carrying the infant Dionysus*, but by transforming the aloof, majestic style of his archaic and classical predecessors into more graceful and sensuous forms he changed the whole culture of Greek art. A few Roman copies of his works exist, including two of the masterpiece *The Aphrodite of Cnidus*, now in the Vatican and the Louvre.

PREMYSLIDS First Czech ruling family, founded by Přemysl, a ploughman, who married the Princess Libuše. They held the throne of Bohemia from c.800 to 1306. In 1198 Přemysl Ottocar I raised the country from a principality to a hereditary kingdom within the **Holy Roman Empire**.

PRESTER JOHN Legendary Christian king, variously believed to rule in central Asia and East Africa. His fabled kingdom, and its riches, captured the medieval imagination between the first **Crusades** and the early 16th century. His story, probably based on garbled reports of the Negus of Abyssinia, played a part in the motivation of many well-financed expeditions, including the final successful efforts of Portugal to reach Asia by sea.

PRODICUS Greek Sophist from the island of Ceos (Kea), active in the 5th century BC and renowned for his precise distinctions between words.

PROTAGORAS (c.485-c.412 BC) Most famous of the Greek Sophists, author of the constitution for the pan-Hellenic settlement of Thurii, and best known for his assertion that 'man is the measure of all things', he taught in Athens and other cities for 40 years. He expressed agnosticism in his text *Concerning the Gods*, but the story of his trial for impiety may be a later invention.

PROTESTANTISM One of the three main branches of **Christianity** since the Reformation of the 16th century. It was originally characterized by belief in justification by grace through faith, the priesthood of all believers and the overriding authority of the Bible. The main early groups were **Lutherans**, **Calvinists**, and **Zwinglians**, with the Church of England including both Catholic and Protestant elements. Other groups from the Anabaptist and Independent traditions, as well as those emerging later such as the Society of Friends (**Quakers**) and the **Methodists**, are also included within the term.

PRUTH, TREATY OF THE A pact signed on 23 July 1711, after the Ottomans had defeated the armies of **Peter I the Great** of Russia on the River Pruth (now the frontier between Romania and Moldavia). Russia agreed to relinquish the fortress of Azov, to demilitarize Taganrog and the Dnieper forts, cease interfering in Poland and the affairs of the Crimean Tartars, and allow safe conduct to **Charles XII** of Sweden. His delay in complying with these terms led to a renewed declaration of war in 1712 and the conclusion of a new, though similar, peace agreement at Adrianople (Edirne) in 1713.

PTOLEMAIC DYNASTY Line of Macedonian kings, founded by **Ptolemy I Soter**. They ruled Egypt from 323 to 30 BC, the last of the line being **Cleopatra**.

PTOLEMY Greek astronomer and geographer of the 2nd century AD. He worked in Alexandria, and wrote a *Geography*, with maps, which became the standard medieval work on this subject; an *Optics*, and a mathematical and astronomical treatise, popularly known as *Great Collection or Almagest*, which pronounced that the Earth was the centre of the Universe. He worked out a close approximation to the value of π in sexagesimal fractions; he divided the degree of angle into minutes and seconds.

PTOLEMY I SOTER (c.367-c.282 BC) Founder of the Ptolemaic dynasty, rulers of Egypt from 323 to 30 BC. He was born in Macedonia, rose to become a general of **Alexander the Great**, and after Alexander's death became satrap of Egypt, Libya and Arabia. He fought off Macedonian attacks (322-1 and 305-04) and in 304 assumed the titles of King and Soter (Saviour). An outstanding administrator, he was also author of a history of Alexander (since lost), and founder of a library and museum.

PUGACHEV, YEMELYAN IVANOVICH (1726-75) Pretending to be Peter III, the murdered husband of **Catherine II**, he led a revolt, in September 1773, among a group of *Cossacks* in the Urals, and was joined by factory serfs, Bashkirs, state peasants and serfs. In August 1774 he sacked the city of Kazan, but then turned south down the Volga, where he was defeated by Russian troops in August 1774. He was executed the following year.

PUNIC WARS Three wars in which Rome and Carthage, hitherto friendly, contested supremacy in the western Mediterranean in the 3rd and 2nd centuries BC.

First Punic War (264-41 BC): the clash came when Carthage threatened to gain control of the Straits of Messina. Carthage was a sea-power, Rome a land-power: to defeat their enemy the Romans had to build a large fleet, which gained a series of brilliant victories. The war, which was also fought by land in Sicily, resulted in the ejection of the Carthaginians from Sicily; Rome made the island its first overseas province.

The Second Punic War (218-1 BC) was caused by **Hannibal**'s advance from Spain into Italy, where after a series of great victories (especially Cannae in 216) he was gradually forced on to the defensive. In 204 Publius Scipio led an expeditionary force to Africa, thus compelling the return of Hannibal, and defeated him at Zama. Scipio had also driven the Carthaginians from Spain, which became a Roman province. Carthage survived but was no longer a great Mediterranean power.

Third Punic War (149-46 BC): Roman suspicions led to the outbreak of a final war. The Romans invaded North Africa; after a desperate siege the city of Carthage was totally destroyed and its territory made into the Roman province of Africa.

PUTTING-OUT SYSTEM Method of industrial production, widely practised in 17th-century Europe. Raw materials were supplied by manufacturers to workers in their own homes or small workshops, and the finished output was then collected and sold, after payment on a piecework or wage basis; it was gradually superseded by the development of the factory system.

PYRRHUS (319-272 BC) King of Epirus, northwest Greece. He fought Macedon, and was then called to help Greek cities in Sicily and southern Italy against the expanding power of Rome. He defeated the Romans, but with crippling losses, at Asculum in 279 BC (hence a 'Pyrrhic victory'), and was forced out of Italy in 275 BC. He died in a street fight in Argos three years later.

PYTHAGORAS (c.580-497 BC) Greek philosopher and mathematician. He emigrated from Samos to southern Italy; founded a school based on the belief that the soul could be purified by study and self-examination; taught transmigration of souls; discovered the numerical basis of the musical scale; taught that numbers form the basis of the universe. Pythagoras' Theorem, which states that the square on the hypotenuse of a right-angled triangle is equal to the sum of the squares on the other two sides, is probably attributable to his school.

QADISIYA, AL- Battle, 636-7, in which the armies of Islam defeated the **Sasanian** Persians, and completed the conquest of Iraq.

QAJARS Iranian dynasty, ruling a unified Persia, 1779-1925. The reign of Fath Ali Shah (1797-1834) saw the beginning of intense European rivalry for control of the country; Nasir ud-Din Shah (1848-96) exploited Anglo-Russian suspicions to preserve its independence, but the Anglo-Russian division of Persia into spheres of influence in 1907, followed by Russian and British occupation of parts of the country in the First World War, led to a *coup d'état* (1921) and the emergence of the **Pahlevi**. Ahmed Shah, the last Qajar, was formally deposed in 1925.

QUAKERS (also known as the Society of Friends). Radical religious movement without clergy or creed, originating in mid-17th century England and rapidly developing in North America from the colony of Pennsylvania, founded by Quaker William Penn under royal charter in 1681. Today Quakers in the world number around 200,000.

QUEBEC ACT One of the Intolerable Acts or Coercive Acts which led up to the American War of Independence. This measure (1774) established a new administration for the Northwest Territory, ceded to Great Britain by France after the **Seven Years' War** (1756-63), and extended its frontiers to the Ohio and Mississippi rivers; the trans-Appalachian claims of the other (largely Protestant) American colonies were thus jeopardized in favour of French Catholics.

QUTBUDDIN AIBAK (d.1210) Muslim ruler in India. Born in Turkestan and sold as a child slave, he entered the service of **Muizzudin Muhammad** where he rose from the position of stableman to that of general. He led many mounted campaigns between 1193 and 1203, and was freed after Muhammad's death in 1206. He laid the foundations for the emergence of the Delhi sultanate under **Iltutmish**.

RABIH ZOBEIR (d.1900) Leader of native opposition to the French in Equatorial Africa from 1878 until his death at the battle of Lakhta.

RADCLIFFE, WILLIAM (1760-1841) An improver of cotton machinery in England. With the aid of Thomas Johnson he invented a cotton dressing machine which enabled the fabric to be starched before the warp was put onto the loom; he went bankrupt in 1807. He started another mill, but this was destroyed by **Luddite** rioters in 1812. He was the author of *Origin of the New System of Manufacture, commonly called Power Loom Weaving* (1828).

RAFFLES, SIR THOMAS STAMFORD (1781-1826) Founder of Singapore. He was appointed Assistant Secretary to the newly-formed government of Penang in 1804, and Lieutenant-Governor of Java in 1811. He was recalled to England in 1816, but returned to the East as Lieutenant-Governor of Benkulen, 1818-24, and in 1819 established a British port at Singapore, henceforth the centre of British colonial activity in Southeast Asia.

RAHMAN, MAJIBUR (1920-75) Usually known as Sheikh Majib. First President of Bangladesh. He founded the East Pakistan Students' League, and during the 1950s was secretary and organizer of the Awami League, seeking autonomy for East Pakistan. He was imprisoned in 1958, and the resulting mob violence led to the breakaway of the province in 1971 as the new state of Bangladesh. Rahman was elected as its first head of state in January 1972. He was assassinated in 1975.

RAJARAJA (d.1014) King of the **Cholas** in southern India, reigning 985-1014. He attacked the alliance between Kerala, Ceylon and the Pandyas, seized the Arab trading centre of Malabar, launched a naval attack on the Arab-held Maldive Islands, devastated Ceylon and its capital Anuradhapura. He was succeeded by his son Rajendra after two years of joint rule.

RAJPUTS Literally, 'Sons of Kings'; members of landowning and military castes, according to one view descendants of central Asian invaders, who dominated large parts of north and western India, especially Rajasthan, from about the 8th to the 18th century.

RAMAYANA Shorter of India's two great epic poems, composed by the poet Valmiki. Its surviving text runs to 24,000 couplets celebrating the birth, education and adventures of Rama, the ideal man and king, and his ideal wife, Sita.

RAMESSES II, THE GREAT (d. c.1237 BC) Third king of Egypt's XIXth Dynasty, son of **Sethos I**. He succeeded c.1304 BC; fought the Hittites in an indecisive battle at Qadesh on the Orontes in the fifth year of his reign; 16 years later he signed a lasting peace treaty with the Hittite king, Khattushilish. He is remembered for his military prowess and vast building activities: he constructed the famous rock-temples of Abu Simbel.

RAMESSES III The last great pharaoh of Egypt, reigning 1198-1166 BC as the second pharaoh of the XXth Dynasty. He fought two major wars against the Libyans and one against a confederation of northerners, who included Philistines, and two minor campaigns in Palestine and Syria. His greatest monument was his funerary temple at Medinet Habu (western Thebes), in which his wars are represented; he also built a small temple at Karnak, which he dedicated to Amun. Late in his reign he survived a palace conspiracy to murder him.

RAMMOHAN ROY (1774-1833) Hindu religious reformer. He published a tract against idolatry in 1790; in 1816 he founded the Spiritual Society in Calcutta, which in 1828 developed into the **Brahmo Samaj** movement. He was active in the campaign to abolish suttee, the ritual burning of Hindu widows; he was granted the title of rajah by the Delhi emperor.

RANJIT SINGH (1780-1839) Known as the Lion of the Punjab, he was the son of a **Sikh** chieftain. In 1799 he seized Lahore, capital of the Punjab, and proclaimed himself maharajah in 1801. His aim to unite all Sikh territories in India was thwarted by the British in 1809. With a modernized army, he inflicted many defeats on Afghans and Pathans in the 1820s and 1830s, and jointly with the British planned to invade Afghanistan in 1838.

RAPALLO, TREATY OF Agreement signed in 1922 between Germany and Soviet Russia, which established trade relations and cancelled pre-1914 debts and war claims.

RASHID ALI AL-GAILANI (1892-1965) Iraqi Prime Minister. He supported German war aims in 1939; resigned his post, January 1941, and then seized power in April; he refused the British permission to move troops through Iraq (agreed under a 1930 treaty), but lost out in a sharp, 30-day war when promised German help failed to arrive, and went into exile in Iran as a pro-British government was formed.

RASHTRAKUTAS South Indian dynasty, founded in the 8th century AD by Dantidurga, a feudatory of the Chalukyas. From their central territory in the north Deccan, they fought wars and formed alliances throughout India. The best-known king, Amoghavarsha (reigned 814-80), patronized **Jainism**. They were eclipsed in the late 10th century by the later Chalukyas.

RASULIDS Muslim dynasty, ruling in Yemen and the Hadhramaut from 1229 to 1454, named after Rasul, a Turkish officer of the **Abbasid** caliph. His grandson Umar I ibn Ali controlled Yemen and Mecca 1229-50; later Rasulid rule was confined to the Yemeni highlands.

RATANA, T W (1870-1939) Maori religious and political leader in New Zealand. In 1920 he founded the Ratana Church, which had widespread popular appeal among Maoris and helped create for them a stronger supra-tribal identity in society and politics, notably through the Ratana-Labour Party alliance.

RATHENAU, EMIL (1838-1915) German industrialist and electrical pioneer. In 1883 he founded Deutsche Edison-Gesellschaft to exploit German rights in the patents of Thomas Edison; the company was renamed Allgemeine-Elektrizitäts-Gesellschaft (AEG) in 1887. With **Werner von Siemens** he founded the Telefunken company in 1903.

RATHENAU, WALTHER (1867-1922) German statesman. He succeeded his father, Emil, as head of the vast electrical engineering firm, AEG. In 1914 he set up the War Raw Materials Department to organize the conservation and distribution of raw materials essential to Germany's war economy. He founded the Deutsche Demokratische Partei (DDP) and advocated industrial democracy and state intervention in industry. He was Minister of Reconstruction, 1921, and as Foreign Minister in 1922 he negotiated the **Treaty of Rapallo** which normalized relations with the Soviet Union. He was assassinated after accusations that he favoured 'creeping Communism'.

RAZIYYA Briefly sultana of Delhi, she succeeded to the throne during the period of anarchy following the death of her father, Iltutmish, in 1236. She provided both political stability and military leadership, but her sex and her unwillingness to share power created growing resentment, and ultimately she was murdered.

REAGAN, RONALD (1911-) US actor, Republican politician and 40th President (1981-9). After acting in over 50 Hollywood films and becoming leader of the actors' union he joined the Republican Party in 1962 and secured the governorship of California for two terms (1967-75). He defeated Democratic incumbent Jimmy Carter in the presidential election of 1980 and served two consecutive terms. As President he supported deflationary policies aimed at reducing taxes and government spending, popularly called 'Reaganomics'. In foreign policy he increased military spending, maintained a tough anti-Soviet posture, authorized US intervention in Grenada (1983), CIA operations in Nicaragua and the bombing of Libya (1986).

RENÉ OF ANJOU (1409-80) Duke of Lorraine, 1431-52, of Anjou, 1434-80, and Count of Provence, 1434-80. He made an unsuccessful bid to become king of Naples, 1435-42; in 1442 he retired to Anjou and later (1473) to Provence, where he patronized poets and artists. In 1481 his lands (except for Lorraine) passed to the French crown.

RESTITUTION, EDICT OF (1629) Decree of the Holy Roman Emperor Ferdinand II (1619-37) that all imperial Church lands taken by secular princes since 1552 should be restored. The measure was brutally enforced by a large imperial army and provoked an alliance of German Protestant rulers against the Emperor. With Swedish aid provided by **Gustavus Adolphus**, the alliance defeated the imperial forces at the battle of Breitenfeld, 1631.

REULEAU, FRANZ (1829-1905) French engineer, best known for his geometric studies on the underlying principles of machine design, set out in his *Theoretische Kinematic*, published in Germany in 1875 and translated into English as *The Kinematics of Machinery* in 1876.

REZA SHAH PAHLEVI (1878-1944) Ruler of Iran, 1925-41. An army officer, he organized a successful revolution in 1921 and deposed the **Qajar** dynasty to become shah in 1925. He instituted a reform and modernization programme; he abdicated in 1941, when British and Russian armies occupied Iran.

RHEE, SYNGMAN (1875-1965) South Korean political leader. Jailed and tortured in his early twenties for his nationalist views, he then studied for six years at American universities until 1910 and lived in exile, working for the Korean Methodist Church in the US (1912-45). As leader of the independence movement, he returned to the newly established Republic of Korea to become its president (1948-60). Known for his dictatorial and militant anti-communist stance, he was forced to resign amid accusations of election fraud and corruption.

RHODES, CECIL JOHN (1853-1902) Financier and imperialist. He emigrated from Great Britain to South Africa in 1870, and made a fortune from Kimberley diamond mines and Transvaal gold. In 1881 he entered the Cape Colony parliament and he strongly advocated British expansion in Africa: he negotiated the annexation of Bechuanaland in 1884, and having sent white settlers into Mashonaland 'founded' Rhodesia. He became Prime Minister of Cape Colony, 1890-6, but resigned after the **Jameson Raid** into the Transvaal.

RICHARD II (1367-1400) King of England, 1377-99. Son of Edward the Black Prince, he succeeded his grandfather, **Edward III**; he was in conflict with a baronial group, the Lords Appellant, to 1397, and was deposed in 1399 by a cousin, Henry of Lancaster, later crowned **Henry IV**; he died in prison, possibly murdered.

RICHELIEU, ARMAND-JEAN DU PLESSIS, DUC DE (1585-1642) French Cardinal and statesman. As Secretary of State (1616-17) and Chief Minister (1624-42) to Louis XIII, he destroyed French Protestant power (the siege of La Rochelle, 1628), undermined Spanish power in Italy (war of Mantua, 1627-31), declared war on Spain, and intervened in the Thirty Years' War against the **Habsburgs** from 1635, although he died before much success had been gained (*see also* **Mazarin**).

RIENZI, COLA DI (c.1313-54) Popular leader in medieval Rome. In 1343 he was sent to Avignon to plead the cause of Rome's new popular party before Pope Clement VI. In 1347 he assumed dictatorial powers with popular acclaim and reformed taxes, courts and political structure, attempting to re-establish Rome as the capital of a 'Sacred Italy'. He successfully suppressed an uprising by the nobles, but was forced to resign before the end of the year; reinstated in 1354 (but for only two months) he was seized and killed trying to quell a riot.

RIGA, TREATY OF (1920) Agreement by which Soviet Russia recognized the independence of Latvia (formerly a Russian province).

RIGA, TREATY OF (1921) Agreement between Poland and Soviet Russia following a war (1919-21) provoked largely by the claim of the new Polish state (created in 1918) that its eastern frontier of 1772 (prior to the first partition) should be restored. The treaty gave Poland large parts of Belorussia and the Ukraine, and lasted until the **Nazi-Soviet Pact** of 1939.

RIM-SIN Last ruler of Larsa, in ancient Mesopotamia, who reigned c.1822-1763 BC. Son of Kudur-Mabuk, probably an **Amorite** chieftain from the borders of Elam, in 1794 he overthrew Isin, the old rival of Larsa, for control of southern Babylonia. He fought frequently with **Hammurabi** of Babylon, who finally defeated him in 1763.

RIPON, GEORGE FREDERICK SAMUEL ROBINSON (1827-1909) 1st Marquis and 2nd Earl of Ripon, Viceroy of India. He was appointed Viceroy in 1880, and attempted many reforms but generated much opposition, resigning in 1884 after the forced withdrawal of his proposal to give Indian judges power over European defendants. He became Secretary for the Colonies, 1892-5, and Lord Privy Seal, 1905-08.

RIZAL, JOSÉ (1861-96) Filipino novelist, poet and patriot, born in Manila. At the University of Madrid he led a movement for reform of Spanish rule in the colony; he returned to the Philippines in 1892 and founded the non-violent Reform society, *Liga Filipina*. Exiled to Mindanao, he was arrested after an insurrection by a secret nationalist group, the Katipunan; although he had no connection with it, he was shot. His martyrdom and his masterly verse-farewell, *Ultimo Adiós*, inspired the fight for Filipino independence.

ROBERT I 'THE BRUCE' (1274-1329) King of Scotland, crowned in 1306 in defiance of the English king, **Edward I**. He consolidated his power during the weak reign of **Edward II**, and inflicted a heavy defeat on the English at Bannockburn in 1314. The title and Scotland's independence were recognized by the English in 1328, the year before his death.

ROBERT OF ANJOU (1278-1343) King of Naples 1309-43; he was the grandson of Charles I, conqueror of Sicily from the **Hohenstaufen** (1268). He unsuccessfully attempted to secure a dominant position in Italy, in alliance with France and the papacy. The kingdom rapidly declined after his death.

ROBESPIERRE, MAXIMILIEN FRANÇOIS MARIE-ISIDORE DE (1758-94) French revolutionary leader. He practised as a provincial lawyer; led the radical **Jacobin** faction, and played a leading part in the 1793 overthrow of the **Girondins** by the extremist Mountain group. As a member of the Committee of Public Safety, 1793-4, he became virtual dictator, establishing the Terror and eliminating his rivals Hébert and **Danton**; he introduced the cult of the Supreme Being. He was overthrown and executed after the *coup d'état* of July 1794.

RODNEY, GEORGE BRYDGES (1718-92) British admiral who commanded in the West Indies in the **Seven Years' War** and again in the American War of Independence. He captured Martinique (from the French) and the neutral islands of St Lucia, Grenada and St Vincent in 1762; and defeated the Spanish fleet to relieve Gibraltar in 1780. His subsequent failures were redeemed by his victory over the French fleet at the battle of the Saints (Dominica) in 1782, for which he was created Baron Rodney.

ROGER II (1095-1154) Founder of the Norman kingdom of Sicily. He succeeded his brother as Count of Sicily in 1105; made Palermo his capital, 1130; acquired Calabria, 1122, and Apulia, 1127; was crowned King of Sicily, 1130. He made Sicily a major meeting place for Christian and Arab scholars.

ROGGEVEEN, JACOB (1659-1729) Dutch explorer. After retirement from law practice in Batavia, he fitted out a private fleet to search for the reputed southern continent in the South Pacific, 1721-2. Though he circumnavigated the globe, his only significant discovery was Easter Island.

ROMANCE The group of languages derived from the spoken Latin of the Roman Empire. Influenced by local languages in the successor states of Rome, the Romance group comprises French, Spanish, Italian, Portuguese, Romanian, Catalan and Romansch.

ROMANOVS Ruling dynasty in Russia from 1613 until the Revolution of 1917. The family came to prominence when Anastasia Romanova married **Ivan IV the Terrible**. In 1613 the grandson of Anastasia's brother, **Michael Romanov**, was elected tsar; the succession thereafter, though remaining within the family, was frequently disorderly. In 1917 **Nicholas II** abdicated in favour of his brother Michael, who refused the throne, thus ending the royal line.

ROMANOV, MICHAEL (1596-1645) First of the Romanov tsars in Russia, reigning 1613-45. Distantly related to Fyodor I (reigned 1584-98), last tsar of the previous Rurik dynasty, he reluctantly accepted popular election to the throne at the end of Russia's 15-year 'Time of Troubles'. The 16-year-old tsar at first shared power with relatives of his mother, who had been forced to become a nun by **Boris Godunov**, and later with his father, who had been forced to become a monk, the Patriarch Filaret.

ROOSEVELT, FRANKLIN DELANO (1882-1945) 32nd President of the United States, first elected 1932. He formulated the **New Deal** policy to combat world depression; inaugurated the Good Neighbour Policy in Latin America; in 1933 he recognized the USSR. He was re-elected in 1936 and again in 1940, when he provided lend-lease support for Great Britain. With **Churchill**, he issued the Atlantic Charter; after the Japanese attack at Pearl Harbor he led the US into the Second World War, and with **Chiang Kai-shek** at Cairo in November 1943 resolved to continue the war until Japan's unconditional surrender. Re-elected for a fourth term, he died after the 1945 **Yalta** conference of Allied leaders.

ROOSEVELT, THEODORE (1858-1919) 26th President of the United States. He worked as a writer, explorer and soldier before entering politics in 1881. He became Assistant Navy Secretary, then led the US **Rough Riders** in Cuba during the Spanish-American War (1898). He was Governor of New York, becoming Vice-President in 1900 and succeeding to the presidency in 1901 after the assassination of **McKinley**. He acquired the Panama Canal Zone in 1903. He left office in 1909, and failed to win back the presidency in 1912.

ROSAS, JUAN MANUEL DE (1793-1877) Dictatorial governor of Buenos Aires, 1829-52. Born into a landowning and military family, he acquired large ranches and controlled a force of *gauchos* (cowboys); in 1827 he was appointed head of the provincial militia, and distinguished himself fighting insurgents (1828-9) and Indians (1833). He accepted the governorship, 1829-32 and from 1835, and ran a ruthless police state. He was overthrown in 1852 by a coalition of Brazilians, Uruguayans and Argentine opponents at the battle of Caseros. He fled to England and died in exile.

ROSES, WARS OF THE Civil war between rival claimants to the English throne: the dynasty of York (whose emblem was a white rose) and that of Lancaster (a red rose). The Yorkists rose against the Lancastrian king, Henry VI, in 1455, and deposed him in 1461. After a series of struggles involving Edward IV, Edward V and Richard III, the conflict was finally resolved in 1485, when Richard was defeated at Bosworth Field by the Lancastrian claimant, Henry Tudor, who was enthroned as **Henry VII** and married the Yorkist princess, Elizabeth, daughter of Edward IV, thus uniting the warring factions.

ROSKILDE, PEACE OF Treaty ending the war between Sweden and Denmark (1655-8) for control of the Baltic; it gave Sweden permanent possession of the strategically important regions of Scania, Blekinge and Bohuslän.

ROUGH RIDERS Popular name for the First Volunteer Cavalry, recruited by **Theodore Roosevelt** from cowboys, police, miners and athletes to fight in the Spanish-American War, 1898.

ROUSSEAU, JEAN-JACQUES (1712-78) Swiss-French writer, born in Geneva. He quarrelled with most of the accepted conventions and established authorities of his time, and explored many of the themes later to form the basis of 19th century Romanticism and modern democracy. His main works include *Du Contrat Social* (1762), setting out a new theory of the relationship between the individual and the state; his autobiographical *Confessions* (published posthumously); and his novels *La Nouvelle Héloïse* (1761) and *Emile, ou l'éducation* (1762).

ROYAL NIGER COMPANY British trading company in West Africa. In 1886 Sir George Goldie's National African Company received a royal charter, changed its name, and was authorized to administer the delta and territories adjoining the course of the rivers Niger and Benue. It engaged in complex struggles with the French, the Germans and local rulers, conquering several emirates; in 1899, after many complaints and disputes, the charter was transferred to the British government.

RUDOLF IV (d.1365) Habsburg Duke of Austria, reigning 1358-65. He forged a charter, the *privilegium majus*, claiming vast lands, privileges and the hereditary title of archduke from his brother-in-law, Emperor **Charles IV**. The document was declared fraudulent by Italian scholar-poet Petrarch; the resulting war ended with the granting of Austria's claim to the Tyrol. He founded the University of Vienna (1365).

RYSWYCK, TREATY OF Agreement, signed September-October 1697, ending the War of the Grand Alliance (1689-97). **Louis XIV** (for France) accepted William III's right to the English throne, restoration of the *status quo* in the French and British colonies, the return of Catalonia, Luxembourg and parts of the Spanish Netherlands to Spain, and a favourable trade treaty with Dutch. The German Emperor recoved many French-fortified places along the Rhine, while Lorraine was restored to Duke Leopold.

SAAD ZAGHLUL *see* **Zaghlul, Saad**

SAADIS Muslim dynasty, claiming to be descendants of the Prophet ('sharifs') and ruling Morocco from the mid-16th to the mid-17th century.

SAAVEDRA, BALTAZAR DE LA CUEVA HENRÍQUEZ ÁRIAS DE (1626-86) Spanish colonial administrator. In 1674 he was appointed Viceroy of Peru, Chile and Tierra Firme (a territory which included the Isthmus of Panama); his prosperous rule ended in outcry in 1678, when he tried to relax commercial monopolies. He was held captive for two years while charges were heard, and was exonerated in 1680. He returned to Spain, and held a seat on the Council of the Indies.

SABINES Ancient Apennine people of central Italy, northeast of Rome. According to legend the Sabine women were abducted by the Romans under Romulus; by the 3rd century the Sabines had become fully Romanized.

SADAT, MOHAMMED ANWAR EL- (1918-1981) Egyptian President. Commissioned in the Egyptian army in 1938, he was one of the group of officers, headed by **Nasser**, who planned the 1952 revolution. He was Vice-President, 1964-6 and 1969-70, and became President after Nasser's death in 1970. In alliance with Syria he launched war against Israel in October 1973. In 1977 he opened a new round of discussions on peace between Israel and Egypt with his visit to Jerusalem; assassinated in 1981 by Muslim fundamentalists.

SAFAVIDS A family of *sheikhs* (heads of a religious order – the Safaviyya) who exercised growing influence in northwest Persia and eastern Anatolia in the 14th and 15th centuries. They married into and succeeded the **Ak Koyunlu** c.1501 as rulers of these regions. Under **Ismail I** (1501-24), who took the title of shah, the **Shia** Safavids extended their rule over most of Persia, coming into conflict with the **Sunni** Ottomans in the west and the **Uzbeks** in Transoxania. Perhaps the most remarkable Safavid ruler was Shah **Abbas** (1587-1629), but from the mid-17th century the dynasty declined. Having capitulated to the Ghilzai Afghans (occupation of Isfahan 1722), the dynasty was finally extinguished by Nadir Shah in 1736.

SAFFARIDS Muslim dynasty ruling much of eastern Persia in the 9th century. By 873 the empire stretched from northeast India to Khurasan; after failing to annex Transoxania in 900 its wider empire collapsed, but Saffarids retained local power in eastern Persia until the 15th century.

SAID, AL BU Muslim dynasty ruling in Oman, c.1749 to the present, and Zanzibar, c.1749-1964. It was founded by Ahmed ibn Said, who displaced the Yarubid imams of Oman to seize power there and in east Africa. In the 18th century they held Bahrain and parts of Persia; at the peak of their power under Said ibn Sultan (1806-56) they established commercial relations with the United States, France and Great Britain. The dominions were divided by Great Britain on the death of Said. The Zanzibar line was overthrown in 1964 when the island became part of Tanzania.

ST BARTHOLOMEW'S DAY MASSACRE Massacre of **Huguenots** (French Protestants) by French Catholics, which began on St Bartholomew's Day, 24 August 1572, and quickly spread from Paris to other French towns.

SALADIN (c.1137-93) Western name of the founder of the **Ayyubid** dynasty, and the Crusaders' most successful foe. He became sole ruler of Egypt and Islamic Syria, 1186; destroyed the Crusaders' army at Hattin, northern Palestine and re-entered Jerusalem, 1187. He also neutralized the gains of the Third **Crusade**.

SALAZAR, ANTONIO DE OLIVEIRA (1889-1970) Dictator of Portugal. He was Finance Minister during the Depression, 1928-32, and became Prime Minister in 1932 after restoring economic order. He established authoritarian rule on Fascist lines in 1933 and maintained personal control until his death.

SALIANS One of many Frankish tribes which moved from central Europe (3rd century AD) and settled in the area north of the Rhine, near the modern Ijsselmeer. Thence, in the 5th century, they expanded south approximately to the River Loire. From them sprang the **Merovingian** dynasty, later superseded by the **Carolingians**, which conquered Aquitaine and Burgundy and reunited most of Gaul. The word is also used of the dynasty which came to power in Germany with Conrad II in 1024; the line died out with his great-grandson in 1125.

SALISBURY, ROBERT CECIL, 3rd MARQUESS OF (1830-1903) British statesman. He entered politics as a Conservative, and became Foreign Secretary 1878-80, a post which he also held through most of his three periods as Prime Minister, 1885-6, 1886-92, 1895-1902. On the whole he inclined towards co-operation with the **Triple Alliance** against Great Britain's imperial rivals, France and Russia, but was reluctant to conclude 'binding alliances' in Europe and was therefore often associated with the so-called policy of splendid isolation.

SALLE, ROBERT CAVELIER SIEUR DE LA (1643-87) French explorer. He emigrated to Montreal in 1666; traded and surveyed along the Illinois and Mississippi rivers from the Great Lakes region to the Gulf of Mexico. He founded Louisiana in 1682.

SAMANIDS Iran's first native dynasty after the Muslim conquests, ruling 819-999. It developed Samarkand and Bukhara as centres of art and culture and assumed the economic leadership of northern Persia, but weakened after the mid-10th century.

SAMNITES Ancient Italian peoples occupying the territory of Samnium, in the southern Apennines in Italy, who were subjugated by Rome in the 4th to the 3rd century BC.

SAMORI (c.1830-1904) Islamic hero and defender of the western Sudan against French colonial expansion in the late 19th century. Between 1865 and 1870 he built up a powerful chiefdom, and by early 1880 ruled an empire stretching from the Upper Volta and Upper Niger to Futa Jallon. In 1890 he set up his own firearms industry. He was finally defeated in 1898 on the Cavalla River, and died in exile.

SAMOYEDS People of the northern coasts of the former Soviet Union, from the White Sea to the Taymyr peninsula. Speaking a Uralic language, they are noted reindeer herders, fishermen and hunters.

SAMUDRAGUPTA (d. c.375) Indian king, succeeding his father Chandragupta I, founder of the **Gupta** dynasty, c.355. From his capital, Pataliputra, in the Ganges valley, he extended control or exacted tribute throughout the greater part of the sub-continent.

SAMURAI Japanese warrior caste. Originally restricted to landed military houses, it became more open to able warriors of all kinds, especially during periods of civil war, such as that which lasted from c.1450 to 1600. After 1603, when the rule of the **Tokugawa** shoguns initiated 250 years of peace, the Samurai became a closed hereditary class, often turning from military to administrative and artistic pursuits. Its feudal privileges were quickly abolished after the **Meiji** restoration of 1868.

SAN (Bushmen) Nomadic people, speaking a distinctive click language, living in the Kalahari Desert area of Namibia and Botswana.

SANDINISTAS Members of Sandinist National Liberation Front, (Frente Sandinista de Liberación Nacional: FSLN), named for César Augusto Sandio (1893-1934), assassinated guerrilla leader of the Nicaraguan resistance against US military occupation (1927-33). The FSLN, founded in 1962, began as a guerrilla campaign and ended in a full scale civil war, resulting in the overthrow of the Somoza regime (1979). They pursued a course of social democracy, with Daniel Ortega as President of the National Assembly (1985-90), in spite of pressure from the US-supplied counter-revolutionary forces throughout the 1980s. In free elections (1989), **Violeta Chamorro**, the opposition candidate was elected President.

SAN-FAN REBELLION see **Wu San-kuei**

SAN MARTÍN, JOSÉ DE (1778-1850) Argentine liberator; with **Simón Bolívar**, he led South America's 19th-century independence struggles from Spain. After service in the Spanish army he returned to Buenos Aires in 1812 and in 1817 led an army of liberation in the epic crossing of the Andes; with **Bernardo O'Higgins** he freed Chile in 1818, and in 1821 invaded Peru from the sea and took the Spanish stronghold of Lima. After a quarrel with Bolívar, he retired to France.

SANSKRIT Classical language of ancient India, in use mainly from c.500 BC to c.AD 1000, but kept alive to the present day as the sacred language of the Hindu scriptures as well as of much secular literature. Also used in early inscriptions in south and southeast Asia, notably in ancient Cambodia. It is an Indo-European language, and hence ultimately related to Greek and Latin.

SAN STEFANO, TREATY OF Agreement ending the Russo-Turkish War, 1877-8. It created a large tributary state of Bulgaria, stretching from the Danube to the Aegean and covering all Macedonia except Salonika, granted independence to and enlarged Serbia, Montenegro and Romania, and gave Russia acquisitions in the Caucasus and a large indemnity. Fiercely opposed by Britain and Austria, the treaty was largely overturned at the **Congress of Berlin** in 1878.

SANTA ANNA, ANTONIO LÓPEZ DE (1794-1876) Mexican *caudillo*. He fought off the Spanish reconquest attempt in 1829, and became President of Mexico in 1834. He quelled Texan resistance at the Alamo, 1836, but was later defeated and captured; seizing power again in 1839 he ruled until 1845, but was routed by US troops in the Mexican War of 1846-8. His services were refused by both Emperor **Maximilian** and his enemies, and Santa Anna died poor and blind.

SANUSI WAR Resistance between 1912 and 1931 to Italian attempts to annex Libya, led by a brotherhood formed among the desert tribes (the 'Sanusis', founded in 1837). While the European powers were involved in the First World War, the Sanusis drove the Italians back to the coast and directed opposition to the French in Tunisia. In the 1920s they were defeated, but after the Second World War their leader became King of Libya.

SAPPHO (born c.612 BC) Greek poetess, who lived at Mytilene in Lesbos. Her affection for a group of young women and girls associated with her in celebrating the cult of Aphrodite is ecstatically described among the surviving fragments from her seven books of poems in the Aeolic dialect. She looks at her emotions honestly and expresses them with a rare gift of verbal music.

SARGON Semitic king of Akkad, reigning c.2371-2316 BC. One of the world's earliest empire-builders, he defeated the Sumerian ruler Lugalzagges of Uruk, seized all southern Mesopotamia, and achieved conquests as far afield as northern Syria, southern Anatolia and Elam in western Persia.

SASANIANS Iranian dynasty, named after Sasan, an ancestor of **Ardashir I**, who founded the family fortunes in AD 224. Under his leadership, Persis defeated the **Parthians** and created a major but frequently fluctuating empire extending from the Roman and Byzantine frontier in the west to central Asia where it absorbed most of the territories of the **Kushans**. They were finally eclipsed by the Islamic invasions of 637-51.

SATAVAHANAS Indian dynasty, controlling the Andhra region in the delta of the Krishna and Godavari rivers. First mentioned in the 1st century AD, when King Satakarni made many conquests, it revived under Gautamiputra and his son Vasishthiputra in the early 2nd century, under whom lands were acquired from Kathiawar on the west coast to northern Madras on the east. They were displaced by the **Vakataka** dynasty.

SATNAMIS Members of one of a group of Hindu sects in India. The oldest, founded by Birbham in the 16th century, was part of an attempt to bring together **Hinduism** and Islam. Another was launched at the end of the 17th century by the Rajput religious leader, Jagji-van Das. Modern Satnamis are found mainly among the Chamars, northern India's hereditary caste of leather-tanners; they follow the teachings of the 19th century Chamar saint, Rai Das.

SAUDI (as-Saud) dynasty Founders and rulers of Saudi Arabia. Originally small rulers in central Arabia, they created their first - but shortlived - large state in the 18th century. The present state was created by Ibn Saud, followed after his death (1953) by four sons in succession: Saud (deposed 1964), Faisal (assassinated 1975), Khaled (d.1982) and Fahd.

SAUNDERS, SIR CHARLES (1713-75) British admiral. He commanded the fleet which carried General **James Wolfe**'s army to conquer French Canada in 1759. He was appointed First Lord of the Admiralty in 1766.

SAXONS German people originating in Schleswig-Holstein and along the Baltic. They responded to the decline of the Roman Empire with a policy of active piracy in the North Sea, developing in the 5th century AD into substantial settlements along the coasts of Britain and Gaul. The Saxon wars, initiated by **Charlemagne**, lasted 32 years and ended with the absorption of the continental Saxons into the Frankish Empire.

SAYYID MUHAMMAD BEN ABDULLAH (d.1920) Known as the 'Mad Mullah', a Somali chief who proclaimed himself **Mahdi** (religious leader) in the 1890s and began systematic raids against British and Italian positions around the Red Sea. He won territorial recognition in 1905 but resumed raids after 1908, keeping Europeans confined to the coast until his death.

SCALA, della Italian dynastic family, also known as Scaligeri, hereditary rulers of Verona, founded by Mastino I (d.1277). Power was built up by his descendants, notably Cangrande I (1291-1329), the patron of **Dante**, but then frittered away in family quarrels. Their power was terminated by the **Visconti** of Milan, who conquered Verona in 1387.

SCANIAN WAR Fought between Sweden and Denmark, 1674-9, over the rich and strategically important province of Scania, or Skåne (at the southern tip of modern Sweden), which had been captured from the Danes in 1658. The Danish army reconquered Scania, but **Louis XIV** vetoed the return of the territory.

SCHLEICHER, KURT VON (1882-1934) Last Chancellor of Germany's Weimar Republic, nicknamed 'the Hunger Chancellor'. He joined the German army in 1900, and in 1919 entered the newly-formed Reichswehr, becoming a major-general in the Ministry of War in 1929. He helped bring down **Brüning**, and succeeded **Papen** as Chancellor in 1932. He offered to aid **Hitler** if he could retain control of the Reichswehr, but was dismissed by **Hindenburg** in January 1933 after Hitler's refusal, and was murdered by the SS during the 'night of the long knives' the following year.

SCHLIEFFEN, ALFRED GRAF VON (1833-1913) German field-marshal, and chief of the German general staff, 1891-1906. In 1905 he devised the Schlieffen Plan, which, in the event of war, would involve the defeat of France by a vast outflanking movement through the Low Countries; in a revised form this provided the basis of German strategy at the outbreak of the First World War.

SCHOUTEN, WILLEM (1567-1625) Flemish navigator, discoverer of Le Maire Strait, between Tierra del Fuego and Staten Island, and of Cape Horn. He was the first captain to traverse the Drake passage, linking the Atlantic and Pacific south of Tierra del Fuego; Drake himself followed the Magellan passage, further north.

SCOTTSBORO BOYS Nine Negro youths from Alabama, USA, charged in 1931 with the rape of two white girls in a railway freight car. The death sentences pronounced by the Alabama courts provoked accusations of racial prejudice from Northern liberals and radicals, and the US Supreme Court twice reversed the Alabama court decisions. In 1937 four were finally sentenced to life imprisonment, and the others released.

SCYTHIANS Nomadic Indo-European people, settling in Scythia, north of the Black Sea, on the lower Don and Dnieper rivers, before the 7th century BC. They were famous for the skill of their mounted archers and their rich gold jewellery; they were displaced by the closely-related Sarmatians in the 3rd century BC.

SEATO see **Southeast Asia Treaty Organization**

SECOND COALITION, WAR OF THE Struggle between France and a combination of Austria, Britain and Russia in support of Turkey, 1799-1802. After initial success in Italy and Switzerland, the alliance was crippled by France's victories over Austria at Marengo and Hohenlinden in 1800. Peace was signed with Austria at Lunéville (1801) and with Britain at Amiens (1802).

SECOND INTERNATIONAL Socialist organization founded in 1889 after the collapse of the First International. One of its main objects was to reconcile the working classes of Germany and France and to prevent war, possibly by means of a general strike, but it broke up when the main socialist parties of Europe decided to support their governments on the outbreak of war in 1914.

SÉGUIN, MARC (1786-1875) Distinguished French engineer who constructed railways, locomotives and suspension bridges. In 1828 he invented a multi-tubular locomotive boiler at almost exactly the same time as - but independently of - a similar invention in England by **Robert Stephenson** and Henry Booth. In 1831 a Séguin locomotive ran on the St Étienne-Lyons line, the first railway in France.

SELEUCID Near Eastern dynasty dominating Syria and Asia Minor from 312 to 63 BC. It was founded by **Seleucus I Nicator** (reigned 312-280 BC), a close associate of **Alexander the Great**. Its capital established at Antioch-on-the-Orontes, the dynasty sought to Hellenize Asia through Greek settlements; it was constantly at war with the Ptolemies. Power in the East was lost in the 3rd century, in Asia Minor in 198; after 129 it became a local dynasty in northern Syria, and it was finally eclipsed during the Roman invasions of Syria and Cilicia, 65-63.

SELEUCUS I NICATOR (c.358-280 BC) Founder of the Seleucid dynasty, rulers of Asia Minor until the region was largely absorbed into the Roman Empire. He fought alongside **Alexander the Great** in Persia and married a Bactrian princess, 324. After Alexander's death he became governor of Babylon, and allied with **Ptolemy I** to prevent Antigonus Monophthalmus of Macedonia from inheriting Alexander's imperial throne; he helped to defeat Antigonus at Ipsus, 301; moved his capital to Antioch-on-the-Orontes. A ruler of high integrity, he was murdered by Ptolemy Ceraunus, son of Ptolemy I.

SELIM I YAVUZ (the Inexorable) (1470-1520) Ottoman sultan, 1512-20. The youngest son of **Bayezid II**, he rebelled against his father in 1511, engineering his deposition and overcoming his own brothers Ahmed and Korkut, 1512-13. He proscribed and massacred the Anatolian Turcoman adherents of the **Safavid** shah, Ismail, defeating him at Chaldiran and occupying Tabriz, his capital. This radical shift in the Middle Eastern balance of power brought Selim into conflict with the **Mamlukes** of Egypt: in 1516-17 he successively conquered Syria and Egypt, abolished the Mamluke sultanate and annexed its territories to the Ottoman state. By the time of his death the Ottomans ruled in Jerusalem, in Cairo and in Mecca and Medina: a vast increase in the size, prestige and wealth of the empire.

SELJUKS Ruling family of the Oghuz branch of the Turkish peoples who began settling in lands of the **Abbasid** caliphate, becoming Muslims, in the 10th century. They established a local power, quickly expanded it and occupied Baghdad, capital of the caliphate, in 1055. They ruled most of the lands of the caliphate, under Abbasid suzerainty, with the title of sultan. The empire split after the death of Nizam al-Mulk, but a branch remained as rulers of part of Anatolia (incorporated in the Muslim world by Seljuk conquest from the Byzantines) from the early 12th century until the Mongol conquest in the 13th century.

SEMINOLE North American Indian tribe. In the early 18th century they separated from the Creek Indians ('seminole' means separate) and moved from Georgia into northern Florida. They fought two wars against the United States to avoid deportation and repel white encroachment (1817-18, while still under Spanish rule, and 1835-42); after the final surrender most of the tribe settled in Indian territory, which in 1907 became the state of Oklahoma.

SEMITES Speakers of the Semitic group of languages, of which Arabic, Hebrew and Amharic are the main languages still current. Akkadian, the language of Babylon and Assyria, was superseded by Aramaic during the 1st millennium BC, though still written for certain purposes down to the first Christian century; Aramaic, once widespread, survives in small enclaves and in the liturgy of the **Jews** and some Eastern churches.

SENDERO LUMINOSO see **Shining Path**

SENGHOR, LEOPOLD SEDAR (1906-) President of Senegal 1960-90. He studied in France (the first black African to obtain his *agrégation*), served in the French army (1939-40) and in the Resistance. He helped to draft the constitution of the Fourth French Republic in 1946 and sat in its Assembly between 1946 and 1958. He formed his own political party in Senegal in 1948, which won power in 1951, and worked in both Paris and Dakar for a federation of independent French West African states; when this failed he ran for office as President of Senegal, and was elected (1960). He resigned in 1980 and became the first African to be accepted by the French Academy (1984).

SENNACHERIB King of Assyria, 704-681 BC. He gained experience as a senior commander during the reign of his father, Sargon II, and on his accession devoted himself energetically to the defence of the empire. The rising strength of Chaldean and Aramaean tribes in Babylonia, backed by Elam, produced a dangerous instability, which Sennacherib made repeated attempts to resolve by both political and military means, finally sacking the capital, Babylon, in 689 BC. A rebellion in the west, politically linked to the disaffection in Babylonia, led to a campaign in 701 BC which included the attack on Jerusalem men tioned in the Bible. Sennacherib had a keen interest in technological innovation; his most enduring work was the replanning of Nineveh as the Assyrian capital. He was murdered by a son or sons.

SEPHARDIM From the Hebrew word *Sepharad* for Spain, it refers to the **Jews** of Spain, and after the expulsion of 1492-7 their descendants down to the present day. It is used in distinction to **Ashkenazim** who have slightly different customs and rites.

SERBS Slav people. Serbia, the largest and most populous republic of Yugoslavia, emerged as a separate principality in the 9th century and an independent kingdom in 1217. It was conquered by the Turks (1389) and incorporated into the **Ottoman** Empire (1459); it regained its independence in 1829. Blamed for the assassination of Archduke **Franz Ferdinand**, which precipitated the First World War, it became part of Yugoslavia in 1918. Serbia backed Croatian and Bosnian Serb separatists in civil war from 1991 to present, after Croatia, Slovenia and Bosnia-Herzegovina declared independence. Formed new Yugoslav state in 1992 comprising Serbia and Montenegro.

SESTERCE A small silver coin, originally worth one-quarter of a Roman denarius. It was the most common unit of Roman currency.

SETHOS I (Seti I) King of Egypt's XIXth Dynasty, he reigned 1318-1304 BC. He campaigned in Syria, continued work on the Temple of Amun at Karnak, and built his own splendid temple at Abydus.

SEVEN YEARS' WAR Complex struggle, fought 1756-63, between Prussia, supported by Britain, and a coalition of Austria, Russia and France. It arose from Austrian attempts to regain Silesia, lost to Prussia in 1748 (War of the Austrian Succession) and extended by colonial rivalries between Britain and France. The untimely death of Elizabeth of Russia saved Prussia from annihilation while, overseas. Britain destroyed French power in North America, the Caribbean and India.

SÈVRES, TREATY OF Agreement between First World War Allies and the Ottoman Empire, providing for dismemberment of the Empire and Greek occupation of part of its Turkish heartland (Izmir and its surrounding region). It was signed reluctantly by the sultan's government on 10 August 1920, but was totally rejected by Turkish nationalists under Mustafa Kemal (**Atatürk**); it was replaced in 1923 by the **Treaty of Lausanne**.

SEWARD, WILLIAM (1801-72) US Secretary of State, 1861-9, best remembered for negotiating the purchase of Alaska in 1867 from Russia, called at the time 'Seward's Folly'. He was a leading anti-slavery agitator; he became governor of New York, 1839-43, and helped to found the Republican Party, 1855. A close adviser to **Lincoln**, he was stabbed by a co-conspirator of Lincoln's assassin, John Wilkes Booth, but survived.

SHAHJAHAN (1592-1658) Mughal emperor of India and builder of the Taj Mahal. Third son of the emperor Jehangir, and grandson of **Akbar**, he rebelled in 1622 in an ineffectual bid to win the succession, was reconciled with his father in 1625, and in 1628 proclaimed himself ruler after his father's death. He created the city of Shahjahanabad, and the Taj Mahal (1632-49), in memory of his favourite wife, Mumtaz Mahal. He was imprisoned in 1657 during a power struggle between his four sons, and died in captivity.

SHAILENDRA DYNASTY Rulers from c.700 to 1293 of the Srivijaya kingdom. Their ardent support of **Buddhism** is reflected in such architectural masterpieces as the great Borobudur complex in Java.

SHAKA (c.1787-1828) Zulu king. He was appointed in 1810 by the **Nguni** leader, Dingiswayo, to train and command the fighting men of northeast Natal; he pioneered the highly disciplined use of the short, stabbing assegai. He established himself as ruler on Dingiswayo's death in 1818 and crushed all rivals in Natal-Zululand before being assassinated by his half-brothers.

SHALMANESER III King of Assyria, 858-824 BC. He was the son and successor of Ashurnasirpal II, whose imperialist policies he continued, although stability and not expansion was his primary objective, as shown in Babylonia where he provided massive military aid to support the ruling dynasty without seeking personal kingship. In a long series of campaigns he broke the power of the Aramaean and Neo-Hittite states of Syria and Cilicia, consolidating control of the routes

from the Mediterranean and Asia Minor. In the north he acted to defend Assyria against the growing power of Urartu (Armenia). He defended the eastern borders by sorties into the Zagros Mountains to secure recognition of Assyrian suzerainty.

SHAMIL (c.1830-71) Caucasian resistance leader. In 1830 he joined the Muridis, a Sufi sect engaged in a holy war against the Russians who had seized the former Persian province of Daghestan. He succeeded as imam in 1834, establishing Daghestan as an independent state; surviving the capture of his main stronghold, Ahulgo, in 1838, he was finally defeated by massive Russian forces in 1859, and was exiled to the Moscow district. He died on a pilgrimage to Mecca.

SHAMSHI-ADAD I A major king in northern Mesopotamia, 1813-1781 BC, and older contemporary and possibly former suzerain of **Hammurabi**. The son of a minor ruler of nomad **Amorite** stock, he first gained control of Assyria, and from that base annexed the kingdom of Mari on the middle Euphrates. This gave him an empire controlling important trade routes, stretching from the Zagros Mountains to the Euphrates and at times beyond, and northwards to the borders of the Anatolian plateau. Much of his correspondence, and that of his two sons appointed as sub-kings, has been found on clay tablets which have been excavated at Mari, and shows his skill and attention to detail in diplomatic, military and administrative matters.

SHANS A Thai people now forming the Shan state of the Union of Burma. The word is a variant of 'Siam', but the Siamese came to call themselves **Thai**, 'free', and their country Thailand. The Shans infiltrated Upper Burma in the 13th century, and when Pagan fell, c.1300, strove for nearly three centuries with the Burmans for dominance; they sacked Ava, the capital, in 1527. In the 1550s the rulers of the Sittang state of Toungoo finally forced the Shan states in the 1550s to accept Burman overlordship. After the British annexation of Upper Burma in 1886 their *sawbwas* (chieftains) accepted British overlordship; later they were joined into the Shan States Federation. After independence in 1948 the Union government abolished the powers of the *sawbwas*.

SHANG CHIH-HSIN (1636-80) Son of Shang K'o-hsi (d.1676), governor of Kwangtung 1650-71, who succeeded his father. In 1673 his father's retirement provoked the rebellion of **Wu San-kuei**; in 1676 he joined the rebels, but the following year submitted to the **Manchus**. In 1680 he was accused of plotting a fresh rebellion, was arrested and ordered to commit suicide.

SHANKARACHARYA (c.788-820) Brahmin philosopher. He was a famous interpreter of *Vedanta* and originator of the Monist (*Advaita*) system of Hindu thought. He established influential religious centres (*mathas*) at Badrinath in the Himalayas, Puri in Orissa, Dwarka on the west Indian coast, and Sringeri in the south; he argued that the visible world is an illusion (*maya*) and that reality lies beyond the senses.

SHARIFIAN DYNASTY Saadi rulers of south Morocco from 1511. They secured Ottoman aid and managed to extend their control over the rest of Morocco in the 1550s and to expel the Portuguese in 1578. In 1591 they sent an expedition of Ottoman-trained troops across the Sahara and destroyed the Songhai empire. Disputed successions after 1610 weakened their authority, and the last Saadi was assassinated in 1660.

SHAYBANIDS Central Asian dynasty, controlling Transoxania in the late 15th and early 16th centuries after defeating the descendants of **Timur**; it was replaced at Bukhara by the Astrakhanids in 1599.

SHENG SHI-TS'AI (1895-1970) Warlord from Manchuria, sent to Sinkiang in 1929. He established control there, 1933-43, with strong support from the USSR, giving extensive concessions to the Soviet Union in return. In 1942 he went over to the Nationalists and demanded Soviet withdrawal, which was completed in 1943. In 1944 he tried to renew Russian links; he was removed from the province.

SHERIDAN, PHILIP HENRY (1831-88) Union general in the American Civil War. He cut off the Confederate retreat at Appomattox in 1865, forcing the surrender of the Southern commander, General **Robert E. Lee** to General **Ulysses S. Grant**. He was army commander-in-chief from 1883 until his death.

SHERMAN, WILLIAM TECUMSEH (1820-91) Union general in the American Civil War. He

entered the army but resigned his commission in 1853; reappointed a colonel in 1861, he was promoted to general after the first Battle of Bull Run. He destroyed the Confederate forces on his famous march through Georgia, 1864; he was appointed commanding general of the army in 1869.

SHER SHAH (c.1486-1545) Afghan emperor of northern India. A soldier under the **Mughal** king of Bihar, he became ruler of Bihar, and conquered Bengal in 1539. He defeated the Mughal emperor, Humayun, in 1539 and again in 1540, and took the royal title of Fariduddin Sher Shah. He effected notable fiscal, social and administrative reforms.

SHIH HUANG TI (c.259-210 BC) Creator of the first unified Chinese empire. He attained the throne of Ch'in, northwest China, in 246 BC. By 221 he had annexed the territories of his six major rivals and proclaimed empire over them. He expanded Chinese control into southern China, establishing centralized administration and a network of roads, extending and consolidating the Great Wall, and unified the Chinese writing system. He entered into bitter controversy with Confucian scholars at his court, culminating in the Burning of the Books in 213.

SHI'ISM One of two main divisions of Islam, which split from the other, the **Sunni**, over the question of succession to the Prophet **Mohammed**, which Shias believe to have gone to his son-in-law **Ali** and then to a line of imams (hence their name, *Shi'at Ali*, party of Ali). They later split into a number of groups recognizing different lines of imams: Zaidis in Yemen, **Ismailis**, and the main or Twelver group recognizing a line of twelve imams, the last of whom is believed to have gone into hiding. This kind of Shi'ism is widespread today in Lebanon, Iraq, India, Pakistan and Iran, where it is the state religion.

SHIMONOSEKI Treaty of agreement ending the first Sino-Japanese war (1894-5). China recognized the independence of Korea, ceded Taiwan, the Pescadores Islands and the Liaotung peninsula (including Port Arthur) to Japan, paid a large indemnity, and opened four new ports to foreign trade. Later in 1895 Russia, France and Germany forced Japan to return south Liaotung to China in return for a larger indemnity.

SHINING PATH (Sendero Luminoso) Peruvian revolutionary movement employing guerrilla tactics and extreme violence in the name of Maoism, founded as the Communist party of Peru in Ayacucho (1970) as an offshoot of other parties. The leader, philosophy professor Abimael Guzmán, and his followers envision revolution as a long-term military offensive aimed at the destruction of all traces of 'bourgeois' influence, including political and military figures, and municipal targets. Expanding their activities from the highlands to the capital city of Lima, they remained a formidable force in Peru despite the capture of Guzmán in September 1992.

SHINTO Ancient religion of Japan. It lacks both an acknowledged founder and an organized body of teaching. It is characterized by worship of ancestors and heroes, a wide variety of local cults, and belief in the divinity of the emperor. It was largely superseded in the 6th century by **Buddhism**, but revived in the 17th century and was the official state religion from 1867 to 1946.

SHIVA Hindu god, combining within himself many apparently contradictory qualities: destruction and restoration, asceticism and sensuality, benevolence and revenge. In Sanskrit the name means 'suspicious one'; he is worshipped as the supreme deity by various Shiva sects in India.

SHUPPILULIUMASH (d. c.1346 BC) King of the **Hittites**, who won the throne c.1380 BC. He successfully invaded northern Syria, driving back Egyptians and Mitannians to add territory as far as Damascus to his empire.

SICILIAN VESPERS Revolt against the French conqueror of Sicily, **Charles I of Anjou**, during the hour of vespers on Easter Monday, 30 March 1282. Encouraged by Peter III of Aragon, the Sicilians massacred 2000 French officials; after long wars between France and Aragon, Peter III's son, Frederick III, won recognition as king under the Peace of Caltabellotta, 1302.

SIEMENS, ERNST WERNER VON (1816-92) German engineer and inventor who discovered a process for galvanic gilding and plating, 1841. He supervised the construction of the first long telegraph line in Europe (Berlin to Frankfurt-am-Main, 1848-9). With Halske he set up a telegraph factory which constructed many telegraph lines

in Russia; his brother Carl ran a subsidiary company in Russia while another brother, William, was in charge of the London branch. A new company (Siemens Brothers) manufactured and laid underwater cables. He invented the electric dynamo in 1866 and was actively concerned with the application of electric power to locomotives, trams, lifts and street lighting.

SIENIAWSKI, MIKOŁAJ HIERONIM (1645-83) Polish general *Voivode* (Army leader) of Volhynia (1680) and *Hetman* of the crown (1682), he fought successfully against **Tartars** and **Cossacks**. In 1683 he led the advance guard of the army led by King **John III Sobieski** to relieve Vienna.

SIGISMUND III (1566-1632) King of both Sweden and Poland, son of John III of Sweden and Catherine of Poland. Sigismund thus belonged to both the Vasa and the **Jagiełło** dynasties, but his efforts to unite the two lines and the two countries ended in disaster. Elected to the throne of Poland, 1587, he also inherited the Swedish crown in 1592, and tried to restore Catholicism to Sweden. When he left Sweden for Poland the regent, his uncle (later **Charles IX**), rebelled, defeating him at Stängebrö, 1598, and deposing him, 1599. The two countries remained intermittently at war until 1660.

SIHANOUK, PRINCE NORODOM (1922-) Cambodian statesman. King of Cambodia from 1941 to 1955, he then became its Prime Minister, 1955-60, and Head of State, 1960-70. In 1970 he was deposed by the National Assembly and Council of the Kingdom, and in Peking set up a Government of National Union. He returned as nominal head of state after the Communist (**Khmer Rouge**) victory in 1975, but was removed from office the following year. He became Cambodian head of state again in 1991.

SIKHS Members of an Indian religious community founded by the 16th-century teacher **Nanak**. Outwardly distinguished by carrying the Five K Symbols: Kesha (uncut hair), Kanga (a small comb), Kara (an iron bangle), Kirpan (a small dagger) and Kacha (a type of underwear), in the 18th and early 19th centuries they emerged as a militant warrior brotherhood, particularly under the leadership of **Ranjit Singh**.

SIMON THE HASMONEAN (d.135 BC) Younger brother of **Judah Maccabee** who in 142 established a new Jewish state independent of the **Seleucid** rulers of the Near East; the state survived until quarrels among the descendants of Simon led to the establishment of Roman control in 63 BC.

SINCLAIR, UPTON (1875-1963) American novelist. His first major success, *The Jungle* (1906), embodied his personal, bitterly controversial investigation into working conditions in the Chicago stockyards; a series of similar works established him as a leading Socialist critic of US capitalism. He ran for governor of California as the Democratic candidate in 1934.

SINDHIAS Ruling dynasty of Gwalior, western India, founded by Ranoji, a **Maratha** official, in the 18th century. Under Sindhia Mahaduji (reigned 1761-94) the family established a virtually independent empire in northwest India, holding off the troops of the **English East India Company**, 1775-82, defeating the **Rajputs** and the **Marathas**, 1793, and taking the **Mughal** emperor, Shah Alam, under their protection. Later Sindhias, however, accepted British pre-eminence (from 1818); their kingdom survived as a native princedom under the British, and was later absorbed into the Indian union.

SIOUX (also called Dakota). North American Indian tribes once occupying vast areas of Minnesota, Montana, the Dakotas and the Western plains. From 1851 to 1876 they organized a resolute and often successful resistance to the advance of white settlers; discovery of gold in the Black Hills of Dakota brought a vast new influx of white fortune-hunters. Despite victory at the Little Big Horn (1876), the Sioux were finally crushed in the Tongue River Valley.

SIVAJI (c.1627-80) Founder of the 17th-century **Maratha** kingdom in west India. He carved out his kingdom from **Mughal** and Bijapur territory and carried on a protracted war against the former. He was enthroned as an independent sovereign in 1674 and he devoted his later life to social reform and the advancement of religious toleration.

SLOVENES South Slav people inhabiting the former Yugoslav province of Slovenia; they number about two million. Gained independence in 1991, after brief opposition from the Yugoslav Army.

SMERDIS Short-lived Persian emperor in 522 BC, son of **Cyrus II the Great** and younger brother of **Cambyses II**, on whose order he was secretly put to death by the king's officer Prexaspes. Subsequently imperial powers were usurped by Gaumata, the majordomo, who put his brother in the place of the vanished prince ('Pseudo-Smerdis') while Cambyses was campaigning in Egypt. After Cambyses' death, 'Smerdis' was recognized as king for eight months before being killed by **Darius I**.

SMETONA, ANTANAS (1874-1944) Lithuanian statesman who signed the Lithuanian declaration of independence, 1918; he became first President, 1919-20, and again after a *coup d'état* from 1926 to 1940. After the Soviet invasion, he fled to western Europe in 1940, and then to the United States.

SMITH, ADAM (1723-90) Scottish economist and philosopher. Professor of Logic, Glasgow University, 1751, and of Moral Philosophy, 1752-64. His *Inquiry into the Nature and Causes of the Wealth of Nations*, 1776, laid the foundations for the new science of political economy.

SMITH, IAN DOUGLAS (1919-) Rhodesian political leader. Served in the British Royal Air Force, 1941-6. He became a member of the South Rhodesia legislative assembly, 1948-53; of the parliament of the federation of Rhodesia and Nyasaland, 1953-61, and of the right-wing Rhodesia Front Party. As Prime Minister of Rhodesia (1964-79) he declared unilateral independence (UDI) in 1965. He retired from politics in 1979 after the transfer of power to a black government.

SOCIALISM Belief in communal or collective ownership of the means of economic production and distribution, and the right of all to share equally in the benefits and opportunities created by society. In Europe it reaches back to the Middle Ages ('when Adam delft and Eva span, who was then the gentilman?') and was influential in the 16th and 17th centuries (e.g. the **Levellers** in England); in the 19th century it broke up into various sub-divisions – Utopian (or Saint-Simonian) socialism, Marxian socialism, Christian socialism, democratic socialism – each differing in the emphasis placed on particular parts of the programme, and the political methods considered acceptable to achieve them.

SOCRATES (469-399 BC) Athenian thinker. None of his own work survives; he is best known through **Xenophon**'s memoirs and the early *Dialogues* of his pupil **Plato**. He was independent but critical of democracy, and was condemned to death by a popular jury. Plato's *Apology* and *Phaedo* purport to be accounts of his defence and last days.

SOLIDUS Byzantine gold coin, first issued by the Emperor **Constantine** in the 4th century AD. One of the most stable units of currency in economic history, it remained important in international trade for over 700 years.

SOLÍS, JUAN DÍAZ DE (c.1470-1516) Spanish explorer. He first visited central America in 1508 with **Vicente Yáñez Pinzón**. In 1515 he left Spain with three vessels and a commission to explore the lands 1700 leagues (5000 miles/8000 km) south of Panama. He reached the Plate River in 1516, sailed up the Uruguay River, and was killed and eaten by Charrua Indians in sight of his crew; the survivors gave valuable information to **Sebastian Cabot**.

SOLOMONIDS Ruling dynasty in Ethiopia from 1770 to 1975. It was founded by Yekuno Amlak, prince of the inland province of Shoa, who claimed direct descent from the biblical King Solomon. Under Amda Sion (1314-44) and Zara Yaqob (1434-68) it consolidated power at home and repelled the Muslims to the north. It was finally eclipsed with the deposition of **Haile Selassie**.

SOPHIST Name applied to itinerant purveyors of higher education for fees in 5th and 4th century Greece. Their leading figures, such as **Protagoras**, were spoken of with much respect, but conservative opinion found their influence disturbing.

SOPHOCLES (c.496-406 BC) Athenian dramatist. Also a statesman, general and priest. He won first prize at Athenian festivals with 24 tetralogies, i.e. 96 of his 123 plays. Seven plays survive: *Ajax*, *The Women of Trachis*, *Antigone*, *King Oedipus*, *Electra*, *Philoctetes*, *Oedipus at Colonus*, and a fragment of *The Trackers*. He said that he created men as they ought to be, whereas **Euripides** wrote about men as they are.

SOTHO/TSWANA One of two main Bantu-speaking groups of southern African peoples, occupying the areas of Botswana, Lesotho, Orange Free State, and the north and east Transvaal since c.1000.

SOTO, HERNANDO DE (c.1500-42) Spanish explorer. He first sailed to Central America, c.1519, and in 1532 took part in the conquest of Peru. He was appointed governor of Cuba in 1537 by **Charles V**, and given a contract to conquer Florida: landing near Charlotte Bay in 1539, he fought his way through today's southern United States as far west as Oklahoma, discovering the Mississippi River in 1541. He died on the return journey.

SOUTHEAST ASIA TREATY ORGANIZATION (SEATO) Set up in 1954 between Australia, France, New Zealand, Pakistan, the Philippines, Thailand, the United Kingdom and the United States to resist possible aggression by Communist China after the Korean War. Pakistan withdrew in 1972; at the 1975 Council meeting it was agreed that the organization should be phased out.

SOVIETS Originally revolutionary councils elected by workers during the Russian Revolution of 1905. They were revived in 1917 to include bodies elected by workers, peasants and soldiers; it signified the primary units of government in the former USSR.

SPARTAKISTS Members of the *Spartakusbund*, a German revolutionary socialist group in the First World War, led by Rosa Luxemburg and Karl Liebknecht, and named after the Roman slave-rebel, Spartacus. It later became the nucleus of the German Communist Party.

SPEER, ALBERT (1905-81) German architect and **Nazi** leader. A member from 1931 of the German Nazi party; as Minister of Armaments between 1942 and 1945 he made widespread use of slave labour from concentration camps for which, at the end of the Second World War, he was sentenced to 20 years' imprisonment. His brilliant organization of industry contributed greatly to German strength. His memoirs, *Inside the Third Reich*, present an intimate picture of life in the entourage of **Adolf Hitler**.

SPEKE, JOHN HANNING (1827-64) British explorer who with Richard **Burton** reached Lake Tanganyika in 1858, and then journeyed alone, becoming the first European to see Lake Victoria and identify it as a source of the Nile.

SPUTNIK First artificial space satellite put into orbit, in 1957, by the USSR. Meaning 'companion', 'fellow traveller', it signalled the Soviet Union's growing technical capability and helped to precipitate a new phase in the US-USSR arms race.

SRIVIJAYA Maritime empire, controlling the Strait of Malacca and much of the Malay Archipelago from the 7th to the 11th century.

STALIN (1879-1953) Born Joseph Vissarionovich Dzhugashvili. Son of a Georgian shoemaker, he trained for the priesthood but was expelled in 1899 after becoming a **Marxist**. In 1917 he became Peoples' Commissar for Nationalities in the Soviet government, and General Secretary of the Communist Party of the Soviet Union from 1922 until his death. He eliminated all rivals after the death of **Lenin** in 1924; promoted an intensive industrialization, the forced collectivization of agriculture, and the development of a police state. He signed a non-aggression pact with Nazi Germany in 1939, resulting in the Russian occupation of eastern Poland and Finland; and led resistance to German invasion, 1941-5. Three years after his death his regime was denounced by **Khrushchev** and a 'destalinization' programme instituted.

STANDARD OIL US company formed in 1870 by John D. Rockefeller to refine and distribute petroleum. By 1879 it controlled almost 95 per cent of all oil refined in the United States and became the first industrial 'Trust', provoking the Sherman Anti-Trust Law of 1890. It was dissolved by the Supreme Court in 1911 and forced to operate as separate corporations chartered in different states. Its principal component, the Exxon Corporation, became the company with the highest turnover in the world in 1975, with annual sales of nearly $50,000 million.

STANISŁAW II PONIATOWSKI (1732-98) Last king of independent Poland, being elected king with the support of **Catherine the Great** after the death of Augustus III in 1763. He failed to counter successive partitions of Poland by Russia, Austria and Prussia, despite the short-lived revival of 1788-94, and abdicated in 1795 as the three countries finally absorbed all Polish territory.

STANLEY, SIR HENRY MORTON (1847-1904) British explorer. As a young war-correspondent, he was sent by a New York newspaper to find the Scottish missionary traveller **David Livingstone**; he met him near Lake Tanganyika in 1871, to secure the 'scoop of the century'. He crossed Africa from Zanzibar to the mouth of the Congo, 1874-7, and founded the Congo Free State in 1879 on behalf of **Leopold II** of the Belgians, after Great Britain had turned down his offer to acquire the territory. He was a Member of Parliament, 1895-1900.

STAUFEN *see* **Hohenstaufen**

STAVISKY, SERGE ALEXANDRE (1886-1934) French financier who founded a credit organization in Bayonne and issued bonds later found to be fraudulent. The scandal that followed his death – said by police to be suicide but widely believed to be murder – precipitated a major political crisis, culminating in the resignation of two prime ministers and a riot outside the Chamber of Deputies in which 15 died.

STEFAN DUSHAN (1308-55) Most famous king of medieval Serbia. He deposed his father and seized the throne in 1331; annexed Macedonia, Albania and large areas of Greece from Byzantium; took the title 'Tsar of the Serbs and Greeks'; granted a major new code of laws.

STEIN, BARON HEINRICH VON (1757-1831) Prussian stateman. As Chief Minister, 1807, he instituted a programme of reform including the emancipation of serfs and municipal self-government; exiled by **Napoleon**, 1808, he became counsellor to Tsar Alexander I, 1812-13, and played a leading part in forming the anti-Napoleonic alliance between Russia and Prussia.

STEPHEN (c.1097-1154) King of England, third son of Stephen, Count of Blois and Chartres, and Adela, daughter of **William I**. Raised by Henry I and given large estates in England and Normandy, he pledged his support to Henry's daughter Matilda, but instead usurped the crown in 1135. Most of his reign was spent in civil war with Matilda (finally defeated 1148); after the death of his son, Eustace, he reluctantly designated Matilda's son, later **Henry II**, as his successor.

STEPHEN I (977-1038) First king of Hungary, a member of the **Árpád** dynasty, and son of the leading Magyar chief, Geisa (Geza). He decisively defeated a pagan uprising after the death of his father in 997, and was anointed king in 1000. He founded bishoprics, abbeys and encouraged church-building; and fought off an invasion by Emperor Conrad I in 1030. He was canonized in 1083.

STEPHEN OF PERM, ST (1335-96) Russian Orthodox bishop who led a mission to the **Zyrians**.

STEPHENSON, GEORGE (1781-1848) English railway pioneer. He built the first successful steam locomotive, 1814: constructed the Stockton and Darlington line, 1825; his *Rocket* won the first open speed contest for railway engines, 1829. With his son, Robert, he built many early track systems both in Great Britain and overseas.

STEPHENSON, ROBERT (1803-59) Civil engineer. He was a partner with his father, George Stephenson, and others in the firm of Robert Stephenson & Co. which built locomotives for British and many Continental railways.

STIMSON, HENRY LEWIS (1867-1950) American statesman. He was Secretary for War, 1911-13, in the Cabinet of William Howard Taft, and went on to serve in the administrations of five presidents, of both parties, up to 1945. He was Secretary for War to **F.D. Roosevelt**, 1940-5, and chief adviser to both Roosevelt and **Truman** on atomic policy: he justified the bombing of Hiroshima and Nagasaki on the grounds that it saved more lives than it cost.

STINNES, HUGO (1870-1924) German industrialist, grandson of **Matthias Stinnes**. He trained as a mining engineer, and founded the Stinnes Combine. Head of German industrial production in the First World War, he took advantage of the post-war hyper-inflation to extend interests in coal, iron, power and transport into timber, insurance, paper manufacture and newspapers. At his death he was probably the most powerful financier in Europe; the company is known now as Stinneskonzern.

STINNES, MATTHIAS (1790-1845) German industrialist who built up large coal mining and river transport interests in the Ruhr; the sinking of a deep shaft in his colliery Graf Beust (near Essen) in 1839-41 began the northward expansion of mining in the Ruhr.

STOICS School of philosophers, founded by Zeno (c.332-264 BC), who taught in Athens at the Stoa. To the Stoics, 'God is all and in all. Call him Zeus, Nature, Universe, Reason – all is in his hands. Virtue is the only good, moral weakness the only evil; to all else – health, wealth, position, pain – man should be indifferent.' Notable Stoics were Zeno's successors, Cleanthes and Chrysippus; Panaetius and Posidonius, who transplanted the philosophy to Rome; and, under the Roman Empire, the statesman Seneca, the ex-slave Epictetus, and the half-agnostic Emperor Marcus Aurelius.

STOLBOVO, PEACE OF Settlement ending the Russo-Swedish war, 1610-17. The Swedes invaded northern Russia and captured Novgorod in 1611; expelled from there, they besieged Pskov. Anglo-Dutch mediation produced an agreement that Sweden would withdraw its troops, but retain Karelia and Ingria, between Finland and Estonia, thus effectively denying Russia any 'window to the Baltic' for the next century.

STOLYPIN, PIOTR ARKADEVICH (1863-1911) Russian statesman. Minister of the Interior and Prime Minister, 1906-11, he tried to save imperial Russia by agrarian reform and the forcible suppression of the revolutionary movement. He was assassinated.

STONE AGE The earliest stage in the development of human culture, characterized by the use of stone, as opposed to metal tools. It is normally sub-divided into an Old Stone Age (**Palaeolithic**), Middle Stone Age (**Mesolithic**) and New Stone Age (**Neolithic**). The Old Stone Age covers the whole of human development during the **Pleistocene** Ice Age; the other two occupy the earlier part of the post-glacial period from 8000 BC onwards.

STROESSNER, ALFREDO (1912-) President of Paraguay; son of a Bavarian immigrant father and Paraguayan mother. He fought in the Chaco War (1932-35); rose to be general in the Paraguayan army in 1951, associated with the Colorado party and became President in 1954 after a palace revolution. He steadily accumulated dictatorial powers, and was voted President for life in 1977. He was deposed by Andrés Rodríguez in a military takeover in 1989.

STRUTT, JEDEDIAH (1726-97) A pioneer in the development of the early English cotton industry. In 1758-59, he patented an improved stocking frame and set up a mill in Derby, England, to manufacture the 'Derby Patent Rib'. In 1768 he entered into partnership with **Arkwright** to exploit Arkwright's new spinning frame.

STUART, JOHN McDOUALL (1815-66) Explorer of South Australia. Born in Scotland, he served as draughtsman in **Sturt**'s expeditions of 1844-46 before making six expeditions (1858-62) to the Australian interior, reaching Van Diemen Gulf.

STURT, CHARLES (1795-1869) Explorer of Australia. Born in Bengal, he was educated in England. Military Secretary to the Governor of New South Wales in 1827, in 1828-9 he traced the Macquarie, Bogan and Castlereagh rivers, then traversed the Murrumbidgee and Murray rivers, 1829-30, and in 1844-6 penetrated north from Adelaide to the Simpson Desert.

SUCRE, ANTONIO JOSÉ DE (1795-1830) Liberator of Ecuador. Born in Venezuela, at the age of 26 he was appointed by **Bolívar** to free the southern part of Gran Colombia, now Ecuador, from Spanish control. He defeated the royalists at Quito, May 1822; won the Battle of Junin, Peru, August 1824, and routed 9,000 Spaniards at Ayacucho, forcing withdrawal. He dislodged the last Spanish survivors from Upper Peru, now Bolivia, whose legal capital carries his name.

SUEBI (SUEVES) Germanic peoples, including the Marcomanni, Quadi, Hermunduri, Semnones and Langobardi (**Lombards**). In the 1st century AD they mostly lived along the river Elbe; apart from the Lombards, who established long-lasting control in northern Italy, their best-known group, dislodged by the **Huns**, entered Spain in 409 and consolidated a quasi-independent kingdom in the northwest (Galicia, Lusitania, Baetica). Their Christian king, Rechiar, was defeated by the **Visigoths** in 456, but the Visigoths finally absorbed the last Suebian territory in 585.

SUEZ WAR Joint military intervention by Great Britain, France and Israel after Egypt nationalized the Suez Canal Company in 1956. After some early success, the action was condemned and halted by the intervention of the **United Nations**, and especially the United States. The Canal, blocked by Egypt during the fighting, was reopened in 1957.

SUHARTO, RADEN (1921-) Indonesian political leader. During World War II he served with the Japanese defence forces and then fought in the anti-Dutch guerrilla movement. After independence (1949) he led the army which in 1965 which slaughtered more than 300,000 communists and leftists after an attempted coup. Suharto took control of the government in 1966 and was elected president five consecutive times. He maintained close ties with Japan and the West, is chair of the Non-Aligned movement, but has been accused of rampant corruption and human rights violations.

SUI Short-lived but important Chinese dynasty, ruling from AD 581. It reunited China in 589, after three centuries of disorder following the collapse of the Han dynasty. The Sui built a great network of canals linking Lo-yang with Yangchow, Hangchow and the northern territories near Peking. It fell in 618, to be replaced by the T'ang dynasty the following year.

SUKARNO (1901-70) Indonesian statesman; he helped to found the Indonesian Nationalist party in 1928. Imprisoned by the Dutch colonial authorities, 1933-42, he was released by, and cooperated with, the Japanese, 1942-5. At the end of the Second World War he proclaimed himself President of an independent Indonesia, and spent the next four years trying to force the Dutch to relinquish their hold on the country. In 1959, after ten years of democratic rule, he assumed dictatorial powers (he declared himself President for life in 1963), and increased contacts with the Chinese Communists. Following a military coup in 1965 Sukarno was deposed (1967) and kept under house arrest until his death.

SÜLEYMAN I (c.1496-1566) **Ottoman** Sultan known as 'the Lawgiver', and to the West as 'the Magnificent'. He succeeded his father **Selim I** in 1520; expanded and reinforced the Ottoman Empire and encouraged the development of art, architecture, literature and law. He conquered Belgrade (1521) and Rhodes (1522); defeated the Hungarians at Mohács (1526); seized large parts of Persia and Iraq. He developed a formidable navy to dominate the Mediterranean, and brought the Ottoman Empire to the practical limits of its power and expansion (unsuccessful siege of Vienna 1529, and of Malta 1565).

SULLA (138-78 BC) Roman general, led the aristocratic party in civil war with the popular leader Marius, and made himself dictator after Marius' defeat. He initiated sweeping constitutional and legal reforms, giving more power to the Senate, but was notorious for cruelty to political and military opponents.

SUMERIANS The predominant people in southern Mesopotamia from the beginning of the 3rd millennium. Immigration of Semites (*see* **Akkadians**, **Amorites**) changed the balance by the end of the millennium, the last Sumerian dynasty collapsing in 2006 BC. Their cultural achievements included the invention of writing and the creation of the first cities. Their language, of agglutinative type, has not been positively related to any other.

SUN CH'UAN-FANG (1884-1935) Warlord who controlled Kiangsu, Chekiang, Anhwei, Fukien and Kiangsi in 1925-7 at the time of the Northern Expedition. He lost control of his provinces in 1927, allowing the Nationalists to capture the lower Yangtze valley. With the aid of **Chang Tso-lin** he attempted to recapture Nanking in August of that year but was routed; he retired from public life. He was assassinated.

SUNNI One of the main two divisions of Islam, and the majority in most Muslim countries. It split from the other main group, the **Shias**, over the question of succession to the Prophet **Mohammed**, which Sunnis believe to have passed to the caliphs. The name is derived from *Sunna*, or words and deeds of the Prophet as recorded in the Hadith or Traditions; Sunnis thus claim to be following the example of the Prophet.

SUNNI ALI Emperor of Songhai in West Africa, who reigned c.1464-92. From his home territories on the Middle Niger he reduced many former Mali provinces to Songhai dependencies; he created a professional army and river-navy; seized Timbuktu, controlled the commerce of the western Sudan, and introduced many advanced administrative reforms.

SUN YAT-SEN (1866-1925) First (provisional) President of the Republic of China (1912). He studied medicine in Hong Kong and Canton; entered politics with the formation of the Revive China Society, 1884, and was exiled in 1896 after instigating an abortive uprising, but attempted to organize a series of further uprisings in south China. He returned from the United States in 1911 during the anti-**Ch'ing** (Manchu) revolution, and was elected provisional head of state but resigned after a few months. In 1923 he gained full control of the country, with Russian support; reorganized the **Kuomintang** to resemble the Soviet Communist Party. His Three Principles of the People inspired both Nationalists and Communists.

SUN YEN-LING (d.1677) Chinese general. His wife was the daughter of a commander in Kwangsi, and in 1660 she was given command of his former army. In 1666 Sun was sent to Kwangsi as its military governor; in 1673 he joined **Wu San-kuei**'s rebellion; wavering in his allegiance after 1676, he was killed on Wu San-kuei's orders.

SUTRI, SYNOD OF Council of the Roman Church held in 1046, convoked at a diocesan seat north of Rome by Pope Gregory VI at the insistence of Henry III, king of Germany. The synod deposed Gregory, who had purchased his post, and two other rival pontiffs; it elected a German as Pope Clement II (1046-7), who inaugurated a thorough reform of the Church culminating in the pontificate of **Gregory VII**.

SVEN ESTRIDSSON (c.1020-74) King of Denmark, nephew of the English and Danish king, **Cnut the Great**. He was chosen as ruler by the Danish nobles in 1047 after the death of **Magnus**; his title was vigorously disputed by Harald Hardrada, but the struggle ended early in 1066, when Harald was killed during an invasion of England (battle of Stamford Bridge). Sven himself sponsored a serious Danish attack on England in 1069, withdrawing after an agreement with **William I** in 1070. His dynasty ruled Denmark for 300 years.

SVEN FORKBEARD (d.1014) King of Denmark, son of the Danish king, **Harald Bluetooth**. After a rebellion against his father, he seized the throne c.986. He unsuccessfully invaded Norway, and in 994 attacked England, being expensively bought off by **Æthelred II**. He was virtual ruler of Norway after 1000. He led a series of expeditions against England, and became king in 1013 after forcing Æthelred into exile.

SVYATOSLAV (d.972) Early Russian hero, Grand Prince of Kiev. He attempted to establish a Russian commercial empire over the steppes from Bulgaria to the Volga, 962-972; crushed the **Khazars**, **Volga Bulgars** and Danubian Bulgars, but was defeated by Byzantine Emperor John Tzimisces in 871. He was ambushed and killed by the **Pecheneg**.

SWAZI Bantu-speaking herdsmen and cultivators, living mainly in the independent African kingdom of Swaziland and in the adjacent South African territory of the eastern Transvaal.

SYAGRIUS Last Roman ruler of Gaul, overthrown by **Clovis** near Soissons in 486.

SYKES-PICOT AGREEMENT Secret pact between the First World War allies for the dismemberment of the Ottoman Empire. It was signed on 7 May 1916, with the assent of imperial Russia, by Sir Mark Sykes for Great Britain and François Georges-Picot for France.

TACITUS, CORNELIUS (c.AD 55-c.120) Roman historian. His works include *Dialogue on Orators* (c.79-81), *Agricola* (c.98), *Germania* (c.98) and fragments of two longer works, the *Histories*, covering the period 68-70 (the original probably went down to 96), and the *Annales*, covering 14-68.

TAJIKS (Tadzhiks) Ancient Iranian people within Tajikistan, a mountainous country adjoining Afghanistan, Pakistan and India. They are mainly livestock keepers by occupation and Muslim by religion.

TALAS, BATTLE OF (751) The prince of Tashkent called upon the Muslims to oust the Chinese after their invasion (747). In this battle the Arabs decisively defeated general Kao Hsien-chih, transferring control of the area west of the Pamirs and Tien Shan mountains (Transoxania) from China to Islam and establishing the boundary between the two civilizations.

TALLEYRAND, CHARLES-MAURICE DE (1754-1838) French statesman and diplomat. Destined for the army but crippled by an accident in childhood, he entered the Church in 1775; became Bishop of Autun in 1788, but was excommunicated for his radical Church reorganization during the French Revolution. Foreign Minister under the Directory, 1797-9, and to **Napoleon I** until resigning in 1807; he intrigued with Tsar Alexander I for Napoleon's defeat, and in 1814 became Foreign Minister to Louis XVIII. At the **Congress of Vienna** (1814-51) he secured favourable terms for France. He was made Duc de Talleyrand-Périgord in 1817, and French ambassador to England, 1830-4.

TALMUD Principal repository of Jewish law and lore. It consists of the **Mishnah** and the Gemarra, an explanation of the Mishnah and a general presentation of the traditions taught and transmitted in the Rabbinical academies and preserved in two versions: the Palestinian, edited around AD 400, and the Babylonian, around 500.

TAMERLANE *see* **Timur**

TAMIL Dravidian language spoken by some 30 million southern Indians, one-third of the population of Sri Lanka (Ceylon), and scattered communities in South and East Africa, Mauritius, Malaysia and Fiji. Tamil literature dates back to the 3rd century BC; it remains the official language in the Indian state of Tamil Nadu (Madras).

TANCHELM (d.1115) Religious radical who criticized the Roman Church, especially its hierarchical organization. He preached to large congregations in the Low Countries (mainly Utrecht and Antwerp) but was eventually murdered by a priest.

T'ANG Imperial Chinese dynasty ruling AD 618 to 907; *see pages* 124-5.

T'ANG CHI-YAO (1881-1927) Chinese military leader. Appointed military governor of Kweichow, 1912, and of Yunnan Province, 1915 until his death, he gave crucial support to rebels opposing **Yüan Shih-k'ai** in his bid to re-establish the empire. After the death of **Sun Yat-sen** in 1925, he made an abortive bid to lead a new national government.

TANGUTS Tibetan-speaking peoples of northwest China, who established the 11th-century kingdom of Hsi-hsia in the area of present-day Kansu and northern Shensi. The Tangut tribes, straddling the main trade route from China to the West, remained tributaries to the Sung dynasty from 960 to 1038; from 1038 to 1044 they attempted, under their emperor, Li Yüan-hao, to conquer the whole of China, but withdrew on payment of an annual tribute; the kingdom then survived until 1227, when it was overrun by the Mongols.

TANTRIC BUDDHISM This form of belief, evolved chiefly between the 6th and the 11th centuries AD, aimed at recreating in the individual the original spiritual experience of Gautama the **Buddha**, and emphasized sexo-yogic practices. Tantric art and sculpture made much use of male and female images to symbolize the process of spiritual growth and fulfilment; *Vajra-Yana* or the 'adamantine path' was its largest school.

TAOISM Ancient cult of China, tracing back philosophically to the legendary **Lao-tzu**, who held that there is a Way (*tao*), a sort of natural order of the universe, and that it is the duty of individuals to ensure that their life conforms to it. It developed as a mass religious movement in the 2nd century AD, with its own church and hierarchy; it emphasizes salvation, aided by magical practices based on the interaction of *yin* and *yang*, the powers of darkness (female) and light (male).

TARTAR (also spelled Tatar) First found in an inscription of 731, the name came to be applied to the forces of **Genghis Khan** and his successors, and in Europe was confused with Tartarus, the classical Hell, which seemed an appropriate place of origin for these dreadful hordes. The name was later loosely and inaccurately applied to some of the Turkic peoples of the Russian Empire for example, Volga Tartars, Crimean Tartars. At the present time there is a Tartar Autonomous Republic within the Russian Federation with its capital at Kazan on the Volga.

TASMAN, ABEL JANSZOON (c.1603-c.1659) Dutch explorer, discoverer of New Zealand, Tasmania, Tonga and the Fiji Islands. He served with the **Dutch East India Company**, 1633-53, carrying out two major voyages in the Indian Ocean and the South Pacific, reaching Tasmania (named after him) in 1642; he circumnavigated Australia without seeing it.

TEHERAN CONFERENCE Meeting held from 28 November 1943 to 12 January 1944 at which the Allied leaders – **Churchill**, **Roosevelt** and **Stalin** – concerted plans for an Anglo-American invasion of France and a Russian offensive against eastern Germany.

TE KOOTI (c.1830-93) New Zealand Maori resistance leader. While imprisoned, he founded the Ringatu cult, which is still extant. After escaping, he conducted skilful guerrilla campaigns (1868-72).

TENNANT, CHARLES (1768-1858) Scottish pioneer industrial chemist. He set up a bleachworks and in 1798 patented a new liquid for bleaching textile fabrics, which was soon widely used by Lancashire bleachers. In 1780 with three partners he set up a chemical plant near Glasgow to manufacture bleaching powder and other alkali products. When he died the firm was operating one of the largest chemical plants in the world.

TENNESSEE VALLEY AUTHORITY (TVA) United States federal agency, formed in 1933 to develop natural resources (particularly hydroelectric power) in the states drained by the Tennessee River system – Tennessee itself, Kentucky, Mississippi, Alabama, North Carolina, Georgia and Virginia.

TEN YEARS' WAR (1868-78) Cuba's first war for independence from Spain. It ended inconclusively with promises of political and economic reform, set out in the Convention of Zanjon, 1878. The nationalist leader, Antonio Maceo, refused to accept the accompanying conditions and fled the island to prepare for renewed struggle.

TERTULLIAN (c.160-c.220) Early Christian theologian. Born in Carthage and trained as a lawyer, he was converted to **Christianity** c.195. Writing in Latin rather then Greek, he provided the Western Church with much of its basic terminology; his *De Praescriptions Haereticorum* (197-8) championed orthodoxy; in *De Testimonio Animae* he claimed that the soul is naturally Christian; in his great *Apology* he praised the martyrs: 'the blood of Christians is seed'.

TEUTONIC ORDER (also called Knights of the Cross). Organization of German crusaders, founded in 1190 at Acre, Palestine. It moved to central Europe in 1211, and in 1226, at the invitation of the Polish duke, Conrad of Masovia, began the conquest of pagan Prussia. Under its Grand Masters, with its headquarters at Marienburg, it controlled the eastern Baltic, conquering Pomerania and other areas of Poland. It absorbed the **Livonian Order** (Knights of the Sword) in 1237. It was defeated by the alliance of Poland and Lithuania at Tannenberg (Grünwald) in 1410, and broken by the Treaty of Torun (Thorn) in 1466. It was secularized as the duchy of Prussia (1525) becoming a fief of Polish kings.

TEWFIK PASHA (1852-92) First khedive of Egypt under the British occupation. He was appointed khedive in 1879 by the Ottoman sultan in succession to **Ismail** Pasha. The growth of tension between England and France, representing the interests of foreign creditors of Egypt, and nationalist sentiment with **Arabi Pasha** as its chief spokesman, led to the weakening of Tewfik's power in favour of Arabi, but British military intervention and occupation in 1882 restored him as a figurehead under British control.

TE WHITI, ORONGOMAI (1831-1907) New Zealand Maori leader. He claimed to be a prophet and refused to take part in the Maori rebellions of the 1860s, preaching instead passive resistance and complete segregation from the Europeans. Imprisoned by the British 1881-3 and 1886, he still exercised great influence on the Maoris.

THATCHER, MARGARET (1925-) British Conservative politician and first woman prime minister (1979-90). With degrees in chemistry from Oxford (1947) and law, she entered parliament in 1959 and served as secretary of state for education and science (1970-4), establishing a reputation for toughness. Following Conservative election defeat (1974), she won the party leadership (1975), and became prime minister in 1979. Her programme of 'Thatcherism' combined a restraint on public spending, privatization of major industries, and fiscal caution. In 1990 she was succeeded as prime minister by her chancellor of the exchequer, John Major.

THEOCRITUS (c.300-250 BC) Pastoral poet from Syracuse, who worked in Cos and Alexandria. His *Idylls* and his lyrical descriptions of country life seem a form of escape from urban Alexandria; he strongly influenced Virgil and, through him, all pastoral poetry.

THEODORET (c.393-c.455) Christian theologian. Born in Antioch, he was appointed Bishop of Cyrrhus in Mesopotamia, and played a prominent part in the **Nestorian** controversy (for long defending Nestorians against **Cyril**), culminating with his appearance at the **Council of Chalcedon** in 451, where he finally agreed to condemn Nestorian beliefs. His works include a *Church*

History and a brilliant defence of **Christianity** against paganism.

THEODORIC THE GREAT (c.454-526) Ostrogothic king of Italy, son of a chieftain. He succeeded his father in 471, led migrations of his people into the Balkans and (in 489, on orders of the Emperor Zeno) Italy. He murdered Odoacer, the previous Italian ruler, in 493, to gain control of the country, though acknowledging imperial supremacy; he issued an edict imposing Roman law on his followers, tolerated Catholicism and sought friendship between Goths and Romans.

THEODORUS Known as Theodorus the Lector, an early Greek Church historian of the 6th century. Though only fragments of his work have survived, it is an essential source for events between the time of **Constantine I** (313) and Justin I (518).

THEODOSIUS I, THE GREAT (c.346-95) Roman emperor, 379-95. Appointed by Gratian to rule the Eastern Empire after the death of **Valens**, he also administered the Western Empire after the death of Maximus in 388. He established Catholicism as the official Roman religion, 380; condemned Arianism and paganism; after the massacre of Thessalonica he submitted in penance to **Ambrose**. After his death the Empire was finally divided into two halves.

THEOPHRASTUS (c.372-c.287 BC) Ancient Greek philosopher taught by **Aristotle** whom he succeeded as head of the Lyceum. Theophrastus was a great teacher, with classes attended by as many as 2000; he influenced the foundation of the Museum at Alexandria. Of his works, the *Enquiry into Plants* and the *Etiology of Plants* survive intact, and his *Doctrines of Natural Philosophers*, reconstructed by 19th century scholars, provide the main foundation for the history of early thought. His entertaining *Characters* has been much enjoyed and imitated.

THIRD COALITION, WAR OF THE Struggle between Napoleonic France and an alliance of Britain, Austria, Russia and Sweden, formed in April 1805. Britain's naval victory at Trafalgar established Allied supremacy at sea, but on land there were only defeats: Austria at Ulm (1805), Austria and Russia at Austerlitz (1805), and Prussia, joining late, at Jena (1806). Further Russian defeats, at Eylau and Friedland (1807) and the elimination of Sweden brought hostilities to an end with the Treaty of Tilsit (1807).

THIRTY TYRANTS Vituperative name given to the men who ruled Athens on behalf of Sparta for eight months after its defeat (404 BC) in the Peloponnesian War. The group included **Socrates'** former associate, Critias, who died in May 403 when a democratic army under Thrasybulus defeated the Tyrants at the Piraeus; the survivors were massacred two years later in Eleusis, where they had taken refuge.

THOMAS, ST One of the twelve Apostles. He doubted the Resurrection until he saw and touched the wounds of **Jesus**; he is traditionally believed to have gone to India as a missionary.

THOMAS, SIDNEY GILCHRIST (1850-85) English metallurgist and inventor, who discovered a new process for making steel which eliminated phosphorus from pig iron. It was applied both to the Bessemer converter (1875) and to the Siemens open-hearth process, perfected by Percy Carlyle Gilchrist.

THREE FEUDATORIES REBELLION *see* **Wu San-kuei**

THUCYDIDES (c.460-c.400 BC) Athenian historian. He served as a general in the Peloponnesian War but was exiled after failing to defend an important strongpoint in Thrace. He had already begun his classic history of the war and completed eight books, breaking off at 411, seven years before the end of hostilities.

THURINGIANS Germanic people, first documented c.AD 350. They were conquered by the **Huns** in the mid-5th century; by 500 their revived kingdom stretched from the Harz Mountains to the Danube, but they were defeated by the **Franks** in 531 and were subsequently ruled by them.

TIBERIUS (42 BC-AD 37) (Tiberius Claudius Nero Caesar Augustus). Second Roman emperor, stepson of the Emperor **Augustus**, he succeeded in AD 14 at the age of 56. In his first years he greatly strengthened Rome's finances and institutions; after his son's death in 23 he gradually withdrew from affairs, retiring to Capri in 27 where he gained the reputation of an arbitrary, cruel and merciless tyrant. In 31 he arranged the execution of Sejanus, to whom he had delegated his authority and who plotted against him.

TIENTSIN TREATIES Agreements forced on the Chinese government in 1858 by Britain and France to allow free access, the posting of resident officials in Peking, and the opening of new trade ports. Similar agreements were then made by Russia and the United States.

TILAK, BAL GANGADHAR (1856-1920) Militant Indian nationalist. He taught mathematics, owned and edited two weekly newspapers, was twice imprisoned by the British; in 1914 he founded the Indian Home Rule League; he signed the Lucknow Pact in 1916 as the basis for a Hindu-Muslim political alliance. His books include *Secret of the Bhagavad-gita*, written in prison between 1908 and 1914.

TIMES, THE London newspaper, founded in 1785 by John Walter under the title *Daily Universal Register*; its present name was adopted in 1788. Known as 'The Thunderer' under the editorship of Delane (1840-79) for its incorruptibility and independence of government.

TIMUR (1336-1405) Known as Timur Lang, from his lame leg, hence Tamerlane. Born near Samarkand, later his capital, he concluded the Mongol age of conquest, although his background was Turkish rather than Mongol, and he was no nomad but a product of the sophisticated Islamic society of Transoxania. He conquered, with legendary barbarity, a vast Asian empire stretching from southern Russia to Mongolia and southwards into northern India, Persia and Mesopotamia. He adorned his capital with splendid buildings, many of which still stand today. He died on an expedition against **Ming** China; after his death the empire soon fell apart.

TIPU (c.1749-99) Indian sultan, known as 'the Tiger of Mysore'; son of **Hader Ali**. He fought frequently against the **Marathas**, 1767-79, despite being publicly caned by his father for cowardice in 1771. He defeated the British on the Coleroon River in 1782 and succeeded to the Mysore throne in the same year. He signed the Treaty of Bangalore with the British in 1784, though he fought several further aggressive and partially successful campaigns against them. He was killed during the final British assault on his capital, Seringapatam; he is remembered in the Mysore saying: 'Haidar was born to create an empire, Tipu to lose one'.

TITO, MARSHAL (1892-1980) (Born Josip Broz). Yugoslav head of state. He led Communist resistance to German occupation of Yugoslavia, 1941-5 and in 1945 became head of the Federal People's Republic with Soviet support; he broke with the USSR in 1948 to pursue a neutralist foreign policy and an independent version of Communism. He served as President from 1953 until his death.

TITUS (AD 39-81) Roman emperor, son of Vespasian. He served in Britain, Germany and under his father in Judaea; on Vespasian's accession as emperor he took charge of the Jewish War, killed many (reputedly one million) Jews and sacked Jerusalem in 70; he was made commander of the Praetorian Guard in 71. He was much criticized for taking Berenice, sister of the Jewish king, Herod Agrippa II, as his mistress. He succeeded his father as emperor in 79, helped to rebuild Rome after the fire of 80, and completed the Colosseum.

TLAXCALANS Indians of the Central Mexican plateau. Relations between the Tlaxcalans and the Aztec confederation were always uneasy, and at the time of the Spanish conquest they joined **Hernán Cortés** as his principal local ally; continued loyalty to Spain brought many privileges.

TOCHARIANS Central Asian peoples, occupying the basin of the upper Oxus River in the 2nd century BC. They were joint founders, with the **Kushans**, of the Kushan Empire. They are not necessarily identical to the speakers of the 'Tocharian' language, one of the Indo-European group, whose main surviving manuscripts, found in Chinese Turkestan (Tarim Basin) date from the period AD 500-1000.

TOJO, HIDEKI (1884-1948) Japanese general and statesman, he was Prime Minister at the time of the Japanese attack on Pearl Harbor. After a military career he became Vice-Minister (1938-9), then Minister (1940-4) of War, and also Prime Minister, 1941-4. He resigned after the fall of Saipan; tried, after the war, by the Tokyo War Crimes Court, he was found guilty and hanged.

TOKUGAWA Dynasty of hereditary shoguns or military dictators, effectively ruling Japan from 1603 to 1868. It was founded by Ieyasu (1542-1616), who mastered the country after the death of **Toyotomi Hideyoshi** and established his capital at the fishing village of Edo (now Tokyo). He organized a new pattern of fiefs and administration which lasted unchallenged until the 19th century. Under his son, Hidetada (1579-1632),

and grandson, Iemitsu (1603-51), Japan eliminated Christianity and virtually closed itself to foreign trade and influence. These three rulers consolidated the family's control, which lasted until the 19th century when Tokugawa Keiki accepted the near-peaceful handing over of power to the emperor, **Meiji**.

TOKUGAWA IEYASU (1542-1616) Founder of the **Tokugawa** shogunate.

TOLTECS Ruling people in Mexico from the 10th to the 12th century. The name is associated with their capital, Tula, or 'place of the reeds', located 50 miles (80 km) north of Tenochtitlán, present-day Mexico City. They captured and sacked the great city of Teotihuacán c.900; under their leader Quetzalcoatl and his successors they established a wide-ranging empire, introducing to it metal-work and ambitious architectural and sculptural techniques. They were overwhelmed by nomad **Chichimec** invaders, including the Aztecs, who destroyed Tula in the mid-12th century.

TOPA (d.1493) Inca emperor, who succeeded to the title in 1471 after the abdication of his father, **Pachacuti**. After an early setback, invading the rain forests near the Tono River, he established a reputation as a great conqueror: he defeated the revolt led by the **Colla** and **Lupaca**, extended the boundaries of his empire to highland Bolivia, northern Chile and most of northwest Argentina; and finally succeeded in incorporating the previously unconquered southern coast of Peru. He devoted the rest of his reign to administration.

TORAH Hebrew name for the Law of Moses, or Pentateuch, the first five books of the Old Testament of the Bible: *Genesis*, *Exodus*, *Leviticus*, *Numbers* and *Deuteronomy*; also the scroll containing these books, used ceremonially in the synagogue.

TORDESILLAS, TREATY OF Treaty between Spain and Portugal, 1494, to determine ownership of lands discovered or to be discovered in the west. It granted Spain exclusive rights west of a north-south line 370 leagues west of the Cape Verde Islands – a 1493 Bull of the Spanish Pope Alexander VI had put the line 270 leagues further east – with Portugal taking lands east of the line. Portugal thus established claim to the so far undiscovered Brazil; but the treaty was never accepted by the other Atlantic powers.

TOTONAC Central American Indians, farming both the highlands and the hot coastal lowlands of eastern Mexico, mainly in the states of Vera Cruz, Puebla and Hidalgo. The two Totonac languages, Totonac and Tepehuan, are believed to be related to ancient **Mayan**.

TOURÉ, AHMED SEKOU (1922-84) President of the Republic of Guinea. A trade union organizer, in 1952 he started a political party, the Guinea Democratic Party; he became vice-president of the government council in 1957, and first President of Guinea on independence in 1958.

TOUSSAINT-L'OUVERTURE (1743-1803) Haitian independence leader, born into a family of African slaves in the part of Haiti which formed the French colony of St Domingue. He joined the slave rebellion and declared in favour of the French Revolutionary government; recognized by the French Directory as lieutenant-governor in 1797, he expelled British and Spanish forces and gained control of the whole island in 1801. The French government, now under Napoleon, sent invasion forces in 1802, and he was defeated and taken to France where he died in prison. The French restored slavery to Haiti.

TOWNSEND, FRANCIS (1867-1960) US doctor who helped lay the foundations for the modern American social security programme. He devised the Old Age Revolving Pension Plan, which mobilized popular support for federal action in this area.

TOYOTOMI HIDEYOSHI (1536-98) Unifier of 16th-century Japan. He served as a chief lieutenant to the feudal general, Oda Nobunaga (1534-82), and after his death became the Emperor's chief minister (1585). In 1590 he conquered the islands of Shikoku and Kyushu to unify the country; he energetically promoted internal peace, economic development and overseas expansion. He died after an unsuccessful invasion of Korea.

TRAJAN (AD 53-117) (Marcus Ulpius Trajanus). First Roman emperor to be born in the provinces – in Italica, near Santiponce, Seville. He served in the army in Syria, Spain and Germany, was named Consul in 91 and chosen as Emperor in 98. He is famous as a builder, social reformer and extender of the Empire in the East and in Dacia, modern Romania (celebrated by

Trajan's Column, still standing in Rome). He died in Cilicia after invading Mesopotamia and taking Ctesiphon, the Parthian capital.

TRASTÁMARA *see* Henry II, King of Castile

TRIPARTITE PACT Agreement signed on 27 September 1940 between Germany, Italy and Japan, setting up a full military and political alliance (the Rome-Berlin-Tokyo Axis) to support one another in the event of a spread of the Second World War to the Far East.

TRIPLE ALLIANCE (1882-1915) Defensive treaty signed on 20 May 1882 pledging Germany and Italy to mutual support in the event of a French attack, and obliging Austria-Hungary to support Italy in such an event in return for a promise of Italian neutrality in the event of a Russian attack on Austria-Hungary. It was extended between 1887 and 1909 by supplementary agreements providing for diplomatic support in the Near East and North Africa.

TROTSKY, LEON (1879-1940) Russian revolutionary leader and theorist. Born Lev Davidovich Bronstein, he spent long periods in prison and in exile before returning to Russia in 1917 to play a major part in bringing the **Bolsheviks** to power. He was Commissar for Foreign Affairs, 1917-18, and Commissar for War, 1918-25. The most prominent revolutionary after **Lenin**, he was an effective organizer of the Red Army during the civil war. After Lenin's death in 1924 he was increasingly in conflict with **Stalin**, and was exiled in 1929. He founded the Fourth International in 1938, and published the *History of the Russian Revolution*. He was murdered by a Soviet agent in Mexico.

TRUMAN, HARRY S. (1884-1972) 33rd President of the United States, 1945-53. The son of a Missouri mule trader, he entered politics as county judge, 1922-4; US Senator, 1935 and re-elected 1940; Vice-President in 1944, succeeding as President in 1945 on the death of **F.D. Roosevelt**. He ordered the atomic bombing of Hiroshima and Nagasaki in 1945; in 1947 enunciated the Truman Doctrine on the 'containment' of the Soviet Union, and established the Central Intelligence Agency (CIA). He inaugurated the **Marshall Plan** and was re-elected, 1948, and supported in 1949 the formation of the **North Atlantic Treaty Organization** (NATO); he ordered the US engagement in Korea in 1950.

TSHOMBE, MOÏSE (1919-69) Congo (Zaire) political leader. He became a member of the Katanga Provincial Council, 1951-3, and president of Conakat (*Confédération des Associations Tribales du Katanga*) in 1959. His plans for a federated Congo after independence were rejected in favour of a central state. He declared Katangan independence in 1960, but was defeated by UN forces in 1963. Appointed by **Kasavubu** as Premier of the Congo in 1964, he was dismissed in 1965 and was sentenced to death *in absentia*, 1967. Hijacked to Algeria in 1967, he died in captivity.

TUAREG Berber nomads from the central and western Sahara; Hamitic-speaking Muslims.

TUDORS English ruling dynasty from 1485 until 1603, founded by **Henry VII** and continued through his descendants **Henry VIII**, Edward VI, Mary I and **Elizabeth I**.

TULUNIDS Muslim dynasty ruling in Egypt and Syria from 868 to 905. It was founded by Ahmed ibn Tulun, a Turk, who arrived in Egypt as vice-governor under the **Abbasids**.

TUNG-MENG-HUI Chinese political party, originally founded as a secret society by **Sun Yat-sen** in 1905.

TUNGUSY People of the sub-Arctic forest in eastern Siberia. Originally nomadic hunters, fishers and reindeer breeders, they moved from the Ob and Yenisey river basins east to the Pacific, and north from the Amur basin to the Arctic Ocean. Since the Russian Revolution (1917) most were settled on collective farms.

TUPAMAROS Members of a Uruguayan urban guerrilla movement. It first came to prominence in 1968, preaching socialist revolution on the Cuban pattern. Its violent campaign of bombing, assassination, robbery, kidnapping – and a spectacular prison break in 1971 when 106 leading Tupamaros escaped from the Uruguayan national penitentiary – brought increasingly severe retaliation; by 1974 over 2000 members were held in a new maximum-security prison and the movement had apparently been crushed.

TUTANKHAMUN (d.1352 BC) King of Egypt's XVIIIth Dynasty. Of uncertain parentage, as a child he succeeded his brother Smenkhkare, who had been co-regent and successor to **Akhenaten**,

During his reign (1361-1352 BC) the worship of the old gods, suppressed by Akhenaten, was restored. In 1922 his long-lost tomb was discovered almost intact by the British archaeologist Howard Carter.

TUTHMOSIS I (died c.1512 BC) Third king of Egypt's XVIIIth Dynasty. He served as general in the army of Amenhotep I, and succeeded in 1525 BC when the pharaoh died without an heir. He re-established military domination in the south and conducted a brilliant campaign in Syria and across the Euphrates.

TUTHMOSIS III (d.1450 BC) Greatest of Egypt's warrior kings of the XVIIIth Dynasty. Son of Tuthmosis II (reigned 1512-1504 BC) and a minor wife named Isis, he ascended the throne as a young boy but was overshadowed for nearly 20 years by his stepmother, Queen Hatshepsut, until her death in 1482 BC. He conducted 17 campaigns in Palestine and Syria, extending Egypt's empire to the banks of the Euphrates; his campaigns in Nubia gave Egypt control over all the gold mines and territory as far as the Fourth Cataract of the Nile.

TWENTY-ONE DEMANDS Claims pressed by Japan on China during the First World War, asking for privileges similar to, but more extensive than, those enjoyed by the Western powers, including railway and mining concessions, coastal access and power to intervene in financial, political and police affairs. An ultimatum, presented on 5 May 1915, forced capitulation on most points by the Chinese President on 25 May and greatly increased anti-Japanese feeling in China.

UIGHURS Nomadic Turkic-speaking peoples of central Asia, who ruled a substantial area north and northwest of China in the 8th and 9th centuries, and later settled in Kansu and the Tarim Basin, establishing a distinct way of life and a literary language. The modern Uighurs live mainly in Sinkiang and the former Soviet Central Asia.

ULFILAS (c.311-c.382) Converter of the Goths to Christianity. In 341 he was consecrated bishop of the Gothic Christians by Eusebius, the Arian patriarch of Constantinople. After initial persecution, the **Visigothic** leaders accepted the **Arianist** doctrine, while Ulfilas created a Gothic alphabet and made the first Germanic translation of the Bible, some of which still survives.

ULMANIS, KARLIS (1877- post 1942) Latvian independence leader. Trained in agronomy, he worked to free Latvia from the century-old Russian control during the 1905 revolution. He fled to the United States, was amnestied in 1913 and founded the Latvian Farmers' Union, 1917. Appointed head of the provisional government by the national independence council, 1918, he held power from 1918 to 1921 and then in 1925-6, 1931-2 and 1934-40. He resigned in 1940 in the face of a Russian military ultimatum; was arrested in July by the Soviet authorities and deported. His fate is unknown.

UMAYYADS Dynasty of caliphs, founded by Muawiya in 661, in opposition to **Ali**, **Mohammed**'s son-in-law and fourth caliph. They were deposed by the **Abbasids** in 750 although a branch continued to rule Muslim Spain from 756 to 1031.

UNION, ACT OF Treaty signed in 1707 under which Scotland and England (which had shared the same rulers since 1603) became jointly the Kingdom of Great Britain. The agreement stipulated a single government, but separate churches and legal systems; Scotland recognized the Hanoverian succession.

UNITARIANS Members of a Protestant Christian denomination, characterized by belief in one God, as opposed to the more orthodox doctrine of the Trinity. It first emerged as a distinct church in Poland and Transylvania in the late 16th and 17th centuries, and was widely followed in England and North America in the 18th and 19th centuries.

UNITED FRUIT COMPANY United States-based multinational company, specializing in the shipment of tropical produce. Founded in 1899 in a merger of Central American shipping, railroad and banana-planting interests, it was merged into the United Brands Company in 1968.

UNITED NATIONS International organization, founded in 1945 as a successor to the **League of Nations**. Its aims are to maintain world peace and security, and to promote economic, social and cultural co-operation among nations. The original membership of 50 had risen to 183 by May 1993. Its main divisions are the Security Council and the General Assembly; special agencies include the World Health Organization (WHO), Food and Agriculture Organization (FAO), United Nations Educational, Scientific and Cultural Organization (UNESCO), etc.

U NU (1907-) Burmese independence leader. He was expelled from Rangoon University in 1936, and in 1940 was imprisoned by the British for sedition. He became Foreign Minister in 1943 in the pro-Japanese government, and was first Prime Minister of independent Burma in 1948-58 and 1960-2, when he was ousted by General **Ne Win** in a *coup d'état*. Released from prison in 1969, he began to organize a resistance movement from abroad.

UPANISHADS Prose and verse reflections on the **Vedas** and forming with them the central corpus of Hindu sacred literature. Numbering 108 in their surviving form, the oldest were composed probably c.900 BC; teaching based on their mystical and philosophic speculations is known as the *Vedanta* – the conclusion of the *Vedas*.

URBAN II (c.1042-99) Pope, 1088-99. He inherited many of **Gregory VII**'s ideas about the freedom of the Church from state interference, and in addition established at Rome the administrative organization to operate it. He preached the First **Crusade** in 1099.

URNFIELD Late Bronze Age culture in central Europe, flourishing from the late 2nd to the early 1st millennium BC. It is characterized by the practice of burying the cremated ashes of the dead in ceramic urns. It was a direct predecessor of the Celtic **Hallstatt** period.

UTHMAN DAN FODIO (1754-1817) Muslim Fulani mystic and revolutionary reformer, and founder of a militant Islamic state in what later became northern Nigeria. He began teaching Sufi doctrines in 1775, and was hailed as deliverer by oppressed Hausa and fellow Fulani peoples. He launched a *jihad* (holy war) from Gabir in 1804, conquering most of northern Nigeria and beyond, establishing the Fulani-ruled Sokoto caliphate before retiring in 1815, disillusioned by the corruption of his supporters.

UTRECHT, PEACE OF Treaties concluded in 1713 which, with those of Rastadt and Baden (1714), ended the War of the Spanish Succession. **Louis XIV**'s grandson Philip was recognized as king of Spain on condition that the kingdoms of France and Spain would never be united and with the cession of the Spanish Netherlands and Spain's Italian territories to Austria and Savoy. Gibraltar and Minorca were ceded to Great Britain, with a 30-year monopoly on supplying slaves to the Spanish colonies. Portugal obtained frontier rectifications in South America at Spain's expense. Louis XIV recognized the Protestant succession in Great Britain (thus abandoning the Stuart cause) and the title of king for the ruler of Brandenburg-Prussia. He also ceded Nova Scotia, Hudson's Bay, Newfoundland and St Kitts to the British, against incorporation of the principality of Orange and the Barcelonette valley into France. The Dutch Republic secured the right to garrison, at Austrian expense, fortresses in the southern Netherlands. At the 1714 treaties between the Emperor Charles VI and Louis XIV, Landau was ceded to France and the electors of Bavaria and Cologne, Louis XIV's allies, were restored to their lands and dignities. Formal peace between Austria and Spain was not made until 1720.

UZBEKS A people of Turkish origin who arrived in the area around Samarkand and Tashkent in the 6th century AD. In the 14th century they became the core of the empire of **Timur**, and in the 16th century the basis for the conquests of **Babur**. Later the area disintegrated into small city-states. Russia annexed the region in the 1860s, although incorporation was not complete until the 1920s; now mostly concentrated in Uzbekistan.

UZKOKS Balkan Christians who fled from the Ottoman conquest in the late 15th century and settled around the Adriatic port of Fiume, whence they attacked both Turkish and Christian (especially Venetian) shipping.

VACA, ALVARO NUÑEZ CABEZA DE (c.1490-1560) One of two Spanish survivors of a voyage of exploration from Florida to New Mexico, 1528-36, who wrote a description of the fabulous riches he claimed to have seen. Many others were thereby encouraged to go to their deaths prospecting there.

VAKATAKAS South Indian dynasty, dominating the western Deccan from the mid-3rd to the later 4th century AD. It achieved its greatest power under King Pravaresena I in the early 4th century; Rudrasena II married the daughter of **Chandragupta II**, and after his death, c.390, the Vakataka territory was absorbed into the **Gupta** empire.

VALENS (c.328-378) Eastern Roman Emperor, who on the death of the Emperor Jovian was appointed co-emperor by his brother, Valentinian I, in 364. He twice devastated the Visigothic lands north of the Danube (in 367 and 369); fought an inconclusive war with Persia 376; was defeated and killed by the **Visigoths** at the battle of Adrianople.

VALERA, EAMON DE (1882-1975) Irish statesman. He was elected President of the Irish Nationalist Party, Sinn Fein, in 1917, and President of the Irish Parliament, the Dáil, while imprisoned in England in 1918-19. He refused to accept the Irish independence treaty in 1921; in 1926 he formed a republican opposition party, Fianna Fáil. He was Prime Minister of the Irish Free State, 1937-48, and again – following full independence – in 1951-4 and 1957-9; and President of the Irish Republic 1959-73.

VALERIAN (c.190-c.260) (Publius Licinius Valerianus.) Roman Emperor. He gained the throne in 253, but left government to his son Gallienus while he led campaigns against the Goths and the Persians. He was captured by the Persians in 260 and died in captivity.

VANDALS Germanic people, displaced from central Europe by the 4th-century incursion of the Huns. They reached North Africa, via Spain, and established their kingdom there in AD 429. At first federated with Rome, they seized their independence in 439 and captured Rome itself briefly in 455. Attacked in 533 by the Byzantine armies under **Belisarius**, they were obliterated in 534.

VARGAS, GETULIO DORNELLES (1883-1954) President and dictator of Brazil. He became state President of Rio Grande do Sul in 1928, and Liberal candidate for national President in 1929, seizing the presidency by force in 1930 after his defeat. Under a new constitution he was re-elected in 1934, and in 1937 he introduced the corporate-style dictatorship of Estado Nôvo (New State). He laid the foundations for the modern nation, and linked Brazil to the Western alliance in the Second World War. He was ousted in 1945, re-elected constitutional President in 1951, and committed suicide during the 1954 political crisis.

VARUS, PUBLIUS QUINTILIUS (d.AD 9) Roman general. He became Consul in 13 BC, Governor of Syria, 6-4 BC, and commander in Germany, AD 6-9. He committed suicide after the destruction of his army by the Germans in the Teutoburg Forest.

VASVÁR, TREATY OF Agreement signed on 10 August 1664, ending an Austro-Turkish war (1663-4) after Austria had been called in to help the then independent principality of Transylvania repel a Turkish invasion. Under its terms Hungary, which had not been consulted, lost numerous fortresses to the Turks, and the resulting fury generated several later anti-Habsburg rebellions.

VAUBAN, SEBASTIEN LE PRESTRE DE (1633-1707) French engineer, military architect and town planner. He revolutionized defensive fortification, building a ring of fortresses on France's frontiers; he planned port fortifications and also towns connected with the many forts. He was made a Marshal of France in 1703.

VEDANTA Most influential among the Six Systems of Hindu philosophy. Decisive in refuting non-Brahminical schools of Hindu thought, it argues the existence of Absolute Soul in all things, and the union of the individual and his Absolute Soul as salvation. It was forcefully promoted by the Brahmin **Shankaracharya**.

VEDAS Collection of ancient Sanskrit hymns, sacred verses and devotional formulae (*mantras*), preserved by Hindu tradition – first oral, then written – since the first appearance of Aryan-speaking peoples in north India, c.mid-2nd millennium BC. The three major compilations – *Rig*, *Yajur* and *Sama* – form the *trayividya* or 'threefold knowledge'; a fourth, the *Atharvaveda*, is made up of more homely chants, spells and incantations, of lesser religious significance.

VENDÉE UPRISING Largest and most successful royalist counterattack against the First French Republic. In 1793 peasant troops, under their own and various aristocratic leaders, scored a number of victories, but were unable to hold the region's coastal ports and establish contact with Britain. Defeat came in October 1793, but the trouble continued sporadically until finally put down by **Napoleon**.

VERONA, LEAGUE OF Alliance of Italian city states (1164), including Vicenza, Verona and Padua, formed to oppose the Emperor **Frederick I Barbarossa**; it was absorbed into the larger **Lombard League** in 1167. Verona was ruled by the da Romano and **della Scala** families from the mid-13th century until conquered by the **Visconti** family of Milan in 1387; it was then subject to Venice from 1404 until 1797.

VERRAZZANO, GIOVANNI DA (c.1485-c.1528) Florentine who in 1524 explored the North American coast from Cape Fear, North Carolina, probably as far north as Cape Breton, Nova Scotia. During his voyage he became the first European to sight New York Bay and Narragansett Bay, and he proved North America to be a continuous landmass. His name is commemorated in New York's Verrazzano-Narrows Bridge, linking Brooklyn and Staten Island.

VERSAILLES, TREATY OF (1783) (also known as the Treaty of Paris) Treaty which ended the American War of Independence. Great Britain recognized US sovereignty to the Mississippi River and ceded Florida to Spain. The agreement also called for payment of debts, US access to Newfoundland fishing-grounds and fair treatment for Americans who had stayed loyal to Great Britain.

VERSAILLES, TREATY OF (1919) Agreement signed on 28 June 1919 between Germany and the Allies after the end of the First World War. Germany was made to accept responsibility for paying heavy war reparations, to give up Alsace-Lorraine to France, yield much territory to Poland, Belgium, Denmark and Japan, and to lose all its overseas colonies. Danzig became a Free City under a **League of Nations** High Commission; the Saar was also placed under League control until 1935, when by plebiscite its citizens voted to be reunited with Germany. The Rhineland was to be permanently demilitarized and occupied by the Allies for 15 years. The Treaty embodied the Covenant of the League of Nations; failing to secure a two-thirds majority in the United States Senate, it was not ratified by the US. The Versailles Treaty with Germany was paralleled by the treaties of Trianon with Hungary, of Neuilly with Bulgaria, of St Germain with Austria and of Sèvres with the Ottoman Empire.

VESPASIAN (AD 9-79) Roman emperor. Of humble parentage, he became Proconsul in Africa, 63-66, led victorious armies in Palestine, 67-68; was proclaimed Emperor by troops during the civil wars following the death of Nero, and was recognized by the Senate in 69. He reorganized provinces in the Eastern Empire; secured the pacification of Wales and much of north Britain; and used tax reform, tolerance and a vast building programme to restore political stability.

VESPUCCI, AMERIGO (1454-1512) Explorer, cosmographer and propagandist. Born in Florence, he moved in 1492 to Seville as the **Medici** representative. He participated in several voyages of exploration, including one along the north coast of Brazil and Venezuela in 1499, and down the east coast of Brazil, possibly as far as Rio de la Plata, in 1501-02. He is credited, on slender evidence, with the first suggestion that America was a continent separate from Asia; even, by some contemporaries, with being its discoverer – hence the name 'America', first used on the world map of Martin Waldseemüller in 1507. From 1508 to 1512 Vespucci was pilot-major of the House of Trade of the Indies.

VICTOR EMMANUEL II (1820-78) First king of united Italy, son of **Charles Albert**, king of Sardinia-Piedmont, whom he succeeded on his father's abdication in 1849. He entrusted government in 1852 to Count **Cavour**, and led Italian troops in the Franco-Piedmontese victories over the Austrians at Magenta and Solferino, 1859. Rather against the wishes of his ministers, he secretly encouraged **Garibaldi** to conquer Sicily and Naples. Proclaimed king of Italy in 1861, he acquired Venetia in 1866 and Rome in 1870.

VICTORIA (1819-1901) Queen of Great Britain and Ireland, 1837-1901, and Empress of India, 1876-1901. She succeeded her uncle, William IV; married in 1840 Prince Albert of Saxe-Coburg-Gotha (1819-61) later styled the Prince Consort. She attached particular signficance to her right to be consulted about foreign affairs and, in the latter part of her reign, identified herself with her people's imperial aspirations. She went through a period of intense unpopularity when she shut herself away from the public after the Prince Consort's death, but re-emerged as the symbol of both national and imperial unity. Her diamond jubilee in 1897 was an ostentatious celebration of the apogee of Great Britain's world power.

VIENNA, CONGRESS OF Convened in fulfilment of Article XXXII of the **First Peace of Paris** and formally opened at the end of October 1814. The principal powers reconstructed Europe following the many territorial changes of the previous two decades, their decisions being embodied in the Final Act of Vienna of 9 June 1815. Legitimate dynasties were restored in Spain, Naples, Piedmont, Tuscany and Modena; the Marches, Legations and other territories were restored to the Holy See; the Swiss Confederation was restored and guaranteed; 39 German states were formed into a Confederation; Belgium, Holland and part of Luxembourg were united under the kingdom of the Netherlands; the kingdom of Lombardy-Venetia was placed under the Emperor of Austria; the Congress Kingdom of Poland was created and placed under the Tsar of Russia, the rest of Poland going to Austria and Prussia; Prussia in addition acquired nearly half of Saxony, Swedish Pomerania and certain territories on both banks of the Rhine; Dalmatia, Carniola and Salzburg went to Austria.

VIET MINH League for the Independence of Vietnam, founded in 1941 by **Ho Chi Minh**. It emerged as a coalition of nationalist and Communist groups, and between 1946 and 1954 successfully fought to expel the French colonial administration. The dominant element of the party in North Vietnam, and since the military victory of 1975 throughout the country, is Lao Dong (Workers Party or Communist Party).

VIJAYANAGAR Powerful Hindu kingdom of southern India, founded in 1336 by a local prince, Harihara, who in 1343 built his new capital of Vijayanagara (City of Victory) to give the state its name. In 1485 a change of dynasty brought the Saluva family to the throne. Its greatest influence was achieved under Krishna Deva Raya (1509-30); the continued struggles with the Muslim Deccan culminated in a crushing defeat at the battle of Talikota in 1565 from which the kingdom never recovered.

VILLA, PANCHO (1877-1923) Mexican revolutionary leader, son of a farm worker. He joined **Madero** in 1909 and led a north Mexican troop in his successful revolution. Imprisoned in 1912, Villa escaped to the United States, returning in 1913 to form his famous División del Norte. He was joint leader of the successful revolt against Madero's successor, the dictator Victoriano Huerta, in 1914, but broke with his co-revolutionary **Carranza**, and fled to the mountains. He was pursued by a United States expedition in 1916 after executing 16 Americans and attacking New Mexico, but was pardoned in 1920. He was assassinated three years later.

VILLAFRANCA, PEACE OF (1859) Preliminary peace between **Napoleon III**, **Victor Emmanuel II** and Francis Joseph I of Austria which brought to an end the Franco-Piedmontese hostilities against Austria. A definitive peace, which provided for the cession of Lombardy to Sardinia-Piedmont, was signed at **Zürich** on 10 November 1859.

VILLARET-JOYEUSE, LOUIS THOMAS (1750-1812) French vice-admiral. He led the French fleet during the Revolutionary Wars; ordered to protect a grain convoy by the Committee of Public Safety in 1794, he suffered severe losses at the hands of the British at the battle of the 'Glorious' First of June, but succeeded in getting the convoy safely home to Brest; recalled by **Napoleon I** to lead the abortive expedition to recover St Domingue. In 1802 he was made Governor of Martinique, which he was forced to yield to the British in 1809. In 1811 he became Governor of Venice, where he died.

VILLENEUVE, PIERRE-CHARLES-JEAN-BAPTISTE-SILVESTRE DE (1763-1806) French vice-admiral. He commanded the French fleet at the battle of Trafalgar in 1805; disgraced in the eyes of **Napoleon I** by his failure, he committed suicide.

VIRACOCHA (d. c.1438) Inca emperor who took his name from the ancient Inca god of creation. He began in the early 15th century to substitute permanent conquest for his predecessors' pattern of intermittent raiding, successfully extending Inca influence into the Titicaca basin. He became embroiled in a civil war with his son, later **Pachacuti** Inca.

VISCONTI Milanese family dominating northern Italy in the 14th and 15th centuries. The family probably became hereditary viscounts of Milan in the 11th century, adopting the title as their surname; by war, diplomacy and marriage they extended their control over large territories between 1300 and 1447. The name died out with Filippo Maria (1392-1447) when he was succeeded by his son-in-law, the *condottiere* Francesco Sforza, who founded his own dynasty, ruling the Visconti domains until the 16th century. Through the female line, Visconti blood was transmitted to almost all the great European ruling houses: Valois in France, Habsburg in Austria and Spain, and Tudor in England.

VISCONTI, GIANGALEAZZO (1351-1402) Lombard ruler. He succeeded his father in 1378 as joint ruler of Pavia and Lombardy with his uncle, Bernabo, whom he put to death in 1385. Recognized as Duke of Milan in 1395, he became master of northern Italy, including Verona, Bologna and Perugia; in 1399 he bought Pisa and seized Siena; he founded Milan cathedral. He died of plague, with the conquest of Florence and his project for a great unified state in northern Italy incomplete.

VISHNU Hindu diety: God the Preserver in the Hindu trinity; the object of special or exclusive worship to Vaishnavas, a major sect of Hindu belief. Traditionally, Vishnu manifested himself in nine incarnations (most recently as the **Buddha**) to save men from evil; his tenth and final incarnation is still to come.

VISIGOTHS Germanic people, closely linked with the **Ostrogoths**, who occupied the former Roman province of Dacia (modern Romania) in the 3rd century AD. Forced by the **Huns** to take refuge in the Roman Empire in 376, they revolted and defeated the Romans at Adrianople in 378 and began the wars and wanderings that included the Sack of Rome in 410 and the establishment of the Visigothic kingdom which, from 418 to 507, covered most of Spain and Gaul. They were defeated by the **Franks** at Vouillé in 511 and retreated to Spain, where their Christian state (first Arian, but Catholic from 589) was finally destroyed in 711 by Muslims invading from North Africa.

VLADIMIR (c.956-1015) Grand Prince of Kiev, saint and first Christian ruler of Russia. Son of **Svyatoslav** of Kiev, he became Prince of Novgorod in 970, and by 980 had linked Kiev and Novgorod, and consolidated Russia from the Ukraine to the Baltic. He signed a pact c.987 with the Byzantine emperor **Basil II** to give military aid and accept Christianity. He agreed to the appointment of a Greek Metropolitan, or archbishop, in Kiev, thus checking Roman influence on Russian religion. During his reign he expanded education, legal institutions and poor relief.

V.O.C. *see* **Dutch East India Company**

VOLGA BULGARS A Turanian people, emigrating northwards from the Black Sea in the 9th century to the junction of the Volga and Kama rivers. They adopted Islam, founded an independent state, and built up a rich fur trade based on the cities of Bulgar and Suvar (early 11th century). They were conquered by the Mongols, 1237; their territory was won by Muscovy after the capture of Kazan (1552) but they themselves seem to have vanished long before.

VOLSCI Ancient Italian people, mainly known for their opposition to Roman expansion in the 5th century BC. Originally related to the Osco-Sabellian tribes of the upper Liris valley, they later moved into the fertile area of southern Latium where for two hundred years they fought against Rome and the Latins. Defeated during the Latin Revolt in 338 BC, they finally submitted in 304, and were quickly Romanized.

WAFD Egyptian nationalist party during the generation after the First World War. The name refers to the delegation, led by **Saad Zaghlul**, which asked the British High Commissioner in Cairo for permission to put the Egyptian case for independence to the British government. Exile of leaders by the British in 1919 led to violence, martial law, and a long crisis which ended in the British declaration of limited Egyptian independence in 1922, the grant of a constitution, 1923, and the assumption of power by the Wafd, now organized as a party, in 1924. It soon lost office, but its leaders, Zaghlul and then Nahas, played an important part in later activities and negotiations which led ultimately to the Anglo-Egyptian Treaty of 1936. Subsequently Nahas was Prime Minister on several occasions, including during much of the Second World War, and the Wafd continued to play the leading role as spokesmen of Egyptian aspirations for complete independence until dissolved after the military revolution of 1952. Reformed in 1978, the party soon dissolved itself. The New Wafd party boycotted the elections in 1990.

WAHABI Member of the Muslim puritan movement founded by Mohammed ibn Abd al-Wahab in the 18th century. Originating in the Nejd district of central Arabia, it was adopted by a local dynasty, the **Saudis**, who created the first Wahabi empire, crushed by **Mohammed Ali** of Egypt acting on behalf of the Ottomans in 1818; revived in the mid-19th century, it was again destroyed, this time by the Rashidis of northern Arabia. The state was reformed, and expanded by Ibn Saud to become the modern kingdom of Saudi Arabia in 1932, with the Wahabi version of Islam as its official faith.

WALDENSIANS (Waldenses) Christian movement founded around 1170 by Peter Waldo (or Valdez) (c.1140-1217), characterized by its poverty, simplicity and evangelism. The Waldensians (also known as the Poor Men of Lyons) exalted personal conduct and the setting of a good example above priestly ordination. Waldo preached no doctrinal heterodoxy (which distinguished his movement from that of the **Cathars** with their dualistic **Manichaeism**), but he was nevertheless critical of the manners of the clerical hierarchy of his time. He was condemned at the Council of Verona (1184) for preaching without licence. As they operated in much the same areas as the Cathars, the Waldensians were also attacked in the Albigensian Crusade of 1209. Although the victim of continual persecution, the Waldensian church still survives in some districts of northern Italy.

WAŁESA, LECH (1943-) President of Poland. The son of a carpenter, he became an electrician at the **Lenin** Shipyard in Gdansk (1967-76), the scene of violent anti-government protest in 1970. Although dismissed for unauthorized labour agitation, he remained active in the underground labour movement, founding Solidarity, a free trade union in 1979. Solidarity was crushed in 1981, by the Communist government, but survived under Walesa's leadership to win recognition again in 1989, in the wake of mass strikes and demonstrations. In 1990, Walesa was elected President of the Polish Republic.

WALLACE, SIR WILLIAM (c.1270-1305) Scottish national hero, son of Sir Matthew Wallace, a landowner near Renfrew. He organized resistance to the claims of the English king, **Edward I**, to rule Scotland, and annihilated a large English army near Stirling in 1297. He ravaged Northumberland and Durham, was badly defeated and discredited at Falkirk in the following year, and was arrested in Glasgow and executed in London in 1305.

WALLIS, SAMUEL (1728-95) Circumnavigator, discoverer of Tahiti, the Wallis Islands and some of the Tuamotu and Society Islands; in 1767 the British Admiralty sent him to survey the extent of Oceania.

WANG FU-CH'EN (d.1681) Chinese general. He was a subordinate of Wu San-kuei in the campaigns against the remnants of Ming forces in southwest China in the 1650s. In 1670 he became governor of Shensi. Wu San-kuei asked him to rebel in 1673 – he refused, and offered to lead his army against Wu. In 1674 he quarrelled with the Manchu commander sent against Wu and murdered him, joining the rebellion. In 1675-6 he controlled much of Shensi and Kansu, but surrendered to the Manchus in 1676 and committed suicide after the final failure of the rebellion.

WANG MANG (d. AD 23) Chinese emperor, known as 'the Usurper', founder of the short-lived Hsin dynasty, AD 9-23, which separated the two halves of the long Han period. He became regent to the imperial throne in 8 BC, at a time when the Han succession was confused; dismissed in 5 BC and reinstated four years later, he finally manoeuvred his way to supreme power in AD 9. By the time of his death a series of natural disasters and widespread rebellion, known as the Revolt of the Red Eyebrows, had precipitated his overthrow. This brought about the restoration of the Han line in AD 25. He instituted many reforms of administration and the economy, for which he claimed Confucian scriptural precedents. These sweeping reforms raised much discontent: for example, he attempted to nationalize land and free all slaves.

WARSAW PACT (Treaty of Friendship, Co-operation and Mutual Aid) Agreement signed in 1955 which formed the basis for mutual defence co-operation within the former Soviet bloc. The original participants were Albania, Bulgaria, Czechoslovakia, East Germany, Hungary, Poland, Romania and the Soviet Union, but Albania withdrew after the Soviet-led invasion of Czechoslovakia in 1968. East Germany withdrew after unification (1990). The Pact was formally wound up in March 1992.

WASHINGTON, GEORGE (1732-99) American soldier and statesman. A farmer and country gentleman of Virginia, as a lieutenant-colonel in the Virginia militia he fought against the French, 1754-8; married 'the prettiest and richest widow in Virginia' in 1759, and became one of the largest landowners in the state. He was a member of the Virginia House of Burgesses, 1759-74, and delegate to the first Continental Congress. Appointed commander of the colonial armies in 1775 on the suggestion of **John Adams**, despite several military defeats in 1777-8 he retained the confidence of Congress, and forced the British surrender at Yorktown in 1781. After the peace of 1783 he resigned his command and returned to farming. He was elected chairman of the Constitutional Convention, 1787, and first President of the United States, 1788 (inaugurated 30 April 1789); he was re-elected in 1792. Declining to serve a third term, he gave his 'Farewell Address' in September 1796.

WATERLOO, BATTLE OF Final defeat in 1815 of **Napoleon I**, Emperor of the French, by the armies of his enemies: Dutch and British forces led by the **Duke of Wellington**, Prussians led by Marshal von Blücher.

WATT, JAMES (1736-1819) Scottish inventor. At the age of 17 he started making mathematical instruments. In 1764, while repairing a model Newcomen pump, he started a series of improvements which transformed the steam engine into the major power unit of the Industrial Revolution: separate condenser (1765), sun-and-planet gear (1781), double-acting engine (1782), centrifugal governor (1788), pressure gauge (1790). He was elected a Fellow of the Royal Society in 1785.

WEDGWOOD, JOSIAH (1730-95) Leading English potter in the 18th century. He introduced great improvements in the manufacturing process, and in 1769 he opened his new Etruria factory; in 1774 he made two dinner services for **Catherine II** of Russia. Wedgwood played an active part in securing the construction of the Trent and Mersey Canal in 1777, which greatly improved the transport facilities of the pottery industry.

WEICHSEL GLACIAL STAGE *see* **Würm Glacial Stage**

WELLESLEY, RICHARD COLLEY (1760-1842) Marquis of Norragh. Anglo-Irish statesman and administrator, brother of the Duke of Wellington. Governor-General of Madras and of Bengal, 1797-1805, he defeated **Tipu**, Sultan of Mysore, but was recalled and threatened with impeachment over the cost and scale of his military annexations. As Lord Lieutenant of Ireland, 1821-8, and 1833-4, he tried to reconcile Protestants and Catholics.

WELLINGTON, DUKE OF (1769-1852) Victor of Waterloo and later Prime Minister of Great Britain. Born Arthur Wellesley, he gained an early military reputation in India, and was raised to the peerage after victories in the Peninsula War (1808-14). With the Prussian Marshal von Blücher he defeated **Napoleon I** in 1815 at Waterloo. A member of various Conservative Cabinets between 1818 and 1827, he became Prime Minister 1828-30, and opposition leader after the passing of the 1832 Reform Act.

WENCESLAS (1361-1419) King of Germany and Bohemia; son of Emperor Charles IV. His drunken and ineffective rule reduced Germany to anarchy between 1378 and 1389; deposed there in 1400, he clung on in Bohemia as a pawn of the aristocracy. He supported **Jan Hus** but failed to protect him from execution.

WESTERN RISINGS A popular English rebellion in 1549 in Cornwall and Devon against the introduction of a Protestant liturgy by Edward VI, which was defeated by government troops; also, in 1628-31, riots in southwest England against the efforts of **Charles I**'s government to enclose and cut down royal forests and thus deprive the local population of common rights.

WESTMINSTER, STATUTE OF (1931) Act of the Parliament of the United Kingdom declaring that the self-governing dominions of Canada, Australia, New Zealand, South Africa, Ireland and Newfoundland were to be regarded equally as 'autonomous communities' within the British Empire, though united by a common allegiance to the Crown. It recognized their sovereign right to control domestic and foreign affairs and to establish their own diplomatic corps.

WESTPHALIA, PEACE OF Name given to 11 separate treaties signed in 1648, after five years of negotiation, to end the Thirty Years' War. The **Habsburg** emperors lost most of their authority over the German princes, promised full toleration for Calvinist states, accepted the secularization of all Church land (carried out 1555-1624), and formally recognized the independence of the Swiss confederation. Sweden and Brandenburg made substantial territorial gains in north Germany; France gained extensive rights and territories in Alsace and Lorraine.

WETTIN Ancient German ruling dynasty, named after the castle of Wettin on Saale below Halle, which played a major role in German eastern expansion. Conrad (d.1156) received the March of Meissen. The dynasty split into two branches in 1485: the Ernestines in Thuringia, the Albertines in Saxony. The latter was a leading territorial state in Germany from 1555 to 1815.

WHITE LOTUS REBELLION The White Lotus was a Buddhist millenarian sect founded before the 13th century. Under the Manchu (**Ch'ing**) dynasty (1644-1911) it became an anti-dynastic movement, aiming to restore the **Ming**. Between 1796 and 1805 White Lotus leaders led a series of large-scale risings in the mountainous regions of central China, using guerrilla tactics; however, there was no coordination of the rebels, who were eventually contained and put down by the organization of local militias at vast expense.

WHITE RUSSIANS Traditional name for the people of Belorussia (White Russia).

WHITES, THE Name used during the Russian Civil War (1918-20) to describe the anti-Bolshevik forces which fought against the Communist Red Army, and after that to describe Russian emigrés.

WILFRID, ST (c.634-c.709) Born in Northumbria, he entered the monastery of Lindisfarne and, after the Synod of Whitby, became bishop of York. He fought to establish Roman customs; helped to convert the **Frisians** and the South Saxons; established monasteries at Ripon and Hexham; and encouraged **Willibrord** and Suidbert to evangelize the Saxons of Germany. His forceful personality and strong principles led to him twice being deposed from his see.

WILKINSON, JOHN (1728-1808) A pioneer English ironmaster who developed a greatly improved method of boring cylinders. The new technique was first used to bore cannon, and was then adapted to the production of boilers for steam engines. In 1779 Wilkinson cast the components for the first iron bridge, over the Severn at Coalbrookedale, and in 1787 built a small iron ship on the Severn.

WILLIAM I, THE CONQUEROR (c.1028-87) First Norman King of England, son of Robert I of Normandy whose dukedom he inherited in 1035, becoming effective ruler in 1042. In 1063 he annexed Maine, and in 1066 successfully invaded England, where he introduced major legal and religious reforms. From 1072 he spent most of his time in Normandy; in 1085 he ordered the compilation of the Domesday Book, a unique survey of English landholdings.

WILLIBALD, ST (c.700-86) Anglo-Saxon missionary in the eastern Mediterrranean and Germany, a nephew and associate of **St Boniface**. He was made Bishop of Eichstätt in 741.

WILLIBRORD, ST (658-739) Anglo-Saxon bishop and missionary, disciple of St Egbert in Ireland, 678-90. He was sent to convert the **Frisians**, and became their archbishop in 695. He worked with the **Merovingian** kings, Pepin II and **Charles Martel**, to extend Christianity in northern Europe. He died at his monastery of Echternach, and was adopted as the patron saint of Holland.

WILLOUGHBY, FRANCIS (c.1613-66) Founder of the British colony of Surinam. He first supported Parliament in the English Civil War, then joined the Royalists. As Lord Willoughby of Parham he was appointed Governor of Barbados in 1650, and the following year successfully implanted settlers in Surinam.

WILSON, WOODROW (1856-1924) 28th President of the United States, an outstanding chief executive whose two terms in office (1913-21) covered the First World War and the Paris Peace Conference. A controversial figure during the first years, Wilson won temporary fame as the world's greatest leader after the war, but his power and influence later declined. The US Senate repudiated the **League of Nations**, which he had ardently advocated, and ill-health sapped his capacity to govern.

WISCONSIN GLACIAL STAGE *see* **Würm**

WITOLD (1350-1430) Grandson of **Gedymin**, Lithuanian Grand Duke and national leader, also known in Lithuania as Vytautas the Great. He fought a long struggle with his cousin **Władysław II Jagiełło**, King of Poland, which ended in 1401 when Władysław recognized him as Grand Duke of Lithuania, while remaining his suzerain. In alliance, the cousins broke the power of the **Teutonic Order** at the battle of Tannenberg (Grünwald) in 1410.

WITTELSBACH Bavarian dynasty enfeoffed with the duchy of Bavaria after the fall of **Henry, Duke of Saxony** in 1180. A collateral line held the Palatinate from 1214 to 1777. The Bavarian Wittelsbachs, imperial supporters in the **Thirty Years' War**, were rewarded with the Upper Palatinate in 1648. Raised to the rank of king by Napoleon in 1806, they continued to rule until 1918.

WITTE, SERGEI YULYEVISH (1849-1915) Russian politician. Promoted the building of the Trans-Siberian railroad (begun 1891), known as the 'Witte system', linking European and Asiatic Russia. Russian minister of Communication (1892) and Finance (1892-1903) and first constitutional prime minister of the Russian Empire (1905-6). He sought to combine authoritarian rule with modernization along Western lines and persuaded Tsar Nicholas II to issue the 'October Manifesto' (1905) supporting a measure of representative government but fell from favour in 1906. He opposed Russia's entury into World War I and died dispirited, foreseeing disaster for the tsarist empire.

WŁADYSŁAW II JAGIEŁŁO (1351-1434) Grandson of Gedymin, son of **Olgierd**, Grand Duke of Lithuania (from 1377). On his marriage to Queen **Jadwiga** of Poland in 1386, he united the two crowns and styled himself Władysław II, King of Poland. At the head of Polish and Lithuanian armies he defeated the knights of the **Teutonic Order** at Tannenberg (Grünwald) in 1410. He gave his name to the **Jagiellonian** dynasty.

WOLFE, JAMES (1727-59) British general. He served in the Low Countries, Scotland and Cape Breton Islands before commanding the British army at the capture of Quebec in 1759; after defeat at Beauport, he climbed the Heights of Abraham to surprise and rout the French army. He thus gained Canada for Britain, but died of wounds during the battle.

WORMS, CONCORDAT OF Agreement concluded in 1122 between Pope Calixtus II and Emperor Henry V, which ended the Investiture Contest in compromise. The Emperor conceded full freedom of election to episcopal office, surrendering the claim to bestow spiritual authority by investiture; but bishops were to be elected in his presence so that he might nevertheless influence the elector's choice. Thus neither side gained all that **Gregory VII** and **Henry IV** had demanded, but each secured valuable concessions from the other; papal headship of the Church was recognized, but the emperor retained some control over its leaders in Germany.

WRIGHT BROTHERS American aviation pioneers. Together Orville Wright (1871-1948) and his brother Wilbur (1867-1912) built the first stable, controllable, heavier-than-air flying machine, which made its first successful flights (the longest of 852 feet, 260 m) at Kitty Hawk, North Carolina, in 1903.

WU P'EI-FU (1874-1939) Chinese warlord. He served with the Pei-yang armies under **Yüan Shih-k'ai**, and with the Japanese army during the Russo-Japanese War of 1904-5. After Yüan's death in 1916, Wu became the most powerful general of the Pei-yang armies, and in 1922 drove back the Manchurian armies of **Chang Tso-lin**. This made him China's most powerful military figure, and he dominated the shaky Peking government from 1922-4. His ruthless suppression of a workers' strike on the Hankow-Peking railway in 1923 cost him much of his popularity and the support of his main ally **Feng Yu-hsiang**. Decisively defeated by Chang near Tientsin in 1924, he retreated to Hupeh; in 1925-6 allied himself with Chang in a war against Feng Yu-hsiang and invaded Honan. In 1926-7 he was defeated by **Chiang Kai-shek**'s Northern Expedition and took refuge in Szechwan; he took no further major part in affairs.

WÜRM GLACIAL STAGE The latest phase of major ice advance in Alpine Europe, starting c.70,000 years ago and ending around 10,000 years ago; it is equivalent to the Wisconsin period in North America and Weichsel in Scandinavia.

WU SAN-KUEI (1612-78) Chinese general. He served in the **Ming** armies, defending the northeast frontier against the **Manchus**, but he appealed to the Manchus for aid when Peking was attacked in 1644 by the rebel **Li Tzu-ch'eng** (c.1605-45), and with their aid drove Li from Peking, where the Manchus set up the **Ch'ing** dynasty. He refused appeals to aid a restoration of the **Ming** emperors, and commanded the southwest province of Yunnan on behalf of the Manchus, growing increasingly powerful and eventually controlling much of southwest and west China. In 1673 he led the Rebellion of the Three Feudatories and attempted to set up his own Chou dynasty; invading central China in 1674. He died of dysentery three years before the rebellion was finally crushed in 1681.

WU-TI (156-87 BC) Powerful Chinese emperor of the former **Han** period, eleventh son of Emperor Ching Ti. He succeeded to the throne in 140 BC; aggressively extended China's frontiers to include much of south and southwest China, north Vietnam, northern Korea and much of central Asia, and established effective defences against the **Hsiung-nu** in the north. He finally established the supremacy of the emperor, created a tightly knit bureaucracy, levied unprecedented taxes and made Confucianism the state religion.

WYATT'S REBELLION English uprising in 1554 against the marriage of Mary Tudor (reigned 1553-8) to Philip II of Spain. Three thousand men from Kent marched on London and reached Fleet Street before surrendering; their leader, Sir Thomas Wyatt (son of the poet of the same name), was executed, and Princess Elizabeth, later Queen **Elizabeth I** (whom Wyatt had wished to place on the throne) was imprisoned in the Tower of London.

WYCLIF, JOHN (c.1329-84) Religious reformer and translator of the Bible into English. As a vigorous anti-clerical he was patronized by John of Gaunt, who continued to support him, but not his views, when he denied the miracle of transubstantiation in the Mass; he was condemned as a heretic in 1381. His followers are known as **Lollards**.

WYNFRITH *see* **Boniface, St**

WYNTER, JAN WILLEM DE (1761-1812) Dutch admiral and politician. In 1785 he led the 'patriot party' which deposed the Stadholder William V, but fled to France when William was restored in 1787. In 1795 he accompanied the French army which conquered the Netherlands, and the French placed him in charge of the Dutch navy; in 1797 he led it to its defeat by the British at the battle of Camperdown.

XENOPHON (c.430-c.355 BC) Greek soldier and author. He studied with Socrates, about whom he wrote the *Memorabilia*, *Symposium* and *Apology*. His *Anabasis* describes the epic retreat of 10,000 mercenaries from Persia after the failure of Cyrus the Younger's expedition against Artaxerxes II. In exile he wrote the *Hellenica*, a history of Greece, and other works on sport and politics.

XERXES I (c.520-465 BC) King of Persia (reigned 486-465 BC). Son of **Darius I** by his second marriage; chosen to succeed over his elder brother. He reconquered Egypt, which had rebelled at the end of Darius' reign; invaded Greece in 480 after digging a canal through the Mount Athos peninsula, forced the pass at Thermopylae and occupied Athens before meeting a crushing defeat at Salamis (480) by sea and at Plataea (479) by land. He was responsible for the finest work at the Persian capital of Persepolis. He was assassinated by conspirators headed by his chief guard, Artabanus.

XHOSA A people, and their Bantu language, in Cape Province, South Africa; now the inhabitants of the Transkei, the first so-called 'independent homeland' inside South Africa.

YAHYA KHAN, AGHA MOHAMMED (1917-82) Pakistan soldier and politician. Commander in East Pakistan (now Bangladesh), 1962-4; commander-in-chief of the Pakistan army, 1966-9, and President of Pakistan and chief administrator of martial law, 1969-71. He was forced to resign after his failure to suppress the revolt in east Pakistan which led to the setting up of the state of Bangladesh.

YALTA CONFERENCE Meeting of Allied war leaders (led by **Roosevelt**, **Churchill** and **Stalin**) at Yalta in the Crimea, 4-11 February 1945. It reaffirmed the decision to demand unconditional Axis surrender, planned a four-power occupation of Germany, and agreed a further meeting to finalize plans for the **United Nations**. It was also agreed that the British and Americans would repatriate all Russians in Allied hands. Stalin, for his part, was prompted to declare war on Japan.

YAO Mountain-dwelling people of south and southwest China and of Southeast Asia, related to the Miao who share a similar heritage of Sino-Tibetan languages. In Kwangtung some have turned to wet-rice cultivation, but most remain in the highlands practising primitive slash-and-burn agriculture.

YEN HSI-SHAN (1883-1960) Chinese general and military governor. A Japanese-trained army officer, he emerged as a warlord in Shansi after the overthrow of the **Ch'ing** (Manchu) dynasty in 1911, and ruled as absolute dictator of the whole region from 1917 until the end of the Second World War. In 1930 he joined **Feng Yu-hsiang** in an abortive northern alliance against **Chiang Kai-shek**, but was afterwards confirmed in command of Shansi, where he instituted a sweeping programme of provincial reforms in 1934. In 1937 he lost most of Shansi to the Japanese, and from 1939 was in constant conflict with the Chinese Communists. He was driven from the province in early 1949; he went to Taiwan and became premier until 1950.

YEZHOV, NIKOLAI IVANOVICH (1894-1939?) Soviet political leader who joined the Communist party in 1917 and served as a political commissar in the Red Army. He was a member of the Central Committee of the Soviet Communist party from 1934 and headed the people's commissariat of internal affairs (NKVD) (1936-8), which under his direction carried out **Stalin**'s purges. As a result, his name became inextricably linked with the Great Terror (Yezhovshchina). He was probably assassinated in 1939, but the circumstances surrounding his death remain unknown.

YORKSHIRE RISING Major revolt in 1489 against the attempts of the English King **Henry VII** to collect a parliamentary grant of £75,000. The king's lieutenant, the Earl of Northumberland, was killed before the rebels were suppressed.

YOUNG TURKS Popular name for the Committee of Union and Progress, an association of army officers and others who compelled sultan **Abdül Hamid II** to restore the 1876 constitution in 1908 and deposed him in 1909. Subsequently it became the Ottoman Empire's dominant political party, in 1914 bringing Turkey into the First World War. It was disbanded after the Central Powers' defeat in 1918.

YÜAN SHIH-K'AI (1859-1916) First President of the Republic of China. He was sent to Korea with the Anhwei army, 1882, and became Chinese commissioner in Seoul, 1885-94; he helped to create a new model army after defeat by Japan in 1895. In 1901 he became viceroy of China's metropolitan province, Chihli, and commander of China's most powerful army, the Pei-yang chün. He was removed from his post in 1907 but exercised power through his former military subordinates, and was recalled by the **Ch'ing** (Manchus) after the outbreak of the 1911 revolution as supreme commander. In 1912 he was recommended by the Emperor to be President, replacing the provisional President, **Sun Yat-sen**; increasingly dictatorial, he precipitated civil war in 1913 by murdering the revolutionary party chairman, and in 1916 tried to create a new imperial dynasty.

YUDENICH, NIKOLAI NIKOLAYEVICH (1862-1933) Russian general. After service in the Russo-Japanese war and the First World War, he took command of the anti-Bolshevik forces in the Baltic after the Russian Revolution. In 1919, with some British support he led an unsuccessful advance on Leningrad (then called Petrograd, now reverted to St Petersburg), and went into exile.

YÜEH-CHIH Central Asian peoples, first identified in Chinese sources in the 2nd century BC, living as nomads in Kansu, northwest China. Under attack by the **Hsiung-nu**, they moved west into Sogdiana and Bactria, displacing the Greek rulers there, c.150 BC. Their descendants, with the **Tocharians**, founded the Kushan Empire, ruling northern India and central Asia until about AD 300. Yüeh-chih and Kushan missionaries helped spread **Buddhism** and Indian culture to China.

YUNG-LO (CHU TI) (1360-1424) Chinese emperor, the third of the **Ming** dynasty, and fourth son of Hung-wu. He rebelled against his nephew in 1399, and seized the throne in 1402 after two years of destructive civil war. He invaded Annam, 1406-7, and began a series of major maritime expeditions into the Indian Ocean. He personally conducted campaigns to crush the Mongols in 1410, 1414 and 1422-4, and expanded Chinese power in Manchuria and the Amur valley. He rebuilt the Grand Canal, and transferred the capital from Nanking to Peking in 1421.

ZAGHLUL, SAAD (1857-1927) Leader of Egyptian nationalism during that period when it first became a mass movement. He became prominent as a minister and politician before 1914; from 1918 he was leader of the **Wafd**, and in 1924 was appointed Prime Minister shortly after the British declaration of limited independence for Egypt; he was, however, forced to resign soon afterwards.

ZAGWE Ethiopian dynasty of Semitic origin which displaced the Axumite kings in the 12th and 13th centuries. It did much to expand and centralize the Christian empire of Ethiopia.

ZAIBATSU Large-scale Japanese business groups, normally organized around the commercial, industrial and financial interests of a single family. The biggest and best known were the Mitsui, Mitsubishi, Yasuda and Sumitomo empires, all of which grew up and flourished in the period from 1868 to 1945. In 1946, after Japan's defeat, the Zaibatsu were ordered to dissolve into their component companies, but most are now, for practical purposes, reassembled and even more formidable than before.

ZAIDI Dynasty of rulers in Yemen, southern Arabia. Founded by imam al-Hadi in northern Yemen in the 9th century, they expanded their power in the 12th century, and again after 1635, when they expelled the Ottoman Turks. Driven back to northern Yemen in the 1710s, they were forced to recognise Ottoman suzerainty in 1849. After the Ottoman collapse in 1918 they became rulers of all Yemen until a military coup in 1962 deposed the last Zaidi imam.

ZANGI (1084-1146) Iraqi warrior who inflicted the first serious defeat on Christian crusaders, recapturing Edessa in 1144. He founded the Zangid dynasty, which ruled northern Iraq and Syria, 1127-1222.

ZANGIDS Muslim Turkish dynasty, ruling northern Iraq and part of Syria from 1127 to 1222. It was founded by Zangi (1127-46), who mounted the first Islamic counterattack against the Christian **Crusades**. **Saladin**, founder of the **Ayyubid** dynasty in Egypt, was a Zangid general, and ultimately brought the family territories under his rule.

ZAPATA, EMILIANO (1879-1919) Mexican revolutionary leader. He supported **Madero** in the 1911 overthrow of **Díaz**; forbidden to redistribute land to the peasants, he issued the Plan of Ayala and renewed revolution under the slogan 'Land and Liberty'. He fought constantly, first against the dictator Huerta in 1913, and then with **Pancho Villa** against the moderate government of **Carranza**. He was ambushed and assassinated.

ZARATHUSTRA *see* **Zoroaster**

ZEALOTS Extremist Jewish resistance party against the Roman domination of Judaea. It played a major part in the **Jewish uprising** of AD 66-73.

ZENO OF CITIUM (c.334-c.262 BC) Ancient Greek philosopher, founder of **Stoicism**.

ZENO OF ELEA (c.490-c.430 BC) Ancient Greek philosopher, best known for his paradoxes demonstrating the unreality of motion.

ZEUS Supreme god of Greek mythology, also identified with the Roman Jupiter; born in Crete (Mount Ida), son of Rhea and Cronus, whom he overthrew.

ZHIVKOV, TODOR (1911-) Bulgarian political leader. He worked as a printer in Bulgarian communist circles in the 1930s. Some claim he led the coup overthrowing the pro-German regime in 1944. He served as secretary of the Bulgarian communist party in 1954, premier in 1962 and president in 1971 but resigned in November 1989 when communist power in eastern Europe collapsed.

ZHUKOV, GEORGIY KONSTANTINOVICH (1896-1976) Marshal of the Soviet Union and leading Russian hero of the Second World War. He served in the Imperial Russian Army, 1915-17, joining the Red Army in 1918; he was cavalry commander in the Civil War. In command of the Mongolian-Manchurian frontier, in 1939, he became General Officer commanding the Kiev Military District in 1940, and in 1941 Chief of the General Staff. He directed the defence of Leningrad and then Moscow after the German invasion; was appointed Marshal in 1943; and led the final assault on Berlin in 1945. He was briefly commander-in-chief of the Soviet forces in Germany, GOC of Odessa Military District 1948-52; Minister of Defence 1955, after supporting **Khrushchev** against Malenkov. He was dismissed in 1957 and retired into private life.

ZIONISM Jewish national movement. It emerged in the latter part of the 19th century, and was placed on a firm and permanent organizational basis by Theodor Herzl, author of *The Jewish State*, who convened the first Zionist Congress at Basle in 1897. It sought the creation of a Jewish national homeland in Palestine which most Jews regarded as their ancestral land; this aim was achieved in 1948 when the United Nations voted to create the state of Israel.

ZIRIDS Muslim Berber dynasty ruling, under various branches, Tunisia, eastern Algeria and Granada from 972 to 1152. They were given a free hand in northwest Africa when their suzerain, the **Fatimid** caliph al-Muizz, moved his capital to Cairo. They were finally conquered by the **Almohads**.

ZOLLVEREIN German customs union established in 1834 when 18 states, some of which had formerly belonged to the Prussian, central German and southern German customs unions, formed, under Prussian auspices, a free trade area. By 1841 most German states had joined; Hanover and Oldenburg joined in 1854; Austria remained outside; Schleswig-Holstein, Lauenburg, Lübeck and the Mecklenburgs joined after the defeat of Austria in 1866 by Prussia, whose power in Germany had been much enhanced by the Zollverein. Hamburg and Bremen joined in 1888.

ZOROASTER (Zarathustra) Prophet and religious reformer of ancient Iran, the founder of Zoroastrianism. His personal writings were the Old Iranian texts known as the *Gathas*, in which he emphasized the ethical aspects of religion against mere conformity with ritual requirements. Theologically, these ideas were expressed in the cult of Ahura Mazda, 'the Wise Lord', as the highest god, in opposition to beliefs never defined but which some have thought included forms of Mithraism. Thus arose the 'dualistic' theology of later Zoroastrianism. which depicts creation not as the immediate rule of an omnipotent just god, but as a long contest between the divine forces of good and evil. This theology provides a simple solution for the problem of suffering, and may have influenced theories concerning the role of Satan in developing Christianity.

ZOSER (Djoser) Second king of Egypt's IIIrd Dynasty; he is traditionally said to have reigned for 19 years during the 27th century BC. With his chief minister and architect, **Imhotep**, he built the first of the great stone pyramids at Saqqara, near his capital, Memphis.

ZULU Nguni-speaking group in Natal, southern Africa. In the early 19th century they joined with related peoples under Shaka, their leader, to form the Zulu empire. They engaged in sporadic warfare with other African peoples and with the advancing European settlers, and were finally defeated in 1879 at Ulundi, now capital of KwaZulu, one of South Africa's Bantu so-called 'independent homelands'.

ZÜRICH, PEACE OF Agreement in 1859 between **Napoleon III** of France and Franz Joseph of Austria to settle the Italian problem after a general rebellion against Austrian rule. Lombardy was ceded to Piedmont, Venetia remained Austrian (to 1866); the central states of Italy voted to join Piedmont, and Nice and Savoy voted to become French (1860).

ZWINGLI, HULDREICH (1484-1531) Swiss religious reformer. He was pastor in Glarus, 1506, and rector and teacher of religion at the Great Minster, Zürich, 1519. He established the Protestant Reformation in Zürich, 1520-3, although failing to agree about doctrine with **Luther** and other German reformers, 1529. He was killed at the battle of Kappel while serving as chaplain in Zürich's army during its campaign against the Swiss Catholics.

ZYRIANS Finno-Ugrian speaking Arctic people, mostly inhabiting the Komi area of northwest Russia.

Index

1 HISTORICAL PLACE NAMES

Geographical names vary with time and with language, and there is some difficulty in treating them consistently in an historical atlas which covers the whole world from the beginning of human pre-history, especially for individual maps within whose time span the same place has been known by many different names. We have aimed at the simplest possible approach to the names on the maps, using the index to weld together the variations.

On the maps forms of names will be found in the following hierarchy of preference:-

a English conventional names or spellings, in the widest sense, for all principal places and features, e.g., Moscow, Vienna, Munich, Danube (including those that today might be considered obsolete when these are appropriate to the context, e.g., Leghorn).

b Names that are contemporary in terms of the maps concerned. There are here three broad categories:-

i names in the ancient world, where the forms used are classical, e.g., Latin or latinized Greek, but extending also to Persian, Sanskrit, etc.

ii names in the post-medieval modern world, which are given in the form (though not necessarily the spelling current at the time of the map (e.g., St. Petersburg before 1914, not Leningrad); whose language reflects the sovereignty then existing, e.g., Usküb (Turkish) rather than Skoplje (Serbian) or Skopje (Macedonian) in maps showing Ottoman rule.

iii names in the present-day world, where the spelling generally follows that of *The Times Atlas of the World*, though in the interests of simplicity there has been a general omission of diacritics in spellings derived by transliteration from non-roman scripts, e.g., Sana rather than Şan'ā'.

On the spelling of Chinese names, readers will be increasingly aware of the Pinyin romanizations that have come into use over the last ten years (e.g., Beijing, Qin dynasty) but the atlas continues to spell Chinese names in the conventional forms and Wade-Giles romanizations that are still more generally found in historical contexts (e.g. Peking, Ch'in dynasty). However, all Chinese names that occur as main entries in the index give the Pinyin spelling in brackets, and there are cross-references from all Pinyin forms to the traditional spellings used in the atlas.

Alternative names and spellings have occasionally been shown in brackets on the maps to aid in identification.

2 THE INDEX

The index does not include every name shown on the maps. In general only those names are indexed which are of places, features, regions or countries where "something happens", i.e., which carry a date or symbol or colour explained in the key, or which are mentioned in the text.

Where a place is referred to by two or more different names in the course of the atlas, there will be a corresponding number of main entries in the index. The variant names in each case are given in brackets at the beginning of the entry, their different forms and origins being distinguished by such words as *now*, *later*, *formerly* and others included in the list of abbreviations (*right*).

"Istanbul (*form.* Constantinople, *anc.* Byzantium)" means that the page references to that city on maps dealing with periods when it was known as Istanbul follow that entry, but the page references pertaining to it when it had other names will be found under those other names.

Places are located generally by reference to the country in which they lie (exceptionally by reference to island groups or sea areas), this being narrowed down by where necessary by location as E(ast), N(orth), C(entral), etc. The reference will normally be to the modern state in which the place now falls unless (a) there is a conventional or historical name which conveniently avoids the inevitably anachronistic ring of some modern names, e.g., Anatolia rather than Turkey, Mesopotamia rather than Iraq, or (b) the modern state is little known or not delineated on the map concerned, e.g., many places on the Africa plates can only be located as W.,E., Africa, etc.

Though page references are generally kept in numerical order, since this corresponds for the most part with chronological order, they have been rearranged occasionally where the chronological sequence would be obviously wrong, or in interests

of grouping appropriate references under a single sub-heading.

All variant names and spellings are cross-referenced in the form "Bourgogne (Burgundy)", except those which would immediately precede or follow the main entries to which they refer. The bracketed form has been chosen so that such entries may also serve as quick visual indications of equivalence. The Bourgogne (Burgundy) means not only "see under Burgundy" but also that Burgundy is another name for Bourgogne.

Reference is generally to page number/map number (e.g., pages 114/2) unless the subject is dealt with over the plate as a whole, when the reference occurs as 114-5 (i.e., pages 114 and 115). All entries with two or more references have been given sub-headings where possible, e.g., Civil War 268/3. Battles are indicated by the symbol ✕.

3 ABBREVIATIONS

Alatri – Argentina

Alatri (Aletrium)
Alawites people of NW Syria, uprising 257/2
Alba Fucens C Italy 87/1
Alba Iulia (anc. Apulum Hung. Gyulafehérvár Ger. Karlsburg) Romania Mithraic site 72/1
Albania Slav settlement 112/4; Black Death 141/1; Ottoman control 183/1; principality 211/2; Ottoman province 225/1; WW1 248-9; Muslim insurrection 263/2; inter-war alliances 260/2, 264/2; annexed by Italy 265/4; WW2 265/5, 268/1, 269/3; withdraws from Warsaw Pact 270/1; Cold War, 293/1; economy 271/4, communism overthrown 290/3
Albania ancient country of Caucasus vassal of Parthian Empire 79/3; 86/3, 89/1, 113/1
Albany (form. Fort Orange) NE USA surrenders to Dutch 157/2
Albany W Australia founded 233/5
Albazinsk SE Siberia founded 158/3
Alberta province of Canada economic development 215/2
Albertville (now Kalémié) E Belgian Congo 280/2
Alborán Island Morocco Spanish occupation 247/2
Ålborg N Denmark flintmine 42/2
Albret region of SW France 147/3
Alcalá S Portugal site 42/2
Alcazarquivir (Al-Kasr-al-Kabir)
Aldeigjuborg (Staraya Ladoga)
Aleksandropol (Leninakan)
Alemanni tribe of C Europe 99/1
Alemannia region of C Europe 156/1, 107/3
Alençon N France fief annexed by France 147/3; provincial capital 189/1
Alep (Aleppo)
Aleppo (anc. Beroea a/c Yamkhad Fr. Alep Ar. Halab) Syria 54/1; bishopric 101/1; Byzantine Empire 113/1,5; early trade 133/1; conquest by Ottomans 137/1; Ottoman centre 166/1; 18C trade 195/1; economy 283/1
Aleria (Alalia)
Alesia (mod. Alise-Sainte-Reine) C France 86/3
Alessandria N Italy Lombard League 119/2; Signorial domain 122/2
Aletum NW France monastery 93/3
Aletrium (mod. Alatri) C Italy 87/1
Aleut tribe of Alaska 35/2
Aleutian Islands W Alaska 243/1; WW2 266-7
Alexander's Empire 76-77; 82/3
Alexandreschata (Alexandria Eschata)
Alexandretta (mod. Iskenderun) E Turkey Achaemenid Empire 79/1; ceded to Turkey 261/1
Alexandria (Ar. Al Iskandariyah) Egypt spread of Christianity 72/1; Alexander's route 76/1; Persian Empire 79/1; Roman Empire 86/3, 89/1, 91/1; Christian centre 92-3; patriarchate 101/2; trade 71/1, 82/4, 133/1, 142/1, 150/2, 195/1; early Jewish community 103/1; Arab conquest 105/1; conquered by Ottomans 137/1; WW2 269/3
Alexandria NW India Alexander's route 77/1
Alexandria (mod. Gulashkird) S Persia Alexander's route 77/1
Alexandria (mod. Charikar) Afghanistan 82/3
Alexandria (mod. Ghazni) Alexander's Route 77/1; 82/3
Alexandria (later Merv since 1937 Mary) C Asia 77/1
Alexandria ad Caucasum Afghanistan Alexander's route 77/1
Alexandria Arachoton (mod. Qandahar Eng. Kandahar) Afghanistan Alexander's route 77/1; Achaemenid Empire 79/1; 82/3
Alexandria Areion (mod. Herat) Afghanistan Alexander's route 77/1; Achaemenid Empire 79/1; 82/3
Alexandria Eschata (a/c Alexandreschata) C Asia Alexander's route 77/1; Achaemenid Empire 79/1; 82/3
Alexandria Opiana NW India Alexander's route 77/1
Alexandria Prophthasia (mod. Farah) Afghanistan Alexander's route 77/1; Achaemenid Empire 79/1
Alexandria Troas W Anatolia Roman Empire 89/1
Al Fas (Fez)
Alger (Algiers)
Algeria under the Almohads 132/1; vassalized by Turks 182/1; Spanish conquests 182/2; economy under French rule 214/1; Ottoman province 224/1; French invasion 235/1; French colonization 236-7, 240/1; immigration from France 205/2; overseas province of France 256/1; under Vichy control 265/5; civil war 280/3; independence 272/2; political development 281/1; economy 295/1
Algiers (Fr. Alger Sp. Argel Ar. Al Jaza'ir anc. Icosium) N Algeria Saharan trade 134/2; Mediterranean trade 142/1; Corsair city 163/1; Ottoman rule 166/1, 224/1; Spanish occupation 182/2; Allied landing WW2 269/3; 281/1
Algonkin (a/s Algonquin) Indian tribe of C Canada 35/2, 145/1
Al Hadhr (Hatra)
Al Hira Mesopotamia town of Parthian Empire 78/3
Al Hoceima (Alhucemas)
Alhucemas (n/s Al Hoceima) N Morocco Spanish occupation 247/2
Al Hudaydah (Hodeida)
Alice Springs C Australia 233/5
Aligarh N India centre of Mutiny 230/1
Ali Kosh Mesopotamia early village 40/1
Ali Murad NW India Harappan site 65/1
Alise-Sainte-Reine (Alesia)
Al Iskandariyah (Alexandria)
Al Jaza'ir (Algiers)
Al-Kasr-al-Kabir (Sp. Alcazarquivir a/c Battle of the Three Kings) Morocco ⚔ 163/1 (inset), 183/2
Al Khalil (Hebron)
Allahabad NE India Mughal province 169/1; Indian Mutiny 230/1; industry 214/1; Hindu-Muslim clashes 279/3
Allahdino NW India pre-Harappan site 65/1
Allenstein (Pol. Olsztyn) W Poland acquired by Germany after plebiscite 261/1
Allifae C Italy early town 87/1
Alma-Ata (until 1921 Vernyy) C Asia urban growth 288/3; industry 289/1
Al Madinah (Medina)
Al Mahdiya Tunisia Mediterranean trade 132/1
Al Makkah (Mecca)
Almalyk Mongolia bishopric 101/1
Almanaza Spain ⚔ 188/3
Al Mawsil (Mosul)
Almería S Spain Mediterranean trade 120/2, 132/1, 142/1
Almizaraque S Spain site 42/2
Almoravids Muslim dynasty of Morocco 133/1; North African empire 135/1
Almohads Muslim dynasty and empire of North Africa 132-3; 135/1
Alpes Cottiae Roman province, France/Italy, 89/1
Alpes Maritimae Roman province, France/Italy 89/1
Alpes Penninae Roman province, France/Italy 89/1
Alpirsbach SW Germany monastery 121/3
Al Qadisiya Mesopotamia ⚔ 78/3, 105/1
Al Qahirah (Cairo)
Al Quds (Jerusalem)
Al Raydaniyya N Egypt ⚔ 137/1
Alsace (anc. Alsatia Ger. Elsass) Magyar invasions 111/1; acquired by Habsburgs, 182/1; Burgundian possession 147/2; acquired by French 188-9; customs union 213/1; WW1 248/2
Alsace-Lorraine (Ger. Elsass-Lothringen) region of E France annexed by German Empire 212/3; ceded to France 261/1
Alsatia (Alsace)
Alsium (mod. Palo) C Italy Roman colony 87/1
Altendorf W Germany Megalithic site 42/2
Altmark region of E Germany 119/1
Altona N Germany customs union 213/1
Altun Ha E Mexico Maya site 46/2
Alwa early Christian kingdom of the Sudan 135/1
Amalfi S Italy Byzantine port 120/2
Amara NW India pre-Harappan site 65/1
Amarapura C Burma early trade centre 173/1
Amasela N Turkey early archbishopric 93/1
Amasia (mod. Amasya) E Anatolia Roman Empire 89/1; Byzantine Empire 112/3
Amastris (earlier Sesamus) N Anatolia Byzantine Empire 112/3
Amasya (anc. Amasia) C Turkey Ottoman town 166/1
Amathus Cyprus ancient Greek colony 75/1
Ambianum (Amiens)
Amboina C Indonesia massacre of English 172/2; trade centre 173/1; WW2 267/2
Ambon E Indies 18C trade 195/1
Ambracia NW Greece 76/4
Ambriz Angola Portuguese settlement 235/1
Amchitka Aleutian Is, Alaska WW2 267/2
Amecameca Mexico on Cortés' route 155/2
America, Central (a/c Mesoamerica) early peoples 36-7; agricultural origins 38/1; early civilizations 46/2, 47/1; Aztec Empire 144/2; Indian tribes 145/1; early voyages of discovery 152/2; colonial expansion 161/1; 18C trade 195/1; exports and foreign investment 222/3; population 222/4; recent development 284-5, 294/1
America, North early man 33/1, 36-7, 37/4; agricultural origins 38/1; early cultures 46/3, 47/1; Indian tribes 145/1; early voyages of discovery 152/1; colonial expansion, 160-1; European colonial rivalry 190-1; 18C trade 194/3; immigration from Europe 205/2; industrialization 215/1; range of buffalo 217/5; Peyote drug cult 217/6; Ghost dance 217/6. See also Canada, United States
America, South early peoples 36-7; agricultural origins 38/1; early civilizations 47/1,4,5; Indian tribes 145/1; Inca Empire 145/3; early voyages of discovery 152/1; colonial expansion 161/1,2; 18C trade 194/3; revolts against Spain 198/1; industrialization 215/1; independence 222-3; immigration from Europe 205/2; economic development 284/2, 294/1; drug trade 294/1; modern politics 285/1; population 285/3
American Colonies trade 195/1
American Samoa (f/c Eastern Samoa) S Pacific 243/1, 273/2 (inset)
Amida (mod. Diyarbakir) E Anatolia 78/3; 89/1; archbishopric and monastery 93/1,3; trade 133/1
Amiens (anc. Samarobriva later Ambianum) N France bishopric 117/1; Burgundian possession 147/2; 17C revolt 181/1; provincial capital 189/1; French Revolution 199/2; industrial development 206/1; WW1 248-9
Amisus (mod. Samsun) N Anatolia Ionian colony 75/1; Roman Empire 86/3; early archbishopric 93/1; Byzantine Empire 112/3
Amiternum C Italy 87/1
Amman (Bibl. Rabbath Ammon anc. Philadelphia) Jordan 225/1, 283/1
Ammon, Sanctuary of Egypt Alexander's route 76/1
Amnisos Crete Mycenaean settlement 67/2
Amöneburg W Germany monastery 100/3
Amorites people of Arabia, kingdom 55/2
Amorium C Anatolia Byzantine Empire, 112-3
Amoy (n/s Xiamen W/G Hsia-men) S China early trade 157/1; industry 214/1; treaty port 228/2; Anglo-French attacks 229/1; Japanese influence 239/2; occupied by Japanese 259/3, 264/3, 267/2
Amphipolis N Greece ⚔ 74/4, 78/3; Roman Empire 91/1; early church 93/1
Amri NW India Harappan site 65/1
Amritsar N India town of Punjab 231/3, 278/1, 279/3; political disturbances under British rule 257/1; police action against Sikh insurgents 279/3
Amselfeld (Kosovo)
Amsterdam Netherlands trading port 176/3; 16C urban development 176/1; 18C financial centre 177/2; imperial trade 194-5; industrial development 206/1, 208/1
Amud Palestine site of early man 32/2
Amur River (Chin. Heilong Jiang W/G Hei-lung Chiang) Russia/China border 158/3; Russian conflict with Japan 264/2; border conflict with China 275/1
Anadyrsk E Siberia founded 158/3
Anagnia (mod. Anagni) C Italy early town 87/1
Anantapur S India ceded to Britain 168/3
Anatolia early settlement 41/1; early trade routes 54/1; ethnic movements 54/3; Muslim conquest 133/2; Ottoman conquest 137/1; Black Death 141/1 See also Asia Minor
Anatolic Theme Anatolia district of Byzantine Empire 112/3
Anazarbus SW Anatolia early archbishopric 93/1; early Jewish community 103/1; Byzantine Empire 112/3
Ancona N Italy Roman Empire 87/1, 91/1
Ancyra (mod. Ankara obs. Eng. Angora) W Anatolia Alexander's route 76/1; Roman Empire 86/3, 89/1, 91/1; early archbishopric 93/1; Byzantine Empire 112-3
Åndalsnes C Norway WW2 265/5
Andalusia (Sp. Andalucía) region of S Spain reconquest by Castile 122/3
Andaman Islands Indian territory of Bay of Bengal 231/3, 241/1
Andegavum (earlier Juliomagus mod. Angers) W France 92/1
Anderab Afghanistan Alexander's route 82/3
Andernach (anc. Antunnacum) W Germany ⚔ 118/2
Andhra region of E India 65/1
Andhra Pradesh state of S India 279/3
Anding (An-ting)
Andorra population growth 294/2
Andover S England Industrial Revolution 197/1
Andredescester S England ⚔ 99/3
Andredesweald Anglo-Saxon region of S England 99/3
Anegray E France early monastery 100/3
Anga region of NE India 65/1, 83/1,2
Angarsk S Siberia urban growth 288/3; industry 289/1
Angers (anc. Juliomagus med. Andegavum) W France 17C revolt 181/1; French Revolution 199/2
Anghelu Ruju Sardinia burial site 43/1
Angkor Cambodia Buddhist site 73/1
Angkor Borei S Cambodia Hindu-Buddhist remains 131/2
Angkor Wat Cambodia temple complex 131/2
Angles tribe of NW Europe, migrations 94/1, 98-9
Anglo-Egyptian Sudan Ottoman territory under British control 241/1; condominium 236/2, 256/1, 272/1
Angola SW Africa early Portuguese trade 155/1; Portuguese exploration 162/2; Portuguese colonization 214/1, 236-7, 241/1; anti-Portuguese risings 245/2; independence 272/2; political development 281/1; economy 295/1
Angora (Ankara)
Angostura Venezuela 222/2
Angoulême (anc. Iculisma) C France provincial capital 189/1
Angoumois C France region annexed to France 147/3
Anguilla island of West Indies settled by English 156/3; independence 273/2 (inset)
Anhalt C Germany principality and duchy 119/1, 187/1; Reformation 178/2; 212/3
An-hsi (n/s Anxi) N China trade 71/1
Anhui (Anhwei)
Anhwei (n/s Anhui) province of E China under the Ming 165/1; Manchu expansion 171/1; T'ai-p'ing control 229/1
Ani Persia Byzantine Empire 113/1
Anjira NW India pre-Harappan site 65/1
Anjou region of NW France British possession 123/1; annexed by France 146/1, 147/3; province of France 189/1
Ankara (anc. Ancyra obs. Eng. Angora) W Turkey ⚔ 126/4, 137/1; revolt against Ottoman rule 166/1; Ottoman Empire 225/3
Ankole Uganda kingdom 163/1, 235/1
Annaba (Bône, Hippo Regius)
Annam N Indo-China under T'ang control 125/2; under Mongol control 127/1; expansion and early trade 173/1; anti-French resistance in 19C 244/1; French protectorate 257/1
Annapolis (until 1654 Anne Arundel Town earlier Providence) NE USA 157/2
Annesoi NW Anatolia early monastery 93/3
Anopolis C Crete Minoan palace 67/1
Ano Zakro E Crete Minoan palace 67/1
An-p'ing (n/s Anping) NE China Han prefecture 81/2
Ansbach S Germany Reformation 179/1; margraviate 187/1
An-shan (n/s Anshan) Manchuria Russo-Japanese War 238/3; industry 259/3, 274/3
Anshan W Persia early city 55/3
Anta da Marquesa Portugal Megalithic site 42/2
Anta dos Gorgiones Portugal Megalithic site 42/2
Antakya (anc. Antioch Lat. Antiochia) E Turkey Ottoman centre 166/1
Antalya (Attalia)
Antananarivo (Tananarive)
Antarctica ozone depletion 295/3
Antibes (Antipolis)
Antietam (a/c Sharpsburg) NE USA ⚔ 219/1
Antigua island of West Indies settlement by British 156/3; colony 223/1; independence 273/2 (inset); population growth 294/2
An-ting (n/s Anding) NW China Han commanderie 81/2
Antinoe L Egypt early trade 70/1
Antioch (Lat. Antiochia mod. Antakya) E Anatolia Mediterranean trade 70/1, 82/4, 133/1; spread of Christianity 72/1; Persian Empire 79/1; Roman Empire 86/3; patriarchate 93/1; archbishopric 101/2; Jewish community 103/1; Byzantine rule 112-3, 121/2; principality 132/3
Antioch C Anatolia early archbishopric 93/1
Antiochia (anc. Antioch mod. Antakya) E Anatolia fortified Roman town 88/3, 91/1
Antiochia Margiana Persia trade 82/4
Antipolis (mod. Antibes) SE France Ionian colony 75/1
Antium mod. Anzio) C Italy Roman colony 87/1
Antofagasta region of N Chile dispute with Peru and Bolivia 223/5
Antrim N Ireland massacre of Catholics 180/2
An-tung (n/c Dandong W/G Tan-tung) Manchuria treaty port 228/2; Russo-Japanese war 238/3; industry 259/3
Antunnacum (Andernach)
Antwerp (Fr. Anvers Dut. Antwerpen) Belgium Hansa city 142/1, 143/3; trade 150/2; 16C and 18C financial centre 176/1, 177/2; town of Spanish Netherlands 181/1; industrial development 208/1; WW1 248-9; WW2 269/3
Anuradhapura Ceylon Buddhist site 73/1
Anvers (Antwerp)
Anxi (An-hsi)
Anxur (later Tarracina mod. Terracina) C Italy 86/2
An-yang (n/s Anyang) N China early urban settlement 53/1; Shang city 62/2
Anyer Lor W Java Iron Age site 130/1
Anzio (anc. Antium) C Italy WW2 269/3
Aocang (Ao-ts'ang)
Aomori N Japan town and prefecture 239/1; industry 239/1
Aornos (mod. Tash-Kurghan) Afghanistan Alexander's route 77/1
Ao-ts'ang (n/s Aocang) C China Han prefecture 81/2
Aozou Strip N Chad occupied by Libya 281/1
Apache Indian tribe of SW USA, 35/2, 145/1
Apache Pass SW USA on trail west 216/1
Apamea Syria Peace of 77/3; Roman Empire 88/3, 91/1; early archbishopric 93/1
Apesokari Crete site 67/2
Aphrodisias SW France Ionian colony 75/1
Apodhoulou Crete site 67/2
Apollonia NE Greece Doric colony 75/1; Roman Empire 86/3, 89/1, 91/1; early church 93/1
Apollonia (mod. Sozopol) Bulgaria Ionian colony 75/1
Apollonia Libya Greek colony 75/1; Roman Empire 91/1; Byzantine Empire 113/1
Apollinopolis (Edfu)
Apologos Persian Gulf port 70/1, 78/2, 79/3
Appenwihr W Germany Hallstatt site 84/1
Appenzell Switzerland Reformation 179/1
Appian Way (Via Appia)
Appomattox SE USA Confederates surrender 219/1
Apremont E France Hallstatt site 84/1
Aptera W Crete Minoan site 67/1
Apulia region of SE Italy unification with Naples 122/2
Apulum (mod. Alba Iulia) Romania Roman Empire 89/1, 91/1
Aqaba (anc. Aela or Aelana) Jordan WW1 249/4
Aqsu (Aksu)
Aquae Sextiae (mod. Aix) France Roman Empire 86/3
Aquileia (med. Aglar) N Italy Latin colony 87/1; Roman Empire 86/3, 89/1, 91/1; early archbishopric 92/1, 107/3; monastery 93/3; invaded by Goths 99/1; Byzantine Empire 112/1
Aquincum (mod. Budapest) Hungary Roman Empire 89/1, 91/1
Aquino (Aquinum)
Aquinum (mod. Aquino) C Italy early town 87/1
Aquisgranum (Aachen)
Aquitaine (anc. Aquitania mod. Guyenne) region of SW France English possession 123/1; Black Death 141/1
Aquitania (mod. Aquitaine later Guyenne) Roman province of Gaul 89/1; invasion by Vandals 98/1; Visigothic territory conquered by Franks 106/1,3; 111/1
Arabaya Arabia satrapy of Achaemenid Empire 79/1
Arabia early trade 70/1; spread of Judaism 72/1; early Christian activity 100/1; centre of Islam 105/1; under Abbasid Caliphate 108/1; Egyptian expedition 235/1; WW1 249/4
Arabia Eudaemon S Arabia port 82/4
Arabian Gulf (Persian Gulf)
Arabia Petraea Roman province of N Arabia, 89/1
Arabissos E Anatolia Byzantine Empire 113/1
Arabs (of Mansura) NW India 129/1
Arabs (of Multan) NW India 129/1
Arachosia (a/c Harauvatish) Afghanistan ancient province of Persian and Alexander's Empires, 77/1, 82/3, 83/1
Aradus (Bibl. Arvad later Arwad Fr. Rouad) Syria Phoenician city 75/1; Alexander's route 76/1; early Jewish community 103/1
Arago S France site of early man 32/2
Aragon (Sp. Aragón) region of E Spain at time of Reconquista 122/3; rural uprisings 141/1; acquired by Habsburgs 146/2; kingdom 182/2
Arakan district of SW Burma Islamic state 131/2,3; British control 173/1; annexed by British 230/2, 231/3; 279/3
Aralsk C Asia 289/1
Aramaeans people of Syria, 56/3, 60-1
Arapaho C USA Plains Indian tribe 145/1
Arapuni N Island New Zealand hydroelectric station 232/1
Arash N Caucasus conquered by Ottomans 167/1
Araucanian S America Andean Indian Tribe 145/1
Arausio (mod. Orange) S France 92/1
Arawak S America Indian tribe 145/1
Araxos S Greece Mycenaean site 67/1
Arbailu (a/c Arbela mod. Arbil) Mesopotamia 54/1
Arbela (a/c Arbailu mod. Arbil) Mesopotamia Alexander's route 76/1; town of Parthian Empire 78/3; under Alexander 82/3; early archbishopric 93/1, 101/1
Arcadiopolis Bulgaria Byzantine Empire 113/1
Archanes (a/s Arkhanes) C Crete Minoan palace 67/1
Archangel (Russ. Arkhangelsk) N Russia founded 153/1, 159/1; Revolution and Allied occupation 255/1; WW2 269/3; growth 288/3; industry 289/1
Archilochori C Crete sacred cave 67/1
Arcole N Italy ⚔ 201/1
Arcot S India ceded to British 168/3; ⚔ 190/2
Arcy-sur-Cure C France site of early man 32/2
Ardabil Azerbaijan early trade 133/1
Ardea N Italy ancient town 87/1
Ardennes forest Belgium/France WW1 248-9; WW2 ⚔ 269/3
Ardmore Ireland early bishopric 92/1
Arelate (mod. Arles) S France Roman Empire 89/1, 90/1; archbishopric 93/1
Arène Candide SE France site 43/1
Arequipa Peru early Spanish city 154/1
Arezzo (anc. Arretium) C Italy medieval city 122/2
Argel (Algiers)
Argentina independence from Spain 222-3, 240/1; exports and foreign investment 222/3; population 222/4; industrialization and economy 215/1; 284-5, 294/1

Argentoratum – Barca

Argentoratum (*mod.* Strasbourg) E France Mithraic site 72/1
Arghun early kingdom of NW India 128/4
Arginusae islands of the Aegean ✕ 74/4
Argissa Greece site 43/1
Argonne NE France WW1 249/3 (inset)
Argos S Greece 67/1, 74/3
Arguin island off NW Africa Portuguese settlement 162/1,2
Århus (*a/s* Aarhus) C Denmark early bishopric 101/2, 116/2
Aria (*a/c* Haraiva) ancient region of Afghanistan 77/1, 82/3
Arica Peru trading post 154/1
Arickara E USA ✕ 217/4
Ariha (Jericho)
Arikamadur S India site 64/3
Ariminum (*mod.* Rimini) N Italy Latin colony 87/1; archbishopric 92/1
Arizona state of USA Depression 263/1; income and population 287/2
Arjunayanas tribe of N India 82/5
Arkansas state of C USA 19C politics 221/2,3; Depression 263/1; income and population 287/2
Arkhanes (Archanes)
Arkhangelsk (Archangel)
Arkines S Greece Mycenaean site 67/1
Arkoudiotissa W Crete sacred cave 67/1
Arlberg Austria tunnel 253/2
Arles (*anc.* Arelate *or* Arelas) S France early archbishopric 106/3; medieval kingdom 119/1; medieval trade 120/1
Arlit N Africa cattle domestication 45/1
Armagh N Ireland archbishopric 92/1, 117/1; monastery 100/3; IRA 291/2
Armagnac region of SW France under English rule 123/1; annexed to France 147/3
Armenia (*anc.* Urartu) country of Caucasus spread of Christianity 72/1; Alexander's Empire 76/1, 82/3; part of Kushan Empire 78/3; Roman province 89/1, 86/3, 91/2; Muslim conquest 105/1; Ottoman Empire 225/1; Independence after WW1 261/1; Soviet Socialist Republic 288/2
Armenia, Lesser region of Asia Minor 132/3
Armeniac Theme Anatolia division of Byzantine Empire 112/3
Armenians emigration from Turkey 261/3; in USSR 288/4
Armorica (*mod.* Brittany *and* Normandy) region of NW France, settlement by Britons 98/1
Arnasco NW Italy principality 183/3
Arnhem Land N Australia Pleistocene site 48/2
Arpachiyah N Mesopotamia early settlement 41/1
Arpi C Italy early town 87/1
Arpino (Arpinum)
Arpinum (*mod.* Arpino) C Italy early town 87/1
Arquata NW Italy principality 183/3
Arrapkha Mesopotamia trading town 54/1
Arras (*anc.* Nemetocenna) N France early bishopric 117/1; fort 189/1; French Revolution 199/2; WW1 248-9
Arretium (*mod.* Arezzo) C Italy Etruscan city 75/1, 86/2; Roman Empire 91/1
Arsamosata E Anatolia city of Kushan Empire 78/3
Arsinoe (*older* Crocodilopolis) Egypt trade 82/4; Roman Empire 89/1; early Jewish community 103/1
Arsinoe Libya ancient town 89/1
Artacoana Afghanistan Alexander's route 77/1
Artajona N Spain Megalithic site 42/2
Ártánd Hungary Thracian/Scythian site 85/1
Artashat Caucasus patriarchate 93/1
Artaxata Armenia Kushan Empire 78/3; Roman Empire 89/1
Artemision (Cape Artemisium)
Artois region of NE France Burgundian possession 147/2,3; province of France 189/1; WW1 248-9
Aruba island of Dutch West Indies 223/1, 240/1, 273/2 (inset)
Arunachal Pradesh (*form.* North East Frontier Agency) NE India frontier dispute with China 275/1, 279/3
Arvad (Arwad)
Arvernis C France monastery 93/3
Arvi E Crete Minoan palace 67/1
Arwad (*anc.* Aradus *Bibl.* Arvad *Fr.* Rouad) Syria Assyrian Empire 57/2; Crusader states 132/3
Arzawans early people of W Anatolia 56/1
Asaak Persia town of Parthian Empire 79/3
Asab Abu Dhabi oilfield 283/4
Asabon SE Arabia early trade 70/1
Asahikawa N Japan 239/1
Asante W Africa early state 163/1, 235/1
Ascalon (*mod.* Ashqelon) S Palestine Egyptian Empire 58/2; Philistine city 75/1; early church 93/1; Venetian naval victory 121/2
Ascension Island S Atlantic British colony 240/1, 272/1,2
Ascoli Piceno (Asculum)
Ascoli Satriano (Ausculum)
Asculum (*a/c* Asculum Picenum *mod.* Ascoli Piceno) N Italy 87/1
Ashdod (*Lat.* Azotus) Palestine Philistine city 75/1
Ash Hollow C USA ✕ 217/4
Ashkhabad (*from 1919-27* Poltoratsk) SW Central Asia industry 289/1
Ashqelon (Ascalon)
Ash Sham (Damascus)
Ash Shariqah (Sharjah)
Ashtishat Caucasus monastery 93/3
Ashur (*mod.* Sharqat) Mesopotamia early urban centre 52/1; 54/1; Assyrian Empire 56-7
Asia early man 33/1,4, 34-5, 37/1; agricultural origins 39/1; early trade routes 70-1; tribal movements 94-5; expansion of Christianity 101/1; early empires 108-9; Chinese expansion 80/3, 125/2, 171/1; Mongol expansion 126-7; religious distribution 131/3; early voyages of discovery 153/1; Russian expansion 158/3; 18C trade 195/1; industrialization 214/1; colonial empires 241/1; anti-colonial resistance 244/1; drug trade 295/1
Asia (*Byzantine name* Asiana) Roman province of Anatolia 86/3, 89/1
Asiago N Italy WW1 249/3
Asia Minor spread of civilization 52/1; conversion to Christianity 72/1, 101/2; Ottoman control 166/1 See also Anatolia
Asiana (Asia)
Asine S Greece Mycenaean site 67/1
Asir SW Arabia Ottoman Empire 225/1
Asisium (*mod.* Assisi) N Italy 87/1
Asmaka ancient kingdom of S India 83/2
Asoka's Empire India 82-3
Aspanvar Mesopotamia town of Sasanian Empire 79/3
Aspendus SW Anatolia Dorian colony 75/1
Aspern/Essling Austria ✕ 201/1
Aspromonte S Italy ✕ 213/2
Assam state of NE India Mongol control 127/1; conquered by Burmese 173/1; British control 228/2; 230/2, 231/3, 278/2, 279/3,4
Assos (*Lat.* Assus) W Anatolia Aeolian colony 75/1; early church 93/1
Assyria empire 56-7; Roman province 89/1
Assyrians people of Middle East 60-61; risings in N Iraq 257/2
Astacus (*mod.* Izmit) NW Anatolia Dorian colony 75/1
Astarac SW France independent fief 147/3
Asti N Italy Lombard League 119/1
Astorga (Asturica Augusta)
Astoria NW USA fur station 216/1
Astrabad Ardashir Mesopotamia town of Sasanian Empire 79/3
Astrakhan S Russia occupied by Mongols 126/4; economy 158/2, 227/1; Tartar khanate 159/1; urban growth 227/1; Bolshevik seizure 255/1; WW2 269/3
Asturias region of N Spain kingdom 106/3, 108/1; part of Castile 122/3; political unrest 260/2
Asturica Augusta (*mod.* Astorga) N Spain Roman Empire 88/1; bishopric 92/1
Asunción Paraguay early Spanish settlement 154/1; 223/1
Asuristan Mesopotamia province of Achaemenid Empire 79/3
Asyut (*anc.* Lycopolis) S Egypt trade 133/1; 282/1
Atacama (*Sp.* Atacameño) S America Andean Indian tribe 47/4, 145/1
Atacama Desert Chile/Peru War of Pacific 223/5
Atacame ño (Atacama)
A-tan (*n/s* Adan *Eng.* Aden) S Arabia
Atapuerca N Spain site of early man 32/2
Atchana (Alakakh)
Athabaskan Indian tribe of Canada 35/2
Athenae (*Eng.* Athens *mod. Gr.* Athinai) Greece Roman Empire 86/3, 89/1, 91/1
Athenopolis SE France Ionian colony 75/1
Athens (*Lat.* Athenae *mod. Gr.* Athinai) Greece Mycenaean palace 67/1; early trade 70/1; Greek parent state 75/1; cultural centre 74/2; Persian wars 74/3; war with Sparta 74/4; 76/1,4; bishopric 93/1; invaded by Goths 99/1; early Jewish community 103/1; Byzantine Empire 112-3; WW1 249/3; WW2 265/5, 269/3
Athinai (Athens)
Athribis N Egypt early Jewish community 103/1
Athura Mesopotamia satrapy of Achaemenid Empire 79/1
Atjeh (*n/s* Aceh *var.* Acheh *a/s* Achin) N Sumatra Islamic state 131/2,3; early trade 172/2
Altanta SE USA ✕ 219/1; strike 263/1; industry 287/1
Atlantic Ocean Viking voyages 111/4; U-Boat warfare WW2 269/2
Atropatene (Azerbaijan)
Attalia (*mod.* Antalya) S Anatolia early church 93/1; Byzantine Empire 112-3
Attica ancient state of SE Greece 74/3, 76/4, 91/2
Attigny NE France Frankish royal residence 106/3
Attirampakkan and Gudiyam Cave S India Stone Age site 64/2
Attleborough E England rebellion 181/1
Attu Island Aleutians, W Alaska WW2 266-7
Atwetwebooso W Africa Iron Age site 45/1
Auch (*anc.* Elimberrum *later* Augusta Auscorum) SE France parlement 189/1
Auckland N Island, New Zealand Maori settlement 49/4; province and second capital 232/1
Audenarde (Oudenaarde)
Auerstädt E Germany 201/1
Aufidena C Italy early town 87/1
Augila (*n/s* Awjilah) Libya early trade 135/1
Augsburg (*anc.* Augusta Vindelicorum) S Germany town of Swabia 118/1; medieval trade centre 143/3; 16C financial centre 176/1; imperial city 187/1
Augusta W Australia early settlement 233/5
Augusta Auscorum (Auch)
Augusta Rauricorum (*mod.* Augst) Switzerland Roman Empire 90/1
Augusta Taurinorum (*mod.* Turin) N Italy early bishopric 92/1
Augusta Treverorum (*mod.* Trier *Eng. Treves*) W Germany Mithraic site 72/1; Roman Empire 89/1, 90/1; archbishopric 92/1; early Jewish community 103/1
Augusta Vindelicorum (*mod.* Augsburg) S Germany Roman Empire 89/1, 91/1
Augustodunum (*mod.* Autun) C France Roman Empire 89/1, 90/1; early bishopric 92/1
Augustów NE Poland WW1 249/3
Auliye-Ata (Dzhambul)
Aulon (*later* Avlona *mod.* Vlorë) Albania Dorian colony 75/1
Auranitis region of Judaea 103/2
Aurelian Way (Via Aurelia)
Aurunci early tribe of C Italy, 86/2
Auschwitz (*correctly* Auschwitz - Birkenau *Pol.* Oświęcim) concentration camp 268/1
Ausculum (*a/c* Ausculum Apulum *mod.* Ascoli Satriano) C Italy early town 87/1
Austerlitz (*mod.* Slavkov) Czechoslovakia ✕ 201/1
Australia (*originally called* New Holland) before the Europeans 48/1,2; early voyages of discovery and exploration 153/3, 233/2,3; early trade 233/4; settlement and development 233/5; emergence of Commonwealth 241/1; dominion status 2 7/1; economy and industrialization 214/1, 262/3, 274/2, 295/1; WW2 266-7
Austrasia the eastern Frankish Empire 107/1
Austria (*Ger.* Österreich) German settlement 119/1; Black Death 141/1; acquired by Habsburgs 139/1, 146/1,2; attacked by Ottomans 166/1; early industry 186/2; archduchy 187/1; Habsburg conquests 192/1, 193/3; opposition to Napoleon 200-1; Alpine tunnels and railways 253/2; inter-war alliances 260/2, 264/1; socio-political change 263/2; annexed by Germany 265/4, 268/1; Allied occupation zones 270/1; EFTA 270/1, 291/1; economy , 271/4, 295/1
Austro-Hungarian Empire agriculture and peasant emancipation 174/1; military Frontier with Ottoman Empire 193/3; population growth 204/3,4; industrial revolution 206/1, 209/1; customs frontier abolished 207/2; ethnic composition 210/1; in Crimean War 226/4; growth in armaments 246; European alliances 246-7; overseas trade 252-3; WW1 248-9; dismantled 261/1
Autesiodorum (*mod.* Auxerre) C France monastery 93/3, 106/3
Autun (Augustodunum)
Auvergne region of C France English possession 123/1; annexed to France 146/1, 147/3; French province 189/1
Auvernier W Switzerland early settlement 43/1
Auxerre (*anc.* Autesiodorum) C France medieval town 120/1, 121/4
Auximum N Italy Roman colony 87/1
Ava C Burma political centre 131/2,3; old capital 173/1
Avanti region of C India 83/1,2
Avaricum (*mod.* Bourges) C France Roman Empire 86/3
Avaris (*a/c* Tanis) Lower Egypt Hyksos capital 58/1
Avars (*Chin.* Juan-juan) ancient people of Asia and Europe 94/1, 98-9; kingdom destroyed 107/3
Avellino (Abellinum)
Avenio (Avignon)
Avennes N France flint mine 42/2
Avesnes N France fort 189/1
Avignon (*anc.* Avenio) S France in Great Schism 141/1 (inset); Papal enclave 189/1; annexed by France 199/3
Ávila C Spain expulsion of Jews 102/3
Avlona (*Gr.* Aulon *mod.* Vlorë *It.* Valona) Albania Byzantine Empire 112-3; Ottoman conquest 137/1
Avranches NW France 17C revolt 181/1
Awdaghost W Africa trans-Saharan trade 134/1,2, 163/1
Awjilah (Augila)
Axel S Netherlands town of Dutch Republic 181/1
Axim Ghana early Dutch settlement 162/1 (inset)
Axum ancient kingdom of NE Africa, 45/1, 71/1, 105/1, 135/1
Ayacucho Peru ✕ 222/2
Aydhab Sudan early trade 133/1
Aydin W Anatolia emirate 136/2, 137/1
Ayia Irini W Aegean ancient site 67/1
Ayia Marina C Greece Mycenaean site 67/1
Ayia Triadha (Hagia Triada)
Ayios Ilias S Greece Mycenaean site 67/1
Ayios Ioannis C Greece Mycenaean site 67/1
Ayios Nikolaos S Greece Mycenaean site 67/1
Ayios Theodhoros N Greece Mycenaean site 67/1
Aylesbury S England Industrial Revolution 197/1
Aymará Andean Indian tribe of S America, 145/1
Ayodhya (*earlier* Saketa) NC India site 64/3; town of Kosala 83/1; Hindu-Muslim clashes 279/3
Ayutthaya (*a/s* Ayuthia *properly* Phra Nakhon Si Ayutthaya) S Thailand early political centre 131/2,3; early trade 173/1
Ayyubids Muslim dynasty, Egypt 133/1; Arabia 135/1
Azad Kashmir district of Pakistan 278/1
Azak (*mod.* Azov) S Russia Ottoman conquest 137/1
Azerbaijan (*anc.* Atropatene) country of the Caucasus province of Achaemenid Empire 79/3; Muslim conquest 105/1; under Abbasid sovereignty 133/1; Ottoman conquest 167/1; acquired by Russia 159/1, 225/1; independence after WW1 261/1; Soviet Socialist Republic 288/2
Azerbaijanis 288/4
Azincourt (Agincourt)
Azores (*Port.* Açores) islands of N Atlantic trade 154/1; Portuguese exploration 162/2; Portuguese colony 240/1
Azotus (*mod.* Ashdod) Palestine bishopric 93/1; in Judaea 103/2
Azov (*Turk.* Azak) S Russia Ottoman town 166/1
Aztalan C USA Hopewell site 46/3
Aztec Empire Mexico growth 144/2; early economy 151/1; conquest by Spain 155/2
Ba (Pa)
Baalbek (Heliopolis)
Babirush Mesopotamia satrapy of Achaemenid Empire 79/1
Babylon Mesopotamia early urban settlement 52/1, 54/1; centre of Amorite kingdom 54/2; town of Parthian Empire 71/1; Achaemenid Empire 79/1; Alexander's route 77/1, 82/3; Jewish community 103/1
Babylonia ancient country of Mesopotamia fall of 56-7; under Alexander 77/1, 82/3
Baçaim (Bassein)
Bactra (*a/c* Zariaspa *mod.* Balkh) Afghanistan silk route 70/1; Alexander's route 77/1, 82/3,4
Bactria (*a/c* Bactriana *Pers.* Bakhtrish *Chin.* Ta-hsia) ancient country of Afghanistan 71/71, 77/1, 82/3
Badajoz SW Spain ✕ 200/1
Badakhshan district of Bactria in N Afghanistan early trade 55/1; under Uzbek khans 167/1
Bad Axe N USA ✕ 217/4
Bad Cannstatt W Germany late Hallstatt site 85/1
Baden S Germany margraviate 187/1,4; state 212/3; German customs union 213/1; 271/2
Baden-Württemberg region of SW Germany 271/2
Badr W Arabia ✕ 105/1
Bad-tibira S Mesopotamia early city 55/3
Baecula SW Spain ✕ 86/3
Baetica S Spain Roman province 88/1
Baffin Island N Canada discovery 152/1
Baghdad Mesopotamia early archbishopric 101/1; Abbasid capital 109/4; Mongol conquest 126/4; early trade 133/1, 150/2; under Ottoman rule 167/1, 225/1; WW1 249/4; anti-British uprising 256/1; oil pipeline 283/3
Bagirmi NC Africa early state 135/1
Bagneux N France Megalithic site 42/2
Bagrationovsk (Eylau)
Bahadarabad NW India site 64/2
Bahal C India site 64/3
Bahamas islands of N Caribbean discovery 152/1; British colony 156/3, 161/1, 195/1, 223/1, 220/1; independence 273/2 (inset)
Bahawalpur native state of NW India under British rule 230/1; joins Pakistan at Partition 278/1
Bahçesaray (Bakhchesaray)
Bahia E Brazil Portuguese control 154/1, 161/1; port 194/3; province 223/1
Bahrain (*f/s* Bahrein *Ar.* Al Bahrayn) island of Persian Gulf Sasanian Empire 79/3; Ottoman siege 167/1; independent sheikhdom 225/1; British control 256/1; independence 273/2; 283/3
Bahr al Ghazal district of C Sudan 235/1
Baile Atha Cliath (Dublin)
Bailén S Spain ✕ 200/1
Baiovarii tribe of S Germany 99/1
Bairat (*a/c* Bhabra) N India site 64/2, 82/3
Bakhchesaray (*Turk.* Bahçesaray) Crimea Ottoman Empire 137/1
Bakhtrish (Bactria) Afghanistan Achaemenid province 79/1
Baku Azerbaijan early trade 133/1; conquered by Ottomans 167/1; Congress of Peoples of the East 254/3; British occupation 255/1; urban growth 227/1, 288/3; Russian Revolution 255/1; WW2 269/3; industry 209/1, 227/1, 289/1
Bakusu tribe of C Belgian Congo 280/2
Balagansk SC Siberia founded 158/3
Balaklava S Russia Crimean War 226/4
Bala-Kot NW India Harappan site 65/1
Balambangan district of Java Dutch control 172/3
Balanovo C Russia early settlement 52/1
Balboa Panama 242/2
Baldissero NW Italy Saluzzo principality 183/3
Bâle (Basle)
Baleares Insulae (*mod.* Baleares *Eng.* Balearic Islands) W Mediterranean Roman province 86/3; Byzantine Empire 112/1
Balearic Islands W Mediterranean attacked by Saracens 111/1; conquest by Pisa 120/2; reconquered by Aragon 122/3
Balestrino NW Italy margravate 183/3
Balikpapan E Borneo recaptured from Japanese 267/2
Balkans rise of nationalism 211/2; alliances 246-7
Balkh (*anc.* Bactra *a/c* Zariaspa) Afghanistan Sasanian Empire 79/3; early bishopric 101/1; Muslim conquest 105/1; Empire of Ghazni 128/2; early trade 133/1
Balkhash C Asia 289/1
Ballarat SE Australia goldfield 233/5
Ballinamuck Ireland ✕ 190/3
Ballynagilly Ireland site 43/1
Baltic Viking trade 110/3; Swedish settlement 111/1; 184-5
Baltic States (Estonia, Latvia, Lithuania)
Baltimore E USA industry 287/1
Balts Indo-European tribe 61/1
Baluba tribe of C and S Belgian Congo, 280/2
Baluchistan region of NW India tribal agency 231/3; joins Pakistan after Partition 278/1, 279/3
Balunda tribe of S Belgian Congo 280/2
Bamako W Africa reached by Mungo Park 234/2; occupied by French 237/1
Bamangwato tribe of S Africa 234/3
Bambala tribe of N Belgian Congo 280/2
Bambara tribe of W Africa 235/1
Bamberg S Germany bishopric 101/2, 117/1, 187/1; medieval trade 120/1
Bamburgh NE England ✕ 99/3
Bamiyan region of NW India 129/3
Bamongo tribe of W Belgian Congo 280/2
Banat region of Hungary/Romania/Yugoslavia conquered by Habsburgs 192/1, 193/3; WW1 249/3
Banbury C England Industrial Revolution 197/1
Ban Chiang N Siam early site 130/1
Bancorna Wales early bishopric 92/1
Bandar Abbas (*form.* Gombroon) SW Persia early trade 157/1; Ottoman siege 167/1
Bandjarmasin (*n/s* Banjarmasin) S Borneo Islamic town 131/3; early trading centre 173/1; WW2 267/2
Bangala tribe of N Belgian Congo 280/2
Bangalore S India industry 214/1
Bangarh E India site 64/3
Banghazi (Benghazi)
Bangka island E Sumatra Dutch settlement 173/1
Bangkok (*Thai.* Krung Thep) S Thailand early trade centre 173/1; captured by Japanese 266/2
Bangladesh (*form.* East Pakistan *or* East Bengal) part of Pakistan 278/2; independence 273/2; 279/3
Bangor N Ireland monastery 100/3
Bangor Wales monastery 93/3, 100/3; bishopric 117/1
Banjarmasin (Bandjarmasin)
Banjul (Bathurst)
Ban Kao SW Thailand early site 130/1
Bannockburn C Scotland ✕ 123/1, 140/2
Bannu (*form.* Edwardesabad) NW Pakistan industry 214/1
Bañolas NE Spain site of early man 32/2
Banpo (Pan-p'o)
Bantam (*form.* Banten) Java Islamic town 131/3; early trade 157/1, 173/1; sultanate under Dutch control 172/3
Banten (Bantam)
Banyu (Pan-yü)
Banzart (Bizerta)
Bao'an (Pao-an)
Baoji (Pao-chi)
Baotou (Pao-t'ou)
Bapaume NW France fort 189/1
Bapende tribe of W Belgian Congo, 280/2
Bar region of NE France/W Germany Burgundian possession 147/3; independent fief 147/2,3; duchy 186/1
Baranovichi (*Pol.* Baranowicze) W Russia WW1 249/3
Barbados island of West Indies settled by English 156/3; British colony 223/1, 240/1; independence 273/2 (inset); population growth 294/2
Barbalissus Syria ✕ 78/3; Roman fort 88/3
Barbaricum port of NW India 70/1, 82/4
Barbuda island of West Indies settled by English 156/3; dependency of Antigua 273/2 (inset); population growth 294/2
Barca Libya ✕ 78/1

Barcelona – Brandenburg

Barcelona (*anc.* Barcino) NE Spain Mediterranean trade 120/2, 132/1, 142/1; urban revolt 141/1; 16C financial centre 176/1; trading port 176/3; 18C urban development 177/2; ✕ 200/1; industrial development 206/1; Civil War 264/3
Barcelonette SE France fort 189/1
Barcino (*mod.* Barcelona) NE Spain early bishopric 92/1
Bardaa NW Persia early archbishopric 101/1
Bardia (*n/s* Bardiyah) Libya WW2 269/3
Bardsey Wales monastery 93/3
Barduli (Barletta)
Bareilly N India Mutiny 230/1
Barga N Italy Tuscan principality 183/3
Barguzinsk (*now* Barguzin) SC Siberia founded 158/3
Bari (*anc.* Barium) S Italy Saracen occupation 111/1; captured by Normans 120/2; WW2 269/3
Barium (*mod.* Bari) S Italy Roman Empire 87/1; Jewish community 103/1
Bar-le-Duc E France 186/1
Barletta (*anc.* Barduli) S Italy medieval city 119/1
Barmen-Elberfeld (*since 1930* Wuppertal) W Germany industrial development 206/1, 208/1
Barnard Castle N England ✕ 181/1
Barnaul C Asia founded 158/3; industry 288/3, 289/1
Barnsley C England Industrial Revolution 197/1
Baroda C India industry 214/1
Barotseland SC Africa early state 235/1
Bar-sur-Aube C France medieval fair 120/1
Barygaza (*Skt.* Bhrigukaccha *mod.* Broach *n/s* Bharuch) NW India trading centre 71/1, 82/4, 83/1
Basel (*Fr.* Bâle *Eng.* Basle) Switzerland bishopric 187/1
Bashkir ASSR C Russia 288/2
Bashkirs Turkic people of C Russia 159/1, 288/4
Basingstoke S England Industrial Revolution 197/1
Basle (*Fr.* Bâle *Ger.* Basel) Switzerland medieval trade 120/1; Reformation 179/1; bishopric 187/1; industrial development 206/1, 208/1
Basonge tribe of C Belgian Congo 280/2
Basque Provinces N Spain reconquest by Castile 122/3
Basque Republic N Spain autonomy 260/1
Basques people of N Spain and SW France 98/2, 210/1
Basra (*Ar.* Al Basrah) Mesopotamia early archbishopric 101/1; ✕ 105/1; trade 133/1; Ottoman conquest 167/1; 18C trade 195/1; British control 224/2, 225/1; oil terminal 283/3; WW1 249/4
Bassano N Italy ✕ 201/1
Bassein Burma early trade centre 173/1
Bassein (*Port.* Baçaim) W India Portuguese settlement 157/1, 169/1
Basse-Yutz E France La Tène site 84/1
Bastar princely state of C India 231/3
Basti district of N India ceded to Britain 168/3
Basutoland (*now* Lesotho) S Africa state 234/3; British colony 236/2, 241/1, 272/1
Batanaea district of Judaea 103/2
Batavi tribe of the Netherlands 89/1
Batavia (*form.* Sunda Kalapa, *since 1949* Jakarta *f/s* Djakarta) Java early trade 157/1, 173/1, 195/1; Dutch control 172/3; port 195/1; WW2 266-7
Batavian Republic (*mod.* Netherlands) state established by French Revolution 199/3
Batelela tribe of N Belgian Congo 280/2
Bath W England Industrial Revolution 197/1
Bathnae E Anatolia monastery 93/3
Bathurst SE Australia founded 233/5
Bathurst (*now* Banjul) Gambia, W Africa British settlement 234/1; 281/1
Bato Caves C Philippines early site 130/1
Baton Rouge S USA ✕ 218/1
Batshokwe tribe of S Belgian Congo 280/2
Batumi (*f/s* Batum) Caucasus British occupation 255/1; economy 289/1
Baudouinville Zaire Congo crisis 280/2
Bautzen E Germany ✕ 201/1
Bavaria (*Ger.* Bayern) conversion to Christianity 100/3; part of Frankish Empire 107/3; Magyar invasions 111/1; Wittelsbach territory 146/1; Electorate 187/1; Napoleonic influence 200/2; German Empire 212/3; customs union 213/1; short-lived soviet republic 254/2; 271/2
Bawit Egypt monastery 100/1
Baxter Spring C USA cow town 216/1
Bayern (Bavaria)
Bayeux N France Scandinavian settlement 110/2; bishopric 117/1
Bayonne (*anc.* Lapurdum) SW France 18C financial centre 177/2; 189/1
Bayreuth S Germany margraviate 187/1
Bayrut (Beirut)
Beans Store C USA cow town 216/1
Bear Island Spitsbergen discovered 153/1
Béarn region of SW France under English rule 123/1; acquired by France 147/4
Bear Paw Mountains C USA ✕ 217/4
Bear Valley W USA mining site 216/1
Beas Valley NW India site 64/2
Beaucaire S France medieval fair 142/1
Beaulieu S England Industrial Revolution 197/1
Beauvais N France bishopric 117/1; 17C revolt 181/1
Beaver NW Canada sub-arctic Indian tribe 145/1
Beç (Vienna)
Becan E Mexico Maya site 46/2
Bechuanaland (*now* Botswana) country of S Africa, British protectorate 214/1, 234/3, 236/2, 241/1, 272/1
Bedcanford S England ✕ 99/3
Bedford S England Viking fort 110/2; Industrial Revolution 197/1
Bedsa (Karli)
Beersheba (*Heb.* Beer Sheva) S Israel WW1 249/4
Beidha S Palestine early village 41/1
Beihai (Pakhoi)
Beijing (Peking)
Beilngries W Germany early Hallstatt site 85/1
Beiqu (Pei-ch'ü)
Beira SE Africa Portuguese occupation 237/1
Beirut (*anc.* Berytus *Fr.* Beyrouth *Ar.* Bayrut) Lebanon Mediterranean trade 133/1, 143/1; French control 225/1; disturbances under French mandate 257/2; civil war 283/4
Beisamoun S Syria early village 41/1
Beiyu (Pei-yü)
Beizhou (Pei-chou)
Bejaia (*anc.* Saldae *Fr.* Bougie *Sp.* Bugia) Algeria Mediterranean trade 142/1
Bekaa Valley Lebanon occupied by Syria 283/4
Belarus (Belorussia)
Belchete NE Spain Civil War 264/3
Belfast N Ireland industrial development 208/1; IRA 291/2
Belfort E France fort 189/1
Belgian Congo (*form.* Congo Free State *now* Zaire) economy 214/1; colony 236/2, 241/1; uprising 245/2; independence 272/1,2
Belgica Roman province of NE France 89/1
Belgium (*form.* Spanish Netherlands *or* Southern Netherlands) industrial revolution 206/1, 208/1; colonial empire 241/1; WW1 248-9; overseas trade 252-3; acquisition of Eupen and Malmédy 261/1; economic and social development 1929-39 262/3, 263/2; inter-war alliances 264/1; WW2 265/5, 268-9; EEC and NATO 270/1, 271/1; economy 271/4, 295/1
Belgorod S Russia founded 159/1; early bishopric 101/2; WW2 269/5; industry 289/1
Belgorod-Dnestrovskiy (Akkerman)
Belgrade (*anc.* Singidunum *S. Cr.* Beograd) C Yugoslavia ✕ 127/1; Ottoman conquest 166/1; 18C urban development 176/1; WW1 249/3; WW2 265/5, 268-9
Belize city of C America founded by British 156/3, 161/1
Belize (*form.* British Honduras) independence 273/2 (inset); economy 295/1
Bellary district of S India ceded to Britain 168/3
Belleau Wood NE France WW1 249/3 (inset)
Belorussia (*a/s* Byelorussia, *a/c* Belarus) independence from USSR 290/3
Belostok (*now* Białystok) Poland in Russian Empire 227/1
Belsen (*correctly* Bergen-Belsen) N Germany concentration camp 268/1
Belzec S Poland concentration camp 268/1
Bemba tribe of Rhodesia 163/1, 235/1
Benares (*anc.* Kasi *now* Varanasi) N India 83/1, 128-9, 168/3; Hindu-Muslim clashes 279/3
Bender (*mod.* Bendery *Rom.* Tighina) S Russia Ottoman conquest 166/1
Bendigo SE Australia goldfield 233/5
Benevento (*anc.* Beneventum) C Italy 111/1; dukedom under Byzantine Empire 113/1; ✕ 122/2
Beneventum (*mod.* Benevento) C Italy Roman Empire 87/1, 89/1
Bengal country of E India 128/4; under Mughal Empire 167/1, 169/1; under British rule 168/3, 190/2, 231/3; anti-colonial revolt 244/1, 257/1; partition between India and Pakistan 278/2, 279/3
Benghazi (*anc.* Berenice *Ar.* Banghazi) Libya Ottoman rule 225/1, 235/1; Italian occupation 237/1; WW2 265/5, 269/3
Benguela Angola Portuguese settlement 163/1, 235/1, 237/1; 18C trade 195/1
Benin early state of Nigeria 135/1, 163/1, 235/1
Benin (*form.* Dahomey) country of W Africa independence 272/2
Benkulen Sumatra trading post 173/1
Benqi (Penki)
Bentheim W Germany country 187/1
Bentonville E USA ✕ 219/1
Bent's Fort C USA fur station 216/1
Beograd (Belgrade)
Beothuk Newfoundland Indian tribe 145/1
Berar C India sultanate 128/4, 169/1; tribal territory 231/3
Berbati S Greece Mycenaean site 67/1
Berbera Somalia Muslim Colony 135/1; British occupation 237/1
Berbers people of NW Africa, attack Roman Africa 94/1; incursions into Morocco 132/1
Berenice Red Sea early trading port 70/1, 82/4; Roman Empire 91/1
Berenice (*mod.* Benghazi) Libya city of Roman Empire 89/1, 91/1; early bishopric 93/1
Berezina river of W Russia ✕ 201/1
Berezov (*now* Berezovo) W Siberia founded 159/1
Berg W Germany Reformation 178/2; duchy 187/1,4, 200/2
Bergama (Pergamum)
Bergamo (*anc. Bergomum*) N Italy medieval city 119/1
Bergen Norway bishopric 101/2; Hanseatic trading post 142/1; WW2 265/5
Bergen (Mons)
Bergen Belsen (Belsen)
Bergomum (*mod.* Bergamo) N Italy invaded by Huns 99/1
Beringia N Pacific land bridge 37/4
Bering Strait N Pacific European discovery 153/3,195/2
Berlin Germany Hanseatic city 142/1; 18C urban development 177/2; urban development 186/2; population growth 205; industrial development 206/1, 208/1; WW1 249/3; Communist uprising 254/2, 260/2; WW2 268-9; divided 271/4; Cold War 292/2
Bermuda British colony in W Atlantic, 240/1
Bern (*Fr.* Berne) Switzerland Zähringen town 121/6; early canton 140/3; Reformation 179/1; industrial development 208/1
Bernicia region of NE England Anglo-Saxon invasion 99/3
Beroea (*mod.* Veroia) N Greece bishopric 93/1; Jewish community 103/1
Beroea (*mod.* Aleppo) Syria Roman fort 88/3
Berri E Arabia oilfield 283/3
Berry region of C France Frankish Royal domain 123/1, 147/3; province 189/1
Bersham N England Industrial Revolution 197/1
Berytus (*mod.* Beirut) Lebanon Roman Empire 89/1, 91/1; early bishopric 93/1
Besançon (*anc.* Vesontio) E France archbishopric 106/3; medieval fair 142/1; gained by France 188/2; French Revolution 199/2
Beshbalik W Mongolia 127/1,3
Besigheim W Germany Mithraic site 72/1
Bessarabia region of Romania/Russia acquired by Russia 159/1; Ottoman province 225/1; lost to Romania 255/1; regained by Russia 261/1, 265/5
Besseringen W Germany La Tène site 84/1
Beth Katraye SE Arabia early bishopric 101/1
Bethlehem Palestine bishopric 93/1
Béthune N France fort 189/1
Betsileo Kingdom Madagascar 235/1
Beverley NE England Industrial Revolution 197/1
Bewdley W England Industrial Revolution 197/1
Beyrouth (Beirut)
Bhabra (Bairat)
Bhagatrav NW India Harappan site 65/1
Bhaja (Karli)
Bhakra-Nangal N India dam 279/3
Bharuch (Broach)
Bhilai C India steel plant 279/3
Bhonsla state of C India 168/3; alliance with Britain 190/2 (inset)
Bhopal C India chemical plant 279/3
Bhota (*mod.* Tibet) 83/2
Bhrigukaccha (Broach)
Bhutan Himalayan kingdom 231/3, 279/3; end of Chinese tributary status 228/2; British influence 273/1
Biache-Saint-Vaast N France site of early man 32/2
Biafra E Nigeria civil war 281/1
Białystok (Belostok)
Biak NW New Guinea captured by US 267/2
Bianzhou (Pien-chou)
Bibi Hakimeh W Iran oilfield 283/3
Bibracte C France Roman Empire 86/3
Bidar sultanate of S India, 128/4
Big Bell W Australia gold town 233/5
Big Hole NW USA ✕ 217/4
Big Mound N USA ✕ 217/4
Bigorre region of SW France under English rule 123/1; independent fief 147/3
Bihar state of E India Muslim expansion 104/2; Sultanate of Delhi 129/3; Mughal Empire 169/1; under British control 168/3, 190/2; 231/3, 279/3
Bijapur sultanate of SW India, 128/4, 169/1
Bilá Hora (White Mountain)
Bilbao N Spain 18C financial centre 177/2; industrial development 206/1, 208/1; Civil War 264/3
Billungmark district of N Germany 117/1
Bilma W Africa early trade 134/2, 163/1; occupied by French 237/1
Biloxi S USA fur station 216/1
Bilston C England Industrial Revolution 196/3
Bilzingsleben Germany site of early man 32/2
Bimlipatan NE India Dutch settlement 169/1
Bindon SW England ✕ 99/3
Bingen W Germany Mithraic site 72/1
Binh Dinh (Vijaya)
Bioko (Fernando Po)
Bird Creek C USA ✕ 217/4
Birka E Sweden Viking trade centre 110/3
Birkenhead N England Industrial Revolution 196/3
Birmingham C England 18C urban development 177/2; Industrial Revolution 196/3, 197/1; industrial development 206/1, 208/1; bombed in WW2 265/5
Birmingham SE USA industry 214/1
Birten N Germany ✕ 118/3
Bisa tribe of C Africa, 235/1
Bishapur S Persia town of Parthian Empire 79/3
Bishopbridge E England Industrial Revolution 197/1
Bishop's Stortford S England Industrial Revolution 197/1
Bisio NW Italy principality 183/3
Bisitun W Persia town of Achaemenid Empire 79/1
Bist Sasanian town 79/3
Biterrae S France bishopric 92/1
Bithynia ancient country of NW Anatolia 75/1, 76/1; Roman province 86/3, 91/2; Byzantine Empire 113/1
Bithynia and Pontus Anatolia Roman province 89/1
Bitlis E Anatolia Byzantine Empire 113/1
Bitolj (*n/s* Bitola *Turk.* Manastir *a/s* Monastir) S Yugoslavia Ottoman control 137/1
Bituricae C France archbishopric 92/1
Biysk Russ. C Asia founded 158/3
Bizerta (*anc.* Hippo Zarytus *Fr.* Bizerte *Ar.* Banzart) Tunisia Mediterranean trade 132/1; Spanish occupation 182/2; WW2 269/3
Bjerre N Denmark Megalithic site 42/2
Blackburn NE England Industrial Revolution 196/3
Blackburn S Africa Iron Age site 45/1
Blackfoot W Canada Plains Indian tribe 145/1
Black Forest SW Germany colonization 121/3; 18C industrial growth 186/2
Blackheath S England ✕ 181/1
Black Patch S England Megalithic site 42/2
Black Sea early trade 52/1
Blagoveshchensk Russ. Far East 227/2; industry 289/1
Blekinge region of S Sweden under Danish rule 116/2; acquired by Sweden 184-5
Blenheim (*Ger.* Blindheim) W Germany ✕ (called Höchstädt by French and Germans) 188/3
Blenheim S Island, New Zealand founded 232/1
Blois region of N France 147/3
Bloody Brook NE USA ✕ 217/4
Bloody Ridge NE USA ✕ 217/4
Bloody Run NE USA ✕ 217/4
Blue Turks tribe of Mongolia 95/1
Bluff S Island, New Zealand aluminium 232/1
Bobangi early state of C Africa 235/1
Bobbio N Italy monastery 100/3, 107/3
Bobriki (Novomoskovsk)
Bodh Gaya NE India Buddhist site 73/1
Bodiam SE England Industrial Revolution 197/1
Bodrum (Halicarnassus)
Boeotia ancient country of C Greece, Persian influence 74/3; League 76/4
Boer Republic S Africa 234/3
Boğazköy (*anc.* Hattushash *Gr.* Pteria) C Anatolia site 66/1
Boğdan (*Eng. Moldavia*) vassal state of Ottoman Empire 137/1
Bohai (Po-hai)
Bohemia (*Ger.* Böhmen) W part of mod. Czechoslovakia occupied by Poland 117/3; medieval German Empire 118/3, 119/1, expansion 139/1; Black Death 141/1; acquired by Habsburgs 146/1,2, 182/2, 193/3; Thirty Years' War 178/2; Reformation 179/1; 18C industrial growth 186/2; kingdom within Holy Roman Empire 186-7; conquest by Prussia 192/4; Austro-Hungarian Empire 193/3, 261/1
Bohuslän province of S Sweden acquired from Denmark 184-5
Bolgar (*a/c* Bulgar) C Russia city of the Volga Bulgars 114/4, 115/1, 126/1; Viking trade 110/3
Bolivia country of S America independence 222-3, 240/1; exports and foreign investments 222/3; population 222/4; 20C revolutions 284-5; economy 215/1, 294/1
Bologna (*anc.* Felsina *later* Bononia) N Italy Mithraic site 72/1; medieval city 119/1, 122/2; 18C urban development 177/2
Bolsheretsk Russ. Far East founded 158/3,195/2
Bolton N England Industrial Revolution 196/3, 197/1
Bombay W India early trade 157/1, 168/2, 195/1; British settlement 169/1; industry 214/1, 231/3; British rule 230/1; Shiv Sena disturbances and Hindu-Muslim clashes 279/3
Bombo Kaburi E Africa Iron Age site 45/1
Bona (*mod.* Annaba *Fr.* Bône) N Algeria acquired by Habsburgs 146/1,2; Spanish occupation 182/2
Bonaire island of Dutch West Indies 223/1, 240/1, 273/2 (inset)
Bonampak E Mexico Maya site 46/2
Bondu early state of W Africa 234/1
Bône (*mod.* Annaba *Sp.* Bona *anc.* Hippo Regius) N Algeria Pisan raids 120/2; Mediterranean trade 142/1; French invasion 235/1
Bonin Islands (*a/c* Ogasawara Islands) N Pacific annexed by Japan 239/2; WW2 266-7
Bonn W Germany capital of Federal Republic 271/2
Bonna (*mod.* Bonn) W Germany Roman Empire 90/1
Bonny W Africa 18C trade 195/1
Bononia (*earlier* Felsina *mod.* Bologna) N Italy Roman Empire 87/1, 89/1
Bonteberg S Africa Iron age site 45/1
Bophuthatswana S Africa independent Bantustan 281/1
Bordeaux (*anc.* Burdigala) SW France early archbishopric 106/3; occupied by English 140/4; medieval fair 142/1; 16C urban development 176/1; trading port 176/3; 18C financial centre 177/2; St Bartholomew Massacre 178/3; Ormée revolt 181/1; industry 189/1; French Revolution 199/2
Border Cave S Africa site of early man 33/1
Borger Holland site 42/2
Borgu States W Africa 163/1
Borneo (*Indon.* Kalimantan) island of East Indies Muslim expansion 104/3, 131/3; Dutch trade 173/1; Dutch and British colonization 241/1; WW2 266-7; confrontation with Malaysia 277/1
Bornhöved N Germany ✕ 119/1
Borno Nigeria early state 163/1, 235/1
Borobudur C Java Buddhist site 73/1; political centre 131/2
Borodino W Russia ✕ 201/1
Bororo forest Indian tribe of S Brazil 145/1
Bosna Saray (*n/c* Sarajevo) C Yugoslavia captured by Ottomans 137/1
Bosnia country of C Yugoslavia vassal state of Ottoman Empire 137/1; under Hungarian Kingdom 139/1; Black Death 141/1
Bosnia-Herzegovina (*S. Cr.* Bosna i Hercegovina) region of S Yugoslavia part of Austria-Hungary 211/2; under Ottoman rule 224/1; Balkan alliances 246-7; after WW1 261/1; independence 290/3
Bosnians people of C Yugoslavia 261/3
Bosporan Kingdom S Russia 86/3, 89/1
Boston E England medieval trade 142/1; Industrial Revolution 197/1
Boston NE USA founded 157/2; British naval base 190/1; trade 194/3; 215/1
Boston Post Road NE USA 216/1
Bostra S Syria Roman fort 88/3, 91/1; early archbishopric 93/1
Botany Bay SE Australia penal settlement 233/5
Botocudo Indian tribe of S Brazil 145/1
Botswana (*form. Bechuanaland*) S Africa independence 272/2; political development 281/1; economy 295/1
Bouchain N France fort 189/1
Bouga S Greece Mycenaean site 67/1
Bougainville one of Solomon Islands, W Pacific WW2 266-7
Bougie (*anc.* Saldae *Sp.* Bugia *mod.* Bejaia) N Algeria Genoese raids 120/2
Bougon N France Megalithic site 42/2
Boulogne (*anc.* Gesoriacum) N France fort 189/1
Boulonnais region of NE France Burgundian possession 147/2
Bouqras SE Syria early village 41/1
Bourbon (*now.* Réunion) island of Indian Ocean French possession 190/2
Bourbon (Bourbonnais)
Bourbonnais (*a/c* Bourbon) region of C France Royal domain 123/1; annexed to France 146/1, 147/3
Boure early state of W Africa 134/1
Bourges (*anc.* Avaricum) C France St Bartholomew Massacre 178/3; 189/1
Bourg-la-Reine C France medieval *villeneuve* 121/7
Bourgogne (Burgundy)
Bourg-St Andéol S France Mithraic site 72/1
Bourne E England Industrial Revolution 197/1
Boussargues S France early settlement 43/1
Bouvines NE France ✕ 119/1, 123/1
Boyacá Colombia ✕ 222/2
Bozeman Trail and Pass NW USA 216/1
Bozzolo N Italy county 183/3
Brabant region of Belgium/Holland medieval German Empire 119/1, 123/1; Burgundian possession 147/2
Bracara (*mod.* Braga) Portugal archbishopric 92/1, 101/2
Bradford N England Industrial Revolution 197/1
Braga (Bracara)
Brahmagiri S India site 64/3
Branč Czechoslovakia burial site 43/1
Branco, Cape W Africa Portuguese exploration 162/2
Brandenburg region of E Germany margraviate under German Empire 117/1; Black Death 141/1; Hohenzollern territory 146/1; Reformation 178/2,

Brass – Caroline Islands

179/1; Electorate 186-7; 18C industrial growth 186/2; part of Prussia 212/3
Brass Nigeria 18C trade 195/1; early European settlement 235/1
Bratislava (*Ger.* Pressburg *Hung.* Pozsony) Slovakia WW1 249/3
Bratsk SC Siberia founded 158/3; industry 288/3, 289/1
Braunschweig (Brunswick)
Brazil discovered 153/1; Portuguese colony 154/1, 161/1; Atlantic trade 194/3; independent Empire 223/1, 240/1; immigration from Europe 205/2; exports and foreign investment 222/3; population 222/4; industrialization and economy 215/1, 262/3, 284-5, 294/1
Brecon W Wales Industrial Revolution 197/1
Brega E Ireland early kingdom 117/1
Breisach W Germany gained by France 188/2
Breitenfeld E Germany ⚔ 178/2
Bremen N Germany bishopric 100/3; archbishopric 117/1, 187/1; Hanseatic city 142/1; Reformation 178/2, 179/1; urban development 186/2; industrial development 206/1; German customs union 213/1; WW1 249/3; short-lived Soviet Republic 254/2; WW2 269/3; city-state 271/2
Bremen and Verden region of N Germany lost by Sweden 184-5
Bremerhaven N Germany WW1 249/3; city-state 271/2
Brenner Austria tunnel 253/2
Brenta, River N Italy ⚔ 111/1
Brescia (*anc.* Brixia) N Italy medieval city 119/1, 122/2
Breslau (*n/c* Wrocław) W Poland Hanseatic city 142/1; 18C financial centre 177/2; Reformation 179/1; urban and industrial development 186/2, 207/1, 209/1; WW1 249/3
Brest NW France English base for 100 Years' War 140/4; fort 189/1; naval base 191/1; French Revolution 199/2
Brest (*a/c* Brest-Litovsk *Pol.* Brześć nad Bugiem) W Russia 227/1, 255/1; WW1 249/3
Bretagne (Brittany)
Bretons Celtic people of NW France, 106/1, 210/1
Bretteville-le-Rabet N France Megalithic site 42/2
Briançon SE France fort 189/1
Bridgnorth W England Industrial Revolution 197/1
Bridgwater W England Industrial Revolution 197/1
Brieg (*Pol.* Brzeg) W Poland Reformation 178/2
Brigantes Britain early tribe 88/1
Brigetio Hungary Mithraic site 72/1; Roman Empire 91/1
Brihuega C Spain ⚔ 188/3
Brindisi (*anc.* Brundisium) S Italy captured by Normans 120/2; WW1 249/3
Briocum NW France monastery 93/3
Brisbane E Australia founded 233/5
Bristol W England trading port 176/3; 18C urban development 177/2; industrial development 197/1, 208/1; bombed in WW2 265/5
Britain conversion to Christianity 72/1; invasion by Germanic tribes 98/1, 99/3; 18C trade 194. See also England, United Kingdom
Britannia (*mod.* Britain) Roman Empire 91/2
Britannia Inferior Roman province of N England, 88/1
Britannia Superior Roman province of S England 88/1
British Bechuanaland S Africa 237/1
British Cameroons (*now part of* Cameroon) W Africa protectorate 272/1
British Columbia province of W Canada economic development 215/2; joins Confederation 240/1; border dispute with Alaska 242/3
British East Africa (*now* Kenya) colony 236/2, 237/1, 241/1, 245/2
British Empire 241/1
British Guiana (*now* Guyana) S America colony 215/1, 223/1, 240/1
British Honduras (*now* Belize) C America colony 223/1, 240/1, 243/4
British North Borneo (*now* Sabah) protectorate 257/1, 273/1
British Somaliland (*now part of* Somalia) E Africa protectorate 214/1, 236/2, 241/1, 256/1, 273/2
Britons tribe of SW England, movement to Brittany 99/1
Brittany (*Fr.* Bretagne) NW France on borders of Frankish Empire 106/3; duchy 117/1; conquered by Normans 123/1; Hundred Years' War 140/4; Black Death 141/1; annexed to France 147/3
Brivas C France monastery 93/3
Brixia (*mod.* Brescia) N Italy attacked by Goths 99/1
Brno (*Ger.* Brünn) Moravia WW1 249/3
Broach (*anc.* Barygaza *mod.* Bharuch) NW India ceded to Britain 168/2
Brody SE Poland WW1 249/3
Brogne S Belgium monastic reform 118/3
Broken Hill SE Australia mining 233/5
Broome W Australia early settlement 233/5
Broseley C England Industrial Revolution 196/3, 197/1
Brouage W France port 189/1
Bruges (*Dut.* Brugge) Belgium medieval city 119/1, 120/1; urban revolt 141/1; Hanseatic city 142/1, 143/3; 16C urban development 176/1; town of Spanish Netherlands 181/1; WW1 248-9
Brundisium (*mod.* Brindisi) S Italy Latin colony 87/1; Roman Empire 89/1, 91/1; Byzantine Empire 113/1
Brunei sultanate of N Borneo spread of Islam 104/3, 131/3; early trade 173/1; recaptured from Japanese 267/2; independence 273/2; British troops 274/2; Azahari revolt 277/1; economy 295/1
Brunete C Spain Civil War 264/3
Brünn (*Cz.* Brno) Czechoslovakia urban and industrial development 186/2, 209/1
Brunswick (*Ger.* Braunschweig) N Germany early city and duchy 119/1; urban revolt 141/1; Hanseatic city 142/1; German state 212/3; WW1 249/3
Brunswick-Lüneburg duchy of N Germany Reformation 179/1; 187/1
Brunswick-Wolfenbüttel duchy of N Germany 187/1
Brusa (Bursa)
Brussels (*Fr.* Bruxelles *Dut.* Brussel) Belgium 16C urban development 176/1; 18C urban development 177/2; city of Spanish Netherlands 181/1, 186/1; industrial development 206/1, 208/1; WW1 248-9; WW2 265/5, 269/3
Bruttii ancient tribe of S Italy 86/2
Bruxelles (Brussels)
Bryansk W Russia bishopric 101/2; town of Novgorod-Seversk 115/1; WW2 269/3,5; industry 289/1
Brzeg (Brieg)
Bubastis Lower Egypt 58/1; Jewish community 103/1
Bucellarian Theme Byzantine province of C Anatolia, 112/3
Bucephala NW India on Alexander's route 77/1, 82/3
Bucharest (*Rom.* București *Turk.* Bükreş) Romania in Ottoman Empire 225/1; WW1 249/3; railway strike 263/2; WW2 268-9
Buchenwald W Germany concentration camp 268/1
Buckingham S England Industrial Revolution 197/1
București (Bucharest)
Buda Hungary Ottoman conquest 166/1
Budapest Hungary 18C urban development 177/2; industrial development 207/1, 209/1; WW1 249/3; WW2 268-9
Budaun region of N India 129/3
Buenos Aires Argentina colonized 154/1, 161/1; trade 194/3, 215/1
Buganda state of E Africa 163/1
Bugia (anc. Saldae *Fr.* Bougie *mod.* Bejaia) Algeria acquired by Habsburgs 182/2
Bu Hasa Abu Dhabi oilfield 283/3
Bujak vassal state of Ottoman Empire in SW Russia 137/1
Bukavu E Belgian Congo Congo crisis 280/2
Bukhara city and province of C Asia limit of Alexander's route 77/1, 822; early bishopric 101/1; Muslim conquest 105/1; under Abbasids 109/1; in Timur's empire 126/4; trade 133/1; khanate 167/1, 225/1, 226/2; People's Republic incorporated into USSR 254/3; industry 289/1
Bukit Tinggi (Fort de Kock)
Bukovina region of Romania gained by Habsburgs 193/3; WW1 249/3
Bükreş (*Eng.* Bucharest *Rom.* București) Romania Ottoman control 137/1
Bukht Ardashir Sasanian town 79/3
Bulandshar N India Indian Mutiny 230/1
Bulgar (Bolgar)
Bulgaria conversion to Christianity 101/2; Empire 108/1, 112/4; Slav settlement 112/2; Mongol invasion 126/2; Christian state 136/2; Black Death 141/1; under Ottoman rule 137/1, 225/1; independence 211/2, 226/4; Balkan alliances 246-7; WW1 248-9; conflict with Greece 261/1; socio-political change 1929-39 263/2; WW2 265/5, 268-9; Warsaw Pact and Comecon 270/1; communism overthrown 290/3
Bulgarians emigration from Greece and Turkey 261/3
Bulgars tribe of Europe 99/1
Bull Run (*a/c* Manassas) SE USA ⚔ 219/1
Buna SE New Guinea recaptured by Allies 267/2
Bunce Island Sierra Leone British settlement 157/1, 162/1
Bundelkhand district of C India 231/3
Bunker Hill NE USA ⚔ 160/3
Buntoto early state of E Africa 235/1
Bunyoro early state of E Africa 163/1
Buqayq (Abqaiq)
Büraburg W Germany bishopric 100/3
Burdigala (*mod.* Bordeaux) SW France Roman Empire 88/1, 90/1; early archbishopric 92/1
Burford C England mutiny of Parliamentary forces 180/2
Burgan Kuwait oilfield 283/3
Burgdorf E Switzerland Zähringen town 121/6
Burgos N Spain Civil War 264/3
Burgundiones (*Eng.* Burgundians) early tribe of Germany 89/1; invade France 99/1,2
Burgundy (*Fr.* Bourgogne) region of E France kingdom 98/2; kingdom conquered by Franks 106/1,3; 111/1; province of medieval German Empire 118-9; French Royal domain 123/1; acquisitions 14C and 15C 140/4; Black Death 141/1; possessions in Low Countries 147/2; annexed to France 146/1, 147/3; province of France 189/1
Burkina Fasso (*f/c* Upper Volta) country of W Africa political development 281/1
Burma spread of Buddhism 73/1; early state 131/2; tributary state of Chinese Empire 171/1, 228/2; conquests 173/1; annexed by Britain 230/2; under British rule 231/3, 241/1, 257/1; anti-colonial resistance 244/1; Japanese support for independence movements 264/2; Japanese occupation 266/1; British recapture 267/2; independence 273/2; boundary agreements with China 277/1, 279/4; economic development 274/2, 279/3, 295/1
Burma Road SW China 264/2, 266/2
Burnley N England Industrial Revolution 197/1
Burnt Corn SE USA ⚔ 217/4
Bursa (*anc.* Prusa *later* Brusa) W Anatolia Byzantine Empire 133/2; centre of Ottoman state 137/1
Burundi (*form.* Urundi) country of C Africa native state 163/1, 235/1; independence 272/2; political development 281/1; economy 295/1. See also Ruanda-Urundi
Burwell E England Industrial Revolution 197/1
Bury N England Industrial Revolution 196/3, 197/1
Buryat-Mongol ASSR E USSR 288/2
Buryats Mongolian tribe 127/1
Bury St. Edmunds E England Industrial Revolution 197/1
Bushehr Bushire)
Bushire (*Pers.* Bushehr) Persian Gulf 128/2
Bushmen tribe of S Africa 35/2, 234/3
Bushy Run NE USA ⚔ 217/4
Busiris Lower Egypt ancient city 58/1
Bussa W Africa reached by Mungo Park 234/2
Buto Lower Egypt early urban centre 52/1; capital 58/1
Buwayhids (Buyids)
Buxar NE India ⚔ 190/2 (inset)
Buxentum S Italy Roman colony 87/1
Buyids (*a/c* Buwayhids) Muslim dynasty of Persia 133/1
Byblos (*mod.* Jubail) Syria early trade 54/1, 57/1, 66/1; Phoenician city 75/1; Alexander's route 76/1
Býčí Skála Czechoslovakia late Hallstatt site 85/1
Byelorussia (Belorussia)
Byelorussian SSR (*a/c* White Russian SSR) 288/2, 289/1
Bylany Czechoslovakia site 43/1, 85/1
Byzantine Empire (*a/c* East Roman Empire) 99/1, 105/1, 112-3, 120/2; conflict with Seljuks 133/1; decline 136/2
Byzantium (*Eng.* Constantinople *Norse* Mikligard *mod.* Istanbul) E Thrace Dorian colony 74-5; Roman Empire 70/1, 89/1, 91/1; Achaemenid Empire 78/1
Cabeço da Arruda C Portugal Megalithic site 42/2
Cabinda coastal district of SW Africa occupied by Portuguese 237/1; part of Angola 272/1
Cacaxtla Mexico Classic site 46/2
Cáceres W Spain Civil War 264/3
Cachar district of E India 230/2
Cacheu W Africa Portuguese settlement 162/1
Caddo S USA Indian tribe 145/1
Cádiz (*anc.* Gades) SW Spain reconquered from Muslims 122/3; Mediterranean trade 142/1; trading port 176/3; 18C urban development 177/2; naval base 191/1; imperial trade 194/3; Civil War 264/3
Caen N France 181/1, 189/1; French Revolution 199/2; WW2 269/3,6
Caere (*mod.* Cerveteri) C Italy Etruscan city 75/1; Roman Empire 87/1
Caerleon (Iscal)
Caernarvon (*Wel.* Caernarfon *anc.* Segontium) N Wales ancient principality 123/1
Caesaraugusta (*mod.* Zaragoza *Eng.* Saragossa) N Spain Roman Empire 89/1, 90/1; early archbishopric 92/1
Caesarea C Israel Roman Empire 89/1, 91/1, 92/2; early archbishopric 93/1; town of Judaea 103/2; Byzantine Empire 112/2
Caesarea (*mod.* Cherchell) N Algeria Roman Empire 89/1
Caesarea (*mod.* Kayseri) C Anatolia Roman Empire 89/1, 92/2; Jewish community 103/1; Byzantine Empire 113/1,5
Caesarea Cappadociae (*mod.* Kayseri) C Anatolia early archbishopric 93/1
Caesarodunum (Tours)
Caesaromagus (Chelmsford)
Cagliari (Carales)
Cahokia C USA early site 46/3; French post 157/2; fur station 216/1
Cahuachi C Andes site 47/4
Cai (Ts'ai)
Caiguá forest Indian tribe of S Brazil 145/1
Cairns E Australia early settlement 233/5
Cairo (*Fr.* Le Caire *Ar.* Al Qahirah and Al Fustat - Old Cairo) Egypt Muslim conquest 105/1; early trade 133/1, 135/1, 150/2; captured by Ottomans 137/1; Ottoman Empire 166/1, 225/1; WW1 249/4
Cajamarca C Andes site 47/4,5; 145/3; Pizarro captures Atahuallpa 154/3
Cajamarqilla C Andes site 47/5
Cajon Pass SW USA 216/1
Calabria region of S Italy part of Kingdom of Naples 122/2
Calagurris (*mod.* Calahorra) N Spain Roman Empire 88/1
Calah (*OT* Kalhu *mod.* Nimrud) Mesopotamia capital of Assyria 57/1
Calahorra (Calgurris)
Calais N France Hundred Years' War 140/4; WW1 248-9; WW2 269/3
Calcutta E India trade 157/1, 195/1; British settlement 169/1; 18C trade 195/1; industry 214/1, 231/3
Çaldiran (*a/s* Chaldiran) E Turkey ⚔ 137/1
Caldy Island S Wales monastery 100/3
Caledonia (*mod.* Scotland) Roman Empire 91/2, 98/1
Cales C Italy Latin colony 87/1
Calgary W Canada growth 215/2
Calicut (*a/c* Kozhikode) SW India trade 147/1, 155/1; Portuguese exploration 162/2; 168/2; industry 231/3
California state of SW USA ceded by Mexico 223/2; 19C politics 231/2,3; Depression 262/1; income and population 287/2; immigration from China and Japan 205/2
Calizzano NW Italy principality 183/3
Callao Peru trade 154/1
Callatis Bulgaria Ionian colony 75/1
Calleva (*mod.* Silchester) S England Roman Empire 88/1
Calliena NW India port 82/4
Callipolis (*mod.* Gallipoli) S Italy Greek colony 75/1
Calne SW England Industrial Revolution 197/1
Calusa Indian tribe of SE USA 145/1
Caluso NW Italy Monferrat principality 183/3
Camarina Sicily Dorian colony 74/4, 75/1; Roman Empire 86/3
Cambaluc Mongolia early bishopric 101/1
Cambay NW India trading centre 168/2
Cambodia (*known formally as* Democratic Kampuchea *earlier* Khmer Republic) early sites 130/1; temple kingdoms 131/2; invaded by Siam and Vietnam 173/1; French protectorate 225/2; independence 273/2; Khmer Rouge 277/1; Vietnamese war 277/3
Cambous S France early settlement 43/1
Cambrai N France early bishopric 117/1; Burgundian possession 147/2; WW1 249/3 (inset)
Cambria (*mod.* Wales) expansion of Christianity 100/3
Cambridge E England Viking fort 110/2; Industrial Revolution 197/1
Camden SE USA ⚔ 160/3
Camerinum (*mod.* Camerino) N Italy Roman Empire 87/1
Cameroon (*f/s* Cameroons, Caméroun *Ger.* Kamerun) country of W Africa 214/1; German colony 236-7, 241/1; revolt 245/2; independence 272/2; political development 281/1; economy 214/1
Cammin (*mod.* Kamień Pomorski) NW Poland founded by Germans 138/2
Campa forest Indian tribe of S America 145/1
Campania region of C Italy Roman Empire 871/1
Campeche province of S Mexico 223/1
Campo NW Italy principality 183/3
Camulodunum (*mod.* Colchester) S England Roman Empire 88/1, 90/1
Cana (*a/s* Cane) S Arabia early port 70/1, 82/4
Canada early trade 195/2; immigration from Europe 205/2; economic development 215/1,3, 262/3, 295/1; Confederation 240/1; boundary dispute with USA 242/3; NATO 293/1; economy 294/1
Çanakkale (*f/s* Chanak) W Turkey Greco-Turkish War 225/3
Çanakkale Boğazi (Dardanelles)
Canal de Briare N France 189/1
Canal Royal S France 189/1
Canal Zone Panama 242/2
Canary Islands on early trade routes 155/1; Portuguese exploration 162/2; Spanish sovereignty 240/1
Canaveral, Cape (*for a short time called* Cape Kennedy) SE USA 152/2
Canberra SE Australia capital territory 233/5
Çandar (*a/c* Kastamonu) early emirate of N Anatolia 137/1
Candelaria W Cuba Soviet missile site 293/6
Candia (*mod.* Iraklion) Crete Mediterranean trade 142/1
Candida Casa S Scotland monastery 93/3, 100/3
Canea (*mod. Gr.* Khania) Crete WW2 265/5
Cangwu (Ts'ang-wu)
Cangzhou (Ts'ang-chou)
Canhasan C Anatolia site 41/1
Çankiri (Gangra)
Canluan (Ts'an-luan)
Cannae S Italy Roman Empire 86/3
Canterbury (*anc.* Durovernum *ecclesiastical Lat.* Cantuaria) S England monastery 100/3 and bishopric 101/2,3; archbishopric 117/1; Industrial Revolution 197/1
Canterbury S Island, New Zealand 232/1
Cantigny NE France WW1 249/3 (inset)
Canton (*n/s* Guangzhou *W/G* Kuang-chou) S China trade 71/1, 125/2, 150/2, 155/1, 157/1, 164/2, 173/1, 195/1; T'ang city 109/1; treaty port 228/2; Anglo-French campaign 229/1; captured by Kuomintang 258/1; captured by Japanese 264/2; industry 214/1, 259/3, 274/3
Canton River S China first European visit 153/1
Cantuaria (*mod.* Canterbury) early archbishopric 92/1
Canusium (*mod.* Canosa di Puglia) S Italy Roman Empire 87/1
Cao (Ts'ao)
Caparcotna Palestine Roman Empire 91/1
Cape Artemisium (*mod. Gr.* Artemision) E Greece ⚔ 74/3
Cape Bojador NW Africa ⚔ 162/1; Portuguese exploration 162/2
Cape Breton Island E Canada French possession 191/1
Cape Coast Castle (*a/c* Cape Coast) Ghana early British settlement 162/1 (inset), 235/1
Cape Colony S Africa captured by British from Dutch 190/2, 235/1; British colony 237/1, 240/1 (inset); immigration from Europe 205/2
Cape Finisterre NW Spain ⚔ 190/3
Capeletti NW Africa cattle domestication 45/1
Cape of Good Hope S Africa first European voyage 153/1; Dutch settlement 157/1
Cape Province S Africa established by Dutch East India Co. 163/1
Cape St. Vincent S Portugal ⚔ 190/3
Cape Town South Africa Dutch settlement 163/1; trade 195/1
Cape Verde Islands W Africa Portuguese exploration 162/1,2; Portuguese sovereignty 240/1; independence 272/2, 281/1; population growth 294/2
Capitanata region of C Italy part of Kingdom of Naples 122/2
Caporetto SW Austria-Hungary WW1 ⚔ 249/3
Cappadocia (*Pers.* Katpatuka) country of E Anatolia Alexander's Empire 76/1, 82/3; independent state 86/3; Roman province 89/1; Byzantine province 112/3
Capsa (*mod.* Gafsa) Tunisia Roman Empire 89/1
Capua S Italy Mithraic site 72/1; Roman Empire 87/1, 91/1; Jewish community 103/1
Carabobo Venezuela ⚔ 222/2
Caracas Venezuela colonized 161/1
Carajá forest Indian tribe of C Brazil, 145/1
Carales (*a/s* Caralis *mod.* Cagliari) Sardinia Roman Empire 86/2, 89/1; archbishopric 92/1
Carapito N Portugal Megalithic site 42/2
Carcare NW Italy principality 183/3
Carchemish (*Turk.* Karkamiş) E Anatolia 54/1, 57/1,2
Cardiff S Wales Industrial Revolution 197/1
Cardigan early principality of Wales 123/1
Caria (*Per.* Karka) country of W Asia Minor Persian province 74/3, 75/1; Roman Empire 91/2
Carib Indian tribe of Caribbean 145/1
Caribbean early voyages of discovery 152/2; European settlement 154/1, 156/3; colonial expansion 161/1; imperial trade 194/3; US involvement 243/4
Carinthia (*Ger.* Kärnten) province of S Austria Frankish duchy 118/2; medieval German Empire 119/1; acquired by Habsburgs 139/1, 182/2, 193/3; Black Death 141/1; Habsburg duchy 187/1
Carlisle N England rebellion against Henry VIII 181/1; Industrial Revolution 197/1
Carmagnola NW Italy Saluzzo principality 183/3
Carmana (Kirman)
Carmania country of E Persia 77/1, 79/3, 83/1,3
Carmarthen early principality of Wales 123/1
Carmathians Muslim sect of Arabia 133/1
Carmaux S France industrial development 206/1
Carnac NW France early trade 52/1
Carnatic (*a/c* Karnata) coastal region of SE India 169/1, 190/2 (inset)
Carniola (*Ger.* Krain) region of Austria/Yugoslavia medieval Germany 119/1; acquired by Habsburgs 139/1, 182/2, 193/3; Habsburg duchy 187/1
Carnuntum ancient town of Austria Mithraic site 72/1; Roman Empire 89/1, 99/1
Carolina N America British settlement 157/2
Caroline Islands C Pacific German sovereignty 241/1; WW2 266-7

Carolingian Empire – Ch'u

Carolingian Empire (Frankish Kingdom)
Carpathos (*It.* Scarpanto) island of E Mediterranean colonization 67/1
Carpi N Italy ⚔ 188/3
Carrawburgh (Procolitia)
Carretto NW Italy margravate 183/3
Carrhae (*mod.* Haran) E Anatolia ⚔ 78/3; in Seleucia 86/3; Roman fort 88/3; Byzantine Empire 113/1
Carrier sub-arctic Indian tribe of NW Canada, 145/1
Carromore N Ireland Megalithic site 42/2
Carrosio NW Italy principality 183/3
Carsioli N Italy Roman Empire 87/1
Carson City W USA mining site 216/1
Cartagena (*anc.* Carthago Nova) SE Spain naval base 191/1; Civil War 264/3
Cartagena Colombia colonial trade 154/1
Carteia S Spain Roman Empire 89/1
Carthage (*Lat.* Carthago) Tunisia Iron Age site 45/1; Mithraic site 72/1; Phoenician colony 75/1; Roman Empire 86/3, 89/1, 91/1; early archbishopric 92/1; Byzantine reconquest 99/1; Muslim conquest 104/1
Carthago Nova (*mod.* Cartagena) SE Spain Roman Empire 86/3, 88/1, 90/1; archbishopric 92/1; Byzantine reconquest 99/1
Casablanca (*Ar.* Dar el Beida) W Morocco Ottoman Empire 224/1; French occupation 247/2
Cascades NW USA ⚔ 217/4
Cashel Ireland bishopric 92/1, 117/1
Caspian Gates N Persia Alexander's route 77/1
Cassano N Italy ⚔ 188/3
Cassian Way (Via Cassia)
Cassino C Italy WW2 269/3 See also Monte Cassino
Castelletto NW Italy principality 183/3
Castellón de la Plana E Spain Civil War 264/3
Castiglione N Italy principality 183/3
Castiglione N Italy ⚔ 201/1
Castiglione NW Italy Tuscan principality 183/3
Castiglione N Italy Venetian principality 183/3
Castile region of Spain at time of Reconquista 122/3, Black Death 140/1; acquired by Habsburgs 146/1, 182/2
Castillo de Teayo Mexico Aztec town 144/2
Castle Cavern S Africa Iron Age site 45/1
Castoria N Greece Byzantine Empire 113/5
Castra Regina (*mod.* Regensburg *form. Eng.* Ratisbon) C Germany German fort 88/2, 91/1
Castrum Novum N Italy Roman Empire 87/1
Castulo (*mod.* Cazlona) S Spain Roman Empire 88/1
Catalans people of NE Spain 210/1
Catalaunian Fields C France ⚔ 98/1
Çatal Hüyük C Anatolia site 41/1
Catalonia (*Sp.* Cataluña *Cat.* Catalunya) region of NE Spain reconquest by Aragon 122/3; under French rule 200/1; autonomous 261/1
Catana (*mod.* Catania) Sicily ally of Athens 74/4; Roman Empire 89/1; medieval German Empire 119/1
Catanzaro S Italy WW1 249/3
Catawba Indian tribe of SE USA 145/1
Cattigara S China early port 71/1
Cattaro (*mod.* Kotor) E Adriatic Venetian territory 183/1, 211/2; WW1 249/3
Caucasus early urban settlement 52/1; Muslim expansion 105/1
Caudium C Italy Roman Empire 87/1
Caulonia S Italy Roman Empire 87/1
Cawahib forest Indian tribe of W Brazil 145/1
Cawnpore (*n/s* Kanpur) N India Indian Mutiny 230/1
Cayapó forest Indian tribe of C Brazil 145/1
Cayenne French Guiana colonization 161/1
Çayönü E Anatolia early village 42/1
Cazlona (Castulo)
Ceará NE Brazil Confederation of the Equator 223/1
Cedar Creek C USA ⚔ 217/4
Cedar Mountain SE USA ⚔ 219/1 (inset)
Cefalù (*anc.* Cephaloedium) Sicily medieval German Empire 119/1
Celebes (*Indon.* Sulawesi) island of East Indies Muslim expansion 104/3; WW2 266-7
Celenderis S Anatolia Ionian colony 75/1
Celts tribe of Europe, France 60/1, 75/1; major settlements 84/3; N Italy 86/2; 98/2
Cempoala Mexico Aztec town 144/2; Cortés' route 155/1
Centallo NW Italy Saluzzo principality 183/3
Central African Federation (Northern Rhodesia, Southern Rhodesia, Nyasaland)
Central African Republic (*form.* Central African Empire *earlier* Ubangi-Shari) independence 272/2; political development 281/1
Central Asian Gasfield USSR 289/1
Central India Agency Indian states under British control, 230-1
Central Provinces (*now* Madhya Pradesh) state of central India 231/3
Ceos (*mod.* Kea) island of the Aegean colonization 67/1
Cephaloedium (Cefalù)
Cephalonia (*mod.* Kefallinia) island of the Ionian Byzantine Empire 113/5; Venetian territory 136/1, 183/1
Cerdagne (*Sp.* Cerdaña) region of France and Spain 189/1
Cerdicesford S England ⚔ 99/3
Ceribon (Cheribon)
Cerigo (*anc.* Cythera *mod. Gr.* Kithira) island S Greece Venetian fort 183/1
Çerkes (Circassia)
Cernăuţi (Czernowitz)
Cerro de Trinidad C Andes early site 47/4
Cerros Belize Mayan site 46/2
Cerveteri (Caere)
Cēsis (Wenden)
Český Těšin (Teschen)
Cetatea Alba (Akkerman)
Ceuta (*Ar.* Sebta) Spanish enclave in N Morocco Portuguese rule 182/1; Spanish occupation 235/1, 247/2, 256/1
Ceylon (*anc.* Taprobane, Sinhala *or* Lanka *a/c* Saylan, Sarandib *Chin.* Hsi-lan) 82/4, 83/1; under Cholas 128/2; trade 150/2, 195/1; captured from Dutch 190/2; under British rule 168/3, 231/3, 241/1, 257/1; independence 273/2; adopted title Republic of Sri Lanka 279/3,4; Tamil insurgency and intervention by Indian Army 279/5; industry and economy 214/1, 295/1
Chad (*Fr.* Tchad) country of C Africa independence from French 272/2; political development 281/1
Chad, Lake C Africa European exploration 234/2
Chaeronea C Greece 74/4
Chafarinas Islands N Morocco Spanish occupation 247/2
Chagar Bazar (Shubat-Enlil)
Chagatai Khanate C Asia 126/4, 127/3
Chagos Archipelago Indian Ocean British control 190/2, 241/1
Chahar former province of N China 171/1; independent of Nanking 258/2
Chaiya S Thailand Hindu-Buddhist remains 131/2
Chakipampa C Andes early site 47/5
Chalcedon (*mod.* Kadıköy) NW Anatolia centre of early Christianity 72/1; Dorian colony 75/1; Roman Empire 86/3; Council 93/1; Byzantine Empire 112/2,3
Chalcidice (*mod.* Khalkidhiki) region of N Greece Persian War 74/3
Chalcis C Greece parent state 75/1
Chaldeans people of Mesopotamia 56/3
Chaldian Theme Byzantine province of E Anatolia, 112/3
Chaldiran (Çaldiran)
Chalon Moulineux C France medieval *villeneuve* 121/7
Chalon-sur-Saône S France medieval fair 142/1
Châlons-sur-Marne N France bishopric 117/1, seat of intendant 189/1; WW1 249/3, WW2 265/5
Chalukyas ancient dynasty of S India 128/2, 129/1
Chambéry SE France medieval fair 142/1
Champa Hindu-Buddhist kingdom of Indo-China 125/2; under Mongol control 127/1, 131/2,3
Champagne region of NE France medieval trade 120/1; French Royal domain 123/1, 147/3; 189/1; WW1 249/3
Champaubert NE France 201/1
Champion's Hill S USA ⚔ 219/1
Chanak (*Turk.* Çanakkale) W Turkey 1922 incident 261/1
Chancelade France site of early man 32/2
Chancellorsville SE USA ⚔ 219/1
Chandellas ancient dynasty of N India 128/2, 129/1
Chandernagore E India French settlement 157/1, 169/1, 190/2 (inset)
Chandigarh N India capital of Punjab 279/3
Ch'ang-an (*n/s* Chang'an) N China trading capital 71/1; Han capital 82/2; T'ang city 108/2, 124/1
Chang-chia-k'ou (Kalgan)
Ch'ang-chih (*n/s* Changchi) N China industry 214/1
Ch'ang-chou (*n/s* Changzhou) E China T'ang prefecture 124/1
Ch'ang-ch'un (*n/s* Changchun) Manchuria treaty port 228/2; railway 238/3, 259/3; industry 274/2
Chang-i (*n/s* Changyi) NW China Han commanderie 81/2
Changkufeng Manchuria Russo-Japanese conflict 264/2
Ch'ang-sha (*n/s* Changsha) C China Han principality 81/2; treaty town 228/2; captured by Kuomintang 258/1; captured by Japanese 266/1; industry 214/1, 259/3, 274/3
Chang-yeh (*n/s* Zhangye) NW China conquered by Han 80/3
Changyi (Ch'ang-i)
Changzhou (Ch'ang-chou)
Chanhu-Daro N India Harappan site 65/1
Channel Islands WW2 269/6
Chansen N Thailand Iron Age site 130/1
Chao (*n/s* Zhao) early state of N China 80/1
Chao-ming (*n/s* Zhaoming) N Korea Han prefecture 81/2
Characene early kingdom of Mesopotamia 78/2; vassal state of Parthian Empire 79/1
Charakopio S Greece Mycenaean site 67/1
Charax early port on Persian Gulf, 70/1, 82/4
Charcas N Mexico Spanish centre 154/1
Chard SW England Industrial Revolution 197/1
Chardzhou (*until 1940* Chardzhuy) Russ. C Asia industry 289/1
Charikar (Alexandria)
Charleroi Belgium industrial development 206/1; WW1 249/3 (inset)
Charles Town Path SE USA settlers' route 216/1
Charleville E Australia railway 233/5
Charolais region of E France Habsburg possession 147/3, 181/1
Charrúa Indian tribe of Argentina 145/1
Charsadda N W India early trade 70/1
Charsianum C Anatolia Byzantine Empire 112/3
Charsinian Theme Byzantine province of C Anatolia 112/3
Chartres C France WW1 249/3
Château-sur-Salins E France late Hallstatt site 84/1
Château-Thierry N France ⚔ 201/1; WW1 248/2, 249/3 (inset)
Chatham SE England Dutch naval raid 181/1; naval base 191/1; Industrial Revolution 197/1; WW1 249/3
Chattanooga SE USA ⚔ 219/1
Chatti Germanic tribe of Roman Empire 89/1
Chauci Germanic tribe of Roman Empire 89/1
Chaul W India Portuguese settlement 169/1
Chavín C Andes site 47/1
Chechen-Ingush ASSR Caucasus 288/2
Che-chiang (Chekiang)
Chedi early kingdom of N India 65/1, 83/2
Chekiang (*n/s* Zhejiang *W/G* Che-chiang) province of E China Ming economy 164/2; Manchu expansion 171/1; T'ai-p'ing control 229/1; Hsin-hai revolution 229/3
Chełm (Kholm)
Chełmno Poland concentration camp 268/1
Chelmsford (*anc.* Caesaromagus) E England Industrial Revolution 197/1
Chelyabinsk C Russia industry 227/1, 288/2, 289/1; urban growth 288/3
Chemin des Dames NE France WW1 249/3 (inset)
Chemnitz (*since 1953* Karl-Marx-Stadt) E Germany industrial development 206/1, 208/1; WW1 249/3
Chemulpo (Inchon)
Ch'en (*n/s* Chen) N China Chou domain 63/4
Chencang (Ch'en-ts'iang)
Cheng (*n/s* Zheng) N China Late Chou domain 63/4
Cheng-chou (*n/s* Zhengzhou *a/s* Chengchow) N China Shang city 62/2; on railway 259/3
Ch'eng-tu (*n/s* Chengdu) W China on trade route 71/1; Han prefecture 81/2; T'ang prefecture 124/1; Ming provincial capital 165/1; industry 274/3
Ch'eng-tu Fu (*n/s* Zhengdufu) W China Sung province 125/5
Chenstokhov (*Pol.* Częstochowa) C Poland in European Russia 227/1
Chen-ting-fu (*n/s* Zhendingfu) N China Sung provincial capital 125/5
Ch'en-ts'ang (*n/s* Chencang) C China Han prefecture 81/2
Chepstow W England Industrial Revolution 197/1
Chera (*mod.* Kerala) region of S India 83/1
Cherbourg N France English base in Hundred Years' War 140/4; French naval base 191/1; WW1 249/3; WW2 269/3,6
Cherchell (Caesarea)
Cherchen (Ch'ieh-mo)
Cheremkhovo S Siberia industry 289/1
Cherepovets NW Russia industry 289/1
Cheribon (*Dut.* Tjeribon *n/s* Ceribon) district of Java Dutch control 172/3
Cherkess AD Caucasus 288/2
Chernigov Ukraine bishopric 101/2; principality 115/1
Chernovtsy (Czernowitz)
Cherokee Indian tribe of SE USA 145/1
Cherokees SE USA ⚔ 217/4
Chersonesus Crimea Ionian colony 75/1; bishopric 93/1
Cherusci Germanic tribe of Roman Empire 89/1
Chesowanja E Africa site of early man 33/1
Chester (*anc.* Deva) C England ⚔ 99/3; Viking trade 110/2; county palatine 123/1; Industrial Revolution 197/1
Cheyenne plains Indian tribe of C USA 49/1
Ch'i (*n/s* Qi) NE China Chou domain 62/3, 63/4; state 80/1, 124/3
Chia (*n/s* Jia) NW China Western Chou domain 62/3
Chia-mu-ssu (Kiamusze)
Ch'iang (*n/s* Qiang) border people of NW China 63/4
Chiang-hsi (Kiangsi)
Chiang-hsia (*n/s* Jiangxia) C China Han commanderie 81/2
Chiang-hsi-an (*n/s* Jiangxi'an) S China early settlement 62/1
Chiang-hsi Nan (*n/s* Jiangxi Nan) C China Sung province 125/5
Chiang-ling (*n/s* Jiangling) C China Western Chou site 62/3; T'ang prefecture 124/1; Sung provincial capital 125/5
Chiang Mai (Chiengmai)
Chiang-nan Hsi-tao (*n/s* Jiangnan Xidao) S China T'ang province 124/1
Chiang-nan Tung (*n/s* Jiangnan Dong) E China Sung province 125/5
Chiang-nan Tung-tao (*n/s* Jiangnan Dongdao) SE China T'ang province 124/1
Chiang-ning-fu (*n/s* Jiangningfu) E China Sung provincial capital 125/5
Chiang-su (Kiangsu)
Chiao (*n/s* Jiao) N China Western Chou domain 62/3
Chiao-chih (*n/s* Jiaozhi) China-Vietnam Han commanderie 81/2
Chiao-ho (*n/s* Jiaohe) Chin. C Asia Han expansion 80/3
Chiao-hsien (Kiaochow)
Chiao-li (*n/s* Jiaoli) NE China Han prefecture 81/2
Chiapa de Corzo C Mexico early site 46/2
Chiapas province of S Mexico 223/1
Chiba C Japan city and prefecture 214/2; industry 239/1
Chibcha Andean Indian tribe 145/1
Chicago N USA industry 215/1, 287/1
Chichén Itzá Mexico Maya site 46/2; Toltec domination 144/2
Chichester S England Industrial Revolution 197/1
Ch'i-ch'i-ha-erh (Tsitsihar)
Chi-chou (*n/s* Jizhou) NE China T'ang prefecture 124/1; Ming military post 165/1
Ch'i-ch'un (*n/s* Qichun) C China Western Chou site 62/3
Chickamauga SE USA ⚔ 219/1
Chickasaw Indian tribe of SE USA 145/1, 217/4
Ch'ieh-mo (*n/s* Qiemo *a/c* Qarqan *n/s* Cherchen) Chin. C Asia Han expansion 80/3
Ch'ien-ch'eng (*n/s* Qiancheng) NE China Han prefecture 81/2
Chien-chou (*n/s* Jianzhou) NE China Ming military post 165/1
Ch'ien-chung (*n/s* Qianzhong) SW China T'ang province 124/1
Chiengmai (*n/s* Chiang Mai) N Thailand early political centre 131/2,3
Chien-nan (*n/s* Jiannan) W China T'ang province 124/1
Ch'ien-t'ang (*n/s* Qiantang) E China Han prefecture 81/2
Chien-wei (*n/s* Jianwei) W China Han commanderie 81/2
Chietao district of Manchuria occupied by Russia 238/3
Chieti (Teate)
Chihli former province of N China Manchu expansion 171/1; Boxer uprising 229/1
Chi-hsi (*n/s* Jixi) Manchuria industry 274/3
Chihuahua province of N Mexico 223/1; US military action 243/4
Chile Spanish colony 154/1, 161/1; 222-3; independence from Spain 240/1; 284-5; exports and foreign investment 222/3; population 222/4; economy 215/1, 294/1
Chilia-Nouă (Kilia)
Chi-lin (Kirin)
Chimkent Russ. C Asia industry 289/1
Chimú Andean Indian tribe 145/1,3
Chin (*n/s* Jin) N China Chou domain 62/3, 63/4; state 124/3; empire conquered by Mongols 127/1
Ch'in (*n/s* Qin) NW China Chou domain 62/3, 63/4; empire 80/1,2,3
China agricultural origins 39/1, 62/1; development of writing 53; beginnings of civilization 62-3; early trade routes 71/1; silk route 71/1; spread of epidemics 71/2; Buddhism and Taoism 73/1; Han expansion 80/3; population growth 80/4, 125/4; early Christianity 101/1; T'ang and Sung 109/1; 124-5; Mongol conquests 127/1,3; Ming Empire 151/1; 164/9; early trade 150/2, 157/1, 173/1; Ch'ing 170/2,3; Manchu expansion 171/1; 18C overseas trade 195/1; Manchu Empire 228-9; Russo-Japanese war 238/3; Japanese influence 239/2; European spheres of influence 241/1; Boxer rebellion 244/1; Empire overthrown 275/1; Communist Party founded 254/3; Japanese occupation 264/2, 266/1, 267/2; Revolution 258-9; Cold War 289/3; emigration to USA 205/2; industry and economy 214/1, 274/3, 295/1; conflict with Vietnam 277/1; conflict with India 279/3; boundary disputes with India, Burma and Pakistan 279/4
Chi-nan (*n/s* Jinan *a/s* Tsinan) N China Ming provincial capital 165/1; industry 214/1
Chin-ch'eng (*n/s* Jincheng) NW China Han commanderie 81/2
Chin-chiang (Chinkiang)
Chin-chou (*n/s* Jinzhou) NE China Ming military post 165/1
Ch'in-feng (*n/s* Qinfeng) NW China Sung province 125/5
Ching-chao-fu (*n/s* Jingzhaof) N China Sung provincial capital 125/5
Ching-chi (*n/s* Jingji) N China T'ang province 124/1
Ch'ing-chiang (*n/s* Qingjiang) SW China Sung provincial capital 125/5
Ch'ing-chou (*n/s* Qingzhou) NE China Sung provincial capital 125/5
Chinghai (Tsinghai)
Ching-hsi Nan (*n/s* Jingxi Nan) C China Sung province 125/5
Ching-hsi Pei (*n/s* Jingxi Bei) C China Sung province 125/5
Ching-hu Nan (*n/s* Jinghu Nan) SW China Sung province 125/5
Ching-hu Pei (*n/s* Jinghu Bei) Sung province 125/5
Ching-kang Shan (*n/s* Jinggang Shan) SE China early Communist soviet 259/3
Chingleput SE India ceded to Britain 168/3
Ching-nan (*n/s* Jingnan) early state of C China 124/3
Ch'ing-tao (*n/s* Qingdao *a/s* Tsingtao) E China industry 274/3
Ching-tung Hsi (*n/s* Jingdong Xi) N China Sung province 125/5
Ching-tung Tung (*n/s* Jingdong Dong) NE China Sung province 125/5
Chinju S Korea industrial centre 275/1
Chinkiang (*n/s* Jinjiang *W/G* Chin-chiang) E China treaty port 228/2
Chinkultic E Mexico Maya site 46/2
Chin-men (Quemoy)
Chinnampo N Korea Russo-Japanese war 238/3
Chinook coast Indian tribe of W Canada, 145/1
Chin Special Division administrative territory of W Burma 279/3
Chinsura Bengal Dutch settlement 157/1, 169/1
Chin-t'ien (*n/s* Jintian) S China T'ai-p'ing rebellion 229/1
Chin-yang (*n/s* Jinyang) N China Late Chou city site 63/4
Chios (*mod. Gk.* Khios) island of E Aegean bishopric 93/1; Byzantine Empire 112/3; to Genoa 137/1, 147/1; gained by Turks 183/1; ceded to Greece 211/2
Chipewyan sub-arctic Indian tribe of N Canada, 145/1
Chisholm Trail C USA cattle trail 216/1
Chishima-retto (Kurile Islands)
Chisimaio (Kismayu)
Chişinău (Kishinev)
Chita E Siberia Trans-Siberian railway 226/2; capital of Far Eastern Republic 254/3; industry 289/1
Chittagong SE Bangladesh trade 231/3, 279/3
Chiu-chang (*n/s* Jiuzhang) E China Han commanderie 81/2
Chiu-chen (*n/s* Jiuzhen) N Indo-China Han commanderie 81/2
Chiu-chiang (Kiukiang)
Chiu-ch'üan (*n/s* Jiuquan) NW China conquered by Han 80/3; Han commanderie 81/2
Chiu-hua Shan (*n/s* Jiuhua Shan) mountain of E China Buddhist site 73/1
Ch'iung-chou (*n/s* Qiongzhou) S China treaty port 228/2
Chiusi (Clusium)
Chi-yang (*n/s* Jiyang) C China Han prefecture 81/2
Chlum Czechoslovakia La Tène site 85/1
Chocó Indian tribe of S America 145/1
Choctaw Indian tribe of S USA 145/1, 217/4
Choga Mami Mesopotamia site 41/1
Choga Mish W Persia early city 55/3
Chola ancient country of S India 83/1
Cholas dynasty of S India and Ceylon 128/2, 129/1
Cholet W France French Revolution 199/2
Cholula C Mexico early site 46/2; Aztec site 144/2; on Cortés' route 155/2
Chongjin N Korea industrial centre 275/1
Chongju S Korea industrial centre 275/1
Chongqing (Chungking)
Chonju S Korea industrial centre 275/1
Chorasmia (*a/c* Khiva, Khwarizm) country of C Asia 82/3
Chorasmii people of C Asia 77/1
Chosen (Korea)
Chota Nagpur district of C India 231/3
Chotin (*n/s* Khotin) Ukraine Thracian site 85/1
Chou (*n/s* Zhou) NC China Western Chou domain 62/3; warring state 80/1
Chou-k'ou-tien (*n/s* Zhoukoudian) N China site 33/1, 37/1, 62/1
Christchurch S Island, New Zealand Maori settlement 49/3; founded 232/1
Christiania (*mod.* Oslo) Norway 185/1
Christiansborg Gold Coast early Danish settlement 162/1 (inset)
Christos C Crete Minoan palace 67/1
Chrysovitsa C Greece Mycenaean site 67/1
Chu (*n/s* Zhu) N China Western Chou domain 62/3
Ch'u (*n/s* Chu) C China Chou domain 62/3, 63/4; warring state 80/1
Ch'u (*n/s* Chu) NE China Western Chou domain 62/3
Ch'u (*n/s* Chu) state of SW China 124/3

Ch'üan-chou – Delaware

Ch'üan-chou (*n/s* Quanzhou) S China Ming trade 164/2
Chud (*a/c* Chudi) early tribe of N Russia 101/2, 115/1
Chudskoye Ozero (Lake Peipus)
Chukchi tribe of NE Siberia, 158/3
Chukchi AD NE Siberia 288/2
Chü-lu (*n/s* Julu) N and S China Han prefectures 81/2
Chumash Indian tribe of W USA 145/1
Chün (*n/s* Jun) C China Western Chou domain 62/3
Chün (*n/s* Jun) N China Western Chou site 62/3
Chunchon S Korea industrial centre 275/1
Ch'ung-ch'ing (Chungking)
Chungking (*n/s* Chongqing *W/G* Ch'ung-ch'ing) C China treaty town 228/2; industry 259/3, 274/3; capital during WW2 264/2,3
Ch'ü-sou (*n/s* Qusou) N China Han prefecture 81/2
Chustenahlah C USA ✕ 217/4
Chuvash ASSR C Russia 288/2
Chuvashi tribe of C Russia, conquered 159/1; 288/4
Ch'u-wo (*n/s* Chuwo) N China Late Chou city site 63/4
Chu-yai (*n/s* Zhuya) S China Han prefecture 81/2
Chü-yen (*n/s* Juyan) NW China administrative centre of later Han 80/3
Chü-yüan-ho-k'ou (*n/s* Juyuanhekou) E China site of early man 33/1
Ciboney Indian tribe of the Caribbean 145/1
Cibyrrhaeot Theme Byzantine province of S Anatolia, 112/3
Cieszyn (Teschen)
Ciglie Gottasecca NW Italy Monferrat principality 183/3
Cilicia (*Hittite name* Kizzuwadna) region of S Anatolia 54/1; Hittite Empire 57/1; early trade 66/4; Persian Empire 75/1; Alexander's Empire 76/1, 82/3; Achaemenid Empire 79/1; Roman province 86/3, 89/1; Byzantine Empire 113/1
Cimmerians people of Asia Minor 56/3, 61/1
Cincinnati N USA industry 215/1
Circassia (*Turk.* Çerkes) region of Caucasus 137/1
Circeii C Italy Latin colony 87/1
Cirencester (*anc.* Corinium) W England Industrial Revolution 197/1
Cirene (Cyrene)
Cirta (*mod.* Constantine) N Algeria Roman Empire 86/3, 89/1, 90/1; early bishopric 92/1
Cisalpine Gaul (Gallia Cisalpina)
Cisalpine Republic N Italy state established by French Revolution 199/3
Cishan (Tz'u-shan)
Ciskei S Africa independent Bantustan 281/1
Cissbury S England Megalithic site 42/2
Cisterna NW Italy principality 183/3
Citium (*OT* Kittim) Phoenician colony 75/1
Ciudad de México (Mexico City)
Civita Castellana (Falerii)
Civitas Nemetum (Speyer)
Clava N Scotland Megalithic tomb 42/2
Clearwater NW USA ✕ 217/4
Cleveland N USA industry 215/1, 287/1
Cleves (*Ger.* Kleve) NW Germany Reformation 178/2; duchy 187/1
Clonard Ireland monastery 93/3, 100/3
Cloncurry N Australia copper mining 233/5
Clonfert Ireland monastery 100/3
Clonmacnoise Ireland monastery 100/3
Clontarf E Ireland ✕ 117/1
Clontibret NE Ireland ✕ 181/1
Cloyne Ireland bishopric 92/1
Cluny C France centre of monastic reform 118/3
Clusium (*mod.* Chiusi) N Italy Etruscan city 86/2
Clysma Red Sea early port 70/1; Roman Empire 91/1
Cnossus (*Gr.* Knossos) Crete Roman Empire 89/1, 91/1
Coahuila province of N Mexico 223/1; US military action 243/4
Coahuiltec Indian tribe of N Mexico 145/1
Coalbrookdale C England Industrial Revolution 196/3
Coba Mexico Maya site 46/2
Coblenz (*n/s* Koblenz) W Germany WW1 249/3, 271/2
Cochimi Indian tribe of W Mexico 145/1
Cochin (*early Chin.* Ko-chih) region of S India Portuguese rule 155/1; Dutch settlement 157/1, 169/1; 18C trade 195/1; British rule 230/1
Cochin-China region of S Indo-China expansion into Cambodia 173/1; French control 240/1 (inset), 257/1; claimed by Cambodia 277/1
Cocos Islands (*now* under Australian administration *called* Cocos-Keeling Islands) Indian Ocean British control 241/1
Coele Roman province of SE Anatolia 89/1
Colchester (*anc.* Camulodunum) Viking centre 110/2
Colchis ancient country of the Caucasus, Ionian colonization 75/1, 76/1; 89/1
Coldizzi Slav tribe of SE Germany 138/2
Colima province of C Mexico 223/1
Colle di Tenda NW Italy tunnel 253/2
Cologne (*anc.* Colonia Agrippina *Ger.* Köln) W Germany medieval city 118/3, 119/1, 120/1, 121/8; Hanseatic city 139/1; archbishopric 107/3, 117/1, 187/1; 18C urban development 176/1; 18C urban development 206/1, 208/1; WW1 249/3; WW2 269/3
Colombia independence from Spain 222-3, 240/1; exports and foreign investment 222/3; population 222/4; political development 284-5; economy 215/1, 294/1
Colombo Ceylon Portuguese trade 155/1; Dutch trade 157/1,195/1; Dutch settlement 169/1; capital of British colony 231/3
Colón Panama Canal Zone 242/2
Colonia Agrippina (*a/c* Colonia Agrippinensis *mod.* Köln *Eng.* Cologne) NW Germany Mithraic site 72/1; Roman Empire 89/1, 90/1; bishopric 92/1; Jewish community 103/1
Colonia Julia Fenestris (Fanum Fortunae)
Colonian Theme Byzantine province of E Anatolia 112/3
Colorado state of W USA 1856 election 221/3; Depression 263/1; income and population 287/2
Colossae W Anatolia town of Achaemenid Empire 78/1
Columbia SE USA burned 219/1
Comacchio N Italy captured by Venice 120/2
Comalcalco Mexico Maya site 46/2
Comana ancient city of E Anatolia 112/3
Comanche plains Indian tribe of S USA 145/1
Comisene region of N Persia vassal state of Parthian Empire 79/3
Commagene region of SE Anatolia state 86/3; Roman province 89/1
Commendah W Africa early British settlement 162/1 (inset)
Commercy C France industrial development 206/1
Comminges independent fief of SW France 147/3
Commonwealth of Independent States 290/3
Como N Italy Lombard League 119/1
Comoro Islands E Africa spread of Islam 163/1; French colonization 241/1, 273/1; independence 273/2, 281/1; population growth 294/2
Compiègne NE France WW1 248/2
Comtat Venaissin S France Papal site 147/3
Conakry W Africa occupied by French 237/1
Condatomagus (*mod.* La Graufesenque) S France Roman Empire 90/1
Confederate States of America 218/3
Confederation of the Rhine 200/2, 201/1
Congo (*form.* Middle Congo *or* French Congo) region of C Africa independence 272/2; political development 281/1
Congo Free State (*later* Belgian Congo *now* Zaire) 237/1
Connaught (*a/s* Connacht) region of W Ireland early kingdom 117/1; Norman-Angevin overlordship 123/1; Presidency 181/1
Connecticut NE USA colony 157/2, 160/3; 19C politics 220/1,2,3; Depression 263/1; income and population 287/1
Connell's Prairie NW USA ✕ 217/4
Conscente NW Italy principality 183/3
Constance (*anc.* Constantia *Ger.* Konstanz) S Germany Frankish Kingdom 118/3
Constanța (*anc.* Tomi *Turk.* Küstence) E Romania WW1 249/3
Constantia (Salamis)
Constantine (*anc.* Cirta) N Algeria Ottoman Empire 224/1
Constantinople (*anc.* Byzantium *Norse* Mikligard *mod.* Istanbul) NW Turkey centre of early Christianity 72/1, 92/2; patriarchate 93/1, 101/2; Arab attacks 105/1; Byzantine Empire 108/3, 113/1,5; conquered 133/2; trade 110/3, 142/1, 150/2; 16C urban development 176/1; 18C urban development 177/2; WW1 249/3
Cooch Behar former state of NE India joins India at partition 278/2
Cooks Islands S Pacific early Polynesian settlement 49/1; New Zealand possession 273/2 (inset)
Cook Strait New Zealand rail ferry 232/1
Cooktown E Australia early settlement 233/5
Copán E Mexico Maya site 46/2
Copenhagen (*Dan.* Koßbenhavn) Denmark 179/1; 185/1; ✕ 190/3; WW1 249/3; WW2 269/3
Coppa Nevigata S Italy site 43/1
Copts Christian people of Egypt, 100/1
Coptus Lower Egypt trading centre 82/4; Roman Empire 89/1, 91/1; bishopric 93/1
Coquilhatville (*now* Mbandaka) NW Belgian Congo 280/2
Cora C Italy Latin colony 87/1
Cora Indian tribe of C Mexico 145/1
Coracesium S Anatolia 75/1
Coral Sea S Pacific ✕ 267/2
Corbie N France monastery 106/3
Corcyra (*mod.* Corfu *Gr.* Kerkira) island of NW Greece Dorian colony 75/1
Cordilleran ice-sheet N America 37/4
Córdoba (*anc.* Corduba) S Spain Muslim conquest 104/1; Umayyad Caliphate and Muslim city 109/5, 120/2; reconquered from Muslims 122/3; Mediterranean trade 132/1; 16C urban development 176/1; 18C urban development 177/2; Civil War 264/3
Corduba (*mod.* Córdoba) S Spain Roman Empire 86/3, 89/1, 90/1; bishopric 92/1; Jewish community 103/1
Corfinium S Italy Roman Empire 89/1
Corfu (*anc.* Corcyra *mod.* Kerkira) island of W Greece Byzantine Empire 113/5; under Venetian rule 136/1, 139/1, 183/1; Ottoman siege 166/1; 1883 incident 261/1
Corinium (Cirencester)
Corinth (*Lat.* Corinthus *Gr.* Korinthos) C Greece parent state 75/1; archbishopric 93/1; Jewish community 103/1; Byzantine Empire 113/1,5; WW2 265/5
Corinth SE USA ✕ 219/1
Corinthus (*Gr.* Korinthos *Eng.* Corinth) C Greece town of Roman Empire 89/1, 91/1
Cork S Ireland monastery 100/3; Scandinavian settlement 110/2, 111/1; bishopric under Scandinavian control 117/1
Cormantin W Africa early Dutch settlement 162/1 (inset)
Corneto (Tarquinii)
Cornwall county of SW England rebellion 181/1
Correggio N Italy county 183/3
Corregidor C Philippines surrender to Japanese 266/1
Corsica island of W Mediterranean Muslim conquest 104/1; Saracen attack 111/1; Byzantine Empire 112/1; Pisan conquest 120/2; Genoese rule 146/1, 182/2; client state of Spain 163/1; rebellion against Genoese rule 198/1; annexed by France 199/3, 213/2; WW2 268-9
Corsica and Sardinia province of Roman Empire 86/3
Corsione NW Italy principality 183/3
Cortanze NW Italy principality 183/3
Cortemilia NW Italy Savoy principality 183/3
Cortona N Italy Etruscan city 75/1, 86/2
Corunna (*Sp.* La Coruña) NW Spain ✕ 200/1
Cos island of E Aegean bishopric 93/1
Cosa N Italy Roman Empire 87/1
Cosentia (*mod.* Cosenza) S Italy Roman Empire 87/1; medieval German invasion 119/1
Cossacks S Russia attacked by Ottomans 159/1, 166/1; anti-Bolshevik activity 255/1
Cossaei tribe of W Russia 77/1
Costa Rica country of C America independence 223/1; political development 284-5; economy 294/1
Costoboci early tribe of SE Europe, 89/1
Cotyora (*mod.* Ordu) N Anatolia Ionian colony 75/1
Courland (*Ger.* Kurland) region of E Baltic occupied by Teutonic Knights 138/3; Reformation 179/1; Swedish rule 184-5
Courtrai (*Dut.* Kortrijk) Belgium ✕ 123/1
Court St. Etienne N France early Hallstatt site 84/1
Coutances NW France bishopric 117/1
Cova Negra SE Spain site of early man 32/2
Coventry C England Industrial Revolution 197/3; bombed in WW2 265/5
Coveta de l'Or SE Spain early farming 42/1
Cozumel island of Mexico Maya trading centre 144/2
Cracow (*Pol.* Kraków) SE Poland bishopric 101/2, 117/3; Hanseatic city 114/1; industrial development 209/1; WW2 268/1
Crayford S England ✕ 99/3
Crécy N France ✕ 140/4
Crediton SW England bishopric 117/1
Cree sub-arctic Indian tribe of N Canada 145/1
Creek Indian tribe of SE USA 145/1, 217/4
Crema N Italy Lombard League 119/1; Venetian principality 183/3
Cremona N Italy Latin colony 87/1; Lombard League 119/1; Signorial domination 122/2; 16C urban development 176/1
Crescent Island E Africa cattle domestication 45/1
Creta (*Eng.* Crete *mod. Gr.* Kriti) Roman province 86/3
Crete (*Lat.* Creta *mod. Gr.* Kriti) settlement 43/1; development of writing 53; migration to Greece and Aegean 66-7; Muslim conquest 104/1; Byzantine Empire 113/1, 120/2, 132/1; Venetian territory 132/2, 137/1; 147/1; Ottoman conquest from Venice 183/1, 192/1; Ottoman province 225/1; cession to Greece 211/2; German capture WW2 265/5, 268/3
Crimea (*Russ.* Krym) S Russia acquired by Russia 159/1; Ottoman vassal khanate 137/1, 166/1; War 226/4; ASSR 288/2
Cristóbal Panama Canal Zone 242/2
Crna Gora (Montenegro)
Croatia (*S. Cr.* Hrvatska) region of N Yugoslavia conversion to Christianity 101/2; Mongol invasion 126/2; under Hungarian Kingdom 139/1; acquired by Habsburgs 182/2, 193/3; forms part of Yugoslavia 261/1; WW2 268-9; acquisition of territory from Italy 271/4; independence 290/3
Croats Slav people of SE Europe, 99/1, 261/1
Crocodilopolis (Arsinoe)
Cromarty N Scotland WW1 249/3
Cromna N Anatolia Ionian colony 75/1
Crooked Creek C USA ✕ 217/4
Cross, Cape SW Africa Portuguese exploration 162/2
Crossmaglen N Ireland IRA terrorism 291/2
Croton (*mod.* Crotone) S Italy Achaean colony 75/1; Roman colony 87/1, 89/1; Mediterranean trade 142/1
Crow plains Indian tribe of W Canada 144/1
Crown Point (*Fr.* Fort St. Frédéric) Quebec capture by British 190/1
Croydon NE Australia early settlement 233/5
Crumlin S Wales Industrial Revolution 197/1
Cruni Bulgaria Ionian colony 75/1
Ctesiphon (*a/c* Tayspun) Mesopotamia early trade 70/1, 82/4; town of Parthian Empire 78/3; Roman Empire 89/1
Cuba discovered 152/2; Spanish colony 156/3, 161/1; independence 222-3, 240/1; exports and foreign investment 222/3; population 222/4; US protectorate 243/4; political development 284-5; Cold War crisis 293/6
Cuddapah S India ceded to Britain 168/3
Cuello Belize Mayan site 46/2
Cuenca Peru Inca site 145/3
Cueva de la Menga S Spain Megalithic site 42/2
Cumae C Italy Ionian colony 74/4, 75/1; Roman Empire 87/1
Cumans (*Russ.* Polovtsy) people of C Russia 126/1
Cumberland county of N England claimed by Scotland 123/1
Cumberland House C Canada fort 195/2
Cuna Indian tribe of C America 145/1
Cunaxa Mesopotamia ✕ 79/1
Curaçao island of S West Indies captured by Dutch from Spanish 156/3; Dutch settlement and colonization 161/1, 223/1, 240/1, 273/2 (inset)
Curium Cyprus Greek colony 75/1
Curlew Mountains NW Ireland ✕ 181/1
Curzon Line Poland 261/1
Cusae Lower Egypt 58/1
Cusco (Cuzco)
Custoza N Italy ✕ 213/2
Cutch (*n/s* Kutch) native state of W India 231/3
Cuttack E India ceded to Britain 168/3
Cuxhaven N Germany 212/3; WW1 249/3
Cuzco (*n/s* Cusco) Peru Inca Empire 145/3, 151/1, 154/1
Cydonia (Khania)
Cyfarthfa S Wales Industrial Revolution 196/3
Cymru (Wales)
Cynoscephalae C Greece ✕ 77/3
Cynossema W Anatolia ✕ 74/4
Cyprus (*Gr.* Kypros *Turk.* Kibris *anc.* Alashiya) early trade 66/4; Greek and Phoenician colonization 75/1; Roman province 86/3; Muslim expansion 105/1; Byzantine Empire 112-3, 121/2, 133/1; Christian kingdom 133/2, 136/2; Venetian territory 137/1; 147/1; acquired by Turks 166/1, 183/1; leased by Britain 241/1; annexed by Britain 225/1, 249/4; WW2 268-9; independence 272/2; invaded by Turkey 272/2, 282/1
Cyrenaica region of N Africa Roman province 89/1; Muslim conquest 105/1, 132/1; Ottoman rule 235/1; Italian conquest 237/1; nationalist resistance to Italian rule 256/1
Cyrene (*It.* Cirene) N Africa Iron Age site 45/1; spread of Christianity and Judaism 72/1; Achaemenid Empire 78/1; centre of Roman province 86/3; early bishopric 93/1
Cyropolis (*a/c* Krukath) C Asia Alexander's route 77/1; Achaemenid Empire 78/1
Cythera (*a/c* Cerigo *mod.* Kithira) *island* S Greece colonization 67/1; captured by Athens 74/4
Cytorus N Anatolia Ionian colony 75/1
Cyzicus NW Anatolia ✕ 74/4; Ionian colony 75/1; Roman Empire 86/3; early archbishopric 93/1; Byzantine Empire 113/5
Czechoslovakia early settlement 42-3; created 261/1; inter-war alliances 260/2; socio-political development 262/3; 263/2; territory lost to Germany and Hungary 265/4; Comecon and Warsaw Pact 270/1; overthrow of communism and dissolution 290/3
Czech Republic separation from Slovakia 290/3
Czechs post-War migration to West 270/1
Czernowitz (*now Russ.* Chernovtsy *Rom.* Cernăuţi) E Austro-Hungarian Empire 193/3; WW1 249/3
Częstochowa (Chenstokhov)
Dabarkot NW India Harappan site 65/1
Dabromierz (Hohenfriedeberg)
Dacca (*n/s* Dhaka) Bangladesh industry 214/1, 231/3; capital of new state 279/3
Dachau S Germany concentration camp 268/1
Dacia (*mod.* Romania) province of Roman Empire 89/1; Byzantine Empire 113/1
Dade Massacre SE USA ✕ 217/4
Dagestan ASSR 288/2
Daghestan region of Caucasus acquired by Russia 159/1, 225/1; ASSR 288/2
Dagon (*mod.* Rangoon) S Burma Buddhism 131/3
Dahae early tribe of Asia 77/1
Dahomey (*n/c* Benin) country of W Africa early state 163/1, 235/1; French colony 237/1, 240/1; independence 272/2; political development 281/1
Dahshur Lower Egypt site 58/1
Dai (Tai)
Daima C Africa Iron Age site 45/1
Dairen (*Chin.* Ta-lien *Russ.* Dalny) Manchuria ceded to Russia and Japan 228/2; Russo-Japanese war 242/2
Daishoji C Japan 171/4
Dai Viet kingdom of N Indo-China 131/3
Dakar Senegal, W Africa French settlement 234/1, 236/1
Dakhlah (Villa Cisneros)
Daleminzi Slav tribe of C Germany 118/2, 138/2
Dali (Ta-li)
Dallas S USA industry 215/1, 287/1
Dalmatia region of E Adriatic Byzantine Empire 113/5; Venetian possession 193/3; 261/1
Dalny (Dairen)
Daman (*Port.* Damão) NW India Portuguese settlement 169/1, 231/3, 273/1
Damascus (*Fr.* Damas *Ar.* Ash Sham *or* Dimashq) Syria Assyrian Empire 57/1; Roman Empire 86/3, 88/3, 91/1; early trade 54/1, 70/1, 133/1; archbishopric 93/1, 101/1; Jewish community 103/1; Muslim conquest 105/1; Byzantine Empire 113/1; Ottoman Empire 137/1, 166/1, 225/1; WW1 249/4; disturbances under French mandate 257/2
Damghan Persia Alexander's route 82/3
Damietta (*Ar.* Dumyat) N Egypt Byzantine Empire 113/1
Damingfu (Ta-ming-fu)
Damman E Arabia oilfield 283/3
Damme Netherlands Hansa trading post 142/1
Da Nang (*Fr.* Tourane) C Indo-China Vietnamese war 277/3
Dandong (An-tung)
Danelaw England under Scandinavian control 110/2, 117/1
Dan'er (Tan-erh)
Danger Cave N America site 47/1
Dantu (Tan-t'u)
Danyang (Tan-yang)
Danzig (*Pol.* Gdańsk) N Poland Hanseatic city 142/1; 16C urban development 176/1; 18C financial centre 177/2; corn shipments 177/4; 185/1; to Prussia 193/5; industrial development 209/1; WW1 249/3; Free City 261/1; WW2 265/5; transferred to Poland 271/2
Dao (Tao)
Dao Tay Sa (Paracel Islands)
Dara Mesopotamia Roman fort 88/3
Dara S Greece Mycenaean site 67/1
Darabgird S Persia town of Sasanian Empire 79/3
Dardanelles (*Turk.* Çanakkale Boğazi *anc.* Hellespont) straits, NW Turkey demilitarized and remilitarized 261/1
Dardani early people of the Balkans 76/1
Dar el Beida (Casablanca)
Dar es Salaam E Africa occupied by Germans 237/1
Dar es-Soltane NW Africa site of early man 33/1
Darfur region of W Sudan stone age culture 45/1; early state 135/1, 163/1, 235/1
Darjeeling N India 231/3
Darlington N England Industrial Revolution 196/3
Dartford SE England Industrial Revolution 197/1
Darwin N Australia early settlement 233/5; Allied base in WW2 267/2
Dascylium NW Anatolia Greek colony 75/1; Achaemenid Empire 78/1
Das Island Persian Gulf oil terminal 283/3
Datong (Ta-t'ung)
Daugavpils (Dünaburg)
Dauphiné region of SE France French Royal domain 123/1, 147/3; province of France 189/1
Davaka NE India tributary state 82/5
Dawenkou (Ta-wen-k'ou)
Dead Buffalo Lake E USA ✕ 217/4
Dęblin (Ivangorod)
Debre Birhan Ethiopia monastery 100/1
Debrecen Hungary WW2 269/3
Debre Markos Ethiopia monastery 100/1
Decapolis Judaea 103/2
Decazeville S France industrial development 206/1
Deccan region of C India Sultanate 167/1; Mughal Empire 169/1
Dego N Italy ✕ 201/1
Deira region of NE England Anglo-Saxon invasion 99/3
Delagoa Bay SE Africa early trade 163/1; Portuguese settlement 157/1, 190/2, 237/1
Delaware state of E USA settled by Swedes 157/2;

Delaware – Etzná

British colony 160/3; 19C politics 220/1, 221/2,3; Depression 263/1; income and population 287/2
Delaware Indian tribe of NE USA 145/1
Delhi city and region of India ✕ 104/2; Mongol invasion 126/4; Sultanate 104/2, 128-9; Mughal Empire 104/2, 167/1, 168/2, 169/1; Indian Mutiny 230/1; British control 214/1, 231/3; independence 279/1; anti-Sikh riots 279/3
Delium E Greece ✕ 74/4
Delos SE Greece in Persian wars 74/3, 77/2
Delphi C Greece Celtic settlement 84/3; Jewish community 103/1
Demetrias E Greece Byzantine Empire 113/1
Denain N France ✕ 188/3
Dendra S Greece Mycenaean site 67/1
Deng (Teng)
Denizli (Laodicea)
Denmark early settlement 42/2; conversion to Christianity 101/2; rise of 116/2; union with Norway and Sweden 141/1, 146/1; Reformation 179/1; break-up of union with Sweden 184; loss of Norway and Schleswig-Holstein 211/3; war with Prussia and Austria 212/1; population growth 204/2,3; emigration 205/1; railway development 206/1; WW1 248/1; N Holstein acquired by plebiscite 261/1; socio-political change 263/2; 1936 declaration of neutrality 264/1; WW2 271/4. 265/5; 268/1; EEC and NATO 270/1, 291/1; economy 271/4, 295/1
Denver W USA industry 215/1, 286/1
Deorham W England ✕ 99/3
Der S Mesopotamia 54/1, 55/3
Derbe S Anatolia early bishopric 93/1
Derbent Caucasus 133/1, 166/1
Derby C England Danish Viking base 111/1; Industrial Revolution 197/1
Derby W Australia early settlement 233/5
Derrynahinch SE Ireland Megalithic site 42/2
Desalpur NW India Harappan site 65/1
Desana NW Italy principality 183/3
Desert, War of the Argentina 223/1
Detroit (form. Fort Pontchartrain) C USA fur station 216/1; ✕ 217/4; industry 215/1, 287/1
Deutscher Zollverein (German Customs Union) 213/1
Deva (mod. Chester) C England Mithraic site 72/1; Roman Empire 88/1, 90/1
Deventer Netherlands Hanseatic town 142/1
Devil's Gate W USA pass 216/1
Devonport SW England WW1 249/3
Dhahran E Arabia oilfield 283/3
Dhali (Idalium)
Dhodhekanisos (Dodecanese)
Dhu'l-Qadr early emirate of SE Anatolia 137/1
Dhu Qar Mesopotamia ✕ 78/3
Dia C Crete Minoan site 67/2
Diaguita Andean Indian tribe of S America 145/1
Dian (Tien)
Dibse (Thapsacus)
Dictaean Cave C Crete Minoan site 67/1
Diedenhofen (now Thionville) NE France Frankish royal residence 107/3
Die Kelders S Africa Iron Age site 45/1
Dien Bien Phu N Vietnam French defeat 277/3
Dieppe N France fortification 189/1; WW1 248-9; WW2 269/3
Dijon E France monastic reform 118/3; parlement 189/1; French Revolution 199/2
Dilmun (a/s Tilmun) Persian Gulf early urban centre 53/1; early trade 55/1
Dilolo C Africa Livingstone's route 234/2
Dimashq (Damascus)
Dina W Anatolia on Persian Royal Road 78/1
Diocaesarea Palestine early archbishopric 93/1
Dioscurias (mod. Sukhumi) Caucasus Ionian colony 75/1; Roman Empire 91/1
Diospolis Magna (Thebes)
Dishley C England agrarian revolution 196/2
Diu NW India Portuguese settlement 155/1, 157/1, 169/1; Ottoman siege 167/1; annexed by India 273/2
Dixcove Ghana early British settlement 162/1 (inset)
Diyarbakir (anc. Amida) E Turkey Safavid Empire 137/1; Ottoman centre 166/1
Djakarta (Jakarta)
Djenné (Jenne)
Djerba island Tunisia Mediterranean trade 142/1; ✕ 166/1
Djibouti (s/s Jibuti) NE Africa occupied by French 237/1
Djibouti (f/c French Territory of the Afars and Issas earlier French Somaliland) country of E Africa independence 273/2, 281/1
Dimitrov W Russia town of Vladimir-Suzdal 115/1
Dmanisi Georgia site of early man 32/2,33/1
Dnepropetrovsk (until 1926 Yekaterinoslav) S Russia urban growth 288/3; industry 289/1
Doab, Lower and Upper districts of N India ceded to Britain 168/3
Dobrin early Prussian state 138/3
Dobruja (a/s Dobrudja) region of Romania/Bulgaria Ottoman Empire 137/1; 211/2; WW1 249/3; 261/1
Dodecanese (Gr. Dhodhekanisos) islands of SE Aegean occupied by Italy, ceded to Turkey 211/2; Ottoman province 211/2; occupied by Italy 225/1, 261/1
Dodge City C USA cow town 216/1
Dogliani NW Italy Saluzzo principality 183/3
Dogrib sub-arctic Indian tribe of NW Canada 145/1
Doha (properly Ad Dawhah) capital of Qatar Persian Gulf 283/3
Dol (anc. Dolus) NW France monastery 93/3; bishopric 117/1
Dolceaqua NW Italy margravate 183/3
Dolmen de Soto SW Spain Megalithic site 42/2
Domfront NE France 17C revolts 181/1
Dominica island of West Indies disputed by England and France 156/3, 191/1; British colony 223/1, 273/1 (inset); independence 273/2 (inset); population growth 294/2
Dominican Republic Caribbean independence 223/1; US military action 243/4; political development 284-5; US intervention 292/1; economy 294/1
Donbass industrial region of S Russia 209/1, 289/1
Doncaster N England Industrial Revolution 197/1
Donets S Russia town of Pereyaslavl 115/1
Donetsk (until 1924 called Yuzovka until 1961 Stalino) S Russia urban growth 227/1, 288/3; industry 289/1
Dong'a (Tung-a)
Dongchuanfu (Tung-ch'uan-fu)
Dong Duong C Indo-China Hindu-Buddhist temple 131/2
Dongpingling (Tung-p'ing-ting)
Dong Son N Indo-China early site 130/1
Donner Pass W USA 216/1
Dorchester S England bishopric 117/1
Dorestad (a/c Duurstede) Netherlands Viking invasion and settlement 110/3, 111/1
Dorostol (n/c Silistra) N Bulgaria ✕ 115/1
Dorpat (form. Yuryev mod. Tartu) W Russia founded by Teutonic Knights 138/3; Hanseatic city 142/1
Dortmund W Germany Hanseatic city 142/1; industry 206/1,3; 208/1
Dorylaeum (mod. Eskişehir) W Anatolia Byzantine Empire 113/5
Douai NE France medieval fair 120/1
Douala Cameroon, W Africa German occupation 237/1
Dove Creek C USA ✕ 217/4
Dover (anc. Dubris) SE England Industrial Revolution 197/1; WW1 249/3
Dowlais S Wales Industrial Revolution 197/1
Down N Ireland bishopric 92/1
Dowth E Ireland Megalithic site 42/2
Doxanii Slavs of E Europe, 138/2
Drangiana (Pers. Zranka) Afghanistan province of Alexander's Empire 77/1, 82/3
Drapsaca (mod. Kunduz) Afghanistan Alexander's Empire 77/1, 82/3
Dresden E Germany ✕ 201/1; industrial development 206/1; WW1 249/3; WW2 269/3; 271/2
Drevlyane Slav tribe of W Russia 115/1
Drobetae (mod. Turnu-Severin) Roman Empire 89/1
Drogheda E Ireland ✕ 180/2
Drogochin W Russia town of Vladimir-Volynsk 115/1
Dubai town and state of E Arabia 283/1
Dublin (Ir. Baile Átha Cliath) Ireland Scandinavian settlement and control 110/2, 111/1, 117/1; bishopric 117/1; taken by England 123/1; 16C urban development 176/1; 18C urban development 177/2; WW1 249/3; 261/1
Dubris (mod. Dover) SE England Roman Empire 90/1
Dubrovnik (Ragusa)
Duisburg W Germany WW1 249/3
Duji (Tu-chi)
Dukhan Persian Gulf oilfield 283/3
Dumfries country of S Scotland acquired by Edward III 140/2
Dumyat (Damietta)
Dünaburg (Russ. Dvinsk n/c Daugavpils) W Russia occupied by Teutonic Knights 138/3
Dunbar S Scotland ✕ 140/2, 180/2
Dunedin S Island, New Zealand Maori settlement 49/3; 232/1
Dungeness S England Dutch naval victory 181/1
Dunhuang (Tun-huang)
Dunkirk (Fr. Dunkerque) N France town of the Spanish Netherlands 181/1; fortification 189/1; WW1 249/1 (inset); WW2 265/5
Dunwich E England bishopric 100/3
Dura-Europos (mod. Salahiyeh) Syria early trade 70/1; Mithraic site 72/1; Parthian Empire 78/3; Roman Empire 86/3, 88/3, 91/1; early church 93/1
Durango province of N Mexico 223/1
Durazzo (anc. Epidamnus later Dyrrhachium mod. Durrës) Albania captured by Normans 120/2; WW1 249/3
Durban S Africa industrialization 214/1; 235/1, 237/1
Durham N England bishopric 117/1, 140/2; palatinate 123/1
Dürkheim W Germany La Tène site 85/1
Durocortorum (mod. Rheims) N France Roman Empire 89/1
Durostorum (mod. Silistra) Bulgaria Roman Empire 89/1, 91/1
Durrës (Dyrrhachium)
Dushanbe (1929-61 Stalinabad) Russ. C Asia industry 288/2, 289/2; urban growth 288/3
Düsseldorf W Germany industrial development 206/1; WW1 249/1; WW2 269/3; 271/2
Dutch East Indies (now Indonesia) early Dutch trade 157/1; early Dutch possession 173/1; industrialization 214/1; national uprisings 257/1; WW2 266-7; independence 273/1
Dutch Guiana (now Surinam) S America 215/1; 223/1, 240/1
Dutch New Guinea (later West Irian n/c Irian Jaya) East Indies transferred to Indonesia 273/2
Dutch Republic (or United Provinces or Holland) revolt against Spain 181/1; wars with England 181/1; in War of Spanish Succession 188/3; 190/3
Dutch West Indies (Netherlands Antilles)
Duurstede (a/c Dorestad) Netherlands Carolingian port 120/1
Dvaravati W Thailand early Mon kingdom 131/2
Dvin Caucasus early archbishopric 93/1
Dvinsk (mod. Daugavpils Ger. Dünaburg) NW Russia 227/1
Dyfed early kingdom of W Wales 117/1
Dyola trading people of W Africa, 134/1, 163/1
Dyrrhachium (earlier Epidamnus mod. Durrës It. Durazzo) Albania Roman Empire 86/3, 89/1, 91/1; Byzantine Empire 113/1,5
Dzaudzhikau (Ordzhonikidze)
Dzhambul (from 1936-8 called Mirzoyan earlier Auilye-Ata) Russ. C Asia industry 289/1
Dzhruchula S USSR site of early man
Dzibilchaltún E Mexico Maya site 46/2
Dzungaria region of C Asia early trade routes 71/1; occupied by Chinese 125/2
Dzungars people of NW China 171/1
East Anglia region of E England conversion to Christianity 100/3; Scandinavian settlement 110/2; under Scandinavian control 111/1
East Bengal (later East Pakistan now Bangladesh) separation from India 278/2
East Cape N Island, New Zealand Maori settlement 49/3
Easter Island E Pacific Polynesian settlement 49/1; discovered by Europeans 153/3
Eastern Rumelia region of Balkans Ottoman province 225/1; ceded to Bulgaria 211/1
Eastern Samoa (American Samoa)
Eastern Solomons ✕ 267/2
Eastern Thrace region of SE Europe occupied by Greeks 261/1
Eastern Turkestan C Asia Chinese protectorate 171/1
East Frisia county of N Germany 186/3, 187/1
East Indies agricultural origins 39/1; spread of Islam 104/3; early kingdoms 131/2,3; early trade 150/2; early European voyages 153/1; 18C trade 195/1. See also Dutch East Indies, Indonesia
East Pakistan (Bangladesh)
East Prussia (Ger. Ostpreussen) region of E Germany unification with Germany 212/3; 261/1; WW2 265/5; divided between Poland and Russia 270/1, 271/2
East Roman Empire (Byzantine Empire)
Ebbsfleet S England ✕ 99/3
Ebla Syria early urban settlement 52/1
Eburacum (mod. York) N England Mithraic site 72/1; Roman Empire 88/1, 90/1; archbishopric 92/1
Eburodunum (Embrun)
Ecbatana (mod. Hamadan) W Persia 57/1; Alexander's route 77/1; Parthian Empire 79/3; Alexander's Empire 82/3; early trade 70/1, 82/4
Echmiadzin (Vagarshapat)
Echternach W Germany monastery 100/3
Eckmühl/Ebersberg S Germany ✕ 201/1
Ecuador independence 222-3, 240/1; population 222/4; political development 284-5; economy 215/1, 222/3, 294/1
Edendale S Island, New Zealand dairy exporting 232/1
Edessa (mod. Urfa) SE Anatolia centre of Christianity 72/1; 78/3; Roman fort 88/3, 91/1; early archbishopric 93/1, 101/1; First Crusade 113/5; Crusader state 132/3
Edfu (a/s Idfu anc. Apollinopolis) Upper Egypt 59/1
Edgehill C England ✕ 180/2
Edinburgh S Scotland medieval trade 142/1; 18C urban development 177/2; National Covenant 180/2; industrial development 208/1
Edirne (Eng. Adrianople) SE Europe Ottoman Empire 137/1
Edmonton W Canada growth 215/2
Edmundston E Canada growth 215/2
Edo (mod. Tokyo) C Japan under Tokugawa Shogunate 171/4
Edremit (Adramyttium)
Edwardesabad (Bannu)
Efes (Ephesus)
Eflâk (Eng. Wallachia) region of S Romania Ottoman vassal state 137/1
Egypt (officially Arab Republic of Egypt form. United Arab Republic Lat. Aegyptus Ar. Misr) early urban settlement 45/1, 52/1; development of writing 53; ancient 58-9; Alexander's Empire 76/1; Ptolemaic kingdom 77/2,3; 86/3; spread of Christianity and Judaism 72/1, 100/1; Arab conquest 105/1; Byzantine Empire 112/2, 113/1; Fatimid Caliphate 121/2, 133/1; conquered by Turks 163/1, 166/1, 183/1; French attack 201/3; Ottoman province 225/1; expansion into Sudan 235/1; anti-colonial incident 245/2, British control 236-41, 241/1, 256/1, 272/1; WW1 249/4; WW2 265/5, 269/3; independence 282/1; political development 281/1; Anglo-French attack (Suez War) 272/2; wars with Israel 283/2, 292/5; economy 214/1, 241/1, 272/1, 295/1
Ehime S Japan prefecture 238/1
Eichstätt SE Germany bishopric 100/3, 187/1
Eigenbilzen Germany La Tène site 84/1
Eilat (Elat)
Eire (Ireland)
Eisenach N Germany industrial development 206/1
El Agheila Libya WW2 269/3
El Alamein Egypt ✕ 269/3
Elam (a/c Susiana or Uvja mod. Khuzistan) state of ancient Middle East 52/1, 56/3, 57/1
El Amarna C Egypt 58/1, 59/4
El Arish Sinai Egyptian-Israeli war 283/2
Elat (f/s Eilat) S Israel port 283/2
Elba (Ilva)
El Barranquete SE Spain Megalithic site 42/2
Elbasan Albania Ottoman Empire 137/1
El Baúl E Mexico Maya site 46/2
Elbing (Pol. Elbląg) W Poland founded by Teutonic Knights 138/3; Hanseatic city 142/1
El Camino Real S USA settlers' route 216/1
Elche (Ilici)
Elea (a/c Velia) S Italy Ionian colony 75/1; Roman Empire 86/2
Elektrostal W Russia foundation 288/3
El Fasher Sudan early trade 135/1, 150/2
El Ferrol NW Spain Civil War 264/3
Elimberrum (Auch)
Elis ancient country of W Greece 76/4
Elisabethville (now Lubumbashi) S Belgian Congo 280/2
El Jadida (Mazagan)
Ellasar (Larsa)
Ellice Islands (now Tuvalu) W Pacific British colony 241/1; WW2 266-7
Elliniko S Greece Mycenaean site 67/1
El Lisht (anc. Itj-towy) Lower Egypt 58/1
Elmedsaete Anglo-Saxon tribe of N England 99/3
Elmenteita E Africa early site 45/1
Elmham E England early bishopric 117/1
Elmina (Port. São Jorge da Mina) Ghana early trade 155/1; Portuguese fort 157/1; Dutch settlement 162/1 (inset); 18C trade 195/1
El Mirador N Guatemala Mayan site 46/2
El Mries N Morocco Megalithic site 42/2
Elne (Illiberris)
El Paso SW USA on trail west 216/1
Elsass (Alsace)
El Tajín Mexico site 47/1, 144/2
Ely E England Industrial Revolution 197/1
Elymais W Persia kingdom 78/2; vassal state of Parthian Empire 79/3
Elymi Carthaginian tribe of Sicily 86/2
Embrun (anc. Eburodunum) S France archbishopric 106/3; fort 189/1
Emden N Germany Reformation 179/1
Emei Shan (O-mei Shan)
Emerita Augusta (mod. Mérida) SW Spain Mithraic site 72/1; Roman Empire 88/1, 90/1
Emesa (mod. Homs) Syria Roman fort 88/3; Byzantine Empire 113/1
Emmaus Palestine town of Judaea 103/2
Emmen N Germany Megalithic site 42/2
Emona (mod. Ljubljana) NW Yugoslavia Roman Empire 89/1; early bishopric 92/1
Emporiae NE Spain Ionian colony 75/1
Enez (Aenus)
Engels (till 1932 Pokrovsk) SE Russia industry 289/1
England Scandinavian settlement 110/2, 111/1; under Scandinavian rule 117/1; Norman kingdom 123/1; medieval urban development 121/5; expansion of Christianity 100/3; expulsion of Jews 102/3; Black Death and religious unrest 141/1; Anglo-Scottish wars 140/2; war with France 140/4; possessions in France 147/4; Reformation 179/1; Civil War 180/2; rebellions 181/1; trade and industry 176/1; Industrial Revolution 196-7, 206-9; WW1 248-9; WW2 265/5, 268-9. See also Britain, Great Britain, United Kingdom
English Harbour Antigua, West Indies British naval base 191/1
Eniwetok Marshall Is, C Pacific captured by US 267/2
Ennedi region of N Africa rock painting 45/1
Enniskillen N Ireland IRA terrorism 291/2
Epernay NE France WW1 249/3 (inset)
Ephesus (Turk. Efes) W Anatolia early trade 54/1; Alexander's route 76/1; Roman Empire 86/3, 89/1, 91/1; Byzantine Empire 113/1; centre of early Christianity 72/1; archbishopric 93/1; Jewish community 103/1
Ephthalites (White Huns)
Epidamnus (later Dyrrhachium It. Durazzo mod. Durrës) Albania Dorian colony 75/1
Epidaurum NW Greece Mithraic site 72/1
Epinal E France WW1 249/3
Epirus ancient country of NW Greece, 75/1; independent state 76/1,4; Roman province 89/1; Byzantine Empire 112/4, 113/1; Despotate 113/5; Serbian Empire 139/1; to Greece 211/2
Episkopi C Crete Minoan palace 67/1
Equateur province of NW Belgian Congo 280/2
Equator, Confederation of the E Brazil 223/1
Equatoria province of S Sudan Egyptian expansion 235/1
Equatorial Guinea (form. Spanish Guinea a/c Rio Muni) country of W Africa independence 272/2; political development 281/1
Eran Asan Kert Kavadh Mesopotamia town of Sasanian Empire 79/3
Eran Khurra Shapur Mesopotamia town of Sasanian Empire 79/3
Erbach county of S Germany 187/1
Erech (Uruk)
Ereğ (Heraclea Pontica)
Eretna Turkoman principality of E Anatolia 136/2
Eretria E Greece parent state 75/1; war with Persia 78/1
Erfurt E Germany bishopric 100/3; Hanseatic city 142/1
Erganos E Crete Minoan site 67/2
Erh-li-t'ou (n/s Erlitou) N China Shang city 62/2
Eridu Mesopotamia 40/1, 52/1, 55/3
Erie Indian tribe of NE USA, 145/1
Eritrea region of NE Ethiopia Italian colony 236/2, 241/1, 256/1, 265/5, 273/1; political development 281/1
Ermeland region of E Germany and Poland occupied by Teutonic Knights 138/3
Erstfeld Switzerland La Tène site 85/1
Eryx Sicily Roman Empire 86/3
Erzerum (Erzurum)
Erzincan E Turkey Ottoman centre 166/1
Erzurum (a/s Erzerum) conquered by Suleiman I 166/1; 225/1
Escuintla E Mexico Maya site 46/2
Esfahan (Isfahan)
Eshnunna (mod. Tell Asmar) Mesopotamia 54/1; Amorite kingdom 54/2; 55/3
Eskimo Indian tribe of Arctic America 35/2, 145/1
Eskişehir (anc. Dorylaeum) W Turkey Ottoman centre 137/1; Greco-Turkish war 225/3
Esna (anc. Latopolis) Upper Egypt 59/1
Esperance W Australia early settlement 233/1
Espirito Santo province of Brazil 223/1
Espiritu Santo New Hebrides, W Pacific US base 267/1
Essaouira (Mogador)
Essen W Germany industrial development 206/1,3; 208/1; WW1 249/3
Essex E England conversion to Christianity 100/3
Es-Skhul Israel site of early man 33/1
Essling (Aspern)
Estonia NW USSR occupied by Teutonic Knights 138/3, 147/1; acquired by Russia 159/1; Reformation 179/1; under Swedish rule 184-5; independence from Russia 255/1, 261/1,3; inter-war alliances 260/2; socio-political change 263/1; 1936 declaration of neutrality 264/1; WW2 268-9; annexed by USSR 265/5, 270/1; constituted SSR 288/2; Estonians in USSR 288/4; independence 1991 290/3
Estrées N France French Revolution 199/2
Estremadura region of W Spain reconquered by Castile 122/3
Ests people of Estonia 115/1
Esztergom (Ger. Gran) N Hungary archbishopric 117/3
Etampes C France medieval villeneuve 121/7
Etaples NE France mutiny WW1 249/3
Ethiopia expansion of Christianity 72/1, 100/1; 16C state 163/1; Tigre Empire of Amhara 235/1; Italian invasion 237/1, 265/5; Italian colony 236/2, 256/1, 273/1; independence regained 273/2; political development 281/1
Etiani Kephala E Crete Minoan site 67/2
Etowah SE USA early site 46/3, 47/1; ✕ 217/4
Etruria ancient country of C Italy 86/2, 87/1
Etruscans ancient people of Italy 67/1, 75/1, 86/2
Etzná Mexico Maya site 46/2

Kassa – La Ferté-Bernard

Kassa (Košice)
Kastamonu C Turkey revolt against Ottoman rule 166/1. See also Çandar
Kastraki N Greece Mycenaean site 67/1
Kastri C Greece Mycenaean site 67/1
Kastri S Greece early settlement 43/1; Cretan colony 67/1
Kastri S Greece Mycenaean site 67/1
Kastro S Greece Mycenaean site 67/1
Katakolou E Greece Mycenaean site 67/1
Katanga (*now* Shaba) province of S Congo anti-colonial resistance 237/1; in Congo crisis 280/2
Kathiawar group of western Indian states under British rule, 230/1,3
Katowice (Kattowitz)
Katpatuka (*Lat.* Cappadocia) country of SE Anatolia satrapy of Achaemenid Empire 79/1
Katsambas C Crete Minoan site 67/2
Katsina Hausa city-state of N Nigeria 135/1, 163/1, 235/1
Kattowitz (*Pol.* Katowice) S Poland industrial development 207/1
Katuruka E Africa early site 45/1
Kaunas (*form. Russ.* Kovno) Lithuanian SSR industry 289/1
Kaupang (Skiringsal)
Kavrochoti C Crete Minoan palace 67/1
Kawasaki C Japan industrial centre 275/1
Kawthule State (*f/c* Karen State) S Burma 277/1
Kaxgar (Kashgar)
Kayah State (*f/c* Karenni State) C Burma 277/1, 279/3
Kayseri (*anc.* Caesarea Cappadociae *or* Mazaca) C Turkey Ottoman Empire 137/1, 166/1
Kazakhs Turkic people of C Asia, conquered by Russians 158/3, 167/1, 226/2; 288/4
Kazakh SSR (*a/c* Kazakhstan) Russ. C Asia 288-9
Kazakhstan economy 295/1
Kazalinsk Russ. C Asia railway 226/2
Kazan C Russia Mongol capital 126/1; urban growth 227/1; Bolshevik seizure 255/1; industry 288/3, 289/1
Kazan Mongol khanate of C Russia conquered by Russia 159/1
Kea (Ceos)
Kebarah Lebanon site of early man 33/1
Kedah state of N Malaya tributary to Siam 172/4
Kediri early state of Java 131/2
Keijo (Seoul)
Keilor Australia site of early man 33/1
Kelantan state of N Malaya tributary of Siam 172/4
Kells E Ireland monastery 100/3
Kemerovo S Siberia foundation 288/3; industry 288/3, 289/1
Kendal N England rebellion against Henry VIII 181/1; Industrial Revolution 197/1
Kenesaw Mountain SE USA ⚔ 219/1
Kenkol C Asia early trade 70/1
Kenora C Canada growth 215/2
Kent early kingdom of SE England 98/1; conversion to Christianity 100/3
Kentish Knock E England English naval victory 181/1
Kentucky state of SE USA Civil War campaigns 219/1, 273/1; 19C politics 221/2,3; Depression 263/1; income and population 287/2
Kenya (*form.* British East Africa) British colony 237/1, 273/1; independence 273/2; political development 281/1; economy 295/1
Kephali C Crete Minoan site 67/1
Keraits Mongol tribe of C Asia 127/1
Kerala (*anc.* Chera) state of S India 279/3
Kerbela (*Ar.* Karbala) Mesopotamia ⚔ 105/1
Kerch (*anc.* Panticapaeum) Crimea industry 289/1; WW2 269/3
Kerkira (Corfu, Corcyra)
Kermadec Islands SW Pacific New Zealand possession 273/2 (inset)
Kerman (*a/s* Kirman *anc.* Carmana) Persia trade 71/1
Kermanshah (*a/s* Kirmanshah) Persia 54/1
Kernstown E USA ⚔ 219/1 (inset)
Ketsk Siberia founded 195/2
Ketton N England agricultural revolution 197/2
Keyukon sub-arctic tribe of Alaska 145/1
Key West Florida US naval base 293/6
Khabarovsk Russ. Far East railway 226/2; industry 289/1
Khafajah (Tutub)
Khakass AD Russ. C Asia 288/2
Khalkha Mongol tribe 165/1
Khalkidhiki (Chalcidice)
Khanbalik (*mod.* Peking) N China Mongol capital 127/1
Khandesh region of W India 129/3, 169/1
Khania (*a/s* Canea *anc.* Cydonia) Crete early palace and city 67/2
Khantsa C Greece Mycenaean site 67/1
Khanty-Mansi AO C Russia 288/2
Khara-Khoja C Persia early bishopric 101/1
Kharg Island Persian Gulf oil terminal 283/3
Kharkov Ukraine founded 159/1; urban growth 227/1; Bolshevik seizure 255/1; WW2 268-9; industry 288/3, 289/1
Khartoum Sudan founded 235/1; British occupation 237/1; 281/1
Khazar Empire S Russia 105/1; 108/1
Khazars Jewish-Turkish tribe of S Russia 101/2, 115/1, 125/2
Kherson Ukraine founded 159/1; bishopric 101/2
Khersones (*a/c* Korsun) Crimea 115/1
Khios (Chios)
Khirokitia Cyprus early village 41/1
Khitan (*a/c* Liao) tribe of Mongolia, raids on China 125/2
Khiva (*a/c* Khwarizm *anc.* Chorasmia) region of C Asia Muslim conquest 167/1; vassal of Russia 216/1; independent khanate 225/1; People's Republic incorporated into USSR 254/3
Khmer (*mod.* Cambodia) SE Asia kingdom under Hindu influence 125/2; temple kingdom 131/2
Khoikhoi early people of S Africa 45/1
Khoisan people of S Africa 135/1, 235/1
Khokand (Kokand)
Kholm (*mod. Pol.* Chełm) W Russia town of Vladimir-Volynsk 115/1
Khorasan (Khurasan)
Khotan (*n/s* Hotan *Chin.* Ho-t'ien) Sinkiang silk route 71/1; Han expansion 80/3; early trade 82/4
Khotin (*Rom.* Hotin) Ukraine Ottoman siege 166/1
Khrisoskalitissa W Crete Minoan palace 67/1
Khurasan (*a/s* Khorasan) region of C Persia early empires 79/3; Muslim conquest 105/1, 125/2; under Abbasid sovereignty 108/1, 133/1; Empire of Ghazni 128/2; Safavid conquest 167/1
Khuzistan (*a/s* Khuzestan *anc.* Susiana *a/c* Elam) region of S Persia province of Sasanian Empire 78/3
Khwarizm (*a/c* Kiva *anc.* Chorasmia) region C Asia under Abbasid sovereignty 133/1; annexed by Empire of Ghazni 128/2; under Khans of Khiva 167/1
Khwarizm Shah, Empire of the Mongol empire of C Asia 127/1, 133/1
Kiamusze (*n/s* Jiamusi *W/G* Chia-mu-ssu) Manchuria 259/3
Kiangsi (*n/s* Jiangxi *W/G* Chiang-hsi) province of SE China under the Ming 164/2, 165/1; Manchu expansion 171/1; T'ai-p'ing control 229/1; Hsin-hai revolution 229/3; Nationalist control 258/2; Soviet under Mao Tse-tung 259/3
Kiangsu (*n/s* Jiangsu *W/G* Chiang-su) province of E China Manchu expansion 171/1; industry 214/1
Kiaochow (*n/s* Jiaoxian *W/G* Chiao-hsien) E China railway 238/3
Kibris (Cyprus)
Kiel N Germany WW1 249/3; 271/2
Kiev (*Russ.* Kyyev *Ukr.* Kyyiv *Norse* Könugard) Ukraine bishopric 101/2; under Khazars 108/1; Viking trade 110/3; principality 115/1; medieval fair 142/1; urban growth 227/1, 288/3; Russian Revolution 255/1; WW2 268-9; industry 288/3, 289/1
Kievan Russia 111/1, 114/5
Kiik-Koba S USSR site of early man 32/2
Kikuyu tribe of E Africa 163/1, 235/1
Kikwit C Belgian Congo 280/2
Kilia (*n/s* Kiliya *Rom.* Chilia-Nouă) Ukraine Ottoman control 137/1; 166/1
Kilkenny S Ireland centre of rebellion 180/2
Killdeer Mountains E USA ⚔ 217/4
Kilwa E Africa early port 45/1; Muslim colony 135/1; Arab-Swahili settlement 235/1
Kilwa Kisiwani E Africa 135/1, 163/1
Kimberley Plateau W Australia goldfield 233/5
Kindu C Belgian Congo Congo crisis 280/2
King's Lynn (*a/c* Lynn) E England medieval trade 142/1; Industrial Revolution 197/1
Kinloss N Scotland limit of Edward I's campaign 140/2
Kinsale S Ireland ⚔ 181/1
Kinshasa (Léopoldville)
Kintampo W Africa cattle domestication 45/1
Kiowa plains Indian tribe of C USA 145/1
Kirensk SE Siberia founded 158/3
Kirghiz Turkic people of C Asia, destroy Uighur Empire 125/2; conquered by Mongols 127/1; conquered by Russians 226/2; 288/4
Kirghiz SSR Russ. C Asia 288/2
Kiribati (*f/c* Gilbert Is) S Pacific independence 273/2 (inset); population growth 294/2
Kirin (*n/s* Jilin *W/G* Chi-lin) province of Manchuria occupied by Russia 238/3; industry 259/3
Kirkby Stephen N England rebellion against Henry VIII 181/1
Kirkuk N Iraq oilfield 283/4
Kirkwall N Scotland bishopric 117/1
Kirman (*a/s* Kerman *anc.* Carmana) region of S Persia Muslim conquest 105/1
Kirovograd (Yelizavetgrad)
Kisangani (Stanleyville)
Kiselevsk C Siberia foundation 288/3
Kish ancient city of Mesopotamia 54/1, 55/3
Kishinev (*Rom.* Chişinău) W Russia urban growth 227/1; Russian Revolution 255/1; industry 289/1
Kishiwada C Japan 171/4
Kiska island of Aleutians, Alaska WW2 266-7
Kismayu (*n/s* Kismaayo *It.* Chisimaio) Somalia under Egyptian rule 235/1
Kistna district of SE India ceded to Britain 168/3
Kita-Kyushu S Japan industrial centre 275/1
Kithira (Cerigo, Cythera)
Kit's Coty SE England Megalithic site 42/2
Kittim (Citium)
Kiukiang (*n/s* Jiujiang, *W/G* Chiu-chiang) C China treaty town 228/2; industry 259/3
Kivu province of E Belgian Congo 280/2
Kiyev (Kiyiv, Kiev)
Kizzuwadna (Cilicia)
Klaipėda (*Ger.* Memel) Lithuanian SSR industry 289/1
Klasies River Mouth S Africa site of early man 33/1
Kleinaspergle C Germany La Tène site 85/1
Kleinklein Austria Hallstatt site 85/1
Kleve (Cleves)
Knossos (*Lat.* Cnossus) Crete 43/1, 52/1, 67/2
Knoxville SE USA ⚔ 219/1; industry 215/1
Kobe C Japan industrialization 175/1, 214/1
København (Copenhagen)
Koberstadt E Germany La Tène site 85/1
Koblenz (Coblenz)
Kochi city and prefecture of W Japan 171/4, industry 238/1
Ko-chih (Cochin)
Koga C Japan 171/4
Koguryo N Korea early state destroyed by T'ang 125/2
Kokand (*a/s* Khokand) C Asia silk route 70/1; Muslim khanate 167/1, 225/1; conquered by Russia 226/2
Kok Charoen C Thailand early site 130/1
Kök Türük (Blue Turks)
Kokura W Japan 170/4
Kola N Russia monastery 101/2
K'o-la-ma-i (*n/s* Karamay *a/s* Karamai) NW China oilfield 274/2
Kolberg (*Pol.* Kołobrzeg) N Poland founded by Germans 138/2; Hanseatic trade 142/1; ⚔ 192/4
Kolhapur SW India industry 214/1
Kolin Czechoslovakia ⚔ 192/4
Köln (Cologne)
Köln-Lindenthal Germany early site 43/1
Kolobeng S Africa 234/2
Kołobrzeg (Kolberg)
Kolomna W Russia 227/1
Kolomoki USA early site 46/3
Kolomyya (*Pol.* Kołomyja *Ger.* Kolomea) Ukraine 115/1
Kolonna E Greece Mycenaean site 67/1
Kolubara river of N Serbia WW1 249/3
Komarów S Poland WW1 249/3
Komi ASSR C Russia 288/2
Komi-Permyak AO C Russia 288/2
Kommos C Crete Minoan site 67/1
Komsomolsk-na-Amure Russ. Far East foundation 288/3; industry 289/1
Kongo early kingdom of W Africa 135/1, 163/1
Königsberg (*since 1946* Kaliningrad) W Russia founded by Teutonic Knights 138/3; Hanseatic city 142/2; 18C financial centre 177/2; corn shipments 177/4; Reformation 179/3; trade 185/1; WW1 249/3; WW2 269/3; ceded to USSR 271/2
Königshofen W Germany Mithraic site 72/1
Konjic C Yugoslavia Mithraic site 72/1
Konstanz (Constance)
Könugard (Kiev)
Konya (*anc.* Iconium) S Anatolia early trade 54/1,133/1; revolt against Ottoman rule 166/1
Koobi Fora E Africa site of early man 33/1
Kophinas C Crete Minoan site 67/2
Kopor'ye NW Russia ⚔ 114/2
Köprüirmaği (Eurymedon River)
Kopys W Russia town of Smolensk 115/1
Korakou S Greece Mycenaean site 67/1
Korea (*anc.* Koryo *or* Silla *Jap.* Chosen) spread of Buddhism 73/1; conquered by Chinese 80/3, 125/2; attacked by Mongols 127/1; invaded by Japan 165/1; invaded by Manchus 171/1; end of Chinese tributary status 228/2; Russo-Japanese war 238/3; acquired by Japan 239/2, 241/1, 258/3; 266-7; 274-5; 1950-3 war 274/2; development after 1941 275/1
Korea, North economy 295/1
Korea, South US bases 293/1; economy 295/1
Koriyama W Japan 171/4
Koroca early people of SW Africa 35/2
Korsun (Khersones)
Kortrijk (Courtrai)
Koryak AD Russ. Far East 288/2
Koryaks tribe of Russ. Far East 158/3
Koryo (Korea)
Kos S Aegean WW2 269/3
Kosala early kingdom of N India 65/1, 83/2
Koselsk C Russia town of Chernigov 115/1
Koshu-kaido early highway of C Japan 171/4
Košice (*Hung.* Kassa) Czechoslovakia industrial development 209/1
Kosogorsk SE Siberia founded 158/3
Kosovo (*properly* Kosovo Polje *a/s* Kossovo *Ger.* Amselfeld) S Yugoslavia ⚔ 137/1, 139/1
Kostienki W USSR site of early man 32/2
Kostroma W Russia Russian Revolution 255/1
Köszeg (Güns)
Kot Diji N India Harappan site 65/1
Kotor (Cattaro)
Koufonisi E Crete Minoan site 67/2
Koukounara S Greece Mycenaean site 67/1
Koumasa C Crete Minoan site 67/2
Kouphia Rachi N Greece Mycenaean site 67/1
Kovno (*Pol.* Kowno *now* Kaunas) W USSR Hanseatic city 142/1; industry 227/1; WW1 249/3
Kowloon S China acquired by Britain 228/2
Kowno (Kovno)
Kow Swamp Australia site of early man 33/1
Kozhikode (Calicut)
Krain (Carniola)
Krak des Chevaliers Syria 132/3
Kraków (Cracow)
Krapina N Yugoslavia site of early man 32/2
Krasnik C Poland WW1 249/3
Krasnodar (*until 1920* Yekaterinodar) Caucasus WW2 268/1; urban growth 288/3; industry 288/3, 289/1
Krasnoi W Russia ⚔ 201/1
Krasnopol'ye S Russia early trade 70/1
Krasnovodsk Russ. C Asia on railway 226/2; Revolution 255/1; industry 289/1
Krasnoyarsk S Siberia founded 158/3; railway 226/2; urban growth 288/3; industry 288/3, 289/1
Kremsmünster Austria monastery 107/3
Krisa C Greece Mycenaean site 67/1
Kristiania (Oslo)
Krivichi E Slav tribe of C Russia 115/1
Krivoy Rog S Ukraine WW2 269/3; urban growth 288/3; industry 289/1
Kromdraai S Africa site of early man 33/1
Kronstadt (*Russ.* Kronshtadt) NW Russia 227/1, 255/1; WW1 249/3
Krukath (Cyropolis)
Krung Thep (Bangkok)
Krym (Crimea)
Ksar Akil Lebanon site of early man 33/1
Ku (*n/s* Gu) C China Western Chou domain 62/3
Kua-chou (*n/s* Guazhou) NW China Ming military post 165/1
Kuala Lumpur Malaya occupied by Japanese 266/1
Kuala Selinsing Malaya early site 130/1, 131/2
Kuan (*n/s* Guan) C China Western Chou domain 62/3
Kuang-chou (*n/s* Guangzhou *Eng.* Canton) S China Sung provincial capital 125/5; Ming provincial capital 165/1
Kuang-chou-wan (*n/s* Guangzhouwan) S China acquired by France 228/2
Kuang-han (*n/s* Guanghan) W China Han commanderie 81/2
Kuang-hsi (Kwangsi)
Kuang-ling (*n/s* Guangling) E China early trade 81/2
Kuang-nan Hsi (*n/s* Guangnan Xi) SW China Sung province 125/5
Kuang-nan Tung (*n/s* Guangnan Dong) S China Sung province 125/5
Kuang-nei (*n/s* Guangnei) N China T'ang province 124/1
Kuang-tung (Kwangtung)
Kuang-wu (*n/s* Guangwu) N China Han prefecture 81/2
Kuba early state of C Africa 163/1
Kubota N Japan 171/4
Kucha (*Chin.* K'u-ch'e) NW China early trade 82/4; Han prefecture 80/3
K'uei (n/s Kui) W China Western Chou domain 62/3
Kuei-chou (Kweichow)
Kuei-lin (n/s Guilin) C China Ming provincial capital 165/1
Kuei-tzu (*n/s* Guizi) N China Han prefecture 81/2
Kuei-yang (*n/s* Guiyang) W China Ming provincial capital 165/1
Kufa Mesopotamia early trade 133/1
Kuhistan Persia province of Empire of Ghazni 128/2
Kui (K'uei)
Kukawa WC Africa Barth's journey 234/2
Kuldja (*n/s* Gulja *Chin.* I-ning) Sinkiang on silk route 71/1
Kullyspell House NW USA fur station 216/1
Kulmerland region of E Germany occupied by Teutonic Knights 138/3
Kůlna Czechoslovakia site of early man 32/2
Kültepe (Kanesh)
Kumamoto city and prefecture of W Japan 170/4, 238/1
Kumasi Gold Coast, W Africa 235/1, 237/1
Kumbi Saleh W Africa possible site of capital of Ghana Empire 135/1
Ku-mu (*n/s* Gumu) NE China Han prefecture 81/2
Kumul (*W/G* Ha-mi) Sinkiang early bishopric 101/1
Kunduz (Drapsaca)
Kunersdorf (*now* Kunowice) W Poland ⚔ 192/4
K'un-ming (*n/s* Kunming *form.* Yün-nan-fu) W China French sphere of influence 228/2; industry 259/3, 274/2; WW2 266/1, 267/2
Kunowice (Kunersdorf)
Kurds people of N Iraq, uprisings 257/2, 282/1
Kurgan Siberia industry 289/1
Kurile Islands (*Russ.* Kurilskiye Ostrova *Jap.* Chishima-retto) acquired by Japan 239/2; reoccupied by Russia 275/1
Kurland (Courland)
Kurnool district of SE India ceded to Britain 168/3
Kurobane C Japan 171/4
Kurs early people of Baltic 115/1
Kursk W Russia 115/1, 159/1; WW2 269/5
Kurukshetra region of N India 83/1
Kuruman S Africa 234/3
Kurume W Japan 170/4
Kusdar NW India tribal state of Ghazni 128/2
Kushan Empire S Asia 70/1, 79/1, 82-3
Kushans tribe of S Asia, migration into Persia 79/1
Kushiya Egypt satrapy of Parthian Empire 79/1
Kusinagara Tibet Buddhist site 73/1
Kustanay Russ. C Asia industry 289/1
Kutch (*f/s* Cutch) region of W India border dispute with Pakistan 279/3
Kutchin sub-arctic Indian tribe of NW Canada 145/1
Kut el Amara (*a/c* Kut) C Mesopotamia WW1 249/4
Kutno C Poland WW2 265/5
Kuwait country of Persian Gulf Ottoman sovereignty 225/1; British protectorate 241/1, 256/1; WW1 249/4; independence 273/2, 282/1; Gulf War 282/1
Kuwana C Japan 171/4
Ku-yüan (*n/s* Guyuan) NW China Ming frontier defence area 165/1
Kuybyshev (*until 1895* Samara) E Russia industry and urban growth 288/3, 289/1
Kuzbass industrial region of Siberia 289/1
Kuznetsk S Siberia founded 158/3; fur trade 195/2
Kwajalein Marshall Islands, C Pacific occupied by US 267/2; US base 293/1 (inset)
Kwakiutl coast Indian tribe of W Canada 145/1
Kwale E Africa Iron Age site 45/1
Kwangju S Korea industrial centre 275/1
Kwangsi (*n/s* Guangxi *W/G* Kuang-hsi) province of SW China Mesolithic sites 62/1; under Ming 164/2, 165/1; rebellion against Ch'ing 170/2; Manchu expansion 171/1; T'ai-p'ing rebellion 229/1; Hsin-hai revolution 229/3; warlords 258/1
Kwangtung (*n/s* Guangdong *W/G* Kuang-tung) province of S China Mesolithic sites 62/1; under Ming 164/2, 165/1; rebellion against Ch'ing 170/2; Manchu expansion 171/1; Hakka-Cantonese war 229/1; Hsin-hai revolution 229/3; autonomous 258/2
Kwantung Leased Territory NE China 239/2
Kwararafa early state of W Africa 135/1, 163/1
Kweichow (*n/s* Guizhou *W/G* Kuei-chou) province of SW China under Ming 164/2, 165/1; rebellion against Ch'ing 170/2; Manchu expansion 171/1; Miao tribal rising 229/1; Hsin-hai revolution 229/3; independent 258/2
Kwidzyn (Marienwerder)
Kyakhta S Siberia Russian trade with China 171/1, 195/1
Kydonia W Crete Minoan site 67/1
Kyongju S Korea Buddhist site 73/1
Kyoto C Japan Buddhist site 73/1; city and prefecture 171/4; industry 175/1, 238/1
Kypros (Cyprus)
Kyushu W Island of Japan 214/2, 238/1
Kzyl-Orda (*form.* Perovsk *earlier* Ak-Mechet) Russ. C Asia industry 289/1
Laang Spean Cambodia early site 130/1
Labici C Italy Latin colony 87/1
Labrador region of NE Canada rediscovered 152/1; to Newfoundland 215/2
Labuan N Borneo British colony 240/1 (inset)
Laccadive Islands (*n/c* Lakshadweep) SW India conversion to Islam 104/2; gained by British 190/2
Lacedaemon (*a/c* Sparta) S Greece Byzantine Empire 113/1
La Chaise W France site of early man 32/2
La Chapelle-aux-Saints C France site of early man 32/2
La Chaussée-Tirancourt N France Megalithic site 42/2
La Clape S France Megalithic site 42/2
Laconia ancient country of S Greece, 74/3, 76/4
La Coruña (*Eng.* Corunna) NW Spain Civil War 264/3
Ladhiqiyah (Latakia)
Ladoga, Lake (*Russ.* Ladozhskoye Ozero) NW Russia waterway trade route 115/1
Ladrones (Marianas)
Lae SE New Guinea retaken by Allies 267/2
Laetolil E Africa site of early man 33/1
La Fère Champenoise NE France ⚔ 201/1
La Ferrassie S France site of early man 32/2
La Ferté-Bernard N France French Revolution 199/2

La Florida – Lusatia

La Florida S Peru early site 47/1
La Forêt-le-Roi C France medieval *villeneuve* 121/7
La Forêt-Sainte-Croix C France medieval *villeneuve* 125/1
La Frebouchère NW France Megalithic site 42/2
Lagash (*a/c* Shipurla) ancient city of Mesopotamia, trade 55/3
Lagny C France medieval fair 120/1
La Gorge Meillet N France La Tène site 84/1
Lagos S Portugal ✕ 191/1
Lagos Nigeria Slave Coast 163/1; taken by British 235/1; British colony 241/1
La Graufesengue (Condatomagus)
Laguna de los Cerros C Mexico Olmec site 46/2
La Habana (Havana)
La Halliade SW France Megalithic site 42/2
La Hogue English Channel Megalithic site 42/2
Lahore NW India in Delhi Sultanate 129/3; trade 168/3; 169/1; industry in British India 231/3; capital of Pakistan Punjab 279/3
Lake Albert W USA ✕ 217/4
Lake Coleridge S Island, New Zealand hydroelectric station 232/1
Lake Mungo Australia site of early man 33/1
Lake of the Woods (Fort Charles)
Lake Okeechobee SE USA ✕ 217/4
Lakhnauti N India district of Delhi Sultanate 129/3
Lalibela Ethiopia monastery 100/1
La Madeleine C France site of early man 22/2
Lamaghan Afghanistan district of Ghazni Empire 128/2
Lamanai E Mexico Maya site 46/2, 144/2
Lambaesis (*mod.* Tazoult) Algeria Mithraic site 72/1; Roman Empire 89/1
Lampaka ancient country of NW India 83/1
Lampsacus (*mod.* Lâpseki) NW Anatolia Greek colony 75/1; early bishopric 93/1; Byzantine Empire 112/3
Lamu Kenya Muslim colony 135/1
Lamuts Siberian tribe 158/3
Lancarvan Wales monastery 93/3
Lanchow (*n/s* Lanzhou *W/G* Lan-chou) NW China early trade 71/1; T'ang prefecture 124/1; Sung provincial capital 125/5; industry 214/1, 259/3, 274/3
Landau W Germany gained by France 188/2; French Revolution 199/2
Langobardi early tribe of NW Germany 89/1. See also Lombards
Lang-t'an-tung (*n/s* Langtandong) E China site of early man 33/1
Languedoc region of S France French Royal domain 123/1, 147/3; province of France 189/1
Lanka (Ceylon)
L'Anse aux Meadows Newfoundland Norse colony 47/1
Lan-t'ien (*n/s* Lantian) C China prehistoric site 33/1; Late Chou site 62/3; Han prefecture 81/2
Lanzhou (Lanchow)
Laodicea (*mod.* Denizli) W Anatolia Roman Empire 89/1; one of seven churches of Asia 93/1; Jewish community 103/1; Byzantine Empire 112/3
Laodicea (*mod.* Latakia *Fr.* Lattaquié) Syria Byzantine Empire 112/3, 113/1
Laodicea in Media (Nehavend)
Laon N France bishopric 117/1; ✕ 201/1
Laos country of SE Asia 131/2; kingdom of Luang Prabang 173/1; end of Chinese tributary status 228/2; French protectorate 257/1; independence 273/2; civil wars 277/1; Pathet Lao 277/3; economy 295/1
Lapland region of Swedish Empire 185/1
Lapps people of N Russia 101/2
Lâpseki (Lampsacus)
Lapurdum (Bayonne)
La Quina SW France site of early man 32/2
Larache Morocco Spanish colony 247/2
Laranda (Karaman)
Lardavif Wales bishopric 92/1
Larisa (*a/s* Larissa *Turk.* Yenişehir) C Greece archbishopric 93/1; Jewish community 103/1; Byzantine Empire 113/1,5
La Rochelle W France 16-17C revolts 181/1; commercial harbour 189/1
Larsa (*Bibl.* Ellasar) Mesopotamia Amorite kingdom 54/2; early city 55/3
Las Bela NW India Alexander's Empire 82/3
Las Haldas N Peru early site 47/1
Lashio E Burma WW2 266/2
Las Navas de Tolosa S Spain ✕ 122/3, 132/1
La Starza S Italy early settlement 43/1
Latakia (*anc.* Laodicea *Fr.* Lattaquié *Ar.* Ladhiqiyah) Syria Mediterranean trade 133/1
La Tène E France site 84/1,3
Later Liang dynasty of N China 124/3
Latin America (America, South)
Latini early tribe of Italy, 86/2
Latin Way (Via Latina)
Lato E Crete Minoan site 67/2
Lattaquié (Latakia)
Latvia country of the Baltic corn shipments 177/4; independence from Russia 255/1, 261/1; inter-war alliances 260/2, 264/1; socio-political change 263/2; WW2 268-9; annexed by Russia 265/5, 270/1; Soviet Socialist Republic 288/2; independence 1991 290/3
Latvians emigration from Russia 261/3; in USSR 288/4
Lauenburg principality of N Germany 187/1
Launceston W England 16C riots 181/1
Launceston Tasmania gold 233/5
Laupen W Switzerland Zähringen town 121/6; ✕ 140/3
Laurentide ice-sheet N America 37/4
Lausanne Switzerland 1924 Conference 261/1
Lausitz (*Eng.* Lusatia) region of E Germany acquired by Poland 117/3
Lava Beds W USA ✕ 217/4
Laval NW France 17C revolts 181/1
Lavan Island S Iran oil terminal 283/3
Lavenham E England rebellion against Henry VIII, 181/1
La Venta C Mexico Olmec site 46/2
Lavinium C Italy Roman Empire 87/1
Lazaret S France site of early man 32/2
Lazica early country of the Caucasus 113/1
Lebanon district of Ottoman Empire 225/1; French mandate 256/1; political disturbances 257/2; independence 273/2, 282/1; US landing 292/5; Middle East conflict 283/4, 293/1; economy 295/1
Lebda (Leptis Magna)
Lechfeld S Germany ✕ 111/1, 118/2
Le Creusot C France industrial development 206/1, 208/1
Ledosus (*mod.* Lezoux) C France Roman Empire 90/1
Leeds N England industrial development 196/3, 197/1, 206/1
Leek C England Industrial Revolution 197/1
Leeward Islands West Indies British and French settlement 156/3
Leghorn (Livorno)
Legionum Urbs Wales early bishopric 92/1
Legnica (Liegnitz)
Le Havre N France trading port 176/3; fortified naval port 189/1; French Revolution 199/2; industrial development 206/1, 208/1; WW2 269/6
Leicester (*anc.* Ratae) C England Scandinavian settlement 110/2, 111/1; Industrial Revolution 197/1
Leiden (Leyden)
Leinster province of SE Ireland early kingdom 117/1; conquered by Normans 123/1
Leipen N Germany Megalithic site 42/2
Leipzig E Germany medieval fair 142/1; 18C financial centre 177/2; industrial development 206/1, 208/1; WW1 249/3; Communist insurrection 254/2
Leipzig (Battle of the Nations) E Germany ✕ 201/1
Le Kef (Sicca Veneria)
Leling (Lo-ling)
Le Mans NW France bishopric 117/1; French Revolution 199/2; industrial development 206/1
Lemberg (*Pol.* Lwów *now* Lvov) N Austria-Hungary medieval trade 142/1; WW1 249/3; E Germany WW2 269/3
Lemnos island of the Aegean Byzantine naval victory 120/2; ceded to Greece 211/2
Le Moustier S France site of early man 32/2
Lenca Indian tribe of central America 145/1
Leng-hui NW China oilfield 274/3
Leninakan (*until 1924* Aleksandropol) Armenian SSR industry 289/1
Leningrad (St Petersburg *Russ.* Sankt-Peterburg, *between 1914 and 1923* Petrograd) NW Russia WW2 265/1, 269/3; urban growth 288/3; industry 289/1
Lens NE France WW1 249/3 (inset)
Lenzen N Germany ✕ 118/2
León early kingdom of C Spain 122/3; city of N Spain, Civil War 264/3
Leontopolis N Egypt early Jewish community 103/1
Léopoldville (*now* Kinshasa) W Belgian Congo 280/2
Lepanto (*mod. Gr.* Navapaktos) C Greece ✕ 166/1
Leptis N Libya Iron Age site 45/1; Phoenician city 74/1
Leptis Magna (*a/s* Lepcis Magna *mod.* Lebda) N Libya Mithraic site 72/1; Carthaginian city 86/3; Roman Empire 89/1, 91/1; early bishopric 93/1
Le Puiset C France medieval *villeneuve* 121/7
Lérida (Ilerda)
Lerinum S France monastery 93/3
Leros S Aegean WW2 269/3
Les Bolards C France Mithraic site 72/1
Lesbos (*mod. Gr.* Lesvos *a/c* Mytilene) island of E Aegean Greek parent state 75/1; acquired by Turks 147/1; ceded to Greece 211/2
Lesotho (*form.* Basutoland) S Africa independence 272/2; political development 281/1; economy 295/1
Letts people of Latvia, NW Russia 255/1
Leubuzzi Slav tribe of C Germany 138/2
Leucas (*mod. Gr.* Levkas *It.* Santa Maura) W Greece Greek colony 75/1
Leucecome early port of W Arabia 70/1
Leucos Limen Red Sea Roman Empire 91/1
Leuthen (*Pol.* Lutynia) SW Poland ✕ 192/4
Leuven (*Fr.* Louvain) town of Sp. Netherlands 181/1
Leu Wiliang W Java early site 130/1
Levkas (Leucas)
Lewes S England ✕ 123/1
Lexington NE USA ✕ 160/3
Leyden (*n/s* Leiden) Netherlands 16C urban development 176/1; 18C urban development 177/2
Leyte SE Philippines US landing 267/2
Lezetxiki N Spain site of early man 32/2
Lezoux (Ledosus)
Lhasa Tibet early trade 71/1; Buddhist site 73/1; seat of Lamaistic patriarch 171/1
Liang NW China Western Chou domain 62/3
Liang-che (*n/s* Liangzhe) E China Sung province 125/5
Liang-chou (*n/s* Liangzhou) NW China early state 124/3; Ming military post 165/1
Liao (Khitan)
Liao-hsi (*n/s* Liaoxi) NE China Han commanderie 81/2
Liao-tung (*n/s* Liaodong) NE China Ming frontier defence area 165/1
Libau (*Latv.* Liepāja) W Russia WW1 249/3; port of Latvian SSR 227/1
Liberia country of W Africa founded 234/1; independent state 236/2, 240/1, 272/1,2; 281/1
Libya Arab conquest 104/1; under the Almohads 132/1; under Ottoman Empire 225/1; Italian colony 214/1, 236/2, 241/1, 256/1; anti-colonial rebellion 245/2; WW2 265/5, 268-9; independence 272/2; political development 281/1; US base 293/1; economy 295/1
Lichfield E England bishopric 117/1
Li-chou (*n/s* Lizhou) W China Sung province 125/5
Liège Belgium bishopric 117/1, 186/1; urban revolt 141/1; 16C urban development 176/1; 18C urban development 177/2; Prince-Bishop expelled 198/1; industrial development 206/1, 208/1; WW1 248-9
Liegnitz (*Pol.* Legnica) W Poland ✕ 126/2, 192/4; Reformation 178/2; industrial development 207/1
Liepāja (*Ger.* Libau) Latvian SSR industry 289/1
Ligny Belgium ✕ 201/1
Ligor S Thailand Hindu-Buddhist remains 131/2
Ligures early tribe of N Italy, 86/2
Liguria country of NW Italy 213/2
Ligurian Republic NW Italy state established by French Revolution 199/3
Lille NE France medieval fair 120/1, 142/1; 18C financial centre 177/2; gained by France 188/2; industrial development 189/1, 206/1; WW1 248/2, 249/3 (inset)
Lilybaeum (*mod.* Marsala) Sicily Phoenician city 75/1
Lima Peru early people 47/4; colonized 154/1, 161/1; imperial state 195/2; attack on 222/2
Limanowa N Austria-Hungary WW1 249/3
Limatambo C Andes Inca site 145/3
Limburg region of Belgium/Holland Burgundian possession 147/2; county 187/1
Limerick Ireland Scandinavian control 111/1; 117/1
Limoges C France annexed to France 147/3; industrial development 189/1,206/1
Limonum (Poitiers)
Limousin region of C France under English rule 123/1; French province 189/1
Li Muri Sardinia Megalithic site 42/2
Lincoln (*anc.* Lindum) E England Danish Viking base 110/2, 111/1; rebellion against Henry VIII 181/1; Industrial Revolution 197/1
Lindisfarne (*a/c* Holy Island) N England monastery 100/3, 101/2; Viking attack 111/1
Lindum (*mod.* Lincoln) E England Roman Empire 83/1, 90/1; bishopric 92/1
Ling N China Ming prefecture 165/1
Lingen district of NW Germany Burgundian possession 147/2; county 187/1
Ling-fang (*n/s* Lingfang) S China Han prefecture 81/2
Ling-ling (*n/s* Lingling) S China Han commanderie 81/2
Ling-nan (*n/s* Lingnan) S China T'ang province 124/1
Ling-yüan (*n/s* Lingyuan) NE China Western Chou site 62/3
Lin-t'ao (*n/s* Lintao) NW China Han prefecture 81/2
Lin-t'ung (*n/s* Lintong) NW China Late Chou city site 63/4
Lin-tzu (*n/s* Linzi) NE China Late Chou city site 63/4; Han trade centre 81/2
Linyanti S Africa on Livingstone's route 234/2
Linz Austria medieval fair 142/1; WW2 269/3
Lipara (*n/s* Lipari) island of S Italy early settlement 43/1; 74/4
Lippe country of N Germany Reformation 178/2; 187/1, 212/3
Lisala Zaire Congo crisis 280/2
Lisbon (*Port.* Lisboa *anc.* Olisipo) Portugal Muslim conquest 104/1; early trade 143/4, 150/2; colonial trade 155/1, 194-5; trading port 176/3; 16C and 18C financial centre 176/1, 177/2; ✕ 200/1
Liscuis N France Megalithic site 42/2
Lismore S Ireland Scandinavian settlement 111/1
Lissa (*S.Cr.*Vis C Adriatic ✕ 213/2
Listem C Ukraine ✕ 115/1
Liternum C Italy Roman colony 87/1
Lithuania country of Europe conversion to Christianity 101/2; Christian empire 136/2; early expansion 139/1; Black Death 141/1; empire of Casimir IV 147/1; acquired by Russia 159/1; corn shipments 177/4; Reformation 179/1; independence 255/1, 261/1; inter-war alliances 260/3, 264/1; socio-political change 263/2; loses Memel territory to Germany 265/4; WW2 268-9; retaken by Russia 265/4; Soviet Socialist Republic 270/1, 288/2; independence 1991 290/3
Lithuanians (*earlier* Litva) people of N Europe emigration from Russia 261/3; in USSR 288/2
Little Armenia early Christian state of S Anatolia 136/2
Little Big Horn N USA ✕ 217/4
Littlehampton S England Industrial Revolution 197/1
Little Poland 117/3
Little Preslav Bulgaria early settlement 112/4
Litva (*mod.* Lithuanians) people of NW Russian border 115/1
Liu C China Western Chou domain 62/3
Liu-ch'eng (*n/s* Liucheng) NE China Han prefecture 81/2
Liverpool N England trading port 176/3; industrial development 197/1, 206/1, 208/1; WW2 265/5
Livonia region of E Baltic occupied by Teutonic Knights 138-1, 147/1; conquered by Russia 159/1; Reformation 179/1; under Swedish rule 185/1
Livonian Order NW Russia 115/1
Livorno (*obs. Eng.* Leghorn) C Italy 18C financial centre 177/2; WW2 269/3
Lixus (*mod.* Larache) Morocco Roman Empire 88/1
Li-yang (*n/s* Liyang) E China Han prefecture 81/2
Lizhou (Li-chou)
Ljubljana (Emona)
Llangollen N Wales Industrial Revolution 197/1
Llantwit Wales monastery 93/3
Lo C China Western Chou domain 62/3
Loano NW Italy principality 183/3
Lobositz (*mod.* Lovosice) Bohemia ✕ 192/4
Locarno Switzerland 1885 Conference 261/1
Loch Garman (Wexford)
Lochhill SW Scotland Megalithic site 42/2
Locri Epizephyrii S Italy Greek colony 75/1, 86/2
Locris W Greece parent state 75/1
Lodi N Italy Lombard League 119/3; Signorial domain 122/2; ✕ 201/1
Lodomeria (Vladimir) region of W Ukraine acquired by Habsburgs 193/3
Lodz (*Pol.* Łódź) Poland industrial development 207/1, 209/1; in Russia 227/1; urban growth 227/1; WW1 249/3
Logan's Fort NE USA ✕ 217/4
Lohumjo-Daro N India Harappan site 65/1
Lo-i (*n/s* Luoyi) N China Western Chou capital 62/3
Lokoja Nigeria taken by British 237/1
Lo-lan Sinkiang Han prefecture 80/3
Lo-lang N Korea Han commanderie 81/2
Lo-ling (*n/s* Leling) NE China Han prefecture 81/2
Lombards early tribe of S Germany 99/1. See also Langobardi
Lombardy region of N Italy kingdom under Frankish dominion 107/3; under medieval German Empire 119/1; medieval trade 120/1; 122/2; acquired by Habsburgs 182/2; unification of Italy 213/2
Lonato N Italy ✕ 201/1
Londinium (*mod.* London) S England Mithraic site 72/1; Roman Empire 88/1, 90/1; bishopric 92/1
London (*anc.* Londinium) S England bishopric 100/3, 117/1; urban unrest 141/1; Hansa trading post 142/1; medieval trade 143/3; trade and industry 16C and 18C 176-7; in Civil War 180/2; 1601 riots 181/1; imperial trade 194/1; industrial development 196/3, 197/1, 206/1, 208/1; WW1 249/3; in Depression 263/2; WW2 265/5, 269/3
London C Canada growth 215/2
Londonderry N Ireland IRA terrorism 291/2
Longreach E Australia railway 233/5
Longwy NE France fort 199/2
Longxi (Lung-hsi)
Longxingfu (Lung-hsing-fu)
Longyu (Lung-yu)
Longzhou (Lungchow)
Loochoo Islands (Ryukyu Islands)
Lookout Mountain S USA ✕ 219/1
Loos NE France WW1 249/3 (inset)
Lopera S Spain Civil War 264/3
Lord Howe Island W Pacific Australian possession 273/2 (inset)
Lorient NW France 189/1
Lorraine (*a/c* Lotharingia *Ger.* Lothringen) region of NE France Magyar invasions 111/1; part of medieval German Empire 118-9; conflict of Church and state 122/2; Black Death 141/1; Burgundian possession 147/2, 186/2; German duchy 187/1; Holy Roman Empire 189/1; German Empire 212/3; WW1 248/2
Lorsch W Germany monastery 107/3
Los Angeles W USA foundation 161/1; industry 287/1; urban development 287/3
Los Millares S Spain site 43/1, 52/1
Lostwithiel SW England ✕ 180/2
Lothagam E Africa site of early man 33/1
Lothal N India early urban settlement 53/1; Harappan site 65/1
Lotharingia (Lorraine)
Lothringen (Lorraine)
Lötschberg Switzerland tunnel 253/2
Loudoun Hill C Scotland ✕ 140/2
Loughborough C England Industrial Revolution 197/1
Louhans E France French Revolution 199/2
Louisbourg Nova Scotia captured by British 191/1
Louisiana region of C North America French rule 156/3, 157/2, 161/1, 201/3; Spanish rule 160/3; purchased by USA 216/3
Louisiana state of S USA Civil War 219/1,3; 19C politics 221/2,3; Depression 263/1; income and population 287/2
Lou-lan (*n/s* Loulan) NW China early trade 71/1
Lourenço Marques (Maputo)
Louth E England rebellion against Henry VIII 181/1; Industrial Revolution 197/1
Louth Ireland bishopric 92/1
Louvain (Leuven)
Lovewell's Fight NE USA ✕ 217/4
Lovosice (*Ger.* Lobositz) Czechoslovakia Hallstatt site 85/1
Lower Burma annexed by British 230/2
Lower California province of N Mexico 223/1
Lower Ob Gasfield N Siberia 289/1
Lower Palatinate W Germany Reformation 178/2
Lower Saxony (*Ger.* Niedersachsen) region of W Germany 271/2
Lowestoft E England English naval victory 181/1; WW1 249/3
Lo-yang (*n/s* Luoyang) N China Shang city 62/2; Chou site 62/3; 63/4; early trade 71/1; Han prefecture 81/2; sacked by Hsiung-nu 95/1; T'ang city 124/1; industry 274/3
Lozi tribe of C Africa, 235/1
Lu E China Chou domain 62/3, 63/4; Han prefecture 81/2
Lü C China Western Chou domain 62/3
Luanda Angola trade 155/1, 195/1; Portuguese settlement 163/1, 235/1, 237/1
Luango early state of W Africa 163/1, 235/1
Luang Prabang SE Asia early political centre 131/2; kingdom 173/1
Luba people of C Africa 135/1, 163/1, 235/1
Lubaantún E Mexico Maya site 46/2
Lübeck N Germany urban revolt 141/1; Hanseatic city 142/1; 16C urban development 176/1; Reformation 179/1; bishopric 187/1; WW1 249/3; WW2 269/3
Lublin Poland medieval fair 142/1; WW1 249/3
Lubumbashi (Elisabethville)
Lubusi S Africa Iron Age site 45/1
Lucani early people of S Italy 86/2
Lucania region of S Italy kingdom of Naples 122/2
Lucca N Italy Republican commune 122/2; independent republic 146/1, 183/1,3, 199/3
Lucedio NW Italy Mantuan principality 183/3
Lucerne (*Ger.* Luzern) early Swiss canton 140/3
Łuck (Lutsk)
Lucknow N India Indian Mutiny 230/1; industry 231/2; Hindu-Muslim clashes 279/3
Lüderitz SW Africa German settlement 237/1
Lugansk (*between 1935-58 and since 1970 called* Voroshilovgrad) Ukraine industry 158/2; urban growth 227/1
Lugdunensis Roman province of N France 88/1
Lugdunum (*mod.* Lyon *Eng.* Lyons) C France Roman Empire 86/3, 89/1, 90/1; archbishopric 92/1; Jewish community 103/1
Luluabourg (*now* Kananga) C Belgian Congo 280/2
Lumbini Tibet Buddhist site 73/1
Luna (*mod.* Luni) N Italy Roman colony 87/1
Lund S Sweden bishopric 101/2, Danish bishopric 116/2
Lunda early kingdom of C Africa 163/1, 235/1. See also Balunda
Lüneburg N Germany Hanseatic city 142/1
Lungchow (*n/s* Longzhou *W/G* Lung-chou) SW China treaty port 228/2
Lung-hsi (*n/s* Longxi) NW China Han commanderie 81/2
Lung-hsing-fu (*n/s* Longxingfu) C China Sung provincial capital 125/5
Lung-yu (*n/s* Longyu) NW China T'ang province 124/1
Luni (Luna)
Lunigiana N Italy Imperial fiefs 183/3
Luo tribe of E Africa, 235/1
Luoyang (Lo-yang)
Lusatia (*Ger.* Lausitz) region of E Germany under

349

Meniet – Nanking

Meniet N Africa cattle domestication 45/1
Menominee (Sauk)
Menorca (Minorca)
Mentese early emirate of SW Anatolia 136-7
Mercia early kingdom of C England 100/3, 108/1, 110/2, 117/1
Meremere N Island, New Zealand ✕ 232/1
Mérida (*anc.* Emerita Augusta) SW Spain Civil War 264/3
Mérida SE Mexico early Spanish city 154/1
Merimde Egypt Iron Age site 45/1
Merina early state in Madagascar 163/1, 235/1
Merioneth (*Wel.* Meirionydd) early principality of N Wales 123/1
Merkits Mongolian tribe 127/1
Meroë Sudan Iron Age site 45/1; monastery 100/1; city of Alwa 135/1
Mersa Matruh (Paraetonium)
Merse (of Berwick) SE Scotland acquired by Edward III 140/2
Merseburg E Germany bishopric 118/2
Mersin (*f/s* Mersina) E Anatolia early trade 54/1
Merthyr Tydfil S Wales Industrial Revolution 197/1
Merv (*since 1937* Mary *anc.* Alexandria) Russ. C. Asia early trade 70/1; spread of Christianity 73/1; Sasanian Empire 79/3; early archbishopric 101/1; Muslim conquest 105/1, 133/1 Safavid empire 167/1
Merya E Slav tribe of C Russia 115/1
Mesas de Asta SW Spain early settlement 43/1
Mesa Verde N America site 47/1
Mesembria Bulgaria Greek colony 75/1; Roman Empire 89/1; Byzantine Empire 113/5
Mesen (Messines)
Meshan Mesopotamia province of Sasanian Empire 78/3
Meshchera E Slav tribe of C Russia 115/1
Meshed (*Pers.* Mashhad) Alexander's Empire 82/3; Safavid Empire 167/1
Mesoamerica classic period 46/2, 47/1; 145/1
Mesopotamia (*mod.* Iraq) earliest settlement 41/1, 52/1; early empires 54-5, 56-7; spread of Mithraism 72/1; Alexander's Empire, 76/1, 82/3; Roman Empire 89/1, 91/2; Muslim conquest 105/1; WW1 249/4
Messana (*mod.* Messina) Sicily Roman Empire 89/1, 91/1; early bishopric 75/1
Messapii early people of S Italy 86/2
Messenia ancient region of SW Greece 76/4
Messina (*anc.* Zancle *later* Messana) Sicily early bishopric 93/1; Norman conquest 120/2; Mediterranean trade 142/1; 16C financial centre 176/1; 18C urban development 177/2; WW2 269/3
Messines (*Dut.* Mesen) Belgium medieval fair 120/1; WW1 249/3 (inset)
Metapontum S Italy Roman Empire 86/2
Methven C Scotland ✕ 140/2
Metz NE France bishopric 117/1; annexed to France 147/3; French Revolution 199/2; WW1 249/3; WW2 269/3
Meuse (*Dut.* Maas) *river* NE France WW1 248/2, 249/3 (inset)
Mexico Aztec Empire 144/2; Spanish colonization 154/1, 155/2; imperial trade 195/1,2; independence 222-3, 240/1; exports and foreign investment 222/3; population 222/4; US intervention 243/4; political development 284-5; economy 215/1, 294-5; population growth 294/2
Mexico City (*Sp.* Ciudad de México) C Mexico industry 215/1
Mi C China Western Chou site 62/3
Mi-ai-t'ing (*n/s* Miaiting) NW China Han prefecture 81/2
Miami Indian tribe of C USA 145/1
Michigan state of N USA 19C politics 221/2,3; Depression 263/1; income and population 287/2
Michoacán province of C Mexico 223/1
Micmac Indian tribe of NE Canada 145/1
Middle Awash Ethiopia site of early man 33/1
Middle East (*a/c* Near East) early Muslim divisions 133/1; WW1 249/4; political disturbances in mandated territories 257/2; WW2 268/3; Cold War 292/5; political development 282-3
Midhen S Greece Mycenaean site 67/1
Midhurst S England Industrial Revolution 197/1
Midland S USA site of early man 33/1
Midnapore district of NE India ceded to Britain 168/3
Midway island of C Pacific US occupation 243/1; WW2 ✕ 266/1; US base 293/1 (inset)
Mie prefecture of C Japan 238/1
Miharu N Japan 171/4
Mihrakert (Nisa)
Mikhaylovka S Russia early settlement 52/1
Mikligard (Constantinople)
Mila C Greece Mycenaean site 67/1
Milan (*It.* Milano *anc.* Mediolanum) N Italy archbishopric 107/3; Lombard League 119/1; medieval trade 120/1; Signorial domination 122/2; 18C urban development 177/2; Spanish Habsburg territory 182/1, 193/3; duchy 183/3; industrial development 206/1, 208/1; railways and tunnels 253/2
Milas (Mylasa)
Milazzo (Mylae)
Miletus W Anatolia Cretan settlement 67/1; 74/2; ✕ 74/3; Greek parent state 75/1; Achaemenid Empire 78/1; Roman Empire 86/3, 89/1; early bishopric 93/1; Byzantine empire 113/1
Milev Algeria early bishopric 92/1
Milford Haven S Wales port 197/1
Military Frontier Hungary 193/3
Milizi Slav tribe of E Germany 118/2
Milk Creek C USA ✕ 217/4
Milwaukee N USA industry 215/1
Min early state of SE China 124/3
Minas Gerais province of C Brazil 223/1
Mindanao island of S Philippines Muslim expansion 104/3, 131/3; Spanish control 173/1; US occupation 242/1; Japanese occupation 266/1; retaken by US 267/2; insurgency 277/1
Mindelheim Germany Hallstatt site 85/1
Minden NW Germany bishopric 117/1, 119/1
Ming Empire China 151/1, 164-5
Minneapolis-St. Paul N USA general strike 263/1
Minnesota state of N USA site of early man 33/1; 19C politics 221/2,3; Depression 263/1; income and population 287/2
Minorca (*Sp.* Menorca) British naval base and ✕ 191/1; Civil War 264/3
Minsk W Russia early town of Polotsk 115/1; 227/1; WW1 249/3; Bolshevik seizure 255/1; WW2 269/3; urban growth 288/3; industry 289/1
Minturnae (*mod.* Minturno) C Italy Roman colony 87/1
Minucciano N Italy Luccan principality 183/3
Minusinsk SC Siberia founded 158/3
Min-yüeh (*n/s* Minyue) region of S China 80/1,3; Han commanderie 81/2
Mirambo's Kingdom early state of E Africa 235/1
Mirandola N Italy principality 183/3
Mirzoyan (Dzhambul)
Misenum C Italy Roman Empire 89/1
Miskito Indian tribe of C America 145/1
Misön C Indo-China Hindu-Buddhist temple 131/2
Mississippi state of S USA Civil War 219/1; 19C politics 221/2,3; Depression 263/1; income and population 287/2
Missouri state of C USA Civil War 219/1; 19C politics 221/2,3; Depression 263/1; income and population 287/2
Mitanni ancient kingdom of Middle East 57/1, 61/1
Mitla Mexico Mixtec site 144/2
Mitla Pass Sinai Egyptian-Israeli war 283/2
Mito C Japan 171/4
Mitropolis C Crete Minoan palace 67/1
Mitylene (Mytilene, Lesbos)
Mixtec early people of C Mexico 46/2, 145/1
Miyagi prefecture of N Japan industry 239/1
Miyako N Japan 171/4
Miyazaki city and prefecture of W Japan 238/1; industry 275/1
Miyazu C Japan 171/4
Mizoram territory of E India separatist movements 279/3
Mladeć Czechoslovakia site of early man 32/2
Mlu Prei Cambodia early site 130/1
Mo border people of N China 63/4
Mobile S USA fur station 216/1; ✕ 219/1
Mobile Bay S USA ✕ 219/1
Moçambique (Mozambique)
Moçâmedes Angola Portuguese settlement 237/1
Mocha (*Ar.* Mukha) SW Arabia trade 157/1, 195/1
Moche C Andes site 47/1
Modena (*anc.* Mutina) N Italy Mithraic site 72/1; Lombard League 119/1; Republican commune 122/2; Reformation 179/1; Duchy 183/3; unification of Italy 213/2
Modjokerto Java site of early man 33/1
Modoc plateau Indian tribe of NW USA 145/1
Modon S Greece captured by Ottomans 137/1; Mediterranean trade 142/1; Venetian fort 183/1
Moesia region of Balkans district of Byzantine Empire 113/1
Moesia Inferior Roman province of the Balkans 89/1
Moesia Superior Roman province of the Balkans 89/1
Mogadishu (*n/s* Muqdisho *It.* Mogadiscio *early Chin.* Mo-ku-ta-shu) Somalia Muslim colony 135/1; early trade 150/2; Italian occupation 237/1
Mogador (*now* Essaouria) Morocco Iron Age site 45/1; French settlement 247/2
Mogilev W Russia Hanseatic trade 142/1; WW1 249/3; Russian Revolution 255/1; WW2 269/3; industry 289/1
Mogontiacum (*mod.* Mainz) W Germany Roman Empire 88/2, 89/1, 90/1
Mohács Hungary ✕ 146/1, 166/1
Mohave Indian tribe of SW USA 145/1
Mohenjo-Daro N India early urban settlement 53/1; Harappan site 65/1
Mohi Hungary ✕ 126/2
Moira Baths C England Industrial Revolution 197/1
Mojos forest Indian tribe of S America 145/1
Mokpo S Korea Russo-Japanese war 238/3; 1950-3 War 274/2; industry 275/1
Moldavia (*Turk.* Boğdan *Rom.* Moldova) region of Romania/Russia Christian state 136/2; Hungarian suzeraínty 139/1; under Ottoman control 137/1, 147/1, 166/1, 183/1; occupied by Russia 201/1; customs union with Wallachia 207/2; part of Romania 211/2; Soviet Socialist Republic 288/2,4; independence 1991 290/3
Mollwitz (*Pol.* Małujowice) SW Poland ✕ 192/4
Molotov (Perm)
Moluccas (*Indon.* Maluku *Dut.* Malukken *form.* Spice Islands) islands of E Indies Muslim expansion 104/3; European discovery 153/1, 157/1; early Portuguese trade 155/1, 172/2; Dutch control 173/1; independent republic 273/2
Molukken (Moluccas)
Mombarcaro NW Italy Saluzzo principality 183/3
Mombasa Kenya Muslim colony 135/1; early trade 155/1, 157/1, 163/1; Arab-Swahili settlement 235/1; British occupation 237/1
Mombercelli NW Italy principality 183/3
Mona (*mod.* Isle of Man) *island* NE England 88/1
Monaco (*anc.* Portus Herculis Monoeci) principality 183/3
Monamore W Scotland Megalithic site 42/2
Monastir (*Turk.* Manastir *S. Cr.* Bitolj *Maced.* Bitola) S Yugoslavia WW1 249/3
Monastiraki Crete palace site 67/2
Monchiero NW Italy principality 183/3
Mondovi NW Italy ✕ 201/1
Monemvasia (*It.* Malvasia) S Greece Byzantine Empire 113/5; Ottoman conquest 166/1; Venetian fort 183/1
Monferrat NW Italy Mantuan margravate 183/3
Monforte NW Italy principality 183/3
Mongiardino NW Italy principality 183/3
Mongol Empire 126-7
Mongolia (*form.* Outer Mongolia) under Turkish empire 95/1; unification of Mongol tribes 127/1; Chinese incursions under Ming 165/1; Chinese protectorate 171/1; autonomy 228/2; Russian sphere of influence 241/1; People's Republic 254/3; limit of Japanese expansion 264/2; economy 214/1, 295/1
Mong-tseu (Mengtze)
Monmouth W England Industrial Revolution 197/1
Mons (*Dut.* Bergen) Belgium industrial development 206/1; WW1 248/2, 249/3 (inset)
Mons people of S Burma early kingdom 131/2; conquest by Burma 173/1
Mons Lactarius S Italy ✕ 99/1
Mon State S Burma 279/3
Montafia NW Italy principality 183/3
Montagnais-Naskapi sub-arctic Indian tribe of NE Canada 145/1
Montana state of NW USA 1896 election 221/3; Depression 263/1; income and population 287/2
Montauban S France 189/1; French Revolution 199/2
Mont Cenis SE France pass 120/1; tunnel 253/2
Montdidier NE France WW1 249/3 (inset)
Monte Albán C Mexico early site 46/2, 47/1; Zapotec centre 144/2
Monte Cassino C Italy monastery 93/3, 107/3. See also Cassino
Monte Circeo Italy site of early man 32/2
Montegrosso NW Italy Savoy principality 183/3
Montenegro (*S. Cr.* Crna Gora) region of S Yugoslavia independent state 211/2; under Ottoman rule 225/1; 19C alliances 246-7; WW1 248-9; forms part of Yugoslavia 261/1; WW2 268/1, 269/3
Montenotte N Italy ✕ 201/1
Montereau N France ✕ 201/1
Monte Verde C Chile early site 47/1
Montevideo Uruguay industry 215/1
Montmaurin S France site of early man 32/2
Montpellier S France Genoese trade 120/2; French Revolution 199/2
Montreal (*Fr.* Montréal) E Canada capture of French fort by British 190/1; industry 215/1,2
Montreux Switzerland 1936 Conference 261/1
Monserrat *island* West Indies English settlement 156/3; British colony 273/2 (inset)
Moransengo NW Italy Mantuan principality 183/3
Morat (*Ger.* Murten) Switzerland 147/2
Moravia (*Czech.* Morava *Ger.* Mähren) region of Czech Republic occupied by Poland 117/3; medieval German Empire 119/1; acquired by Bohemia 139/1; Hussite influence 141/1; acquired by Habsburgs 146/1, 182/2, 193/3; Reformation 179/1; 18C industrial growth 186/2; Margravate 187/1; conquered by Prussia 192/4; forms part of Czechoslovakia 261/1
Mordva (*n/c* Mordvins) people of C Russia 114/4, 115/1; conquered 159/1; 288/4
Mordvinian ASSR C Russia 288/2
Morea (*a/c* Peloponnese) region of S Greece Byzantine Empire 113/5; Despotate 136/2; conquered by Ottomans 137/1, 147/1; under Turks 183/1
Morelos province of C Mexico 223/1
Moreton Bay E Australia penal colony 233/5
Morgarten E Switzerland ✕ 140/3
Mori W Japan clan territory 164/4
Morioka N Japan 171/4
Mormon Bar W USA mining site 216/1
Mormon Trail N USA settlers' route 216/1
Morocco (*Fr.* Maroc *Sp.* Marruecos) under Almohads 132/1; Sharifian dynasties 162/1; Spanish conquest 182/2; independent sultanate 224/1; French and Spanish protectorates 236/2, 237/1, 241/1, 247/2, 256/1; immigration from France 205/2; WW2 265/5, 268/1; independence 272/2; conflict with Algeria 281/1; US bases 293/1; economy 214/1, 295/1
Morotai *island* N Moluccas, E Indies captured by Allies 267/2
Mortsani Slav tribe of E Europe 138/2
Moscha S Arabia early trade 70/1, 82/4
Moscow (*Russ.* Moskva) W Russia early bishopric 101/2; Mongol attack 114/4; city of Vladimir-Suzdal 115/1; early trade 147/1, 159/1; 18C urban development 177/2; captured by Napoleon 201/1; urban growth 227/1, 288/3; WW1 249/3; Bolshevik seizure of power 255/1; WW2 268/1, 269/3; industrial development 207/1, 209/1, 227/1, 288/2; 289/1
Moshesh tribe of S Africa 234/3
Moskva (Moscow)
Mosquito Coast C America English settlement 156/3; to Nicaragua 223/1
Mossel Bay S Africa Portuguese exploration 162/2
Mossi early states of W Africa 135/1, 157/1, 163/1
Mossi-Dagomba early states of W Africa 235/1
Mostaganem Algeria Mediterranean trade 142/1
Mostar Herzegovina, Yugoslavia Ottoman Empire 137/1
Mosul (*Ar.* Al Mawsil) Iraq early archbishopric 101/1; Muslim conquest 105/1, 133/1; Ottoman Empire 137/1; WW1 248/4; oilfield 283/3
Moudon W Switzerland Zähringen town 121/6
Mouliana E Crete Minoan palace 67/2
Moulmein S Burma occupied by Japanese 267/1
Mound City USA Hopewell site 46/3
Moundville SE USA early site 46/3
Mount Athos N Greece monastery 93/3
Mount Carmel Israel site of early man 33/1
Mount Isa N Australia copper 233/5
Mount's Bay SW England Megalithic site 42/2
Mount Sinai E Egypt monastery 93/3
Mouri W Africa early Dutch settlement 162/1 (inset)
Mousehold Heath E England ✕ 181/1
Mozambique (*form.* Portuguese East Africa *Port.* Moçambique) early trade, 155/1, 157/1, 195/1; Portuguese settlement 163/1, 235/1; Portuguese colony 236-7, 241/1; independence 273/2; political development 281/1; economy 214/1
Mtskheta Caucasus early archbishopric 93/1
Mubarran United Arab Emirates, Persian Gulf oilfield 283/3
Muchic Andean Indian tribe of S America 145/1
Mudraya Egypt satrapy of Achaemenid Empire 78/1
Mud Springs C USA ✕ 217/4
Mughal Empire India 151/1, 167/1, 168-9
Mukden (*Chin.* Shenyang) Manchuria treaty town 228/2; Russo-Japanese war 238/3; Japanese occupation 264/2
Mukha (Mocha)
Mülhausen (*Fr.* Mulhouse) W Germany industry 208/1
Mulhouse (*Ger.* Mülhausen) E France industrial development 206/1
Multan district of NW India ✕ 104/2; Muslim conquest 105/1; Empire of Ghazni 128/2; Mughal Empire 169/1; industry under British rule 231/3
München (Munich)
Munda S Spain Roman Empire 86/3
Mundurucú forest Indian tribe of N Brazil 145/1
Munhata S Palestine early village 41/1
Munich (*Ger.* München) S Germany in medieval Bavaria 119/1; in Thirty Years' War 178/2; industrial development 206/1, 208/1; 212/3; WW1 249/3; WW2 269/3; 271/2
Munster early kingdom of SW Ireland 117/1; conquered by Normans 123/1; Presidency 181/1
Münster N Germany bishopric 117/1, 187/1
Muqdisho (Mogadishu)
Murakami N Japan 171/4
Murban United Arab Emirates oilfield 283/3
Murcia region of S Spain reconquest by Castile 122/3
Mureybat Mesopotamia early village 41/1
Murfreesboro SE USA ✕ 219/1
Murmansk N Russia Allied occupation 255/1; industry and urban growth 288/3; industrial development 289/1
Muroma E Slav tribe of C Russia 115/1
Murom-Ryazan early principality of C Russia 115/1
Muroran N Japan 239/1
Murten (*Fr.* Morat) C Switzerland Zähringen town 121/6
Murviedro (Saguntum)
Murzuk Libya early trade 134/2; 163/1; Barth's journey 234/2
Muscat (*Ar.* Masqat) town and district of SE Arabia early trade 133/1; Ottoman siege 167/1; oil 283/3
Muscat and Oman (*now* Oman) SE Arabia British protectorate 225/1, 256/1
Muscovy early principality of W Russia 147/1, 159/1
Mushki early people of Anatolia 56/3
Mutina (*mod.* Modena) N Italy Roman Empire 87/1, 89/1, 91/1
Muza SW Arabia early trade 82/4
Muziris S India early trade 71/1, 82/4
Mwenemutapa early state of SE Africa 163/1
Mycale W Anatolia ✕ 74/3, 78/1
Mycenae ancient city of S Greece 52/1; 66-7
Mylae (*mod.* Milazzo) Sicily Roman Empire 86/2,3
Mylasa (*mod.* Milas) SW Anatolia Alexander's route 76/1
Mymensingh Bangladesh 279/3
Mynydd Rhiw N Wales Megalithic site 42/2
Myos Hormus ancient port on Red Sea 70/1, 91/1
Myra S Anatolia Byzantine Empire 112/3
Myrsini E Crete Minoan site 67/2
Myrtos E Crete Minoan palace 67/1
Mysia ancient country of W Anatolia 75/1, 76/1
Mysians ancient people of Anatolia 56/3
Mysore (*now* Karnataka) region of S India Maratha state 168/3; alliance with Britain 190/2 (inset); state under British rule 231/3
Mytilene (*a/s* Mitylene) W Anatolia early church 93/1. See also Lesbos
Mzêrib Lebanon medieval fair 143/1
Mzilikazi tribe of S Africa 234/3
Nabateans ancient people of Palestine 103/2
Nagaland state of E India separatist movements 279/3
Nagano city and prefecture of C Japan 239/1
Nagaoka N Japan 171/4
Nagappattinam (Negapatam)
Nagasaki W Japan early European trade 155/1, 157/1, 170/4, 195/1; industry 214/1, 238/1, 275/1; bombed by US 267/1
Nagidus S Anatolia Greek colony 75/1
Nagorno-Karabakh AD Caucasus 288/2
Nagoya C Japan 171/4, 175/1, 214/1, 238/1
Nagpur city and region of C India 214/1, 231/3
Nahuatl Indian tribe of C Mexico 145/1
Naimans Mongolian tribe 127/1
Nairobi Kenya occupied by British 237/1
Naissus (*Mod.* Niš) S Yugoslavia Roman Empire 91/1; bishopric 93/1
Najd (Nejd)
Najran SW Arabia early bishopric 100/1
Nakamura N Japan 171/4
Nakasendo *highway* C Japan 171/4
Nakatsu W Japan 170/4
Nakhichevan Caucasus conquered by Ottomans 167/1; ASSR 288/2
Nakhodka Russ. Far East industry 289/1
Nakhon Pathom S Thailand Hindu-Buddhist remains 131/2
Nakhon Ratchasima C Thailand Vietnam war 292/4
Nambicuara forest Indian tribe of W Brazil 145/1
Namibia (*a/c* South West Africa) 272/2, 281/1
Namsos C Norway WW2 265/5
Namu N America site 47/1
Namur Belgium Burgundian possession 147/2; town of Spanish Netherlands 181/1; industrial development 206/1; WW1 248/6, 249/3 (inset)
Nan C China Han commanderie 81/2
Nan-ch'ang (*n/s* Nanchang) S China Ming provincial capital 165/1; under warlord control 258/1; anti-Nationalist insurrection 259/3; occupied by Japanese 264/2
Nan-chao (*n/s* Nanzhao *mod.* Yunnan) SW China independent kingdom 124-5, 131/3
Nan-cheng (*n/s* Nanzheng) N China Han prefecture 81/2
Nan Chih-li (*n/s* Nan Zhili) E China Ming province 164/2, 165/1
Nan-ching (Nanking)
Nancy E France ✕ 147/2; French Revolution 199/2; industrial development 208/1; WW1 248-9
Nandi tribe of E Africa, 235/1
Nan-hai (*n/c* Canton) S China trade centre 81/2
Nan-hai (*n/s* Nanhai) S China Han Commanderie 81/2
Nan-hsing-t'ang (*n/s* Nanxingtang) N China Han prefecture 81/2
Nanking (*n/s* Nanjing *W/G* Nan-ching) N China ; Ming provincial capital 165/1; British influence 228/2; T'ai-p'ing capital 229/1; Nationalist capital 258/1,2;

Nan-ning – Obdorsk

occupied by Japan 264/2, 266/1; industry 259/3, 274/3
Nan-ning (*n/s* Nanning) S China treaty port 228/2
Nantes NW France Scandinavian settlement 111/1; 17C revolt 181/1; trading port 176/3; 18C urban development 177/2; French Revolution 199/2; industrial development 206/1
Nantwich C England ✕ 180/2
Nanxingtang (Nan-hsing-t'ang)
Nan-yüeh (*n/s* Nanyue) SW China independent kingdom 80/3
Nanzhao (Nan-chao)
Nanzheng (Nan-cheng)
Nan Zhili (Nan Chih-li)
Napata U Egypt Iron Age site 45/1
Napier N Island, New Zealand founded 232/1
Naples (*anc.* Neapolis *It.* Napoli) early city 119/1; Mediterranean trade 132/1, 142/1; under Spanish rule 182/2, 183/1; industrial development 206/1; WW2 269/3
Naples, Kingdom of Black Death 141/1; to Aragon 146/1; acquired by Habsburgs 146/2, 166/1; to Austria 188/3; satellite of France 200-1; unification of Italy 213/2
Napoli (Naples)
Naqada Upper Egypt 59/1
Nara C Japan Buddhist site 73/1; prefecture 238/1
Narasura E Africa cattle domestication 45/1
Narbo (*mod.* Narbonne) S France Roman Empire 86/3, 89/1, 90/1
Narbonensis (*a/c* Gallia Narbonensis) Roman province of S France, 89/1
Narbonne (*anc.* Narbo) S France Muslim conquest 104/1; early archbishopric 106/3; medieval trade 120/1,2
Nariokotome E Africa site of early man 33/1
Narnia (*mod.* Narni) N Italy Latin colony 87/1
Naroch *Lake* W Russia WW1 ✕ 249/3
Narraganset Indian tribe of NE USA 145/1
Narragansett Fort NE USA 217/4
Narva Estonia, W Russia early trade 185/1; WW2 269/3
Narvik N Norway WW2 265/5
Narym W Siberia 158/3
Nasca C Andes site 47/1,4
Naseby C England ✕ 180/2
Nashville SE USA ✕ 219/1
Nashville Road C USA settlers' route 216/1
Nasrids Muslim dynasty of Spain 133/1
Nassau principality of C Germany 187/1; Reformation 179/1; unification with Germany 212/3
Natal province of S Africa annexed by Britain 234/3; British colony 235/1, 237/1, 240/1 (inset); immigration from India 205/2
Natchez S USA site of early man 32/1; Indian tribe 145/1
Natchez Trace S USA settlers' route 216/1
Natchitoches S USA fur station 216/1
Natick NE USA Protestant mission 216/1
National Road C USA settlers' route 216/1
Nations, Battle of the (Leipzig) E Germany ✕ 201/1
Naucratis Egypt Iron Age site 45/1; Greek colony 75/1
Nauplia (*mod. Gr.* Navplion) S Greece Venetian fort 183/1
Nauru *island* W Pacific independence 273/2 (inset)
Nautaca (*mod.* Karshi) C Asia on Alexander's route 77/1
Navajo Indian tribe of SW USA 145/1
Navarino (Pylos)
Navarre (*Sp.* Navarra) region of N Spain/SW France kingdom 122/3; acquired by Habsburgs 182/2; acquired by France 146/1, 189/1
Navpaktos (Lepanto)
Navplion (Nauplia)
Naworth Castle N England ✕ 181/1
Naxos island of Aegean gained by Turks 183/1
Naxos Sicily Greek colony 75/1
Nazca Andean Indian tribe of S America 145/1
Nazlet Khatir NE Africa site of early man 33/1
Ndebele (*a/c* Matabele) tribe of S Africa 234/3, 235/1
N'Djamena (Fort Lamy)
Ndonga early state of SW Africa 235/1
Neanderthal Germany site of early man 32/2
Neapolis (*mod.* Napoli *Eng.* Naples) S Italy Greek colony 75/1; Roman Empire 87/1, 89/1; early bishopric 93/1; Jewish community 103/1
Neapolis Sardinia Roman Empire 86/2
Near East (Middle East)
Neath S Wales Industrial Revolution 197/1
Nebraska state of C USA 1896 elections 221/3; Depression 263/1; income and population 287/2
Neerwinden Belgium ✕ 199/2
Nefertara N Greece Mithraic site 72/1
Negapatam (*n/s* Nagappattinam) S India Dutch settlement 157/1, 169/1; ✕ 190/2 (inset); industry 231/3
Negri Sembilan state of Malaya 172/4
Negritos people of SE Asia, 35/2
Negroponte (Euboea) Venetian possession 139/1
Neh S Persia town of Parthian Empire 79/3
Nehavend (*anc.* Laodicea in Media) W Persia ✕ 79/3, 105/1
Nejd (*Ar.* Najd) region of C Arabia 225/1
Nellore district of SE India ceded to Britain 168/3
Nelson county and town of S Island, New Zealand founded 232/1
Nelson Bay S Africa Iron Age site 45/1
Nemausus (*mod.* Nîmes) S France Roman Empire 89/1; early bishopric 92/1
Nemetocenna (Arras)
Nemours region of N France 147/3
Nenets AO N Russia 288/2
Neocaesarea N Anatolia early archbishopric 93/1; Byzantine Empire 113/1
Nepal tributary state of Chinese Empire 171/1; 228/2; British influence 257/1, 273/1, 279/3; economy 214/1
Nepala (*mod.* Nepal) tributary state of the Guptas 82/5
Nepete N Italy Latin colony 87/1
Nerchinsk SE Siberia founded 158/3
Nesvizh (*Pol.* Nieśwież) W Russia town of Turov-Pinsk 115/1
Netherlands (*a/c* Holland *form.* Dutch Republic, United Provinces) Burgundian possession 147/3; acquired by Habsburgs 146/1, 181/2, 183/1; agriculture and land reclamation 174-5; trade and industry 176-7; independence in north 181/1, 183/1; losses to France 188/2; gains by Austrian Habsburgs 188/3; struggle for power 198/1; industrial revolution 206/1, 208/1; colonial power 241/1; overseas trade 252-3; socio-political development 262/3, 263/2; EEC and NATO 270/1, 291/1; economy 271/4, 295/1. See also Belgium, Flanders, Holland
Netherlands, Austrian (*Mod.* Belgium) revolt against Emperor 198/1; occupied by French 199/3
Netherlands, Spanish (*later* Holland *or* United Provinces; and Belgium) Reformation 179/1; part of German Empire 187/1; 181/1; territory lost to and gained from France 182/2, 188/2
Netherlands, United 187/1
Netherlands Antilles (*a/c* Dutch West Indies) 273/2 (inset)
Netherlands East Indies (*now Indonesia*) occupied by Japanese 267/1 See also East indies, Borneo, Java, Moluccas, Sumatra
Neuengamme N Germany concentration camp 268/1
Neuenheim W Germany Mithraic site 72/1
Neustria the Frankish lands of N France 106/1
Neuchâtel Switzerland Reformation 179/1
Neuve-Chapelle NE France WW1 249/3 (inset)
Nevada state of W USA 1896 elections 220/1; Depression 262/1; income and population 287/2
Nevers C France independent fief 147/3; industrial development 206/1
Neville's Cross N England ✕ 140/2
Nevis *island* W Indies English settlement 156/3; British colony 223/1; self-government with St Christopher 273/1 (inset); 273/2 (inset)
New Amsterdam (*earlier* Fort Amsterdam *now* New York City) colonized by Dutch 157/2
New Britain *island* Papua New Guinea early Melanesian settlement 49/1; WW2 266-7; to Papua 273/2 (inset)
New Brunswick province of E Canada joins Confederation 215/2, 240/1
New Caledonia *islands* S Pacific early Melanesian settlement 49/1; French colony 241/1, 273/2 (inset); US base 267/1
Newcastle SE Australia penal settlement 233/5
Newcastle-under-Lyme C England Industrial Revolution 197/1
Newcastle-upon-Tyne N England medieval trade 142/1; Civil War 180/2; industrial development 196/3, 197/1, 208/1
Newchwang (*n/c* Yingkou) Manchuria treaty port 228/2; Russo-Japanese war 238/3
New England NE USA British settlement 157/2; industry 287/1
Newfoundland province of E Canada rediscovered 152/1; British settlement 157/2, 161/1, 191/1; British colony 240/1; economic development 215/2. See also Vinland
New France French possession in Canada 157/2, 191/1
New Galicia Spanish colony of C Mexico 154/1
New Granada (*mod.* Colombia) Spanish colony 154/1, 161/1; vice-royalty in rebellion against Spain 198/1
New Grange Ireland early site 42/2
New Guinea (*now part of* Papua New Guinea) early settlement 48/1; Dutch/German/British control 241/1; WW2 266-7. See also West Irian, Papua New Guinea
Newham N England ✕ 181/1
New Hampshire state of NE USA colony 157/2, 160/3; urban growth 204; 19C politics 220/1, 221/2,3; Depression 263/1; income and population 287/2
New Haven NE USA founded 157/2
New Hebrides (*Fr.* Nouvelles Hébrides *n/c* Vanuatu) *islands* S Pacific early Melanesian settlement 49/1; British/French condominium 241/1; US base 267/1
New Holland (*now* Australia) early voyages 153/3
New Ireland *island* Papua New Guinea early Melanesian settlement 48/1; WW2 266-7
New Jersey state of E USA colony 157/2, 160/3; urban growth 204; 19C politics 220/1, 221/2,3; Depression 263/1; income and population 287/2
New Lanark S Scotland Industrial Revolution 196/3
New Malton N England Industrial Revolution 197/1
New Mexico state of SW USA ceded by Mexico 223/1; Depression 263/1; income and population 287/2
New Netherland (*now* New York City) Dutch colony 157/2
New Orleans S USA French/Spanish occupation 160-5; Civil War 218/1; industry 215/1
New Plymouth N Island, New Zealand founded 232/1. See also Taranaki
Newport S Wales Industrial Revolution 197/1
Newport Pagnell S England Industrial Revolution 197/1
New Sarai S Russia Mongol capital 126/1
New South Wales state of SE Australia early exploration 153/3; settlement and development 233/5; statehood 240/1 (inset)
New Spain (*mod.* Mexico, C America and Caribbean) early voyages of discovery 152/1; Spanish vice-royalty 154/1, 161/1,2; rebellion against Spain 198/1
New Territories S China acquired by Britain 228/2
Newton C USA cow town 216/1
Newton C Wales Industrial Revolution 197/1
Newton le Willows NW England Industrial Revolution 196/3
New Ulm N USA ✕ 217/4
New York (*form.* New Netherland) colony 157/2, 160/3; trade 195/1
New York state of E USA 19C politics 221/2,3; Depression 263/1; income and population 287/2
New York City (*1653-64 called* New Amsterdam *earlier* Fort Amsterdam) 157/2; British naval base 190/1; population growth 204; industry 215/1; 287/1
New Zealand early Polynesian settlement 49/1,3; early voyages 153/3,233/2; settlement and development 232/1; end of colonial status 241/1, 273/1; industrialization 215/1; economy 262/3, 295/1
Neyshabur (*a/s* Nishapur) N Persia 55/1
Nez Perce plateau Indian tribe of W Canada 145/1
Ngandong Java site of early man 33/1
Ngaruawahia N Island, New Zealand 232/1
Ngatapa N Island, New Zealand ✕ 232/1
Ngazargumu W Africa capital of Kanem-Borno 135/1
Nguni (*a/c* Ngoni) tribe of S Africa 163/1, 234/1, 235/1
Nha Trang S Indo-China Hindu-Buddhist temple 131/2
Niah Cave Borneo site of early man 33/1; Bronze Age caves 130/1
Niani W Africa early capital of Mali Empire 135/1
Nicaea (*mod.* Iznik) W Anatolia centre of early Christianity 72/1; Roman Empire 89/1, 91/1, 93/1; Slav settlement 112/4; Byzantine Empire 113/5
Nicaea NW India Alexander's route 77/1
Nicaragua country of C America early exploration 153/1; independence 223/1; US protectorate 243/4; political development 284-5
Nicarao Indian tribe of C America 145/1
Nice (*It.* Nizza) S France Mediterranean trade 142/1; annexed from Italy 199/3, 213/1
Nicephorium (*mod.* Raqqa) Syria Roman Empire 89/1, 91/1
Nichoria S Greece Mycenaean site 67/1
Nicobar Islands Indian Ocean territory of British India 231/3, 241/1
Nicomedia (*mod.* Izmit) W Anatolia Roman Empire 86/3, 89/1, 91/1; early archbishopric 93/1; Byzantine Empire 113/1
Nicopolis Lower Egypt 91/1
Nicopolis W Greece archbishopric 93/1; Byzantine Empire 113/5
Nicopolis E Anatolia Roman Empire 86/3, 89/1
Nicopolis (*mod.* Nikopol) Bulgaria Byzantine Empire 113/1
Nida W Germany Mithraic site 72/1
Nidaros (*n/c* Trondheim) C Norway bishopric 117/1
Niedersachsen (Lower Saxony)
Nieśwież (Nesvizh)
Niger country of W Africa French colony 237/1; independence 272/2, 281/1
Nigeria country of W Africa British colony 236/2, 237/1, 240/1; independence 272/2, political development 281/1; economy 214/1, 295/1
Nihommatsu N Japan 171/4
Niigata E Japan 171/4, 175/1, 239/1
Nijmegen (Nimwegen)
Nikki Dahomey, W Africa occupied by French 237/1
Nikko-kaido old highway of C Japan 171/4
Nikolayev S Ukraine founded 159/1; Russian Revolution 255/1
Nikopol (Nicopolis)
Nilgiris district of SW India 231/3
Nilotes people of E Africa 135/1, 163/1
Nîmes (*anc.* Nemausus) S France French Revolution 199/2
Nimrud (*anc.* Calah *Bibl.* Kalhu) Mesopotamia 57/2
Nimwegen (*a/s* Nymwegen, *mod.* Nijmegen) Netherlands Frankish royal residence 106/3; 119/1
Nina S Mesopotamia 55/3
Nindowari N India Harappan site 65/1
Nineveh Mesopotamia early trade 54/1; Assyrian Empire 56/7; Alexander's Empire 76/1, 79/1
Ningbo (Ningpo)
Ning-hsia (*n/s* Ningxia) NW China early bishopric 101/1; Ming frontier defence area 165/1
Ningpo (*n/s* Ningbo) E China early trade 125/2, 164/2; treaty port 228/2
Ningxia (Ning-hsia)
Ninus (Nineveh)
Nippur Mesopotamia 41/1, 54/1, 57/1
Nirou Khani C Crete Minoan palace 67/1
Niš (Naissus, Nish)
Nisa (*a/c* Mihrakert) N Persia town of Parthian Empire 79/3
Nish (*S. Cr.* Niš *anc.* Naissus) E Yugoslavia Ottoman Empire 137/1; WW1 249/3
Nishada ancient kingdom of W India 65/1
Nishapur (*Pers.* Neyshabur) W Persia early bishopric 101/1; Muslim conquest 105/1; Mongol conquest 127/4; trade 133/1; Safavid conquest 167/1
Nishio C Japan 171/4
Nisibis (*mod.* Nusaybin) E Anatolia Alexander's route 76/1, Roman Empire 86/3; fortification 88/3; early archbishopric 93/1, 101/1; Jewish community 103/1; Muslim trade 133/1
Nivernais region of E France Royal domain 123/1
Nizhne-Kamchatsk Russ. Far East founded 158/3
Nizhne-Kolymsk NE Siberia founded 158/3
Nizhne-Udinsk C Siberia founded 158/3
Nizhniy Novgorod (*since 1932* Gorkiy) C Russia town of Vladimir-Suzdal 115/1; industry 227/1; Bolshevik seizure 255/1
Nizhniy Tagil W Siberia founded 159/1; urban growth 288/3; industry 289/1
Nizza (Nice)
Nkope E Africa Iron Age site 45/1
Nobeoka W Japan 170/4
Noemfoor (*n/s* Numfor) island of NW New Guinea retaken by US 267/2
Nogai Tartars tribe of C Russia, 159/1
Nohmul Belize Mayan site 46/2
Noirmoutier W France Scandinavian settlement 111/1
Noisy N France Megalithic site 42/2
Nok W Africa Iron Age site 45/1
Nola S Italy monastery 93/3
Nombre de Dios Panama early Spanish port 154/1
Nomonhan (*a/c* Khalkin Gol) E Mongolia Russo-Japanese conflict 264/2
Non Nok Tha N Thailand early site 130/1
Nootka coast Indian tribe of W Canada 145/1
Norba C Italy Latin colony 87/1
Norcia (Nursia)
Nördlingen S Germany medieval fair 142/1; ✕ 178/2
Nordmark N Germany region of Brandenburg 117/1, 118/2
Nordrhein-Westfalen (North Rhine-Westphalia)
Norfolk E USA industry 215/1
Norfolk Island S W Pacific Australian territory 241/1, 273/2 (inset)
Noricum Roman province of C Europe 89/1, 91/2
Norilsk NW Siberia urban growth 288/3; industry 289/1
Normandy region of N France Scandinavian settlement 110/2; dukedom 117/1; English rule 123/1; French Royal domain 147/3; province of France 189/1; WW2 invasion 269/6 (inset)
Normans in Sicily and S Italy 113/5, 120/2
Normanton E Australia early settlement 233/5
Northampton C England Viking fort 110/2; Industrial Revolution 197/1
North Battleford C Canada growth 215/2
North Cape N Island New Zealand Maori settlement 49/3
North Carolina state of E USA colony 157/2, 160/3; Civil War 219/1; 19C politics 220/1, 248/2,3; Depression 263/1; income and population 287/2
North Dakota state of N USA 1896 elections 221/3; Depression 263/1; income and population 287/2
North East Frontier Agency (Arunachal Pradesh)
Northern Ireland IRA terrorism 291/2
Northern Rhodesia (*now* Zambia) British colony 236/2, 237/1, 241/1, 272/1; part of Central African Federation 272/2
Northern Sarkars (*a/s* Circars) territory of E India 168/3, 190/2 (inset)
Northern Territory Australia settlement and development 233/5
Northern Wei (Toba)
North Island (*Maori* Te Ika-a-Maui) New Zealand settlement and development 232/1
North Ossetian ASSR Caucasus 288/2
North Rhine-Westphalia (*Ger.* Nordrhein-Westfalen) region of NW Germany 271/2
Northumberland N England claimed by Scotland 123/1
Northumbria early kingdom of N England conversion to Christianity 100/3; Scandinavian settlement 110/2; under Scandinavian control 117/1
North Vietnam independence 273/2; military growth 274/2. See also Vietnam, Indo-China
North West Frontier Province N Pakistan in Indian Empire 231/3; joins Pakistan 278/1
Norway conversion to Christianity 101/2; emergence as medieval state 117/1; Black Death 141/1; Union of Kalmar 146/1; union with Sweden 141/1, 211/3; Reformation 179/1; population growth 204/3,4; emigration 205/1; railway development 206/1; socio-political change 263/2; WW2 265/5, 268-9; NATO and EFTA 270/1, 291/1; economy 271/4, 295/1
Norwich E England Scandinavian settlement 110/2; rebellion 181/1; Industrial Revolution 197/1
Noshiro N Japan 171/4
Notgrove C England Megalithic site 42/2
Notium W Anatolia ✕ 74/4
Nottingham C England Danish Viking base 111/1; Industrial Revolution 197/1
Nouvelles Hébrides (New Hebrides)
Novae Bulgaria Mithraic site 72/1; Roman Empire 91/1
Nova Goa (*later* Pangim *now* Panaji) W India 231/3
Novara N Italy Lombard League 119/1; Signorial domination 122/2 ✕ 213/2
Nova Scotia (*form.* Acadia) province of E Canada ceded by France 157/2; British possession 160-1, 191/1; joins Confederation 240/1; economy 215/2
Novaya Zemlya region of Arctic Russia discovery 153/1
Nové Košariská Czechoslovakia Hallstatt site 85/1
Novellara N Italy county 183/3
Novello NW Italy principality 183/3
Novgorod (*Norse* Holmgard) NW Russia bishopric 101/2, 114/2, Viking trade 110/3; Hanseatic trade 142/1; Baltic trade 185/1; Russian Revolution 255/1; WW2 269/3
Novgorod Empire NW Russia 115/1; conquered by Muscovy 159/1
Novgorod-Seversk early principality of W Russia 115/1
Novibazar, Sanjak of Ottoman province of Yugoslavia 211/2
Novocherkassk S Russia industry 227/1; Bolshevik seizure 255/1
Novokuznetsk (*1932-61 called* Stalinsk) C Siberia foundation and development 288/3; industry 289/1
Novomoskovsk (*until 1934* Bobriki *until 1961* Stalinogorsk) C Russia development 288/3
Novonikolayevsk (*since 1925* Novosibirsk) C Siberia on railway 226/2
Novorossiysk S Russia industry 227/1; Bolshevik seizure 255/1
Novosibirsk (*until 1925* Novonikolayevsk) C Siberia development 288/3; industry 289/1
Novosil W Russia early town of Chernigov 115/1
Ntereso W Africa early site 45/1
Nubia region of NE Africa introduction of Christianity 100/1; Christian kingdom 135/1
Nuestra Señora de la Soledad W USA Catholic mission 216/1
Nuevo León province of N Mexico 223/1; US military intervention 243/4
Numantia N Spain Roman Empire 86/3
Numazu C Japan 171/4
Numfor (Noemfoor)
Numidia Roman province of N Africa 86/3, 89/1, 91/2
Nupe Nigeria early Hausa state 135/1, 163/1, 235/1, 237/1
Nuremberg (*Ger.* Nürnberg) S Germany Reformation 179/1; 16C urban development 176/1; industrial development 206/1
Nuri U Egypt Iron Age site 45/1
Nursia (*mod.* Norcia) C Italy Roman Empire 87/1; monastery 93/3
Nyamwezi tribe of E Africa 235/1
Nyasaland (*now* Malawi) British protectorate 235/1, 236-41, 241/1, 273/1; part of Central African Federation 273/2
Nymwegen (Nimwegen)
Nysa Afghanistan Alexander's route 77/1
Nyssa W Anatolia early bishopric 93/1
Oakham C England Industrial Revolution 197/1
Oaxaca province of S Mexico 46/2, 223/1
Obama C Japan 171/4
Obdorsk (*since 1933* Salekhard) W Siberia founded 159/1

Persian Gates – Ragusa

Christianity 101/1; Muslim conquest 105/1; under Abbasid sovereignty 108/1, 133/1; Mongol conquest 126/4; Safavid Empire 167/1; independent kingdom 225/1; economy 214/1; British and Russian spheres of influence 225/2, 241/1; revolution 244/1; oil under British control 256/1
Persian Gates SW Persia Alexander's route 77/1
Persian Gulf (*a/c* Arabian Gulf *or* The Gulf) WW1 249/4; oil 283/3
Persians attack Assyria 56/3
Persis (*a/c* Fars, Parsa) S Persia Alexander's Empire 77/1; vassal kingdom of Parthian Empire 79/3
Perth W Australia early settlement 233/5
Peru Spanish colonization 154/3, 161/1; exports and foreign investment 222/3; population 222/4; independence 222/2, 223/1, 240/1 (inset); war with Chile 223/5; political developments 284-5; economy 294/1
Perusia (*mod.* Perugia) N Italy Roman Empire 87/1, 89/1
Pesaro (Pisaurum)
Peshawar Pakistan industry under British rule 231/3; capital of NW Frontier Agency 279/3
Peshwa (*a/c* Peishwa) native state of W India 168/3, 190/2
Pessinus W Anatolia Jewish community 103/1
Pesto (Poseidonia)
Peterborough E England Industrial Revolution 197/1
Peterlingen (Payerne)
Peterwardein (*mod.* Petrovaradin *Hung.* Pétervárad) Serbia ✕ 193/3
Petra Jordan Assyrian Empire 57/1,2; Roman Empire 89/1, 91/1; early archbishopric 93/1
Petralona Greece site of early man 32/2
Petrograd (*before 1914* St. Petersburg *since 1924* Leningrad) WW1 249/3; Russian Revolution 255/1
Petropavlovsk (*now* Petropavlovsk-Kamchatskiy) Russ. Far East founded 158/3; fur trade 195/2; industry 289/1
Petrovaradin (Peterwardein)
Petrozavodsk NW Russia Russian Revolution 255/1
Petsamo (*Russ.* Pechenga) NW Russia Russian conquest from Finland 265/5
Petsophas E Crete Minoan site 67/2
Pettau (Poetovio)
Pfalz (Palatinate)
Pfalz-Sulzbach W Germany principality 187/1
Phaistos Crete palace site 67/2
Phalaborwa SE Africa early state 45/1; 135/1
Phanagoria S Russia Greek colony 75/1
Phan Rang S Indo-China Hindu-Buddhist temple 131/2
Pharsalus (*Gr.* Pharsalos) C Greece Roman Empire 86/3
Phaselis SW Anatolia Greek colony 75/1; Alexander's route 76/1
Phasis Caucasus Greek colony 75/1; Roman Empire 89/1
Phazania (*mod.* Fezzan) region of S Libya 89/1
Philadelphia (*mod.* Alaşehir) W Anatolia early church 93/1
Philadelphia N Egypt Jewish community 103/1
Philadelphia E USA founded 157/2; industry 215/1, 287/1
Philadelphia (Amman)
Philiphaugh S Scotland ✕ 180/2
Philippi N Greece Roman Empire 86/3; 89/1; Jewish community 103/1
Philippines early sites 130/1; spread of Islam 104/3, 131/3; early trade 155/1, 157/1; Spanish conquest 172/2, 173/1; imperial trade 195/1; acquired by US 241/1, 242/1; anti-colonial revolts 244/1; occupied by Japanese 264/2, 266/1; retaken by US 267/2; insurgency 277/1; US bases 273/1, 293/1; industry and economy 214/1, 274/2, 295/1
Philippine Sea ✕ 267/2
Philippopolis (*mod.* Plovdiv *Turk* Filibe) Bulgaria Roman Empire 89/1; Byzantine Empire 113/1; Ottoman Empire 166/1
Philistines displaced 67/3
Philomelium (*mod.* Akş ehir) C Anatolia Byzantine Empire 113/5
Phnom Laang Cambodia early site 130/1
Phnom Penh Cambodia early political centre 131/2; Khmer capital 173/1; Vietnam war 292/4
Phocaea W Anatolia Greek colony 75/1
Phoenicia at time of Greeks 75/1, 76/1; Roman province 89/1; 102/2
Phoenicians move into Africa 45/1; colonization 61/1,2
Phylakopi SE Greece early settlement 43/1
Phrygia ancient country of W Anatolia 75/1, 76/1, 92/2; spread of Christianity 72/1; Roman province 86/3, 91/2; Byzantine Empire 113/1
Phrygians early people of Anatolia 56/3, 67/3
Phylakopi Aegean Mycenaean palace site 67/1
Piacenza (*anc.* Placentia) N Italy Lombard League 119/1; Signorial domination 122/2; medieval fair 142/1
Piauí state of NE Brazil 273/1
Picardy (*Fr.* Picardie) region of N France annexed from Burgundy 147/3; 189/1; WW1 249/3 (inset)
Picentes early tribe of N Italy 86/2
Pichincha Colombia ✕ 222/2
Pictavi W France early bishopric 92/1
Picton S Island, New Zealand railway 232/1
Picts early tribe of Scotland 98/1
Piedmont (*It.* Piemonte) region of N Italy occupied by France 199/3; 213/2
Pien-chou (*n/s* Bianzhou) N China T'ang prefecture 124/1
Pietrasanta N Italy Tuscan principality 183/3
Pigs, Bay of Cuba CIA invasion 293/6
Pilbara W Australia early settlement 233/5
Pilos (Pylos)
Pilsen (*Cz.* Plzeň) Czechoslovakia industrial development 206/1
Pima Indian tribe of N Mexico 145/1
Pinega N Russia town of Novgorod Empire 115/1
P'ing-yin (*n/s* Pingyin) C China Han prefecture 81/2
P'ing-yüan (*n/s* Pingyuan) NE China Han prefecture 81/2
Pinsk W Russia town of Turov-Pinsk 115/1; WW1 249/3
Piombino N Italy Mediterranean trade 142/1; French rule 201/1
Piqillacta C Andes early site 47/5
Pirna E Germany ✕ 192/4
Piro forest Indian tribe of S America 145/1
Pisa (*anc.* Pisae) N Italy medieval city 119/1; Mediterranean trade 120/1, 132/1; raids and conquests 120/2; Republican commune 122/2; 146/1
Pisae (*mod.* Pisa) N Italy Roman Empire 87/1, 89/1; bishopric 92/1
Pisaurum (*mod.* Pesaro) N Italy Roman colony 87/1
Piscataway Fort NE USA ✕ 217/4
Pishpek (Frunze)
Pisidia ancient country of C Anatolia 76/1, 113/1
Pistoia (*anc.* Pistoriae) N Italy Roman Empire 87/1; medieval city 119/1
Pitcairn Island C Pacific British colony 273/2 (inset)
Pithecusa S Italy Greek colony 75/1
Pit River W USA ✕ 217/4
Pittsburgh E USA industry 215/1
Pittsburg Landing (Shiloh)
Pityus Caucasus Greek colony 75/1; early bishopric 93/1
Placentia (*mod.* Piacenza) N Italy Latin colony 87/1
Plassey E India ✕ 168/3, 19/2 (inset)
Plataea C Greece ✕ 74/3, 78/1
Platanos C Crete Minoan site 67/2
Plate River (*Sp.* Rio de la Plata) Argentina explored 152/1
Platěnice Czechoslovakia Hallstatt site 85/1
Plati E Crete Minoan site 67/2
Plenty, Bay of N Island, New Zealand Maori settlement 49/4
Plevna (*now* Pleven) Bulgaria WW1 249/3
Pliska Bulgaria early city 108/1
Pločnik S Yugoslavia early settlement 43/1
Ploeşti (*n/s* Ploieşti) Romania WW2 269/3
Plovdiv (Philippopolis)
Plussulien NW France Megalithic site 42/2
Plymouth SW England naval base 191/1; Industrial Revolution 197/1; WW1 249/3; WW2 265/5
Plymouth NE USA founded 157/2
Plzeň (Pilsen)
Pobietto NW Italy Mantuan principality 183/3
Poço da Gateira S Portugal Megalithic site 42/2
Podolia region of S Ukraine acquired by Lithuania 139/1
Poduca S India early port 71/1
Poetovio (*mod.* Ptuj *Ger.* Pettau) N Yugoslavia Mithraic site 72/1; Roman Empire 89/1; early bishopric 93/1
Po-hai (*n/s* Bohai *Kor.* Parhae *mod.* Manchuria) NE China early state 125/2
Pohang S Korea 1950-3 war 274/2; industry 275/1
Point of Rocks C USA ✕ 217/4
Poitiers (*anc.* Limonum) C France ✕ 104/1, 123/1; ✕ 140/4; monastery 106/3; 17C revolts 181/1; seat of intendant 189/1; centre of French Revolution 199/2
Poitou region of W France English possession 123/1; French Royal domain 147/3; province of France 189/1
Pola (*mod.* Pula) N Yugoslavia Roman Empire 89/1; WW1 249/3
Polabii Slavic tribe of N Germany 118/3, 138/2
Poland conversion to Christianity 101/2; under Boleslav Chrobry 117/3; Mongol invasion 126/2; union with Lithuania 139/1; Black Death 141/1; Empire of Casimir IV 147/1; acquired by Russia 159/1; agriculture and peasant emancipation 174/1; Reformation 179/1; Baltic trade 185/1; Partitions 192/1; 193/5; revolt against Russia 198/1; industry under Russian rule 227/1; independence after WW1 255/1, 261/1; socio-political development 262/3, 263/2; WW2 265/5; Warsaw Pact and Comecon 270/3; communism overthrown 295/1
Poles post-WW1 migration to Poland 261/3; post-WW2 migration to West 270/1
Polish Corridor 261/1
Polochaney NW Russia E Slav tribe 115/1
Polotsk W Russia bishopric 101/2; early city and principality 115/1; Hanseatic trading post 142/1
Polovtsy (*a/c* Cumans) tribe of C Russia 114-5
Poltava Ukraine town of Pereyaslavl 115/1; industry and urban growth 227/1; Bolshevik seizure 255/1
Poltoratsk (Ashkhabad)
Polyane Slav tribe of the Ukraine, 115/1
Polynesia island group of C Pacific early settlement 49/1
Pomerania (*Ger.* Pommern *Pol.* Pomorze) region of N Europe acquired by Poland 117/3; medieval German Empire 119/1; Black Death 141/1; Reformation 179/1; unification of Germany 212/3; 271/2
Pomerania, East part of Germany 187/1
Pomerania, Swedish 192/4; ceded to Prussia 211/3
Pomerania, West to Sweden 184-5, 187/1,4
Pomeranians Slav tribe of N Europe 138/2
Pomerelia (*Ger.* Pommerellen) region of N Europe occupied by Teutonic Knights 138/3
Pomo Indian tribe of NW USA 145/1
Pompeii S Italy Jewish community 103/1
Pompeiopolis S Anatolia Roman Empire 89/1
Pondicherry (*Fr.* Pondichéry) SE India French settlement 157/1, 169/1; captured by British 190/2 (inset); imperial trade 195/1; French enclave 231/3; returned to India 273/2
Pondo region of SE Africa British administration 234/3
Pons Saravi E France Mithraic site 72/1
Ponthieu region of NE France Frankish royal residence 106/3; under English rule 123/1; Burgundian possession 147/2
Pontia (Ponza)
Pontiae (*a/c* Pontine Islands *mod.* Isole Ponziane) C Italy Roman Empire 87/1
Pontianak W Borneo Dutch settlement 173/1
Pontine Islands (Pontiae)
Pontnewydd N Wales early man 32/2
Pontremoli N Italy Spanish principality 183/3
Pontus district of N Anatolia 77/3; Roman province 86/3, 89/4; Byzantine Empire 113/1
Ponza (Pontia) *island* C Italy Mithraic site 72/1
Ponziane, Isole (Pontiae)
Poona W India industry 214/1, 231/3
Populonia N Italy Etruscan city 75/1, 86/2
Pornasso NW Italy principality 183/3
Porolissensis Roman province of E Europe 89/1
Porolissum Romania Roman Empire 89/1
Portage la Prairie (Fort La Reine)
Port Arthur (*Chin.* Lüshun *Jap.* Ryojun) Manchuria ceded to Russia and Japan 226/2, 228/2, Russo-Japanese war 238/3; 259/3
Port Arthur (*now* Thunder Bay) C Canada growth 215/2
Port Arthur Tasmania penal settlement 233/5
Port Augusta S Australia settlement 233/5
Port Chalmers S Island, New Zealand 232/1
Port Elizabeth SE Africa British settlement 234/3
Port Essington N Australia founded 233/5
Port-Francqui (*now* Ilebo) C Belgian Congo 280/2
Port Hedland W Australia early settlement 233/5
Port Hudson S USA ✕ 218/1
Porti C Crete Minoan site 67/2
Port Jackson (Sydney)
Portland S England WW1 249/3
Portland SE Australia founded 233/5
Port Lincoln S Australia settlement 233/5
Port Macquarie SE Australia penal settlement 233/5
Port Moresby SE New Guinea Allied base in WW2 267/1
Porto Novo SE India ✕ 190/2
Porto-Novo W Africa French settlement 235/1
Porto Pisano N Italy Mediterranean trade 142/1
Port Pirie S Australia settlement 233/5
Port Royal Jamaica British naval base 190/1
Port Said N Egypt Egyptian-Israeli war 283/2
Portsmouth S England naval base 191/1; Industrial Revolution 197/1; WW1 249/3
Portsmouth NE USA settlement 157/2
Portugal (*anc.* Lusitania) early settlement 42-43; Jewish migration 102/3; Muslim conquest 104/1; reconquest 122/3; 152-3; expansion overseas 154-5; annexed to Spain 182/1; agriculture 175/1; trade and industry 176-7, 194-5; population growth 204/3,4; emigration 205/1; railway development 208/1; colonial empire 241/1; 19C alliances 246-7; WW1 248/1; inter-war alliances 260/2; general strike 263/2; NATO and EEC 270/1, 290/3, 291/1; US bases 293/1; economy 271/4, 295/1
Portuguese East Africa (*now* Mozambique) 241/1
Portuguese Guinea (*now* Guinea-Bissau) W Africa Portuguese colony 236/2, 240/1, 272/1; independence 272/2
Portuguese Timor E Indies annexed by Indonesia 273/2, 277/1
Portus Herculis Monoeci (*a/c* Herculis Monoeci *mod.* Monaco) S France Greek colony 75/1
Porus early kingdom of NW India 77/1
Poseidonia (*later* Paestum *mod.* Pesto) S Italy Greek colony 75/1
Posen (*Pol.* Poznań) W Poland medieval fair 142/1; industrial development 207/1; North German Confederation 212/3; WW1 249/3; ceded by Germany 261/1
Potaissa Romania Roman Empire 91/1
Potawatomi Indian tribe of C USA 145/1
Potentia (*mod.* Potenza) N Italy Roman colony 87/1
Potidaea N Greece Dorian colony 75/1
Potosí Peru Spanish silver mine 154/1
Potsdam E Germany 271/2
Pouey-Mayon SW France Megalithic site 42/2
Poverty Point N America site 47/1
Powhatan Indian tribe of E USA 145/1
Pozsony (Bratislava)
Poznań (*Ger.* Posen) W Poland bishopric 117/3; 139/1
Pozzuoli (Puteoli)
Praeneste (*mod.* Palestrina) C Italy Roman Empire, 87/1
Prague (*Cz.* Praha) Czechoslovakia bishopric 101/2, 117/3; medieval trade 120/1; Hanseatic trade 142/1; 16C urban development 176/1; ✕ 192/4; industrial development 206/1, 209/1; communist coup 292/2
Praia das Maçãs C Portugal burial site 43/1
Praisos E Crete Minoan palace 67/1
Prambanan C Java Hindu-Buddhist temple 131/2
Pratiharas early dynasty of N India 128/2
Pravdinsk (Friedland)
Preah Vihear district of Cambodia claimed by Thailand 275/1
Preanger district of Java Dutch control 172/3
Předmosti Czechoslovakia site of early man 32/2
Preslav Bulgaria early city 108/1
Pressburg (*mod.* Bratislava) 111/1
Preston N England ✕ 180/1; Industrial Revolution 197/1
Prestonpans S Scotland Industrial Revolution 196/3
Pretoria S Africa on Boer trek 234/3
Preussen (Prussia)
Preussisch-Eylau (Eylau)
Preveza C Greece ✕ 166/1
Prilep S Yugoslavia medieval fair 142/1
Primorskiy Kray (Maritime Province)
Prince Edward Island (*form.* Ile St. Jean) E Canada joins confederation 215/2
Prince's Town Ghana early French settlement 162/1 (inset)
Principe *island* W Africa Portuguese settlement 163/1, 237/1
Prinias E Crete Minoan site 67/2
Priniatiko Pyrgos E Crete Minoan site 67/2
Prizren Serbia WW1 249/3
Procolitia (*mod.* Carrawburgh) N Britain Mithraic site 72/1
Prome C Burma Buddhist site 73/1
Prosymna S Greece Mycenaean site 67/1
Provence region of S France Frankish Empire 106/1,3; medieval German Empire 119/1, 123/1; Arabs expelled 120/2; annexed to France 147/3; province of France 189/1
Providence NE USA founded 157/2
Provins C France medieval fair 120/1
Prusa (*mod.* Bursa) W Anatolia Byzantine Empire 113/1
Prussia (*Ger.* Preussen) region of E Germany conquest by Teutonic Knights 138/3; Reformation 179/1; Baltic trade 185/1; rise of 186/3; Duchy 187/1; Kingdom 187/4; conquests in Europe 192/1,4; 193/1; opposition to Napoleon 200-1; unification of Germany 212-3
Przemyśl Austria-Hungary WW1 249/3
Pseira E Crete Minoan site 67/2
Pskov W Russia town of Novgorod Empire 115/1, 159/1; Hanseatic trading post 142/1; acquired by Muscovy 147/1; Russian Revolution 255/1
Pteria (*mod.* Boğazköy) C Anatolia ✕ 79/1
Ptolemais Egypt Roman Empire 89/1
Ptolemais (*mod.* Tulmaythah *It.* Tolmeta) Libya Roman Empire 89/1, 91/1; early archbishopric 93/1
Ptolemais (*Eng.* Acre *mod.* Akko) Palestine early archbishopric 93/1
Ptuj (Poetovio)
Puebla C Mexico early Spanish city 154/1; province 223/1
Pueblo Indian tribe of SW USA 145/1; 46/3
Pueblo Bonito N America site 47/1
Puelche Indian tribe of Argentina 145/1
Puerto Rico W Indies Spanish settlement 156/3; conquered by US 223/1, 243/4
Puig Roig NE Spain Megalithic site 42/2
Pukow (*n/s* Pukou *W/G* P'u-k'ou) E China British influence 228/2
Pula (Pola)
Pulicat SE India Dutch settlement 169/1
Pundra region of E India 83/1
Punjab region of NW India Muslim expansion 105/1; limit of Abbasid sovereignty 133/1; state of British India 231/3; partition between India and Pakistan 279/1, 280/3; water dispute with Haryana 279/3
Puri district of NE India cession to Britain 168/3
Purushkhaddum early town of C Anatolia 54/1
Pusan (*Jap.* Fusan) S Korea Russo-Japanese war 238/3; 1950-3 war 274/2; industry 275/1
P'u-shan (*n/s* Pushan) Sinkiang Han expansion 80/3
Pushkari W USSR site of early man 32/2
Putaya Libya satrapy of Achaemenid Empire 78/1
Puteoli (*mod.* Pozzuoli) C Italy Roman colony 87/1; Roman Empire 91/1; early bishopric 93/1
P'u-t'o Shan (*n/s* Putuo Shan) *mountain* E China Buddhist site 73/1
Pyatigorsk Caucasus 159/1
Pydna C Greece ✕ 77/3; Roman Empire 86/3
Pygmies people of C Africa 35/2
Pylos (*a/s* Pilos *It.* Navarino) SW Greece Mycenaean palace site 67/1
Pyongyang (*Jap.* Heijo) N Korea Russo-Japanese war 238/3; 1950-3 war 274/2; industry 275/1
Pyramid Lake W USA ✕ 217/4
Pyrgi C Italy Roman colony 87/1
Pyrgos C Crete Minoan palace 67/1
Pyrgos C Greece Mycenaean site 67/1
Pyrgos E Crete Minoan palace 67/1
Pyu S Burma Buddhist kingdom 125/2
Qadi Burhaneddi Turcoman principality of C Anatolia 136/2
Qandahar (Kandahar)
Qarabagh region of the Caucasus conquered by Ottomans 167/1
Qarakhanids (*a/s* Karakhanids) Muslim dynasty of Central Asia 133/1
Qarqan (Ch'ieh-mo)
Qatar sheikhdom of Persian Gulf 225/1, 283/3
Qatif E Arabia oilfield 283/3
Qatna Syria Amorite kingdom 54/2
Qi (Ch'i)
Qiancheng (Ch'ien-ch'eng)
Qiang (Ch'iang)
Qiantong (Ch'ien-l'ang)
Qianzhong (Ch'ien-chung)
Qichun (Ch'i-ch'un)
Qiemo (Ch'ieh-mo)
Qin (Ch'in)
Qinfeng (Ch'in-feng)
Qingdao (Tsingtao)
Qinghai (Tsinghai)
Qingjiang (Ch'ing-chiang)
Qingzhou (Ch'ing-chou)
Qiongzhou (Ch'iung-chou)
Qiqihar (Tsitsihar)
Quadi Germanic tribe 89/1
Quanterness N Scotland Megalithic site 42/2
Quanzhou (Ch'üan-chou)
Quebec city, E Canada capital of New France 157/2; captured by British 190/1
Quebec province, E Canada 160/5; joins Confederation 240/1; economic development 215/2
Quechua Andean Indian tribe of S America, 145/1
Queen Adelaide Province SE Africa 234/3
Queensland state of NE Australia 233/5; 240/1 (inset)
Quelimane Mozambique Portuguese settlement 163/1, 235/2, 237/1
Quemoy (*W/G* Chin-men) *island* SE China Nationalist outpost 277/1
Quentovic (*a/s* **Quentowic) N France** 110/3
Querétaro state of C Mexico 223/1
Quetta Pakistan 231/3, 279/3
Quiberon Bay W France ✕ 191/1
Quierzy N France Frankish royal residence 106/3
Quimper NW France bishopric 117/1
Qui Nhon S Vietnam 1945-75 war 277/3
Quiriguá E Mexico Maya site 46/2
Quito Ecuador Inca Empire 144/3; colonized 154/1, 161/1
Qumis (*a/c* Hecatompylos) city of Parthian Empire 79/3
Qunaytirah SW Syria Arab-Israeli war 283/2
Qusou (Ch'ü-sou)
Rabat Morocco early trade 134/2; French occupation 247/2
Rabaul Papua New Guinea Japanese base in WW2 267/1
Rabbath Ammon (Amman)
Rabih's State C Africa 237/1
Radimichi W Russia E Slav tribe 115/1
Rafah (*anc.* Raphia) Sinai Egyptian-Israeli war 283/2
Raffles Bay N Australia settlement 233/1
Rages (Rai)
Ragusa (*now* Dubrovnik) Croatia Byzantine Empire 113/5; Venetian conquest 120/2, 137/1; in Reformation 179/1; Ottoman vassal republic 183/1;

Rai – Samara

under French rule 201/1
Rai (*anc.* Rhagae *Bibl.* Rages *Gr.* Europus) N Persia early archbishopric 101/1; Muslim conquest 105/1; Mongol conquest 126/4; early trade 133/1
Rainy Lake (Fort Pierre)
Rajasthan (*form.* Rajputana Agency) state of N India 279/3
Rajputanaregion of NW India Muslim expansion 104/2; Mughal conquest 167/1; in alliance with Britain 190/2
Rajputana Agency (*now* Rajasthan) state of British India 231/3
Rajput Confederacy NW India 128/4
Rajputs people of NW India, 169/1
Raleigh E USA Civil War ⚔ 219/1
Ram Hormizd W Persia town of Sasanian Empire 79/3
Ramillies Belgium ⚔ 188/3
Ramla Palestine ⚔ 105/1
Ramsbury S England bishopric 117/1
Ramsey E England Industrial Revolution 197/1
Ramshög S Sweden Megalithic site 42/2
Randelia E Anatolia Roman Empire 89/1
Rangiriri N Island, New Zealand ⚔ 232/1
Rangoon (*anc.* Dagon) Burma Buddhist site 73/1; early trade centre 173/1; industry 231/3; WW2 266/1; 267/2; capital of independent state 279/3
Rangpur NW India Harappan site 65/1
Ranians E Germany Slavonic tribe 138/2
Rann of Kutch region of W India boundary dispute with Pakistan 278/1, 279/3
Rapallo N Italy 1922 Conference 261/1
Raphanea Syria Roman Empire 91/1
Raphia (*mod.* Rafah) N Sinai Roman Empire 86/3
Raqqa (*anc.* Nicephorium) Syria 137/1
Ras el-`Amiya C Mesopotamia early settlement 41/1
Ras al Khaimah United Arab Emirates Persian Gulf 283/3
Ras Hafun Somalia Muslim colony 135/1
Rashtrakutas dynasty of C India 128/2, 129/1
Ras Shamra (*anc.* Ugarit) Syria early village 41/1; early trade 66/1
Ras Tanura E Arabia oil terminal 283/3
Rasulids Muslim dynasty of SW Arabia 133/1
Ratae (*mod.* Leicester) C England Roman Empire 88/1
Ratiaria Bulgaria early archbishopric 93/1
Ratisbon (*Ger.* Regensburg) S Germany ⚔ 201/1
Ravenna N Italy Roman Empire 91/1; early archbishopric 93/1; 107/3; Byzantine occupation 99/1; exarchate 113/1; captured by Venice 120/2; medieval city 122/2
Ravensberg N Germany Burgundian possession 147/2; county 186/3, 187/1
Ravensbrück N Germany concentration camp 268/1
Raynham E England agrarian revolution 197/2
Reading S England Industrial Revolution 197/1
Reate (*mod.* Rieti) N Italy Roman Empire 87/1
Rechitsa W Russia town of Turov-Pinsk 115/1
Recife (Pernambuco)
Recuay early people of C Andes 47/4
Redarii N Germany Slav tribe 11/3, 118/2, 138/2
Redwood Ferry E USA ⚔ 217/4
Regensburg (*anc.* Casra Regina *obs. Eng.* Ratisbon) S Germany bishopric 100/3, 187/1; Frankish royal residence 107/3; 120/1
Reggio (*a/c* Reggio di Calabria *anc.* Rhegium) S Italy Norman conquest 120/2; Ottoman siege 166/1
Reggio (*a/c* Reggio Emilia *anc.* Regium Lepidum) N Italy Republican commune 122/2
Regina C Canada growth 215/2
Regium Lepidum (Reggio Emilia)
Reichenau S Germany monastery 107/3
Reii S France early bishopric 92/1
Reims (Rheims)
Remedello N Italy burial site 43/1
Remi (*mod.* Rheims) N France early bishopric 92/1
Remojadas C Mexico early site 46/2
Rennes NW France bishopric 117/1; 17C revolt 181/1; French Revolution 199/2
Rethel NE France independent fief 147/3
Réunion (*form.* Bourbon) *island* Indian Ocean French colony 241/1
Reval (*Russ.* Revel *mod. Est.* Tallinn) E Baltic German colonization 138/3, Hanseatic city 142/1; Swedish Empire 185/1; Russian Empire 227/1; Russian Revolution 255/1
Rewardashur Persia early archbishopric 93/1, 101/1
Rhaeti early tribe of N Italy 86/2
Rhaetia (*mod.* Switzerland) Roman province 89/1; Frankish Empire 106/1
Rhagae (*Per.* Rai *Bibl.* Rages *Gr.* Europus) N Persia Alexander's Empire 77/1, 79/1; early trade 82/4
Rhambacia NW India early trade 82/4
Rhegium (*mod.* Reggio di Calabria) N Italy Greek colony 75/1; Roman Empire 87/1, 89/1, 91/1
Rheims (*Fr.* Reims *anc.* Durocortorum *later* Remi) N France sacked by Vandals 99/1; archbishopric 106/3, 117/1; French Revolution 199/2; ⚔ 201/1; industrial development 206/1; WW1 248-9; WW2 269/3
Rheinheim Germany La Tène site 84/1
Rheinland (Rhineland)
Rhenish Prussia W Germany unification of Germany 212/3
Rhesaenae E Anatolia Roman Empire 91/1
Rhine, Confederation of the Napoleonic creation 187/4, 200/2, 201/1
Rhineland (*Ger.* Rheinland) region of W Germany 18C industrial growth 186/2; remilitarized 261/1, 265/4
Rhineland Palatinate (*Ger.* Rheinland-Pfalz) region of NW Germany 271/2
Rhode Island state of NE USA colony 157/2, 160/3; 19C politics 220/1, 221/2,3; Depression 263/1; income and population 287/2
Rhodes (*mod. Gr.* Rodhos *Lat.* Rhodus *It.* Rodi) *island* SE Aegean Greek state 75/1, 77/2,3; archbishopric 93/1; ⚔ 105/1; under Knights of St John 137/1; Ottoman conquest 166/1; gained by Turks 183/1. See also Dodecanese
Rhodesia (*form.* Southern Rhodesia *n/c* Zimbabwe) Matabele/Mashona revolt 245/2; independence (UDI) 272/2; 281/1; economy 295/1. See also Zimbabwe
Rhodus (*mod. Gr.* Rodhos *Eng.* Rhodes) *island* SE Aegean Roman Empire 86/3, 89/1, 91/1
Riade C Germany ⚔ 117/1
Ribe Denmark bishopric 101/2, 116/2
Rich Bar W USA mining site 216/1
Richmond N England rebellion against Henry VIII 181/1
Richmond E USA burned 219/1; industry 215/1
Ricken Switzerland tunnel 253/2
Ricomagus (Riom)
Rieti (Reate)
Rif mountain region of Morocco resistance to French 256/1
Riga Latvia, N Europe founded by Teutonic Knights 138/3; Hanseatic city 142/1; early bishopric 101/2; Swedish Empire 185/1; Russian Empire 227/1; urban growth 227/1; short-lived Communist control 254/2; WW2 268-9; industry 289/1
Rijeka (Fiume)
Rijkholt S Holland Megalithic site 42/2
Rile (Jih-le)
Rimini (*anc.* Ariminum) N Italy Lombard League 119/1; Signorial domination 122/2; WW2 269/3
Rinaldone C Italy early settlement 43/1
Rinan (Jih-nan)
Rio Barbate Spain ⚔ 104/1
Rio de Janeiro Brazil colonized 161/1; imperial trade 194/3; industry 215/1; state 223/1
Rio de la Plata (*mod.* Argentina) early Spanish colony 161/1; vice-royalty in rebellion against Spain 198/1
Rio de Oro (later Spanish Sahara *now* Western Sahara) NW Africa Spanish colony 236/1,2, 240/1, 256/1
Rio Grande do Norte state of N Brazil Confederation of the Equator 223/1
Rio Grande do Sul state of S Brazil 223/1
Riom (*anc.* Ricomagus) C France seat of intendant 189/1
Rio Muni (*a/c* Spanish Guinea *now* Equatorial Guinea) W Africa Spanish colony 236/1,2, 272/1
Rio Negrostate of W Brazil 223/1
Ripon N England monastery 100/3; revolt against Henry VIII 181/1
Rithymna C Crete Minoan palace 67/1
Rivara NW Italy Monferrat principality 183/3
Rivoli N Italy ⚔ 201/1
Riyadh C Saudi Arabia oil 283/3
Roccaverano NW Italy principality 183/3
Rochdale N England Industrial Revolution 197/1
Rochefort W France naval base 189/1, 191/1
Rochester SE England bishopric 117/1
Rochford E England Industrial Revolution 197/1
Rockhampton E Australia early settlement 233/5
Rocroi NE France ⚔ 178/2
Rodenbach Germany Hallstatt site 84/1
Rodhos (Rhodes)
Rodi (Rhodes)
Rogoźnica (Gross-Rosen)
Rogue River W USA ⚔ 217/4
Rohri N India Harappan site 65/1
Rojadi N India Harappan site 65/1
Roma (Rome)
Romagna region of N Italy unification of Italy 213/2
Roman Empire 70/1, 82/4, 86/3, 88-91, 94/1, 99/1
Romania (*f/s* Rumania, Roumania) on break-up of Ottoman Empire 225/1; independence 211/2; European alliances 246-7; WW1 248-9; inter-war alliances 260/2; acquisition of Transylvania 261/1; emigration of Hungarians and Turks 261/3; economic and socio-political development 209/1, 262-3; WW2 268-9; Warsaw Pact and Comecon 270/1; communism overthrown 290/3. See also Moldavia, Wallachia
Roman Republic 77/2,3; 199/3
Rome (*anc.* Roma *It.* Roma) C Italy Celtic settlement 84/3; Roman Empire 86-91; early trade 70/1; arrival of Christianity 72/1; economy under Empire 91/2; sack by Vandals and Visigoths 94/1, 99/1; patriarchate 92/1, 101/2; Jewish community 103/1; 107/3; Magyar raid 111/1; papal patrimony 119/1; 122/2 papal schism 141 (inset); medieval finance 143/3; 18C urban development 176-7; under French rule 201/1,2; annexed by Italy 213/2; industrial development 206/1; WW2 269/3
Romeral SE Spain Megalithic site 42/2
Romilly N France French Revolution 199/2
Roncesvalles N Spain ⚔ 106/3
Ronco NW Italy principality 183/3
Rong (Jung)
Rongyang (Jung-yang)
Roosebeke Belgium class unrest 141/1
Rorke's Drift S Africa ⚔ 235/1
Rosebud C USA ⚔ 217/4
Rostock N Germany founded by Germans 138/2; Hanseatic city 142/1; WW1 249/3
Rostov (-on-Don) S Russia industry and urban growth 227/1, 255/1, 288/3; WW2 268-9; 289/1
Rotomagus (*mod.* Rouen) N France Roman Empire 90/1; archbishopric 92/1
Rotterdam Netherlands industrial development 206/1; 208/1; WW2 265/5, 269/3
Rotuma island of Fiji, C Pacific 273/2 (inset)
Rouad (Arwad)
Roubaix N France industrial development 206/1
Rouen (*anc.* Rotomagus) N France Scandinavian settlement 110/2, 111/1; archbishopric 106/3, 117/1; urban revolt 141/1; medieval fair 142/1; 16C and 18C financial centre 176/1, 177/2; St Bartholomew Massacre 178/3; 16- 17C revolts 181/1; parlement 189/1; French Revolution 199/2; WW1 249/3
Rouergue region of S France 147/3
Rough and Ready W USA mining site 216/1
Roumania (Romania)
Round Mountain C USA ⚔ 217/4
Roundway S England burial site 43/1
Rourkela E India steel plant 279/3
Roussillon region of S France acquired from Spain 146/1, 183/1; 189/1
Rouvray-St Denis C France medieval *villeneuve* 121/7
Roxburgh country of S Scotland acquired by Edward III 140/2
Roxolani tribe of E Roman Empire 89/1
Royale, Ile (*now* Cape Breton island) E Canada French settlement 157/2
Rozwi early native state of SE Africa 163/1
Ruanda-Urundi (*now* Rwanda *and* Burundi) C Africa Belgian colony 272/1
Ruanruan (Juan-juan)
Ruapekapeka N Island, New Zealand ⚔ 232/1
Ruffec C France French Revolution 199/2
Rugii German tribe of E Europe 99/1
Ruhr region of NW Germany industrial expansion 206/3, 208/1; occupied by French 261/1
Rui (Jui)
Ruicheng (Jui-ch'eng)
Ruijin (Jui-chin)
Rumaila S Iraq oilfield 283/3
Rumania (Romania)
Runan (Ju-nan)
Runnymede S England 123/1
Runzhou (Jun-chou)
Rupar N India Harappan site 65/1
Rupert House N Canada Hudson Bay Company post 157/2
Rubert's Land region of N Canada fur-trading area 157/2; Hudson's Bay Company 161/1,2; British possession 190/1
Rusaddir (*mod.* Melilla) Morocco Roman Empire 88/1
Ruschuk (*mod.* Ruse) Bulgaria Ottoman control 166/1
Rusellae N Italy Etruscan city 86/2
Rush Creek C USA ⚔ 217/4
Russell N Island, New Zealand first capital 232/1
Russia (in Europe) conversion to Christianity 101/2; Jewish immigration 103/3; Kievan Russia 115/1; Mongol Invasion 114/4, 126-7; Viking trade 110/3; Black Death 141/1; expansion 158/3, 159/1; agriculture 175/3; economic development, trade and industry 158/2, 176-7; European conquests 192/1; Cossack revolt 198/1; opposition to Napoleon 200-1; population growth 204/3,4; emigration 205/2; industrial revolution 207/1; railway development 209/1; expansion into Asia 226/2; growth in armaments 246; 19C European alliances 246-7; WW1 248-9; overseas trade and investment 252-3; Revolution 254-5; Allied intervention 255/1; WW2 268-9; economy 295/1; population growth 294/2. See also USSR
Russia (in Asia) expansion 158/3, 226/2; acquisition of Maritime Province from China 228/2; 19C spheres of influence 241/1; revolt in C Asia 244/1; population growth 294/2
Russian Federation successor to USSR 290/3
Russian Soviet Federated Socialist Republic 288/2
Ruthenia region of SW Ukraine acquired by Poland-Lithuania 139/1; incorporated into Czechoslovakia 261/1; occupied by Hungary 265/4
Ruyin (Ju-yin)
Rwanda (*form.* Ruanda) early state of C Africa 163/1; independence 272/2; political development 281/1
Ryazan C Russia early bishopric 101/2; town of Murom-Ryazan 115/1; acquired by Muscovy 159/1; industry 289/1
Rye SE England Industrial Revolution 197/1
Rylsk C Russia town of Novgorod-Seversk 115/1
Ryojun (Port Arthur)
Ryukyu Islands (*f/c* Loochoo Islands) E China Sea acquired by Japan 228/2, 239/2
Rzhev C Russia WW2 269/3
Saadids Muslim dynasty of Morocco 133/1
Saar (*Ger.* Saarland *Fr.* Sarre) district of W Germany industrial development 208/1; League of Nations mandate and plebiscite 261/1; 265/4; 271/2
Saba Dutch island of W Indies 156/3, 223/1
Sabae C Japan 171/4
Sabaea ancient of SW Arabia 45/1
Sabah (*form.* British North Borneo) incorporated into Malaysia 273/2; claimed by Philippines 277/1
Sabbioneta N Italy principality 183/3
Sabini early tribe of C Italy 86/2
Sabiri early tribe of the Caucasus 99/1
Sabrata (*a/c* Abrotonum) Libya Punic city 74/1; Roman Empire 89/1, 91/1; early bishopric 93/1
Saccopastore Italy site of early man 32/2
Sachsen (Saxony)
Sachsenhausen C Germany concentration camp 268/1
Sacramento City W USA mining site 216/1
Sado *island* N Japan 171/4
Sadowa (*a/c* Königgrätz) Bohemia ⚔ 212/3
Sadowara W Japan 170/4
Sadras S India Dutch settlement 169/1
Saena Julia (Siena)
Safaniya E Arabia oilfield 283/3
Safavid Empire Persia 133/1, 137/1, 151/1, 167/1
Safavids Muslim dynasty of Persia 133/1
Saffarids Muslim dynasty of Persia 133/1
Safi Morocco French control 247/2
Saga prefecture of W Japan industry 238/1
Sagres SW Portugal early trade 147/2; base for exploration 162/2
Saguntum (*med.* Murviedro *mod.* Sagunto) E Spain Greek colony 74/1; Roman Empire 86/3, 89/1; Jewish community 103/1
Sahara region of N Africa early settlement 44-45; trade 134/2; slave routes 162/2
Sa Huynh C Indo-China Iron Age site 130/1
Saïda (Sidon)
Saidor New Guinea retaken by US 267/2
Saigon (*a/c* Ho Chi Minh City) S Vietnam early trade centre 173/1; 1945-75 war 277/3
St. Albans (Verulamium)
St. Andrews E Scotland bishopric 117/1
St. Anthony Egypt monastery 100/1
St. Augustine (*form.* San Agostín) SE USA Spanish fort 190/1
St. Barthélemy W Indies French settlement 156/3, 273/2 (inset)
St. Blasien SW Germany monastic reform 118/3
St. Brieuc N W France bishopric 117/1
St. Catherine, Cape W Africa Portuguese discovery 147/2, 162/2
St. Césaire W France site of early man 32/2
St. Christopher *island* W Indies English settlement 156/3
St. Christopher and Nevis W Indies British colony 223/1; independent 273/2 (inset); population growth 294/2
St. Clair's Defeat N E USA ⚔ 217/4
St. David's (*anc.* Menevia) SW Wales bishopric 117/1
St. Denis N France medieval fair 120/1, 142/1
Saint-Domingue (*now* Haiti) French colony 156/3, 161/1, 190/1
Ste. Colombe France Hallstatt site 84/1
Ste. Geneviève C USA fur station 216/1
Ste. Marie Madagascar French settlement 190/2
St. Etienne S E France industrial development 206/1, 208/1
St. Eustatius *island* West Indies Dutch settlement 156/3; colony 223/1
St. Florentin N France French Revolution 199/2
St. Gallen (Sankt Gallen)
St. Germans SW England bishopric 117/1
St. Gotthard Switzerland tunnel 253/2
St. Gotthard (*Hung.* Szentgotthárd) Hungary ⚔ 193/3
St. Helena *island* S Atlantic British colony 241/1, 272/1,2
St. Helens N England Industrial Revolution 197/1
St. Ives SW England medieval fair 120/1
St. James's Day Fight SE England English naval victory 181/1
St. Jean, Ile (*Eng.* Isle St. John *now* Prince Edward Island) E Canada French settlement 157/2, 191/1
St. Jean-d'Acre (Acre)
St. John Novia Scotia growth 215/2
St. John's Newfoundland growth 215/2
St. Joseph C USA fur station 216/1
St Kitts and Nevis (St. Christopher and Nevis)
St. Lawrence River E Canada exploration 152/1
St. Louis C USA fur station 216/1; industry 287/1
St. Louis Senegal French settlement 162/1, 234/1, 236/1; 18C trade 194/1
St. Lucia *island* W Indies disputed between French and English 156/3, 191/1; British colony 223/1; independence 273/2 (inset); population growth 294/2
St. Macarius Egypt monastery 100/1
St. Malo N France bishopric 117/1; naval base 189/1
St. Martin (*Dut.* Sint-Maarten) *island* West Indies French settlement 156/3; shared by French and Dutch 273/2 (inset)
St. Mary, Cape SW Africa Portuguese discovery 147/2, 162/2
St. Michel-du-Touch France site 43/1
St. Mihiel NE France WW1 249/3 (inset)
St. Neots C England Industrial Revolution 197/1
St. Omer N France medieval fair 120/1
Saintonge et Angoumois region of SW France under English rule 123/1
St. Pachomius Egypt monastery 100/1
St. Petersburg (*1914-24* Petrograd *1925-92* Leningrad *now* St. Petersburg) W Russia 18C urban development 177/2; founded 185/1; industrial development 207/1, 209/1; urban growth 227/1
St. Pierre et Miquelon Newfoundland French colony 191/1, 240/1
St. Pol N France fief 147/3
St. Quentin N France WW1 249/3 (inset)
St. Riquier N France monastery 106/3
St. Samuel Egypt monastery 100/1
St. Simeon Egypt monastery 100/1
St. Vincent *island* West Indies disputed by French and English 156/3, 191/1; British colony 223/1; independence 273/2 (inset); population growth 294/2
Saipan *island* Marianas, C Pacific Japanese base in WW2 266/1; occupied by US 267/2
Sais NE Egypt Iron Age site 45/1
Saitama prefecture of C Japan 239/1
Saka Haumavarga C Asia satrapy of Achaemenid Empire 79/1
Sakalava tribe of Madagascar 235/1
Sakas early people of W India 82/4
Sakata N Japan 171/4
Saketa (*later* Ayodhya) N India 83/1
Sakhalin (*Jap.* Karafuto) *island* Russ. Far East north acquired by Russia 226/2, 254/3; south acquired by Japan 239/2; south reoccupied by Russia 267/1
Saksiny tribe of S Russia 115/1
Sakura C Japan 171/4
Sala Morocco Roman Empire 88/1
Sa-la (*mod.* Zeila) Somalia early trade with China 146/1
Salahiyeh (Dura-Europos)
Salamanca N Spain ⚔ 200/1
Salamantica (*a/c* Helmantica *mod.* Salamanca) N Spain Roman Empire 88/1
Salamis (*later* Constantia) Cyprus Greek colony 75/1; Roman Empire 89/1; archbishopric 93/1; Jewish community 103/1
Salamis C Greece ⚔ 74/3, 78/1
Salankayanas people of SE India 82/5
Saldae (Bougie)
Salé NW Africa site of early man 33/1; trans-Saharan trade 134/2
Salekhard (Obdorsk)
Salem district of S India ceded to Britain 168/3
Salernum (*mod.* Salerno) S Italy Roman colony 87/1; Byzantine port 120/2
Salinelles SE France Megalithic site 42/2
Salisbury S England Industrial Revolution 197/1
Salisbury S Rhodesia 237/1
Salish House NW USA fur station 216/1
Salonae (*a/s* Salona) Albania Mithraic site 72/1; Roman Empire 89/1, 91/1; early archbishopric 93/1; Byzantine Empire 113/1
Salonika (*a/s* Salonica *a/c* Thessalonica *Gr.* Thessaloniki *Turk.* Selanik) N Greece bishopric 101/2; occupied by Ottomans 137/1, 211/2, 18C urban development 177/2; WW1 249/3
Saltillo N Mexico early Spanish city 154/1
Salt Lake City W USA early trails 216/1; industry 215/1
Saluzzo NW Italy French margravate 183/3
Salzburg Austria bishopric 100/3; archbishopric 107/3, 187/1; Habsburg acquistion 193/3
Samanids Muslim dynasty of Persia 133/3
Samara (*since 1895* Kuybyshev) C Russia founded 159/1; on railway to east 226/1; Bolshevik seizure 255/1

Samaria – Sidon

Samaria region of C Palestine 103/1; Israeli settlement 283/2
Samarra Mesopotamia early village 41/1
Samarkand (*anc.* Maracanda) C Asia early trade 71/1,2; early archbishopric 101/1; Muslim conquest 105/1; under Abbasids 109/1; Timur's Empire 126/4, 147/1; Soviet Union 289/1; industry 289/1
Samasobriva (Amiens)
Samatata early state of E India 82/5
Sambat (*n/c* Kiev) Ukraine Khazar city 108/1
Sambor Prei Kuk Cambodia Hindu-Buddhist temple 131/2
Samborzec Poland early site 43/1
Sambre *river* NE France WW1 249/3 (inset)
Samnites early people of C Italy 86/2
Samoa *islands* S Pacific early settlement 49/1; German colony 241/1; annexed by US 243/1. See also Western Samoa
Samogitia (*Lith.* Žematija) region of E Baltic occupied by Teutonic Knights 138-9
Samory's Empire W Africa 237/1
Samos *island* Aegean Sea Greek parent state 75/1; bishopric 93/1; gained by Turks 183/1
Samosata E Anatolia Roman Empire 89/1, 91/1; Jewish community 103/1; Byzantine Empire 113/1
Samoyeds people of N Siberia, 115/1, 158/3
Sampford Courtenay W England ✕ 181/1
Samrong Sen Cambodia early site 130/1
Samsun (*anc.* Amisus) N Turkey Ottoman town 166/1
Samudra NW Sumatra 131/3
Sana SW Arabia early bishopric 100/1; trade 133/1, 256/1
San Agostín (*now* St. Augustine) SE USA Spanish fort 154/1
San Agustín Colombia early site 47/1
San Antonio S USA early Catholic mission 216/1
San Antonio SE USA Spanish fort 190/1
San Benigno Montanaro NW Italy principality 183/3
San Candido (Aguntum)
Sanchi C India Buddhist site 73/1
San Cristóbal W Cuba Soviet missile base 293/6
Sand Creek C USA ✕ 217/4
San Damiano NW Italy Monferrat principality 183/3
San Diego (*form.* San Diego de Alcalá) SW USA early Catholic mission 216/1
Sandwich Islands (*now* Hawaii) C Pacific discovered 153/3
San Felipe S USA early Catholic mission 216/1
San Fernando Rey de España W USA early Catholic mission 216/1
San Francisco (*form.* San Francisco de Asís) W USA Spanish settlement 161/1; early Catholic mission 216/1; general strike 263/1; industry 286/1
Sanga early state of C Africa 45/1; 135/1
San Gabriel Arcángel SW USA early Catholic mission 216/1
Sangela NW India Alexander's route 77/1
San Gimignano C Italy Republican commune 124/2
Sangiran Java site of early man 33/1
San José Magote C Mexico Olmec site 46/2
San Juan del Puerto Rico W Indies Spanish fort 154/1
Sankt Gallen Switzerland monastery 100/3, 107/3, Reformation 179/1
Sankt Peterburg (St. Petersburg)
San Lorenzo C Mexico Olmec site 46/2
San Luis Obispo de Tolosa W USA early Catholic mission 216/1
San Luis Potosí state of C Mexico 223/1
San Sebastián N Spain industrial development 206/1, 208/1; Civil War 264/3
San-shui NW China Han prefecture 81/2
San Stefano NW Italy margravate 183/3
Santa Bárbara W USA early Catholic mission 216/1
Santa Catarina state of S Brazil 223/1
Santa Cruz W USA early Catholic mission 216/1
Santa Cruz Islands S Pacific limit of Japanese advance 266/1
Santa Fe SW USA on trail west 216/1
Santa Fé de Bogotá (*n/c* Bogotá) Colombia Spanish capital of New Granada 154/1, 161/1
Santa Marta Colombia Spanish port 154/1
Santa Maura (Levkas)
Santander N Spain industrial development 206/1, 208/1; Civil War 264/3
Santa Rita Mexico Maya site 46/2, 144/2
Santa Severina S Italy Saracen occupation 111/1
Santiago Chile founded 154/1; industry 215/1
Santiago de Compostela NW Spain bishopric 101/2; 111/1
Santiago del Estero Argentina early settlement 154/1
Santignone NW Italy principality 183/3
Santo Domingo (*now* Dominican Republic) W Indies founded 154/1; Spanish colony 156/3, 161/1, 191/1
Santorini (Thera)
Santos S Brazil industry 215/1
San-tu-ao E China treaty port 228/2
San Xavier del Bac SW USA early Catholic mission 216/1
São Jorge da Mina (Elmina)
São Paulo S Brazil imperial trade 194/3; state 223/1
São Salvador Angola Portuguese settlement 235/1
São Tomé *island* W Africa Portuguese colony 155/1, 163/1, 237/1, 241/1; independence (with Principé) 273/2, 281/1; population growth 294/2
Sapporo N Japan industrial centre 275/1
Saqqara Lower Egypt 58/1
Saracens invasion of S Europe 111/1
Saragossa (*anc.* Caesaraugusta *mod.* Zaragoza) N Spain bishopric 101/2; Mediterranean trade 132/1; 16C financial centre 176/1; ✕ 188/3; captured by French 200/1; Civil War 264/3
Sarai S Russia early trade 146/1. See also New Sarai, Old Sarai
Sarajevo (*Turk.* Bosna Saray) C Yugoslavia captured by Ottomans 137/1; Ottoman administrative centre 166/1; WW1 249/3; WW2 265/5; 269/3
Sarandib (Ceylon)
Saratoga NE USA ✕ 160/3
Saratov C Russia founded 159/1; industry 227/1, 289/1; urban growth 288/3; Bolshevik seizure 255/1
Sarawak country of N Borneo Brooke becomes rajah 173/1; British protectorate 241/1; 257/1; WW2 267/2; incorporated into Malaysia 273/2; insurgency 277/1
Sarbinowo (Zorndorf)
Sarcee plains Indian tribe of W Canada 145/1
Sardes (Sardis)
Sardica (Serdica)
Sardinia (*It.* Sardegna) *island* W Mediterranean Muslim conquest 104/1; Saracen attacks 111/1; Byzantine Empire 112/1; Pisan conquest 120/2; to Aragon 146/1; acquired by Habsburgs 182/2; under Spanish rule 183/1; rebellion against Piedmont 198/1; Kingdom 213/2
Sardinians migration 67/3
Sardis (*a/s* Sardes) W Anatolia Alexander's route 76/1; Persian Royal Road 78/1; Roman Empire 86/3, 89/1; one of seven churches of Asia 93/1; Jewish community 103/1; Byzantine Empire 113/1
Sariwon N Korea industrial centre 275/1
Sarkel S Russia under Khazars 108/1; ✕ 115/1
Sarmatia ancient country of S Russia 91/2
Sarmatians (*Lat.* Sarmatae) tribe of Caucasus and S Russia 75/1, 89/1
Sarmizegetusa Romania Mithraic site 72/1; Roman Empire 89/1
Sarnath E India Buddhist site 73/1
Sarre (Saar)
Sarsina N Italy Roman Empire 87/1
Saruhan early emirate of W Anatolia 136-7
Sasanian Empire Western Asia 79/3, 82/5, 94-5
Sasayama C Japan 171/4
Sasebo W Japan 238/1,3
Saskatchewan province of C Canada economic growth 215/2
Saskatoon C Canada growth 215/2
Sassoferrato (Sentinum)
Satala NE Anatolia Roman Empire 89/1, 91/1; early archbishopric 93/1
Satara princely state of W India 231/3
Satavahana ancient kingdom of India 83/1
Satgoan Bengal trade 147/1
Saticula C Italy Latin colony 87/1
Satricum C Italy Latin colony 87/1
Saturnia N Italy Roman colony 87/1
Saudi Arabia Kingdom of Arabia 256/1, 273/1,2, 282/1, 292/5, 293/1, 295/1; Gulf War 282/1
Sauerland W Germany 18C industrial growth 186/2
Sauk (*a/c* Menominee) Indian tribe of C USA 145/1
Sault Ste. Marie C Canada French fort 157/2, 190/1
Saumurois region of W France English possession 123/1
Savannah SE USA evacuated 219/1; industry 215/1
Savenay NW France French Revolution 199/2
Savo one of Solomon Is, SW Pacific ✕ 267/2
Savoy (*Fr.* Savoie *It.* Savoia) region of France/Italy medieval state 146/1; Calvinism 179/1; independent duchy 183/1; 188-9; annexed by France 199/3; ceded to France 213/2
Saxons Germanic tribe of NW Europe, 94/1, 98-9
Saxony (*Ger.* Sachsen) region of N Germany conversion to Christianity 100/3; Frankish Empire 107/3; Magyar invasions 111/1; medieval German Empire 117/1, 118-9; Black Death 141/1; Wettin territory 146/1; Reformation 179/1; 18C industrial growth 186/2; Electorate and Duchy 187/1,4; occupied by Prussia 192/4; Napoleonic influence 200/2; unification of Germany 212/3; 271/2
Saxony-Anhalt (*Ger.* Sachsen-Anhalt) region of E Germany 271/2
Say W Africa Muslim revival 235/1; occupied by French 237/1
Sayda (Sidon)
Saylac (Zeila)
Saylan (Ceylon)
Sayn county of C Germany 187/1
Scandia (*mod.* Scandinavia) region of N Europe 89/1
Scandinavia (*anc.* Scandia) Viking invasions of Europe 111/1; emigration 205/1; 211/3
Scania (*Sw.* Skåne) region of S Sweden acquired from Denmark 184
Scapa Flow N Scotland WW1 249/3
Scarborough N England WW1 249/3
Scarpanto (Carpathos)
Schlesien (Silesia)
Schleswig (*Dan.* Slesvig) S Denmark Reformation 179/1; plebiscite 261/1
Schleswig-Holstein region of N Germany customs union with Denmark 207/2; ceded to Prussia 211/3; unification of Germany 212/3; 271/2
Schooneveld I and II S North Sea Dutch naval victories 181/1
Schussenried Switzerland early site 43/1
Schuttern SW Germany Zähringen monastery 121/3
Schwaben (Swabia)
Schwarzburg country of E Germany 119/1
Schwarzerden W Germany Mithraic site 72/1
Schwerin N Germany WW1 249/3; 271/2
Schwyz Switzerland original canton 140/3
Scodra (*mod.* Shkodër *It.* Scutari) Albania Roman Empire 89/1
Scolacium S Italy Roman colony 87/1
Scone S Scotland Edward I's campaign 140/2; Civil War 180/2
Scotland (*anc.* Caledonia) Scandinavian settlement 110/2, 111/1; early kingdom 117/1; feudal monarchy 123/1; Anglo-Scottish wars 140/2; Black Death 141/1; acquires Shetland, Orkney and Hebrides 146/1; Reformation 179/1; in English Civil War 180/2; trade and industrial development 176-7, 196-7, 206/1, 208/1
Scots 210/1
Scots Celtic tribe of N Ireland 98/1
Scupi (*mod.* Skoplje *Mac.* Skopje *Turk.* Üsküb) early archbishopric 93/1; Byzantine Empire 113/1
Scutari (*mod.* Shkodër *anc.* Scodra) Albania conquered by Ottomans 137/1
Scylacium S Italy Greek colony 75/1
Scythia ancient country of C Asia 77/1
Scythians ancient tribe of S Russia 61/1, 75/1, 76/1
Scythopolis N Palestine city of the Decapolis 103/1
Seattle NW USA ✕ 217/4; industry 286/1
Sebaste Palestine bishopric 93/1; town of Judaea 103/2
Sebastopol (*Russ.* Sevastopol) Crimea, S Russia urban growth 227/1; WW1 249/3; WW2 268-9
Sebta (Ceuta)
Sech S Ukraine 159/1
Sedan N France ✕ 212/3; WW1 248/2; WW2 265/5
Sées N France bishopric 117/1
Segesta Sicily ally of Athens 74/4
Segontia (*a/c* Segontium *mod.* Caernarvon) Wales Mithraic site 72/1; Roman Empire 89/1
Ségou (*Eng.* Segu) French Sudan 237/1
Segovia C Spain Roman Empire 88/1
Segu (*Fr.* Ségou) early city-state of W Africa 163/1, 234-5
Seibal E Mexico Maya site 46/2
Seistan (*a/s* Sistan) province of E Persia Muslim conquest 105/1; under Abbasid sovereignty 133/1
Sekiyado C Japan 171/4
Selangor state of Malaya 172/4
Selanik (Salonika)
Seleucia (*a/c* Veh-Ardashir) Mesopotamia early trade 71/1, 82/4; Seleucid kingdom 77/2; Sasanian Empire 78/3
Seleucia (*a/c* Seleucia Tracheotis) SE Anatolia early archbishopric 93/1; Jewish community 103/1; Byzantine Empire 112/3
Seleucia-Ctesiphon Mesopotamia early patriarchate 93/1, 101/1
Seleucian Theme S Anatolia province of Byzantine Empire 112/3
Seleucid Kingdom Anatolia-Persia 77/2,3
Selinus (*mod.* Selinunte) Sicily Greek colony 74/1; Roman Empire 86/2
Seljuks (*a/c* Seljuk Turks) Turkish Muslim dynasty of Middle East 113/5, 133/1
Selkirk country of C Scotland acquired by Edward III 140/2
Sellasia S Greece ✕ 76/4
Selsey S England bishopric 117/1
Selymbria SE Europe Greek colony 75/1; Byzantine Empire 112/4
Semendire (*mod.* Smederevo) N Serbia conquered by Ottomans 137/1
Semgallen (*obs. Eng.* Semigallia) region of E Baltic occupied by Teutonic Knights 138/3
Seminole Indian tribe of SE USA 217/4
Semipalatinsk S Siberia industry 289/1
Semites early migrations 61/1
Semmering Austria tunnel 253/2
Sempach C Switzerland ✕ 140/3
Sena N Italy Roman colony 87/1
Sena Mozambique Portuguese settlement 163/1
Senas dynasty of India 128/2
Sendai N Japan 171/4, 175/1
Senegal W Africa French colony 236/1, 240/1; independence 272/2; political development 281/1
Senegambia region of W Africa source of slaves 162/1, 194/3
Senegambian Confederation W Africa 281/1
Senigallia C Italy Mediterranean trade 142/1
Senlis N France bishopric 117/1
Sennar Sudan early town 135/1; Saharan trade 163/1
Sens NE France archbishopric 106/3
Senta (Zenta)
Sentinum (*mod.* Sassoferrato) N Italy Roman Empire 87/1
Seoul (*Jap.* Keijo) S Korea Russo-Japanese war 238/3; Korean war 274/2; industry 275/1
Sepphoris town of Judaea 103/2
Septimania ancient region of S France part of Frankish Empire 106/3
Serampore (*form.* Frederiksnagar) NE India Danish settlement 169/1
Serbia (*now part of* Yugoslavia) country of SE Europe conversion to Christianity 101/2; Byzantine Empire 113/5; Mongol invasion 126/2; Christian state 136/1; empire under Stephen Dushan 139/1; Black Death 141/1; Ottoman province 137/1, 193/3, 198/1, 225/1; independence 211/2; industrial development 209/1; WW1 248-9; forms part of Yugoslavia 261/1; WW2 268-9
Serbs Slav tribe of SE Europe 98-9
Serdica (*a/s* Sardica *mod.* Sofia) Bulgaria Mithraic site 72/1; Roman Empire 89/1, 91/1; early archbishopric 93/1; invaded by Huns 99/1; Byzantine Empire 113/1
Seres (*mod.* Serrai) N Greece medieval fair 142/1
Serpukhov C Russia town of Muscovy 159/1
Serrai (Seres)
Serralungo NW Italy Savoy principality 183/3
Sesamus (*later* Amastris) N Anatolia Greek colony 75/1
Sesheko S Africa on Livingstone's route 234/2
Sestus SE Europe Greek colony 75/1; Roman Empire 91/1
Setaia E Crete Minoan site 67/2
Setia (*mod.* Sezze) C Italy Latin colony 87/1
Settiva Corsica Megalithic site 42/2
Sevastopol (*Eng.* Sebastopol *med. Turk.* Akhtiar) Crimea founded 159/1; Crimean War 226/4; Russian Revolution 255/1
Severyane E Slav tribe of S Russia 115/1
Seville (*Sp.* Sevilla *anc.* Hispalis) S Spain Emirate of Córdoba 111/1; reconquered from Muslims 124/3; early trade 132/1; colonial trade 154/1; 16C urban development 176/1; 18C urban development 177/2; Civil War 264/3
Seychelles *islands* Indian Ocean captured from French 190/2; British colony 241/1; population growth 294/2
Sezze (Setia)
Shaanxi (Shensi)
Shaba (Katanga)
Sha-ch'e (Yarkand)
Sha-chou (*n/s* Shazhou) NW China early state 124/3; Ming military post 164/1
Shaheinab Sudan Iron Age site 45/1
Shahr-i Sokhta C Persia early urban settlement 52/1, 55/1
Shama W Africa early trade 147/2; Dutch settlement 162/1 (inset)
Shan N China Late Chou site 63/4
Shandong (Shantung)
Shanghai E China treaty port 228/2; Nationalist control 258/1; occupied by Japanese 266/1; British military presence 273/1; industry 214/1, 259/3, 274/2
Shanidar Persia site of early man 32/2
Shan-nan Hsi-tao (*n/s* Shannan Xidao) C China T'ang province 124/1
Shan-nan Tung-tao (*n/s* Shannan Dongdao) C China T'ang province 124/1
Shans people of E Burma 131/2
Shansi (*n/s* Shanxi *W/G* Shan-hsi) province of N China invaded by Hsiung-nu 94/1; Ming province 164-5; Manchu expansion 171/1; T'ai-p'ing northern expedition 229/1; Hsin-hai revolution 229/1,3; warlord control 258/1,2
Shan State(s) Burma annexed by British 230/2; part of India 231/3; province of independent Burma 279/3; insurgency 277/3; Shan revolts 279/3
Shan-t'ou (Swatow)
Shantung (*n/s* Shandong) province of E China under Ming 164-9; Manchu expansion 171/1; Hsin-hai revolution 229/3; Japanese influence 239/2; warlord control 258/2; Japanese invasion 258/1
Shanxi (Shansi)
Sharjah (*Ar.* Ash Shariqah) United Arab Emirates 283/3
Sharm-el-Sheikh S Sinai Egyptian-Israel war 283/2
Sharon SE USA ✕ 217/4
Sharpsburg (*a/c* Antietam) E USA ✕ 219/1
Sharqat (Ashur)
Shavante forest Indian tribe of NE Brazil 145/1
Shawnee Indian tribe of E USA 145/1
Shawnee Trail C USA cattle trail 216/1
Shaybanids Muslim dynasty of C Asia 133/1
Shazhou (Sha-chou)
Sheffield N England Industrial Revolution 196/3, 197/1; industrial development 206/1
Shefford C England Industrial Revolution 197/1
She C China Western Chou domain 62/3
Shensi (*n/s* Shaanxi) province of N China invaded by Hsiung-nu 95/1; under Ming 164-5; Manchu expansion 171/1; Hsin-hai revolution 229/3
Shenyang (*a/c* Mukden) Manchuria Ming military post 165/1; industry 274/3
Sherborne S England bishopric 117/1
Shetland (*form.* Hjaltland) NE Scotland Norwegian settlement 110/2; 111/1; under control of Orkney 117/1; acquired by Scotland 146/1
Shibata N Japan 171/4
Shiga prefecture of C Japan industry 238/1
Shihr S Arabia early Chinese trade 146/1
Shih-ta (*mod.* Jidda) W Arabia early Chinese trade 146/1
Shikoku island of SW Japan 238/1
Shikotan *island* S Kuriles claimed by Japan 274/1
Shillong NE India capital of Assam 231/3
Shiloh (*a/c* Pittsburg Landing) SE USA ✕ 219/1
Shilsk SE Siberia founded 158/3
Shimabara W Japan 170/4
Shimane prefecture of W Japan 238/1
Shimazu clan of W Japan 164/4
Shimoda C Japan 171/4
Shimonoseki (*f/c* Akamagaseki) W Japan 170/4, 238/1,3
Shinjo N Japan 171/4
Shipibo forest Indian tribe of S America 145/1
Shipovo S Russia silk trade 70/1
Shipurla (Lagash)
Shirakawa N Japan 171/4
Shiraz S Persia trade 133/1
Shiroishi N Japan 171/4
Shirwan region of Caucasus conquered by Ottomans 167/1
Shizuoka (*form.* Sumpu) C Japan industry 238/1
Shoa tribe of Ethiopia 163/1, 237/1
Sholapur C India industry 214/1, 231/3
Shona tribe of SE Africa 235/1
Shonai (*now* Tsurugaoka) N Japan 171/4
Shongweni S Africa Iron Age site 45/1
Shortughai C Asia early urban settlement 33/1
Shoshone Indian tribe of NW USA 145/1
Shou-ch'un-fu (*n/s* Shouchunfu) C China Sung provincial capital 125/5
Shouf Mountains Lebanon Civil War 283/4
Shrewsbury W England Industrial Revolution 197/1
Shu border people of W China 63/4
Shu W China conquered by Chin 80/1; Han commanderie 81/2
Shu SE China Western Chou domain 62/3
Shubat-Enlil (*a/c* Chagar Bazar) Mesopotamia Amorite kingdom 54/2
Shuo-fang (*n/s* Shuofang) N China Han commanderie 81/2
Shuruppak (*mod.* Fara) Mesopotamia 55/3
Shuswap plateau Indian tribe of W Canada 145/1
Siam (*now* Thailand) spread of Buddhism 73/1; conquests 172-3; European and Chinese influence 257/1; economy 214/1, 295/1; under Japanese influence 264/2
Sian (*n/s* Xi'an *W/G* Hsi-an) N China industry 259/3
Siberia Russian expansion 158/3; fur trade 195/2; West Siberian oilfield 289/1; industrial development 289/1
Sicani early tribe of Sicily 86/2
Sicca Veneria (mod. Le Kef) Tunisia Roman Empire 89/1; early bishopric 92/1
Sichuan (Szechwuan)
Sicily (*Lat. and It.* Sicilia) *island* C Mediterranean Greek colonization 75/1; province of Roman Empire 86/3; Muslim conquest 104/1; Saracen raids 111/1; Byzantine Empire 113/1; German attacks 119/1; Norman conquest 120/2, 132/1; under the Almohads 132/1; rural uprisings 141/1; to Aragon 124/2, 146/1; acquired by Habsburgs 182/2; corn shipments 177/4; under Spanish rule 183/1; to Savoy 188/3; Kingdom of the Two Sicilies annexed to Piedmont/Sardinia 213/2; WW2 269/3
Siculi early tribe of Sicily 86/2
Sidama Kingdoms E Africa 135/1; 235/1, 237/1
Side S Anatolia Greek colony 75/1; Roman Empire 91/1
Sidi Abderrahman Morocco site of early man 33/1
Sidi Barrani Egypt WW2 265/5
Sidi Ifni Morocco Spanish control 247/2
Sidon (*mod.* Saïda *Ar.* Sayda) Lebanon Assyrian Empire 57/2; Mithraic site 73/1; Phoenician city 75/1; Alexander's route 76/1; early bishopric 93/1; Jewish community 103/1; Crusades 132/3

Swansea – Timor

Swansea S Wales Industrial Revolution 197/1
Swartkrans S Africa site of early man 33/1
Swatow (W/G Shan-t'ou) S China treaty port 228/2; industry 259/3; Japanese occupation 264/2
Swazi tribe of SE Africa 234/3, 235/1
Swaziland country of SE Africa British protectorate 236/2, 241/1; independence 273/2, 281/1
Sweden conversion to Christianity 101/2; Viking expansion 111/1; emergence as a state 117/1; Black Death 141/1; Union of Kalmar 146/1; Thirty Years War 178/2; Reformation 179/1; empire in the Baltic 184-9; losses to Russia and Prussia 192/1; population and emigration 204-5; industry 176-7, 207/1; customs union 207/3, 209/1; loss of Denmark and Norway 211/3; 20C economic and socio-political development 262/3, 263/2; EFTA 270/1; economy 271/4, 291/1, 295/1
Swift Creek/Santa Rosa Group early Indians of USA 46/3
Swindon W England Industrial Revolution 197/1
Swiss Confederation (a/c Helvetia) formation 140/3; agriculture and peasant emancipation 174/1
Switzerland early settlement 42/2; Zähringen towns 121/6; medieval cantons 146/1; Reformation 179/1; Industrial Revolution 206/1, 208/1; neutral in WW1 249/3; Alpine tunnels and railways 253/2; socio-political change 263/2; EFTA 270/1, 291/1; economy 271/4, 295/1; neutral in WW2 265/5, 268-9. See also Swiss Confederation
Sword Beach NW France Allied invasion point 269/6
Sybaris S Italy Greek colony 75/1, 86/2
Sybrita C Crete Minoan site 67/1
Sycae S Anatolia Byzantine Empire 112/3
Sydney (form. Port Jackson) SE Australia founded 233/5; industry 214/1
Sydney Nova Scotia growth 215/2
Syene (mod. Aswan) Upper Egypt 59/1
Syktyvkar (until 1930 Ust-Sysolsk) N Russia industry 289/1
Sylhet district of Bengal votes to join Pakistan 278/2
Synnada W Anatolia early archbishopric 93/1; Byzantine Empire 112/3
Syracusa (a/s Syracusae mod. Siracusa Eng. Syracuse)
Syria earliest settlements 41/1, 52/1; centre of ancient civilizations 56-7; at time of Alexander 76/1; Roman Empire 86/3, 91/2; expansion of Christianity 101/1; Arab conquest 105/1; under Abbasids 132/3; conquered by Turks 183/1; Ottoman province 225/1; French attack on 201/3; WW1 249/4; French mandate 256/1; political disturbances 257/1; WW2 268/1; independence 273/2; war with Israel 283/2, 292/5; occupation of Lebanon 283/4
Syriam S Burma early trade centre 173/1
Syrmia (S Cr. Srem Hung. Szerém Ger. Sirmien) district of Austria-Hungary now part of Serbia WW1 249/3
Syzran C Russia founded 159/1
Szczecin (Stettin)
Szechwan (n/s Sichuan W/G Ssu-ch'uan) province of W China under Ming 164-5; rebellion against Ch'ing 170/2; Manchu expansion 171/1; T'ai-p'ing rebellion 229/1,3; politically fragmented 258/1; Nationalist control 258/2; industry 274/3
Szemao (n/s Simao W/G Ssu-mao) SW China treaty town 228/2
Szentes-Vekerzug Hungary Thracian site 85/1
Szentgotthárd (St. Gotthard)
Szerém (Syrmia)
Sztutowo (Stutthof)
Tabasco state of S Mexico 223/1
Tabennesis Egypt monastery 100/1
Tabert Algeria Arab conquest 104/1
Tábor Moravia Hussite centre 141/1
Tabora E Africa Livingstone's travels 234/2
Tabriz NW Persia early archbishopric 101/1; occupied by Mongols 126/4; early trade 133/1; conquered by Ottomans 137/1, 167/1
Tabun C Israel site of early man 32/2
Ta-ching Manchuria oilfield 274/3
Tadcaster N England Industrial Revolution 197/1
Tadmekka NW Africa early town 134/2, 135/1; trade 163/1
Tadmor (Palmyra)
Tadzhik SSR (Tajik SSR)
Taegu S Korea industry 275/1; 1950-3 war 292/2
Taejon S Korea industry 275/1; 1950-3 war 292/2
Taganrog Crimea acquired by Muscovy 159/1
Taghaza (n/c Terhazza) NW Africa trans-Saharan trade 134/2, 135/1, 162/2, 163/1
Tagliacozzo C Italy ⚔ 119/1, 122/2
Tagliolo NW Italy principality 183/3
Tahiti island S Pacific Polynesian settlement 49/1; European discovery 153/3
Ta-hsia (Bactria)
Tai (n/s Dai) N China Han prefecture 81/2
Taimyr AO C Siberia 288/2
T'ai-hsi-ts'un (n/s Taixicun) N China Shang city 62/2
Taira N Japan 171/4
Taiwan (a/c Formosa) Mesolithic sites 62/1; Japanese pirate invasions 165/1; occupied by Ch'ing 170/2; rising of aboriginals 171/1; acquired by Japan 228/2, 239/2, 258/1,2, 264/2; conflict with mainland China 277/1
Taixicun (T'ai-hsi-ts'un)
T'ai-yüan (n/s Taiyuan) N China; early bishopric 101/1; T'ang city 124/1; Sung provincial capital 125/5; Ming provincial capital 165/1; French railway 228/2; industry 259/1, 274/3
Taizz Yemen trade 133/1
Tajik SSR (a/s Tadzhik) C Asia 288/2,4
Takada C Japan 171/2
Takamatsu W Japan 171/4
Takasaki C Japan 171/4
Takeda C Japan clan territory 164/4
Takedda NW Africa trans-Saharan trade 134/2
Takeshima (Kor. Tok-do) island Sea of Japan claimed by Korea 275/1
Takht-i-Sulaiman (Adhur Gushnasp)
Takkola Malaya early trade 71/1
Takla Makan Desert 71/1,2
Takoradi W Africa early Dutch settlement 162/1 (inset)
Takrur early empire of W Africa 134/1
Takua Pa S Thailand Hindu-Buddhist remains 131/2
Talas river C Asia ⚔ 105/1, 109/1, 125/2
Talavera S Spain ⚔ 200/1
Talgai SE Australia site of early man 33/1
Ta-li (n/s Dali) N China site of early man 33/1
Tal-i Ghazir W Persia early city 55/3
Ta-lien (Dairen)
Tallinn (Ger. Reval Russ. Revel) Estonian SSR industry 289/1
Talladega SE USA ⚔ 217/4
Tamanrasset S Algeria Saharan trade 134/2, 163/1; French occupation 237/1
Tamar (Palmyra)
Tamaulipas state of N Mexico 223/1
Tambov C Russia founded 159/1; Bolshevik seizure 255/1
Tambo Viejo C Andes early site 47/4
Tamil Nadu (form. Madras) state of S India 279/3
Tamils people of Ceylon 279/5
Ta-ming-fu (n/s Dumingfu) N China Sung provincial capital 125/5
Tamluk E India early trade 71/1
Tamsui (W/G Tan-shui) N Taiwan treaty port 228/2; Anglo-French attacks 229/1
Tamuín Mexico Huastec site 144/2
T'an (n/s Tan) E China Chou domain 62/3, 63/4
Tana S Russia Mongol conquest 126/4, 127/3
Tanais S Russia Greek colony 75/1
Tanakura N Japan 171/4
Tanana sub-artic Indian tribe of Alaska 145/1
Tananarive (n/s Antananarivo) Madagascar centre of Merina kingdom 235/1, 237/1
Tancáh Mexico Maya site 46/2
T'an-chou (n/s Tanzhou) C China Sung provincial capital 125/5; T'ang prefecture 124/1
Tan-erh (n/s Dan'er) S China Han prefecture 81/2
Tanga E Africa Arab-Swahili settlement 235/1
Tanganyika (form. German East Africa now part of Tanzania) 235/1; anti-German rising 245/1; British mandate 273/1; industry 214/1; independence 273/2; political development 281/1
T'ang Empire China 109/1, 124-5
Tangier (a/c Tangiers Fr. Tangier Sp. Tánger Ar. Tanjah anc. Tingis) Morocco early trade 132/1, 134/2, 162/2, 194/1; Portuguese rule 182/1; French and Spanish influence 247/2; international control 256/1
T'ang-shan (n/s Tangshan) NE China industry 259/1, 274/3
Tanguts tribe of S Mongolia 127/1
Tanis (a/c Avaris) Lower Egypt 58/1
Tanjah (Tangier)
Tanjore district of S India ceded to Britain 168/3
Tannenberg (Pol. Stębark) E Prussia ⚔ Teutonic Knights defeated 138/3; ⚔ 249/3
Tannu Tuva (now Tuvinskaya ASSR) C Asia independence from China 228/2; People's Republic under Soviet protection 254/3
Tan-shui (Tamsui)
Tanta Egypt medieval fair 143/1
Tan-t'u (n/s Dantu) E China Western Chou site 62/3
Tan-yang (n/s Danyang) E China Han commanderie 81/2
Tan-Zam Railway E Africa 281/1
Tanzania (formed by amalgamation of Tanganyika and Zanzibar) 273/2, 281/1. See also German East Africa
Tanzhou (T'an-chou)
Tao (n/s Dao) C China Western Chou domain 62/3
T'ao-chou (n/s Taozhou) W China Ming military post 165/1
Taodeni (a/s Taoudenni) NW Africa trade 135/1; French occupation 237/1
Taprobane (Ceylon)
Tara W Siberia founded 158/3
Tarabulus al Gharb (Tripoli)
Tarabulus ash Sham (Tripoli)
Tarahumara Indian tribe of N Mexico 145/1
Tarakan NE Borneo recaptured from Japanese 267/2
Taranaki (a/c New Plymouth) province of N Island, New Zealand Maori settlement 49/3; development 232/1
Taranto (anc. Tarentum) S Italy Saracen occupation 111/1; WW2 269/3
Tarapaca S Peru acquired by Chile 223/5
Tarapur NE India atomic energy plant 279/3
Tarasco Indian tribe of C Mexico 145/1
Tarawa Gilbert Islands, S Pacific ⚔ 267/2
Tarentaise SE France archbishopric 107/3
Tarentum (mod. Taranto) S Italy Greek colony 75/1; Roman Empire 86/3, 87/1, 89/1, 91/1
Tarim Basin C Asia occupied by China 125/2
Tarnopol (now Russ. Ternopol) E Austria-Hungary WW1 249/3; WW2 269/3
Tarnow (now Pol. Tarnów) E Austria-Hungary WW1 249/3
Tarquinii (later Corneto mod. Tarquinia) C Italy Etruscan city 75/1
Tarracina (earlier Axur mod. Terracina) C Italy Roman colony 87/1, 91/2
Tarraco (mod. Tarragona) NE Spain Greek colony 75/1; Roman Empire 86/3, 89/1, 90/1; Jewish community 103/1
Tarraconensis Roman province of N Spain 88/1
Tarragona (anc. Tarraco) NE Spain Civil War 264/3
Tarsus S Anatolia early trade 52/1, 54/1; Assyrian Empire 57/2; Alexander's route 76/1; Achaemenid Empire 79/1; Roman Empire 89/1; 91/1; early archbishopric 93/1; Jewish community 103/1; Byzantine Empire 113/1
Tărtăria C Romania early settlement 43/1
Tartars (a/s Tatars) Turkic people of E Russia, 127/1, 147/1, 158/3, 192/1, 288/4
Tartu (Dorpat)
Taruga C Africa Iron Age site 45/1
Tarvisium (Treviso)
Tashi-lhunpo S Tibet seat of Lamaistic patriarch 171/1
Tashkent Russ. C Asia on Alexander's journey 77/1; Mongol conquest 126/4; centre of Bolshevik activity 254/3; industry 289/1; urban growth 288/3
Tash-Kurghan (a/s Tashkurgan anc. Aornos) C Asia early trade 82/4
Tasmania (until 1856 Van Diemen's Land) island state of SE Australia settlement and development 233/5 (inset), 240/1 (inset)
Tassafaronga Solomon Is, SW Pacific ⚔ 267/2
Tassili Massif N Africa rock painting 45/1
Tatanagar NE India industry 279/1
Tatar ASSR C Russia 288/2
Tatars (Tartars)
Tatebayashi C Japan 171/4
Tatsuno W Japan 171/4
Ta-t'ung (n/s Datong) N China Ming frontier defence area 165/1; railway 259/3; industry 274/3
Tauern Austria Alpine tunnel 253/2
Taung S Africa site of early man 33/4
Taunum W Germany Mithraic site 72/1
Ta-wen-k'ou (n/s Dawenkou) NE China early settlement 62/1
Taurasia (Turin)
Taxila (Skt. Takshasila) NW India Alexander's route 77/1; early trade 70/1, 82/3,4, 83/1,2
Taxiles early kingdom of NW India 82/3
Tayadirt N Morocco Megalithic site 42/2
Tayasal E Mexico Maya resistance to Spaniards 144/2
Tazoult (Lambaesis)
Tbilisi (f/s Tiflis) Georgian SSR economy 289/1
Tchad (Chad)
Teanum Apulum C Italy Roman Empire 87/1
Teanum Sidicinum (mod. Teano) C Italy Roman Empire 87/1
Teate (mod. Chieti) C Italy Roman Empire 87/1
Tebessa (Theveste)
Tegnapatam SE India Dutch settlement 169/1
Teheran (Pers. Tehran) C Persia 225/1; oil pipeline 283/3
Tehuelche Indian tribe of S Argentina 145/1
Te Ika-a-Maui (North Island, New Zealand)
Teke early state of C Africa 235/1
Teke SW Anatolia region of Ottoman Empire 136/2, 137/1
Tel-Aviv C Israel 283/2
Telingana region of C India under Delhi Sultanate 129/3
Tell Agrab (a/s Tell Ajrab) S Mesopotamia 55/3
Tell Asmar (Eshnunna)
Tell Aswad S Mesopotamia 55/3
Tell Brak E Syria early settlement 41/1
Tell el'Ubaid S Mesopotamia early settlement 41/1, 55/3
Tell-es-Sawwan Mesopotamia early village 41/1
Tell es-Sultan (Jericho)
Tell Halaf Mesopotamia early village 41/1
Tellicherry SW India English settlement 157/1
Tell Ramad W Syria early village 41/1
Tell Shemshara C Mesopotamia early settlement 41/1
Tell Uqair S Mesopotamia 55/3
Tell Wilaya S Mesopotamia 55/3
Telo Martius (Toulon)
Tembu region of SE Africa 234/1
Temirtau W Siberia foundation 288/3; industry 289/1
Tempsa S Italy Roman colony 87/1
Tenasserim district of S Burma territorial dispute with Siam 157/1; British control 173/1; annexed by British 230/2; insurgency 277/1
Tenetehara forest Indian tribe of NE Brazil 145/1
Teng (n/s Deng) N China Chou domain and city-state 62/3, 63/4; warring state 80/1
Tengyueh (n/c Tengchong W/G T'eng-ch'ung) SW China treaty town 228/2
Ten Kingdoms China 124/3
Tennessee state of SE USA Civil War 219/1; 19C politics 221/2,3; Depression 263/1; income and population 287/2
Tenochtitlán Mexico Aztec capital 144/2; conquest by Spaniards 155/2
Teotihuacán early culture of C America 46/2, 47/1
Teotitlán Mexico site 144/2
Tepe Gawra N Mesopotamia early settlement 41/1
Tepe Hisar N Persia 55/1
Tepehuan Indian tribe of N Mexico 145/1
Tepexpan Mexico site of early man 32/1
Tepic state of N Mexico 223/1
Te Porere N Island, New Zealand ⚔ 232/1
Teramo (Interamna)
Terebovl W Russia town of Galich 115/1
Teremembé forest Indian tribe of NE Brazil 145/1
Terezin (Theresienstadt)
Tergeste (mod. Trieste) N Italy Roman Empire 89/1
Terhazz (Taghaza)
Ternate Moluccas, East Indies Islamic town 131/3; Portuguese settlement 172/2
Ternifine Algeria site of early man 33/1
Ternopol (Tarnopol)
Terracina (Anxur, Tarracina)
Terranova di Sicilia (Gela)
Teruel E Spain Civil War 264/3
Teschen (Cz. Těšín or Český Těšín Pol. Cieszyn) city and district divided between Poland and Czechoslovakia 261/1; Czech part retaken by Poland 265/4
Teshik-Tash C Asia site of early man 33/1
Těšín (Teschen)
Tete Mozambique Portuguese settlement 163/1; Stanley's travels 234/2
Tetuán Morocco Spanish control 224/1, 247/2
Teutonic Order Baltic 115/1; conquest of Prussia 138/3, 139/1; territory lost to Poland 147/1
Teverya (Tiberias)
Te Waiponamu (South Island, New Zealand)
Tewkesbury W England Industrial Revolution 197/1
Texas state of S USA independent 223/1; 19C politics 221/2,3; Depression 263/1; income and population 287/2
Texel I and II N Netherlands English/Dutch naval battles 181/1, 190/3
Thailand (f/c Siam) early Iron and Bronze Age sites 130/1; Theravada Buddhism 131/3; occupied by Japanese 266/1, 267/1; militarization and insurgency 277/1; US bases 293/1; economy 274/2, 295/1. See also Siam
Thais people of SE Asia, expansion 131/2
Tham Ongban W Siam early site 130/1
Thames N Island, New Zealand gold rush 232/1
Thames Valley N Island, New Zealand Maori settlement 49/3
Thamugadi (a/c Timgad) Algeria ancient city 89/1
Thang Long (mod. Hanoi) N Indo-China major political centre 131/2,3
Thapsacus (Bibl. Tiphsah mod. Dibse) Syria Alexander's route 76/1; Achaemenid Empire 79/1; Alexander's Empire 82/3
Thapsus Tunisia Punic city 74/1; Roman Empire 86/3, 89/1
Thara N Persia Alexander's route 77/1
Tharro NW India Harappan site 65/1
Thasos island N Greece ancient city 75/1
Thaton S Burma early Hindu-Buddhist temple 131/2
Thebes (mod. Gr. Thivai) C Greece Mycenaean palace 67/1; Jewish community 103/1
Thebes (Lat. Thebae earlier Diospolis Magna) Upper Egypt Iron Age site 45/1; 59/1; Roman Empire 89/1, 91/1
Thenae Tunisia Punic city 74/1
Theodosia (mod. Feodosiya) Crimea Greek colony 75/1; Roman Empire 89/1
Theodosiopolis E Anatolia early bishopric 93/1; under Seljuks of Rum 113/5
Thera (mod. Thira a/c Santorini) island of S Aegean 67/1; Greek parent state 75/1
Theresienstadt (now Cz. Terezin) C Germany concentration camp 268/1
Thermopylae C Greece ⚔ 74/3, 78/1
Thessalonica (a/c Salonika Gr. Thessaloniki) N Greece Roman Empire 86/3, 89/1, 91/1; Jewish community 103/1; Byzantine Empire 113/1; medieval fair 142/1; WW2 265/5
Thessaly (Gr. Thessalia) region of C Greece 76/4; Slav settlement 112/4; district of Byzantine Empire 113/1; ceded to Greece 211/2
Thetford E England Scandinavian settlement 110/2, 111/1; Industrial Revolution 197/1
Theveste (mod. Tebessa) Algeria Roman Empire 89/1, 91/1
Thiel (Tiel)
Thionville (Diedenhofen)
Thira (Thera)
Thirsk N England rebellion against Elizabeth I 181/1
Thirteen Colonies N America 190/1, 198/1
Thivai (Thebes)
Thomas Quarries NW Africa site of early man 33/1
Thonburi Thailand early trade centre 173/1
Thorikos E Greece Mycenaean site 67/1
Thorn (Pol. Toruń) N Poland founded by Teutonic Knights 138/3; Hanseatic city 142/1
Thrace (anc. Thracia) region of SE Europe 75/1, 76/1; divided between Bulgaria and Turkey 211/2; East occupied by Greece 261/1
Thracesian Theme W Anatolia district of Byzantine Empire 112/3
Thracia (Eng. Thrace) SE Europe Roman province 89/1,4; Byzantine Empire 113/1
Thracians early people of SE Europe 61/1, 67/3
Three Days Battle S England English naval victory 181/1
Three Forks NW USA fur station 216/1
Thrimbokambos C Crete Minoan palace 67/1
Thun C Switzerland Zähringen town 121/6
Thunder Bay (Fort William)
Thurgau Switzerland Reformation 179/1
Thurii Copia S Italy Latin colony 87/1
Thuringia (Thüringen) region of E Germany Frankish Empire 107/3; Magyar invasions 111/1; medieval German Empire 119/1; 18C industrial growth 186/2; amalgamation of petty states 187/4; German unification 212/3; 271/2
Thuringians E Germany Germanic tribe 98/2
Thyatira (mod. Akhisar) W Anatolia one of seven churches of Asia 93/1
Tiahuanaco Empire C Andes site 47/1,4,5; 145/3
Tianjin (Tientsin)
Tianshui (T'ien-shui)
Tiantai Shan (T'ien-t'ai Shan)
Tiberias (Heb. Teverya) Israel town of Judaea 103/2
Tibesti Massif N Africa rock painting 45/1
Tibet (anc. Bhota Chin. Hsi-tsang n/s Xizang form. T'u-fan) C Asia spread of Buddhism 73/1; early expansion 95/1; unified kingdom 125/2; part of Mongol Empire 127/1; Chinese protectorate 171/1; British sphere of influence 228/2, 241/1; absorbed by China 273/2; economy 214/1
Tibur (mod. Tivoli) C Italy Roman Empire 87/1
Tichitt W Africa early site 45/1
Ticinum (Pavia)
Ticonderoga (Fr. Fort Carillon) NE USA British capture of French fort 190/1
Tidore island Moluccas, E Indies Islamic town 131/3; Portuguese settlement 172/2; Dutch settlement 173/1
Tiel (f/s Thiel) Netherlands early market 110/3; 119/1
Tien (n/s Dian) early state of W China 80/1
T'ien-chin (Tientsin)
T'ien-fang (Mecca)
T'ien-shui (n/s Tianshui) NW China Han commanderie 81/2
T'ien-t'ai Shan (n/s Tiantai Shan) mountain E China Buddhist site 73/1
Tientsin (n/s Tianjin W/G T'ien-chin) NE China treaty port 228/2; Boxer uprising 229/1; Japanese occupation 264/2; industry 214/1, 259/1, 274/3
Tieum N Anatolia Greek colony 75/1
Tievebulliagh N Ireland Megalithic site 42/2
Tiflis (n/c Tbilisi) Caucasus Muslim conquest 105/1, 133/1; Mongol conquest 126/4; Safavid Empire 137/1; Ottoman conquest 167/1; urban growth 227/1, 288/3
Tighina (Bender)
Tigliole NW Italy principality 183/3
Tigranocerta (mod. Siirt) E Anatolia Parthian Empire 78/3; Roman Empire 86/3, 89/1
Ti-hua (Urumchi)
Tikal E Mexico Maya site 46/2
Tilmun (Dilmun)
Tilya-tepe C Asia treasure 79/1
Timbira forest Indian tribe of N Brazil 145/1
Timbuktu (Fr. Tombouctou) W Africa trans-Saharan trade 134/2, 135/1, 150/2, 162/2; conquered by Al Hajj Umar 235/1; occupied by French 237/1
Timgad (Thamugadi)
Timor island of E Indies early Portuguese colony 155/1, 157/1, 173/1; Dutch/Portuguese control 241/1; WW2 266-7; resistance to Indonesian occupation of E Timor 275/1